NEW TESTAMENT HISTORY

ACTS

A CRITICAL AND EXEGETICAL
COMMENTARY

———————————— by ————————————

GARETH L. REESE

HEAD OF NEW TESTAMENT DEPARTMENT
CENTRAL CHRISTIAN COLLEGE OF THE BIBLE
MOBERLY, MISSOURI

Scripture Exposition Books, LLC
803 McKINSEY PLACE
MOBERLY, MISSOURI
65270

Copyright 1976 by College Press Publishing Company.
Copyright 2002 by Scripture Exposition Books.

The information in this book is intended for personal study, for classroom, and for pulpit use by Bible students and teachers. Therefore, readers who wish to reproduce any of the comments or Special Studies in the form of free handouts to students or listeners or in sermon outlines as they are being preached, are encouraged to do so with no need to seek prior permission. We ask that you simply include a line giving credit to the source you have copied. No other reproduction of this book in any form or by any means is allowed without prior written permission from the publisher.

Third Printing 2008
Fourth Printing 2015

ACKNOWLEDGEMENT

The Scripture quotations contained herein, unless otherwise noted, are from the *New American Standard Bible,* copyrighted 1960, 1962, 1963, 1968, 1971, 1972, 1973, 1975, 1977, by the Lockman Foundation. Used by permission.

Suggested Cataloging Data

Reese, Gareth L., 1932-
    New Testament History : a critical and exegetical commentary on the book of Acts / by Gareth L. Reese. – Scripture Exposition Books, c.2002.

    xxxviii, 1017 p. : ill., maps ; 26 cm.
    Cover title: New Testament History-Acts.
    Spine title: Acts.
    "Third edition" – Pref.
    Includes bibliographical references and index.
    ISBN 0-971-76523-5 (Previously ISBN 0-8990-0055-X)

    1. Bible. NT. Acts.-Commentaries. I. Bible. NT. Acts. English. New American Standard. II. Title. III. Title: New Testament History—Acts, rv. Title: Acts.

    BS2625.3.R38 2002

To my helpmeet

KATHLEEN

who first typed stencils when this material was distributed in mimeographed form, and who has encouraged me to put it in book form, and has diligently helped in its production.

PREFACE

"Need is the mother of invention," someone has said. This volume has arisen out of the need for a book to serve as a source of materials for a study of the book of Acts for a freshman college class.

The study opens with a brief survey of the dates of the major events of New Testament history, in the Gospels, as well as in Acts. This examination of the way that the dates are arrived at will serve as a basic framework into which to locate the historical materials of Acts. It will also give opportunity to make a brief survey of the whole book of Acts at once, before the study begins in detail.

The second part of the introductory studies is concerned with the matters usually studied in the field of Higher Criticism, that is, such things as authorship, purpose, trustworthiness, date and place of writing, as well as the destination to which it was addressed. Though some of these materials are difficult for freshmen to see the value of, still, with the great, massive attack being made on the Christian faith in these days, this commentator believes that such a detailed study of "critical" matters will prove to be a most needed source of evidence on which to build a continuing faith in the divine origin of the Christian Religion.

The exegetical notes which follow have been gleaned from many sources over the years that this commentator has taught Acts at Central Christian College of the Bible. He acknowledges an indebtedness to his teacher in college days, L. Edsil Dale. Further, much information has been taken from commentaries, such as *Pulpit Commentary, Barnes Notes, Alford's Greek Testament, Ellicott's Commentary,* and individual works on Acts by McGarvey, DeWelt, Bruce, Boles, Meyer, Rackham, and others.

This book is presented to its readers with the prayer that our merciful God will bless this work with His divine favor, and that His revealed truth may be brought more and more home to the hearts of the readers of His Holy Word.

Moberly, Missouri, June, 1966

PREFACE TO THE SECOND EDITION

Ten years have passed since this volume grew out of its mimeographed format into the first edition of a printed format. It has been used in greater numbers and in more places than the author ever dreamed.

As the years passed, certain weaknesses kept calling for a newer printing which would correct those weaknesses. With Don DeWelt's encouragement and the help of College Press, that newer printing is now presented.

The American Standard Version of 1901 was the text followed in the first edition. Fewer and fewer copies of this excellent translation of the New Testament are available for purchase in the present decade. A decision was made to use the New American Standard Bible as the text upon which comments would be made in this new edition.

The current edition has a new format, and readable type. Materials that have been quoted are better documented. Two new Special Studies, one on "The Faith that Saves," and one concerning "The World of the Occult," have been included because of growing interest in what Acts says on both subjects. Finally, one of the most useful features of this new edition, the author believes, will be the detailed index that has been included at the close of the volume.

Acts of Apostles is a pivotal book in New Testament studies, giving us information about how the Church began and developed in those key years after the ascension and glorification of Jesus. It is this commentator's prayer that the new printing of this commentary on Acts will encourage further study not only of Acts but of the whole New Testament.

Moberly, Missouri, April, 1976

PREFACE TO THE THIRD EDITION

After publishing this work for a quarter of a century, College Press has relinquished the publishing of this book back to its author.

In the more than half-century this commentary has been in print, not only has it been used in the English-speaking world, but it has been translated into Russian, Portuguese, and now also is being translated into Chinese. It has served as the textbook for college and church classes on the book of Acts. Continuing requests for the book for use as a text by American Bible College and Seminary teachers has made keeping it in print a pleasant responsibility.

The verse by verse comments included in this printing closely follow those in the earlier College Press printing, but the present format has been updated to match the author's other volumes on New Testament Epistles. The scholarly literature cited in the Special Studies is still germane and helpful, and the Special Studies themselves are still timely. The internet and periodical indexes make the retrieval of current scholarly literature, where it is desired, easily available.

The author still holds the view that faithfulness to what one reads in the pages of the New Testament is what the Lord expects of His people. That being true, this work is offered to Bible students with the prayer that together we may think God's thoughts after Him, and live and worship and serve the way people redeemed by the blood of the Lamb should.

Moberly, Missouri, January, 2022

TABLE OF CONTENTS

PREFACE

INTRODUCTORY STUDIES   Page
   NEW TESTAMENT CHRONOLOGY
      Chronology of the Gospels i
      Chronology of the Apostolic Age x

   INTRODUCTORY STUDIES TO ACTS
      1. Title xxii
      2. Purpose xxii
      3. Authorship xxiv
      4. Trustworthiness xxvi
      5. Dependence xxxiii
      6. Language xxxv
      7. Date of Writing xxxv
      8. Place of Writing xxxvi
      9. Destination xxxvi
      10. Integrity xxxvii
      11. Characteristics xxxvii
      12. The Value of Introductory Studies xxxvii

COMMENTARY
   Chapter One 1
   Special Study #1 — Diverse Opinions About the Kingdom of God... 34
   Special Study #2 — The Brothers of the Lord 39
   Chapter Two 43
   Special Study #3 — The Person and Work of the Holy Spirit 89
   Special Study #4 — Speaking in Tongues 102
   Special Study #5 — The Doctrine of Inspiration 127
   Special Study #6 — Predestination and Foreknowledge 130
   Special Study #7 — Hades and the Intermediate Place of the Dead 135
   Special Study #8 — What is Repentance? 145
   Chapter Three 150
   Chapter Four 171
   Special Study #9 — The Sects of the Jews 196
   Chapter Five 201
   Special Study #10 — Church Discipline 230
   Special Study #11 — Demons and Demon Possession 235
   Chapter Six 247
   Special Study #12 — A Method of Selection of Elders and Deacons 264

Table of Contents, *cont'd*

Chapter Seven 271
    Special Study #13 — Difficulties in Acts 7 306
Chapter Eight 313
Chapter Nine (with chapters 22 and 26 harmonized) 345
    Paul's Youth 345
    Paul in Jerusalem 347
    Paul's Trip to Damascus 351
    Paul's Conversion in Damascus 357
    Paul in Arabia 364
    Paul Back in Damascus 365
    Paul Again in Jerusalem 366
    Paul Goes to Tarsus and Antioch 368
Chapter Ten 378
Chapter Eleven 407
Chapter Twelve 426
    Special Study #14 — Was Peter Ever in Rome? 447
Chapter Thirteen 453
    Special Study #15 — The Synagogue and its Services 494
Chapter Fourteen 497
Chapter Fifteen 527
Chapter Sixteen 564
    Special Study #16 — The Faith that Saves 598
Chapter Seventeen 611
Chapter Eighteen 638
Chapter Nineteen 666
    Special Study #17 — The World of the Occult 701
Chapter Twenty 726
    Special Study #18 — The Lord's Supper 759
Chapter Twenty-one 779
Chapter Twenty-two 808
Chapter Twenty-three 815
Chapter Twenty-four 836
Chapter Twenty-five 857
Chapter Twenty-six 872
Chapter Twenty-seven 889
Chapter Twenty-eight 919

EPILOGUE: THE LAST LABORS AND LETTERS OF PAUL 951

MAPS 526, 955

INDEX 965

Charts, Diagrams, and Outlines

TITLE	Page
A Comparison of Information from Acts and Galatians	xix
Key Dates in the Life of Paul	xx
Summary of the Dates of the Apostolic Age	xxi
Outline of the Book of Acts	xxxix
Post-Resurrection Appearances of Jesus	4
Five Baptisms in the New Testament	8
The Mode of Baptism	75
The Different Activities of the Holy Spirit	101
The World of the Dead	144
Diagram of the Temple Area at Jerusalem	151
Diagram of the Floor Plan of a Middle-class Home	435
The General Outline of Paul's Sermons to Jewish and Gentile Audiences	510
Two Kinds of Law in the New Testament	554
The Unknown God	634
The Conversion of a Preacher	664
Paul's Address to the Ephesian Elders	743
Thanatos Inscription Stone	801
Paul's Message to Herod Agrippa II	872

NEW TESTAMENT CHRONOLOGY

HOW DID THE ANCIENTS RECKON TIME?

The Greeks dated historical events by Olympiads. The first of these was in 776 BC. The Romans reckoned time in two manners. They dated many things from the date of the founding of the city of Rome in 753 BC. In some chronologies, therefore, numbers like 726 AUC appear. The initials AUC stand for the Latin *ab urbe condita*, which means "from the founding of the city." Some articles on chronology give a double set of figures, like 750/4. The first number stands for the number of years from the founding of the city; the second is the equivalent year on our calendar. 750 AUC is reckoned to be the same as 4 BC. The Romans also used the names of rulers as a fixed point from which to reckon time. This method is used in the New Testament. The calendar used in our day, reckoned from the birth of Jesus, is based upon the calculations of Dionysius (6th century AD). Subsequent investigations have shown the Dionysian date to be at least four years in error.[1]

Chronology of the Gospels

There are three points from which to date the events recorded in the Gospels: the birth, the baptism, and the death of Jesus.

THE BIRTH OF JESUS

A. Biblical Data

Augustus was the Roman emperor. An enrollment of the empire was being made at his direction when Jesus was born, Luke 2:1.

Quirinius was exercising authority in the province of Syria, Luke 2:2. Judea was a part of the Roman province of Syria.[2]

Herod the Great was king of Judea, Matthew 2:1. Judean kings were subordinate to the governor or proconsul of Syria.

Summarizing the Biblical data as to the time of the birth of Jesus: He was born before the death of Herod the Great, at the time of a census or enrollment made in the territory of Herod in accordance with a decree of Caesar Augustus, the census being made at a time when Quirinius was exercising authority in the province of Syria.

B. Historical Data

1. *Augustus*

Augustus, the Roman emperor, ordered several enrollments. These are dated 726/28, 746/8, and 767/14. The enrollment of 746/8 (i.e., 8 BC) best fits the Biblical data. History tells us that it took a year before the enrollment of 28 BC was carried out in Gaul. Therefore,

---

[1] See this error explained in *Christianity Today*, 12-18-64, p.277.

[2] See notes at Acts 25:1 where it is explained that Judea was a part of Syria

if the enrollment was ordered in Rome at 8 BC, it could conceivably be two years before it would be carried out in the outlying provinces such as Palestine, 1500 miles from Rome. So we might tentatively date the census as being carried out in Palestine about 6 BC.

Would Herod the Great be expected to enroll the area over which he was king? Herod was a *rex socius* (an associate king – i.e., associate to Augustus), and as such would have certain rights that would be respected. It is asked whether it would be at all probable that Augustus would think of exposing Herod to a mark of subjection and dependence so humiliating as a census of Judea. And the answer is yes! These *reges socii* were not so independent of Rome as one might think. They had to pay tribute to the Romans. And Herod, especially because of his cruelties, was hated by the Jews, and more and more, particularly in his later life, had to look to Rome for protection.

It appears that Augustus commanded the enrollment to be made, but that the census was conducted by Herod in the Jewish form. That it was a "Jewish-type" enrollment is evident from the fact that (as everyone went to this own city) Joseph had to go to Bethlehem "because he was of the house and lineage of David."[3] Another evidence that this first enrollment made when Quirinius was governor of Syria was a "Jewish-type" enrollment is the fact that at the time of the next census (which was collected by the Romans) there was a revolt in Galilee under the leadership of Judas the Galilean.[4] The Jews revolted because they felt the taxation (i.e., money going to the emperor who claimed to be a god) to be an infringement and an imposition on their laws and liberties. However, at the census mentioned by Luke in his Gospel, there seems to have been no such resistance or revolt on the part of the Jews, which fact leads us to believe that this first enrollment was a "Jewish-type" enrollment.

2. *Death of Herod the Great*

According to Matthew 2:1-19, the death of Herod the Great is the *terminus ad quem* for the birth of Jesus. From secular history, we learn of the date of Herod's death. He died at Passover time, after reigning 37 years. Josephus tells us he began to reign in the 184 Olympiad, or 41-40 BC.[5] Or, figured from another starting point, he reigned 34 years after the death of Antigonus, which happened in September or October of 38 BC. Just before Herod's death there was an eclipse of the moon.[6] Of the several eclipses that would have been visible in Palestine between 5 BC and the turn of the century, that of March 12, 4 BC fits in best with the other information we have. This being the case, Jesus must have been born somewhere between 6 BC and 4 BC. Remember, Herod had all the babes under two years old killed. Two years is, therefore, the longest before Herod's death that Jesus could have been born.

This date of 4 BC for Herod's death is confirmed by the evidence for the duration of the reigns of his three sons. Archelaus was deposed in AD 6, after a reign of 10 years. Antipas was deposed in AD 39 after a reign of 43 years. Philip died in AD 34 after reigning 37 years. All of these men must have begun to reign in 4 BC; therefore, Herod must have died in 4 BC.

---

[3] Luke 2:4.

[4] Acts 5:37.

[5] *Antiquities*, XVII.8.1.

[6] *Op. cit.*, XVII.6.4.

3. *Quirinius, an Official in Syria*

Josephus says that Quirinius became governor of Syria in AD 6, after the deposition of Archelaus and the annexation of Judea to Syria. But this is ten years *after* Christ's birth, which preceded Herod's death in 4 BC. The negative critics have used this fact to say that Luke's record of the birth of Jesus under Quirinius is just a hoax, or "... just a tricky attempt to get Jesus to Bethlehem to get him born there to fulfill prophecy." How are we to solve and explain this apparent discrepancy?

We reject the following three attempted solutions as inadmissible. 1) The attempt to remove the difficulty in a critical way – whether by rejecting the whole verse (Luke 2:2) as an erroneous gloss, or by altering the well-supported reading as we find it in both the KJV and ASV. 2) The explanation that this enrollment took place "before" Quirinius was governor of Syria. Luke writes better Greek than to use *prōtē* ("first") in the sense of *prōtera* ("before"). 3) The supposition of Schleiermacher that it was merely a priestly taxing that took the parents of Jesus to Bethlehem, and that Luke confounded this priestly census with a Roman census. Why should they go to Bethlehem to pay the priestly tax when the temple was at Jerusalem?

The solution seems to lie in the following facts, which answer the question, Who ruled in Syria previous to Herod's death in 4 BC? From 9-6 BC, Sentius Satuminus was governor. From 6-4 BC, Quinctilius Varus was governor of Syria. From here, there is a gap in the extant records that covers the years down to AD 6, when P. Sulpicious Quirinius becomes governor. How can it be, then, that Luke is correct when he says that Quirinius was governor when Jesus was born in the days before the death of Herod the Great? Recent archaeological discoveries indicate that Quirinius was apparently twice governor of Syria (4-1 BC and AD 6-11). But even this does not solve our problem, for 4 BC is too late. It has been satisfactorily demonstrated that, strangely enough, Quirinius – who in AD 6-11 was governor (*legatus*) of Syria – at the time of the birth of the Savior, held high office in Syria, either as "governor" (*praeses*) or as "imperial commissioner" (*quaestor*). The Greek word *hegemon* (translated "governor") would have been used for either of these offices. So, we can say that Quirinius held important offices in Syria from 12 BC to AD 11.

4. *Other Historical Data* (sometimes used to date the birth of Jesus)

The Star

Some have attempted to identify the star that guided the wise men with a conjunction of Saturn and Jupiter in 747/7 and 748/6. It does not seem to be proper to identify the star with any natural heavenly phenomena. The star went before them, the Bible says, and then stood over the place where Jesus lay.[7] A star, as we know them, does not so act.[8]

The Course of Abijah

Zacharias, the father of John the Baptist, was a priest of this course, and was serving about 6 months before Jesus was conceived (Luke 1:5ff). Some attempt to reckon back

---

[7] Matthew 2:9.

[8] For further information, see the article, "What was the Star of Bethlehem?" in *Christianity Today*, 12-18-64, p.277.

from the time of the destruction of Jerusalem (at which time, according to tradition, the course of Jehoiarib was functioning), and thus determine the approximate time of the announcement to Zacharias of the birth of John the Baptist, but it is not possible to do so with any degree of certainty.

The Day of the Month

There is great uncertainty as to the day of Jesus' birth. The New Testament gives no definite data on this point. The earliest reference to this subject in early Christian literature is from Clement of Alexandria (about AD 190).[9] He states that some thought the date of Christ's birth was April 21; others thought April 22; and still others May 20. The Eastern Church argued that Christ must have been born on January 6 because he was the "second Adam"[10] and therefore should have been born on the sixth day of the year, because the first Adam was created on the sixth day of creation."[11] The celebration of December 25 can be traced back as far as the 4th century AD. It seems to have arisen in the West. The predominance of the Roman church led to its well-nigh universal acceptance. But the fact that shepherds were feeding their flocks at night when Jesus was born (Luke 2:8) makes it improbable that the season of the year was winter. The uncertainty of the date of Jesus' birthday should not disturb us. If it had been an essential feature of the Christian faith, the New Testament would have given more specific information.

C. Conclusion as to the Date of the Birth of Jesus

The information gained from the Biblical and historical data leads us to a date of about 5 or 6 BC for the birth of Jesus.

THE BAPTISM OF JESUS

A. Biblical Data

Jesus was about 30 years old when He began His ministry.[12] He thus could have been anywhere between the ages of 28 and 32. If Jesus were born between 6 and 4 BC, the beginning of His ministry would be somewhere between AD 22 and AD 28.

Luke, using a recognized method of dating events, names a number of government and religious officials in power at the time Jesus began His ministry.[13] Tiberius Caesar was in the 15th year of his reign. Pontius Pilate was governor of Judea. Herod Antipas was tetrarch of Galilee. Philip was tetrarch of Iturea and Trachonitis. Lysanias was tetrarch of Abilene. Annas and Caiaphas were the high priests.

At the time when Jesus was in His first year of ministry (which was just shortly after his baptism), we learn that Herod's workmen had been in the process of rebuilding the temple for 46 years.[14]

---

[9] Plummer, Alfred, "Luke," *International Critical Commentary* (Edinburgh: T&T Clark, 1908), p.55.

[10] 1 Corinthians 15:47.

[11] Genesis 1:26-31.

[12] Luke 3:23.

[13] Luke 3:1,21.

[14] John 2:20.

B. Historical Data

According to His age ("about 30"), Jesus' ministry began somewhere between 22 and 28 AD. Does the information that history gives us about the leaders and rulers fit this limitation?

1. *Tiberius Caesar*

Tiberius was the second Roman emperor, succeeding Caesar Augustus. Augustus reigned from 31 BC to August 19 of AD 14. If we were to figure Tiberius' 15th year from this date, we would be taken to AD 29 for the beginning of Jesus' ministry. This does not fit the limitations noted above for the beginning of Jesus' ministry.

However, it should be noted that Tiberius ruled jointly with Augustus for several years. Around AD 6 he was made Tribune. In AD 11, by a special law, Tiberius was given the sole authority in the provinces with the title Imperator (co-regent). Since Jesus and Luke were in the provinces, this would appear to be the time from which Luke dates Tiberius' rule. Fifteen years after he became co-regent would be AD 26. A date of AD 26 for the baptism of Jesus falls within the limitations noted above. We can accept this date for the baptism of Jesus, if it fits other information from Luke and John. Does it?

2. *Pontius Pilate*

Pilate was the fifth Roman procurator (governor) in Judea after the deposition of Archelaus. Pilate followed Valerius Gratus in the position. He came into office in AD 26;[15] in the year AD 36, after ten years of crookedness and corruption, Pilate was recalled to Rome to answer to Tiberius concerning his conduct while in office.

Pilate's government ended abruptly. A Samaritan imposter promised his countrymen that, if they would go to the top of Mt. Gerizim, he would show them where Moses had hidden certain golden vessels of the tabernacle. Although Moses never was at Mt. Gerizim, nor had he crossed the Jordan River, yet a deluded multitude gathered at a village at the foot of the mountain in order to go up. Unfortunately for them, they carried arms. Pilate, therefore, seized all the ways to Mt. Gerizim with horsemen and foot-soldiers, attacked the mass of professed treasure seekers, slew many, and made prisoners of others and sent them to execution. The Samaritans forwarded a complaint against Pilate to his immediate superior, Vitellius, the legate of Syria. Vitellius appointed a new procurator and ordered Pilate to proceed to Rome to answer to the emperor for his conduct. Before Pilate arrived, Tiberius died on March 16 of AD 37. The new emperor banished Pilate to Vienne, in southern France, and there Pilate later ended his own life in suicide (so tradition tells us).

The AD 26 date for Jesus' baptism would put it during the first year of the governor's term in office in Judea.

3. *Herod, Tetrarch of Galilee and Perea*

Herod the tetrarch was a son of Herod the Great and his Samaritan wife, Malthace. This made the boy half Idumaean and half Samaritan, and therefore "Galilee of the Gentiles"

---

[15] *Antiquities*, XVIII.4.3 and 5.3.

seemed a fit domain for such a prince. His name is often given as Herod Antipas.

He ruled as tetrarch of Galilee and Perea from 4 BC until AD 39. In Herod the Great's second will, all his kingdom was willed to Antipas. However, in Herod's final will, Antipas received only a fourth of the kingdom. Antipas contested the will against his brother Archelaus, but the final will was allowed to stand by the Emperor Augustus.

Antipas' first wife was a daughter of Aretas IV, king of Nabatea, whose capital was Petra. But he divorced her, and married Herodias. Before her marriage to Antipas, Herodias had been the wife of Philip, one of Antipas' half- brothers. While he was visiting with Philip and his wife in Rome, Antipas seduced Herodias, and then arranged to divorce the daughter of Aretas and marry Herodias instead. Aretas repaid this insult to his daughter by a destructive war against Antipas.[16]

Antipas' wife Herodias, and her daughter Salome, were the ones responsible for the death of John the Baptist. John rebuked Antipas for his gross immorality and defiance of the laws of Moses (Leviticus 18:16), and John paid for his courage with his life.[17]

The Gospel picture of Antipas does little to leave the reader with a favorable impression of the tetrarch. He was superstitious,[18] "foxlike in his cunning,"[19] and wholly immoral. Yet the tetrarch had a following, for mention is made of the leaven of Herod,[20] and of the sect of the Herodians.[21] When the fame of Jesus began to spread abroad, the uneasy conscience of Herod made him fear that John the Baptist had arisen from the dead.[22] He was present at Jerusalem at the time of the crucifixion, and Jesus was sent to him by Pilate. Herod thought that now he would have the opportunity of seeing a miracle performed, but he was disappointed. The same day he was reconciled to Pilate, whereas they had before been at variance.[23]

The advancement of Herodias' brother, Herod Agrippa I, to be king, while her husband remained only tetrarch, aroused the envy of this proud woman; and she prevailed upon Herod to go with her to Rome and ask for a crown. Agrippa I, however, sent letters after them to the emperor Caligula, accusing Herod of being secretly in league with the Parthians; and Herod Antipas was in consequence banished to Lyon in France, in AD 39.

4. *Philip, the Tetrarch*

Philip was the son of Herod the Great and Cleopatra of Jerusalem. At the death of his father, Herod the Great, Herod Philip inherited Gaulonitis, Trachonitis, and Paneas. His reign began in 4 BC right after the death of Herod the Great.

Philip was apparently unlike the rest of the Herodian family. He was dignified, moderate, and just. He was also wholly free from the intriguing spirit of his brothers. He married Salome, the daughter of Herodias, the same girl who danced and then asked for the Baptist's head. He enlarged the town of Paneas, and renamed it Caesarea Philippi. He reigned until AD 34.

---

[16] *Op. cit.*, XVIII.5.1; 2 Corinthians 11:32.

[17] Matthew 14:10; *Antiquities*, XVIII.5.2.

[18] Matthew 14:1ff.

[19] Luke 13:32ff.

[20] Mark 8:15.

[21] Matthew 22:17; Mark 3:6.

[22] Matthew 14:1,2.

[23] Luke 23:7-15; Acts 4:27.

5. *Lysanias, the Tetrarch (and contemporary of Philip and Antipas)*

Josephus mentions a Lysanias who was put to death about 36 BC by Mark Antony at the instigation of Cleopatra of Egypt. The negative critics say that Luke made another mistake here. Josephus mentions only one Lysanias, and he lived 60 years before the "15th year of Tiberius;" therefore Luke must be in error, the critics insist. Doesn't it seem strange that every time the critics find an apparent discrepancy between the Biblical writers and the secular historians of the ancient world, that it is always assumed that the Biblical writers must have been wrong? If there is a mistake, why must it always be the Biblical writers who were in error?

In fact, it is merely an assertion by the critics that Josephus mentions only one Lysanias (i.e., one who lived prior to 36 BC)! Davidson, in his New Testament Introduction, shows that it is most probable that Josephus mentions two men by the same name.[24] Josephus speaks of the Lysanias killed by Antony and calls him "ruler of Chalcis," and never is this person called "tetrarch" or "ruler of Abilene." Importantly, Palestine was not divided into "tetrarchies" until after the death of Herod the Great. So when Josephus also speaks of a "Lysanias the tetrarch," it must be a reference to the Lysanias of New Testament times, rather than the one of Antony and Cleopatra's time.

There is substantial evidence that two rulers of Abilene were indeed called Lysanias. The heading of this part of our study of the historical data speaks of a Lysanias who was a "contemporary of Philip and Antipas." Archaeological evidence has been found that there was a Lysanias who was tetrarch of Abilene subsequent to the death of Herod the Great. In modern times a coin was found bearing the inscription, "Lysanias, tetrarch and high priest," and the coin belongs to a period after Herod the Great's death. An inscription was also discovered at the remains of a Doric temple, called by the Arabs "the tomb of Nebi Abel," i.e., the ancient Abilene, which makes mention of "Lysanias, tetrarch of Abilene." The inscription at the temple ruins also comes from a period subsequent to Herod the Great.[25]

Lysanias the tetrarch ruled from 4 BC until c. AD 37, when his tetrarchy was given to Herod Agrippa I.

6. *Annas and Caiaphas, High Priests*

Annas

Annas was elevated to the high priesthood by Quirinius, governor of Syria, in AD 7. At this time in Jewish history, the office was filled and vacated at the caprice of the Roman governors.

Though Annas was deposed of official status by Valerius Gratus in AD 15, he continued to wield great power as the dominant member of the hierarchy. The fact that he wielded great power, even though having been deposed, is shown by the fact that he was able to maneuver five of his sons and his son-in-law, Caiaphas, into the favor of the Roman

---

[24] Davidson, Samuel, *An Introduction to the New Testament* (London: Samuel Bagster and Sons, 1848), Vol. I, p.215.

[25] *Ibid.*, p.218.

governors, and into the office of high priest.[26] Another mark of his continued influence is that long after he was deposed he was still called "high priest" – and his name appears first whenever the names of chief members of the Jews are given.[27]

He belonged to the Sadducean aristocracy, and like others of that class he seems to have been arrogant, astute, ambitious and enormously wealthy. He and his family were proverbial in their rapacity and greed. The chief source of their wealth seems to have been the sale of necessities for the temple sacrifices, such as sheep, doves, wine and oil, which they carried on in the famous "booths of the sons of Annas" on the Mount of Olives, with a branch in the precincts of the temple itself. During the great feasts of the Jews they were able to extort high monopoly prices for their goods. Hence, as He cleansed the temple twice of this market, Jesus denounced those who had made the house of prayer a "house of merchandise" and a "den of robbers."[28]

Caiaphas

Joseph Caiaphas, son-in-law of Annas, was appointed to the office of high priest by Valerius Gratus in AD 18. This is the man who suggested that Jesus should be killed so they could at once get rid of a dangerous rival and propitiate the frowns of Rome.[29] Caiaphas was deposed by Vitellius at Passover season in AD 36.[30]

7. *The 46th Year of the Building of Herod's Temple*

In the first year of Jesus' ministry, and perhaps as much as 4 or 6 months after his baptism, Jesus was in Jerusalem for the Passover Feast. While he was there, the religious leaders spoke of that as being the 46th year of the work of rebuilding the Temple.

Herod the Great began the temple in the 18th year after his accession to Jerusalem.[31] His accession to Jerusalem came in 37 BC, and thus the work on the temple began in 19 BC. Forty-six years later would bring us to the year AD 27. Since Jesus was baptized sometime before his visit to the temple in AD 27, his baptism would have been in AD 26. This checks with the 15th year of Tiberius, which we have above shown to also be AD 26.

Notably, the rebuilding of the temple was completed in AD 68, just two years before the Romans leveled it during the destruction of Jerusalem.

C. Conclusion as to the Date of the Baptism of Jesus

Two dates – namely, the 15th year of Tiberius Caesar, and the year before Jesus' first visit to the temple during His ministry – have centered on the same year of AD 26 as being the year when Jesus was baptized. None of the other historical data is violated when this date is affirmed for the baptism of our Lord.

---

[26] John 18:12; *Antiquities*, XX.9.1

[27] Acts 4:6; Luke 3:2.

[28] John 2:17; Mark 11:15-19.

[29] John 11:48-50, 18:14.

[30] *Antiquities*, XVII.2:2 and 4.3.

[31] *Antiquities*, XV.11.1.

THE DEATH OF CHRIST

A. Biblical Data

The length of Jesus' ministry has been variously figured. Taking the Synoptic Gospels as a starting point, we are shown that Jesus' ministry must have been at least two years in length. In Mark's Gospel, chapters 2-6 cover one year and chapters 7-10 comprise a second. In Luke's Gospel, one year would be needed for the Galilean ministry (chapters 4-9) and another for the later Judean ministry (chapters 10-19). From the Synoptics we learn that Jesus' ministry had to be at least two years long.

The length of Jesus' ministry is best determined by the Passovers mentioned by John in his Gospel.[32] Accepting the conclusion that John records Jesus' activities at four different Passovers, and also starting from the conclusion that the first was in AD 27,[33] we arrive at the date of AD 30 for the death of Jesus.

Scripture	*Passover*	*Event*	*Date*	
1) John 2:23	First	-- Cleansing of Temple	AD 27	1st Year
2) John 5:1	Second	-- Healing of Lame Man	AD 28	2nd Year
3) John 6:4	Third	-- Feeding of 5000	AD 29	
4) John 11:55	Fourth	-- Crucifixion	AD 30	3rd Year

When we remember that some of Jesus' activities occurred before His first visit to Jerusalem in AD 27, and that some followed His crucifixion and resurrection, then the total length of His ministry can be estimated at three and a fraction years' long.

Further Biblical data helping to date the death of Jesus are these: Pilate was governor;[34] Herod Antipas was tetrarch of Galilee and Perea;[35] Annas and Caiaphas were high priests;[36] and Jesus died at Passover time.[37]

B. Historical Data

1. *Pilate, the Governor*

The tenure of Pilate as governor of Judea has already been given above in our study of the date of Jesus' baptism. It extended from AD 26 to AD 36. Thus, an AD 30 date for the death of Jesus falls within these limits.

---

[32] That John 5:1 is indeed a Passover feast is disputed by some Bible students, and it is true that John does not in fact call it "a Passover." He simply writes, "*the* feast of the Jews." (Note the presence of the definite article in the Greek.) For further arguments that John 5:1 is indeed a Passover feast, see Hendriksen, William, *The Gospel of John* (Grand Rapids: Baker Book House, 1953), p.188-189.

[33] The AD 27 date for the first cleansing of the temple was figured by counting back from the "46th year of the building of the temple," John 2:20. See the AD 27 date figured in the paragraph about the date of the baptism of Jesus earlier in these chronological studies.

[34] Matthew 27:2; Mark 15:1.

[35] Luke 23:7ff.

[36] Matthew 26:3; John 18:13.

[37] Matthew 26:2ff.

2. *Herod Antipas, Caiaphas, Annas*

The pertinent information about these men has also already been given. As far as dating the death of Jesus by important persons is concerned, Jesus' death could have occurred anywhere between AD 26 (the earliest year for Pilate) and AD 36 (the last year of both Pilate and Caiaphas). Thus, we are driven back to reckoning the date of Jesus' death by counting the Passovers in John's Gospel.

C. Conclusion as to the Date of the Death of Christ

Taking the date of AD 26 for His baptism, and allowing for a ministry of a little over three years, we have Jesus being crucified in the year AD 30. This date fits with the historical and Biblical data without contradicting any element.

Chronology of the Apostolic Age

DATES IN THE BOOK OF ACTS

There are several places where Biblical information and historical records can be compared. First, we shall examine the book of Acts in search of famous people who also might be mentioned in secular history. Then we shall go to that secular history to learn what there is to know about the dates of these same people.[38]

A. Biblical Data
1. Pentecost, Acts 2
2. Annas and Caiaphas, Acts 4:6
3. Gamaliel, Acts 5:34
4. Candace, queen of Ethiopia, Acts 8:27
5. Paul's escape from Damascus during the reign of Aretas, Acts 9:25; 2 Corinthians 11:32, 33. (This was some time after Paul's conversion.)
6. Famine while Claudius was the Roman emperor, Acts 11:28-30
7. Death of Herod Agrippa I, Acts 12:1-23
8. Proconsulship of Sergius Paulus in Cyprus, Acts 13:7
9. Edict of Claudius against the Jews, Acts 18:2
10. Proconsulship of Gallio in Achaia, Acts 18:12
11. Tyrannus, Acts 19:9
12. The Egyptian, Acts 21:38
13. Ananias, Acts 23:2
14. Governorship of Felix, Acts 23:24, 24:1ff
15. Governorship of Festus, Acts 24:27
16. Reign of Herod Agrippa II, Acts 25:13, 26:32
17. Publius, the chief man of Malta, Acts 28:7
18. Two years in a Roman prison, Acts 28:30

---

[38] As readers look up the chapters and verses noted for the various Biblical events, they are encouraged to make a brief survey of the book of Acts, noting the major themes recorded in each chapter. This will serve as an effective preview of our study of Acts itself, once the introductory studies are completed.

19. Other helpful dates:
    - Burning of Rome (and resulting persecution of Christians)
    - Destruction of Jerusalem
    - John on the Isle of Patmos, Revelation 1:9

B. Historical Data

For Jewish information we are indebted to the writing of Josephus. From the writings of Tacitus and Suetonius we learn the pertinent information about non-Jewish people and events.

1. *Pentecost*

The church began, just as the history of the book of Acts begins, in the same year Jesus died. In the Chronology of the Gospels, this date has been determined to be AD 30.

2. *Annas and Caiaphas*

It has been shown above that Caiaphas was put out of office in AD 36. Therefore, Peter's experience before the Sanhedrin (recorded in Acts 4) took place somewhere between AD 30 and 36.

3. *Gamaliel*

There were many sects of the Jews in the apostolic age.[39] Two of the more prominent were the Pharisees and the Sadducees, and by far the more prominent of these two was the Pharisees. In Jesus' day there were two rival schools within the sect of the Pharisees – the school of Hillel and the school of Shammai. The school of Hillel upheld the honor of tradition as even superior to the Law of Moses. The school of Shammai despised tradition when it clashed with Moses. The antagonism between these rival schools was so great that it was said that even "Elijah the Tishbite would never be able to reconcile the disciples of Hillel and Shammai." Of these two schools, that of Hillel was by far the more influential in its day; its decisions have been held authoritative by the greater number of Rabbis.

The greatest teacher in the school of Hillel was Gamaliel, the grandson of Hillel. Gamaliel's learning was so great that he is considered to be one of the seven greatest teachers of all Judaism. It is even said in the Talmud that "since Rabban Gamaliel died, the glory of the Law is departed." Gamaliel died 18 years before the destruction of Jerusalem, i.e., he died in AD 52.

He is called "Gamaliel the elder" to distinguish him from his very famous grandson. The fearfully bitter prayer[40] against heretics and apostates (i.e., against Christians) which Conybeare and Howson attribute to Gamaliel the elder[41] is more correctly assigned to the grandson.

---

[39] See Special Study #9, "The Sects of the Jews," which provides more detailed information than is needed at this present point.

[40] *Mishna Sota*, 9:15.

[41] Conybeare and Howson, *The Life and Epistles of St. Paul* (London: Longman and Green and Co., 1873), p.48.

4. *Candace*

We receive no help here in dating the events in the book of Acts. Strabo, Dio Cassius, and Pliny all concur in stating that Ethiopia in the 1st century AD was governed by a succession of queens, each called Candace.

5. *The Reign of Aretas IV*

It was while Aretas was king over the area in which Damascus is situated that Paul was let out the window in the wall. Aretas IV was of the Nabatean line; in the time of Christ, Nabataea included most of the territory from the Red Sea to the River Euphrates, and its capital city was Petra. Aretas IV reigned within the rough limits of 9 BC to AD 40. The exact dates are uncertain, but he reigned longer than 47 years.

Aretas IV was enraged, as we have already seen, by Herod Antipas' disgraceful treatment of his daughter, and so made war against Herod. By AD 32 he had utterly defeated Antipas. Antipas complained to the Roman emperor Tiberius, who in a rage sent Vitellius (the Syrian *Legate*, under whose jurisdiction Damascus fell) to capture Aretas, and either bring him in alive or send in his head. Vitellius had no love for Antipas, and so made no great haste to march against Aretas. In the course of his march against Aretas, he came to Jerusalem about the time of Pentecost in AD 37. While he was in Jerusalem, word came to him of the death of Tiberius, so he at once stopped the expedition against Aretas because Caligula, the new Emperor, disliked Antipas as much as did Vitellius. We have been led to this point thus far: Paul's escape from Damascus must have been between the years AD 32 and 40, while that city was ruled over by Aretas.

Is it possible to be any more precise in the dating of Paul's escape from Damascus? At this point, a brief survey of Roman Imperial chronology is needed.

Augustus	-- d. AD 14	
Tiberius	-- AD 14-37	*(smothered to death)*
Caligula	-- AD 37-41	*(assassinated)*
Claudius	-- AD 41-54	*(poisoned)*
Nero	-- AD 54-68	*(suicide)*
Vespasian	-- AD 68-79	
Titus	-- AD 79-81	
Domitian	-- AD 81-96	
Nerva	-- AD 96-98	
Trajan	-- AD 98-117	

Now that we are acquainted with the names and dates of the Roman emperors, we are ready to proceed in our attempt to date more precisely the escape of Paul from Damascus. Acts 9:23-24 reads the "Jews plotted against Paul and guarded the gates of the city." 2 Corinthians 11:32-33 says that "In Damascus the ethnarch under Aretas the king was guarding the city." There is no contradiction involved, but there are some strange items to be noted here. 1) Damascus was under control, not of the governor of Syria in which province it normally was, but under the "ethnarch."[42] 2) The ethnarch was appointed, not by the Roman emperor, but by Aretas, the king of the Nabatean Arabs. 3) The ethnarch lent himself to the enmity of the Jews and stationed troops at each gate of the city to prevent Paul's escape. One more fact must be noted, and then we shall attempt to piece all these things together. The Romans captured the Nabatean area in 64 BC, and coins found at Damascus show Damascus still under the Roman empire (the coins have Caesar's picture on them) until AD 33 or 34. But from AD 34 to 62, no coins found at Damascus have Caesar's picture on them. After AD 62, the coins of Damascus show Nero's picture. Here is what we suggest may have happened.[43] We picture Aretas as becoming king over Damascus about the time of Tiberius' death in AD 37. Either he captured it while there was a power vacuum in the area immediately following the emperor's death, or the new Emperor Caligula bestowed the area on Aretas. Since the Romans often allowed areas with a large Jewish population (and Damascus had a large Jewish element) to keep their own method of worship and their own leaders – such leaders were called "ethnarchs" – we suppose that Aretas, copying the practice of the Romans and in order to conciliate the Jews, allowed them to have their own "ethnarch" to rule the city as his viceroy. When the Jews plotted against Paul, the ethnarch, especially if he were just new on the job, would do what he could to please his new subjects. So, having pictured Aretas as becoming "king" over Damascus about the time of Tiberius' death, we also date Paul's escape at about the same time, namely, AD 37.

6. *The Famine Under Claudius*

The imperial chronology above shows that Claudius' reign extended from AD 41-54. This famine, predicted by Agabus,[44] began in the fourth year of Claudius (i.e., AD 44) and lasted until AD 48. Josephus places it after the death of Herod Agrippa I, and during the procuratorships of Cuspius Fadus and Tiberius Alexander, which stretched from the death of Herod Agrippa I to the coming of Cumanus to be the new procurator in the 8th year of Claudius (AD 48).[45]

7. *The Reign and Death of Herod Agrippa I*

Agrippa I came into his kingdom by stages. When Philip the tetrarch died, his tetrarchy was given to Agrippa I by the emperor Tiberius. Philip died in AD 34, and his tetrarchy included Batanea, Trachonitis, and Auranitis. In AD 37 the tetrarchy of Lysanias (Abilene) was given to Agrippa I, along with the title of "king," by Caligula. In AD 40 the tetrarchy of Antipas (Galilee and Perea) was also given to Agrippa I by Caligula. In AD 41, when Claudius became emperor, he gave Judea and Samaria to Agrippa I, and Agrippa's kingdom was now more extensive than that of his grandfather Herod the Great.

---

[42] "Ethnarch" was about this time a common title of a subordinate official under Roman provincial governors. 1 Maccabees 14:45, 15:1,2; Josephus, *Wars,* II.6.3.

[43] There is a considerable difference of opinion among Bible scholars as to how to piece together all the known facts about Aretas IV being "king" of Damascus. For further arguments both for and against the position outlined in this commentary, see R.J. Knowling, "Acts," *The Expositor's Greek Testament* (Grand Rapids: Eerdmans, 1967), Vol. II, p.240.

[44] Acts 11:28.

[45] *Antiquities,* XX.5.

Agrippa I ruled over "all Judea" for three years, and then died in the spring of AD 44.[46] According to Acts 12:4ff, it was near Passover time that he died.

8. *Sergius Paulus, the Proconsul of Cyprus*

When Paul visited Cyprus with Barnabas during the first missionary journey, the island was administered by one Sergius Paulus. From an inscription data in the 12th year of Claudius (AD 52) we learn that L. Annius Bassus was proconsul then. A proconsul's normal tenure of office was one year, but the Roman senate usually elected a man for a second term. Too, it is most probable that Julius Cordus was Bassus' predecessor. Therefore, Sergius Paulus must be dated sometime before AD 50.

Thus, Paul's first missionary journey came somewhere between AD 44 (i.e., the date of Agrippa's death) and AD 50 (i.e., the latest possible date for Sergius Paulus).

9. *The Edict of Claudius Against the Jews*

When Paul came to Corinth for the first time, in the midst of his second missionary journey, he met Aquila and Priscilla, who had just lately left Rome because of an edict of the Emperor Claudius, expelling the Jews from the city.[47]

Suetonius mentions an expulsion of the Jews from Rome by Claudius, but gives no date. His account is that in consequence of frequent disturbances and riots among the Jews in Rome, Claudius drove them out. His account reads, *"Iudaeos impulsore Chresto assidue tumultuantes Roma expulit."*[48] When we combine Tacitus' account of the spread of Christianity in the city before the time of Nero,[49] it seems most likely that *Chresto* is a corruption of "Christ." If this be true, then these riots may well have been attacks made by the unbelieving Jews upon the Jewish Christians – similar to those at Jerusalem,[50] at Antioch,[51] at Iconium and Lystra,[52] and at Thessalonica and Berea.[53] At this midpoint of the 1st century, the Romans did not differentiate between Jews and Christian Jews, but considered Christianity to be simply a new type of Judaism.

Tacitus, too, speaks of an expulsion of astrologers from Italy in AD 52,[54] and some mistakenly have tried to identify that expulsion with the edict mentioned in Acts. Orosius (AD 417) dates the edict in the 9th year of Claudius (AD 49),[55] but how trustworthy this date is, is not known.

10. *Proconsulship of Gallio in Achaia*

During Paul's sojourn in Corinth (in the midst of the second missionary journey), he is brought before the proconsul Gallio. If we can date Gallio, we'll have help dating a number of events in Acts.

---

[46] *Antiquities*, XVIII.5.
[47] Acts 18:2.
[48] *Life of Claudius*, ch.25.
[49] *Annals*, XV.44.
[50] Acts 8:1-4.
[51] Acts 13:50.
[52] Acts 14:1ff.
[53] Acts 17:1ff.
[54] *Annals*, XII.52.3.
[55] *History*, VII.6.15.

There were two types of provinces in the Roman empire. If there was an army in the province to keep law and order, the province answered to the Emperor, and was governed by a "Governor" (procurator), who was appointed by the Emperor. If there was no army in the province, the province answered to the Roman Senate, and was governed by a "Proconsul," who was elected by the Senate. From AD 15-44, the province of Achaia was under a procurator, but in AD 44 the army was withdrawn, and so the province answered to the Senate thereafter. Gallio would not have been proconsul in Corinth before AD 44.

There is a fragmentary inscription from Delphi containing a letter from Claudius in which Gallio is mentioned. Scholars have dated the letter AD 52. We have noted that the Senate usually elected the proconsuls to two one-year terms. Therefore, Gallio could have been in Achaia anytime between AD 50 and 54. Sometime in those years, perhaps AD 52, Paul was brought before Gallio to be tried; and Gallio threw the case out of court.

11. *Tyrannus*

It is uncertain whether Tyrannus was a Gentile or a Jew. If he was a Gentile, he would have been a philosopher or rhetorician. If he was a Jew, he was probably a Rabbi. The Jews had their private schools in one of the two rooms of the synagogue buildings, or in the largest room of the Rabbi's home. But in either case, there is no information available regarding the dates of Tyrannus.

12. *The Egyptian*

The Egyptian was a false prophet. In the reign of Nero (AD 54-68) he stirred up his followers, and advanced from the desert to the Mount of Olives, intending to overpower the Roman garrison at Jerusalem. He promised his followers that the walls of Jerusalem would fall down before them, just as did the walls of Jericho before Joshua. However, the walls did not fall, and the Roman garrison under Felix defeated the army of the Egyptian, who fled into the wilderness.

It is not known exactly in what year the insurrection took place, but the memory of it is still in Lysias' mind. For a moment he thought that perhaps Paul was that Egyptian who had returned and, instead of being able to deceive the people again, has fallen into popular fury.

13. *Ananias*

This man was high priest when Paul was tried in Jerusalem following his arrest just after the completion of the third missionary journey. Ananias was appointed to office in AD 48 by Herod of Chalcis, a brother of Agrippa I.

During Ananias' high priesthood there were bitter quarrels between the Jews and the Samaritans. Some Galileans were massacred by the Samaritans, so the Samaritans were attacked and many of their villages plundered by the Jews. Ananias was accused of complicity in these acts of violence, and so was sent by Quadratus (who was governor of the province of Syria) to stand trial at Rome.[56] This was in AD 52. Several things resulted from the trial. Powerful influences were at work at the imperial court on the side of both

---

[56] Josephus, *Wars*, II.12:6.

the Samaritans and the Jews. But thanks to Herod Agrippa II, the Emperor Claudius gave his decision in favor of Ananias, who thereupon returned to Jerusalem to continue to discharge the functions of the office of high priest. Another result was a change of governors in Judea. The one who was governor before AD 52, Cumanus, had listened to the accusations of the Samaritans against Ananias; when Claudius decided in favor of Ananias, Cumanus was banished and Felix was appointed governor in his place. A third result of the trial concerned Jonathan. Jonathan, who had been made high priest in Ananias' absence, was murdered at the order of Felix, who had become tired of Jonathan's repeated admonitions.[57] So Ananias, on his return to Jerusalem, and without any express sanction, it seems, resumed his office; thus, he was functioning as high priest when Paul was on trial before the Sanhedrin.

Ananias was a typical Sadducee, wealthy, haughty, unscrupulous, filling his sacred office for purely selfish and political ends. It was no uncommon thing for him to send his servants to the threshing floors to take the tithes by force, while he defrauded the inferior priests of their dues and left some of them to die of starvation. His rapacity and greed became a byword, so much so that he was lampooned in a parody of Psalm 24. It went, "The temple court cried out, 'Lift up your heads, O ye gates; and let Yochanan (Ananias) ... enter and fill his stomach with the divine sacrifices.'"[58]

Ananias was put out of office in AD 59 by Agrippa II, who transferred the office to Ishmael, son of Fabi.[59] The immediate reason for Ananias' removal from office was his treatment of the lesser priests and his forceful taking of the tithes. After his disposition, Ananias retained great influence by lavishing wealth he had accumulated on those he wished to influence.

Years later, when the rebellion broke out which ended in the destruction of Jerusalem, Ananias concealed himself, but was discovered during the siege, and was murdered by the fanatical Jews (in AD 67).[60]

Somewhere before the year AD 59, Paul was on trial before the court of the Sanhedrin, presided over by Ananias.[61]

14. *The Governorship of Felix*

The event which led to the introduction of Felix into the narrative of Acts was the riot at Jerusalem (Acts 21:27). There, Paul, being attacked at the instigation of the Asiatic Jews for alleged false teaching and profanation of the temple, was rescued with difficulty by Lysias, the chief captain of the Roman garrison at Jerusalem. But Lysias, finding that Paul was a Roman citizen, and that therefore the secret plots against the life of his captive might entail serious consequences upon himself, and finding also that Paul was charged on religious rather than political grounds, sent him to Felix at Caesarea for trial.

M. Antonius Felix was a freedman of the emperor Claudius. The date of his appointment to office as governor of Judea is disputed, but it is somewhere around AD 52, after Cumanus was banished. Felix may have ruled in Samaria before his tenure over Judea.

---

[57] *Antiquities*, XX.8.5.

[58] Babylonian Talmud, *Pesachim* 57a.

[59] *Antiquities*, XX.8.8.

[60] *Wars*, II.17.9.

[61] Acts 23:1ff.

Felix seems to have obtained this appointment partly through the influence of his brother, Pallas, who was a great man in the court of Claudius.

Felix was a cruel and tyrannical ruler. He had Jonathan, the high priest, murdered by the Sicarii (a band of murderous men who carried concealed daggers, killing all who offended them).[62] Felix' wife, Drusilla, was a Jewess, whom he had seduced from her lawful husband. The only reason he kept Paul in jail was because he hoped to be bribed.[63]

Somewhere about AD 60, Felix was ordered back to Rome by Nero to stand trial for his cruelties. He would have been punished if it had not been for Pallas' intervening on his behalf. We therefore date Paul's trial before Felix about AD 58.[64]

15. *The Governorship of Festus*

Paul had been in prison for two years at Caesarea when Festus became governor in Felix' place.[65] The exact date of Festus' accession to office is uncertain; it has been placed anywhere from AD 55 to 61. There is evidence in Acts 21:38 (the Egyptian) that Paul's arrest could not have been earlier than the spring of AD 55. Thus, the accession of Festus two years later (Acts 24:27) could not have been earlier than AD 57. The latest possible date would be the summer of AD 60, for Albinus, the successor of Festus, came into office in AD 62, and Festus would hardly have ruled less than two years.

It is probable that we should take the latest date possible, for Paul said to Felix (who had begun to govern around AD 52), "You've been judge many years." An AD 60 date fits this statement better than an AD 57 date, so we date Festus' accession to office at AD 60. This would then become the date of the end of Paul's two years in prison at Caesarea.

16. *The Reign of Herod Agrippa II*

Shortly before the beginning of the voyage to Rome, Paul was tried before Herod Agrippa II in Caesarea. Agrippa II was the son of Agrippa I and Cypros (a grand-niece of Herod the Great), and was the great-grandson of Herod the Great. He was the brother of two notorious women, Bernice and Drusilla. Drusilla, as we have seen, was married to Felix.[66] Bernice was first married to her uncle, Herod, ruler of Chalcis, who soon died. She was so much with her brother Agrippa II, that scandal arose in consequence. She was suspected of living in incest with her brother.[67] She tried to allay the scandal by a marriage with Polemo, king of Cilicia; but she soon tired of him, deserted him, and returned to be with her brother. She afterward became the mistress of Vespasian, then of Titus.[68]

---

[62] *Antiquities*, XX.8.5.

[63] Acts 24:26.

[64] Some say Felix had to be in Rome before AD 60 for Pallas, they say, was not in favor after AD 55. While it is true that Pallas was not in office much after AD 52, he did not drink poison until the year AD 62. So the AD 60 date for Felix' trial before Nero is probably not far wrong.

[65] Acts 24:27.

[66] At Acts 23:24, we shall meet Drusilla again, and there we shall give more of her life story.

[67] *Antiquities*, XX.7.3.

[68] Tacitus, *History*, II.2.81; Suetonius, *Titus*, 7.1.2. Because Bernice had such a bad reputation among the

When Agrippa I died, Agrippa II was 17 years old, and was living in Rome, being brought up in the imperial household. Because of his youth, the emperor Claudius was dissuaded from appointing him to the throne of his father.[69] Judea was placed under a procurator, and Agrippa II remained in Rome. When his uncle, Herod of Chalcis, died in AD 48, his kingdom was given to Agrippa II. In the year AD 52, Claudius also gave him Batanea, Trachonitis, Gaulonitis, and Abilene, together with the control of the Temple and its treasury, and the power of appointing and displacing the high priest.[70] In AD 54 or 55, Nero added much of Galilee and Perea to his kingdom.[71]

When Festus succeeded Felix as governor of Judea, Agrippa II and his sister Bernice went to Caesarea to salute him and welcome him to Palestine. This is where the trial of Paul comes in.

Agrippa II ruled until the outbreak of the war against Rome (AD 66-70) that culminated in the destruction of Jerusalem. He first tried to persuade the Jews not to rebel. Then, when war broke into its fury, he fought on the side of Vespasian and was wounded in the siege of Gamala.[72] After the capture of Jerusalem, he moved to Rome (with his sister Bernice accompanying), where he was invested with the dignity of praetor (a court judge or governor in the provinces). He died in AD 100.

17. *Publius*

While Paul was on the isle of Melita, he healed the father of the ruler of the island. That ruler's name was Publius. His name suggests that he was a Roman. His title, which is also found in inscriptions relating to Malta, seems to mean that he was the highest Roman official on the island. No other information is known.

18. *Two Years in the Roman Prison*

If the AD 60 date is correct for the trial before Festus and the end of Paul's imprisonment at Caesarea, the dates of Paul's first Roman imprisonment would be AD 61-63.

19. *Other Helpful Dates*

The burning of Rome took place in AD 64.

The destruction of Jerusalem took place in AD 70, after a two-year siege.

We are told in early Christian literature that John was banished to the isle of Patmos in the 14th year of the reign of Domitian, which would be AD 94-95.[73] We therefore date the writing of Revelation in AD 96.

Roman people, Titus was prevented from marrying her; he finally sent her from Rome, possibly when he became emperor.

[69] *Antiquities*, XIX.9.2

[70] *Antiquities*, XX.1.3, 5.2, 8.8; *Wars*, II.12.1, 12.8, 13.2.

[71] *Antiquities*, XX.8.4

[72] *Wars*, II.16.4; IV.1.3.

[73] Jerome, *Lives of Illustrious Men*, ch.9.

C. Summary of Key Dates in the Book of Acts

From among the above historical dates, several prove to be helpful when it comes to dating the events of Acts with confidence:

AD 30 -- Pentecost
AD 37 -- Aretas IV, king of Damascus
AD 44 -- Death of Herod Agrippa I
AD 52 -- Gallio, proconsul in Corinth
AD 60 -- Festus becomes governor of Judea
AD 64 -- Burning of Rome
AD 70 -- Destruction of Jerusalem

DATES IN THE LIFE OF PAUL

Before we can make use of the above dates and finish our chronology of the apostolic age, we must know more details about Paul's life.

A. Evidence from the Book of Galatians

Paul tells about himself only in passages where he is trying to meet the objections of those who cast doubt and aspersions on his motives and work. That is what he is doing in Galatians. He is rehearsing his story because the Judaizers have attacked him.

In Galatians 1:12-13, Paul tells of his conversion. In 1:17, he tells us that after his conversion he went away into Arabia, and returned again to Damascus. Then "after three years I went up to Jerusalem," he says in 1:18. We interpret this to mean that three years after his conversion he went up to Jerusalem for the first time, and stayed 15 days. While in Jerusalem, Paul saw only Peter and James. From there he went to "Syria and Cilicia." The major cities of these countries, respectively, are Antioch and Tarsus. Galatians 2:1 then says, "After 14 years I went up again to Jerusalem." Fourteen years after what? After his conversion is one possibility. But after his first trip is the more probable interpretation.[74] Thus, adding the 3 years and the 14 years together, we find that 17 years after his conversion, Paul attends the Jerusalem Conference, as recorded in Galatians 2 and Acts 15.

B. A Comparison of Information from Acts and Galatians

Event	*Where the Event is Recorded*	
1) Damascus (saw Christ)	Acts 9:3ff	Galatians 1:12-16
Ananias		
"certain days there"	Acts 9:19-22	
Preached Christ	Acts 26:20	

---

[74] There is no way to know for certain whether the Jerusalem Conference is 14 or 17 years after Paul's conversion; we just have to see which fits best the narrative of Acts. To this commentator, the 17 years – 14 + 3 – fits best. Yet there is the possibility that the Jerusalem Conference recorded in Galatians 2:1ff was but 14 years after Paul's conversion. Many Bible students have worked out chronologies using the 14-year length of time, and their chronologies date the Jerusalem Conference at AD 48. Since we prefer the 17-year period between Paul's conversion and the Conference, our chronology shows the Jerusalem Conference in AD 51.

Event	Where the Event is Recorded	
2) To Arabia		Galatians 1:17
3) Returned to Damascus Preached Christ "Out through the window"	Acts 9:23-24	Galatians 1:17 2 Corinthians 11:33
4) First trip to Jerusalem 3 years after his conversion Saw Peter and James Warned to leave the city	Acts 9:26 Acts 9:27 Acts 22:17	Galatians 1:18 Galatians 1:18 Galatians 1:18
5) To Tarsus	Acts 9:30	Galatians 1:21
6) To Antioch (Syria)	Acts 11:26	Galatians 1:21
7) To Jerusalem Offering to the elders Apostles not there Herod's Persecution	Acts 11:30 Acts 12:25	
(1st Missionary Journey)		
8) To Jerusalem Conference 17 years after his conversion	Acts 15:1ff	Galatians 2:1ff

C. Summary of Key Dates in the Life of Paul

Having figured several dates from historical data, and using the information gleaned from the comparison of information about Paul in Acts and Galatians, we are able to construct the following chronology, beginning from Festus and working backwards:

AD 60	-- Festus comes into office
AD 58	-- Paul is arrested in Jerusalem
AD 54-58	-- 3rd Missionary Journey *(The 3rd missionary journey was 3-4 years long. Paul spent 3 months in Achaia, Acts 20:3. He spent 2-3 years in Ephesus, Acts 19:8-10 & 20:31.)*
AD 51-54	-- 2nd Missionary Journey *(On the 2nd missionary journey Paul spent 18 months in Corinth, Acts 18:11. He was tried before Gallio in Corinth somewhere about AD 52.)*
AD 51	-- Jerusalem Conference *(This event was 14 years after Paul's escape from Aretas IV, and his escape was dated in AD 37.)*
AD 45-48	-- 1st Missionary Journey *(The 1st missionary journey started after the death of Herod, Acts 12:21-25 and 13:1. Herod's death is precisely dated in AD 44.)*
AD 40-42	-- Paul is brought by Barnabas to work at Antioch *(Acts 11:25ff shows this was before Herod's death.)*
AD 37	-- Paul's escape from Damascus *(Aretas became "king" of Damascus c. AD 37, near the time of Tiberius' death.)*
AD 34	-- The Conversion of Paul *(The conversion of Paul was 3 years before his escape from Aretas, and 17 years before the Jerusalem Conference.)*

SUMMARY OF THE DATES OF THE APOSTOLIC AGE

1. The Church was begun in AD 30, the same year Jesus died.
2. Paul's conversion – AD 34.

   After his conversion in Damascus, Paul went away to Arabia, returned to Damascus, from which he made his ignominious escape in AD 37. After his escape from Aretas, Paul went to Jerusalem. After a short visit there, he went to Tarsus.

3. Paul was brought by Barnabas to Antioch – AD 40-42.

   This is after the conversion of Cornelius. And during this residence in Antioch, the Disciples are called Christians for the first time.

4. The 1st Missionary Journey – AD 45-48.

   It is about ten years after Paul's conversion that this journey begins. The Galatian churches are established during this tour. At its close, Paul and Barnabas report back to Antioch (Syria).

5. The Jerusalem Conference – AD 51.
6. The 2nd Missionary Journey – AD 51-54.

   Paul revisits the Galatian churches. He goes to Macedonia, after the vision and the call to "Come, help us!" Then he visits Berea, Thessalonica, and Athens. Then he is in Corinth and we have the trial before Gallio. He moves to Ephesus where Priscilla and Aquila are left, then he goes to Palestine, visits the Jerusalem church, and closes the journey by reporting to the church in Antioch of Syria.

7. The 3rd Missionary Journey – AD 54-58.

   The major centers visited are Ephesus and Corinth. The journey closes with the trip to Jerusalem to deliver the offering to the poor there.

8. Paul's arrest in Jerusalem – AD 58.
9. Two years in prison in Caesarea – AD 58-60.
10. Voyage to Rome – AD 60.
11. Two years in the First Roman Imprisonment – AD 61-63.

    For the rest of Paul's life, see the "Epilogue to the Book of Acts" at the close of this commentary, or see the introductory materials to the Pastoral Epistles.

12. The burning of Rome – AD 64.
13. The destruction of Jerusalem – AD 70.
14. The writing of the Book of Revelation – AD 96.

    The whole New Testament was written between about AD 45 and AD 96. As we study Acts, we shall note where the epistles of Paul are fitted in, as well as date some of the other books of the New Testament.

INTRODUCTORY STUDIES

Title of the Book

The title "The Acts of the Apostles" is generally assumed not to have been given to his work by Luke himself. We do not know what Luke's inscription (if any) was. The present title ("Acts of Apostles") is of high antiquity, found in Codices Vaticanus and Beza. Codex Sinaiticus has simply "Acts." The book is often quoted in the Early Church Fathers as "Acts." In the Muratorian Canon, "Acts of Apostles" is the recognized designation.

Such titles were added to the books after the books of the New Testament were collected.[1] The titles were written on the outside of the books, so it would be easy to pull them out of the cases where they were kept – easy in the sense of being able to tell immediately what book was being picked up. In time, each congregation of Christians would have their own collection of scrolls, the collection being kept at the place where the congregation met. Whole books were read out loud during the worship service, and thus the need for identification of what scroll was being picked up.

The propriety of the designation "The Acts of the Apostles" has often been questioned. The book is not *all* the acts of *all* the apostles. It is not even the acts of *part* of the apostles. The book is primarily the acts of Peter and Paul. Thus, other titles have been suggested in an attempt to arrive at a name that will fairly well represent the contents of the book. "Acts of the Holy Spirit (i.e., a book of conversions and non-conversions)" was suggested by McGarvey. The ASV has simply "The Acts." But there is also a book titled "The Acts" which records the life of Alexander the Great. Someone has said it may well be called "The Road to Rome." Still another has suggested the title "The Coming of the Kingdom," for the book tells of the beginning and spread of the Church.

We shall utilize the title found in our versions, knowing that such titles are the work of men, and often do not tell the whole story.

Purpose for Which the Book was Written

It was considered wise in liberal circles, a century or less ago, to doubt the historical value of the book of Acts.[2] Having cast aside the idea the book was a history of what hap-

---

[1] Conservative scholars, marshaling evidence from both the New Testament and Early Christian Literature, insist that the collecting of the books of the New Testament was accomplished in the period of AD 60-140.

[2] "Religious liberalism, liberalism, religious modernism, and modernism mean approximately the same thing. Liberalism refers more specifically to a spirit of inquiry to which nothing is sacrosanct. Modernism speaks more of the higher achievements of man in knowledge, especially critical and scientific, in the modern era. Religious liberalism is a product of modern philosophy, modern science, and modern enlightenment, which attempts to conserve the essence of Christianity in the modern or scientific or enlightened age. It strives to do this by a radical re-interpretation of the Christian faith.

"There were three movements of religious liberalism in the 19th century. The first stems from German identity-philosophy or pantheism and is represented by Schleiermacher. The second stems from the Kantian philosophy and is represented by Ritschl. The third stems from Hegelian philosophy and is represented by Biedermann.

"The religious liberals agreed in applying without reservations the critical methods used in the study of literature, history, and philosophy to the Scriptures. They generally accepted the uniformity of nature, the rejection of the supernatural, and the continuity of the human and the divine. They reinterpreted Christ

pened, F.C. Baur, of the Tubingen School, thought the book was an *eirenicon*; that is, Acts is a document of peace. His theory was this: According to Galatians 2:7ff and Acts 15:7ff, Peter and Paul had an argument, and this argument led to a split in the ancient church. Some churches followed Paul's doctrine and became known (in the terminology of the liberals) as the Pauline churches. Other churches followed Peter, rejecting Paul's teachings, and these churches became known as the Petrine churches. "Acts" was then thought to have been written by some teacher in the 2nd century AD for the purpose of showing that there was actually "peace" between these two great leaders. We reject Baur's theory.[3] The argument between the two was over Peter's actions, not his teaching. And according to Galatians, the two were in agreement. There was no split between the two that caused a rift in the church, or that led to the churches taking sides. Further, Paul and Peter taught the same doctrines. Finally, we deny that Acts is to be dated in the 2nd century (a date necessary if Baur's theory is to be sustained).

Conservative scholars have suggested several reasons why Acts came to be written.

- One thinks "Acts" was intended to be a brief for Paul's trial at Rome. This would make an excellent record of Paul's activities to be presented to the court, for it would show that he had never been found guilty in a Roman court. However, the idea that Acts was intended to be a brief has not received wide acceptance. Still, see how many times the life of Paul comes into contact with the Roman government. Felix, Festus, Gallio, Sergius Paulus, the time at Philippi, and the Roman soldiers at Jerusalem – all of these underscore the fact that no Roman ever found Paul guilty.

- Thiessen suggested that Acts meets a fourfold need: 1) The need of authoritative information concerning the activity of the leading apostles. How were they related to each other in the spread of Christianity? 2) The need to show that the Christian movement was one movement, whether the believers were Jews, proselytes, Samaritans or Gentiles. Acts shows how Jewish and Gentile believers are related to each other in the church. 3) The need to set Paul's experiences (especially his arrest and imprisonment) in the right light. 4) The need to show that God bore witness with the apostles.[4]

- Ellicott believed that Luke's purpose in writing was to show the spread of the Gospel from Jerusalem to Rome.[5]

The primary purpose, we believe, was to give the world a record of the establishment of the church, and also information on how to become a Christian. How greatly in need of material on these two subjects we'd be if we did not have Acts. We wouldn't know of Pen-

---

not as God the Son incarnate in Jesus of Nazareth but as a specially and specifically divinely filled man who perfectly reflected in terms of this earth the life of God in the soul." Bernard Ramm, *A Handbook of Contemporary Theology* (Grand Rapids: Eerdmans, 1966), p.80.

[3] Baur attempted to use Hegelian philosophy as a framework in which to explain the Scriptures. Hegel made popular the Thesis-Antithesis-Synthesis idea. Paul's theology might be called Thesis. Peter's theology might be called Antithesis. And Acts and certain other books, which take a mediating position between the two (he affirmed), could be called Synthesis. Such an attempt to interpret the Scriptures through philosophical "glasses" is to be rejected as a wrong method of hermeneutics.

[4] Henry C. Thiessen, *Introduction to the New Testament* (Grand Rapids: Eerdmans. 1954). p.185-86.

[5] C.J. Ellicott, "Acts" in *Layman's Handy Commentary of the Bible* (Grand Rapids: Zondervan, 1957), p.2.

tecost. We wouldn't know where the writer of over one-half of the New Testament came from. Where could one turn to find information on how to appropriate the results of Christ's atoning death, like the passages found in Acts?

Authorship – Who Wrote Acts?

There are two lines of evidence used to determine the identity of the human penman of the books of the New Testament.[6] One is called internal evidence – the information the book itself gives as to its author. The other is external evidence – the evidence from other sources outside the book as to the identity of the human author.

A. EXTERNAL EVIDENCE

Allusions to the book of Acts do not appear in early Christian literature as early or as frequently as they do for the Gospels or the Pauline epistles. But the allusions are ample enough to show that Acts was early recognized as an authoritative book. There are allusions in the Epistle to Diognetus (AD 130)[7] and the Didache (AD 140).[8] The words of Stephen, "Lay not this sin to their charge," appear in the Epistle of the Churches of Vienne and Lyon (AD 177), so Eusebius tells us.[9]

Quotations, not naming the author or the source, are another type of external evidence. Irenaeus (AD 180)[10] and Clement of Alexandria (AD 190) quote from Acts, the latter citing Paul's speech at Athens.[11] Tertullian (AD 200),[12] Eusebius (AD 325),[13] and Jerome (AD 400)[14] also quote from Acts.

A third type of external evidence is called annotated quotations. Such evidence is abundant. Any testimony in early Christian literature that the Third Gospel is written by Luke is testimony that Acts is by Luke, for the opening of Acts, "the first account," shows that both books are by the same author. Not fewer than fifty words are common to the two books, and are not found elsewhere in the New Testament. The Muratorian Canon (AD 170) includes this note:

---

[6] We are not at this place discussing how we arrive at the belief in the Divine inspiration of the books of the New Testament. While believing that the author of Acts had the spiritual gift of prophecy through the laying on of Paul's hands and thus would be "inspired," the thing discussed under "authorship" has to do with the human instrument used by the Holy Spirit.

[7] *Epistle to Diognetus*, ch.3, seems to have an allusion to Acts 17:24, 25.

[8] *Didache*, ch.4. has an allusion to Acts 4:32.

[9] Eusebius, *Church History*, II.5

[10] *Against Heresies*, III.15.1, quotes Acts 22:8 and 26:15. III.12.1 quotes Acts 2:30-37. And III.12.3 quotes Acts 3:6.

[11] *Stromata*, I.18, quotes Acts 2:41. I.23 quotes Acts 5:1. VI.18 quotes Acts 17.

[12] *An Answer to the Jews*, ch.7, quotes from Acts 2:9,10. *A Treatise of the Soul*, ch.57, quotes from Acts 8:9. *On Idolatry*, ch.24, quotes from Acts 15:1-31.

[13] *Church History*, III.25.

[14] Philip Schaff and Henry Wace, *A Select Library of Nicene and Post-Nicene Fathers of the Christian Church*, Second Series (Grand Rapids: Eerdmans), Vol.6, p.521, lists Acts passages referred to by Jerome.

> But the Acts of all the Apostles were written in one volume. Luke compiled for "most excellent Theophilus" what things were done in detail in his presence, as he plainly shows by omitting both the death of Peter and also the departure of Paul from the city, when he departed for Spain.[15]

Irenaeus wrote the following paragraph, which references Acts 15:39, 16:8ff, and 20:6.

> And that Luke was inseparable from Paul, and his fellow-worker in the gospel, he himself shows; not indeed boasting of it, but impelled by truth itself. For, says he, when Barnabas and John who was called Mark separated from Paul, and they sailed to Cyprus, "we came to Troas;" and when Paul had seen in a dream a man of Macedonia, saying, "Come over into Macedonia, Paul, and help us," "immediately," says he, "we endeavored to go into Macedonia, assuredly gathering that the Lord had called us to preach the gospel to them; therefore, loosing from Troas, we came in a straight course to Samothrace." And then he carefully relates all the rest of their course till they arrived in Philippi, and how they spoke their first discourse. "And we sat down," says he, "and spake to the women that resorted thither;" and who believed, and how many. And again, he says, "And we sailed away from Philippi after the days of unleavened bread, and came to Troas, where we abode seven days." And many other things he relates in order while he was with Paul.[16]

Clement of Alexandria wrote:

> As Luke, in the Acts of Apostles, records Paul to have said, "Ye men of Athens ...."[17]

Tertullian quotes Acts 2:15 and says that Luke wrote it.[18] Eusebius tells us that:

> Luke has left us two inspired volumes, viz., the Gospel and the Acts.[19]

Jerome, in his catalogue of Ecclesiastical writers, expressly attributes Acts to Luke.[20]

Thus, Irenaeus and the Muratorian Canon testify to the Lucan authorship of Acts in the Western church; Tertullian in the African church; and Clement of Alexandria in the Egyptian church.

B. INTERNAL EVIDENCE

Nowhere does the author sign his name. But the "we" sections indicate the author was one of Paul's companions.[21] All the book was written by the same author. The internal evidence thus agrees with the external – saying that the author is Luke the physician, who

---

[15] Quoted by Thiessen, *op. cit.*, p.178.

[16] *Against Heresies*, III.14.1.

[17] *Stromata*, V.

[18] *On Fasting*, X.

[19] *Amphiloch quaest*, 145.

[20] B.F. Westcott, *On the Canon of the New Testament* (London: MacMillan & Col., 1870), p.530-531.

[21] E.g., Acts 16:10ff.

was indeed one of Paul's companions, as we learn from his being named in the epistles.[22]

C. ATTACKS ON THE LUCAN AUTHORSHIP

In the last 100 years, various objections have been raised to the Lucan authorship of Acts. Let us briefly examine several of these.

It is said that Paul's companions are expressly named in Acts,[23] but that Luke is never so named, and so, evidently, he was not a companion of Paul, and therefore (it is urged) could not be the author of the "we" sections. We reply to this attack that the assertion made is too sweeping. All who appear as Paul's companions are not always named in Acts. For example, Titus is never mentioned in the book of Acts, yet he was a companion of Paul.[24] The epistles show that Luke, too, was a companion of Paul. While it is true that Paul's companions are usually named in Acts, it is not uncommon for writers to omit their own names, and to indicate their presence by another method. For example, see how the Apostle John indicates his presence in his epistles and in the Gospel especially.[25]

Some have claimed that certain portions (e.g., 20:1-15) show evidence that they were written by Timothy. But, we reply, that it is necessary to tamper with the text to make 20:1-5 look like this – in verse 4, "Timothy" must be changed to "I" – and it is supposed that when the author of this "history" incorporated this portion he changed the "I" to "Timothy." We reject such arguments as aspersions on the character of the author.

No legitimate reason has yet been advanced that would lead us to the need to abandon the traditional conclusion that Luke is the author of Acts.

Trustworthiness

In Introductory Studies, this word "trustworthiness" is used in a technical sense, meaning that the record is accurate and may be believed. It is not a sly or tricky attempt on the part of someone to deceive the readers.

A. ATTACKS UPON THE TRUSTWORTHINESS OF ACTS

Attacks upon the trustworthiness (and consequently upon the Lucan authorship) of Acts have been made at several points.

1. *Paul's Conversion (cp. Acts 9:1-19, 22:6-16, and 26:12-20)*

The negative critics maintain that there is a discrepancy within the accounts. In 9:7 the men with Paul "hear." In 22:9 it is said that they do *not* "hear." However, there is no real discrepancy here. The two Greek words at issue in the passages, "hear" (*akouō*) and "sound" (*phonē*), can each bear different connotations. The men with Paul did indeed hear (*akouō*) a sound (*phonē*), but they did not understand (*akouō*) the words (*phonē*).

The critics also maintain that there is a contrast between Luke's account and Paul's

---

[22] 2 Timothy 4:11; Colossians 4:10,14; Philemon 24.

[23] Acts 13:2,5; 15:2,40; 16:3; 18:18; 20:4.

[24] Galatians 2:3; 2 Corinthians 2:13.

[25] John 13:23, 19:26, 20:2. I.e., as "the disciple whom Jesus loved."

own claims when Acts 26:13 is compared with 1 Corinthians 15:8. It is asserted that Luke indicates Paul saw only a blinding light and heard a voice, but did not actually see a person; whereas Paul affirms that he actually saw the Lord. In reply to this attack, note Acts 9:7, which says the *companions* of Paul heard, but saw no one. The implication is that *Paul* did indeed see someone, as well as heard what was said.

2. *The Silence in Acts about the Collection for the Saints in Jerusalem*

From the epistles we learn that this offering was a thing of great importance to Paul.[26] It is argued that if Acts were a true record, it would also mention this collection as the 3rd missionary journey is reported.

However, it is not true that the book of Acts contains no specific mention of the offering for Jerusalem. See 24:17! And there are several passages that are not easily understood without being aware of the offering. For example, in Acts 20:3, Luke lists men from all the churches who were with Paul. What were they doing? 1 Corinthians 16:3 gives the answer. Each church was to send a representative, who would carry the monies collected by that congregation, so no one could say that Paul absconded with the funds. Further, note that it was at this time that Paul changed his plans as to itinerary, because of a plot of the Jews.[27] It would have been a good time for their plot, especially if Paul had all the money of the collection mentioned in Romans 15:31.

Also, note Acts 24:26. Felix was hoping for a bribe. While this is not a direct allusion to the offering, it is still an interesting aside. Perhaps Felix has heard of the tremendous amount of money Paul brought to Jerusalem, and was trying to get a bit of it.

Finally, it was not necessary for Luke to mention the collection in Acts, if he chose not to. The collection simply did not fall within the scope of his purpose for writing.

3. *The Failure to Hint that Paul Wrote Letters to the Churches*

This need not sway our confidence in the trustworthiness of Acts. It is a poor critic, who, because he finds something in one source, thinks he should find it in another. One way of responding to this objection, then, is to suggest that such information also was outside the scope of Luke's purpose. Luke is concerned about Paul's missionary labors. To say Paul wrote a letter, Luke would then have to describe the setting and occasion where Paul wrote, and how it was received. All this would have led him away from his purpose.

Another means of replying is to speculate on the question, Was Luke planning a third volume? In the book of Acts, how much is there about the life of Jesus? Only a little before the ascension, and some words of Jesus as recorded in the sermons. Luke knew that the life of Christ had been recorded in his first volume, so he little needed to refer to it in the second. It is possible that he was planning a third volume, and so did not include in Volume 2 what was to be in Volume 3.

Did Luke ever publish a third volume, perhaps a collection of Paul's epistles? What happened to Luke after Acts was written? He was with Paul some years later when 2 Timothy was written, but we do not know what happened to Luke after Paul was martyred.

---

[26] 1 Corinthians 16:1ff; Romans 15:25ff; 2 Corinthians 8:9; Galatians 6:6-10.

[27] Acts 20:3.

There are traditions that he went on preaching tours over several areas.[28] We also do not know when Paul's epistles were first collected, but it was not long after he wrote.[29] Ignatius (an early Christian writer) had an amanuensis who wrote for him. After Ignatius' death, the people wanted a collection of his writings. The amanuensis collected Ignatius' writings. If this was done for Ignatius, might it have been done for Paul's letters by Luke?

Why did Luke not say something about Paul's letters in Acts? Perhaps it was because Luke was collecting them, and was intending to publish them as Volume 3 of his history. There is some evidence that tends to substantiate such a theory. The Pastoral Epistles have a different manuscript history than the rest of Paul's epistles, which might suggest that Paul's epistles were collected in two different groups.[30]

At least, this much is true: Luke's failure to mention the letters of Paul is no strong objection to the trustworthiness of the book of Acts.

4. *The Asserted Disharmony Concerning Paul's Visits to Jerusalem*

Another objection raised against the trustworthiness of Acts, and thus against the Lucan authorship, is the assertion of a disharmony concerning Paul's visits to Jerusalem when the records of Acts and Galatians are compared. While it is certainly true that Acts 11 records a trip made by Paul to Jerusalem that Galatians does not record, the difference is related to the underlying purposes of the two documents. In Galatians Paul is arguing that his message has its source in divine revelation, and that he has not learned it from men, least of all from the apostles. Thus, in Galatians, he very carefully points out every time he had any communication with the original apostles, showing that at no time was there ever enough time spent together with them that he could have learned his gospel from them. The Acts 11 journey is omitted in Galatians, we suggest, because Paul saw no apostles on this trip. The fact that this trip to Jerusalem, about the time Herod died, is not mentioned in Galatians is because there was no possibility of learning any of his gospel on that trip.[31]

5. *The Alleged Difference in Paul's Attitude Toward the Jews*

It has been asserted that Paul's relationship to Judaism is different in the epistles than in Acts. It is said that in the epistles he is vehement in his fight against Judaism, but not so in Acts. What evidence is given to substantiate such a reconstruction? The Galatian letter is probably the most severe against Judaizers, though there are other places in his letters where he attacks the Judaizers. In Acts, the last time Paul came to Jerusalem, he even went into the temple and sponsored some men who had a vow (i.e., he paid certain fees charged to other worshipers as he was in the process of completing his own vow).[32] Chronological-

---

[28] J.M. Bebb, "Luke, The Evangelist," *Hastings' Dictionary of the Bible* (New York: Scribners, 1908), Vol. 3, p.161-162.

[29] 2 Peter 3:15ff implies that, by the time 2 Peter was written in AD 66 or AD 68, at least some of Paul's letters have already been collected.

[30] Lewis A. Foster, "The Earliest Collection of Paul's Epistles" in *Seminary Review* XIV (1967-68), #2, p.41-56.

[31] Further discussion about the apparent disharmony in the accounts of Paul's visits to Jerusalem will be found in the notes at Acts 11:30.

[32] Acts 21:17ff.

ly, the event of Acts 21 happened after the Galatian letter was written. Was Paul being consistent? Was Paul in the wrong in his actions in Jerusalem?

Paul never objected to Jewish practices as long as they were not made a matter of Christian faith. Did Paul ever forbid the offering of sacrifice, the taking of vows, the rite of circumcision? Timothy he circumcised,[33] Titus he did not.[34] Christ is the one final, complete sacrifice for sins.[35] The emphasis of Paul's teaching was that the Jew did not have to give up the ceremonies he held dear, as long as the Jew did not try to force these ceremonies on someone else as matters of faith. 1 Corinthians 9:19ff is a helpful passage in this regard. Paul was free. He had a certain liberty in Christ. Yet he became all things to all men, in order to win them.[36] (Of course, he did not do things that would compromise the faith.) Paul combated Judaizers and Judaistic tendencies when this emphasis was a specific problem in the churches, as it was in Galatia. Paul, who was a Jew before his conversion, did not ridicule and trample the Law of Moses, as was slanderously reported to the Jews at Jerusalem. Paul never said that one could not go to the temple to pray. But Paul did say this – that the keeping of the Law of Moses was no longer necessary to salvation. The New Testament nowhere says that the Old Testament (which had been revealed by God) was false, or that the Old Testament practices were now "taboo." Paul did not compromise when his freedom in Christ was at stake. But he did try to be all things to all men, wherever possible with consistent Christian principles.

There are those who say Paul made a mistake in his actions in the temple (Acts 21). The Scripture is very accurate in what it records. It also points out what is right and wrong. The Scripture does not say Paul was wrong. Therefore, we hesitate to affirm that he made a mistake in his actions here. And it is difficult to find the alleged differences between Paul's attitude as depicted in Acts and as depicted in the epistles as far as his treatment of the Jews was concerned. Believers were his brothers, unbelievers were not. And he was as generous toward all as Christian principles would permit.

6. *The Charge that Paul's Theology Does Not Match*

It has been asserted that Paul's theology in Acts does not match his theology in the Epistles, and thus the trustworthiness and genuineness of Acts is questioned. For example, some critics claim that Acts indicates that Christ's death was a simple crime wrought by the Jews, "one more act of infamy by those who always opposed the truth." But in his epistles, they claim, Paul presents Christ's death as a vicarious atonement.[37]

In fact, Acts contains very little of Paul's theology with reference to the cross in particular, so both the critics' argument and a refutation of it are based on meager evidence. Suffice it to say that Acts does not contradict what Paul writes in his letters.[38]

---

[33] Acts 16:3.

[34] Galatians 2:3.

[35] Hebrews 7:9.

[36] 1 Corinthians 9:19-23.

[37] Morton S. Enslin, "The Atoning Work of Christ in the New Testament" in *The Harvard Theological Review* (New York: Cambridge University Press, Vol. 38, Jan 1945), p.50-53.

[38] Since there rise of Liberalism some 100 years ago, just as there have been claims against the

B. ASSURANCES ACTS PROVIDES FOR ITS TRUSTWORTHINESS

Having examined the attacks made upon the trustworthiness of Acts, it is well to look at the points which serve to assure us of the trustworthiness of this book. The following points are adapted from Henry J. Cadbury, *The Book of Acts in History* (Harper, 1955). Luke wrote orderly and carefully.

1. *Fixed Dates*

Luke realizes the importance of fixed dates and connects the events given in the book of Acts with the history of the world in this time. It does not begin, "Once upon a time." In the second half of the book, Luke mentions the passage of days, more than is done in the first half – but this was because he was present for the events recorded in the latter part of the book.

2. *Geographical Knowledge and Accuracy*

We know there are differences of civilizations in different nations, and different peoples have different moral rules, political conditions, activities, etc. In all the intricacies of the different nations and peoples, Luke never makes a mistake. And this is not just a general accuracy, like would be found in a writer who avoids wording his production in such a way as to make it impossible to say he is wrong. In other words, Luke does not avoid being technically accurate. Why was he so accurate and correct? He was there! He was an accurate historian! He was inspired!

Examples of this accuracy (verisimilitude, it is called) are found all through the book. In Acts 13:7, Sergius Paulus is called proconsul of Cyprus. This is the proper term for the ruler of Cyprus, though it was denied by the negative critics for years. But inscriptions recently found show Luke to be exactly correct in the title he gives to Sergius Paulus. In Acts 13:50, he speaks of the chief men ("leading men") of Antioch of Pisidia. Archaeology has shown that "chief men" was actually the title for the city leaders of Antioch.

In Acts 16:20, 23, 35, the terms "magistrates" (*praetors*), "jailer," and "policemen" (*lictors*) are exactly correct. In 17:6, we have Paul on trial before the "city authorities" (*politarchs*). For many years the critics said there was no such title ever given to city leaders in the ancient world. Now, after some years of research, Thessalonica, thus far, is one of only two cities in the world (Monastir, Turkey, being the other) where archaeologists have found this title. An ancient inscription has been found at Thessalonica showing that that city was governed by seven politarchs.[39] In Acts 17:22, "Areopagus" is the proper term for the gathering place in Athens.

"Asiarchs" (Acts 19:31) and "town clerk" (19:35) are also exactly right terms. The Asiarchs, ten in number, were officers annually chosen from all the cities of proconsular Asia to preside over all sacred rites, and to provide at their own expense the public games

---

trustworthiness of Acts, similar attacks are made against other Bible books. These attacks are a common method used by critics in an attempt to cast doubt on the Biblical record. And not a few preachers educated in Liberal seminaries believe and preach such "assured conclusions." The reader will likely find it helpful to have a book such as DeHoff's or Halley's *Alleged Discrepancies in the Bible* in his library, in order to become acquainted with the most common of these attacks, and some of the possible answers to them.

[39] There is a picture of the inscription from Thessalonica in *Zondervan Pictorial Dictionary of the Bible* (Grand Rapids: Zondervan Publishing House, 1963), p.848.

in honor of the gods and the deity of the emperor. This necessitated their being men of high rank and great wealth.[40] The town- clerk was the city secretary. His office was to read public documents to the people, and to be chief registrar, to draft the laws, and to have custody of the archives.

Luke gives to Publius his peculiar official term, designating him as "leading man of the island" (Acts 28:7). The "soldier that guarded him" (28:16) would have been the captain of the guard, the "prefect of the Praetorian camp." There were usually two great officers so called, and it was their special duty to take charge of prisoners sent from the provinces to be tried at Rome.

Luke was an intricate observer. James Smith, who was a seaman, in his *Voyage and Shipwreck of St. Paul,* shows that Luke is accurate even in the storm and wreck. They cast goods out of the hold, threw off the rigging, bound the ship around – and precisely the proper term in Greek is used for each activity.

Every place where Luke's accuracy can be checked, he has been found to be exactly right. Verisimilitude argues for Luke's trustworthiness.

3. *Luke's Orderly Manner of Presentation is Magnificent*

In his use of speeches, Luke balances them between Peter's and Paul's just the way that a good historian of that age did. There were standards and forms to be followed in writing a history, and every good historian followed these forms. The quality of the history was judged from how adept he was in fitting the speeches into the narrative, to hold the interest of the reader. In Luke's history, the speeches are not just strung along with nothing between. Everything falls into place as we are led up to each speech. Not only this, but Luke uses seven speeches from Peter, and the same number from Paul, as well as speeches made by others, such as Gamaliel, Stephen, James, Demetrius, the Town clerk, Festus, and Tertullus. Peake has pointed out that Peter's speeches are in harmony with the language and thought of the Petrine epistles. Paul's speeches are also in harmony with his epistles.[41] Lightfoot has shown the appropriateness of Stephen's speech, and Paul's in Lycaonia.

There is a balance also in Luke's method of presenting the lives of Peter and Paul. The similarities are not forced, nor do the two men rival each other. Such a balance was the regular way of presenting a history in the 1st century. (Compare Plutarch's *Lives.*)

Peter's ministry –
   a) Began his ministry with the healing of the lame man, 3:6
   b) People sought for Peter's shadow to fall on them for healing, 5:15
   c) Peter and the sorcerer, Simon Magus, 8:20
   d) Tabitha raised from the dead, 9:32
   e) Cornelius worshiped him, 10:25
   f) Peter in the Sanhedrin, supported by Gamaliel, a Pharisee, 5:34

---

[40] It has been shown that it could cost an Asiarch the average of 3000 day's wages for a working man to help produce one of the public games. No one who had served his appointed one-year term was obliged to hold appointment a second time. Once a man had held the office of Asiarch, he retained the title for life.

[41] A.S. Peake, *A Critical Introduction to the New Testament* (London: Duckworth & Co., 1909), p.129.

g) Stephen stoned,[42] 7:58
h) Peter miraculously released from prison, 5:19
i) Peter's vision of the sheet recorded three times. Acts 10
j) Peter beaten, Acts 5:40

Paul's ministry –
a) Helped the lame man at Lystra, 14:8ff
b) People took aprons and handkerchiefs away from Paul for healing, 19:12
c) Paul and the sorcerer, Bar-Jesus, 13:8
d) Eutychus raised from the dead, 20:9-12
e) Paul worshiped at Lystra, 14:13
f) Paul supported by the Pharisees in the Sanhedrin, 23:6, 7
g) Paul stoned, 14:19
h) Miraculously released from prison, 16:26
i) His vision of Christ recorded three times, 9:22, 26
j) Paul beaten, Acts 16:22, 23

The early church noted this parallel, and carried it on. They said that both died in Rome on the same day.[43] Just because a certain parallel outline seems to be followed as the lives of Peter and Paul are presented is not reason to doubt the truthfulness of Luke. As we have said, Plutarch's *Lives* presents history by comparing the lives of great men. It cannot be said that such a practice of comparison falsified the story for either character being compared. Neither can it be said that the Acts record is falsified.

4. *From General to Particular*

Luke gives a generality, and then gives incidents, both good and bad, to illustrate the generality. For example, "They had all things common," he writes. And then he gives Barnabas as the good example, and Ananias and Sapphira as the bad example.

5. *Luke is Very Exact*

In the first twelve chapters there are Semitisms (i.e., Hebrew idioms or manners of expression showing through the Greek), and this is natural since these chapters deal with events in Palestine. After Acts 12, the Semitisms stop. Some argue this indicates a change of source, that Luke is now copying from a different source. Not so! Luke, a master writer, does this deliberately. Aristotle speaks of such a change as being *katechon* – appropriate. It would detract from the value of a modern history if a man from Brooklyn talked like a southern belle. Luke too knew the differences, and he very carefully put them in.

---

[42] Note, it is Stephen, not Peter, who is stoned. The pattern is not artificially adhered to. You cannot say this is manufactured, as some liberal critics tried to do in the 19th century. These are examples of these apostles' work. Both are preaching the same gospel and doing the same work, so you would expect some similarities.

[43] The illustration on the front cover of this book is another example of carrying on the parallelism between Peter and Paul. It is the oldest known picture of the two, same size as the original. It is taken from the bottom of a gilded cup found in the catacombs of St. Sebastian at Rome. It is estimated to come from the 3rd century, and it pictures Christ presenting a crown of life to the two apostles. The inscriptions say, "Friendship's blessing: May you live forever with thy (Savior)."

6. *Candor*

There is honesty and fidelity to the truth, in that Luke records the shortcomings of the church. He unblushingly tells of the hypocrisy of Ananias and Sapphira, the contention between Paul and Barnabas over Mark, the discontent at Jerusalem among the Hellenistic widows, and of the conflicts with the Judaizers.

7. *The Characters are Introduced Before They Become Prominent*

First we see a glimpse of a person, and then later in the book the details are filled in. Saul is introduced in Acts 8:1, before he becomes prominent at 9:1ff and 13:1ff. The same is true of Barnabas, Stephen, Philip, and John Mark.

8. *Acts is a Book of Particulars*

Luke is careful and particular details he gives. For example, 110 names are given.

Indeed, Luke provides a trustworthy history! Clear evidence points to this fact.

Dependence

The question as to the sources from which Luke derived his information concerning the events recorded in the first 15 chapters of Acts will, of course, be answered differently by those who look upon Acts as a late composition, versus those who accept it as Luke's genuine work.

The negative critics have introduced several hypotheses in an attempt to account for Luke's material on a purely naturalistic basis. Eichhorn thought Luke composed the speeches and put them into the mouths of the characters, and it has been shown that perhaps some ancient writers did indeed make up speeches.[44] While it is true that Luke is a marvelous historian, it is highly unlikely that he had the ability to do as Eichhorn suggests. Few men who have ever lived have had the creative genius necessary to do a job of manufacturing like Luke is supposed to have done. For example, Peter's speeches use the same vocabulary, and have the same theology as do Peter's epistles. Likewise, Paul's language is the same in the epistles as in the "sermons" in Acts. It would take real genius not only to make up the speeches, but to employ the same vocabulary.

Other negative critics have suggested that Luke was dependent on Josephus for some of his materials.[45] But note how these widely divergent hypotheses soon become ridiculous. One author tells us that Luke is such a genius that he is to be ranked with the great creative thinkers of all time. Another tells us that he was so dumb that he thought he could get away with taking names and places he read in Josephus, and weaving church his-

---

[44] A.T. Robertson, "Acts of the Apostles," *International Standard Bible Encyclopedia* (Grand Rapids: Eerdmans, 1949), Vol. I, p.42.

[45] R.J. Knowling, "The Acts of the Apostles," *The Expositor's Greek Testament* (Grand Rapids: Eerdmans), Vol. II, p.30ff.

tory around them to fool the people. If further reply is needed to such hypotheses, note that the evidence is sufficient to show Luke had independent, and often personal, knowledge of the events he records.

Baur, who thought Acts was an *eirenikon*, spent little time with the question of dependence. Within Baur's theory, it mattered little what sources a compiler used if that compiler merely took what material he had, changed it to suit himself, and thus accomplished his intention by giving false coloring to the lives he professes to describe. Baur's theory, as has been said, has fallen into disrepute, so his contempt for the question of "sources" has also come upon hard times.

Upon what, then, was Luke dependent? Where did he get his information? He was not there to witness for himself much of what he records in the first fifteen chapters.

Harnack, himself a liberal critic, has shown that in no part of Acts can the use of sources be proven simply on the basis of linguistic investigation.[46] It is not possible to look at a word or a phrase, and say, "This was copied from such-and-such a document." Harnack has also devastated the theory that chapters 13 and 14 and some of the "we" passages were copied from a diary of one of Paul's companions. It is possible that Luke himself kept a diary and used it as he wrote the latter part of Acts, but this is far from saying that some later writer found a diary, and copied from it as he was falsifying the record.

The book of Acts contains the text of several letters.[47] Luke probably saw these letters himself, or copies of them, or examined people who had seen the letters and knew the contents. This would be his source for these letters.

But, again, what of the events and speeches recorded in the first fifteen chapters? Where did he get his information? Most of the events were matters of public knowledge, known to all Christians. The speeches of Peter were of great importance. They would have been written down, or preserved in the retentive and practiced mind of Hebrew disciples. Likewise, Paul could have told Luke, his friend and companion, full accounts of all that he himself knew as a pupil of Gamaliel and as an agent (if not a member) of the Sanhedrin.

Luke was constantly examining eyewitnesses.[48] From Barnabas and John Mark, Luke could have learned about the origin of the church. Luke was acquainted with Philip the evangelist and could have learned from him about the events in Samaria, and on the road that led from Jerusalem down to Gaza. From James, the Lord's brother, he could have learned of the events in the Jerusalem community. Luke could have learned of some of Paul's labors from Silas, especially the journeys when Luke himself was not in the missionary party. Timothy could have told Luke of a portion of Paul's first and second missionary journeys.

So the sources on which Luke is dependent boil down to his own examination of eyewitnesses, his own experience, and the speeches of Peter and Stephen (whether in written or oral form). Many immediately appeal to a revelation from God as the source of

---

[46] Robertson, *op. cit.*, p.40.

[47] Acts 13:23-29, 23:25-30.

[48] Luke 1:1-4.

the whole of Luke's information. We would not deny the presence of such a factor (we indeed affirm the revelation and inspiration through Luke), but God has seldom done for man what man could do for himself. As far as dependence is concerned, Luke could have learned a great part of the information he records by examining the eyewitnesses of the events he was not himself a participant in. And then the Holy Spirit would have helped him choose the right words to record the truth for generations to follow.

Language

The language of Acts is good Greek, better than in the third Gospel. In Codex Beza there is an interesting variation in the Greek at Acts 11:28. It reads, "And when we had come together, a certain one of them named Agabus ...." Codex Beza is an example of what textual critics call the Western Text, which has a number of peculiarities.[49] Most textual scholars currently reject the Western readings as being interpolations, but the study of the value and place of the Western text continues, and some believe it may one day be recognized as most nearly like Luke's autograph.

Date of Writing

According to Acts 1:1, this book was written after the third Gospel was written. Luke's Gospel is conservatively dated c. AD 60, since Paul's two years in prison at Caesarea (which ended in AD 60) would have given Luke the time needed to examine the eyewitnesses to what the Gospel records (Luke 1:1-4).

Acts must have been written after the accession of Festus in AD 60. It must have been written within the lifetime of Luke, for internal and external evidence both point to this fact.

The "abrupt ending" of the narrative, after Paul's two years' abode at Rome, infers that the book was written at that time. However, various other explanations are offered for the abrupt ending.

- One idea is that Paul was killed at the end of the two years, and Luke did not want the record to end in a defeat for Paul. Certainly, it is improper to affirm that Paul died at the end of his first Roman imprisonment.[50] But even if he did die at that time, his death would not be a defeat, but a glorious entrance into life eternal, and a very fitting end to a life of service.
- Some negative critics suggest that the end of Acts was deliberately cut off so that the forgers could have time in Paul's life for him to have written the Pastoral Epistles.
- Another idea is that Paul's fate was already known to Theophilus, and therefore Luke did not include it. But this proves too much, for on the same principle, many things specified in the course of the history might have been omitted.

---

[49] Knowling, op. cit., p.41ff.

[50] See the Epilogue at the close of this commentary for a rehearsal of Paul's later life and travels.

- Another attempted explanation for the abrupt ending is that Luke stops where he does because he has shown that the command of Christ (Acts 1:8) has been executed, and because the promise given to Paul (23:11) has been fulfilled by Paul's arrival in Rome and his preaching there. But it has not at all been proved that these passages delineate Luke's specific plan for writing, or they comprise the exact compass to which he meant to carry his history.

- Recently, it has been suggested that Luke died, and that his work was published posthumously, and this accounts for the abrupt ending.

The effective way in which the narrative of Acts ends[51] is a sufficient answer to those who try to explain the abrupt ending in some other way. The simplest explanation for the abrupt ending is that Luke has recorded all the events that have happened up to the time he wrote.

- Luke does not tell us about Paul's death because, it appears, Paul was not put to death at this time. The Pastoral Epistles indicate that Paul was released from the first Roman imprisonment and traveled extensively.

- The book of Acts does tell (indirectly) what happened to Paul. He has waited two years for his prosecutors from Palestine to come. A fragment has been found in Egypt that shows the practice of the courts. If a man's accusers didn't come within two years' time, the accused was set free.[52] There was the possibility that the accusers would be put to death if they brought a false case, or if Nero thought they had wasted his time in the court. The Jews hadn't been able to prove their case in Palestine in courts that might be inclined to be favorable to them. How could they expect to prove their case before Nero in Rome? It seems likely that Paul's accusers just weren't willing to risk their own necks to prosecute the case in Rome.

- Furthermore, the epistles written from the first Roman imprisonment sound as if Paul soon expects to be free.[53]

So we tend to believe that the prosecutors didn't arrive, and after Paul had waited the two years, he was released from his first Roman imprisonment. About at that time, Luke wrote the Acts record.

Paul's two years in Rome would have ended in AD 63, and we give this date to Acts as the date of writing.

Place of Writing

Acts was written in Rome. Even those who deny the authenticity agree with the conclusion that Rome is the place of writing.

---

[51] See notes at 28:31 on the effectiveness of the close of the book.

[52] H.J. Cadbury, "Roman Law and the Trial of Paul," *Christian Beginnings*, edited by F.J. Foakes-Jackson and Kirsopp Lake (Grand Rapids: Baker, 1966), Vol. 5, p.297ff.

[53] Cf. Philemon 22; Philippians 1:24-26.

Destination

Acts 1:1 addresses the letter to Theophilus, who probably was the patron of this book, just as he was of the Gospel. The patron bore the cost of having the book published.

The book also, in the providence of God, is intended for all the church (as is evidenced by its inclusion in the New Testament Canon), in order that the church would have an inspired history of her beginning, and of the early spread of Christianity.

Integrity

"Integrity" deals with the wholesome preservation of the text substantially as it proceeded from the pen of Luke. Worded another way, does Acts appear in substantially the same form in all the manuscripts that are extant of it, and in the same form that it appears in our versions? If various portions are missing consistently in the manuscripts, there might be reason to suggest that it was not all written at once, or that some verses have been included that were not in the autograph.

Concerning the matter of integrity, scholars are agreed that the book of Acts is substantially in the same condition as that which proceeded from the author. True, the extant works of the Early Church Fathers do not contain many quotations from Acts. But the book was evidently not much read in the early church, perhaps because it was not so much about Christ as some of the other books which were regularly read.

There are a few interpolations in the book, but not many of any length or consequence. The most notable is probably 8:37.

Characteristics

There are a number of striking features about the book. It is a great missionary book. It recounts the founding of the church. It tells of the spread of Christianity from Jerusalem to Rome. It is the inspired history of the first thirty years of the church's growth.

Acts is also the inspired record of the advent, mission, and operations of the Holy Spirit.

And the book furnishes the background for at least ten of Paul's epistles. We find here the historical setting for 1 and 2 Thessalonians, 1 and 2 Corinthians, Galatians, Romans, Colossians, Philemon, Ephesians, and Philippians. It is also likely that Paul is the author of Hebrews; if so, the book of Acts furnishes the background for the writing of Hebrews, written we suppose from the first Roman imprisonment.

The Value of Introductory Studies

Why spend so much time on the introductory problems? Why not just plunge into a verse-by-verse study of the book? Why not just take the Bible (and in this case. Acts in particular) as inspired? Well, can one put inspiration into a test tube and isolate it, and thus exhibit it? No! Does the fact that a certain quire of paper has the words on it, "The Holy Bible," make that quire any more valuable than the quire that reads, "Romeo and Juliet"?

Here is why we spend so much time on introductory studies. First, where the Bible crosses history, we are historical. Where faith is necessary, we will believe, provided there is evidence on which to base that belief. What is belief? Carnell has said, "Faith is whole-soul trust in God's Word as true because of the sufficiency of the evidence."[54] Christians are not afraid to examine the evidence on which their faith is based. Christianity is not a religion made up of a group of credulous, thick-headed, and unenlightened ignoramuses. We are pleased to examine the evidence on which our faith rests! If the Bible can be proved to be true in all points where it can be tested, then who can say it is false in the points where it cannot be tested? And it has been shown to be true where it can be tested. So although the Bible's claims to inspiration cannot be tested per se, we believe that claim because the Bible is true in all the places where it can be tested.

Second, we spend time on introductory studies because the effort of men to deny God's record is incredible! We wish each Christian to be familiar with these attempts. If men are spending so much time trying to deny the trustworthiness of the record, we must be able to meet their false teaching and refute it so that men may know the truth. Christians must have a firm knowledge of the Living Word.

Third, the method of interpretation believed most likely to present to us the Word of God is the method called grammatico-historical. By means of introductory studies, we can arrive at the historical situation out of which a letter came, and to which it is addressed. Knowing these facts helps us to understand the book and to make proper application of it to our day and time.

Finally, the Restoration Movement is built upon the book of Acts. If the book of Acts is false, as some claim, then so is much of the Restoration Movement. We must know upon what kind of foundation our convictions rest. This is why time must be spent on the problems presented as part of the introductions to the New Testament books.

---

[54] E.J. Carnell, *An Introduction to Christian Apologetics* (Grand Rapids: Eerdmans, 1952), p.66.

Outline of the Book of Acts

I. THE CHURCH IN JERUSALEM. 1:1-7:60

   A. The Preface. 1:1-5
   B. The Ascension of Christ. 1:6-11
   C. The Waiting in Jerusalem. 1:12-14
   D. The Place of Judas Filled. 1:15-26
   E. The Apostles Baptized with the Holy Spirit. 2:1-4
   F. The Effect on the Multitudes. 2:5-13
   G. Peter's Pentecost Sermon. 2:14-36
   H. Effect of Peter's Sermon. 2:37-41
   I. The First Days of the Church of Christ. 2:42-47
   J. The Lame Man Healed. 3:1-11
   K. Peter's Second Sermon. 3:12-26
   L. The First Persecution by the Sanhedrin. 4:1-31
      1. The Men Arrested. 1-4
      2. Peter's Defense Before the Council. 5-12
      3. A Private Consultation. 13-17
      4. Further Preaching Forbidden. 18-22
      5. Report of the Two Apostles and Prayer of the Twelve. 23-31
   M. Unity and Liberality of the Early Church. 4:32-37
   N. The First Church Discipline. 5:1-11
   O. A Period of Peaceful Growth. 5:12-16
   P. Second Persecution by the Sanhedrin. 5:17-42
      1. Peter and All the Apostles are Imprisoned. 1-25
      2. Peter's Address to the Sanhedrin. 26-32
      3. The Speech of Gamaliel. 33-42
   Q. Seven Men Chosen to Serve Tables. 6:1-7
   R. Stephen Arrested and Falsely Accused. 6:8-15
   S. Stephen's Defense Before the Sanhedrin. 7:1-58
      1. The Case of Abraham & the Patriarchs – An Emphasis on God. 1-16
      2. The Case of Moses in Egypt – An Emphasis on Moses. 17-29
      3. The Case of Israel in the Wilderness – An Emphasis on the Law. 30-43
      4. The Case of the Tabernacle and Temple – An Emphasis on the Temple. 44-50
      5. The Application. 51-53
   T. Stephen Stoned to Death. 7:54-60

II. THE CHURCH IN JUDEA AND SAMARIA. 8:1-12:25

   A. The Jerusalem Church Dispersed. 8:1-4
   B. The Labors of Philip. 8:5-40
      1. Philip in Samaria. 5-13

2. Peter and John in Samaria. 14-25
3. Philip and the Eunuch. 26-40
C. A Harmony of the Early Life of Paul. 9:1-30, 22:3-21, 26:4-20, and Galatians 1:11-21
   1. Paul's Youth.
   2. Paul in Jerusalem
   3. Paul's Trip to Damascus.
   4. Paul's Conversion in Damascus.
   5. Paul in Arabia.
   6. Paul Back in Damascus.
   7. Paul Again in Jerusalem.
   8. Paul in Tarsus and Antioch.
D. Another Period of Peaceful Growth. 9:31-43
   1. The Church Edified. 31
   2. Peter Cures Aeneas at Lydda. 32-35
   3. Peter Raises Dorcas at Joppa. 36-43
E. The Conversion of the First Gentile (Cornelius) to Christianity. 10:1-11:18
   1. Peter at Caesarea. 10:1-48
      a. Cornelius sends to Joppa for Peter. 1-8
      b. Peter has a vision about clean and unclean things. 9-16
      c. The delegation from Cornelius finds Peter in Joppa. 17-23a
      d. Peter meets Cornelius. 23b-33
      e. Peter's sermon. 33-43
      f. The results. 44-48
   2. Peter at Jerusalem Defends His Preaching to the Gentiles. 11:1-18
F. The Church Established in Antioch. 11:19-26
   1. Beginning of the Work in Antioch. 19-21
   2. The Jerusalem Church Sends Barnabas to Antioch. 22-24
   3. Barnabas Brings Paul to Antioch. 25-26
G. The Judean Famine and Relief from Antioch. 11:27-30
H. Persecution of the Church by the Civil Government. 12:1-25
   1. James Beheaded and Peter Imprisoned. 1-11
   2. Peter Leaves the City and the Guards are Slain. 12-19
   3. The Death of Herod and the Return of Barnabas and Paul. 20-25

III. THE CHURCH IN THE UTTERMOST PART OF THE EARTH. 13:1-28:31

A. The First Missionary Journey. 13:1-14:28
   1. At Antioch of Syria. 13:1-3
   2. At Seleucia. 13:4
   3. In Salamis. 13:5
   4. At Paphos. 13:6-12
   5. In Perga. 13:13
   6. In Antioch of Pisidia. 13:14-52

7. At Iconium. 14:1-6
  8. In Lystra. 14:7-20
  9. At Derbe, Then Back to Lystra, Iconium, and Antioch. 14:21-23
  10. Through the Provinces of Pisidia and Pamphylia. 14:24
  11. At Perga and Attalia. 14:25
  12. In Antioch of Syria. 14:26-28
B. The Conference in Jerusalem. 15:1-35
C. The Second Missionary Journey. 15:36-18:22
  1. In Antioch of Syria. 15:36-40
  2. In Syria and Cilicia. 15:41
  3. At Derbe and Lystra. 16:1-3
  4. Through Iconium and Pisidian Antioch. 16:4-5
  5. Through Phrygia and Galatia Toward Troas. 16:6-8
  6. At Troas. 16:9-10
  7. Through Samothrace and Neapolis. 16:11
  8. In Philippi. 16:12-40
  9. Through Amphipolis and Apollonia. 17:1a
  10. At Thessalonica. 17:1b-9
  11. At Berea. 17:10-14
  12. At Athens. 17:15-34
  13. At Corinth. 18:1-17
  14. At Cenchrea. 18:18
  15. At Ephesus. 18:19-21
  16. At Caesarea and Jerusalem, and the Syrian Antioch. 18:22
D. The Third Missionary Journey. 18:23-21:16
  1. In Antioch of Syria and Through the Provinces of Galatia and Phrygia. 18:23
  2. Apollos in Ephesus and Corinth. 18:24-28
  3. Paul's Ministry in Ephesus. 19:1-41
    a. Paul corrects some on the baptism of John. 1-7
    b. Paul preaches in the synagogue and school of Tyrannus. 8-10
    c. Miracles worked. 11-20
    d. Paul's future plans and the two sent to Corinth. 21-22
    e. The riot of Demetrius and the silversmiths. 23-41
  4. From Ephesus to Troas to Macedonia. 20:1-2
  5. At Corinth. 20:3
  6. From Corinth to Philippi to Troas. 20:4-6
  7. In Troas. 20:7-13
  8. At Assos and at Mitylene. 20:14
  9. A Voyage Past the Islands of Chios and Samos to Miletus. 20:15
  10. In Miletus. 20:16-38
  11. At Cos, Rhodes, and Patara. 21:1-2
  12. Sail by Cyprus and Stay at Tyre. 21:3-6
  13. In Ptolemais. 21:7
  14. At Caesarea. 21:8-14
  15. To Jerusalem. 21:15-16

E. The Last Years of the Apostle Paul. 21:17-28:31
   1. Paul's Last Visit to Jerusalem. 21:17-23:30
      a. His reception by the church. 21:17-26
      b. Paul is arrested. 21:27-36
      c. Paul obtains permission to address the mob. 21:37-40
      d. Paul's defense in the Hebrew language. 22:1-21
      e. The response of the mob, and Paul imprisoned. 22:22-30
      f. Paul's defense before the Sanhedrin. 23:1-10
      g. The Lord encourages Paul. 23:11
      h. The plot to kill Paul. 23:12-30
   2. At Antipatris. 23:31-32
   3. Paul's Two-Year Imprisonment at Caesarea. 23:33-26:32
      a. Paul is presented to Felix. 23:33-35
      b. Paul's trial before Felix. 24:1-23
      c. Paul before Felix and Drusilla. 24:24-27
      d. Paul's trial before Festus. 25:1-12
      e. Paul's defense before Herod Agrippa II. 25:13-26:32
         1) Herod Agrippa II visits Festus. 25:13-22
         2) Paul appears before Herod Agrippa II. 25:23-27
         3) Paul's sermon to Herod Agrippa II. 26:1-23
         4) Interchange between Paul, Festus, and Herod Agrippa II. 26:24-29
         5) Agreement about Paul's innocence. 26:30-32
   4. The Voyage to Rome. 27:1-28:15
      a. From Caesarea to Sidon. 27:1-3
      b. Under the lee of Cyprus to Myra. 27:4-6
      c. To Cnidus and under the lee of Crete. 27:7
      d. At Fair Havens. 27:8-15
      e. Under the lee of Clauda. 27:16-17
      f. Storm and shipwreck. 27:18-44
      g. At Malta. 28:1-10
      h. At Syracuse. 28:11-12
      i. At Rhegium and Puteoli. 28:13-14
      j. At the Market of Appius and the Town of the Three Inns. 28:15
   5. Paul's First Roman Imprisonment. 28:16-31
      a. Paul arrives at Rome. 16
      b. Paul preaches to the Jews. 17-29
      c. Paul spends two years in custody. 30-31

COMMENTS ON THE ACTS OF THE APOSTLES

I. THE CHURCH IN JERUSALEM – Acts 1:1-7:60

A. The Preface. 1:1-5

1:1 – *The first account I composed, Theophilus, about all that Jesus began to do and teach,*

The first account. The word "account" (literally, "word" or "discourse") had been used by Xenophon as Luke uses it, of what we would call "volumes."[1] As noted in the Introductory Studies, the reference is to the first volume written by Luke, the Gospel of Luke.

I composed. The author of both this book and the third Gospel is Luke. See the discussion on "Authorship" in the Introductory Studies.

Theophilus. What or who is designated by this word? When translated, the Greek word means "friend of God" or "lover of God." Because of this, it has been supposed that Luke did not refer to any particular individual, but that the third Gospel and the book of Acts are addressed to anyone who is a "friend" or "lover of God." However, there are several lines of evidence which show that such a generalization need not be made, that Theophilus was indeed a man living in the 1st century. The title, "most excellent,"[2] given to him in the preface of the Gospel is strongly in favor of this opinion. The name itself was very common among both among Jews (Jedidiah) and Gentiles. It was an ordinary personal name in use from the 3rd century BC onwards.

The title "most excellent" perhaps tells us about this man. By some, this title has been supposed to express the *character* of Theophilus. But its use in the 1st century would lead us to suppose that it denoted *rank* or *office*. The word appears only three other times in the New Testament, and each time is given to men of high *office*.[3] The title was often used to denote a member of the Roman equestrian order. It is therefore probable that Theophilus was some distinguished Roman or Greek, who had been converted to Christianity. He was most likely, from Luke's connection with Antioch (Luke was probably from Antioch of Syria), a nobleman of Antioch (though some Bible students believe he was from Alexandria or Rome).

Josephus tells us that the High Priest Jonathan (who succeeded Caiaphas in AD 36) had a brother named Theophilus. Jonathan had not been in office very long when he was deposed by Vitellius.[4] Theophilus was then given the office of high priest of the Jewish

---

[1] *Anabasis*, II.1; *Cyrop.*, VIII.1.2.

[2] Luke 1:3.

[3] The three cases where the title "most excellent" appear in the New Testament are Acts 23:26 and Acts 24:3 where the Roman governor Felix is so addressed, and Acts 26:25 where the Roman governor Festus is similarly addressed.

[4] *Antiquities*, XVIII.5.3.

people. He held this position from AD 37-41. Some writers affirm that Luke's two volumes were addressed to this man after he somehow had been converted to Christianity, but such a conclusion is more than we can know for certain. Despite the evident apologetic motive in Luke's history, it is equally outstripping the evidence to regard Theophilus as the defense lawyer for the hearing of Paul's appeal to Caesar. Actually, we know little about this man, even were we to credit the old tradition that he eventually became bishop of Caesarea Philippi.

What was Luke's purpose in addressing this book to Theophilus? One purpose might be to give Theophilus a history of the early Church. A more likely suggestion is that Theophilus was the patron of the book. He would see to the circulation of a large number of exact copies. He would pay for the publication of the book. It was common to name the patron who was sponsoring the book in the prologue.

> Such dedications were common form in contemporary literary circles throughout the Roman Empire. For example, Josephus dedicated his *Autobiography*, his *Jewish Antiquities*, and his treatise *Against Apion* to a patron of the name of Epaphroditus. At the beginning of his first volume *Against Apion*, he addresses him as "Epaphroditus, most excellent of men"; and he introduces the second volume of the work with the words, "By means of the former volume, my most honored Epaphroditus, I have demonstrated our antiquity." These opening words are remarkably parallel to those of Luke's second volume.[5]

About all that Jesus. The "all" is evidently not absolute. We do not have recorded in Luke's Gospel, or in any other Gospel, absolutely *all* the things Jesus did. Each Gospel omits some materials that the other evangelists included in their Gospels. Jesus' earthly life lasted about 35 years. Of these years the Gospel writers are mainly concerned with the last 3½ years. And of these last years, there are recorded events from only about 40 days.

The name "Jesus" means "salvation is of Jehovah." Jesus is His name. Christ is His title; it means "the anointed One" and is the New Testament equivalent to the Old Testament word "Messiah."

Began to do and teach. This is a Hebrew form of expression, meaning the same thing as "what Jesus did and taught." Some have read more into the word "began" than Luke intended. A.T. Robertson, for example, makes Acts the continuation of the work of Christ, picturing Jesus as carrying on His work from His throne in Heaven.

> The Acts, according to Luke, is a continuation of the doings and teachings of Jesus. "The following writings appear intended to give us, and do, in fact, profess to give us, that which Jesus *continued* to do and teach after the day in which he was taken up."[6]

This commentator doubts that we should read so much into this word "began" as Robertson wishes to do. Certainly, Acts is a record of the continuation of the redemptive plan of God that involved the incarnation and the cross, and we also believe that Jesus is involved in God's providential acts even in our world. But the word "began" in Acts 1:1 is likely not the proof text for either of these doctrines.

---

[5] F.F. Bruce, *The Book of the Acts*, NICC (Grand Rapids: Eerdmans, 1956), p.32.

[6] A.T. Robertson, *Word Pictures in the New Testament* (Nashville: Broadman, 1930), Vol. III, p.4.

The verb "begin" is specially characteristic of Luke's Gospel, in which he uses it not less than 31 times. So its occurrence at the beginning of Acts is, accordingly, as far as it goes, an indication of the identity of the author.

"To do" would refer to Jesus' miracles and acts of benevolence, and includes all that He did for man's salvation. It probably includes His sufferings, death, and resurrection as part of that which He did to save man.

"To teach" speaks of His doctrines. This whole phrase, then, is a simple summary of the contents of volume one of Luke's books. Verse 2 continues this summary statement.

1:2 – *until the day when He was taken up, after He had by the Holy Spirit given orders to the apostles whom He had chosen.*

Until the day. The ascension took place on the 40th day after the resurrection (Acts 1:3). Luke 24:51, which is the close of Luke's first volume, also speaks of the ascension. Luke reminds Theophilus that in the first volume, the narrative ended with the ascension of Jesus.

When he was taken up. "Taken up" refers to the ascension of Jesus into Heaven. He was taken up in a cloud, and is represented as having gone up into Heaven (Acts 1:9).

After. Jesus ascended after He gave the commandment about to be mentioned.

He ... by the Holy Spirit. What exactly was done by the help of the Holy Spirit depends on with which verb this phrase is taken. It can be taken with "chosen," meaning He chose the apostles by the help of the Holy Spirit, and this is the way the Syriac and Ethiopic versions translate the verse. It can be taken with "taken up," meaning Christ was taken up to Heaven by the power of the Holy Spirit. Or it can be taken with "given orders," meaning Christ acted by the special aid of the Holy Spirit when He gave the Great Commission, and this is the way the NASB translators have handled the verse. It is repeatedly declared in the Scriptures that the Holy Spirit was abiding in Christ and empowering Him,[7] so the NASB rendering is in harmony with what the Bible teaches elsewhere.

Had given orders. The "orders" evidently in Luke's mind are those in what we call the Great Commission, the command to preach the gospel to all nations. Before His death, Christ was not ready to have His name proclaimed to the world,[8] but here in Acts the commission is no more limited. It might even be said that the Great Commission is the key to Acts.[9]

To the apostles whom He had chosen. The apostles are the eleven who remained after the treason and death of Judas Iscariot. An account of His choosing the 12 apostles is found in Matthew 10:2-4; Mark 3:13-19; and Luke 6:13-19.

---

[7] Isaiah 61:1; Luke 4:18; Acts 10:38; Matthew 12:28; Hebrews 9:14.

[8] Matthew 16:20.

[9] Matthew 28:18-20; Mark 16:15-18; Luke 24:44-49; John 20:21. 22.

1:3 – *To these He also presented Himself alive, after His suffering, by many convincing proofs, appearing to them over* **a** period of *forty days, and speaking of the things concerning the kingdom of God.*

To these He also presented Himself alive. Jesus appeared to the eleven apostles, and to others, inhabiting the same body He lived in before He was crucified, save it was now a glorified body. The resurrection of Jesus from the dead was the great fact on which the truth of the Gospel was established.

After His suffering. Luke thus reminds us of the torture and anguish that preceded the crucifixion, and the exquisite pain and pressure involved in the suffering and death on the cross.

By many convincing proofs. This word does not occur elsewhere in the New Testament. In Greek authors it denotes an infallible sign or argument by which anything can be certainly known.[10] The word speaks of proofs that carried a certainty of conviction, as contrasted with those that were only probable or circumstantial.

The evidence that Jesus was alive after his death was such as could not deceive or could not be mistaken. That evidence consisted in His eating with them, talking with them, meeting them at various times and places, working miracles,[11] and uniformly showing Himself to be the same friend with whom they had associated for more than three years. He was touched and handled by those who knew Him.[12] And in the age in which we live, to date a letter or sign a check is to indirectly acknowledge the resurrection of Jesus, for the date we put on our correspondence is an "A.D." date ("in the year of our Lord"). The facts of the life, death, and resurrection of Jesus as the only begotten Son of God are so well written into the fabric of two thousand years of history that to deny them would be to disengage oneself from history, society, and the very institutions in which he now lives. It would be as easy, if not easier, to deny the historical facts supporting the life of Julius Caesar as it would be to deny the historical facts of the resurrection of Christ. Jesus appeared at intervals to His apostles in a manner which could leave no doubt in their minds that He was alive again, risen from the dead!

Appearing to them over *a period of* **forty days.** There are no less than 13 different appearances of Jesus to His disciples recorded in the New Testament.

Appearances on the day of the Resurrection (the Lord's Day)
1) Mary Magdalene – Mark 16:9-11; John 20:11-18
2) The Women – Matthew 28:9-10
3) Two on the way to Emmaus – Luke 24:13-22
4) Peter – 1 Corinthians 15:5; Luke 24:36-43; John 20:19ff
5) The Ten – Mark 16:14; Luke 24:36; John 20:19ff

---

[10] The word *tekmērion* is defined by Aristotle as "the necessarily convincing proof," in *Rhet.* I.2.16.

[11] John 21:6,7.

[12] Matthew 28:9.

Appearance on the Lord's Day, one week after the resurrection
1) The Eleven – John 20:26-31

Other Appearances
1) The Seven by the Sea of Galilee – John 21:1-23
2) The 500 (Great Commission) – 1 Corinthians 15:6; Matthew 28:16-20
3) In Jerusalem (Commission repeated) – Mark 16:15-18
4) James – 1 Corinthians 15:7
5) The Disciples (further commission) – Acts 1:3-8; Luke 24:44-49
6) The Ascension – Acts 1:9-12; Mark 16:19-20; Luke 24:50-53
7) Stephen – Acts 7
8) Paul – Acts 9

The idea conveyed by the Greek verb and preposition here is that our Lord was not with the apostles constantly, as He was before the resurrection, but that He came and again disappeared (Chrysostom). They were intermittent appearances, spread over 40 days.

Notably, it is this verse that tells us there were 40 days between Jesus' resurrection and ascension. And it is this verse, too, that tells us there were less than 10 days between His ascension and the day of Pentecost.

And speaking of the things concerning the kingdom of God. He was not only *seen* by them, but he continued the same topics of teaching as before His sufferings (thus showing He was the same person, and that His heart was still intent on the same great work). What did he teach during these 40 days? The Gnostic schools which flourished in the 2nd century claimed that He gave certain esoteric (confidential) teachings to His disciples, teachings not recorded in the canonical literature, teachings of which they themselves were the custodians and interpreters. On the contrary, Luke here plainly says that Jesus taught concerning the kingdom of God. This implies, it is obvious, much unrecorded teaching of Jesus. Yet, the close of the Gospels points out the general character of these teachings of Jesus. After we have discussed what the "kingdom of God" is, we shall list some of these teachings.

The kingdom of God. Are the terms "kingdom of God" and "kingdom of heaven" merely different ways of saying the same thing? Some say no, asserting that the "kingdom of heaven" refers to the redeemed in heaven (or in a Millennial kingdom), whereas the "kingdom of God" refers to the redeemed who are still living on earth. However, there is abundant evidence that very often the terms are synonymous. Compare Matthew 4:17 and Mark 1:14-15, both of which tell of the beginning of Jesus' ministry. Compare also Matthew 5:3 and Luke 6:20, both of which tell of the Sermon on the Mount. Or compare Matthew 10:7 and Luke 9:1-2, both being instructions to the disciples.[13] "Kingdom of heaven" and "kingdom of God" are but different terms signifying the same thing.

---

[13] For a more complete listing of such passages showing how the kingdom of heaven and the kingdom of God and the church are the same thing, see Jesse W. Hodges, *Christ's Kingdom and Coming* (Grand Rapids: Eerdmans, 1957), p.121ff.

Further, in many passages, the Kingdom ("of heaven" or "of God") and the "Church" are merely different ways of referring to the same thing. Consider the language of Matthew 16:18-19, where the terms are used evidently synonymously. The way the "kingdom" is spoken of before and after Pentecost is another evidence. Through the Gospels, and up until the day of Pentecost, it is predicted that the kingdom is still future ("at hand"). But through Acts and the Epistles, after Pentecost when the church was established, the kingdom is spoken of as being in existence (cf. Colossians 1:13; Revelation 1:6).[14]

Things concerning the kingdom. What were these things Jesus discussed? Jesus gave the apostles instructions about the organization, spread, and edification of His church. Among those things that Jesus taught His disciples during this period of 40 days was that "repentance and remission of sins should be preached in His name unto all the nations, beginning from Jerusalem ... You are to stay in the city until you have been clothed with power from on high."[15] Jesus would have pointed out the true interpretation of the Old Testament prophecies concerning the Messiah.[16] He spoke of the disciples' mission to the whole world, and the admission of penitent believers into the church by baptism.[17] He spoke of His own perpetual presence with His church.[18] He promised supernatural powers and divine protection for the apostles.[19]

1:4 – *And gathering them together, He commanded them not to leave Jerusalem, but to wait for what the Father had promised, "Which,"* **He said,** *"you heard of from Me;*

And gathering them together. Note the reading given in the margin, "eating with them," a reading found also in the Latin Vulgate, Syriac, and Ethiopic versions. There is a manuscript variation in this place, with the better reading being the one found in our text.

The apostles had scattered after the death of Christ. This verse tells us He assembled them together in order to give them instructions regarding their conduct after His ascension. When this meeting took place does not appear from Luke's account. It is not, apparently, the day of the ascension, but rather some days before, for verse 6 begins the record of the day of the ascension. The place where they were (Jerusalem) tends to indicate that this event did not happen on the day of the ascension.

He commanded them not to leave Jerusalem. Why did Jesus command them not to depart from Jerusalem? According to the Old Testament prophets, the first preaching of the gospel and the beginning of the church were to take place in Jerusalem. The law was to go forth from Zion, and the word of God from Jerusalem (Isaiah 2:3).

---

[14] See notes at Acts 14:22 for a further discussion of the "kingdom."

[15] Luke 24:47-49.

[16] Luke 24:26, 44-45.

[17] Matthew 28:19.

[18] Matthew 28:20.

[19] Mark 16:15-18; Luke 24:49; Acts 1:4.

But to wait for what the Father had promised. The thing promised was the descent of the Holy Spirit. Jesus came to earth, and then went back to the Father. To take His place, He sent the Holy Spirit, the Comforter. The coming of the Holy Spirit had been promised by the Father in the Old Testament, and by God through the mouth of Jesus during His earthly ministry. When Jesus promised it, it was just as though God Himself had spoken.[20]

Which, *He said,* you heard of from Me. Several times before His death, Jesus promised the coming of the Holy Spirit. Especially on the night of His betrayal, as He and the apostles were about to leave the upper room on their way to the Garden of Gethsemane, Jesus had promised this coming of the Spirit to them.[21]

1:5 – *for John baptized with water, but you shall be baptized with the Holy Spirit not many days from now."*

For John baptized with water. These are the words Jesus spoke to His apostles at the time He charged them not to leave Jerusalem, but rather to wait there until the promised Holy Spirit had come. These words are a repetition of what John the Baptist had said earlier when he compared his baptism with the baptism Christ would administer.[22] When John was speaking, he was predicting that when Messiah came He would baptize with the Holy Spirit and with fire. Now, as Jesus spoke to His apostles, a few days before His ascension, He is telling them that the time is drawing near when that prediction made by John would be fulfilled.

On the following page is a chart that will help us distinguish between the different "baptisms" we find in the New Testament. To help in understanding the chart, several words of explanation are needed:

1) *John's Baptism* – It was an immersion in water. It was a baptism unto repentance (i.e., into a life characterized by repentance), to get the people prepared for the coming of the Messiah. It was superseded by the baptism of the Great Commission (Acts 19:1-6).

2) *The Baptism of Suffering* – This not only happened to Christ, but also happens to Christ's followers. The baptism of suffering refers to the suffering and death of Christ, and to the suffering (and often the death, too) of the ones who are faithful to Christ – a suffering resulting from severe persecution by the enemies of Christ and the enemies of Christians. It is paying for one's faith with his own blood. Many early Christians and thousands through the years have made this supreme sacrifice. From their blood came the blossom of Christ's body, the Church, which now bears fruit throughout the earth, for "The blood of the martyrs is the seed of the church" (Tertullian). Is it possible for us to be baptized of the baptism of suffering? It is! All that is needed is for wicked men to believe there is profit for them in opposing the church, and then the people of God will suffer.

---

[20] John 5:19, 12:49.

[21] John 14:12,25, 15:25, 16:7-13.

[22] Matthew 3:11; John 1:33.

FIVE BAPTISMS OF THE NEW TESTAMENT

	NATURE	PURPOSE	BY	SUBJECTS	ELEMENT	ACT	DURATION
GREAT COMMISSION	Commandment Mt. 28:19 Acts 2:38	Forgiveness Acts 2:38 1 Pet. 3:21	Disciples Mt. 28:19	Penitent Believers Mk. 16:18 Acts 2:38	Water Acts 8:36-39	Immersion Rom. 6:3-5	Till the end Mt. 28:19-20
JOHN'S	Commandment Lk. 7:29-30	To prepare for Messiah Jn. 1:31 Lk. 3:3-6 Acts 19:4	John Mk. 1:5	Penitent Jews Mk. 1:4-5	Water Jn. 1:26	Immersion Mk. 1:10 Jn. 3:23	Ceased before cross Acts 19:3-5
SUFFERING	Experience Mk. 10:38-39	1. Bring salvation 1 Peter 2:24, 2 Cor. 1:5-6 2. Resulting glory Heb. 12:2, 2 Tim. 2:12	Wicked Men Acts 2:23 2 Thes. 3:1-2	1. Jesus Mk. 10:38 2. His followers Mk. 10:39	Suffering Mk. 10:39	Overwhelming Mt. 27:46,50	1. On the Cross Mt. 27:50 2. Until Jesus returns 2 Tim 3:12
HOLY SPIRIT	Promise Acts 1:4-5	1. Empower for special work Acts 1:8 Jn. 16:13 2 Cor. 12:12 2. Prove God's acceptance of Gentiles Acts 11:15-18	Christ Mt. 3:11	1. Apostles Acts 2:1-4 2. Cornelius & Household Acts 11:15-16	Holy Spirit Mt. 3:11	Overpowering Mt. 10:19-20 Acts 2:4	Occurred but twice Acts 2, 10 *(each a special case)*
FIRE	Warning Mt. 3:11-12	Punishment Mt. 25:45-46	Christ Mt. 3:11	Wicked Mt. 3:10 2 Thes. 1:7-8	Fire Mt. 3:11	Overwhelming Rev. 20:15	Everlasting Mt. 25:41

3) *Baptism of the Holy Spirit* – In this passage in Acts, something is promised especially to the apostles, and the promise was fulfilled in the events on Pentecost as recorded in the next chapter. Special Study #3, "The Person and Work of the Holy Spirit," is at the close of chapter 2; we shall save most of our discussion of the Baptism of the Holy Spirit until then. When the apostles were baptized of the Holy Spirit, they were enabled to speak in languages they had never studied, proclaim the full gospel (as the Spirit brought to their minds all things Jesus said and did), and perform miracles to substantiate their message. Is it possible for Christians to be "Baptized with the Holy Spirit" today? Evidently not! In Special Study #3 we will see how what is called "Baptism in the Holy Spirit" today differs in purpose from what the apostles received. Early Christians (not every individual one, however) received "spiritual gifts" by the laying on of an apostle's hands, and thus could work miracles, or speak in tongues, or prophesy, etc. Such "spiritual gifts" were temporary for the early church, just as the office of apostle was temporary. It is possible that "Baptism with the Holy Spirit" was the measure of the Spirit that empowered a man to be an apostle; and when the last apostle died, that was the end of the divine activity called "Baptism with the Holy Spirit."

4) *Baptism of Fire* – The baptism of fire is yet to be administered by Christ as the punishment to sinners after the final judgment. Matthew 3:12 indicates that the baptism of fire is Hell. Admittedly, not all Bible students agree with this handling of Matthew 3:12, and therefore believe that the baptism of fire is something needed by Christians today; in fact, they pray for the baptism of fire. In this commentator's opinion, that is a misguided prayer, and it would be a fearful thing if God should answer these prayers. Because something like fire appeared to the apostles on the day of Pentecost, some interpreters suppose that the "baptism with the Holy Spirit and with fire" all has reference to Pentecost's happenings, but such an interpretation does not align with John's own explanation of the "baptism of fire" in Matthew 3:12. John said to his audience that some of them would receive the baptism with the Holy Spirit, and some of them would be baptized with fire because of their rejection of his message and the One who came after him. Is it possible for a man to be baptized with fire in this age? Yes. All sinners shall be cast into the lake of fire if they have not repented and surrendered to Christ.

5) *The Baptism of the Great Commission* – This is the baptism Jesus commanded men to submit to as part of their response to the Gospel. This baptism is for the remission of sins. It is in water. Other than the possibility of experiencing the baptism of suffering, the baptism of the Great Commission is the only baptism a man may experience in this life. God has left it for his messengers to administer this baptism to penitent believers, who in turn may become one of his messengers, and in turn immerse others who respond to the invitation.[23]

---

[23] The baptism of the Great Commission is sometimes called "Christian Baptism," a title that is fine if it is only used to distinguish this from John's baptism, but a title that is misleading if it causes one to think a man is already a Christian and then later submits to the ordinance of baptism. To avoid this possible misunderstanding, some scholars prefer to call the baptism of the Great Commission by the title "Believer's Baptism," which indicates this ordinance is for people old enough to make a personal confession of their faith in Jesus, as opposed to infants who cannot make any such declaration or have any such belief.

But you shall be baptized with the Holy Spirit. This "baptism" gave the recipient, among other things, the power to work miracles. For other information, see the Special Study #3, "The Person and Work of the Holy Spirit," at the close of chapter 2.

Not many days from now. These words of Jesus were probably spoken not long before His ascension, and not long before the day of Pentecost when the apostles were baptized with the Holy Spirit. This prophecy was soon to be fulfilled in a remarkable manner.

B. The Ascension of Christ. 1:6-11

1:6 – *And so when they had come together, they were asking Him, saying, "Lord, is it at this time You are restoring the kingdom to Israel?"*

And so when they had come together. It is another day than the one spoken of in the previous verses. The apostles are together with Jesus on the Mount of Olives (Acts 1:9,12).

They were asking Him, saying, Lord. A "lord" is one who rules, or who has power and authority. In the feudal systems of Medieval times, the one who ruled the feud (the whole farm), the one to whom everyone else bowed in subjection, was called the "lord." That the apostles should call Jesus "Lord" shows their convictions about His deity, convictions that have become even stronger since His resurrection. The verb translated "were asking" is an imperfect tense verb, a technical term that signifies that they asked Him over and over again as they were walking along the mountain side. One can almost feel their excited impatience for an answer as they keep pounding Jesus with this question.

Is it at this time You are restoring the kingdom to Israel? "Restore the kingdom." The apostles, all through Jesus' ministry, had held the same opinions most Jews held, namely, that the reign of the Messiah predicted in the Old Testament was a *temporal dominion*, rather than spiritual. Their use of the word "restore" shows that they were still looking back to the glorious days gone by – the days of David and Solomon, when the Jewish nation was the ruler of the world – and were still hoping for such days to return. The apostles expected that the Messiah would reign as a prince and a conqueror, and would free the Jews from being a captive nation under the Roman authority. Many instances occur in the Gospels, where this expectation of the people is pressed upon the attention of Jesus, in spite of all the efforts He made to explain to them the true nature of His coming kingdom. The apostles themselves had entertained ideas that in the restored kingdom they themselves would have places of honor.[24] This false expectation was checked, and almost destroyed by His death,[25] but His return to life again excited their hopes. They beheld Him with them again, and they were assured He was the same Savior. They saw now that His enemies had no power over Him. If they killed Him, He would just come back to life. They could not doubt that a being who could rise from the dead could easily accomplish His plans, and establish the kingdom He had been promising all along.

---

[24] Mark 10:35ff.

[25] Luke 24:21.

"At this time?" The disciples, still wrong in their ideas concerning the kingdom, and not doubting that Christ would restore the ancient glory to the nation Israel, were asking whether or not He was going to do it at the very time they were speaking. It might be noted that Lightfoot has given a different interpretation. He thinks there was a tone of indignation against the Jews in the voices of the apostles as they asked the question. He suggests that the force of the question is this, "Will you confer dominion on a nation which has just put you to death?" But the answer Jesus gives shows that such was not the design of the apostles' question at all. The fact that the apostles still entertain wrong ideas about the kingdom is proof that they very much needed the help of the Holy Spirit ("what the Father had promised") before they could spread the message of Christ. It was not possible for them to preach the gospel of the kingdom until they understood the nature of the kingdom – that it was spiritual and heavenly, and not earthly and temporal. (Further notes on this disputed phrase appear in Special Study #1, "Diverse Opinions about the Kingdom of God," at the close of chapter 1.)

1:7 – *He said to them, "It is not for you to know times or epochs which the Father has fixed by His own authority;*

He said to them. In verse 7, Jesus answers the first part of their question. The apostles had asked, "Is it at this time?" Jesus answers, "It is not for you to know the times or epochs." In verse 8, Jesus will address the second part of their question, and will again seek to correct their mistaken ideas of the nature of "the kingdom."

It is not for you to know times or epochs. What can be signified by the use of the different words "times" and "epochs"? As far as the Greek words are concerned, "times" speaks of periods of considerable length, while "epochs" speaks of the particular moments fixed for particular events. Thus, most commentators suggest that "times" may refer to the ages (dispensations) before the consummation, and "epochs" may mark the critical periods by which the ages are marked.

What is Jesus talking about when He says it is not for the apostles to know the times or epochs? Some would refer it to the second advent of Christ, and at time Jesus certainly used similar language in speaking about His return.[26] However, the context here shows that the establishment of the church at Pentecost is the thing foremost in the mind of Christ. Jesus' full answer to the apostles was, "It is not for you to know ... but wait in Jerusalem." In other words, the day is not too far in the future.

Which the Father has fixed by His own authority. It is true that the Father has reserved for Himself the knowledge of the time of the second advent, so that even Jesus Himself did not know the time.[27] But the point here being discussed evidently is that the Father had set by virtue of His own authority the time when the kingdom would be established. The implication in Jesus' words then is this: 'It is the business of the Father to determine the times and epochs, and it is your job (you apostles) to watch, pray, and wait.' God has fixed

---

[26] Matthew 24:36.

[27] Mark 13:32.

the time of the great kingdom events, and He will bring them to pass in His own time and His own way.

1:8 – *but you shall receive power when the Holy Spirit has come upon you; and you shall be My witnesses both in Jerusalem, and in all Judea and Samaria, and even to the remotest part of the earth."*

But you shall receive power when the Holy Spirit has come upon you. Literally, "You shall receive the power of the Holy Spirit coming upon you." (The power and the Spirit were not something separate.) Here begins Jesus' attempt to correct the false impressions of the kingdom held by the apostles. It was not to be a political power such as had formerly been the object of their ambitions. It was to be a spiritual kingdom, where the chief interest was the forgiveness of sins which is now available to men through Jesus. The "power" Jesus here speaks of and the "baptism with the Holy Spirit" of verse 5 are the same thing. What they were to receive would empower them to do their work as His chosen apostles.

And you shall be My witnesses. Jesus says they are to be witnesses (*martures*, from which we get "martyrs"), not princes. The reason the name "martyr" was given to those who suffered for Christ in times of persecution is because they "bore witness" to the life, instructions, death, and resurrection of Christ – even in the midst of persecution and death. Nearly all the apostles ended their sojourn here on earth as martyrs; all but John died violently at the hands of persecutors. The apostles testified with their lives.

For this very purpose, to witness what they knew, the apostles had been chosen. To prepare them to be witnesses, they had been with Jesus about three years. They had seen His manner of life, His miracles, His meekness, His sufferings. They had listened to His instructions. They had conversed and eaten with Him as a friend. They had seen Him ascend to heaven. A "witness" tells what he knows. These men were thus qualified to tell to all parts of the world the things they knew about Jesus.

It has often been noted that verse 8 is a sort of outline for the book of Acts, and is in fact the verse from which the three-part outline adopted in this book has been taken.

> It has often been pointed out that the geographical terms of verse 8 provide a sort of "Index of Contents" for Acts. "Ye shall be my witnesses" might be regarded as the theme of the book; "in Jerusalem" covers the first seven chapters; "in all Judea and Samaria" covers chapters 8:1 to 11:18; and the remainder of the book deals with the progress of the gospel outside the frontiers of the Holy Land until at last it reaches Rome.[28]

Both in Jerusalem. The first gospel sermon was preached here on the day of Pentecost, AD 30. Most of the *disciples* remained in Jerusalem until the persecution that arose about the death of Stephen;[29] but the *apostles* remained there even longer, until Herod put James to death.[30] The apostles were soul-winners and church planters. They started where they were and moved out in all directions teaching and preaching Christ.

---

[28] Bruce, *op. cit.*, p.39.

[29] Acts 8:3-4.

[30] Acts 12:1-2.

And in all Judea. Judea is the southern division of the Holy Land, and included Jerusalem as the capital.

And Samaria. Samaria was the middle portion of the Holy Land.

And even to the remotest part of the earth. There may be times when the word "earth" is used in the Bible to denote only the land of Palestine, but there does not seem to be a necessity for limiting it thus here. If Christ had intended that, He could have said "Galilee" as this was the only remaining division of the country. It seems best to understand the expression "earth" as referring to all the Gentile lands. Jesus expressly directed the apostles to preach the gospel to all nations, and the rest of the book of Acts is evidence that the apostles did as they were directed.

Someone has suggested that this verse gives us an ideal missionary program for the local church. It suggests four areas of God's world, and the local church should have a vital interest in each one of these areas. Jerusalem would be similar to the community in which the congregation today is located. Judea would suggest that the congregation should have a vital interest in some mission work in the state in which it is located. Samaria would remind us to have a particular interest in a third area, in some state adjacent to ours. And "the uttermost parts" tells us to have a vital interest in a mission field on foreign soil. A living link in each of these four areas should be minimum goal to strive for.

1:9 – *And after He had said these things, He was lifted up while they were looking on, and a cloud received Him out of their sight.*

And after He had said these things. In Luke 24:50-52, Jesus left them while He was speaking a blessing on them, and they in turn "worshiped him, and returned to Jerusalem with great joy." Putting the two accounts together, we learn that Jesus began to rise even while He was yet speaking. It is His ascension into Heaven.

While they were looking on. It was important for Luke to state that the apostles witnessed His ascension. It is not affirmed in the New Testament that anyone actually saw Jesus as He was coming out of the tomb at His resurrection, because the evidence of that fact could be better established by their seeing Him after He was risen. But the truth of the ascension to heaven could not be confirmed in that manner. Hence, it was so arranged that Jesus should ascend in open daylight, in the presence of the apostles. Had Jesus vanished secretly or just stopped making post-resurrection appearances, the apostles would have had difficulty understanding, and might even have been tempted to believe they had been deceived about His resurrection and His plans. Where was He? What was He doing? Many questions could flood their minds. Instead, their minds were set at ease by this ascension which began even while He was talking to them and their attention was fixed on Him.

He was lifted up. If the Savior was taken up to heaven, it settled the question about the nature of the kingdom. It was clear that it was not designed to be a temporal kingdom. Several reasons have been advanced in order to make it plain that it was better that He ascend rather than remain on earth.

1) Christ had finished the work which God gave Him to do on the earth.[31]
2) It was proper that Christ should ascend in order that the Holy Spirit might descend and perform His part of the work of redemption.[32]
3) A part of the work of Christ was yet to be performed in heaven – the work of intercession.[33]

Both natures of our Lord are recognized in this passage. He ascended with His glorified body, and there in Heaven He awaits the time of His return to earth as Judge.[34]

And a cloud received Him out of their sight. Several ideas can be gleaned from this phrase. Christ is pictured as being carried away by a cloud chariot. The song "Christ is King" has the words, "At His feet on Old Olivet's hill, they say, cloud chariots halted, took Christ away ...." The same picture is presented in Codex Beza, where it reads, "And after He said these things, a cloud received Him, and He was taken up from their eyes." Another picture these verses present is that Christ slowly rose off the face of the ground up to the region of the clouds, and then a cloud came across between Jesus and the apostles, hiding Jesus from their view. Something similar had happened at the transfiguration.[35] On that occasion, a cloud covered those on the mountain; and when it finally left, Jesus was still there. Perhaps some of the apostles remembered that previous event, and expected that when the cloud passed, Jesus would still be visible. But this was not to be. Now that Jesus had ascended to heaven, no further appearances were granted to the apostles of the kind they had experienced for the preceding 40 days. Jesus had made His commission to them sufficiently plain. Now the task was theirs to witness to the world, beginning at Jerusalem.

1:10 – *And as they were gazing intently into the sky while He was departing, behold, two men in white clothing stood beside them;*

And as they were gazing intently into the sky while He was departing. The apostles continued to peer into the sky at the spot where Jesus was last seen in hopes of catching one last glimpse of Him. They fixed their eyes on the spot, and were so intent on catching another glimpse of Him that they didn't notice when two angel messengers took their stand beside the apostles.

Behold, two men ... stood beside them. From their dress and the nature of their message, it seems clear these were angels in human form. As angels had appeared at the tomb in hu-

---

[31] John 17:4-5, 19:30; Philippians 2:6,9,10.

[32] John 16:7.

[33] Hebrews 7:25.

[34] Philippians 2:9. The phrase in Philippians "highly exalted Him" also suggests that Christ now has His glorified body in heaven. See this matter explained by William Hendriksen, "Philippians" in *New Testament Commentary* (Grand Rapids: Baker, 1962), p.105ff.

[35] Mark 9:26; Matthew 17:5; Luke 9:34. Because in one place where the Master is telling about His second advent the word "cloud" is singular (Luke 22:27), and because of the similarity of the ascension with the Transfiguration, many believe that the cloud which took Christ away, and on which He will return, is nothing other than the Shekinah, the visible symbol of God's presence, the pillar of cloud and fire that led the Israelites in the Old Testament.

man form, so we assume it is angels who appear here as "men."[36] The past perfect active tense of the verb means "had taken their stand by them" – an act completed in the past time with results for some time in the past. It is because of this verb tense that we suggest that the apostles did not see the two angels until the angels spoke to them, "Men of Galilee ...." Those words would have caused the apostles to turn their heads from their intense peering into the sky to staring awestruck upon these two heavenly strangers.

In white clothing. Angels are commonly represented as wearing white clothing. Some Bible students have developed an elaborate symbolism of colors, finding each color (red, pale green, black, etc.) mentioned in the Bible as symbolizing some truth. Within such color schemes, the color "white" is held to be an emblem of the purity of heaven.

1:11 – and they also said, "Men of Galilee, why do you stand looking into the sky? This Jesus, who has been taken up from you into heaven, will come in just the same way as you have watched Him go into heaven."

And they also said. That is, the angels spoke these words.

Men of Galilee. Galilee was the place of their former residence, and they were commonly known by the name Galileans. It usually is affirmed that all the apostles except Judas were Galileans since Iscariot has regularly been taken to be equivalent to *Ish-Kerioth*. i.e., "a man of Kerioth," a village in Judea.[37] The others were Galileans, and five of them were from the same village, Bethsaida.

Why do you stand looking into the sky? There seems to be a slight degree of censure implied in these words, as the angels call the apostles away from their vain attempt to see the departed Savior one more time.

This Jesus. This was said to comfort the apostles. The same tried friend who had been so faithful to them would return. They ought not, therefore, look with despondency on His departure. Note that neither the coming of the Spirit on Pentecost, nor the destruction of Jerusalem, nor the death of the believer, is the "second coming." Jesus Himself is to return!

Who has been taken up from you into heaven. This expression denotes that Jesus was ushered into the immediate presence of God. We shall learn in future verses that Jesus is now seated at the right hand of the Father on high (Acts 2:33).

Will come in just the same way as yon have watched Him go into heaven. These, too, are comforting words. Jesus would not be separated from them forever. There is to be a second coming of Jesus to earth, followed by a judgment. And He shall return just as He ascended, visibly and bodily. When the return of Jesus is mentioned, it is uniformly said

---

[36] Luke 24:4; Mark 15:5. The Greek word for "angel" is masculine, so we should perhaps picture angels as being masculine, rather than feminine form as artists have often pictured them.

[37] Oscar Cullman, *The State in the New Testament* (New York: Scribners, 1956). p.15 urges that "Iscariot" means Judas was a member of a revolutionary group of zealots, in particular one of the *sicarii* (assassins).

that He will return in the clouds.[38] Every eye shall see Him when and as He comes.

C. The Waiting in Jerusalem. 1:12-14

1:12 – *Then they returned to Jerusalem from the mount called Olivet, which is near Jerusalem, a Sabbath day's journey away.*

Then they returned to Jerusalem. Luke 24:52 tells us they worshiped Jesus before they returned. Some think the act of worship to which Luke refers in the Gospel is the thing mentioned in this section of Acts, i.e., their gazing intently after their departing Lord.

From the mount called Olivet. The usual name for this mountain in the Bible is "Mount of Olives." The Greek word translated "Olivet" means "olive orchard," or "olive grove."[39]

Which is near Jerusalem. The Mount of Olives is located to the east of Jerusalem. Between the East wall of Jerusalem and the mount, there runs a small stream called the brook Kidron. The stream is dry throughout most of the year, but swells to a considerable size during the rainy season. On the western slope of the mountain was the Garden of Gethsemane. On the eastern slope were the villages of Bethpage and Bethany.

A Sabbath day's journey away. A "Sabbath day's journey" was a distance of about 2000 cubits, or about 3/5 of a mile. According to Jewish thinking in the 1st century, this was as far as one might travel on a Sabbath; to travel further would be to violate the prohibition about working on the Sabbath. In fact, no such distance limitation was fixed by the laws of Moses; Jewish religious teachers had fixed the distance. Hence it was a tradition, not a law. Where did the Jewish teachers get such a figure? This measure was determined on because it was a tradition that in the camp of the Israelites, when coming from Egypt, no part of the camp was more than 2000 cubits from the tabernacle. In the wilderness, the Israelites would be allowed to travel this distance as they were coming to worship.

Attempts have been made to locate the spot on the side of the Mount of Olives from which Jesus ascended, and the spot has been the subject of dispute for some time. There is a spot marked by the Church of the Ascension, including a rock with a depression like a man's foot (Jesus supposedly made the depression as He "pushed off" for Heaven), but the location is questionable. Luke tells us that Jesus led the disciples out toward Bethany just prior to His ascension,[40] but he does not tell us if Jesus went up over the hill, or took the long route around the southern end of the mount. Because the route directly over the top is such a strenuous climb, perhaps we should picture Jesus and the apostles taking the easier-to-climb southern route. If so, the ascension would have taken place as they were about half-way from Jerusalem to Bethany.

The ascension evidently took place on Thursday, for the 40th day after the resurrection would fall on a Thursday.

---

[38] Acts 1:11; Matthew 24:30, 26:64; Mark 13:26; Revelation 1:7. See also footnote #35 on previous page.

[39] See *Zondervan Pictorial Bible Dictionary*, p.607 for a picture of the Mount of Olives.

[40] Luke 24:50.

1:13 – *And when they had entered, they went up to the upper room, where they were staying; that is, Peter and John and James and Andrew, Philip and Thomas, Bartholomew and Matthew, James the son of Alphaeus, and Simon the Zealot, and Judas the son of James.*

And when they had entered. That is, when the apostles had returned and entered into the city of Jerusalem.

They went up to the upper room. Not all 1st century homes would have such a room. Those that did belonged to the wealthier. Such rooms could be used for a guest room, for large family gatherings, or for entertaining. Many friends and relatives from a distance came to attend the feasts of the Jews, and such rooms would afford them a place to stay.

Where was this particular room? One idea is that it was a room in the temple since Luke says they were continually in the temple praising God.[41] But there are several reasons for thinking the upper room mentioned here was not part of the temple. It would not likely be said of this group that they were "staying" (living) in the temple area. Further, such a room as this could have been part of any better home in Jerusalem, and it is reasonable to assume the disciples would pick a location where they might be together, yet remain relatively safe from the Jews. A second idea is that this particular upper room was a room in the home of Mary, the mother of John Mark,[42] and perhaps the very same room that had been used at the institution of the Lord's Supper, for the Greek reads "*the* upper room." Objection has been raised to this second idea based on the claim that the room of the paschal supper (*anagaion*)[43] was on the ground floor, and the upper room in Acts (*huperōon*) was on the second floor. However, the Lexicons do not support such a distinction in the words used for the "room." A third idea is that the room intended was simply "a room in some home or building where all these faithful followers were normally staying while in Jerusalem." This commentator sees no reason why the second suggested identification should be rejected, and is thus the one he prefers.

Where they were staying. The upper room was not their permanent residence, but a place to stay at night while they were visiting Jerusalem, and, in this instance, while they were waiting for the coming of the Holy Spirit. Upon a number of occasions Jesus and His apostles came to Jerusalem. We know they were often entertained at the home of Mary and Martha and Lazarus in Bethany, outside Jerusalem. Subsequent events point strongly toward other friends who entertained the group while they were visiting in Jerusalem.

That is, Peter ... Judas *the son* of James. All the apostles were there whom Jesus had first chosen, except Judas Iscariot, who had committed suicide. James the son of Alphaeus is sometimes said to be the author of the book of James in the New Testament. It is also said that James the son of Alphaeus and James the Lord's brother are the same person. This commentator is of the opinion that both of these identifications are wrong. For detailed information about this issue, see the Special Study #2, "The Brothers of the Lord," at the close of chapter 1.

---

[41] Luke 24:53.

[42] Mark 14:15; Luke 22:13; Acts 12:12.

[43] Mark 14:15.

The names of the apostles have been given many times in the Gospel record. Here is the final roll call as they are about to go into all the world witnessing what they know about Jesus. G. Campbell Morgan suggests the men's names are given according to the way they were paired into teams for world evangelism. He calls one team, "Peter the doer and John the dreamer – the practical man and the poet." Another he calls "James and Andrew – courteous and curious ones." Again, he speaks of "Philip the believer and Thomas the skeptic." etc. However, we do not know whether or not such an idea was in fact followed in the arrangement of names.

This is the last mention in the New Testament of many of these apostles. It certainly would be wrong to assume that the unsung service of most of them proved their lack of interest and sacrifice in the new evangelistic endeavor. Early Christian tradition leaves a record of the work of most of the men here named.

1:14 – *These all with one mind were continually devoting themselves to prayer, along with the women, and Mary the mother of Jesus, and with His brothers.*

These all with one mind. The "one mind" denotes the entire harmony of their views and feelings. There were no schisms, no divided interests, no discordant purposes. Because they were in harmony with Jesus' instructions about waiting to be empowered to be witnesses, they were in harmony with each other.

Were continually devoting themselves to prayer. "Continually" denotes persevering and constant attention; they let nothing interfere with their prayers. According to Luke 24:53, this praying was done, not in the upper room where they were staying, but in the temple at the hours of prayer (the Greek here in verse 14 is "*the* prayer"). They had been told to wait for the fulfillment of the promise, and that it would not be many days, so they spent their time in prayer. Since early in the 20th century, some have tried to use this verse to prove that it took the apostles ten days to "pray down" the Holy Spirit. They picture the apostles in a ten-day crescendo of emotional hysteria climaxing at Pentecost, and would further assert such a "Pentecostal experience" is available to all Christians following conversion. But did the apostles' prayers *cause* the Holy Spirit to come on the day of Pentecost? It is doubtful! This prayer practice was part of their lives, and it continued after Pentecost.[44] They are doing what devout Jews did at the daily hours of prayer.

Along with *the* women. Who were the "women"? Perhaps Luke here again mentions the women who had followed Jesus from Galilee:[45] Mary Magdalene, Salome, Johanna, Susanna, Mary and Martha of Bethany, and others. These women would have been mentioned in this informal way because they would be remembered by one who, like Theophilus, had read the first volume of Luke's history. Most were relatives of the apostles or of Jesus, and it is not improbable that some of them were wives of the apostles.[46]

---

[44] Acts 6:4; Romans 12:12. The subject of "praying down the Holy Spirit" will be examined in greater detail in the Special Study #4, "Speaking in Tongues," at the close of chapter 2.

[45] Luke 23:49-55; Matthew 28:9; Mark 15:14.

[46] 1 Corinthians 9:5 and Matthew 8:14 tell us that Peter was married and had his wife along with him on his evangelistic crusades. So did other apostles. Perhaps some of the wives were already accompanying

And Mary the mother of Jesus. Jesus' mother is here particularly mentioned to show that she now cast her lot with the apostles. She had, besides, been specially entrusted to the care of John,[47] and had no other home. This is the last time she is mentioned in the New Testament. Contrary to what the Roman Church teaches as they have evolved an elaborate system of Mariolatry, L. Edsil Dale writes:

> She has a position of respect, but there is no halo about her head. She is loved but not worshipped. The shadow of the cross and her deep sorrow have now turned to a song in her heart. At this point we bid Mary adieu and leave it to later generations to corrupt the memory of her humble and faithful life.[48]

The legends of some apocryphal books present her as staying at Jerusalem with John until her death, 22 years after the ascension. The legends of other apocryphal books represent her as going with John to Ephesus, and dying there; the apostles gather around her death-bed, she is buried, and the next day the grave is found emptied, and sweet flowers have grown around it; Mary also had been taken into Heaven. It has now become a doctrine of faith in several large communions to affirm the "Bodily Assumption of Mary." The festival of the Assumption, which owes its origin to the legend in the apocryphal books, dates from the 6th or 7th century AD. All these legends are fanciful.

And with His brothers. In Mark 6:3 and Matthew 12:46, four brothers and (at least) two sisters are mentioned.[49] These brothers and sisters (really half-brothers and half-sisters) were born to Joseph and Mary after Jesus was born. The fact that the brothers of Jesus were in the company of the believers (according to this verse) is proof that a great change had come over them since their Divine brother had closed His labors in Galilee. When Jesus finished His Galilean ministry 6 or 8 months prior to His death, His brothers did not believe on Him.[50] But a number of things had happened in the last six months to convert them. Lazarus had been raised from the dead. The resurrection of Jesus Himself was the miracle of miracles. Jesus even appeared to James, His brother.[51] So it is only natural that these brothers are now found standing in the front line, ready for Christian action and service.

The theological world is not at all in agreement as to the actual relationship between these "brothers" and Jesus. An extended discussion of the problem is included at the close of this chapter, entitled "The Brothers of the Lord." Two of the books of the New Testament were penned by His brothers – James and Jude.

---

their husbands before Pentecost. Whoever the women were, we find no real evidence that they lived together (as one author suggests), perhaps in Bethany, in a kind of sisterhood.

[47] John 19:26-27.

[48] L. Edsil Dale, *Acts Comments* (Cincinnati: published by the author, 1952), p.20,21.

[49] Matthew 13:55-56 imply there were more sisters than one.

[50] John 7:5.

[51] 1 Corinthians 15:7.

D. The Place of Judas Filled. 1:15-26

1:15 – *And at this time Peter stood up in the midst of the brethren (a gathering of about one hundred and twenty persons was there together), and said,*

And at this time. This verse begins an account of an event that took place on one of the days in the ten-day period between the ascension of Jesus and Pentecost. The text indicates this is a different meeting than the "prayer meeting" mentioned in verse 14 since verse 15 refers to a multitude of about 120 persons gathered; in verse 14, we found only the Eleven, the women, Mary, and the brothers of Jesus.

Peter stood up. Why Peter? It may be that Peter was the oldest of the apostles, which would, among Jews, give him a position of spokesman or leader. Or it may be as in any group today, there is one or more who would naturally step forward and be the first to suggest actions. One group of theologians, seeking any evidence they can find of the primacy of Peter (as they call it), believe he already is functioning as Christ's vicar on earth. Since the whole theory of the primacy of Peter is suspect, such an explanation of this verse is also suspect. Dale reminds us it was Peter's nature to be a leader.

> Peter was first among equals. He spoke out first in Matthew 16:16,17. He was of an impetuous and impulsive nature. In any group today one or more would naturally step forward as first among equals. All the apostles were outstanding leaders, but each in a different way and with his own personality and ability.[52]

In the midst of the brethren. The word "brother" is used in several senses in the New Testament. We have just had mention of the blood brothers of Jesus. In this verse the word brother is used in the sense of a "spiritual brother."

(A gathering of about one hundred and twenty persons were together), and said. One writer says, "This was the first assembly convened to transact the business of the church, and it is not a little remarkable that the vote in so important a matter as electing an apostle was by the entire church."[53] However, had the church been established yet? We believe not. The church is not begun until the day of Pentecost, some days later. And, was this the whole church electing an apostle? Again, we believe not. Verse 24 tells us that the Holy Spirit (or God) chose the new apostle. While it is true that the New Testament teaches local autonomy of the church, this verse is not one of the passages that show it. And while it is true that no ecclesiastical body has the authority to place a minister in a given congregation, this is not the verse to use to show that either.

Were these 120 all the believers in Christ there were at this time, several days before Pentecost? The number seems to include all the faithful in and around the city of Jerusalem, but there were other believers, especially in Galilee.[54]

---

[52] Dale, *op. cit.*, p.21.

[53] Albert Barnes, "Acts" in *Barnes' Notes on the New Testament* (Grand Rapids: Baker, 1953), p.11.

[54] 1 Corinthians 15:6.

Where was there room for a group of people this size to meet as they make such a choice? They apparently are in the temple area, for it was their habit to resort there for daily worship. It is not likely that such a crowd could gather in the upper room where just the few of verse 14 had been lodging.

1:16 – *"Brethren, the Scripture had to be fulfilled, which the Holy Spirit foretold by the mouth of David concerning Judas, who became a guide to those who arrested Jesus.*

Brethren. This was a customary form of address, implying affection and respect, and intended to get the attention of the audience.

The scripture had to be fulfilled. This is saying that the predictions that God made would certainly come to pass. Not that there was any physical necessity or compulsion in what Judas did, but that it could not but occur that a prediction of God would be fulfilled. God, with all knowledge, could look ahead and see what was going to happen.

What "Scripture" does Peter have in mind? Some think he had Psalm 41:9 in mind, which reads "Yea, mine own familiar friend ... hath lifted up his heel against me." This verse is expressly applied to Judas by Jesus.[55] And if Peter is referring to Psalm 41, then he also informs us that David wrote that Psalm. (Absent this reference, we do not know the author of Psalm 41.) Others argue that the Scripture Peter had in mind is Psalm 69, which will be quoted in verse 20.

Which the Holy Spirit foretold by the mouth of David. This is a strong affirmation of the inspiration of David. This claim accords with the testimony of Peter that the Old Testament writers spoke (and wrote) as they were moved by the Holy Spirit.[56]

Concerning Judas. See notes at verses 11 and 20 for information about Judas Iscariot.

Who became a guide to those who arrested Jesus. *Pulpit Commentary* states that these are Luke's words (not Peter's) because the 120 gathered in Jerusalem would know this, and Peter would not need to tell them, whereas Luke might well need to tell his readers. Note Luke uses the verb "became," a verb that suggests what Judas did was his own act; it wasn't something Judas was predestined to do, and had to do contrary to his own will.

1:17 – *"For he was counted among us, and received his portion in this ministry."*

For he was counted among us. These again are Peter's words, and Peter says Judas was chosen by Jesus to be an apostle (versus the idea that Jesus chose Judas because there had to be a betrayer). Those writers, we believe, are wrong who suggest Jesus purposely chose a spy and traitor to be one of His disciples. It was after a long night of prayer that Jesus chose the Twelve,[57] and He picked men of promise to be His apostles. Judas was not likely

---

[55] John 13:18.

[56] 2 Peter 1:21.

[57] Luke 6:12.

already a thief when Jesus selected him. Perhaps Judas was a very smart, intellectual business man, or at least a man with talents in that direction. (Certainly, many a man has been tempted most severely in the very area of his talents. Right while he handles money, a task that he does well, is when he is tempted to be a thief.) On multiple occasions, Jesus tried to rescue Judas from his sin; however, Judas didn't listen and only became more entangled. Why would Jesus attempt such a rescue if Judas was purposely chosen for the express purpose of being a spy and a traitor? Notice some of the times Jesus tried to rescue Judas. At the close of the sermon on the bread of life (i.e., the day of the feeding of the 5000), the people began to go away and not follow Jesus. Jesus said to His disciples, "Will you also go away?" Peter replied, "Lord, to whom shall we go? You (and You alone) have the words of life." Jesus then spoke, "Did I not choose you the twelve, and yet one of you is a devil?" (In other words, "One of you will go away, I'm afraid, because you listen to the Devil's allurements.")[58] While the rest of the apostles received the teaching of Jesus and grew better, Judas rejected it and grew worse. Judas even used his apparent zeal for economy as a cloak for hypocrisy.[59] His love for money not only increased his deceit but also destroyed his faith.[60] Judas had heard Jesus' teaching to beware of the leaven of the Pharisees, which was hypocrisy. Jesus warned His disciples to lay up treasures in heaven rather than seeking the things of this earth. Even the night of the betrayal, Jesus tried to rescue Judas, when He said, "What you do, do quickly!"[61] In other words, 'If you are going to betray Me, then do it. If you are going to repent, then do it now. Whatever you are going to do, do it quickly.'

> Judas' sin of greed was a cancer of progressive degeneration (James 1:14,15), from avarice, thievery, deceit, betrayal, remorse, to suicide and to his own place. What a biography! What is the motive of the minister today for serving the Lord? Does it offer an easy life of things without real service and sincerity? Every man must constantly examine his motives while serving Christ. Judas did not properly repent. He was sorry, but he did not properly repent and instead committed suicide. What a contrast between Judas and Peter! Both had been rebuked as Satan by Jesus. Both turned against the Lord at the end of His ministry. Both had deep sorrow – Judas with his bitter remorse and Peter in his dark night of weeping. But Peter had godly sorrow which leads to true repentance (2 Corinthians 7:10); whereas Judas had only worldly sorrow – sorrow that he was caught or finally shown up (2 Corinthians 7:10b). Judas could have come back as Peter did, if he had had real repentance. It is a fearful thing to be a free moral agent, free to choose one's way![62]

And received his portion in this ministry. Judas had been selected by Jesus and had the same commission and miraculous powers as the rest of the Twelve. The word "portion" carries the idea of an appointment by God. This phrase has a direct bearing on Judas' selection by Jesus. Jesus intended that Judas have a place in the apostleship of the church just as did any of the other apostles. Instead, he turned out to be a traitor and a false prophet.

---

[58] John 6:66-71.

[59] John 12:3-6.

[60] 1 Timothy 6:8-10.

[61] John 13:27.

[62] Dale, *op. cit.*, p.22.

1:18 – *(Now this man acquired a field with the price of his wickedness; and falling headlong, he burst open in the middle and all his bowels gushed out.*

(Now this man. Judas is the one Luke speaks of. Note that verses 18 and 19 form a parenthetical statement. These are the words of Luke, who is explaining to Theophilus whom Peter was talking about. It is not likely that Peter would introduce a narrative like this in an address to the 120 disciples, a circumstance with which they were already familiar. Before Luke reports the actual passages from the Psalms which Peter quoted to establish his point, he inserts a parenthetical note so that his readers may understand the background of Peter's words.

Acquired a field with the price of his wickedness. The "price" is the payment Judas received for betraying Jesus, i.e., the 30 pieces of silver. (Remember, this was equivalent to 3 months' wages for the working man.) Yet since Judas killed himself, how can it be said that he obtained a field? Yet still, Judas had returned this money to the priests.[63] When they would not take it from him as he tried to hand it to them, he probably rushed right into the Holy Place – an act punishable by death – and threw the money down on the floor. Perhaps he hoped that the temple guard would kill him. But the temple guard did not lay a hand on him. Either they had been instructed not to harm the apostles, or they were afraid that after the condemnation of Christ, to kill one of the apostles would have thrown all Jerusalem into a riot. Having failed to be killed, Judas went out and hanged himself.

The hypocritical priests could not use the money in the treasury of the temple, so they bought a potter's field in which to bury the poor (since some could not afford to bury their own dead) or the strangers (pilgrims who came to Jerusalem, died there, and no one could identify them). In reality then, Judas purchased the field because the priests used his money. Apparently, the field was purchased after the death of Judas; and when it was given closer inspection, they found Judas' body. Why was the field so cheap? Because as a potter's field,[64] it was a worthless piece of real estate. A potter was a person who made pottery out of clay, so all the good earth was gone from this field, and it was therefore worthless.

And falling headlong. What caused Judas' body to fall? Some suggest that he hung so long the rope rotted and broke. Others suggest that perhaps in his terrible state of mind, he failed to properly tie the rope, and fell 50 or 100 feet onto the rocks below. In either case, his body fell head first onto the rocks at the bottom of the valley of Hinnom.

He burst open in the middle and all his bowels gashed out. Matthew tells us that Judas hanged himself.[65] Harmonizing what Matthew and Luke tell us, we suppose that Judas' body hung till his body decayed somewhat. Then when the rope gave way, he fell and was mangled as here described by Luke.

---

[63] Matthew 27:3-10.

[64] Matthew 27:7.

[65] Matthew 27:5.

1:19 – *And it became known to all who were living in Jerusalem; so that in their own language that field was called Akeldama, that is, Field of Blood.)*

And it became known to all who were living at Jerusalem. "Living" (*katoikeō*) speaks of those dwelling permanently at Jerusalem.[66] Someone found the body, and by and by, the scene in the temple, the acts of the priests in purchasing the field, and the discovery of Judas' body in that very field, all would have become known.

So that in their own language. The language was Aramaic, a corrupted form of the Hebrew, and was spoken in Palestine in the 1st century AD.

That field was called Akeldama, that is, Field of Blood.) Akeldama is an Aramaic word and in works written to Greek speaking people (people unfamiliar with the Aramaic language), such words are transliterated and then explained. "Field of blood" is a good translation, for the word Akeldama is composed of two Aramaic words which mean, literally, field of blood. Why would the name of the field be changed from "potter's field" to "field of blood"? Perhaps because Judas' blood was shed there. Perhaps because the field was purchased with blood-money (it was there that the price of the innocent Redeemer ended).

Where was this field located? The traditional site, dating from the time of Jerome in the 4th century AD, is on the south side of the Valley of Hinnom. Consult a map of Jerusalem and the traditional site can be located. The identification is not improbable, for the locality is one which can furnish potter's clay, and has long been surrendered to burial purposes.

1:20 – *"For it is written in the book of Psalms, 'LET HIS HOMESTEAD BE MADE DESOLATE, AND LET NO MAN DWELL IN IT'; and, 'HIS OFFICE LET ANOTHER MAN TAKE.'*

For it is written in the book of Psalms. After the parenthetical statement in verses 18-19, Luke now resumes his record of Peter's speech. Peter quotes from two different Psalms. The first part of verse 20 is taken from Psalm 69:25. This Psalm is repeatedly quoted with reference to the Messiah.[67] When David spoke the words originally, his primary reference was to his enemies. Thus, the Psalm probably does not have reference to Judas alone, but to any enemy of Messiah, of which Judas was one. The latter part of verse 20 comes from Psalm 109:8.[68]

---

[66] Compare notes on Acts 2:5, where the word *katoikeō* appears, evidently with a different meaning.

[67] Psalm 69:9, "The zeal of thine house hath eaten me up," is applied to Jesus in John 2:17, and is also quoted by Paul in Romans 15:3. Psalm 69:21, "They gave me also gall for my meat; and in my thirst they gave me vinegar to drink" was the thing done to Jesus on the cross (Matthew 27:34; John 19:28-30). The Psalm was Messianic

[68] The translators of both the ASV and NASB have used a different type style for quotations from the Old Testament, and in most cases have set them off by indentation, to help the New Testament readers to recognize the verses quoted from the Old Testament.

LET HIS HOMESTEAD BE MADE DESOLATE, AND LET NO MAN SWELL IN IT. This quotation is not made literally from either the Hebrew or the LXX (Septuagint). In the Hebrew, the Psalm reads, "Let their habitation (Heb., fold, enclosure for cattle, tower, palace) be desolate, and let none dwell in their tents." The term "homestead" in the Psalm evidently refers to the dwelling-place of the enemies of the writer of the Psalm, and the verse presents an image expressive of those enemies' overthrow and defeat by a just God. Paraphrased, what the Psalmist prayed for is, 'Let their families be scattered, and the places where they have dwelt be without an inhabitant, as a reward for their crimes.' Peter sees something similar to what happened to David in the case of Judas. When Judas became an enemy of Christ, he forfeited his right to his "homestead" too, just as did the enemies of the Psalmist.

And, HIS OFFICE LET ANOTHER MAN TAKE. This phrase comes from Psalm 109:8. The margin reads "his position as overseer" instead of "office." The KJV reads "bishoprick." The Greek word means "care, charge, business, oversight" of anything. The word, *episkopēn*, is very similar to the word translated "bishop," which is *episkopos*. It scarcely needs to be said that Peter here is not affirming that Judas (and the other apostles) sustained any office corresponding to what is now commonly understood by the term "bishop" (in a Diocesan Episcopate).

Psalm 109 was written during the difficult times when Saul, or Shimei, or another was rebelling and persecuting David. David deemed his enemy, whoever he was, unworthy of his office (position), and desired that it be given to another. In the case of David, the idea of the prayer is that those who were hounding him, men who were entrusted with military or other offices, had treacherously perverted them, and had thus shown themselves unworthy of the office. David therefore prays that the enemy be removed from his office and replaced by someone else. The application to the case at hand, Judas, is easy to see. Peter is saying that through his traitorous act, Judas had rendered himself unworthy of the position to which Christ had called him, and therefore it was proper that another should be found to take the position. Peter was simply taking the Biblical example and applying it to the situation at hand.

1:21 – *"It is therefore necessary that of the men who have accompanied us all the time that the Lord Jesus went in and out among us –*

It is therefore necessary that of the men who have accompanied us. Peter probably refers to the 70 disciples when he speaks of "men who have accompanied us."[69]

All the time that the Lord Jesus went in and out among us – . That is, those who had witnessed the life and miracles of Jesus, and who therefore were well qualified to discharge the duties of the "office" from which Judas fell. "Went in and out" is a phrase signifying that He was their constant companion. It expresses in general all the actions of life.

---

[69] Luke 10:1,2.

1:22 – *"beginning with the baptism of John, until the day that He was taken up from us – one of these should become a witness with us of His resurrection."*

Beginning with the baptism of John. These men (from whom one was to be selected to take Judas' place) must have accompanied and personally witnessed the greater part of the ministry of Christ, from the time He was baptized by John in the Jordan River.

Until the day He was taken up from us –. I.e., the day of Jesus' ascension. The successor to an apostle had to possess certain high qualifications. We have these given in Acts 1:21, 22 and 1 Corinthians 9:1. Peter tells us that such a successor had to have been with Jesus from the time of His baptism until His ascension. Paul tells us that such a person had to have personally seen the risen Christ. In the case of Paul, perhaps only the second requirement is met, but Paul himself recognizes that he is an exception, as he speaks of himself as "one untimely born."[70] But Paul was called personally and directly by the Lord Himself to be an apostle.[71] Because it is not possible for a man to meet these qualifications today, it does not appear possible for any man to claim to be an apostle today.[72]

One of these should become a witness with us. It was fitting, and following a Biblical example, that one should be chosen to fill the vacancy. The 70 would have witnessed most of Jesus' public ministry, and many of them would have seen the risen Lord, and so could be "witnesses" of what they had seen.

Of His resurrection. The great cardinal truth of apostolic teaching is that in Jesus there has been a resurrection from the dead. Involved in this statement is the whole of their testimony (4:23), apart from which fact preaching and faith were vain (1 Corinthians 15:14).

1:23 – *And they put forward two men, Joseph called Barsabbas (who was also called Justus), and Matthias.*

And they put forward two men. We would say that they nominated two men. But who is meant by "they"? Did all 120 who were assembled have part in the nominating process? Was it only the eleven apostles who did the nominating? Since Peter has given the qualifications, perhaps the 120 nominated the two. The two nominated were probably so nearly equal in qualifications that they could not further determine which was the best fitted for the office.

---

[70] 1 Corinthians 15:8.

[71] Acts 26:16.

[72] The notes given for Acts 21:18 contain a further discussion of the office of apostle in the early church. Not only were there "apostles of Christ" (i.e., chosen by Christ), but in the New Testament there were "apostles of churches" (chosen by local congregations to carry out a mission for that congregation), such as is seen from 2 Corinthians 8:23 where the NASB has "messenger" but the Greek has "apostle." When we say no one meets the qualification for apostle, we are speaking of apostles of Christ, and the particular doctrine we are objecting to is the doctrine of apostolic succession.

Joseph called Barsabbas (who was also called Justus). "Barsabbas" means "son of Sabbas" or "born (son of) on the Sabbath." Perhaps he was a brother of Judas Barsabbas (Acts 15:22). Lightfoot, who held the Epiphanian view concerning the Lord's brothers,"[73] comes up with the peculiar notion that this man was a son of Alphaeus, and that he was chosen on account of his relationship to the family of the Lord. If we reject the Epiphanian view, and we do, we'll have to look elsewhere for a reason why he was nominated.

Not only was he known as Joseph, but he was also called Justus. The former is a Hebrew name; and Justus is a Roman name. The name Justus was probably given to him because of his integrity and justness. There is a tradition that he one day drank snake's venom in the Lord's name, and suffered no evil consequences.[74]

And Matthias. Little is known of this man, his family, or of his character further than that he was numbered with the apostles, and shared their lot in the toils, the persecutions, and the honors of preaching the gospel. A tradition preserved in Eusebius represents him as one of the 70.[75] It is said by Nicephorus that Matthias preached and suffered martyrdom in Ethiopia.

1:24 – And they prayed, and said, "Thou, Lord, who knowest the hearts of all men, show which one of these two Thou hast chosen

And they prayed and said. Barnes writes, "As they could not agree on the individual, they invoked the direction of God in their choice ...."[76] This sounds like, 'After they tried everything else, and failed, they prayed.' Rather, they are wisely leaving the decision to God, allowing God to pick the man He wanted. They would agree with God's decision.

Thou, Lord, who knowest the hearts of all men. Is "Lord" a reference to Christ or God? It could well be a reference to Christ. The name "Lord" is commonly applied to Christ by the apostles (e.g., Acts 1:6). This was a matter which pertained especially to the church – the body for which Christ came to give His life – and since He chose the apostles originally, why not ask Him now to choose the replacement? The prayer of Stephen[77] shows that direct prayer to the Son was not foreign to the minds of the disciples, and omniscience is attributed to Christ elsewhere in the New Testament.[78] On the other hand, this prayer might well be addressed to God. In 1 Chronicles 28:9 and Jeremiah 17:10, it is said of the Father that He knows the hearts of men, the very thing predicated here.

---

[73] See Special Study #2, "The Brothers of the Lord," where this term is explained. Also, the reader must be careful not to confuse Barsabbas with Barnabas, whom we shall meet at Acts 4:36.

[74] Eusebius, *Church History*, III.39.9

[75] *Ibid.*, I.12; III.25

[76] Barnes, *op. cit.*, p.25.

[77] Acts 7:59-60.

[78] John 2:24-25 is one example where we are told Jesus could read men's hearts.

Barnes believes that this thought of knowing the hearts of men is included in the prayer because in the background is the matter of Judas' treachery. Since one apostle of fair external character had proved a traitor, they appealed to God Himself to select one who would be true, and not bring dishonor to the cause of Christ. The apostles knew only the qualifications, but God knew the heart; the apostles wanted God to make the choice so that the right one would be chosen.

Show which one of these two Thou hast chosen. That is, point out by some visible or other means which of the two He had chosen to take the place of Judas.

1:25 – *to occupy this ministry and apostleship from which Judas turned aside to go to his own place."*

To occupy. The NASB does not translate two Greek words that the Nestle text carries. The ASV reads "to take the place" and does translate the words *ton topon*.[79] The meaning of the word "place" here in the first part of the verse is "position, office."

This ministry and apostleship. This is likely an instance of the figure of speech hendiadys, where two words are used to express one thing. It means "the apostolic ministry," or "the apostolic service."[80]

From which Judas turned aside. Judas turned aside instead of adhering faithfully to the character and service which his apostleship required of him. The transgression (for such is the literal meaning of *parabē*, here translated "turned aside") referred to was his treason and suicide.

To go to his own place. First it must be determined about whom this is speaking.

- Some have said it speaks of Matthias (or Joseph) going to his own place. The idea would be that Judas Iscariot fell in order that Matthias or Joseph might fill the place for which he was predestined and qualified by God. There are several objections to this interpretation. The apostolic office could with no propriety be called, in the case of Matthias, his own place, until it was actually conferred on him. There is no instance (so far as this commentator knows) where the expression "to go to his own place" is applied to a successor to an office. It surely is not true that God causes one man to transgress just so that another might take his office. It may be true that God removes a man who has sinned, but never is the reason for the sin the fact that God wants another

---

[79] The KJV reads "part of this ministry," following Codex Sinaiticus and the Textus Receptus. Nestle's test follows the readings of Codices A, B, C, D, and the Vulgate

[80] The Greek construction is a case where Sharp's Rule of Grammar helps understand the meaning. Sharp says that when two words in the same case are connected by "and," and the first has an article and the second doesn't, both words refer to the same thing, and the second is further explanation of the first. Ephesians 4:11 is another example, where "pastoring teachers" is the right idea — just one office, not two, being intended.

in the sinner's place. Finally, if the reference were to Matthias, then it would be merely repetition of what was said in the first part of this verse, that someone must take the place of Judas.
- The proper answer is that this phrase is speaking of Judas. It was Judas who went to his own place.

Second, what is the meaning of "to his own place"?
- Some suppose it refers to his own house. According to this idea, the meaning is that Judas left the apostolic office to return to his own home. Appeal is made to Numbers 24:25 as a parallel example. An objection to this idea is the fact that there is no evidence Judas merely went home rather than travel any longer with Jesus. In fact, the only thing we are told is that Judas went to find a place to hang himself.
- Another suggestion is that the phrase "his own place" refers to the grave. The idea is that the grave is the place of man, where all must lie, and in particular as an ignominious place where it was proper that a traitor like Judas should lie. There are also objections to this idea. There is no example where the word "place" is so used of the grave. There is no instance in ancient literature where a man, by being buried, is said to have returned to his own or proper place.
- Yet another suggestion is that the phrase in question speaks of the manner of Judas' death, i.e., by hanging. The key objection to this idea is that the word "place" does not apply to an act (suicide); it refers to a habitation, abode, situation in which to remain.
- The best explanation for the meaning of this phrase here in Acts is that it refers to the fact that Judas' soul went to a place of punishment in the intermediate world, and ultimately will be consigned to Hell. Such an interpretation accords with the crimes of Judas that such should be his eternal destiny. The expression "to go to his own place" is one which was used by ancient writers to denote going to an eternal destiny,[81] and such is the best explanation of its meaning here in Acts.

It is important to note that this passage does not teach Calvinistic predestination. The theory of predestination, according to Calvin, is that each man is predestined to either heaven or hell by the sovereign God. Each man's destiny is fixed, regardless of how he lives. Verse 25 does not say that Judas went to his predestined place. Rather, it indicates that he went to the proper place such a character as he should go.[82]

How would Peter know of the destiny of Judas, so as to make a statement like this? By comparing his knowledge of the man's character with the teaching of the Word of God. We doubt that Peter is speaking by inspiration at this point, for the day of Pentecost, with its coming of the baptism of the Holy Spirit, is still some days in the future.

---

[81] The Jewish tract, Baal Turim, on Numbers 24:25, says, "Balaam went to his own place, that is to Gehenna (Hell)." The Targum on Ecclesiastes 6:6 has, "Although the days of a man's life were 2000 years, and he did not study the Law, and do justice, in the day of his death his soul shall descend to hell, to the *one place* where sinners all go." Ignatius in *ad Magnesians* says, "Because all things have an end. the two things death and life shall lie down together, and each one shall go to his own place."

[82] See notes at Acts 16:28 concerning the nature of suicide, and whether or not it is sin. Also, Special Study #6 deals in greater detail with the problem of "Predestination and Foreknowledge."

1:26 – *And they drew lots for them, and the lot fell to Matthias; and he was numbered with the eleven apostles.*

And they drew lots for them. "They" likely speaks of the apostles as being the ones who drew the lots, rather than having all 120 voting on the matter. Indeed, the word "lot" does not express voting, or suffrage. This method of choosing is an Old Testament idea, just as was Peter's idea that someone should be chosen.

> The Jews were familiar with the process of casting lots; this method of decision by lot was an Old Testament custom. The land of Canaan was divided and assigned to the different tribes by lot, Numbers 26:55. The guilt of Achan seems to have been determined by lot, Joshua 7:14. The first king of Israel, Saul, was selected by lot, 1 Samuel 10:20,21. The same method was used to determine the "scapegoat," Leviticus 16:8. Proverbs 16:53 indicates how the lot was cast.[83]

A specially marked stone was placed among other stones in a cloth (like we place slips of paper in a hat), or in a container of some kind, and then drawn out, or shaken out. Another way of casting lots was to write each name on a tablet, place the tablets in an urn, and shake the urn till one came out.[84] Proverbs 16:33 tells us, "The lot is cast into the lap, but *the whole disposing thereof is of the Lord.*"[85]

This is the only instance of the use of lots in the New Testament. It occurs between the Lord's ascension and the coming of the Spirit on Pentecost. The church evidently dispensed with the use of lots after the coming of the Holy Spirit, who was to guide the apostles into all truth. The drawing of lots was not used in the choosing of later leaders, from which we gather the inference that now there is a better way.[86]

And the lot fell to Matthias. God chose Matthias to take the place of Judas Iscariot.

---

[83] H. Leo Boles, *Acts of Apostles* (Nashville: Gospel Advocate. 1941). p.31.

[84] Leviticus 16:8.

[85] Because a number of men who have developed a like for the habit of gambling have appealed to Acts 1:26 as Biblical sanction for continuing their indulgence, it would be well to paraphrase what Dale has written about gambling. "Casting lots does not authorize gambling in the church. The choice of Matthias is God's choice without chance in the casting of lots." "Chance" would be a "wager" or a "gamble." "God does not act by chance, and men do not live by chance." To insist that men live simply by chance is to deny God's providence. "It is wrong to gamble because God has ordained that man must live by honest work (Genesis 3:17-19; Ephesians 6:6 where 'eyeservice' is working only when watched, cheating; 1 Thessalonians 4:17, 2 Thessalonians 3:10-12). It is wrong to gain by tricking the other fellow, and getting his money from him without an honest effort in reciprocity. Life is not a gamble (as some would say). There is a vast difference between running the ordinary risks of life and living a life of trickery and stealth. The nickel and dime chances bought on everything from turkeys to cars are no less gambling than betting on the horses. Gambling is wrong because it is the attempt to get something valuable for little or nothing. The love of gambling is part of a materialistic philosophy that pervades much of our 20th century culture. Get money and things any way you can, except by honest work. Such a philosophy is an idea that the Scriptures abhor." Dale, *op. cit.*, p.23.

[86] Acts 6:1ff, and Titus 1:5ff. give several ways for choosing church leaders now that the Comforter has come.

And he was numbered with the eleven apostles. Nothing further is known of Matthias in the New Testament. There is a tale that one day he was forced to drink a hallucinogenic drug and was not harmed by it.[87] Other traditions from early church history concerning Matthias have been noted at 1:23.

Was Peter in the wrong in suggesting that one be chosen to take the place of Judas? The argument that Peter was wrong goes like this:

- Peter was not Holy Spirit-inspired as yet, and Paul was the one God intended to become the twelfth apostle. Since the Holy Spirit had not descended onto the apostles, and would not until the day of Pentecost, therefore Peter was mistaken because he was not Spirit-led at this point.
- It is also suggested that the choice of Matthias was a mistake because the idea and methodology were put forward by Peter, a man known to be hasty and impetuous. (Again, the belief is that God in His own good time planned to fill the office held by Judas by calling Paul.)

Before we accept the conclusion that Peter was running ahead of God and made a mistake, let us look at the indications that the choice, and the leadership of Peter in the matter, was not contrary to the will of God.

- The method used by Peter for determining the Lord's will was an accepted method; namely, finding a teaching or parallel example in the Scriptures, and then doing things according to the pattern found in Scripture.
- We are told Matthias "was numbered with the eleven apostles." If the choice of Matthias was contrary to the will of God, Luke had about 30 years after the choice to make the correction. Instead, Luke tells us that Matthias was numbered with the eleven. If Peter was wrong, and Luke does not tell us, how can we believe the rest of the narrative? Does not the Bible faithfully point out men's mistakes, lest we inadvertently make the same mistakes?
- It is conceivable that one of the things Jesus told the apostles to do (while He was telling them the things concerning the kingdom of God, Acts 1:3) was to select one to fill the place of Judas, and to do it before the promised Holy Spirit came in His baptismal measure (as He would do on the day of Pentecost).

We believe Bible students should be hesitant about accusing Peter of error in his suggestion that one be chosen to fill the place of Judas' apostleship. He took his idea from a principle in the Old Testament, and even the method of choosing was a common Old Testament method of determining the Divine will.

This discussion about whether or not Peter was acting in harmony with the will of God leads us to a related question: How do we know the Lord's will for our lives? We do not wish to run contrary to God. The following steps by which to learn the will of God are found in Dale's *Acts Comments:*

---

[87] *Acts of Andrew and Matthias. Ante-Nicene Fathers,* Vol. VIII, p.517.

According to Major Verval L. Smith, a soldier of many years in the U.S. Army (a student at the Cincinnati Bible Seminary, '45-'46), an elder in the Church of Christ (a man who, according to Smith, had been a veteran of the Spanish American War) passed this bit of information along to him: When we wish to know God's will, there are three things which always concur:

(1) The inward impulse [i.e., what would you really like to do, remembering that your talents are God given and are an indicator of His will];
(2) The Word of God;
(3) The trend of circumstances

God in the heart impelling you forward, God in His Book corroborating whatever He says in the heart, and God in circumstances, which are always indicative of His will. NEVER start until these things agree.[88]

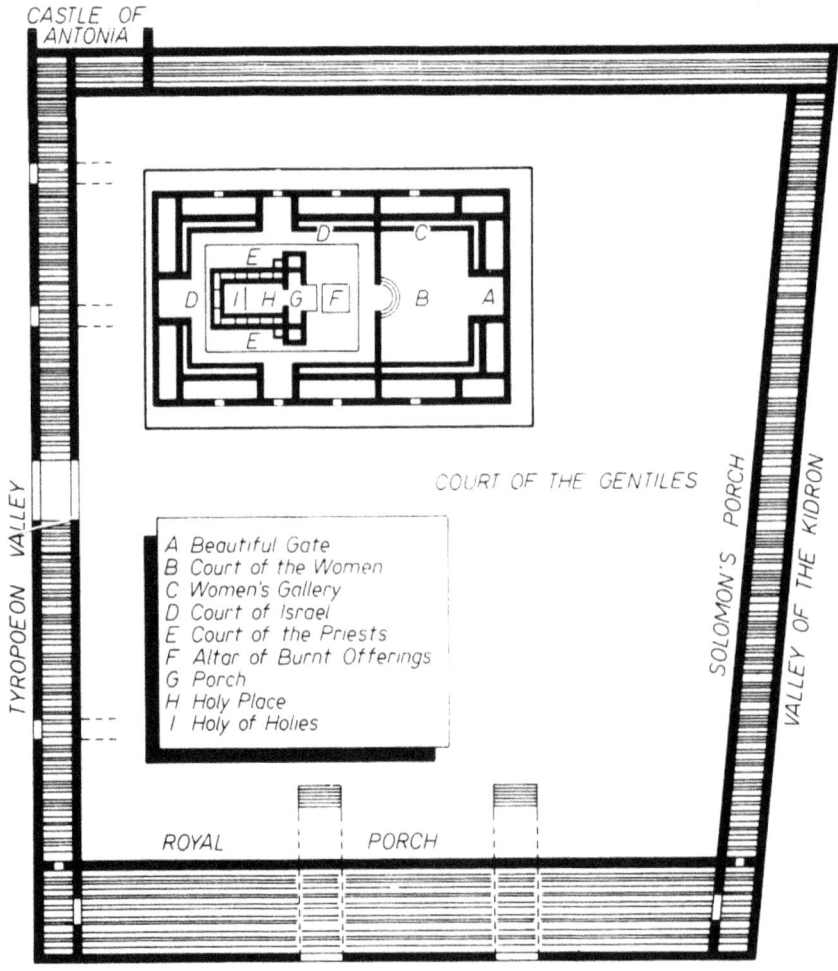

---

[88] Dale, *op. cit.*, p.17.

SPECIAL STUDY #1

DIVERSE OPINIONS ABOUT THE KINGDOM OF GOD

In the exegetical notes at Acts 1:3 and 1:6, the following points have been made:

(1) The disciples embraced the same erroneous ideas that most of their Jewish contemporaries held, namely, that the kingdom was to be a temporal, political, and earthly thing, when Messiah finally ushered it in.

(2) The "church" and the "kingdom" are but different terms for the same thing.

A dominant topic of discussion in the theological world is about the nature of the Kingdom of God. And this subject is but one of the many places in the New Testament where one's eschatology tends to influence, if not determine, his "exegetical" notes.

A brief survey of some of the current eschatological schemes will show how a variety of interpretations is given to the question asked by the disciples (Acts 1:6), and each of the interpretations is more or less exclusive of all the others.

Before we can study the diagrams of the various eschatological theories, we must read some key passages and note some terms.

Key Passages	*Key Terminology to be Noted*
Matthew 25:31-46	▪ Sheep and Goat Judgment
1 Thessalonians 4:13-18	▪ "Rapture" of the Church ▪ Resurrection of the righteous
2 Thessalonians 2:1-12	▪ Man of sin (Antichrist?)
1 John 2:18ff	▪ Antichrist
Revelation 16:16	▪ Battle of Armageddon
Revelation 20:1-10	▪ Binding of Satan ▪ Thousand years (Millennium) ▪ Satan loosed ▪ 1,000-year reign of Christ ▪ First resurrection ▪ Gog and Magog
Revelation 20:11-15	▪ Great White Throne Judgment
Revelation 7:14	▪ Great Tribulation *(Matthew 24:14 is erroneously used to speak of the alleged "Great Tribulation" at the end of the world. We believe that the verse in Matthew talks not of the end of the world, but of the destruction of Jerusalem in AD 70.)*

Now that we've been reminded of some of the key passages and have learned some of the key terminology used, let's examine some of the various eschatological schemes and their concepts of the "kingdom." We are not giving approval, at the present, to any of these theories. Rather, we are merely presenting them, to learn how the "kingdom" is understood and presented by the different eschatologies.

I. POSTMILLENNIAL IDEA OF THE "KINGDOM"

"Postmillennial means that the second coming of Christ is after (i.e., post) the millennium. A chart depicting the postmillennial theory might look like this:

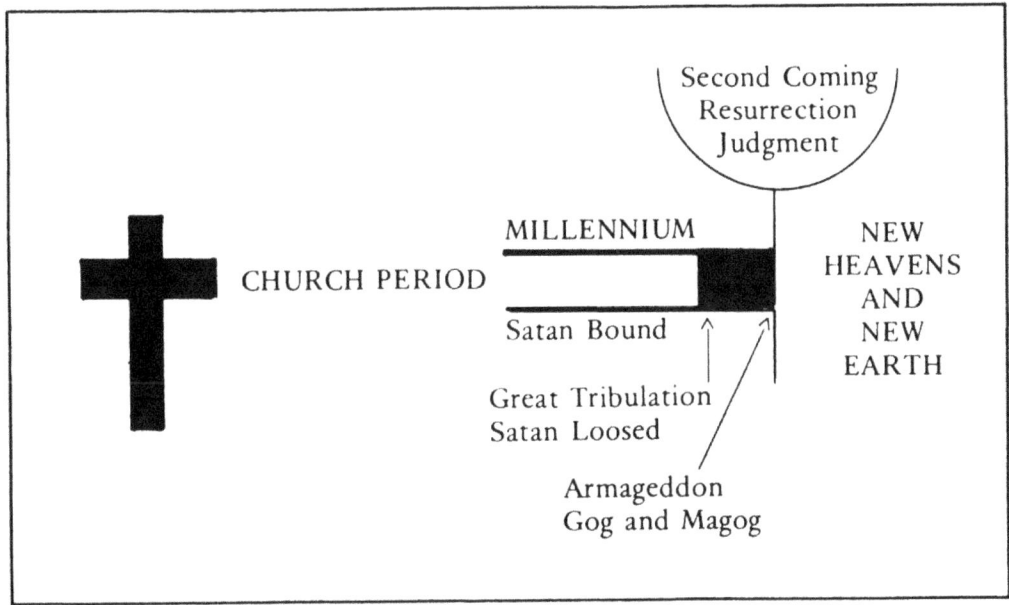

An explanation of the chart's chief ideas: (1) The time covered by the diagram is from the death of Christ (i.e., i.e., the cross) till the second coming. (2) According to postmillennialists, the kingdom (labeled "Millennium" on the chart) gradually comes into being, to be ushered in as mankind becomes better and better. (3) Following the 1000 years of the golden age of the kingdom, Christ will return, and (4) eternity (in Heaven or Hell) will begin.

The "kingdom" of Acts 1:6 and the "millennium" are the same thing, if you are postmillennial in your eschatology.

II. HISTORIC PREMILLENNIAL IDEA OF THE "KINGDOM"

"Historic" means that this system of eschatology is very ancient, being taught by some of the early church fathers. For example, see the Epistle of Barnabas, and the writings of Papias, Justin Martyr, Irenaeus, Tertullian, and Victorinus. Of course, not all of the early church fathers were premillennial in eschatology. Gaius of Rome and Origen, just to name two, strongly opposed premillennial doctrines.

"Premillennial" means the second coming of Christ is thought to be before (i.e., pre) the millennium. A chart depicting the postmillennial theory might look like this:

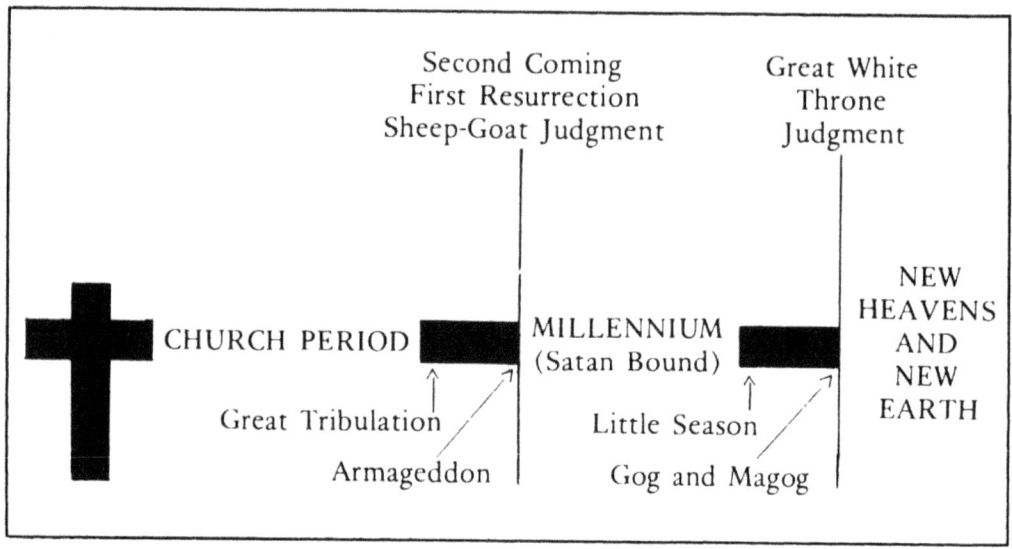

An explanation of the chart's chief ideas: (1) The kingdom, a thousand years of peace and prosperity, is to be ushered in at the second coming. (2) It is to be an earthly kingdom in which Christians are reigned over by Christ.

The "kingdom" of Acts 1:6 and the "millennium" are the same thing, if you are historic-premillennial in your eschatology.

III. THE DISPENSATIONAL PREMILLENNIAL (i.e., Modern Premillennial) IDEA OF THE "KINGDOM"

According to this theory, a "dispensation" is a period of time during which man is tested in respect of obedience to some specific revelation of the will of God. According to the most popular version of dispensationalism, there are seven such dispensations distinguished in Scripture (see note 5, page 5, of the *Scofield Reference Bible*). A chart depicting the dispensational theory is shown on the following page.

An explanation of the chart's chief ideas: (1) According to dispensationalists, Christ really intended to set up an earthly, temporal kingdom, just as the Jews supposed Messiah would. However, unforeseen by God, the Jews rejected Christ, and so the coming of the kingdom had to be postponed until the second coming (this idea is shown on the chart by the dotted semi-circular line). (2) As a stop-gap measure, the Church age (which was unforeseen by the Old Testament Prophets) was ushered in. (3) The Jewish star at the left of the chart indicates that God has always intended for the Jewish people to be His special people. When the kingdom comes, the Jewish people will again be His special people, and the millennium will be an earthly reign over the Jews by Christ.

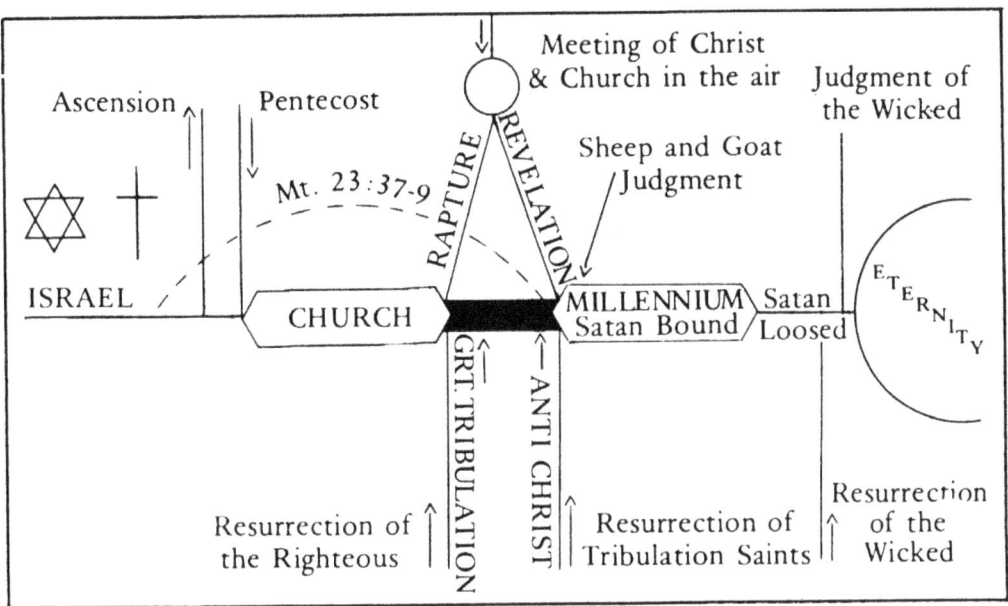

The "kingdom" of Acts 1:6 and the "millennium" are the same thing, if you are modern premillennial in your eschatology.

IV. THE AMILLENNIAL IDEA OF THE "KINGDOM"

"Amillennial" means "no literal 1,000-year period" as such – i.e., there is no literal 1000-year reign of Christ on earth from a rebuilt city of Jerusalem. (*Note:* This commentator is amillennial in eschatology, and the interpretation given in the exegetical notes at Acts 1:6 is from an amillennial standpoint.)

A chart depicting the amillennial theory looks like this:

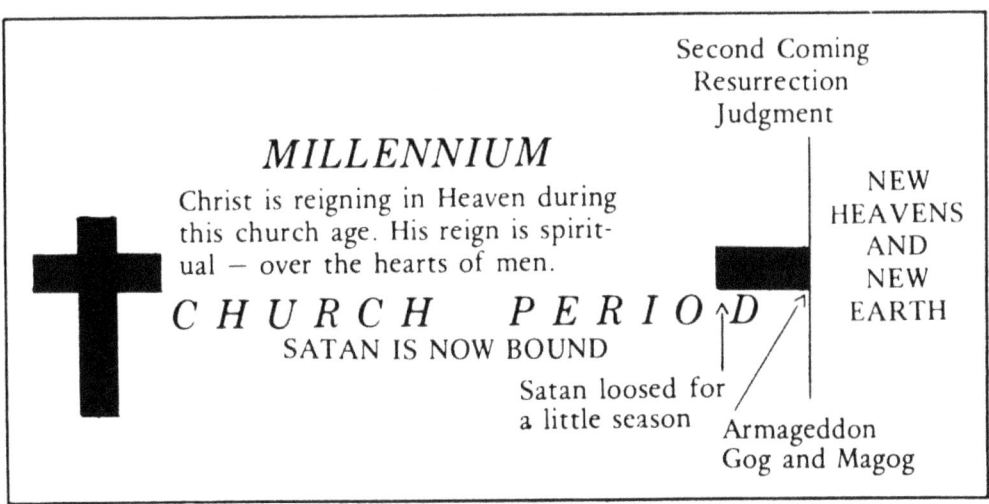

An explanation of the chart's chief ideas: (1) The Scriptures appear to teach one second coming, one general resurrection, one general judgment. (2) The millennium of Revelation 20 is understood to be figurative language, and represents the whole Church age. (3) Satan being "bound" means that his powers are limited. (See, for example, Jude 6.) (4) The reign of Christ is spiritual and is going on right now. (5) When the second coming takes place, Christ will not set up an earthly kingdom, but will turn the kingdom which already exists over to God (1 Corinthians 15:20-28).

(This commentator realizes that there are some passages that are difficult to fit into an amillennial system of eschatology. But this fact is true of each of the four systems. He finds fewer problem passages with the amillennial approach than he does with any of the other systems, and has therefore embraced the amillennial system as being the most probable system of eschatology.)

CONCLUSION

What is the kingdom of God? It is not easy to give a single, definite, brief answer which would be satisfactory to all students, or true to all Scriptural uses of the phrase. Its essential idea is the reign or government of God over the lives of men. Sometimes it comprehends the characteristics and advantages of the complete submission of the individual life to the rule of God. Sometimes it refers to the whole community of people (i.e., the church) who obey God on earth. Sometimes it has reference to heaven itself as a place where God reigns in perfect peace, wisdom, and glory.

One thing seems evident: the kingdom that Jesus set up is not a worldly, materialistic, or military kingdom. He said, "My kingdom is not of this world" (John 18:36). It also seems clear that the "kingdom" is not to be equated with the millennial ideas of a literal 1,000-year reign of Christ on earth from a rebuilt city of Jerusalem, after Jesus has returned the second time.

References for further study:
Books
   Allis, O.T., *Prophecy and the Church*
   Boettner, Loraine, *The Millennium*
   Brown, David, *Christ's Second Coming*
   Foster, R.C., *The Final Week* (Chapters 11 and 12)
   Hamilton, Floyd, *The Basis of the Millennial Faith*
   Hendriksen, William, *More than Conquerors*
   Hodges, Jesse W., *Christ's Kingdom and Coming*
   Kik, J. Marcellus, *Revelation Twenty*
   Kromminga, D.H., *The Millennium*
   Ladd, George E., "Kingdom of God," in *Baker's Dictionary of Theology* Murray, George C., *Millennial Studies*
   Orr, James, *The Christian View of God and the World* (appendix)
   Ramm, Bernard, "Kingdom of God," in *A Handbook of Contemporary Theology*

Periodicals
   Martin, Ralph P., "The Kingdom of God in Recent Writing," *Christianity Today,* Jan. 17, 1964, p.347ff. (This is a good survey of the scholars' treatment of the "kingdom" in the last 50 years.)
   Wilson, Seth, "The Kingdom of God among Men," *Christian Standard,* 1948, p. 159.

SPECIAL STUDY #2

THE BROTHERS OF THE LORD

In Mark 6:3 and Matthew 12:46, four "brothers" of Jesus are mentioned. Matthew 13:55-56 tells of at least two "sisters." The theological world has been sharply divided as to the exact relationship of these people to our Lord.

I. THE HELVIDIAN VIEW

This statement of belief is so called because of the very clear statement of Helvidius (c. AD 380) that the "brethren" of Jesus were sons of Joseph and Mary. Helvidius was not the first to believe this way; this view was clearly held in the church of the 2nd century.

When Helvidius wrote, he was merely restating the belief of many generations before his time. But as the beginnings of the Roman Catholic Church developed, the gradual growth of the worship of Mary led to the doctrine that Mary was perpetually a virgin, and to the various efforts to explain away *adelphos* (Grk. for "brother") as "cousin."

II. THE EPIPHANIAN VIEW

Epiphanius (c. AD 380; bishop of Salamis on Cyprus) held the view that Mary had no other children than our Lord. The "brethren" were Joseph's children by a former marriage.

The earliest form of this view seems to be in the apocryphal gospels. (Apocryphal = of doubtful authenticity, spurious, counterfeit.) In the *Protevangelium Jacobi,* Joseph is represented as a widower of more than 90 years, with a number of children, when he takes Mary for his wife. The *Gospel of Peter* adds the thought that Mary is a child of 12 when she is betrothed to Joseph. Origen inclined to the Ephiphanian view, although he admitted it had no backing other than the legendary apocryphal gospels and had only a dogmatic or sentimental basis. The Greek Orthodox and the Eastern sects have generally held to this view. Many Protestants have also held to the Epiphanian view, among them Luther, Lightfoot, and others.

On the one hand, "no conclusive objection can be brought against the Epiphanian view. It is not intrinsically improbable, nor contrary to anything in the Scriptures, that Joseph should have married, lost his wife, and had a family of children by his former wife, when he became betrothed to Mary." (Ropes, "James" in *International Critical Commentary*, p.60.) On the other hand, no real evidence speaks for it. The Epiphanian view does not agree with Matthew 1:25, "knew her not *until* she brought forth a son." Nor does it agree with the use of "firstborn" in Luke 2:7, which implies Jesus was not the only child of his mother. Indeed, the apocryphal gospels afford no trustworthy tradition. In fact, it seems likely "the Epiphanian view had its roots in the dogmatic assumptions of ascetic theology." (Ropes, p.60.)

III. THE HIERONYMIAN VIEW

"Hieronymian" means "composed by Jerome." Jerome (AD 385), while studying in Rome, wrote a reply to Helvidius affirming the perpetual virginity of Mary. This view reduces the number of persons in the New Testament by the name of "James" to two – both apostles – James the son of Zebedee, and James the son of Alphaeus. The "brothers" and "sisters" of Jesus were held to be "cousins" of Jesus, the children of His mother's sister, Mary the wife of Clopas.

"Jerome's theory appears to have been wholly original with him, and both his own efforts and those of later Roman Catholic writers to find support for this view in earlier ecclesiastical tradition have failed." (Ropes, p.58.) It seems Jerome invented the view to protect the doctrine of the perpetual virginity of Mary, a doctrine which arose from pagan environs and caused the church to change from the early and natural view as to the identity of the "brethren" to the later, ascetic view. Augustine adopted Jerome's view, and it generally has held sway in the Roman Catholic Church. Some Protestant commentators (e.g., Barnes) have been unduly influenced by Jerome and Augustine.

Among the weighty objections against the Hieronymian view are these: (1) *Adelphos* cannot mean "cousin." This is, in fact, impossible, and is fatal to the whole theory. There is no New Testament or Classical Greek example, as far as this commentator knows, of *adelphos* being used to denote "cousin." (2) Jerome's interpretation of John 19:25 is very unlikely. He said that Mary of Clopas is the sister of the virgin Mary. (3) It is not proper to identify "Clopas" and "Alphaeus," as must be done, if one is to hold to Jerome's views. (4) To hold this theory of Jerome's, one must make an unwarrantable distinction between the James of Galatians 1:19 and the James of Galatians 2:9.

IV. FURTHER DETAILED STUDY

Having briefly defined the three views concerning the "brothers" of the Lord, there is need to give attention, in detail, to some of the questions that arise as one tries to settle the problem of their relationship to Jesus.

> A. May we identify "James, the son of Alphaeus" and "James, the Lord's brother" as being the same person?

A listing of the women who watched the crucifixion will have a bearing on our answer to this question.

Matthew 27:56	Mark 15:40	John 19:25
		His mother
Mary Magdalene	Mary Magdalene	Mary Magdalene
Mary, the mother of James & Joses	Mary, the mother of James the less and Joses	Mary, the wife of Clopas
The mother of the sons of Zebedee	And Salome	The sister of Jesus' mother

Matthew and Mark each name three women, whence it is thought that Salome was the name of the wife of Zebedee. Much of our problem lies with John 19:25. Does John name three or four women?

- If *three*, then Mary, the wife of Clopas, was Jesus' mother's sister. (James the less and Joses would be cousins of Jesus, and Jerome would appear to be correct.) But it seems unlikely that two sisters would have the same name, i.e., Mary.
- If John names *four* women, then Salome, the wife of Zebedee, was Jesus' mother's sister. Thus, James and John, sons of Zebedee, would be Jesus' cousins.

There is much in favor of the idea that John lists *four* women: (1) John would be giving two pairs of women, each coupled by "and." The first pair is kindred to Jesus, and is unnamed. It is paralleled by the other pair, which is not kindred, and whose names are given, as was the custom of John. (2) It accords with John's custom to withhold the names of himself and all his kindred. In his Gospel he nowhere gives his own, his mother's, or his brother's name, nor does he even give the name of our Lord's mother, who was his aunt. (3) This relationship would explain in part why Jesus, when dying, left the care of His mother to John. It was not an unnatural thing to impose such a burden upon a kinsman.

The conclusion to this first question then is this: If John names but three women, then very probably "James the son of Alphaeus" and "James the Lord's brother" are the same people. But if, as seems more likely, John names four women, there is no reason to say they are the same man.

> B. *What are the arguments, pro and con, concerning Jerome's theory that the "brothers of the Lord" are really "cousins" – being in truth the children of Alphaeus?*

Two key arguments have been advanced in favor of identifying "the sons of Alphaeus" and "the brothers of the Lord."

(1) If the two men named James (James the son of Alphaeus, and James the brother of the Lord) are distinct, then one of them (the son of Alphaeus, one of the Twelve apostles) disappears altogether from the New Testament after Acts 1:13. It is argued, therefore, "Would we have James the apostle disappear, and another James – almost unintroduced, which is contrary to Luke's custom – suddenly taking a prominent position in the church at Jerusalem?" (By way of reply: Several of the apostles disappear after Acts 1:13 – e.g., Simon the Zealot, Bartholomew, and Thomas. And James, the leader of the Jerusalem church, may be considered to have been sufficiently introduced at Acts 1:14, where it speaks of "His brethren.")

(2) If James the son of Alphaeus and James the brother of the Lord are distinct (it is argued), we have certainly *two*, and in all probability *three*, sets of brothers bearing the same names: (a) James, Joseph, and Simon, the Lord's brothers; (b) James, Joses, and Symeon, the sons of Clopas; and (c) James, Joses, and Symeon, the sons of Alphaeus. (By way of reply: These names were common ones, so not much stress should be laid upon this argument.)

Whether or not Alphaeus and Clopas are the same man, one being his Hebrew name, the other being the Aramaic equivalent, is another problem. See McGarvey, *Fourfold Gospel,* p.224; and Ropes, *International Critical Commentary on James,* p.58.

On the other hand, the arguments against making the identification that Jerome did are weighty. (1) If we say "the sons of Alphaeus" and the "brothers of Jesus" are different people, it enables us to give the term *adelphos,* "brother," its natural meaning. There is a distinct Greek word (*suggenēs*) for "cousin." As Ropes suggested (p.61), absent the need to support the dogma regarding Mary's perpetual virginity, no one would have thought of trying to make *adelphos* mean 'cousin' instead of 'brother.' (2) To make the identification that Jerome did, one must say that some of the "brothers" of Jesus were also His "apostles." But the New Testament regularly distinguishes between the "apostles" and the "brothers" of the Lord. (See John 2:12, 7:15; Mark 3:21,31; Acts 1:14.) In fact, the "brother of the Lord" could not have been one of the original apostles, for the brethren of the Lord did not believe on Him (John 7:5). (3) Finally, the "Lord's brethren" are mentioned in the Gospels in connection with Mary (His mother) or with Joseph (His reputed father). Never once are they mentioned in connection with Mary (the wife of Clopas), as would surely be the case if Jerome's theory were true.

CONCLUSION

We conclude that Helvidius had things exactly right; namely, that the "brothers" of Jesus were actually half-brothers, the sons of Joseph and Mary, born after Jesus.

We also conclude that the "brothers" of the Lord and the "sons" of Alphaeus are distinct sets of people. And if Alphaeus and Clopas are not the same man, then we have three sets of children with the same names.

Further, we conclude that the "brothers" of Jesus and the apostles are two distinct groups of people.

The Mount of Olives

**Drawing by Horace Knowles
from the British and Foreign Bible Society**

E. The Apostles Baptized with the Holy Spirit. 2:1-4

2:1 – And when the day of Pentecost had come, they were all together in one place.

And when the day of Pentecost. "Pentecost" is a Greek word signifying the fiftieth part of a thing, or the fiftieth in order. The word came to have a technical meaning, referring to one of the feasts of the Jews. This feast had several other names. It was also called "the feast of weeks" because of the seven weeks that intervened between it and the Passover.[1] Because the wheat harvest occurred in that 50-day interval between Passover and Pentecost, it was also called "the feast of harvest."[2] And on account of the offering peculiar to it, it was also called the "feast of first fruits."[3] But after the Greek language became known in Palestine, in consequence of Alexander's conquest of Asia and Syria, it acquired the name Pentecost (fiftieth), because it was the fiftieth day after the Passover sabbath.

God's people, the Jews, were required by Law to keep three annual festivals – the feast of Passover, the feast of Pentecost, and the feast of Tabernacles.[4] The PASSOVER feast commemorated the deliverance of Israel from Egyptian bondage.[5] At the time of the Exodus, when the first Passover was held, the lamb was slain and roasted during the afternoon of the 14th of the Jewish month Nisan, and then eaten just after the 15th of Nisan began. (Remember, Jewish days began at sunset.) Blood from the lamb was sprinkled on the door posts and lintel of the house in which the lamb was to be eaten. Every house that had no blood on the door posts was visited by the Angel of Destruction during that night, and the first-born of both man and beast was slain. Each house with blood on the posts was passed over – hence, the name "Passover." Following this tenth of the plagues brought by God on Egypt, Pharaoh released the Jews from the bondage in Egypt. In New Testament times, Passover began on the 10th of Nisan (a month roughly equivalent to our March or April, depending on the vernal equinox, and varying just as our "Easter" does), on which day the lamb was selected, followed by the sacrifice and celebration on the 14th and 15th of Nisan, just as of old. This was followed by a week-long feast of "unleavened bread" which completed the Passover celebration. The feast of PENTECOST came next in the Jewish calendar. This feast was a kind of thanksgiving day, a feast of thanking God for the bountiful crops that were just beginning to be harvested ("first fruits"). It was celebrated, according to the Mosaic Law, by the special service of offering the first-fruits of the wheat harvest in the form of two loaves of bread.[6] The last of the three annual feasts was that of TABERNACLES. It was celebrated after the harvest had all been gathered in,

---

[1] Deuteronomy 16:10.

[2] Exodus 23:16.

[3] Leviticus 23:17; Numbers 28:26.

[4] 2Chronicles 8:12-13; 1 Kings 9:25, 12:32-33.

[5] Exodus 12:3-20.

[6] Leviticus 23:15-21; Numbers 28:26-31. In Old Testament times, Pentecost was a harvest feast. In later Judaism, Pentecost came to be reckoned as the anniversary of the giving of the Law at Mt. Sinai since it happened to be 50 days after Passover that the Law was given. See *Jubilees* 1:1 and 6:17; *Babylonian Talmud,* Pesachim 68b; and Midrash *Tanchuma* 26c. There is no evidence that Jews in New Testament times looked on Pentecost as the anniversary of the giving of the Law.

and so also came to be called "the Feast of the Ingathering."[7] This feast also commemorated the Jews' deliverance from Egypt and their wandering in the wilderness, when they had to dwell in "tabernacles"[8] (i.e., a lean-to kind of structure). This festival also lasted seven days, and it began after the Day of Atonement, a day that usually falls in our month of September.[9]

On what day of the week did Pentecost fall in New Testament times? Some commentaries say Pentecost always fell on Sunday. Others, that it fell on any day of the week in any given year. Which are correct? Is it of any importance? Barnes, for one, says it is of little importance on what day of the week Pentecost fell.[10] We reply that it is of great importance, for if Pentecost did not fall on Sunday, we lose one of the great reasons (i.e., the church began on Sunday) for worshiping on Sunday. (Another reason for worshiping on Sunday is that the resurrection of Jesus took place on Sunday, and ever since, the church has celebrated His resurrection each first day of the week.)

The answer to the problem of which day of the week Pentecost fell on rests upon the interpretation of Leviticus 23:1-16 (especially verse 15). We shall state the problem, study the history of the interpretation of the passage, and then draw our conclusion.

- The problem is this. Some allege the first day of the feast of unleavened bread (Passover) was called a "sabbath," regardless of the day of the week on which it fell. Then, the 50-day count until Pentecost began the day after the first day of unleavened bread. Thus, Pentecost could fall on any day of the week. Others assert that the sabbath talked about in Leviticus 23:15 is the regular weekly sabbath. Counting from the day after the regular weekly sabbath, Pentecost would always fall on Sunday.

- Historically, the Leviticus passage was variously interpreted. The *Sadducees,* who were in power in the 1st century AD, interpreted the sabbath of verse 15 to be the regular weekly sabbath. Until the destruction of Jerusalem, at which time the Sadducean aristocracy lost their control over Jewish religious practices, the interpretation of the Sadducees would have been normative. Thus, until the fall of Jerusalem, Pentecost always fell on Sunday. It would have been a Sunday when the events of Acts 2 took place. The *Pharisees,* however, took the other position, believing the sabbath of Leviticus 23:15 to be the first day of unleavened bread. After the fall of Jerusalem, the Pharisees became the recognized religious authorities, and from that time on their interpretation would have been normative.[11] Josephus follows the interpretation of the Pharisees when he explains that the 50 days were counted from "the second day of un-

---

[7] Exodus 34:22.

[8] Leviticus 23:40-44.

[9] Leviticus 16:1ff, 23:26, 23:32; Numbers 29:7-11.

[10] Barnes, *op. cit.*, p. 20.

[11] The Pharisaic reckoning became normative in Judaism after AD 70; thus, in AD 1953 the first day of unleavened bread falls on Tuesday, March 31 (Nisan 15, 5713), and the first day of the feast of weeks falls on Wednesday, May 20 (Siwan 6, 5713), on the fiftieth day by inclusive reckoning from the second day of unleavened bread. Cf. Mishnah *Menachoth* x. 3; Tosefta *Menachoth* x.3.528; Babylonina. Talmud *Menachoth* 65a; see also L. Finkelstein, *The Pharisees* (Philadelphia, 1946), p.115ff. Bruce, *op. cit.*, p.53.

leavened bread, which is the 16th day of the month."[12] If the Pharisees misinterpreted the Leviticus text, then Josephus' explanation too is a misinterpretation, and those many modern commentators who appeal to Josephus for proof will find that their conclusions rest on shaky evidence.

- The conclusion as to the day of the week on which Pentecost fell: the correct opinion is that Pentecost always fell on the first day of the week in New Testament times. McGarvey writes:

> The language [of Leviticus 23] is not easily misunderstood – for even if the first clause, the words "from the morrow after the sabbath" (v.15) could be construed as meaning from the morrow after the first day of unleavened bread; the latter part of the sentence precludes any such interpretation; for the count was to be "unto the morrow after the SEVENTH SABBATH," and the word here unquestionably means a weekly sabbath (i.e., Saturday).[13]

If McGarvey is correct, then the first day of unleavened bread – even though in it no servile work was to be done – is never called a "Sabbath;" and not even Leviticus 23:15 can be used to prove that it is.

Had come. The marginal reading is "was being fulfilled." The day of Pentecost was an ideal time for the coming of the Holy Spirit. Of the three Jewish feasts, this is the one likely to be the best attended. Jews were dispersed over the Mediterranean World, and it would not be possible for many to attend all three feasts during the year. Travel, especially on the sea, would be hazardous, were one to attempt to come to Passover or Tabernacles, but to come to Pentecost would not have nearly as many dangers. So if a Jew had to choose which of the feasts he would attend, it was naturally Pentecost. Another reason it could be said to be an ideal time is because God has been pointing all of history toward this day. If Jesus came in the fullness of time, and He did, and if His death and resurrection were the "good news" for which the world had been waiting, then this Pentecost following His suffering and glorification was the right time for the Holy Spirit to come. As they have been instructed to do, the apostles are waiting in Jerusalem for the empowering that will aid them to witness to what they know.

They were all together in one place. Who is meant by "they"? Some answer, "The 120 mentioned in Acts 1:15."[14] While this explanation was first advanced by Chrysostom (AD 347-404), it is without support in the context. The fact that the prophecy about to be quoted from Joel contains "universal language" is sometimes proffered as evidence that surely more than the apostles (i.e., that all 120) received the baptism with the Holy Spirit. However, before we are swayed by the argument from Joel's "universal language," it should be observed that not *all* of Joel's prediction was fulfilled on Pentecost. According to the record in Acts 2, none present was seeing visions, or dreaming dreams. What hap-

---

[12] *Antiquities*, III.10.5.

[13] J.W. McGarvey, *New Commentary on Acts of Apostles* (Cincinnati: Standard, 1892), Vol. I, p.19.

[14] A partial list of interpreters who believe all 120 are involved in Acts 2 are Hervey, Barnes. Meyer, Wordsworth, Alford, Lange, Farrar, Ellicott.

pened on the day of Pentecost was only the beginning of the fulfillment of that which Joel predicted.[15] We need not, therefore, postulate that it *must* have been all 120 who received the baptism with the Holy Spirit, for Joel's language is more inclusive of the early days of the church than simply what happened on Pentecost. The apostles received the baptism with the Holy Spirit on Pentecost, and the "sons and daughters, young men and old," received the Spirit in the days immediately following.

"They" in Acts 2:1 evidently is limited to the twelve apostles. Several lines of proof point to this conclusion.

- Verse 7 says that all who were baptized with the Holy Spirit (and subsequently were speaking in "tongues") were Galileans. This note of identification would fit the Twelve, but it might be difficult to show that all 120 in that upper room in Judea were Galileans.

- Again, it was the apostles to whom Jesus was speaking in Acts 1:5 when He promised that they would receive the baptism with the Holy Spirit. By what means do we now include others as involved in the fulfillment of that promise, without ignoring some of the basic rules of hermeneutics, rules as old as Wycliffe, or older?

- The grammatical construction of 1:26 and 2:1 points *only* to the apostles as the recipients of the baptism with the Holy Spirit on the day of Pentecost. When we remember that the original manuscripts did not contain the chapter and paragraph divisions that our English translations do, and when we read from chapter 1 to chapter 2 without pausing between them, it becomes very clear who Luke wanted us to understand were baptized with the Holy Spirit. The antecedent of any pronoun is generally found by referring back to the nearest noun with which it agrees in person, number, and gender. This clinches the argument that the baptism with the Holy Spirit was something that happened *only* to the apostles, as far as Acts 2 is concerned.

Where was the "one place" where they were "all together"? Verse 2 tells us about "the house where they were sitting." Some think the place where the apostles were was the same home in which they were staying (Acts 1:13). But it is improbable that a multitude of over 3000 (verses 14 and 41) to whom the apostles preached could gather even in the courtyard of such a home. Others have thought they were in one of the synagogues in Jerusalem. Probably the best opinion is that they were in the temple area. We learn that this event took place at an hour of prayer (verse 15), and the apostles were continuing steadfast in prayer at the temple during the hours of prayer.[16] Since this was a great feast day for the Jews, and since the temple was the central place for such a celebration, it does not seem logical that the apostles would be in their homes upon such an occasion. However, if we picture the apostles as being in the temple area, say one of the rooms along the wall, rooms which would be open toward the temple court, all they needed to do was to turn to the patio side of the room, and there were many acres of the temple area to accommodate the crowd drawn together by the strange phenomena which happened.

---

[15] See notes at Acts 2:17-20, where explanation is advanced concerning that which Joel predicted, including a discussion of the concept of "Mountain Peak Prophecies."

[16] Acts 1:14.

2:2 – *And suddenly there came from heaven a noise like a violent, rushing wind, and it filled the whole house where they were sitting.*

And suddenly there came from heaven. The events happened unexpectedly, and therefore were a startling phenomena. "From heaven," i.e., appearing to rush down from the sky. Winds blow horizontally. This sound came down (vertically?), and thus would attract attention from its unusual *direction* as well as the *suddenness*.

A noise like a violent, rushing wind. Literally, "as of a violent blast borne along" (*pheromenēs*, 'rushing along'). It does not appear that there was any wind, only the sudden sound like a violent wind. Observers in our time have described the sound of a tornado as being like the sound of a number of railroad trains all passing at once. And in a gale, the wind is sometimes borne along so violently and with such noise as to make it difficult to hear even the thunder in the gale. Some such noise should be thought of as rushing down out of the sky on the day of Pentecost.

The Greek word "wind" is not the one commonly so translated (*anemos*) but is one from the same root as the Greek for "spirit" (*pnoē*). It perhaps is here used as better fitted than the more common word for the supernatural inbreathing which was then taking place.

And it filled the whole house where they were sitting. What filled the house? Not the wind! There is no evidence there was even a breeze stirring. It was the sound that filled the house! In fact, the grammatical structure of the sentence admits no other conclusion since *ēchos* ("noise" or sound) is the only word in the nominative (subjective) case in the sentence. A phenomenon like this, so unusual, would attract attention. When all was still, when there was no storm, no wind, no rain, no thunder (it being the dry season), such a rushing sound must have arrested people's attention, and directed all minds to this unusual and unaccountable happening. People would begin to wonder how to account for a sound like that, when not a breeze was stirring. Shortly, the apostles, who have been sitting in the temple, waiting for the events of the day's celebration to begin, will stand up and explain to the wondering multitude the meaning of the unusual sound.

2:3 – *And there appeared to them tongues as of fire distributing themselves, and they rested on each one of them.*

And there appeared to them tongues ... distributing themselves. The "fire-like appearing" thing first was seen by the apostles and others gathered in the Temple area before it rested in the form of "tongues" on the apostles. It seems there was one great sheet of light, and that this broke up into different parts called "tongues" which rested on each of the twelve. They are called "tongues" because they were tongue-shaped. The verb "distributing themselves (mg. being distributed)" does not mean that each flame was forked; that is, it was not "cloven tongues" as the KJV renders it. Our mental picture probably should be of one great flame splitting up and a part going to each of the apostles. Thus, we have the symbolic picture of the Holy Spirit imparting Himself to each of the apostles, or dividing Himself to each so each had His presence and guidance.

As of fire. The "tongues" were not actual fire, but something that looked like "fire." Early in the Introductory Studies, we became acquainted with a method of interpretation designated as "religious liberalism." So the student will be better acquainted with the results of this method, we reproduce Renan's interesting (and blasphemous) treatment of this event.

> One day when the brethren were come together there was a tempest. A violent wind burst open the windows, and the sky was one sheet of fire. In that climate tempests are often accompanied by an extraordinary amount of lightning. The atmosphere is on all sides furrowed with jets of flame. On that occasion, whether the lightning actually passed through the room, or whether the faces of all present were suddenly lit up by an extremely bright flash of lightning, all were convinced that the Holy Spirit had entered their assembly, and had sat upon the head of each in the shape of a tongue. In these moments of ecstasy, the disciples possessed by the Spirit uttered sounds inarticulate and incoherent, which the hearers fancied were the words of a strange language, and in their simplicity tried to interpret. They listened eagerly to the medley of sounds, and explained them by their own extemporaneous thoughts. Each of them had recourse to his native *patois* to supply some meaning to the unintelligible accents, and generally succeeded in affixing to them the thoughts that were uppermost in his own mind.[17]

And they rested on each one of them. That is, the tongue rested for a moment, in the form of a lambent or gentle flame, on each of them, and then vanished. The verb tense expresses momentary, not continuous, action.

2:4 – *And they were all filled with the Holy Spirit and began to speak with other tongues, as the Spirit was giving them utterance.*

And they were all filled with the Holy Spirit. This is the third event. The first was the sound from heaven which affected the ear. The second was the "tongues like fire" which would be seen by the eyes. And now the third. Whether these three came close together, or all at the same moment, cannot be determined with certainty. "Entirely under His power" is what Barnes thinks "filled with the Spirit" means.[18] But this does not seem to be quite correct, for the spirits of the prophets are subject to the prophets.[19] For detailed information as to what "filled with the Spirit" means in the case of the apostles, see Special Study #3, "The Person and Work of the Holy Spirit," at the close of this chapter. Suffice it to say here that this filling gave those men the endowments they needed to qualify them to do the work of an apostle. In fact, it would appear that it was the thing that made an apostle, as compared to, say, a prophet.

---

[17] *Les Apotres*, p.65-68, as quoted in *Pulpit Commentary* on Acts. We remind the reader that at Acts 1:5 we rejected the idea that the "tongues as of fire" was a fulfillment of John's prediction about "baptized with ... fire."

[18] Barnes, *op. cit.*, p.22.

[19] 1 Corinthians 14:32.

And began to speak with other tongues. In the apostles' case, this is one result of the baptism with the Holy Spirit – they began to speak with other tongues as the Spirit gave them utterance. What does "speaking in tongues" mean? Some would say it was only the uttering of unintelligible sounds, the using of a mere jargon of syllables with no meaning. Verses 6 and 8, however, indicate that speaking in tongues in the Bible means speaking in a foreign language which one has never studied. What the apostles spoke was a foreign language, in words clear and distinct to the hearers, for "every man heard them speaking in his own language." See the Special Study #4, "Speaking in Tongues," at the close this chapter.

It has been proposed by some that the loss of unity of language at Babel, as recorded in the book of Genesis, is restored in the Gospel message.

> In Genesis 11, the whole world was of one language. In their pride they proposed to build a tower that would reach to heaven. God came down and confused their language so they could not understand one another's speech. Sin ruined the unity of language. Babel brought darkness, discord, and separation. Pentecost brought light, understanding, and unity.[20]

The speaking in tongues, or languages, was for the childhood state of the church (1 Corinthians 13:8-13). When the baptism with the Holy Spirit (and the spiritual gifts) ceased, that was the end of speaking in tongues like one reads about in the New Testament.

> The mere fact of glossolalia or any ecstatic utterance is no evidence of the presence of the Holy Spirit. In apostolic times it was necessary to provide criteria for deciding whether such utterances were of God or not, just as it had been necessary in Old Testament times (Deuteronomy 18:12; 13:1ff). "Believe not every spirit," says John, "but prove the spirits whether they be of God" (1 John 4:1), and the test he indicates is the testimony which the spirit bears to Christ. Paul had already laid down a similar test (1 Corinthians 12:3). We should do well to pay heed to these apostolic injunctions today.[21]

As the Spirit was giving them utterance. The apostles spoke by inspiration, and they continued to speak as the Spirit helped them to do so (the verb "was giving" is an imperfect tense, "went on giving"). They spoke, by inspiration, languages they had never studied. The doctrine of inspiration is discussed in some detail in Special Study #5, "The Doctrine of Inspiration," at the close of this chapter. Verse 11 tells us what they were saying as they went on speaking – they were telling the mighty works of God.

F. The Effect on the Multitudes. 2:5-13

2:5 – *Now there were Jews living in Jerusalem, devout men, from every nation under heaven.*

---

[20] Dale, *op. cit.*, p.29

[21] Bruce, *op. cit.*, p.57-58.

Now there were Jews living in Jerusalem. The word translated "living" (*katoikeō*) often means to have a fixed and permanent home in a certain place, in distinction to *paroikeō* which means to have a temporary or transient residence in a place.[22] But the word *katoikeō* also sometimes is used of visiting, and we suppose that is the meaning here. These men about to be listed as having come from various countries appear to have been only temporary visitors to Jerusalem. Their actual homes were in one of the many communities of Jews in foreign lands, communities that resulted from the scattering (dispersion) during the captivities in Old Testament times.[23] They had settled in the foreign lands, and many just never did return to the promised land to live.

Devout men. The term *eulabēs* is applied to men who were cautious about offending God, men who were careful to observe His commandments. Used of these Jewish worshipers, it characterizes them as the best of the adherents to the Jewish religion. They were so anxious to avoid offending God that they traveled, some of them, thousands of miles to attend the feast at Jerusalem, just as the Old Testament prescribed.

From every nation under heaven. That is, they have come from all over the Roman empire, and even from some countries that never were conquered by Rome's legions. The exact countries will be specified in verses 9-11. Feasts like Pentecost attracted thousands of pilgrims. We are told that when Titus besieged Jerusalem in AD 68-70, an event which occurred about Passover time, there were no less than three million people in the city.[24]

2:6 – *And when this sound occurred, the multitude came together, and were bewildered, because they were each one hearing them speak in his own language.*

And when this sound occurred. There has been much discussion as to the meaning of this phrase. The word "sound" here is a different Greek word than "sound" in verse 2. Still, some believe the "sound like a violent, rushing wind" is what was heard that brought the multitude together. Because the word is different, others think the "sound" was the "speaking in tongues," and this is what the multitude came to see and hear. A third explanation is that "sound" here has the sense of "rumor," and that the multitude drew together because the rumor of what was happening spread like wild fire among the worshipers in the Temple. Against this latter idea is the fact that *phonē* isn't much used in the sense of "rumor, report." So, perhaps, we should combine the first two ideas, and picture the multiple miraculous happenings as being the circumstance which brought the curiosity-seeking multitude together.

---

[22] See also notes at Acts 1:19 on the verb *katoikeō*.

[23] How did the Jews come to be scattered or dispersed? There had been three principal dispersions: 1) The ten tribes under Shalmaneser, 721 BC, were carried to the lands of the Parthians, Medes, and Elamites. 2) Judah and Benjamin were carried by Nebuchadnezzar, 606 BC, to Mesopotamia. 3) Ptolemy Lagus took great numbers of Jews to Egypt, 329 BC. See further notes under "men of Cyrene" at Acts 2:10.

[24] *Wars*, V.3.1.

The multitude came together, and were bewildered. After the act of God led the crowd to assemble, Luke tells us the people were bewildered, full of consternation. They did not understand what was happening, nor could they come up with any reasonable explanation for it.

Because they were each one hearing them speak in his own language. "Were hearing" catches the force of the Greek imperfect tense, which indicates the continuance of their "speaking" over a period of time. Note the marginal note on "language": it is "dialect." Those in the multitude were each hearing their own dialects being spoken by these Galileans, the very dialects those in the crowd had learned in the foreign countries from which they had each come to the feast.[25]

2:7 – *And they were amazed and marveled, saying, "Why, are not all these who are speaking Galileans?*

And they were amazed and marveled. Luke wields his vocabulary in an attempt to describe the effect on the hearers. He says, "they were bewildered," "they were amazed," "they marveled," "they were perplexed" – and they questioned one another as to what could come of this. The sound of the violent, rushing wind has been heard over a large area. It seemed to come down at the very place where the apostles were. When the crowd ran together to see what had happened, here were these Galileans speaking in foreign languages they could not have been expected to know. What did it all mean? What was happening?

Saying, "Why, are not all these who are speaking Galileans? There is a tone of disbelief in the question. Galilean men came from a despised district (John 7:52) where education was scanty, the standard of culture low, and the spoken dialect was peculiar (Mark 14:30). Their Galilean accent was easily recognized, even though the apostles were speaking languages other than Greek or Aramaic, for Galileans had difficulty with certain guttural sounds (similar to the Japanese who have trouble with "L" in English). In addition to their speech, the apostles' dress would have aided in their identification by the devout men who had been drawn together at the place. "They are Galileans! How can they be doing that?" was the thought going through the minds of the listeners.

Those who believe that more than the twelve apostles were baptized with the Holy Spirit on the day of Pentecost are hard pressed by this expression. Were all the 120 Galileans? It is regularly stated that many of the 70 who were sent on a missionary journey late in Jesus' Judean ministry (Luke 10:1-24) were included in the 120 of Acts 1:15. Were all of the 70 from Galilee? This seems unlikely. If so, it is hard to accept the idea that all 120 were baptized of the Spirit on Pentecost. But if we posit that those who were baptized with the Holy Spirit on Pentecost were the apostles only, this verse gives us no trouble, for all of those were Galileans!

---

[25] Some have supposed that the only "dialects" spoken were modifications to the Hebrew language that these foreign Jews gradually would have made to their language after long years away from the home country of Palestine. And it is possible that the miracle could have been that the apostles spoke in the dialects of Hebrew used in the foreign countries. But this seems to be less than what Luke says was actually done. He seems to speak of foreign languages other than Hebrew.

2:8 – *"And how is it that we each hear them in our own language to which we were born?*

And how is it that we each hear *them*. Was the miracle performed on the tongues of the speakers, or on the ears of the hearers? Some say the apostles all spoke one language, but the hearers heard in their own language (i.e., the miracle was performed on the ears of the hearers). If all we had were this verse, we might understand the account in this way. But if we put all the verses together, the record plainly shows that the miracle was wrought on the tongues of the apostles. It says, "they began to speak with other tongues." It is not proper to transfer the miracle from those who had the baptism of the Holy Spirit to those who (as yet) did not have Him.

In our own language to which we were born? Greek was almost universally spoken over the whole of the eastern part of the Roman empire, but still most districts had their old dialects, too. Proof? Aramaic was spoken in Palestine. The people of Lycaonia had a language all their own.[26] Hence Luke is saying that the utterances by the apostles, inspired by the Holy Spirit, were in a variety of dialects of languages.

2:9 – *"Parthians and Medes and Elamites, and residents of Mesopotamia, Judea and Cappadocia, Pontus and Asia,*

Parthians and Medes and Elamites. Luke enumerates the different nations that were represented at Jerusalem to show the surprising extent and power of this miracle of speaking in tongues. The countries mentioned here are in geographical order, starting from the far east and working westward. Since it was a Jewish feast, we must understand that the people listed from the various countries are either Jews or proselytes. *Parthia* was a part of Persia, and was located between the Persian Gulf and the Caspian Sea on the west and the river Indus on the east. The language spoken in Parthia was Persian. *Medes* came from Media, a country situated south and west of the Caspian Sea. The language spoken there was Persian. The country of *Elam* was bounded by Persia on the east, by Media on the north, by Babylonia on the west, and by the Persian Gulf on the south. The language spoken by this people was Persian.

And residents of Mesopotamia. The name *Mesopotamia*, which is Greek, is a compound word meaning "between the rivers," that is, the region lying between the Tigris and Euphrates rivers. The language spoken here was probably Syriac (or perhaps including a mixture of the Chaldee).

Judea and. In a list of foreign countries from which visitors came to Jerusalem, why should Judea be listed? It is a matter that has troubled Bible students for years. Some have supposed there is an error in our manuscripts, and have proposed that instead of "Judea" we should read "Armenia" or "India" or "Lydia" or "Idumea" or "Kurdistan," but there is precious little evidence that would support such a conjectural emendation of the text. Others

---

[26] Acts 14:11.

have proposed the idea that the language of Galilee was so different from that of Judea as to render it remarkable that the apostles could speak like a Judean (i.e., without the usual Galilean peculiarities of pronunciation), but this seems to contradict what was just implied in verse 7 about how the speakers were recognized as Galileans. Still others insist there is nothing out of the ordinary in listing Judea among the nations from which people had come up to Jerusalem, but this attempted explanation appears to miss the point that we are listing different languages spoken by naming the country where the dialect was indigenous. As far back as the time of Jerome, he used "Syria" in his translation where our Bibles have "Judea." Bruce writes, "If 'Judea' could be understood here in its widest possible sense, it might denote the extent of the land from the Egyptian frontier to the Euphrates, controlled directly or indirectly by … David and Solomon. This would explain the absence of Syria from the list."[27]

Cappadocia, Pontus and Asia. Next in order are mentioned five provinces in Asia Minor (three in this verse, and the first two names in the next). *Cappadocia* is the southeastern portion of the land we call Turkey. The language which was spoken here is not certainly known, though their neighbors, the Lycaonians, had their own peculiar dialect. *Pontus* is the northeastern part of Asia Minor bordering on the Black Sea. The language which was spoken here is not certainly known, either. *Asia* refers to the Roman province of Asia (which included the little countries of Mysia, Lydia, and Caria) bordering on the Aegean Sea and opposite to Greece. The language spoken here was perhaps Greek.

2:10 – Phrygia and Pamphylia, Egypt and the districts of Libya around Cyrene, and visitors from Rome, both Jews and proselytes,

Phrygia and Pamphylia. These two countries were located a little south of the central part of Asia Minor. The language of these places was probably Greek.

Egypt and the districts of Libya around Cyrene. *Egypt* is that extensive country in the southeast corner of the Mediterranean, through which the Nile River flows. The language used there was Demotic. *Libya* was a general name for that part of the African continent immediately across the Mediterranean to the south of Greece and Italy. *Cyrene* was originally a Greek colony in the land of Libya, located about 500 miles west of Egypt (an expanse of Libyan desert is in between). In New Testament times it was an important city. The language spoken here is not certainly known.

And visitors from Rome. There was a large Jewish population in *Rome*, and some of these have come to Jerusalem for the feast of Pentecost. The language spoken in the capital of Italy was Latin.

In passing, some have supposed these visitors returned to Rome and planted the church there. And it is true that when Paul writes to the Romans in AD 58, no apostle has yet been there, but there is a church in Rome. However, it seems better to suppose the congregations to whom Paul writes were founded by some of his own converts who have

---

[27] Bruce, *op. cit.*, p.62.

found their way to Rome and whose names appear in Romans 16, rather than to believe the Roman church dates to Pentecost. Even if a church were planted by these visitors when they returned to Rome, there is reason to believe it was decimated when Claudius issued his decree expelling all Jews from Rome.[28]

Both Jews and proselytes. "Jew" speaks of a person born of Jewish parents. A "proselyte" is a Gentile who has been converted to the Jewish religion. Dale reminds us there were two kinds of proselytes.

> There were two classes of proselytes: 1) a *proselyte of the gate* was one who limited his obedience to the Jewish law and was not circumcised. His worship at the temple was also limited. 2) A *proselyte of righteousness* was one who accepted the full responsibility of the Law, and was circumcised. Such a Gentile enjoyed the full privileges of the temple.[29]

How broad or limited is the expression "Jews and proselytes"? Is it limited only to those visiting from Rome, or are we to understand that among those visiting from all the nations would be found both those who were Jews by birth and those who had become converts to the Jewish religion? Hervey insists it is limited. He writes:

> If it were to apply to the whole preceding, we would not expect to find the two nations (Crete and Arabia) following in the next verse.[30]

2:11 – *Cretans and Arabs – we hear them in our **own** tongues speaking of the mighty deeds of God."*

Cretans and Arabians. *Crete* was an island in the Mediterranean Sea, south of the Aegean Sea, off Greece and Asia Minor. There were many Jews living on Crete, and Josephus took his third wife from among them.[31] The language spoken there was probably Greek. *Arabia* is the great peninsula which is bounded on the north by part of Syria, on the east by the Persian Gulf, and on the west by the Red Sea. The language spoken here was Arabic.

We hear them in our *own* tongues. The languages spoken by the apostles were nine or ten different languages, but this total is still less than the number of apostles. Perhaps we should picture each apostle as speaking one dialect, different from the dialects spoken by each of the other apostles. It would not take long for the visitors to gather in groups around the apostle who was speaking their native language. Here would be a group of Medes, there a group of Jews from Egypt, and there again, those from Cappadocia, etc.

---

[28] Acts 18:2.

[29] Dale, *op. cit.*, p.29.

[30] A.C. Hervey, "The Acts of the Apostles" in *The Pulpit Commentary* (Grand Rapids: Eerdmans, 1962). p.51.

[31] Josephus, *Life*, 76.

Speaking the mighty deeds of God. The "mighty deeds of God" are what the apostles talked about as they spoke in tongues, including the things God had done in sending His Son in the Incarnation, in raising Him from the dead, in His miracles, His ascension, etc.

If all the apostles spoke of the mighty works of God, as indeed we picture them doing, each to his own group of hearers, can it be said Peter preached the first gospel sermon, as it is sometimes affirmed? Perhaps there might be a difference between "mighty deeds" and the "gospel," though this is not easy to accept, since the mighty deeds we have listed above are a part of the gospel. What we can say is that Peter's is the first *recorded* gospel sermon. And we can also say Peter was the first to tell men what to do to be saved, once those men have heard and believed the message about the mighty deeds of God.

2:12 – *And they all continued in amazement and great perplexity, saying to one another, "What does this mean?"*

And they continued in amazement and great perplexity. The effect of the amazing phenomena and of the narration by the apostles of God's mighty deeds is here briefly described. Luke, after listing the nations from which the hearers came, now takes up the narrative that was interrupted at verse 7.

Saying one to another. In their amazement, they turned to each other, trying to find an explanation for the astounding events – the rushing of the wind, the flames of fire, the speaking in tongues.

"What does this mean?" Literally, "What will this be?" or "What will this become?" They recognized it was enough out of the ordinary to be a miracle, and they knew that miracles credentialed the messengers; but they could not at the moment determine what this meant, or for what purpose the miracle had been wrought. In their amazement, there were several different reactions. Some said, "What does this mean?" Others (verse 13) said, "They are drunk!"

2:13 – *But others were mocking and saying, "They are full of sweet wine."*

But others were mocking and saying. The word translated mocking means to deride, to scoff. Who are these "others" who mock and ignore all the supernatural things that have been observed? McGarvey suggests they were irreverent men. Perhaps so. Is it possible that these mockers were the scribes and Pharisees, who were so opposed to Christ and His followers? A slight evidence of this might be found in the fact that "others" is *heteros* (not *allos*), i.e., another class of hearers of a different kind than those just named. Rather than visitors, they were different – different in the sense that they were permanent dwellers at Jerusalem. Compare 2:14 where both classes are addressed.

"They are full of sweet wine." I.e., these men are drunk! The ASV translated the Greek word *gleukos* as "new wine," but that is misleading, for it carries the idea it was just freshly squeezed. That cannot be, for at the time of year when Pentecost falls the only wine available was last year's vintage. The vintage of the current year is still some months off. "Sweet wine" was artificially prepared to retain its sweetness and extra strength and was very intoxicating.[32] Perhaps we are to understand that there was something about the behavior or appearance of the apostles that would cause the mockers to make such a charge.

G. Peter's Pentecost Sermon. 2:14-36

2:14 – But Peter, taking his stand with the eleven, raised his voice and declared to them: "Men of Judea, and all you who live in Jerusalem, let this be known to you, and give heed to my words.

But Peter, taking his stand with the eleven. Why Peter? Is it to be explained simply that it was in accordance with the natural temperament of Peter? As Barnes suggests, "He was bold, forward, ardent; and he rose now to defend the apostles of Jesus Christ, and Christ himself, from an injurious charge"?[33] No, there is much more. Christ told Peter that he would be given the KEYS OF THE KINGDOM and allowed to bind and loose on earth with the approval of heaven itself.[34] Keys are for opening doors, and the door of entrance into the church was opened by Peter at Pentecost. For the first time in history men are about to be told the gospel plan of salvation. The keys had reference to faith, repentance, confession, and baptism. The binding and loosing had reference to the response of the sinner to the gospel invitation. If the convicted sinner rejected the gospel, his sins were bound on him by his own willful act of rejection. If he accepted the Christ in complete obedience, his sins were loosed through forgiveness. Every gospel preacher then and now had and has this same power to bind and loose when he presents the gospel, but only Peter had keys. Through the miraculous manifestations the multitude had assembled and were anxious to know the cause of these manifestations. Peter is thus given the opportunity to turn the keys and open the door to the kingdom.

Matthias was now one of the apostles, and so there are "the eleven" who are standing with Peter, as they all appear as witnesses for the truth. The language implies that all twelve took part in the preaching. Perhaps we should picture Peter as speaking first, and the others acting as interpreters for the people gathered round each of them. Or perhaps all preached in a different place in that 35-acre temple area, each preaching his own sermon under the influence of the Holy Spirit, and only Peter's is recorded.

Raised his voice and declared to them. The large crowd, each with their own native language, all buzzing in excitement, demanded that Peter speak out if he were to be heard. By this means he captured their attention in order that he might speak to them what the Spirit prompted him to speak.

---

[32] *Gleukos* can also mean mere "grape juice" (i.e., must) as opposed to fermented juice, as most of the Greek lexicons show. Some have even worked this fact into the mockery. "They're drunk! And what are they drunk on? *Grape juice!*" And then all would laugh at the joke. However, Job 32:19 shows that *gleukos* can be fermented, and thus our comments have been based on the idea that the apostles are accused of drinking fermented juice which would intoxicate. The ancients did have a way of preserving juice without fermenting. See this documented in the article on "Wine" in *Zondervan Pictorial Bible Dictionary*, p.894.

[33] Barnes, *op. cit.*, p.29.

[34] Matthew 16:19. No *keys* were given to the other apostles, but power to bind and loose was (John 20:22,23).

Men of Judea, and all you who live in Jerusalem. "Men of Judea" in the original carries more the idea that they were Jews than that they lived in Judea, though both ideas are included. "You who live in Jerusalem" speaks of the visitors who have come to the feast of Pentecost. Though some had just mocked, Peter did not return railing for railing (1 Peter 3:9), but sought by a respectful address to lead them to the truth.

Let this be known to you, and give heed to my words. The audience may be perplexed and unable to explain what has just happened, but not Peter. He proceeds calmly to explain to them the real significance of the day's events. We are not to suppose that what Luke has recorded here is the whole of Peter's sermon, but we are given just the main points of Peter's presentation.[35]

2:15 – *"For these men are not drunk, as you suppose, for it is* **only** *the third hour of the day;*

For these men are not drunk, as you suppose. With a sweep of his hand (we may suppose), Peter points to the apostles as he says, "these men." Peter includes himself with the others for the charge of drunkenness extended to all the apostles. "Not drunk!" he says, for he must clear themselves of such a charge before he can expect the audience to listen to the rest of the message which the Spirit was to speak through him. If they were indeed drunk, the "devout men" (verse 5) would have been little inclined to listen, for it was a strict violation of Jewish law to drink intoxicants on a feast day, especially before noon, for on feast days devout Jews did not even eat their first meal till after the sixth hour, let alone drink.[36]

For it is *only* **the third hour of the day.** By Jewish reckoning of time the third hour is about 9 A.M.; their day was divided into 12 equal parts between sunrise and sunset. How would the fact to which Peter calls attention, that it was still early in the morning, show that the apostles were not drunk? It is the morning hour of prayer, only the third hour of the day: no Jew, certainly no devout Jew, would eat or drink before this hour was past.

> This was the custom of pious people in ancient times, that each one should offer his morning prayers with additions in the synagogue, and then return home to take refreshment ... The fourth is the hour of repast, when all eat.[37]

It was not usual in those days for even drunkards to become drunk in the daytime.[38] The charge of drunkenness was so absurd that Peter meets it without any more proof than an observation that all present could make.

2:16 – *"but this is what was spoken of through the prophet Joel:*

---

[35] Acts 2:40 plainly tells us that we have only an abbreviated edition of Peter's first recorded sermon.

[36] Knowling, *op. cit.*, p.57.

[37] Maimonides, *Shabb.*, ch.50.

[38] 1 Thessalonians 5:7.

But this is what was spoken of through the prophet Joel. Peter says the events that had just happened were a fulfillment of that which was predicted in Joel. He will quote (though not literally from either the LXX or the Hebrew) Joel 2:28-32.

Before looking at the prophecy in detail, it is useful to be aware of the general outline followed in Peter's sermon. The same major points were regularly made by the apostles when preaching to Jewish audiences.

I. An affirmation that the time of the fulfillment of the Old Testament prophecies had come
II. A rehearsal of the ministry, death, resurrection, and ascension of Jesus
III. An appeal to relevant Old Testament Messianic prophecies, for their fulfillment in these events is evidence that Jesus is Himself the Messiah
IV. A call to repentance

2:17 – 'AND IT SHALL BE IN THE LAST DAYS,' God says, **'THAT I WILL POUR FORTH OF MY SPIRIT UPON ALL MANKIND; AND YOUR SONS AND YOUR DAUGHTERS SHALL PROPHESY, AND YOUR YOUNG MEN SHALL SEE VISIONS, AND YOUR OLD MEN SHALL DREAM DREAMS;**

AND IT SHALL BE IN THE LAST DAYS,' God says. Here begins the quotation of Joel's prophecy. The "last days" from Joel's standpoint would be the whole time from Christ until the judgment day. To the Old Testament prophets, the "last days" had reference to the entire Christian age.[39] We still are living in the "last days" about which the Old Testament prophets made predictions. Because the "last days" refer to the entire Christian age, the fulfillment of Joel's prophecy is not limited to one day – like to Pentecost itself, or to the destruction of Jerusalem, or to some other day. Yet Peter affirms that what happened on Pentecost is included in what Joel predicted.

THAT I WILL POUR FORTH OF MY SPIRIT UPON ALL MANKIND. As seen in the light of its fulfillment, this must speak of the manifestation of the Holy Spirit called the baptism with the Holy Spirit. In addition, Joel's language might also be a prediction of "spiritual gifts" in the opening days of the Christian age. But Barnes does not appear to be correct when he implies that this is something common to all Christians;[40] rather, as the context indicates, this pouring forth of the Spirit was a measure of the Spirit that resulted in miraculous manifestations (prophecy, visions, dreams).

How shall we harmonize the verb "pour forth" with the verb ("baptism," *baptizō,* to dip) used in the prediction of this event by John and Jesus as they spoke of a "baptism with the Holy Spirit"? The power which the Spirit Himself exerted over the minds of the apostles after He entered into them is figuratively called a "baptism," while the term "pour forth" expresses the act of Christ in sending the Spirit from heaven. It is doubtful that the terminology used of Christ's action from heaven has any bearing on the meaning of the word "baptism."

---

[39] Isaiah 2:2; Micah 4:1.

[40] Barnes, *op. cit.*, p.31.

"Of my Spirit" implies a distribution. Portions of the Holy Spirit were meted out to various individuals. Gifts, administrations, operations of the Spirit may vary, but the Spirit from whom they all come is the same.[41] Another verse that implies that there were different measures of the Holy Spirit given to the spiritually gifted and those baptized with the Spirit is John 3:34. That Jesus had the Spirit "without measure" implies that others had the Spirit "by measure."

"All mankind" refers to "Jews and Gentiles." At Pentecost the Spirit was poured out on the Jews. In the case of Cornelius (Acts 10) the Spirit was poured forth on the Gentiles. And in the early days of the church, both Jews and Gentiles were recipients of the spiritual gifts (1 Corinthians 12-14). But the expression "all mankind" does not refer to "every human being." Not even every Christian received the baptism with the Holy Spirit, nor did all receive spiritual gifts.[42] Again, the reason many are led to think of spiritual gifts being included in the scope of Joel's prophecy is the fact that contemplated in the prophecy are men and women prophesying, seeing visions, and dreaming dreams. As far as Luke's record is concerned, no women were included in the activities of the Spirit on the day of Pentecost. All but the first part of the prophecy of Joel was yet to be fulfilled (even after the events of Pentecost were past), but all of the first part of Joel's prophecy was fulfilled in the course of events that are about to be recorded by Luke in the rest of the book of Acts.

AND YOUR SONS AND YOUR DAUGHTERS SHALL PROPHESY. This did not happen on Pentecost (as far as the record goes), but did happen during the early years of the "last days." Philip the Evangelist, for example, had four daughters who did prophesy.[43] The word "prophesy" has a broad meaning: it can include predicting future events (Matthew 11:13, 15:17); it can mean to tell what happened in the past (Matthew 26:68); it can mean to teach or preach right at the present moment (1 Corinthians 14:1-5). To prophesy, then, is to *speak by inspiration of the Holy Spirit in the vernacular of the people,* no matter what the content of the message – whether prediction, rehearsal, or exhortation for the present.

AND YOUR YOUNG MEN SHALL SEE VISIONS. In the Old Testament, God would, from time to time, make known His will to His servants by means of visions. In fact, the old Prophets were called "seers" because they received revelations through visions. God would cause the appearance of the objects or events to pass before their minds, and the prophet would "see" what God wished to reveal. There were no visions on Pentecost (as far as Luke's record goes), but during the "last days," during the Church age, there were.[44]

---

[41] 1 Corinthians 12:4-5.

[42] Acts 8:14ff is an example of Christians who did not have spiritual gifts until an apostle came and laid hands on them. Even then, not all Christians were included, for Simon was a Christian, but was not included in the group on whom hands were laid.

[43] Acts 21:9. These apparently held the function, but not the office, of prophet.

[44] Post-Pentecost visions were seen by Ananias (Acts 9:10), by Paul (Acts 9:16, 16:9), by Peter (Acts 10:11) and by Cornelius (Acts 10:3). See Barnes, *op. cit.,* p.32, and *Zondervan Pictorial Bible Dictionary,*

AND YOUR OLD MEN SHALL DREAM DREAMS. The fourfold repetition of "your" in these verses implies that these gifts would be bestowed on Jews in the first instance. Later they would also be given to Gentile believers. As God had used visions to make His will known, so in Old Testament times He had used dreams. Dreams and visions differ apparently in this particular: visions would pass before the mind while the man of God was awake, whereas dreams were revelations made while he was asleep. There are no post-Pentecost examples in Scripture of revelations being given to men by means of dreams, yet they likely happened, for so it had been prophesied.

2:18 – '*EVEN UPON MY BONDSLAVES, BOTH MEN AND WOMEN, I WILL IN THOSE DAYS POUR FORTH OF MY SPIRIT and they shall prophesy.*

EVEN UPON MY BONDSLAVES, BOTH MEN AND WOMEN. The Holy Spirit would be poured forth on both male and female servants of God, Joel predicted.

I WILL IN THOSE DAYS POUR FORTH MY SPIRIT. Notice it is during "those days" (plural). The prophecy is not limited just to Pentecost. Joel is predicting a great extension of the work of the Spirit in the Church age, as compared to the operations of the Spirit in the Mosaic age.

And they shall prophesy. There was prophecy on the day of Pentecost by male servants (inspired preaching by the apostles). The careful reader will have observed that this one phrase (in the midst of all those quoted from Joel) is not a part of Joel's prediction. It likely is Peter's application of the prophecy, and by it he explains what the apostles were doing. They were God's bondslaves, and were preaching as they were because they were prompted to do so by God's Spirit.

2:19 – '*AND I WILL GRANT WONDERS IN THE SKY ABOVE, AND SIGNS ON THE EARTH BENEATH, BLOOD, AND FIRE, AND VAPOR OF SMOKE.*

AND I WILL GRANT WONDERS IN THE SKY ABOVE, AND SIGNS ON THE EARTH BENEATH. "Wonders" is the common word in the Bible to denote a miracle. That these were to take place "in the sky above" leads us to harmonize these words of Joel with those which speak of the cosmological changes in sun, moon, and stars at the time of the second coming of Jesus. When we compare verses 19 and 20 with 2 Peter 3:10-12 and Matthew 24:29-31, we find that the language of Joel is similar to Peter's and Matthew's description of the second advent. Joel's prophecy covers the whole "last days," i.e., clear up to the close of the age. No such cosmological changes as are about to be enumerated happened on Pentecost. It speaks rather of the close of the age.

BLOOD, AND FIRE, AND VAPOR OF SMOKE. Those who think that all of Joel's prophecy was fulfilled on Pentecost say, "The blood must have flowed from the altars like rivers as thousands of animals were sacrificed. The fire and vapor of smoke ascended from

---

p.884, for additional notes on visions.

the altars as the same sacrifices were burned."[45] But since it is not possible to limit the previous verses to the day of Pentecost, why try to squeeze this verse into such a mold? Other commentators (because of a misinterpretation of Matthew 24) see a reference to the destruction of Jerusalem in AD 70. Barnes informs us he thinks the blood refers to the slaughter of battle, that fire is an image of war in the conflagration of towns and villages, and that the smoke is pillars of smoke rising from the burning towns and villages.[46] But he appears to be inconsistent, for he says, "The great and notable day of the Lord (v. 20)" is "the final judgment." How then can these events which immediately precede the final judgment refer to the destruction of Jerusalem? It is evident that this part of Joel's prophecy is yet to be fulfilled, and will not be fulfilled till the second coming of Christ. The "blood, fire, and vapor of smoke" have to do, not with the day of Pentecost, but with the day of the consummation of this age.

2:20 – 'THE SUN SHALL BE TURNED INTO DARKNESS, AND THE MOON INTO BLOOD, BEFORE THE GREAT AND GLORIOUS DAY OF THE LORD SHALL COME.

THE SUN SHALL BE TURNED INTO DARKNESS. The reference is to the actual sun, and the time is the second advent of Christ. The heavenly bodies (sun, moon, stars, planets) shall be dissolved. This is not a reference to the darkness of the day of crucifixion (Boles), for that event happened before the "last days" began. Likewise, there is no need to take the passage as figurative (Barnes)[47], because elsewhere we learn that such momentous events will take place when Jesus returns.[48]

AND THE MOON INTO BLOOD. Compare the similar language of Revelation 6:12ff, which speaks, likely, only of the second coming of Christ.

BEFORE THE GREAT AND GLORIOUS DAY OF THE LORD SHALL COME. The "day of the Lord" is the final judgment day,[49] the day of judgment on man that follows Christ's return at the close of the age. The day is called "great" because on that day Jesus will most impressively and strikingly judge His enemies. There may have been judgments on enemies from time to time in history, but those will seem insignificant next to the final, great judgment on that day. In Joel the word is "terrible" or "fearful;" the NASB has "glorious." It will be a glorious day for the redeemed, but a day of terror for the unrepentant.

Once more, note that the prophecy of Joel has been a description of the "last days" – the whole Church age. There are many similar prophecies in the Old Testament, prophecies that have been called "Mountain Peak Prophecies."[50] As one looks out across the mountains, he sees only the peaks, and not the long distances between the peaks. The two

---

[45] Don DeWelt, *Acts Made Actual* (Joplin, MO: *College Press*, 1953), p.13.

[46] Barnes, *op. cit.*, p.34.

[47] Boles, *op. cit.*, p.40. Barnes, *op. cit.*, p.34

[48] 2 Peter 3:7-10.

[49] Luke 17:24ff; 1 Thessalonians 5:2, 2 Peter 3:12. See also "Day of the Lord" in a Bible dictionary.

[50] W. Kay, Commentary on Isaiah in *The Bible Commentary,* edited by F.C. Cook, (London: John Murray, 1898). p.19, has an excellent discussion on what he calls "the law of perspective shortening."

peaks Joel saw as he looked out into the future were Pentecost and the final judgment day. Part of Joel's prophecy was fulfilled at the beginning of the period called "last days;" part will not be fulfilled until the second coming of Christ and the end of the age.

2:21 – 'AND IT SHALL BE, THAT EVERYONE WHO CALLS ON THE NAME OF THE LORD SHALL BE SAVED.'

AND IT SHALL BE. Peter is still quoting Joel, and both are saying that in the days of grace, the days of the Church age, the age in which we are now living, that whosoever shall call upon the name of the Lord shall be saved.

THAT EVERYONE WHO CALLS ON THE NAME OF THE LORD. Salvation is not limited to Jews alone anymore. It is for "everyone" ("whosoever" ASV). He who would be saved must "call" in the appointed time and in the appointed way. Of course, we are not to understand that the mere act of speaking the name of the Lord will save. This same prophecy is cited by Paul in Romans 10:10-17, and there we learn that hearing the gospel, faith, and confession are included in "calling on the name of the Lord." That is the appointed way. Peter will explain further about the appointed way in verse 38 at the close of his sermon. When is the appointed time? Not at the second coming of Christ, it will not do any good to repent then. Instead of repenting, men are pictured as looking for a place to hide from the wrath of God.[51] During this life is the time to call – during this life, as we live in the "last days" of the prophets. To Peter's audience (as well as to us) the time was now. There is danger and death in delay. As this passage is quoted in the New Testament, "Lord" evidently is a reference to Christ, whereas it was a reference to God when Joel first spoke it. This is one of the many evidences of the deity of Christ we find in the New Testament. At first glance, it might seem as if "calling on the Lord" and "calling on the name of the Lord" might mean the same thing. But the addition of the words "the name of" draws attention to the character and work of the person whose name follows. Thus, when a man calls on the name of the Lord, he is making appeal to the character and work of Jesus, both in time and eternity, as a basis of his plea for salvation.

SHALL BE SAVED. Saved from what? The calamities that attended the destruction of Jerusalem?[52] No! The reference is to being saved from Hell. In the day of judgment, while the wicked will call on the rocks and mountains to shelter them from the wrath of God, those who have called on the Lord in the appointed time and in the appointed way shall find favor and mercy and deliverance.

2:22 – *"Men of Israel, listen to these words: Jesus the Nazarene, a man attested to you by God with miracles and wonders and signs which God performed through Him in your midst, just as you yourselves know –*

Men of Israel, listen to these words. It would be difficult for us to realize the blow on the

---

[51] Revelation 6:12ff.

[52] In AD 70, Christians did escape the destruction of Jerusalem by fleeing to a city named Pella in Perea. But that is not the meaning of "shall be saved" here.

listeners' thinking the next words of Peter must have made. We have come to the second part of Peter's message, where he tells about the ministry of Jesus. (See outline given at verse 16.) We are coming to the first public announcement of what happened since the day Jesus was crucified.

Jesus the Nazarene. Since many men had the name "Jesus" (the Old Testament equivalent was "Joshua"), our Savior was designated by Peter as being the Jesus who came from Nazareth, so the listeners would fully understand about Whom he was speaking. In Acts 4:10, Peter uses this designation for Jesus again. It must have been the designation in popular use, and it even formed part of the inscription Pilate had put on the cross.

A man attested to you by God. Jesus, says Peter, was a man who had had it demonstrated and shown that He had been sent by God, and that He had the approval of God. God have given this approval via the miracles Jesus wrought.

With miracles and wonders and signs. By these three terms, Peter does not mean three classes of actions; but he uses three terms to describe the same miracles worked through Jesus. "Miracles" translates *dunamis* – powerful deeds, works that demonstrated the mighty power of God. They are called "wonders" because they excited wonder in those who witnessed them. They are called "signs" because they were designed to present evidence to convince the people concerning Jesus' person and message.[53]

Which God performed through Him in your midst. The Lord Jesus Himself often traced His power to do miracles to His commission from the Father.[54] The miracles were done in the personal presence of many of those who were now listening to Peter's sermon.

Just as you yourselves know. What did they know? Many in the crowd of listeners knew by experience that God's power was behind the miracles that Jesus had performed.

2:23 – *"this Man, delivered up by the predetermined plan and foreknowledge of God, you nailed to a cross by the hands of godless men and put Him to death.*

This *Man*, delivered up. Jesus was given over to His enemies. Peter does not here name the human agents involved. Perhaps Peter had the wicked Jews in mind. Perhaps it was God Himself who gave His Son. Perhaps Peter has in mind the fact that Jesus willingly, when His hour came, gave Himself into the hands of His enemies, and let them do what they would with Him. Peter does not name the agent involved in the giving over, but he does tell us why it was done.

By the predetermined plan and foreknowledge of God. The death of Jesus was "resolved on by God before it took place." The Old Testament and the Savior Himself had predicted His death. The death of Christ was not something that was unseen by God, or

---

[53] John 5:36, 10:35, 20:30-31 and Hebrews 2:4 all show that Biblical miracles had as their purpose the credentialing of the messenger.

[54] John 5:19,30.

that came as an afterthought in God's redemptive program. It was part of God's predetermined plan, a plan made back in eternity before even the earth was created. "Foreknowledge" denotes the seeing beforehand of an event yet to take place, and even of approving of what is seen beforehand. Taking the two words together, we in no way impinge on the freedom of Christ to act as He wished. Had He wished, as a free moral agent, He could have avoided the cross. (See Special Study #6, "Predestination and Foreknowledge," at the close of this chapter.) God determined ahead of time the plan to be followed in the redemption of man, but He did not force Christ to go through with it. Christ went to the cross of His own free will.

You nailed to a cross by the hands of godless men and put *Him* to death. The Jews were the instigators of the crucifixion of Jesus. The "godless men" to whom they delivered Jesus to be crucified are the Roman soldiers and Pilate. For "godless men" the marginal reading is "men without the Law." The men into whose hands Jesus was delivered were not violators of the laws of the state. Rather the expression speaks of those who were not under the Law of Moses, i.e., Gentiles. Peter here charges the Jews with the crime of having killed their own Messiah. Their guilt was not diminished because they had employed others to do the actual killing.[55]

2:24 – *"And God raised Him up again, putting an end to the agony of death, since it was impossible for Him to be held in its power.*

And God raised Him up again. This is the main point of this part of Peter's sermon – the resurrection of Jesus Christ from the dead. It is likely there had been rumors of His resurrection spreading through Jerusalem, but now Peter stands and without equivocation declares that what had been only rumored is actually the fact! One must believe in the bodily resurrection of Jesus to be a Christian.[56] Anyone who denies the bodily resurrection is not a Christian in the New Testament sense of the term. In this message by Peter, the death of Christ occupies only one verse, but resurrection occupies nine! It was the great point of Peter's sermon.

Putting an end to the agony of death. The margin has "the birth pangs of death." A.T. Robertson wrote, "Early Christian writers interpreted the resurrection of Christ as a birth out of death" – and so use the term "pangs,"[57] i.e., birth pains. Whether or not Robertson was right, we are not to understand that Jesus suffered after His death. In fact, the suffering

---

[55] A dispute, much in the news these days, revolves around the question, Who crucified Christ? It is often considered a mark of anti-Semitism to accuse the Jews of guilt in the crucifixion of Christ, as Peter did in his sermon. Fruitful references to stimulate one's thinking are found in *Christianity Today*, 3-13-54. p.535, "The Anatomy of Anti-Semitism"; and in R.C. Foster's book. *The Final Week* (Grand Rapids: Baker, 1962), p.186ff. If there is a breach between Christian and Jewish peoples today, it is not caused by ill feelings over who crucified Jesus. It is because there is no agreement between unbelief and belief – in the case of the Jew who rejects Jesus and on the part of the Christian who accepts Jesus as Savior.

[56] Romans 10:9.

[57] Robertson, *op. cit.*, p.30. See also Barnes, *op. cit.*, p.39.

was finished before He died. When Jesus said, "It is finished,"[58] His sufferings were completed. The idea, then, in this verse may be best described as "death being pictured as a cord or rope that binds a man or confines him."[59] God loosed this "bond" in Jesus' case.

Since it was impossible for Him to be held in its power. The circumstances of the case were such that He could not remain dead. Why this was not possible, Peter goes on to show. The Old Testament prophecies could not be fulfilled and have Jesus yet remain dead, for those prophecies spoke of a resurrection. The Greek word translated "held" might be rendered "overpowered." It was not possible for death to overpower Jesus!

> Filled with amazement as the hearers already were, by a visible and audible manifestation of the Spirit of God, they now see that the whole of this amazing phenomenon is subservient to the name of the Nazarene whom they had despised and crucified. In one breath they are reminded of the wonderful miracles and signs which Jesus had wrought among them; they are charged with knowing that these were done by the power of God; they are informed that it was in accordance with God's pre-ordained purpose that Jesus was delivered into their hands, and not through His own impotence; and they are boldly told that God had raised Him from the dead, it being impossible that such a being should be permanently held down among the dead. Never did mortal lips announce in so brief a space so many facts of import so terrific to the hearers. We might challenge the world to find a parallel to it in the speeches of her orators, or the songs of her poets. There is not such a thunderbolt in all the burdens of the prophets of Israel, or among the voices which echo through the Apocalypse. It is the first public announcement to the world of a risen and glorified Redeemer.[60]

2:25 – *"For David says of Him, 'I WAS ALWAYS BEHOLDING THE LORD IN MY PRESENCE; FOR HE IS AT MY RIGHT HAND, THAT I MAY NOT BE SHAKEN.*

For David says of Him. Two of Peter's affirmations in the above announcement needed further proof: (1) that Jesus had been delivered up in accordance with the predetermined plan of God, and (2) that God raised Him from the dead. (The other statements made about Jesus by Peter needed little proof. The crowd knew that Jesus had worked miracles by the power of God, and that they by the hands of godless men put Him to death.) Peter quotes Psalm 16:8-11 as evidence that what happened to Jesus was in harmony with God's will and purpose.[61] The word translated "of" in this clause ("concerning" in the ASV) is *eis*. This preposition is used when the language of the quotation is applicable, not strictly, but by way of accommodation. Such is the case with Psalm 16.

I WAS ALWAYS BEHOLDING THE LORD IN MY PRESENCE. "Beholding" means "looked up to, fixed my attention on, as my helper and advocate." This verb is in

---

[58] John 19:30.

[59] Barnes, *op. cit.*, p.39-40.

[60] McGarvey, *op. cit.*, p.30.

[61] Note Peter's clear statement in verse 25 about the Davidic authorship of Psalm 16. Compare also verse 34 in regard to Psalm 110. To deny David's authorship of these Psalms is tantamount to denying the inspiration and truthfulness of Peter.

the imperfect tense, expressing habit. As applied to Jesus, the words show that Jesus regarded God as present with Him; that He could put His confidence in the Father; that He could expect assistance from the Father, for the Father was one who always was present to help, and to deliver the Son out of all troubles, because (it is implied) the Son was doing things of which the Father approved. In other words, the Psalm is quoted to show that what happened to Jesus was in accordance with God's will.

FOR HE IS AT MY RIGHT HAND, THAT I MAY NOT BE SHAKEN. The right hand is mentioned because that was the place of dignity and honor. Jesus has a place of exalted dignity at the right hand of the Father, and so He is not affected by evil or calamity. In the courts of justice, advocates stood at the right hands of their clients.[62]

2:26 – 'THEREFORE MY HEART WAS GLAD AND MY TONGUE EXULTED; MOREOVER MY FLESH ALSO WILL ABIDE IN HOPE;

THEREFORE. Peter is ascribing these words to Messiah, though they were originally spoken by David.

MY HEART WAS GLAD. The reason Jesus rejoiced was that He would be preserved amidst the sorrows that were coming upon Him, and He could look forward to the triumph that awaited Him. Compare Hebrews 12:2. "Heart" here stands either for the man's thoughts, or for his whole person. The Hebrews often used different members of the body to stand for the whole person.

AND MY TONGUE EXULTED. The Hebrew reads, "My glory exults," or "My honor exults." The LXX reads as Peter quotes it, i.e., "My tongue exults." One thing that makes man more exalted than the beasts is his tongue – his ability to speak and communicate. Perhaps that is why "tongue" and "glory" have something in common.

MOREOVER, MY FLESH ALSO WILL ABIDE IN HOPE. Paraphrased, this phrase has Jesus saying, "In addition to my heart being glad and my tongue rejoicing, my body I commit to the grave, with the confident expectation that before it begins to decay, it will be raised up."

2:27 – 'BECAUSE THOU WILT NOT ABANDON MY SOUL TO HADES, NOR ALLOW THY HOLY ONE TO UNDERGO DECAY.

BECAUSE THOU WILT NOT ABANDON MY SOUL TO HADES. This is the reason Jesus' body could rest in the grave in hope. The soul is the immortal part of a man. (That is, I am a soul; I live in a body.) Soul and body are not to be equated. Often, the "body," "soul," and "spirit" may overlap in describing the animated body. The Jehovah's Witnesses, at this point, have a "hidden and damning heresy." Holding the preconceived doctrine of annihilation (i.e., that for the wicked there is no life beyond the grave), they try to equate body and soul. Dale has well stated it:

---

[62] Psalm 109:31.

When there is a deliberate effort to destroy by denial the eternal part of the body while living in the flesh, it becomes necessary to deny the whole Messianic and prophetic scheme of redemption. The hidden and damning heresy of the Jehovah's Witnesses sect is the dogmatic denial of the deity of Christ under the cover of a complicated argument in an effort to be logical. To make soul mean the flesh of man alone leads directly to the denial of the incarnation of Christ, His atonement for sin, and His deity.[63]

The word "soul" is used in the Bible, at times, in the sense of a "disembodied soul"; i.e., disjoined from a body.[64] When a man dies, his body is buried in a grave somewhere, but the thing that animated that body, the soul, still conscious, enters the intermediate state. Hades, before the resurrection and ascension of Christ, was the intermediate place (state) of all the dead, and it was a disembodied state. The passage Peter quotes asserts a return of the soul of Jesus from the intermediate place of the dead. (For more details about "Hades" see Special Study #7, "Hades and the Intermediate Place of the Dead," at the close of this chapter.)

NOR ALLOW THY HOLY ONE TO UNDERGO DECAY. The reference in "Holy One" is to God's Son, i.e., to His body. The Greek word speaks of one not corrupted by sin, for the Greek word here for "holy" (*hosion*) is different from the word commonly rendered "holy" (*hagios*). Involved in *hosion* is the idea of personal piety and godliness. The whole phrase asserts that the body of Jesus would be re-animated by the return of the soul to it, before decay could set in.

2:28 – 'THOU HAST MADE KNOWN TO ME THE WAYS OF LIFE; THOU WILT MAKE ME FULL OF GLADNESS WITH THY PRESENCE.'

THOU HAS MADE KNOWN TO ME THE WAYS OF LIFE. In relation to Messiah, the words mean, "You will restore me to life." McGarvey felt this verse indicates the resurrection was made known to Jesus before He died. In any case, the Psalmist predicted Messiah would be restored to life again, restored to the actions, doings, and ways of living.

THOU WILT MAKE ME FULL OF GLADNESS WITH THY PRESENCE. Gladness expresses the feelings of the Messiah in view of the resurrection and ascension. This phrase, especially the words "with Thy presence," speaks of the ascension, and how the Raised One would be full of gladness when He returned again to the presence of God via the ascension.

Let us summarize the points of this prophecy made by David and appealed to by Peter. (1) The Messiah would die, (2) yet his soul would not be abandoned in Hades, (3) nor would His body stay in the grave long enough to begin to decay. (4) Furthermore, He would be raised from the dead and would ascend to sit on the heavenly throne at the right hand of God. J.W. McGarvey's note prepares us for the next verse.

---

[63] Dale, *op. cit.*, p.45.

[64] Revelation 6:9.

That this passage predicts the resurrection of some person from the dead previous to the corruption of his body, is undeniable; and the only question between Peter and his hearers would have been, Of whom did David speak? This question Peter now answers in the following verses.[65]

2:29 – *"Brethren, I may confidently say to you regarding the patriarch David that he both died and was buried, and his tomb is with us to this day.*

Brethren. Peter now shows that the Psalm did not refer to David.

I may confidently say to you regarding the patriarch David. That is, 'I wish to speak with boldness, openly, respecting David.' Because Peter uses the word "confidently," some have interpreted this as though Peter is apologizing for using Psalm 16 as a reference to Messiah when Jews (later on, in the Targum and in Rabbinical commentaries) did not. But one wonders if after Messiah came the Jews didn't change their interpretations of Old Testament passages that Christians now used as Messianic proof texts, a change eventually reflected in the Targum and Rabbinical writings. Peter's confidence in the case came from the facts that everyone was acquainted with; namely, David was dead and buried. That was something that could not be gainsaid. "Patriarch" means the head or ruler of a family, and then the founder of a family, or an illustrious ancestor. David is called a patriarch in 1 Chronicles 24:31 (LXX) because he was the founder of a line of royalty.

That he both died and was buried. The record of these facts they had in the Old Testament.

And his tomb is with us to this day. David's tomb was on the south side of Mount Zion (the western hill of the two hills on which Jerusalem was built), the city of David.[66] David's was the only tomb inside the walls of Jerusalem. Hyrcanus (134 BC) opened it and took out 3000 talents of silver, and used a tenth of that sum to induce Antiochus Sidetes to raise the siege he had around Jerusalem. David's tomb was again violated by Herod the Great, who carried off much wealth.[67] It fell into ruin in the time of Hadrian. Present-day visitors to Jerusalem are shown a location on Mt. Zion where David is said to be buried.[68] Peter is saying that David had not been raised from the dead. Therefore, the Psalm could not apply to David since his body was still in the tomb.

2:30 – *"And so, because he was a prophet, and knew that GOD HAD SWORN TO HIM WITH AN OATH TO SEAT* one *OF HIS DESCENDANTS UPON HIS THRONE,*

And so, because he was a prophet. Since the body of David was still in the tomb, and he therefore was not speaking about himself, he must have been speaking of someone else. In this case, David had predicted a future event when he prophesied.

---

[65] McGarvey, *op. cit.*, p.32.

[66] 1 Kings 2:10; Nehemiah 3:16.

[67] Josephus, *Wars*, I.2.5; III.15.3; XVI.7.1.

[68] *Zondervan Pictorial Bible Dictionary*, p.203.

And knew that GOD HAD SWORN TO HIM WITH AN OATH. The prediction that David made, he could make because he knew what God had said to him about his descendants. The places where it is recorded that God "swore" to David are found in Psalms 89:3-4, 132:11; and 2 Samuel 7:11-16 (where Nathan gives assurance to David). An "oath" is not anything like using "curse words," a connotation we sometimes give to the word "oath," but is something like "As God lives ... such and such is true." Because God could not swear by any greater than Himself, He swears by Himself.

TO SEAT *one* OF HIS DESCENDANTS UPON HIS THRONE. Taking an oath, God made a solemn promise to David that one of David's descendants would be made head of the spiritual kingdom (for Messiah's kingdom is not of this world). Some have suggested that the Psalms originally envisioned Solomon as the one who would sit on David's throne. Perhaps so, but Peter, speaking by inspiration, declared the oath had reference to the coming Messiah (see verse 31).

2:31 – *"he looked ahead and spoke of the resurrection of the Christ, that HE WAS NEITHER ABANDONED TO HADES, NOR DID His flesh SUFFER DECAY.*

He looked ahead. David, seeing out into the future, and observing what was to happen in the days of Messiah, spoke what he did, Peter boldly says.

And spoke of the resurrection of the Christ. This is Peter's conclusion from his reasoning about what David predicted. David was speaking about the Christ. Peter, beginning at verse 25, has now proved what he set out to prove – that Christ, according to a predetermined and expressed plan of God, was to suffer death, and to rise again speedily from the dead.

That HE WAS NEITHER ABANDONED TO HADES, NOR DID His flesh SUFFER DECAY. It is from this verse that we have drawn the conclusion that Psalm 16 predicted the resurrection of Christ. To Hades His soul did go (i.e., it was part of God s plan that Messiah die), but He did not languish there evermore. He returned from Hades, and reanimated His body, now transformed into a spiritual, resurrection body.

2:32 – *"This Jesus God raised up again, to which we are all witnesses.*

This Jesus God raised up again. Having shown from Scripture that it was predicted that Messiah would rise from the dead, Peter now affirms such a resurrection has indeed occurred in the case of Jesus.

To which we are all witnesses. What proof does Peter offer that Jesus had risen from the dead? He says, "We twelve apostles are all witnesses of the fact!" And their testimony is not false testimony. It has all the earmarks of truthful testimony. Psychologically, men will not endure great hardships or even die for something they know is a lie. Yet the apostles all endured years of toil and hardships in order to tell the resurrection story. In fact, they were tortured, and most of them were martyred, because they knew the resurrection of Jesus was true; they refused to back away from their testimony just to be saved the agony of a martyr's death. Furthermore, there were too many witnesses for all of them to be deceived. In case any should ask, "If Jesus has risen from the dead, where is he now?" Peter goes on to tell where He is and what He is doing.

2:33 – *"Therefore having been exalted to the right hand of God, and having received from the Father the promise of the Holy Spirit, He has poured forth this which you both see and hear.*

Therefore having been exalted to the right hand of God. Peter is now telling where the risen Jesus is. "To the right hand" might also be translated "*by* the right hand exalted." Thus, Peter may be saying that God, by His own right hand, lifted Jesus to His present place in Heaven. But when we consider verse 34, it would appear that "*to* the right hand" is correct. David's throne is not on this earth then, but is located "at the right hand of God in heaven." The word "exalted" might mean more than "lifted up." It could also include the idea that Christ has been glorified, crowned as king. Christ is king, and Peter is about to tell them how to become subjects of the kingdom.

And having received from the Father the promise of the Holy Spirit. The promise, made by the Holy Spirit, was the one made to David, that one of David's descendants would sit on his throne.[69] Peter here clearly declares in language that is hard to misunderstand that *Jesus now reigns on David's throne.* The ascension and coronation of Christ fulfill the prophecy made through David.

He has poured forth this which you both see and hear. The amazing phenomena manifested that hour on the day of Pentecost, the things the assembled multitude had seen and heard that were out of the ordinary (verses 2-4), these were the actions of Jesus from His throne on high. The apostles were not drunk. Drink could not produce what the crowd had just seen. These day's events had been predicted in the Old Testament, and now were done by the power of Jesus. 'The glorified Jesus is responsible for what you have seen and heard this day,' says Peter, 'and what you've seen and heard is proof that He is glorified.' The Father gave the authority over the Spirit to the Son, and the Son distributed the gift to men. John 14-16 shows the return of Christ to heaven was an indispensable preliminary to the coming of the Spirit.

2:34 – *"For it was not David who ascended into heaven, but he himself says: 'THE LORD SAID TO MY LORD, "SIT AT MY RIGHT HAND,*

For it was not David who ascended into heaven. David himself is not the one who David predicted would ascend to heaven, Peter argues. Peter reminds his listeners that David even bore testimony to the fact that Messiah would ascend to Heaven and be exalted.

---

[69] *The Living New Testament,* translated by men who are premillennial in their eschatology and who therefore believe that Jesus' reign on David's throne is something reserved for the future millennium, have mangled their handling of this verse. Otherwise, they would have to abandon one of the key doctrines of the whole premillennial scheme of things.

But he himself says. Psalm 110:1 is quoted in this verse and the next. This is explicit testimony to the Davidic authorship of Psalm 110, and both Jesus and Peter set forth an argument that hinges on the Davidic authorship.

> Some in that audience would have been able to recall that a few weeks before this time, the Pharisees had been confused by a question about the meaning of this same passage, and they dared not answer Jesus; if they had answered Him truly, they would have conceded His claim to deity, Matthew 22:42-45.[70]

Those who were then silenced by Jesus are now taught how it was that David's Son was also David's Lord.

THE LORD SAID TO MY LORD. In the Hebrew, "Jehovah said to Adonai;" that is, "the Father said to the Messiah." Paraphrased, the quotation is, "Jehovah said to Him whom I, David, acknowledge to be my superior and sovereign ...." The One whom David acknowledged to be his Lord was none other than Jesus the Messiah.

SIT AT MY RIGHT HAND. This was a prediction made by David respecting the exaltation of Christ. The Father (Jehovah) invited Jesus to a place at His right hand, a place of favor, trust, and power.

2:35 – "UNTIL I MAKE THINE ENEMIES A FOOTSTOOL FOR THY FEET."

UNTIL I MAKE THINE ENEMIES A FOOTSTOOL FOR THY FEET. In olden days, when a king conquered an enemy, the enemy was often made to lie down on his back on the floor in front of the conqueror's throne. The victor would then use the one on the floor for a footrest, even putting his feet on the victim s neck, symbolizing his complete control over the conquered one. So Christ shall one day finish God's grand plan for the ages. All those who have rebelled against God will be subdued. The last enemy that shall be abolished is death,[71] and then we shall have arrived at the consummation of the ages and ushering in of eternity.

2:36 – "Therefore let all the house of Israel know for certain that God has made Him both Lord and Christ – this Jesus whom you crucified."

Therefore let all the house of Israel know for certain. "Know for certain" means "be assured, know without any hesitation or possibility of mistake." Barnes has quoted someone on this verse:

> Convinced by the prophecies, by our testimony, and by the remarkable scenes exhibited on the day of Pentecost, let all be convinced that the True Messiah has come and has been exalted to heaven.[72]

---

[70] Boles, *op. cit.*, p.44.

[71] 1 Corinthians 15:25-26.

[72] Barnes, *op., cit.*, p.49.

Peter is urging his audience to believe the evidence that has been presented to establish the fact that Jesus of Nazareth was the Messiah, the now-exalted Son of God.

That God has made Him both Lord and Christ. "Made" has the force of "appointed" or "constituted." "Lord" denotes "master, sovereign," one who has all authority in heaven and on earth. God has shown that Jesus is the Lord (spoken of in the Psalm just quoted) by causing Him to sit on His own throne to rule over angels and men. And today, when a man confesses that "Jesus is Lord," he is saying that he believes Jesus sits at the right hand of the throne of the universe, actively controlling all things for the good of God's children. The exaltation of Jesus by the Father also shows that He is the Messiah predicted in the Old Testament. In words as clear as language can be, Peter affirms that Jesus is now sitting on David's throne. We should not then, as some millennial schemes picture, look for Jesus to sit on some earthly throne out in the future, in the belief that He is not yet sitting on David's throne.

– This Jesus whom you crucified. The very person who suffered was raised from the dead, and exalted and glorified by the Father. Peter has now shown these men assembled before him their guilt. The Son of God, and the hope of their nation, they had put to death. He was not an imposter, nor a man interested only in revolution against the established government, nor a blasphemer. He was the Messiah of God! And they had stained their hands with his blood!

H. Effect of Peter's Sermon. 2:37-41

2:37 – Now when they heard **this***, they were pierced to the heart, and said to Peter and the rest of the apostles, "Brethren, what shall we do?"*

Now when they heard *this.* When they heard this declaration by Peter, and the proof that Jesus was actually the Messiah, they admit their belief of what Peter has said by asking the question, "What shall we do?"

They were pierced to the heart. The marginal reading is "smitten in conscience." The verb means "to pierce, to sting, to stun, to smite." It implies the idea of sudden and acute grief. They were stunned with anguish and alarm at what Peter had said. Barnes has listed several possible causes for their grief: their sorrow that the Messiah had been put to death by His own countrymen, their deep sense of guilt in having done this, and fear of his wrath.[73] Christ's declaration recorded in John 16:8,9 was being fulfilled for the first time.

> The Holy Spirit convicts of sin (John 16:8) through the Word, spoken or written. Peter had completed his part, the Holy Spirit had completed His part, and the rest was left in the hearers. Having a will to act, the decision was entirely in the hands of the hearers.[74]

---

[73] *Ibid.*, p.50.

[74] Dale, *op. cit.*, p.46.

And said to Peter and the rest of the apostles. Again it appears that all twelve have been speaking, else why would the listeners address "all" the apostles?

Brethren, what shall we do? This is an expression of earnestness. They want to know what to do to avoid the wrath of God upon them. When we look at the answer given to them, we find they were asking what to do to obtain forgiveness for their sins.

> This is the first time under the reign of Christ that this momentous question was propounded, and the first time, of course, under the new covenant, that it received an answer. Whatever may have been the proper answer under any previous dispensation, or on any previous day in the world's history, the answer given by Peter on this day of Pentecost, the day in which the reign of Christ on earth was first announced, is the true and infallible answer for all such inquirers in all subsequent time.[75]

If we want to avoid the wrath of God upon our sins, we'll have to do what Peter tells his hearers to do, for we live in the same dispensation that began on the day of Pentecost.

2:38 – *And Peter* **said** *to them, "Repent, and let each of you be baptized in the name of Jesus Christ for the forgiveness of your sins; and you shall receive the gift of the Holy Spirit.*

And Peter *said* to them. Peter had been the chief speaker, though the others had also addressed the crowd. He now, in the name of all, directs the hearers what to do. They are commanded to do two things: to repent, and to be baptized in the name of Jesus. And they are promised two blessings which would follow on the doing of those two things: the remission of sins, and the gift of the Holy Spirit.

Repent. Repentance results from a godly sorrow for the sins committed against God (or fellow men), with a purpose to forsake those sins. Repentance means to turn around and go the other way. True repentance involves restitution where possible.[76]

And let each one of you be baptized. "Let each one of you" represents the change of verbs in the Greek. "Repent" is plural, while "Let each one of you be baptized" is singular. There is also a change from the second to the third person. This change implies a break in the thought. The first thing to do when you are convicted of your sins is to make a radical and complete change. This is done in repentance, and is to be done by all. The next thing to be done is an individual thing. "Let each one of you be baptized ...." The direction that Christ gave to His apostles was that they should baptize all who believe.[77]

A word needs to be said about the *origin* of the ordinance of baptism. A popular, modern approach to the origin of the act is to say that it has a Jewish origin, perhaps in the

---

[75] McGarvey, *op. cit.*, p.37-38.

[76] At Luke 19:8, Zacchaeus vows to make restitution as a result of his repentance. This is one place where we learn that repentance involves restitution where possible. Detailed information on repentance is given in Special Study #8, "What is Repentance?," at the close of this chapter.

[77] Matthew 28:19; Mark 16:16. The Greek construction is such in Matthew that it says that one "makes disciples ... by baptizing." "Baptizing them" in Matthew is a circumstantial participle, being one of the things involved in "discipling."

days of the Babylonian captivity, and that John the Baptist merely appropriated for his own a Jewish custom he already found in use.[78] The idea that proselytes to the Jewish religion were baptized, even during Old Testament times, is based on a reference found in the Talmud. However, since the Talmud was not put into written form until 300 to 500 years after Christ, it is very difficult to affirm that all the things now found in the Talmud were in the oral form of the Talmud in Old Testament times. As Beasley-Murray noted, "there is not one clear testimony to [Jewish baptisms prior to the Christian era] in pre-Christian writings, and [the practice is completely unmentioned in] the writings of Philo, Josephus, and the Bible, particularly the New Testament." Importantly, there are several indications that the act of baptizing people in water originated with John the Baptist. First, John was called "the baptizer" because his practice of immersion was something new – something the people had never seen before. Further, Matthew 21:25ff is clear evidence that John's baptism was not of human origin. Finally, it is also likely that early Jewish baptisms were primarily for female proselytes; male proselytes to Judaism submitted to actual circumcision. (However, there is some evidence that both male and female proselytes to Judaism eventually submitted to immersion as an ablution, as part of a cleansing ritual.) Thus, it does not seem at all probable that Christianity learned about and simply copied the practice of baptizing from Judaism.

A word needs to be said about what it means to be "baptized." What *action* is signified by this verb? The Greek verb *baptizō,* in our version transliterated "baptize," means "immerse" or "dip."[79] That it actually has this meaning can be learned from those verses where it is translated rather than transliterated. For example, there is the time in the upper room, at the institution of the Lord's Supper, when Jesus speaks these words, "He that dips (*baptizō*) his hand with me in the dish ...."[80]

> The word baptize means immerse in the original. One may ask any Greek working in this country and learn this simple fact. The Greek Catholic church has always known this fact and still practices immersion to this day. Jesus walked about sixty-five miles to be immersed in the Jordan River. John baptized at Aenon because there was "much" water there (John 3:23). Philip took the eunuch "down into the water" and both of them "came up out of the water" (Acts 8:38,39). Paul tells us that we are buried in baptism (Romans 6:4-6).[81]

The chart at the top of the next page helps us visualize the point that the action signified in the Bible as being "baptism" is only immersion.

---

[78] G.R. Beasley-Murray, *Baptism in the New Testament* (Grand Rapids: Eerdmans, 1973), p.1-44, discusses the Jewish antecedents of Christian baptism, and has well summarized all the standard arguments for a human origin of the practice of immersion. The Beasley-Murray quote in the paragraph above is found on p.19 of his work.

[79] Alexander Campbell, *The Campbell-Rice Debate on Christian Baptism* (Lexington, KY: A.T. Skillman & Son, 1844), p.1-272, has answered all the standard arguments that have been asserted in the past 150 years to the effect that one can "baptize" by pouring or sprinkling (as well as by immersion), because the word *baptizō* merely means "to apply water in some fashion or another." Campbell effectively shows that the New Testament requires "immersion" if it is to be called a baptism!

[80] Matthew 26:23.

[81] Dale, *op. cit.*, p.48.

New Testament Baptism Requires	**Sprinkling Requires**	**Pouring Requires**	**Immersion Requires**
Water, Acts 10:47	✓	✓	✓
Much water, John 3:23		✓ (?)	✓
Going to water, Matthew 3:13			✓
Administered in water, Mark 1:9			✓
Down into water, Acts 8:38			✓
Coming out of the water, Matthew 3:16			✓
A burial, Romans, 6:4			✓
A resurrection, Colossian 2:12			✓
Bodies washed, Hebrews 10:22			✓

The baptism Peter commands here in verse 38 is a baptism in water, even though Peter does not specifically say so. That it is a baptism in water can be discerned from several different points of logic.

- By way of elimination, it is not the baptism of the Holy Spirit that Peter commands his hearers to submit to.[82] Remember, the subjects of the baptism of (with) the Holy Spirit were the apostles, and that the purpose of that baptism with the Holy Spirit was to empower them to do their witnessing work. This should show that the baptism commanded now by Peter is not the same as the baptism with the Holy Spirit, for Peter's hearers were not involved in the promise of the baptism with the Holy Spirit.

- A second way to learn what baptism Peter was commanding is to consult other passages in the New Testament which tell about people becoming Christians. Those passages, like Acts 10:44-48, will show that it is a baptism in water that is universally involved in the initiation into the Christian religion.

- It has been properly said that whenever the word "baptism" appears in the New Testament, it is a baptism in water unless the immediate context makes it plain it is one of the other baptisms. (Reference again the chart on "Baptisms in the New Testament" at Acts 1:5.) After the listeners have repented, Peter is admonishing them to submit to an immersion in water. "Let each one of you be baptized!"

In the name of Jesus Christ. There is a manuscript variation concerning the preposition translated "in." Some ancient manuscripts read *epi*, "upon"; and some read *en*, "in" or "by." Therefore, commentaries offer different notes, depending on which textual reading they follow:

---

[82] Many commentators, because of a faith-only background or persuasion, in an attempt to evade the force and necessity of baptism for salvation as taught by Acts 2:38, will insist that it is not a baptism in water that is necessary, but a "baptism of the Holy Spirit." They will then give "baptism of the Holy Spirit" a peculiar twist, as though it were synonymous with the new birth, and will then say this is what is necessary for salvation, but not a baptism in water. Beware! Not even 1 Corinthians 12:13a teaches a "spirit baptism" into the body of Christ. That verse says that by the *agency* of the Holy Spirit a man is led to the place where he wants to be baptized into the body.

- Some who follow the reading *en* understand this to mean "by the authority of Christ," like "Stop in the name of the King" means "By the authority of the king I command you to stop." I.e., 'Repent and be baptized because Christ commands it.'
- Commentators who follow the reading "upon" (*epi*) are divided in their explanations. Some think there is a reference to confession. "Upon the confession of Jesus Christ," i.e., having made a confession of Jesus as Messiah, they were to be baptized.
- Others following the reading "upon" think there is a reference to a prayer as the candidate is being baptized, similar to Acts 22:16 ("calling on the name of the Lord").
- Still others see a reference to the "baptismal formula" – i.e., the words spoken by the baptizer as he immerses the candidate. As he immerses the penitent believer, the baptizer says something like, "I now baptize you in the name of Jesus Christ."[83]

For the forgiveness of your sins. The Greek preposition translated "for" is *eis*. Over the meaning of this little word a great battle is being waged. Involved is the question of whether or not a person must be baptized in order to have his sins forgiven. A large part of Christendom holds to a doctrine that has been commonly categorized as "faith only." The faith-only doctrine is that baptism is *not* necessary for salvation. All that men are required to do to be saved is to believe. Then, of course, once a man is saved, he will want to go ahead and be baptized. Among Bible students of this persuasion, baptism is often called "an outward sign of an inward grace;" it is merely a token to others of what has already happened in the heart, it is believed. If baptism is merely a token, how do the faith-only teachers explain this little preposition *eis* ("for")?

(1) Some follow Baptist scholar A.T. Robertson who, believing that salvation comes before baptism, translates *eis* "because of." That is, he appeals to what is called a "causal use of *eis*." His argument proceeds in this fashion: You put a man in jail *for* murder. The "for" in that sentence means (not in order that he might commit murder, but) "because he already has." So those translations, like the KJV and NASB, which read "*for* the remission of sins" are interpreted to mean "be baptized *because* your sins have already been forgiven." Robertson insisted that the verse did not mean a man is baptized *in order to* have his sins forgiven, but rather because they already had been forgiven. REPLY to this first faith-only explanation of *eis*: Many lexicons do not even give a "causal use of *eis*." Out of 1,773 occurrences of *eis* in the New Testament, only 4 might mean "because." Those lexicons that do list a "causal use of *eis*" admit that such a translation is at best controversial.[84]

(2) Since the argument for the "causal use of *eis*" has not been convincing, faith-only teachers have tried another approach to explain what *eis* means here in verse 38. They appeal to what is called the "static use of *eis*." In New Testament times, there was a prepo-

---

[83] Further discussion of the "baptismal formula" will be found in notes at Acts 10:4b.

[84] Examining the material in the Arndt-Gingrich *Greek-English Lexicon of the New Testament* and other Early Christian literature (Chicago: University of Chicago Press, 1957), p.131 and 229, we find these significant facts: (1) Arndt-Gingrich give no examples of causal *eis* in the church fathers. (2) A scholarly article in *The Journal of Biblical Literature*, by Marcus, referred to by Arndt-Gingrich, notes that there is no example of causal *eis* in the papyri of the 1st century. Are we then to find examples of causal *eis* in the New Testament?

sition *en* meaning "in," and also a preposition *eis* meaning "into." *Eis*, the second, was used more and more, even invading the use of *en,* till in modern Greek *eis* is used for both "in" and "into," and *en* has disappeared from use. Those who assert the "static use of *eis*" would thus render Acts 2:38 as "be baptized ... *in respect to* the forgiveness of sins." This is just another way of saying because your sins are forgiven already, you need to be baptized. REPLY to this second faith-only explanation of *eis*: Few reputable Greek scholars who would stake their reputations on such a rendering of Acts 2:38. Indeed, there was a static *eis* in *koine* Greek, but not even the Arndt-Gingrich lexicon, which does list a number of places where *eis* is static, gives that as a meaning for Acts 2:38. That highly regarded lexicon says that *eis aphesin tōn hamartiōn* in verse 38 "indicates the purpose of baptism."[85]

The various faith-only arguments marshaled to prove that baptism is not necessary for the forgiveness of sins have not been convincing. Thus, by a process of elimination, we have been led to agree with those scholars who say that this passage means that forgiveness *is contingent on* repentance and baptism. It would be rightly translated, "baptized ... in order to have your sins forgiven."[86] Edgar J. Goodspeed (also a Baptist scholar), in his version of the Scriptures, translated the verse, "You must repent and be baptized every one of you *in order to* have your sins forgiven." When asked about this very un-Baptist translation (since it certainly does not uphold the doctrine of faith-only as the way of salvation), Goodspeed replied, "I am first a Greek scholar, and then a theologian."[87] In other words, the faith-only theology will just have to suffer, for Acts 2:38 makes baptism essential to salvation.[88]

Peter has commanded two things: repentance and immersion. And he promises his hearers, first, that upon compliance with these conditions they shall have as a result the forgiveness of sins. The sins that are forgiven when a penitent is scripturally immersed are

---

[85] Arndt-Gingrich, *op. cit.*, p.131.

[86] A number of excellent articles on the necessity of immersion for salvation have appeared in journals. We would call attention to two: Don Nash, "For the Remission of Sin," *Christian Standard,* CX, (March 30, 1975), p.270-72, and R.L. Aldrich, "Baptism – For Remission of Sins?" *Restoration Herald,* January 1963, p.7ff.

[87] Basil Holt. "New Evidence on an Old Question" in *Christian Standard,* LXXVII (June 20, 1942). p.605. James Earl Ladd, "The Purpose of Christian Baptism" in *Christian Standard,* LXXXIII (September 6, 1947), p.611,624.

[88] For the reader who needs further confirmation of the necessity of immersion for salvation, there are the following items. (1) "The endless controversy over baptism as necessary, or not necessary, for salvation could have been avoided. If Christ commanded baptism, and He did (Matthew 28:19; Mark 16:16); and if one believes it is necessary to keep a command of Christ to be saved, then baptism is necessary to salvation." (Dale, *op. cit.*, p.47.) (2) Both repentance and baptism have the same relationship to remission of sins here in Peter's instructions. If there is no remission before repentance (and I know of no faith-only teacher who would so hold), then there is no remission before baptism. Peter said, "Repent and be baptized ... for the forgiveness." If repentance is "unto" (in order to) the remission (rather than "because of"), the same must be said for baptism. And if there is no remission before baptism, then baptism is essential to salvation, as essential as repentance. (3) Consider Galatians 3:26,27. In studying this passage, remember that verses beginning with "for" give an explanation of something just said. Verse 26 says men are "justified by faith" and then verse 27 begins "*for* as many as are baptized into Christ have put on Christ." In other words, "baptism for remission of sins" is "justification by faith." (4) J.W. McGarvey. *op. cit.*, p.243ff, has an excellent article, "The Connection between Baptism and the Remission of Sins."

the sins he has committed up to the time of that baptism. This is the law of pardon for the non-Christian.[89]

And you shall receive the gift of the Holy Spirit. At the outset, it must be observed that this phrase can mean either "a gift from the Holy Spirit" (i.e., a gift which He gives) or "a gift which consists of the Holy Spirit" (i.e., if I give you a gift of candy, what did I give you? Candy, of course. If we receive the gift of the Holy Spirit, what do we receive? The Spirit!). Since the Greek itself is ambiguous, we must choose which of the two ideas is best. In the light of parallel passages, which teach that obedient believers receive the indwelling gift of the Holy Spirit at the time of their conversion, we find no objection to so understanding the words of Peter's promise.[90]

Perhaps this conclusion, that Peter is promising the indwelling gift of the Holy Spirit, needs to be reinforced. We've already referred to Special Study #3, "The Person and Work of the Holy Spirit," which is found at the close of this chapter. In that study, we learn of several activities of the Holy Spirit. Is there any other measure of the Holy Spirit, besides the indwelling gift, that would fit what Peter promises to all those who obey?

- Can Peter be promising every new convert that he or she automatically receives "spiritual gifts"? Those miraculous spiritual gifts were received by the laying on of an apostle's hands, and not every baptized believer received spiritual gifts. In verse 38, Peter makes a promise to all baptized believers, and there is no mention of laying on of hands. Therefore, it is doubtful he is offering the measure of the Spirit called "spiritual gifts."

- Can Peter be promising every new convert that he will receive the "baptism with the Holy Spirit"? This too is most unlikely, for in our studies on the Holy Spirit and Glossolalia we have emphasized that this measure of the Spirit is not something every Christian receives.

So, we are limited to the idea that what Peter is promising to every penitent, obedient believer is the indwelling presence of the Holy Spirit.[91]

2:39 – *"For the promise is for you and your children, and for all who are far off, as many as the Lord our God shall call to Himself."*

For the promise is for you. "To you Jews to whom I'm speaking" is the sense of Peter's words. But the promise of what?

- One group of commentators believes Peter is promising the "baptism with the Holy Spirit." In order to arrive at this surprising conclusion, they refer back to the promise made by Jesus to the apostles (Acts 1:4,5) and to the word "promise" in the middle of Peter's sermon (verse 33), and then affirm that the word "promise" here in verse 39 refers to the same promised Holy Spirit. Even if we were to admit that all 120 (rather

---

[89] A Christian does something different to find forgiveness for his sins, as we shall learn at Acts 8:22

[90] Galatians 3:2; Ephesians 1:13.

[91] See Part VII of Special Study #3, "The Persons and Work of the Holy Spirit," for details about the indwelling of the Holy Spirit.

than just the apostles) received the baptism with the Holy Spirit, as this interpretation requires, it still would be a hard position to sustain, for it requires ignoring the context in order to put the passages together that these interpreters attempt to put together. Once the whole context (not just the word "promise") is taken into account, it becomes clear Peter is not promising the "baptism with the Holy Spirit."

- A second group of commentators believes Peter is promising "spiritual gifts," but Barnes and Ellicott confuse the "gift of the Spirit" (verse 38) with "spiritual gifts." Once this is seen, there is little to recommend this interpretation.

- The fact that verse 39 begins with "for" shows that something said in verse 38 (something there promised) is here being further explained. Taken in its context, what Peter means when he says "the promise is to you" is that the promise of salvation and the gift of the indwelling Holy Spirit are for all who will obey.

And your children. Bible teachers will interpret this phrase in the light of what they did with the first phrase of this verse. Those who think the "promise" refers either to the baptism with the Holy Spirit or to spiritual gifts immediately think of the "sons and daughters" of Joel's prophecy. Alford even finds a proof text for infant baptism here![92] If the last suggestion given in the explanation of "promise" is correct, then Peter is promising to his hearers that the blessings of salvation shall not be confined to their generation, but shall be extended to their posterity (generation after generation).

And for all who are far off. Peter is saying, 'Not only is this salvation for you Jews (you and your children), but it is also for the Gentiles (those far off).' Compare Ephesians 2:13,17 and Isaiah 57:18. It would seem that Barnes is mistaken when he tries to limit what Peter says to Jews who were scattered in other nations. Barnes argues as he does because he does not think Peter has a world-wide vision yet, and will not till after the vision of the sheet and the preaching to Cornelius in Acts 10.[93] But what Peter may or may not have thought has nothing to do with what he said, for he was speaking by inspiration! Compare 1 Peter 1:10 where it is also taught that prophets often spoke more than they personally understood as they were speaking. So it was with Peter.

As many as the Lord our God shall call to Himself. How does God call? He calls people by His Gospel.[94] The call presupposes understanding, which rules out infants. The call includes the power and right to reject, which rules out Calvinistic predestination and what is called (by Reformed theologians) "effectual calling."[95]

---

[92] Henry Alford, *The New Testament for English Readers* (Chicago: Moody Press, 1950), p.664. (The note about infant baptism does not appear in the 1871 edition of *Alford's Greek Testament*, published In London by Rivingtons.)

[93] Barnes, *op. cit.*, p.54.

[94] In 2 Thessalonians 2:14, Paul says God called the Thessalonians through the gospel Paul preached. See also Romans 10:13,14 and John 6:45.

[95] James I. Packer, "Call, Called, Calling" in *Baker Dictionary of Theology* (Grand Rapids: Baker Book House, 1960), p.108.

2:40 – *And with many other words he solemnly testified and kept on exhorting them, saying, "Be saved from this perverse generation!"*

And with many other words he solemnly testified and kept on exhorting them, saying. This sermon, though one of the longest in the New Testament, is but an outline. Luke did not record all that Peter said. Jesus had said they would be "witnesses" (*martureō*), and now Peter has solemnly witnessed (*diamartureō*) by the help of the Holy Spirit. He witnessed to God's great redemptive acts in history. "Exhort" means to "entreat, plead with, urge." The fact that there is a variation in the tense of these two verbs in this phrase has led many to believe that "testify" refers to what preceded, and "exhort" to what follows.

Be saved from this perverse generation! The Greek is passive, "Be saved" – by obedience to the will of the Lord. This is how one may be preserved from the influence and fate of the godless people about him. Peter is urging them to submit to God's way of salvation, the way which he has just explained. The word "perverse" speaks of people who are not easily guided or taught, people who are wicked. If it was the priests or scribes that accused the apostles of being drunk, perhaps Peter pointed to them as he said, "Be saved from *this* perverse generation!"

2:41 – *So then, those who had received his word were baptized; and there were added that day about three thousand souls.*

So then, those who had received his Word were baptized. "Received" is equal to, "They were persuaded by it. They believed what Peter said."[96] The "Word" is the message which Peter had spoken about the Messiah and the means of pardon for sin through Him. Those who believed Peter's preaching were immersed on that same day.[97]

Some writers, trying to defend a sprinkling or pouring mode of baptism, have argued that 3,000 people could not have been immersed during the remainder of that day, nor could a sufficient supply of water have been found near Jerusalem to accommodate a crowd like that. (1) Would there have been time left in that day to baptize 3,000 people? Peter's sermon started about 9 A.M. (verse 15). The sermon conceivably could have lasted three hours, though the length is not given. Thus, Peter's appeal to them to respond to God's call could have been given about noon, or shortly after. There still was time for the 3,000 to be immersed. Baptizing one person per minute, which can be done by immersion. twelve persons could baptize 3,000 people in 4½ hours. And, of course, any Christian could baptize. The act of baptizing does not have to be limited to the apostles. Long before evening fell, the 3,000 could have all been immersed! (2) Would there have been a sufficient amount of water nearer than the Jordan River (which is 20 miles away) in which

---

[96] John 1:12 shows that "receiving" and "believing" are synonymous ideas in the New Testament.

[97] Barnes, who tries to defend his faith-only beliefs wherever he can in his *Notes,* writes, "Their conversion was instantaneous." (Barnes, *op. cit.*, p.56.) The idea that conversion is instantaneous is part of the doctrine that a man is saved the moment he believes. However, the New Testament presents conversion – a term that includes regeneration and repentance and obedience – as a process. Individuals are not saved by faith only. If it takes more than mental assent to save a person, then conversion must be described as a process.

to immerse? McGarvey and other reliable scholars have proved long ago, by the simple process of measuring the pools in and around the city of Jerusalem, that a supply of water was not a problem. The pool of Siloam (immediately south of the Temple enclosure) is still used today for the immersion of believers. The pools of Upper Gihon and Lower Gihon are located in the Valley of Hinnom, west of the city of Jerusalem. Upper Gihon measures 316' x 218' and averages 20' deep. Lower Gihon measures 592' long, and was made by damming up the valley. The Pool of Bethesda and the Pool of Hezekiah are within the walls of the city. Since a knowledge of ancient Jerusalem has been spread abroad by the writings of archaeologists in the last 100 years, it has become indefensible to raise an objection regarding the availability of the quantity of water needed.

And there were added that day about 3000 souls. The verb translated "added" means "to join together, to gather with." The older translations that have "there were added *unto them* ... " have understood that this verse means the 3,000 who were converted that day were added to the number already following Christ (the Twelve and the 120). But what the Greek tells us is that the 3,000 were joined together into a community, a society, a congregation. It does not mean that they were "added to the Church," for there was no Church until this beginning was made.

Our study of later verses in Acts will persistently show that men were baptized the same day they came to belief and confessed that belief in Christ, just as was done on Pentecost. It reads "there were added ... *that day*"! In Acts, we find no delay in the timing of the actual immersion of a penitent believer.

"3000 souls." Likely those who responded to the invitation were but a small part of the great crowd that heard Peter's sermon.

> The 3000 who responded were only a part of the great crowd that heard the message of salvation. These 3000 exercised their own free will and accepted without compulsion the gospel plan of salvation. Many others likely rejected the invitation.[98]

Should we pray for another "Pentecost" today, as many religious people do? Barnes seems to think, for example, that we can have such revivals. It appears to this commentator to be improper to pray for such an outpouring of the Spirit as the apostles received. However, it certainly is appropriate to pray for revival, and to pray that individuals will respond to the call given and promises offered by God.

I. The First Days of the Church of Christ. 2:42-47

2:42 – *And they were continually devoting themselves to the apostles' teaching and to fellowship, to the breaking of bread and to prayer.*

And they were continually devoting themselves. The early Christians were regular in their worship together. Barnes, attempting to read his "once saved, always saved" doctrine into this verse, writes, "That any of these apostatized is nowhere recorded, and is not to be

---

[98] Dale, *op. cit.*, p.51.

presumed."[99] However, he surely can find a better proof text than this, if the doctrine indeed be true. These new Christians, having been baptized on the same day in which they first became believers, had many objects of faith to become acquainted with and many duties yet unknown in which to be instructed. By devoting themselves to the apostles' teaching, fellowship, and other activities noted here, they would soon be "taught to observe all things whatsoever Jesus commanded."[100]

To the apostles' teaching. The apostles were teaching the new converts all the doctrines of Christianity. In the Great Commission, Jesus had instructed that the converts were to be further instructed (Matthew 28:20), and this is what is being done by the apostles. The apostles, aided by the Holy Spirit, would be sharing with the new converts the wonderful truths they themselves had learned from Jesus during His earthly ministry. In due course, the apostolic teaching took written shape in the New Testament scriptures.

And to fellowship. Fellowship speaks of that common interest and mutual participation in those things which concern the welfare of each other. *Koinōnia* is often translated "communion." It denotes having things in common, or participation in a common cause. Among other things, it includes offerings for the poor and for the spread of the Gospel.[101]

To the breaking of bread. This language is sometimes used of a common meal, and sometimes of the Lord's Supper; it must be determined from the context each time just which is meant. Some writers urge that the thing spoken of here is a common meal, or perhaps even a love feast. But it would be difficult to interpret this of an ordinary meal, for the Greek reads, "THE breaking of THE bread" (i.e., there is an article in both places in the original). The context evidently is speaking of the worship services of the church. The apostles' teaching, fellowship, and prayers completely circle "the breaking of bread." Everything about the thought must be spiritual, making it improbable to say that verse 42 speaks of a common meal. In several New Testament passages the Lord's Supper is called "the breaking of bread,"[102] and by analogy it appears that such is the proper meaning here.

And to prayer. The marginal reading is plural, "prayers." The Greek reads "in THE prayers." Whether these were private or public prayers[103] is disputed. The use of the plural seems to indicate recurring times of prayer at fixed hours. It may speak of prayers together as a congregation, and/or attendance at the public Jewish prayers, as at Acts 3:1.[104]

---

[99] Barnes, *op. cit.*, p.56. A beginning book, to learn about the Bible's teaching on the doctrine sometimes called "eternal security" is Guy Duty, *If Ye Continue* (Minneapolis: Bethany Fellowship, 1966).

[100] Matthew 28:20.

[101] Romans 15:26; 2 Corinthians 8:4; Philippians 1:5.

[102] 1 Corinthians 10:16. Special Study #18, "The Lord's Supper," at the close of chapter 20 lists the Scriptural names given for this meal, as well as a host of other details.

[103] Matthew 6:6 speaks of private prayer. Acts 20:36 is an example of public prayer. Both types are recognized as proper in God's Word.

[104] Acts 2:42 is not the first time we have met the concept of "prayer" in the book of Acts. By this time, the typical reader is usually caused to think seriously about his own prayer life, for this passage is an example for Christians of what congregational life is like. The Model Prayer (Matthew 6:9-13) contains many helpful

The ASV reads "they continued steadfastly" where the NASB reads "continually devoting themselves." How often is "steadfastly"? What regularity is indicated by "devoting themselves"? The Greek word is a present participle, a tense that indicates continuous action. Remember, this speaks of the days and weeks immediately following Pentecost. How often did these new converts go to hear the apostles preach? (Was it only quarterly, or was it more regularly than that?) How often did they share in the fellowship? (Once a month, or quarterly, or was it more regularly than that?) How often did they pray? (Was it quarterly, or more often than that?) It soon becomes evident that those groups who are having the Lord's Supper only quarterly (or even yearly) are not doing things the way they were done in the early church. The early church was just as steadfast in partaking of the Lord's Supper as they were in doing the other things listed in verse 42. There just is no basis for claiming that the Lord's Supper was any less frequent than weekly. If the early church was steadfast in each of these things, then so should we be today.

In verse 42 we have a good picture of the elements that were included in a worship service in the apostolic age, and it thus forms an example for us, too. Those elements were apostles' doctrine, fellowship (offering), the breaking of bread, and prayers. From 1 Corinthians 14:15,26 it is learned that singing also was a part of the services in the church at Corinth, and from that passage we get the idea for singing as part of the congregational participation in our present-day worship.

2:43 – *And everyone kept feeling a sense of awe; and many wonders and signs were taking place through the apostles.*

And everyone kept feeling a sense of awe. "Everyone" might speak of people outside the church, as well as church members. Just after the brief sketch of the regular public worship of the church, we have a statement about the effect of the new life in Christ on both members and outsiders. There was a sense of awe at what God was doing in His world.

And many wonders and signs were taking place through the apostles. "Wonders" and "signs" are miracles, as was explained in verse 22. Examples of the kinds of miracles done will be found in the following chapters. And notice carefully – they were done through the apostles who had been promised an empowering by Jesus. If all the 120 were baptized with the Holy Spirit, as some insist, why were the miracles done only through the apostles? "Were taking place" represents an imperfect tense verb, speaking of continual action.

2:44 – *And all those who had believed were together, and had all things in common;*

And all those who had believed were together. In verse 41, we learned that "received the word" is the same as "believed what Peter had preached about Jesus being the Messiah." "Were together" speaks of the marvelous unity of this congregation. It does not seem to

---

ideas for our own prayer life regarding what to say when we are talking to God. The posture taken during prayer is a matter of personal preference. Jesus knelt and then bowed His face to the ground during prayer in the Garden (Mark 14:35). Paul knelt during prayer once (Acts 20:36). David prayed while lying on his bed at night (Psalm 63:6). Standing is also proper (Mark 11:25; Luke 18:11-13). Not the posture, but the attitude of the heart (reverent, humble), is the important thing.

mean they were all living together in the same house, for it would be hard to conceive of over 3,000 living in the same house. Rather, it speaks of unity in mind, in purpose, in faith, in heart, in action. They were united because they were obedient believers in Jesus Christ. This is the only way to the unity for which Christ prayed.[105] Not in the Ecumenical Movement, or in the Pope's Encyclical on Church Unity, is the way to unity to be found. Men cannot manufacture such unity; they can only endeavor to keep the unity they already have in Christ. The following verses will help us understand what it is to be "together" (*epi to auto*). We shall see described an unselfishness, a mutual interest in the needs of brothers and sisters in Christ, and a joy and satisfaction found in everyday tasks, all capped off by voices lifted in praise to God. This unity with God and with one another caused them to daily worship God, not only in the Temple, but also in the home. Their reverence for God made the common tasks of the day a joy to perform, and the final and inevitable result of this divine oneness was the salvation of more souls.

And had all things in common. "All things," that is, their property and possessions.[106] This is not absolute communism, where everything is confiscated and placed in a central storehouse and then doled out equally to all. None of the early Christians was required to give his goods or sell his property. Not even while the Twelve were with Jesus, and they had a common treasurer, did they relinquish personal property rights, for each evidently still owned personal property. And after the church began, there is abundant evidence of private property held as a stewardship for God among even the most devout.[107] So it is a mistake to say the early church practiced absolute communism. "Having all things common" does not mean that everyone sold everything he possessed, or gathered up his title to houses and lands, and presented it all to the church leaders. Verse 44 does say the Christians were willing to use whatever they had when others had need. "It's yours if you need it" was the prevailing attitude about possessions. Christianity teaches that we are responsible for the welfare of our brothers in Christ, and that we should render service, money, and everything if need be, for the welfare of our brethren. This was unlimited giving in an unlimited and united way to save as many people in as short a time as possible. Another reason for such a practice (besides the evangelistic one) was that many of those who came from abroad to the feast of Pentecost may have stayed longer than anticipated, and they would now be denied the hospitality by the Jews who had not yet embraced Christianity. In these circumstances, it would be natural and proper that the Christians share their means while they fellowshipped together.

2:45 – *and they began selling their property and possessions, and were sharing them with all, as anyone might have need.*

And they *began* selling their property and possessions. They sold as much as was neces-

---

[105] John 17:20ff.

[106] Compare Acts 4:34-35.

[107] Acts 5:4. Ananias and Sapphira did not have to sell their possessions; they could have kept them as private property. Mary did not have to sell her house (Acts 12:12). Mnason still owned property (Acts 21:16). The Hebrew Christians still had property of which they could be despoiled (Hebrews 10:34 and 13:2,5.16). At Corinth, Christians could lay in store each week (1 Corinthians 16:2). See also 1 John 3:17.

sary to meet the needs, as the rest of the verse shows. "Property" speaks of real estate, and "possessions" speaks of personal items. Whatever they had of value was gladly relinquished and the money given from time to time as the need arose. The verbs throughout this section are in the imperfect tense, expressing the constant recurrence of this act. The sale and distribution took place from time to time as special occasions of distress or want called for them.

And were sharing them with all, as any one might have need. The ready cash received from the sale of the real estate and personal possessions was distributed according to need (not on an equality, as is done in most 20th century communistic societies). "As anyone had need" limits what was before said about "having all things in common."

2:46 – *And day by day continuing with one mind in the temple, and breaking bread from house to house, they were taking their meals together with gladness and sincerity of heart,*

And day by day. Through the weeks that followed the day of Pentecost, the things described in verses 42-45 were daily occurrences.

Continuing with one mind in the temple. At the hours of prayer the Christians would go up to the Temple to pray. For a number of years, the Hebrew Christians will continue many of the old religious practices learned from Moses and the Prophets. Even the Romans, for a number of years, will consider the Christian religion just another sect of the Jews, and so allowed the religion to grow. The real break with Jewish practices will not come until the Temple is destroyed, along with the city of Jerusalem, in AD 70.

And breaking bread from house to house. Does this speak of the Lord's Supper, or of common meals?
- Some think the Lord's Supper is intended. It is urged that this phrase speaks of the Lord's Supper, while the next phrase here in verse 46 speaks of the love feast which was often held in connection with the Lord's Supper. If this phrase is so interpreted, it follows that in the early days of the church the Lord's Supper was shared daily. (More will be said about the frequency of the Lord's Supper in notes at Acts 20:7.)
- This commentator is of the opinion that both phrases in verse 46 speak of common meals. The reference appears not to be to the Lord's Supper, for the next clause seems to be further explanation of what it meant to "break bread from house to house."

If verse 46a is understood to be a reference to the Lord's Supper, then "house to house" tells us that not only did the first Christians meet in the Temple, but they also met in each other's homes (since there were as yet no church buildings) for the celebration of the Lord's Supper (an act of worship for which the Temple enclosure was unsuitable). If the reference is to common meals, then "house to house" speaks of the hospitality extended by the brethren in Christ – part of the marvelous unity of the early church. Such association of Christians together is an integral part of the life of the congregation, for without it, new converts will not get a sense of belonging to the family of believers, and soon are likely to drift into new associations seeking that sense of belonging.

They were taking their meals together with gladness and sincerity of heart. This seems to be an explanation of the previous phrase in verse 46, and shows that "breaking of bread" here is not a reference to the Lord's Supper. "Gladness" is rejoicing, a very strong word in the original, "exultation." Those who contributed of their means to those who had not, rejoiced in the opportunity to help others. Those who received help rejoiced that there were those who loved them and were able to help. They all rejoiced because Messiah had come, and they had been privileged to believe on Him and become part of the family of God. "Singleness of heart" says they were satisfied and thankful, open-handed and liberal.

2:47 – praising God, and having favor with all the people. And the Lord was adding to their number day by day those who were being saved.

Praising God. Giving thanks to God is the idea.

And having favor with all the people. With the great mass of the Jewish people, for the time being, the Christians had favor. This does not mean that all the Jewish people looked favorably on the Christians, for the following chapters will show that the Jewish religious leaders were very antagonistic toward the early believers.

And the Lord was adding to their number. The "Lord" here (as in verse 39) is a reference to God, rather than to Christ. No person can "join church" like he might join some human fraternal society. He must be added by the Lord. Men are added to the body of believers when they become obedient. Paul and Apollos (and we) may plant and water, but God gives the increase. Again, the verb tense pictures continuous action; i.e., God went on adding.

Barnes interprets this to mean "caused, or inclined them to be joined to the church."[108] Is this so? It sounds suspiciously like the idea of a "first work of grace," where God must first operate on the sinner's heart to make him either want to or be able to believe. Such a doctrine is part and parcel of the larger concept called "total depravity and total inability," a doctrine not taught in the Scriptures, but one made popular by Augustine and Calvin. "Adding" is the same Greek word that was used in verse 41, and such an idea as Barnes tries to give it here would not fit there. Rather, these words of Luke's are expressive of the fact that when a man is obedient, his name is added to the Lamb's book of life.[109] Where the NASB has "to their number," the KJV reads "to the church." The words "to the church" are not in the Greek. The Greek is *epi to auto*, the very same phrase translated "were together" in verse 44. The idea is that daily men and women who became believers were joined together into the one body, and included in the daily fellowship and hospitality and helpfulness of that one body.

Day by day. There were daily additions to the church in those early months and years. Why is it not so today? There was no open membership in the early church. Only those who are saved (whose sins have been forgiven, who have been obedient to the faith) are entitled to church membership. Perhaps today men are demanding less of alien sinners in

---

[108] Barnes, *op. cit.*, p.59.

[109] Hebrews 12:24; Revelation 3:5, 20:12,15.

an effort to swell the church rolls here on earth, only to find that the truncated version of Christianity which they have offered men does not satisfy, and so, more and more, the church is passed by.

Those who were being saved. The question has already been raised whether conversion is an act or a process. Here is further evidence that the conclusion given (i.e., that conversion is a process) was correct, for the Greek here pictures a process – those who were in the process of being saved. The translation of the KJV ("such as should be saved") takes its place among the few passages in which the KJV translators have, perhaps, been influenced by a Calvinistic bias. What Luke states is that those individuals who complied with the exhortation in verse 40, and obeyed the commands given in verse 38, placed themselves in a state of salvation, a condition of progress. The present participle ("were being saved") expresses a continuous or progressive state. Not only is salvation a process, but continuing salvation (sanctification) is also a process (Hebrews 10:14).

In Jerusalem

Drawing by Horace Knowles
from the British and Foreign Bible Society

SPECIAL STUDY #3

THE PERSON AND WORK OF THE HOLY SPIRIT

What is the average Christian's concept of the Holy Spirit? Is He too mysterious to be understood? Is He as well known as the other two members of the Godhead? Should He be any more mysterious than the Father or the Son?

A working knowledge of the Holy Spirit is important, because we are living in the age of the Holy Spirit.

Divine guidance is surely needed when one comes to a study of this topic. Personal spiritual experience cannot furnish the beginning point for our inquiry into this subject, for our experiences may not be shared by others. Hence, our source of knowledge must be the Word given us.

The Holy Spirit has been neglected in our thinking, teaching, and preaching. Many preachers, otherwise faithful, propound many erroneous views upon this subject. May God then help us in our thinking, that we may show forth such great care and caution as required, and that we may receive much good from this study.

"The Holy Spirit is much more prominently mentioned in the Word of God than the average reader realizes: someone has pointed out that in the 66 books of the Bible, He is mentioned in 47 of them; more than 250 times in the New Testament, more than 400 times in the entire Bible, and by more than 40 different names."

I. HOLY SPIRIT IDENTIFIED

A. *Care in identification of terms is required*

Remember that the mere use of the term "spirit" *(ruah,* Heb.; *pneuma,* Grk.) does not necessarily determine what is meant in any one passage.

"Spirit" is a name for the divine self-consciousness (1 Corinthians 2:10-11). It is a name for the glorified Christ (1 Corinthians 15:45; 2 Corinthians 3:17-18). It is a name for God's indwelling presence (Acts 2:38). *Ruah* and *pneuma* are sometimes translated "wind" (John 3:8; Exodus 10:13). "Spirit" is a name for a distinct Divine person, i.e., the Holy Spirit (1 Corinthians 12:11; Romans 8:9,14,16,26; 2 Corinthians 13:14; Ephesians 4:4-6). And "spirit" sometimes speaks of the human spirit (1 Corinthians 2:11).

B. *The personality of the Holy Spirit (the third member of the Godhead)*

The Holy Spirit is a person, not an inanimate force. He possesses mind (Romans 8:27; John 16:14; 1 Corinthians 2:10). He possesses knowledge (1 Corinthians 2:11). He possesses affection (Romans 15:30; 1 Corinthians 2:4; Isaiah 63:10). He possesses a will (Acts 16:7; 1 Corinthians 12:11).

The Holy Spirit is a person. He can be grieved (Ephesians 4:30). He can be resisted (Acts 7:51; Genesis 6:3). He can be blasphemed (Matthew 12:31-32). He can be quenched (1 Thessalonians 5:19).

The Holy Spirit is a person because He acts as a person. He speaks (1 Timothy 4:1). He bears testimony (John 15:26). He reveals the truth (John 16:12-13; 1 Corinthians 2:9,10). He restrains (Acts 16:6-7). He has influence (Luke 24:44-49; Romans 8:26).

The personality of the Holy Spirit is seen in the benediction of 2 Corinthians 13:14 and in Ephesians 4:4.

Admittedly, the Greek word *pneuma* is neuter (from which some have argued that the Holy Spirit is not a person). However, whenever a pronoun is used to refer to the Holy Spirit, it is usually a masculine pronoun (not neuter). For example, see John 14:26. Once, at Romans 8:26, the neuter pronoun is used.

C. *The deity of the Holy Spirit*

The Holy Spirit is a divine being, partaking of and sharing God's nature. He is eternal (Hebrews 9:14). He is omnipresent (Psalm 139:7-10). He is omnipotent (Micah 3:8; Romans 15:19). He is omniscient (1 Corinthians 2:10-11; Isaiah 40:13-14). He is placed on an equal with the Father and Son (Matthew 28:19; Romans 15:13; 2 Corinthians 13:14).

The Holy Spirit is the third person in the Godhead.[1] But being the "third" person of the Godhead does not imply that the Holy Spirit is inferior to God or Christ in wisdom, power, or knowledge. He is deity.

II. HOLY SPIRIT IN THE OLD TESTAMENT (adapted from G.M. Elliott)

A. *The difficulty with the word Ruah*

The Hebrew word *ruah* is variously translated "air, anger, blast, breath, cool, courage, mind, quarters, side, tempest, wind, vain, windy" as well as "spirit."

B. *The personality and Godhead of the Holy Spirit in the Old Testament*

Isaiah 63:10-14 is an excellent passage for study in this regard. It is one of the best in the Old Testament to show the nature of the Spirit.

C. *The work of the Holy Spirit in the Old Testament*

---

[1] "Godhead" is sometimes spoken of as "the Trinity," although the word "Trinity" does not occur in our English versions. "Godhead" is used, at Colossians 2:9. Some people, because they cannot understand the "Trinity," deny the doctrine of the pluralistic-unity of the Godhead. But it is best to realize at the start that we cannot fully explain God. If we could fully understand the Godhead, we would be God! Instead, we shall find peace and happiness and contentment if we acknowledge our humanity and His divinity. There is much we do not understand while on earth; we would do well not fret over things that are solely in the realm of divine wisdom and reserved for eternal concern and comfort.

The creative and providential functions of the Holy Spirit are set forth in the Old Testament. Genesis 1:1-2 presents the Holy Spirit as continually hovering over the creation in an intense, vibrant, perhaps vitalizing movement in bringing order and beauty out of chaos. The Father, Son, and Holy Spirit were active in the creation. See also Psalm 104:30 and Job 26:13. In Genesis 1:26, do we have communication within the Godhead? Are they counselling together as to the making of man in the image of God? Then compare Genesis 2:7 and Job 33:4. In Isaiah 34:16, Isaiah spoke, but the Holy Spirit was in the fulfillment. Isaiah 63:14 records praise to God for both the revealed and unrevealed activities of the Holy Spirit in creation and in divine providence. Hebrews 10:5 and Luke 1:35 also are references showing the creative and providential functions of the Holy Spirit.

The Holy Spirit's activity in providence in the Old Testament is suggested by verses such as Job 33:4; Isaiah 34:16; and Isaiah 63:14. Providence is that preservation, care, and government which God exercises over all things that He has created, in order that they may accomplish the ends for which they were created. Providence is God's *everyday* activity in his world.[2]

The work of the Holy Spirit in clothing servants of God with might, courage, and wisdom is suggested in Judges 6:34 (note the marginal reading); Judges 11:29, 14:6,19, and 15:14; Exodus 31:1ff; 1 Samuel 16:12-14; Nehemiah 9:20,30. Men chosen to be God's spokesmen were endowed with the gifts appropriate to their God-given work.

The Old Testament scriptures themselves are the work of the Holy Spirit (2 Samuel 23:1-2; Zechariah 7:12; 2 Timothy 3:16; 2 Peter 1:21). The Holy Spirit was behind the inspired writing of this text – He is the reason for the origin, order, unity, and inherent power seen in the Old Testament scriptures.

The Old Testament prophets foresaw a large extension of the operations of the Holy Spirit in the days of the Messianic Kingdom (Ezekiel 36:26ff; Joel 2:28). An indwelling gift of the Holy Spirit was not available to the average man of God in the Old Testament times like He is available to all God's New Testament people (John 7:27-39; Acts 19:2; Galatians 3:2).

III. HOLY SPIRIT IN THE MINISTRY OF JESUS

A. *The Holy Spirit and the Incarnation*

The Holy Spirit had something to do with the conception of Jesus (Matthew 1:18-21; Luke 1:34-35).

B. *The Holy Spirit in the Ministry of Jesus*

---

[2] Miracle, on the other hand, is not something that happens every day. There are only 4 or 5 epochs of miracle in all of Bible history – at the time of the Flood; at the time of the Exodus and the establishment of the nation in Canaan; during the life and death struggle of the true religion with heathenism in the days of Elijah and Elisha; during the Captivities; and then at the time of Jesus' ministry and introduction of Christianity into the world. C.S. Lewis has defined miracle in these words: "The divine art of miracle is not the art of suspending the pattern to which events conform, but of feeding new events into that pattern." Be careful about what is called "miracles" – it may simply be God's everyday providence we are seeing!

At His baptism by John, we are told that the Holy Spirit came upon Jesus in the form of a dove, and after that He was "full" of the Holy Spirit (Luke 3:21-22, 4:1ff).

He was anointed of the Holy Spirit (Acts 10:38). He was helped during His ministry by the Holy Spirit (Luke 4:14; Acts 1:2). His miracles were done in the power of the Holy Spirit (Luke 4:18ff; John 14:10).

C. *Jesus was Filled with the Holy Spirit*

He possessed the power of the Holy Spirit without limit and without measure (John 3:34; see also Luke 1:35 and Isaiah 61:1-2).

D. *The Holy Spirit and the Death of Jesus*

Hebrews 9:14 tells us that when Jesus went to Calvary, He "by the Eternal Spirit offered Himself." The Holy Spirit had something to do with the sacrificial death of Christ.

E. *The Holy Spirit and the Resurrection of Jesus*

Several passages attribute the resurrection of Jesus' body from the dead to the Holy Spirit (for example, Romans 8:11 and 1 Peter 3:18).

IV. THE BAPTISM OF THE HOLY SPIRIT

A. *Definitions and Synonyms*

"The expression 'baptism of the Holy Spirit' is based on a number of predictions found in our four Gospels and, in connection with these, the record of their fulfillment in the book of Acts ... The gift of the Holy Spirit on the Day of Pentecost and the miraculous manifestations which followed are clearly the chief historical fulfillment of the prediction of the baptism of the Holy Spirit."[3] The apostles, we know, were: (1) baptized of the Holy Spirit, Acts 1:5; (2) endued, clothed upon, with power from on high, Luke 24:49; (3) filled with the Spirit, Acts 2:4. Thus what Biederwolf has said is true,[4] namely, that in the case of the apostles, the words "baptism," "enduement," and "filling" refer to one and the same experience.

B. *The Baptism of the Holy Spirit was Prophesied and Promised*

Long before the Spirit was given to the apostles, the event was predicted (for example, Joel 2:27-32; Matthew 3:11; Luke 24:44-49; John 1:29-34; Acts 1:1-2:5).

---

[3] E.Y. Mullins, "Baptism of the Holy Spirit" in *International Standard Bible Encyclopedia*, ed. By James Orr (Grand Rapids: William B. Eerdmans Publishing Co., 1960), Vol. 1, p.399-400.

[4] William E. Biederwolf, *Study of the Holy Spirit* (Grand Rapids: Kregel Publications, 1903), p.64,67.

C. *The Administrator of this Baptism*

Christ (God) was the administrator (i.e., the one doing the baptizing), as Luke 3:16; Acts 1:15ff; and John 20:22 plainly show.

D. *The Purpose of the Baptism of the Holy Spirit*

Supernatural claims demand supernatural evidence (Hebrews 2:3-4). Divine guidance was needed during the time preceding the revealing of the New Testament scriptures (1 Corinthians 13:9). The Jewish Christian leaders needed evidence to convince them the gospel was to be preached to the Gentiles (Acts 10:47, 11:1-18, 15:8). The completion of the revelation of God's will required that the apostles be under the control of the Holy Spirit (John 20:21-22, 16:13; Luke 24:44-49; Acts 1:8).

E. *The Whom was the Promise Made?*

The promise is made only to the apostles (Matthew 10:19-20; Luke 21:13-14, 24:49; John 14:26, 16:13; Acts 1:8). The Joel passage does not contradict this statement, for Joel's prophecy was not exhausted by the phenomena known as "baptism of the Holy Spirit."

F. *Specifically-Recorded Cases of the Baptism of the Holy Spirit*

There are only two cases where we are specifically told that the thing that happened was none other than the baptism of the Holy Spirit. These are the case of the apostles and the case of Cornelius.

The apostles were baptized of the Holy Spirit (Acts 2:1-5). On that occasion there was the sound from heaven as of the rushing of a mighty wind, there was the appearance of tongues like as of fire parting asunder and resting upon each one of the apostles, there was the filling with the Holy Spirit, and this resulted in the speaking with other tongues as the Spirit gave them utterance.

Cornelius and his household were baptized of the Holy Spirit (Acts 10). In Cornelius' case, Spirit baptism did not bring pardon from sins (Acts 15:9, 11:18, 10:47-48). It did not take the place of baptism in water (Acts 10:47-48), and this, even though the baptism of the Spirit preceded the baptism in water. What happened to Cornelius was the same that happened to the apostles at Pentecost (Acts 11:15).

Several reasons might be given why the case of Cornelius is not an example for Holy Spirit baptism today. (1) The purpose of the baptism of the Holy Spirit on that occasion denotes it as a special act of God. Hence, it could not be a general example for all Christians. Acts 11:15-18 states in plain words the purpose for this event: to convince Peter and all other Jews that the Gentiles are to have the benefit of the gospel. There is an axiom that applies very well at this point: "The exception proves the rule." The rule here is that "only the apostles were baptized of the Holy Spirit." The exception is the household of Cornelius, and this is an exception because it accomplished a special purpose, and thus proves the rule. (2) Those of the household of Cornelius were baptized of the Holy Spirit before their sins were washed away (Acts 10:48, compared with Acts 22:16, 2:38; 1 Peter 3:21). This again points to the fact that it was a special case, and not an example for us today. If this were an example, then Holy Spirit baptism would precede baptism for the remission of sins, and thus would God grant to sinners a greater blessing in the Spirit than to saints.

Paul, the apostle to the Gentiles, was evidently also baptized of the Holy Spirit, but it is nowhere specifically recorded that he was. The fact that he had all the powers the other apostles did points to the conclusion that he received all they received.

G. *Powers that Accompanied the Baptism of the Holy Spirit*

Inspiration (Acts 2:1-4) and revelation (Acts 2:1-4; John 14:26) are two of the special powers a person received when baptized of the Holy Spirit. He was also enabled to work miracles, like the casting out of demons (Acts 16:16-18); healing the sick (Acts 3:6-10); raising the dead (Acts 9:40-41); and power over serpents and poison (Mark 16:17-20; Acts 28:1-6).

V. THE MISSION OF THE HOLY SPIRIT IN THE PRESENT AGE

A. *A Comforter and Guide to the Apostles*

The Holy Spirit was given to be a comforter to the apostles (John 16:7,13). The original word translated "comforter" is *paraclete,* meaning "one who walks along beside." This is the mission of the Holy Spirit – He was to go with the apostles as helper and advocate.

The Spirit, coming from God and Christ, was to complete the divine revelation established through Christ, bringing all the words of Christ to their remembrance (John 14:26). The result of this operation of the Holy Spirit is the infallible, inerrant, final Word of God. Thus, the Spirit of God came before the church was established or could be established. The church had to be led of the Holy Spirit through men as they spake "being carried along by the Holy Spirit" (2 Peter 1:21)

B. *To Convict the World of Sin*

The Holy Spirit was to bear witness of Christ through the apostles (John 15:26-27). "There is not an example recorded in the Bible of the Holy Spirit testifying otherwise than in words spoken (or written) by those moved by His power, and in the lives of those in whom He dwells."[5]

The Holy Spirit finds the world guilty before God (John 16:8-11). Guilty of sin – the greatest of sins being the rejection of the Lord Jesus Christ, the lover of your soul. Guilty of false judgment – the world declared Christ to be an imposter and a sinner, when He was the Righteous and the Holy One of God. Guilty of rebellion – against God and Christ, and found in alliance with the Devil.

---

[5] Barton W. Johnson, *The New Testament Commentary: A Commentary for the People* (St. Louis: Christian Board of Publication, 1886), Vol. III, notes at John 15:26.

C. *The Holy Spirit is to Glorify Jesus Christ*

The Holy Spirit continues the revelation of God's will to man which Christ had established (John 16:14). He builds upon the completed work of Christ (1 Corinthians 2:10-12).

VI. SPIRITUAL GIFTS

A. *Identification*

Certain members (other than apostles) of the early Church, chosen by the Spirit, were specially enabled by the Spirit for various kinds of supernatural work. This special endowment was called a "spiritual gift" (1 Corinthians 12:1ff; Romans 12:6-8).

B. *A Listing of Some of the Spiritual Gifts*

1. Words of wisdom – 1 Corinthians 2:6-7; 12:8
2. Words of knowledge – 1 Corinthians 12:8
3. Faith – 1 Corinthians 12:9, 13:2; Matthew 17:19-21
   (Listed among the miraculous spiritual gifts, this "faith" is something other than the faith that comes by hearing.)
4. Healing – 1 Corinthians 12:9; Acts 5:15-16; James 5:14
5. Workings of miracles – 1 Corinthians 12:10
6. Prophecy – 1 Thessalonians 5:19; Acts 11:27-28, 21:8-11; 1 Corinthians 12:10
7. Discerning of spirits – 1 Corinthians 12:10; 1 John 4:1
8. Speaking in tongues – Acts 2:1-15; 1 Corinthians 12:10
9. Interpretation of tongues – 1 Corinthians 12:10

C. *Purpose of These Spiritual Gifts*

Those who were spiritually gifted could help reveal the truths of the Gospel (1 Corinthians 12:8-10). The New Testament was not in written form at first, and in the absence of an apostle, some such help to know the will of God was needed in the infant churches.

Teachers and preachers needed the inspiration of the Holy Spirit.

The miracles wrought would help confirm the Gospel (Hebrews 2:3-4), proving that the Gospel came from heaven. The spiritual gifts served as a "sign ... to the unbelieving" (1 Corinthians 14:22).

Gifted persons would be able to give guidance to the Church in her life and worship (1 Corinthians 14:12-15). The early Church was in especial need of such supernatural guidance.

D. *To Whom Were the Gifts Given?*

Not every individual member of the early Church received spiritual gifts (Romans 1:11). In 1 Corinthians 14:16, the "unlearned" are distinguished from those who possessed a gift. Those individual members selected by the Holy Spirit through the apostles were the ones who received these gifts (1 Corinthians 12:28).

Some of the Christians who were so gifted include the seven (Acts 6:1-8), the Samaritans (Acts 8:14-23), the twelve at Ephesus (Acts 19:1-7), Timothy (2 Timothy 1:6), and many of the leaders in the early Church (Acts 11:27, 13:1, 15:32, 21:8-14; 1 Corinthians 12-14; Romans 1:11).

Generally, we find each individual Christian had one spiritual gift which he could exercise. This is shown in 1 Corinthians 12:29-30 where not all individuals had miraculous powers, gifts of healing, tongues, or interpretation. 1 Corinthians 12:14 likens each spiritual gift to one part of a human body, which would also point in the direction that one gift per person was the norm. 1 Corinthians 14:1-2 indicates that a person with the gift of tongues did not also have the gift of prophecy. 1 Corinthians 14:5,28 shows that the one who had the gift of tongues could sometimes interpret, and sometimes not. So, a spiritually gifted person with more than one ability was perhaps the exception to the rule (as, for example, in the case of Philip the evangelist).

E. *How Were These Spiritual Gifts Received?*

The passages that give any hint at all seem to indicate that spiritual gifts were received only through the laying on of an apostle's hands. The first notice of these spiritual gifts is in Acts 8, in relation to the church at Samaria. Verse 17 plainly says it is through the laying on of hands by an apostle. Following the baptism of the twelve men at Ephesus, Paul laid his hands on them and imparted to them the miraculous gifts spoken of in Acts 19:1-7. The "gift of God" came to Timothy by the hands of Paul (2 Timothy 1:6). And Paul longed to go to Rome that he might impart some spiritual gift to them (Romans 1:11). This too points to the fact that the gifts were received through the laying on of an apostle's hands.

F. *When Did Spiritual Gifts Cease?*

When the apostles and those on whom they had laid their hands died, so early Christian literature tells us, the gifts ceased.

When that which was perfect was come (1 Corinthians 13:8-10; Psalm 19:7; 2 Timothy 3:17), the spiritual gifts ceased.

G. *Biblical Phenomena v. Modern-day Faith Healers*

If the supernatural gifts have ceased, then there would be no miracles (in the Bible sense) today. The modern-day faith-healer has no answer for the question, "What was the especial, unique purpose of the spiritual gifts in New Testament times, if, as you say, you still have such gifts?"

VII. THE INDWELLING GIFT OF THE HOLY SPIRIT

A. *What is it?*

In Acts 2:38 a gift is promised to those who obey the gospel. The gift they receive is the indwelling presence of the third person of the Godhead (Romans 8:9-11; 1 Corinthians 6:19). It is called the "indwelling gift" (to distinguish this from the other activities of the Holy Spirit) because the Spirit dwells in our human bodies, making them His home, as it were.

B. *To Whom is the Indwelling Gift of the Holy Spirit Given?*

The Holy Spirit comes to live in the bodies of everyone who obeys the gospel (Acts 2:38; Galatians 3:2).

C. *Where Does He Dwell?*

In the bodies of men (the temple), (1 Corinthians 6:19; Romans 8:9,11; James 4:5; 1 John 3:24).[6] In the 1 Corinthians 6 passage, the body is referred to as "the temple of the Holy Spirit."

D. *The Purpose of the Indwelling Gift of the Holy Spirit*

That our lives may bear fruit (Galatians 5:22; Romans 6:20-22). To lead us, and enable us to walk as children of God ought to walk (Galatians 5:16-18; Ephesians 4:1). To give spiritual power to the servants of God (Ephesians 3:16ff; Acts 4:31).

E. *The Results of Having the Indwelling Gift of the Holy Spirit*

You will be a new creature (2 Corinthians 5:17; Galatians 6:15; 1 Corinthians 3:1-10). He will seal your salvation (Ephesians 1:13-14; Romans 8:11; 2 Corinthians 5:1-22). The fruit of the Spirit will become manifest (Galatians 5:22-24). By the Holy Spirit the Christian is to "put to death the deeds of the body" (Romans 8:13). The believer is led of the Spirit (Romans 8:14; Ephesians 6:17). He helps us pray (Romans 8:26-27). The Holy Spirit sanctifies (Romans 15:16; 1 Corinthians 6:11). The faithful will be raised from the dead by the Holy Spirit (Romans 8:11).

F. *How to Have the Assurance of the Indwelling Gift of the Holy Spirit*

Can a Christian know that he has the indwelling gift of the Holy Spirit? One can be assured that he has the indwelling gift of the Holy Spirit if: He has been obedient to the conditions of the new covenant (Acts 2:38). He loves and obeys God's Word (Acts 17:11). He wants to see souls saved, he desires worldly things less than he desires God's things, his life bears fruit of the Spirit, he does not quench the Spirit (1 Thessalonians 5:17-19).

---

[6] Don DeWelt, *Acts Made Actual* (Joplin, MO: *College Press*, 1953), p.358ff.

G. *General Statements*

It was necessary for a time to confirm the gospel by signs, and wonders, and mighty works of power, wrought by the Holy Spirit. Such a necessity does not in any way alter the fact that on the day of Pentecost, God bestowed upon men the (natural) gift of the Holy Spirit to abide forever in the hearts of obedient and true believers on the Lord Jesus Christ.

Failing to distinguish these facts, "men, in their blind exaggeration of signs and sensible demonstrations, lose their way, and run then into either the extravagance of fanaticism on the one hand, or the skeptical frigidity of rationalism on the other. The vain and ignorant enthusiast who prays for a baptism in fire, and hopes for dreams and visions, and sensible signs and wonders, as attendant upon the impartation of the Spirit, is not a whit farther from the truth than the errorist who affirms that miracles are a necessary and invariable accompaniment of the Spirit's presence, and that, because such demonstrations are not now given, therefore no Holy Spirit whatever is now received, and Christ's promise to be with His people to the end of the world has totally failed."[7]

VIII. THE BIRTH (OR BEGETTING) OF THE HOLY SPIRIT

Before a man is converted, there must be the begetting work of the Spirit (John 1:12-13, 3:3,5). This is not to suggest that there is such a thing as, so-called by some, "the first work of grace." Rather, the Holy Spirit leads a man to the place where he submits to baptism, and thus becomes a member of the body of Christ (1 Corinthians 12:13; Colossians 1:18, 2:12). Such a person is said to have been begotten by the Holy Spirit (1 Peter 1:23; 1 Corinthians 4:15; Ephesians 6:17).

The work of the Holy Spirit through the written Word in conversion has been explained in this fashion:

> The Holy Spirit works through his divinely authenticated word, as the instrumental cause, or efficient means, of his saving operations. For the very same saving effects that are ascribed to the Spirit are also ascribed to the Word – born by the Word, nourished by it, enlightened by it, converted by it, made wise by it, to live by it, to be sanctified by it, to be saved by it.[8]

Campbell also makes the point that if the Holy Spirit works apart from the Word in the conversion of a man (as some religious teachers affirm that He does), why are there no Christians where the Gospel has never gone?

> Moreover, were we to attempt to separate the Spirit from the Word, or the Word from the Spirit, the consequences must prove fatal; for it would not only be separating what God has

---

[7] Robert Richardson, *A Scriptural View of the Office of the Holy Spirit* (Cincinnati: Chase & Hall Publishers, 1875), p.169-169.

[8] Thomas Campbell, *The Millennial Harbinger*, November 1841 (Joplin, MO: College Press Publishing Co., 1987), 1941, Vol. V, No. XI, p.496.

constitutionally and solemnly united, saying, "As for Me, this is My covenant with them, saith the Lord; My Spirit is upon them, and My words which I have put in thy mouth, shall not depart out of thy mouth, nor out of the mouth of thy seed, nor out of the mouth of thy seed's seed, saith the Lord, henceforth forever," Isaiah 59:21. But moreover, to separate these, would also be depriving ourselves of that blissful certainty of our salvation, which the Word and the Spirit of God, only when united, can give. ... Again, if either the Word or the Spirit separately, had been sufficient to have answered the divine purpose, why give us both? Do not we learn from the uniform tenor of the Good Book, that the Word without the Spirit could not save us? For "no man can say that Jesus is the Lord, but by the Holy Spirit," 1 Corinthians 12:3. Also, it is evident, that the Holy Spirit without His divinely authenticated Word, would be inaccessible to us.[9]

After conversion, the Holy Spirit may work apart from the Word, to comfort, and bless us, but in conversion, He works only through the Word.

IX. REJECTING THE HOLY SPIRIT (DRIVING HIM FROM OUR LIFE)

All true believers have received the Holy Spirit, and He indwells them (Acts 2:38). And the Spirit is not a respecter of persons; He doesn't aid one person more than another. Why then are there so many inconsistencies, and so much lack of power in the believers? It is because of a failure to obey the commandment found in Ephesians 4:30, "And grieve not the Holy Spirit, whereby ye were sealed unto the day of redemption."

Someone has said there are four downward steps in the path to spiritual death for the believer: Grieving the Spirit (Ephesians 4:30); Resisting the Spirit (Acts 7:51); Quenching the Spirit (1 Thessalonians 5:17-19); and Blaspheming of the Spirit (Matthew 12:31-32; Hebrews 10:26).

It seems to this commentator that several other passages must be included in this downward path: Despising the Holy Spirit (Hebrews 6:4-6; Numbers 15:30); Lying to the Spirit (Acts 5:3-9); Defiling the temple of the Holy Spirit (1 Corinthians 6:19-20).

The insults, the despising, the lying, the defiling, the resisting, are like drops that fill a cup. When the cup is full, the Holy Spirit will leave (Genesis 6:3).

CONCLUSION

The Holy Spirit is a person and is divine. We should not refer to the Spirit as "it." We do not speak of Christ or God as "it;" rather, we use "He." So should it be done in the case of the third person of the Godhead.

The Holy Spirit is not schizophrenic; he is not a split personality. Any feeling or teaching a man holds that is out of harmony with the Holy Scriptures is not of the Holy Spirit. The Holy Spirit will not deny Himself. Note this: many who claim supernatural power and guidance today reject the simple teaching of Acts 2 with reference to salvation. Do they thus in fact actually then have the power and guidance that the Spirit gives?

---

[9] Campbell, *op. cit.*, p.498-499.

"There are two abiding monuments to the work of the Holy Spirit in and through believers in Christ: these are the Bible and the Church."[10]

The following chart, "The Different Activities of the Holy Spirit," is intended to help visualize what has been set forth in this Special Study.

A street in Jerusalem

Drawing by Horace Knowles
from the British and Foreign Bible Society

---

[10] H. Leo Boles, *The Holy Spirit* (Nashville: Gospel Advocate. 1942). p.243.

THE DIFFERENT ACTIVITIES OF THE HOLY SPIRIT

Designation	Greek Word Involved	How Imparted	To Whom Imparted	When Imparted	For What Purpose	With What Result	Temporary/Permanent
INDWELLING GIFT OF THE HOLY SPIRIT (Romans 8:9)	dōrea Acts 2:38	God-given Galatians 4:6 2 Corinthians 1:21-22	To all who become Christians Galatians 3:2 Acts 2:38 John 7:39 1 Corinthians 6:19	At the time of one's baptism in water Acts 2:38 Romans 6:3 1 Corinthians 6:11 Galatians 3:2 (At the time of one's justification)	Comfort, encouraged Acts 9:31 Guidance Romans 8:13,14 Help overcoming desires of the flesh Romans 8:12 Help with prayers Romans 8:26	Fruit of the Spirit produced Galatians 5:22,23 Salvation assurance Romans 5:5 1 John 4:13 2 Corinthians 5:5-16	Permanent throughout the whole Church age Acts 2:38
SPIRITUAL GIFTS (1 Corinthians 12:1)	charismata 1 Corinthians 12:4 2 Timothy 1:6 dōrea Acts 8:20	The laying on of an apostle's hands Acts 8:17-19 2 Timothy 1:6 Romans 1:11 Acts 6:6	Selected Christians chosen by the Holy Spirit Himself 1 Corinthians 12:11 1 Corinthians 14:16	After one's baptism in water Acts 19:1-7 1 Corinthians 12:13	To reveal truth 1 Cor. 12:8-10, 14:6,26 To confirm the gospel Hebrews 2:3,4 Guide infant church in absence of NT canon 1 Corinthians 12:28	Infant church grew, becoming strong and vital 1 Corinthians 13:8-12 Acts 8:12	Spiritual gifts were temporary for the infancy of the church 1 Corinthians 13:8
BAPTISM OF THE HOLY SPIRIT (Acts 1:5)	baptizō Acts 1:5 pimplēmi Acts 2:4 enduō Luke 24:49 dōrea Acts 10:45, 11:17	Directly given by God or Christ Matthew 3:11 Acts 11:17	The Apostles Acts 2:1-4 Cornelius' House Acts 10:44-48 Paul 2 Corinthians 12:11-12	Pentecost Acts 2:1-4 Before conversion Acts 10:47,48 After conversion Galatians 1 (implied)	Revelation and inspiration Acts 2:1-4 Enable to work miracles Acts 3:1ff Convince Peter salvation is for Gentiles Acts 11:17	Divine Manifestation (fire, sound of wind) Acts 2:1ff Speak foreign languages Acts 2:8 Miracles worked Acts 9:40,41; 16:18 Recall of Truth John 14:26, 16:17	Temporary ... Scripture seems to imply that this special measure of the Holy Spirit was intended only for the apostles
BEGETTING (Birth) OF THE SPIRIT (Philemon 10, 1 Corinthians 4:15)	gennaō John 3:3-5	Through the Word 1 Corinthians 4:15 John 3:8	The Word is the "seed" sown in those who hear Matthew 13:18ff Luke 8:11ff 1 Corinthians 4:15	When one receives the Word 1 John 5:1 Titus 3:5 John 1:12,13	Convict world of sin, righteousness, and judgment to come John 16:8-11 Help to become a Christian 1 John 5:1 John 1:12	Beginning of the new life, beginning of the death of the "old man" Romans 6:1ff 1 Corinthians 6:11 1 Corinthians 12:13	Permanent ... the Holy Spirit works in this fashion throughout the whole Church age

SPECIAL STUDY #4

SPEAKING IN TONGUES

E. Mansell Pattison, writing in *Christian Standard*,[1] presented the matter succinctly.

> Everybody in religious circles these days seems to be talking *about tongues*, if not *in tongues*. So-called tongues-speaking, or glossolalia, is variously said to be psychotic babbling, neurotic fakery, or the deception of the devil, on the one hand; or claimed on the other hand as an absolutely necessary experience for all Christians before they can consider themselves wholly sanctified.

Since about 1900, "glossolalia" (from the Greek *glossa,* tongue or language, plus *lalia,* a talking, speech, or dialect) is the term often used to describe the religious exercise practiced today which advocates insist is like the "speaking in tongues" one reads about in the Bible.

People in the church are going to be called upon more and more to arrive at a conclusion concerning "charismatic gifts" (i.e., the ability to work miracles, miracles affirmed to be similar to the "spiritual gifts" the Bible speaks about) and "glossolalia" in particular as the days go by, if recent developments give us any criteria to judge by. To help us in our thinking, this study shall briefly show the spread of the Charismatic Movement, what the present tongues-speakers are advocating, a study of some of the relevant Scriptures involved, and finally some evaluations of the present phenomena.

I. THE OUTBURST OF TONGUES IN THE PAST 70 YEARS

A. 20th Century Pentecostalism

The roots of Pentecostalism can be traced back to John Wesley and the beginnings of Methodism in the 1780's. Wesley placed great emphasis on an experience that every Christian should have after conversion. He called it "perfect love," and meant by that term what today is called sanctification, or a second work of grace. Charles G. Finney (1792-1876), a famous revival preacher, took Wesley's idea and modified it a bit. He was the first to say that the "experience after conversion" is the same as "the baptism of the Holy Spirit" that one can read about in the Bible. About the time of the Civil War, Methodism's emphasis on perfect love had fallen into decline, and as a reaction the Holiness Movement was born in an effort to re-iterate the emphasis on the forgotten second experience. However, the Holiness people had difficulty deciding on the criteria by which to judge if a person was "holy" or not. This is where the peculiar emphasis of the Pentecostals comes in. Pentecostals, once the movement was born, began to teach that "speaking in tongues" is evidence a man has been baptized of the Holy Spirit, that he has experienced the sanctifying work of the Holy Spirit after conversion.

---

[1] E. Mansell Pattison, "Speaking in Tongues and About Tongues" in *Christian Standard*, February 15, 1964, p.99.

In the early 20th century, one of the first places where one finds considerable emphasis on tongues-speaking, then, is in the Pentecostal Churches.

> The modern tongue-speaking movement had its beginning around the turn of the century. Richard G. Spurling, a Baptist preacher in the Great Smoky Mountain region, left the Baptist church and began working as an independent preacher. In 1896 while he held a revival in Cherokee County, North Carolina, there was an extensive outburst of ecstatic "speaking in tongues." It is to this experience that the Church of God (Cleveland, Tenn.) traces its beginning.[2]

"The father of the modern Pentecostal movement" is usually given as Charles F. Parham (1873-1929), the founder of Bethany Bible College, Topeka, Kansas. In the fall of 1900 he led his student body of about 40 students to seek the baptism in the Holy Spirit with speaking in tongues as its evidence. After several weeks of intense seeking, one of the students, Agnes Ozman, a former Methodist student associated with the Holiness movement, on New Year's Day in 1901, after having hands laid on her, spoke in syllables no one could understand. The reason this is such an important event in modern Pentecostalism is pointed out by one of the historians of that movement, Klaude Kendrick.

> Although Agnes Ozman was not the first person in modern times to speak in 'tongues,' she was the first person to have received such an experience as a result of specifically seeking a baptism in the Holy Spirit with the expectation of speaking in tongues. From this time Pentecostal believers were to teach that the baptism in the Holy Spirit should be sought and that it would be received with the evidence of 'tongues.' For this reason, the experience of Agnes Ozman is designated as the beginning of the Modern Pentecostal Revival.[3]

Here we have emphasized the seeking of the baptism in the Holy Spirit, and also tongues as the initial evidence that the baptism in the Holy Spirit has been received. These two points are the distinctives of the modern Pentecostal movement.

Parham later moved to Houston and there established a Bible school. One of his students was a Holiness preacher, W.J. Seymour, who became a convert to Parham's teaching. Seymour was invited to hold a meeting in a small Nazarene church in Los Angeles in 1906, but when he began to advocate the particular points of the Pentecostal doctrine, he met with strong opposition from the Nazarenes, and his meeting was closed down. However, there were some Baptists who invited him to preach in their home at 214 North Bonnie Brae Street. On April 9, 1906, while meeting in this house, seven persons "received the baptism in the Holy Spirit and spoke in tongues." Others, attracted by the shouts of praise and the noise of the meetings, came to attend the services, and as the group increased in number a former Methodist church building located at 312 Azuza Street was obtained for holding the meetings. Thus, the Azuza Street Mission came into existence, and for three years the meetings continued.

The Azuza Street Mission became a radiating center for the spread of modern Pente-

---

[2] Charles W. Conn, *Like a Mighty Army Moves the Church of God, 1886-1955* (Cleveland, TN: Church of God Publishing House, 1955), p.1-55.

[3] Klaude Kendrick, *The Promise Fulfilled: A History of the Modern Pentecostal Movement* (Springfield, MO: Gospel Publishing House, 1961), p.53.

costalism across America and throughout the world. Both men and women preachers led the services, and people had visions and spoke in tongues. As other persons heard about this interesting mission, they visited it, and some went back to their home communities to spread the movement.[4]

The Pentecostal movement now encompasses such large bodies as the numerous independent Churches of God, the Assemblies of God, and the International Church of the Foursquare Gospel (founded by Aimee Semple McPherson). In addition, there are well over 100 sects in America which practice glossolalia, not all of them Pentecostal, such as Father Divine's Peace Missions, and the United Pentecostal Church.

B. Penetration into Many Denominations since 1950

Frank Farrell in *Christianity Today* noted the spread amongst the denominations:[5]

> Some 2000 Episcopalians are said to be speaking in tongues in Southern California ... also speaking in tongues are upwards of 600 folk at the First Presbyterian Church of Hollywood, the world's largest Presbyterian church; James A. Pike, Episcopal Bishop of California, confronts the practice in the Bay Area to the accompaniment of front-page headlines in San Francisco newspapers; a journal relates that in the entire state of Montana only one American Lutheran pastor has not received the experience of speaking in tongues; Dr. Francis E. Whiting, director of the Department of Evangelism and Spiritual Life of the Michigan Baptist Convention (American Baptist) speaks in support of present charismatic works of the Spirit at a Northern Baptist Seminary evangelism conference, declaring the choice is Pentecost or holocaust; a Minneapolis Evangelical Free Church splits over the issue; a United Presbyterian minister who wishes to ask youth to repent and receive the Holy Spirit at the First Northern American Reformed and Presbyterian Youth Assembly is stopped by a church officer before he reaches the Purdue University stage and is escorted out by a campus policemen; members of the Inter-Varsity Christian Fellowship at Yale speak in tongues, as does also a Roman Catholic student, a daily communicant at St. Thomas More chapel; and echoes of the penetration come from evangelical institutions and organizations such as Fuller Seminary, Wheaton College, Westmont College, Navigators, and Wycliffe Bible Translators.

Toward the end of the 1960's the neo-Pentecostal movement made another stride. It entered the new youth culture and became known as the Jesus Movement. It is estimated that some 90% of the Jesus people, as they are called, have had some form of Pentecostal experience. In the late 1960's, neo- Pentecostalism entered the Catholic Church, beginning at Duquesne University, Notre Dame, and Michigan State University. Fr. Edward O'Connor and Cardinal Suenens of Belgium are leading spokesmen for the Charismatic Movement among the Roman Catholics. The early 1970's brought on what is called an ecumenical phase of Pentecostalism (i.e., an effort to unite all believers in Christ on the basis of the Pentecostal experience while ignoring all doctrinal and liturgical differences). 1971 saw the Charismatic Movement enter the Greek Orthodox Church.

Some organizations and personalities are in the forefront of this penetration of Pente-

---

[4] Frank Pack, *Tongues and the Holy Spirit* (Abilene, TX: Biblical Research Press, 1972), p.10-12.

[5] Frank Farrell, "Outburst of Tongues: The New Penetration" in *Christianity Today*, Sep. 13, 1963, p.1163.

costalism into the religious world at large. The Full Gospel Business Men's Fellowship, Women's Aglow Fellowship, and Melody Land Christian Center of Anaheim, California, are three such organizations. Personalities involved are John Sherrill, Harald Bredesen, George Otis, Kathryn Kuhlman, Dennis Bennett, Demos Shakarian, David Wilkerson, Jamie Buckingham, David J. DuPlessis, and J. Rodman Williams. Book publishing houses such as Logos, Whitaker House, Harvest House, and Living Waters Productions are also actively involved in the spread of Pentecostalism.

C. The Restoration Movement Has Been Impacted by the Phenomenon

Students have been expelled from Bible colleges over the issue. Student preachers have been asked to resign from pulpits because of "speaking in tongues." A new publication, called *The Spiritual Witness*, is being sent to preachers of the Restoration Movement, and tells of the experiences of various preachers who have "received the baptism in the Holy Spirit" and "begun to speak in tongues." This publication urges that all members of the Christian Church need this "filling of the Holy Spirit."

Pat Boone became involved in the Charismatic Movement and published a book, *A New Song*, in which he answers the standard arguments regularly used in the Restoration Movement to prove that miracles ceased about the time the last apostle died. Boone's book has had a powerful influence among many, being the catalyst that caused them to become involved in neo-Pentecostalism. One of Boone's college teachers, James Bales, has written of his own efforts to dissuade Pat from his growing interest in Pentecostalism. Bale's book is called *Pat Boone and the Gift of Tongues* and should be read in conjunction with *A New Song*, if one is going to read Boone's book. Bales shares dimensions to the story that Boone himself did not give as he wrote his own account, including a rehearsal of how Boone was "led" to deceive his own brethren about his involvement in charismatic activities.

II. PRESENT-DAY CHARISMATIC CLAIMS

To understand the Charismatic Movement, it is needful to state some of the main doctrinal emphases found in almost every writer and teacher involved in the Movement.

A. "Baptism *of* the Holy Spirit" v. "Baptism *in* the Holy Spirit"

To most Pentecostals, "Baptism *of* the Holy Spirit" (where the Holy Spirit is the agent who does the acting) is the thing which makes a man a Christian, while "Baptism *in* the Holy Spirit" (where the Holy Spirit is the element into which the Christian is inundated) is the second work of the Holy Spirit.

B. Baptism in the Holy Spirit is for All Believers

While some divergence of doctrine exists, one basic position unites Pentecostals – their common belief that "the baptism in the Holy Spirit" is a distinct experience which all believers may and should have following conversion.[6]

> Common to all Pentecostals is the one basic belief that "the baptism in the Holy Spirit" is an experience subsequent to conversion — all believers should have it, and the initial physical evidence for this baptism or infilling is the speaking of tongues.[7]

C. Baptism in the Holy Spirit Follow Conversion

Both the above quotations state that this experience is something that "follows conversion." While Charismatics do not agree on the number of prerequisites a believer must have before he receives the baptism in the Holy Spirit, there are four oft-mentioned conditions: *conversion* (with Acts 2:38 being made to read as though "the gift of the Holy Spirit" follows sometime after repentance and baptism in water); *prayer* (Luke 11:13 and Acts 1:14 are proof texts that one must pray for the baptism in the Holy Spirit); *obedience* (with Acts 5:32 is alleged to show that following conversion a life of careful obedience is necessary if one would receive the Holy Spirit); and *"faith"* (believe you will get the baptism in the Holy Spirit, or desire the gifts, 1 Corinthians 12:31 and 14:1).

D. Speaking in Tongues is the Initial Evidence of Having Been Baptized in the Holy Spirit

Those who insist "baptism in the Holy Spirit" is for every believer also allege that "speaking in tongues" is the initial physical evidence of such a baptism. "Tongues is the sign of the initial infilling of the Spirit."[8] "Tongues as initial evidence is distinguished from the gift of tongues (1 Corinthians 12:12), which was not granted to all."[9] Harold Horton makes the same point:

> Everybody speaks in tongues at least once at his baptism in the Spirit (Acts 2:4, 10:45, etc.), but apparently all do not retain this power to speak in tongues (1 Corinthians 12:30), though there seems to be no Scripture reason why they should not retain it (1 Corinthians 14:5,23). The only Scriptural distinction between the sign of tongues and the gift of tongues is that when tongues are first employed by an individual, the utterance is the SIGN of the baptism in the Spirit; every subsequent use of the supernatural tongue by this same individual is the GIFT of tongues in operation.[10]

E. The Nature of Tongues

Among modern Pentecostals, there is no agreement as to the nature of the "tongues" one speaks after he is baptized in the Holy Spirit. To some, the tongues are a foreign language. To others, the tongues are a heavenly language (and not at all like any language

---

[6] Thomas F. Zimmerman, "Pleas for Pentecostalists" in *Christianity Today*, January 4, 1963, p.319ff

[7] Farrell, *ibid.*

[8] Gene Birney, *The Spiritual Witness*, I.2.8.

[9] Farrell, *ibid.*

[10] Harold Horton, *The Gifts of the Spirit* (Springfield, MO: Gospel Publishing House, 1975), p.155.

spoken somewhere on this earth). Horton offers this explanation of the nature of tongues:

> It is supernatural utterance by the Holy Spirit in languages never learned by the speaker – not understood by the mind of the speaker – nearly always not understood by the hearer. It has nothing to do with linguistic ability, nor with the mind or intellect of man. It is a manifestation of the Mind of the Spirit of God employing human speech organs. When a man is speaking with tongues his mind, intellect, understanding are quiescent. It is the faculty of God that is active. Man's will, certainly, is active, and his spirit and his speech organs; but the Mind that is operating is the Mind of God through the Holy Spirit. The linguistic skill of man is no more employed in speaking with tongues than the surgical skill of man was employed when at Peter's word, "Rise and walk," the lame man instantly arose and leaped and walked! It is in short a miracle. It is not a mental miracle; the mentality is God's. It is a vocal miracle.

Some tongues-speakers have claimed that modern "tongues" are intelligible foreign languages. McCandlish Phillips states that at times those speaking in tongues speak in foreign languages they have never studied.[11] And Birney *(op. cit.,* 1.1.8) writes:

> In answer to the question are these tongues languages that are known or unknown, they can be both. The tongues on the day of Pentecost were unknown to the Apostles (Acts 2:7), but were known by many that heard (Acts 2:8). This is sometimes the case today. It is not unknown for a tongue to be understood by someone in the audience who happens to know the language being spoken by the Spirit ... The Spirit chooses the language, and while most seem to be the languages of men, i.e., languages that have been or are spoken by men, it can also be a heavenly or angelic language (1 Corinthians 13:1).[12]

F. The Duration of Spiritual Gifts

Both Thomas Zimmerman[13] and Carl Brumback[14] refer to scattered instances throughout church history as evidence the gift of tongues has continued all through the Church age. In fact, it is affirmed that all the spiritual gifts have continued through the centuries. Birney[15] points out clearly that tongues, prophecy, and knowledge as special gifts will definitely continue until the second coming, and bases this on an interpretation of 1 Corinthians 13:8,9, which makes the word "perfect" refer to the second coming of Christ.

It is obvious that in the view of the tongues-speakers, this gift of tongues is to persist until the return of Christ, and that all believers must receive the baptism in the Spirit in this day with its attendant evidence of tongues, or be sadly deficient in many graces.

---

[11] McCandlish Phillips, "And There Appeared to Them Tongues of Fire" in *Saturday Evening Post,* May 16,1964.

[12] Birney, *op. cit.,* I.1.8.

[13] Zimmerman, *op. cit.,* p.12.

[14] Carl Brumback, *What Meaneth This? A Pentecostal Answer to a Pentecostal Question* (Springfield, MO: Gospel Publishing House, 1947), p.89-96.

[15] Birney, *op. cit.,* I.1.7.

G. Purpose of Speaking in Tongues

Most charismatics make a distinction between two kinds of tongues. One kind of tongues is for private devotions. This is likely to be a "heavenly language," and is used when men wish to speak supernaturally with God. The other kind of tongues is for public use, and is more likely to be a "foreign language" such as was the case on the Day of Pentecost.

The purpose of tongues, alleged as being set forth in the Scripture, are enumerated by Horton and Birney:

1. Scriptural evidence of the baptism in the Holy Spirit
2. That men may speak supernaturally with God (1 Corinthians 14:2)
3. To magnify God (Acts 10:46)
4. Personal edification of the believer
5. That our spirits, as distinct from our understanding, may pray (1 Corinthians 14:14), a sort of spiritual cathartic
6. Coupled with the gift of interpretation, that the church may be edified (read 1 Corinthians 14:12,13,5,26, in this order)
7. For a sign to the unbelievers of the fulfillment of prophecy (1 Corinthians 14:21-22 and Acts 2:16-18)

H. The Effects of the Baptism in the Holy Spirit

The Spiritual Witness offers the following list of effects of the baptism in the Holy Spirit among the churches:

> I had power in my preaching that was never present before. I used the same sermons and illustrations that I normally used in such meetings, but the effects were noticeably different. People were moved, hearts were touched. During the meeting one woman was gloriously healed by the Lord, others were blessed, and two members of the church received the baptism of the Holy Spirit ... In the past few weeks I have witnessed numerous healings, heard many prophecies, tongues and interpretations. I have witnessed the gifts of wisdom, knowledge and discernment in action night after night. I have heard and seen demons cast out screaming and tearing just as the Gospels state, cast out in the name of Jesus.
> I have witnessed people gloriously delivered and sent on their way rejoicing with a new joy never known before.
> The Park Road Christian Church has become revitalized due to the changes in the life of Bro. Ivan Correll since he received the baptism of the Holy Spirit. Bro. Correll states that before his baptism he was completely wrapped up in the affairs of his own church, but now the Holy Spirit has changed his attitudes as well as his Spiritual outlook and greatly broadened his ministry.
> One person was miraculously healed and two filled with the Spirit, and a revival started that has changed the entire church as a result of a recent revival conducted here by Gene Birney.
> An evangelist reports that the Lord is now confirming his ministry with signs following, since his recent baptism of the Spirit. An elderly lady, with her entire right side

paralyzed from a severe stroke, was healed and walked, after being carried to church. She was delivered by the prayer of faith, after being anointed with oil.

Since that time I have had a positive leading everywhere I go. If God has a particular task for me, whenever I ask Him, at night, morning or anytime, He can give me that leading. I could not start to cite a few of the multitude of times that God has thus led me since I received the greater filling of the Holy Spirit. God thus talks to me and tells me specifically what He wants me to do.

Brother Alvin Ball, Christian minister and graduate of Manhattan Bible College, reports many signs and wonders following the ministry of himself and Bro. Kent Newman, also a Christian minister, in recent revivals conducted in Carrizo Springs, Texas, and Chicago, Illinois. Bro. Ball has been assisting with the revival here in San Antonio for the past week. He has a fine gift of prophecy.

We have seen the Book of Acts in action. We have seen people healed, demons cast out, the gift of knowledge and other spiritual gifts in action.

III. WHAT DOES THE BIBLE TEACH ABOUT SPEAKING IN TONGUES?

Several passages are important to any discussion of speaking with tongues. The plan of this section of the study is to offer a series of brief notes on these relevant passages.

A. Mark 16:17

The passage promises that one of the "signs" that would follow believers was the ability to "speak with new (*kainos*) tongues." The fact that *kainos* is used rather than another word for new (*neos*) is easily explainable if the "tongues" are foreign languages unfamiliar to the speaker. *Neos* has the implication of "new in time, never existing before;" whereas *kainos* simply means "fresh, recently made, unused." "New tongues" are a language unused by the speaker before.

Behm's article on "tongues" in Kittel's *Theological Dictionary of the New Testament* shows four different meanings for the word *glossa* ("tongue"). (1) The tongue, as an organ of the body, as in James 3:5. (2) A language or dialect, including foreign words that need translation or explanation, as Acts 2:6. (3) Anything shaped like a tongue, like the tongue of a shoe, or a tongue of land jutting out into the sea, as in Acts 2:3. (4) The ecstatic utterances of pagan priestesses as at Delphi. Thus, any time "tongue" appears in Scripture, it must be determined which of the four ideas was in the writer's mind.

There is no reason to understand Mark 16:17 as being other than foreign languages, as Thayer's *Lexicon* defines this word in the article under "Glossa (2)."

B. Acts 2:1-11

1. The filling of the Holy Spirit was accompanied, in the case of the apostles, by utterances given by the Spirit, so that those from throughout the Roman empire heard what was being said in their own native *languages*.
2. The things the apostles talked about, when they spoke these native languages, were "the mighty works of God" (verse 11).

3. Luke is not describing ecstatic speech. It was a "language."
4. There is no evidence these men have been praying for the coming of the Holy Spirit, or that they were desiring the "sign" of His coming.
5. Various objections have been raised to the idea that Acts 2:1-11 teaches that the "tongues" on Pentecost were actual foreign languages.
    a. Some deny the reliability of Acts. It is said that Acts is a much later book than 1 Corinthians, and that the tradition about Pentecost as recorded in Acts 2 is perverted; therefore. Acts 2 cannot be used to interpret 1 Corinthians.
    Reply: The date of 1 Corinthians is AD 57. The date of Acts is AD 63. Six years would not make that much difference. Further, Luke is an A-1 historian. He conversed with many of the eye and ear witnesses of the events of the day of Pentecost. The account of Acts 2 is reliable.
    b. Some hold that Acts is not clear and understandable. It is claimed that a reader must interpret Acts 2 in the light of 1 Corinthians 12-14. Doing this, the scholars lead us to the place that the "tongues" of Acts is made to be "unintelligible babblings" (such as the scholars believe were spoken at Corinth).
    Reply: This does not fit the record of Acts 2, particularly verses 6-8,11.
    c. Some have held that the hearers just imagined they heard their own language on the day of Pentecost.
    Reply: This theory also does not fit the record of Acts 2.
    d. Others question the need for the apostles to speak in unlearned foreign languages, since it is supposed the whole world was bilingual. I.e., everyone knew Greek.
    Reply: It is true that Greek was a universal language in the early days of the church. But it is also true that many would understand their mother tongue better than Greek.
    e. Another difficulty is found in Acts 2:13. It is said, "If the apostles were actually speaking in foreign languages, what was the occasion for the accusation of drunkenness?"
    Reply: We are not told who made the accusation. Could it have been the Jewish religious leaders? These men on numberless occasions had tried to put Jesus in a bad light, saying He acted by the power of the devil. It is unlikely they have had a change of heart. Now, they are making similar slanderous remarks about the apostles, in an attempt to discredit them.

C. Acts 8:14-19

1. There is no direct reference made in these verses to speaking in tongues. But since it is said that at the laying on of the apostles' hands, Christians received "spiritual gifts," it might be assumed that some received the gift of tongues.
2. "The Spirit fell on them" at some time subsequent to their baptism into the body of Christ (verse 16).

3. This "gift" was imparted by an apostle laying his hands on some of the Christians at Samaria (verses 17,18).
4. Spiritual gifts were not received by every individual Christian – Simon didn't.

D. Acts 10:44-48

1. This "falling of the Spirit" was similar, if not identical, to Pentecost. See Acts 11:15-17.
2. "Speaking with tongues" appears to have signified that Cornelius and his household had been baptized of the Holy Spirit.
3. Note that in this case the baptism of the Spirit *preceded* the conversion of these people. They were not baptized into Christ until later (verses 47,48).
4. There was no seeking of such a gift or manifestation on the part of Cornelius or his household.
5. A question arises – What language did Cornelius and the others speak? Being a Roman soldier, he would know Latin and probably Greek. Peter and the others recognized the language. It seems possible, then, that the language Cornelius spoke was Aramaic – a language which a Roman soldier, particularly an officer, would not normally know nor take the trouble to learn, since it would be a provincial language.

E. Acts 19:1-6

1. After these people became Christians, Paul laid his hands upon them, and they received spiritual gifts, one of which was "speaking with tongues."
2. It was Paul who desired these Ephesian men to receive the gifts. The men themselves did not seek the gift; they did not so much as know that the Spirit had been given to individuals.
3. This passage would be parallel to 1 Corinthians 12-14, for not only did the Ephesians receive the gift of "speaking with tongues" but also the gift of "prophesying."

F. 1 Corinthians 12-14

1. Though most scholars agree that Acts 2 speaks of foreign languages, a number of present-day scholars favor the idea that 1 Corinthians 12-14 speaks not of languages, but of ecstatic or unintelligible utterances. This commentator sees no reason for making this distinction!
    a. Comparing the accounts in Acts 2 and 1 Corinthians 12-14, several points are identical. In both the Corinthian and Pentecostal cases, an extraordinary influence and gift of the Holy Spirit was responsible for the speaking. In both, the people were speaking as the Spirit led them to speak. In both, the intention of speaking in tongues was to bring praise and honor to God, and to edify the hearers.

b. In 1 Corinthians 12-14, those verses that are alleged to show that "tongues" in Corinth were different than the "languages" of Pentecost, when interpreted under the hypothesis that "tongues" at Corinth were "foreign languages," make marvelous sense.

1) It is said that the speaking of the apostles (Acts 2) was intelligible, and consequently was understood by the hearers without assistance from others (verses 8,11); whereas the Corinthian speaking with tongues was not understood without the aid of an interpreter (1 Corinthians 14:2,13,16,27,28). (*Reply*: It seems rather that 1 Corinthians 14 is saying, "Why desire the gift of tongues when there may be only a few present in the services who understand the language you're speaking? If you did use your gift of speaking, an interpreter would have to make clear to most of the congregation what you have said. Why not desire one of the other, more broadly useful gifts?")

2) 1 Corinthians 14:14 is not an evidence that "tongues" is unintelligible babbling. A man could pray, using a language he had never learned or studied, and it might still be said of him that he did not understand what he was saying.

3) Nor can 1 Corinthians 14:23 be used to show that what was happening at Corinth was ecstatic syllabication. The verse reads, "If therefore the whole church be assembled together, and all speak in tongues, and there come in men ungifted or unbelievers enter, will they not say that you are mad?" The point being made is not that there is a bedlam of all believers speaking at once. Rather, Paul is assuming an extreme case for the sake of argument: that everyone present in the worship service had the gift of tongues, and that one after another they get up and speak a foreign language. Suppose a visitor comes to the service. The Christians, one after another, get up, and instead of speaking the language of the locale, uttered a speech in a foreign language that the visitor did not understand (he was "unlearned"). On his way home, after hearing a whole service of nothing but words in languages he did not understand, he would conclude that the Christians were crazy.

4) 1 Corinthians 14:27-28 gives the instruction that if there is no interpreter present, the one speaking in tongues is to "keep silent" or "speak to himself." Rather than being evidence that "tongues" at Corinth was ecstatic speaking, these verses point in the other direction, that "tongues" at Corinth were foreign languages. The supposition is that, at Corinth, there might be days when no visitor would come to the services whose native tongue was the same as the language of the one who had the "gift of tongues." (Each person who spoke in tongues evidently was able to speak one foreign language, 1 Corinthians 14:18). Since

his gift was not really needed that day, there would be no "edifying" of those present, unless someone could interpret what he said – and there were other Christians who had the gift of understanding when someone else spoke in a foreign language. Such an ability was called "the gift of interpretation."

    5) Finally, 1 Corinthians 14:2 need not be so interpreted as to prove that "tongues" in Corinth was unintelligible babbling. The verse reads, "For one who speaks in tongues does not speak to men, but to God; for no one understands, but in *his* spirit he speaks mysteries." In the context, this verse is designed as an explanation of why men ought to desire the gift of prophecy rather than the gift of tongues. Men who were prophesying in the vernacular of the people would edify the church, whereas men speaking in a language that none of the church members understood (unless an interpreter was present, verse 5) would leave the hearers "in the dark" as to what was said. And this would be true, even when the speaker was guided by the Holy Spirit in what he said.

  c. So, this commentator has no reason to say that speaking in tongues in Acts 2 differs fundamentally from the speaking in tongues in 1 Corinthians 12-14. *In both cases, foreign languages are referred to.*

2. Now that this issues has been answered, let us examine several other pertinent points to be found in 1 Corinthians 12-14.
   a. The Holy Spirit has given and does give gifts to the members of the body of Christ. In the Corinthian church he gave "spiritual gifts" to some, in addition to the "talents" which He gives to every Christian.
   b. The purpose of these "spiritual gifts" (including tongues) was that the whole congregation might be benefited (1 Corinthians 12:7,31; 14:12,26).
   c. In 1 Corinthians 12:4 we note that there are "varieties of gifts." The chapter then lists nine of these: wisdom, knowledge, faith, healing, miracles, prophecy, discerning of spirits, tongues, and interpretation of tongues. In verse 28, a similar list is given in the following order: first, apostles; second, prophets; third, teachers; after that, workers of miracles; then healers, helpers, administrators and speakers in tongues. It is noteworthy that the gift the Corinthians most wanted (and the gift most want today) is put last in all the listings.
   d. When the context is considered, 1 Corinthians 14:5, "Now I wish that you all spoke in tongues," is in no way intended to show that Paul believed that the ability to speak in tongues was a sign of spiritual maturity. Paul's expressed desire that all might speak with tongues is immediately qualified in verse 5 by "but *even* more that you would prophesy; and greater is one who prophesies than one who speaks in tongues, unless he interprets, so that the church may receive edifying." Of course, if one "prophesied" (i.e., spoke by inspiration in the vernacular of the people), more people would

be edified, than if one spoke the same message by inspiration, but in a foreign language. This is not the only time in which Paul has contrasted the relative unimportance of tongues to the obvious importance of preaching the Word for the edification of the church. Furthermore, Paul has already told us that ALL would NOT speak in tongues (1 Corinthians 12:10,30). It must be remembered that this gift (like all the others) is imparted by God as it pleases Him; not to all, but to whomever He wills.

e. 1 Corinthians 14:16 speaks of the "ungifted." Perhaps this means that not all the Corinthian Christians had received spiritual gifts. Note the marginal reading in the NASB, "unversed in spiritual gifts."

f. Nor is Paul's statement in 14:18 to be taken as proof that all the Corinthian Christians had spoken in tongues. His statement of thankfulness that he is able to speak with tongues is qualified by the statement that immediately follows, "However, in the church I desire to speak five words with my mind, that I may instruct others also, than 10,000 words in a tongue." Paul's idea is, 'If you are just getting up to show off, I could put on a better show than all of you put together who have the gift of tongues, for I (an apostle) have the ability to speak more foreign languages than all of you (who have only spiritual gifts) put together.' This strongly worded corrective places the gift of tongues in a relatively unimportant position. It is always wise to place importance where God places it, and dangerous to overemphasize the relatively unimportant.

g. As Paul closes his treatise on spiritual gifts, he says, "Do not forbid to speak in tongues" (14:39). This, too, he qualifies by a preceding statement, "Desire earnestly to prophesy," and by a statement that follows, "Let all things be done properly and in an orderly manner." Here Paul seems to be correcting a possible false conclusion. The gift of tongues was useful, and had its place, because it, as well as prophecy, was Spirit inspired. He says, 'One gift is to be greatly longed for, i.e., the power to preach by inspiration. The other, speaking with tongues, was not to be forbidden so long as the proper conditions were met and the rules of decency and decorum were observed.' In its own place, the gift of tongues was a valuable endowment; on proper occasions it was to be exercised.

h. Between the first and second listing of gifts (1 Corinthians 12:4-11 and 28-30), Paul carefully and emphatically illustrates the relationships of these gifts by using the human body as an analogy.

He says, "For as the body is one, and hath many members, and all the members of that one body, being many, are one body; so also is Christ" (1 Corinthians 12:12). Paul then points out that the various members of the body are interdependent upon one another. No organ of the body is independent of the body as a whole. No single organ of the body stands as ultimate proof that the body is either alive or healthy. The combined labors of all the organs contribute to the life and health of the body.

As no one member of the body can claim to be the whole body, so no single gift of the Spirit can claim to be the whole ministry of the Spirit.

Nor is one gift of the Spirit given to every member of the Body of Christ, any more than the faculty of seeing is given to every organ of the physical body. No single gift of the Spirit is for every Christian. All are not apostles. All are not prophets. All are not teachers. All are not workers of miracles. Much less then do all speak with tongues or all have the gift of interpretation of tongues (1 Corinthians 12:29,30).

i. It is important to remember that the gifts of the Spirit are gifts. One does not dictate to another when, how, or what gifts he is to receive. Gifts are given when, how, and to whom the giver pleases. The apostle strongly emphasizes this point. He tells us that the diversity of gifts has been made by God Himself (12:4-6). It is also clear that the Holy Spirit is sovereign in the distribution of these gifts, "dividing to every man severally as He will" (12:11).

j. 1 Corinthians 12:13, properly interpreted, is not a reference to the "baptism of the Holy Spirit" as being for everyone. The verse reads, "By one Spirit have we all been baptized into one body, and have been made to drink of one Spirit." Paraphrased, it reads, 'By the influence of the Holy Spirit we have all been led to be baptized (in water) into Christ. And the spiritual gifts that are in the church are the result of the activity of the Holy Spirit, too." So understood, the verse harmonizes beautifully with all Scripture elsewhere, and fits into this context very beautifully, too. And it says nothing at all about people becoming members of the church through the baptism of the Holy Spirit.

k. Whatever else 1 Corinthians 14:34 may mean, it clearly forbids wives to speak in tongues in the public assembly. As one is able to observe the present situation, women are quite prominent in the performance of tongues-speech and interpretation in the public assembly. To say that verse 34 was valid only in a 1st century culture is to cause all other commands of the Lord (e.g., 14:37) to be subjected to the whims of culture and circumstance. This clearly will not do.

l. There are indications that tongues are associated with the infancy of the church (see 1 Corinthians 13:11 and 14:20).

G. Conclusions Drawn from the Basic Scriptures

Acts 2 is the key passage. It is clear that in the New Testament speaking in tongues had reference to foreign languages; and this is true, we believe, even in Corinth! If the tongues of the New Testament passages were unstudied foreign languages, then much of the current tongues movement is not like what one reads about in the Bible.

IV. EVALUATION OF SELECTED PRESENT-DAY CHARISMATIC CLAIMS

A. *What about the distinction between "Baptism of" and "Baptism in" the Holy Spirit?*

If the distinction were true, we would expect passages addressed to non-Christians to read "baptism of the Holy Spirit," and passages addressed to those already Christians to read "baptism in the Holy Spirit," when we find instructions addressed to these different groups. How reads the original? Acts 1:5 (which according to Pentecostal theology is addressed to men already Christians, since they had received the new birth at John 20:21 according to Pentecostal interpretation) reads *en pneumati*, "in the Holy Spirit." Acts 11:16, addressed to non-Christians (by anybody's interpretation of Acts) reads *en pneumati*, "in the Holy Spirit." 1 Corinthians 12:13a, which tells how the Holy Spirit leads a man to the place he wants to be baptized into Christ, reads *en pneumati*, "in the Holy Spirit." In other words, what is to be expected if the Pentecostal distinction is true does not appear at all in the Greek. In passages where the Greek ought to be different (so as to read "of the Holy Spirit"), it reads *en pneumati*. This first of Pentecostalism's major claims does not stand inspection.

B. *What about the claim that "baptism in the Holy Spirit" is for all believers?*

The only way charismatics can affirm such a doctrine is Biblical is to take all the passages in Acts that speak about the Holy Spirit and insist that they all deal with the activity of the Spirit that is called "baptism in the Holy Spirit." This is hard to accept when it is observed that some passages speak of the Spirit's work before conversion, and some speak of His post-conversion work.

C. *What about the claim that "baptism in the Holy Spirit" follows conversion?*

Acts 10-11 is a hard passage for Charismatics to harmonize with their doctrine of subsequence.

Charismatics try to prove their doctrine of subsequence by appealing to verses where "filling with the Spirit" appears, insisting that all speak of the same phenomenon that occurred on Pentecost which is called a "filling" (Acts 2:4). Ephesians 5:18 is a passage often alluded to, but it is a mistaken allusion. In the Greek, the verb "filling" is a present tense verb, which implies a continuous filling. For Pentecostal doctrine to be true, it should be an aorist tense, a one-time filling thus being implied. In fact, Ephesians 5:18 also gives some tests by which one can determine if he is constantly being filled ("speaking to one another," "singing," "making melody," "giving thanks," and "submitting" are all participles in the Greek, giving examples of what a Spirit-filled life does).

In addition to the above weaknesses in the doctrine of subsequence, there is the fact that when the proof texts given for the prerequisites to receiving the "baptism in the Holy Spirit" are studied, it is soon evident that they will not bear the interpretation put on them by Charismatics.

D. *What about the claim that speaking in tongues is the initial evidence of the "baptism in the Holy Spirit"?*

In this place it is much easier to see that the modern Pentecostals are exactly contrary to what Scripture teaches. Pentecostals claim that every Christian should speak in tongues at least once in his life, at the time of his baptism in the Holy Spirit. 1 Corinthians 12:30 shows such a doctrine just cannot be true, for it indicates that *not* all are expected to speak in tongues.

E. *What about the claim that spiritual gifts last all through the Church age?*

The New Testament looks forward to the cessation of the spiritual gifts. 1 Corinthians 13:8-13 says the spiritual gifts will cease "when that which is perfect is come." The context says that when the gifts are exercised, their exercise only gives the recipients a partial picture of God's revelation. But there was coming a day when the completed revelation would remove the need for partial explications of God's will through the gifts. (This argument is based on the fact that in any context the word *teleios*, "perfect," must receive its meaning from its context. Here we are plainly told that the "partial" is the opposite of the "perfect.") Further, Paul says the graces – faith, hope, and love – will abide *after* the gifts have ceased. The graces faith and hope will *not* last beyond the second coming of Christ (i.e., faith gives way to sight, and hope to fruition); therefore, there is no way to say the spiritual gifts will last *until* the second coming. "That which is perfect" must be something other than the second coming of Jesus, for the graces last long after the spiritual gifts have ceased.

Corroboration of this interpretation of 1 Corinthians 13:8-13 is found in several avenues. (1) If Paul has predicted that the gifts will soon cease, early church history ought to tell us they did. And this is exactly what early church history says. (See documentation of this in the first paragraph of the next part of this Special Study.) (2) If we still have spiritual gifts today, then too we must have apostles in the church today (see how apostles are listed in the same verses as spiritual gifts, 1 Corinthians 12:28, for example). Ephesians 2:20 shows that "apostles and prophets" were temporary, for the foundation of the church. (3) If there are apostles today, then logically one would have to insist that there are continuing revelations. Such a claim of continuing revelations would make a liar out of Jesus, who said that the original apostles would be led into all truth (John 14:26). In passing, 2 Peter 1:3 tells us that Christ's promises about the apostles being led into all truth have not failed, for Peter says that Jesus' divine power had already granted to the apostles all things pertaining to life and godliness. (4) In another passage, Peter implies that the special, miraculous gifts were ceasing. During the early days of the church, the people were to take no thought what they would say when hauled before judges. It would be given them in that hour what to say. The Holy Spirit would speak through them (Matthew 10:17-20). But 30-some years later, Peter gives his readers instructions that they are indeed to take thought what they will say, being ready always to give an answer to whoever asks them concerning the hope they have within them (1 Peter 3:15). This apparent contradiction in instructions is easily explained on the supposition the gifts are ceasing. It is not so easily explained if the gifts were for all believers in every age.

F. *What about the claim for the purpose of tongues?*

The purpose of the spiritual gifts, including tongues, was to credential the message or the messenger (Mark 16:17-20; Hebrews 2:3-4; John 20:30-31; 1 Corinthians 14:22).

How different is the claim of some today that "tongues" are for a devotional purpose. Charismatic theology books which have tried to find proof texts for this claim must chop up 1 Corinthians 12-14, making some verses refer to a public use of tongues, and making some verses in the same context refer to a devotional use of tongues in private. Further, Acts 2 must be made to speak of "devotional tongues" in spite of the fact that we are told in that chapter that the apostles were talking foreign languages to foreigners who were there and heard "the mighty works of God" (not praise!) being expounded to them in their own languages and dialects.

G. *Conclusion of this Part of the Special Study*

It would be possible to take the other claims made by the modern Pentecostals and show how they fail to harmonize with plain verses in the Word of God. Because the Pentecostal doctrine fails to agree with Scripture in each of its main claims, the whole system must be rejected!

V. EVALUATION OF CURRENT TONGUES MOVEMENT BY EXTRA-BIBLICAL CRITERIA

A. The Criterion of Religious History

In the above discussion about the duration of the gifts, we prepared for this part of the study by suggesting that Paul teaches the gifts were temporary. We introduce this study by observing that the question is asked over and over again, *How long do the gifts remain?*

> Perhaps the most common view relates the gifts of the Spirit to the founding of the New Testament Church, their cessation during the second century taking place after it was well established under the authority of the completed New Testament Canon. Presbyterian theologian B.B. Warfield believed the *charismata* (spiritual gifts) to be given for authentication of the apostles as God's messengers, a sign of apostleship being possession of the gifts and the ability to transmit them. Gradual cessation of the gifts thus came with the death of those who had received the gifts through the apostles (see his *Miracles: Yesterday and Today*).[16]

Advocates of glossolalia reply that Warfield's theory flies in the face of history, and they assert that all through history there have been examples of tongue-speaking. So let us look at history.

Although several passages are cited in the *Apostolic Fathers and Justin Martyr* with reference to tongues-speaking, there is no direct reference to them in the Fathers or in Justin as being still in existence when those Fathers wrote.

- Justin Martyr does write, "For the prophetical gifts remain with us, even to the present time. And hence you ought to understand that [the gifts] formerly among your nation

---

[16] Farrell, *op. cit.*, p.1164.

have been transferred to us."[17] Although he does not specifically mention tongues, it would be hard to exclude this gift from Justin's language.

- Two passages from Clement of Rome are cited: "Thus a profound and abundant peace was given to you all, and ye had an insatiable desire for doing good, while a full outpouring of the Holy Spirit was upon you."[18] "Having therefore received their orders, and being fully assured of the resurrection of our Lord Jesus Christ, and established in the word of God, with full assurance of the Holy Ghost, [the apostles] went forth proclaiming that the Kingdom of God was at hand. And thus preaching through countries and cities, they appointed the first fruits, having first proved them by the Spirit, to be bishops and deacons of those who should afterward believe."[19]

- Irenaeus, born about AD 130, wrote five books against heresies about AD 185. In one of these (Book 5, chapter 6, section 1) he speaks of a passage in 1 Corinthians 2:6, and says, "those persons ... who through the Spirit of God do speak in all languages, as [Paul] used himself also to speak. In like manner we do also hear many brethren in the church who possess prophetic gifts, and who through the Spirit speak all kinds of languages ...." This is often cited as evidence of the existence of tongues as late as AD 185. The translator, however, footnotes the words "do also hear," and points out that the verb here is actually in the perfect tense and shows that the action has been completed in the past. The interval is indefinite, but if Irenaeus were aware of his Latin, he was saying that he used to hear this, but does not necessarily hear it now.

- Tertullian, writing c. AD 204, has this statement, "For apostles have the Holy Spirit properly, who have Him fully, in the operations of prophecy, and the efficacy of [healing] virtues, and the evidences of tongues; not partially as all others have."[20] It would be difficult to defend the idea that this quotation can only mean that the gift of tongues was still something every Christian received in the year AD 204.

- Finally, Origen says this, writing c. AD 210, "This is He who places prophets in the church, gives powers and healings, does wonderful works, offers discriminations of spirits, affords powers of government, suggests counsels, and orders and arranges whatever other gifts that are of Charismata; and thus make the Lord's church everywhere, and in all, perfected and complete."[21] In context, Origen is speaking about the Holy Spirit as one of the persons of the Godhead, as He appears in Scripture, and not necessarily as He acted in the days that Origen was living and writing.

Leaving the Early Church Fathers, and going to the age of the *Nicene and Post-Nicene Fathers*, we find examples alleged as proof that tongues-speaking was still continuing in that time.

- Examples from the Montanists are cited, as evidence of continuing glossolalia, since the practice was attacked by Celsus. However, Cutten points out that Epiphanius, a 4th

---

[17] *Ante-Nicene Fathers,* Vol. 1, p.240.

[18] *First Epistle of Clement,* ch. 2, p.8.

[19] *First Epistle of Clement,* ch. 42, p.16, in the Eerdmans' edition of the *Ante-Nicene Fathers.*

[20] *Ante-Nicene Fathers,* Vol. IV, p.53.

[21] *Ante-Nicene Fathers,* Vol. IV, p.254.

century bishop, comments that the tongues-speech of the Montanists is quite different from that described in Corinthians.[22] Hayes further points out, "The Montanists represented a reaction in the church against the growing Ecclesiasticism and the dependence upon forms instead of the spiritual power of the primitive times. It was a protest against the domination of a hierarchy in favor of individual liberty and personal inspiration which the Montanists preached, and they strove to come into direct communion with the Divine."[23]

- As early as the 4th century, Chrysostom (AD 345-407) expressed puzzlement at Paul's account of the Corinthian situation: "The whole passage is exceedingly obscure and the obscurity is occasioned by our ignorance of the facts and the cessation of the happenings which were common in those days but unexampled in our own."[24]

Charismatic gifts were unknown between the 2nd and 17th centuries. R.A. Knox, in his historical study, *Enthusiasm: A Chapter in the History of Religion,* traces outbreaks of "charismatic gifts" – tongues, healings, miraculous signs, etc. He concludes that, except in Biblical times, such charismatic gifts were unknown in church history before the 17th century.

Since the 17th century, such phenomena have been connected with a particular theological attitude. During the 17th and 18th centuries, protest movements rose against the cold, rigid, formal, rational church institutions. These reactive movements stressed the importance of the indwelling of the Spirit, the subjective awareness of religious dedication, and the overriding importance of "holy behavior." Whenever such an outbreak occurred it was accompanied by the appearance of tongues, healings, ecstatic bodily experiences, etc. It is noteworthy that the current wave of "charismatic phenomena" has arisen in just such a context. To further cloud the issue, commentators remind us that the degree of similarity between the New Testament phenomenon of glossolalia and current ones is uncertain. New Testament scholar Leon Morris points to the obscurity of present-day understanding of the exact nature of some of the gifts, such as "helps" and "governments" (1 Corinthians 12:28): "We may make ... conjectures ... But when we boil it all down, we know nothing about these gifts or their possessors. They have vanished without leaving visible trace."[25]

In the *modern era*, prophecy and languages are claimed for the persecuted French Huguenots called the Little Prophets of Cevennes – very young children sharing the gifts.[26] There were also outcroppings among the Jansenists and Shakers. Mother Ann Lee, founder of the latter sect, is said to have testified in 72 different languages before Anglican clergymen who were also noted linguists. Certain emotional phenomena among early Methodists and Quakers have been linked to glossolalia. The 19th century was relatively quiescent, presenting only the Irvingites and the Mormons who claimed to speak in tongues. And then we come to the outburst, previously noted, in the 20th century.

---

[22] G.B. Cutten, *Speaking With Tongues* (New Haven, CT: Yale University Press, 1927), p.34-35.

[23] D.A. Hayes, *The Gift of Tongues* (Cincinnati: Jennings and Graham, 1913), p.63.

[24] Quoted by Farrell, *ibid.*

[25] Leon Morris, *Spirit of the Living God* (Grand Rapids: InterVarsity Press, 1961), p.63.

[26] Robert C. Dalton, *Tongues Like as of Fire* (Springfield, MO: Gospel Publishing House, 1945), p.15ff.

Finally, as we look at history, phenomena very similar to the present-day tongues movement have not been confined solely to religious groups. Zilboorg has pointed out these same phenomena in secular groups, especially during medieval times when demonic superstitions flourished.[27] Linton has demonstrated that such phenomena are frequently seen today in secular groups,[28] although we are loath to recognize it.

Thus, in terms of religious history, it would seem that today's tongues-speaking is not the same as the tongues-speaking of the Apostolic age, for the apostolic phenomena died out by the close of the 2nd century.

B. The Criterion of Cultural Anthropology

Another important observation comes from the field of anthropology. Anthropologists have amply documented that during periods of social distress, a primitive tribe may suddenly develop a new movement; a leader emerges, and the authenticity of his movement is validated by "tongues," healings, miracles, and signs.

In Africa and Melanesia these have been studied repeatedly.[29] Identical phenomena are described as occurring in primitive tribes, are recorded in European history, religious and secular; and are current in America today.[30]

Experiences similar to what happened in primitive tribes and in medieval Europe are happening in American church services, in all parts of the country. The data merely demonstrates that normal people, given the motivation and appropriate situation, can and do react in somewhat predictable fashion. For instance, stereotyped action may be seen in crowd situations, such as football games or on some sales days in retail stores. Usually it reflects intense emotional situations where people are given social sanction to participate in expressing their feelings *in action* rather than *in words*.

Applying these criteria to modern-day glossolalia, it might be said that instead of being similar to the New Testament speaking in tongues, modern-day tongues are more similar to what happens many times in a completely non-religious situation.

C. The Criterion of Speech Psychology

Speech is a complex phenomenon involving both conscious, willful elements and unconscious, automatic patterns in psychological and physiological circuits. We are all aware of common distortions of normal speech. When we get excited we stutter, forget what we were saying, say something other than intended (slip of the tongue), or are rendered speechless! We can talk to one person, listen to another, and think about a third. Sometimes when starting to talk we get confused and tongue-twisted, saying a garble of sounds and syllables. People talking in their sleep often utter unintelligible jargon. So also do patients under sedation or anesthesia, or in partial coma.

---

[27] G. Zilboorg, *A History of Medial Psychology* (New York: Norton, 1941).

[28] R. Linton, *Culture and Mental Disorders* (Springfield, IL: Thomas Press, 1956).

[29] Peter Worsley, *The Trumpet Shall Sound: A Study of 'Cargo' Cults in Melanesia* (London: Macgibbon and Kee, 1957).

[30] L. Festinger, N.W. Riecken, & S. Shacter, *When Prophecy Fails* (Minneapolis: Univ. of Minnesota Press, 1959).

All of these examples indicate aberrations of our usual and normal speech patterns. We can observe that if our attention is diverted from our speech we may continue talking under the control of unconscious mechanisms which may or may not produce intelligible speech. Any of us could "speak in tongues" if we adopted a passive attitude about controlling our body and speech and had an emotional tension pressing for expression. A familiar example is the explosive, contagious laughter of a group which reaches a point where everyone is "too weak to move" from laughing. Trying to talk while thus laughing results in vocalizations which have all the characteristics of present-day glossolalia. Religious mystics throughout history have been able quite willfully to enter such states and experience "tongues" (Underhill, *Mysticism*). Most people need the appropriate motivation, group setting, and examples before they can develop such experiences.

Again, glossolalia is an experience quite normal people can and do experience. It is not the malcontent, emotionally disturbed, or socio-economically deprived who necessarily seeks out such experiences. Currently many earnest, sincere Christians, desiring the will of God for their lives, are seeking to deepen their spiritual vitality. It is not surprising that they come to such an experience.[31]

Applying this criterion to our study, it is possible to show that very natural mechanisms can produce what today are called "glossolalia." Why suggest that the unintelligible syllabication is the product of the Holy Spirit, when such "glossolalia" can be produced and can be readily understood on a natural plane?

D. The Criterion of Linguistics

It is occasionally claimed that some modern tongue-talker is actually speaking in a foreign language which is unknown to the speaker, and usually unknown to all of his audience.

Instances of actual languages spoken are almost without exception found to be xenoglossic (or evidence is insubstantial when one begins to examine specific instances). Xenoglossia is the repeating of utterances in languages to which the speaker has been exposed but has not mastered. Under self-hypnosis or trance these utterances may be recalled. Martin R. Pope and G.B. Cutten both state that no case of speaking in tongues in a language which has never been heard by the speaker has yet been verified.[32]

There is also evidence that most of modern "glossolalia" is not a language at all.

Since I am not a professional linguist, I shall refer to recent reports on linguistic analysis of tape recordings made from glossolalia: (1) Russell Hitt, in *Eternity* magazine (August, 1963, "The New Pentecostalism"), reports a study by Dr. Eugene Nida of the American Bible Society; (2) Dr. Frank Farrell, in *Christianity Today* (9-13-63, p.1166) refers to a study by a group of United States government linguists; (3) Dr. William Welmers, linguistics professor of UCLA. submits several analyses ("Letters to the Editor," *Christianity Today*, 11-8-63), and (4) Dr. Weston LaBarre, an anthropologist, presents comparative linguistic material (in his book *They Shall Take Up Serpents*, 1962).

---

[31] Pattison, *op. cit.*, p.100.

[32] Martin R. Pope, "Gift of Tongues" in *Dictionary of the Apostolic Church* (New York: Charles Scribner's Sons, 1922), Vol. II, p.598-599. Cutten, *op. cit.*, p.35.

In summary, they all report that the various samples of glossolalia are structurally not a "language"; that it would be linguistically impossible to derive the alleged "interpretations" from the glossolalic message; and most significantly, that the glossolalia was linguistically a decomposed form of English.

To this I can add my own observations from clinical experiences with neurological and psychiatric patients. In certain types of brain disorders resulting from strokes, brain tumors, etc., the patient is left with disruptions in his automatic, physical speech circuit patterns. If we study these "aphasic" patients we can observe the same decomposition of speech that occurs in schizophrenic thought and speech patterns, which is structurally the same as modern-day glossolalia.[33]

What conclusion then are we to draw from the application of this criterion? We can say that certain stereotypes of speech will result whenever conscious, willful control of speech is interfered with, whether by injury to the brain, by psychosis, or by passive renunciation of willful control. We believe it can be shown that modern glossolalia is a stereotyped pattern of unconsciously controlled vocal behavior, and is not at all like what one finds in the pages of the New Testament.

E. The Criterion of Pagan Mythology

The ancient classical descriptions are found in Virgil *(Aeneid*, vi. 40-106) and Plato (*Timaeus*). Virgil draws a lifelike picture of the ancient prophetess allegedly speaking in tongues, and Plato described the power of the *mantis*, or prophet. One may consult the works of Nilsson for further descriptions. Seers, oracles, and the ecstatic elements of Greek religion are described in passages in *Greek Popular Religion,* p.121ff., and in *A History of Greek Religion.* p.205-211.

If the pagan Greek religions at 500 BC had a "speaking in tongues" which was very similar to what we have in the modern-tongues movement, how do we say that the modern-tongues movement is Holy Spirit inspired? Would anyone be so hardy as to say that either the pagan or the modern tongues movement is like what the Holy Spirit produced at Pentecost or at Antioch or at Corinth?

VI. THE WORK OF THE HOLY SPIRIT IN THE LIVES OF CHRISTIANS

The vitality that the Holy Spirit can give to the lives of God's children is sorely missed in much of today's religious world. People are looking for something to distinguish the church from the Rotary Club. Thousands of people can be corralled into church membership at various times, and many of them, we believe, may never have received the indwelling gift of the Holy Spirit. Desperately looking for something – happiness, joy, power – these people are in the proper emotional state for the modern-tongues experience. However, this experience is not the "speaking in tongues" that one reads about in the New Testament.

Still, there are also born-again people who do not experience the vitality offered by

---

[33] Pattison, *op. cit.*, p.100ff.

the Holy Spirit. Why is that? Several suggestions might be made.

In Ephesians 5:18 we read, "Be filled with the Spirit." The context suggests three things. One, being filled with the Spirit is a process. Two, the fulness of the Spirit is evidenced by the control and authority of the Spirit over the life. These first two factors are seen in the opening portion of the verse, "And be not drunk with wine, wherein is excess; but ...." Being drunk is the result of a process and continues only as long as one drinks. It leads to control by the "spirits" consumed, and the drunkard begins to walk in the spirit of drunkenness.

On the positive side of the picture we are introduced to a third point. The behavior of the Spirit-filled life is described in Ephesians 5:19-6:19. That walk which is under the control of the Holy Spirit is one in which there is singing and making melody in the heart to the Lord. There is the giving of thanks for all things; the submitting of ourselves one to another in the fear of the Lord; love between husband and wife; obedience of children to parents; mutual consideration between management and labor; victory in the face of spiritual conflict; and prayer and supplication in the Spirit for all saints – in short, the vital happiness, joy, and power that Christians are looking for.

The command to be filled with the Spirit stands in contrast to the order, "And grieve not the Holy Spirit of God" (Ephesians 4:30). And how are we to understand this order? Again, the context gives the clue. Immediately preceding verse 30, we have the following instructions: do not let the sun go down on your wrath; do not give place to the devil; do not steal; and do not let any corrupt communication proceed out of your mouth. In the concluding two verses of chapter 4 we read, "Let all bitterness, all wrath, and anger, and clamor, and evil speaking, be put away from you, with all malice: and be kind one to another, tenderhearted, forgiving one another, even as God for Christ's sake hath forgiven you."

We grieve the indwelling Holy Spirit by overt acts of sin, by the unrighteous things we do, say, and think. However, true holiness is something more than avoiding unholiness. The full-orbed life into which the Holy Spirit desires to lead us is filled with positive demonstrations of goodness. These are possible only as we "grieve not the Spirit."

It is the nature of the Spirit of God to speak the things of Christ. It is His purpose to glorify Christ through spoken testimony. Any refusal on our part to be His witnesses, via the spoken word, is to grieve (smother) His ministry.

He is also the Spirit of intercession. He is the author of all true prayer. It is for this reason we are exhorted to pray in the Spirit. Any refusal on our part to allow Him liberty in this ministry of prayer and supplication quenches the Spirit. Prayerlessness in our lives bears irrefutable testimony to the fact that we are grieving (quenching) the work of the Holy Spirit in our lives.

The Third Person of the Godhead is also the Spirit of unity. It is His nature to love the brethren. It is through Him the love of God is shed abroad in our hearts. A lack of love on our part for the brethren, any party spirit, any spirit of divisiveness, is not of Him. Any such spirit within us serves to grieve the Spirit.

The children of Israel were accused of limiting "the Holy One of Israel" (Psalm 78:14). Nor is the church any less guilty of limiting (grieving) the Person and work of the

Holy Spirit. The Spirit of God is "straitened" within us. His ministry is unlimited, unhampered, and unquenched only as we walk in obedience to Him. The fulness of the Spirit is enjoyed by those who are responsive to Him. There is no gift of the Spirit (not even speaking with tongues) that can be considered a substitute for the Spirit-controlled life.

CONCLUSION

There has been a renewed interest in the work of the Holy Spirit in our day, and for this we are grateful. And the new outburst of "tongues" in many religious groups has led people to once again search the Scriptures, and for this we are grateful.

Such a search of the Scriptures, we believe, will reveal that the speaking in tongues that took place in Bible times was the uttering of a foreign language never learned or before studied by the speaker. And if this is true, then what is seen on every hand today is something different than what one finds in the Bible.

The modern tongues movement can be explained in a number of naturalistic ways. Normal, devout religious people may have this experience during states of intense spiritual emotion. The experience does not indicate the presence of any valid spiritual experience.

Since the modern phenomena is occurring in so many groups (including even many high church groups like "God's frozen people," the Episcopalians), can it be that men who found themselves in religious groups that had no vital "spiritual program" have turned to this experience of glossolalia because there was a spiritual vacuum that needed to be filled?

And it is a serious indictment of the Restoration Movement that we have fallen into the same lethargic rut that is grieving and quenching the Spirit in Christendom at large. We need to emphasize the need of restoring the Spirit to the lives of church members.

It is entirely possible that God can use an extremist movement to help awaken a sleeping church. The glossolalic movement is in demand because people are hungry for a genuine spiritual experience with God. A Spirit-less life and church cannot fill this need. May God give all of us that constant and ready obedience to the Holy Spirit which will result in holiness, courage, unity, liberality, prayerfulness, Bible study, and a witness for Christ which is accompanied by life-transforming power.

BIBLIOGRAPHY

A. Books

Bales, James, *Pat Boone and the Gift of Tongues*. Searcy, AR: published by the author, 1970.

Boone, Pat, *A New Song*. Carol Stream, IL: Creation House, 1970.

Brumback, Carl, *What Meaneth This?* Springfield, MO: The Gospel Publishing House, 1947.

Bruner, Frederick D., *A Theology of the Holy Spirit*. Grand Rapids: Eerdmans, 1970.

Burdick, Donald, *Tongues: To Speak or Not to Speak?* Chicago: Moody Press, 1969.

Cutten, G. B., *Speaking With Tongues*. New Haven: Yale University Press, 1927.

Dalton, Robert. Chandler, *Tongues Like as of Fire*. Springfield, MO: The Gospel Publishing House, 1945.

Festinger, L., Riecken, N.W., and Shacter, S., *When Prophecy Fails*. Minneapolis: University of Minnesota Press, 1959.

Hayes, D.A., *The Gift of Tongues*. Cincinnati: Jennings and Graham, 1913.

Horton, Harold, *The Gifts of the Spirit*. Harrow, Middlesex, Great Britain: n.d.

Knox, R.A., *Enthusiasm: A Chapter in the History of Religion*. London: Oxford, 1950.

LaBarre, W., *They Shall Take Up Serpents*. Minneapolis: University of Minnesota Press, 1962.

Linton, R., *Culture and Mental Disorders*. Springfield, IL: Thomas Press, 1956.

Nilsson, Martin P., *Greek Popular Religion*. New York: Columbia University Press, 1940.

------, *A History of Greek Religion*. Oxford: Clarendon Press, 1949.

Underhill, E., *Mysticism*. New York: Meridian, 1955.

Worsley, P., *The Trumpet Shall Sound: A Study of 'Cargo' Cults in Melanesia*. London: Macgibbon and Kee, 1957.

Zilboorg, G., *A History of Medical Psychology*. New York: Norton, 1941.

B. Articles

Farrell, Frank, "Outburst of Tongues: The New Penetration," *Christianity Today*, September 13, 1963, p.1163ff.

Hillis, Don, "Speaking in Tongues," *Sunday School Times*, April 6, 1963, p.249ff.

Mayfield, Wm. H., "Response to the 'Tongues' Movement," *Christian Standard*, August 1, 1964, p.485ff.

Pattison, E. Mansell, "Speaking in Tongues and about Tongues," *Christian Standard*, February 15, 1964, p.99ff.

Phillips, McCandlish, "And There Appeared Unto Them Tongues of Fire," *Saturday Evening Post*, May 16, 1964.

Zimmerman, Thos. F., "Pleas for Pentecostalists," *Christianity Today*, January 4, 1963, p.11ff.

SPECIAL STUDY #5

THE DOCTRINE OF INSPIRATION

The process of inspiration (of men "being carried along by the Holy Spirit," 2 Peter 1:21) is explained by Paul in the classic passage found at 1 Corinthians 2:9-16.

First, Paul declares that the message spoken by the apostles has not come from human reason, but by divine revelation. He begins the treatment of this subject by telling the Greeks that neither scientific investigation nor human reason has ever been able to discover a sure foundation upon which a religious system could be built ("It never entered into the heart of men ...," verse 9). The message brought by God's envoys was not something that mere human thinking had conjured up.

Then, Paul proceeds to describe the three successive steps in the transmission of truth from the heart of God to the heart of man. These are:

1) *REVELATION*, the act of the Holy Spirit imparting to God's messengers truth incapable of being discovered by man's unaided mind (verses 10-12).

2) *INSPIRATION*, the act of the Holy Spirit enabling the messengers to speak in God-chosen words, infallibly, the truth revealed (verse 13).

3) *ILLUMINATION*, the act of the Holy Spirit enabling believers to understand the truth given by revelation and spoken by inspiration (verses 14-16).

It is assumed in the remainder of this study, since there is no cogent argument against the conclusion, that what is said in these verses in 1 Corinthians 2 about the "speaking" of the apostles would hold equally true of their writing, especially when what they were writing were the same truths they had been speaking.

I. REVELATION

Paul explains that the Bible did not come by way of scientific investigation and human reason, but that it came in another way, by revelation (verse 10). Then, by use of pure logic, Paul proves to these Greeks the impossibility of discovering God's Word through scientific investigation or human reason (verse 11). The first step, therefore, in the transmission of truth from the heart of God to the heart of the believer is revelation. God must reveal His mind if men are to know His thoughts and will.

II. VERBAL INSPIRATION

After the Bible writers had been given the truth by means of the act of the Holy Spirit in uncovering that truth to them, the apostle says they were *not* left to themselves to make a record of it. It is one thing to know a certain fact. It is quite another to find the exact words which will give someone else an adequate understanding of that fact. This is where the need of verbal inspiration comes in.

Paul first makes the negative statement, "Which things we speak (i.e., put into words), not in the words taught by human wisdom." That is, the words which the Bible writers used were not dictated by their own human reason or wisdom. The Bible is not (as some men say) a record of man's search for God.

Then the apostle makes the positive statement, "but in words taught by the Spirit." *He says that the words which the Bible writers used were taught them by the Holy Spirit.* That is, as they wrote the Scriptures, the Holy Spirit who had revealed the truth to them now chose the correct word out of the writer's vocabulary, whose content of meaning will give to the believer the exact truth God desires him to have. This, however, does not imply mechanical dictation nor the effacement of the writer's own personality. It is not that the Holy Spirit used the writers as though they were typewriters.

Perhaps an example of how the Holy Spirit worked is found in Acts 16:6-10. In that passage the Holy Spirit guided the missionary party. It would appear that He didn't do anything as long as they were going toward the right town. But the moment they began heading in the wrong direction, the Holy Spirit somehow hindered them (we are not told exactly how). Perhaps in the same way the Spirit worked in the matter of inspiration.

Thus, we have in the original Hebrew and Greek autographs of our Bible manuscripts the very words that God taught the writers to use as they recorded the truth, which they had received by revelation. This is what is meant by verbal inspiration.

In the words of verse 13, "comparing spiritual things with spiritual words" (ASV), Paul explains this process of choosing the right word in each case. This is the procedure which the Bible writers went through in writing their books. As led by the Holy Spirit, they searched through their vocabularies for the exact word which would adequately express the truth they wished to record. By the process of comparing the word with the truth they wished to write down, they rejected all those words which the Holy Spirit showed them would not correctly express the thought, and finally chose the word to which the Holy Spirit led them.

III. ILLUMINATION

Not only did the Holy Spirit have something to do with the revelation and the inspiration of the will of God, but He also helps the hearer to understand it. Paul says, "The natural man receiveth not the things of the Spirit of God." The "natural man" is the man who is devoid of the influence of the Spirit of God; the man who is governed by his physical nature alone. Paul then finishes by saying that spiritual things are Spiritually discerned. In other words, when one hears (or reads) the Word, and in his heart really desires to understand it, the Holy Spirit will aid him in his quest. The Holy Spirit works through the preached word (written word) – not directly on the heart (apart from the word).

CONCLUSION

We should be heedful to distinguish carefully between revelation and inspiration, so that we do not mix up or conflate the terms. "Revelation" is God making His will known.

"Inspiration" is the help that God gave the Bible preachers (and writers) to speak the exact words that would convey the truth He wanted men to know.

BIBLIOGRAPHY

Alexander, Archibald, *Evidences of the Authenticity, Inspiration, and Canonical Authority of the Holy Scriptures*. Philadelphia: Presbyterian Board of Publication, 1836.

Gaussen, S.R.L., *Theopneustia, the Plenary Inspiration of the Holy Scriptures*. London: Francombe and Son, 1912.

Harris, R. Laird, *Inspiration and Canonicity of the Bible*. Grand Rapids: Zondervan Publishing Co., 1957.

McGarvey, J.W., "Grounds on which We Receive the Bible as the Word of God, and the Only Rule of Faith and Practice" in *The Old Faith Restated*, edited by J.H. Garrison. St. Louis: Christian Publishing House, 1891, p.11-48.

Milligan, R., *Reason and Revelation*. Rosemead, CA: Old Paths Book Club, 1953.

Warfield, Benjamin B., "Inspiration" in *International Standard Bible Encyclopedia*. Vol. III, p.1473-1483.

------, *Revelation and Inspiration*. Philadelphia: Presbyterian and Reformed Publishing Co.

Wuest, Kenneth S., *In These Last Days*. Grand Rapids: Eerdmans, 1955, p.36-42.

SPECIAL STUDY #6

PREDESTINATION AND FOREKNOWLEDGE

The whole problem of how to harmonize the ideas of divine sovereignty and human freedom of will is difficult and complicated. We define *Predestination* as that theological doctrine primarily associated with Calvinism, which holds that from eternity God has foreordained all things which come to pass, including the final salvation or reprobation of men. "Predestination" among theologians has both a broad and a narrow sense. Broadly, it covers all of creation, the idea being that God ordained (i.e., determined before creation) all that would come to pass in that creation. Technically, however, the word is used specially of God's will respecting the eternal destiny of intelligent creatures. We define *Sovereignty* as being the supreme authority of God, who is "Almighty," "the blessed and only Potentate, the King of Kings and Lord of Lords," who "works all things according to the counsel of His own will." He is God and Creator, and can do with His creation as He wishes. *Freedom of the will* is explained as meaning that men are not irrevocably programmed to act or choose in a certain way, but are free to choose or reject the Divine overtures.

The problem is this: if God has foreordained all things which will come to pass, how can there be any freedom on the part of man? Is not man just a puppet, who does what God has predetermined him to do?

> The philosophical problem of freedom is further complicated in Theology by the ideas of God's providence, omniscience, and omnipotence, as well as the ideas of sin and grace. The idea of God's providence, especially when joined with the ideas of foreknowledge and predestination, raises acute questions concerning the independence of the will. If all human events are foreseen, or if all actions are but expressions of one infinite action, in what sense is human decision really free? Or if, since the fall of Adam, it is impossible for man to will the good, in what sense is choice real and significant? These issues have led to theological controversy again and again in church history ... Augustine argued that, although Adam (before the fall) possessed both the ability not to sin (*posse non peccare*) and the ability to sin (*posse peccare*), he lost the former when he exercised the latter. This original freedom of man, he believed, could only be restored by an act of divine grace. This, however, raises the question whether man has the ability to accept or reject that grace ... Augustine argued that grace was irresistible and prevenient; that is, that an act of God is itself required to enable the will to accept grace, and that it is this grace which is irresistible to those whom God wills to give it ... This problem is complicated, however, by the notion of predestination ... because if God decrees from all Eternity what will happen and who will be saved, in what sense is it meaningful to speak even of Adam's freedom to choose before the fall? Is not one driven to say that even this choice was predetermined?[1]

---

[1] Van A. Harvey, *A Handbook of Theological Terms* (New York: Macmillan, 1968), p.101-103.

I. THE DOCTRINE AS TAUGHT IN SCRIPTURE

The idea of predestination is set forth with great power and clarity in Romans 8:29-30.

The idea also occurs in Ephesians 1, where verses 4 and 5 say that God has chosen us in Christ "before the foundation of the world," having "predestined [or foreordained] us to adoption as sons through Jesus Christ." Further, verse 9 says our salvation is "according to His good pleasure which He purposed in Christ." This eternal purpose to save man "in Christ" is referred to again in Ephesians 3:11.

See also Acts 4:27-28; 13:48; 1 Corinthians 2:7; Psalm 139:16; etc.

II. HISTORIC RISE AND DEVELOPMENT OF THE CALVINISTIC DOCTRINE OF PREDESTINATION

During the first three centuries of the church, Christian writers left this doctrine largely undeveloped.

Augustine gave the doctrine of predestination its first full exposition about AD 400, making the doctrine of a special predestination the foundation of his opposition to Pelagius. He gave new prominence in his theory to the absolute will of God: he made divine grace the only ground of man's salvation. Grace was, to him, the irresistible power (the Holy Spirit?) working faith within the heart, and bringing freedom as its result. Further, God's grace was given only to a limited number of people, the others perishing eternally. Augustine held predestination as an inference from his concept of the Fall and of grace.

> Augustine taught that infants who died without baptism were eternally damned (a teaching which followed from his conclusion that all mankind must be punished for the sin of one man, Adam; a concept later to be titled "the Doctrine of Original Sin"). He taught that the infants would not likely suffer in torment, but rather be deprived of the presence of heaven. This led to the doctrine of the Roman Catholic Church, which placed unbaptized infants in a special compartment (called *Limbus Infantum*) just at the border of Heaven where they are deprived of Heaven's blessings but kept from Hell's torments, a condition called "sorrow without torment."[2]

In the Middle Ages, Anselm, Peter Lombard, and Thomas Aquinas followed the Augustinian view to a certain extent, more or less identifying predestination with God's broad providential control over things. In pre-Reformation times, Wycliffe and Huss set forth strict predestination views. Roman Catholicism did not yet endorse a particular doctrine on the matter, but it officially tolerated both the teachings of Molina (1535-1600), who taught that the gift of divine grace is given in the light of God's foreknowledge of free human cooperation, and the more rigorous Thomistic view, although the latter does not approach the harshness of the Calvinistic view.

During the Protestant Reformation, the doctrine of predestination was set forth with emphasis by Luther, Calvin, Zwingli, Melanchthon, Knox, and all the outstanding leaders

---

[2] L. Edsil Dale, *Acts Comments* (Cincinnati: published by the author, 1952), p.41.

of that period. The Reformation leaders built upon the doctrine and theology of Augustine, rather than going back to see what the Scriptures themselves had to say on the subject.

> Luther, in later life, moved away from the doctrine of total depravity, somewhat Zwingli rejected fatalism and believed in an all-ruling providence which left no room for accidents. Melanchthon later modified his views, and under his leadership the Lutheran Church came to oppose the strict doctrine of predestination. Melanchthon's position made possible the later development of Arminianism, which was the foundation of Methodist doctrine on the problem.[3]

Arminianism, summarized briefly, believes that (a) God elects or reproves on the basis of foreseen faith or unbelief, (b) Christ died for all men, but only believers will be saved, (c) man is so depraved that the divine grace is necessary unto faith or any good work, (d) this grace may be resisted, and (e) whether all who are truly regenerate will certainly persevere in the faith is a point which needs further clarification.

Calvin (1509-1564) was the one who most systematically developed the doctrine believed by many denominations and reformed theologians in this day.

> Calvin stood firmly on divine sovereignty, emphasizing the supreme will of God and His eternal decrees, which caused some to be lost and some to be saved, no matter what they should do. Calvin concluded that most infants were predestined to salvation, thus avoiding that "horrible doctrine" (as he called it) of Augustine's. Otherwise, said Calvin, God would be engaged in an endless process of creating souls for children, whom He "hurries from the womb to the tomb, and from the tomb to everlasting doom." (*History of the Christian Church*, vol. 8, p.545-582).[4]

Preachers of the early Restoration Movement roundly rejected the Calvinistic doctrines. They did not, on the other hand, accept (c) and (e) of the above summary of Arminianism, either. Cochran's book, *Raccoon John Smith*, is a popular presentation of those Restoration preachers' struggles with the doctrines of Calvinism as they tried without success to harmonize them with Scripture.[5] Since they could not be harmonized, they rejected the doctrine of Calvin with reference to predestination.

Certain Neo-orthodox theologians in the 20th century also have rejected the Calvinistic doctrine as being not Biblical. Karl Barth and Emil Brunner, although not agreeing with each other as to the reason for so doing, are united in asserting that Calvin's doctrine is to be rejected.

III. BRIEF SUMMARY OF THE BIBLICAL TEACHING ON PREDESTINATION

Both Scripture and men's reason suggest men are free moral agents. Many verses say, in effect, "whosoever will may come." Thus, it is difficult to deny freedom of the will.

---

[3] Dale, *ibid.*

[4] Dale, *ibid.*

[5] Louis A. Cochran, *Raccoon John Smith* (New York: Duell, Sloan & Pearce, 1963).

Had God made man without freedom to choose, the death of Christ would have been in vain.

> One may struggle a lifetime amidst the lights and shadows of infralapsarianism (predestined after sin entered the world) and supralapsarianism (predestined from before the creation), and still find himself responsible for his own decisions and acts.[6]

> There are two main ways in which the doctrine has been formulated ... Supralapsarianism (antelapsarianism) is that starker form of the doctrine which holds that even before the creation and Fall (*lapsus*) of man, God eternally willed some men to salvation without any consideration of their merits or worthiness. Infralapsarianism (sub- or postlapsarianism) is that form of the doctrine – some would call it a milder form – which holds that God's decree is subsequent to the Fall; that is, after the Fall of man, God elects to save some who would otherwise have perished. The infralapsarian argues that the supralapsarian view is not consistent with the love and justice of God, who would not condemn some men to damnation before their creation and the exercise of their freedom. The supralapsarians argue that the infralapsarian position is logically and theologically indefensible because an omnipotent and omniscient deity necessarily foreordains all that happens, even the Fall.[7]

The predestination of plants and animals (i.e., the irrational part of God's creation) is an absolute predestination. They do not have freedom of choice.

> The part of God's creation which has no rational nature has been absolutely predestined. From the Garden of Eden until this day, birds have built their nests from their predestined blueprints with the same materials and patterns. Bees have stored their honey and followed the same type of labor union as God fixed for them by creation. The regularity of life and action in insects and animals amazes man; but what God has fixed by the laws of nature remains fixed, allowing no new methods and no departure from the routine.[8]

However, when we come to man (and angels?), which are the rational part of God's creation, God's predestination is not so absolute. God created man a free moral agent, with the power (within limits) to choose his own way.

> The foreknowledge of God in no way predestines the free will of man. A father may clearly see the outcome bound to result from certain acts of the child, but his foreknowledge in no way determines the child's actions. The plan of salvation and the way to heaven are fixed and predestined by God from before the creation, but the traveler has within his will the power to depart from the way and doom his own soul. The omniscience of God has nothing to do with the obedience of man. Foresight and free choice stand alone and separate.[9]

As in the illustration above, the father's foreknowledge does not control the son's choice, still, we can imagine the father putting gentle pressure on the boy to do as the father

---

[6] Dale, *ibid.*

[7] Harvey, *ibid.*

[8] Dale, *ibid.*

[9] Dale, *ibid.*

knows is best, urging the boy to make the right decision. So it is with God!

God, by providence and revelation, points the way and pleads to man; but He, in no case, takes over man's free will. Whatever divine influence may bear on one's life, one can safely say that His influence never overwhelms the choice of man as man exercises his own free will (1 Corinthians 10:1-13; 14:32). Examine, too, all these passages which teach the freedom of man's will, and that the death of Christ was for all mankind – it was not just a limited atonement: Ezekiel 18:23,32; 33:11; John 1:29, 3:16, 12:32, 15:1-2; Romans 11:16-24; 1 Corinthians 9:27; Galatians 5:4; 1 Timothy 2:4; Titus 2:11; Hebrews 3:16-18; 2 Peter 1:1-10, 3:9; 1 John 2:2, 4:14.[10]

CONCLUSION

God, in eternity, determined that those "in Christ" should be saved. He also determined that those not "in Christ" should be damned. God brings various influences to bear on a person's life, but He never forces a person to go against his own free will. The sovereign God determined there would be two, and only two, ways a man could walk: either a life of belief, or one of disbelief. Each individual is free to choose whether he will be "in Christ" or not.

Irrational creation is predestined as God willed it, with no freedom to choose its own way. Rational creatures, however, do have a choice. God has predestined the plan to be followed, but He does not predestine individuals (in the Calvinistic sense of the word).

BIBLIOGRAPHY

Berkouwer, G.C., *The Providence of God*. Grand Rapids: Eerdmans, 1952.

------, *Divine Election*. Grand Rapids: Eerdmans, 1957.

Boettner, Loraine, *The Reformed Doctrine of Predestination*. Philadelphia: Presbyterian and Reformed Publishing Co., 1968.

Dale, L. Edsil, *Acts Comments*. Cincinnati: published by the author, 1952.

Harvey, Van A., *A Handbook of Theological Terms*. New York: Macmillan, 1968.

Hodge, Charles, *Systematic Theology*. Grand Rapids: Eerdmans, 1960, Vol. I, p.535-549.

Schaff, Philip, *History of the Christian Church*. Grand Rapids: Eerdmans, 1960, Vol. 8, p.545-582.

Steele, David N., and Thomas. Curtis C., *The Five Points of Calvinism*. Philadelphia: Presbyterian and Reformed Publishing Co., 1963.

Warfield, B.B., *Biblical and Theological Studies*. Philadelphia: Presbyterian and Reformed Publishing Co., 1952, p.3-67.

------, "Predestination" in *Hastings' Dictionary of the Bible*. New York: Scribner's Sons, 1909, Vol. 4, p.47-62.

---

[10] Dale, *ibid*.

SPECIAL STUDY #7

HADES & THE INTERMEDIATE PLACE OF THE DEAD

The relationship of "Hades," "Heaven," "Hell," and the "Intermediate Place of the Dead" is an issue that has been raised many times by Bible students. The refusal of the King James Version translators to distinguish between the Greek words *gehenna*, *haidēs*, and *tartarus* has led to much confused theology. This study is intended to help readers get a better understanding of this important topic.

I. DEFINITION OF TERMS

The "Intermediate Place of the Dead" speaks of the place (or state) where a person is between his death and the second coming of Christ. It is, of course, a "disembodied state," since at death the person leaves his body,[1] and the body is buried in a "grave." Each person will receive a resurrection body when the Lord Jesus returns.[2]

"Heaven" is the place where God dwells. In "Heaven," with God in the midst, is where the redeemed will spend eternity future.

"Hell" is the final state of the wicked, their place of punishment after the judgment.

The American Standard Version (1901) helpfully distinguished between the different Greek words, using "Hell" to translate *gehenna*, "Hades" to translate *haidēs*, and "Hell" to translate *tartarus*, also adding a footnote that it might be translated "Tartarus" (2 Peter 2:4). Most translations subsequent to the ASV have largely maintained these distinctions.

II. PROPOSITION

This study will show that "Hades" is (1) not the grave; (2) not Hell; (3) not Tartarus; (4) not Heaven; and (5) not merely the "state" of the dead.

"Hades" will be shown to be (1) a *place* in the unseen world distinct from Heaven and Hell; (2) having, before the ascension of Christ, two compartments – one of comfort, the other of misery; (3) to which, before Christ's ascension, the souls of all who died (whether good or bad) were carried; (4) into which Christ, at His death, descended, delivering the souls of the righteous; (5) to which, since the ascension of Christ, the souls of the wicked, and the wicked only, have been consigned; (6) in which they are reserved in misery against the day of general judgment; (7) from which they are then to be brought

---

[1] See notes at Acts 5:5. See also 2 Timothy 4:6; Ecclesiastes 12:7; 2 Peter 1:13-14.

[2] 1 Corinthians 15:33-57, especially verses 51-52; 1 Thessalonians 4:13-17.

for public judgment previously to their being cast into Hell.

III. HADES IS NOT THE GRAVE

A. *Old Testament references showing that "Hades" is not the grave.*

In Old Testament times, the Hebrews had a word for grave (*kever*), and in at least two instances "Hades" is clearly distinguished from the "grave." In Genesis 37:35, the word for "Hades" first appears in the Bible, when Jacob declares, "I shall go down into Sheol[3] to my son." Yet in verse 33 we learn the Patriarch was under the impression that Joseph had not, and could not have, a grave, for he is there represented as exclaiming, "An evil beast devoured him." Isaiah 14:15 declares that Lucifer (the Babylonian king) shall be "brought down to Hades," while verse 19 represents him as being "cast out of his grave (*kever*)."

In the poetical books, "Hades" never occurs in one of two parallel clauses, answering to *kever* in the other, which shows again that "Hades" and "grave" are not synonymous in the Old Testament.

"Hades" is used synonymously with "nether (lower) parts of the earth,"[4] and this, too, shows that "Hades" and the grave are not synonymous.

Given the foregoing, it seems reasonable to conclude that, in the Old Testament, the term "Hades" (Sheol) is not used to designate the literal grave.

B. *New Testament references showing that "Hades" is not the grave.*

In New Testament times, the Greek language had a word for grave (*mnēma* and *mnēmeion*), and there are instances in the New Testament that show that "Hades" is clearly distinguished from the grave.

For example, Peter manifestly spoke of both the body and the soul of our Lord, asserting that the body did not see corruption although placed in the grave, and that His soul was not abandoned in Hades[5] (implying, of course, that His soul went to Hades). Unless we adopt the conclusion that the soul sleeps with the dead body in the tomb – a conclusion which is contradictory to the whole tenor of the Word of God – Hades must be a distinct place from the grave.

In the KJV, at 1 Corinthians 15:55, the KJV translators rendered the Greek word *haidēs* by "grave." (In the best manuscripts, *haidēs* does not appear; instead, "death" is the subject of both clauses. See ASV, *in loc.*) It is true, however, that Hosea 13:14, of which 1 Corinthians 15:55 is a loose quote, has "Hades" (Sheol). Dr. Charles Hodge, who believes "grave" is a proper translation of *haidēs*, writes, "Here, where the special reference is to the bodies of men and to the delivery of them from the power of death, it is properly

---

[3] Sheol is the Hebrew; the Greek equivalent is Hades.

[4] See Ezekiel 31:14-15; Psalm 43:9; Isaiah 44:23.

[5] Acts 2:27-31.

rendered 'the grave.' The apostle is not speaking of the delivery of souls of men from any intermediate state, but of the redemption of the body."[6] In reply to Hodge, we agree that it is indeed true that Paul's special reference in the whole context is to the glorification of the body. But this does not forbid the idea that there should also be a reference to the soul. In the moment of the body's glorification, and essential to that glorification, the soul is needed to reanimate the body. If indeed there be, or has been, no place of the soul's imprisonment, of course, there can be no reference to such a place. But if there is, or has been, such a place of the soul's imprisonment, what is more natural than for Hosea 13:14, in view of the redemption of the body, which also involves the complete deliverance of the soul, to reference the deliverance of both body and soul?

It seems that the New Testament confirms the teaching of the Old as to the distinction between Hades and the literal grave.

IV. HADES IS NOT HELL

Hades cannot be synonymous with Hell, as is made clear from the fact that, before the ascension of Christ, it is represented as the dwelling place of all the dead (including the righteous dead). Such Godly men as Jacob (Genesis 37:35), Job (Job 17:13), David (Psalm 16:10), and Hezekiah (Isaiah 38:18) all expected to go to Hades. If these worthies went to Hades, so did all the rest of the righteous of the Old Testament age. In Genesis 49:33, we read of Jacob, one of the righteous of the Old Testament age, being "gathered to his people." This language is not speaking of burial. Jacob was "gathered to his people" immediately upon his death, but he was not buried till long after (Genesis 50:13). If he went to Hades, and if "gathered to his people," the people must have been in Hades also.[7]

A further indication that "Hades" is not "Hell" is the fact that, in Revelation 20:14, "'Hades" is spoken of as being cast into Hell (the lake of fire). It is not possible for Hades to be Hell, and be cast into Hell, too.

The everlasting destruction threatened in 2 Thessalonians 1:9 is to be inflicted after the second coming of Christ (i.e., after the Judgment). The ungodly do not go to Hell until after the Judgment. Those who go to Hades before the Judgment cannot, therefore, be in Hell. Here is another indication that Hades and Hell are not synonymous.

V. HADES IS NOT TARTARUS

A. *2 Peter 2:4*

"Hell" in 2 Peter 2:4 is a translation of the participle *tararōsas*, i.e., "cast down to Tartarus" (cp. ASV margin). The verse reads, "... God did not spare angels when they sinned, but cast them into hell (Grk., *tartarōsas*) and committed them to pits of darkness,

---

[6] Charles Hodge, *An Exposition of the First Epistle to the Corinthians* (Grand Rapids: Eerdmans, 1965). p.198.

[7] See also Genesis 25:8-9, 35:39; 2 Kings 22:20.

reserved for judgment." Fronmüller, in *Lange's Commentary*, writes,

> ... Grotius rightly remarks that [*tartarōsas*] denotes in Classic Greek, 'to cast down into Tartarus,' not 'to condemn to Tartarus' ... It is [parallel to] *abussos,* while *haidēs* describes the abode of the dead in general, and *gehenna* denotes the final place of punishment, the lake of fire ...Consequently, [Tartarus is] the preliminary place of confinement ... of spirits, similar to what Sheol [i.e., *haidēs*] is for men.[8]

Tartarus is rightly understood to be the place of detention of wicked angels (i.e., the Devil and his demons) until the Judgment.

B. *The Abyss and Tartarus May Be Synonymous*

From the way the word "abyss" is used, it appears that it is but another name for the preliminary place of confinement of the evil spirits. In Luke 8:31, where the legion of demons is cast out from the possessed man in the country of the Gadarenes, the evil spirits are represented as beseeching our Lord "that he would not command them to go out into the deep (Grk., *abusson*, abyss). If the abyss is a preliminary place of confinement, their request is easily understandable.

In Revelation 9:1-3, when the angel opens the bottomless pit of the abyss, out come the devil's helpers (called locusts in this vision).

In Revelation 17:8, reference is made to a beast that ascends out of the abyss, and who is destined to go into perdition (Hell).

In Revelation 20:3, Satan is represented as being shut up in the abyss for 1,000 years; after his imprisonment he is loosed again for a little season, and then, per verse 10, is cast into Hell.

These passages indicate that the abyss is a preliminary place of confinement of evil spirits, and therefore is synonymous with the "Tartarus" of Peter's epistle.

C. *Tartarus is Not the Same as Hell*

In the Old Testament there is occasionally and dimly set forth the existence of a place of darkness and woe (other than Hades) – called in Hebrew *abaddon*, and translated "Destruction" or "Abaddon." Job 26:6 says, "Sheol (Hades) is naked before God, and Abaddon hath no covering." Job 28:22 reads, "Destruction (*abaddon*) and death say, 'We have heard a rumor thereof with our ears.'" Job 31:12 speaks of "a fire that consumes unto destruction (*abaddon*)." Psalm 88:11 also speaks of *abaddon* in these words, "Shall lovingkindness be declared in the grave? Or thy faithfulness in Destruction (*abaddon*)?" Proverbs 15:11 declares that "Sheol and Abaddon are before Jehovah ...."

The book of Revelation shows that Abaddon (Grk., *apōleia*,[9] destruction) is but another name for Hell, and that the "abyss" and "Abaddon" are different places.

---

[8] G.F.C. Fronmüller. 2 Peter, in Lange's *Commentary on the Holy Scriptures* (Grand Rapids: Zondervan, n.d.), p. 27.

[9] In the LXX, the Hebrew work *abaddon* is translated into Greek by the *apōleia* word family.

- In Revelation 17:8, reference is made to a beast that ascends out of the abyss and who is destined to go into perdition (*apōleia*). In Revelation 19:20, this beast is represented as being cast into the lake of fire, and manifestly this lake of fire (Hell) into which the beast is cast is the *apōleia* into which he was destined to go.

- In Revelation 20:3, Satan is represented as being shut up in the abyss for 1,000 years. After his imprisonment, he is loosed again for a little season, and then is cast into "the lake of fire and brimstone where the beast and false prophet are" (verse 10). Then follows the account of the general judgment (verses 11-13), after which "death and hades" (or those detained in them) were to be cast into the same lake of fire (verses 14-15). It seems this "lake of fire" (Abaddon or destruction, *apōleia*) is Hell, regarded as the place of final and everlasting punishment of devils and wicked men.

In view of the use of *abaddon* in the Old Testament and *apōleia* in the book of Revelation, may there not be some reference to the place of final punishment when Jesus says (Matthew 7:13), "Broad is the way that leadeth to destruction *(apōleian)*"?

Other verses where *apōleia* speaks of the place of final punishment are Romans 9:22; Philippians 3:19; Hebrews 10:39; 1 Timothy 6:9; 2 Peter 2:1,3 and 3:7.

Since Tartarus (viz., abyss) and *abaddon* (i.e., destruction, the place of final punishment) are different places, so the conclusion seems inevitable that Tartarus (viz., abyss) is not the same as Hell. Therefore, we should follow the marginal reading at 2 Peter 2:4 and rightly conclude that Tartarus is the preliminary place of confinement of evil spirits.

D. *Hades is Not Synonymous with Tartarus*

Hades cannot be synonymous with Tartarus. While men go to Hades, there is no evidence that men go to Tartarus.

- In points III and IV above, it has been documented that in Scripture men are represented as going to Hades.

- That men evidently do not go to Tartarus is established by the context the only time *tartarōsas* appears in the New Testament. In 2 Peter 2:4, the apostle is proceeding to prove that wicked men and false teachers shall be punished, and he does so using three examples: the angels that sinned, the wicked world at the time of the flood, and Sodom and Gomorrah. In the case of the angels that sinned, neither their former rank, their dignity, nor their holiness saved them from being cast into Tartarus. If God punished the angels so severely, then false teachers could not hope to escape. Likewise, when God cut off the wicked race in the time of Noah, He showed the world that He punishes the guilty. And by saving of Lot out of the midst of Sodom and Gomorrah, we see that God makes a distinction between the righteous and the wicked; while the wicked will be destroyed, the righteous will be saved. In verse 9, Peter then draws his conclusion: "The Lord knows how to deliver the godly out of temptation, and to *keep the unrighteous under punishment* unto the day of judgment." When commentators attempt to make Peter say that God is "confining wicked men in Tartarus" (as well as confining wicked angels there), it seems they are missing the point of Peter's argument. In chapter 2, Peter is affirming that God knows how to punish the wicked, but Peter says nothing about where wicked *men* are to be confined to await judgment.

We have thus shown that Hades is probably not synonymous with Tartarus.

VI. HADES IS NOT HEAVEN

This deduction reflects the following logic:

God, angels, and Christ (save during the time between His death and resurrection) never are represented as abiding in Hades. Therefore, Hades and Heaven are not the same, for God is often represented as abiding in Heaven.

Hades is distinguished from Heaven. It is placed in antithesis to Heaven in multiple passages (e.g., Job 11:8; Psalm 130:8; Amos 9:2). The approach to Hades is a descent (Numbers 16:33), whereas the approach to Heaven is an ascent (Acts 1:11).

That Hades is not Heaven is also evident from the fact that Hades is always spoken of as a place to be delivered from (Psalm 49:15-16, 16:10; Hosea 13:14).

The New Testament teaching accords with the Old Testament teaching. When our Lord referred to the condition of Lazarus, He did not speak of Lazarus as enjoying the fulness of His Father's house, but as being "comforted" (Luke 16:25), a term never used in reference to the joys of Heaven. When Paul spoke of the condition of the Old Testament saints previous to the ascension of Christ, he makes manifest reference to the incompleteness of their blessedness (Hebrews 11:39-40).

The key argument, however, that Hades was not Heaven is to be found in the fact of the deliverance of the righteous from Hades at the resurrection and ascension of Christ (see point VIII below).

VII. HADES IS NOT MERELY THE "STATE" OF DEATH

The opinion that Hades is merely a "state," and not a "place," is widely held in theological circles. The primary basis for this opinion is the difficulty of harmonizing those Old Testament texts which speak of the righteous going to Hades, with those New Testament texts which, on the one hand, declare that the righteous are taken to Heaven and those, on the other hand, which declare that Hades will be cast into the lake of fire. (Point VIII gives a better way to harmonize these texts rather than saying that Hades is only a "state.")

Every Scripture we have discussed that speaks of Hades treats it as a place, not merely as a state or condition. Certainly, the state or condition of things in Hades is different than the state or condition of things we are accustomed to here in this life. But Hades is not just the "state" of death; it is a place.

VIII. HADES IS A PLACE IN THE UNSEEN WORLD DISTINCT FROM HEAVEN AND HELL

A. *Before Christ's Ascension*

Previous to the death of Jesus, there are several allusions to what is called the "intermediate place of the dead." At death, good and bad alike went to Hades.

- That the wicked went into Hades is shown by the fact that the rich man after death was in Hades, being in torment (Luke 16:23).
- That the righteous were also in Hades prior to Christ's ascension is shown by the previously cited Old Testament passages which speak of the righteous going to Hades at their death.

Jesus' conversation with the penitent thief is crucial to our understanding of this topic of Hades and the intermediate place of the dead. While on the cross, Jesus said to the penitent thief, "Today you shall be with Me in Paradise" (Luke 23:43). Yet Acts 2:27-32 indicates Christ was in Hades while His body was in the grave. We also know that Christ did not go to the Father (in Heaven) while His body was in the grave because on the day of His resurrection He said to Mary, "Stop clinging to Me, for I have not yet ascended to My Father" (John 20:17). If Jesus went to Paradise as He told the thief He would, yet was also in Hades as Peter says He was, it would seem that before the ascension Paradise was a compartment of Hades.

We have thus shown that, previous to the ascension of Christ, Hades had two compartments – one of comfort, the other of misery – to which the souls of *all* who died, righteous and wicked alike, were carried.

B. *Christ's Descent into Hades*

Ephesians 4:8-9 indicates that Christ, between His death and resurrection, delivered from Hades a captivity detained therein. The verses read, "Therefore it says, 'WHEN HE ASCENDED ON HIGH, HE LED CAPTIVE A HOST OF CAPTIVES, AND HE GAVE GIFTS TO MEN.' (Now this *expression*, 'He ascended,' what does it mean except that He also had descended into the lower parts of the earth?)"

- None deny that the place to which the Lord "ascended on high," leading "captivity captive," was Heaven. This ascension took place on the day of the resurrection. (Compare John 20:17, where Jesus said, "Stop clinging to Me, for I have not yet ascended to My Father" and Matthew 28:9, where the women "came up and took hold of His feet." These verses suggest Jesus ascended to the Father and returned in the time between the appearance to Mary Magdalene and the appearance to the women who were on their way back to Bethany).
- In point IIIA, it was noted that the "lower parts of the earth" and "Hades" are synonymous terms. It was evidently while He was in Hades that Peter records that Christ "went and preached to the spirits in prison" (1 Peter 3:19).
- The "captivity" which our Lord delivered from Hades and took with Him to Heaven consisted of the righteous dead. Based on Scriptural usage elsewhere, it seems that the phrase "led captivity captive" has reference to the deliverance of captured friends. Compare Judges 4:16 with Judges 5:12. The first declares that Barak took no prisoners; he annihilated the enemy. So the captivity that Barak led (5:12) must have been Israelites that he had delivered from the enemy – Israelites who had, previous to their deliverance, been captured by the enemy. See also Psalm 68:18.

This, then, is the Scripturally suggested interpretation of Ephesians 4:8, 9 – after His death, Christ descended into Hades, and then ascended into Heaven, leading a multitude of the souls of the righteous whom He had delivered (i.e., captured) from captivity.

Since the souls of the righteous were delivered from Hades by Christ after His death, it stands that Hades no longer has two compartments.

C. *Since Christ's Ascension*

Since the ascension of Christ, the souls of the wicked, and the wicked only, have been consigned to Hades. In fact, every time the word Hades is used in the New Testament following the ascension of Christ, it speaks only of the wicked. See passages such as Revelation 20:14 where Hades (and those detained therein) are cast into Hell.

That Hades now has only one compartment (that of misery) is also shown by the fact that since the ascension of Christ, the righteous, at death, go to be *with the Lord*.

- Numerous Scriptures show that Christ is presently in Heaven, at the right hand of the Father.[10]

- Numerous Scriptures also show that, now that Christ has ascended, when the righteous die they go to be with Christ. 2 Corinthians 5:8 says, "To be absent from the body and to be present with the Lord." Philippians 1:23 has "To depart and be with Christ." 2 Corinthians 12:1-4 talks about "caught up to the third heaven ... caught up into Paradise."[11] Revelation 6:9 shows that, before the judgment (verse 16), souls are under the altar.[12] The souls[13] under the altar are martyred saints, and are in Heaven while righteous men are still on the earth. 1 Thessalonians 4:14 implies that the righteous dead are with Christ, for when Christ returns He will bring the souls of the righteous dead with Him, so that they may receive their resurrection bodies.

Hades no longer has two compartments, for the righteous have been delivered from it. Paradise was the abode of the righteous in Hades until the ascension of Christ., but at the ascension it was moved to Heaven. Hades has only one compartment now. Thus, since the ascension of Christ, only the souls of the wicked have been consigned to Hades.

The Scriptures indicate that Hades (after the ascension) is a place of misery, from which the wicked are to be brought for public judgment previous to their being cast into Hell (Revelation 20:13-14, etc.).

---

[10] Acts 1:11, 3:21, 7:56; John 17:24.

[11] The Jews had three heavens: (1) *Rakiah,* the atmospheric regions around us. (2) *Shamayim,* the starry heavens. (3) *Shamayim Hashamayim,* the dwelling place of God, into which Christ ascended after His resurrection, but which is not subject to man's senses as *Rakiah* and *Shamayim* are. Paul can speak of "Paradise" and "the third heaven" as being one and the same since, when Paul's experience took place, Paradise had been moved to heaven itself, out of Hades.

[12] The account of the Seer does not actually say so, but one's impression is that the altar is very near the throne on which God is sitting.

[13] There is no disagreement between this note and one given earlier. The intimation of Revelation 6:9 is that at death the righteous go to Heaven, but are disembodied *spirits.* The word "souls" has as one of its six various meanings, "disembodied spirit, the soul freed from the body, a disembodied soul." Revelation 6 pictures the disembodied souls in heaven while saints were still on the earth.

CONCLUSION

Hades is a place in the unseen world distinct from Heaven and Hell. Before the ascension of Christ, Hades had two compartments – one of comfort, the other of misery — to which the souls of all who died were carried. At His death, Christ descended to Hades, delivering the souls of the righteous. Since the ascension of Christ, the souls of the wicked, and the wicked only, have been consigned to Hades, in which they are reserved in misery against the day of general judgment. At the final judgment, the wicked will be brought forth from Hades for public judgment previous to their being cast into Hell.

Since the ascension of Christ, the righteous at death go to be with the Lord in Heaven, but do not enjoy all the bliss they shall have after the Lord returns, for until His return, they are disembodied spirits. Once Christ has returned, and the righteous have received their resurrection bodies, then they will, upon their return to Heaven, be able to enjoy Heaven to its fullest.

Some object to the conclusion that the righteous dead now go to be with Christ in Heaven, and that the wicked are in Hades (ultimately to be cast into Hell), since this seems, in their thinking, to do away with any need for a final judgment. However, the Bible never did teach that the purpose of the final judgment was to determine where eternity would be spent. Luke 16:19ff indicates that a person knows his eternal destiny the moment he dies! The final judgment then is "the final vindication of God for the rewards and penalties already in part bestowed." That is, the purpose of the final judgment is to determine *why* one is to spend eternity where he does, and to show that God is absolutely just in His dealings with each individual.

The chart on the next page is intended to help visualize what has been set forth in this Special Study.

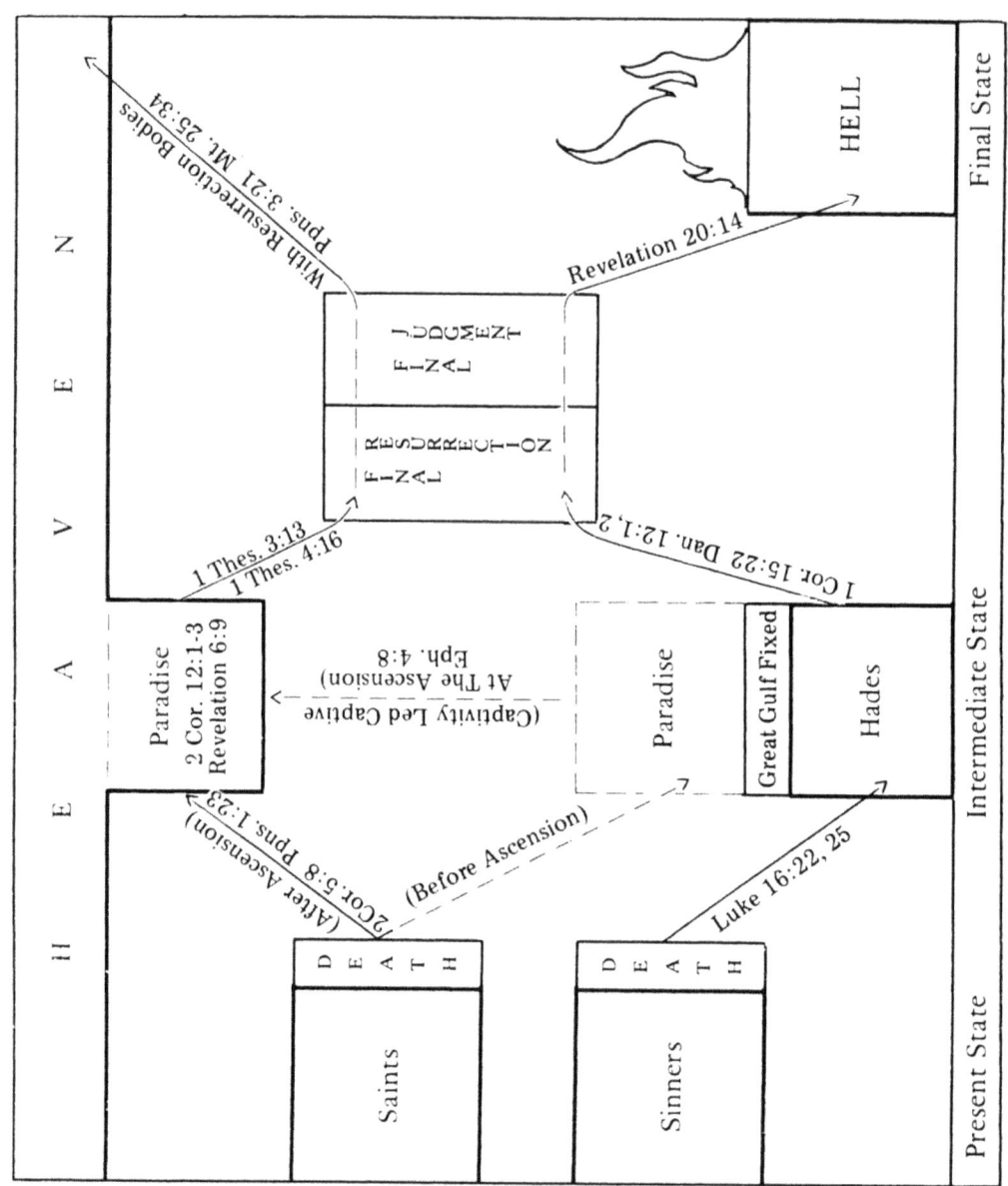

SPECIAL STUDY #8

WHAT IS REPENTANCE?

This study will examine repentance from four different angles. Repentance is individual, inclusive, indispensable. What does repentance involve? How is repentance brought about? What are the results of repentance?

I. REPENTANCE IS INDIVIDUAL, INCLUSIVE, AND INDISPENSABLE

A. *Repentance is individual.*

"Except ye repent," said Jesus.[1] "Repent and be baptized every one of you," said Peter.[2] Repentance cannot be done by proxy; it is something each individual must do for himself. No parent can repent for his children. No priest can repent for his people. Repentance is individual.

We may overlook our need for repentance because we sometimes think our sins are not so great as those committed by others. In Luke 13:1-5, Jesus clearly points out this fact. Some people had informed him of the terrible sins committed by the Galileans whose blood Pilate had mingled with their sacrifices. But Jesus declared, "You need not think that these Galileans were sinners above all Galileans. You must repent of your sins or you will perish." Just because you think your sins are not as great as others does not excuse you of your need to repent. The eighteen who were killed when the tower of Siloam fell upon them were offenders, but the Lord implied they were not sinners above all those who dwelt in Jerusalem. Some no doubt thought that since they had not done as badly as those offenders, that they were all right and did not need to repent. But that was a mistake. Jesus declared, "Except you repent, you shall likewise perish."

We sometimes think, "My sins are little sins, but yours are big sins." Your sins are so big (as I view them), and mine are so little, I overlook my need of repentance. I think, "You are the one who needs to repent; not I." While some sins are more grievous than others, the Bible does not speak of big sins and little sins as far as person's need for repentance is concerned.

Every man must repent of his own sins, regardless of what others' sins might be. Repentance is individual.

B. *Repentance is inclusive.*

---

[1] Luke 13:3.

[2] Acts 2:38.

"God commands all men everywhere to repent" (Acts 17:30). There is no exception. ALL MEN EVERYWHERE are to repent. God has commanded it. Repent or perish!

We have all sinned and come short of the glory of God. A part of the remedy for sin is genuine repentance. There is no use in stewing around in fuming futility. There is little value in seeking escape through consultations with psychiatrists, unless we are ready to repent. All must repent. Repentance is inclusive.

C. *Repentance is indispensable.*

Repentance is a MUST; it is a necessity. God commands every man to repent. Repentance is essential to salvation (Acts 2:38). Individuals have no choice. When God has commanded, we each must do it, or perish!

II. WHAT DOES REPENTANCE INVOLVE?

Since it is imperative that every individual repent of his sins, it is needful that we each know what repentance is. Biblical repentance involves three things: a change of intellect, a change of emotions, and a change of will.

A. *Repentance involves a change of intellect.*

Repentance includes a knowledge of our personal sinfulness – a conviction of personal sins committed. This is the change of intellect. When Isaiah was convicted of his sins, he said, "Woe is me ... I am a man of unclean lips" (Isaiah 6:5). When Job was convinced that he was a sinner, he said, "I abhor myself" (Job 42:6). When Peter was convicted of his sins, he said, "I am a sinful man" (Luke 5:8). When Paul was convicted of his sins, he called himself "the chief of sinners" (1 Timothy 1:15). We must be aware that death awaits us if we continue in our sins. "The wages of sin is death" (Romans 6:23). We must also be aware that we cannot help ourselves. All the good deeds and acts of morality we do will not rid us of the fact that we have sinned.

Repentance includes a change of intellect. Where once we ignored our sins, now we must be acutely aware of them.

B. *Repentance involves a change of emotions.*

There must be a Godly sorrow because we have broken the laws of our loving Father. There is a difference between Godly sorrow and worldly sorrow. Paul wrote, "Godly sorrow produces a repentance without regret, *leading* to salvation; but the sorrow of the world produces death" (2 Corinthians 7:10). Godly sorrow leads to repentance; worldly sorrow leads to death.

An illustration of the difference between Godly sorrow and worldly sorrow would be this. Suppose that while I am visiting your home, I find your wallet and remove from it a $10 bill. Soon the visit is over and I go home. Soon I receive a letter from you saying you saw me take the $10, and would I please return it. Would I be sorry? Well, I might only be sorry that I was caught. That is worldly sorrow. The jails and penitentiaries are full of people with worldly sorrow. Yes, they are very sorry, but sorry they were caught. Now let's think of Godly sorrow. Suppose I had taken the $10 from the wallet; later, after I was home, I begin to think of the evil I had done to my friend. I become very sorry for what I did. Finally, my sorrow leads to repentance. I write you a letter explaining that I stole the $10 and am very sorry. I return the $10. I ask your forgiveness. That would be Godly sorrow – a sorrow that leads to repentance.

Repentance includes a change of emotions. Where I once thought nothing of stealing the $10, now I am sorry I wronged a friend. Where once I thought nothing of sinning against my God, now I am sorry I have wronged Him.

C. *Repentance involves a change of will.*

It is when we come to the will that we find the very heart of repentance. Included in Biblical repentance is a determination to forsake sin. This must be a whole-hearted decision to forsake sin. We must love the Lord our God with our whole heart, soul, mind, and strength. This attitude to forsake sin will be a day-by-day series of decisions. "He said unto them, 'If any man would come after me. let him deny himself, and take up his cross daily and follow me'" (Luke 9:23).

Biblical repentance includes a change of the will — a whole-hearted decision and determination to forsake sin.

III. HOW DOES REPENTANCE COME ABOUT?

A. *The Holy Spirit in involved.*

It is the work of the Holy Spirit to bring about this repentance. It is the Holy Spirit who convicts the world of sin, righteousness, and judgment (John 16:7-11). It is the Holy Spirit working through the preached and written Word (Luke 24:45-47; Matthew 12:41; Jonah 3:1-10).

B. *Godly sorrow leads to repentance.*

Godly sorrow *leads to* repentance. That is why Paul wrote, "Godly sorrow produces a repentance leading to salvation." Note, Godly sorrow and repentance are not equated.

The most prevalent conception of repentance is godly sorrow for sin; but according to Paul, godly sorrow for sin stands related to repentance as cause to effect. "Godly sorrow," he says, "worketh repentance unto salvation, a repentance which bringeth no regret." He says further to the Corinthians, "Now I rejoice, not that ye were made sorry, but that ye were made sorry unto repentance," (2 Corinthians 7:8-10). These remarks show that it is godly sorrow that brings men to repentance; and the last implies that there may be sorrow for sin without repentance. The same distinction is implied in commanding those on Pentecost who were already "pricked in heart" to repent. It is illustrated in the case of Judas, who experienced the most intense sorrow for sin; but instead of working repentance, it drove him to suicide.[3]

We hear the Gospel, and we believe what we hear about God and His love to us. With Godly sorrow, we are sorry we have offended Him, and we determine to forsake the ways of sin.

    C. *The goodness of God is involved.*

The goodness of God leads us to repentance. Romans 2:4 throws light on the subject of how repentance is brought about: "Do you think lightly of the riches of His kindness and forbearance and patience, not knowing that the kindness of God leads you to repentance?" The goodness of God includes everything God has done for us: life, friends, loved ones, food, clothing, opportunities for every material progress, and best of all, His only begotten Son.

O, how good and patient, kind and loving, our Heavenly Father has been! O, how that goodness should melt our stony hearts. With what earnestness we should all cease our evil ways. The goodness of God leads us to repentance.

    D. *The thought of promised judgment is involved.*

The thought of promised judgment also leads us to repent. "Having overlooked the times of ignorance, God is now declaring to men that all everywhere should repent, because He has fixed a day in which He will judge the world in righteousness through a Man whom He has appointed, having furnished proof to all men by raising Him from the dead" (Acts 17:30-31). Because we have no desire to go to Hell, the thought of the approaching judgment leads us to repentance.

This repentance that is so needed by us all – this change of intellect, emotion, and will – is brought about by the work of the Holy Spirit through the Word, Godly sorrow, the goodness of God, and the thought of the approaching judgment.

IV. WHAT ARE THE RESULTS OF REPENTANCE?

Repentance brings a hatred of sin in my life. "Thou hast loved righteousness, and hated iniquity" (Hebrews 11:8). "Hating even the garment spotted by the flesh" (Jude 23).

Repentance brings us to the place we no longer want to live in sin. There is not one verse of Scripture that indicates that we can be a Christian and yet live any kind of life we want to. We have the warning from Christ that He will not receive us into His kingdom until we are ready to give up all – until we are ready to turn from all sin in our lives. Half-

---

[3] McGarvey, *op. cit.*, p.59.

way repentance is no repentance at all! We cannot say, "I'll give up some of my sins, and hang on to others." Jesus demands complete surrender. When that is accomplished – when we are determined to renounce and forsake sin and yield all to Christ – we have gone a long way towards finding peace with God.

Repentance also brings joy in heaven. After telling the parables of the lost sheep, the lost coin, and the lost son, Jesus emphasized the point of all three by saying, "I say unto you, there is joy in the presence of the angels of God over one sinner that repents" (Luke 15:10).

CONCLUSION

Repentance is individual, inclusive, and indispensable. It is a change of intellect, emotion, and will. It is brought about by the work of the Holy Spirit, a Godly sorrow, the goodness of God, and the thought of the approaching judgment. Repentance brings a hatred of sin, no longer living in sin, and joy in heaven among the angels.

Note, repentance itself is not forgiveness. Many honest people have believed that because they have repented of their sins, they were forgiven of their sins. This is not necessarily true. Repentance is a change of a person's own heart. Forgiveness is something that takes place in the mind of him who was offended. Remember the illustration about the $10: I stole it, thus offending you. I repented of my offense, and asked for your forgiveness. You may or may not forgive me, as you see fit. Repentance is not forgiveness. Man has sinned against God, and must repent and seek God's forgiveness. But we must remember that repentance is not forgiveness; it is a condition of forgiveness.

Repentance leads us to confess before men that Christ is God's son, and that we wish Him to be our Savior. Repentance leads us to be baptized for the remission of our sins.

J. The Lame Man Healed. 3:1-11

3:1 – *Now Peter and John were going up to the temple at the ninth hour, the hour of prayer.*

Now Peter and John. How much time has passed since Pentecost? No hint is given, but we may presume some weeks or months have passed. Through those days we may suppose the evangelistic work of the apostles was little opposed. With the introduction of the healing of the lame man, Luke now records a series of conflicts and opposition related to the spread of the gospel.

We often find Peter and John associated together. They have evidently been friends from their youth upward. They had been partners as fishermen on the Sea of Galilee before Jesus called them.[1] They had been sharers in looking for the consolation of Israel, and had together been baptized by John the Baptist.[2] The brothers James and John are associated with Peter in the inner circle of Jesus' disciples at the transfiguration, at the raising of Jairus' daughter, and at the agony in the garden.[3] They had been sent together to prepare the Passover meal the night Jesus instituted the Lord's Supper.[4] Later that night, John took Peter into the palace of the High Priest, where Jesus had been taken for trial after His arrest.[5] It was Peter and John who ran together to the tomb on the resurrection morning.[6] These two were in the group fishing together after the resurrection.[7] After the account here in Acts 3, they will together be involved in the mission to Samaria,[8] and in recognizing the work that had been done among the Gentiles by Paul and Barnabas.[9] When it was that they parted, never to meet again on this earth, we have no record.

Were going up to the temple. The temple area, including its various courts and buildings and porches, looked something like the chart on the next page.[10] Note the locations of such features as the Beautiful Gate, Solomon's Porch, the Court of the Gentiles, the Court of the Women, the Court of Israel, the Court of the Priests, the Holy Place, and the Holy of Holies.

There were no church buildings as yet. Christians continued to worship in the temple area and to meet in the synagogues along with the Jews, and in the homes of individual

---

[1] Luke 5:10.

[2] John 1:41.

[3] Matthew 17:1; Mark 5:37; Matthew 26:37.

[4] Luke 22:8.

[5] John 18:16.

[6] John 20:3.

[7] John 21:7. There may at times have been passing rivalries between Peter and John, especially at those times when there were disputes among the disciples as to who was the greatest (Matthew 20:20; Mark 10.35). But the idea maintained by Renan (*Vie de Jesus*, Introduction) that John wrote his Gospel to exalt himself at the expense of Peter must take its place among the *delirantium sommia,* the morbid imaginations, of inventive interpretation.

[8] Acts 8:14.

[9] Galatians 2:9.

[10] Emil G. Kraeling, *Rand McNally Bible Atlas* (New York: Rand McNally Co., 1956), p.400.

members. In fact, through most of the pages of the New Testament, meetings take place in members' homes. The first church buildings were not constructed until after AD 125, at Edessa and Arbella, towns east of Damascus.[11]

Why were the apostles going to the temple? Were they going in order to keep the requirements of the Old Testament Law? Acts 2:46 and Luke 24:53 indicate the followers of Christ continually went up to the temple at the hours of prayer. Keeping such Old Testament elements of worship apparently was not wrong; it was merely no longer a necessity since Christ, the final sacrifice, had been sacrificed. However, this continual conformity to the Jewish ritual was favorable to the success of apostolic teaching. The Jerusalem Conference (Acts 15) indicates that "circumcision" (and the keeping of other parts of the Law of Moses which were not reiterated in the teaching of Christ) was now in the realm of Christian liberty. At the temple, during the hours of prayer, the apostles would find a ready-made audience to whom they might preach, and preach they did, in addition to their own worship and prayers.

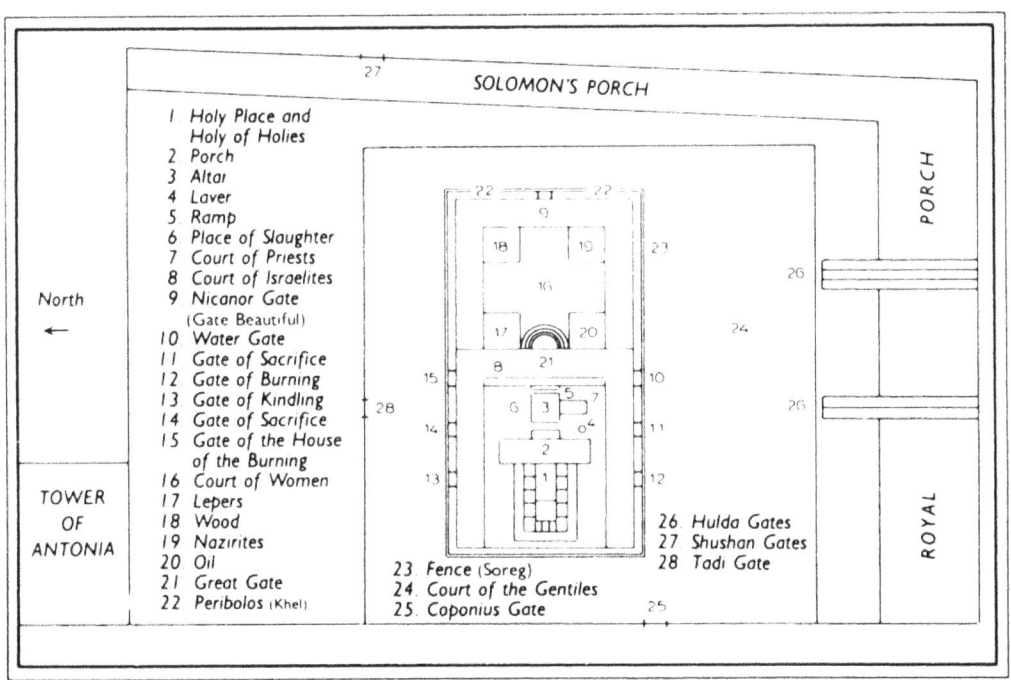

At the ninth *hour*, the hour of prayer. The notes at Acts 2:15 introduce the Jewish method of counting time. The ninth hour would be roughly equivalent to 3 p.m. our time. The traditions of the Jews (rather than any specific Old Testament commandment) had fixed the third, the sixth, and the ninth hours as times for private prayer. Daniel's practice of praying three times a day[12] seems to imply that the practice was prevalent in his day, and Psalm 55:17 ("evening and morning and noon will I pray") carries the practice as far

---

[11] Compare notes at Acts 11:26.

[12] Daniel 6:10.

back as the time of David. "Seven times a day" for prayer was, perhaps, the rule of those who aimed at a life of higher devotion.[13] Both practices passed into the usage of the Christian Church, early in her history. The three hours were observed by many at Alexandria in the time of Clement.[14] The seven became the "canonical hours" of the Western church during the time of Benedict (AD 542). The ninth hour was the time of the evening sacrifice, and the temple would be thronged with people.[15]

3:2 – *And a certain man who had been lame from his mother's womb was being carried along, whom they used to set down every day at the gate of the temple which is called Beautiful, in order to beg alms of those who were entering the temple.*

And a certain man who had been lame from his mother's womb. This person had been lame from birth. There was no deception here; this was not one of those pseudo-"miracles" where a person with an imaginary or psychosomatic ailment is "cured." It truly was a miracle. For over 40 years the man had been lame, having been born with some malformation of his ankles and feet.[16]

Was being carried along. The only way the lame man could get where he wished to go was to have his friends carry him. Many commentators suggest that the tense of the Greek verb indicates that he was in the process of being carried to his usual place of begging when this miracle was performed.

Whom they used to set down every day at the gate of the temple which is called Beautiful. Since he was there daily, the lame man would be well known to the people who were entering the temple. He had been placed at the gate for many years.

In the first centuries there were no hospitals for the sick, and no homes for the poor or the aged. The poor were dependent on the charity of those who were in better circumstances. It thus became an important matter for the poor to be placed where they would see many people. Hence, it was customary to place them at the gates of rich men, or they sat by the side of the highway to beg where many persons would pass.[17]

Many attempts have been made to identify which gate it was that Luke calls "Beautiful." No gate of this name is mentioned by any other writer whose works are extant; therefore, it is difficult to be sure about the identification of the gate. The weight of available evidence is in favor of identifying it with the gate called Nicanor in the Mishna,[18] a gate which led from the Court of the Gentiles into the Court of the Women. Josephus describes the Nicanor Gate as made of Corinthian bronze,[19] and it was adorned with silver

---

[13] Psalm 119:164.

[14] *Stromata*, VII, p.722.

[15] Exodus 29:41; Numbers 28:3-4.

[16] Acts 4:22.

[17] Luke 16:20; Mark 10:46; Luke 18:35; John 9:1-8.

[18] *Middoth*, II.3.

[19] *Wars*, V.5.3.

and gold plates. 75 feet high and 60 feet wide, it was located on the east where the sunlight presented a bright reflection to the constant crowds entering for worship.[20]

In order to beg aims of those who were entering the temple. Alms would be charity in the form of gifts of money. The entrance of the Court of Women would be an ideal place for begging. Women are often more likely to show compassion than men, and people going to worship might tend to be more liberal than when going about their everyday tasks.

3:3 – *And when he saw Peter and John about to go into the temple, he began asking to receive alms.*

And when he saw Peter and John. Perhaps this lame man knew Peter and John. He had been placed at this gate for many years. He might have seen Jesus and His disciples enter the temple many times.

About to go into the temple, he *began* asking to receive aims. "To receive alms" is another way of saying that, being lame, he was asking for gifts of charity.

3:4 – *And Peter, along with John, fixed his gaze upon him and said, "Look at us!"*

And Peter, along with John, fixed his gaze upon him and said. The word means to fix attention on, to look intently at; it is the same word used at Acts 1:10. The typical thing is to turn the head away or avert the eyes when passing a beggar, and not look at him. However, Peter seems to be a man of compassion. It is doubtful that the language implies, as some have thought, that Peter is looking on the man's heart by miraculous insight to see if he is worthy of healing.

Look at us. Peter wants the man's undivided attention. What was Peter doing? Was he raising the man's hopes? If the man knew Peter and John, was Peter trying to produce hope on the part of the lame man?

3:5 – *And he began to give them his attention, expecting to receive something from them.*

And he *began* to give them his attention. This is an imperfect tense verb, implying the man kept giving heed to Peter and John. The man followed the instructions he had been given.

---

[20] The Nicanor Gate identification seems more satisfactory than to identify the "Beautiful Gate" with the Shushan Gate that led from the Court of the Women into the Court of Israel, or with the Hulda Gate that led from the Court of the Gentiles into the Valley of Kidron (the gate now called the Golden Gate).

The whole dispute arises from a seeming contradiction in Josephus, whose writings give one of the two extant descriptions of Herod's temple. In *Wars*, V.5.3, Josephus says distinctly that there were ten gates – four on the north, four on the south, and two on the east. In *Antiquities*, XV.11, he says there were seven gates – three on the north, three on the south, and one on the east. These accounts are not easy to harmonize, but it seems probable that there were two gates on the east side – one the beautiful and costly Nicanor Gate, of Corinthian bronze, between the Court of Women and the Court of the Gentiles; the other (Shushan) a greater gate between the Court of Women and the Court of Israel. Shushan is described as 87 feet high, covered with lilies in high relief. The Hulda Gate is also identified by some as being the "Beautiful Gate." But Hulda, on the south side of the temple compound, does not seem as likely a location.

Expecting to receive something from them. People who looked away as they passed the beggar, he must have long ago learned, were people from whom he would receive no alms. People whose eyes met his were people who would be helpful. Since he has been asking for money, and since God had instructed Israel to care for the poor,[21] he undoubtedly thought he would receive money from these two men who had stopped where he was sitting. And if he recognized Peter and John as followers of the Christ who had worked miracles, maybe his hope, too, was kindled.

3:6 – *But Peter said, "I do not possess silver and gold, but what I do have I give to you: In the name of Jesus Christ the Nazarene – walk!"*

And Peter said, "I do not possess silver and gold. The narrative of Acts 2:45 shows that the apostles were treasurers and stewards of the sums of money committed to their charge by the generous self-denial of the Christians. What then do Peter's words mean? It may be that the words mean that they had no money with them at the time. It may be that the words mean that Peter did not regard the common fund as available for cases of charity to unbelievers (assuming the lame man was an unbeliever). Or, putting Peter's whole answer together with the man's request, Peter could be saying that he did not have money to keep him in his present condition, but he did have something to get him out of his present condition.

But what I do have I give to you. This does not say that Peter originated the power to heal. It is not a case of Peter, by his own power, working the miracle. The miracle was worked through Peter. That which Peter had to give was more valuable than all the silver and gold which, had he been carrying it with him, he might have given to the lame man.

In the name of Jesus Christ the Nazarene – walk! The expression "in the name of" means "by the authority of" or "by virtue of the power derived from Him." We were told in Acts 2:43 that many signs and wonders were done by the hands of the apostles. This miracle is selected from among the many because it brought the apostles into conflict with the authorities. Opposition and persecution started at this time; as Jesus predicted, this was a continuation of the opposition that had been raised against Him. The Greek word "Walk!" is *peripateō*, and literally means "walk around." To be able to do this would be evidence of a great miracle, and also would be an evidence credentialing Peter and John as messengers of God. As the man who used to be lame continued to walk around in obedience to this command he would continue to draw more attention.

3:7 – *And seizing him by the right hand, he raised him up; and immediately his feet and his ankles were strengthened.*

And seizing him by the right hand. The NASB translation seems to have a connotation of forceful action on Peter's part, as though Peter had to pull the man up before he would even attempt to walk. The same word is used of catching fish, in which case it would picture enough force to overcome the resistance the fish put up to being taken. However,

---

[21] Leviticus 14:21, 19:10, 23:22; Deuteronomy 15:4.

it is possible the word only pictures Peter's offer of his hand to help the lame man up. When the lame man makes his effort to respond, right at that moment he is healed! Peter was following the example he had seen in Jesus when He had healed his mother-in-law.[22]

He raised him up. As Peter helped him up, the miracle was performed.

And immediately his feet and his ankles were strengthened. Note that miracles in the New Testament are instantaneous. Luke the physician tells us the exact cause of the trouble. The long unused muscles and tissues were now firm and vigorous and usable.

3:8 – *And with a leap, he stood upright and* **began** *to walk; and he entered the temple with them, walking and leaping and praising God.*

And with a leap, he stood upright and *began* **to walk.** The first word is a present middle participle. He was leaping up and down repeatedly. This would be the natural expression resulting from his joy at being healed. The verb "walk" is in the imperfect tense. He continued to walk around, just as he had been commanded to do.

And he entered the temple with them. The man had been healed as he was being carried to his place by the gate. Now that he is healed, he went on in with Peter and John to offer his praise to God.

Walking and leaping and praising God. The man kept repeating the new physical actions, things he had never done. That he should give praise to God was natural and appropriate, and expressed his joy to God. Does this not show some faith on the part of the man? He is not bubbling over with enthusiasm and thanks to the apostles. Rather, he is directing his praises and thanks in the proper direction, to God!

3:9 – *And all the people saw him walking and praising God;*

And all the people saw him walking and praising God. This was the hour of prayer in the afternoon. We can imagine the usual silence of the worshipers being rather surprisingly interrupted by the leaping and cries of praise to God from this one who for so long had been lame. Perhaps we might picture the worshipers coming into the temple quietly, reverently – and then into their midst comes this man shouting at the top of his voice and leaping about? He would be seen and noticed!

3:10 – *and they were taking note of him as being the one who used to sit at the Beautiful Gate of the temple to* **beg** *alms, and they were filled with wonder and amazement at what had happened to him.*

And they were taking note of him as being the one who used to sit at the Beautiful Gate of the temple. The word "take note" (*epiginōskō*) speaks of the kind of knowledge that comes by experience. Out of their past experience, the witnesses of this event knew that this was the very same man who for years sat lame, begging from them as they came

---

[22] Mark 1:31.

through the Gate Beautiful. This matter of identification will be important later on. The Sanhedrin could not deny that a healing had taken place because the people had seen him. This very man for years was lame, and now was walking.

To *beg* alms. The Greek has "to beg *the* alms." The article seems to be the article of previous reference, reminding us of what Luke has already recorded in verse 2.

And they were filled with wonder and amazement at what had happened to him. The word "wonder" is a word that denotes "shock." They were shocked to see this man, who for many years had been a cripple, now walking and leaping all through the temple area. The word translated "amazement" denotes "astonishment." They were astonished at what had happened to him, the kind of astonishment that arises when something never before seen now is so evident and actual and undeniable.

3:11 – And while he was clinging to Peter and John, all the people ran together to them at the so-called portico of Solomon, full of amazement.

And while he was clinging to Peter and John. Before this, the verses have pictured the man as continually walking and leaping and praising God as he was on his way into the temple. Now he is pictured as walking with Peter and John, holding on to them, perhaps with his arms linked in theirs. It evidently describes all three men as leaving the temple after they have finished their worship inside. By walking arm in arm with the apostles the man would be letting all know to whom he was indebted for his great blessing. He has offered praise to God for his healing, but he also is thankful to Peter and John through whom the miracle was worked.

All the people ran together to them. The apostles and the healed man, after worshiping in the temple, emerged (probably through the Beautiful Gate) into the Court of the Gentiles, and made their way toward the east side. The fact of the cure and the conduct of the man would soon tend to draw a crowd together, and this in turn produced a favorable opportunity to preach the gospel. A huge crowd of people who had come for the afternoon prayer now gather around the three men as they approached Solomon's porch.

At the so-called portico of Solomon. Along the whole eastern side of the temple enclosure was a porch, or roof, extending from the top of the wall back into the temple area. This roof was held up by two rows of columns, 37 feet high. The whole porch was 60 feet wide.[23] This covered porch would provide protection for the worshipers during the rainy season and shade during the hot summer months. Jesus had taught here the year or so before at the Feast of Dedication,[24] and this porch evidently became a regular meeting place for the Jerusalem Christians.[25] It was called "Solomon's Porch" because, when the temple was rebuilt by Zerubbabel, fragments of Solomon's temple were used in the construction

---

[23] As a comparison, the Royal Porch across the southern end of the temple area was 90 feet wide.

[24] John 10:23. The date of Jesus' teaching in this porch at the Feast of Dedication was AD 29. It thus has been one or two years ago, as the text suggests.

[25] Acts 5:12.

of this porch. The Jewish people later tried to persuade Herod Agrippa I to pull it down and rebuild it, but he shrank from the risk and cost of such an undertaking.[26]

Full of amazement. Even though they have had some time to reflect on the cause behind the lame man's recent miraculous healing, the people still are struggling in their minds to explain what has happened to him.

K. Peter's Second Sermon. 3:12-26

3:12 – *But when Peter saw this, he replied to the people, "Men of Israel, why do you marvel at this, or why do you gaze at us, as if by our own power or piety we had made him walk?*

But when Peter saw this, he replied to the people. Peter sees the crowd of people assembling, and sees that they still are at a loss to explain the source of the miracle, or the reason for it, and so Peter "replies" to the questions that seem to have been in everyone's mind. The word "replied" (also translated "answered" when it appears elsewhere in the New Testament) is used in modern narrative for a response to a question that has been asked, although there apparently had been no questions directed to Peter on this occasion. Rather, Peter is responding to the questions he sees in their minds and expressions to each other, as in amazement they continue to stare at the man now healed.

Men of Israel. "Jews, listen to me!" Cf. 2:14. Again, Luke apparently has not given all of Peter's sermon. What we have is likely only a brief outline. The chief points of emphasis in this message are: (1) the miracle was the work of God to glorify Jesus; (2) the Jews denied Jesus from ignorance; (3) Jesus fulfilled the Old Testament prophecies; (4) therefore, they should repent and be saved through the gospel.

Why do you marvel at this? The ASV reads "at this man?" though there is no word for "man" in the Greek; still, yet many Bible students believe Peter pointed to the healed man standing there with them as he spoke. The NASB, which omits "man," is a translation which represents the interpreters' idea that Peter is speaking of the miracle itself, rather than the healed man. Jews were sufficiently acquainted with miracles to interpret them, and to know whence they came. Peter intimates they should have understood it better. The people ought not have been thinking so much about *how* did it happen, but ought to have been asking *why* God had performed the miracle.

Or why do you gaze at us. Peter includes John in the "us." He is telling them to look to God at once. 'You ought to know that we did not do this,' he says. 'The miracle could be done only by God.'

As if by our own power or piety we had made him walk? "Power" is a word sometimes used of "miracles," and "piety" implies that a man is careful lest he fail either in his duties to God or in his duties to his fellow men. The miracle was not done because Peter and John

---

[26] Josephus. *Antiquities*, XX.9.7.

themselves had such powers as their own peculiar possession, or because they were eminently pious and holy men. Don't give credit to Peter and John for the deed. It was God who worked the miracle!

3:13 – *"The God of Abraham, Isaac, and Jacob, the God of our fathers, has glorified His servant Jesus,* **the one** *whom you delivered up, and disowned in the presence of Pilate, when he had decided to release Him.*

The God of Abraham, Isaac, and Jacob, the God of our fathers. Peter is here making his first point. The miracle was the work of God to glorify Jesus. It was the very same God the Patriarchs had known and worshiped. It was important to show that it was the same God that the Old Testament Scriptures spoke about. The apostles were not introducing any new religion ("new" in the sense that it was different from what had been predicted in the Old Testament).

Has glorified His Servant Jesus. The Greek word *pais* may be translated either "child" or "servant." Here it would seem that there is an allusion to the Suffering Servant poems of the Old Testament, especially Isaiah 42:1ff, 52:13ff, etc. Peter is saying that God did this miracle so that Jesus might be honored (glorified).

***The one* whom you delivered up, and disowned in the presence of Pilate.** Jesus was delivered up to the Romans, who put Him to death. That Peter could say "you" delivered Jesus implies that in his audience were some of the very men who had been present at Jesus' trials and who had cried out, "Crucify! Crucify Him!" That same crowd had rejected Jesus, affirming He could not be their king, for they had no king but Caesar.[27]

When he had decided to release Him. There were two different trials before Pilate, with a hearing before Herod Antipas in between. During the early stages of his investigation, Pilate clearly tried to defend Jesus' innocence. According to Luke 23:16-20, Pilate had indeed determined he would release Jesus because of His lack of guilt in the charges placed against Him. But Pilate was a man who could be swayed by the wishes of the people he ruled, and after the multitude had been persuaded by the rulers of the Jews to ask Pilate to release Barabbas and crucify Jesus, Pilate acceded to the popular clamor.[28]

3:14 – *"But you disowned the Holy and Righteous One, and asked for a murderer to be granted to you,*

But you disowned the Holy and Righteous One. As he did in his previously recorded sermon, Peter compares what wicked men did to Jesus with what God did to Him.[29] The words "Holy One" would have caused a Jewish hearer to immediately think of the Messiah.[30] And Jesus was "righteous" in that He was innocent, one who was free from any

---

[27] John 19:15.

[28] Matthew 27:20; Mark 15:11-14.

[29] Compare Peter's statements at Acts 2:36.

[30] Psalm 16:10 and Isaiah 43:3 use "Holy One" in a Messianic context.

of the crimes the persecutors claimed He was guilty of. They had charged Him with blasphemy during His trial before the Sanhedrin,[31] and they charged Him with sedition during His trial before Pilate,[32] but neither of the charges could be proved.

And asked for a murderer to be granted to you. The reference is to Barabbas, a terrorist and murderer, whom Pilate had suggested along with Jesus as being one of two possible prisoners who would be released at Passover.[33] Pilate likely believed they would ask for Jesus' release since people could be expected to want the miracle-working Good Man released rather than the murdering revolutionary. Pilate, however, had failed to realize what this mob (persuaded by the religious leaders) would do.

3:15 – *"but put to death the Prince of life,* **the one** *whom God raised from the dead,* **a fact** *to which we are witnesses.*

But put to death the Prince of life. *Archēgon* is a word capable of several different meanings. It may be translated "prince" or "leader" (as is done in the KJV of Hebrews 2:10) when the context suggests the idea is one of authority over something. It may be translated "author" (as is done in the ASV of Hebrews 2:10, 12:2) when the translator believes the context is speaking of the source or origin of something. So when the translator comes to this word *archēgon*, he must determine whether Jesus is pictured as the One having dominion over life ("captain of salvation," "prince of life") or whether He is pictured as the one who is the source of life ("author of salvation," "author of life"). Perhaps here the latter idea is best, as if Peter were saying Jesus is the source from which life and salvation flow.

"Life" could be physical or spiritual life, or both. This is quite a contrast that Peter gives. They had killed the author of their own lives. Think of it – to have killed the giver of life! Some have objected to Peter's doctrine here since the Bible affirms that Jesus willingly gave His life as a ransom for men. If He gave his life, how can Peter claim here that they killed Him? Peter is speaking of what was in their hearts; it was their intention to kill Him. What they did would have killed an ordinary man, but Jesus died only when He was ready to.

The one whom God raised from the dead. The fact of the resurrection of Jesus was the cardinal point emphasized in sermon after sermon. It is the thing that makes Christianity unique among the religions of the world.

Notice carefully, "YOU" is emphatic in the Greek. The sentence reads something like this: 'God glorified Jesus; YOU delivered Him up.' 'Pilate determined to release Him; YOU denied Him.' 'He was holy and just; YOU preferred a murderer.' 'He was the author of life; YOU killed Him.'
- Peter says, "You betrayed Him, but God glorified Him." Peter has already identified the God of whom he speaks as "the God of our fathers." It is the very God the crowd

---

[31] Matthew 26:65.

[32] Luke 23:2.

[33] Matthew 27:21; Mark 15:7; Luke 23:12.

- claims to be worshiping. *You have worked in opposition to the God whom you worship.*
- Peter says, "Pilate determined to release Him, but you disowned Him." Not only did you deliver Him up, but you disowned Him in the face of Pilate when that man was determined to release Him. You are not only in opposition to the God you claim to worship, *you are also in opposition to the state that is over you.*
- Peter says, "You denied the holy and righteous One and asked for a murderer to be granted to you." He was not only the Messiah, but He was an innocent man. They demanded the release of one everyone knew was guilty of great crimes. *They were opposing morality and justice* when they demanded the release of a man they knew was a murderer.
- Peter says, "You killed the prince of life." Here is an enigma, if ever there was one. *You are opposed to life itself because you killed the author of life.*

However, in spite of everything they did to oppose God, the state, morality and justice, and even life itself, God raised Him from the dead. From God came the source and power of His resurrection.

A fact to which we are witnesses. Here is the word "witnesses" again.[34] As proof of the resurrection, Peter and John are offering themselves as the official witnesses. The "we" is emphatic (i.e., the pronoun is stated, besides being in the personal ending of the verb form). 'We ourselves (Peter and John) are witnesses,' witnesses of His glorious resurrection. Once again, be sure to observe the historical details which are the basis for faith. Jesus was delivered up and denied, killed, and raised – these are all facts, historical facts to which the people were contemporaries and, in many cases, actual participants. Peter's audience was not confronted with mere human theories or theologies, but with historical facts! This is the gospel – there are facts to be believed as well as commands to be obeyed.

3:16 – *"And on the basis of faith in His name,* **it is** *the name of Jesus which has strengthened this man whom you see and know; and the faith which* **comes** *through Him has given him this perfect health in the presence of you all.*

And on the basis of faith in His name. Since the turn of the century a number of learned studies have been done on the words "in his name."[35] These have generally emphasized that "the name stands for the person," and often there is a contrast implied. Thus, Peter is saying, "Because of a faith in the *risen Jesus* (the name stands for the person, and pay special attention to that person in particular!), this once-lame man has been healed." Since the "faith" Peter has in mind seems not to be the saving faith that includes baptism, "on the basis of faith" is not referring to the healed man. Rather, this "faith" seems to be similar to the spiritual gift called "faith,"[36] a faith that includes the power to work miracles.[37] In

---

[34] "Witnesses" was explained in notes at Acts 2:32.

[35] Lars Hartman has a short study of "Into the name of Jesus" in *New Testament Studies,* XX, p.432-440, in which he outlines the efforts during much of the 20th century to determine the meaning of this phrase.

[36] 1 Corinthians 12:9.

[37] Matthew 17:20; 1 Corinthians 13:2.

the apostles' case, this "faith" (an ability to work miracles) appears to have been one of the results of the baptism with the Holy Spirit which they experienced on the previous Pentecost. The first use of the word "faith" in this verse speaks of something the apostles had.[38]

It is the name of Jesus which has strengthened this man whom you see and know. This is equivalent to saying "the *risen Jesus* (emphasis again) has made this once-lame man strong." Peter is declaring that the very Jesus whom they had denied and rejected and killed, the very Jesus whom God had raised from the dead – that Jesus was involved in this miracle. The power of the apostles was not the cause; Jesus was.

Peter reminds the onlookers that the healed man was known. There could be no mistake. Luke noted the man was known to them through past experience (verse 10), and Peter says they can know (*oida*, a different Greek verb than was used in verse 10) through mental perception that it is the same man. Peter's word for "see" is also notable. He uses the word *theōreō* – not just an indifferent spectator, but one who looks at a thing intently and for a purpose. Peter is saying that his audience could "inspect" this man, and see for themselves he was healed.

And the faith which *comes* through Him has given him this perfect health. While the first part of the verse made mention of a "faith" the apostles had, this part of the verse seems to speak of a faith which the lame man himself had. In almost every case of healing in the New Testament, we find the healer attempting to draw the sick person to a measure of faith before the miracle was performed. While there does *not* have to be "faith" on the part of the patient in Bible times for a miracle to be worked,[39] in this case there seems to have been. This man was healed, then, because of a miraculous faith the apostles had which enabled them work the miracle, and because of a faith the lame man had. In both cases the faith was directed toward Jesus. They apostles had faith in His power, and that He would give the power to heal. The lame man, recognizing Peter and John to be followers of the Christ, had faith in the apostles and in Jesus, for he praised God (not the apostles) for his healing.

---

[38] The idea that if our faith were strong enough we also could work miracles has no foundation in Scriptures. Do not confuse the results of the baptism of the Holy Spirit, or the reception of spiritual gifts, with the indwelling of the Holy Spirit. The effects of these different measures of the Spirit are not synonymous.

[39] Some contemporary "faith healers" (so-called) claim the reason they sometimes fail to heal is because the patient does not have enough faith. One searches almost in vain in the New Testament for such a hindrance to miracles. The fact that Jesus could do not many mighty works at Nazareth because of their unbelief (Matthew 13:58) is certainly not a parallel case to the lack of faith cited by the "faith-healer." In the case of the people of Nazareth, it was complete rejection of Jesus as Messiah, not just lack of confidence that they could be healed.

Unbelief or lack of belief on the part of the patient in the possibility of being healed was no hindrance to miracle in the Bible. There are several cases of miracle where no faith on the part of the patient is manifested at all. Paul healed a dead man and brought him to life (Acts 20:9-10). Did the dead man show faith? Or did Dorcas (Acts 9.36ff)? Jesus cursed the fig tree and calmed the waves, and certainly no faith could be manifested by the tree or the waves. Paul performed a miracle on Elymas, the sorcerer, who sought to destroy the faith (Acts 13:8-11). Jesus healed Malchus' ear (John 18:10). So, to demand faith on the part of the patient before one works a miracle – and to appeal to lack of faith as an excuse for failure to work the sought-for sign – is hardly an excuse that present-day pretenders can use.

"Perfect health" is a word which denotes integrity of parts, freedom from any defect. The cure performed on the man was instantaneous, perfect, and entire. The man had the complete use of his limbs restored.

In the presence of you all. 'You are witnesses of it; you can judge for yourselves.' This miracle was done in the open, out in public, in "the presence of you all."

3:17 – "And now, brethren, I know that you acted in ignorance, just as your rulers did also.

And now. Peter here begins his second point – the fact that Jesus was denied through ignorance. "Now" (*nun*) can be either temporal or logical in its connotation. Here it seems to be logical, equivalent to "since what I have just said is indisputable."

Brethren. Though he has just accused them of being guilty of an enormous crime, yet Peter shows tenderness as he addresses them still further. Peter is not brow-beating his audience nor trying to club them into submission. He has exposed their opposition to all good and decency in no unsparing terms, but his tone is one of compassion and his aim is to win his listeners to Christ.

I know that you acted in ignorance. Peter does not mean to affirm that they were innocent. He says "ignorant, not knowing." Deeds done in ignorance are still sin, and need forgiveness. Their ignorance is admitted; and in fact, that makes the sin forgivable. In the Old Testament, God made provisions for two kinds of sin; namely, for presumptuous sins and for unwitting sins. Those who sinned presumptuously (i.e., sins of commission) or with a "high hand" were to be cut off from the people (Numbers 15:30-31). But those who sinned unwittingly (i.e., sins of omission), or as they are here called "sins of ignorance," were to make the proper sacrifices and could be forgiven (Numbers 15:27-29).[40] Peter is saying that their sin of denial of Jesus was a sin of ignorance, and therefore there was forgiveness for it. Their ignorance did not excuse them, but it was ground for calling them to repentance.

Just as your rulers did also. Other passages also speak of the ignorance of the religious leaders.[41] How the religious leaders could have been ignorant of the fact that Jesus was the long-awaited Messiah is hard to see. They had countless opportunities to learn and to know the truth for themselves. However, they let their prejudice and passion overpower the witness borne by reason and conscience. By inspiration, the sacred writers affirm the religious leaders did not know He was the Messiah when they killed Him.

3:18 – "But the things which God announced beforehand by the mouth of all the prophets, that His Christ should suffer, He has thus fulfilled.

But the things which God announced beforehand by the mouth of all the prophets, that His Christ should suffer. Here is summarized the third part of Peter's message, that

---

[40] Leviticus 4:2,27 and 5:18 also give instructions about sacrifices for sins of ignorance.

[41] Luke 23:34; 1 Corinthians 2:8.

what happened to Jesus was just as was predicted in the prophets would happen to Messiah when He came. "The things" which God indicated in type and prophecy would happen to the Messiah has reference particularly to the sufferings and death of Messiah, the very things just listed by Peter as done by the Jews to Jesus. But the Jews somehow missed these predictions, and instead of a suffering Messiah they expected the Messiah to be a grand, political, earthly ruler. As in Acts 1:12 and 2:33, we have here an echo of the method of interpretation of the Old Testament prophecies which the apostles learned from Jesus.[42] Peter's statement about God speaking by the mouth of all the prophets is an inspired affirmation of the inspiration of a large portion of the Old Testament.

He has thus fulfilled. It turned out that Christ died, just as the prophets said He would. Peter is removing all the obstacles that might be in the way of faith in his listeners' minds. They had stumbled over Jesus' life, sufferings, and death, thinking them to be un-Messiah-like. But there is no need to stumble longer. Now, they too can see the Old Testament prophecies like Jesus taught His apostles to see them. This fact just stated – that in the Jews' mistreatment of Jesus, God was fulfilling what He had predicted through the prophets – is not easily reconciled by human philosophy with the assertion of their guilt. But this is no more difficult than Peter's assertion of God's sovereignty and man's free moral choice in the last chapter (Acts 2:23). Peter's affirmation in essence is, 'You people are *guilty*. God saw what you would do; in fact, He predicted it via the prophets; but you did not have to do it. You *are* guilty. Therefore, you need to repent.'

3:19 – *"Repent therefore and return, that your sins may be wiped away, in order that times of refreshing may come from the presence of the Lord;*

Repent therefore and return. Concerning the nature of repentance, see Special Study #8. Here, as in Acts 2, Peter makes no mention of faith; but having labored from the beginning of his sermon to convince the hearers, his command to repent carries the assumption that they believed. This second sermon by Peter certainly does not contradict what he said in his first sermon on the day of Pentecost. At the close of that first recorded sermon, he told the listeners what to do to be saved (Acts 2:38). He gave two commands and made two promises. It would seem likely that as Peter is now telling this audience what to do to be saved, he gives the same instructions and promises. Let us compare his instructions:

	COMMANDS		PROMISES	
2:38	Repent	Be baptized	Remission of sins	Gift of Holy Spirit
3:19	Repent	Return	Sins wiped out	Time of refreshing

"Therefore" tells us this is a conclusion drawn from what has just been said. 'Because of your sin of putting the Christ to death, you should repent, etc.'

In the command, "repent and return," the word "return" speaks of something to be done after they have repented, and something to be done different from repentance. The word *epistrephō* means to "turn," "to return to a path from which one has gone astray," and then "to turn away from sins," or "to forsake them." There was one act uniformly enjoined

---

[42] Luke 24:44ff is an example of Jesus' interpretation of the Old Testament prophets.

upon each penitent believer, an act by which he became dead to sin, and arose to walk in newness of life; that act is baptism. When we consult the comparison of Acts 2:38 and 3:19, it would appear that baptism is that act by which a man "returns" to the path he had gone away from. It is the point at which one enters upon the new and better life.

Unfortunately, the KJV translators gave this verb a passive sense, i.e., "be converted." This has given some support to the Calvinistic concept that in conversion the individual sinner is wholly passive and that conversion is a miraculous act brought about by the direct influence of the Holy Spirit upon the heart. In the original, the verb is an aorist active imperative, and indicates that the "returning" is a responsibility each individual person has. The Lord makes salvation possible and gives us the invitation, but the responsibility is always the individual's.

That your sins may be wiped away. The two things commanded were to be done in order that their sins might be "wiped away." This expression is similar to "remission of sins" in Acts 2:38. The expression "to wipe away" (or "to blot out") is taken from the practice of creditors charging their debtors, and when the debt is paid, the record is canceled or blotted out, removed from the record. The word used here refers to the practice of writing such records on tablets covered with wax. By inverting the stylus (or other writing instrument), the blunt end is used to again smooth the wax, thus removing every trace of the writing. A similar concept is contained in the word "propitiation" (Romans 3:25). The blood of Christ has so worked that God doesn't "see" the sins of the believer when it comes time for justification.

In order that. This is a translation of the word *hopōs*, a word which denotes a reason why a thing is done. The NASB's "in order that" is exactly right. The KJV translation "*when the times of refreshing come*" is misleading; the Greek adverb never has the meaning "when." The Greek does not mean that the refreshing (renewal) will come at the time of the second coming of Christ, as the KJV's wording would lead the reader to believe.

While the command to repent and return was for the primary purpose that their sins might be wiped away, two other consequences are mentioned, as further reasons why the listeners should repent and return: 1) So that times of renewal could come. 2) So that God may send Jesus.

Times of refreshing may come. From reading such Old Testament passages as Isaiah 28:12 and 40:1ff, the Jews anticipated that the Messianic age would be a time of rest, ease, and prosperity. They pictured the Messianic age as a period when they would have rest from their enemies, a respite from the evils of oppression and war, and great national prosperity and peace. Perhaps Peter has such prophecies in mind when he tells his audience that if they turn to God through faith and obedience to Christ, those blessed days of righteousness and peace and universal joy and rest would be theirs. If our comparison of Acts 2:38 and 3:19 is correct, then this renewal of soul was to be brought about by the work of the indwelling Holy Spirit in the lives of Christians.

From the presence of the Lord. God was the author of the renewal.

3:20 – *"and that He may send Jesus, the Christ appointed for you,*

And that he may send Jesus. The second coming of Christ seems to be the event referred to here. Peter seems to be saying that this is another reason his hearers should repent and return; namely, so that the Father may send Jesus back to earth the second time. Such an interpretation has been objected to, for it seems to imply, in a general way, that a certain amount of evangelistic work must be done before His second coming. In spite of the objection, that seems to be exactly the thrust of the passage, and such an interpretation is in harmony with verses elsewhere in the New Testament which speak of a certain number of redeemed people that is to be filled before Christ returns.[43]

The Christ appointed for you. There is a manuscript difference here. The KJV reads "Christ, who before was preached unto you," a reading found in the Textus Receptus and many minuscules. The better supported reading (found in *Aleph*, A, B, C, D, E, and others) is that found in the NASB, "Christ who has been appointed for you." How was Jesus "appointed" as the Christ? Jesus was "appointed" (i.e., designated, marked out, shown to be) the "Christ" by the resurrection from the dead, and by the miracles He performed.[44]

3:21 – *"whom heaven must receive until **the** period of restoration of all things about which God spoke by the mouth of His holy prophets from ancient time.*

Whom heaven must receive. The Greek is plural, "heavens," and speaks of the third heaven where God dwells;[45] it is regularly translated as though it were singular in order to distinguish it from the starry heavens in the reader's mind. Why was it necessary for Jesus to ascend to heaven ("heaven must receive Him")? So that our eternal High Priest might enter the heavenly, true holy of holies with His blood.[46] So that the Comforter could come.[47] So that He might direct the welfare of the Church.[48] So that prophecy might be fulfilled.[49] No earthly kingdom, no temporal sovereignty, such as some Jews expected, was to be looked for.

Until *the* period of restoration of all things. "Until" tells us that Jesus will remain in heaven until the restoration of all things. Just what time is denoted by this expression "restoration of all things?" This does not appear to be a reference to a Millennial Kingdom,

---

[43] 2 Peter 3:12 also speaks of a certain number of redeemed that must be reached before Christ returns. That verse speaks of men living holy lives (i.e., remaining true to Christ), and thus hastening the day of His return. Romans 11:12,25 speak of the "fulness" (fulfillment, NASB) of the Jews and Gentiles, an expression which also suggests a number to be reached before Christ returns.

[44] Romans 1:3.

[45] See footnote #11 in Special Study #7 on "Hades and the Intermediate Place of the Dead" where this language "third heaven" is explained.

[46] Hebrews 9:24ff.

[47] John 16:7.

[48] Ephesians 1:20-22.

[49] Ephesians 4:7.

as though Jesus would stay in heaven until it was time for such to begin.[50] The word translated "period" is plural in the original, and speaks of more than one season of time. It seems best to understand this expression in the light of the explanation that follows. Peter goes on to explain that he is speaking of the fulfillment of the Old Testament prophecies. Peter seems to be saying, 'Jesus will remain in heaven until all the things the prophets predicted are fulfilled.'

In the beginning of creation, things were in their proper order. It was a paradise. Then sin entered and threw the whole creation out of joint. Now men are being restored through the gospel.[51] We are living in the times of the restoration of all things. This restoration which is already in progress will culminate in the creation being delivered from the bondage of corruption into the glorious liberty of the sons of God.[52] Peter says in verse 24 (as he quotes the prophets to prove his point), "They told of these days." The times of the restoration of all things is not some future millennial period. Peter says the days he was living in (and the days we are living in) were these days. The first coming of Jesus marked the beginning of these times, and His return will mark the end of the restoration of all things.

That Peter says "all things" are to be restored should not be taken as evidence that all men will ultimately be saved. Such an interpretation would be contrary to Peter's just spoken exhortation to "repent and return in order to have sins wiped out." All of nonrational creation will be restored as this age comes to a close, but only those men who have obeyed the gospel will find themselves restored in both body and soul. Not all men are promised salvation, only those in Christ!

About which God spoke by the mouth of His holy prophets. "About which" points to "the period of the restoration of all things." Peter is saying that the Old Testament prophets spoke about the days when such restoration was to be accomplished.[53]

From ancient time. That is, during the Old Testament age. This expression takes in the promises to Adam (Genesis 3:15), to Abraham (Genesis 22:18), and to Moses (see the next verse) and those prophets that came after him.

3:22 – *"Moses said, 'THE LORD GOD SHALL RAISE UP FOR YOU A PROPHET LIKE ME FROM YOUR BRETHREN; TO HIM YOU SHALL GIVE HEED in everything He says to you.*

Moses said. The quotation about to be repeated is recorded in Deuteronomy 18:15-19. The authorship of Deuteronomy is here attributed to Moses. Several different ideas have been advanced in an attempt to discern Peter's object in making this quotation. One com-

---

[50] Concerning a "Millennial Kingdom," see the notes at Acts 1:6 and Special Study #1, "Diverse Opinions About the Kingdom of God."

[51] Matthew 19:28; Titus 3:5.

[52] Romans 8:19:21.

[53] Peter's language again affirms the inspiration of the Old Testament prophets. He says that God spoke through the prophets, and that can only be by inspiration.

mentator thinks these verses from Deuteronomy were quoted for the purpose of showing that the heavens must receive the Messiah (see verse 21). This interpretation would be reached by emphasizing the words "God shall *raise up* a prophet like me ...." Another thinks the quotation is made for the purpose of showing that the prophets had spoken of the days of refreshing (i.e., the Church age), the very things that were then taking place (see verse 24). This latter seems the more likely of the two ideas.

THE LORD GOD SHALL RAISE UP FOR YOU A PROPHET LIKE ME. The Jews acknowledged that this passage in Deuteronomy was a Messianic prophecy. They had asked John the Baptist, "Are you the prophet?"[54] and John replied that he was not the Messiah. Here Peter identifies "the prophet" with the Christ (Messiah); that is exactly what the Jews had done when speaking to John. A prophet is one who speaks by inspiration as he delivers the message from God.[55] He would be one who would infallibly guide the people in their religious affairs. Through Moses, God was promising He would not leave the people to grope for the right way by themselves, but would raise up One to lead them. God was the one who would raise up Jesus; and the words "raise up" here do not speak of the resurrection, but merely speak of God's appointing or commissioning the Christ to do a specific job.

"Like me." In what sense were Moses and Christ alike? Here are some of the ways the two have been compared. God sent both. Both were lawgivers. Both were saviors (Moses of a particular people; Christ of all people). Both delivered others from bondage (Egypt in Moses' case; sin in Christ's). Both were prophets (both revealed God's will). Both were mediators (Moses for the people of Israel; Christ stands between all men and God). God raised up both to do their particular job. Of all these suggested parallels, is not the salvation activity of each the great point of resemblance?

FROM YOUR BRETHREN. The "prophet" (Messiah) was to be a Jew, one of the very countrymen to whom Peter was speaking.

TO HIM YOU SHALL GIVE HEED in everything He says to you. This is not an exact quotation of Deuteronomy by Peter; it sounds more like a quotation from memory. The gist of what Peter is saying is this: 'Moses was talking about the Jesus whom I am preaching to you. And Moses (an accepted authority among you people) commanded you to listen to this Jesus whom I am preaching.' "Give heed" equals "obey."

3:23 – *'And it shall be that every soul that does not heed that prophet shall be utterly destroyed from among the people.'*

And it shall be that every soul that does not heed that prophet. This is still part of the inexact quotation from Moses, who himself warned that every person who did not obey the instructions of Jesus ("that prophet") would suffer suitable recompense.

Shall be utterly destroyed from among the people. Where the Greek reads "utterly de-

---

[54] John 1:21ff.

[55] John 12:48-49.

stroyed," the Hebrew in Deuteronomy 18:19 speaks of being responsible for one's actions ("I will require it of him"). The usual mode of punishing such offenses was by cutting the offender off from the people.[56] The idea which Peter is expressing was that the Jews had exposed themselves to the severest punishment in rejecting and crucifying the Lord Jesus, and that they should, therefore, repent of this great sin and seek for mercy. Unless they repent and return, God Himself would visit punishment upon them.[57]

3:24 – *"And likewise, all the prophets who have spoken, from Samuel and* **his** *successors onward, also announced these days.*

And likewise, all the prophets who have spoken. "Likewise" suggests that the burden of the prophets was the same as that prediction given by Moses: give heed to the Messiah, or perish! In the writings of each Old Testament prophet, you find such information about the coming Messianic age.

From Samuel and *his* successors onward. Why pick Samuel? He was not the first prophet. Actually, Enoch was the first prophet,[58] and Moses also preceded Samuel. Perhaps Samuel is picked because he was the founder of the school of the prophets (i.e., those whom Peter calls "his successors"). Or perhaps the reason Samuel is named next after Moses (verse 22) is because after the settlement of Canaan, there was no prophetic voice (save two special messages, delivered by men whose names are not even recorded[59]) for almost 400 years. Samuel was the next, after Moses, to be named as a prophet. We could say there was no prophet between Moses and Samuel.

Also announced these days. The people listening to Peter preach could not reject his message without rejecting the Christ; and if they were to reject the Christ, they would be rejecting all their prophets, for those prophets had looked forward to the very age Peter and his listeners were living in. Dispensationalism, one of the modern systems of eschatology, says the Church age is not predicted in the Old Testament. Dispensationalism, in this assertion, is exactly contrary to what Peter said by inspiration! Peter says that the events happening then (and that was the early part of the Church age) were predicted in the Old Testament Prophets, in Moses, Samuel, and all his successors.

3:25 – *"It is you who are the sons of the prophets, and of the covenant which God made with your fathers, saying to Abraham, 'AND IN YOUR SEED ALL THE FAMILIES OF THE EARTH SHALL BE BLESSED.'*

It is you who are the sons of the prophets. Not in the sense that they were all literal descendants of the prophets. Rather, the language is idiomatic of the idea that they were

---

[56] Exodus 30:33; Numbers 15:31; Leviticus 7:20-27. To be cut off from the people was one of the most severe punishments a Jew could suffer. He was no longer able to sacrifice in the Temple. He would be treated like a Gentile. Thus, it speaks of a severe punishment when Peter uses the language

[57] Compare Matthew 8:12 and 2 Thessalonians 1:8-9.

[58] Jude 14.

[59] Judges 6:8-10; 1 Samuel 2:27.

the disciples, pupils, followers of the teachings of the prophets. Peter is saying to his listeners that they could inherit all the promises and blessings that were the subjects of those prophecies of old, if they would but repent and return.

And of the covenant which God made with your fathers. The sense is, "you are the sons of the covenant ...." There are two different Greek words translated "covenant" in our versions. *Suntheke* speaks of an agreement or compact between equals, an agreement in which both parties have an equal voice in drawing up the terms of the compact. *Diatheke* generally speaks of an agreement or compact or disposition between unequal parties. God, who is greater than men, makes the rules and conditions. Men may agree to the terms, but the man has no voice in drawing up the terms of the compact. The word used here is *diatheke*. It is not man's provenance to attempt to change or make up terms of pardon. It is man's place to submit to the terms given by an all wise and loving God.

Saying to Abraham. The covenant here before Peter's mind was first made to Abraham[60] and later to Isaac and Jacob.[61]

AND IN YOUR SEED ALL THE FAMILIES OF THE EARTH SHALL BE BLESSED. In Galatians 3:15-29 Paul indicates that the reference in the word "seed" is to Christ. (The Jewish nation are not the "seed" through whom the world was to be blessed. It was Christ. The Lord said not "seeds" plural, but "seed" singular.) "All families" includes Jews and Gentiles both. Though the Old Testament reads, "All the nations (i.e., Gentiles)," this word was avoided as possibly distasteful to the Jewish hearers. Instead, Peter substitutes "families" (*patriai*) where the LXX has *ethne*. All families were to be made happy or blessed – spiritually blessed. We have here an apostolic interpretation of the promise made to Abraham. It was fulfilled, according to Peter, in the Messiah; and men would be made spiritually prosperous if they would repent and turn away from their sins to service for Christ.

3:26 – *"For you first, God raised up His Servant, and sent Him to bless you by turning every one of you from your wicked ways."*

For you first. Christ came to His own people, the Jews, first. The Jews were given first opportunity to obey the Gospel.[62] The new covenant religion was to begin at Jerusalem.

God raised up His Servant. Again, though the English translation reminds us of the resurrection, the reference is apparently not to that event. The language and meaning are similar to verse 22. As the Old Testament predicted that Messiah would do, Jesus did. "Servant" (as previously noted) is a term the people were familiar with from Isaiah 40-53. This Servant (none other than Jesus) had been sent first to the very people whom Peter was addressing.

---

[60] Genesis 12:3, 18:18, 22:18.

[61] Genesis 26:4, 28:14.

[62] Compare Acts 13:46 and Romans 1:16. In God's providence, the Jews did have a priority when it came to who heard the gospel first.

And sent Him to bless you. To make you spiritually happy. It is a blessing indescribable to have one's sins forgiven! The blessings promised to all families are available to all through the offers of salvation made in the preaching of the gospel as is here being done by Peter.

By turning every one *of you* from your wicked ways. By His preaching, example, death, and glorification, Christ would make provision for men to turn from their iniquities. "Wicked ways" (iniquities) is one of the regular words used for sin in the New Testament. It emphasizes the side of sin that delights in injury, doing evil to others.

Allusion has previously been made to the matter of whether or not man is wholly passive in salvation. This verse in the NASB is translated in such a way that it implies man is passive. Christ turns men from sin, it says. It is also possible to translate it "providing each one of you turns from your wicked ways," and this would match the commands Peter has already given as recorded in verse 19.[63]

---

[63] There is a technical problem involved in the translation of this verse. It is this – whether the verb has an object or not.

- In Greek, there is a grammatical rule, sometimes used, that says the subject of the infinitive is in the accusative case. The word "each" (*hekaston*) is in the accusative case, and thus could be the subject of the infinitive "turn." This is the way the final sentence of our notes has rendered it, and is also the way English versions before 1611 (with the exception of the Geneva Bible) handled it. Those older versions were following the lead of the Syriac and Vulgate, and Luther.
- The translation found in the NASB, which repeats the word "you" (*humas*) and makes it the object of the verb "turn," is also a possible translation. In this approach, the object of the infinitive is in the accusative case also.

Thus, this is one place where the theology of the translator is likely to determine how his English translation reads. We prefer to understand that "turn" is an intransitive verb in the light of the fact that the Bible presents men as active agents in salvation, rather than as wholly passive.

L. The First Persecution by the Sanhedrin. 4:1-31

1. The Men Arrested. 4:1-4

4:1 – *And as they were speaking to the people, the priests and the captain of the temple guard, and the Sadducees, came upon them,*

And as they were speaking to the people. Does Luke's account, by saying "they" were speaking, suggest Peter addressed one portion of the multitude, while John was speaking to another? Chapter 4 continues the account of the events that began with the healing of the lame man by Peter and John as they were entering the temple at the 3 p.m. hour of prayer. Peter's sermon to the crowd that gathered that afternoon has been outlined by Luke. We presume Peter would have closed with an immediate exhortation to obedience (similar to the exhortation in Acts 2:38-40), but before Peter could finish his sermon, a group of men are bearing down upon the crowd at Solomon's Porch. Peter's sermon was cut short.

The priests. The priests in the group of men who interrupt the preaching are probably those who were serving in the temple for the week, priests from whichever one of the twenty-four courses was serving the worshipers that week.[1]

And the captain of the temple *guard.* Some believe the commander of the Roman soldiers stationed in the Tower of Antonia is here called the captain of the temple guard. But it is more probable that the man intended is a Jewish officer, whose duty it was to command the guard of Levites stationed in the temple.[2] This temple guard was first appointed under the name of porters by David, and in New Testament times numbered 400 men.[3] The captain of this guard was an officer of high rank in Jewish circles.[4] These Levitical soldiers acted as sentinels at night in the temple area, and during the day the temple guard was to preserve the orderly, worshipful atmosphere in the temple and to see that the wishes of the religious leaders were carried out. Since the leaping and shouting of the healed man had attracted attention, and since the crowd that had gathered was still present in the temple area, this body of men was vitally interested in what was going on.

And the Sadducees. See Special Study #9, "The Sects of the Jews," at the close of this chapter for information about the Sadducees. We are especially interested here in the teaching of the Sadducees. Importantly, Sadducees denied any idea of a future resurrection of the body for any man. So the preaching of the apostles about Jesus' resurrection was obnoxious to them.

---

[1] In the "Chronological Studies on the Gospels" in the introduction to this book we've already been introduced to the "course of Abijah." It was one of these twenty-four courses of priests. "David divided the priests and Levites into 24 groups, called courses in Luke 1:8, each with its own head (1 Chronicles 24:1ff). These courses officiated for a week at a time, the change being made on the sabbath before evening sacrifice." *Zondervan Pictorial Bible Dictionary*, p.185.

[2] 1 Chronicles 9:11; 2 Chronicles 31:13; Nehemiah 11:11.

[3] 2 Chronicles 16:1-19.

[4] Acts 5:24; Luke 22:4,52; Josephus, *Antiquities*, XX.6.2.

Came upon them. This expression gives the mental image of a large group of men suddenly bearing down on the apostles who were preaching to the multitudes. Their sudden appearance, their unexpected interruption of the sermon, would take the people by surprise; even if any might have been tempted to resist, the sudden appearance of the temple guard would cause them to be cautious. It is interesting to speculate why each group came. The priests were likely there because of the fact the apostles were teaching. Teaching was the official position and duty of the priests; if anyone were going to preach in the temple, the priests were going to do it. The captain and the temple guard were likely there because any activity that disturbed the routine of temple worship was their responsibility. Their duty was to preserve the law and order prescribed by the religious leaders. The Sadducees were likely there because Peter and John were teaching the resurrection doctrine.

4:2 – *being greatly disturbed because they were teaching the people and proclaiming in Jesus the resurrection from the dead.*

Being greatly disturbed because they were teaching the people. "Being greatly disturbed" is a mingled emotion of indignation and anger. Their positions of leadership had been threatened by the apostles, and their response is one often seen of anger. They were offended that unlearned Galileans, in no way connected with the priestly office, and unauthorized by them, should presume to set themselves up as religious teachers.

And proclaiming in Jesus the resurrection from the dead. The Sadducees would be particularly opposed to this doctrine since they denied the doctrine of the resurrection (not just in Jesus' case, but in general). Some men, when their teachings are opposed, take the opposition as a personal attack against them, and strike out in anger. The fact that Jesus has risen from the dead would be a difficult argument for them to answer as they attempted to maintain their denial of the idea of any resurrection at all.

> It is particularly striking that neither on this occasion nor on any subsequent occasion (as far as our information goes) did the Sanhedrin take any serious action to disprove the apostles' central affirmation – the resurrection of Jesus. Had it seemed possible to refute them on this point, how readily would the Sanhedrin have seized the opportunity! Had they succeeded, how quickly and completely the new movement would have collapsed.[5]

4:3 – *And they laid hands on them, and put them in jail until the next day, for it was already evening.*

And they laid hands on them. Arrested them, we would say. Who all was arrested? Just Peter and John? Or was the healed man also included? When the next morning comes, and the trial begins, the lame man is there before the Sanhedrin (see verses 10,14).

And put them in jail until the next day. They were put in jail overnight as no trial could take place before the next day. The Law spoke of an overnight cooling-off period[6] so that

---

[5] Bruce, *op. cit.*, p.103.

[6] Jeremiah 21:12.

no one was lynched in anger or thoughtlessness or haste. This law was violated in the trial of Jesus, but it is not violated in the case of the apostles and the healed man.

For it was already evening. "Evening" must mean the second of the two Jewish evenings, i.e., from 6 to 9 p.m.[7] Peter and John had gone up to the temple at 3 p.m. They had apparently been preaching for two or three hours after the lame man was healed. Then they are arrested at evening, perhaps as late as 7 or 8 p.m. Much more must have occurred than is recorded here by Luke.

4:4 – *But many of those who had heard the message believed; and the number of the men came to be about five thousand.*

But many of those who had heard the message believed. In contrast to the opposition from the Jewish leaders, many of those that heard the sermon became believers. In spite of the arrest, and the attempt to silence the message by the religious authorities, still the people believed. In full knowledge that they too might be harassed and pressured, still they believed. Here is another example of the doctrine of Romans 10:17, that "faith comes by hearing." It is impossible to expect a man to believe without hearing, whether by the preached message or by reading the written Word.

And the number of the men came to be about five thousand. Barnes thinks "men" means "persons," that the number of people – men and women together – now came to 5000. But it is very probable that Luke's count included men only. McGarvey has worded the reason for such a comment:

> True to custom of oriental nations even to the present day, the number of the men alone is here given, the women not being counted.[8]

Did the 5000 believe for the first time that day? This is one possible way to understand Luke's figure, and this is the way Chrysostom and Augustine understood the passage. Or did the whole number of Christian men (since the day of Pentecost when the church began) now come to total 5000? This latter is the usual interpretation. How long this is after the day of Pentecost is not known, but as was suggested in notes at the beginning of chapter 3, perhaps a month or less had passed since Pentecost.

2. Peter's Defense Before the Council. 4:5-12

4:5 – *And it came about on the next day, that their rulers and elders and scribes were gathered together in Jerusalem;*

And it came about on the next day. The meetings of the Sanhedrin customarily began at 10 a.m.

---

[7] Exodus 12:6.

[8] McGarvey, *op. cit.*, p.68.

That their rulers and elders and scribes. These three groups of officers made up the body called the Sanhedrin. "Sanhedrin" comes from the Greek *sun* and *hedra,* which means "to sit together." Composed of 72 members (authorities vary from 70 to 72 members for the Sanhedrin), the Sanhedrin was the high court of the Jewish people. It would have its counterpart in our American society in the Supreme Court. So Peter, John, and the healed man were brought before the supreme court of the Jewish people.

As to the origin of this body, the Sanhedrin was constituted by Moses.[9] Moses himself had tried to rule in all points of dispute among the people of Israel while they were wandering through the wilderness. Because of the fact that there were so many points of dispute, the work became overburdening. Jethro, Moses' father-in-law, suggested he appoint several men to do the job, which Moses did. Such a body continued to function through the years. The Sanhedrin was reorganized by Ezra after the exile in Babylon.[10]

What is the distinction between "rulers," "elders," and "scribes"? Rulers would be the chief priests, the heads of the 24 courses. The elders were 24 elderly men picked by the people to sit on the court; these were likely men of age, influence, and position. The scribes were 24 lawyers, men who transcribed the Law. Scribes in New Testament times were the learned men, the men skilled and familiar with the Law because they worked with it constantly, making copies of it. Scribes also kept the records of the courts of justice and the family registers in the synagogues, wrote articles of contract and sale, and bills of divorce. They were called "scribes" because they wrote the public records. Scribes were not themselves a religious sect; they might be either Pharisee or Sadducee by belief.

The jurisdiction of the Sanhedrin was limited, in New Testament times, to cases not involving capital punishment, for the Romans had taken away from the Jews the right of capital punishment. There seems to be only one instance when the Sanhedrin could pronounce capital punishment upon anyone, and that was in the case where a Gentile crossed the inner fence dividing the temple proper from the Court of the Gentiles. It was sure death for a Gentile to cross into the court where Gentiles were not to go. In such cases the Sanhedrin could pronounce the death penalty and the Roman authorities pretty nearly always carried out the wishes of the Sanhedrin.[11] In all other cases involving capital punishment, the disposition of the whole case had to be turned over to Roman courts.

Were gathered together in Jerusalem. Jerusalem was the usual place where the Sanhedrin assembled. However, on account of the great increase in crime, from AD 30 onward, the Sanhedrin moved from place to place and held court. The declaration that they were now in Jerusalem is corroboration of the idea that they moved the location of the court from time to time.

---

[9] Exodus 24:1.

[10] Ezra 5:9, 6:7, 10:8; Nehemiah 2:6, 11:1.

[11] At chapter 21:29, Luke records that Paul was charged with violating this law about taking Gentiles across the wall into the Court of Israel. Those were grave charges, and if shown to be true, would have meant Paul's speedy execution. Further information about this law is given in notes at 21:29.

4:6 – *and Annas the high priest* **was there,** *and Caiaphas and John and Alexander, and all who were of high-priestly descent.*

And Annas the high priest *was there.* On page *vii-viii* of the New Testament Chronology, information has been given about Annas. Annas was the legal high priest (according to family succession), but he had been deposed from his priestly duties by the Roman governor. Though he was no longer recognized by the Romans as high priest and not allowed to officiate in the temple, he still kept the presidency of the Sanhedrin.

And Caiaphas. See page *viii* of the New Testament Chronology concerning this man. Between Pentecost in AD 30 and his deposition in AD 36, he was the man recognized as high priest by the Roman authorities. Both Annas and Joseph Caiaphas were Sadducees.

And John and Alexander. Little is known for sure of these men, for the names are common. Because the context suggests they were very influential men in the Sanhedrin, Farrar has suggested that they are "Johanan Ben Zakkai; and Alexander, perhaps the wealthy brother of the learned Philo,"[12] but such an identification is not certain. Because it is a possibility, a word or two about these men is in order. Johanan Ben Zakki was one of the seven great Rabbans. He became president of the Sanhedrin after Simeon, son of Gamaliel. He would, in later years, become a favorite of the Roman general, Titus. Thirty years before the destruction of Jerusalem he had expounded Zechariah 11:1 as foretelling the coming destruction of the city. The Alexander who was the brother of Philo became Alabarch (chief magistrate of the Jews) at Alexandria.[13] It has been questioned whether the Alexander named by Luke and the brother of Philo are to be identified, since it is not easy to see how a man who was powerful in Jerusalem could also become a civil officer in Egypt. Josephus seems to explain this problem by stating that Philo's brother was an old friend of the emperor Claudius.[14]

And all who were of high-priestly descent. This might have included some ex-high priests, since there had been three in office between Annas' high priesthood, and that of Caiaphas.[15]

4:7 – *And when they had placed them in the center, they* **began to** *inquire, "By what power, or in what name, have you done this?"*

And when they had placed them in the center. Each member of the Sanhedrin was seated (in a semicircle) so as to be able to see the other members, and also to see the prisoners. Prisoners, when on trial, were made to stand in the center of the semicircle of seated Sanhedrin members.

---

[12] Frederic W. Farrar, *The Life and Work of St. Paul* (New York: E.P. Dutton & Co., 1880), p.60.

[13] Josephus, *Antiquities*, XVIII.8.1.

[14] *Antiquities*, XIX.5.1.

[15] A listing of the Jewish high priests can be seen in a footnote in Josephus, p.596

They *began to* inquire. It would appear the Sanhedrin members were trying to intimidate the apostles, to scare them into retirement and silence. Literally, it says "were inquiring." They put the question repeatedly, in many and varying forms.

By what power, or in what name, have you done this? "By what power" suggests they were asking the apostles whether their power was divine or demonic. "In what name" equals "by whose authority?" Did the questioners point to the healed man who was in the midst (verses 10, 14) when they said "this"? Or was "this" indefinite, phrased so that perhaps by their answer the apostles might say something for which they could be condemned?

"Done what?" might have been Peter and John's answer. Done this preaching? this miracle? this what? The question posed by the Sanhedrin specified nothing, and the obvious reason is that there was no particular thing done by Peter and John on which the Sanhedrin could base a charge of wrongdoing.[16] It would seem the chief priests cunningly framed an indefinite question in hope that the defendants, in their confusion, would furnish a ground of accusation by speaking unguarded words. "You" is in an emphatic position in the Greek. The religious leaders will not admit God has wrought any miracle. 'It was YOU, you apostles who did it. Where did the power come from? It was demonic, wasn't it?' This is the implication of the question put over and over again to the defendants.

4:8 – *Then Peter, filled with the Holy Spirit, said to them, "Rulers and elders of the people,*

Then Peter, filled with the Holy Spirit, said to them. The tense of the verb "filled" is aorist. The filling happened sometime before Peter spoke, but whether it refers back to the Pentecostal filling, or whether it was an immediate, sudden inspiration right at this moment, cannot be absolutely determined. In any case, the promises made by Jesus were being fulfilled. He had promised His disciples such aid, whenever they might be brought before rulers for the sake of Christ.[17] One such promise was made in these words:

> Beware of men: for they shall deliver you up to councils, and they will scourge you in their synagogues, and you shall be brought before governors and kings for My sake, for a testimony to them and the Gentiles. But when they deliver you up, be not anxious how or what you shall speak; for it shall be given you in that same hour what you shall say. For it is not you who speaks, but the Spirit of your Father who speaks through you.[18]

Rulers and elders of the people. A few weeks earlier, Peter had quailed before the soldiers and servants in the high priest's palace.[19] He could not have forgotten that before this very Council, and these very men, his Master had been arraigned and condemned. Now he stands before the Sanhedrin and speaks, in respectful language, but with unflinching boldness. Only the resurrection of Christ and the guidance of the Holy Spirit can account for such a change.

---

[16] A very similar thing was done when Jesus was arrested. He was arrested without a charge, and then the Jewish leaders held several trials to try to find something for which they could punish Him.

[17] Mark 13:11; Luke 12:12, 21:14-15.

[18] Matthew 10:17-20.

[19] John 18:25ff.

4:9 – *"if we are on trial today for a benefit done to a sick man, as to how this man has been made well,*

If we are on trial today. The word "trial" is used in its technical sense of "investigate, interrogate, examine one who is accused," as in Luke 23:14.

For a benefit done to a sick man. Surely these honorable judges will not object to the apostles doing a good deed to help a sick man! If they were to object to doing good, they would be destroying the very basis of any judicial system which ever hopes to be respected. This is a tacit condemnation of the unrighteousness course the Sanhedrin was following.

As to how this man has been made well. The fact that he had been healed was not denied, even by the religious leaders. The man was present in the court room with the apostles, and there was no doubting that he was "well."[20]

4:10 – *"let it be known to all of you, and to all the people of Israel, that by the name of Jesus Christ the Nazarene, whom you crucified, whom God raised from the dead – by this name this man stands here before you in good health.*

Let it be known to all of you, and to all the people of Israel. Peter wants everyone to know the source of the miracle, especially since such miracles as this credential the good news of salvation which is available in Jesus. Peter was anxious for the entire membership of the Sanhedrin to recognize who Jesus is, and become His followers. The indefinite question asked by the court gave Peter a wide-open opportunity, and he made use of it.

That by the name of Jesus Christ the Nazarene. Jesus Christ – the juxtaposition of these two names is based on the fact that Jesus of Nazareth is none other than the Messiah predicted in the Old Testament. The Sanhedrin members have not yet come to the place where they can admit that Jesus was the Messiah, but Peter was affirming that He was. And it is by the authority of Messiah Jesus, Peter says, that the lame man had been healed.

Whom you crucified, whom God raised from the dead. Is this the first instance where the rulers themselves are accused to their faces of crucifying the Messiah, or were they present in the audience on previous occasions when this same charge had been made?[21] Peter was most bold, to accuse them of murder – the murder of Jesus of Nazareth.

> Instead of the Sanhedrin placing Peter and John on trial, these apostles now put the Sanhedrin on trial. The Sanhedrin is forced to defend the crime which they had committed, or they could acknowledge their guilt.[22]

---

[20] The word translated "well" can also be translated "saved." It can mean saved from danger, saved from sickness, saved from eternal punishment. Anytime the word appears, the translator must decide which sense is correct. Some commentators have supposed that in this place the word speaks not so much of salvation from lameness as it does salvation from sins. But this does not seem likely.

[21] Compare Acts 2:23 and 3:17.

[22] Boles, *Acts of the Apostles*, p.67.

Again, as in each recorded sermon thus far, Peter drives home the point of the resurrection. God raised Jesus Messiah from the dead, Peter affirms.[23]

By this *name* this man stands here before you in good health. They had asked, "By what power, or in what name …?" Peter now tells them that it was by the authority of Jesus Christ. And the healed man was standing right there in the court room. Evidently, he was arrested at the same time as the apostles; he would have been arrested because he had been the one running and leaping and shouting, the one who caused the crowd to gather.

4:11 – *"He is the STONE WHICH WAS REJECTED by you, THE BUILDERS,* but *WHICH BECAME THE VERY CORNER stone.*

He is the STONE WHICH WAS REJECTED by you, THE BUILDERS. This language is taken from Psalm 118:12. In letters they will write years after this, both Peter and Paul refer to this prophecy and apply it to Christ.[24] It was a Messianic Psalm, and Christ himself referred to it as He was speaking to these very Sanhedrin members on the great day of questions a few weeks before.[25] Jesus spoke of them as being builders who rejected the cornerstone right after He had told the story about the wicked husbandmen who killed the son of the vineyard owner – a very thinly veiled allusion to what they were doing to Him! The verb "rejected" indicates that the Jews had considered the stone, but rejected it as not worthy of being in the building they were erecting.

But* WHICH BECAME THE VERY CORNER *stone. There is some disagreement concerning the exact significance of the word rendered "cornerstone." It might be any of three stones, stones we give the names "capstone," "keystone," or "cornerstone." Perhaps in this place it speaks of "cornerstone" (as the NASB translators have rendered it), that huge stone in the foundation from which the walls get their direction and angle. Such stones differed from the "cornerstones" of present-day buildings. Ours are added after much of the building is constructed; those that Peter spoke of were laid first, and often reached the dimensions of 7x14 feet. The entire building must await the cornerstone, it was of such importance. Christ is as important to Christianity as the cornerstone to an ancient building.[26]

Quoting these words from David, Peter has painted a rather startling picture of his judges. They are like builders trying to build an edifice without using the stone the master-builder had cut out for the corner. At best, such a building would be a tumble-down affair! More likely, without the stone, there wouldn't even be a building. DeWelt has outlined for us the marvelous progression of thought in Peter's defense:

---

[23] Perhaps this emphasis on the resurrection made by the New Testament preachers is an element lacking from present-day preaching. If so, let's restore the emphasis and the hope it inspires.

[24] Ephesians 2:20; 1 Peter 2:4-6.

[25] Matthew 21:42.

[26] Some critics accuse Peter and Paul of contradicting one another, because Paul speaks of Christ as the foundation (1 Corinthians 3:11), whereas Peter uses the term "cornerstone." There is, however, no contradiction. The writers merely use different figures of speech as they illustrate the truth of the central and indispensable place of Christ in the Christian religion.

First, he calls attention to the man who was healed and was standing with them. How did he become whole? Through Jesus of Nazareth. And who is He? He is the one whom you crucified and whom God raised from the dead. Yea, He is the stone which is set at nought of you the builders.[27]

4:12 – *"And there is salvation in no one else; for there is no other name under heaven that has been given among men, by which we must be saved."*

And there is salvation in no one else. Since the word translated "salvation" in this verse is the same as was translated "well" in verse 9, Whitby and others have affirmed that Peter's statement means that "healings" are found only in Jesus. Such an affirmation plainly denies the fact that the devil can work lying miracles, including healings. Peter's use of "saved" here must speak of salvation from the penalty of sin, rather than salvation from some bodily infirmity, and therefore the NASB translators have used "salvation" in their version. Such salvation, including the forgiveness of sin and the opportunity for eternal life with God in heaven, says Peter, is available in no one else save Jesus Christ of Nazareth.

There is salvation in no other person – only in Jesus. There is emphasis upon the negative, which in the Greek stands in the very first part of the sentence. 'There is NO chance. There is NO other way.' By Peter's inspired statement, every other world religion, including the Jewish, stands impoverished when it comes to saving a person from his sins. No other religions are equal to Christianity. None are valid at all! None put a man right in God's sight!

For there is no other name under heaven that has been given among men. There is salvation in no other person (the name, remember, stands for the person). Peter is saying, 'There is no one who can save you but Jesus!'[28] The expression "under heaven" does not materially differ from the expression immediately following, i.e., "among men." They are both designed to emphasize that salvation is to be obtained in Christ alone, and not in any patriarch, or prophet, or teacher, or king, or false Messiah. "Given among men" shows that salvation is not now limited to Israel only, but is intended for mankind at large.

By which we must be saved. In the Greek, the "we" is emphatic, since it is the last word in the sentence.[29] It means '*We all* – whether we are priests, elders, scribes, fishermen, or ex-beggars – must be saved by faith and obedience to Christ if we are to be saved at all!' "Must" does not imply the necessity of salvation, as though everyone has to be saved (and as if they have no choice in the matter). Rather, "must" implies the necessity of having Christ if we are to have salvation. To be saved, you must come the way Jesus instructed. Similarly, in Romans 1-3, Paul shows the failure of all other ways, pointing to the fact that salvation is only through faith in Christ. This truth must be faced and accepted by us all

---

[27] DeWelt, *op. cit.*, p.28.

[28] On the basis of this verse, some say that the name is "Christian." However, it does not appear to be a proper use of this verse to find in it a proof text for the doctrine that "Christian" is the only proper name for a believer to be called. However true that may be, this verse is not a verse to prove it.

[29] There is no contradiction between this note about the emphatic position of a word in the Greek and the note given in the first paragraph of notes on verse 12. There were two emphatic positions where words might be placed in Greek writing – at the very beginning of a sentence and at the very end.

before we will see the eternal value in Christianity, and especially before we will ever be motivated to take the gospel to adherents of any of the other major religions in the world. As sure as Jesus of Nazareth is the Messiah, and has been raised from the dead, none of the other world religions are just as good for their followers as Christianity is!

3. A Private Consultation. 4:13-17

4:13 – *Now as they observed the confidence of Peter and John, and understood that they were uneducated and untrained men, they were marveling, and* **began** *to recognize them as having been with Jesus.*

Now as they observed the confidence of Peter and John. This is a present participle, better translated "they were observing." As Peter is preaching, and as the Sanhedrin is looking on, this is the thing that was going on in their minds. One by one they are coming to the awareness that these men have been with Jesus. "Confidence" is the opposite of hesitancy, the opposite to equivocation in declaring one's sentiments. In spite of the anger of the arresting body the day before, in spite of their intimidation in this very hearing, Peter and John have spoken without any attempt to conceal or disguise what they really believed. How was it that the Sanhedrin saw the confidence of John? As far as the record is concerned, John had not spoken during this trial. But by look and bearing, by a nodding of the head in agreement with what Peter spoke, or perhaps by his own defense in words unrecorded by Luke, John showed that he, too, shared Peter's courage and convictions.

And understood that they were uneducated and untrained men. The word translated "uneducated" means without technical training in the school of Hillel, or the school of Shammai. Jesus Himself was regarded as "uneducated,"[30] for He, like His apostles, had not attended the schools of the rabbis. "Untrained" speaks of one who is from a private place in life, as opposed to one who is used to appearing and speaking in public. The Greek word for "understand" could be translated "having ascertained." It implies, not direct perception, but the grasp with which the mind lays hold of a fact after inquiry.[31]

They were marveling. There was an amazement that men who had not been educated in the schools, and who were not accustomed to speaking in public, should be able to speak their convictions with such boldness and confidence.

And began to recognize them as having been with Jesus. The verb translated "began to recognize" is an imperfect tense verb, which implies that one after another the rulers "began to realize" the reason for the boldness of Peter and John. "With Jesus" is where the apostles received their education.[32] Then as now, those who tried to mandate and maintain human

---

[30] John 7:15.

[31] In Acts 25:25, the same Greek word appears and is translated "found." In that context the idea of "ascertaining by inquiry" is plainly implied.

[32] "They had attended the school of Jesus for more than three years, often day and night, and twelve months a year. If actual hours were counted, we might find that they had more semester hours of training under the greatest Teacher of all time than the average man with a degree of today." Dale, *op. cit.*, p.62.

standards were grieved when men without meeting such standards dare to teach the people. Peter and John gave evidence they had been with Jesus, and they knew what they were talking about, when they claimed that the lame man was healed through the power of Jesus of Nazareth, the Messiah, whom God had raised from the dead.

4:14 – *And seeing the man who had been healed standing with them, they had nothing to say in reply.*

And seeing the man who had been healed standing with them. The healed man was standing there before their eyes in the midst of the semicircle of judges; he was unanswerable proof of what Peter had said. In fact. he was "Exhibit A" for the defense.

They had nothing to say in reply. The Sanhedrin never did deny the miracle, but neither were they prepared to acknowledge that the risen Jesus was the real source of the healing. The miracle had been done in a public place and was obviously a miracle. The man who was healed was well-known because of his long-time begging at the same place while a cripple, so there was no way to evade the conclusion to which Peter had conducted them.

> At the close of Peter's remarks there seems to have been a total silence for a time, for "they could say nothing against it." None of them was ready to contradict anything Peter had said. They were not ready to rebuke him for saying it. Their embarrassment was painful.[33]

In substance, Peter's defense was this: 'We have done a good deed. Are you who are guilty of murdering the Messiah going to punish us?' No wonder the rulers were in a place of great embarrassment. They had had no charge against the apostles in the first place, and they could find no flaw in Peter's defense. The Sanhedrin did the only thing they could do if they were going to save face – they stalled for time in order to consider their dilemma.

4:15 – *But when they had ordered them to go aside out of the Council, they* **began** *to confer with one another,*

But when they had ordered them to go aside out of the Council. During the great day of questions, whenever the religious leaders found themselves in a tight spot, they went aside for consultations, hoping to find a face-saving way out of their situation.[34] The defendants, then, are cleared from the court room so that the judges may confer amongst themselves as to what was the best thing to do.

They *began* **to confer with one another.** One would have expected them to ask what to do to be saved, as honest men would have done when convinced of the facts of the case.

Some have cited verse 13 as Biblical basis to advocate for "unlearned, untaught ministers;" i.e., that formal education for ministers is unnecessary and extra-Biblical. However, that would not be the intent nor the thrust of this verse. Certainly, not every preacher must have a college degree in order to be qualified to preach; many great preachers have been self-taught. The idea we are objecting to is the old fundamentalist idea that any education is a bad thing, liable to lead a preacher into religious liberalism.

[33] McGarvey, *op. cit.*, p.73.

[34] Matthew 21:25.

But these men deliberately closed their minds against the truth. In their private conference, they tried to come up with some way of rationalizing the situation and cutting their losses to the minimum.

4:16 – *saying, "What shall we do with these men? For the fact that a noteworthy miracle has taken place through them is apparent to all who live in Jerusalem, and we cannot deny it.*

Saying, "What shall we do with these men? The object which the Sanhedrin had in mind was to prevent the preaching of the apostles, and thus prevent too many people from becoming followers of the gospel. A miracle had been performed, but the judges do not want more people being led into belief in Christ through more preaching.

For the fact that a noteworthy miracle has taken place through them is apparent to all who live in Jerusalem. They would have denied a miracle had been done if anyone would have believed them. But there was no way to get the people to believe such a lie. To tell such would have merely discredited them more.

And we cannot deny it. After the raising of Lazarus, these same religious leaders had admitted that Jesus was working miracles, but still they would not submit to His lordship.[35] These same men now admit the apostles have worked a genuine miracle, but it only drives them further into rebellion. In the case of Jesus, they had refused to submit because they believed it would cost them their places of leadership.[36] That same fear is the motive that drives them now to try to silence the apostles.

4:17 – *"But in order that it may not spread any further among the people, let us warn them to speak no more to any man in this name."*

But in order that it may not spread any further among the people. They did not want the knowledge of the miracle and the resulting belief in Jesus as Messiah to spread any further, either at Jerusalem where it was more and more becoming known, nor outside the city. While the religious leaders admit that there has been a miracle, and while they knew that only God worked such miracles, yet they are attempting to keep God's message from being known. They view the teaching of the apostles about the resurrection of Jesus as if it were the spread of a contagious disease that must be quarantined and arrested at all costs.

Let us warn them. The Greek reads, "Let us threaten them with a threat." Hebrew idioms express intensity via reduplication. Thus, this was a most solemn threat. On the next occasion, which will occur soon after (Acts 5:40), since this solemn threat did not quiet the apostles, the Sanhedrin will add beating to their threats, as they attempt to intimidate the apostles further in order to cause them to stop preaching.

To speak no more to any man in this name. Literally, "Not to make a sound any longer." They are not to be teaching at all about Jesus. How did Luke learn about the secret proceed-

---

[35] John 11:47.

[36] John 11:48.

ings of the Sanhedrin? We are not informed, but it is not difficult to imagine. Gamaliel, Saul's teacher, was no doubt present; perhaps even Saul himself was there. So perhaps the information came through this channel. If this conjecture seems unsatisfactory, remember that "a great company of the priests" (Acts 6:7) afterward became obedient to the faith; they would not hesitate to confess the villainy of their previous beliefs and actions.

4. Further Preaching Forbidden. 4:18-22

4:18 – *And when they had summoned them, they commanded them not to speak or teach at all in the name of Jesus.*

And when they had summoned them. All during the consultation between the Sanhedrin members, the apostles have been outside the court room. Now that the judges have decided upon a course of action, the defendants are summoned back to their position in the semicircle in the midst of the judges. Once they have returned, they will hear the decision.

They commanded them not to speak or teach at all in the name of Jesus. The Greek is very forceful, "absolutely not to let the name of Jesus pass their lips again." They severely threatened them and charged them that they were not to speak about Jesus in their private conversation or in any public teaching.

4:19 – *But Peter and John answered and said to them, "Whether it is right in the sight of God to give heed to you rather than to God, you be the judge;*

But Peter and John answered and said to them. The Holy Spirit, just as Jesus promised He would, suggested the same answer to both apostles.

> This reply of the apostles shows the strong ground which they took; God spoke by the miracle which they had done; and the Sanhedrin, however authorized, had no right to contradict God. This was also an implication that the authority of the Sanhedrin was in defiance of the authority of God.[37]

Whether it is right in the sight of God to give heed to you rather than to God. The idea is, 'Which is right, to obey you or God?' We have here given a great principle on which Christians may act. Christians are always to act in such a way as to be pleasing to God. If what we propose to do will please Him, then it is right; if it will not please Him, then it is wrong. And the way we know what is pleasing to Him is to learn from His word what pleases Him. The same doctrine is more explicitly stated in Acts 5:29, "We must obey God rather than men!"

Not only is this a passage on which the great doctrine of Christian liberty is based, but also the doctrine of the separation of church and state rests on this passage. Both religion and government have their ultimate beginnings in the will and decree of God. Both duty to God and duty to civil government are clearly taught in God's word. That God has

---

[37] Boles, *op. cit.*, p.70.

regularly given instructions concerning worship and service for Him is a fact admitted by all who have read the Bible. But that God has ordained human government is a fact not so readily admitted. Yet it is plainly taught (e.g., Romans 13:1ff) that the idea of government originated in the mind of God. Since both church and state are God-given, both are to be given their proper allegiance by the Christian. Someone may ask just where Acts 4:19 teaches the separation of church and state, for they cannot see the "state" anywhere in this passage. The "church" they can see in Peter and John as typical representatives, but where is the "state"? Remember that the Sanhedrin was not only a religious authority, but it was also a quasi-political authority. They represented human government as they performed their judicial functions.

In secular thought, the prevailing belief seems to be that the state gives a man his freedom; Biblically, it seems that God's intention for the state is to guard the freedom given to man by God. That is, the real function of the state is to guard the personal liberties of the individual citizen, permitting him to worship and serve his Creator as the Creator has commanded. However, instead of guarding liberties, human governments tend more and more to the control of the individual's thoughts and actions. Both state and church have their sources in God, so neither has the right to conclude that one side versus the other has all the authority and rights; it is an error when either tries to coerce the other.

Certainly, the Christian recognizes the superiority of God's claims over those of the state. If the two ever conflict, the Christian subjects himself to God rather than the state, just as Peter and John did in this case. Since the Sanhedrin's command to be silent was in exact opposition to God's Great Commission, Peter and John elected to obey God.

You be the judge. The Sanhedrin was in a dilemma. If the Sanhedrin said it was right to obey God when God commands a thing to be done, then the apostles would continue to speak and teach in the name of Jesus. But if the Sanhedrin should say that it was absolutely necessary to keep silent and not utter the name of Jesus as they had commanded, they would be guilty of rebellion against God. Since the Sanhedrin had been in rebellion to God since before the condemnation of Jesus to crucifixion, we can expect their rebellion likely to continue.

4:20 – *"for we cannot stop speaking what we have seen and heard."*

For we cannot stop speaking. The pronoun "we" is emphatic: "*We*, for our part ...." DeWelt has caught the essence of the apostles' answer to the decision of the Sanhedrin:

> Put yourselves in our place: suppose God told you to do one thing, and man told you to do another – which one would you obey? Well, that is exactly our situation. Jesus Christ whom we beheld risen from the dead, commissioned us to tell of His resurrection and saving power; now you tell us not to speak the very thing the risen Lord told us to speak. You be the judge. To whom should we hearken?[38]

Peter then answers his own question. He said, "We will do as Jesus told us to do."

---

[38] DeWelt, *op. cit.*, p.29.

What we have seen and heard. Throughout the three years of Jesus' ministry they had seen His miracles, sufferings, death, and resurrection. They heard His explanation of the Law and the Prophets, and His declarations concerning His kingdom. They had been commanded to pass these on, and they were going to obey their Lord.

4:21 – *And when they had threatened them further, they let them go (finding no basis on which they might punish them) on account of the people, because they were all glorifying God for what had happened;*

And when they threatened them further. When a person continues for a time in a path of rebellion, it is hard to break that pattern of rebellion to God. The Sanhedrin members continue to rebel. They repeat with emphasis their demand that the apostles be silent about Jesus.

They let them go. The apostles are allowed to go free, not because the Sanhedrin members are reconciled to what the apostles reasoned, but simply because they were unable to find a legal way how they might punish them.

(Finding no basis on which they might punish them) on account of the people. The motive behind their actions against the apostles is "How will it set with the people?" If the people were to become convinced that the Sanhedrin had acted without due cause, then the very thing the religious leaders were trying to avoid would have happened: they would have lost their place among the people. Since at this moment the people were ready to side with the apostles against the Sanhedrin because of the good deed done to the crippled man, for the Sanhedrin to take any strong action against the apostles would have been to endanger their own authority among the people, the very thing they did not want to do.

Because they were all glorifying God for what had happened. The verb tense implies continued action. The people were continually praising God for the miracle.

4:22 – *for the man was more than forty years old on whom this miracle of healing had been performed.*

For the man was more than forty years old on whom the miracle of healing had been performed. There was a reason why Luke gives the age of the man: he had been lame all his life. At the time of his healing, the man was more than forty years old. In that length of time many in Jerusalem would become acquainted with him and his condition. This is part of the evidence which shows the certainty and genuineness of the miracle. There was no possible way deception could have been practiced.

5. Report of the Two Apostles and Prayer of the Twelve. 4:23-31

4:23 – *And when they had been released, they went to their own* **companions,** *and reported all that the chief priests and the elders had said to them.*

And when they were released, they went to their own *companions*. Who is included among the "companions" to whom they came? One group of commentators suggests the whole church is intended. But where could over 5,000 believers assemble, save in the temple area? Especially since Luke will shortly use the contrasting phrase "the congregation" (verse 32), it therefore appears that the twelve apostles are "their own companions" to which the two came to report. On another occasion, the upper room was the place where the apostles were staying,[39] so perhaps this was the place to which Peter and John came upon this occasion. Luke's account seems to imply a recognized place of meeting.

And reported all that the chief priests and elders had said to them. "Chief priests" would include the families of Annas and Caiaphas, as well as the heads of the twenty-four courses of priests, as has been explained above in the comments at verse 5. What the Sanhedrin said has been recorded in verse 18.

4:24 – *And when they heard* **this,** *they lifted their voices to God with one accord and said, "O Lord, it is Thou who DIDST MAKE THE HEAVEN AND THE EARTH AND THE SEA, AND ALL THAT IS IN THEM,*

And when they heard *this*, they lifted their voice to God with one accord and said. "Lifting the voice" was a phrase found regularly in the Old Testament, and could denote either (1) an address to the people,[40] (2) weeping,[41] or (3) prayer. Lifting up the voice to God here means they prayed to Him. It is a public prayer, and an audible prayer. But how is it that they all prayed together? Did they repeat the words after him who prayed aloud? Did they sing Psalm 2 (from which the words come)? Did one lead and the others join mentally, or by the responses of "Amen"? Was there a general form of prayer already in use in the church?

O Lord. The Greek word used is *despota*, from which is derived our word despot. It is not *kurios*, the common word usually translated Lord. *Despota* denotes one who rules over others, and was applied to the highest magistrate or officer. It denotes authority in ruling, power, absoluteness.

It is Thou who DIDST MAKE THE HEAVEN AND THE EARTH AND THE SEA, AND ALL THAT IS IN THEM. God made the universe, and therefore He has the right to rule. God is all powerful, and therefore He is surely able to help His servants.[42]

---

[39] Acts 1:13. From the accounts of Jesus' resurrection appearances, as well as from tradition, there is some evidence that Zebedee had a house in Jerusalem as well as one up in Galilee. If the upper room of Mary's house is not the meeting place for this prayer meeting, then perhaps we could look to a meeting in Zebedee's home.

[40] Judges 9:7.

[41] Genesis 29:11; Judges 2:4

[42] The NASB uses the archaic "thee" and "thou" forms of the pronoun when language is addressed to God. This is merely a personal choice made by the translators; it is not at all evidence that such forms of the pronoun should be used by us in our prayers. When the forms "thee" and "thou" were written in the KJV and by this means made familiar to generations of Bible readers, those were the regular forms used in the people's everyday speech. They were not a special form to be used only in prayer language.

4:25 – *who by the Holy Spirit,* **through** *the mouth of our father David Thy servant, didst say,* 'WHY DID THE GENTILES RAGE, AND THE PEOPLES DEVISE FUTILE THINGS?

Who by the Holy Spirit. Here is another claim in the book of Acts concerning the inspiration of the Old Testament, in this case for David, the human author of the Psalm about to be quoted. As they opened their prayer, they appealed to God's right to rule His creation (verse 24). In this part of their prayer, they appeal to the fact that God has foreseen the very thing that has just been done by the Sanhedrin, and therefore they plead for His protection.

Through the mouth of our father David Thy servant, didst say. Psalm 2 is here ascribed to David. In their prayer, the apostles are quoting Scripture and are using it as a basis for their appeal. They are asking God to do as He had promised He would in Psalm 2:1,2.

WHY DID THE GENTILES RAGE. "Gentiles" is likely a reference to the Romans in particular, for their part in the crucifixion. "Rage" is a translation of *ephruaxan*, which literally means "to neigh like a horse, to prance or stamp the ground, to put on lofty airs." The Psalmist sees Jehovah on His throne and the Messiah entering upon His dominion. The enemies of both rise up against them in frantic tumult, and vainly strive to cast off their rule. Hence the sudden question, "What ails the Gentiles?" Don't they know that if they oppose God and His Messiah, they will come to naught?

AND THE PEOPLES DEVISE FUTILE THINGS? Probably the "peoples" should be identified with the tribes of Israel, as they attempted the destruction of Jesus, and the cause for which He died. "Devise" is a rendering of *emeletēsan*, which means "to ponder meditatively" and to practice like orators in order to perfect their style. It includes the ideas of meditating, thinking, proposing. The Jewish people used thought, plan, purpose, in opposing the Messiah. *Kena* ("futile things") means "empty," as a vessel which is not filled; then "useless," as of labors which result in nothing, or which do not succeed at that which is attempted. The Jews attempted an opposition to God which the Psalmist sees could not succeed. Their efforts, whether in the case of Christ or in the case of His church, were futile because they were not strong enough to oppose God.

4:26 – *'THE KINGS OF THE EARTH TOOK THEIR STAND, AND THE RULERS WERE GATHERED TOGETHER AGAINST THE LORD, AND AGAINST HIS CHRIST.'*

THE KINGS OF THE EARTH TOOK THEIR STAND. The "kings" are Herod and Pilate as verse 27 will indicate. The word picture in "took their stand" is that of battle lines drawn up opposite each other. The earthly rulers were acting like hostile enemy soldiers taking their stand in the battle line as they offered their resistance to the Messiah.

AND THE RULERS WERE GATHERED TOGETHER. The Sanhedrin would be included in this term "rulers." "Gathered together" often implies the joining together of those who previously were separated, in order that they might oppose a common enemy. These verses are a very fine example of the parallelism often used in Hebrew poetry, where the second phrase speaks nearly the same thing as the first, but in different words.[43]

AGAINST THE LORD, AND AGAINST HIS CHRIST. The Psalmist sees both God the Father and the Messiah as being opposed by the enemies, but by an opposition which is ill-fated and destined to fail. Again, notice how the apostles prayed. Their model shows us it is proper to quote Scripture as we pray, and then base our petitions on the statements just quoted.

4:27 – "For truly in this city there were gathered together against Thy holy servant Jesus, whom Thou didst anoint, both Herod and Pontius Pilate, along with the Gentiles and the peoples of Israel,

For truly in this city there were gathered together. The apostles, still in prayer, declare they see in the Jerusalem events the fulfillment of Psalm 2. The one leading in prayer says, "Now we understand what the words of David mean. They not only opposed God then, but they just did it today when they told us never more to speak the name of Jesus."

Against Thy holy Servant Jesus. The word *pais*, translated "servant" has already been explained at Acts 3:13. It could possibly be translated "Holy Child" here, but "servant" seems the likely idea.

Whom Thou didst anoint. Is the reference to the coming of the Holy Spirit at the time of Jesus' baptism? Or was there some other time when God "anointed" Jesus?

Both Herod. Of the several Herods who appear in the pages of the New Testament, this is Herod Antipas, the tetrarch of Galilee and Perea.[44] Luke is the only Gospel writer who records the part taken by Herod Antipas in conjunction with Pilate in the condemnation of Jesus. See page *v-vi* of the New Testament Chronology concerning this man.

And Pontius Pilate. See page *v* of the New Testament Chronology concerning this man.

Along with the Gentiles and the peoples of Israel. Based on how Psalm 2 was applied in verse 25, the Romans and the Jews are denoted by these two phrases.

4:28 – "to do whatever Thy hand and Thy purpose predestined to occur.

To do whatever Thy hand and Thy purpose. "To do" is to be taken with the verb "gathered together" of verse 27, not with "predestined." "Purpose" speaks of the plan God made back in eternity before He ever created, a plan to redeem man if the man He was about to make sinned. That plan included the death of Christ. The Gentiles and Jews, the government and religious officials, who took part in His crucifixion were acting of their own free will, yet they were doing just as God had planned for them to do.

---

[43] Consult the *Westminster Dictionary of the Bible,* p.486-87 for a study concerning Hebrew parallelism in poetry.

[44] Luke 23:1-12.

Predestined to occur. Predestination has already been discussed in notes at Acts 2:23 and 3:18. "To occur" (*ginesthai*) is a different verb than the one translated "to do" (*poiesai*). The latter speaks of man's agency, the former of God's providence. The Bible everywhere suggests that the sovereign God is in full control of His creation, so that it accomplishes the purpose for which it was created. Nothing happens in this universe apart from His permission, nor will anything that happens defeat His purposes for His creation.

4:29 – *"And now, Lord, take note of their threats, and grant that Thy bond-servants may speak Thy word with all confidence,*

And now, Lord, take note of their threats. Does this mean "Take note in order to deliver us"? Or does it mean "Take note in order to frustrate their plans"? If the latter, then this is a New Testament example of what has been called imprecatory prayer.

And grant that Thy bond-servants may speak Thy word with all confidence. The apostles are praying for courage to go ahead and preach the Gospel in spite of official opposition. They are praying for protection by God from the devices of the enemies of the gospel. This is a good example for us. When we are harassed by those in power; when we are persecuted for righteousness' sake, we should commit our way unto God, lest we be deterred from the path of duty.

4:30 – *"while Thou dost extend Thy hand to heal, and signs and wonders take place through the name of Thy holy servant Jesus."*

While Thou dost extend Thy hand to heal. The apostles were not only asking for courage to speak, but they were also asking God to continue to work miracles through them. The miracles would furnish continuing evidence to the people that God was with apostles, and also confirm the truth of the message the apostles were delivering.

And signs and wonders take place through the name of Thy holy Servant Jesus. On the words "signs and wonders" see the comments at Acts 2:22. The words Peter used when he spoke to the lame man ("In the name of Jesus of Nazareth – rise up and walk around!") would be an example of a miracle taking place through the name of Jesus.

The apostles, between Pentecost and now, had been steadfastly teaching concerning Jesus, seemingly with little opposition from the authorities. Now, having worked this miracle on the lame man, they found themselves in trouble with the authorities. Nevertheless, they pray that the miracles may continue to be performed as they continue to speak the Word with boldness.

4:31 – *And when they had prayed, the place where they had gathered together was shaken, and they were all filled with the Holy Spirit, and began to speak the word of God with boldness.*

And when they had prayed. That is, when their prayer was ended.

The place where they had gathered was shaken. "Shaken" commonly denotes an earthquake. A part of God's answer to their prayer was this physical manifestation. A similar instance of an answer to prayer by an earthquake is recorded in Acts 16:25-26. From certain Old Testament events it could even be affirmed that an earthquake was regarded by the Jews as a striking and impressive evidence of the immediate presence of the Lord.[45]

And they were all filled with the Holy Spirit. This is probably to be understood as a renewal of the Holy Spirit received at Pentecost. Ford comments, "I think that this is a reoccurrence of the thing that happened at Pentecost, though nothing can absolutely be proven on this point."[46] It would appear that the apostles are the only ones assembled, and the only ones involved in this gift.[47] Why the need for this second empowering? It is not possible to answer why, with certainty. Some suggest that the presence of the baptismal power of the Holy Spirit was not an abiding thing, but each recipient was empowered from time to time as the occasion demanded.

And *began* to speak the word of God with boldness. In the days and months that followed this first opposition by the religious leaders, the apostles went right on evangelizing. Their prayers had been answered. They had prayed for boldness, and with boldness they continued to witness.

M. Unity and Liberality of the Early Church. 4:32-37

4:32 – *And the congregation of those who believed were of one heart and soul; and not one of them* claimed that anything belonging to him was his own; but all things were common property to them.

And the congregation of those who believed were of one heart and soul. The use of the word "multitude" (congregation) here, whereas Luke has previously spoken about "their own company" in verse 23, is further evidence that the "company" included only the apostles. In contrast to that group, Luke now speaks of the congregation of believers as a whole. "Believed" is a past tense verb. The 3,000 of Acts 2:41 and the 5,000 of Acts 4:4 are the ones intended, as well as those who may have been converted by the confident witness of the apostles after their release by the Sanhedrin. All these converts are still in and around Jerusalem. "One heart and one soul" indicates the marvelous unity of the early

---

[45] Isaiah 29:6; Psalm 68:8. This commentator objects to Barnes' language at this place. He writes. "They probably regarded this as an answer to their prayer." (Barnes, *op. cit.*, p.89.) These apostles were not superstitious; they were followers of the living God, and not left to follow their own blind imaginations.

[46] Harold W. Ford, *Notes on Acts of the Apostles* (Transcribed course notes, Lincoln Bible Institute, 1953), p.67-68.

[47] Modern Pentecostalism uses Acts 4:31 as proof that all who were baptized into Christ since Pentecost now receive the baptism in the Holy Spirit. Even were we to agree that more than the apostles are included here in verse 31, the passage still would not square with Pentecostal doctrine. That doctrine states that "tongues" are the initial evidence of having been baptized in the Holy Spirit. Verse 31 is not about the use of devotional tongues after people are filled with the Holy Spirit. The people are not pictured as praying to God in tongues, but as speaking the Word of God to men with boldness as a result of this filling. The passage thus proves as difficult for Pentecostal pneumatology as it does for the non-Pentecostal.

church. "One heart" indicates they felt alike, and were interested in the same things. The word represents the intellectual side of their Christian life.[48] "One soul" indicates the close and loving union of the early believers. This word speaks of the emotional side of their Christian life.[49]

> Considering the large number of persons in this congregation, and the variety of social relations from which they had suddenly been drawn together, it is truly remarkable, and well worthy of a place in the record, that they were "of one heart and soul." The unity for which the Savior prayed (John 17) was now enjoyed by the church, and witnessed by the world.[50]

An example of their oneness is shown in their liberality and complete lack of selfishness.

And not one *of them* claimed that anything belonging to him was his own. "Not even one" is the way the Greek has it. Because they were so filled with the desire to see souls saved there was, for the time being, no opportunity for disharmony and dissensions, nor any selfish assertions.

But all things were common property to them. Compare comments made on Acts 2:44-45. The rights of property ownership have not been abolished, nor is the individual holding of property declared to be wrong. Rather, we find all of the brethren willing and anxious to use whatever they possessed for the eternal benefit of each and any of their brethren. They loved so much they were willing to give all they had if it would help the other fellow.

4:33 – *And with great power the apostles were giving witness to the resurrection of the Lord Jesus, and abundant grace was upon them all.*

And with great power. Some think this speaks of "powerful preaching." Boles so thinks, for he writes, "Great power means the force of argument accompanied with spiritual power."[51] And Barnes has, "It refers to their preaching."[52] But the word could also be a reference to miracles performed by the apostles. After all, the apostles had prayed to be so empowered (verse 30).

The apostles were giving witness to the resurrection of the Lord Jesus. The Greek reads "went on giving." This is the main point of apostolic preaching, the very thing objected to by the Sadducees. The resurrection of Jesus was the chief apologetic for the truth of Christianity, and was the indisputable demonstration that He was sent from God. Over and over again, through the book of Acts, we shall hear the ringing claim concerning the resurrection!

---

[48] Mark 2:6, 8; 11:23; Luke 2:35; 3:15; 6:45.

[49] Luke 2:35, 12:22; John 12:27.

[50] McGarvey, *op. cit.*, p.79.

[51] Boles, *op. cit.*, p.75.

[52] Barnes, *op. cit.*, p.90.

And abundant grace was upon them all. Some Bible scholars believe this language signifies that "the entire membership of the church was finding *favor* with each other and with outsiders."[53] Their oneness of heart and soul, their benevolence and liberality in supplying the wants of the needy, would be the thing that won the hearts of the people so that they looked on the Christians with favor. However, since the passage does not specify the author of the grace, many believe Luke means that "the favor *of God* was upon them" because they were doing His will. He was pleased with them, and was a blessing to them. The majority of English versions translate the word "grace" as if accepting the highest meaning, that God's grace is the thing spoken of.

4:34 – *For there was not a needy person among them, for all who were owners of land or houses would sell them and bring the proceeds of the sales,*

For. Does this "for" explain the "abundant grace," the context then deciding that "favor" is the idea? Or is this verse giving a reason why God was pleased with them?

There was not a needy person among them. Because of their good will toward each other, no Christian brother was allowed to go without. Compare Acts 2:44ff.

For all who were owners of lands or houses would sell them. A number of 20th century interpreters have used this passage, as well as chapter 2, to try to show that only "communism" is Christian, and that private ownership of property is contrary to the way things were done in New Testament times. We believe that such a handling of these chapters is misguided. It mistakes "communism" for "fellowship." Both communism and fellowship (*koinōnia*) have a root idea of "common," but after that, the two ideas markedly diverge. Communism says, "What is yours is mine, and I'll take it!" Fellowship says, "What is mine is yours; I'll share it!" The one forcibly invades the right of private property; the other voluntarily relinquishes the right of private property where it sees a need. The modern attempts at communal living, in the belief that it is the only Christian way, fall short of New Testament concepts. And certainly, the atheistic forms of communism are even more at variance with New Testament Christianity.

And bring the proceeds of the sales. Evidently, as there had been among the apostles when they traveled with Jesus, so now, there is a common treasury into which such benevolent funds were channeled.

4:35 – *and lay them at the apostles' feet; and they would be distributed to each, as any had need.*

And lay them at the apostles' feet. The brethren committed the money received from the sales of goods and property into the care of the apostles, and the apostles would distribute it, wherever it was needed among the poor members of the congregation. This soon became burdensome and inconvenient for the apostles; in chapter 6, other men will be chosen to have special responsibility for this distribution.

---

[53] Boles, *op. cit.*, p.76.

And they would be distributed to each, as any had need. Were those with needs other Christians? Yes! The church is not told that it is to provide for all the poor even among the heathen. Did these people only sell the excess of possessions they had, or did they also sacrifice? They probably did both. The idea should not be drawn from this that they did not sacrifice. Later in Acts, we shall find the Gentile churches of Greece and Asia Minor sending an offering to Jerusalem, and for them it was a sacrificial offering.[54] They had learned such a concept from the Jerusalem church, which years before had given herself poor so that the gospel might rapidly spread.

4:36 – *And Joseph, a Levite of Cyprian birth, who was also called Barnabas by the apostles (which translated means, Son of Encouragement),*

And Joseph, a Levite of Cyprian birth. Many manuscripts read "Joses," but the better reading is "Joseph." This man is mentioned as an illustration of an early Christian selling his possessions and placing the money at the disposal of the apostles. As was Luke's custom, this also serves as an introduction of this man, whom afterwards will be regularly called Barnabas. Luke introduces each of the main characters in his history before their main part was played.

Barnabas was a Levite. What was the difference between "priests" and "Levites"? The whole tribe of Levi was set apart to the service of the temple, and anyone descended from Levi would be a Levite. Luke is telling us that Barnabas was of the tribe of Levi. Levi had three sons – Gershon, Kohath, and Merari. Aaron was of the family of Kohath, and all the sons of Aaron were the "priests." (Thus, all priests would be Levites, but not all Levites would be priests.)

Cyprus was an island in the Mediterranean Sea. The distance was 80 miles from the mouth of the Orontes River across the Mediterranean Sea to Cyprus. The lofty mountains of Cyprus are visible from the mainland. "Cyprus" means "copper." There were Jewish settlers on Cyprus in the 2nd century BC,[55] and their numbers were increased after Cyprus' copper mines were assigned by Augustus to Herod the Great's control. Barnabas was a descendant of some of these Jews, for he was not a Cypriot, but a Jew by blood. Today there is a monastery called St. Barnabas near the ruins of Salamis on the eastern end of the island, and it traditionally marks the spot where Barnabas was buried. Once we have learned that Cyprus was Barnabas' home, it appears to be more than just coincidence that Cyprus was the first place to which Paul and this very same Barnabas went on the first missionary journey.

Who was also called Barnabas by the apostles (which translated means, Son of Encouragement). Note the marginal reading, "son of consolation." The difficulty is that this Greek word *paraklēsis* cannot be easily translated into English. Sometimes it seems to mean "exhortation" and sometimes it seems to mean "encouragement, consolation, or comfort." Joseph is given this name Barnabas because it expresses some of the things he did best. If it is translated "consolation," we are reminded of how he helps introduce Paul

---

[54] 2 Corinthians 8:1ff.

[55] 1 Maccabees 15:23.

to the Jerusalem Christians after Paul was converted.[56] That act would have been a great encouragement to Paul at that particular time in his life. On the other hand, if we translate it "exhortation," we are reminded that Barnabas was an outstanding speaker and preacher.[57]

4:37 – *and who owned a tract of land, sold it and brought the money and laid it at the apostles' feet.*

And who owned a tract of land. This statement has caused problems for some Bible commentators. When the promised land was divided among the tribes, the tribe of Levi received no lands. In fact, the Law of Moses made provision that the Levites were to be supported by the tithes from the "other tribes."[58] No little surprise has been expressed, then, that Luke tells us a Levite was the owner of a tract of land. But it should be taken into consideration that the original division of the land among the tribes, with certain cities to the Levites, was no longer observed after the Captivity, for it was only remnants of certain tribes that returned from the exile. Further, there was no law that forbade the Levites from acquiring real estate. Josephus, a Levite himself, owned lands near Jerusalem,[59] so why could not Barnabas?

Sold it and brought the money and laid it at the apostles' feet. Where was the property that Barnabas owned? Was it near Jerusalem? Was it located on Cyprus? And how shall we explain the presence of Barnabas in Jerusalem? Was he there as the result of his service in the ministries of the temple? Was he there as a result of having come to the Feast of Pentecost? Was he a settled resident of Jerusalem who had witnessed even the ministry of Jesus? Was he one of the 3,000 who responded to Peter's preaching on Pentecost?

---

[56] Acts 9:22-26.

[57] Acts 11:23.

[58] Numbers 18:20,24; Deuteronomy 10:9, 18:2; Joshua 13:14,33.

[59] Josephus, *Life*, 76.

SPECIAL STUDY #9

THE SECTS OF THE JEWS

The Jewish people of New Testament times were divided into five major parties. Following is a brief outline of the origin, doctrines, and history of each of those parties.

I. THE PHARISEES

A. *Origin of the Party*

In all probability the Pharisees originated in the period before the Maccabean War, in a reaction against the Hellenizing spirit which appeared among the Jews, and manifested itself in the readiness of a part of the people to adopt Greek customs. Those who regarded these Hellenizing practices with abhorrence, and their spread with alarm, were incited to strict and open conformity to the Mosaic Law. They were driven yet more closely together as a party by the fierce persecutions of Antiochus Epiphanes, 175-163 BC. Antiochus persecuted those faithful Israelites who would not abandon Judaism and accept the Greek faith. He attempted to destroy the Holy Scriptures, and commanded that whosoever was found with any Book of the Covenant, or consented to the Law, should be put to death (1 Maccabees 1:56-57).

The Hasidim – the pietists who were mighty men of Israel, and who participated in the revolt against Antiochus – were probably the forerunners of the Pharisees, although they did not wear that name. When the war ceased to be a struggle for religious liberty and became a contest for political supremacy, they ceased to take an active interest in it.

The Pharisees are not mentioned during the time that Jonathan and Simeon were the Jewish leaders, 160-135 BC, but they appear under their own name in the time of John Hyrcanus, 135-105 BC. Hyrcanus was a disciple of theirs, but left them and joined the Sadducees.[1] Hyrcanus' son, Alexander Jannaeus, endeavored to exterminate the Pharisees by the sword. His wife, Alexandra, who succeeded him in 78 BC, recognizing that physical force was powerless against religious conviction, favored the Pharisees. Thenceforth, the Pharisees' influence was paramount in the religious life of the Jewish people.

B. *Doctrines of the Pharisees*

The Pharisees held the doctrine of foreordination and considered it consistent with the free will of men.[2] They believed in the immortality of the soul, in the resurrection of the body, and in the existence of spirits (angels and demons). They believed that men are

---

[1] Josephus, *Antiquities*, XIII.10.5-6.

[2] See Special Study #6, "Predestination and Foreknowledge."

rewarded or punished in the future life according as they have lived virtuously or viciously in this life. They believed that the souls of the good men become reincarnated in body after death, while the souls of the wicked are detained forever in everlasting punishment in a prison under the earth. There are references to these beliefs, especially in transmigration of souls, in Matthew 16:14; Luke 9:8; Acts 23:8, *Antiquities* XVIII.1.3; *Wars* II.8.14.

These doctrines distinguished them from the Sadducees, but did not constitute the essence of later Pharisaism. Pharisaism is the final and necessary result of that conception of religion which makes religion consist of conformity to the Law. They believed God promised grace only to the doers of the Law. Thus, religion became external; the disposition of the heart was less vital than the outward act, in their estimation. The interpretation of the Law and its application to the details of ordinary life accordingly became a matter of grave consequence. Lawyers acquired increased importance, and expositions of the Law by recognized authorities grew to be a body of binding precepts. Josephus, himself a Pharisee, tells us that they delivered to the people a great many observances by succession from the fathers, which were not written in the Law of Moses,[3] these being the traditional interpretations of the elders, which Jesus pronounced of no binding authority (Matthew 15:2-3,6).

C. *Subsequent History of the Sect*

At first, when one incurred great danger in joining the party, the Pharisees were men of strong religious character; they were the best people in the nation. Subsequently, Pharisaism became an inherited belief; the profession of it was popular; and the character of its later adherents very inferior to that of the original members. With the lapse of time, an essentially vicious element in the system developed and laid the Pharisees, as commonly represented by the members of the party, open to scathing rebuke. John the Baptist called them and the Sadducees a generation of vipers.[4] Jesus denounced their self-righteousness, their hypocrisy, their inattention to the weightier matters of the law, and other faults.[5]

The Pharisees always numbered in their ranks men of perfect sincerity. Paul, in his early life was a Pharisee.[6] Gamaliel was of this sect.[7]

II. THE SADDUCEES

A. *Origin of the Party*

The rabbis say that the party took its name from its founder, Zadok (*Sadouk*, Greek), who lived about 300 BC. But since it appears that the members and adher-

---

[3] Josephus, *ibid*.

[4] Matthew 3:7.

[5] Matthew 5:20; 16:6,11,13; 23:1-39.

[6] Acts 23:6, 26:5-7; Philippians 3:5.

[7] Acts 5:34.

ents of the highest priestly aristocracy constituted the party, it is now generally believed that the name refers to the high priest Zadok, who officiated in David's reign, and in whose family the high priesthood remained until the political confusion of the Maccabean times – his descendants and partisans being called Zadokites, or Sadducees.

In the 3rd and 4th centuries BC, the Sadducees began, unconsciously perhaps, to place political above religious considerations. In the time of Ezra and Nehemiah, the family of the high priest was worldly and inclined to resist the strict separation of Jew from Gentile (see the case of Eliashib). In the time of Antiochus Epiphanes, a large number of priests were friendly to Greek culture (2 Maccabees 4:14-16), and the high priests Jason, Menelaus, and Alcimus were pronounced to be Hellenizers. The people took a determined stand under the Maccabees for the purity of Israel's religion; when the Maccabean party triumphed and secured the high priesthood, the Sadducees were forced into retirement and driven to politics. It seems they continued to be ready to neglect the customs and traditions of the elders and favor Greek culture and influence. John Hyrcanus, Aristobulus, and Alexander Jannaeus (135-78 BC) were Sadducees, and the conduct of political affairs was largely in the hands of the Sadducees during the time of the Roman domination and the reigns of the Herods. The high priests met in the New Testament period were Sadducees.[8] The Sadducees, with the Pharisees, were active in the trial and death of Jesus. Both parties were to be found among the Sanhedrin members.

B. *Doctrines of the Sadducees*

In opposition to the Pharisees, who laid great stress on the traditions of the elders, the Sadducees limited their creed to the doctrines which they could find in the sacred text itself. They held that the written Law of Moses alone was binding.[9] They maintained the right of private interpretation.[10] In distinction to the Pharisees, the Sadducees denied the resurrection and future retribution in Sheol, asserting that the soul dies with the body.[11] They denied the existence of angels or spirits.[12] They denied fatalism, contending for the freedom of the will, teaching that all actions are in our own power, so that the individual himself is the cause of what is good and receives what is evil from his own folly. They affirmed that God is not concerned in our doing good or not doing what is evil.[13]

In denying immortality, they were relying on the absence of explicit statements of these doctrines in the Mosaic Law. The Sadducees failed to hold the faith of the Patriarchs regarding the existence of Sheol.[14]

---

[8] Acts 5:17; Josephus, *Antiquities*, XX.9.1.

[9] *Antiquities*, XIII.10.6.

[10] *Antiquities*, XVIII.1.4.

[11] Matthew 22:23-33; Acts 23:8; Josephus. *Antiquities*, XVIII.14; *Wars*, II.8.14

[12] Acts 23:8.

[13] *Antiquities*, XIII.5.9; *Wars*, ibid.

[14] See Special Study #7, "Hades and the Intermediate Place of the Dead." The reality of Sheol, though not fully developed as a doctrine, is indeed taught in the Old Testament. Those rudimentary teachings were the seed of later revelations regarding the resurrection of the body and future retribution.

In affirming that there was neither angel nor spirit, the Sadduccees were setting themselves against the elaborate angelology of the time, but they fell short of the Law's actual teaching (Exodus 3:2; 14:19).[15]

The Sadducees probably at first emphasized the truth that God directs affairs with respect to man's conduct, punishing or rewarding in this life according as man's deeds are good or evil. If they actually taught, as Josephus affirms they did, that God is not concerned in our doing good or refraining from evil, they rejected the clear teaching of the Mosaic Law which they professed to believe (see, for example, Genesis 3:17, 4:7, 6:5-7). It is probable they began by denying what is expressly taught in the letter of Scripture; but as they yielded more fully to Greek influence, they adopted the principles of the Aristotelian philosophy and refused to accept any doctrine which they could not prove by pure reason.

III. THE ESSENES

A. *History of the Sect*

The earliest note of the existence of the Essenes, as is also true of the Pharisees and the Sadducees, is under the high priesthood of Jonathan (1 Maccabees 2:5,9-13). It would seem that during the early Maccabean struggles, the pietist Hasidim supported the Maccabees, but that they later deserted the Maccabeans when the Maccabeans made alliances with heathen powers like Rome. The Essenes were scattered over Palestine, maintaining their own communities. They perhaps numbered about 4,000 in Judea in Jesus' time. The sect of the Essenes disappears about AD 70-100.

Our knowledge of the sect has increased considerably since the momentous discovery of the Dead Sea Scrolls in 1947.[16] From the silence of the Scripture concerning the Essenes (or for that matter, any sect from the Dead Sea area), one of two conclusions can be reached: (1) The role the Essenes played in the ministry of Jesus and the beginning of the Church was so small and insignificant that there was no need to mention it. So God in His wisdom, and the Holy Spirit in His guidance, purposely omitted any reference to the Essenes. (2) The Essenes' role was so great that their name was purposely left out, because everyone knew all the leaders of the New Testament institutions were Essenes. (That is, if the Essenes were important and yet are not mentioned, they must have been deliberately left out of the record.) Both the trustworthiness of the Biblical narratives and the remoteness of the Essene beliefs make this second possibility untenable.

B. *Doctrines of the Essenes*

---

[15] Some modern critics have said that the Jews learned their ideas about angels while they were in Babylon during the exile, and that the Sadducees were rejecting such wild notions as the Babylonians held. We reject such purely naturalistic approaches to explaining the source of Old Testament doctrines.

[16] Some helpful references for study about the Dead Sea Scrolls are: William S. LaSor, *Amazing Dead Sea Scrolls and The Christian Faith* (Chicago: Moody. 1956); Millar Burroughs, *The Dead Sea Scrolls* (New York: Viking Press, 1955); A.D. Tushingham and Peter V. Bianchi, "The Men Who Hid the Dead Sea Scrolls" in *National Geographic*, Vol. 114, No. 6 (December, 1958), p.785-808.

The Essenes practiced a form of communism (i.e., they had all things common), which has caused some scholars to attempt to show that Jesus, John the Baptist, and the apostles were Essenes. Some have even tried to equate the "communism" of the early church with the practices of the Essenes. But the two practices were entirely different – too much so for identification.

Some Essene communities repudiated marriage. They did, however, welcome the opportunity to adopt young children who could then be reared in accord with Essene teaching. They also appealed to those who were tired of the way most of the world was living to come and join them. In this way the sect kept alive from generation to generation.

In work, the Essenes labored as farmers or craftsmen. They would not go to war, or make instruments of war, or engage in commerce.

Their discipline was severe and ritualistic. They had long periods of silent meditation and worship. Their various religious observances were strictly kept. They practiced baptism in sand (i.e., each morning they would cover themselves with sand, and watch for the rising of the sun). They had many ceremonial ablutions.

They did not offer animal sacrifices, and were excluded from the temple at Jerusalem. Whether they withdrew, or, as is more probable, were put out, is not known with certainty. The Essenes were probably put out at Jerusalem because of their heterodox teaching. After their exclusion, they repudiated the temple practices which they were no longer allowed to attend.

The Essenes studied and searched the ancient writings, preferring moral application or a prophetic significance to a literal or philosophical treatment. Essene religion was moralistic; one of their most important doctrines was the morality of the two ways – the way of life and the way to destruction. Essene interpretation was eisegetic, versus exegetic.

IV. THE HERODIANS

The Herodians were apparently a political party of rich and influential people who were well disposed to the Herodian rule, and consequently also that of the Romans, who supported the Herods. They were on the side of Herod in a land where many people were decidedly opposed to that regime.

V. THE ZEALOTS

"Zealot" is the Greek equivalent of the Aramaic "Cananean." This was a Jewish patriotic party, interested in the overthrow of the Roman domination of Palestine. This party was a movement started by Judas the Galilean in the time of Quirinius (Acts 5:37) to resist Roman aggression. The increasing fanaticism of this party eventually led to the abortive revolution which ended in the destruction of Jerusalem by the Romans in AD 70. Simon the apostle was distinguished from Simon Peter by his title, Simon the Zealot (Luke 6:15, Acts 1:13). Judas of Galilee was a revolutionary who had been scattered after the uprising that had occurred at the time of the census (Acts 5:37).

N. The First Church Discipline. 5:1-11

5:1 – But a certain man named Ananias, with his wife Sapphira, sold a piece of property,

But a certain man named Ananias. Perhaps the division of chapters at this place is unfortunate. It would have been well if chapter 5 had started at 4:32. Luke has spoken of the liberality of the early church and he gave a good example of that liberality, Barnabas. Now he gives an example of how not to practice liberality, Ananias and Sapphira – a quite striking case of insincerity and hypocrisy, and of the just judgment of God on those who were guilty of such.

Chapter 5 introduces a second type of conflict which the early church faced. The first conflict was from without – the first persecution by the Sanhedrin. This second conflict was from within.

The case of Ananias and Sapphira stands as a warning for all the people who live in the New Testament era, for this case illustrates God's attitude toward hypocrisy. A person today may not suffer immediately as did Ananias and Sapphira, but God will repay all that is due.

Ananias (the Greek form of the Hebrew name Hananiah) was a rather common name among the Jews.[1] The name means "Jehovah has been gracious."

With his wife Sapphira. The name Sapphira means "beautiful" or "jewel," but her actions, in collusion with her husband, were not beautiful. They intentionally attempted to deceive the church, so they were not living a life in harmony with their profession of faith; in fact, their attempt to deceive was a matter of agreement between them. We can almost imagine them talking over the situation, and agreeing between themselves what they will do. Their besetting sins likely were a love of money and a love of the praise of men.

Sold a piece of property. Verse 3 tells us it was land, and the NASB translators have used that information when they rendered *ktēma* here by the words "a piece of property."

5:2 – and kept back some of the price for himself, with his wife's full knowledge, and bringing a portion of it, he laid it at the apostles' feet.

And kept back *some* of the price for himself. The verb "kept back" sometimes carries the idea of "surreptitiously" or "clandestinely,"[2] and in the middle voice here, emphasizes that the clandestine action was a selfish thing, done for Ananias' own benefit. They secretly kept back part of the sale price for themselves, while professing to be giving the whole amount received from the sale to the work of the church.

---

[1] Not only do we meet an Ananias here in Acts 5, but a disciple in Damascus is also named Ananias (Acts 9:10-19), as is a high priest before whom Paul is tried (Acts 23:1-5).

[2] The word translated "kept back" is translated "pilfering" (purloining, ASV) at Titus 2:10. This choice of English words in Titus is based on the fact the word has a connotation of stealth or dishonest appropriation in it. The word is also used in the Septuagint at Joshua 7:1 to describe the sin of Achan.

With his wife's full knowledge. The margin reads "with his wife's collusion." It is thus emphasized that Ananias took the lead in this hypocrisy, but his wife knew about what he planned to do and entered into the sin with him. They had decided together beforehand that this was the course they would pursue.

And bringing a portion of it, he laid it at the apostles' feet. Remember that Barnabas earlier had sold his land, and brought the money and laid it at the apostles' feet (4:37). Ananias and Sapphira were apparently looking for the praise of the people. No doubt Barnabas had received the praise and acclaim of the people for his generosity, and Ananias and Sapphira wanted some of the same kind of praise. Barnabas received praise because of his self-sacrifice. Ananias and Sapphira thought they could have the same result more cheaply.

5:3 – But Peter said, "Ananias, why has Satan filled your heart to lie to the Holy Spirit, and to keep back some of the price of the land?

But Peter said. Peter must have known about the plans of Ananias and Sapphira because of a revelation from God. Through the power of the Holy Spirit, Peter could read men's hearts. Such a gift would be very similar to the spiritual gift called "discerning of spirits."[3] Whether it was a temporary and recurring ability, or whether it was something Peter had permanently as a result of being baptized with the Holy Spirit, the Scriptures do not tell.

Ananias, why has Satan filled your heart. "Filled your heart" is Biblical language for "planted the thought in your mind." The devil does have the ability both to plant thoughts in men's minds and to stir up the desires of their bodies.[4] The question "why" implies that resistance to the temptation had been possible in Ananias' case. But Satan had tempted them, and they allowed the temptation to take root and grow.[5]

To lie to the Holy Spirit. "To lie to" here equals "to attempt to deceive." The deception which Ananias attempted to get by with was to keep back for himself part of the sale price, and yet pretend to be giving it all. Two ideas have been advanced as to exactly how Ananias would have been lying to the Holy Spirit. (1) Either he lied to Him who dwelt in the apostles, or he lied against Him who dwelt in Ananias (i.e., the indwelling gift of the Holy Spirit).[6] (2) Or it may be that Ananias' lie was an injury to Him who dwelt in the congregation.[7] It is not possible to tell for certain from the context which is intended.

---

[3] 1 Corinthians 12:10.

[4] A helpful, readable book about temptation and how to meet it is C.S. Lovett's book, *Dealing with the Devil* (Baldwin Park, CA: Personal Christianity, 1967).

[5] James 1:14-15 tells how sin grows from the initial temptation till it brings forth death.

[6] For more information on the Holy Spirit's role and activities, see Special Study #3, "The Person and Work of the Holy Spirit."

[7] 1 Corinthians 3:16-17 pictures the congregation as a place where the Spirit of God dwells.

And to keep back *some* of the price of the land? Hypocrisy is "play acting." Hypocrisy consists in attempting to imitate the people of God, or to assume the appearance of being religious without actually surrendering wholly to the will of God. This is what Ananias was doing as he surreptitiously attempted to keep part of the money for himself.

5:4 – *"While it remained unsold, did it not remain your own? And after it was sold, was it not under your control? Why is it that you have conceived this deed in your heart? You have not lied to men, but to God."*

While it remained *unsold*, did it not remain your own? Peter's question means, 'Before you sold it, you could do with it what you wanted, could you not?' This passage proves that there was no obligation imposed upon the early Christians to sell all their property and pool their resources in a common fund. Absolute communism did not exist in the early church. Those who did sell, did it voluntarily; and it does not appear that selling goods and possessions was something expected to be done by all.

And after it was sold, was it not under your control? Even after the land had been sold, and Ananias had received the money for it, he was still free to do with the money as he wished. There was no compulsion on him to bring any of it and give it to the apostles for distribution to the poor and needy. He could have put it in the bank, had there been one, and saved it for old age pension, if he had wished. He could have saved part, and brought part, and given it to the care of the apostles, as long as he only represented it as part. Had he brought part and said, 'This is a part of what we received when we sold our field,' things would have been perfectly all right. He did not have to bring any, for that matter. The point Peter is making is that Ananias had no excuse for his sin.

Why is it that you have conceived this deed in your heart? Notice how Peter words it, as recorded in verses 3 and 4. In verse 3 the question was, "Why has Satan filled your heart?" Now in verse 4 the question is, "Why have you conceived this deed in your heart?" The comparison shows what is involved in the sin they committed – the temptation by the devil, and their acquiescence to his suggestions. Actually, there are three things involved in any sin: (1) A knowledge of what God has commanded, for sin is transgression of God's law, whether by omission or commission. (2) Satan and his temptation (verse 3). (3) The will of the person who submits to the temptation (verse 4).

You have not lied to men, but to God. Probably we should understand this to mean, 'You have not only lied to men, but also to God.' The parallelism between this phrase and "lying to the Holy Spirit" (verse 3) has often been used, and perfectly so, as an evidence that the apostles did not shrink from speaking of the Holy Spirit as God. This is in harmony with what we have learned about the deity of the Holy Spirit in Special Study #2, "The Person and Work of the Holy Spirit."

5:5 – *And as he heard these words, Ananias fell down and breathed his last; and great fear came upon all who heard of it.*

And as he heard these words, Ananias fell down and breathed his last. This is more than just dying from the shock that Peter knew all about his secret plans, or having a heart attack. This man's death is not just a natural occurrence. It is an act of God. That the deaths of both are more than just natural can be seen from the fact that Peter even prophesies the death in the case of Sapphira. "Breathed his last" is a rendering of the Greek *ekpsuchō* (from *ek*, out, and *psuchē*, soul), a word which means "soul out." Death is separation of the soul from the body, the leaving of the body by the soul.

And great fear came upon all who heard of it. It was manifestly such an awesome act of God that all who heard about it were caused to pause and consider his own life, and to live more circumspectly, lest the same thing happen to him. This statement by Luke appears to have reference to a longer time period than just that time between the deaths of Ananias and Sapphira. The impression that resulted from their deaths would be lasting for some time. And evidently "all who heard" would encompass people outside the church as well as people who were already believers.

Why should God deal so severely with this couple? This thing in which Peter and these New Testament Christians are involved at this time concerns not them alone, nor their age alone, but all the centuries to follow. God knew the church could stand persecution from the outside, for Jesus had overcome, and was available to help them when they needed help in time of persecution. But one thing the infant church could not stand was fifth column activity from within. May we not believe that in the early days it was so necessary that everything be right that God just simply takes out of the new congregation those undesirable elements that would have sapped her strength and led to her extinction. This commentator has thought about this act of God and the church today: what would happen to us if God sought to purify His church, and suddenly would strike dead all the hypocrites? How many of us would be left alive? Let each of us be apprised of the fact that at the judgment the wheat and tares will be separated!

5:6 – *And the young men arose and covered him up, and after carrying him out, they buried him.*

And the young men arose. Mosheim says that very probably these young men were "deacons" in the early church;[8] it was their business to attend to the needs of the congregation and to perform various helpful services when Christians celebrated their worship. Can we agree with Mosheim that already in the church men have been chosen to the function of "deacons," similar to the office that is found in later pages of the New Testament? Ellicott believes we can. He writes that the Greek reads "the younger men," the article implying the existence of a distinct body as contrasted with the "elders" of the church.[9] However, Hervey writes that this does not seem to be sufficient ground for supposing that a definite class of church officers is meant here.[10] Meyer thinks Peter just instructed several

---

[8] Johann L. Mosheim, *An Ecclesiastical History Ancient and Modern Vol. I*, trans. by Archibald Maclaine (Rosemead, CA: Old Paths Book Club, 1959), p.29.

[9] Charles J. Ellicott, "Acts" in *Layman's Handy Commentary on the Bible* (Grand Rapids, MI: Zondervan, 1957), p.83.

[10] Hervey, *op. cit.*, p.157.

of the young men standing by to do the job.[11]

While they are not specifically called deacons, perhaps they were. That we have not been told of any selection of such leaders is no real objection, for neither does Luke tell us about the selection of the elders who are present in Jerusalem (see chapter 11).

And covered him up. Poor men simply had their own garments wrapped tightly about their bodies as a preparation for burial. Among the richer class of Jews, it was done as in Lazarus' case.[12] The body would be wound in many layers of linen before it was buried, and the layers were interspersed with dry spices which served to slow the decay of the body. The use of coffins evidently was unknown in Palestine at this time.

And after carrying him out. The implication is that the burial was ordered by Peter. "Out" means "outside the walls of the city." It was customary to bury outside the walls. They may have used the regular Jewish cemetery, or they may have used the Potter's Field. It is doubtful that the church already had its own private burial plot.

> It is scarcely conceivable that young men in the audience would have felt at liberty to do anything, unless it would be to go and tell the dead man's wife what had happened, if they had received no orders from the apostle.[13]

They buried him. Why bury him so soon? The ancient Persians buried bodies almost immediately after death. Did the Jews adopt this practice during the exile? Or was quick burial the result of the idea of ceremonial defilement as the result of touching a corpse (Numbers 19:11-16)? Perhaps the hot dry climate necessitated burial, for decomposition would set in quickly. Yet none of these suggestions satisfy as to why the burial was so hasty that not even the nearest of kin was notified. There must be more to the case that we must read between the lines.

5:7 – *Now there elapsed an interval of about three hours, and his wife came in, not knowing what had happened.*

Now there elapsed an interval of about three hours. Such a lapse of time could bring us to the next hour of prayer.

And his wife came in. Came into where? Was this a public worship service where the deaths of Ananias and Sapphira took place? Or was it merely at the place where the apostles were staying, into which Sapphira came? Whichever it is, Sapphira came to the place, prepared to act out the deception that she had agreed on with her husband.

Not knowing what had happened. She did not know her husband had been stricken dead, having been caught in his hypocrisy. How was she kept from knowing for three hours?

---

[11] H.A.W. Meyer, *Critical and Exegetical Handbook to the Acts of the Apostles* (New York: Funk and Wagnalls, 1883), p.107.

[12] John 11:44.

[13] McGarvey, *op. cit.*, p.85.

One of the first things done in the case of a death is to notify the next of kin. That she has not been notified leads us to suppose that some command from Peter or one of the other apostles had been given to the people to keep the miraculous event quiet. Especially is this true if Ananias had been stricken dead in a public assembly. The only other explanation why someone present had not gone to inform Sapphira might be that those present were wholly given to some silent self-examination. The power of God to reveal the intents and thoughts of the heart struck home with such force that every person just might concern himself with his own secret thoughts and be fervently seeking the favor of divine mercy.

5:8 – *And Peter responded to her, "Tell me whether you sold the land for such and such a price?" And she said, "Yes, that was the price."*

And Peter responded to her. The word "responded" does not necessarily imply that she had asked some question, but could speak of Peter's response to her unasked thoughts. She at least can be pictured as wondering what people were thinking of the amount of money her husband brought. Perhaps she was even expecting to find him held in high honor in the midst of the assembly.

Tell me whether you sold the land for such and such a price? Peter's question gave her an opening for repentance. The moment Peter's question struck her conscience, she would have an inner struggle with herself whether to repent and tell the truth, or whether to attempt to lie and bluff her way through. "Such and such a price" would be the sum which Ananias had presented. Perhaps we may picture Peter as pointing to the pile of money which had been carried in by Ananias as he asks the question of Sapphira. After a moment she makes her choice of how she will answer.

And she said, "Yes, that was the price." At the time the plan was formed she could have warned her husband that any deception was wrong, and possibly have saved him. It is now in her power to tell the truth, and save herself through repentance and confession. But she misses this new opportunity as she had missed the other. The hypocrisy which she and her husband had agreed upon comes glibly from her tongue, and her fate is fixed.

5:9 – *Then Peter said to her, "Why is it that you have agreed together to put the Spirit of the Lord to the test? Behold, the feet of those who have buried your husband are at the door, and they shall carry you out as well."*

Then Peter *said* to her. Sapphira had been given an opportunity to repent and to confess her wrong, but she continued persistently in the premeditated sin. Peter therefore predicts God's judgment upon her.

Why is it that you have agreed together to put the Spirit of the Lord to the test? "Agreed" speaks of "conspiring" or "laying a plan." To "put the Spirit of the Lord to the test" means to endeavor to deceive the Spirit, to see if they could get by without being challenged by the Spirit, or to act as if the Spirit of the Lord could not detect the crime.[14]

---

[14] "Spirit of the Lord" is probably equivalent, here, to the Old Testament name "Spirit of Jehovah. This

Here it seems the "Spirit" intended is the Spirit who empowered the apostles, and may in particular have reference to the spiritual gift called "discerning of spirits."

Behold, the feet of those who have buried your husband are at the door. It must have come as quite a shock to Sapphira to learn for the first time that her husband was dead. And she would understand that he had put the Spirit of the Lord to the test, and been punished for it. She, too, was about to be stricken by the hand of God. "At the door" gives us the mental image that the young men are just now stepping back into the assembly room, having completed their burial detail for Ananias. Whether or not Peter knew Ananias would be stricken for persisting in the lie, he knows that the same thing will be true in Sapphira's case; and he declares it.

And they shall carry you out *as well.* As Sapphira had been no less guilty in the sin than her husband, so it was ordered in the providence of God that the same judgment should come upon her.

5:10 – *And she fell immediately at his feet, and breathed her last; and the young men came in and found her dead, and they carried her out and buried her beside her husband.*

And she fell immediately at his feet, and breathed her last. Her death, like her husband's, was clearly an act of God. It is not possible to put the Lord to the test and get away with it.

And the young men came in and found her dead. Can we imagine how awe-stricken the young men must have been as they buried Ananias? Can we imagine what they said to each other as they worked? And then can we imagine what they must have felt when they returned to the assembly room, only to find another body?

And they carried her out and buried her by her husband. "Out" likely means outside the walls of the city. The Greek reads "face to face to her husband," but it likely means that she was simply buried beside her husband in the same plot of ground.

5:11 – *And great fear came upon the whole church, and upon all who heard of these things.*

And great fear. People's conduct is likely to be much more wholesome when they realize the God of the universe sees and hears and knows all that goes on, even their thoughts and motives, and the things they thought no one knew about. If God knew what Ananias and Sapphira secretly planned, then He knows our secrets, too; and we'd best be circumspect in our thoughts and behavior. This act of God reminds us that one purpose of church discipline is to keep the church pure. In the case of Ananias and Sapphira, the discipline was supernatural. But there are abundant instructions in the New Testament concerning discipline that every congregation is to practice.[15]

---

name for the Holy Spirit is rare in the New Testament; it is also used at 2 Corinthians 3:17. But it is common in the Old Testament, e.g., Isaiah 61:1 (quoted in Luke 4:18); 1 Kings 22:24; 2 Kings 2:16.

[15] See Special Study #10, "Church Discipline," at the close of chapter 5.

Came upon the whole church, and upon all who heard of these things. Both those inside the church and those who were not yet Christians were impressed with the discipline. It accomplished its intended purpose, namely, causing men to have respect for the church.

This is the first occurrence of the word "church" in the New Testament since the two recorded instances when Jesus used the word.[16] The word *ekklēsia* was already in use; the word was not newly minted for use in the Bible. It is frequently used in the Septuagint for the "assembly" or "congregation" of Israel,"[17] and it was used in a political sense by the Greeks of the assembly (town meeting) where every citizen had a voice in their own government.[18] However, Jesus and the Gospel writers did with this word as they did with many other words they found already in use. They took the words, filled them with a new content, and used them to express spiritual truths which would be comprehendible to their hearers. The word *ekklēsia,* as has often been pointed out, refers not to a building, but to a group of believers called out for a special purpose.

O. A Period of Peaceful Growth. 5:12-16

5:12 – And at the hands of the apostles many signs and wonders were taking place among the people; and they were all with one accord in Solomon's portico.

And at the hands of the apostles many signs and wonders were taking place among the people. It is significant that the signs and wonders came by "the hands of the apostles"! If, as some affirm, the 120 were involved in the baptism with the Holy Spirit on the day of Pentecost, why do we read constantly and consistently in Acts that signs and wonders were done by the apostles (and not by the others)? This wording is confirmation of the conclusion reached in chapter 2 concerning just who received the baptism with the Holy Spirit.

It is also significant that the word "wonders" (miracles, see notes at Acts 2:43) is never used by itself in the New Testament, but instead always appears with the word "signs." It would seem that the New Testament is not concerned with miracles except as they are "signs." And this is exactly in harmony with the doctrine that miracles were intended to confirm the message. We never find Jesus or the apostles ever performing a miracle just for the miracle's sake. Rather, a miracle was always a sign!

Some commentaries suggest verse 12b is the beginning of a parenthesis, with the thought of verse 12a continued at verse 15. In fact, such is the handling in the KJV. Others see no need to think of a parenthesis at this place.

And they were all with one accord in Solomon's portico. Shall we find the antecedent of "they" in the near word "people" or in the far word "apostles"? Both choices have found defenders. Some think Luke speaks of the apostles as being regularly in Solomon's porch. Others think the verse says that the miracles were worked on the people who were meeting

---

[16] The KJV has "church" in the text at Acts 2:47, but the reading is doubtful. Jesus' use of "church" is recorded in Matthew 16:18 and 18:17.

[17] Deuteronomy 18:16, 23:1; Psalm 26:12. etc.

[18] See notes at Acts 19:41 for the use of *ekklēsia* in its political sense.

regularly in Solomon's porch. Hermeneutical principles would urge us to find the antecedent of pronouns in the nearest antecedent (unless such an interpretation would make the Bible contradict itself), and so we shall do that here. "Solomon's portico" has been explained in notes at Acts 3:11.

See notes at 1:14 on the meaning of "one accord." If "all" refers to the people, then we must stop to note that even after all the difficulty from outside the church and within the church, the church is still one. And it would appear that the Christians are coming to the temple at the regular hours of prayer, and are using Solomon's porch as a pulpit from which to proclaim the gospel to the crowds who are not yet converted.

5:13 – *But none of the rest dared to associate with them; however, the people held them in high esteem.*

But none of the rest dared to associate with them. Who "them" is depends on what one understands by the word "all" in verse 12, since the "them" and the "all" are evidently the same. But who are the "rest" who are afraid to associate with them? A great variety of interpretations for this verse will be found among the commentaries.

- Lightfoot says, "The remainder of the 120 of whom Ananias had been one" is what is meant by "rest,"[19] but it might be hard to prove that Ananias was one of the 120.
- Bruce suggests "All of those who had not yet become believers" were the ones afraid to join the body of Christ,[20] but this is contrary to what is written in the very next verse.
- Hervey thinks the reference is to the Jews because the "rest" are distinguished from the "all" in verse 12. He thinks that the meaning is that the Jews looked with awe upon the apostolic church because of the miracles, and none dared associate with them simply out of mere curiosity or idle purpose.[21]
- Barnes writes that the "rest" refers to the Jewish leaders, of whom Ananias was one,[22] but it might be difficult to demonstrate that Ananias was one of the Jewish leaders (say a Sanhedrin member).
- Boles suggests that "rest" refers to the "apostles," and that the meaning is that the other Christians stood in awe of them and did not come near them,[23] but this requires "them" at the end of the verse to be handled in a peculiar fashion. If Boles had said that "them" is apostles, and "rest" referred to Christians in general, then we might accept his idea, for the "rest" of the brethren might be apprehensive to associate with the apostles after what happened to Ananias and Sapphira in Peter's presence.
- Dale thinks that "rest" refers to the "rest of the enemies of Christ," and the meaning is thought to be that the manifestation of the power of God in taking the lives of Ananias

---

[19] Quoted by R.J. Knowling, "Acts" in *Expositor's Greek Testament* (Grand Rapids: Eerdmans. 1967), p.145.

[20] Bruce, *op. cit.*, p.118.

[21] Hervey. *op. cit.*, p.158.

[22] Barnes, *op. cit.*, p.98.

[23] Boles, *op. cit.*, p.82.

and Sapphira gave boldness to the apostles, but it struck fear into the hearts of the enemies of Christ.[24]

- Given the context, this commentator is of the opinion that "rest" refers "to the rest of the people like Ananias and Sapphira (i.e., the rest of the hypocrites).

However, the people held them in high esteem. By "the people" Luke evidently intends the people outside of the church. The people on the outside looked upon them (either the apostles or the church), and they weighed and balanced the things that were transpiring before their very eyes in the city of Jerusalem. The Christians were looked up to, they were respected by those outside the church.

5:14 – *And all the more believers in the Lord, multitudes of men and women, were constantly added to their number;*

And all the more believers in the Lord ... were constantly added to *their number*. "Believers" is the name by which disciples were designated, because one of the main things that distinguished them was that they believed that Jesus was the Christ. The effect of the miracles was to confirm the message, and the effect of the message was that the number of believers increased. Faith comes by hearing! Although the judgment of God on Ananias and Sapphira had the effect of deterring hypocrites from trying to associate with the church, and though it produced awe and caution, yet still the number of true converts was increased. An effort to keep the church pure by wholesome discipline, rather than weakening the true strength of the congregation, tends to increase its numbers and its consecration to the Lord. "Lord" here is a reference to the Lord Jesus Christ. "More" means "many more" than was counted at Acts 4:4. In the NASB, "to their number" is in italics, indicating there is nothing corresponding to this in the Greek text. DeWelt has suggested it should be rendered "believers were added to the Lord," and he then explains with these words:

> What is the meaning of the expression "added to the Lord?" When we refer to Ephesians 1:22-23 (and other passages) we find the church is referred to as "the body of Christ," thus we can draw the logical conclusion that the thought of being "added to the Lord" was in reference to the action of being added by their conversion and baptism to the Lord's body, His Church.[25]

Multitudes of men and women. They came into the church in such numbers that they lost count. To the 3,000 in the beginning (Acts 2:41) more were added daily (2:47); then the number was 5,000 men (Acts 4:4); and now they can no longer count the total number of members. McGarvey believes that this special mention of women among the converts is a probable indication that among the converts there was now a greater relative number of women than before.[26] The notation about women converts also prepares us for the introduction of "widows" (chapter 6) who are members of the church.

---

[24] Dale, *op. cit.*, p.71.

[25] DeWelt, *op. cit.*, p.35.

[26] McGarvey, *op. cit.*, p.89.

5:15 – *to such an extent that they even carried the sick out into the streets, and laid them on cots and pallets, so that when Peter came by, at least his shadow might fall on any one of them.*

To such an extent that they even carried the sick out into the streets. The connection of verse 15 to the previous statements depends on whether or not we make verses 12b-14 a parenthesis. If we do, then verse 15 is connected to the fact that "wonders" were being done through the apostles. If we do not, then verse 15 is connected to the fact that the Christians were held in such high honor (verses 13-14). The word "streets" carries the connotation of a wide avenue, as opposed to a narrow lane or alley.[27] The verb tense in "carried" implies continuous action, and the friends of the sick people are the ones who did the carrying. It is possible the phrase pictures Christians bringing their sick to the apostles to be healed, but it is also possible the phrase includes even non-Christians bringing their sick to the apostles. For some days or weeks, the sick were laid all along the streets down which the apostle Peter was known to walk.

And laid them on cots and pallets. "Cots" represents the Greek *klinē*, which speaks of a bed, a couch for reclining at meals, such as those who were relatively rich might own. "Pallets" represents the Greek *krabbatos*, which speaks of a camp bed, a pallet, a mattress, such as poor people would have. "The rich came, they on little beds; the poor came, they only on a blanket," comments Ford.[28]

So that when Peter came by, at least his shadow might fall on any one of them. The sick people were laid out in the street, in hopes that as Peter walked by his shadow might pass over them. Were the sick healed in this manner? The implication of verse 15 is that they were. Otherwise, why were the sick continually laid in the streets? The news of these events evidently traveled widely, for people were brought from miles around and Luke explicitly says these were healed (verse 16).

> Assuming that miracles are possible, and that the narratives of the Gospels indicate generally the laws that govern them, there is nothing in the present narrative that is not in harmony with those laws. Christ healed sometimes directly by a word, without contact of any kind (Matthew 8:13; John 4:52); sometimes through material media – the fringe of His garment (Matthew 9:20), or the clay smeared over the blind man's eyes (John 9:5) becoming channels through which the healing virtue passed. All that is wanted was the expectation of an intense faith, as the subjective condition on the one side, the presence of an objective supernatural power on the other, and any medium upon which the imagination might happen to fix itself as a help to faith.[29]

An instance somewhat similar is recorded in Acts 19:12. There, it is expressly said that the sick were healed upon contact with aprons and handkerchiefs that were brought from Paul. The apostles' prayer (from Acts 4:30) continues to be answered.

---

[27] See Matthew 6:5. The word "streets" is *plateia*, which means avenue, or broadway.

[28] Ford, *op. cit.*, p.76.

[29] Ellicott, *op. cit.*, p.85.

5:16 – *And also the people from the cities in the vicinity of Jerusalem were coming together, bringing people who were sick or afflicted with unclean spirits; and they were all being healed.*

And also the people from the cities in the vicinity of Jerusalem were coming together. As with the word "carried" from verse 15, the verb tense in "came together" also points to continuous action over a period of time. The people came continually, attracted by the fame of Peter's miracles. With a few brief sentences Luke summarizes what must have occurred over a period of several months. Multitudes (see the marginal reading) are coming from the neighboring cities around Jerusalem – cities such as Hebron, Bethlehem, Emmaus, Jericho, perhaps also Lydda and Joppa.[30]

Notice, we are entering upon Luke's record of the spread of the gospel outside of Jerusalem (Acts 1:8). It would seem that many of the people who came were healed, baptized, and then went home and started congregations in those cities.

Bringing people who were sick or afflicted with unclean spirits. Be sure to see that sickness is something different than being afflicted by unclean spirits.[31] What are here called "unclean spirits" are called "demons" elsewhere in Scripture.[32] They are "unclean" because the doctrines and practices they encourage are regularly unmoral or immoral.

And they were all being healed. Does "all" include those of verse 15 as well as those of verse 16? There is no reason why it cannot be inclusive. It is significant that after Pentecost the apostles were successful in every case they tried to heal.[33] Unlike the "faith healers" of today, the apostles never had to make any excuses for being unable to heal someone. Luke tells they were *all* healed. Power to deliver those possessed of demons was twice promised by Jesus to the apostles.[34]

Do men today have the power to heal miraculously as the apostles had power to heal? Such miraculous abilities were received either by the baptism with the Holy Spirit or by the laying on of hands by the apostles (Acts 8). It has been a long time since any apostles were here in the flesh, and it has been a long time since any believer has had hands laid on him by an apostle. We affirm that the Holy Spirit is not a split personality. The New Testament, written by inspiration of the Holy Spirit, reveals to us the way God does things. We further affirm that the Holy Spirit would not contradict Himself by doing something today contrary to what He has revealed about the way God does things. When we find a man today who claims to be a faith healer (i.e., working cures by the power of God), and who does not even preach the simple gospel message, what can we conclude but (in love) to say, "He is deceived!"?

---

[30] In the comments at chapter 9:32,36, we will suggest another source for the planting of Christianity in Lydda and Joppa and the plain of Sharon. Thus, it is not certain these cities should be included here.

[31] This is important to note in a time when certain popular preachers and radio-TV personalities try to attribute all sickness to demon possession.

[32] See Special Study #11, "Demons and Demon Possession," at the close of chapter 5.

[33] Apostolic powers at this time exceeded what they previously had been, Matthew 17:16.

[34] Luke 9:1; Mark 16:17.

P. Second Persecution by the Sanhedrin. 5:17-42

1. Peter and All the Apostles are Imprisoned. 5:17-25

5:17 – *But the high priest rose up, along with all his associates (that is the sect of the Sadducees), and they were filled with jealousy;*

But the high priest rose up. Does this speak of Annas or Caiaphas? The commentators are divided in their attempts to answer this question. Perhaps we are to see Caiaphas as the mover behind this persecution, just as he was behind the opposition that led to the crucifixion of Jesus. "Rose up" is an idiom that means he began active opposition again. The high priest and the Sadducees would have especially disliked challenges to their doctrine of no bodily resurrection. So they were stimulated to action by what was taking place in the city because of the preaching and miracles in the Christian community.

Along with all his associates (that is of the sect of the Sadducees). Acts 4:5-6 has already introduced several of these "associates" during the first persecution by the Sanhedrin. Not all the Sanhedrin members were Sadducees by belief, but those who were are involved, along with their leader, in this persecution.[35] The word "sect" is a translation of the Greek *hairesis*, which meant "something one chooses to do or believe;" later, it came to mean "party to which one belongs by choice." To the people of the 1st century, the word "sect" did not have the harsh connotation it does to our ears. For example, different schools of philosophy were called "sects" by the Greek writers, and Galen used the word to speak of the different schools of medicine.

And they were filled with jealousy. The same word is elsewhere translated "zeal" or "envy." The KJV has "indignation." The motives behind the action of the Sadducees may have been an attempt to jealously guard their own beliefs from attack. Or they may have been angry that the apostles had so little regarded their authority and had disobeyed their solemn injunction against preaching in the name of Jesus. Or they may have been envious of the popularity of the apostles.

5:18 – *and they laid hands on the apostles, and put them in a public jail.*

And they laid hands on the apostles. The Greek word used here has the meaning "to throw upon." We might say in our idiom, "They grabbed them by the nape of the neck and threw them in jail." All twelve apostles were arrested this time (verse 29). The Sadducees want to give the impression that they really mean business this time. Lenski thinks the apostles were caught and arrested when there were no crowds of people around them,[36] drawing this implication from what happens when the same authorities capture the apostles again and bring them without violence, for they feared the people (verse 26).

---

[35] See notes at Acts 4:1 and Special Study #9, "The Sects of the Jews," for further information about the Sadducees.

[36] R.C.H. Lenski, *Interpretation of Acts of the Apostles* (Philadelphia: Wartburg Press, 1944), p.214.

And put them in a public jail. "Jail" was used before at Acts 4:3. The addition of the word "public" perhaps indicates a greater severity of treatment. They were not merely put in custody, but they were roughly treated as common criminals and held in the same confinement as were robbers and murderers. Prisoners were kept in jail overnight because they could not be tried on the same day they were arrested, according to the Law of Moses.

5:19 – *But an angel of the Lord during the night opened the gates of the prison, and taking them out he said,*

But an angel of the Lord. The release, as recorded by Luke, was obviously supernatural. An angel, whose very existence was denied by the Sadducees who had arrested the apostles, is the one who did it! Those who do not accept what Luke says at face value, and yet who wish to maintain the general historical character of the record, are driven to the hypothesis that the "angel" was some zealous and courageous disciple, and that the apostles, in the darkness of the night and the excitement of their liberation, ascribed their rescue to the intervention of an angel.[37] Such a loose handling of the account impinges on its trustworthiness and its inspiration, and is to be rejected!

During the night. We shall learn in the following verses that there were guards on duty at the jail. Was something done to their eyes that they didn't see what the angel was doing?

Opened the gates of the prison, and taking them out he said. Critics have sometimes asked, 'What was the use of such a deliverance as this, when the apostles will be arrested again on the very next day?' The answer to such a question is straightforward. Such a release would serve as a rebuke to the Sadducees. It would help increase the faith of the apostles. And when the people heard of it, it would tend to convince them all the more of God's power and presence and providential care of His own.

5:20 – *"Go your way, stand and speak to the people in the temple the whole message of this Life."*

Go your way, stand and speak to the people in the temple. The angel instructs the apostles to be in a conspicuous public place. If the authorities wish to arrest them again, they will have to do it publicly. In the meantime, the apostles can be demonstrating forcefully their purpose to obey God rather than men.

The whole message of this Life. The Greek word translated "message" is plural; i.e., it is "words." However, the word is not *logos* but *hrēma*, which has the connotation of an ordered discourse. Thus, the NASB "message" is a suitable translation. Compare John 6:68. "Life" is emphatic in the Greek sentence structure. "This life" probably speaks of the eternal life about which they taught, a life available to all because of the resurrection of Jesus. The angel has instructed the apostles to go about telling the conditions of salvation from sins.

---

[37] Charles J. Ellicott, *Ellicott's Commentary on the Whole Bible* (Grand Rapids: Zondervan Publishing House, 1959), Vol. VII, p.29. In notes at Acts 7:30ff, we shall have more detailed information about the "angel of the Lord."

5:21 – *And upon hearing* **this,** *they entered into the temple about daybreak, and* **began** *to teach. Now when the high priest and his associates had come, they called the Council together, even all the Senate of the sons of Israel, and sent* **orders** *to the prison house for them to be brought.*

And upon hearing *this*, they entered into the temple about daybreak. During a great part of the year in Palestine, especially during the dry season, the heat becomes oppressive soon after sunrise. The morning sacrifice was offered at sunrise. Jesus taught early in the morning (John 8:2). So it would not be surprising that a large crowd of people would be found listening to the apostles in the temple area this early in the morning. Furthermore, Luke has just introduced this second persecution by telling of the popularity of the apostles. Once news spread that the apostles were teaching in the temple area, the crowd would soon swell in size.

And *began* to teach. Soon the apostles are back preaching and telling the conditions of salvation. McGarvey suggests that the sermons which were interrupted the previous day were renewed as if the interruption had been but momentary, but his comment is true only if their arrest on the previous day was not done secretly, as Lenski has suggested.

Now when the high priest and his associates had come, they called the Council together. The leaders convened the Sanhedrin for the purpose of trying the apostles for their disregard of the injunction against further preaching. Remember, it was customary for the Sanhedrin to begin their meetings at 10:00 a.m. The Sadducees are taking the lead in this second persecution, since the same "associates" introduced at Acts 5:17 are involved here. McGarvey suggests these religious leaders have spent a troubled night as they await the time for the Council to convene.

> To the high priest and his coadjutors, the night had doubtless been one of troubled thought, for they knew that in the morning they would have to confront once more the men who had defied them, and who, in the course of defiance, had won to their side vast multitudes of the best people in the city and surrounding country.[38]

And all the Senate of the sons of Israel. What is the difference between "Senate" in this phrase and "Council" in the previous phrase? The word translated "Senate" is "elders" in the Greek, men of age and experience. Twenty-four elders were already members of the Sanhedrin (the "Council"), but this verse suggests another group of elderly men in addition. The "senators" here introduced may be identical with "the Council of the Elders" who are named at Luke 22:66 and Acts 22:5.[39] The Senate seems to have been a body of men – how chosen we do not know – who acted as advisers to the Sanhedrin on special occasions.

And sent *orders* to the prison house for them to be brought. The high priest and his associates did not yet know the apostles were gone and were again in the temple preaching.

---

[38] McGarvey, *op. cit.*, p.92.

[39] Extra-Biblical references to the "senate" may be found in 1 Maccabees 12:6; 2 Maccabees 1:10, 4:44: and Judith 4:8, 15:8.

5:22 – *But the officers who came did not find them in the prison; and they returned, and reported back,*

But the officers who came did not find them in the prison. These "officers" would be Jewish officers, rather than Roman, perhaps part of the temple guard, or other servants of the Sanhedrin. When they opened the door of the cell where the apostles had been imprisoned and did not find them, was there a search made of the premises? We can imagine a thorough search being made, as implied in their report back to the Sanhedrin.

And they returned, and reported back. After making a search, they return to the meeting place where the Sanhedrin and Senate are assembled. They report all they found.

5:23 – *saying, "We found the prison house locked quite securely and the guards standing at the doors; but when we had opened up, we found no one inside."*

Saying, "We found the prison house locked quite securely. Every precaution had been taken to prevent the apostles from escaping. The door was locked, just as the night before. There were no marks to indicate the door had been pried or forced open. Everything was in good order. The verb "locked" is in the perfect tense, a tense that indicates past action with present continuing results. The door, having been locked, remained so. As far as they could tell, the door had not been unlocked; it looked to them like it had remained locked all night until they had arrived to bring the prisoners back for trial.

And the guards standing at the doors. The guards were those who were on duty during the various watches of the night. The officers report that they were still present, and keeping watch, as if unaware that anything had happened. As far as the guards knew (until the door was opened), the prisoners were still in the jail.

But when we had opened up, we found no one inside." This must have been quite a shock. We can see them looking all around, and then looking at each other. Would not some of the better men among them think of the possibility of some miraculous intervention from God on the part of the apostles?

5:24 – *Now when the captain of the temple guard and the chief priests heard these words, they were greatly perplexed about them as to what would come of this.*

Now when the captain of the temple *guard* and the chief priests heard these words. In the comments at Acts 4:1,5,23, these terms have been explained.

They were greatly perplexed about them as to what would come of this. "Perplexed" denotes the state of anxiety which arises when a man has lost his way, when he does not know what to do to escape from a difficulty. The Jewish leaders were staggered by the announcement; for a time they did not know what to do or say, and they were concerned about what was to be the final outcome of these events. Their own authority has been disregarded. There is this unusual disappearance of the prisoners from the jail, which suggests God has opposed them by a miracle. The apostles' teachings are gaining converts.

All their efforts thus far to oppose and quiet the apostles have been in vain. Where was it all going to end?

5:25 – *But someone came and reported to them, "Behold, the men whom you put in prison are standing in the temple and teaching the people!"*

But someone came and reported to them. Who brought the report is not further identified. He knew about the arrest the previous night, and he knows that it is surprising that the apostles are now where they are. So he comes to report to the Sanhedrin.

"Behold, the men whom you put in prison are standing in the temple and teaching the people!" First there had been the astonishing report that the prisoners were gone! They were not in the prison house. Now comes another announcement of astonishing impact. "Those men are in the temple and they are doing the very thing for which they have been arrested twice already!" The jealousy and zeal and envy that had led to the arrest of the apostles on the previous day would be all the more stirred up, once the religious leaders get over their initial surprise at the reports.

2. Peter's Address to the Sanhedrin. 5:26-32

5:26 – *Then the captain went along with the officers and* **proceeded** *to bring them* **back** *without violence (for they were afraid of the people, lest they should be stoned).*

Then the captain went along with the officers. The captain of the temple guard and some of his Jewish soldiers at once went to retrieve the escaped prisoners. The captain himself accompanies this arresting party to ensure there are no slip-ups. He personally will see to it that the apostles are taken into custody.

And *proceeded* **to bring them** *back* **without violence.** Does "without violence" suggest a different handling of this arrest than the one the day before? Did they roughly handle the apostles, doing them violence, when they seized them a day earlier? Perhaps so. But this arrest, because it was in public and because the officers feared the people, was done in a rather kindly manner. They came to lead the apostles away, and the apostles offered no resistance, even though with all the popular feeling running in their favor, they could have raised a tumult and likely prevented the arrest from being carried out. Christians are law-abiding citizens. The command of the Sanhedrin was sufficient to secure their presence.

For they were afraid of the people, lest they should be stoned. As the Jewish soldiers looked into the faces of the people, and as they looked at the size of the crowd, they could see that what they were doing could be a dangerous thing. The people were on the side of the apostles. If violence had been attempted, or if any of the apostles should be injured during the arrest, the soldiers knew they would have a riot on their hands. Notice that the Jewish leaders are fearful! Here are officers of the supreme court of the Jews making an arrest of twelve men who are teaching in defiance of the court's orders, yet that court's representatives are afraid. This offers insight into the standing which the apostles were gaining, not only in the eyes of the church people of the city, but also in the eyes of the people not yet converted, but who were eager to listen to what the apostles had to say.

5:27 – *And when they had brought them, they stood them before the Council. And the high priest questioned them,*

And when they had brought them, they stood them before the Council. Compare the comments at Acts 4:7. The Sanhedrin sat in a semicircle, and the prisoners were in the midst. We can picture them meeting in the hall Gazith, the regular meeting place for the Sanhedrin.

And the high priest questioned them. See verse 17 regarding the identification of the high priest. This time, as he accuses all twelve apostles, the speaker is not so indefinite about the grounds of accusation as he was in the case of Peter and John alone (Acts 4:7).

5:28 – *saying, "We gave you strict orders not to continue teaching in this name, and behold, you have filled Jerusalem with your teaching, and intend to bring this man's blood upon us."*

Saying, "We gave you strict orders not to continue teaching in this name. See 4:17-18,21. The Council had threatened Peter and John, ordering them not to speak again in the name of Jesus. They had said the name was not so much as to cross the lips of the apostles again.

And behold, you have filled Jerusalem with your teaching. "Filled" implies that there has not been just one act of disobedience to the order of the Sanhedrin, but many. Though not designed to be so, this was a tribute to the zeal and faithfulness of the apostles. When Christians are arraigned or persecuted, it is well if the only charge which their enemies can bring against them is that they have filled the whole city with the Christian faith. We hear a tone of indignation as the high priest speaks. If Jesus had risen from the dead, then obviously the Sadducees' doctrine of "no resurrection" was false; and the Sadducees did not like it that they were publicly being shown to be wrong! He contemptuously speaks about "your teaching," as though it were merely the wild ideas of mentally unstable men.

And intend to bring this man's blood upon us." Not only have the apostles been contradicting the Sadducean belief of "no resurrection," but they have been saying that the Jewish religious leaders have had something to do with the death of Jesus.[40] "To bring one's blood on another" is a phrase that signifies to accuse him of being guilty of murdering an innocent man. Have the religious leaders forgotten what they said at the time of Jesus' trial before Pilate?[41] They were willing enough to accept the responsibility at the time, but now they do not wish to accept the responsibility of murdering the Christ.

---

[40] Peter's words recorded in Acts 2:36, 3:13-14, and especially 4:10 provide the background of this charge being made by the conscience-stricken Council members. In their preaching, the apostles had indeed been telling the part played by the religious leaders in the crucifixion of Jesus.

[41] "All the people answered and said, 'His blood be upon us and on our children'" (Matthew 27:25).

5:29 – *But Peter and the apostles answered and said, "We must obey God rather than men.*

But Peter and the apostles answered and said. The opening statement by the high priest contained two specific charges against the apostles: (1) disobedience to the injunction by the Sanhedrin, and (2) an attempt to show the Sanhedrin to be guilty of the murder of an innocent man. Peter now acts as spokesman for the whole group of apostles, and they affirm they agree with what Peter says.

"We must obey God rather than men. Compare comments at Acts 4:19. At the time of the first persecution, Peter and John had courageously answered their judges. Now, with the command of the angel who released them from jail to back up their present preaching, the apostles courageously respond to the charges against them. To the first charge, that of disobeying the Sanhedrin, they plead guilty. And it is explained why they have disobeyed: "When God and men both command, and the commands contradict, we have to obey God! He told us to preach, and preach we have!"

5:30 – *"The God of our fathers raised up Jesus, whom you had put to death by hanging Him on a cross.*

The God of our fathers raised up Jesus. Now Peter takes up the second charge made by the high priest, that of accusing the Sanhedrin of the murder of an innocent man. He refers to what the God of their fathers (see comments on this expression at Acts 3:13) had demonstrated when He raised Jesus from the dead, namely, that Jesus must have been an innocent man. Would God have accepted His sacrifice and raised Him from the dead if He were the blasphemer the religious leaders insisted He was? Hardly! Peter uses what God did for Jesus as proof of His innocence.

Whom you had put to death by hanging Him on a cross. Of the death of Jesus there had been no doubt, for the religious leaders had been at pains to certify it.[42] And according to the Gospel record, this was only one act in a long list of deeds instigated by the Sanhedrin members in their attempt to get rid of Jesus. Peter answers the second charge against the apostles by saying, "It's the truth! You did kill Jesus. You did deliver Him to the Romans and then clamored for His death till the Romans, at your insistence, crucified Him."[43]

5:31 – *"He is the one whom God exalted to His right hand as a Prince and a Savior, to grant repentance to Israel, and forgiveness of sins.*

He is the one whom God exalted to His right hand. Notice how Peter again places the Sanhedrin in opposition to God. Peter says, 'You are telling us to stop preaching this gospel message? Well, you were opposing God when you told us this before; and you are still in opposition to Him. God wants everyone to know about the salvation available to all men through the exalted Jesus!' Peter also used this language about Jesus being "exalted to (or by) the right hand of God" at Acts 2:33. In addition to the comments offered at that verse,

---

[42] John 19:31-34.

[43] Concerning the nature of the cross (a "tree"), see comments at Acts 10:39.

it is also noteworthy that the only place Peter's word *hupsoō* appears in the Gospels is in John's Gospel, at John 3:14 and 12:32 (translated "lifted up"). *Hupsoō* was used of God's Suffering Servant in Isaiah 52:13 (LXX), and Paul will later use this word for the ascended and glorified Christ at Philippians 2:9. By wording this phrase as he did, Peter is saying that the Messiah predicted in the Old Testament has come and has been "lifted up" and "exalted," and is thus the source of salvation – a salvation that must be preached to all men.

As a Prince and a Savior. Peter is saying that God has exalted Jesus because He views Him as men's hope for salvation. It is part of God's provision for the salvation of men. God has exalted Him who is none other than a Prince and a Savior. On the word "prince" see notes at Acts 3:15. "Savior" was a name given by the ancients to deities (especially tutelary deities), to princes, kings, and in general to men who conferred special benefits upon their country. The word means deliverer, preserver, savior. The benefits Jesus bestows are about to be named by Peter.

To grant repentance to Israel. Concerning the nature of repentance, consult Special Study #8. How can God grant repentance to men? Isn't repentance something that each man must do for himself? God grants repentance by giving men the *opportunity* to repent. He does not bestow it apart from the exercise of the man's own will, for repentance is, as has been shown in the Special Study, an act of man's will. Because Christ has been "exalted," a foundation has been laid by which repentance is made possible, and that repentance is then also connected with forgiveness, too. For their part in the rejection and crucifixion of Jesus, Israel and her rulers deserved to be stricken and punished. Instead, they had been given opportunity by God to repent. "Israel" would speak of the Jewish nation in general, and, since Peter is speaking to them, to the Sanhedrin in particular. Of course, repentance is not for the Jews only; the gospel is also for the Gentiles (Luke 24:47).

And forgiveness of sins. See comments at Acts 2:38 for the explanation of this phrase, which speaks of being pardoned of sin. This is another of the special benefits bestowed because Jesus has been exalted as Savior. Just as repentance involves the exercise of the man's will, so forgiveness is not something just granted arbitrarily. Forgiveness is granted to those who obey God's will. Someone has rightly said that salvation has two parts – God's part and man's part. We must not read into Peter's statement any idea that would ignore or make unnecessary either part.

5:32 – *"And we are witnesses of these things; and so is **the Holy Spirit, whom God has given to those who obey Him.**"*

And we are witnesses of these things. If the Sanhedrin is still in doubt of the fact of the resurrection, or that a way of salvation is now granted to men through the exalted Prince and Savior, Peter repeats what he has said before – that he and his fellow apostles were witnesses of these things.[44] Although the Sanhedrin judges may close their minds to the truths Peter is affirming, we must remember that this testimony comes from men whose teaching has been credentialled, not only by miracles (such as Luke has just recounted ear-

---

[44] See Acts 2:32 for comments on Peter's claim that the apostles are "witnesses."

lier in this chapter) but also by a marvelous delivery from a guarded prison. There is no reason to doubt what Peter affirms.

And *so is* the Holy Spirit. From the context, it appears this reference is to the baptism of the Holy Spirit (Pentecost), which gave to the apostles the power to work miracles. Peter is saying that the preaching of the apostles has been credentialled.

Whom God has given to those who obey Him. Peter is saying, 'We have been obeying God rather than you men. Do you want proof of that? God gives the power to work miracles only to those who obey Him.[45] We have the power to work miracles. Therefore, it follows that we have been obeying Him!'[46]

3. The Speech of Gamaliel. 5:33-42

5:33 – But when they heard this, they were cut to the quick and were intending to slay them.

But when they heard this. The "this" which the Sanhedrin heard was the plea of guilty to both charges, plus a defense of their actions by the apostles, for whom Peter has acted as spokesman.

They were cut to the quick. This is not the same expression as translated "pierced to the heart" in Acts 2:37; this expression is stronger. The word picture involved speaks of "cutting with a saw;" when applied to a man's thoughts, it means to be agitated with rage and indignation. It is the irritation that comes when one is struggling against his conscience. Luke will use the same word again at Acts 7:54. Peter's defense has exasperated the Sanhedrin members beyond measure, nearly turning the court into a mob.

And were intending to slay them. The Sanhedrin members were so angry that they have already made up their minds to kill the apostles. The formal decree had not been passed, but they had decided what to do. There was only one way to silence these men – kill them!

5:34 – But a certain Pharisee named Gamaliel, a teacher of the Law, respected by all the people, stood up in the Council and gave orders to put the men outside for a short time.

But a certain Pharisee named Gamaliel. Notes about the sect of the Pharisees have been given in Special Study #9, "The Sects of the Jews." At this point in time, the Pharisees seem

---

[45] While it is true that the indwelling Holy Spirit is given to each person who becomes a Christian, an appeal to that activity of the Holy Spirit hardly fits the context. Such an appeal would be little evidence of the obedience to God on the apostles' parts. "The Holy Spirit, whom God gives to those who obey Him" must be understood as something that would overtly credential the apostles as obedient to God.

[46] Pentecostal and Charismatic interpreters of Acts have used verse 32 as a proof text that the baptism in the Holy Spirit is for all men who are believers. While many in the early church had spiritual gifts, in addition to the apostles who had received the baptism with the Holy Spirit, not every Christian had spiritual gifts. To attempt to use verse 32 to show that men today may expect to be baptized in the Holy Spirit is to draw from the passage more than Peter intended.

to be not as determined as the Sadducees in the persecution of the disciples. Detailed information about Gamaliel is given on pages *xi* and *xii* of the Introductory Studies. Gamaliel was an important leader of the sect of the Pharisees. He was the fourth in a dynasty of Jewish scholars which began with Hillel, and that dynasty continued for several centuries. Paul was one of Gamaliel's students (Acts 22:3); had Paul remained with the Jews, he could very probably have been the next in the line of this dynasty of scholars.

A teacher of the Law. "Scribe" and "teacher of the Law" and "lawyer" are synonymous terms in the Bible. A "lawyer" may have been a "scribe" who specialized in legal questions involving interpretation of the Law, while "teacher of the Law" was a scribe who specialized in preserving and transmitting the Law of Moses as well as the tradition-based laws of the Pharisees. But all were men who had spent many hours studying and mastering the Law of Moses. Gamaliel was such a wonderful teacher that Jewish young men came from all over the world to study under him.

Respected by all the people. This is the fourth of the things that Luke tells us about Gamaliel. He was a member of the Sanhedrin, a Pharisee, a teacher of the Law, and he was respected by all the people. He was so respected that he was one of only seven men to receive the highest of honorary titles Jewish people gave their teachers, "Rabboni."

Stood up in the Council and gave orders to put the men outside for a short time. "Stood up" pictures Gamaliel as rising to speak to the Council. It was customary, when the Council deliberated, to command the accused to retire from the court room.[47] The statement that Gamaliel commanded the apostles to be taken from the court has been taken as evidence that this was the privilege of any member of the Sanhedrin to so command in New Testament times.

5:35 – And he said to them, "Men of Israel, take care what you propose to do with these men.

And he said to them. Gamaliel is probably to be pictured as holding his position on the floor until the officers had removed the accused. The report of his speech which follows may have come to Luke from some member of the Sanhedrin, or perhaps from Paul himself (who we may assume heard it from his teacher Gamaliel, either when it was delivered in the court room, or as rehearsed by Gamaliel in the classroom sometime later).

Men of Israel, take care what you propose to do with these men. 'Be careful (or cautious) about reaching a decision. Let us not act hastily, for there may be something that we have not considered in this matter. Let us carefully think through this before we act.'

5:36 – "For some time ago Theudas rose up, claiming to be somebody; and a group of about four hundred men joined up with him. And he was slain; and all who followed him were dispersed and came to nothing.

For some time ago Theudas rose up. Gamaliel's advice is akin to the old proverb about

---

[47] See a similar action at Act 4:15.

giving a man enough rope and he will hang himself. To show how regularly this happens, he gives first the example of Theudas, and then that of Judas the Galilean. How long before this date it was that Theudas appeared on the scene of history cannot be determined with certainty. However, since Gamaliel mentions Theudas before Judas of Galilee (who lived about AD 6), it is probable that Theudas lived about the time Jesus Christ was born, i.e., about 5 BC. "Rose up" means that Theudas incited and attempted revolution.

There is a Theudas mentioned by Josephus,[48] but he does not appear to be the same man that Gamaliel is speaking about.

- The Theudas of Josephus' account lived about 10 or 15 years after the events Luke records in Acts 5.
- The Theudas of Josephus' history "persuaded a great part of the people to take their effects with them and follow him to the Jordan." The "400" mentioned by Gamaliel certainly is not similar to Josephus' "a great part of the people."
- The Theudas recorded by Josephus told the people to follow him to the Jordan River, that he was a prophet, and that he would divide the waters and lead them over.
- Fadus, the procurator of Judea, however, came suddenly upon them, and slew many of them. Theudas was captured, taken to Jerusalem, and beheaded.

Because of the alleged discrepancies between Gamaliel's speech and Josephus' record, it has been inferred by some New Testament critics that here at Acts 5:36 we have a blunder so egregious as to prove that the speech supposedly given by Gamaliel was actually made up long years after its alleged date by some writer who was ignorant of history. In fact, it is claimed that the entire narrative of this part of Acts is accordingly untrustworthy, and that the book as a whole must be sifted with a suspicious caution.

The easiest solution is to suppose that there were two men, living at some interval apart, who had the same name, and who both attempted to stir up revolution against Rome. The name Theudas, whether considered as a form of the Aramaic name Thaddeus (see Matthew 10:3) or the Greek Theodorus, was common enough to make it probable that there had been more than one rebel of that name. Further, Josephus mentions no less than three insurrections as occurring shortly after the death of Herod the Great.[49]

Claiming to be somebody. That is, Theudas claimed to be the Messiah, or some eminent prophet, or made pretensions to royalty. About the time Jesus was born, a number of false prophets appeared who claimed to be the Messiah.

And a group of about four hundred men joined up with him. There were several bands of robbers and revolutionaries, some more and some less numerous than this, with whom the Roman authorities continually had to deal.

And he was slain. Theudas was killed during the insurrection he attempted.

And all who followed him were dispersed and came to nothing. The word translated

---

[48] Josephus, *Antiquities*, XX.5.1.

[49] *Antiquities*, XVII.10.

"followed" is *peithō*, and is the word commonly used to denote "belief." *Peithō* can also be translated "persuaded," or "obeyed." It speaks of people who believed Theudas' pretensions. Gamaliel makes the point that Theudas' pretensions were hollow, and the movement died out. It appears Gamaliel deliberately uses this language to cast doubt on those who have "followed" what the apostles have been teaching.

5:37 – *"After this man Judas of Galilee rose up in the days of the census, and drew away some people after him, he too perished, and all those who followed him were scattered.*

After this man Judas of Galilee rose up. Josephus has given an account of this man.[50] He says the revolt took place under Quirinius, at a time when an enrollment was being made. "In one passage,[51] Josephus calls him a Gaulonite, i.e., of the country east of Galilee. Had this [been the only extra-Biblical reference to the man,] Luke might have been charged here also with inaccuracy. But in other passages Judas is described as a Galilean,"[52] and therefore Luke's account here has not been questioned.[53]

In the days of the census. This is the second enrollment under Quirinius.[54] The date of this second enrollment was about AD 6, at the time when Judea became a province under a Roman governor.[55]

And drew away *some* people after him. Ellicott affirms, "The insurrection of Judas was by far the most important of the attempts to throw off the yoke of Rome. He was assisted by a Pharisee named Sadduk, and the absolute independence of Israel was the watchword of this revolutionary party. [Among Judas' followers] it was unlawful to pay tribute to Caesar in any form, and it was lawful to use any weapons in defense of freedom."[56]

He too perished, and all those who followed him were scattered. "The war [Judas and his followers] waged was a 'holy war.' Josephus, writing long after the movement had collapsed, but obviously giving the impressions of his own early manhood, enumerates them as being (along with the Pharisees, Sadducees, and Essenes) one of the four great sects of Judaism."[57] The scattered followers could still be found in Galilee and were called Zealots (or Canaanites) in the New Testament times. Judas perished, but his sons Jacob and

---

[50] *Antiquities*, XVII.10.5.

[51] *Antiquities*, XVIII.1.

[52] *Antiquities*, XX.5.2.

[53] Ellicott, *op. cit.*, p.31.

[54] In his first volume, Luke speaks about the fist census under Quirinius (Luke 2:2). The enrollment of Acts 5:37 is not to be confused with the "first enrollment made when Quirinius was governor of Syria." That first census took place about 6 BC.

[55] Compare notes in commentaries at Matthew 2:22 and in the Introductory Studies of this book where the record of Herod the Great's sons is recounted, especially the information about the first census and the problems connected with it.

[56] Ellicott, *ibid*.

[57] *Ibid*.

Simon continued to be looked on as leaders after his death, and were crucified during the procuratorship of Tiberius Alexander.[58]

5:38 – *"And so in the present case, I say to you, stay away from these men and let them alone, for if this plan or action should be of men, it will be overthrown;*

And so in the present case, I say to you, stay away from these men and let them alone. Gamaliel's advice is to cease opposing or threatening them. The reasoning behind this advice is drawn from his two illustrations. If what the apostles were doing was of men, it would fade away just as did the movements of Theudas and Judas.

For if this plan or action should be of men. If the apostles had originated it for purposes of imposture, or if the apostles were fake leaders like Theudas and Judas, the Council did not need to worry about this movement.

It will be overthrown. Gamaliel's advice is uninspired; he is giving human advice; his guidelines for dealing with various movements are not to be adduced as Biblical guidelines to be followed today. For example, apply the principle to any of the world's great religions. Many of them have stood a long time, even when they plainly are not of God. It would be foolish to allow one of the Eastern sects or cults to come into our congregational meetings and teach and make disciples over a period of time, while at the same time we defend our permissiveness by saying "If it is of men, it will come to nought!" The Bible gives a different standard by which to measure truth – namely, how does a man and his doctrine compare with the inspired Word of God?[59]

5:39 – *"but if it is of God, you will not be able to overthrow them; or else you may even be found fighting against God."*

But if it is of God, you will not be able to overthrow them. 'If God is the author of this religion, you will not be able to suppress it, because God is almighty and He is unchanging.' The conditional sentence in verse 38 implies that the condition is "probable" – Gamaliel is saying he thinks the apostolic movement "probably" is of men. The conditional sentence here in verse 39 implies nothing. Together, Gamaliel's words suggest, 'I really think it is of men. But suppose for the sake of argument it is of God. It would be hopeless to be found fighting against God. You'd only lose!" Both the historical examples Gamaliel has used illustrate his real thinking that Christianity was only of human origin.

Or else you may even be found fighting against God. In the Greek this is "lest at any time" – at some future time, when it will be too late to retract your doings, you will have been found to have been fighting against God. Not only would such resistance be hopeless, it would be tragic, Gamaliel argues. "Fighting against God" is a phrase that recurs in the reasoning of the Pharisees who took Paul's side in a later scene in this same court room.[60]

---

[58] Ellicott, *ibid.*, and Josephus, *Antiquities*, XX.5.2.

[59] 1 Timothy 6:3ff.

[60] Acts 23:9.

5:40 – *And they took his advice; and after calling the apostles in, they flogged them and ordered them to speak no more in the name of Jesus,* **and** *then released them.*

And they took his advice. The Greek says, "They were persuaded by him." The Sadducees were the recognized leaders of the Jewish religious activities, but the Pharisees commanded much more popular respect. The Sadducees had to have the approval and support of the Pharisees or their decisions would be disobeyed and their leadership ignored. In the case at present, where the defendants were as popular as the apostles were, it was especially important to have the Pharisees' support. Gamaliel stated the position for the Pharisees in this trial, so the others must abandon their design of putting the apostles to death.

And after calling the apostles in. The apostles are called back into the courtroom to hear the verdict.

They flogged them. Beating or whipping was a common method of punishment for minor offenses among the Jews. It was intended to be disciplinary rather than a means of capital punishment. The usual number of lashes inflicted on offenders was thirty-nine.[61] To be beaten was a considerable disgrace. A Roman citizen could not be beaten by Roman authorities, but the Jews had no restrictions against beating, so this disciplinary punishment was often meted out. In this case, all twelve apostles were flogged.

Gamaliel had advised, "Let them go, let them alone." Although they abandoned their already fixed plan to execute the defendants, the Council did not fully follow Gamaliel's advice. Why? Several answers have been suggested. Boles has written:

> The members of the Sanhedrin may have felt that their honor was at stake, and that, if the apostles departed untouched, they themselves would be regarded as having proceeded against innocent men. Hence, to save their honor and the honor of the court, and to make the impression that the apostles were guilty of some offence, they were beaten.[62]

Another writer has expressed it this way:

> The physical torture of beating – which was likely administered with exceptional vigor (especially since the previous warning had been ignored, Acts 4:18-21) – would have left the persons who received the lashes bleeding and torn, and would serve to remind the apostles for many days of the order to be silent.[63]

Perhaps the Pharisees, influenced by Gamaliel, agreed to these disciplinary measures demanded by the Sadducees in exchange for averting the more violent punishment that had earlier been determined by the infuriated members of the Sanhedrin.

---

[61] 2 Corinthians 11:24.

[62] Boles, *op. cit.*, p.83.

[63] W.S. LaSor, *Church Alive* (Glendale, CA: Gospel Light, 1972), p.84.

And ordered them to speak no more in the name of Jesus, and *then* released them.

5:41 – *So they went on their way from the presence of the Council, rejoicing that they had been considered worthy to suffer shame for* **His** *name.*

So they went on their way from the presence of the Council. The apostles had prayed for protection from these religious leaders. The prayer has been answered – not perhaps in the exact way they had expected, for they had been flogged; but their lives had been spared, and they can preach another day.

Rejoicing that they had been considered worthy to suffer shame for *His* **name.** What is the usual effect of a beating? To most men, nothing would be more disgraceful than a public whipping. Why then are the apostles rejoicing? Perhaps because they were permitted by this to imitate the example of Christ (who had been beaten by Roman soldiers, and also possibly by the Jews[64]), and thus show they truly were followers of Christ. Perhaps because in this beating they have another evidence that they have been doing as God expected them to do, for Jesus Himself had promised them they could expect such treatment if they were "peacemakers."[65] "Considered worthy" by whom? In the eyes of God? In the eyes of the Sanhedrin? And in whose eyes was it a "shame"? In the eyes of the Sanhedrin, or in the eyes of the people?

5:42 – *And every day, in the temple and from house to house, they kept right on teaching and preaching Jesus* **as** *the Christ.*

And every day. See comments at Acts 2:46. The apostles continued to disregard the threats of the Sanhedrin, and they continued to obey God.

In the temple and from house to house. They taught right under the noses of the men who had just told them not to speak in the name of Christ. It is probable that they continued to use Solomon's porch, and the captain of the temple would act on the suggestion of Gamaliel (agreed to by the whole Sanhedrin)[66] that they let the movement take its course without interruption.[67] And the apostles entered into the homes of those who would hear

---

[64] The scourging of Jesus by Roman soldiers is recounted in John 19:1 and elsewhere. That He was flogged by the Jews is a possible understanding of the word "beating" in Luke 22:63ff.

[65] Matthew 5:11-12, 10:17,22.

[66] What happened to some of the chief members of the Sanhedrin after this point in Acts has been told in the Introductory Studies. In addition to what is said there about Annas and Caiaphas, a further word about Gamaliel might be of interest. Gamaliel was allowed to preside over the Sanhedrin under the reigns of Caligula and Claudius. Christian traditions have represented him as having been a secret disciple of Jesus (Pseudo-Clement, *Recogn.* I.65). Photius (*Cod.* 171) has Gamaliel baptized by Peter and Paul, along with Nicodemus (represented as his nephew) and his son Abibas. In a legendary story, purporting to come from Lucian, a priest of Syria, Gamaliel is involved in the burial of Stephen and other Christians, and to have been himself buried in the same tomb with Stephen and Nicodemus (Augustine, *Civ. Dei* XVII.8 and *Serm.* 318).

[67] Ellicott, *op. cit.*, p.32.

them. This type of evangelism is needed today – everyday, preaching the gospel publicly, and from house to house.

They kept right on teaching and preaching Jesus *as* the Christ. Nothing could stop them from preaching and teaching that Jesus was the Messiah!

In this present-day, when Biblical critics and scholars attempt to distinguish between the *kerygma* and the *didache,* the combination of these two terms in verse 42 has an important part to play in opposing those efforts which purport to "distill from the present Bible narratives to the original *kerygma.*"

**Drawing by Horace Knowles
from the British and Foreign Bible Society**

SPECIAL STUDY #10

CHURCH DISCIPLINE

In the Scriptures we have the divine law of admission into the church, the divine law of organization of the church, the divine law of regulation of the church, and the divine law of exclusion from the church. Men have no right to be more lax on one than on another.

There are, properly, two sides, or two phases, of church discipline. There is what is called *formative* (constructive, or preventive) church discipline. And there is also what is called *corrective* church discipline.

By "formative" discipline is meant teaching. Church members cannot be expected to know what is right and what is wrong if they are not first instructed in righteousness. The New Testament shows that in the church such formative teaching is to be done by the evangelist and the elders. Sin is to be rebuked. Righteousness is to be inculcated. Corrective discipline should never be urged or practiced until there has first been the formative discipline.

Throughout the years, and even at present, there are those in the congregations who object to the idea of a local congregation practicing corrective church discipline. Two of the most common objections are these:

1) Some object to the practice of discipline because the Bible says, "Judge not, that ye be not judged" (Matthew 7:1ff). But this verse certainly does not prohibit church discipline, for Paul wrote to the Corinthians that they were to judge concerning sinful deeds (1 Corinthians 5:12-13). The Scripture harmony is retained, and only accomplished, when we let both scriptures speak in their proper settings. The Matthew 7:1 passage does not prohibit corrective discipline; it prohibits hypocritical judging.

2) Other objectors say, "Jesus said, 'Let both (good and bad) grow together until the harvest'" (Matthew 12:24-30). However, this verse is not a prohibition of discipline, either. Jesus explained that the field in which these were growing together was the world, not the church. Naturally, church members are not to go out and weed bad men out of the world. But church members are taught to remove certain individuals from the fellowship of the congregation because of their sins.

Finally, by way of introduction, a word is needed about the spirit of the church members as they undertake the disciplining of a sinning member. A wrong spirit on the part of the congregation might be as great a sin as the one continually committed by the person being excluded. Corrective discipline must be done in the spirit of fierceness and tenderness and love. There must be sorrow that such action has become needful. And it is to be done with the hope of winning the sinner back to repentance.

I. AUTHORITATIVE TEACHING ENJOINING CORRECTIVE DISCIPLINE

A. All penitent, immersed believers are to be recognized as brothers in Christ.

This is the teaching of the Great Commission (Matthew 28:18-20; Mark 16:15-16). This is the teaching of the apostles (Acts 2:37-41,47, etc.). Those penitent believers who are immersed in the name of Christ are recognized as members of the body of Christ, His Church. All such are to be esteemed as brethren. This is Christ's delivered plan. In this matter, all are to conform to Christ's will. We have no right either to widen or constrict the gate into the Church, or into Heaven.

B. Scripture teaches the necessity of corrective discipline.

If all other means of corrective discipline have not brought a sinning brother to repentance, many Scriptures teach a withdrawal of fellowship (e.g., 1 Corinthians 5:11,13; Matthew 18:15-18). The church is to conform to these plain instructions just as obediently as she does to the instructions concerning receiving people into the fellowship. Why preach loud and long on the steps of admittance (because they are clearly set forth in the Scriptures), and refuse to emphasize the divine law of exclusion (which is just as clearly set forth)?

II. THE SCRIPTURAL PURPOSE OF CORRECTIVE CHURCH DISCIPLINE

A. To warn others lest they fall into sin also (1 Timothy 5:20)

One purpose of discipline is to keep the Church pure. God could not allow sin within the flock to go unpunished. If people could get by with sin, the entire foundation of the Church would be at stake. People would be no different after becoming members of the church than before.

B. To save the transgressor (1 Corinthians 5:5; 1 Timothy 1:20)

C. To save the Church from pollution (1 Corinthians 5:6-7; Hebrews 12:16; 2 Timothy 2:17-18)

D. To demonstrate our obedience to Christ (2 Corinthians 2:9, 7:11a)

E. To impress favorably those outside the Church (Acts 5:14)

III. THE SCRIPTURAL PROCEDURE OF DISCIPLINE

The following Scriptures may be helpful in regard to the steps to be taken in discipline: Matthew 18:15-18; 1 Corinthians 5:1ff; 1 Timothy 5:19-22; 2 Corinthians 2:5-11; and 1 Corinthians 12:12-30. As indicated above, that there are two types of discipline – formative and corrective.

A. Formative discipline

Formative discipline is the first step. Each Christian is to be instructed in righteousness, so that each learns what it is to be in relationship to Christ and a member of His Body. When the gospel is properly taught, most disciplinary problems will adjust themselves.

B. Corrective discipline

However, there are some cases that no amount of formative discipline via teaching will solve. Such obstinate cases must then be dealt with by the progressive steps of corrective discipline outlined in Matthew 18:15-18.

Private Counsel. Often the only correction needed for an erring brother is to take him quietly aside, and make known to him his error and the means for adjusting it. It is possible for a sincere Christian to be living in sin, or teaching falsely, without being aware of it. If this brother is truly serving God, he will welcome your correction, and will immediately correct himself when his mistake is known. This manner of church discipline is vividly illustrated in the case of what Aquila and Priscilla did with Apollos. When disciplining an erring brother, the first step is private counsel.

Public Rebuke. Private instruction is often effective, but it does not always convict the erring one of his mistake. A stronger form of discipline is needed in such cases – a rebuke by several witnesses. Jesus instructed us to take with us two or three witnesses, that every word may be established. If he then repents, the brother is gained. The second step in corrective discipline is a visit from several in the church body.

A Called Meeting of the Congregation. If the erring one still refuses to repent after being confronted by two or three witnesses, then the matter is taken before the whole congregation. There is a good example of this type of action from the ministry of Paul, where he withstood Peter before the whole congregation (Galatians 2:11ff). By the public rebuke in front of the congregation, Peter was led to repent. If the erring brother is trying to do the Lord's will, this third step in corrective discipline will prove effective in drawing him back into the Way. But if he is seeking to serve his own will, more drastic methods of discipline must be used.

Disfellowship, i.e., *Expulsion from the Congregation.* Paul again has provided us with an example of this extreme step in corrective church discipline (1 Corinthians 5:1-13). Perhaps if we used this form of correction as the Lord intended, we would see an aroused membership walking more discretely, having respect for their fellowship in the church body. If after private counsel and public rebuke and a confrontation of the congregation the erring one still refuses to repent, the next step – separation – must be taken by those who serve and love the Lord and His Church.

IV. THE SINS WHICH REQUIRE AN EXERCISE OF CORRECTIVE CHURCH DISCIPLINE

A. All sins are to receive proper discipline.

Repentance, prayer, and confession are necessary for all sins. However, there are some sins, which if continued in and unrepented of, require the congregation to take action against the transgressor.

B. Factious persons who cause dissension and trouble (Titus 3:10-11; Romans 16:17)
C. The sins of fornication, covetousness, idolatry, railing, drunkenness, and extortion (1 Corinthians 5:11)
D. Those who willfully disobey and disregard the apostles' teaching (2 Thessalonians 3:6,14)

V. THE CONGREGATION'S ATTITUDE AND RESPONSIBILITY TO THE DISFELLOWSHIPPED MEMBER

A. The Church is to seek to restore the disciplined member by helping him overcome the sin into which he has fallen.

As the church seeks to restore the disciplined member and to overcome his sin, it is to be done in the spirit of meekness and gentleness (Galatians 6:1-2). Those who have been disfellowshipped are not to be considered personal enemies, but as sinning brothers (2 Thessalonians 3:14-15).

Every action should be taken with the constant purpose of saving the soul of the erring one. Too often, the misuse of church discipline drives the erring one to further sin and destruction. Discipline is not to be thought of as "a church fighting among themselves," or "striking a member from the roll," or as a "quarrel between some stubborn officer and a member." This impression of discipline has left fear and confusion in the minds of people. Discipline, done Biblically, is the attempt to restore a wayward child of God before he is completely lost.

B. There comes a time when the disfellowshipped member is to be considered as an "Outsider."

According to Matthew 18:15-18, there seems to be a time when the expulsed man is to be considered no longer to be a brother, but is instead to be considered as an "outsider." Or as Paul puts it, "We are not to eat" (1 Corinthians 5:11) with the one who has been disfellowshipped.

C. Restore the one who repents.

When the disciplined person repents, he is to be received back into fellowship, forgiven, and comforted (2 Corinthians 2:6-8).

CONCLUSION

"To cut off an offender is good; to cure him is better; but to prevent him from falling is best of all." *Alexander Campbell*

"Discipline is medicine for curing, not poison for killing; it is not to gratify the hatred of the judge, but to admonish the offender who is being judged." *J.W. McGarvey*

Properly ordered church discipline is an act that is recognized in the courts of Heaven. After giving His instructions about the method to be followed, and telling them that some would have to be disfellowshipped, Jesus said, "Truly I say to you, whatever you shall bind on earth shall have been bound in heaven, and whatever you shall loose on earth [i.e., including disfellowship] shall have been loosed in heaven" (Matthew 18:18, NASB).

Drawing by Horace Knowles
from the British and Foreign Bible Society

SPECIAL STUDY #11

DEMONS AND DEMON POSSESSION

One wonders if we are not inclined to shrug off the thought of demons and spirits today, ignoring in the process the tremendous volume of references to these beings found in both the Old and New Testaments. The very thought of unseen agents of Satan involves a concept to which not a few are unwilling to subscribe. Surely, it's thought, such things have no place in this age of scientific research and reason. Or do they?

The apostle Paul, writing to the church in Ephesus, speaks of the warfare of the Christian and describes the situation in these words, "For our fight is not against any physical enemy: it is against organizations and powers that are spiritual. We are up against the unseen power that controls this dark world, and spiritual agents from the very headquarters of evil."[1] If we are confronted with an "unseen power," if that power "controls" the world in which we live, and if he sends out "spiritual agents," are we not being utterly foolish to ignore their reality and the means whereby they may be defeated?

The etymology of the term "demon" (*daimonion*), in the earlier language *daimōn*, is not too certain. Both words are translated "devil" in the KJV, but they are carefully distinguished in the original from the term *diabolos*. In the ASV the words are rendered by the word "demon," and both words are used as synonymous both by pagan and sacred writers. As far, then, as the derivation is concerned, Plato derived it from *daemon*, an adjective formed from *dao*, and signifying "knowing" or "intellect."[2] Eusebius derived it from the word *deimaino*, "to be terrified."[3] Proclus derived it from *daio*, "to distribute," because demons were supposed to assign the lots or destinies of men.[4]

I. DEMONS – THEIR IDENTITY

A. In the Pagan Writers

The term went through several changes and modifications in the time between Homer and the writing of the Septuagint.

1. In Homer, where the gods are but supernatural men, "demon" is used interchangeably with *theos* (gods).[5] Demons were thought to be the souls of good men, which upon their departure from the body were called heroes, and were afterwards raised to the dignity of demons, and subsequently to that of gods.[6] And Plato says, "The poets speak excellently who affirm that when the good men die, they attain great honor and dig-

---

[1] Ephesians 6:12, Phillips translation.

[2] *Cratylus* I.398.

[3] *Proep. Evang.* IV.5.

[4] Hesiod, *Works and Days*, trans. by Richard Lattimore, p.109-126.

[5] *Iliad*, XVII.98,99

[6] Plutarch, *De Defac. Orac.* and Hesiod, *ibid.*

nity, and become demons."[7]

2. A second stage in the development of the term "demon" appears in post-Homeric usage when demons were conceived as being intermediaries between the gods and men. When the idea of gods had become more exalted and less familiar, the demons are spoken of by Hesiod as intermediate beings, the messengers of the gods to men.[8] After writing, "Every demon is a middle being between God and mortal," Plato went on to explain what he meant by "middle being." "God is not approached immediately by man, but all the commerce and intercourse between gods and men are performed by the mediation of demons." Then Plato enters into further particulars, saying, "Demons are reporters and carriers from men to the gods, and again from the gods to men, of the supplications and prayers of the one, and of the injunctions and rewards of the other."[9]

3. A third stage of development came when the estimate of demons was lowered even more, as the philosophers attempted to exalt the gods. Demons were now held to be malignant by nature, and not merely so when provoked. It was also now believed that the souls of bad men became evil demons.[10] Plutarch wrote, "It is a very ancient opinion that there are certain wicked and malignant demons, who envy good men, and endeavor to hinder them in the pursuit of virtue, lest they should be partakers of greater happiness than they enjoy."[11] Pythagoras held that certain demons sent diseases to men and cattle.[12]

B. In Jewish Thought

1. Rabbinic demonology is full of distortion of Biblical truths. "The fall of Satan and his angels, in rabbinic demonology, is strangely imagined as subsequent to the creation of man, and was occasioned by their jealousy of him. And various gross ideas are entertained as to the origin of demons, ranging from their creation on the eve of the first Sabbath, before their bodies could be finished (this is supposed to account for their being spirits), to generation of multitudes of them as the offspring of Eve and male spirits, and of Adam and female spirits, or with Lilith, the queen of female spirits. Still grosser ideas link them to transformations from vipers, or as springing from the backbone of him who did not bow in worship. Fully sexed, they multiply rapidly, and are innumerable. A thousand at your right hand, ten thousand at your left."[13] Rabbinic methods for managing demons varied – such as torchlight by night, ablutions, phylacteries, amulets, magic formulae, fumigations, etc.

2. In most cases, the translators of the Septuagint did not allow the wild superstitions of the day to enter their translation. In the LXX, the terms *daimōn* and *daimonion* are not found very frequently, yet they are used to translate certain Hebrew words consistently. The Hebrew language has no precise equivalent for the single Greek term *daimōn*; indeed, no fewer than five different Hebrew words are translated by it. (Of note, only one of these Hebrew words was rendered "demon" by our English translators).

---

[7] *Cratylus, ibid.*

[8] Hesiod, *op. cit.*, p.121

[9] *Sympos.*, III.202,203

[10] Chalcid, *Platon. Tim.*, p.135

[11] Plutarch, *Dion.*, I.958.

[12] Diog. Laert., *Vit. Pythag.*, p.514

[13] Merrill Unger, *Biblical Demonology* (Wheaton IL: Scripture Press, 1952), p.33.

- "Demon" (*daimōn, daimonion*) was used by the LXX translators at Deuteronomy 32:17 and Psalm 106:37 of the "idols" worshiped by the heathen, for the Hebrew word *sheddim* (and its derivatives).
- The LXX translators used "demon" at Leviticus 17:1-7 for the Hebrew word *seirim*, "he-goats" or "hairy satyrs." These were another object of idolatrous worship.
- "Demons" was used for the Hebrew word *elilim,* "idols," at Psalm 96:5.
- "Demons" was used for the Hebrew word *gad,* a god of fortune, at Isaiah 65:11. *Gad* was another idol worshiped by the Babylonians, elsewhere also called Baal.
- The use of "demon" at Psalm 91:6, where the Hebrew word is "destruction," seems to be a trace of the popular notion creeping into the translators' minds, that "hard luck" or "tragic reverses" were the results of malignant demons.

3. In Josephus we find the word demon used always of evil spirits; and he says expressly, "Demons are no other than the spirits of the wicked, that enter into men and kill them, unless they can obtain some help against them."[14] He speaks of their exorcism by fumigation (as in *Tobit* 8:2,3), or by means of roots and using the name of Solomon. Josephus also believed the origin of the demons to be found in the offspring of the union of the "sons of God" and the "daughters of men" at Genesis 6:2.[15]

4. Philo, in *De Gigantibus*, used the word demon in a more general sense, as equivalent to "angels," and referring to both good and evil beings. Philo also held to the "angel hypothesis" (similar to Josephus) as explaining the origin of the demons.

C. In Scripture

1. *As to their existence*, Scripture presents demons as really and truly existing. Jesus and the Scripture writers speak of them, without any hint of the slightest doubt as to their actual existence.

In the Old Testament, as noted in the previous point, the *sheddim* and the *seirim*, which were both objects of idolatrous worship, were demonic conceptions.

> That the New Testament writers believed firmly in the existence of demons is capable of ample proof. They declare their existence (James 2:19; Revelation 9:20), describe their nature (Luke 4:33, 6:18) and their activity (1 Timothy 4:1; Revelation 16:14), mention their expulsion from human bodies (Luke 9:42), suggest their organization under Satan (Matthew 12:26; Ephesians 6:12), indicate their abode (Luke 8:31; Revelation 9:11), and point out their final doom (Matthew 25:41). That Christ Himself shared the identical views of the Biblical writers, though this fact is extensively denied, is subject to the same ample proof. He commanded His disciples to cast out demons (Matthew 10:1), cast them out Himself (Matthew 15:22,28), rebuked them (Mark 5:8), had complete power over them (Matthew 12:9), and viewed His conquest over them as a conquest over Satan (Luke 10:17, 18).[16]

---

[14] *Wars*, VII.6.3

[15] *Antiquities*, VI.8.2; VIII.2.5.

[16] Unger, *op. cit.*, p.36.

Demons are presented as believing the power of God and "trembling" (James 2:19); they recognize Jesus as the Son of God (Matthew 8:29; Luke 4:41), and acknowledge the power of His name used in exorcism, in the place of the name of Jehovah, by his appointed messengers (Acts 19:15); and they look forward in terror to the judgment to come (Matthew 8:29). In 1 Corinthians 10:20-21; 1 Timothy 4:1; and Revelation 9:20, the word *daimonia* is used of the objects of Gentile worship; and in the 1 Corinthians 10 passage *daimonia* is placed in juxtaposition to the word *theos* (with a reference to Deuteronomy 32:17), as it also is by the Athenians in Acts 17:18. The same identification of the heathen deities with the evil spirits is found in the description of the damsel having "a spirit of divination" at Philippi (Acts 16:16). Importantly, in 1 Corinthians 10:20-21, as Paul is arguing with those who declared the idol to be a pure nullity, and he declares that all which is offered to the idol is really offered to a "demon." Indeed, it can be said that the Bible gives considerable evidence for the actual existence of beings called demons.

2. *As to their nature*, demons are spirits. In the four Gospels generally (Matthew 8:16, 10:1, 12:43-45; Mark 9:20; Luke 10:20, etc.), in James 2:19, and in Revelation 16:14, the demons are spoken of as spiritual beings at enmity with God and having power to afflict man with bodily diseases. In Acts 19:12-13, they are exactly defined as "evil spirits." Hence, there is ascribed to them intelligence and will (Mark 1:24; Luke 4:34; James 2:19, 3:14), as well as great power (Matthew 9:28-32; Mark 9:25; Ephesians 6:12).

Whether demons are to be reckoned as belonging to a class of spirit beings on the level of angels, or as having fallen from the original condition of angels, does not clearly appear from any statement of the Scriptures. They are the messengers or agents of Satan; as such, they could be either "angelic" in nature, or "lesser than angels" in nature.

3. *As to their origin*, because the Scriptures make no specific statements, scholars have advanced all sorts of ideas.[17] Demons are apparently fallen angels – i.e., angels who sinned at the time the devil did (Jude 6; 2 Peter 2:4; Luke 8:29-31; Revelation 12:7-9). Satan is called the prince of demons. The demons whom our Lord cast out are collectively called Satan (Matthew 12:24-29; Luke 13:16). And the phrase "unclean spirits," which is applied to demons (Matthew 10:1; Mark 3:11; 6:7, etc.), is applied also to the fallen angels (Revelation 16:13, 18:2), and even in the singular to Satan himself (Mark 3:30; cp. verse 22). These considerations, in this commentator's opinion, render it probable that the demons of the New Testament belong to the number of angels "who kept not their first estate," and that they must be the same as the "angels of the devil" (Matthew 25:41; Revelation 12:7-9). They are "the principalities and powers" against whom we "wrestle" (Ephesians 6:12, etc.).

4. *As to their abode and their sphere of operation*, the evidence with Scripture is abrupt and fragmentary. Sometimes the demons are pictured as being in bondage, and sometimes as being free spirits, and it is not an easy problem to attempt to harmonize the two ideas.

- As to their sphere of operations – sometimes we read of demons in the "heavenly places" (Ephesians 6:12); sometimes in the "air" (Ephesians 2:2); sometimes "in the earth" (Job 1:7); sometimes "in waterless places" (Luke 11:24); sometimes in "swine"

---

[17] For the ideas that demons are the disembodied spirits of inhabitants of a pre-Adamic earth, or that demons are the monstrous offspring of angels and antediluvian women, see the extended discussion in Unger, p.42ff.

(Mark 5:13); sometimes "in the kings of the earth" (Revelation 16:14); sometimes as being behind idols and idol worship (1 Corinthians 10:20).

- Yet, when it comes to the question of their abode – demons are represented as "reserved in everlasting chains under darkness unto the judgment of the great day" (Jude 6; cp. 2 Peter 2:4); and they are said also to be in the abyss (Luke 8:31; cp. Revelation 9:1-11).

Such descriptions, however, could be understood as intimating nothing more than their being in a state of punishment, or under control, for the activities ascribed to them are incompatible with the idea of their being in a state of confinement. Indeed, such passages as Ephesians 2:2 and 6:12 would lead to the conclusion that a sphere of extended physical freedom is allowed to these fallen spirits.

(Some suggest a different method to harmonize the ideas of bondage v. freedom for demons. Some suggest there are two classes of demons. One class sinned a horrible sin after being expelled from heaven, a sin for which they are now bound in chains of darkness. A second class, though expulsed along with the devil, are not guilty of this horrible sin, and so are free to operate as the Ephesian passages imply. See this idea developed by Herbert Lockyer in a series of articles in *Sunday School Times,* beginning April 2, 1958.)

5. *As to their destiny*, the demons' future is the same as that of their leader – namely. everlasting Hell. Jesus spoke of the "eternal fire which is prepared for the devil and his angels" (Matthew 25:41). This is unquestionably the terrifying doom the demons had in mind when they cried out to Jesus, "What have we to do with you, Jesus of Nazareth? Have you come to destroy us?" (Mark 1:24) "Have you come here to torment us before the time?" (Matthew 8:29)

D. In the Early Christian Writers

Early Christian writings abound with references to demons. Unger writes, "Justin Martyr (*De Defectiona Oraculorum* XIII), for example, obviously following clear Old (Deuteronomy 32:17; Psalm 106:37) and New Testament teaching (1 Corinthians 10:19-20; 1 Timothy 4:1; et al.), asserts that demons inspired Greek mythology, raised up evil men like Simon Magus, heretics like Marcion, and energized Christian persecutions."[18]

- By some early Christian writers, the demons are represented as angels who, originally created holy, fell into rebellion and sin.[19] Others represent them as the fruit of the intercourse of angels with women.[20] Yet others represent them as the souls of the giants whom the daughters of men bore to devils.[21]

- All describe them as evil, as deceiving and destroying men, as being the object of worship to the heathen, and as used by God to punish the wicked.[22]

- They also teach that the demons are *asomata* (without bodies), yet not in such a sense as to be absolutely immaterial, but as *skia onto* (having shadows, having adumbrations, having a slight sketchy shape).[23]

---

[18] Unger, *op. cit.*, p.58.

[19] Joan. Damasc., *Expos. Fidei*, II.4.

[20] Justin Martyr, *Apol.*, II.4.

[21] *Pseudo-Clementine Homilies*, VIII.18.

[22] Origen, *Cont. Celsius*, V.234; VIII.399.

[23] See Clem. of Alexandria, *Stromata*, VI.7. Cp. Chrys., *Hom.* CXVV and Theodoret, *In Jes.*, XIII.

II. DEMON POSSESSION

A. The Biblical Record

Both the Old and New Testaments not only speak of demons, but they present the demons as entering into people's bodies and possessing those people. The word demoniac (*daimonizomenous*, rendered "possessed with a demon"), and the words "having a demon" (*daimona echon*), are frequently used in the New Testament, and are applied to persons suffering under the possession of an evil spirit – such possession generally showing itself visibly in bodily disease or mental derangement. In the New Testament, demonized persons are those who were spoken of as having a demon (or demons) occupying them. Further, the demons suspended the faculties of the person's mind and governed the members of the person's body, so that what was said and done by the demoniac was ascribed to the indwelling demon. Especially in the Gospels and Acts, almost every time demons are mentioned it is in connection with some human into whom they have entered.

Though there is no evidence that demons could cause a man to sin or make him a sinner, the person in whom the demon lived was to an extent ruled by the demon (Matthew 4:24). The inhabitation of such a person in some cases created physical effects, and produced certain ordinary diseases. Thus, one possessed boy is described as having a deaf and dumb spirit, and as being affected at intervals with physical symptoms resembling epilepsy (Mark 9:14-29; Matthew 17:15-18; Luke 9:37-41). The ordinary and literal interpretations of these demoniac passages in the Scriptures is that there are evil spirits, subjects of the Evil One, who, especially in the days of our Lord and His apostles, were permitted by God to exercise a direct influence over the bodies of certain people. The distinguishing feature of possession is the complete (or almost complete) loss of the sufferer's reason or power of will: his actions, his words, and almost his thoughts are mastered by the demon (Mark 1:24, 5:7; Acts 19:15), till his personality seems to be destroyed, or if not destroyed, so overborne as to produce the consciousness of a twofold will within him.

In one key passage, the person himself seemingly was responsible for his hideous visitor (Luke 11:24-26). Probably not until a person was degraded and weakened by his own sin might he be taken captive by a demon (cp. 1 Samuel 16:14 with 13:8-14 and 15:10-31).[24]

B. Modernistic Attacks on the Biblical Record

With regard to the frequent mention of demoniacs in Scripture, several lines of denial of the historicity of the record have been advanced.

1. *That of Strauss and the Mythical School*

To David Friedrich Strauss (in his two-volume work on *The Life of Jesus*), whatever in the Gospel narratives was supernatural or abnormal was "mythological" (though he never

---

[24] However, it is difficult to hold this point dogmatically since the Gospel writers also report at least one case of a demon's possessing a child. Yet the implications of involuntary possession by demons raises its own set of difficulties.

defined "myth"). For example, he felt most readers of the story of Gideon would recognize the purely human and historical features in it. It is a story of courage and adventure, of a self-taught military genius and his achievements. But, Strauss suggested, the imagination of Israel transformed this tale so that it became a part of the dealings of God with His chosen people. When the event is finally recorded in the Bible (so the mythological theory suggests), God was made to be the deliverer, and Gideon was the instrument in the hands of the Most High God. In a similar fashion, there was a fellow named Jesus. The admiration of the early Christians for Jesus found expression in the fashioning of myths about Him, as also being an instrument in the hands of God. In reality, there weren't really any such beings as demons. This was just a vivid symbol of the presence of evil in the world, and the "casting out of demons by our Lord" was a corresponding figure of triumph over evil by His doctrine and life.

This notion stands or falls with the mythical theory as a whole – and the mythical theory has long ago fallen aside, because it never had a Jesus big enough to account for the existence of the 1st century Church. If Jesus was not really divine, there is no way to account for the origin of the body called the Church. The Gospel accounts are plain narrations of the incidents, and they are in a prosaic style, rather than poetic. To say that in the midst of pure prose there is "myth" makes the statements not a mere symbol or figure, but a lie. It would be as reasonable to expect to find a myth or figurative fable from Thucydides or Tacitus in their accounts of contemporary history as to expect to find a "myth" in the Gospel accounts.

2. *Jesus was mistaken.*

The theory goes that Jesus so acted, and went through the form of casting out demons, because in this matter He was mistaken – and in this He shared the erroneous opinions of His contemporaries.

Such an opinion impinges upon the truthfulness of the Savior, and the salvific nature of His work. Since His resurrection provides clear proof of His other claims about Himself and His work, this theory is to be rejected.

3. *Jesus spoke by way of accommodation.*

The theory that Jesus and the Gospel writers spoke by way of accommodation says that what was called "demon possession," we now call "disease" or "insanity," and that Jesus so spoke and acted (as His hearers thought and expected Him to act), although He knew there were no actual demons to be cast out. That is, He accommodated Himself to His hearers' ignorance and superstition, without making any assertion as to the actual existence or nonexistence of the phenomena described.

The idea that "demon possession" is really the same as what we call "disease" or "insanity" is based on the following facts and arguments: (1) The symptoms of demon possession were often the same as those of physical disease (e.g., blindness and dumbness, Matthew 12:22; or epilepsy, Mark 9:17-27). (2) At times, "demon possession" seems to have been synonymous with "madness" or dementia (e.g., Matthew 8:28; Mark 5:1-5; John 7:20, 8:48, 10:20). (3) It is (erroneously?) assumed that cases of actual demon possession are not known to occur in our day; instead, we call it by other names. In the same way what the Bible calls palsy, we call paralysis or polio, what in Biblical times they called "demon possession," we call insanity or disease. Some even claim that what the Bible calls "demon possession" is the mental disorder we call "dual personality," or schizophrenia.

However, this ingenious theory is completely incompatible with the simple and direct attribution of personality to the demons (e.g., Mark 1:23ff). It is rather hard to conceive of Jesus speaking to a disease or to insanity, and having the disease talk back! And what of the idea that demon possession is the mental disorder we call "dual personality," or schizophrenia? Well, it is difficult to square this theory with the case of the Gadarene demoniac. Was he afflicted with four or five thousand (i.e., a legion) personalities? Further, this theory also denies the existence of demons as real beings, which places it at odds with the straightforward presentation in the Gospel records.

Demon possession is more than physical or mental illness. Demons were able to speak and were addressed as persons (Mark 1:23-24, 3:11-12, 5:7; Acts 19:15). The demons recognized their own distinct individuality independent of Jesus, and independent of the person possessed (Matthew 8:31). The distant herd of swine became frenzied when the demons were cast out of the Gadarene demoniac and allowed to enter them (Matthew 8:30-32). Jesus recognized the demons as actually existing, and instructed His disciples saying. "This kind can come out by nothing save prayer" (Mark 9:29; Luke 10:17-20).

Possession and its cure are recorded plainly and simply. Jesus distinguished between demons and diseases, and so did the apostles (Matthew 10:8; Mark 1:32, 16:17-18; Luke 6:17-18, 10:17-20; Acts 5:16; 19:12). Demoniacs are even distinguished from epileptics (*selēniazomenoi*, Matthew 4:24) and paralytics (*paralutikoi*, Matthew 4:24). The same outward signs are sometimes attributed to possession, sometimes merely to disease (compare Matthew 4:24 with 17:15; Matthew 12:22 with Mark 7:32). The demons are represented as speaking in their own persons with superhuman knowledge, and acknowledging our Lord to be, not as the Jews generally called Him, son of David, but son of God (Matthew 8:29; Mark 1:24; 5:7; Luke 4:41, etc.). All these speak of a personal power to evil, and, if in any case they refer to what we might call mere disease, they at any rate tell us of something more in the disease or in the insanity than just a sickness of bodily organs, or a self-caused derangement of the mind.

But the essential idea of the accommodation theory is in itself unsound. Jesus did not speak of demons only to the ignorant and superstitious and uninitiated multitudes, but also in His private instruction to His own disciples (Matthew 17:19-21), as He declares to them the means and conditions by which power over the demons could be exercised. Twice He distinctly connects demon possession with the power of the Evil One: once to the seventy disciples, where He speaks of His powers and theirs over demoniacs as a "fall of Satan" (Luke 10:18); and once when He was accused of casting out demons through Beelzebub (Matthew 12:25-30). In Matthew, rather than giving any hint that the possessed were not really under any direct and personal power of evil, Jesus uses an argument about the division of Satan against himself, which, if possession be unreal, becomes inconclusive and almost insincere.

Notice also that simply labeling a case as one of disease or insanity gives no real explanation of its cause; it assigns the circumstance to a class of cases which we know to exist, but that labeling gives no answer to the further question, How did the disease or insanity arise? Even in diseases in which the mind acts upon the body (e.g., in nervous disorders, epilepsy, etc.), the mere derangement of the physical organs is not the whole cause of the malady; there is a deeper cause lying in the mind. Insanity may indeed arise, in some cases, from the physical injury or derangement of those bodily organs through which the mind exercises its powers. But is this the only cause of insanity? Might not there be cases when insanity is due to metaphysical causes. To call it "only insanity" is to give up all attempts at explanation of its cause. The truth is that here, as in many other instances, the Bible, without contradicting ordinary experience, advances to a region where human science cannot follow. The Bible connects the existence of mental and bodily suffering in the world with the introduction of evil by the Fall, and it refers certain cases of bodily and mental disease to the influence which demons are permitted to exercise over people's bodies and minds. While the action of spirit on spirit may be inexplicable to us, no one can pronounce *a priori* whether it be impossible or improbable, and no one has the right to disregard or disdain the strong expressions of Scripture in order to reduce its declarations to a level with our own ignorance.

One other important comment needs be said about this theory of accommodation. Language can be used by way of accommodation only in cases where things are not alike, and the words used, though etymologically or scientifically inaccurate, express or convey a true impression; or in cases where the things are alike, and the words used are precise and correct as far as they go, but the impression conveyed is imperfect and partial, because of the arrested or stunted progress of the hearers. Concerning the language of accommodation. Trench has written this interesting paragraph:

> [There is no harm in our] speaking of certain forms of madness as *lunacy*, not thereby implying that we believe the moon to have or to have had any influence upon them; but if we began to describe the cure of such as the moon's ceasing to afflict them, or if a person were solemnly to address the moon, bidding it abstain from injuring this patient, there would be here a passing over to quite a different region [than accommodation] ....[25]

There is a very similar gulf between truth and the idea of accommodation in this matter of miracles. Jesus is actually addressing the demons, bidding them to cease injuring this person. If there were no real demons there, what Jesus is doing is not accommodation. It is bordering on the essence of a lie!

The opinion that Jesus spoke merely by way of accommodation does not match the evidence. That age in which He lived and spoke was one of scant faith and appalling superstition. Would Jesus sanction, and the Gospel writers be permitted to record, an idea which was essentially false, which has since that time become a stronghold of superstition? It would not seem that He would, since in another place our Lord denounced superstitions associated with things far more trivial (Matthew 23:5, 16-20)

---

[25] Richard C. Trench, *Notes on the Miracles of Our Lord* (New York: Revell, 1953), p.153ff.

C. The Problem of the Duration of Demon Possession

Some assert there are no cases of demon possession now, and they offer several lines of argument:

- In an age of science and enlightenment, who can believe in demons?
- There can be no demon possession today because we do not have the miraculous powers (spiritual gifts) to deal with them.
- The frequency of demon possession in the time of Christ is probably due to the fact that His advent formed a great crisis in the spiritual order of things, with the devil and his hosts making a concerted effort to thwart Jesus.

Many others argue that there are still cases of demon possession prevalent today.

- If there were such all through the Old Testament age, and examples are found all through the New Testament, what caused them to cease?
- If there is no possibility of demon possession today, why do we have warnings in the Bible against magic, against divination, against necromancy, and spiritism?[26]
- Perhaps our real issue is that we do not have any inspired person to tell us whether or not certain phenomena we see today are actually cases of demon possession. Missionaries in many countries experience things that they believe only "demon possession" can satisfactorily account for. (For example, compare the experiences of the Morse family in Tibet and Burma. They have seen a child who fell into fires and water ponds, just as the demoniac boy in Scripture, and who was healed when the church elders laid hands on him and prayed. See also the documentation of similar cases in the Orient in the series of articles in *Sunday School Times*, beginning July 27, 1957. See also Unger, *op. cit.*, page 81ff.)
- Does demonism have anything to do with heresies and cults, or with world governments, or with moral degeneracy, and the appearance of the man of sin in the last days?[27]

D. Deliverance from Demon Possession

Special Study #17, "The World of the Occult," continues the subject of demons and demon possession. At that place is an outline of the method of deliverance from demon obsession and possession.

---

[26] Unger, *op. cit.*, p.107ff.

[27] See Special Study #17, "The World of the Occult," for a development of these ideas. See also Unger's fine treatment of these matters, *op. cit.*, p.165ff.

CONCLUSION

The Scriptures give no clear testimony as to the origin of demons, just as they give no clear testimony as to the origin of the Satan, (e.g., how he could be tempted before there was a devil to tempt him). But concerning other phases of demonic activity, Scripture passages are abundant and quite suggestive.

Paul's warning in Ephesians 6:12, that "our struggle is not against flesh and blood, but against the rulers, against the powers, against the world forces of this darkness, against the spiritual *forces* of wickedness in the heavenly *places*," need not be looked at with a raised eyebrow, as though it were something old-fashioned and outdated. If we believe in spirits, we must make room in our theological system for evil spirits (demons) as well as for good spirits (angels).

The Streets of Jerusalem

Drawing by Horace Knowles
from the British and Foreign Bible Society

BIBLIOGRAPHY

A. Books

    Alexander, William Menzies, *Demonic Possessions in the New Testament: Its Relations Historical, Medical, and Theological.* Edinburgh: T&T Clark, 1902.

    Campbell, Alexander, "Demons and Demon Possession," *Millennial Harbinger*, published by the author, Bethany, VA, 1841, p.457 and 480ff. 1842, p.65ff and 124ff.

    Davis and Gehman, "Demons, Demoniac," *Westminster Dictionary of the Bible.* Philadelphia, PA. Westminster Press, 1924.

    Gilmore, George W., "Demon, Demonism," *New Schaff-Herzog Encyclopedia of Religious Knowledge*, Vol. III, p.399-401. New York: Funk and Wagnalls, 1909.

    Hastings, James. editor. *Encyclopedia of Religion and Ethics*, Vol. IV, p.565-635. New York: Charles Scribner's Sons, 1939.

    McClintock and Strong, *Cyclopedia of Biblical Literature*, Vol. II, p.638-42. New York: Harper and Brothers, 1891.

    Needham, Mrs. George C., *Angels and Demons.* Chicago: Moody Colportage Library, n.d.

    Trench, R.C., *Notes on the Miracles of Our Lord.* New York: Fleming H. Revell Co., 1895.

    Unger, Merrill F., *Biblical Demonology.* Wheaton, IL: Scripture Press, 1952.

    ------, *Demons in the World Today.* Wheaton, IL: Tyndale House Publishers, 1971.

    ------, "Demons," *Zondervan Pictorial Bible Dictionary.* Grand Rapids: Zondervan, 1963.

    ------, "Demons," *Baker's Dictionary of Theology.* Grand Rapids: Baker Book House, 1960 and author, 1952.

    Weiss, Johann, "Demoniac," *New Schaff-Herzog Encyclopedia of Religious Knowledge,* Vol. III, p.401-403. New York: Funk and Wagnalls, 1909.

B. Articles

    Almquist, David, "Demonic Possession in our Day," *Sunday School Times*, February 28, 1942.

    Gruenthaner, Michael J., "The Demonology of the New Testament," *The Catholic Biblical Quarterly*, January 1944, 6-27.

    Lockyer, Herbert, "Doctrine of Angels and Demons," *Sunday School Times*, April 5, 1958, and issues following, (p. 250ff).

    Tharp, Edwin J., "Demonology," *Sunday School Times*, July 27, 1957, and issues following, (p. 579ff).

C. Encyclopedias

    Sweet, Louis M., "Demon, Demoniac, Demonology," *International Standard Bible Encyclopedia*, Vol. II, p,827-29. Grand Rapids: Eerdmans Publishing Co., 1939.

    Whitehouse, Owen C., "Demon, Devil," in *Hastings' Dictionary of The Bible*, Vol. I, p.590-94. New York: Scribners & Sons Publishing Co., 1908.

Q. Seven Men Chosen to Serve Tables. 6:1-7

6:1 – *Now at this time while the disciples were increasing* **in** number, *a complaint arose on the part of the Hellenistic* **Jews** *against the* **native Hebrews, because their widows were being overlooked in the daily serving** of food.

Now at this time. It is now about AD 33 or 34. It is very near the time that Paul was converted (cf. chapter 9), and from our study of New Testament Chronology we have dated this conversion in AD 34.

While the disciples were increasing *in number.* Compare comments at Acts 5:14. By this time some estimate that, counting men, women, and young people, there would have been close to 20,000 Christians in and around the city of Jerusalem.

A complaint arose on the part of the Hellenistic *Jews* **against the** *native* **Hebrews.** This "complaint" sounds as if there had been some partiality shown in the distribution of the common fund. We see in this complaint the first symptom of a loss of the harmony and oneness and unanimous good will noted by Luke earlier.[1] While it is lamentable that what was probably an accidental oversight led to such complaining, it should be remembered that even so, such murmuring or whisperings of discontent is a sin, and is frequently condemned in the New Testament.[2] Who were these "Hellenistic Jews"? In the time when the gospel was first preached, there were two classes of Jews. The Hebrews were those who were born in Palestine and who spoke the Hebrew language. The Hellenists were those who were born of Jewish parentage outside of Palestine, who spoke the Greek language, and who used the Septuagint in their synagogues. The Hellenistic Jews, to a greater or lesser degree, had adopted more of the Greek ideals and customs after Alexander the Great had carried that Greek culture over the world when he had conquered it about 300 years earlier. In Jewish communities the Hebrews, who had not adopted the Greek customs, tended to look down on the Hellenists as being somewhat less holy. Perhaps some of the old feelings are in the background of this present dispute. Hellenistic Jews were also known as "those of the Dispersion."[3]

Because their widows were being overlooked in the daily serving *of food.* We learn incidentally from this verse that very early in the history of the Church there was a special provision made for widows (and probably orphans, too) of the congregation to be provided for out of the common fund. We find them in the church at Joppa[4] and at Ephesus.[5] It is

---

[1] Acts 4:32.

[2] Philippians 2:14; 1 Peter 4:9.

[3] See notes at Acts 2:5 on how this Dispersion took place. In our English translations at James 1:1, when "Dispersion" (with a capital "D") is used, it indicates that the translators think Jewish people are addressed. When "dispersion" (with a lower-case "d") is used, it indicates the translators think Christians (who are the new "dispersion") are addressed.

[4] Acts 9:41.

[5] 1 Timothy 5:3ff. Notice that this passage gives qualifications that must be met if a widow were to be

clear from the Epistles that widows were objects of special attention in the early church, and that the first generation of Christians regarded it as a matter of indispensable obligation to provide for their needs.[6]

In the Jerusalem area, with so many thousands to care for, it became an easy matter for the apostles to accidentally overlook some whose needs were greatest in the physical realm. The words "daily serving of food" imply something of an organized administration of the common fund described in Acts 4:32-37.[7] The funds raised by the sale of property and goods (and laid at the apostles' feet) were understood to be designated for the equal benefit of all those in need. When some were accidentally overlooked, the overlooked ones began to complain about those "Hebrews."[8]

6:2 – *And the twelve summoned the congregation of the disciples and said, "It is not desirable for us to neglect the word of God in order to serve tables.*

And the twelve summoned the congregation of the disciples and said. "The twelve" is the name for the apostles. Matthias has been added to the apostolic college after the apostasy of Judas, and thus the original number was still whole. This mention of the apostles indicates that for the first three or four years of the Church, all twelve of the apostles were still in and around Jerusalem. Was the whole Church included in the "congregation" called together? If so, this would be quite a group assembled! Or were just the Grecians assembled? Perhaps only those who had been engaged in the complaint are called together, and they themselves are given opportunity to themselves be the means of satisfactorily removing all cause of complaint.

It is not desirable for us to neglect the word of God. "Not desirable" means "not satisfactory." The gospel is here called the "word of God." The twelve who had been with Jesus had been chosen to proclaim what they had seen and heard. For such eyewitness tes-

---

eligible for support from the common fund.

[6] James 1:27. A clear present-day need is for an in-depth study of local benevolence practices and principles. As various government welfare and assistance programs have proliferated, has not the Church been allowing someone else to do for her elderly and needy what she has a responsibility of doing herself? Christians ought to consider it a blessing to care for the needy, especially for a saint who has been loyal to the Lord. Instead, much of the time, the needy are turned over to the (impersonal) state. There is a world of difference between welfare set up by the state for the care of the elderly people, and benevolence provided by the Church. Some of our brethren are making it their special ministry to become administrators or volunteer helpers in nursing homes, and the elderly and needy respond to such loving care. It does take money and time to provide such a ministry, but given the Scriptural commands involved, and the early church example recorded in Acts, and when precious souls are in the balance, dare the Church afford anything else?

[7] The word "food" in the NASB of verse 1 is in italics. The Greek reading is simply "the daily serving." The same word "serving" appears at Acts 11:29 and is translated "relief." It can mean alms or food, or whatever "service" is needed by the widows.

[8] Up to this time, all care of the needy had been in the hands of the apostles (Acts 4:35, 5:2). The comments on verse 1 are written with the thought that the apostles are still trying to do the distribution themselves. Mosheim has suggested that some Christians of Hebrew background had been delegated by the apostles to see that the daily distribution was made; therefore, they are the ones complained against, because they had been oversolicitous about their own needy. The majority of commentators, however, feel that the apostles are the ones complained against.

timony there were no substitutes. Therefore, nothing must interfere with their proclamation. Before their earthly service is over, the twelve must spread the "word of God" far and wide – first by the spoken word, and then by putting it in written form for future generations. They had found that the daily responsibility of distributing the common fund was causing them to neglect the preaching and teaching to the extent that their primary task was being limited. They were not wholly forsaking the preaching, but they found their time severely infringed upon.

In order to serve tables. The word "table" is used with several different connotations. It may speak of the table off which a family would eat its food, at times even being equivalent to the food which is set on the table. The word was also used for the table on which a moneychanger kept the different kinds of money he used for exchange purposes.[9] So in this context, which speaks of the receipt and disbursement of the common fund, the word is well suited whether it speaks of food being put on the table of the poor, or simply of the distribution of funds so the poor can purchase their own needs.

It is well to give attention to what is here said. The apostles acknowledge a place for the daily ministration. It is needful. But it was not the primary thing in the life of these early church leaders. They were not willing to neglect the preaching just to serve tables. Note that this is opposite to the emphasis of the "Social Gospel."[10]

It is from the word "serve" (and "minister" in verse 4) – i.e., from the work they did – that we determine these seven men were chosen as "deacons." Although the word "deacon" is not found in the book of Acts as an official designation, and although we are not told in any definite language that these men were "deacons," still they did the work of deacons.[11]

The Jerusalem church of Acts 6 is now three or four years old. Why had no deacons been appointed before this?

- Perhaps there had been deacons appointed already. Note the discussion in Acts 5:6 concerning the "young men," as to whether or not they were deacons.
- Barnes answers this question by saying that up to this time there was no need for any such officers; therefore, none were yet chosen.[12]

---

[9] Matthew 15:27; Acts 16:34; Matthew 25:27; John 2:15.

[10] "Social Gospel" is a name given to the central idea of a widely influential movement within American Liberal Protestantism in the late 19th and early 20th centuries. That central idea was that the chief interest of the gospel lay in the social area: business, government, economics, the family, community, national and international problems. "Sin" was defined as whatever was evil and unjust in these social institutions. So the main emphasis of men like Joseph Parker, Walter Rauschenbusch, and Harry Emerson Fosdick was diverted from salvation of men's souls by restoring a right relationship to God through obedience to Jesus, to emphasis on social progress. In the Bible order of things, social progress is a by-product of salvation from personal sin.

[11] Some writers, trying to justify the episcopal type of church organization of which they are a part, believe that the "young men" referenced in chapter 5 were "*deacons*" and that these "seven" in chapter 6 were, so to speak, "*archdeacons*," appointed to superintend and guide the "deacons." In reply to such a contention, there is no evidence elsewhere in records from the 1st century church of an order of "archdeacons."

[12] Barnes, *op. cit.*, p.112.

- McGarvey says, "The Spirit guided them into additional truth as additional truth was needed."[13]
- It should not be thought strange that we perhaps have no mention of the original appointment of deacons, for we also have no record of the first appointment of elders. Yet in Acts 11:30, around AD 44, we find elders in the Jerusalem church. And it does not appear these elders have been just chosen at the time they are first mentioned in Acts. So we could likewise presume that elders were chosen when the need arose. The apostles would have served as "elders" (overseers) until they left Jerusalem; and at that juncture, perhaps, the elders were first chosen, for a need had arisen.

6:3 – *"But select from among you, brethren, seven men of good reputation, full of the Spirit and of wisdom, whom we may put in charge of this task.*

But select from among you, brethren. "From among you" means "from among you Grecians," if we have interpreted "congregation" correctly in verse 2. The method suggested by the apostles would ensure that there was no more accidental neglect of a segment of the congregation's needy, and thus there would be no further cause for complaint. The Hellenistic Christians had been contributing their own offerings to the common fund for the care of the needy, so it was proper that they should be permitted to choose such men as they could confide in to superintend the distribution. By this means the apostles would be free from all suspicions.

Briefly stated, here is the process by which these men were chosen. The apostles suggested the course of action and stated the qualifications. The people selected the men, and then the apostles prayed and laid hands on those whom the people had chosen. It follows from this example that the right of selection of deacons resides in the congregation, and does not belong exclusively to the ministry. No ingenuity of argument can evade the conclusion that this gives the authority of apostolic precedent for the popular election of church officers by members of the congregation voting.[14]

Seven men. That is, enough to meet the needs. It does not follow that seven deacons must now be chosen by any local congregation.[15]

Of good reputation. As the apostles gave instructions about the method of selection, they also gave several qualifications the men *must* meet before they are to be considered as pro-

---

[13] McGarvey, *op. cit.*, p. 104.

[14] For further information, see Special Study #12, "A Method of Selection of Elders and Deacons," at the close of chapter 6. The method of selecting church officers by the congregation is important. The method should in some way require the qualifications to be considered, give the congregation a voice, and the election be followed by a "laying on of hands." The people of the churches must be led away from the "popularity contest" type of election of men to serve as elders and deacons. Rather, the churches must be led to the place where only qualified men are ordained into the places of spiritual leadership.

[15] Yet, from "seven" having been the number of the first deacons, arose the custom of some congregations always having seven deacons. This custom continued some centuries in the Roman Church. One of the Canons of the Council of Neo-Caesarea (AD 314) enacted that "there ought to be but seven deacons in any city." (Hervey, *op. cit.*, p.193.) Mark is said by tradition to have ordained seven deacons at Alexandria. (Bingham. *Christ. Antiq.*, Vol.I, p.232. quoted by Hervey, *ibid.*)

spective candidates for office. Compare 1 Timothy 3:8-10 where Paul gives Timothy a similar list of qualifications for men aspiring to the office of deacon. First, say the apostles to the congregation, they must be of fair reputation, regarded as men of integrity (both by those in the church, and those without).

Full of the Spirit. Some commentators think this refers to "spiritual gifts and miraculous powers," but there are certain objections to this opinion. McGarvey argues that, because we have had no account thus far of any except the apostles having received the miraculous powers from the Spirit, the historian Luke cannot be fairly understood as referring, by this expression, to such powers.[16] "Full of the Spirit" must then mean "full of the fruit of the Spirit as respects a holy life," men whose lives are bringing forth the fruit of the Spirit.[17]

And of wisdom. As before, some interpreters see a reference to the spiritual gift called "wisdom,"[18] a gift that perhaps gave men the power to reveal the whole plan of salvation. We object to this interpretation on the same grounds as we did in the previous qualification. Instead, the idea seems to be of prudence, or skill, to be able to make a wise and equitable distribution so as to give no offense in their ministrations.[19]

Whom we may put in charge of this task. Does "we" speak of only the apostles who were making the suggestion (cf. verse 2), or does it include the entire congregation? Apparently, it speaks of the apostles only. "We" in this context, since verse 2, has referred to the apostles. There is no reason to take it differently here. The deacons were selected by the congregation, yet the power of ordaining them, or setting them apart, was retained by the apostles. The way in which this "putting them in charge" was done was by prayer and the laying on of hands (verse 6).

"This task" is the distribution of the alms of the Church. Two observations ought to be made in this regard:

- In the ancient synagogues of the Jews there were men to whom was entrusted the care of the poor. Perhaps the idea for the choice of men to serve tables is a carry-over from the synagogue. This is, however, not saying that all of Christianity is just copied from the Jewish or heathen religious customs. We firmly believe the origin of Christianity to be divine, not human.

- The service these seven men performed was not limited only to serving tables. We know that two of them (and probably all) also taught and preached.[20] Thus today, when men are chosen to the function of deacon, we should make no attempt to shut them off from any area of usefulness for which they have talent and desire. In fact, one of the most rewarding areas of the ministry is the encouragement of men to develop and use their abilities for the growth of the congregation's life and health.

---

[16] McGarvey. *op. cit.*, p.105.

[17] Galatians 5:22ff.

[18] 1 Corinthians 12:8; 2 Peter 3:15.

[19] Cp. James 1:5, 3:13-17.

[20] See the activities of Stephen and Philip in Acts 6:8-8:1.

6:4 – *"But we will devote ourselves to prayer, and to the ministry of the word."*

But we will devote ourselves to prayer. Again, "we" seems to refer to the apostles, just as in the last verse. The verb in the Greek speaks of perseverance in a thing, giving constant attention to a thing. It is the same verb used at Acts 2:42. Whether the apostles are speaking of private or public prayer cannot be certainly determined. The Greek does read "*the* prayer," which might support the idea of prayer at the hours of prayer rather than private devotions. The general consensus of opinion in the commentaries is that public prayer is the thing intended.

And to the ministry of the word. That is, the apostles would continue preaching and teaching the gospel. The Greek work is again *diakonia*, the same word used in verse 1 for "the daily *serving*." However, here it does not refer to the diaconate; rather, the reference is to preaching as a special ministry (service) with which the apostles were concerned.

6:5 – *And the statement found approval with the whole congregation; and they chose Stephen, a man full of faith and of the Holy Spirit, and Philip, Prochorus, Nicanor, Timon, Parmenas and Nicolas, a proselyte from Antioch.*

And the statement found approval with the whole congregation. The course of action suggested by the apostles was approved as a solution for uprooting the causes of the complaining.

And they chose Stephen. As is Luke's custom, Stephen is introduced here, and will come on the stage to play his part later. This man had what Barnes calls the distinguished honor of being the first Christian martyr. Of Stephen's previous life or training, we know nothing of certainty. Two conjectures have been defended in recent times.

- One is that the Stephen who was a goldsmith in the imperial court is the same person who became the first martyr. In the background behind this attempted identification are the following items. The name Stephanus was not a common name; in fact, it appears in only a few inscriptions. One place where it does appear is in the Columbarium, or burial place, of Empress Livia. Among the many who are buried there is a Stephen who was a goldsmith, an *immunis* (i.e., one exempted from the pagan religious obligations of the trade union) and a *libertinus* (i.e., a freedman). What is known about the Stephen buried in Rome could fit, in general, what we know about Stephen the martyr. It would be possible that the goldsmith was among the "visitors from Rome" who came to the feast of Pentecost (Acts 2:10). A consecrated Jew would be interested in being exempted from pagan religious obligations. And when Stephen begins to preach, the most prominent scene of his activity is the synagogue of the Freedmen.[21]

- A second conjecture concerning the previous life of Stephen is that he was one of the

---

[21] Against the identification of Stephen the martyr with Stephen the goldsmith is the question of how his remains got to Rome after his martyrdom in Palestine. Still, even if we question or deny the identification, the material has served to introduce the reader to the idea that a knowledge of contemporary history can throw light on the understanding of the background of the books of the New Testament.

Seventy who were sent shortly after last Feast of Tabernacles in our Lord's ministry into every city and village where He himself would shortly come.[22] This suggestion was an early tradition, and was accepted by Epiphanius in the 4th century AD.[23]

A man full of faith and of the Holy Spirit. Stephen was a man who had a good grasp of the doctrines of Christ, a man of settled convictions. This is what "full of faith" means. Consult the notes at verse 3 concerning his being "full of the Holy Spirit."

And Philip. Just as later chapters in Acts tell us more about Stephen, so subsequent chapters in Acts give us a record of some of Philip's activities in the later church. The man here chosen as a "deacon" is to be distinguished from Philip the apostle.[24] This Philip is called "Philip the evangelist"[25] to so distinguish him. Some of Philip's labors in Samaria and elsewhere are recorded in Acts 8.

Of his previous history we know nothing, except a tradition that he also had belonged to the Seventy.[26] The chief scene of the mission of the Seventy was Samaria, and it is interesting to note that Philip shortly will be working in Samaria as an evangelist. If the tradition is true, then Philip's earlier work there would have something to do with his present choice of that area as a place in which to evangelize.

Prochorus, Nicanor, Timon, Parmenas. The names of all seven of the deacons who were chosen are Greek names, and this fact may indicate the generosity of the native Hebrews in putting this matter into the hands of the Hellenists from whom the complaint had arisen in the first place.[27] Of these four men, nothing is known, nor are there any materials even for making a probable conjecture.

And Nicolas, a proselyte from Antioch. Barnes notes that Irenaeus and Epiphanius, two of the Early Church Fathers, connect the rise of the sect of the Nicolaitans, which is mentioned with so much disapprobation in Revelation 2:6,7, to this man. However, the evidence for this is not clear.[28] Victorinus of Pettau (c. AD 300), in the earliest extant Latin commentary on the book of Revelation, has this note at Revelation 2:6:

---

[22] Luke 10:1-20.

[23] *Heresies*, XX.4.

[24] Not only is there an apostle named Philip, but two of Herod's sons had this name; and these are indications that Philip was as common a name as that of Stephen was rare.

[25] Acts 21:8.

[26] Epiphanius, *ibid*.

[27] Some contend that the Greek names of the seven do not prove these were all Grecian Jews. When a corroborative argument is drawn from the fact that even some of Jesus' apostles had Greek names (e.g., Andrew, Peter) and were still Jews, it should be remembered that these men came from Galilee, which did have Greek influences in times past. Those who question the idea that all seven were Hellenists often suggest that three of the seven were Hebrews to serve the Hebrews, three were Hellenists to serve the Hellenists, and one was a proselyte to serve the proselytes.

[28] Barnes, *op. cit.*, p.112.

> Before that time factious and pestilential men had made for themselves a heresy in the name of the deacon Nicolas, teaching that meat offered to idols could be exorcized, so that it might be eaten, and that one who had committed fornication might receive absolution the eighth day.[29]

Victorinus, who gives more details in his account than does Irenaeus, and who appears to absolve Nicolas from personal responsibility for Nicolaitanism (i.e., "a heresy *in the name of*"), probably drew his information from Papias. Because of his closer proximity in time to the events of 1st century, the likelihood is that Papias was correct. And what Victorinus says matches Revelation 2:14ff, where the Nicolaitan teaching is represented as a breach of the decisions handed down by the Jerusalem Conference recorded in Acts 15. That one of the seven men chosen to be deacons should become a backslider or an apostate from the faith is not in itself inconceivable, but we would prefer to believe that Nicolas remained true to Christ and to this place of trust to which he has just been appointed.

Nicolas is called a proselyte.[30] This shows he had been converted from paganism to Judaism at some time before he became a convert to Christianity. Evidently, he had been a proselyte of righteousness. Otherwise, his conversion would have precipitated the same crisis that was afterward met in the conversion of Cornelius (Acts 11).

Antioch of Syria (not Antioch of Pisidia) is apparently meant as being Nicholas' home. Where was Nicolas converted to Judaism? Some suggest that one time he lived in Antioch, and after moving to Jerusalem was converted to Judaism there. Others think he was converted to Judaism while still living in Antioch, and upon coming to Jerusalem, became a Christian. Whichever the case, just as Luke introduces characters who later become important to the historical record in Acts, so here he introduces Antioch, a city which will play such a large role in later chapters in Acts.

> That the only member of the Seven to have his place of origin named should belong to Antioch is a mark of Luke's special interest in that city, which helps to confirm the tradition that he himself was an Antiochene (see notes at Acts 11:28) ... As a parallel to this passage, James Smith, *Voyage and Shipwreck of St. Paul*, p.4, points out that out of eight accounts of Napoleon's Russian campaign – three by Frenchmen, three by Englishmen, and two by Scots – only the two Scots mention that the Russian General Barclay de Tolly was of Scots extraction.[31]

6:6 – *And these they brought before the apostles; and after praying, they laid their hands on them.*

And these they brought before the apostles. This "bringing" was done after the congregational vote that selected these men. It was the congregation as a whole that selected these seven men and presented them to the apostles for their installation or ordination.

---

[29] See Irenaeus, *Against Heresies*, I.26.3, III.11.1.

[30] See the explanation concerning proselytes at Acts 2:10.

[31] Bruce, *op. cit.*, p.129.

And after praying. Who prayed? Was it the apostles, or the men about to be ordained? The nearest antecedent is the apostles. The prayer would have invoked the blessing of God to attend these Seven in the discharge of the duties and responsibilities to which they are being appointed.

They laid their hands on them. This is the first mention of laying on of hands in the New Testament.

> The ceremony of imposition of hands was used in the Old Testament for the bestowal of a blessing (cf. Genesis 48:12ff); to express identification, as when the sacrificer laid his hands on the head of the sacrificial victim (cf. Leviticus 1:4, 3:2, 4:4, 16:21, etc.); for commissioning a successor (cf. Numbers 27:33), and the like. According to the Mishna (*Sanhedrin* IV.4) members of the Sanhedrin were admitted by the imposition of hands.[32]

The only question in verse 6 is whether or not there was an impartation of miraculous powers as the apostles laid their hands on these seven men.

- Some commentators would say, "There were no miraculous powers imparted." Dale, for example, feels the laying on of hands here in verse 6 is no different than the act in 13:3, and did nothing but serve as an announcement and approval of the appointment made by the congregation. He goes on to say that the apostles imparted the "spiritual gifts" to Stephen and Philip at another time.[33] It should be noted, however, that it was not the apostles, but the congregation who did the laying on of hands in Acts 13:3, and therefore the two examples cited by Dale are not quite synonymous.

- Not a few of the commentators are of the opinion that through this laying on of hands, the seven deacons were given spiritual gifts.[34] The probability is that this is more than a mere ordination service, because it seems from the New Testament practice of the laying on of the apostle's hands that it was for the purpose of passing on the ability to perform miracles (spiritual gifts). By studying all the cases where the apostles laid their hands on anyone, one arrives at the conclusion that miraculous power is involved here, especially in the light of the narrative Luke shares, beginning in verse 8.

6:7 – *And the word of God kept on spreading; and the number of the disciples continued to increase greatly in Jerusalem, and a great many of the priests were becoming obedient to the faith.*

And the word of God kept on spreading. The verb tense indicates gradual and continuous growth. More and more people hear the message, and the Church kept on increasing all the more, because the apostles were now relieved from the daily responsibility of distribution of aid to the needy. We may also think of the seven involved in evangelistic work, as we later have specific examples of Stephen and Philip doing.

---

[32] Bruce, *op. cit.*, p.130.

[33] Dale, *op. cit.*, p.80.

[34] See the immediate activities associated with Stephen in Acts 6:8. Compare also Acts 8:18 and 2 Timothy 1:6.

And the number of the disciples continued to increase greatly in Jerusalem. This is the third instance where, after telling us about some difficulty faced and overcome by the Church, Luke tells us the heartening news that the difficulty was but a stepping stone to greater growth for the Church.[35]

And a great many of the priests were becoming obedient to the faith. How many of the priests were converted is uncertain. There were, of course, many priests in Jerusalem. The priests were so numerous that they were divided into twenty-four courses, with each course working a week at a time in the temple services. We are probably to think of hundreds of this "great company" which became converts.[36]

In the course of church history, when leaders of other religions were won, whole groups of their followers too became converts. In the early days of the Restoration Movement whole denominational churches were won in this fashion. We think something similar happened to the Jews of Palestine at this time.

The word "faith" is here evidently put for the Christian religion. Faith is one of the main requirements of the gospel, and by a figure of speech is put for the gospel itself. Luke's statement that they became "obedient to the faith" is noteworthy as being an example in the New Testament that there is something to the faith to be obeyed.[37] This obedience is done not simply when one comes to faith. A man's initial salvation requires more than "faith only." It requires an expression of that faith, an expression here called "obedience," before we would say that a man has been justified by his faith. We naturally think of repentance and confession and immersion for the remission of sins as being involved in this "obedience to the faith."

R. Stephen Arrested and Falsely Accused. 6:8-15

6:8 – And Stephen, full of grace and power, was performing great wonders and signs among the people.

And Stephen, full of grace and power. The death of the first Christian martyr, and the causes which led to it, serve as an introduction to Paul's connection with early Christianity, for it is in the events surrounding Stephen's death that we first meet Paul.

Before this time, the opposition by the Jews, whether Pharisee or Sadducee, had been limited to threats and imprisonment and beating. But now the frustration and anger will burst forth, to be satisfied only by shedding the blood of the Christians. This is but the first of a whole series of persecutions against Christians that the world has witnessed, persecutions which have called for the believers to be faithful even when it means physical death.

---

[35] Compare notes at Acts 2:41; 4:4,32; and 5:14.

[36] There are times when the word "company" speaks of a smaller group, i.e. the 120 at Acts 1:15. and the publicans present as Matthew's guests at Luke 5:29.

[37] The same expression "obedience of faith" is found in Romans 1:5 and 16:26. A similar thought is expressed in the words "the steps of Abraham's faith" in Romans 4:12ff.

"Grace" here seems to be used chiefly in its sense of favor with God. "Power" was shown in the working of miracles.

Was performing great wonders and signs among the people. "Was performing" indicates a continuous exercise of the spiritual gifts which had been received at the time of the laying on of the apostles' hands. This is the first time Luke has told of miraculous signs done by anyone other than the apostles.[38]

6:9 – *But some men from what was called the Synagogue of the Freedmen,* **including** *both Cyrenians and Alexandrians, and some from Cilicia and Asia, rose up and argued with Stephen.*

But some men ... rose up. That is, they began to actively oppose Stephen's work. Verse 9 gives the reaction to Stephen's ministry. There must be a lot more involved in verse 8 than there appears to be on the surface. We must see Stephen as working and laboring in the city of Jerusalem through a considerable length of time. As a result of his ministry, his influence is felt in Jerusalem; and the Jews begin to rise up in opposition against him.

From what was called the Synagogue of the Freedmen. Special Study #15, "The Synagogue and Its Services," follows the comments on chapter 13. Since the leaders of the synagogues were invariably Pharisees, Luke is noting a change in the identity of the persecutors. Up to this point in the history of the church, the persecutors have been Sadducees. Now the opposition comes from the synagogues and their Pharisee leaders.

"Called" (*legomenēs*) is the word Luke uses when he introduces some foreign word into the narrative. Here the word is "Libertines" (translated "freedmen" in the NASB). What is meant by this word? (a) Perhaps it speaks of *people*, i.e., freedmen. In the Roman empire there were a number of ways a slave could gain his freedom, and the freed slave and his descendants would be classed as freedmen. The Latin name for these was *Libertini*, the word here transliterated into Greek. (b) Perhaps it is the name of a *place*. In the first printing of this commentary, following the suggestion of Barnes, Clarke, and Pearce, we argued that since the other four names in this verse are places, it could be expected that "Libertines" were people from a place called Libertum or Libertina, a town or district in North Africa near Carthage. And, in fact, a place of this name did exist. Victor, bishop of the church at Libertina, was present at the Council of Carthage (AD 411). Suidas in his Lexicon also wrote that *Libertini* is the "name of a people" (*onoma tou ethnos*). However, further study has caused this commentator to have second thoughts about identifying this word with a place. Suidas may have based his lexical note on an interpretation of Acts 6:9. And granting that there was a place called Libertum, was it sizable enough to have a Jewish

---

[38] See comments at Acts 2:43 concerning these different words for miracle. We live in what has been labeled a "scientific age," when many men tend not to believe in miracles. Sometimes the Bible's record of miracle is explained away by modern critics by saying that people back then didn't understand all that we now know about the scientific causes of things; what to them was mystifying is now explainable by us. But remember that Luke was a physician. From what we know of 1st century physicians (i.e., Hippocrates, the "father of medicine," lived c. 430-360 BC; and Galen, whose medical writings are well-known, lived c. AD 130-200), we can say that Luke lived at a time when medical knowledge was in one of its great ages. Remember also that Luke investigated carefully before he wrote, even about "miraculous healings." It is difficult to believe that Luke the physician would call something a "miracle" unless it really was.

population like was found in Cyrene and Alexandria (with which it is connected here in 6:9), and thus also have enough of those Jews removed back to Jerusalem to be included in the groups here named? This last question has caused this commentator the most doubts.

Who were the "Freedmen"? There were several kinds of freedmen. (1) There were *Jews* who had been carried off as slaves and who in time had been freed. Ptolemy Lagus (312 BC) had taken many Jews captive into Egypt. As time passed, these and their descendants had settled in Alexandria and Cyrene (see notes below). There were also great numbers of Jews carried to Rome by Pompey (63 BC). Many later became freedmen, and in the time of Augustus were settled in the trans-Tiberene quarter of Rome.[39] Chrysostom, c. AD 400, first suggested the interpretation that "Freedmen" in Acts 6:9 referred to these Jewish freedmen at Rome, some of whom had returned to Jerusalem and built a synagogue. (2) There were *men from many lands* who, like the Jews, had been carried to Rome. Many of these had become proselytes to the Jewish religion as well as freedmen in the Roman empire. Tacitus tells how 4000 of these proselytes were transported to Sardinia, and the rest expelled from Rome in AD 19.[40] Did some of these expelled proselytes go to Jerusalem and settle and build "the Synagogue of the Freedmen"?

Further complicating the explanation of verse 9 is the matter of how many synagogues are denoted. The answer might aid in the interpretation of "Libertines," but the Greek is ambiguous and the translation is doubtful. Therefore, several explanations have been defended. (a) There was a synagogue for each party named. A similar situation would be found in our larger cities, where each nationality of immigrants would settle in a section of town and have its own place of worship. "Libertines" in this case could be either "freedmen" or people from Libertum.[41] (b) There were three synagogues – one for the Freedmen, one for the African Jews, and one for the Asian Jews.[42] (c) There were two synagogues – one for the Freedmen (from Alexandria and Cyrene) and one for the Asian Jews.[43] The idea of two synagogues has appeal. It is what the Greek with two articles in the genitive plural after the subject "certain ones" would first imply (though we admit that the Greek would fit some of the other hypotheses, too). Besides, the insertion of "which is called" could be understood to mark the term "Libertines" as an exception to the other local designations. (d) There was one synagogue – made up of Hellenistic Jews, whether slave or free, from the four provinces named.[44]

As noted in the comments at verse 1, Hellenistic Jews, to a greater or lesser degree, had adopted Greek ideals and customs during their years living outside Palestine. In Jewish communities the Hebrews, who had not adopted the Greek customs, tended to look down on the Hellenists as being somewhat less holy. Therefore, when any Hellenistic Jews would return to the homeland, they would tend to be unwelcome in the synagogues of the Hebrews; thus, the necessity for their own synagogues.

---

[39] Philo, *Leg. ad Caium*. 23

[40] *Annals*, II.85.

[41] See Boles, Meyer, Schurer.

[42] See *Alford's Greek Testament*.

[43] See Lake and Cadbury, *Beginnings*. Notice too that the NASB opts for this interpretation

[44] See Bruce, *ibid*.

However many synagogues Luke actually mentions, it is certain that Stephen entered each and preached Jesus as the Messiah; and in each he met opposition. Perhaps Hausrath is right when he suggests that the Jews were often freed because their value as slaves was greatly lessened by their tenacious adherence to their national customs.[45] Having returned to Jerusalem, after so suffering for their religion, they were foremost in the opposition to Stephen whom they looked on as impugning the sacredness of all that they held dear. From his leadership of later persecution, perhaps it can be concluded that Paul was leading and coordinating the opposition at this time.[46]

Including both Cyrenians. Cyrene was the chief city in North Africa, and a large Jewish colony was located there.[47] Numbers of Jews were settled there by Ptolemy Lagus,[48] and are said by Josephus (quoting Strabo) to have been a fourth part of the inhabitants of the city.[49] Many times the Jews at Cyrene are alluded to in the New Testament.[50] A synagogue for these people at Jerusalem was a natural thing.

And Alexandrians. Next to Jerusalem and Rome, there was perhaps no city in which the Jewish population was so numerous and influential as at Alexandria in Egypt. As in Rome and Cyrene, the Jews in Alexandria had their own quarter, assigned to them by Ptolemy Philadelphus. They were governed as if they were a free republic by an Alabarch of their own.[51] The Jewish population of Alexandria in New Testament times has been put at about 100,000, or about 2/5 of the whole city. From Alexandria, in 285 BC, came the Greek translation of the Old Testament, known as the Septuagint (LXX), so called because it was the work of seventy translators. In New Testament times, the LXX was version of the Hebrew Scriptures read by all Hellenistic Jews, and even in many parts of Palestine itself by the Hebrews. Philo, the great teacher, was living in fame and honor in Alexandria at the time of the events recorded in Acts 6.

And some from Cilicia and Asia. The transition from the African Jews to those of Asia is marked by changing the form of the Greek construction into *kai tōn apo kilikias*. There were many Jews in Cilicia. Cilicia was a province of Asia Minor (the land we now call Turkey), on the sea coast, just north of Cyprus. The capital of this province was Tarsus, the

---

[45] Adolph Hausrath has the article on "Libertines" in Schenkel's *Bibel-Lexicon*.

[46] Saul also has the name Paul (Acts 13:9). Because he is better known as the apostle Paul, we shall use that name as consistently as we can in our comments. This decision also has the happy result that we can more easily distinguish this man from the king in the Old Testament whose name was Saul.

[47] Concerning Cyrene, see notes at Acts 2:10.

[48] *Cont. Apion*, II.4.

[49] *Antiquities*, XIV.7.2.

[50] Jews from "the parts of Libya around Cyrene" are named (Acts 2:10). Simon who bore the Savior's cross was a "man from Cyrene" (Matthew 27:32). There were "men of Cyrene" at Jerusalem at the time of the persecution that arose about Stephen (Acts 11:19). "Lucius of Cyrene" is named (Acts 13:1). Compare also Mark 15:21.

[51] *Antiquities*, XIV.7.2.

hometown of Paul.[52] As Paul was from Cilicia and doubtless would have worshiped in this synagogue, we can likely suppose that he was one who was engaged in this dispute with Stephen.[53] "Asia" speaks of the Roman province of Asia.[54] Asian Jews are in the forefront of opposition to the gospel, not only here, but later on through the book of Acts.[55]

Argued with Stephen. Though this verse speaks of "arguing" in opposition to what Stephen preaches, still there is some truth to the assertion that "arguing" is a new method of teaching the gospel, a method which will be used quite extensively by the Christians, and especially by Paul. The Greek word *suzēteō* means "to examine together, to discuss, dispute, question." Stephen, being himself a Hellenist, must have been a member of one of these synagogues before he became a Christian. When people became Christians, they looked on their fellow worshipers in the synagogues as excellent prospects for evangelization. Because they needed to obey Jesus, Stephen would "discuss" their need for conversion. One of the chief questions they disputed was likely whether or not Jesus was the Messiah predicted in the Old Testament. Men tend to hold dear that which has cost them greatly either in labor or suffering, and they resent anything which suggests that they have wasted their labor or suffered in vain. When Stephen suggests that a new covenant has replaced the old, and that the temple and its services were passing away, it is no wonder that he met hostile opposition.

6:10 – *And yet they were unable to cope with the wisdom and the Spirit with which he was speaking.*

And *yet* they were unable to cope. The Greek is very forceful, and literally reads, "They had no strength to withstand." They were not able to answer Stephen's arguments.

With the wisdom and the Spirit with which he was speaking. Perhaps "wisdom" refers merely to his knowledge of the Old Testament Scriptures. Or perhaps instead it may speak of the spiritual gift of wisdom.[56] Note that the word "spirit" is not capitalized in the KJV. If we so take it, the word speaks of Stephen's own natural abilities – his energy, power, and zeal. The word is capitalized in the ASV and NASB, for the translators think Luke is telling us Stephen spoke as he was inspired to speak by the Holy Spirit. If so, no wonder the Jews in the synagogue were not able to answer his arguments.

6:11 – *Then they secretly induced men to say, "We have heard him speak blasphemous words against Moses and against God."*

Then they secretly induced men to say. That is, they bribed men to be false witnesses. The Greek word speaks of bringing another under one's control by suggestion or money.

---

[52] Acts 9:11.

[53] Compare Acts 7:58.

[54] See comments at Acts 2:9.

[55] Acts 21:27ff.

[56] Compare 1 Corinthians 12:8.

By some means or other, they induced men to lie in court about what Stephen had actually said.

We have heard him speak blasphemous words against Moses and *against* God. Moses was regarded with profound reverence. Among the Jews his laws were held to be unchangeable. And if Stephen has been urging anything at all like what will be later written down in the book of Hebrews – e.g., that there was a greater lawgiver than Moses, that the priesthood and tabernacle were mere shadows and types of things to come, that now that Christ had died the old covenant was no longer binding – it is easy to see how devout Jews would regard it as blasphemy. Of course, Stephen (following Jesus' example) spoke not of the destruction of the Law, but of its fulfillment in the fuller revelation of Christ. He had been putting the Law in its proper place as a schoolmaster to bring men to Christ. But the Jews did not hear him clearly or carefully. What they heard they insisted was "blasphemy," words spoken against someone or something. It must be remembered that at this time the whole Jewish people were in a state of ill-suppressed agitation because of the Roman domination, and they were sensitively jealous for the honor of the Mosaic institutions. The Law was about all they had left of their former glory. What Stephen was arguing sounded very much like this too was no longer to be held dear.

How they could accuse Stephen of blasphemy of the Law is not hard to see. But how can it be said he was blaspheming God? God had given the Law, and anyone guilty of tampering with the Law might be thereby guilty of blaspheming God the Giver. Or perhaps Stephen was charged with blasphemy because he said that if the Jews continued in unbelief that their temple would be destroyed. The temple was regarded as God's holy place, and so to speak against it was perhaps tantamount to speaking against God.

6:12 – *And they stirred up the people, the elders and the scribes, and they came upon him and dragged him away, and brought him before the Council.*

And they stirred up the people, the elders and the scribes. They (the leaders of the Hellenists?) excited the people, and alarmed their fears.[57] This "stirring up the people" was the same tactic used when Jesus was condemned to death.[58]

This is the first time the people of Jerusalem have been represented as being against the apostles or the Church. Hitherto the people have been on the side of the apostles; in fact, fear of the people restrained the violence of the early persecutors. This change in the sentiment of the people is accounted for by the fact that this persecution is led by the Pharisees, who had much more influence with the masses than did the Sadducees. The Sadducees, in charge of the Jerusalem temple, had comparatively little influence with the people. The Pharisees, being the synagogue teachers and leaders, were men of authority in every community and were much more popular with the people. The Pharisees would have to distort the speeches of Stephen only a little to make them sound like blasphemous charges against the institutions of the Old Testament.

---

[57] Refugees, who had returned to settle in Jerusalem, would be open to such fears. As noted earlier in the comments, they would be especially fanatical about their religion, and therefore more easily excitable.

[58] Matthew 27:20.

"Elders and scribes" seems to indicate that the members of these Hellenistic synagogues even stirred up the Sanhedrin against Stephen. Perhaps they wanted the high court of the Jews to pass the death sentence against Stephen, since that was the regular sentence for blasphemy.

And they came upon him and dragged him away. The synagogue leaders, having stirred up the attitude of the crowd to fever pitch, then went after Stephen.

And brought him before the Council. Stephen was placed on trial, in the midst of the semicircle of judges who sat on the Sanhedrin. And Luke has told us that the court has already been prejudiced against the defendant, having been stirred up by the synagogue members. Was there a crowd of people around the fringes of the courtroom also?

6:13 – *And they put forward false witnesses who said, "This man incessantly speaks against this holy place, and the Law;*

And they put forward witnesses who said. These "secretly induced" men (verse 11) perverted the meaning of Stephen's words. The similarity of Stephen's trial to that of our Lord is striking. The same purpose of silencing the truth of Stephen's words by putting him to death; the same dishonest use of false witnesses; the same wresting of good words into criminal acts; the same meekness and patience of the accused in the face of death.

This man incessantly speaks against this holy place. "This holy place" would be the temple. When the Sanhedrin sat in their chambers, they were just across the valley to the west of the temple area.

And the Law. The Law of Moses.

6:14 – *"for we have heard him say that this Nazarene, Jesus, will destroy this place and alter the customs which Moses handed down to us."*

For we have heard him say. These false witnesses, like those who distorted our Lord's words,[59] doubtless based their accusation upon some semblance of truth. If Stephen had said anything like what Jesus said to the woman of Samaria,[60] or to his disciples,[61] or what the writer of Hebrews wrote,[62] or what Paul wrote to the Colossians,[63] his words might easily be misrepresented by false witnesses. There was real truth behind the half-truths the false witnesses spoke against Stephen.

That this Nazarene, Jesus, will destroy this place. Several times in His preaching, Jesus

---

[59] Matthew 26:61; John 2:19.

[60] John 4:21.

[61] Mark 13:2.

[62] Hebrews 8:19.

[63] Colossians 2:16-17.

spoke about the future of Jerusalem. He warned (with tears) that Jerusalem – city and temple – would be destroyed if they persisted in their rejection of Him. All the false witnesses would have to do is omit the "if clause" and they could make Stephen sound as if he were announcing Jesus' unconditional threat against the holy place. Or perhaps it is possible that Stephen was quoting Jesus' words about His death, burial, and resurrection; and as was done before, so now these words are twisted.[64]

And alter the customs which Moses handed down to us. "Alter" by introducing others in their place. "Customs" are the ceremonial rites and observances – sacrifices, festivals, clean and unclean meats, etc. The word "customs" seems to be almost a half-technical word, including the whole complex system of the Mosaic Law – its rituals, symbolism, regulations for daily living, circumcision, Sabbath-keeping, etc.[65]

6:15 – *And fixing their gaze on him, all who were sitting in the Council saw his face like the face of an angel.*

And fixing their gaze on him. That is, the Sanhedrin members looked intently at Stephen. With this look, they said, "What do you have to say for yourself in answer to these charges?"

All who were sitting in the Council. Was Paul there, observing? The case for the prosecution has been fully stated. The testimony of the false witnesses has been elicited. There is a momentary pause, and all eyes are turned toward Stephen as he stood there before his accusers.

Saw his face like the face of an angel. Some have questioned how these people would know what the face of an angel looked like, so as to be able to compare the expression they see on Stephen's face. Some have tried to avoid this problem by saying the language is figurative, indicating the peace and composure of Stephen (even when under the fire of false accusations). Such a peaceful expression was not characteristic of most defendants when treated as Stephen had been. Others have urged that many of them could have known what an angel looked like, and what they saw in Stephen's expression was similar. It has even been suggested that Stephen's face took on a glow, a radiance similar to what Moses' face had after he had been in the presence of God.[66]

---

[64] Matthew 26:61; John 2:19.

[65] Acts 15:1ff, 21:21, 26:3, 28:17.

[66] Exodus 34:30; 2 Corinthians 3:7ff.

SPECIAL STUDY #12

A METHOD OF SELECTION OF ELDERS AND DEACONS

The New Testament gives no specific instructions concerning *how* to select men to serve as elders and deacons. All that is done is to give certain guidelines within which the Church must stay, but the details are left up to the choosing of each individual congregation.

For the sake of an orderly presentation, our study is divided into three general areas: Qualifications, Method of Selection, and the Matter of an Ordination Service.

I. QUALIFICATIONS FOR ELDER AND DEACON

The fact that qualifications are given which men *must* meet[1] is evidence that the Lord intended the offices or functions of elder and deacon to continue in the churches throughout the age. It is wrong to argue on the basis of Acts 6 that the function of deacon was only temporary, and that when the job of waiting on tables was finished, so was the need for deacons. If that were true, why are qualifications given in passages besides Acts 6 to guide congregations other than the one in Jerusalem as they select men for the office or function?[2]

The qualifications for an elder are as follows:[3]

1. The bishop must be above reproach
2. The husband of one wife
3. Temperate
4. Prudent
5. Respectable
6. Hospitable
7. Able to teach
8. Not addicted to wine
9. Not pugnacious
10. Gentle
11. Uncontentious
12. Free from the love of money
13. He must be one who manages his own household well, keeping his children under control with all dignity (for if a man does not know how to manage his own household, how will he take care of the church of God?).
14. Not a new convert, lest he become conceited and fall into the condemnation incurred by the devil

---

[1] 1 Timothy 3:1ff; Titus 1:5ff.

[2] The word "function" denotes there is more to the eldership and to the diaconate than just filling an office. There is a *task* to be done.

[3] 1 Timothy 3:2-7; Titus 1:6-9.

15. He must have a good reputation with those outside the church, so that he may not fall into reproach and the snare of the devil.
16. Having children who believe
17. Not self-willed
18. Not quick-tempered
19. A lover of what is good
20. Just
21. Devout
22. Self-controlled
23. Holding fast the faithful word which is in accordance with the teaching, that he may be able both to exhort in sound doctrine and to refute those who contract

The qualifications for a deacon are as follows:[4]
1. Of good reputation
2. Full of the Spirit
3. Full of wisdom
4. Men of dignity
5. Not double-tongued
6. Not addicted to much wine
7. Not fond of sordid gain
8. Holding the mystery of the faith with a clear conscience
9. Tested and beyond reproach
10. The husband of one wife
11. Good manager of his children and his own household

There are several ways these qualifications have been applied. (a) Ignore them, and select whomever you please. (b) Think of them as only ideals, and select the men who most nearly qualify. (c) Consider them to be "musts," and select only those who are qualified. Is not this third way the Biblical way? Paul in fact said "must" (i.e., the Greek is *dei*, "it is necessary") when he gave the qualifications?[5] If Paul said "must," how can we say anything less?

The first thing, then, when it comes to choosing a method of selecting leaders, is to pick a method that will assist the membership of the congregation to consider carefully each man in the light of the Biblical qualifications.

II. THE METHOD OF SELECTION

Whatever method is finally adopted, it must permit the congregation to have a voice in the choice. Some religious leaders would affirm that the way to appoint leaders over a congregation is for the preacher, acting like a dictator, to appoint whatever man he sees fit to appoint. But this is not the way it was done in the Jerusalem church. The apostles did

---

[4] Acts 6:3; 1 Timothy 3:9-12.

[5] 1 Timothy 3:2.

not ride roughshod over the congregation's wishes and franchise.

Milligan is right when he says "that it is the law of Christ that the Church should elect her own officers ...."[6] So the method adopted should reflect the fact that the Bible does not give the leaders the right to autocratically appoint elders and deacons. The members of the Jerusalem church choose their own deacons, notwithstanding the presence of the most august and impartial body of Christian ministers (i.e., the apostles) ever found in any one congregation on earth. Surely, if ever there was an occasion when the congregation's vote might, with propriety, be suspended, and the officers of a congregation selected by the leaders, that was the time when the first deacons were chosen in Jerusalem. There was evidently danger that party spirit would be excited unless the whole matter were disposed of with great prudence. Might we not expect such prudence to be found in the apostles? They knew all the members well, and their respective qualifications. Surely to the eye of sense and finite reason, the shortest and best way to settle the whole matter would seem to be that the apostles themselves should choose and appoint men to wait on the poor and needy. But, no! Under the infallible guidance of the Holy Spirit, the apostles thought very differently. The apostles did not appoint these seven men; but they said, "You select from among you ... seven men ... whom we may put in charge of this task." And then we read a few verses later, "The statement found approval with the whole congregation, and [the congregation] chose Stephen ... Philip ... etc." (Acts 6:3ff).

Several times, the apostles or evangelists are said to "ordain" or "appoint" leaders for the congregations. Acts 14:23 is one such example. At the close of Paul's first missionary journey, elders were appointed in every congregation. How was this appointment made? The word "appoint" comes from a verb which is a compound of two words, "hand" and "to stretch." In some way or another, there was a stretching of the hands as these elders were put into office. Perhaps this means that the apostles stretched forth their hands as they ordained the men chosen by the congregation. Or perhaps it means that the congregation "stretched forth their hands" as they voted in the assembly on certain men to be their spiritual leaders. Whichever meaning is given to this verb "appoint," it is certain that in Pauline churches, the people had a part in selecting their servants.[7] It is certainly possible that the "appointment" done by the apostles in the churches of Asia Minor was no more than approval of the actions of the people, just as was done in Jerusalem.

Compare also the example described in Titus 1:5, about which Dale has written:

> "Ordain" or appoint does not violate the inspired example already set by the apostles [in Acts 6]. It must include as much as Luke gives in Acts 6, which allows for local autonomy. The leadership of an evangelist in selecting elders and deacons does not exclude the right of the congregation to "stretch forth" their hands, as they are approving men for their leaders. If the evangelist usurps this freedom by appointing without congregational approval, he exercises more power than the apostles did over the rights of the congregation. Elders, evangelists, teachers must point the way by faithful teaching; but the people must be allowed freedom to walk or not to walk therein.[8]

---

[6] Robert Milligan. *Scheme of Redemption* (St. Louis: Christian Board of Publication, nd). p.344.

[7] 2 Corinthians 8:19.

[8] Dale, *op. cit.*, p.77.

Scripture shows that the leaders – the apostles and evangelists – have a part in the selection of elders and deacons: they impress the necessary qualifications upon the congregation. Scripture also shows that the people have a part in the selection of elders and deacons: they have a right to vote or choose as did the Jerusalem congregation. Further than this, the Scriptures are silent as to the details of how an election of officers is to be done.

The details of one method that has proved successful are as follows:

- The evangelist carefully explains the qualifications of elders and deacons, and then the congregation is encouraged to nominate by ballot the men they believe to be qualified for the function.
- Following the meeting of the congregation in which the nomination ballots are filled out, the elders meet together to consider the men nominated on the largest number of ballots. If, in the knowledge of the elders, the men nominated are qualified, the next step is to go to the men nominated to see whether they are willing and desirous to serve.
- The names of those desiring the service are then placed on an election ballot, which is distributed to the membership at the next congregational meeting. The election ballots are so printed that they must be marked either "yes" or "no" for each individual man. If a church member marks "no" behind any man's name, that member must then write the Scriptural reason for such a vote in the space provided, and then sign his name at the bottom of the ballot. (There are several reasons for having the voter sign his name. If a member knows something about a man that would disqualify the man from office, something that the elders did not know about, the elders may want to talk to the voter, or even take the voter and go to the man in question to see if there is any truth to the objection, especially if the thing objected to has the nature of sin about it and needs to be repented of. Again, the offices of the church are not to be filled on the basis of popularity. Nor does the church want men in places of leadership who would bring disrepute on the congregation.)
- The ones elected on a majority of election ballots are then (in a special service?) installed into office. This installation, or ordination, would be similar to the "appointment" done by the apostles, and is no more than approval of the actions of the people.

This method, though certainly not the only one that could be used, is one that permits the leaders to have their Scriptural part in the selection, and one that gives the congregation its Scriptural part in the selection. This method helps the people to see the seriousness of the privilege of selecting men to oversee and serve the church of Jesus Christ on earth.

III. THE ORDINATION OF ELDERS AND DEACONS

It is not enough that the elders and deacons be elected by the suffrages of the people. The common-sense of mankind requires that all candidates for important offices, whether civil or ecclesiastical, shall be installed with some solemn and impressive ceremonies. And hence the apostles said to the disciples at Jerusalem, "You choose ... We will appoint (ordain)."[9] This is all that is meant in the Scriptures by ordination. It is simply a solemn setting apart of such persons to their respective offices as have been previously elected by the congregation, according to the standard of qualifications laid down by the Holy Spirit.

That this was done by the imposition of hands, with prayer and fasting, seems clear from the following Scriptures: (1) Acts 6:5-6, "And the saying pleased the whole congregation. And they chose Stephen etc. ... Whom they set before the apostles; and when they had prayed they laid their hands on them." (2) Acts 13:1-3, "Now there were in the church which was at Antioch certain prophets and teachers ... Barnabas and Saul ... And when they had fasted and prayed and laid their hands on them, they sent them away." (3) Acts 14:23, "And when they ordained them elders in every church, and had prayed with fasting, they commended them to the Lord, on whom they had believed."

Dale wrote, "Neither ecclesiastical nor extraordinary powers are imparted by ordination. There can be no 'direct succession' by the laying on of hands. The claims of religious groups to pass on powers has made possible tyranny in the name of piety."[10] And this conclusion is right. Ordination is the ceremony that inducts the elected person into the office, but no ecclesiastical rights or privileges are imparted by ordination. While it is true that when the apostles laid on hands, they often passed on special powers (spiritual gifts),[11] there are no apostles in the flesh today to pass on such powers. While it is true that the laying on of an apostle's hands often imparted special powers, it is also true that the laying on of hands in the Bible was often only symbolic.[12]

> An ordination service with prayer and fasting for elders, deacons, and evangelists is an act of public acknowledgement of their fitness and worthiness for service; but it in no way qualifies them, or authorizes their service by ecclesiastical claims.[13]

G.H. Cachairas has written concerning the ordination of elders and deacons that the vote of the congregation does not put them into office; it is the ordination service that does.

> It is true that the seven deacons were selected by the church in accordance with apostolic instructions which prescribed the requisite qualifications. And it is reasonable to conclude that elders were also selected in the same way. The Holy Spirit prescribes the qualifications, and the congregation should select persons who possess the required qualifications. But this election by the church does not put the person thus elected into office. After they are elected, they are appointed to office by an evangelist. This is the divine method of induction into office.
>
> It is an error, then, to hold that election of officers by the congregation is a scriptural appointment to office. Their appointment belongs to the work of an evangelist. In civil

---

[9] Acts 6:3.

[10] Dale, *op. cit.*, p.77.

[11] Acts 8:17; 2 Timothy 1:5. It shall be shown in the commentary in chapter 8 that the passing on of special powers did not go beyond the apostles.

[12] Genesis 48:13-14; Deuteronomy 34:9; Numbers 27:8, 8:9-13; Leviticus 16:21; Acts 13:3; 1 Timothy 4:14; 5:22.

[13] Dale, *op. cit.*, p.78.

affairs, a distinction is recognized between election and appointment or induction into office. There follows sometime after the election the induction into the office by means of a special ceremony. Just so, it is in the church. The congregation may select for elders and deacons persons possessing the scriptural qualifications for these offices; these persons are then to be appointed to office by an evangelist. This appointing is done by fasting, prayer, and the laying on of hands.[14]

CONCLUSION

The qualifications are stated distinctly. Several guidelines are given in the New Testament to help the congregation in its selection of officers. Much is left to be determined by the churches themselves concerning the actual mechanics of the selecting process. Milligan has shown the impracticability of trying to govern the church in all cases by any more specific laws. He put it this way:

> Had the Divine Founder of Christianity attempted to govern His church in all cases simply by specific rules and precepts, truly, indeed, the world itself would not have contained the books which would have been written. The *lex scripta,* or written code of England, consists of thirty-five large quarto volumes, besides cart loads of local and private acts of parliament. And yet it very rarely happens that an existing law can be found which in all respects is applicable to a given case. Almost every new case of law and equity differs, in some respects, from every antecedent one. Every lawyer knows that it is only by analogy the courtroom decisions are generally applied to new cases of litigation. What, then, would have been the magnitude of the Divine code had God attempted to govern His people in all ages and under all circumstances by specific rules and regulations! Surely we cannot too much admire that wisdom which for such a code has substituted a little volume of a few hundred pages, and which, notwithstanding its great brevity, has made it a perfect rule of faith and practice for every accountable being in every kindred, and tongue, and nation, and people while time endures! In doing so He has, in the first place, made the whole Bible, and especially the New Testament, *a book of motives*; secondly, He has enacted some very *general laws and regulations*; thirdly, He has illustrated these laws and the general principles of His government by a great variety of *authoritative examples*; and finally, He has given to us such specific laws and ordinances as are necessary to make the Bible a perfect rule of faith and practice.[15]

---

[14] G.H. Cachairas' article "Errors Concerning Church Officers" was reprinted in a mimeographed study on elders and deacons distributed to his class of students by Prof. George M. Elliott of Cincinnati Bible Seminary in 1954.

[15] Milligan, *op. cit.,* p. 349.

BIBLIOGRAPHY

DeWelt, Don, "The Ordination of Officers," in *The Church in the Bible* (Rosemead, CA: Old Paths Book Club), 1958.

Hayden, W.L., *Church Polity* (Kansas City, MO: Old Paths Book Club), nd.

McGarvey, J.W., *Treatise on the Eldership* (Murphreesboro, TN: DeHoff Publishing House), 1956.

Milligan, Robert, *The Scheme of Redemption* (St. Louis, MO: The Christian Board of Publication), nd.

Phillips, H.E., *Church Officers and Organization* (St. Petersburg, FL: Cypress Press), 1948.

Walker, W.R., *A Functioning Eldership* (Cincinnati, OH: Standard Publishing Co.), 1942.

Entrance to the City

Drawing by Horace Knowles
from the British and Foreign Bible Society

S. Stephen's Defense Before the Sanhedrin. 7:1-58

1. The Case of Abraham & the Patriarchs – An Emphasis on God. 7:1-16

7:1 – And the high priest said, "Are these things so?"

And the high priest said. The high priest usually presided in the meetings of the Sanhedrin. Since Joseph Caiaphas was not deposed until AD 36, it is probable that he was the one who put the question. We call this chapter "Stephen's Defense," but it actually is not a defense of himself at all; rather, it is a defense of the gospel he preached. It might be better called an "apology," but the word apology today has come to have quite a different meaning than it once had. Originally, it meant to make a statement showing you were right. Today, it has become an admission you were wrong.

Are these things so? To wit, all things that Stephen was supposed to have blasphemed. He had been accused of speaking against Moses, against God, against the temple, and against the Law.[1] The accused was called on to plead guilty or not guilty, and he then had an opportunity to make his defense. On that defense we now enter.

> If Caiaphas was indeed high priest, presiding over the Sanhedrin in virtue of his office, there may be a sinister implication in his question, "Are these things so?" For Caiaphas had been president of the Sanhedrin on the occasion when Jesus was arraigned before that body on very similar charges to those now brought against Stephen. On that occasion the witnesses who tried to reproduce in court Jesus' words about destroying and rebuilding the temple presented conflicting evidence, and when Jesus was asked to give His account of the matter, He refused to say anything in answer to this charge. Now, when similar charges are brought against Stephen, he in his turn is asked to reply. If the Master could not be convicted of disparaging the temple, it might be possible to convict the servant, and thus to discredit the whole new movement in the eyes of pious Jews.[2]

7:2 – And he said, "Hear me, brethren and fathers! The God of glory appeared to our father Abraham when he was in Mesopotamia, before he lived in Haran,

And he said, "Hear me, brethren and fathers. "Brethren" perhaps shows that a crowd of bystanders lined the walls of the judgment hall. But "brethren and fathers" also is a proper way of addressing the judges, too. It has been questioned whether Stephen spoke in Greek or Hebrew. It seems probable that Stephen, as a Hellenistic Jew, spoke in Greek, which seems to be borne out by the quotations of Scripture being from the LXX. However, Meyer and others think he spoke in Hebrew, for every Jew would be able to speak this language also.

Why did Stephen introduce such a long history of the Jews? is another question often asked. In what way would this be a defense against the charges made against him by the false witnesses? In fact, this is a magnificent way to answer the charges of blasphemy as he shows reverence toward the history and institutions of the Jews. A recitation of the his-

---

[1] Acts 6:11,13,14.

[2] Bruce, *op. cit.*, p.144.

tory of the Jews was a favorite topic among the Jews, and would secure their rapt attention. They loved to hear their history recounted. Stephen, however, is very selective. A common procedure in trials is to appeal to cases similar to yours in order to substantiate the verdict you wish to be handed down. Stephen does this. Starting first with the case of Abraham and the patriarchs, he is proceeds to show that his accusers had the same characteristics as their forefathers.

The God of glory appeared to our father Abraham. "God of glory" is a Hebrew form of expression denoting the God who is characterized by glory. This unusual phrase identifies God, of whom Stephen speaks, with the God whose visible glory was seen by the patriarchs.[3] The words contain an allusive reference to the Shekinah, or cloud of glory, which was the symbol of the presence of Jehovah. Paul's language "the Lord of glory" is a very similar phrase.[4] These opening words are an implied answer to the charge of blaspheming God. In what manner (vision, dream, etc.) God appeared to Abraham is not said. In Genesis it is merely reported that God spoke to Abraham, though this particular call of Abraham while he still resided in Haran is not recorded in the Old Testament. Stephen calls Abraham "*our* father." He identifies himself with his judges as long as there was any hope of influencing them.[5] Compare how Stephen speaks *after* it is clear how the case will go.[6]

When he was in Mesopotamia, before he lived in Haran. Mesopotamia means "between the rivers" – i.e., the Tigris and Euphrates rivers.[7] Genesis 11:31 speaks of Ur of the Chaldees, and Acts 7:4 speaks of "the land of the Chaldeans." Here, from Stephen, we learn that Abraham was called out of Ur of the Chaldees. The Old Testament does not record this call.[8] The Genesis 12 record tells us of Abraham's call out of Haran, but all that can be said about the Old Testament record of a call out of Ur is that it is implied.[9]

7:3 – *and said to him, 'DEPART FROM YOUR COUNTRY AND YOUR RELATIVES, AND COME INTO THE LAND THAT I WILL SHOW YOU.'*

And said to him, 'DEPART FROM YOUR COUNTRY AND YOUR RELATIVES. God wants Abraham to get away from his relatives who lived in Mesopotamia. Abraham

---

[3] Genesis 12:7; 18:1; 26:2; 28:12,13; 35:9; Exodus 24:16, 17; Numbers 16:19; Isaiah 6; John 12:41.

[4] 1 Corinthians 2:8.

[5] See how Stephen includes himself with his listeners in Acts 7:11,12,15,19,29.

[6] See how he no longer includes himself with his hearers in Acts 7:51,52.

[7] It can be a helpful habit to study the Bible with a Bible map at hand. This geographical knowledge helps to make the stories come alive, and reinforces the historicity of the Scriptures.

[8] This is one of several instances in the New Testament where we learn facts that supplement our Old Testament knowledge. See also the prophecy of Enoch (Jude 14), the names of the Egyptian magicians (2 Timothy 3:8), the hope that sustained Abraham as he offered Isaac (Hebrews 11:19), the acknowledgment of Moses of his own fear in the face of God's manifestation (Hebrews 12:21), the motive which caused Moses to leave the court of Pharaoh (Hebrews 11:24,25), and the prayer of Elijah (James 5:17).

[9] Genesis 11:31, 15:7; Nehemiah 9:7.

is given notice that he is to leave his family behind and go almost alone to a new land. Joshua's words, many years later, tell us why God wanted Abraham to leave his relatives behind.[10] God wanted to get Abraham away from the influence of idolatrous surroundings, lest he too be contaminated.

AND COME INTO THE LAND THAT I WILL SHOW YOU.' Abraham did not know, as he journeyed westward, to what country it was that he was going. "By faith Abraham went out, not knowing whither he went."[11]

7:4 – *"Then he departed from the land of the Chaldeans, and settled in Haran. And from there, after his father died,* **God** *removed him into this country in which you are now living.*

Then he departed from the land of the Chaldeans, and settled in Haran. "Land of the Chaldeans" is obviously synonymous with "Mesopotamia" of verse 1. Archaeologists have shown that Haran was a flourishing city early in the second millennium BC. Stephen has summarized Genesis 11:27-31.

And from there, after his father died, *God* **removed him into this country in which you are now living.** Stephen's speech is remarkable because it brings together within a comparatively small compass a considerable number of real difficulties or seeming inaccuracies in the details of the history which is called to the judges' attention. "When his father died" is one of these. Does this speak of Terah's physical death or spiritual death? Those who think it speaks of Terah's spiritual death note that the Jews unanimously affirm Terah relapsed into idolatry before Abraham left Haran, and this relapse they denominate "death" (the same word here used by Stephen). Further, it is supposed by some that if Stephen is speaking of Terah's physical death, then Stephen is making a mistake in chronology.[12] But having considered the evidence, this commentator concludes verse 4 does indeed speaks of Terah's physical death. Terah was 130 years old when Abraham was born, not 70 as might appear upon a superficial reading of Genesis 11:26. The death mentioned by Stephen was Terah's physical death, when he was 205 years old.

7:5 – *"And He gave him no inheritance in it, not even a foot of ground; and* yet, *even when he had no child, He promised that HE WOULD GIVE IT TO HIM AS A POSSESSION, AND TO HIS OFFSPRING AFTER HIM.*

And He gave him no inheritance in it. Abraham led a nomadic life, and this passage means that he did not himself receive a permanent possession or residence in that land (of Canaan). The only land which he owned was a field which he purchased of the children of Heth for a burial place,[13] called the Cave of Machpelah. This apparent exception was not a real exception. The field and cave were purchased for a special purpose, for use after this earthly life was over.

---

[10] Joshua 24:2.

[11] Hebrews 11:8.

[12] In Special Study #13, "Difficulties in Acts 7," see the discussion of *Alleged Mistake Number One*.

[13] Genesis 23:1ff.

Not even a foot of ground. This is a proverbial expression, denoting in an emphatic manner that Abraham owned no land.

And *yet*, He promised that HE WOULD GIVE IT TO HIM AS A POSSESSION. God did promise Abraham that Canaan would be his own land one day.

AND TO HIS OFFSPRING AFTER HIM. The land was promised to Abraham's children, when there was no human probability that he would ever have any children.[14]

7:6 – *"But God spoke to this effect, that his OFFSPRING WOULD BE ALIENS IN A FOREIGN LAND, AND THAT THEY WOULD BE ENSLAVED AND MISTREATED FOR FOUR HUNDRED YEARS.*

But God spoke to this effect. Verses 6 and 7 are taken from Genesis 15:13-14 in the LXX.

That his OFFSPRING WOULD BE ALIENS IN A FOREIGN LAND. The "foreign land" is a reference to Egypt. An "alien" is a citizen of another country who has temporary residence in a land other than his homeland.

AND THAT THEY WOULD BE ENSLAVED AND MISTREATED. God was predicting that Abraham's descendants would be made slaves, and would be oppressed and afflicted in Egypt.

FOR FOUR HUNDRED YEARS. Stephen is here alleged to be in contradiction to Paul and also to some passages in the Old Testament when he seems to set the length of the bondage in Egypt at 400 years.[15] Perhaps through the years interpreters have misunderstood the exact import of Genesis 15:13-14, and the captivity was but 215 years in duration. In any case, this alleged mistake is highlighted so that the reader may be aware that there are certain problems, and supposed discrepancies, and alleged contradictions in the Bible, and to make him aware that there are reasonable answers to these – reasonable enough that they need not shake one's faith!

7:7 – *'AND WHATEVER NATION TO WHICH THEY SHALL BE IN BONDAGE I MYSELF WILL JUDGE,' said God, 'AND AFTER THAT THEY WILL COME OUT AND SERVE ME IN THIS PLACE.'*

'AND WHATEVER NATION TO WHICH THEY SHALL BE IN BONDAGE I MYSELF WILL JUDGE.' As noted above, verse 7 is still part of Stephen's quotation of Genesis 15. "Judge" often has the sense of executing judgment; that is, punishing the offender. God is promising Abraham that in due time He would punish the Egyptians. And just as God said, the Egyptians were judged by the plagues and the overthrow at the Red Sea.

---

[14] Genesis 15:2-3, 18:11-12. Compare also Romans 4:18. See also the paragraph concerning Stephen's alleged mistake about the incredulity of Abraham in Special Study #13, "Difficulties in Acts 7," in *Alleged Mistake Number One*.

[15] In Special Study #13, "Difficulties in Acts 7," see the discussion of *Alleged Mistake Number Two*.

Said God. This verse actually combines the promise to Abraham in Genesis 15:16 along with a free rendering of the sign given to Moses (Exodus 3:12) which referred not to Canaan but to Horeb. What Stephen does is to substitute with the natural freedom of a narrative given from memory the words "they shall serve me" for the simpler phrase "they shall come hither again" of Genesis. He can do this without being accused of making a mistake because the latter phrase implies what the other one specifically states.

AND AFTER THAT THEY WILL COME OUT AND SERVE ME IN THIS PLACE.
"After that" equals after the Egyptians are punished. "Serve" has the idea of 'worship Me, and be regarded as My people.' "This place" is the place where God made the promise to Abraham, i.e., the land of Canaan.[16]

7:8 – *"And He gave him the covenant of circumcision; and so* **Abraham** *became the father of Isaac, and circumcised him on the eighth day; and Isaac* **became the father of** *Jacob, and Jacob* **of** *the twelve patriarchs.*

And He gave him the covenant of circumcision. God appointed or commanded this covenant.[17] On the word "covenant," see notes at Acts 3:25. The word here is *diathēkē*, a contract made between parties unequal in authority. God gave all the specifications and rules to Abraham; Abraham merely agreed to God's plan. Circumcision was appointed as a mark, or indication, that Abraham and those thus marked were the persons included in the gracious purpose and promise of God.

Perhaps here we can trace an indirect reference to the charge that he had spoken "against the customs." Stephen does not deny the specific charge that he has said Jesus would change them. In fact, that change had come when the Law of Moses was nailed to the cross. Stephen does assert that, though never intended to be permanent through all future ages, circumcision came from God's appointment, and therefore was to be spoken of with all reverence. It served the purpose and the age for which it was given.

And so *Abraham* became the father of Isaac, and circumcised him on the eighth day.
The covenant of circumcision was given to Abraham the year before Isaac was born. The argument suggested here by Stephen's words is apparently the same as Paul's in Romans 4:10-17. There it is affirmed that circumcision had nothing to do with Abraham's justification, for Abraham was justified before the seal of circumcision was ever given. Thirteen or more years before he received the covenant of circumcision from God, Abraham had already been reckoned as righteous because of his continuing obedient faith.[18] The "eighth day" was the regular day, according to the covenant's provisions, for the male babies to be circumcised.

And Isaac *became the father of* Jacob, and Jacob *of* the twelve patriarchs. The word

---

[16] The whole context is at variance with the assumption made by some that Stephen meant by the last words of this verse that Abraham worshiped God on the same mount at Jerusalem where the trial was then taking place. Stephen is speaking of the whole land Canaan, not one specific location in that country.

[17] Genesis 17:9-13.

[18] Romans 4:1ff; Galatians 3:17.

"patriarch" denotes one who is father and ruler of a family.[19] Here the word is applied to the sons of Jacob as being, each of them, the founder of a *patria*, or family.

7:9 – *"And the patriarchs became jealous of Joseph and sold him into Egypt. And yet God was with him,*

And the patriarchs became jealous of Joseph. Here begins that part of Stephen's argument which went on to show how the Israelites had always ill-used their greatest benefactors, and resisted the leaders sent to them. The other brothers were dissatisfied with the special favor which their father Jacob showed toward Joseph. They were envious at what Joseph's dreams indicated, namely, that he was to be exalted to a place of honor above his parents or his older brothers.[20]

And sold him into Egypt. Reuben prevented Joseph's being killed by suggesting they throw him in a pit. Judah suggested they sell Joseph to some passing caravan in order to keep him from starving to death.[21] Joseph's brothers knew that the result of the sale of Joseph would be that he soon would be a slave in some house in Egypt. And Joseph himself in later years says, "Ye sold me hither."[22]

And *yet* God was with him. God was with Joseph in Egypt – another proof that His presence and favors were not restricted to the land of Israel. God protected him, and in His providence overruled all the evil things that happened. Soon Joseph was in the very position his dreams had suggested he would one day be. He was made ruler over Egypt. The evil plans of men cannot frustrate God's gracious purpose. They didn't in Joseph's day, and they will not in Stephen's day, may be what Stephen is implying.

7:10 – *"and rescued him from all his afflictions, and granted him favor and wisdom in the sight of Pharaoh, king of Egypt; and he made him governor over Egypt and all his household.*

And rescued him from all his afflictions. God saw to it that Joseph was restored from prison and humiliation to a place of freedom and service. The afflictions did not derail God's plans. The afflictions the Church was suffering from the Sanhedrin would not derail them either.

And granted him favor and wisdom in the sight of Pharaoh, king of Egypt. Joseph's wisdom was evidenced not only in the interpretation of Pharaoh's dreams, but in his administration of surplus food stores in preparation for the coming famine. "Pharaoh" is not the name of a king, but a title, like "President" is in the United States. The Egyptian word meant "a great house."

---

[19] See Acts 2:29 for comments on the word "patriarch."

[20] Genesis 37:3-11.

[21] Genesis 37:28.

[22] Genesis 45:5.

And he made him governor over Egypt and all his household. Joseph's position was second in all of Egypt, and in addition he had rule over the court (house) of Pharaoh.

7:11 – *"Now a famine came over all Egypt and Canaan, and great affliction with it; and our fathers could find no food.*

Now a famine came over all Egypt and Canaan. The famine came, just as God had helped Joseph predict. Canaan was the place where Jacob was living at the time of the famine.[23]

And great affliction *with it*. It speaks of the distress and difficulties and hard times that came upon those hit by the famine.

And our fathers could find no food. The marginal reading is "no fodder." In the New Testament this word includes food for either man or animals; in fact, Boles thinks that in Genesis 24:25,32, it speaks of fodder for the cattle, as being a first necessity for owners of herds of cattle. Before long, when the herds are being decimated by starvation, the owners too will feel the pinch. Plumptre has attempted to help us see the application of the illustration Stephen has just used.

> So far as we can trace the sequence of thought, there seems to be the suggested inference that as those who, in the history of Joseph, had persecuted him, came afterwards to be dependent on his bounty, so it might prove to be, in the last parallel which the history of Israel presented. In the coming famine, not of bread, but of sustenance of their spiritual life, they would have to turn to Him of whom they had been the betrayers and murders.[24]

7:12 – *"But when Jacob heard that there was grain in Egypt, he sent our fathers there the first time.*

But when Jacob heard that there was grain in Egypt. The original speaks of wheat or barley (not "corn" as per the KJV).

He sent our fathers *there* the first time. Ten sons were sent, Benjamin remaining with Jacob.[25]

7:13 – *"And on the second visit Joseph made himself known to his brothers, and Joseph's family was disclosed to Pharaoh.*

And on the second *visit* Joseph made himself known to his brothers. The second visit speaks of the second time they went to Egypt to buy food.[26] Joseph controlled the distribu-

---

[23] Genesis 41:54.

[24] E.H. Plumptre, "A Commentary on Acts" in *Layman's Handy Commentary* (Grand Rapids: Zondervan Publishing House, 1957), p.110.

[25] Genesis 42.

[26] Genesis 45:4

tion of the grain, and had a cup hidden in Benjamin's sack. The brothers were finally told by Joseph who he was, and then they recognized him.

And Joseph's family was disclosed to Pharaoh. That is, Joseph's relatives, his family background, became known to Pharaoh.[27]

7:14 – *"And Joseph sent word and invited Jacob his father and all his relatives to come to him, seventy-five persons in all.*

And Joseph sent *word* **and invited Jacob his father and all his relatives to come to him.** Pharaoh assisted Joseph in making arrangements to bring his father and his relatives into Egypt.

Seventy-five persons *in all.* Stephen is here accused of making his third mistake, for the Old Testament (in Hebrew) mentions that 70 was the number that went down into Egypt.[28] Stephen, a Hellenist, is merely quoting the LXX, the version with which he would have been familiar. How the LXX came to read "75" where the Hebrew reads "70" is not known.

7:15 – *"And Jacob went down to Egypt and there passed away, he and our fathers.*

And Jacob went down to Egypt and *there* **passed away, he and our fathers.** On Jacob's death, see Genesis 49:33. The time spent in Egypt was long enough that all the sons of Jacob also died before the Jews went out of that land under the leadership of Moses toward the land of Canaan.

7:16 – *"And from there they were removed to Shechem, and laid in the tomb which Abraham had purchased for a sum of money from the sons of Hamor in Shechem.*

And *from there* **they were removed to Shechem.** Shechem is about 30 miles north of Jerusalem. A fourth mistake has been charged to Stephen in this phrase.[29] The words appear to include Jacob, who was buried not at Shechem, but at Machpelah (Hebron).[30] But if we limit the verb "they were removed" to the twelve sons of Jacob, which is a tenable limitation, we are met by the fresh difficulty that the Old Testament contains no record of the burial of any of the sons of Jacob, with the exception of Joseph, whose bones were laid in Shechem at the time of the occupation of Canaan by the Israelites.[31] When we give thought to what probably happened, we can accept the suggestion that the example set in Joseph's case was followed for the other sons of Jacob, too. Since Shechem was far more prominent than Hebron as the center of the civil and religious life of Israel in the time of

---

[27] Genesis 45:16.

[28] Genesis 47:26; Exodus 1:5; Deuteronomy 10:22. In Special Study #13, "Difficulties in Acts 7," see the discussion of *Alleged Mistake Number Three* for a more detailed explanation of the problem and its proposed solution.

[29] In Special Study #13, "Difficulties in Acts 7," see the discussion of *Alleged Mistake Number Four*.

[30] Genesis 50:13.

[31] Joshua 24:32.

Joshua, it is understandable why this place was chosen for the burial of the twelve patriarchs rather than Machpelah.

And laid in the tomb which Abraham had purchased for a sum of money from the sons of Hamor in Shechem. Stephen is here charged with his fifth mistake.[32] The better explanation of the alleged contradiction is that Abraham had indeed purchased a tomb at Shechem, which Jacob later had to retake (as recorded in Genesis 33:19). The KJV has added the words "the father" in the verse, so that it reads "of the sons of Emmor *the father* of Sychem." This must be looked on as an effort of the translators to meet the difficulty which this verse presents, but it may be noted that this is the only English version to add these words to the text. If the Greek read "of Shechem," such a reading could be defended; but the better manuscripts, including Vaticanus and Sinaiticus, have the reading "*in* Shechem" rather than "*of* Shechem."

We have finished the first part of Stephen's speech, "The Case of Abraham and the Patriarchs." What did it have to do with the charges brought against Stephen? The emphasis in this section has been upon God. We may surmise that Stephen had taught that God did not have to be worshiped in the temple or in Jerusalem (a statement similar to the one Jesus made to the Samaritan woman in John 4). Stephen backs up his statement by reminding the Sanhedrin that God was active in Mesopotamia, Haran, Canaan, and Egypt. Yahweh was not a little tribal deity, limited to the confines of the promised land.

2. The Case of Moses in Egypt – An Emphasis on Moses. 7:17-29

7:17 – *"But as the time of the promise was approaching which God had assured to Abraham, the people increased and multiplied in Egypt,*

But as the time of the promise was approaching. The time of the fulfillment of the promise, that is. Several promises were made to Abraham concerning the land of Israel. "Unto thy seed will I give this land,"[33] God had promised to Abraham, and this was now to be fulfilled. More likely Stephen has in mind the promise he himself has just quoted: "And in the fourth generation they shall come hither again."[34]

Which God had assured to Abraham. "Assured" is another word for "promised," and suggests that God "promised with an oath."[35]

---

[32] In Special Study #13, "Difficulties in Acts 7," see the discussion of *Alleged Mistake Number Five*.

[33] Genesis 12:7.

[34] Genesis 15:17. Compare comments at Acts 7:7.

[35] Involved in Stephen's argument is the concept of "progressive revelation," which means that God makes His will known little by little, in more detail this time than He did before. The idea of progressive revelation is abhorrent to some. Although it is clearly taught in Hebrews 1:1-2, many reject it, insisting that it is a hypothesis put forward to explain what would otherwise be contradictions in the Bible. Nothing could be

The people increased and multiplied in Egypt. Stephen is now telling what Moses has recorded in Exodus 1:6-9.

7:18 – *"until THERE AROSE ANOTHER KING OVER EGYPT WHO KNEW NOTHING ABOUT JOSEPH.*

Until THERE AROSE ANOTHER KING OVER EGYPT. "Another" is *heteros*, "different," rather than *allos*, "another of the same kind." The Hyksos rulers, sometimes called "shepherd kings," who looked upon the children of Israel with sympathy and favor, were displaced by another dynasty who brought suffering and sorrow to God's people in Egypt. There was a change of dynasty which brought back as king of Egypt the first native sovereign in many years.[36]

> The "Shepherd kings" were Asiatic Semites who had invaded Egypt many years before and naturally favored the family of Joseph. The other king that arose was most likely one of pure Egyptian blood, who displaced the sovereignty of the Hyksos rulers and reestablished the Theban kings.[37]

The identification of the Pharaoh who knew not Joseph is disputed. Those who hold to a 1225 BC date for the Exodus identify the Pharaoh as being Rameses II, the fourth king of the 19th dynasty. He came to power about 1300 BC.[38] Those who hold to a 1447 BC date for the Exodus identify the Pharaoh as being Ahmes (sometimes spelled Ames), the first king of the 18th dynasty. This man came to power in 1580 BC. For the record, Thotmes I, 1539-1514 BC, was the Pharaoh when Moses was born.

WHO KNEW NOTHING ABOUT JOSEPH. The Hebrew idiom means "not caring for." It can hardly be supposed that the verb is to be taken literally, i.e., that Pharaoh literally knew nothing of the name and deeds of Joseph. This expression must be understood as meaning that he did not show special favor to the people of Joseph. Because of the change of dynasties, the promises of the Shepherd kings of a previous generation were ignored and the contracts made were deliberately broken by this new Pharaoh. Whenever there is a revolution, gratitude for great deeds done by the leaders who are thrown out of power is forgotten. The old class of favored people is often oppressed by the new rulers.

7:19 – *"It was he who took shrewd advantage of our race, and mistreated our fathers so that they would expose their infants and they would not survive.*

---

further from the truth! The Bible itself claims that the things not clearly revealed in the Old Testament are made more clear in the New (see the word "mystery"). God did not reveal all truth at once, but has been unfolding if down through the ages until His final revelation in the New Testament. Stephen points out that God did not give the final form of revelation to Abraham, but only a promise; and then through the ensuing ages, different men had a part in God s eternal purpose as it came time for Christ to come into the world.

[36] Josephus, *Antiquities*, II.9.1.

[37] McGarvey, *op. cit.*, p.84.

[38] This commentator rejects the late date for the Exodus, and prefers the 1447 BC date. The late date does not allow sufficient time for the events that the Old Testament records as happening between the Exodus and the time of David, who can be dated precisely.

It was he who took shrewd advantage of our race. He acted deceitfully, cunningly. Probably Stephen has reference to the attempt by Pharaoh to weaken or destroy the Hebrew people by causing their male children to be put to death.[39]

And mistreated our fathers. He was cruel, unjust, and oppressive toward them.

So that they would expose their infants and they would not survive. Note the marginal explanation of "expose" as meaning "put out to die." There is a difference of manuscript readings here that is interesting. According to the reading adopted by the translators, the idea is that Pharaoh dealt with the Israelite people in this cruel manner, hoping that the *they* themselves would expose their own sons, rather than having them grow up to experience the same cruel and inhuman treatment as their fathers had. The other reading is "that *he* should expose their infants," and the idea is that the infants were killed by the Egyptians acting as agents of Pharaoh.

7:20 – *"And it was at this time that Moses was born; and he was lovely in the sight of God; and he was nurtured three months in his father's home.*

And it was at this time that Moses was born. Right when the mistreatment was harshest is when Moses was born.[40] Amram (Moses' father), a Levite of the family of Kohath, had married Jochebed. They had at least two children, Miriam and Aaron, before Moses was born.[41] It is not known whether Miriam and Aaron were born before Pharaoh's decree was issued, but it is known that Moses was born while this decree (about exposure) was in force.

And he was lovely in the sight of God. The Greek reads "He was fair to God," a way of stating, "He was a very handsome baby."[42] So attractive was this baby that he captured the hearts of his parents and they determined to preserve him alive.

And he was nurtured three months in his father's home. Moses was hidden at home for three months, in defiance of the new Pharaoh's decree.

7:21 – *"And after he had been exposed, Pharaoh's daughter took him away, and nurtured him as her own son.*

And after he had been exposed. The record in Exodus is that Moses was put in a basket of rushes which had been made watertight and set afloat on the Nile River near the place where Pharaoh's daughter was known to come to bathe.[43]

Pharaoh's daughter took him away. When the daughter of Pharaoh, accompanied by

---

[39] Exodus 1:22.

[40] Exodus 2:2ff.

[41] Exodus 6:20.

[42] Josephus describes the beauty of the infant Moses as such that those who met him turned to gaze in admiration. *Antiquities*, I.9.6.

[43] Exodus 2:3.

some of her handmaidens, came to bathe in the river, Moses' sister was standing at a distance waiting to see what would happen. The maidens found the baby boy in the rushes. The infant was presented to Pharaoh's daughter, and she decided on the spot to adopt him. Moses' sister offered to find a nurse and the child's own mother was engaged to nurse the baby. God works in mysterious ways His wonders to perform! Pharaoh and his daughter were being used to train and protect the one who would eventually become the leader who would deliver Israel from their hands. The name of Pharaoh's daughter is often given as Hatshepsut.[44]

And nurtured him as her own. She adopted him, and treated him as her own. She herself could never become ruler of Egypt, but her oldest son (Moses in this case) would be in line for the throne.

7:22 – *"And Moses was educated in all the learning of the Egyptians, and he was a man of power in words and deeds.*

And Moses was educated in all the learning of the Egyptians. The Egyptians had advanced markedly in the study of astrology, the interpretation of dreams, medicine, mathematics, and music. Philo, in his *Life of Moses*, says he was skilled in music, geometry, arithmetic, and hieroglyphics, and the whole circle of arts and sciences.[45] Moses also learned from his mother while she served as his nurse.

> The most striking thing about his education was the power and influence of his mother. Amidst all the wealth, sin, and culture of the court life and the learned of the day, Moses was held in the mighty power of religious training and love of devout parents. There could hardly be a more concrete illustration of the influence and power of godly parents over the life of a sincere and talented child. Again, could there be a more vivid example of the power and place of a woman in the leadership of a nation and true service in society? All that wealth and learning had to offer could not throttle nor thwart the faithful training of the home. If parents were worried about the danger of public education – as well they may be – perhaps they should look to their own home teaching of their child first. The time and place to save a child must be from crib to college "in the home" under the daily teaching by word and example of devout parents who love Christ and know His Word.[46]

And he was a man of power in words and deeds. Since Stephen is giving a chronological presentation, this means that Moses was distinguished in Egypt before he ever fled to Midian or was called to lead the children of Israel out of Egypt.[47] Josephus, following tra-

---

[44] See the article on 'Pharaoh" (#3) in *Zondervan Pictorial Bible Dictionary*, p.645. In distinction to this article, Josephus calls the daughter's name Thermuthis (*Antiquities*, II.9.5,7)

[45] *Vita Moys*, II.83.

[46] McGarvey, *op. cit.*, p.85.

[47] It appears to be out of context to try to explain these words of Stephen by appealing to words or actions of Moses years later during the time of the Exodus. Thus, it would seem to be in error to say that "in words" has reference to Moses' speaking through Aaron. Rather, this statement by Stephen is evidence that

ditional history, relates that Moses commanded the Egyptian army in a campaign against the Ethiopians, and protected the land of Egypt against serpents that infected the country by transporting large numbers of ibis into Egypt (the ibis being a bird that feeds on serpents).[48]

7:23 – *"But when he was approaching the age of forty, it entered his mind to visit his brethren, the sons of Israel.*

But when he was approaching the age of forty. The age of Moses when this event happened is not recorded in the Old Testament, but it was a constant tradition of the Jews that Moses was 40 years old when he undertook to deliver the Jews the first time.

It entered his mind. The distinct purpose Moses had in mind when he went to visit his Jewish brethren is stated by Stephen somewhat more emphatically than it is in Exodus 2:11. But there is no contradiction to the record in the Old Testament.

To visit his brethren, the sons of Israel. "Visit" has the connotation of "helping" or "relieving," as it does elsewhere in the New Testament.[49] The Israelites were in the land of Goshen at this time, and Moses went with the purpose in mind of delivering them from their oppressive bondage.[50]

7:24 – *"And when he saw one* of them *being treated unjustly, he defended him and took vengeance for the oppressed by striking down the Egyptian.*

And when he saw one *of them* **being treated unjustly.** The "unjust treatment" the Israelite was suffering was that the Egyptian taskmaster was striking the Hebrew.[51]

He defended him and took vengeance for the oppressed. There is no praise of Moses' actions in the word "vengeance." All it says is that Moses was violent in his treatment of the Egyptian taskmaster. "Oppressed" pictures the Hebrew as being on the point of being worn out and overcome in the struggle.

By striking down the Egyptian. Moses killed the Egyptian, and buried him in the sand.

7:25 – *"And he supposed that his brethren understood that God was granting them deliverance through him; but they did not understand.*

Moses was making an excuse when he told God at the burning bush some years later that he could not talk, so did not feel he was the one who should be sent to be the deliverer (Exodus 4:10). Barnes comments that "works" has reference to miracles (the plagues, etc.), but this too seems to be inconsistent with the chronological approach Stephen is using.

[48] *Antiquities*, II.10.

[49] Matthew 25:36; Luke 1:68; James 1:27.

[50] See what Stephen says, recorded in Acts 7:25.

[51] Exodus 2:11-12.

And he supposed that his brethren understood. In light of the purpose for which Moses went to visit the Hebrews, Moses looked upon the slaying of the Egyptian as being a signal for his countrymen to rise up and strike for liberty under his leadership. We are not told in the Scriptures how Moses was impressed with the thought of delivering his brethren from the Egyptian bondage. Josephus has preserved a tradition that Moses' mother, Jochebed, had a divine revelation that her son was to rise and deliver the children of Israel.[52]

That God was granting them deliverance through him. When they saw Moses contending with the Egyptian, and being victorious over him, Moses thought the Israelites would understand that their promised deliverer was here. After all, hadn't he shown that the Egyptians were mortal? With courage, and God's direction and help on their behalf, they were as good as delivered!

But they did not understand. Just as those to whom Stephen was speaking failed to understand the character and conduct of the greater Deliverer sent to them, and so rejected Him, the Hebrews fail to respond to Moses' act. They do not rise up and follow him.

7:26 – *"And on the following day he appeared to them as they were fighting together, and he tried to reconcile them in peace, saying, 'Men, you are brethren, why do you injure one another?'"*

And on the following day he appeared to them as they were fighting together. According to Exodus 2:13, two Hebrews were fighting with each other when Moses came upon the scene.

And he tried to reconcile them in peace, saying. Moses urged them to cease fighting with each other, and he particularly remonstrated with the one who was at fault.

Men, you are brethren, why do you injure one another. Moses reminds the combatants that they are both Hebrews, and both were oppressed by a common master; therefore, they ought to be united in their opposition to the Egyptian master, rather than fighting among themselves. 'If you are going to injure someone,' Moses implies, 'let it be an Egyptian!'

7:27 – *"But the one who was injuring his neighbor pushed him away, saying, 'WHO MADE YOU A RULER AND JUDGE OVER US?"*

But the one who was injuring his neighbor pushed him away. The Hebrew who had started the quarrel shoved Moses away when Moses tried to separate the two men who were fighting. His mind filled with rage, the one who was at fault rejected all interference from Moses. He wanted to finish the purpose he had in mind when he started the fight.

Saying, 'WHO MADE YOU A RULER AND JUDGE OVER US? "Ruler" seems to have the idea, 'Who gave you the right to boss us around?' "Judge" seems to mean, 'What makes you think you should settle differences and arbitrate cases that are really none of your business?'

---

[52] *Antiquities*, II.9.

7:28 – 'YOU DO NOT MEAN TO KILL ME AS YOU KILLED THE EGYPTIAN YESTERDAY, DO YOU?'

YOU DO NOT MEAN TO KILL ME. 'What are you going to do, if I don't listen to you?' the one at fault says to Moses.

AS YOU KILLED THE EGYPTIAN YESTERDAY, DO YOU?' How was it known that Moses had killed the Egyptian? Was the man who started the fight the one who had been rescued on the previous day? Or had the Hebrew man Moses defended spread the news of his rescue at the hands of Moses?

7:29 – *"And at this remark MOSES FLED, AND BECAME AN ALIEN IN THE LAND OF MIDIAN, where he became the father of two sons.*

And at this remark Moses fled. The Hebrews hadn't taken his "signal" to rise in revolt to the Egyptian masters. Perhaps Moses thought the news of his killing the Egyptian hadn't gotten around, and thus the Hebrews didn't rise up. But when the one combatant spoke of the act of the previous day, Moses now knew that what he had done was no secret.[53] And when it dawned on him that the knowledge of the act might reach the ears of Pharaoh, and that he himself was in danger of being arrested and punished, he became a fugitive. And he judged correctly, for as soon as Pharaoh heard of it, he sought to take Moses' life.[54]

And became an alien in the land of Midian. Midian was the southern part of the Arabian peninsula, and included land on the eastern side of the Red Sea also. The descendants of Midian, the fourth son of Abraham and Keturah,[55] occupied a considerable territory, some 300 miles along the Eastern shore of the Red Sea, and stretching deep into the interior. They were a nomadic people, and had very few towns.

Where he became the father of two sons. Moses married Zipporah, the daughter of Jethro (also named Reuel).[56] Jethro was a priest of Midian. The names of Moses' two children were Gershom ("a stranger in the land") and Eliezer ("my help is God").[57]

How does this second case related by Stephen pertain to the charges levied against him? Stephen had been accused of blaspheming Moses, so he refutes the charge by reverently rehearsing the history of Moses. Perhaps the Sanhedrin could also see this further inference: the Israelites in Moses' day rejected his leadership. Stephen may have been inferring that the Israelites (including the Sanhedrin) are still rejecting Moses' leadership,

---

[53] Exodus 2.12 tells us that before Moses killed the Egyptian, he looked both ways to see if anyone was about; and he struck the Egyptian only when it appeared no one was looking.

[54] Exodus 2:15.

[55] Genesis 25:2.

[56] Exodus 2:18; Numbers 10:29.

[57] Exodus 18:3-4.

for Moses pointed to Christ. Indeed, the whole history of Israel was marked by the rejection of those who were, at each successive stage, God's ministers and messengers for its good.

3. The Case of Israel in the Wilderness – An Emphasis on the Law. 7:30-43

7:30 – *"And after forty years had passed, AN ANGEL APPEARED TO HIM IN THE WILDERNESS OF MOUNT Sinai, IN THE FLAME OF A BURNING THORN BUSH.*

And after forty years had passed — Moses would then have been 80 years old. The Pharaoh from whom he had fled had died.[58]

AN ANGEL APPEARED TO HIM IN THE WILDERNESS OF MOUNT Sinai. Lenski and other commentators think that the angel who appeared to Moses was none other than Jesus Christ in angelic form. In fact, in many passages in the Old Testament, this messenger from God is called "the angel of Yahweh."[59] Also, there are passages in the New Testament where the same person is thought to be indicated.[60] It is a study in itself whether or not the angel of Yahweh who appeared to Moses and to other Old Testament leaders was really Christ. In an effort to cause the Bible student to be hesitant of accepting the identification every place the language "angel of Yahweh" appears, we offer these two lines of thought: (1) R.C. Foster argued that the angel of Jehovah cannot be Christ, for to so say would destroy the force and argument of the book of Hebrews;[61] and (2) there is some evidence that the angel who appeared to Moses was not Christ. In both the Hebrew and the LXX of Exodus 3:2, the word "angel" is, as here in Stephen's speech, anarthrous. If the reference were to Christ (as the angel of Yahweh), one would expect the Greek to read "*the* angel." Any angel commissioned by God to do a special task could be denominated by the Bible writers as "an angel of Jehovah."

In the Old Testament, it is said that this event concerning the burning bush occurred at Mount Horeb. But there is no contradiction, for Horeb and Sinai are but different peaks or elevations of the same mountain.

IN THE FLAME OF A BURNING THORN BUSH. Barnes thinks it just appeared to be a flame of fire; the bush just seemed to be ablaze.[62] But there seems no reason to say it

---

[58] Exodus 2:23.

[59] *Zondervan Pictorial Bible Dictionary,* p.40, lists some Old Testament passages where the angel of the Lord is distinguished from Jehovah, yet regarded as deity. Among these are Genesis 16:7-14, 22:11-18, 31:11, 31:13; Exodus 3:2-5; Numbers 22:22-34; and Judges 6:11-23.

[60] In the New Testament we have "an angel of the Lord" spoken of as active around the time of the birth of Jesus (Luke 1:11; Matthew 1:20; Luke 2:9; Matthew 2:13). In Acts the angel appears five times: (Acts 5:19, 7:30, 8:26, 12:7ff, 12:23). Not all of these could be Christ appearing as an angel, for in some instances He is already present in His incarnate form.

[61] One of the key arguments of the book of Hebrews is that the New Testament is superior to the Old Testament because the Messenger who gave it (i.e., Christ) is superior to the messengers who gave the Old Testament (i.e., angels, prophets, etc.).

[62] Barnes, *op. cit.*, p.128.

wasn't really burning. Again, Barnes suggests that it was really a grove, or clump of trees, rather than a single bush. The Hebrew word *seneh* is used for a species of thorny acacia, which still grows in the wilderness of Sinai. The Greek word, in the LXX and here in verse 30, is singular, and was used commonly for the bramble, or any prickly shrub. It is hard to see why Barnes wants to make it plural.

7:31 – *"And when Moses saw it, he* **began** *to marvel at the sight; and as he approached to look* **more** *closely, there came the voice of the Lord:*

And when Moses saw it, he *began* **to marvel at the sight.** What particularly attracted his attention was the fact that the bush did not burn up.[63]

And as he approached to look *more* **closely.** "Look more closely" is the regular word meaning "to examine and contemplate" the phenomena.

There came the voice of the Lord. God the Father spoke to him from the midst of the burning bush. Moses did not see God; He merely heard His voice. Stephen's speech agrees with Exodus 3:4, where the voice is attributed to the Lord, while the visible manifestation was that of an angel of the Lord.

7:32 – *'I AM THE GOD OF YOUR FATHERS, THE GOD OF ABRAHAM AND ISAAC AND JACOB.' And Moses shook with fear and would not venture to look.*

'I AM THE GOD OF YOUR FATHERS. This name for God has already been explained in comments at Acts 5:30.

THE GOD OF ABRAHAM AND ISAAC AND JACOB.' It is probable that Stephen knew that this designation for God had been cited by Jesus in answer to one of the Sadducees' questions on the Great Day of Questions.[64] In any case, the Sadducees would hardly have forgotten that Moses is being told the One speaking to him was the same God who made revelations to the Patriarchs before him.

And Moses shook with fear and would not venture to look. It always is a fearful thing to stand in the presence of God. Moses looked no longer in the direction of the bush.

7:33 – *"BUT THE LORD SAID TO HIM, 'TAKE OFF THE SANDALS FROM YOUR FEET, FOR THE PLACE ON WHICH YOU ARE STANDING IS HOLY GROUND.*

BUT THE LORD SAID TO HIM, 'TAKE OFF THE SANDALS FROM YOUR FEET. In Exodus 3, this is introduced in a different order, as being spoken *before* God said, "I am the God ...." To take off one's shoes or sandals was an act of reverence. The Jewish priests were barefoot in the tabernacle and temple, lest anything should have attached itself to their sandals that would defile the holy places. Moslem mosques, even

---

[63] Exodus 3:2-3.

[64] Matthew 22:32.

today, are not entered till the worshiper has removed his shoes. People in the Western world have a similar custom. They remove their hats as an act of respect and worship.

FOR THE PLACE ON WHICH YOU ARE STANDING IS HOLY GROUND. The ground was rendered sacred by God's presence. It had been set apart for a sacred purpose.

7:34 – *'I HAVE CERTAINLY SEEN THE OPPRESSION OF MY PEOPLE IN EGYPT, AND HAVE HEARD THEIR GROANS, AND I HAVE COME DOWN TO DELIVER THEM; COME NOW, AND I WILL SEND YOU TO EGYPT.'*

I HAVE CERTAINLY SEEN THE OPPRESSION OF MY PEOPLE IN EGYPT. The Hebrew in Exodus reads: "Seeing, I have seen." Repetition like this was the regular Hebrew method by which a thing was emphasized. God is aware of what happens in His world, not only to whole nations, but to individuals. He had seen the cruel treatment the Israelites were receiving since the change in government had occurred.

AND HAVE HEARD THEIR GROANS. Their cries of pain and anguish of the Israelites because of the oppression is what God continually heard.

AND I HAVE COME DOWN TO DELIVER THEM. This is spoken in accordance with human conceptions. When God moves in the unseen world there often are reverberations in our physical world. In this case, God was going into action, and shortly there would be a deliverance of His people from Egypt.

COME NOW, AND I WILL SEND YOU TO EGYPT. We have here a concise summary of what is expressed in much greater detail in Exodus 3:7-10.

7:35 – *"This Moses whom they disowned, saying, 'WHO MADE YOU A RULER AND A JUDGE?' is the one whom God sent* to be *both a ruler and a deliverer with the help of the angel who appeared to him in the thorn bush.*

This Moses whom they disowned. In the Greek, four verses in a row (verses 35-38) begin with the demonstrative pronoun "This (man)." This repeated pointing to Moses is a very emphatic way for Stephen to drive home his point of the contrast between his Divine mission and the people's repeated rejection of him.

The Israelites rejected Moses' leadership when he first presented himself to them as a leader 40 years before. Stephen introduces and dwells upon the rejection of Moses in order to emphasize the point that this had always been the character of the Jewish nation. It is preparation for the charge he will bring against them at the close of his defense.[65]

Saying, 'WHO MADE YOU A RULER AND A JUDGE.' See comments at verse 27.

Is the one whom God sent *to be* both a ruler and a deliverer. A military leader, or a governor in civil matters, is the force of the word "ruler" here. Redeemer is one aspect of

---

[65] See Stephen's charges as recorded in verses 51-53.

the word "deliverer." The word appears to have been chosen by Stephen to emphasize the parallel which exists between the work of Moses and the work of Christ. In a yet higher sense than Moses, Christ also had been made a "ruler and a deliverer."

With the help of the angel who appeared to him in the thorn bash. Under the direction and the help of that angel, Moses was able to deliver the Hebrews from Egyptian bondage. The Council must have seen the parallel suggested in Stephen's words. Their fathers had rejected Moses even though he had been sent by God; so now they rejected Jesus, even though He had been sent and credentialed by God to deliver them. These Sanhedrin members were in the process of rejecting another Heaven-sent messenger and message.

7:36 – *"This man led them out, performing wonders and signs in the land of Egypt and in the Red Sea and in the wilderness for forty years.*

This man led them out, performing wonders and signs in the land of Egypt. At Acts 2:22 we learned that "wonders and signs" refer to miracles. Here Stephen likely has in mind the ten plagues. Psalm 78:12 talks of the district around the city of Zoan (afterwards called Tanis by the Greeks) as being the particular place that saw these miracles.

And in the Red Sea. The dividing of the Red Sea so the Israelites could walk across in safety, and the overthrowing of the Egyptians who tried to follow, are the events in Stephen's mind.[66] It may be worthwhile noting that the familiar name ("Red Sea") comes to us, not from the Hebrew but from the LXX. Greek travelers from the time of Herodotus have called the particular body of water the "Red Sea" (*Erythean Sea*). The Hebrew reads *yam suph*, "Sea of Reeds," or "Marsh Sea." Modern negative critics attempt to deny the miracle by emphasizing that the place where the crossing was made was a shallow, marshy place, a "sea of weeds." This denies the clear statement of Stephen ("wonders and signs"), and it denies the clear statement of Exodus that the water stood on both sides in a wall, and was deep enough to drown the pursuing Egyptians.[67] Why the body of water was called "the Reed Sea" or "the Red Sea" is an unsolved problem. Some have referred to the color of the coast. Others have referred to the papyrus reeds that abound in places nearby.

And in the wilderness for forty years. Not only in Egypt and at the Red Sea, but also in the wilderness, during their forty years' journey toward the promised land, miracles were performed. The miracles include: providing manna each day; providing quail for meat on occasion; drinking water from a rock; deliverance from poisonous serpents, etc. The Israelites' clothing did not wear out, nor did their feet swell.[68]

---

[66] See Exodus 14.

[67] This commentator prefers to identify the place of crossing as being the northwestern arm of the Red Sea (the Gulf of Suez), a location also preferred by J.W. McGarvey, *Lands of the Bible* (Cincinnati: Standard Publishing Co., nd), p.438ff. This commentator prefers this as the probable site rather than either the Great Bitter Lakes or Lake Timsah, the latter of which is defended in *Zondervan Pictorial Bible Dictionary*, p.709.

[68] See Exodus 16ff and Deuteronomy 8:4.

7:37 – *"This is the Moses who said to the sons of Israel, 'GOD SHALL RAISE UP FOR YOU A PROPHET LIKE ME FROM YOUR BRETHREN.'*

This is the Moses who said to the sons of Israel. The speech made by Moses that Stephen is about to quote is recorded in Deuteronomy 18:15-18. If the Jews had really felt the reverence they professed toward Moses, they would have gladly welcomed the Prophet to whom Moses directed their attention.

GOD SHALL RAISE UP FOR YOU A PROPHET LIKE ME FROM YOUR BRETHREN. As noted in comments at Acts 3:22, Peter appealed to this Deuteronomy passage in one of his early sermons. The early Christians, by inspiration, applied it to Christ. The Sanhedrin must have been familiar with this Messianic application of the passage. Stephen refers to Moses' prediction in order to show why he believed as he did about Jesus. Rather than blaspheming Moses, Stephen has been paying the greatest respect to Moses' teachings. It is the Sanhedrin, in their rejection of Jesus as the Prophet, that is opposing Moses, not Stephen!

7:38 – *"This is the one who was in the congregation in the wilderness together with the angel who was speaking to him on Mount Sinai, and who was with our fathers; and he received living oracles to pass on to you.*

This is the one who was in the congregation in the wilderness. Note the marginal reading of "church" or "assembly." The Greek is *ekklēsia*, the word at times translated "church."[69] This verse is not to be taken to show that the church such as we know it was in existence in the time of Moses. The Hebrews indeed were a "called out people," having been called out of Egypt. But the church of Christ was not in existence in Old Testament times, as is seen from the future tense of Jesus' words at Caesarea Philippi, when he predicted, "I *will* build my church …."[70] The NASB helps guard the reader from any wrong impressions by using the word "congregation" here for *ekklēsia*, rather than church.

Together with the angel who was speaking to him in Mount Sinai. Some understand Stephen to be referring to the same angel of the Lord who appeared to Moses before the Exodus (Acts 7:30). Others understand Stephen as referring to the angel through whom the Law was given (Acts 7:53). As we have observed before, Stephen is giving a chronological recounting of Jewish history, and so at this place we see him as speaking of the angel who had something to do with the giving of the Law on Mt. Sinai.

And *who was* with our fathers. The Greek construction shows that it is Moses who was with the fathers, not the angel. 1 Corinthians 10:1ff does tell how Christ was with the Hebrews in their wilderness wanderings; and some have tried to put that passage together with this one from Stephen, as they try to show that the angel of Yahweh was none other than Christ. But Stephen is not speaking of an angel being with our fathers. Rather, it was Moses ("this man") who was with them.

---

[69] Compare what is said about the use of *ekklēsia* in the comments on Acts 5:11.

[70] Matthew 16:18.

And he received living oracles to pass on to you. An "oracle" is an inspired message from a deity. They were called "living" oracles because the doing of them meant life.[71] They were not mortal words which would die when Moses did, but they had an abiding vitality and force for ages after his death, until a new covenant should take their place. Moses went up on the Mountain while the Hebrews waited at its base. While there, God gave to Moses the Ten Commandments and the other laws and commandments that make up the Law of Moses. These are what Moses received that he was to pass on to the Hebrews when he returned to where they were encamped.

7:39 – *"And our fathers were unwilling to be obedient to him, but repudiated him and in their hearts turned back to Egypt,*

And our fathers were unwilling to be obedient to him. Stephen here is likely recounting what we can read in Exodus 32:1-23. While Moses is up on the Mountain for days longer than the Hebrews expected him to be gone, they turned to Aaron to be their leader. They rejected Moses as their leader. The Hebrews rejected Moses then, Stephen implies, just as the Sanhedrin was rejecting Christ now, even after He had shown Himself to be their redeemer from a worse than Egyptian bondage.

But repudiated him and in their hearts turned back to Egypt. They began to feel sorry that they had ever left Egypt, and they desired again the comforts which they had back in Egypt as being preferable to the privation they were experiencing in the wilderness.[72] They weren't, we believe, truly anxious to go back to a life of servitude; but they did yearn for some of the creature comforts they had known. Even the idolatry of the Egyptians had a certain influence over the morals and habits of the Hebrews. Not knowing how to worship Yahweh aright, and being familiar with all the gods of Egypt, they imitated the idolatries of the Egyptians.

7:40 – *"SAYING TO AARON, 'MAKE FOR US GODS WHO WILL GO BEFORE US; FOR THIS MOSES WHO LED US OUT OF THE LAND OF EGYPT – WE DO NOT KNOW WHAT HAPPENED TO HIM.'*

SAYING TO AARON, 'MAKE FOR US GODS WHO WILL GO BEFORE US. The Hebrews asked Aaron to make idols for them to worship. The word "gods" in the Hebrew is *elohim* (a plural form). The word is regularly translated as though it were singular when it refers to Yahweh, but it is translated as plural when it speaks of the gods of the heathen. Stephen's speech here follows the LXX of Exodus 32:4, which does have a plural form. "To go before us" seems to reflect the pagan practice of carrying their idols in the forefront of their army's marching columns.

FOR THIS MOSES WHO LED US OUT OF THE LAND OF EGYPT – WE DO NOT KNOW WHAT HAPPENED TO HIM.' Moses was on the mountain forty days. The people thought perhaps he was dead, and so they would get no further guidance from him.

---

[71] Leviticus 18:5; Deuteronomy 4:40; Luke 10:28.

[72] Numbers 11:5.

7:41 – *"And at that time they made a calf and brought a sacrifice to the idol, and were rejoicing in the works of their hands.*

And at that time they made a calf. They constrained Aaron to make the idol.[73] It was made from the golden earrings and ornaments which the people had brought from Egypt. Just why they made a *golden* bull has been variously explained. Boles wrote:

> It is thought that they made a "calf" of gold because they were accustomed to seeing the Egyptians worship the bull Apis at Memphis as a symbol of Osiris, the sun. The Egyptians had another sacred bull, Mnevis, at Heliopolis.[74]

Jacobsen suggests that Aaron tried to make a visible likeness of one of the angels[75] he had seen when he ascended Mt. Sinai with Moses and others (Exodus 24:9, 10), or that he was trying to make a likeness of the angel whose guidance was promised (Exodus 23:20-24).[76]

And brought a sacrifice to the idol. If this idol worship was anything like present-day idol worship, an animal was killed, roasted, and feasted upon, as part of their worship of the idol.

And were rejoicing in the works of their hands. The tense "were rejoicing" expresses the frequency or continuance of the sin. They rejoiced in the calf they had made, as if it were Yahweh whom they professed to worship. Idolatry is so foolish.[77] Still, we must remember that it had been years since men had received any revelations of God's will. All these people had to live by was oral tradition passed down from their forefathers. As time passed, such men remembered less and less about the true God and how to worship Him, and more and more invented their own ways (often as they were tempted and prompted by the devil). The Israelites danced around the idol,[78] and perhaps indulged in sensual acts, as indicated by "rose up to play" in 1 Corinthians 10:7.

7:42 – *"But God turned away and delivered them up to serve the host of heaven; as it is written in the book of the prophets, 'IT WAS NOT TO ME THAT YOU OFFERED VICTIMS AND SACRIFICES FORTY YEARS IN THE WILDERNESS, WAS IT, O HOUSE OF ISRAEL?*

But God turned away. That is, God turned His face away from them. Some of the older translations render this same word "gave them up"[79] – an expression which indicates that

---

[73] Exodus 32:1-4.

[74] Boles, *op. cit.*, p.113.

[75] Some cherubim look like bulls (Ezekiel 1:4-28, 10:1-22; Revelation 4:6-11).

[76] William Jacobsen, "Commentary on Acts" in *The Bible Commentary*, edited by F.C. Cook (New York: Charles Scribner's Sons, 1886), p.402.

[77] Isaiah 44:9-20.

[78] Exodus 32:19.

[79] See Romans 1:24,26,28.

God withdrew His gracious aid, permitted the appropriate punishment to be administered, and allowed them to go deeper into degradation than they would have otherwise.

And delivered them up to serve the host of heaven. Sun, moon, and stars are the "host of heaven." The worship of the stars, Sabaism, was one of the earliest forms of idolatry.[80] Astrology is an ancient form of pagan worship. God allowed the Israelites to become worshipers of the planets as a punishment for their rejection of Him. Actually, there is a permissive (God allowed them to have their own way), a privative (God withdrew His gracious aid), and a judicial (the appropriate punishment for their sin came into effect) sense in the words "God turned away."

As it is written in the book of the prophets. The quotation following is from Amos 5:25-26. The twelve minor prophets were commonly included in one book (one scroll). Josephus counted all twelve as one book when he spoke of the Old Testament canon as having 22 books.[81] Using language that was regularly used in the 1st century AD, Stephen speaks of the book containing the several prophecies, Jonah, Hosea, Micah, etc.

IT WAS NOT TO ME THAT YOU OFFERED VICTIMS AND SACRIFICES FORTY YEARS IN THE WILDERNESS, WAS IT, O HOUSE OF ISRAEL. The Israelites certainly did kill the animals prescribed in the Law of Moses, and on the days they were prescribed, and they did it through all those years of wilderness wanderings. But they did not have the right heart and attitude as they went about their worship. Though they kept up the form of worship generally, they frequently forsook God and offered worship to idols, and thus obviated the sacrifices they were ostensibly making to God. The round number "forty" is used here by Stephen, as in Numbers 14:33-34, for the exact 38 ½ years.[82]

7:43 – 'YOU ALSO TOOK ALONG THE TABERNACLE OF MOLOCH AND THE STAR OF THE GOD ROMPHA, THE IMAGES WHICH YOU MADE TO WORSHIP THEM. I ALSO WILL REMOVE YOU BEYOND BABYLON.'

YOU ALSO TOOK ALONG THE TABERNACLE OF MOLOCH. "Took along" might mean they carried the tabernacle of Moloch with them when they traveled, or it might mean they "elevated" it at their halting places in order that they might have a place to worship Moloch. The word "tabernacle" properly means a "tent," but it is also applied to the small container in which the image was carried. The idols were carried wherever they went because they thought it would act as a sort of "good luck charm," a talisman or amulet to defend them from evil. "Moloch" comes from the Hebrew word meaning "king." Moloch, King, Baal, and Lord were all names for the sun-god worshiped by the pagans, especially the Ammonites, who offered human sacrifices to this god. The image of this idol, made of brass, resembled a bull sitting up on its back legs with its front legs extended so as to form a sort of platform. On this platform, once the statue had been heated till it

---

[80] Job 31:26-28.

[81] Josephus, *Against Apion*, I.8.

[82] See also Acts 13:18.

was burning hot, infants were placed to fry to death. Part of the worship consisted of the priests' beating drums and cymbals to drown out the screams of the burning child.

AND THE STAR OF THE GOD ROMPHA. Exactly what star was being worshiped is not certain. In Amos 5:26, the name is given as Chiun in the Hebrew, and as Rompha (Rephan or Raiphan) in the LXX. The most satisfactory explanation of this seems to be that Rompha is the Coptic name of the star while Chiun was the Hebrew or Arabic name. The star is usually said to be the planet Saturn. Both Moloch and Rompha were forms of ancient astrology – a substitute for worship of the true God.

THE IMAGES WHICH YOU MADE TO WORSHIP THEM. The Israelites made little images of the gods. The same word "images" is used by Josephus of Laban's images, which were stolen by Rachel.[83]

I ALSO WILL REMOVE YOU BEYOND BABYLON. This is still part of the quotation from Amos 5 that Stephen was using as part of his defense. Where Stephen has "beyond Babylon" the Hebrew has "beyond Damascus." Amos had reference to the Assyrian captivity of Israel (not the Babylonian captivity of Judah) when he predicted a carrying away because of their sin and idolatry. Because Stephen says "beyond Babylon," some have supposed at this place he is no longer quoting Amos but Jeremiah 20:4-5, which does speak of the Babylonian captivity of Judah. Still others have asserted that "beyond Damascus" to the Jewish mind meant to go to Babylon, and Stephen is simply giving an inspired commentary on what the Hebrew of Amos meant.

How did this section, "The Case of Israel in the Wilderness," pertain to the charges against Stephen? The emphasis in this section was upon the Law. Those who did not keep the Law were punished. Stephen indicates his horror and dismay that the Law was not kept, and his approval of the divine punishments that accompanied the breaking of the Law. He also points out that the Law looked forward to its own abrogation (verse 37).

   4. The Case of the Tabernacle and Temple – An Emphasis on the Temple. 7:44-50

7:44 – *"Our fathers had the tabernacle of testimony in the wilderness, just as He who spoke to Moses directed* **him** *to make it according to the pattern which he had seen.*

Our fathers had the tabernacle of testimony in the wilderness. It was the tabernacle of testimony[84] because: 1) it was the visible symbol of God's presence, where the Shekinah rested; 2) the two stone tables of the law were kept there inside the ark of the covenant; and 3) it was visible evidence that God had revealed how He wished men to worship.

---

[83] *Antiquities*, I.9-10; Genesis 31:19.

[84] This is the title found in the LXX of Numbers 9:15, 17:7.

Stephen is now going to argue that God is not necessarily worshiped in any one particular spot to the exclusion of all other places in the world. His argument is this: the place of worship in the Old Testament age was the tabernacle, but as the tabernacle was moved around, the place of worship changed. Stephen is preparing to show that the religious leaders are the ones who changed from the customs of Moses. Stephen is now answering the charges that he spoke against the temple. He admitted and asserted that Divine sanction had been given to the tabernacle and temple. What he denied was that that sanction involved perpetuity.

Just as He who spoke to Moses directed *him*. The first place of worship for the Hebrews was not the temple. Nor was it erected in Jerusalem, but in the wilderness according to God's specific command. This command was given to Moses while he was upon the slopes of Mt. Sinai.

To make it according to the pattern which he had seen. While upon Mt. Sinai, Moses was shown a pattern, and this pattern he was to follow (like one would follow a blueprint) as he led in the construction of the tent.[85] The word translated "pattern" here was translated "images" in verse 43. There is the very good possibility that Moses saw a vision of Heaven as it now appears,[86] and the tabernacle he was to make was a miniature model of the real thing. Since God showed Moses the "pattern" to be followed, that was evidence that the tabernacle had God's sanction. Against that Stephen was not about to speak.

7:45 – *"And having received it in their turn, our fathers brought it in with Joshua upon dispossessing the nations whom God drove out before our fathers, until the time of David.*

And having received it in their turn. None of the generation that came out of Egypt, and who participated in the building and dedication of the tabernacle, was alive when the children of Israel finally entered the promised land, except Joshua and Caleb.[87] A new generation was in possession of the tabernacle when it came time to enter Canaan, and thus it is said "in their turn."

Our fathers brought it in with Joshua. The KJV has "Jesus" where the ASV and NASB have "Joshua." "Jesus" is the Greek way of spelling the Hebrew name "Joshua." Thus, in the New Testament, the translator must be careful to distinguish between Jesus and Joshua. The context indicates that Joshua (the Old Testament leader) is the person intended, not our Lord.

Upon dispossessing the nations whom God drove out before our fathers. After Moses has died and Joshua became leader of the children of Israel, they crossed the Jordan River and began conquering the land already occupied by several nations. God gave them victory over these peoples, and the land that had been promised to Abraham 400 years before now

---

[85] Exodus 27:9,40; 26:30.

[86] Revelation 4:1-8:1 describes Heaven as it now appears, and there are many features similar to the features of the tabernacle Moses built.

[87] Numbers 14:22-24, 32:11-12.

was in possession of Abraham's descendants. The same word in the original is sometimes translated "nations" and sometimes "Gentiles." Here the "nations" driven out are the Canaanites, Hivites, Amorites, Perizzites, Hittites, Girgashites, and Jebusites.[88]

Until the time of David. This may mean that God continued to drive out the nations until the time of David,[89] or it may mean that the tabernacle was in possession of the Israelites and was the appointed place of worship until the time of David.

7:46 – *"And **David** found favor in God's sight, and asked that he might find a dwelling place for the God of Jacob.*

And *David* found favor in God's sight. That is, God's approval and help were regularly granted to David. In his early life, with God's help, there were victories over Goliath, the lion and the bear, and over Israel's enemies. David was delivered from Saul's hand and the evil intent of others.

And asked that he might find a dwelling place for the God of Jacob. David asked permission to prepare a more permanent dwelling place for the ark of the covenant than the tabernacle was (which was a structure which could be transported from place to place); he sought to build a house that would be permanent, where the ark might be deposited.[90] "Might find" seems to imply that the site for the building was left to human selection, but it was not. God Himself even chose the site.[91]

Again, we see Stephen providing, though still in the form of a narrative, an indirect answer to the accusations brought against him. He shows that the temple was planned by the man after God's own heart (i.e., David), but it was not built by him. Perhaps Stephen is suggesting that if the temple had been as important as the Jew maintained, God would have allowed David to build it. After all, David was the one who "found favor in God's sight." And whether or not that building was the place of the final and perfect worship was a point yet to be demonstrated.

7:47 – *"But it was Solomon who built a house for Him.*

But it was Solomon who built a house for Him. God did not grant David's request to build the more permanent building because he had been a man of war.[92] David was allowed to prepare and collect the building materials for the temple, but it was Solomon who built it.[93]

---

[88] Joshua 24:11.

[89] 2 Samuel 5:6; 1 Chronicles 11:6.

[90] "Dwelling place" is a translation of *skēnōma*, a word implying more permanence than *skēnē* ("tabernacle"). See 2 Samuel 17; 1 Chronicles 17:1-12,22:7.

[91] 2 Samuel 17:2, 24:18; 1 Chronicles 21:26, 22:1.

[92] 1 Chronicles 22:8.

[93] 1 Chronicles 22; 1 Kings 6.

7:48 – *"However, the Most High does not dwell in* **houses** *made by* **human** *hands; as the prophet says:*

However. Stephen was charged with speaking against the temple. He has shown due respect for it, by declaring that it had been built by the command of God. But he goes on to show that God does not need such a temple. Heaven is His throne; the universe in His dwelling place. So the temple might be destroyed without hurting God Himself, or even the worship of Him. The truth being spoken by Stephen is that God is not confined in His worship to any age, people, or nation.

The Most High does not dwell in *houses* **made by** *human* **hands.** The words "Most High" are simply another of the many names of God. This very same idea about where God dwells was spoken by Solomon when the temple was first dedicated.[94] Stephen's argument here reflects Jesus' teaching during His conversation with the woman at the well.[95] And it is interesting to see how Paul, who was likely now listening to Stephen's defense, could take these same words which originally were applied to the temple of God in Israel and show how they have force against the temples of Zeus and Athena.[96]

As the prophet says. The quotation in verse 49 is from Isaiah 66:1-2. The very idea for which Stephen appeals to Isaiah for proof had been uttered by Solomon himself in his dedicatory prayer at the completion of the temple. But Stephen turns to what, to Stephen's hearers, might be considered a higher authority – to the great prophet Isaiah. The Sanhedrin would have known their Old Testaments well enough to remember that Isaiah had closed his mission with the utterance of the truth that, whatever glory and greatness might be attached to the temple in Jerusalem, the prayer of the man who had a "broken and contrite heart" was equally acceptable wherever it might be offered. This, too, has bearing on the charges made against Stephen of blaspheming the temple.

7:49 – *'HEAVEN IS MY THRONE, AND EARTH IS THE FOOTSTOOL OF MY FEET; WHAT KIND OF HOUSE WILL YOU BUILD FOR ME?' says the Lord; 'OR WHAT PLACE IS THERE FOR MY REPOSE?*

HEAVEN IS MY THRONE. Verses 49 and 50 are Isaiah's statement about God's dwelling place. God is pictured as being so vast that the whole universe is needed for a place for Him to sit.

AND EARTH IS THE FOOTSTOOL OF MY FEET. Yahweh cannot be confined to a material building when He is so vast that the universe is His seat and the earth is a mere footstool. If the universe which God made could not contain Him, how much less this temple which had been made by the hands of men.

WHAT KIND OF HOUSE WILL YOU BUILD FOR ME? says the Lord. What house

---

[94] 1 Kings 8:27; 2 Chronicles 6:18.

[95] John 4:21-23.

[96] Acts 17:24.

can be large or magnificent enough to be the dwelling of Him who made all things?

OR WHAT PLACE IS THERE FOR MY REPOSE? That is, where is there a place suitable for God to rest, like a man sits down and rests in the comfort of his own home?

7:50 – *'WAS IT NOT MY HAND WHICH MADE ALL THESE THINGS?'*

WAS IT NOT MY HAND WHICH MADE ALL THESE THINGS? Scriptures over and over again assert that God has created this world and the entire universe.

What did this section, "The Case of the Tabernacle and Temple," have to do with answering the charges made against Stephen? The emphasis was on the temple. Instead of either admitting or formally denying the charge, Stephen has gone to great lengths to carefully explain just what he does teach about the temple. This building was part of God's revelation to a people who only a few years before had come out of an atmosphere of idolatry. The tabernacle served as a place of worship, but was supplanted by the temple. And as even the builder and worshipers in the temple recognized that, grand as it was, it was not at all the real place where God dwelt, so Stephen shows that the temple wasn't the final revelation of God's will about how men should worship. How could it then be called blasphemy if Stephen, in harmony with the Old Testament prophets, shows there is a better way to worship than the worship conducted in the physical, temporary, man-made temple?

5. The Application. 7:51-53

7:51 – *"You men who are stiff-necked and uncircumcised in heart and ears are always resisting the Holy Spirit; you are doing just as your fathers did.*

You men who are stiff-necked and uncircumcised in heart and ears. Stephen's defense has every appearance of having been interrupted. There is a sudden change in tone from the calm argument he has been following to a charge as sharp to the ears of the Sanhedrin as "heretic" or "infidel" would be today. We would piece together what has happened like this. The Sanhedrin has seen the general application of Stephen's defense and have been enraged by it. More and more by their actions and expressions, and perhaps even outcries against Stephen, they have shown their disinclination to be swayed by his arguments. In righteous indignation Stephen addresses them in the language of this verse.

"Stiff-necked" is a figure taken from an animal that is refractory, and that will not submit to being yoked or bridled. The word had been applied to the sins of Israel in an earlier time.[97] In applying this expression to his hearers, Stephen was using the identical language of Moses when he conveyed God's rebuke to Israel. Considering that the Sanhedrin members professed to be standing on Moses' side against Stephen, this must have made Stephen's words doubly cutting to them.

---

[97] Exodus 33:3, 33:5, 34:9.

Circumcision was the external sign of being a Jew – of acknowledging the authority of the Law of Moses. The expression "uncircumcised in heart" denotes those, then, who were not willing to acknowledge that Law or submit to it. "Uncircumcised in ears" means they were unwilling to hear what God says.

> On account of the feeling with which Jews came to look upon all uncircumcised persons, the term uncircumcised was used by them as a term of reproach and contempt. Moses emphasized his lack of eloquence by speaking of his "uncircumcised lips" (Exodus 6:12-13); and speaks of Israel in apostasy as having "uncircumcised hearts" (Leviticus 26:41). David denounces Goliath as "this uncircumcised Philistine" (1 Samuel 17:26), while Jeremiah says of the people, "their ear is uncircumcised, and they cannot hearken" (Jeremiah 6:10). Ezekiel speaks of Elam as "uncircumcised in heart, and uncircumcised in flesh" (Ezekiel 54:7,9). Adopting this usage of Scripture, Stephen denounces his judges in the terms hurled at heathen nations and apostate Israel by Moses and the prophets. No words could have been severer in their estimation, and none could have been more just.[98]

Are always resisting the Holy Spirit. The Holy Spirit was active in Old Testament times, helping to reveal and inspire the messages given through Moses, the prophets, and the Savior. In New Testament times, He helped reveal and inspire the messages given through the apostles and prophets. All of these messengers the Jews and their fathers had opposed, insists Stephen. That opposition is not just the opposition of men, it is also opposition to the Holy Spirit.

You are doing just as your fathers did. Joseph, the divinely selected savior of his brethren, had been sold into Egypt. Moses, the divinely selected savior to deliver Israel from bondage, was at first rejected by them to become a fugitive in the land of Midian; then, after leading them out of Egypt, was again rejected by them. All the prophets had met with similar treatment. Their fathers had resisted the Holy Spirit and persecuted the divinely appointed messengers. And so now, these very people, before whom this trial was being conducted, had rejected Jesus, the divinely selected Savior and Messiah, and were violently opposing the messengers who had come to share with them the good news.[99]

7:52 – *"Which one of the prophets did your fathers not persecute? And they killed those who had previously announced the coming of the Righteous One, whose betrayers and murderers you have now become;*

Which one of the prophets did your fathers not persecute? By putting his charge in the form of a question, Stephen rather forcibly states that they had persecuted *all* the prophets. It was the characteristic of the Jewish nation to persecute the prophets and messengers sent

---

[98] McGarvey, *op. cit.*, p.130. In the current generation, among our own people, there is a similar condition of "unbaptism" among the baptized. Could not this accusation be made against many in our time, that they are unbaptized in heart and ears? Theirs has been only a fleshly baptism. They do not know the truth and do not want to hear the truth. This unbaptism is demonstrated in many phases of their lives. So, before we are too harsh in our condemnation of the Sanhedrin to whom Stephen spoke, we should carefully examine our own hearts and lives.

[99] See Acts 4:21, 5:23 and 40, and the present persecution of Stephen.

to her by God. In making this charge, Stephen is simply echoing our Lord's own words.[100]

And they killed those who had previously announced the coming of the Righteous One. Stephen reminds his judges that their fathers had killed those prophets whose main message was that the Messiah was to come. It was a great aggravation of their offense that they put to death the very messengers who foretold the greatest blessing that their nation would ever receive. "The Righteous One" is the Messiah. This name for Messiah, suggested perhaps by Isaiah 53:11, appears in two other passages in Acts (3:14 and 22:14) and in James 5:6. These passages are all addressed to Jews who understood the title to be a name for the Messiah. There is an implied charge against the judges that just as their fathers had persecuted and killed the prophets, so they were still persecuting the prophets who had been sent by God.

Whose betrayers and murderers you have now become. By using the name "Righteous One" for Jesus, and right alongside of it speaking of how they had betrayed and murdered Him, Stephen accuses the Sanhedrin of murdering an innocent man. More than that, he accuses them of murdering the world's only "Righteous One." 'You have gone beyond your fathers in guilt because you have betrayed and murdered Messiah Himself.' Perhaps Stephen has in mind how the religious leaders employed Judas to betray Jesus. Perhaps Stephen has in mind how persistent the religious leaders were as they urged Pilate over and over again to pronounce the death sentence. They were not merely accessories; they were principals in the death of Jesus.

7:53 – *"you who received the law as ordained by angels, and* yet *did not keep it."*

You who received the law as ordained by angels. "Law" is the Law of Moses – the law they professed to be keeping and which they had accused Stephen of blaspheming. Some think "ordained by angels" means that angels *were present* when God gave this Law through Moses.[101] Others think it means that angels *were the instruments* through whom the Law was given to Moses.[102] Still others believe we should translate the word "messengers," and understand it to refer to *the human messengers* Moses, Aaron and Joshua. There is emphasis on the word "you." For one to kill Christ accidentally would be bad. 'But you – you who had the Law – for you to kill the Christ was a terrible crime.'

And *yet* **did not keep it.** Those who had accused Stephen of blaspheming the Law are now accused by Stephen of themselves blaspheming the Law, and persecuting the disciples of Christ. Instead of trying Stephen, Stephen had put the Sanhedrin on trial. It has been suggested that a good title for Stephen's defense would have been "History Repeats Itself." As the Jewish people responded negatively to the will of God in the past, so now these Jewish people in Jerusalem, represented by the Sanhedrin, are again responding negatively to God's divinely planned Messiah. History has been shown to repeat itself throughout Stephen's entire speech. His main point has been that the Jews have always resisted the

---

[100] Compare Matthew 21:33, 5:12; Luke 13:34.

[101] Psalm 68:17; Deuteronomy 33:2.

[102] Compare Hebrews 2:2, Galatians 3:19.

Holy Spirit, and now they are doing it again.

How did Luke know the text of Stephen's speech? He may have learned it from Paul, who was most probably present at Stephen's trial; or he may have learned it by revelation, and reproduced it by inspiration.

T. Stephen Stoned to Death. 7:54-60

7:54 – *Now when they heard this, they were cut to the quick, and they* **began** *gnashing their teeth at him.*

Now when they heard this. What had begun as an orderly trial (e.g., witnesses, though false, were called) now degenerates into mob action.

They were cut to the quick. Compare comments on a similar expression at Acts 5:32. The Council members were exceedingly angered by the charges made by Stephen. This was not a case of a speaker "just laying them in the aisles," of Stephen intentionally using extravagant or inflammatory language simply to get his audience's attention. We see Stephen as using drastic measures in an effort to win the Sanhedrin to the Lord.

And they *began* gnashing their teeth at him. When men get exceedingly angry, they double up their fists and grit their teeth and bare them in an effort to convey to the object of their anger the fact of their displeasure. Like an angry dog they bared their teeth in rage at Stephen.

7:55 – *But being full of the Holy Spirit, he gazed intently into heaven and saw the glory of God, and Jesus standing at the right hand of God;*

But being full of the Holy Spirit. This expression "full of the Holy Spirit" has been commented upon before in Acts.[103] The permanent character of Stephen's spiritual endowments is strongly indicated by the use of *huparchōn* ("being") instead of *ōn*. A special filling to meet this emergency would likely have been expressed by *genomenon*.

He gazed intently into heaven. When a man is in extreme circumstances, he just automatically looks up toward heaven, as if imploring heaven's help or protection or encouragement. Stephen is in such circumstances. He was aware that his final statement had triggered such a response that there was no safety or justice possible at the hands of the Sanhedrin. What he sees as he looks toward heaven was more than most mortal men are granted to see at such moments.

And saw the glory of God. The word "glory" is often used of the Shekinah, as we have noted earlier in our study of Stephen's speech.[104] Whenever mortal men have been given a glimpse into the heavenly throne room, and then try to tell us what they saw, the One who

---

[103] See Acts 6:6, 8:6.

[104] Acts 7:2.

sits on the throne of the universe is seldom described, save that what is seen is a splendor, a light, a glowing sphere surrounding and emanating from Him who sits on the throne.[105] This sphere of light is what Stephen saw and calls "glory."

And Jesus standing at the right hand of God. Stephen saw Christ in His glorified humanity, and Jesus was in an exalted place.[106] Jesus' standing is likely to be understood as expressing His readiness to sustain and welcome Stephen home.

> In Acts 2:34, Jesus is pictured as seated at the right hand of God. The same thought is carried out in Matthew 26:64; Mark 16:19; Ephesians 1:20; Colossians 3:1; and Hebrews 1:3. Many interpretations have been placed on this expression "standing." Some think that Jesus, out of great interest in the death of the first martyr, stood to cheer him on to victory. Others have made Jesus subject to the Father, and standing ready to do the Father's bidding.[107]

7:56 – *and he said, "Behold, I see the heavens opened up and the Son of Man standing at the right hand of God."*

And he said, "Behold, I see the heavens opened up. Stephen speaks as if the skies had parted and his eyes had penetrated beyond to the third heaven where God dwells. It is probable that what Stephen saw was visible only to the inward spiritual eye, and not to his physical eyes. Since no member of the Sanhedrin (as far as the record goes) saw the opened heavens, the words which declared what Stephen saw seemed only an aggravation of the offenses of which they had already determined he was guilty.

And the Son of Man standing at the right hand of God." This is one of only three places outside the Gospels where the title "Son of Man" is applied to Jesus, and thus it is a matter of special notice. Jesus regularly used this title when speaking of Himself[108] because it was a recognized Messianic title.[109] Stephen's use of the title here is one of those little confirmations of the truth of the Gospel record, for Stephen delivered his defense some years before any of the Gospels were written. Furthermore, all the apparent inaccuracies and contradictions are other than what we would expect to find if Luke had simply made up the speech and put it into the mouth of Stephen. Thus, the occurrence of the Messianic title here is evidence in favor of the truthfulness of the Gospel narrative, for it shows that "Son of Man" was a title familiar to the people and to the Sanhedrin even at this early time. Would some of the Sanhedrin members remember that Jesus Himself had spoken similar words when He was on trial before this same body?[110]

---

[105] Revelation 4:2. 3; 1 Timothy 6:16

[106] See Acts 2:25.

[107] Dale, *op. cit.*, p.90.

[108] See Matthew 8:20, etc.

[109] Revelation 1:13 and 14:14 are the other two New Testament occurrences of this title outside the Gospels. See Guldenhuys, Commentary on Luke" in the *New International Critical Commentary* series (Grand Rapids: Eerdmans, 1951), p.352-353.

[110] Matthew 27:64-65.

7:57 – *But they cried out with a loud voice, and covered their ears, and they rushed upon him with one impulse.*

But they cried out with a loud voice. Who is "they"? The people or the Sanhedrin members?[111] Probably the Sanhedrin members. Such words as Stephen had just spoken about the Son of Man had been condemned as blasphemy when Jesus spoke them, and the Sanhedrin would view them as simply a repetition of blasphemous words. The title was offensive in that it proclaimed that Jesus was equal with God. In Stephen's case, it was further offensive in that it proclaimed Jesus to be the risen and exalted Lord (else how could He be at the right hand of God?).

And covered their ears. They thus indicated they wanted to hear no more blasphemy. They wanted to shut out any more of such evil words as they believed they were hearing.

And they rushed upon him with one impulse. The scene has now turned into a riot and mob action. No longer is Stephen getting a fair trial, if indeed it was fair in the first place. This is violence! All restraint has been removed, and the shameful outrage is about to be carried out that will make Stephen the first martyr for the cause of Christ.

7:58 – *And when they had driven him out of the city, they began stoning him, and the witnesses laid aside their robes at the feet of a young man named Saul.*

And when they had driven him out of the city. This was in accordance with the Law of Moses, which instructed that the one to be stoned was to be taken outside the camp.[112]

They began stoning him. This was the appointed punishment for cases of blasphemy.[113] The Greek imperfect tense verb might emphasize the beginning of the action, as the NASB translators have explained it. Or it might picture a continuous action; after pelting him with large rocks, they would rush up, pick up the rocks again, and hurl them at Stephen again and again.

And the witnesses. In this case, the witnesses would have been the false the witnesses who testified against Stephen at the trial.[114] It was required by the Law that the witnesses in a given case should be the first ones to hurl stones at the condemned man. The intention of such a requirement was to discourage false accusations, for if the accused is found guilty, the accusers knew they would be employed as the executioners. After the witnesses threw the first stones, all the rest would join in.

Laid aside their robes at the feet. They laid aside their outer garments, those long, flowing robes, in order to have free access and use of their arms. Their action is more than

---

[111] In the comments at verse 2 we weighed the two possibilities concerning the make-up of the audience for this trial.

[112] Leviticus 24:14

[113] Leviticus 24:16; John 10:31.

[114] Acts 6:13

"Here, hold my coat!" Paul was taking responsibility for the action that day upon himself. If the Roman authorities should call the Jews to account for the deeds of the day, Paul was taking personal responsibility for it.

Of a young man named Saul. By Jewish modes of reckoning, a young man was anyone between the ages of 24 and 40.[115] Here Luke introduces the main character of the last half of the book of Acts.

> There was at least one in the audience upon whom, we have reason to believe, the impression made by this whole procedure was deep and lasting. Saul never forgot it; but long afterward, bending under the weight of years, he made sad mention of the scene. Acts 22:19, 20; II Timothy 1:12-17.[116]

7:59 – *And they went on stoning Stephen as he called upon* **the Lord** *and said, "Lord Jesus, receive my spirit!"*

And they went on stoning Stephen. This time, we believe, the NASB has caught the idea in the imperfect tense verb. As the stoning continues, Stephen offers his memorable prayer.

Did the Jews have the right of capital punishment? Was what they were doing legal? No, for the Romans had taken away, except in the case of the violation of the temple courts, the Jews' authority to execute prisoners. But this was mob action, and such actions are typically unlawful, for they usually disregard the established authority of the day. Did the Sanhedrin even cast a vote in this case? Boles, for example, thinks they did. The majority of commentators think they did not. In the "rush" of verse 57, they did not take time to cast a formal vote.

As he called upon *the Lord.* That is, Stephen was praying while they were stoning him, and he was addressing his prayer to Jesus. Stephen, full of the Holy Spirit, knew well to whom it was right to address prayer. Here in the New Testament we have an example of what Pliny, many years later, tells us Christians did; namely, they addressed prayer "to Christ as God."[117]

And said, "Lord Jesus, receive my spirit." This prayer is very similar to one that Jesus prayed from the cross – "Father, into thy hands I commend my spirit."[118] "Receive" means to receive it to yourself; i.e., 'Take my spirit to where You live in heaven.'

7:60 – *And falling on his knees, he cried out with a loud voice, "Lord, do not hold this sin against them!" And having said this, he fell asleep.*

And falling on his knees. This seems to be something that Stephen did voluntarily. He

---

[115] Philo gives the ages as 21 to 28 for a "young man," but all other authorities give it as under 40. Chrysostom in *Sermons on Peter and Paul* gives Paul's age as 35.

[116] McGarvey, *op. cit.*, p.133.

[117] *Epistle*, X.97.

[118] Luke 23:46.

chose to die in this position, while offering prayer.

He cried out with a load voice. Note the change in posture, and the loudness of the cry, even after they had been stoning him for a period of time.

"Lord, do not hold this sin against them." That is, forgive them. This is also very similar to a prayer Jesus prayed from the cross.[119] The resemblance to the prayer of Jesus seems hardly to have been accidental. Either Stephen witnessed the crucifixion of Christ, or the sayings on the cross were widely published as the early preachers recounted the death of Christ.[120]

And having said this, he fell asleep. This is the usual mode of describing the death of the saints in the Bible. Death is simply like a sleep. Such passages that speak of death being a "sleep" must not be understood as teaching that death is an unconscious state (i.e., the theory of soul-sleep). Luke 16:19ff; Revelation 6:9ff; and Hebrews 12:1ff show that the dead souls are conscious of their own state, and of what is going on in the world they have left. What is asleep is the body, not the soul.

Drawing by Horace Knowles
from the British and Foreign Bible Society

---

[119] Luke 23:34.

[120] Conybeare and Howson (*Life and Epistles of St. Paul*, Vol. I, p.82) attribute Paul's conversion to the prayer of Stephen. See also Augustine's *Sermons*, p.314-318.

SPECIAL STUDY #13

DIFFICULTIES IN ACTS 7

In the exegetical notes of the opening verses of Acts 7, it has been observed that Stephen has been charged with making several very glaring mistakes. This Special Study will examine the alleged mistakes, and the solutions that have been suggested.

I. ALLEGED MISTAKE NUMBER ONE – ACTS 7:4

The problem: Stephen seems to make the Old Testament contradict itself. Abraham left Haran when his father had died, Stephen says. On first appearances, Genesis 11:26 seems to say that Terah was 70 years old when Abraham was born. Further, in Genesis 12:4 there is a statement to the effect that Abraham was 75 years old when he left Haran. If we add these two figures, Terah would have been 145 years old when he died. However, and here comes the seeming contradiction, Genesis 11:32 tells us that Terah was 205 years old when he died in Haran. How do you explain this apparent discrepancy?

Proposed solutions to the problem

(1) Some suggest that errors at the hands of copyists are likely in recording numbers. It is noted that the Samaritan Pentateuch, in fact, at Genesis 11:32 gives the age of Terah as 145 when he died. However, the Hebrew Scriptures uniformly give 205.

(2) Some suggest Abraham left Haran 60 years before Terah's death. This is where the speculation arises that Stephen speaks of Terah's spiritual death, not his physical death; i.e., Abraham was called to leave Haran and his relatives when they lapsed into idolatry.

(3) The whole calculation and the alleged resulting discrepancy depend upon the correctness of the assumptions from which it starts.

- Genesis 11:26 only says Terah was 70 years old before he had any sons – the sons being Abraham, Nahor, and Haran. Being named first does not necessarily mean that Abraham was the first-born.

- Nowhere is it said that Abraham was the oldest son. Why then was he mentioned first, if he is not the oldest? Perhaps because he was the most important son. He might be named first because the chosen people were descended from him.

- There are many Old Testament examples where a son other than the oldest is mentioned first. The three sons of Noah are commonly listed as Shem, Ham, and Japheth,[1] yet Ham is the youngest and Japheth is the oldest.[2] Isaac's name takes prece-

---

[1] Genesis 5:32, 6:10, 9:18, and 10:1.

[2] Per Genesis 9:24, Ham at the very least is younger than Shem, and the Hebrew can also bear the

dence over Ishmael's (1 Chronicles 1:28). Judah is placed first in the list of the sons of Jacob (1 Chronicles 4:1 v. 5:1-2). Moses is named before his elder brother, Aaron. So, a son's being named first is no proof that he is the oldest. Rather, the first-listed is the one through whom God is carrying out His plans and purposes in the world.

- There are indications that Abraham was *not* the oldest son. (a) Unless we assume that these three sons were triplets, we cannot assert that Terah was just 70 when all three were born. (b) Haran was apparently the oldest of the sons, for Nahor's wife was a daughter of Haran (Genesis 11:29). Further, Haran's son, Lot, appears to have been about the same age as Abraham given the later history of the two. (c) Abraham's son, Isaac, married Rebekah, the granddaughter of Abraham's brother, Nahor (Genesis 24:15).

In other words, the author of Genesis, in his brief record, gives merely the age of the father at the birth of the oldest son, and while doing so, mentions the births of the other sons, without necessarily stipulating the birth-order of the sons.

The conclusion to the problem

Stephen may be relied on when he says that God removed Abraham from Haran into Canaan after the death of Terah at age 205 (Genesis 11:32). And if so, then the age of Terah when Abraham was born was 130 years (205 - 75 = 130).

Alford objects to this conclusion. "Terah, in the course of nature, begets his son Abram at 130; yet this very Abram regards it as incredible that he himself should beget a son at 99 (Genesis 17:1,17); and on the birth of Isaac out of the course of nature, most important Scripture arguments and consequences are founded (cf. Romans 4:17-21; Hebrews 11:11-12)."[3] However, Abraham's incredulity in Genesis 17 can be otherwise explained: (a) The New Testament tells us Sarah was barren, or sterile (Romans 4:19). (b) Abraham's incredulity regarding himself could reflect the fact that, at age 99, he had now been living 13 years with a young concubine, Hagar, since the birth of Ishmael, and she had not borne him other sons (Genesis 17:24-25). (c) The "proper time of life" mentioned in Hebrews 11:11 cannot simply refer to Abraham's age since "in the course of nature" this same Abram, long after he was 99, and apparently after the death of Sarah when he was 137, took a younger wife and begat six other sons (Genesis 23:1 v. 25:1-4).

So, when the evidence is examined, we find that the modern critics are not justified in accusing Stephen of making a mistake.

II. ALLEGED MISTAKE NUMBER TWO – ACTS 7:6

The problem: Stephen's words are interpreted so as to make him say that the captivity in Egypt was 400 years in duration. In fact, some parallel texts seem to agree with this,

---

meaning "youngest." Per Genesis 11:10, Abraham was 502 when Shem was born. Since Genesis 5:32 indicates Abraham was 500 when he had his first son, Japheth must have been born before Shem. This accords with the KJV translation of Genesis 10:21, and the marginal reading of the ASV, NASB, NIV, etc.

[3] Henry Alford, "Acts" in *Alford's Greek Testament* (London: Rivington's, 1871), Vol. II, p. 68-69.

including Genesis 15:13-14 according to the traditional interpretation and Exodus 12:40-41 in the Masoretic text. However, there is considerable evidence that the captivity was but 215 years in length. Is Stephen right or wrong? Is the traditional interpretation wrong?

There is strong evidence for a 215-year captivity

(1) In Galatians 3:17, Paul says that it was 430 years from the time the promise was given to Abraham until the Exodus and the giving of the Law on Sinai. 215 of those years would have elapsed from the time the promise was given until the entry into Egypt. (Isaac was born 25 years after the promise was given, per Genesis 12:4 and 21:5. Jacob was born when Isaac was 60, per Genesis 24:26. Jacob was 130 when he entered Egypt, per Genesis 47:9. Add these figures, 25 + 60 + 130, and you get 215.)

Josephus says the Israelites left Egypt 430 years after Abraham came to Canaan, but 215 years after Jacob removed to Egypt.[4]

(2) The correctness of the Hebrew text at Exodus 12:40 has been questioned. The LXX, according to the Vatican codex, inserts "and in the land of Canaan," so that the whole verse makes the stay in Egypt and in Canaan to be but 430 years. A similar reading (though not verbatim) is to be found in the Alexandrian codex, in the Coptic version, and in the Samaritan Pentateuch (the latter reads "in the land of Canaan and the land of Egypt").

(3) The genealogical listings are somewhat troublesome if the period of the sojourn in Egypt is more than 215 years. It is said that from the account which Moses has given of the lives of certain persons it would seem clear that the time which they spent in Egypt was not 400 years. For example, (a) It appears Kohath was born before Jacob went into Egypt (Genesis 46:8,11). Kohath lived 133 years (Exodus 6:18). Amram, Kohath's son and the father of Moses, lived 137 years (Exodus 6:20). Moses was eighty years old when he was sent to Pharaoh (Exodus 7:7). The entire time period thus included, counting the time which each father lived AFTER his son was born, is but 350 years. (b) Alford calculates that Levi lived in Egypt about 88 years. Jochebed is expressly stated to have been the daughter of Levi (Numbers 26:58), and so must have been born within 88 years of the entrance into Egypt. Moses was 80 at the Exodus. If we have "x" as Jochebed's age when Moses was born, then 88 + 80 + "x" = the length of the captivity in Egypt. "X" would have to be 232 if the captivity were 400 years long, or 262 if the stay were 430 years. It is doubtful that Jochebed was 232 or 262 years old when Moses was born. If the stay in Egypt was but 215 years, then Jochebed would have been about 47 when Moses was born.

There is, on the other hand, just as strong evidence for a 400-year captivity

(1) Both Genesis 15:13-14 and Acts 7:6 – according to traditional interpretation – speak of a 400-year captivity. The terminology in both places appears to apply to Egypt, and not to Canaan, for the patriarchs were not enslaved or afflicted in Canaan. If the Hebrew text of Exodus 12:40-41 be taken as it stands (and only one late Hebrew manuscript reads differently), it fixes the duration of the captivity at 430 years.

(2) The expression "fourth generation" in Genesis 15:16 is taken to be identical with

---

[4] *Antiquities*, II.15.2.

the preceding time period ("400 years" of verses 13-14). Gesenius and other Hebrew scholars understand the term to be equivalent of a century. Leupold writes, "... we see the word reckons a hundred years to a generation. Such a computation, according to chapter eleven, is not out of place, especially if one considers that Abram himself lived to the age of 175 years."[5] Gesenius says, "... from the longevity of the patriarchs, in their time [a generation] was reckoned at a hundred [years]; and in like manner amongst the Romans, the word *seculum* originally signified a generation, and was afterwards applied to a century ...."[6]

(3) The Vulgate and Syriac versions, and the Targum of Onkelos agree with the Hebrew text of Exodus 12:40.

(4) There is some evidence that the genealogical tables in the Pentateuch are incomplete. For example, at the first numbering there were 8,600 male Kohathites (Numbers 3:28). Kohath was a son of Levi, and the grandfather of Moses. Kohath had four sons (Exodus 6:18, 1 Chronicles 6:18). One of these sons was Amram, who in turn had two sons and six grandsons, as far as the Scripture record goes. In order to reach the 8,600 total, are we to believe the other three sons of Kohath averaged 2,866 male descendants, or are we to recognize that the genealogies are abbreviated (cp. Matthew 1)?

(5) Some allege that there is still a problem with age, even if the 215-year captivity is accepted. For example, Cook's note reads, "... in order to make out 215 years [for the sojourn in Egypt] it is necessary to assume that Levi was 95 years old when Jochebed was born, and that Jochebed was 85 years old when she became mother of Moses. This ... involves two miracles, for which there is no authority in Scripture."[7]

(6) Interestingly, Josephus twice speaks of a 400-year captivity,[8] and some take this as an indication that many in his day believed the captivity was long rather than short.

(7) It is asserted that Paul's statement in Galatians 3:17 can be harmonized with the idea of a 400-year captivity, even though he expressly states that it was 430 years from the promise to Abraham to the Exodus (a calculation which would make the captivity itself but 215 years in length). It is suggested that Paul simply quotes from the LXX of Exodus 12:40 as he writes to the Galatians. The LXX, it will be remembered, favors the 215-year captivity. The supposition is that Paul quoted the LXX, rather than the Hebrew text, so that he would not surprise or perplex his readers by referencing a number of years different from that which they were accustomed to find in their Greek Bible, even though a quotation from the Hebrew might have added to the force of his argument.

---

[5] H.C. Leupold, *Exposition of Genesis* (Columbus, OH: The Wartburg Press, 1942), p.486.

[6] William Gesenius, *Gesenius' Hebrew-English Lexicon to the Old Testament*, trans. by S.P. Tregelles (Grand Rapids: Eerdmans, 1952), p.194.

[7] F.C. Cook, "Commentary on Exodus" in *The Bible Commentary* (London: John Murray, 1871), Vol. II, p.301. However, Cook's statement appears to go too far. Accepting Cook's calculations (and indeed the ages could be figured in the manner he suggests) does not necessitate the need for two "miracles." Terah begat a son at the age of 130, and Abraham begat sons after he was 137. Were we to take Alford's suggestion that Jochebed was 47 when Moses was born, that would make Levi about 130 when Jochebed was born, and even this would not be miraculous. We are thus led to the conclusion that there are not the age problems with the 215-year captivity that there are with the 400-year captivity.

[8] *Antiquities*, II.9.1; *Wars*, V.9.4. However, footnote #4 above has shown that Josephus also speaks of the 215-year period. The most that can be said is that Josephus gives evidence that in his day both opinions were held, just as is true today.

Proposed solutions to the problem

(1) A great number of commentators decide in favor of the Hebrew reading of Exodus 12:40, and therefore reject the LXX reading. Thus, Paul's statement in Galatians 3:17 is taken to be a deliberate understatement of the duration of the captivity. Such a line of argument makes the Genesis 15 passage normative, and then interprets all passages in its light. The result is a 400-year captivity.

(2) Some writers recently have begun to question the traditional interpretation given to Genesis 15:13ff. Starting with the assumption that Paul is right in assigning a period of 430 years from the time the promise was made until the giving of the Law at Sinai, they then interpret all the Old Testament passages in that light. Such an approach suggests that the LXX of Exodus 12:40 is correct. The key problem passage to this approach is the Genesis 15 passage itself, which must be interpreted so as to harmonize with a 215-year captivity. For example, Atkinson has written, "How then are we to read the four hundred years of this verse? It seems difficult to take the words [of verse 13] 'a land [that is not theirs]' as referring to anything wider than Egypt ... [Thus,] the meaning of the words 'four hundred years' seems to be, 'and they shall afflict them until a time, which is four hundred years from now.'"[9] 400 years from the time God was speaking to Abraham would include but a 215-year captivity. Perhaps Atkinson is pointing us in the right direction as he interprets Genesis 15:13-14 and the way Stephen quotes it in Acts 7:6 in light of Paul's clear statement in Galatians 3:17. Likely, this is the right way to harmonize and understand the various Biblical passages.

In any case, Stephen was merely quoting the Old Testament as it read in the Hebrew Scriptures, and should not be held accountable for a mistake, when the mistake may be merely in our interpretations of certain relevant passages.[10]

III. ALLEGED MISTAKE NUMBER THREE – ACTS 7:14

The problem: Stephen is said to make a mistake in putting the number of Jacob's family at 75, whereas the text of Genesis 46:27 makes the number 70, including two who had died in Canaan before they went down into Egypt.

Proposed solution to the problem

Many conjectures have been advanced to account for the difference, while the most logical answer has often been overlooked.

- Stephen was a Hellenist, and being familiar with the LXX, he quoted what he had read in that translation. The LXX at Genesis 46:27 reads, "All the souls of the house of Jacob who went with Jacob into Egypt, were 75 souls." Versus the "70" reading in the

---

[9] Basil F.C. Atkinson, "Genesis" in *The Pocket Commentary of the Bible* (Chicago: Moody Press, 1957), p.145.

[10] It should be further noted that if the captivity was really 430 years in length, then the 400-year figure (in Genesis 15 and quoted by Stephen) is just a round number, and is not really an error of 30 years.

Hebrew text, the LXX makes up this extra five by listing the names of two sons of Manasseh, two of Ephraim, and one grandson of Ephraim, at verse 20 of Genesis 46.

- When a study is made of the total number of people who went down into Egypt, it soon becomes clear that there is a great diversity in the way the number is figured. Josephus gives the total as 70.[11] Philo, including 3 sons of Ephraim and a son and grandson of Manasseh, gives the figure as 75.[12]

- Before one accuses the LXX of being mistaken in its total, observe also that even the Hebrew accounting makes use of a bit of poetical license. The actual number of *living* people who entered Egypt was 68 (see Genesis 46:12).

IV. ALLEGED MISTAKE NUMBER FOUR – ACTS 7:16

The problem: In the phrase "they were removed to Shechem," Stephen appears to say that Jacob was carried over to Shechem and buried there, whereas Jacob himself was actually buried in the field of Machpelah by Joseph and his brethren (Genesis 50:13).

Proposed solution to the problem

McGarvey argues that the subject of the verb "were removed" is "our fathers," and that there is no reference to Jacob being carried to Shechem and buried there.[13] It is expressly stated in Joshua 24:32 that Joseph's bones were carried by the Israelites when they came into the land of Canaan and were buried in Shechem. Stephen then is telling us that the bones of all twelve patriarchs were laid to rest after the example of Joseph. With such an interpretation Jerome agrees.[14]

Complicating the question is the fact that Josephus[15] and also *Jubilees* (46:9) relate the burial of Jacob's sons (except Joseph) at Hebron, not Shechem; and the same tradition appears to underlie the *Testament of the Twelve Patriarchs*. Hervey rejects the testimony of Josephus and the others on the basis of the fact that there are no tombs of the patriarchs at Hebron, save one for Joseph; and the idea of even having a tomb for him at Hebron is completely contradictory to the Old Testament record.[16]

V. ALLEGED MISTAKE NUMBER FIVE – ACTS 7:16

The problem: Stephen spoke of the tomb "that Abraham bought ... from the sons of Hamor in Shechem." Who actually purchased the tomb? Genesis 33:19 and Joshua 24:32

---

[11] *Antiquities*, II.7.4; IX.3; VI.5-6.

[12] *De Migratione Abrahami*, 36.

[13] McGarvey, *op. cit.*, p.121.

[14] *Epistol.*, 86.

[15] *Antiquities*, II.8.2.

[16] Hervey, *op. cit.*, p.217.

indicate the purchase of that tomb at Shechem was made by *Jacob*, not by Abraham.

Proposed solutions to the problem

(1) Some suggest this is evidently a scribal mistake. That is, some scribe, familiar with the story of Abraham's purchase of the cave of Machpelah at Hebron, confused the purchase of the tomb at Shechem by Jacob, and instead of writing Jacob as should have been done here, wrote Abraham. The scribe, not Stephen, really made the mistake.

(2) A second suggestion is according to Genesis 12:6. Abraham was in Shechem a long time before Jacob was there. It is suggested that perhaps Abraham purchased this tomb at that time, and that Stephen is talking of that purchase. After Abraham left Canaan, the tomb was retaken by aliens, and then was repurchased by Jacob when they made their return to the promised land. This latter would be the purchase spoken of in Genesis 33:19.

CONCLUSION

Five mistakes are charged to Stephen in the first sixteen verses of Acts 7. In the face of such accusations against Stephen's defense, it is important for us to keep in mind that Stephen is not accused of error by those to whom he was speaking. Nor was he accused of error by any of the friends or enemies of Christianity in the early church.

We do not have sufficient materials, in some cases, to judge with certainty whether Stephen made any errors. More importantly, obvious and defensible solutions can be supplied for every supposed error that Stephen made.

The only mistake Stephen made, from the point of view of the Sanhedrin, was the mistake of accusing them of killing Jesus. For this, they stoned him as a blasphemer.

Roman Soldiers

Drawing by Horace Knowles
from the British and Foreign Bible Society

II. THE CHURCH IN JUDEA AND SAMARIA – Acts 8:1-12:25

A. The Jerusalem Church Dispersed. 8:1-4

8:1 – And Saul was in hearty agreement with putting him to death. And on that day a great persecution arose against the church in Jerusalem; and they were all scattered throughout the regions of Judea and Samaria, except the apostles.

And Saul was in hearty agreement with putting him to death. The first clause of this verse concludes the account given in chapter 7, and would be better included as part of chapter 7. (Notice, the NASB begins the new paragraph in the middle of verse 1 where the new thought begins.)[1] Paul, being a dedicated Jew, believed the sentence carried out in Stephen's case was exactly as ought to have been done, for such was the teaching in the Law of Moses. Moses had taught that anyone who came teaching men to ignore the Law was to be executed.[2] The same phrase here used by Luke of Paul's feelings in the matter is used by Paul himself in Acts 22, during his speech from the castle steps at the close of the third missionary journey.

And on that day a great persecution arose against the church in Jerusalem. The words "And on that day" are the beginning of the second major division of the book of Acts. The day Stephen was killed saw the beginning of the first of a number of waves of persecution that swept over the church. The tumult did not subside when Stephen was dead. The persecutors went looking for others to "discipline" until they either recanted of this new heresy or were dead! The following verses indicate that this persecution involved much suffering, imprisonment, the confiscating of men's goods and property, the believers being made "a public spectacle through reproaches and tribulations,"[3] and even death for many.

And they were all scattered. This "scattering" is a key point in time as far as the history Luke is writing is concerned. He will return to it several times,[4] to take up various facets of the church's history, each of which is initiated by this persecution.

How much of the Church was scattered? Just the Hellenistic portion, or the whole congregation, both Hellenistic and Hebrew? At times the word "all" is not absolute in the Scriptures, so if we were to make it mean "all the Hellenists," we would not be wresting Scripture. Still the context here, which exempts only the apostles from the scattering, has a universal sound to it.[5]

---

[1] Compare the notes at Acts 2:1 concerning the original division of our Bible into chapters and verses.

[2] Deuteronomy 13:7-10. Stephen is not actually guilty of turning the Jews to "another god," but that is how Paul viewed it at the time and so heartily consented to the stoning of Stephen.

[3] Hebrews 10:33-34.

[4] Acts 8:4, 9:1, 9:31, 11:19.

[5] The only reason some have hesitated to take the "all" at face value is that later in the book of Acts we find a church still in Jerusalem (Acts 9:26, 11:2, 12:1, 12:5; 15:1ff). How is this possible if they were "all" scattered? However, even the presence of a church in Jerusalem after the scattering of chapter 8 is not

Throughout the regions of Judea and Samaria. The neighboring Judean towns of Hebron, Gaza, Lydda, and Joppa became places of refuge.[6] And in Samaria they would find a welcome simply because they were being persecuted by the Jewish religious leaders.

Jesus had said that the gospel was to be carried from Jerusalem to Judea and Samaria, and then to the uttermost parts of the earth.[7] Some have suggested that a reason why God permitted this persecution was because the early Christians were becoming settled and contented in Jerusalem, so God permitted the persecution to get them out of the nest and to exercise their fullest strength and talents. However, before we unhesitatingly accept this explanation, we should also consider the possibility that before a mission work can be undertaken in another place (e.g., Judea and Samaria) there has to be a foundation laid (e.g., Jerusalem). Once this foundation is laid, then we are ready to spread to other places.

Except the apostles. Why the apostles did not flee, we are not told, so various speculations have been advanced.

- Some suggest the apostles' lives were not in danger. The Sanhedrin had seen that it would fail to stamp out the church by persecuting its leaders, so it turned toward the individual members.

- Others suggest the work of the apostles was not yet completed in the city of Jerusalem, so they stayed behind to convert more of the city. Jerusalem was the very center of activity – people coming there to the feasts – so the apostles braved the danger to stay and preach Christ. A tradition is recorded by both Clement of Alexandria[8] and Eusebius[9] that the Lord had commanded the apostles to remain in Jerusalem for twelve years, giving their testimony, lest any should say, "We have not heard," and only after that date were they to go forth to other places in the world with the message.

- Others suggest that the Sanhedrin took Gamaliel's advice and left the apostles alone.

- Others suggest that the persecution which was now raging seems to have been directed especially against those Hellenists like Stephen who even before their conversion had been cool toward the "traditions" of the Pharisees, and who after their conversion paid even less attention to such customs. Part of this suggestion too is the idea that the apostles have not yet broken with many Jewish practices since they were still regularly worshiping in the temple, keeping themselves from all that was common and unclean, and aloof from close fellowship with the Gentiles.[10]

- Others suggest that because of the miracles wrought by the apostles, they had great popularity in the eyes of the people so that the Sanhedrin was afraid to harm them.

---

in itself conclusive that the "all" is not universal. We could reasonably suppose that the apostles who remained behind when the church was scattered have had more converts and that these new converts make up the church we find in those later passages in Acts.

[6] Does the fact that the fleeing Christians are welcomed in the towns of Judea reflect a goodwill that resulted from the healings performed on the sick people who had earlier been brought to Jerusalem (Acts 5:16)?

[7] Act 1:8.

[8] *Stromata*, VI.5.43.

[9] *Church History*, V.13.

[10] Acts 10:14,28.

8:2 – *And some devout men buried Stephen, and made loud lamentation over him.*

And *some* devout men. Who were these "devout men"?

- It has sometimes been asserted that these were proselytes to Judaism. Perhaps so, but the word used here is *eulabēs*,[11] while the word used by Luke when he is speaking of such proselytes is usually *sebomenē*.[12]
- Some believe that Christians buried Stephen. Against this idea is the matter that the Christians are being persecuted and dispersed. And would not Luke have likely used "believers" or "brethren" if he meant that Christians buried Stephen? On the other hand, the whole church would not have been so quickly dispersed that it would of necessity have been Jews that had to bury Stephen's body.
- In favor of the idea that devout Jews buried Stephen is the great respect people had for the Christians about which Luke has told us earlier. Further, the word "devout" has already been used by Luke for consecrated Jews like Simeon,[13] the multitude of Jews who had come from a considerable distance to be present on the day of Pentecost,[14] and Ananias the preacher.[15] One further point in favor of devout Jews is the fact that there is an ancient tradition, already noted,[16] that Nicodemus and Gamaliel were active in the burial of Stephen.

Buried Stephen. That these devout men would bury Stephen's body is equivalent to an avowal of their belief that he was innocent. Commonly, when a man was stoned to death on a charge of blasphemy, he would have no funeral honors, but instead would have been buried with "the burial of an ass."[17]

And made loud lamentation over him. Such lamentation was a usual thing among Jews at a funeral.[18] Jewish funeral services were very interesting – very formal, and very widely announced. This seems to be the description of the fact that Stephen's body was properly prepared for burial, and the proper days of mourning and lamentation carried out.[19]

8:3 – *But Saul began ravaging the church, entering house after house; and dragging off men and women, he would put them in prison.*

---

[11] Luke used the same word at Acts 2:5.

[12] Acts 13:43,50; 16:14; 17:4,17; 18:7.

[13] Acts 2:25.

[14] Acts 2:5.

[15] Acts 22:12.

[16] See footnote #66 in chapter 5.

[17] Jeremiah 22:19.

[18] " Genesis 50:9, 10; 1 Maccabees 2:70, 4:39, 9:20.

[19] See the article on "Mourning" in the *Zondervan Pictorial Bible Dictionary,* p.561, where the mourning and lamentation is shown to last a week or more in Jewish funerals.

But Saul *began* ravaging the church. The verb used here by Luke gives a very vivid word picture. It is the word used to speak of the devastation caused by wild beasts (lions, wolves, etc.). Luke tells us that Paul raged against the church like a wild beast. The tense of the verb indicates continuous action. He was authorized, as he himself tells us,[20] by the chief priests. He was acting as their agent in the persecution of the Christians.

Entering house after house. The language conveys the idea of a house to house search, seeking for those who were known or suspected of being Christians. Those who were found were dragged off to prison as the next phrases indicate.

And dragging off men and women. That women were included as victims of the persecution is emphatic proof of Paul's violence and bitterness. Until World War II with its concept of "total war," women were usually not victims of the strife between men; since then, we are not surprised to hear that women and innocent children have been victims of senseless violence. Because of this latter fact, we must not read back into the 1st century our present-day attitudes or we'll misunderstand what God's Word is trying to tell us.

He would put them in prison. In the 1st century world, men were put in prison to await trial. The ancients did not give prison sentences, as courts today do. In those days, when the trial was completed, the prisoner was either freed, beaten and freed, or executed. It is an interesting thing to note the complete determination of Paul in his opposition to the church during this part of his life. Later, after his conversion, we will see him equally zealous and determined to promote the cause of Christ.[21]

8:4 – *Therefore, those who had been scattered went about preaching the word.*

Therefore, those who had been scattered. The word Luke uses for "scattered" comes from the same root as the word for Dispersion or Diaspora. However, there is a difference. The Diaspora of the Jews had not resulted in evangelization; the dispersion of the church did result in evangelism. Luke's history will show that these scattered Christians, fleeing the persecution, shared the Good News in Judea, Samaria, Galilee, and beyond.[22]

Went about preaching the word. The Greek word is "evangelizing," or announcing the good news of the message of God's mercy.

> The people doing this evangelizing were not elders, deacons, and preachers. They were the disciples, great hosts of them, seeking a place of refuge from the destruction of Saul. As they found places to sleep or stay for a few days, they would have to explain the purpose of their plight and flight. In so doing, they went everywhere telling the bad news of their

---

[20] Acts 26:10.

[21] This type of 180-degree change is typical of New Testament Christianity. If you can convert a denominationalist or someone who is zealous in his paganism to simple New Testament Christianity, he will become as zealous, or more so, for the cause of Christ in the New Testament way as he was in his denominational way beforehand. Many times, such who are thoroughly converted become the strongest Christians afterwards, just as it was with Paul.

[22] Acts 9:31, 11:19.

persecution and the good news of salvation in Christ.[23]

Barnes, in commenting on this verse, tries to defend the denominational distinction between "clergy" and "laity." According to such thinking, a man must be ordained in order to be a public teacher, administer baptism, and plant congregations. But such an idea is surely not in harmony with Acts 8:4, for the preaching here referred to was doubtless both public and private teaching – the latter being participated in by women as well as men, McGarvey suggests.[24] And be apprised of this fact, that it is not possible to preach the good news without telling a person about the need and place of baptism, and administering it to those penitent believers who present themselves for it.[25]

Until the love of Christ and the gospel of Christ so fills the heart of the average church member that he goes out to proclaim the Word – until he is so sold on the gospel that he will do that – the Church will never reach the pinnacle of success that Christ intended for her to have. It is an obligation resting on everyone who is a Christian to herald the Word, however he or she can. Some try to excuse themselves from this responsibility by saying, "I can't do anything," or "I don't know what to say." One wonders how that person would have become a Christian in the first place if everyone in the world had acted and spoken in this way. When a person makes such a statement as "I can't" or "What do I say?" he is admitting his ignorance of the plan of salvation. And he is admitting his ignorance of how he himself became a Christian.

The axiom that "the blood of the martyrs is the seed of the Church" held true from the beginning. The attempt to stamp out the new faith in fact gave that new faith a wider scope of action, and urged it on to pass the limits within which it might otherwise have been confined for a much longer period.

B. The Labors of Philip. 8:5-40

A. Philip in Samaria. 8:5-13

8:5 – *And Philip went down to the city of Samaria and* **began** *proclaiming Christ to them.*

And Philip. This is Philip the deacon (Acts 6), not Philip the apostle, for the apostles stayed in Jerusalem (verse 1). Luke's plan is to follow the travels of Philip and describe his evangelistic labors, then Peter,[26] then others. Perhaps the need for Philip to function as a "deacon" was terminated by the scattering of the Jerusalem church. As he leaves Jerusalem, he becomes an evangelist, the title by which he is called in Acts 21:8. There does not seem to have been a special commission in order for him to become an evangelist. He simply went, evangelizing, because he saw a need he could fill.

---

[23] Dale, *op. cit.*, p.91.

[24] McGarvey, *op. cit.*, p.134.

[25] See notes at verses 12 and 35.

[26] The section of Luke's history about Peter begins at 9:32, and his account of others is found at 11:19ff.

Went down to the city of Samaria. Because of the absence of the article in some manuscripts, there was in years past some question whether Philip went to *the* city of Samaria, or to the region of Samaria (i.e., *a* city in the Samarian region). The question of the article was settled by the finding of the Codex Sinaiticus in 1850, which reinforced the previously known evidence of Codex Alexandrinus and Codex Vaticanus, and overbalanced all evidence for the omission of the article. The definite article "the" enjoys integrity and the reading of the NASB is correct. The city of Samaria on some maps is called Sebaste, the name given to the city by Herod after he fortified it.[27]

And *began* proclaiming Christ to them. He was preaching that Messiah had come. The verb tense implies continuous action extending, it may be, over weeks and months. Samaritans were a mixed-race people, the result of marriages between poor Israelites and relocated foreigners, years before, when Assyria captured the world. Partially because of their mixed blood there was animosity between the Jews and the Samaritans.[28] Perhaps this background of the Samaritans helps explain why God used a Hellenist to evangelize the area. He would be received more openly than a Hebrew.

8:6 – *And the multitudes with one accord were giving attention to what was said by Philip, as they heard and saw the signs which he was performing.*

And the multitudes with one accord were giving attention to what was said by Philip. The same word here translated "give attention to" is translated "respond" in Acts 16:14. In present-day terminology, we would say that multitudes of the Samaritans were responding to the invitation offered as the gospel was preached (verse 12).

As they heard and saw the signs which he was performing. The verb tense is another imperfect tense, indicating continuous action; i.e., Philip kept on working miracles. Philip was able to confirm the message he was preaching by miraculous deeds ("signs"). Philip had the power to work miracles. This reminds us of what Acts 6:6 said concerning the laying on of an apostle's hands. That laying on of an apostle's hands was done, not as a simple ordination service, but for the passing on of spiritual gifts. A number of New Testament verses show that miracles wrought through men like Philip were for the purpose of confirming the message preached.[29]

8:7 – *For* **in the case of** *many who had unclean spirits, they were coming out* **of them** *shouting with a loud voice; and many who had been paralyzed and lame were healed.*

For *in the case of* **many who had unclean spirits, they were coming out** *of them* **shouting with a loud voice.** "Unclean spirits" are beings Luke has already introduced to

---

[27] Josephus, *Antiquities*, XV.8.5. In intertestamental times the city had been reduced to ruins by Hyrcanus (*Antiquities*, XIII.10.3).

[28] John 4.9. See the article on "Samaritans" in the *Zondervan Pictorial Bible Dictionary*, p.746.

[29] Passages in the New Testament which show the evidential nature of the miracles are John 3:2, 20:30-31; Mark 16:17-20; and Hebrews 2:3-4, among others.

his readers.³⁰ These demons caused the people in whom they resided to cry out (in pain?) as the demons themselves left the people. The outcry as the demons left would attract the attention of the multitude to the one who was afflicted, but now healed. The cry may have been caused by the demons' desire to hurt the one in whom they had lived just once more.

And many who had been paralyzed and lame were healed. Note that here in verse 7 demon possession is clearly distinguished from physical infirmity. Under the general name "paralyzed" several infirmities were included: disabled, enfeebled, and paralyzed (from a failure of the nerves to respond to motor messages from the brain). On the word "lame," see notes at Acts 3:2.

8:8 – And there was much rejoicing in that city.

And there was much rejoicing in that city. Do you see the causes for the rejoicing in the context? There was rejoicing because so many persons who before had been sick and paralyzed are now healed. There is rejoicing because the old subjugation to demons that some used to suffer is now broken. There is rejoicing because sins have been forgiven when these Samaritans responded to the gospel.

8:9 – Now there was a certain man named Simon, who formerly was practicing magic in the city, and astonishing the people of Samaria, claiming to be someone great;

Now there was a certain man named Simon. The early church fathers have written much about this man, some of their accounts being highly imaginative; however, nothing is certainly known of him more than what Luke tells us in this place. Luke tells us nothing about his life prior to his arrival in Samaria. He is known as "Simon Magus" and "Simon the Sorcerer."³¹ His name "Simon" has been taken to suggest he was of Jewish or Samaritan origin.³²

Who formerly. That is, before Philip came to Samaria. According to Luke's custom of giving a general truth and then illustrating it, we understand that the paragraph about Simon is an illustration of the truth Luke has just given in verses 6-7.

Was practicing magic in the city, and astonishing the people of Samaria. "Magic" has to do with *power* over and beyond what is human, power derived from the help of the demons.³³ Some of the older translations use "sorcerer" at this place, and that was a good word, but it is only one facet of "magic."³⁴ Both what are popularly known as white witch-

---

³⁰ See notes at Acts 5:17 concerning "unclean spirits."

³¹ He is called "the Sorcerer" because that was what he used to practice before becoming a Christian. He is called "Magus" because he used to claim he "was somebody great," or perhaps because "Magi" was a regular term for one who practiced such magical arts.

³² Some of the information found in Early Christian Literature about Simon the Sorcerer is included following the comments on verse 24.

³³ On "magic," more information is given in Special Study #17, "The World of the Occult."

³⁴ The English word "sorcerer" comes from a French word which speaks of casting lots for the purpose of

craft and black witchcraft are a part of the world of the occult commonly denominated by the word "magic." The practice of witchcraft has always been a substitute for divinely revealed religion. Involved, some more and some less, would be occultic practices such as astrology, fortunetelling, spiritism (i.e., the alleged communication with the souls of the dead), psychokinesis, astral projection, and many others; all of these were expressly forbidden to the Jews on pain of death.[35] Since this paragraph about Simon the Sorcerer clearly shows that "magic" is inferior to real Christianity, the Christian should refuse to meddle in table tipping, occult hypnosis, fortune telling, or dealing with the dead (seances), ouija boards, and the like.[36] The word translated "astonished" can mean to be "out of one's mind," and this is exactly what it is to get involved in the occult. A man's judgment has been confounded by the devil, or he wouldn't get involved.

Claiming to be someone great. Simon boasted and pretended to be a "great one." The next verse defines the nature of the claims more clearly; at least, verses 10-11 give what the Samaritans believed him to be, and their beliefs likely reflected what he himself had claimed. According to Irenaeus,[37] Simon claimed to combine in himself the three persons of the trinity, alleging that he appeared to the Jews as the Son, to the Samaritans as the Father, and among the Gentiles as the Holy Spirit. Perhaps this was a claim to have been reincarnated several times, a common doctrine found in the occult.

8:10 – *and they all, from smallest to greatest, were giving attention to him, saying, "This man is what is called the Great Power of God."*

And they all, from smallest to greatest, were giving attention to him. He deceived a great multitude of the people, both the common people and the leaders of the community.

Saying, "This man is what is called the Great Power of God." The word "power" is a name of one order of angels, whether good or demonic.[38] Thus, some have suggested that Simon was claiming to be an angel who had become incarnate. As the ASV has it, "he is that power [i.e., an angel] of God that is called Great [i.e., an archangel]."

8:11 – *And they were giving him attention because he had for a long time astonished them with his magic arts.*

And they were giving him attention. This verb tense pictures something that happened over and over again, over a period of time. The word used here in verse 10 and 11 of the

---

divination (fortune-telling).

[35] A number of Old Testament passages specifically forbid dabbling in the occult, most of which are listed in Special Study #17 at the close of chapter 19. For the present, such passages as Exodus 22:18 ("You shall not permit a witch (medium) to live"), Deuteronomy 18:10-11, and Jeremiah 27:9 and 29:8 should be consulted.

[36] This thought concerning the Christian's attitude toward the occult is more forcefully driven home at Acts 19, where it is shown to be a sin that Christians are to confess and utterly repudiate.

[37] *Against Heresies*, I.23.1.

[38] Ephesians 1:21.

people's response to Simon was the same word Luke used in verse 6 of their response to the gospel. There is a bit of truth to the saying that both God and the devil appeal to man in the same way: if man responds to God, it is called faith; if he responds to the devil, it is called sin.

Because he had for a long time. The time frame could perhaps be as long as five to seven years. In the year AD 27, Jesus had been to Sychar which is near the city of Samaria.[39] There is the possibility that Simon the Sorcerer arrived in the area just after Jesus left. Finding the people still influenced by the impressions of the Master's visit, he capitalized on their excited feelings for his own purposes.

Astonished them with his magic arts. Again, let it be especially fixed in the mind that magic arts (the world of the occult) is a means used to confound people's good sense. Such a conviction will greatly dissuade present-day individuals from becoming involved in these magic arts. The magic arts may appear innocent enough to begin with, but the end is absolute bondage to the devil, a fearsome end indeed! Beware lest we too be "astonished" and respond to the siren song of the Evil One!

8:12 – *But when they believed Philip preaching the good news about the kingdom of God and the name of Jesus Christ, they were being baptized, men and women alike.*

But when they believed Philip preaching the good news about the kingdom of God. In verse 9, Luke has told us that the Samaritans "gave attention" (responded) to what Philip said. Now he details what they did as they responded, and became subjects in the kingdom of God (the Church).[40]

And the name of Jesus Christ. Philip's preaching included the recounting of the redeeming mission and work of Jesus Christ, His death, resurrection, and exaltation.

They were being baptized, men and women alike. One topic we are paying special attention to in the early part of Acts is the question of what did individual people do to become Christians? Here, as in Acts 2:38-41, when men become believers they are baptized. Time and again in Acts, when we see a case of conversion, we shall be told by Luke that the believers were baptized. It is a part of discipling a person to baptize him or her.[41] The tense of the verb here points to a continual procession of converts into the baptistry. And when Luke tells us that women were included, we think of the woman of Samaria (John 4:7), and wonder whether she was one of them.

---

[39] John 4.

[40] See notes at Acts 1:3,6 and Special Study #1 at the close of chapter 1 where explanatory notes about the "kingdom of God" have been given.

[41] The words "baptizing" and "teaching" following the command to "make disciples" in the Great Commission of Matthew 28:18-20 are circumstantial participles, and suggest that one makes disciples by baptizing and teaching.

8:13 – *And even Simon himself believed; and after being baptized, he continued on with Philip; and as he observed signs and great miracles taking place, he was constantly amazed.*

And even Simon himself believed. The Reformation leader John Calvin exerted a great influence on the thinking of the Protestant religious world of the 20th century. One of his five major doctrines has been called "the doctrine of eternal security," popularly called "once saved, always saved."[42] Commentators who have been influenced by Calvin's teaching have real difficulty with this paragraph about Simon the Sorcerer, for it is one of several passages in the New Testament that is diametrically opposed to the doctrine of eternal security as propounded by Calvin. Barnes,[43] for example, explains to us that Simon did not have saving faith (even though Luke writes "Simon also believed," ASV). Barnes wants us to believe that all Simon had was a faulty belief about Jesus being a miracle worker and having been raised from the dead. According to Barnes, Simon wasn't really saved since Peter plainly says, later, that he was not a Christian ("you have no part nor lot in this matter").

However, the better, more straightforward understanding of verse 13 emerges when we do not attempt to read the Calvinistic doctrine of eternal security into the narrative. In fact, verse 13 is a clear argument against the type of eternal security Calvin conceived. Luke plainly shows by the use of "even" (*kai,* also, even) that there was no difference between the faith of Simon and the faith of the other Christians in Samaria. He believed the same thing the others believed, and he was baptized just as were the others. Not only did he have the kind of faith that motivated him to action and obedience, but he continued in the fellowship of Philip, the preacher.

And after being baptized, be continued on with Philip. It was customary for disciples to remain with their teachers. New converts, remaining like this with their teachers for a period of time, would be trained for the ministry in a sort of apprenticeship program.

And as he observed signs and great miracles taking place, he was constantly amazed. He was amazed that Philip could really perform so much greater miracles than he had even pretended to do. Philip's power (via the Holy Spirit) was greater than that demonic power which Simon had exercised over others.

---

[42] The acrostic TULIP is used to help fix in mind the five points of Calvinism. T = total depravity; U = unconditional election; L = limited atonement; I = irresistible grace; and P = perseverance of the saints (what is also called "eternal security"). The reader should be acquainted with each of these terms and be aware that each of the ideas is unbiblical, at least in the form taught by Calvin. The reason for the necessity of knowing these ideas is that any churchgoer who worships in the Reformed tradition will be taught them, and will need to be re-taught if he is to be won away from denominational ideas.

[43] Barnes, *op. cit.,* p.140.

B. Peter and John in Samaria. 8:14-25

8:14 – *Now when the apostles in Jerusalem heard that Samaria had received the word of God, they sent them Peter and John,*

Now when the apostles in Jerusalem heard that Samaria had received the word of God. The apostles were still in Jerusalem (verse 1) though the Church had been scattered. News came to Jerusalem that the harvest had occurred in Samaria. The phrase "word of God" is used by Luke for the whole sum and substance of the gospel of Christ.

They sent them Peter and John. The apostles ("they") delegated two of their own number to go to Samaria. This indicates rather conclusively that there was no chief ruler among them, no one acting as pope. They acted as being equal to each other in authority under Christ. The two men who were sent had been to Samaria before. John had been the one who sought to call down fire on a Samaritan village.[44] The purpose of these men's visit is indicated in what they did, as recorded in the following verses.

8:15 – *who came down and prayed for them, that they might receive the Holy Spirit.*

Who came down. This is the usual language for someone leaving Jerusalem, for this required the traveler to descend ("go down"), no matter what direction of the compass you were journeying as you left Jerusalem. Samaria actually is north of Jerusalem, but it is still "down" from Jerusalem.

And prayed for them. The bestowal of the spiritual gifts was not at the discretion of the apostles; they prayed previously. And the restriction of the conveyance of such gifts to the apostles is very strong presumptive evidence in favor of the view that miraculous powers ceased with the generation on whom the apostles had laid their hands. Romans 1:11 is a similar example, in this commentator's opinion, of spiritual gifts being passed on only by the apostles.

That they might receive the Holy Spirit. The reference is to spiritual gifts, such as speaking in tongues, working miracles, etc.[45]

8:16 – *For He had not yet fallen upon any of them; they had simply been baptized in the name of the Lord Jesus.*

For He had not yet fallen upon any of them. The NASB is an improvement here on the ASV, which reads "*it* had fallen." The Holy Spirit is a person, and the proper pronoun therefore is "He." The word "fall" may express the idea of the sudden advent of *special* powers, whether the baptismal measure (as in Acts 10:44, 11:15), or the measure called spiritual gifts (Acts 19:6 has "fall" rather than "came" in some manuscripts).

---

[44] John 4:1ff; Luke 9:5.

[45] The context so limits our explanation of verse 15 to "spiritual gifts." Neither the baptism with the Holy Spirit nor the indwelling gift were accompanied by prayers to receive them.

They had simply been baptized in the name of the Lord Jesus. This is Luke's way of telling us they had received the indwelling gift of the Holy Spirit, given at the time a penitent believer is baptized.[46] Some measure of the Holy Spirit they already had, but the measure called "spiritual gifts" they did not yet have, is what Luke is saying.

8:17 – *Then they began laying their hands on them, and they were receiving the Holy Spirit.*

Then they *began* laying their hands on them. Even though Luke uses the word "fallen" (verse 16) in this context, just as he does in Acts 10 in the case of Cornelius, it does not appear that the measure of the Spirit received in both cases is the same. There was no laying on of hands at Pentecost,[47] nor in the case of Cornelius,[48] both of which are called "baptism with the Holy Spirit." What the Samaritans receive appears to be different. Apparently, the Holy Spirit given by the laying on of the apostles' hands was a measure of the Holy Spirit not so full as the baptismal measure of the Holy Spirit.[49] That spiritual gifts were a measure of the Spirit given by the laying on of the apostles' hands has already been indicated in Acts 6:6. Therefore, that is what we believe Luke is telling us that the Samaritans received.

How many of the Samaritan Christians received spiritual gifts is not stated, but it is evident that it was not bestowed on all, for Peter and John did not thus lay hands on Simon. Perhaps it was done on a few of the brethren who then would be employed particularly in places of leadership and instruction in the Samaritan church.

And they were receiving the Holy Spirit. Both the verbs "laying" and "receiving" are in the imperfect tense in the Greek, which implies the repetition of the acts and of the reception of the Holy Spirit by several individuals. In contrast, "prayed" in verse 15 is in the aorist tense, indicating a single act. Thus, this passage does not harmonize with certain modern practices, where *every* time there is a laying on of hands that some people might receive what is called the "baptism in the Holy Spirit," there is also a time of prayer by the leader of the charismatic study group. Churches which practice a rite called "confirmation" appeal to this passage (plus Hebrew 6:2 and Acts 19:6) as a proof text authorizing the rite. But the practice finds no support in these or other Acts passages.[50]

8:18 – *Now when Simon saw that the Spirit was bestowed through the laying on of the apostles' hands, he offered them money,*

Now when Simon saw that the Spirit was bestowed through the laying on of the apostles' hands. That Simon was able to see something is a strong indication that the result of

---

[46] See verse 12 and Acts 2:38.

[47] Acts 2:4,33.

[48] Acts 10:44.

[49] In 1 Corinthians 12, it is indicated that each who had spiritual gifts generally had but one miraculous thing he could do, whereas the apostles could work a multitude of different phenomena.

[50] This verse is hardly to be appealed to as evidence that the "confirmation" rite traces to apostolic times. Where is there anything in Acts similar to infant sprinkling followed twelve or so years later by the rite of confirmation, which is supposed to confer the indwelling gift of the Holy Spirit? Cp. also notes at Acts 14:22.

the Samaritans' receiving the Spirit was something extraordinary and visible, namely, miraculous spiritual gifts. When the apostles' hands laid on believers, the result was that spiritual gifts were imparted, and the effects of these gifts could be seen by the eye.

This passage has a considerable bearing on the question of whether or not there are "faith healers" today exercising the same powers as were available to the apostolic church.

> The purpose of Peter and John's trip to Samaria must be found in what they did when they arrived. Philip, who was not an apostle, had the power to perform miracles, but he evidently did not have the power to pass such an ability on to other people. Had he possessed such power, it would have been unnecessary for Peter and John to make the trip to impart the power. It was the purpose of Christ and His apostles to establish in every community the work of spreading the gospel. In order to accomplish this task, it was necessary to have "diversities of gifts" for the performance and perfection of the body of Christ (1 Corinthians 12:4-11 and Ephesians 4:11-16). In every congregation these gifted leaders cared for the work and spread of the Word. One person had the gift of the "word of wisdom," which was perhaps the ability to present the Word of God and the plan of salvation through the guidance of the Holy Spirit (for they as yet had no New Testament written to guide them). Another leader had the gift of knowledge. Another possessed the gift of healing, which was to prove the power of God and to extend mercy to the suffering. Still others were enabled to speak in the necessary language for those of other tongues. Some could discern the spirits, or tell if one's teaching were true or false. Having all these gifts enabled the workers to safeguard the new flocks until the revealed Word had been written by the apostles and presented to the congregations for their guidance. Had they possessed the New Testament at that time, as we now have it, these special gifts would have been unnecessary. Upon the death of the apostles and of those upon whom they had laid their hands for the granting of special gifts, the power to perform miracles ceased. By that time, the miracles that had been performed were recorded in His revealed Word. By that time the New Testament had been completed; and every congregation had the written Word to guide them in the teaching and telling of the story of Christ. Miracles established the work and the Word. Once established, the need for special powers and gifts ceased.[51]

It is not to be expected that a man will receive miraculous powers at the time of his baptism; the believers in Samaria did not. Miraculous powers do not come with baptism into Christ. They are not involved in the indwelling gift of the Spirit that comes to us at baptism.

He offered them money. In the days before Christianity came to Samaria, Simon had exercised an extended influence over the Samaritans; and a man who uses the occult to get power for himself has a hard time breaking himself of the desire for such position. Likely this is what is behind his desire for the power to pass on the Holy Spirit. It would increase and perpetuate his influence. The idea that such knowledge could be purchased also would have come from his background in the occult. It was the custom of the time for novice enchanters to purchase the secrets of magic from previous masters in the magic art. Simon evidently looked upon the apostles as "enchanters" with a higher knowledge than he possessed. After the custom of the time, he thought that he might obtain it from them just the way he had obtained his previous magical knowledge from others; namely, by purchasing it.

---

[51] Dale, *op. cit.*, p.93-94.

8:19 – *saying, "Give this authority to me as well, so that everyone on whom I lay my hands may receive the Holy Spirit."*

Saying, "Give this authority to me as well. Simon is asking for the knowledge needed to be able to do what the apostles did. In the light of the context, those commentators who have Simon asking for the indwelling gift of the Holy Spirit have surely missed the point. Simon wants to be a "master enchanter" like he conceives the apostles to be.

So that everyone on whom I lay my hands may receive the Holy Spirit." From the act of Simon's attempting to buy this knowledge about the Holy Spirit, we have derived our word "Simony," which is the buying and selling of positions or offices in denominational church hierarchies.

8:20 – *But Peter said to him, "May your silver perish with you, because you thought you could obtain the gift of God with money!*

But Peter said to him, "May your silver perish with you. This rather startling statement is expressive of the horror and indignation of Peter at the base offer of Simon.[52]

Because you thought you could obtain the gift of God with money. The measure of the Spirit called spiritual gifts is here called "the gift of God." Any measure of the Spirit that a Christian received, whether he be an apostle and received the baptismal measure, or a believer who received the indwelling gift at baptism, or some spiritual gift received through the laying on of an apostle's hands, what he received was a gift from God.

8:21 – *"You have no part or portion in this matter, for your heart is not right before God.*

You have no part or portion in this matter. Barnes thinks "this matter" has reference to "the Christian religion." He says that Simon was not a Christian.[53] However, as noted in comments at verse 13, Simon was as much a part of the body of Christ as were all the other baptized believers in Samaria. "This matter," in the context, is the ability to pass on the supernatural powers of the Holy Spirit by the laying on of hands, like the apostles have just recently done in Samaria.

For your heart is not right before God. "Heart" usually stands for a man's thoughts; but here is speaks, it seems, of Simon's motives or principles of conduct. *Euthus* (translated "right") has both the sense of "being as it ought to be" and "straightforward, sincere." This is why we think "heart" here is a reference to motives. Peter did not need to miraculously search Simon's heart to know this. "Out of the abundance of the heart the mouth speaks" (Luke 6:45). Even if his heart had been right, Simon still would have had no part in the bestowing of spiritual gifts. Acts 8:18 and 19:1-7 indicate that only apostles could pass the

---

[52] The Early Church Fathers understood Peter's words to be a prediction of what would happen to Simon in the future. We believe our translators are right when they take his words to be an imprecation.

[53] Barnes, *op. cit.*, p.142. the reader will remember that Barnes is a writer in the Calvinistic tradition, who tries regularly to defend the doctrine of eternal security

gifts on, and Simon hardly qualified to be an apostle. "Before God" means that God is able to see and judge Simon's motives, and He sees they are not right.

8:22 – *"Therefore repent of this wickedness of yours, and pray the Lord that if possible, the intention of your heart may be forgiven you.*

Therefore repent of this wickedness of yours, and pray the Lord. This verse addresses the topic of forgiveness for the erring Christian. When a Christian sins, how is he to be forgiven? Is he to be baptized for the forgiveness of his sins again? According to this passage, when a Christian sins, he is commanded to repent and pray for forgiveness. "Pray the Lord" in some manuscripts has been altered to "Pray God," but the better manuscripts read as does the NASB. "Lord" has either the Old Testament sense of the word (i.e., as a reference to God) or, as often is the case in the New Testament, it has reference to Christ.

That if possible, the intention of your heart may be forgiven you. "If possible?" Peter has no allusion to the unpardonable sin, as several commentators suppose,[54] for he knew very well what that sin is (Mark 3:28-30), and he would have known that Simon had not committed *that* sin. Many writers think that "if possible" indicates some doubt whether Simon might be forgiven.[55] But if God is faithful that promised – and He has promised to forgive our sins if we meet certain conditions – "if possible" cannot indicate such a doubt. If there is any doubt expressed by this language, it is doubt as to whether Simon would repent. "Intention of your heart" speaks of Simon's selfish desire to be able to deceive the people in order to continue in his place of power and influence over them.

8:23 – *"For I see that you are in the gall of bitterness and in the bondage of iniquity."*

For I see that you are in the gall of bitterness. Peter could "see" by observing the offer Simon had made, which displayed a state of mind wholly inconsistent with true Christianity.[56] Thayer's *Lexicon* says that "gall of bitterness" means "extreme wickedness." "Gall" is a word that is used for bile, that yellow-greenish fluid that is secreted by the liver.

> The ancients considered that the gall of noxious snakes was the source of their venom, and Peter warns Simon that unless repentance comes he will be worse and worse until he becomes all venom.[57]

And in the bondage of iniquity. 'You are bound by iniquity,' says Peter. Even after a man becomes a Christian, it is possible to go back into servitude to the old sin master.[58] Simon, by repentance, needed to offer himself to God, to be His servant, in order to break the bondage he was in. This expression used by Peter may be based on Isaiah 58:6.

---

[54] Plumptre, Alford, and others make similar comments.

[55] Barnes, *op. cit.*, p.143.

[56] Peter's expression may have been suggested by Deuteronomy 29:18.

[57] Boles, *op. cit.*, p.131.

[58] Romans 6:16.

8:24 – *But Simon answered and said, "Pray to the Lord for me yourselves, so that nothing of what you have said may come upon me."*

But Simon answered and said. Barnes suggests that Simon is hypocritically asking Peter to pray for him.[59] However, this commentator thinks Simon was sincere in his request, because he saw the danger he was in. It seems that he has been led to repentance by Peter's words, and is asking Peter to pray for him, as though his own prayer were not sufficient to obtain forgiveness.

Pray to the Lord for me yourselves. There is an emphasis to Simon's language as he pleads, *"You* pray for me (too)!" Prayer for others is efficacious, especially when they too are praying for their own needs.

> Seldom, today, do men ask others to pray for them. Paul said, "Brethren, pray for us" (1 Thessalonians 5:25; 2 Thessalonians 3:1; Hebrews 13:18). Years ago, Christians often shook hands and asked their brethren to pray for them.[60]

So that nothing of what you have said may come upon me. "You" is plural, so that we must understand that John's concurrence with Peter's assessment of the situation must have been clearly shown.

At this point, Simon disappears from the history of Acts, and this seems accordingly the right place for stating briefly the later traditions as to his history. In those traditions Simon occupies a far more prominent position than in Luke's narrative. He becomes almost a hero of heresy. The tradition has it that he was born at Gittom, in Samaria,[61] and received his education at Alexandria, where he picked up the language of a mystic Gnosticism from Disitheus.[62] Again, tradition has it that Simon had for a short time been a disciple of John the Baptist.[63] He is said to have murdered a boy that the soul of his victim might become his familiar spirit, and give him insight into the future.[64] It is said that a woman of great beauty accompanied him. Her name was Luna or Helena, and he represented her as a kind of incarnation of the wisdom or thought of God.[65] He identified himself with the promised Paraclete and the Christ, and took the name of "He who stands," as indicating divine power.[66] He boasted that he could turn himself and others into the form of brute beasts, and that he could cause statues to speak.[67] Tradition also has it that after the episode here related in Acts, Simon went to Caesarea, so that James the brother of

---

[59] Barnes, *op. cit.*, p.144.

[60] Dale, op. cit., p.95.

[61] Justin Martyr, *Apology*, I.26.

[62] Pseudo-Clementine *Homilies*, II.c.22; *Apost. Constit.* VI.8.

[63] *Homilies*, II.c.23.

[64] *Homilies*, II.c.26; Pseudo-Clementine *Recognitions*, II.9.

[65] Justin Martyr, *Apology*, I.56.

[66] *Recognitions*, II.7.

[67] *Homilies*, IV.c.4; *Recognitions*, II.9 and III.6.

the Lord and an apostle (Galatians 1:19), sent Peter there to confront him and hold a debate with him on various points of doctrine. From Caesarea, Simon made his way to Tyre and Tripolis, and then to Rome, and was there worshiped by his followers, so that an altar was seen there by Justin Martyr that had this inscription, "SIMONI DEO SANCTO."[68] Tradition then indicates that Peter followed him, and in the reign of Claudius the two met, once more face to face, in the imperial city.[69] According to one legend, Simon offered to prove his divinity by flying in the air, trusting that the demons whom he employed would support him. But through the power of the prayers of Peter, he fell down, and his bones were broken, so he committed suicide.[70] Another legend represents Simon as being buried alive at his own request, in order that he might show his power by rising on the third day from the dead, and so met his death (since he couldn't get out of the grave).[71]

8:25 – *And so, when they had solemnly testified and spoken the word of the Lord, they started back to Jerusalem, and were preaching the gospel to many villages of the Samaritans.*

And so, when they had solemnly testified and spoken the word of the Lord. This summary statement by Luke involves a stay of some duration, long enough to strengthen and organize a congregation of disciples, building on the work already done by Philip.

They started back to Jerusalem. The apostles, Peter and John, are the ones returning to Jerusalem.

And were preaching the gospel to many villages of the Samaritans. The return trip to Jerusalem evidently took many days. When they came to Samaria, Peter and John seem to have come directly from Jerusalem to the place where Philip was preaching. On their return to Jerusalem, they traveled more at leisure, and preached to many villages and towns. We shall see later that the apostle Paul revisited cities where he had preached at an earlier time, in order to establish and strengthen the disciples in the faith. Perhaps Peter and John are doing this very same thing in villages where Philip and others (remember those who were scattered by the persecution) have started congregations.

The curtain falls at the close of this narrative on the Christians of Samaria, and we know very little of their after-history. One glimpse we get of them is of some special interest. After the first missionary journey, when Paul and Barnabas come up to Jerusalem for the Jerusalem Conference, they passed "through Phoenicia and Samaria" (Acts 15:3). Luke records that the Samaritans heard with joy about the conversion of the Gentiles. One

---

[68] Justin Martyr, *Apology*, I.56. An altar, now in the Vatican Museum, was discovered in Rome in 1574, on the island in the Tiber River, with the inscription SEMONI SANCO DEO FIDIO. Archaeologists, however, agree in thinking that this altar was dedicated to the Sabine Hercules, who was known as Semo Sancus; and it has been thought by many commentators that Justin may have seen this or some similar altar, and, in his ignorance of Italian mythology, have imagined that it was consecrated to the sorcerer from Samaria named Simon. Justin's statement is repeated by Tertullian (*Apol.*, c.13) and by Irenaeus (*Adv. Heresies*, I.20).

[69] Note that this tradition says in the reign of "Claudius"! It is doubtful Peter was in Rome as early as the reign of Claudius. Special Study #14, "Was Peter Ever in Rome?", at the close of chapter 12 will take up this matter in more detail.

[70] *Apost. Constitutions*, II.14, VI.9.

[71] Irenaeus, *Adver. Heresies*, VI.20.

other note about the church in Samaria comes from the fact that Justin Martyr's birthplace was Samaria.

With the exception of Acts 12:2, this is also the last mention of the apostle John in the book of Acts. We know from Galatians 2:9 that he was still at Jerusalem at the time of the Jerusalem Conference. Probably he did not leave Palestine until after the period of time covered by Acts. There is no evidence of John's being in Asia Minor during the life of Peter or Paul, but there is considerable evidence for his ministry there in the closing years of the 1st century, including traditions about the writing of the fourth Gospel, the three epistles that bear his name, and the book of Revelation.

C. Philip and the Eunuch. 8:26-40

8:26 – *But an angel of the Lord spoke to Philip saying, "Arise and go south to the road that descends from Jerusalem to Gaza." (This is a desert road.)*

But an angel of the Lord spoke to Philip saying. The tense of the verbs in the preceding verse and here implies that the events that follow synchronized with the journey of Peter and John through Samaria. Some modern translations read "*the* angel of the Lord,"[72] but there is more likelihood that the NASB has it right when it reads "*an* angel of the Lord." That is, he is one of many messengers God uses from time to time to reveal His will to men.

Arise and go south. The congregation in Samaria has been endowed with spiritual gifts so that it has inspired leadership, so men like the apostles or Philip are no longer needed there. They were free to go to another field of labor. "South" means "south of the city of Samaria," where Philip was when the angel appeared to him.

We are entering the study of the paragraph of the conversion of the Ethiopian eunuch. It deserves special attention, for it is one of what have been called "pattern conversions" in the book of Acts. All the conversions follow a certain pattern; and the pattern is very clearly delineated in these following verses, which makes them especially helpful today when we would tell someone what to do to be saved.

To the road that descends from Jerusalem to Gaza. As Philip journeyed to the place where he would meet the Ethiopian, he would travel the "ridge road" which passes west of Jerusalem and which intersects the Jerusalem-Gaza road somewhere southwest of the city of Jerusalem. Much question and confusion about this road is found in the older commentaries, many of which were written before the recent thorough explorations of the land. Archaeology has shown that there was a road built by the Romans that led from the southwestern corner of Jerusalem in a westerly and southerly direction toward Gaza, some traces of which are still visible, though the route for the most part is impassable for modern vehicles. McGarvey describes the traces of the road, which he himself traveled, about 100 years ago.

---

[72] Compare comments at Acts 7:30 concerning the import of the name "the angel of the Lord."

Some five or six miles from Jerusalem the road begins to descend from the central ridge, which it follows that far, through a rough and narrow ravine known in the Old Testament as the Valley of Elah. After traversing this valley a few miles nearly due south, the road turns west, and rises through another wadi, i.e., creek, to the level of the Philistine Plain, which it follows the rest of the way to Gaza.[73]

Gaza is one of the oldest cities in the world (Genesis 10:19). Travelers to and from Egypt used to supply themselves with provisions there. Joshua could not subdue it.[74] It was assigned to Judah, but even that warlike tribe was unable to subdue it.[75] It passed into the hands of the Philistines, and became one of their chief cities.[76] About 300 BC, it took Alexander the Great five months' siege to take it, and when he finally took it, he did not destroy Gaza. So at the date of the eunuch's travels, it was a flourishing city.[77]

(This is a desert *road*.) See the marginal reading, "This city is deserted." Either is a possible translation, and which is correct depends on whether these are the words of the angel who is speaking to Philip, or whether they are a comment by Luke. "Desert" means "uninhabited." Perhaps Luke is telling his readers that the city of Gaza is uninhabited. If so, it means that Acts was written after the city had been laid waste during the Jewish war (AD 65). If it is the angel who speaks, then the angel is telling Philip to go to the Jerusalem-Gaza road which passes through no populated areas (i.e., the route other than the one through Hebron). It seems best to understand that this parenthetical note is part of the angel's instructions to Philip.

It was "desert" in the sense that it was unpopulated, and not in the sense that there was no water there. Before men knew the geography of Palestine, many said that the eunuch could not have been immersed because he was in a dry, arid region where there was no water. But this is a misunderstanding of the word "desert."[78]

8:27 – *And he arose and went; and behold, there was an Ethiopian eunuch, a court official of Candace, queen of the Ethiopians, who was in charge of all her treasure; and he had come to Jerusalem to worship.*

And he arose and went. It would take some faith on the part of Philip to leave the promising field in Samaria and go to a road which did not even pass through any villages in its whole length from Jerusalem to Gaza. But God had spoken, and off he went!

---

[73] For greater detail, see McGarvey's *Commentary on Acts*, p.150-151, or his *Lands of the Bible*, p.46. Present-day visitors to the Holy Land are led to believe the eunuch traveled south to Hebron, and thence westerly to Gaza. However, see notes at verse 36.

[74] Joshua 10:41.

[75] Joshua 15:47.

[76] Judges 16:21; 1 Samuel 6:17.

[77] Josephus, *Antiquities*, XIII.13.3, XIV.5.3, XV.7.8.

[78] It is true that "desert" (*erēmos*) could speak of a sandy, rocky area, like the wilderness of Judea or the desert of Arabia, even the Negeb of southern Palestine. However, that does not seem to be the meaning here in Acts 8.

And behold, there was an Ethiopian eunuch. The Old Testament looked forward to the admission of the Ethiopians among the citizens of Zion,[79] and the conversion of the eunuch was the beginning of the fulfillment of this prophecy.

Ethiopia was one of the great kingdoms of Africa. It lay south of Egypt, on the Nile River. It was bounded on the north by Egypt, on the east by the Red Sea and Indian Ocean, on the south by the (then) unknown regions of the interior of Africa, and on the west by Libya and the great Libyan deserts. This kingdom was north of the land that is today known as Ethiopia. The Ethiopia of New Testament times stretched from modern Aswan to modern Khartoum, and the principal cities were Maroe (the Sheba of the Old Testament) and Naphta.

"Eunuch" has been taken by some commentators as meaning no more than "chamberlain" or "palace official," which is, indeed, the strict etymological sense of the word. However, the use of the word in Matthew 19:12, and indeed in the Greek writers generally, is in favor of the literal sense of the word here, of a man who had been emasculated and rendered impotent. Eunuchs were commonly employed in the attendance and supervision of the females of a king's court in Oriental countries.

A court official of Candace, queen of the Ethiopians. "Candace" is said to have been the common name given to all queens of Ethiopia (i.e., as "Pharaoh" was a dynastic name or title for the kings of Egypt).[80] Eunuchs often obtained high position and great authority.[81] The position this Ethiopian held is explained later in the verse; he was treasurer of the land.

Who was in charge of all her treasure. This would be a position of great trust and great responsibility. Because the word translated "treasure" (*gaza*) is the same word that is the name of the town (Gaza), some have made a play on words here. They speak of the man in the parable of Matthew 13:44, who found a treasure in a field and sold all he had to buy the field. So this Ethiopian, in charge of one treasure, and headed toward a town whose name means "treasure," finds a treasure worth more than all the others.

And he had come to Jerusalem to worship. The Ethiopian was, then, either a Jew or a proselyte.

- If he was a proselyte, he was a proselyte of righteousness.[82] This must be the case, for his baptism was not, like that of Cornelius, the admission of a Gentile into the Church. Many who believe he was a proselyte also have very definite convictions that he was a

---

[79] Zephaniah 3:10; Jeremiah 38:7-13, 39:16-18; Psalm 87:4, 88:31.

[80] See Strabo, *Geography*, XVII, p.820; Pliny, IV.35; *Dio Cass.*, LIV.5; Eusebius, *Church History*, II.1.

[81] Examples of eunuchs rising to high positions are the captain of the guard of Pharaoh and his chief butler and chief baker (Genesis 37:36, 40:2,7).

[82] See notes at Acts 2:10 on the two types of proselytes. Some early writers, Eusebius (*Church History*, II.1) among them, speak of the eunuch as being the first convert among the Gentiles (i.e., he was neither proselyte nor Jew). This opinion does not appear to be correct, for there was no controversy about his acceptance, as there was in the case of Cornelius (Acts 11).

black man.[83] The word "Ethiopia" means "burned countenance." But it would be difficult to show positively that the Ethiopian was a black man.

- It is possible the man was a Jew, for there was a Jewish colony in Ethiopia. There is reason to believe the Judean king Manasseh sent a considerable body of Jews south to protect the outposts of his kingdom. (According to a statement in the narrative of Aristeas, which he made on the LXX translation, Manasseh had formed an alliance with Psammetichus, king of Egypt.) Thus, by the mid-30's AD, Jews had been in Ethiopia for some centuries. Given the historical Jewish skillfulness at handling money, it is not unthinkable for one to have become a government treasury official.

This man had taken a very long trip to Jerusalem to worship. There is a probability that he had been up to Jerusalem for one of the great pilgrimage festivals, perhaps Pentecost (in AD 34?). During the time of Moses (Deuteronomy 23:1), eunuchs were excluded from the worship services of the tabernacle, but the removal of this ban is announced in Isaiah 56:3ff and Jeremiah 38:7.

8:28 – *And he was returning and sitting in his chariot, and was reading the prophet Isaiah.*

And he was returning. He was on his way back to Ethiopia, after having been to Jerusalem to worship.

And sitting in his chariot. The exact form of this vehicle is not known. It may have been on wheels, or it may have been a litter (palanquin).

And was reading the prophet Isaiah. Just like Deuteronomy 6:7 taught, so this Ethiopian was doing, as he traveled: he was reading from the Word of God. There is the possibility that he had just purchased this manuscript of Isaiah during his visit to Jerusalem, and was reading the wonderful utterances for the first time from his own copy of Isaiah. Given the way Isaiah is quoted in verses 32-33, it was a copy of the LXX that he was reading. After the manner of most Eastern nations, to whom silent reading is almost unknown, the Ethiopian was reading out loud (see verse 30).

8:29 – *And the Spirit said to Philip, "Go up and join this chariot."*

And the Spirit said to Philip. The Holy Spirit is here evidently intended. The Spirit spoke[84] to Philip, not to the Ethiopian, and this is significant. Many people today think that conversion is achieved by the direct action of the Holy Spirit on the heart (mind) of the unconverted sinner, but this notion is without precedent and without example in the Scripture.[85] Here the Spirit is working through the evangelist. The Holy Spirit operates through the Word in conversion, not directly upon the heart apart from the Word.

---

[83] Dale, *op. cit.*, p.97, notes that today in New York City there is a Black Jewish sect composed of some 3000 members who teach that blacks are actually Hebrews from Ethiopia. They even teach that Adam was a black man.

[84] In passing, notice this evidence of the personality of the Holy Spirit, namely, his ability to speak.

[85] This "without precedent and without example" statement excludes the one incident in Acts 10 involving Cornelius, who is a special case and will be discussed later.

Only God could plan such a meeting as this one. It was necessary for God to call Philip away from the work in Samaria before the eunuch left Jerusalem. It was necessary for God to properly time the arrival of Philip, so that the eunuch would be reading this particular passage. Philip must have started from Samaria at least as early as the day previous to that on which the Ethiopian left Jerusalem. The Lord knew how long it would take the Ethiopian to reach the point at which Philip came in behind him, and how long it would take Philip to reach the same point.

Go up and join this chariot. "Join" is a word that pictures "be glued to."[86] Evidently the Spirit wants Philip to walk (or run) alongside the chariot, and stay with it.

8:30 – *And when Philip had run up, he heard him reading Isaiah the prophet, and said, "Do you understand what you are reading?"*

And when Philip had run up. What does this indicate? Some think it speaks of the fact that he was behind and had to run to catch up.[87] Others think his running shows Philip's desire to preach. Think of the impression it must have made on the Ethiopian. Here is a man running up to the side of the chariot; and his first words are, "Do you understand what you are reading?" (Philip in effect is saying, "I've come on the run to help you, if you want the help.")

He heard him reading Isaiah the prophet. The Ethiopian must have been reading out loud. Reading in ancient times was almost invariably aloud. In his *Confessions,* Augustine mentions as something worthy of note that Ambrose of Milan read silently.[88]

And said, "Do you understand what you are reading?" One of the first things to be done whenever a prospect is met, is to find out where he is on the road to salvation. By this question, Philip can learn where the Ethiopian is spiritually.

> Considering the relative positions of the parties, Philip's question, "Dost thou understand what thou readest?" strikes us as a rather abrupt, if not an impertinent, method of introducing himself to the treasurer. It was, however, an appropriate question and wisely propounded. Philip as yet knew not his man; he knew not whether to approach him as a fellow disciple or as an unbeliever. He knew that if he were an unbeliever he could not tell the meaning of the well-known prediction which he was reading, one of the plainest predictions in all the prophets concerning the sufferings of Christ. (The Jews, not willing to apply it to the Christ because they expected him to be a great earthly king, knew not what to do with it.) On the other hand, Philip knew that if the man were a believer, the passage would be unmistakably clear to him. The purpose of the question, then, was to draw out the religious position of this man, so as to determine how to proceed with him further.[89]

---

[86] The same word was used at Acts 5:13.

[87] McGarvey, *op, cit.*, p.153, speaks of the chariot as being some distance ahead, almost ready to pass out of sight.

[88] Augustine, *Confessions*, VI.3.

[89] McGarvey, *op. cit.*, p.153-154.

This is one of the verses used by the Roman Church to prove that the only infallible interpreter of Scripture is the Church (and the Roman hierarchy in particular). Further, it is said that the average man cannot read and understand the Scriptures for himself. 'Didn't the Ethiopian have to have help from an ecclesiastic?' the Roman argument goes.[90] However, Tomlinson has listed several Scriptures (among them Acts 17:11; 1 Peter 2:2; 2 Peter 1:19; Revelation 1:3) which show that the Scriptures are for all, and are understandable to any spiritual man.[91] Further, 1 Corinthians 2:14-16 indicates that the Holy Spirit helps the "average Christian" to understand the Scriptures; the illumination there spoken about is not something that is for the ecclesiastical leaders only. A detailed discussion of interpretation can be found in M.S. Terry's *Biblical Hermeneutics*.[92]

8:31 – *And he said, "Well, how could I, unless someone guides me?" And he invited Philip to come up and sit with him.*

And he said, "Well, how could I, unless someone guides me?" By these words the Ethiopian acknowledges his need of help. It is evidence of a humble state of mind, one who was willing to be taught. It is an acknowledgment, too, that the passage he was reading did not harmonize with the usual Jewish idea of a conquering Messiah. He had trouble understanding how the description of humiliation and condemnation could be reconciled with Jewish ideas of a conquering prince.

And he invited Philip to come up and sit with him. Now we picture the chariot going down the road, with Philip and the Ethiopian intently reading and commenting upon the passage of Scripture from Isaiah.

8:32 – *Now the passage of Scripture which he was reading was this: "HE WAS LED AS A SHEEP TO SLAUGHTER; AND AS A LAMB BEFORE ITS SHEARER IS SILENT, SO HE DOES NOT OPEN HIS MOUTH.*

Now the passage of Scripture which he was reading was this. The quotation about to be given is from the Septuagint version of Isaiah 53:7-8. It comes from a section of Isaiah in which are found what have been called "Suffering Servant Poems." There are five of them, all of which picture the work of the coming Messiah.

HE WAS LED AS A SHEEP TO SLAUGHTER. Messiah is the person being spoken of by Isaiah. Isaiah pictures Him as being led by others to be killed. The reference is to the crucifixion.

AND AS A LAMB BEFORE ITS SHEARER IS SILENT. That is, patient, still, unresisting.

---

[90] The Roman Church's use of this passage to support their theology is questionable. The Holy Spirit leading a Christian to understand the Old Testament is considerably different from claiming that only ecclesiastical leadership is qualified to interpret the New Covenant to satisfy Roman dogma.

[91] Lee G. Tomlinson, *Churches of Today* (Nashville: Gospel Advocate Co., 1955), p.18.

[92] Milton S. Terry, *Biblical Hermeneutics* (Grand Rapids: Zondervan, nd), p.151ff.

SO HE DOES NOT OPEN HIS MOUTH. Jesus did not complain or cry out harsh words against His tormenters. He yielded patiently to whatever was done to Himself by others. Each of the phrases from Isaiah's prophecy refer to some event or attitude during the passion of Jesus. Philip could take each of the phrases from Isaiah and show exactly what the prophet had predicted did come true; namely, the silent patience of the Sufferer; His previous life and work; the proofs which both had given that He was none other than the one He claimed to be – the Christ, the Son of God.

8:33 – *"IN HUMILIATION HIS JUDGMENT WAS TAKEN AWAY; WHO SHALL RELATE HIS GENERATION? FOR HIS LIFE IS REMOVED FROM THE EARTH."*

IN HUMILIATION HIS JUDGMENT WAS TAKEN AWAY. The Hebrew reads, "He was taken from prison and judgment." There is not much difference between the Hebrew for "prison" and the Hebrew for "humiliation," as the latter word was understood by the LXX translators. It speaks of the time during Jesus' trial when He had no one to speak in His defense, no friends in the court. And "judgment" being taken away means that justice, a just sentence, was denied Him; He was cruelly condemned after an unfair trial.

WHO SHALL RELATE HIS GENERATION? Because the Hebrew of Isaiah is open to so many different explanations, a number of interpretations have been given to this phrase; indeed, the same is true of each of the phrases in the Suffering Servant Poem. Lowth translates it, "His manner of life who would declare?" Lowth supposes this refers to the fact that when a prisoner was condemned and led to execution, it was customary for a proclamation to be made by a crier in these words, "Whoever knows anything about his innocence, let him come and declare it."[93] Calvin referred this question to His deity, or His divine generation, intimating that no one could explain the mystery of His eternal generation.[94] Meyer has seen in it a reference to His own spiritual posterity, "Who shall declare (who can count) His spiritual offspring?"[95] Still another explanation has been, "Who can describe the character and wickedness of the generation in which He lived – the enormous crime of the age in putting Him to death?"[96] Barnes offers the suggestion, "Who will stand up for him, declaring who He is? Who will appear in court on His behalf? Who will vindicate Him?" – meaning that at His trial all would forsake Him, and that there would be none to plead His case.[97]

FOR HIS LIFE IS REMOVED FROM THE EARTH. The Hebrew admits of no other

---

[93] Barnes, *op. cit.*, p.148. This comment is based on the Babylonian *Gemara*, a Jewish work written 200 or so years after Christ. It tells how before the death of Jesus, this proclamation asking for a defender to come forward was made for 40 days, but no one came forward. It sounds suspiciously like a Jewish attempt to relieve themselves of the guilt which the Christian preachers have been openly declaring them to be guilty of in the crucifixion of Jesus.

[94] John Calvin, *The Gospel According to Isaiah* (Grand Rapids: Eerdmans, 1953), p.71.

[95] H.A.W. Meyer, *Critical and Exegetical Handbook to the Acts of Apostles* (New York: Funk and Wagnalls, 1883). p. 176.

[96] Barnes, *op. cit.*, p.148.

[97] *Ibid.*

meaning than the Sufferer was hurried to a violent death. The fact that in being thus taken from the earth the Sufferer was exalted to heaven, though true in itself, cannot be found in the words of this phrase of the prophecy. It would take many pages to give a detailed and critical explanation of each of the phrases of Isaiah's prophecy, and that is beyond what is needed for this commentary. However, it is not difficult to think of Philip as pointing to the words of the context, and unfolding in full, not only the suffering of Jesus, but its purpose – namely, to atone and redeem, as set forth in Isaiah's marvelous prediction.

8:34 – *And the eunuch answered Philip and said, "Please tell me, of whom does the prophet say this? Of himself, or of someone else?"*

And the eunuch answered Philip and said, "Please *tell me*, of whom does the prophet say this? Of himself, or of someone else?" This was a very natural question, for there was nothing in the book of Isaiah which would determine to whom reference was made. True, many Jews considered the Suffering Servant Poems to be a reference to the Messiah, but many did not.[98] The answers given to this question in modern times have been numerous, especially when unbelievers try to answer it. But Philip had no difficulty, nor did he hesitate between a number of alternative answers. Isaiah himself might not have known (1 Peter 1:11), but now that the prophecy had come true, Philip knew that it referred to Jesus; and so he began with this passage as a background and told the Ethiopian the Good News about Jesus.

8:35 – *And Philip opened his mouth, and beginning from this Scripture he preached Jesus to him.*

And Philip opened his mouth. This phrase, when it occurs in the New Testament,[99] implies something like a set discourse (i.e., a sort of standard sermon with certain points being emphasized, whenever this passage of Scripture was explicated), or it calls attention to the importance of what was about to be said.

And beginning from this Scripture. A personal evangelist soon learns just what the prospect's understanding of the Scriptures is. He then uses that understanding as a foundation on which to build a greater understanding in the heart of the prospect, till the prospect is led on to a full obedience. Philip, by his questions and the Ethiopian's answers, has learned where his prospect is, and now uses the Isaiah passage to teach the prospect what is required of him for salvation.

He preached Jesus to him. This was the very theme of the text from Isaiah. That text told all about Jesus – His life and death and exaltation and the beginning of the Church. Philip showed the Ethiopian that Jesus of Nazareth exactly answered the description made by Isaiah years before, and therefore the prophet must have been referring to Jesus of Nazareth. In a time when the only Scriptures in written form were the Old Testament scrolls,

---

[98] See Bruce, *op. cit.*, p.193, where Jewish attitudes are expounded and documented.

[99] Acts 10:34, 17:14.

8:36 – And as they went along the road they came to some water; and the eunuch said, "Look! Water! What prevents me from being baptized?"

And as they went along the road they came to some water. In the comments at verse 26, we have already noted the problem of identifying the exact road along which the Ethiopian was traveling. Bound up with the problem of which road is the identification of the body of water they were coming to. Eusebius and Jerome have stated that the "water" was the spring at Bethsoron, 20 miles south of Jerusalem and 2 miles from Hebron, on the more heavily traveled road from Jerusalem to Gaza. Such an identification seems opposed to "desert" in verse 26. McGarvey, who himself traversed the old Roman road which passed through no villages the whole distance from Jerusalem to Gaza, makes this identification of the "water" to which the chariot has now come.

> The first natural water to which they would come (unless it were a spring or pool on the wayside) was the brook which flows through the valley of Elah. It is a mountain stream, which goes dry in summer, but flows with a strong current through the winter and spring. If the chariot had already crossed the valley of Elah when the Eunuch requested baptism, there is another stream in the plain of Philistia, now called the Wady el-Hasy, where the baptism could have taken place. It is a perennial stream and suitable for baptizing at any season of the year. There were also a multitude of pools in the area. They have a rainless season of seven months each year; and the country would have to make provision of water for the stock, and for irrigating the summer crops – and no country was ever so well supplied in this way as Judea.[101]

And the eunuch said, "Look! Water! What prevents me from being baptized?" Preaching Jesus must include instruction on what to do to become a Christian. A question expressing a desire to be immersed would not have occurred to the Ethiopian unless he had been previously instructed concerning the ordinance of baptism. There is a lesson to be learned in this passage that needs to be heard today:

> No inspired preacher of the Gospel ever preached Jesus without preaching the baptism that Jesus commanded; no Gospel preacher today can preach Jesus without preaching the command to be baptized.[102]

Philip asked the Ethiopian, "Do you understand what you are reading?" From the answer that Philip received, he was able to judge as to the gospel needs of the eunuch. When the eunuch answered as he did, he showed that he knew nothing of Jesus as the promised Messiah. He certainly also, then, had learned nothing definite concerning the baptism which Jesus had commanded; and we are consequently forced to the conclusion that what the Ethiopian now requested (i.e., to be baptized) he had learned from Philip's preaching.

---

[100] In this century, we too could use Old Testament passages as we teach prospects about Jesus; but we have a much better source of reliable truth in the New Testament, and wisdom would rely on it much more than Old Testament Scriptures in the work of personal evangelism.

[101] McGarvey, *op. cit.*, p.157.

[102] Boles, *op. cit.*, p.138.

The suggestion that the Ethiopian learned about baptism from the words "so shall He sprinkle many nations" (Isaiah 52:15) has been advanced by some teachers in an effort to prove the validity of sprinkling. But such an opinion has not been approved by any of the critical commentators, and is shown to be without much to commend it when it is known that the LXX, which the eunuch was reading, has "astonish" at this place instead of "sprinkle." Philip must have told the eunuch, as Peter told his audience in Jerusalem on the day of Pentecost, that the appropriate response to such good news was repentance and baptism for the remission of sins and the reception of the Holy Spirit.

As Philip preached Jesus, he also preached baptism, for the eunuch asked for it. Not only that, but the eunuch understood that it was to be a baptism in water. "Here is water! What prevents me from being baptized?" he said. It was not a Spirit baptism into the body of Christ that Philip preached. Philip, the inspired preacher, preached a message different than many of the preachers of this day who preach only a Spirit baptism (in an effort to avoid the force of the passages which speak of baptism as being necessary for salvation). The Ethiopian's asking to be baptized was equivalent to a profession of acceptance of all the instructions given by Philip.

[8:37 – *And Philip said, "If you believe with all your heart, you may." And he answered and said, "I believe that Jesus Christ is the Son of God."*]

[*And Philip said, "If you believe with all your heart, you may."* Observe that in the NASB, this verse is in the margin. In the older ASV, it is a footnote.

- Footnotes and/or marginal notes very often indicate a variant reading in the major manuscripts which underlie the translations of the Scriptures. Very often, where the divergent readings are almost equally supported in the ancient manuscripts, the translators would vote on which reading to incorporate into the text. If the majority voting for one reading was just one or two over half of those voting, the minority opinion was included in the form of a footnote.

- Another reason for footnotes is to show that verses and phrases that have become very familiar to us (because of our acquaintance with the KJV) do not really have enough evidence behind them to warrant their inclusion in the text of our present-day versions. *Textual scholars are pretty well agreed that Acts 8:37 is an interpolation.* That is, it did not appear in the autograph copy of Acts, but was early written onto the margin of copies that had been made from the original. Later it was transcribed as part of the original text. Evidence that Acts 8:37 was not in the original autograph is seen in the fact that the following manuscripts do not carry it: *Aleph,* A, B, C, G, H, P46. But if it is an interpolation, it is a very early interpolation. It was found in a text which Irenaeus (AD 170 to 210) used.[103] Cyprian (AD 200-258) also was familiar with the reading of verse 37.[104] The verse was introduced into the modern printed Greek texts by Erasmus, who thought it had been omitted through scribal error and that it originally belonged to what Luke wrote. From Erasmus' text, it was included in the KJV.

---

[103] *Against Heresies*, III.12.8.

[104] *Testimonies*, III.43.

Even if the verse is an interpolation and should be left out of the New Testament, it does not change in any way the thought; nothing is added by retaining the verse so far as doctrine is concerned, and nothing certainly is lost by omitting the verse.

- The same idea of confession of belief in Christ can be found in Matthew 10:32, Romans 10:9, and 1 Timothy 6:12-13.[105] What the early scribes wrote in the margin of Acts 8 was merely a reflection of what was practiced at the time they added the note. There was a step of salvation called "confession." Just what the exact words were when this confession was made is not specifically stated, but it had to do with belief in who Jesus was, namely, the Christ, the son of the living God.[106]

- Further evidence that no doctrine is lost if we omit Acts 8:37 can be seen in another area besides confession. When the verse is included, it states the necessity of faith preceding baptism; but that idea is also taught in Mark 16:16ff. When the verse is omitted, the Ethiopian's desire to comply with the conditions of salvation are an evidence of his faith. He is a believer, and is thus a suitable candidate for immersion.

So no doctrine is lost, even if we agree with the textual scholars who say the verse does not enjoy integrity.

And he answered and said, "I believe that Jesus Christ is the Son of God."] This statement doubtless summarizes all the instructions given by Philip to the Ethiopian, and by his confession the Ethiopian is expressing his own convictions about Jesus, now that he has been taught. Such a statement as this includes all there is to know about Christ; it includes all one will ever learn about Christ, even though he is not aware of some of the facets included in it at the time he makes such a confession. As we have affirmed above, there was a practice of making a confession of belief about Jesus in the process of conversion. Before a man was admitted to Christian fellowship by baptism, he made a public confession of his new faith, probably in response to some definite question asked of him about his beliefs. Likewise today, some kind of confession is needed so that the evangelist knows that the prospect is a suitable candidate for baptism, just as some such indication was needed in the early days of the Church.

8:38 – *And he ordered the chariot to stop; and they both went down into the water, Philip as well as the eunuch; and he baptized him.*

And he ordered the chariot to stop. Evidently the Ethiopian had a chariot driver (or some litter carriers), since he commanded the chariot to stop.

And they both went down into the water, Philip as well as the eunuch. The primary meaning of the Greek word *eis* is "into" – and if Barnes were not prejudiced in favor of

---

[105] Some have urged that the Matthew passage speaks of a life-long confession, rather than just one of the steps of salvation. But Romans 10:9 likely speaks of initial salvation, and 1 Timothy 6:12, 13 surely does.

[106] Matthew 16:16 gives the example of the confession made by Peter, and the words of Jesus that such a confession would be the "rock" on which the Church was built, thus implying others would make a similar confession. 1 Timothy 6:12-13 speaks about the confession Jesus made before Pilate as being the example followed by Timothy at his conversion. That is, when Jesus was asked if He were the Christ, He said. "I am!"

sprinkling, he would not have his long discourse at this place trying to prove otherwise.[107] This verse, along with Acts 2:38, has long proven difficult for those who insist sprinkling or pouring is just as good as immersion. Attempts to evade the force of this passage vary from one paedo-Baptist to another.

> One insists that the problem rests with the word "both." If it is immersion, then "both" would have to go under the water, he insists. Another man approaches it from the word "into." He argues that the same word in John 11:38 can mean only "to" and not "into," and therefore Acts 8:38 says no more than they went "near to" the water.[108]

Indeed, the Greek preposition might mean simply "near the water," but the universality of immersion in the practice of the early Church supports the translation of our version. In spite of the many attempts at evading the meaning of the term, there is no getting around the idea that baptism is like a burial and a resurrection.[109]

And he baptized him. That is, Philip baptized the Ethiopian. The Ethiopian would have laid aside his outer garments on the bank, descended till he was about chest-deep into the water, and would then have been plunged under it "in the name of the Lord Jesus." No other form of baptism except immersion was practiced for 200 or more years in the early Church.[110]

In this day when "faith-only" teachers are so prominent, saying, "Only believe! That is the way of salvation!" it is helpful to remember that the "faith-only" doctrine is no older than Martin Luther. Before Luther wrote the word *sola* (Latin for "only") in the margin of his Bible at Romans 3:28 (making it read, "man is justified by faith *only*"), no one ever taught *fides sola* (faith-only). And not even Luther meant to exclude baptism when he taught "faith only." Modern-day faith-only teachers have distorted Luther's meaning. He was combating the meritorious works idea he found in the Roman Catholic penance and indulgence system. He was not attempting to exclude such things as the Bible includes in what is called "the obedience of faith."

8:39 – *And when they came up out of the water, the Spirit of the Lord snatched Philip away; and the eunuch saw him no more, but went on his way rejoicing.*

And when they came up out of the water. The primary meaning of the word *ek* is "out of," and there is no reason for not so interpreting it here. They went down into the water before the baptismal service, and exited from up out of the water after the service.

The Spirit of the Lord snatched Philip away. One manuscript, Codex Alexandrinus, reads, "And the Spirit of the Lord fell upon the eunuch, but the angel of the Lord caught Philip away." This alteration evidently was made because of the feeling that without more

---

[107] Barnes, *op. cit.*, p.150.

[108] Dale, *op. cit.*, p.99.

[109] Romans 6:4; Colossians 2:12.

[110] Moses E. Lard, *Commentary on Romans* (Nashville, TN: Gospel Advocate Co., 1914), p.198ff.

help (e.g., spiritual gifts, miraculous help), the eunuch would not have lasted long as a Christian. We might reply that there was no absolute need of further instruction from a fellow-creature for one like the Ethiopian who had the Word of the Lord in his hands and the indwelling Spirit in his life. Still, without a New Testament to study, his faith will be greatly limited.

In the words "snatched away" some picture a miraculous transport away from the presence of the Ethiopian for Philip, similar to Elijah's being caught up into the air and carried out of sight.[111] Others think that the Spirit spoke to Philip, as before, directing him to go to another place.[112]

And the eunuch saw him no more, but went on his way rejoicing. Notice that the rejoicing comes after obedience. If there are any feelings (experiences) connected with salvation, they follow, not precede, becoming a Christian. The Ethiopian's rejoicing sprang from the fact that his sins had been forgiven on the condition of his obedient faith.

> It is impossible that Philip failed to tell him, as Peter did his converts, the connection of remission of sins with repentance and baptism. Now that he had complied with the conditions of pardon, he rejoices in the experience of it.[113]

Irenaeus says this eunuch became a missionary to the Ethiopians. With this agree Eusebius and Jerome.[114]

> The eunuch continued his trip back to Ethiopia. It is to be noted that the Spirit would not have directed Philip to the conversion of the eunuch had it not been for the purpose of even a greater work of saving souls in another country. The eunuch was a man of great influence, and no doubt, of ability. His conversion made it possible for him to carry the good news to thousands in his own land.[115]

For several hundred years we find a strong church in Ethiopia (though indeed, our records of the Ethiopic church are no earlier than the 4th century). His lack of further instruction in the Christian religion has left its imprint on the Ethiopic church. That church, throughout its history, was the most strongly Jewish, in its worship and in the tone of thought, of all Christian communities.[116]

---

[111] 1 Kings 18:12; 2 Kings 2:11.

[112] Certain occultists delight in pointing to passages like verse 39 as proof that what they are doing is the same as was done in the Bible, and arguing from the similarity that what they are doing must not be criticized or condemned. The occultic practice of apport is what they believe they are seeing in this passage. But there is a considerable difference between the Spirit of God who acts here in Acts and the evil spirits who help the occultist. The two are not the same!

[113] McGarvey, *op. cit.*, p.161.

[114] *Adv. Heresies*, III.12.8.

[115] Dale, *op. cit.*, p.100.

[116] Arthur P. Stanley. *Lectures on the History of the Eastern Church* (London: John Murray, 1884), p.12.

McGarvey's long paragraph about this pattern conversion deserves our attention. He wrote:

> Our conception of this case of conversion will lack completeness if we fail to look at it from another point of view which the account enables us to take. Should a friend have met the eunuch after he parted from Philip, and inquired as to the cause of the joy so manifest in his countenance, the recital would have presented the facts of the conversion from this point of view, rather than from that of the historian. He would not have begun the story, as our author does, with the visit of the angel to Philip; for of that he knew nothing; he would not have mentioned the command of the Holy Spirit, "Go join thyself to this chariot"; for of this he was equally ignorant; but his story would have been about this: I had been to Jerusalem to worship. I started for home, and as I rode in my chariot I opened the book of Isaiah and commenced reading. I came upon the passage so much puzzling to our scribes, in which the prophet speaks of humiliation and death of some one for the good of the world; and I was laboring hard to determine in my own mind of whom the prophet wrote those words, when suddenly there appeared running by the side of my chariot a footman, who inquired, "Understandest thou what thou readest?" His manner indicated that he understood it, and it seemed providential that he came to me at the very moment when I needed his help. I invited him to take a seat with me; I pointed to the passage, and stated to him my difficulty. In a short time, he made it perfectly plain to me that the passage referred to the long looked for Messiah: and that this great personage, instead of reigning here on earth, as our scribes have taught us, was to die a sacrifice for our sins; to rise from the dead, ascend to heaven from whence He came, and to establish His kingdom over both men and angels. He convinced me of the truth of all this, and showed me that through that man's blood, by faith in Him and repentance and baptism in His name, we are to receive the remission of sins which the Law could not give us. While he was still speaking to me these good tidings of great joy, we came to a certain water, and I requested the baptism in which he had instructed me. He baptized me; and then turned away as abruptly as he had come to me; but I have come on my way rejoicing in the forgiveness of sins, and in the assured hope of everlasting life. – Such was the experience of this man up to the moment that the curtain of history drops and hides him from our view. Happily, as we lose sight of him, the sounds that come back to us are notes of joy, and we may hope to meet him at the point where all our journeys end, and to rejoice with him forever. His ready faith and prompt obedience give evidence of such a character that we may believe he will bring many sheaves with him in the great harvest.[117]

8:40 – *But Philip found himself at Azotus; and as he passed through he kept preaching the gospel to all the cities, until he came to Caesarea.*

But Philip found himself at Azotus. Azotus is the city called Ashdod in the Old Testament. Then it was the capital of one of the five states of the Philistines, and the chief seat of the worship of Dagon. It once withstood a siege of 29 years from the Egyptian Pharaoh Psammetichus.[118] It had been destroyed in the time of the Maccabees,[119] and was

---

[117] McGarvey, *op. cit.*, p.162-163.

[118] *Herod*, II.157.

[119] 1 Maccabees 5:68, 10:77-85.

rebuilt by Gabinus in 55 BC.[120] It is located near the Mediterranean Sea, about 20 miles north of Gaza and about 35 miles from Jerusalem. In later years there was a church at Azotus, for a bishop from Azotus was present at the councils of Nicea and Chalcedon.

Though the NASB is generally excellent in its rendering of verb tenses, it appears that the handling of the verb "found" here is faulty. In the original Greek, it is an aorist passive verb, and the attempt of the NASB to translate it as if it were a middle voice verb is highly suspect. Philip "was found" is the proper rendering of it. Some writers have put emphasis on the word "found" as though it were proof of a miraculous transport away from the eunuch. However, there seems to be nothing more than a contrast in the text. The eunuch went on his way to Ethiopia, whereas Philip next preached in Azotus.

And as he passed through he kept preaching the gospel to all the cities. It was about 60 miles from Azotus to Caesarea. The plains of Philistia and Sharon are included in this area, as are many towns including Lydda and Joppa. Perhaps we can trace some of the effects of Philip's evangelistic work in the appearance later in Acts of flourishing churches in both Lydda and Joppa.[121] It was a field of evangelism sufficient to occupy many years of Philip's time. In addition to Lydda and Joppa, other towns of importance were Askelon, Arimathea, and Antipatris.

Until he came to Caesarea. It appears from Acts 21:8 that Philip settled down to live at Caesarea, and stayed there as an evangelist for upwards of 20 years. At Acts 10:1 there will be notes on Caesarea's history.

---

[120] Josephus, *Antiquities*, XIV.5.3.

[121] Acts 9:32,36.

C. A Harmony of the Early Life of Paul. 9:1-30, 22:3-21, 26:4-20, and Galatians 1:11-21

1. Paul's Youth

Paul was a Jew, born of descendants of Benjamin. In Philippians 3:5 he writes of himself: **circumcised the eighth day, of the nation of Israel, of the tribe of Benjamin, a Hebrew of Hebrews; as to the Law, a Pharisee.**[1]

He was the son of a Pharisee; in fact, his ancestors for several generations had been Pharisees.[2] Did a man have to be a Pharisee by birth to be a Pharisee? No. Did a man have to be a Sadducee by birth? Yes! The Sadducees were the priestly family. The Sadducees lived in Jerusalem where the temple was. However, the Pharisees were scattered over the world, where they often were the teachers in the synagogues. Thus it was that Jesus ran into the Pharisees all over the land, but the Sadducees only when He was near Jerusalem. A man became a Pharisee by belief and training, not by birth. It is not at all improbable that Saul's father was the religious leader of Tarsus' Jews. Being a Pharisee, Saul's father may well have been the ruler of the synagogue in Tarsus.

Twice in the epistles Paul calls himself a "Hebrew of Hebrews." He was born of Jewish parents, and they were not proselytes to the Jewish religion (i.e., not of Gentile background). He was a real Hebrew, of Hebrew parents, from a long line of Hebrews for that matter. "Circumcised the eighth day" distinguishes Paul from the Edomites who circumcised at age 13, and from proselytes who were circumcised at whatever age they became converts to Judaism.

Paul's birthplace was Tarsus of Cilicia.[3] Tarsus was then a center of Greek learning, almost rivaling Athens and Alexandria. Also, on account of its location on a navigable river (the Cydnus River), near the mountain passes leading into the interior of Asia Minor to the north and of Syria to the east, it was the center of an extensive commerce.

What were the schools like that a boy would attend? In Greek schools, the teachers were peripatetics, and emphasized Greek philosophy. They met their students on porches, in the market place, or in street recesses. The students would then walk up and down the place of meeting, being taught and reciting the day's lessons. The Jewish schoolhouse was one of the two rooms of the synagogue, and the ruler of the synagogue was also the teacher. At the age of 6, the Jewish boys took up the study of the Pentateuch, writing, and arithmetic. At the age of 10, the Mishna was added to the curriculum. The Mishna was in oral form in Paul's day, and the teacher would recite the lesson to the pupil; then, the pupil was to recite the lesson back to the teacher verbatim. The rabbis had a saying that "a good pupil was like a cistern that doesn't leak." At the age of 15, the *Gemara* was added. The *Gemara* was a still later and more extensive development of the Midrash, which was a part of the Mishna; the *Gemara* contained the discussions of the rabbis down through the centuries.

---

[1] Throughout "A Harmony of the Early Life of Paul," phrases printed in bold are Scripture quotations.

[2] Acts 23.6.

[3] Acts 22:3.

Did Paul have *a Jewish or a Greek education,* or both?

- Several lines of argument have been advanced that he had a Greek education. Paul reflects high training in Greek, especially in the polished Greek style in his letters. (But even in the Jewish educational system outside of Palestine, the children learned Greek.) His examples and illustrations reflect a Greek background. Note the contrast between Jesus' and Paul's illustrations. Jesus used illustrations from country life – farmer, shepherd, vineyard. Paul uses illustrations from the Greek world – the races, boxing, military figures, builders of buildings, debtors, slaves, etc. And a final argument that Paul had a Greek education is found in the fact that he quotes the Greek poets.[4]

- On the other hand, a good case can be made for the idea that Paul had a Jewish education. Paul mentions his Jewish background and education,[5] but he never makes mention of any Greek background. Of course, this argument is somewhat weakened by the fact that when Paul mentions his background, he is talking to Jews who are prejudiced against Greeks and Hellenistic ways. The fact that Paul was familiar with the theatre does not necessarily prove that he was of Greek schooling, for there was a theatre in Tarsus.

- If given a choice between whether Paul had a public *or* a parochial school education, this commentator would pick the parochial school as the type attended by Paul. (Whether or not his father was the teacher has little bearing on this point.)

- However, it appears Paul was educated in both public and parochial schools. In later years Christians sent their children to public school to learn math, rhetoric, science, etc., but they had their own parochial schools to teach the Bible. In Paul's case, it is felt that he attended both the Jewish school to study the Law, Prophets, and all things pertaining to religion, and that he attended the public schools for his secular education.

Besides his religious instruction, *every Jewish boy was taught a trade* or a craft. Paul was taught the trade of tent-maker.[6] The goat's hair which was used for the manufacture of rude garments and tent cloth was produced in great quantities in the mountains of Cilicia, and the manufactured article acquired the Greek name *kilikion* (Lat., *cilicium),* from the name of the province. The fact that Paul afterward received an expensive intellectual education proves that his father put him to this trade, not out of necessity, but in compliance with the Jewish concept that some form of manual labor was an important part in the education of every boy. In the Talmud, Gamaliel is quoted as saying, "Learning of every kind, unaccompanied by a trade, ends in nothing, but leads to sin." Rabbi Meir is quoted as saying, "Let a man always teach his sons pure and easy trades," and Rabbi Judah, "Not to teach one's son a trade is like teaching him robbery."[7] Paul's knowledge of this trade was of great service to him in his later ministry.[8]

---

[4] Acts 17:28; 1 Corinthians 15:53; Titus 1:12.

[5] Acts 22:3.

[6] Acts 18:3.

[7] F.W. Farrar, *Life and Work of Paul* (New York: E.P. Dutton & Co., 1880), p.14, note 1.

[8] Acts 18:3, 21:34; 1 Thessalonians 2:9.

Paul also was *a Roman citizen.*[9] On what occasion and for what service the Roman citizenship had been conferred on one of Paul's ancestors we cannot say; this only we know, that before his birth his father possessed this coveted privilege. There were several ways to get a Roman citizenship. One might be born in a Roman colony; thus, all the townspeople were granted the privilege for some service to the emperor. One might buy his citizenship. Or one could be born of Roman parents.

2. Paul in Jerusalem

In Acts 22:3 and 26:4, Paul tells us he was *brought up in Jerusalem*. Conybeare and Howson, in their *Life and Epistles of St. Paul*, reconstructed the journey and the sights and the thoughts that might well have filled the mind of Paul as he made his first trip to the Holy Land. Paul's age when he came to Jerusalem cannot be determined with any degree of certainty. Boles suggests, "Paul probably lived in Tarsus until he was eleven years of age, not later than thirteen years of age, as the Jewish parents put their sons in training at the age of twelve."[10] Others suggest he was just a lad of six or seven when he came to Jerusalem. Still others suggest he was fifteen to eighteen when he came to study. It is not probable that Paul was in Jerusalem at the time of the crucifixion of Jesus, or for several years previous, for that matter. If Paul had known Jesus during His earthly ministry, it is unaccountable that in all his speeches and epistles he makes no allusion to a personal knowledge of the events of Jesus' life. Evidently, even 2 Corinthians 5:16 does not mean that Paul had seen Jesus during His earthly ministry. In the context, that passage seems to say that at one time, (before his conversion) Paul used to look for a Messiah that would satisfy his earthly plans and anticipations; but now, he no longer has such a view of Messiah.

In Jerusalem, Paul studied **at the feet of Gamaliel**.[11] The phrase "to sit at the feet of one" is expressive of the condition of a disciple, or learner, or student. It is probable that it arose from the fact that the students occupied a lower place or seat than the teacher. It was like going to college at Jerusalem for Paul to be Gamaliel's student. What kind of student was Paul? In Galatians 1:14 he himself says he advanced beyond many of his own age. It is not at all improbable that Paul was distinguished in the school of Gamaliel for zeal in the Jewish religion.

His *course of studies* while in Jerusalem would have been varied. (1) He was instructed **strictly according to the law of our fathers**.[12] "Strictly" speaks of the utmost rigor and severity of this instruction. No pains were spared to make him understand and practice the Law of Moses. The Law is called "the law of our fathers" because it had been received by the fathers and handed down by them orally. It is also possible that this term includes the study of the Prophets of the Old Testament age. (2) He was instructed **in the doctrines (traditions) of the Pharisees**.[13] Remember, a man became a Pharisee by choice

---

[9] Acts 22:28.

[10] Boles, op. cit., p.351.

[11] Acts 22:3. Review also the notes about Gamaliel found in the Introductory Studies and at Acts 5:34.

[12] Acts 22:3.

[13] Acts 26:5; Galatians 1:14.

and by training.[14] Josephus tells us "that the Pharisees have delivered to the people a great many observances by [oral tradition] from their fathers which are not written in the law of Moses."[15] All of these more than 600 rules were part of Paul's studies. (3) He was instructed **in the Jews' religion**.[16]

Galatians 1:14 tells us that Paul **advanced in Judaism beyond many of my contemporaries**. At the time of Stephen's death, Paul must have been at least thirty years of age, and he perhaps had been out of Gamaliel's school for eight or ten years. The supposition that he had returned to Tarsus previous to the beginning of the ministry of John the Baptist, and had returned to Jerusalem after the ascension of Jesus, agrees with all the known facts in the case. "Advanced" may mean that he advanced in favor with the high priest and the Sanhedrin faster than others of his own age, even to the place where before he reached the age of maturity (40), he was given a responsible position (i.e., chief persecutor of the church).

In later life, Paul could look back on those days, and think of himself **as earnestly serving God day and night**.[17] He was zealous for God. He had a constant burning zeal for God and His law which expressed itself not only by scrupulous adherence to its forms and ceremonies, but in persecuting all who opposed the Law. "Serving God" speaks of the ordinances and observances in the Temple. "Day and night" tells of constant and intense devotion. He was at all the temple services; he was a conscientious and very religious man.

He did *many things contrary to Jesus of Nazareth*. In Acts 26:9 it is recorded, **I thought to myself that I had to do many things hostile to the name of Jesus of Nazareth**. Paul thought he was duty bound to oppose and suppress Christianity. He thought he owed it to his country, to his religion, to his God, to oppose in every manner the claims of Jesus of Nazareth to be the Messiah. Some of the things he did are explained in Acts 9:1ff.

Acts 9:1 tells us that even after some time had elapsed since the death of Stephen, Paul was **still breathing threats and murder against the disciples of the Lord**. "Still" recalls the record at Acts 7:58 and 8:1-3. We do not know the length of time occupied by the events in Samaria and Philip's mission, but all during that interval the persecution continued.

> When the church in Jerusalem had been scattered abroad, Saul doubtless thought that he had effectually destroyed the hated sect. But the news soon began to filter back from various quarters that the scattered disciples were establishing congregations in every direction. One less persistent than Paul might now have despaired of success in suppressing a faith which had thus far been promoted by every attack made upon it, and which seemed to gather renewed life from apparent destruction, but he had a will that rose to higher resolve as obstacles multiplied before it.[18]

---

[14] See Special Study #9, "The Sects of the Jews," for specifics concerning the doctrines of the Pharisees.

[15] *Antiquities*, XIII.10.6.

[16] Galatians 1:14.

[17] Acts 22:3, 26:7.

[18] McGarvey, *op. cit.*, p.168.

The Jerusalem church has been scattered, but Paul is not satisfied with that. The verb "breathing" is expressive of deep, agitating emotion, as when men breathe rapidly and violently under the weight of emotion. Every breath that Saul breathed encouraged him on to persecute the disciples of Christ. Every time he took a breath it seemed that new threats against the followers of Christ were uttered. And in the word "murder" is the idea that he intensely desired to put to death as many Christians as possible, thinking that in doing this he was doing God a service.

At Paul's direction his followers **bound and put both men and women into prison**.[19] The verb "lock up" in 26:10 speaks of "shutting down like a trap door." Saul's persecutions were of such a nature that he showed no mercy, even toward the women. Note that live Christians are called "saints" in 26:10.[20]

One thing Paul did was to try to make the arrested Christians speak words of blasphemy.[21] The tense of the verb **"force them to blaspheme"** implies the effort was repeatedly made. He did what he could to compel the Christians to say that they no longer believed that Jesus was the Messiah, but was rather an imposter. Or perhaps it means that he tried to get the Christians to utter words that could be termed "blasphemy" by the Jews, as had been done in the case of Stephen,[22] because the sentence of death could be passed by the Sanhedrin on anyone who was guilty of blasphemy.

I persecuted this Way unto death, he tells us in Acts 22:4. Luke frequently uses "Way" as a title or designation for Christianity. We have here the first occurrence of a term which seems to have been used familiarly as a synonym for the followers of Christ.[23]

- It may have originated in the words in which Christ claimed to be Himself the "Way," as well as the truth and the life.[24]
- It may refer to His language about the straight and narrow way that leads to life.[25]
- Perhaps it originated in Isaiah's prophecy, cited by the Baptist, about preparing the way of the Lord.[26]

Prior to the general use of the term "Christian," the designation "Way" served as a neutral, convenient name by which the followers of Christ could designate themselves, and which others might use who wished to speak of the followers of Christ. In this commentator's mind, it is doubtful that Paul personally put any Christians to death, but rather he committed them to prison, from which they would be taken, judged, and sentenced.

When the Christians were killed, Paul says, **I cast my vote against them**.[27] There

---

[19] Acts 22:4, 26:10.

[20] See notes at verse 14 on "saints."

[21] Acts 26:11.

[22] Acts 6:13ff.

[23] Acts 19:9,23; 22:4; 24:14,22.

[24] John 14:6.

[25] Matthew 7:13.

[26] Isaiah 40:3; Matthew 3:3; Mark 1:3.

[27] Acts 26:10.

is no specific account in Acts of any Christian being put to death, except Stephen, but there is no improbability in supposing that the same thing which first happened to Stephen also occurred in other cases. The Greek words (*katēnegka psēphon*) underlying "vote" literally mean "I cast down my pebble." The ancient Greeks (and Sanhedrin, too?) used white pebbles for acquittal, and black ones for conviction or condemnation. They literally cast the pebbles into an urn. Many think from this statement that Paul was a member of the Sanhedrin, and actually voted with them.[28] However, it is possible to take this language in a figurative sense, meaning "I gave my approval to the actions," without meaning that he was actually a voting member of the Sanhedrin. It may not be possible to determine whether or not Paul was a member of the Council, but this commentator leans against it. When he was standing over the garments at the time of Stephen's death, he was a young man, i.e., under 40, and thus would not have been eligible for membership in the Sanhedrin, unless he had really advanced beyond those of his own age.

In the course of doing many things contrary to Jesus of Nazareth, *he carried the persecution* **to many foreign cities**.[29] Paul's words seem to imply that Damascus is merely one of the cities outside Judea to which he carried the persecution. When he found Christians in any of those cities, they were either punished in the synagogues[30] or brought to Jerusalem to be punished.[31] Bringing Christians to Jerusalem implied the offense, since it was against the Holy Place and against the Law, was beyond the jurisdiction of the local courts that met in the synagogue buildings, and must be reserved for the Sanhedrin. After a trial before the Sanhedrin, the prisoner was freed, or beaten and freed, or killed.

As part of his preparations to go to Damascus, Paul **went to the high priest** (and to the Sanhedrin) **and asked for letters**.[32] "Went" indicates that Paul volunteered for the task. If our chronology is correct (see Introductory Studies), and the year is about AD 34 or 35, then the high priest is Joseph Caiaphas.[33] The letters were written and signed in the name and by the authority of the Sanhedrin. The high priest, as president of the council, signed them; but the authority of the Council lay behind the letters. The letters amounted to warrants for the arrest of Christians. The letters were credentials (i.e. authority),[34] implying a commission to Paul, that he had the right of requesting the aid of those addressed in ferreting out the Christians, and bringing them back to Jerusalem for trial and punishment.

The letters were addressed to the synagogues in Damascus.[35] The city of Damascus was located about 120 miles northeast of Jerusalem. One of the oldest cities in the world,

---

[28] A man had to be married and at least 40 years old to be a member of the Sanhedrin. If Paul were a member of the Sanhedrin, he was married at the time, and must then have been divorced (his Jewish wife divorcing him because he became a Christian?) or a widower by the time he wrote 1 Corinthians 7:7ff, for he was not married at that time.

[29] Acts 26:11.

[30] *Ibid*.

[31] Acts 9:2, 22:5.

[32] Acts 9:1-2, 22:5, 26:10.

[33] Barnes gives a different name for the high priest, but it would seem Barnes' chronology is in error.

[34] Acts 26:10.

[35] Acts 9:2.

Damascus was the ancient capital of Syria.[36] It was captured and brought under the dominion of Rome by Pompey, 64 BC.[37] The plurality of synagogues in Damascus indicated in Acts 9:2 suggests that the city contained a very large Jewish population. The Jews were so numerous in Damascus that 10,000, shut up unarmed in a gymnasium, were slain within an hour, and 18,000, with their wives and families, perished in a massacre during the reign of Nero.[38] The Jewish population in the mid AD 30's has been estimated at 40,000, with synagogues numbering 30 or 40. Julius Caesar and Augustus had granted the high priest and the Sanhedrin jurisdiction over Jews in foreign cities, as well as at Jerusalem. Christianity must have made considerable headway in Damascus in order for this persecution to be undertaken. By whom the gospel was preached there is unknown. Were there some present on the day of Pentecost? Did some of those persecuted Jerusalem Christians flee to Damascus and preach as they went?

3. Paul's Trip to Damascus

Paul started to Damascus **with the authority and commission of the chief priests**.[39] We are not told the method of travel Paul used in making this journey to Damascus. Artists have pictured him on horseback, camelback, or in a chariot. But the fact that, after the Lord appeared to him, they led him by the hand on into Damascus, indicates that they probably were on foot. There were several roads by which Paul could have made the journey. One was the Via Maris, the caravan road which led from Egypt to Damascus and kept near the coast line of Palestine till it struck eastward to cross the Jordan River at a point north of the Sea of Galilee. To connect with this road, Paul would first have had to go west from Jerusalem toward the Sea, till he intersected the road. A second road, the Way of the Patriarchs, led north from Jerusalem through Neapolis and crossed the Jordan south of the Sea of Galilee, and passed through Gergesa and on northeastward to the city of Damascus. A third possible route would be the road on the east side of the Jordan Valley by which the Galilean pilgrims sometimes traveled in order to avoid Samaria.[40]

He and those with him were **approaching Damascus about noon time**.[41] Assuming the journey to have been continuous, the approach to Damascus would come five to seven days after leaving Jerusalem.

Suddenly **a light out of heaven, brighter than the sun**, shown around him and those who were journeying with him.[42] The light must have been intensely brilliant to be brighter than the sun at noon in the Syrian desert. This does not appear to be a flash of lightning, as

---

[36] 2 Samuel 8:6; Isaiah 7:8.

[37] Josephus, *Wars*, II.20.2; *Antiquities*, VII.8.7.

[38] Josephus, *Antiquities*, XIV.2.3.

[39] Acts 26:12.

[40] The Way of the Kings, a highway which crossed the highlands east of the Jordan River, is perhaps too far east to be a possible choice for a route to Damascus.

[41] Acts 22:6, 26:13.

[42] Act 9:3, 22:6, 26:13.

some commentators suggest in an attempt to explain this as a naturalistic event. Nothing in the narrative suggests the thought of a sudden thunderstorm. In such a case, the gathering gloom and the dark rolling clouds would have prepared the traveler for the lightning flash. In fact, it is farfetched to suppose that Paul mistook a thunderclap for Jesus speaking to him, for the word Paul uses for "light" (*phōs*) is never used of lightning. The naturalistic suggestion that Paul was struck by a lightning bolt does not fit the record.

> A few radical scholars have tried to make the conversion of Saul nothing but a sunstroke, saying that in the heat of his anger and the heat of the desert he was overcome by a stroke! On the contrary, most fair-minded men see one of the most marvelous miracles of all revelation in the conversion of Saul. It is one of the greatest proofs for the resurrection of Jesus Christ, for Paul's conversion cannot be explained apart from the resurrection of Christ.[43]

The miraculous light was brighter than the sun. If men would attempt to disprove Christ's resurrection by finding a naturalistic explanation for the great change in Paul, they will have to come up with a better hypothesis than any put forward so far.

All of *the group* **fell to the ground**.[44] Here is another indication that Paul did not merely suffer sunstroke. The light was of such a nature that, when it shone upon them, the entire group was driven off their feet down onto the ground. It is unlikely that the kind of men traveling with Paul on their avowed purpose would have been unnerved without adequate cause. If he only had sunstroke, how is the fact that all fell to be explained?

A voice spoke to Paul in the Hebrew language.[45] That the voice spoke in Hebrew we learn only from Paul's speech to Agrippa and Festus in chapter 26. When Paul is speaking some other language than Hebrew (as he would have been before the assembly in Caesarea), he tells us in what language the voice spoke. The "Hebrew language" can be either Aramaic or pure Hebrew, as the one Greek word is used for both. The voice said, **"Saul, Saul, why are you persecuting Me?"** The order of words in Jesus' question is such that there is emphasis on "Me." "Me – why are you persecuting me?" The repetition of his name would fix Paul's attention. The particular interrogative form "why" implies "for what reason?" The Lord had done Paul no injury, had given him no provocation. For what reason, then, was Paul acting the way he was? Christ and His people are one.[46] To persecute Christians, as Paul was doing, is to persecute Him.[47]

Jesus continued to address Paul by asking, **"Is it hard for you to kick against the goads?"**[48] This is evidently an idiom, as Barnes shows,[49] listing the many Greek and Latin

---

[43] Dale, *op. cit.*, p.101.

[44] Acts 9:4, 22:7, 26:14.

[45] *Ibid*.

[46] John 15:1-6.

[47] Matthew 25:40,45.

[48] The words are genuine in Acts 26:14. The are a gloss in those manuscripts that also include them at 9:5 and 22:7.

[49] Barnes, *op. cit.*, p.156.

writers who used a similar expression. An ox-goad was a sharp piece of iron stuck onto the end of a heavy stick, with which the ox is urged on. The other end of the stick was flat, for cleaning the plowshare. It was also capable of being used as a formidable weapon.[50] The expression "to kick against the goad" is derived from the action of a stubborn and unyielding ox kicking against the goad. As the ox would gain nothing by the struggle and would injure no one but itself by the kicking, it comes to denote an obstinate and refractory disposition and course of conduct. In Paul's case, he was resisting the authority of Him who has a right to command, and opposing the leadings of Providence, to the injury of the one making the resistance. What was Paul kicking against? It was not a tortured conscience! The fact that he thought he was doing God a service prevents us from interpreting the remark about kicking against the goad as referring to the goading of conscience.[51] Elsewhere, Paul makes it clear that he had acted in all good conscience, even amidst his opposition to Christianity.[52] What was he kicking against then? A popular explanation is that he was resisting grace in his effort to keep the Law of Moses. In his effort to make men adhere to the letter of the Law, he was kicking against the grace of God which had been revealed in Christ. Yet the more he kicks (i.e., persecutes), the more the church grows!

To this question, *Paul answered,* **"Who art Thou, Lord?"**[53] Should the Greek word *kurios* be translated "Lord" or "sir" in this verse? Either is a proper translation of the word.[54] The general opinion of the commentators is that the word would be best translated "sir" – "Who are you, sir?" It is argued that it is evident Paul did not as yet know that it was the Lord Jesus speaking to him. He heard a voice as of a man; he heard his own name called; but by whom the words were spoken he was not sure. Paul seems to be saying, "Whose voice do I hear? Who is speaking to me?"

Paul is now informed that this was *Jesus revealing Himself to Paul.*[55] **"I am Jesus the Nazarene, whom you are persecuting,"** was the reply to Paul's question. This was a personal appearance of the Jesus the Savior to Paul; he actually saw the risen Lord.[56]

> It is impossible for us, who have been familiar with the story of the risen Christ from infancy, to fully realize the thoughts and feelings which flashed through the soul of Saul upon hearing these words. Up to this moment he had held Jesus to be an imposter, cursed of God and man, and His followers blasphemers worthy of death. But now this hated being is suddenly revealed to him in a blaze of divine glory. The evidence of eyes and ears cannot be doubted! There stands Jesus, with the light of heaven and the glory of God around Him, and He says, "I am Jesus." Stephen was right then, and I have shed innocent blood. "O wretched man that I am, who shall deliver me from the body of this death?"[57]

---

[50] Judges 3:31; 1 Samuel 13:19,21.

[51] Acts 26:9.

[52] Acts 23:1; 1 Timothy 1:13; 2 Timothy 1:3.

[53] Acts 9:5.

[54] For example, see John 4:15.

[55] Galatians 1:12, Acts 9:5, 22:8, 26:15.

[56] 1 Corinthians 9:1, 15:8.

[57] McGarvey, *op. cit.*, p.171.

Again, it should be noted that it was not the Christians alone whom Paul was persecuting. What was done to them, the Lord counted as done to Himself. And again let it be emphasized that Paul saw the risen Lord. Jesus appeared to Paul, not to convert him, but to qualify him to be an apostle (see below).

After they arose from the ground, **the men who traveled with Paul stood speechless.**[58] Who were these men with Paul?

- Some think they were Jewish soldiers. It is possible that these were a part of the Temple guard, which has been appointed to travel with Paul.
- Others suggest that they were Roman soldiers. Since the men with Paul **heard the voice but did not understand** what was said,[59] it has been asserted that they were Romans, else they would have understood what the voice said in Hebrew.[60]
- A third suggestion is that those with Paul were just chance travelers.
- A final suggestion is that those with Paul were men of the synagogue of the Hellenists who have volunteered to assist in the extermination of the Christians.

There is no contradiction in the record, as Luke in one place tells us they all *fell* to the earth at the appearance of the light, whereas he here tells us they *stood* speechless. In Acts 26:14, when the narrative refers to the immediate effect of the appearance of the light, they were all driven to the ground together. This was before the voice spoke to Paul. In Acts 9:7, Luke records what occurred after the first fright. There is no improbability that they rose from the ground immediately, and surveyed the scene with silent amazement. The word speechless (*eneoi*) properly denotes those who are so astonished or stupefied as to be unable to speak. They had seen the light but were not blinded by it as was Paul.[61] They had heard the voice of the Lord, but did not understand the words spoken to Paul.[62]

Paul now wants to know from the Lord what is expected of him. He asks, **"What shall I do, Lord?"**[63] Barnes, in error from thinking that Paul's conversion was instantaneous, understands this question of Paul's to mean, "Now that I am converted, what is it that I am to do with my life?"[64] It is better to understand that Paul is asking, "What shall I do

---

[58] Acts 9:7.

[59] Acts 9:7, 22:9.

[60] It is possible for even Jews to hear a voice speaking in Hebrew and not understand it. Those around the cross when Jesus was crucified did not understand when He spoke in the Hebrew language (Mark 15:34). So the fact the travelers did not understand the voice speaking to Paul is no proof one way or another whether they were Roman or Jewish.

[61] Acts 22:9.

[62] In the Introductory Studies, p.*xxvi-xxvii*, the alleged contradiction in Acts 9:7 v. 22:9 is explained. A similar instance occurs in John 12:28,29, when the voice of God came from heaven to Jesus. "The people who stood by and heard it said it thundered." They heard the sound, the noise — but they did not distinguish the words addressed to Jesus. So it is here in the case of the voice speaking to Paul.

[63] Acts 22:10.

[64] *Conversion is a process — not instantaneous.* The seed was planted in Paul's heart by the discussions with Stephen, and by Stephen's appearance as he died. Paul was impressed by and seriously thought on the death of Stephen. That Paul was not converted as yet will be seen clearly from the work Ananias will soon do with Paul. A person's conversion is not complete until he has been obedient in baptism. Baptism is the point at which there has been a change of state (see Romans 6:1ff).

to be saved?" The experience on the road was the turning point in Paul's life, but it did not make him a Christian. He was subdued but not saved. The surrender of a man's will in no way clears his case. Even Paul understood that there was something for him to do other than acknowledge the fact of the presence and power of Christ. Furthermore, Jesus is going to tell him to go into the city, and there it would be told him what to do to be saved. Paul must hear the gospel, which is God's power unto salvation. Paul is instructed to go to Damascus, and there it would be told him what to do. Jesus did not appear to Paul to make him a Christian; this task was left for men to do. Jesus sent him to a human agent, Ananias in Damascus, for the plan of salvation.

The Lord answered Paul's question by saying, **"Arise, (stand on your feet), and go into Damascus, and there you will be told all that has been appointed for you to do."**[65] Paul was not converted on the Damascus road, but in Damascus, through preaching and obedience to the gospel. Faith comes by hearing the Word of God, not through personal appearances by Jesus Himself.

Christ appeared to Paul for the following reasons: (1) To make him a minister and a witness of the things that would be subsequently revealed to him by God, and (2) to qualify him to be an apostle to the Gentiles. Let's examine both of these reasons.

- Acts 26:16 reads, **"For this purpose I have appeared to you, to appoint you a minister and a witness, not only to the things which you have seen, but also to the things in which I will appear to you."** "For this purpose" – not to take vengeance on Paul for his hostility to the gospel, but for the purpose about to be explained. "Appoint" is a word that carries the connotation of "chosen beforehand." "Minister," as used here, means a servant through whom the gospel is broadcast. A "witness" tells what he knows, what he has personally experienced. Jesus here promised to reveal Himself further to Paul, and Paul did later receive further revelations of the person and work of Christ, and of His purposes and will.[66] It is probable that many of these revelations occurred while Paul was in Arabia. Galatians 1:12ff tells us that Paul did not get his gospel from men, but through revelations – and the implication is that the time spent in the land of Arabia is the time when he received those revelations.

- Before one could be an apostle, he had to have seen the risen Lord.[67] He must also have been a witness of the earthly ministry of Jesus. Perhaps the revelations given in Arabia met this qualification in Paul's case.[68] We repeat, Jesus did not appear to Paul to save him. Had Jesus appeared to Paul to make him a Christian, He would have been saying, in effect, that His death and resurrection as proclaimed by the mouth of trustworthy witnesses could not save a sinner such as Paul. This would be contrary to Romans 1:16, 17 which says that, throughout this whole Church age, the gospel is the power of God unto salvation. This second reason for Jesus' appearance to Paul is more fully stated in Acts 26:17-18: **"Delivering you from *Jewish* people and from the**

---

[65] Acts 9:6, 22:10, 26:16.

[66] Acts 18:9, 22:18, 23:11; 2 Corinthians 12.1-7.

[67] Acts 1:22.

[68] See 1 Corinthians 11:23. Paul had detailed knowledge about the institution of the Lord's Supper, and he got his information directly from the Lord.

Gentiles to whom I am sending you, to open their eyes so that they may turn from darkness to light and from the dominion of Satan to God, in order that they may receive forgiveness of sins, and an inheritance among those who have been sanctified by faith in Me." "Delivering" is from the Greek word *exairoumenos*, which means both "to choose out, to select" one from many, and also "to rescue, to deliver." The "people" are the Jewish people (the NASB addition of "Jewish" in italics is a correct interpretation); and if the word is translated "delivering," then the idea is that God would rescue Paul when he was persecuted by the Jews. But if it is translated "to choose out," then the idea is that God has chosen Paul from among the Jews for a special purpose. "Delivering" is probably the right idea, for the rest of verse 17 seems to say that Paul would also be rescued from the Gentiles when persecuted by them. In fact, the word occurs four other times in Acts, and is uniformly rendered "deliver."[69] See also that Paul is being promised sufferings, dangers, and persecutions if he becomes the minister Christ wants him to be. The words "Gentiles to whom I send you" are Paul's commission to the Gentiles, and he later speaks of himself as the apostle to the Gentiles. "To open their eyes" means to instruct them, to help them see the truth of God. Ignorance is represented by the eyes being closed, and the instruction of the gospel by the opening of the eyes. Paul's preaching would help to turn the Gentiles from the darkness of heathenism and sin, to the light and purity of the gospel. "Darkness" in the Bible is often an emblem of sin and ignorance, and the heathen nations (in idolatry) are often represented as sitting in darkness.[70] In addition, the Gentiles are pictured as being under the dominion of the Devil.[71] The Bible tells us that the Devil is the prince of this age, the prince of the darkness of this world, the prince of the powers of the air, etc. The heathen world, lying in sin and superstition, is said to be under his control.[72] Now, Jesus says, Paul is going to be the vessel through whom the Gentiles learn about and receive forgiveness of sins. Compare "forgiveness of sins" at Acts 2:38 – forgiveness comes when a man is obedient to the preached word. The "inheritance" they would receive through Paul's labors was an heirship, or lot – that is, they were going to be entitled to the privileges and favors that pertain to the children of God. None but Jews were in the church at the time of Paul's conversion. Gentiles, also, Paul is being told, are to have a part in the blessings of the church and of heaven, along with the Jews who already had been sanctified.[73] And finally, Jesus tells Paul that these blessings and forgiveness are conditioned on faith in Himself.

Rising from the ground, and finding that he was blind, Paul was **led by the hand into Damascus**.[74] This commentator disagrees with Barnes at this place. Barnes does not seem to think the blindness was miraculous, but it would appear from Luke's record that it was. Paul was stricken blind by God. It was not just from his own attempts to look into

---

[69] Acts 7:10,34; 12:11; 23:27. Further, it would be difficult to construe how Jesus would be "choosing" Paul from among the Gentiles. So "deliver" is the better choice to translate this word.

[70] Matthew 4:16; John 8:12; Romans 2:14.

[71] Compare Colossians 1:13, 1 Peter 2:9.

[72] John 12:31; 2 Corinthians 4:4; Ephesians 2:2.

[73] Ephesians 1:3 works out this idea of joint heritage in greater detail.

[74] Acts 9:8, 22:11.

the light as long as he could that he is now unable to see, once the appearance of Jesus has ended.

> Saul at this time presents a sad and pathetic picture. Saul, the proud persecutor, clothed with authority from the Sanhedrin, now becomes the convicted, blind, and helpless one, and has to be led into the city of Damascus to wait for further instruction.[75]

The mission he had started out from Jerusalem to accomplish in Damascus is abandoned, and the letters to the synagogues are not delivered.

4. Paul's Conversion in Damascus

Paul was three days without sight, and neither ate nor drank.[76] The three days are likely to be understood according to the Jewish way of counting time, as including the rest of the day he arrived, the entire day following, and the portion of the day after that till the arrival of Ananias. He neither ate nor drank, probably because he was overwhelmed because of his sins, and thus gives no thought to any physical needs.[77] When a man is brokenhearted over his sins, and the way of duty is not clear, fasting is one natural action that follows. Verse 11 tells us that Paul spent much of this three-day period in prayer.

> Saul was no longer his own, so he was praying for further light and leading. He was not praying to "get religion" for religion is something one does, not something one gets! (See James 1:27.) He was in sorrow over his mistaken past and waited in prayer to the God he had always trusted and followed for the information Jesus had told him he would get in Damascus.[78]

A certain disciple named Ananias lived at Damascus.[79] We know him only as a "certain disciple," but he must have been a strong worker and perhaps a leader in the church at Damascus. Luke does not tell us when Ananias became a Christian. Perhaps he was one of those converted on the first Pentecost (Acts 2). Since at verse 13 Ananias speaks of Paul's persecuting career in Jerusalem as a matter of hearsay, we infer that he was not one of those who fled from Jerusalem because of the persecution that arose after the death of Stephen. He must have been a Christian before that. The special description of Ananias in Acts 22:12 was obviously given with a view to conciliate those who were listening to Paul's speech. Ananias is called **devout by the standard of the Law and well-spoken of**

---

[75] Boles, *op. cit.*, p.144.

[76] Acts 9:9.

[77] When comparing the notes in other commentaries, notice at this place the perplexity of denominational commentators who believe Paul was converted on the Damascus road. If Paul was converted on the road, why is he thus still overwhelmed? As in the case of the Ethiopian eunuch in chapter 8, once a man is converted, he goes on his way rejoicing. The only conclusion we can draw from Paul's actions is that he is not yet a Christian; he is still in his sins. The express statement of Ananias in Acts 22:16 indicates this to be the case.

[78] Dale, *op. cit.*, p.104.

[79] Acts 9:10, 22:12.

by all the Jews who lived in Damascus. Perhaps in earlier years Ananias was one of the 70 who had been sent out by Jesus, but this cannot be proved.[80] It may be that Ananias was simply an ordinary disciple – that is, not an evangelist or elder or deacon.[81] Still, it may be best to picture Ananias as a leader in the church at Damascus. He may well have been on Paul's list of known Christians, one who would have been punished or brought back to the city of Jerusalem in chains save for what happened on the Damascus road. God's wisdom can be seen in the selection of Ananias to be the one to go to Paul with the gospel message. A man well thought of by the Jews would help keep a breach from arising unnecessarily between the unconverted Jews and those who had been converted. One such as Ananias was not likely to connect himself with a profane blasphemer, nor to receive the repentant persecutor except on evidence that the change was God-approved.

Jesus appeared to Ananias in a vision, and called him by name.[82] The context in verses 10-16 clearly indicates that it was Jesus who appeared to Ananias. Luke first identifies the One who appeared in the vision simply as "the Lord." In reply to the Lord's call, **Ananias said, "Behold, here am I, Lord."**

The Lord told Ananias to go to the house of Judas, and restore Paul's sight. Verse 11 reads, **"Arise and go to the street called Straight, and inquire at the house of Judas for a man from Tarsus named Saul, for behold, he is praying."** Barnes gives a description of the city of Damascus, but we must remember that things today are not as they used to be, for the city has been captured and sacked and plundered many times since Paul visited it. The Greek word "street" speaks of a narrow lane (as in Luke 14:21). It is not the word for "broad thoroughfare" that we met in Acts 5:15.[83] Nothing further is known of Judas with whom Paul was staying. He may have been one of the Christians, or he may have been one to whom Paul had letters. "Behold he is praying" gives us a good indication of the manner in which Paul passed the three days. It is doubtful that the words imply that Paul never prayed before. Paul had grown up a strict Hebrew, a Pharisee who observed all rules, so he would have been a man of prayer.[84] Paul has prayed before, but the content of his prayer is different now. What was Paul praying about during these three days? Estimating the content of his prayer by what comes as an answer to it, we may think of Paul as requesting pardon for the past, light and wisdom for the future, strength to do the work to which he had been called, and intercession for those whom he had before persecuted unto the death. At any rate, Paul was no longer the persecuting Pharisee; and Ananias could feel free to make the trip down to Straight street, and to call at the home of

---

[80] Luke 10:1-24.

[81] If this be the case, Paul's thus becomes an example of a baptism performed by unofficial hands. It would show that the validity of the ordinance of baptism by no means depends upon its administration by an (ordained) officer of the church.

[82] Acts 9:10. The exact nature of the "visions" we find spoken of several times in Acts (e.g., 2:17; 9:10,12; 10:3,17,19; 11:5; 12:9; 16:9,10; 18:9; 26:19) cannot be completely determined, but see Kittel's *Theological Wordbook of the New Testament*, Vol. 5, p.350-352, 371-372.

[83] There is no street now called "Straight" in Damascus, except one so called by the Christians. It runs upward of a mile from east to west through the city, but it does not contain the traditional home of Judas which is shown elsewhere to visitors to the city.

[84] Some suggest, because of his Pharisaic background, that Paul's prayers before he met Jesus may have been like those of the proud Pharisee that Jesus used as an illustration of how not to pray (Luke 18:10).

Judas, where Paul was in prayer.

Jesus' instructions to Ananias continue, **"He has seen in a vision a man named Ananias come in and lay his hands on him, so that he might regain his sight."**[85] This tells us that while Paul was praying during those three days he had a vision – a vision of Ananias the preacher coming to visit him. Perhaps the vision was simultaneous with the one that Ananias had; i.e., Jesus appeared to Paul and to Ananias at the same time. In any case, Paul had been shown the answer to his prayer: Ananias was to come, lay his hands on him, and restore his sight. No doubt Ananias was one of those upon whom the apostles had laid their hands (in order to impart to him spiritual gifts), and thus he had the power to be able to correct the blindness of Paul.

Luke records in verses 13 and 14 what Ananias' answer to Jesus was. **"Lord I have heard from many about this man, how much harm he did to Thy saints at Jerusalem; and here he has authority from the chief priests to bind all who call upon Thy name."** In the Greek there is a "but" – "but Ananias answered." Ananias didn't want to have anything to do with Paul. The "many" from whom Ananias had heard of Paul's persecuting activities are probably fugitives who had fled from Jerusalem and taken refuge in Damascus. The words are of interest, for they show the duration and intensity of the persecution of which Paul had been the leader. It was so intense that report of it had spread far and wide. Verse 13 is the earliest use of the name "saint," a term that came to be a regular name for the Christians still living on earth.[86] How did the people in Damascus know the purpose for which Paul had come there? Perhaps running messengers had spread the news that the great persecutor was on his way to Damascus. It may well be that such men as Joseph of Arimathea and Nicodemus (identified as members of the Sanhedrin during the ministry of Jesus) would let the news out so that the people might be warned. At Acts 2:21 the expression "all that call upon Thy name" was explained as meaning prayer to the Lord Jesus, or total obedience to Him.

To Ananias' objection about going to Paul, Jesus replies, **"Go, for he is a chosen instrument of Mine, to bear My name before the Gentiles and kings and children of Israel; for I will show him how much he must suffer for My name's sake."**[87] Such is often the only answer given to the doubts and hesitations we voice about duty. Ananias found, as all others have who have ventured to argue against a command of God, that He listens to no such argument. McGarvey has an excellent paragraph on "chosen instrument."

> Jesus compares Saul to a carefully selected casket, in which a jewel rich enough for a present to a king has been deposited. Jewelers always keep costly gems in caskets of corresponding value; and so, when Jesus is about to send His name to kings and the great ones of the earth, He chooses this persecuting Saul as the fittest vessel in which to enclose it. The selection was a most surprising one to Ananias; but subsequent events proved its wisdom. Long afterward, Saul himself employed the same figure of speech, having doubtless caught it from the lips of Ananias; but he changes it materially, saying, "We have this treasure in earthen vessels, that the exceeding greatness of the power may be of God,

---

[85] Acts 9:12.

[86] Note, this usage of the word "saint" is contrary to the Roman doctrine of canonization of dead people into sainthood. All Christians are called saints because they are holy, or consecrated to God.

[87] Acts 9:15,16.

and not of us (2 Corinthians 4:6,7).[88]

Jesus chose Paul for service before Paul chose Jesus as his Lord. The word "chosen" (the same word is often translated "election") afterwards became a prominent word in the teaching of Paul. Paul the chosen instrument is to communicate knowledge about Jesus and the way of salvation to the Gentiles, and kings, and to the Jews, Ananias is told. Paul comes to be known as the apostle to the Gentiles,[89] and he did preach to kings,[90] and to the Jews too.[91] Wherever Paul went, he preached the gospel first to the Jews, then to the Gentiles. He had made others suffer for Christ; he had persecuted them even unto death. Now he is to suffer as he had caused others to suffer, Jesus tells Ananias. This prediction was fully carried out.[92]

After the vision was ended, as Jesus commanded him to do, *Ananias came to where Paul was staying.* His mission was twofold: to restore Paul's sight, and to see that Paul received the Holy Spirit. Verse 17 reads, **"And Ananias departed and entered the house, and after laying his hands on him said, 'Brother Saul, the Lord Jesus, who appeared to you on the road by which you were coming, has sent me so that you may regain your sight, and be filled with the Holy Spirit.'"** The use of the word "brother" by Ananias has caused some comment. Barnes thinks this is an expression recognizing Paul as a fellow Christian,[93] but this does not seem to be correct, for Paul has not yet been immersed for the remission of his sins. The address as "brother" must then be no more than a term of endearment intended to allay Paul's fears. Paul was not converted until he was baptized into Christ (as he himself taught to be true in all cases of conversion, Romans 6:3,4), and a man should not be called a Christian until he is converted. Since Paul had not been baptized into Christ when Ananias first addressed him, "brother" can hardly be an "expression recognizing him as a fellow Christian." Notice also that Ananias clearly indicates that Paul actually saw the risen Lord on the Damascus road. "The Lord Jesus, who appeared to you on the road," Ananias says.

The first thing that Ananias came to do for Paul was accomplished, for verse 18 indicates, **"And immediately there fell from his eyes something like scales, and he regained his sight."** Years later, Paul recounts the incident in these words, **"And at that very time I looked up at him."**[94] The Greek word translated "scales" is *lepides*, which comes from a verb meaning "to peel." Luke does not say that actual "scales" came off his eyes, but that it felt to Paul like something was peeled off his eyes. This is a miraculous healing, just as the blindness was miraculously caused. Some have suggested that this left a permanent defect in Paul's eyesight, and often appeal to Galatians 4:15 as evidence that Paul's eyesight was poor. But if there was a defect after the healing, it is the only case in

---

[88] McGarvey, *op. cit.*, p.176.

[89] Romans 11:13, 15:16; Galatians 2:8.

[90] Acts 25:23, 26:32, 27:24; 2 Timothy 4:16.

[91] Acts 9:20-22, 13:46, 28:17.

[92] Acts 20:23; 2 Corinthians 11:23-27; 2 Timothy 1:11-12.

[93] Barnes, *op. cit.*, p.161.

[94] Acts 22:13.

Scripture record where a person miraculously healed was left with any after-effects or defects.[95]

The second part of Ananias' mission to Paul was to see that Paul received the Holy Spirit. Ananias put it this way when he spoke to Paul, **"Jesus ... sent me so that ... you may be filled with the Holy Spirit."** Barnes thinks this refers to the baptism with the Holy Spirit (like at Acts 2:4), but he fails to distinguish between the indwelling gift of the Holy Spirit and the baptism of the Holy Spirit. Instead, Ananias is apparently talking about the indwelling gift of the Holy Spirit (like at Acts 2:38). We have learned in Peter's first recorded sermon that all who repent and are baptized receive the Holy Spirit. Now, immediately after restoring Paul's eyesight, Ananias preached the gospel to Paul and urged him to **"be baptized, to wash away his sins."** In fact, here in verse 18, right after saying he received his sight, Luke tells us that Paul was baptized. The parallelism in verses 17 and 18 is most elucidating. In verse 17, Ananias says, "regain your sight and be filled with the Holy Spirit." Then in verse 18, Luke tells us it happened. But instead of saying it in wording as we might expect (i.e., 'he regained his sight, and was filled with the Spirit'), Luke actually writes, "he regained his sight and was baptized." Surely, by this, Luke is saying that the baptism of Paul had something to do with his being filled with the Spirit![96]

Before Paul comes to an obedient faith and receives the Holy Spirit, he must hear the gospel. This is the same process that any one goes through who becomes a Christian, for faith comes by hearing the word of God (Romans 10:17). So Ananias preached to Paul, ending the message by telling him to be baptized (Acts 22:14-16). Ananias also said, **"The God of our fathers has appointed you to know His will, and to see the Righteous One, and to hear an utterance from His mouth."** Jesus had used this same word "appointed" as He was speaking to Paul on the road, and it carries the idea of "choosing beforehand."[97] God's "will" could be the plan of salvation, or, perhaps, God's plans for Paul's future life here on earth, that Paul was to be a chosen instrument to the Gentiles. "The Righteous One" he was to see was the Christ. Since Paul was to be an apostle, and since it was the peculiar function of an apostle to bear witness to the person and deeds of the risen Lord, it was necessary that Paul should see the risen Lord, that thus he might be a competent witness of His resurrection. Ananias speaks of Paul's "hearing an utterance from His mouth," which means that Paul should hear and obey the commands of Christ. Then Ananias continued, **"For you will be a witness for Him to all men of what you have seen and heard."** The words Ananias is now speaking to Paul are the very words that Jesus had earlier spoken to Ananias, and are similar to what Jesus had told Paul on the Damascus road. The only way Ananias could be repeating such language, Paul would know, was that Ananias had been divinely instructed concerning Paul's case. That Paul should be a "witness" is exactly identical with the commission given to the Twelve (Acts 1:8), and it placed Paul on a level with them. And what had Paul seen and heard, about which he could witness? There was the proof of his own divine mission to the Gentiles which he himself

---

[95] And there certainly are other ways to explain Paul's large handwriting in the Galatian letter (Galatians 6:11) and the Galatians' willingness to pluck out their eyes and give them to Paul, than attributing these to poor eyesight.

[96] See this problem discussed in detail in McGarvey, *op. cit.*, p.177-178.

[97] See notes at Acts 9:7, and the reference to the parallel passage in Acts 26:16.

had experienced. There was the inescapable proof of Jesus' resurrection from the dead (had not Paul seen the risen Lord?), which also served to show that He was the Messiah of the Old Testament prophets. Ananias concludes his exhortation to Paul by saying, **"And now why do you delay? Arise, and be baptized, and wash away your sins, calling on His name."** 'Why wait any longer,' Ananias asks. 'You believe in Jesus as the Christ (proof of Paul's belief is found in that he is not carrying out his intended persecution); you have repented of your sins (three days in prayer and fasting). You are a suitable candidate for baptism. Why wait any longer to receive forgiveness of your sins?' "Be baptized" literally means "cause yourself to be baptized," i.e., allow someone to dip you (i.e., the verb is middle voice in the Greek). Baptism is connected with the washing away of sins. This verse is strongly indicative of the fact that a person's sins are not forgiven in God's mind until the time that person is obedient in baptism. A person's sins are washed away (forgiven), not previous to, but at the time of baptism. Here is further evidence, were it needed, that Paul was not saved on the Damascus road, for a person is not saved until his sins are forgiven. Paul still had his sins, three days after his Damascus road experience, as is evident from the fact that Ananias is here telling him how to have them now forgiven. Note also that Ananias instructs Paul to be in prayer while he was being baptized ("calling on the name of the Lord"). A prayer for pardon, evidently, is intended.

Paul did as the Ananias exhorted him to do. Verse 18 tells us, **"He arose and was baptized."** The place where he was immersed is not specified by Luke, but the river Abana runs through Damascus, and would be a likely place for a baptism.[98] Ananias was probably the one who did the dipping of Paul so that Paul's sins might be forgiven. Now the Holy Spirit part of Ananias' coming has been taken care of, too, for the indwelling gift of the Holy Spirit was connected with the baptism for the forgiveness of sins (Acts 2:38).

Verse 19 then says, **"And [Paul] took food and was strengthened."** During the three days since Jesus appeared to him on the Damascus road, because he has been overwhelmed with a sense of his sins, Paul has eaten nothing. That he now eats following his baptism implies that the sense of burden and remorse is gone – and this agrees with the promise of forgiveness of sins in baptism.

Paul, now a Christian, spent some days with the Christians in Damascus, also preaching Jesus in the synagogues there.[99] Luke records it on this fashion, **"Now for several days he was with the disciples who were at Damascus."** Ananias was far from being the only Christian in Damascus. The section we are now entering causes not a little difficulty to those attempting a harmony of the life of Paul.

- Based on Paul's use of the word "immediately" at Galatians 1:16, Lightfoot thinks Paul left for Arabia immediately after his conversion. He thus places this paragraph about Paul's preaching in the synagogues at a time after his return from that country.[100]
- Meyer puts Paul's departure into Arabia after the "several days" of verse 19, and also after Paul's preaching Christ in the synagogues of Damascus in verse 20.[101]

---

[98] J.W. McGarvey, *Lands of the Bible*, p. 551-558 tells about the rivers and the pools of Damascus.

[99] Acts 9:19-22.

[100] J.B. Lightfoot, *The Epistle of St. Paul to the Galatians* (Grand Rapids: Zondervan, 1957), p.90.

[101] Meyer, *op. cit.*, p.190. Verse 20 says Paul's preaching in the Damascus synagogues took place

- This commentator is inclined to agree with Meyer. Verse 23, where Luke says "many days," is the likely place in the Acts account to insert Paul's three years in Arabia (Galatians 1:17). If this is correct, then verses 19-22 tell us that for perhaps a month or so after his conversion Paul has fellowship with the Christians at Damascus.

And immediately he *began* to proclaim Jesus in the synagogues, saying, "He is the Son of God." Earlier in these comments, we noted the plurality of synagogues in Damascus. Paul visits several of these during their Sabbath meetings, and in each one he speaks about Jesus being the Son of God.[102] How is it that Paul was invited to speak? It was customary to invite distinguished guests to address the assembled worshipers.[103] Some think that at this time Paul was already speaking by inspiration of the Holy Spirit.[104] Perhaps he was, but Paul could have preached at this juncture without being inspired. He could have referred to the Old Testament prophets in which he had been schooled. He could repeat the sermons that Stephen preached.[105] He could well testify to the resurrection and glorification of Jesus of Nazareth. And if any man in Damascus doubted Paul's truthfulness, he had but to ask Paul's traveling companions about the reality of the light which had flattened all of them to the ground. And his physical blindness (perhaps better known to the Jews than to the Christians, if Judas with whom he stayed was a Jew) certainly was not the result of imagination. From personal experience Paul could preach some powerful sermons, all without needing to be aided by Holy Spirit inspiration. At this time, of course, he would not know all the facts of the gospel (many of which he will learn during his stay in Arabia). But even without those later revelations, Paul knew enough to do some powerful preaching; and he makes an intense effort to convert the Jews of Damascus to the faith.

The *reaction of the Jewish hearers* to Paul's sermons is now documented. **And all those hearing him continued to be amazed, and were saying, "Is this not he who in Jerusalem destroyed those who called on this name, and who had come here for the purpose of bringing them bound before the chief priests?"**[106] This was asked by Jews who heard his preaching, not by Christians, whose inquiries about him had already been answered, else he would not have been welcome among them. The worshipers in the synagogues were amazed at the sudden and complete change in this one-time persecutor. Somehow, this verse tells us, the Jewish sector of Damascus had become aware of why Paul had left Jerusalem and headed for their city. Perhaps the reason they had all come was shared with the Jewish population by those who had accompanied Paul. He intended

---

"immediately" after his conversion.

[102] "Son of God" as a title for Jesus is used only here in Acts by Luke. It was the designation of the Messiah commonly received among the Jews (John 1:49).

[103] Remember how Jesus was the speaker in the synagogue at Nazareth (Luke 4:14ff). For further information, see Special Study #15, "The Synagogue and Its Services," at the close of chapter 13.

[104] Paul was, doubtless, baptized with the Holy Spirit – a measure of the Spirit that would enable and qualify a man to do the work of an apostle. But we do not know at just what point in his life this occurred. This commentator's idea from the records is that it took place while he was in Arabia.

[105] During his time as a student, Paul would have developed his ability to memorize as a speaker was speaking. Further, men have a hard time forgetting those arguments advanced by others which they cannot answer. Paul would have remembered what he heard preached by Stephen and others.

[106] Acts 9:21. Luke has already told us about Paul's attempts at destroying the Church in Acts 8:3, though the word used there is different than the one here.

to destroy the Church, if possible. And now he is preaching in behalf of Christ and His Church! Astounding!

But Saul kept increasing in strength and confounding the Jews who lived at Damascus by proving that this Jesus is the Christ.[107] Paul's preaching, which kept becoming better and better, would necessarily excite opposition in those who had not accepted Christ. Paul would give the reasons for the change he had made, the reasons for believing that Jesus was the Messiah, the Son of God. As he did so, opposition would increase against him, and Paul would necessarily have to increase "the more in strength" if he were going to be convincing and demonstrate that he had no doubt that Jesus was the Christ. Luke tells us that Paul "confounded" them. This is one translation of the word *sugchunō*, and would mean that Paul bested them in the discussion over the Old Testament Scriptures and the identity of Jesus as the long-awaited Messiah. The word can also mean "tumult" or "excitement," so that it is possible that Paul, by his preaching, did exactly the same thing in Damascus that Stephen did by preaching in the synagogues at Jerusalem. The unbelieving Jews were not able to meet his arguments, so they rose up against him. The phrase "proving that this Jesus is the Christ" is instructive. "Proving" is from the verb *sumbibazō*, which means to unite, to compare, to put things together. What Paul did was to make a comparison of the Old Testament prophecies and the facts from the life of Jesus; and then he would draw the inescapable conclusion that Jesus must be the promised Messiah, else how could the perfect agreement between the two be accounted for?

5. Paul in Arabia

Paul went away to Arabia and stayed about three years, he himself tells us in Galatians 1:17-18. We place this break in Paul's life into the Acts narrative at verse 23, where Luke tells us that **"many days had elapsed."**[108] The capital city of Arabia would have been the rock city of Petra. Some think Paul went there, but the exact place to which he went is in dispute. Lightfoot suggests El Belka (northeast of the Dead Sea), or the region about Damascus, or the region near Mt. Sinai.[109]

Why did Paul go to Arabia? The hypothesis that Paul's journey into Arabia was not for the purpose of preaching, but for the purpose of meditating on his new relationship to Christ and for clearly thinking through what his new theology will be (though adopted by Alford, Lightfoot, Farrar, etc.) may not be the whole truth. We are not to picture Paul as forging and hammering out his own theology by sheer mind power. It was during this time that Paul was receiving revelations from God that determined his theology for him. Galatians 1:11ff, in which Paul tells us about the trip to Arabia, has this as its thesis that he

---

[107] Acts 9:22.

[108] In the Introductory Studies, we dated Paul's conversion a full three years before his escape from Damascus in AD 37. It is possible that there was less time between his conversion and escape than a full three years, for according to Jewish reckoning, a part of the year in which he was converted, a whole year, and a part of the one in which he escaped, would be "three years." Since "three years" could actually be little more than 18 months, Paul's conversion could be dated in AD 35 or AD 36, rather than in AD 34 as we have dated it.

[109] J.B. Lightfoot, *The Epistle of Paul to the Galatians* (Grand Rapids: Zondervan, 1957), p. 87ff.

did *not* get his gospel from men, but by direct revelation from God. The implication is that many of the revelations about Jesus that he received happened while he was in Arabia. It is also very possible that Paul spent much of the time there preaching and evangelizing.

6. Paul Back in Damascus

Returning to Damascus from Arabia, Paul again preached in the synagogues that Jesus is the Christ.[110]

The Jews plotted together to do away with Saul, but their plot became known to him.[111] They designed a scheme to capture and kill Paul. He was a powerful preacher before he went to Arabia; and now, with further knowledge about Jesus as a result of all the revelations he had received, Paul's skill and success would enrage the Jews. They knew of no other way to silence him and free themselves from the effects of his arguments and influence than to kill him. Just as in Stephen's case, the Jews were not able to withstand the arguments of God's preacher, and hence resorted to persecution and violence and intimidation.

The *governor of the city,* under Aretas, *guarded the city,* in order to capture Paul.[112] At this time in history, cities were surrounded by high walls pierced at intervals by gates through which men and animals could enter and leave the city. Not being aware that Paul knew of the plot, his enemies suspected that one day Paul would attempt to leave the city through one of these gates; so they stationed guards at the gates to intercept him. If, as we have suggested in the Introductory Studies, Aretas has just recently captured Damascus, it may be that the governor he appointed was a Jew. This would explain how the governor would be party to the plots of the Jews in the city. Or if he were not a Jew, the Jews who were there might easily represent Paul as a criminal, and demand that he be captured. Thus, a guard would be furnished to them for their purpose. The date of these activities, as shown in the Introductory Studies, cannot have been before AD 37.

The plot became known to Saul, and he in turn evidently communicated the intelligence to the *disciples, who helped him escape from the city* during one night. **His disciples took him by night, and let him down through an opening in the wall, lowering him in a basket.**[113] "His disciples" would be those who became Christians because of Paul's preaching. The Greek word translated "basket" commonly is used to denote the basket in which food was carried.[114] It was a wicker basket or a rope-work hamper. Other ropes would have been attached to the basket; and then with Paul in it, it would have been lowered out through the opening in the wall, and down to the ground.[115] Thus Paul avoided

---

[110] Galatians 1:17; Act 9:23.

[111] Acts 9:23-24.

[112] 2 Corinthians 11:32.

[113] Acts 9:25.

[114] The same word *spuris* is used in the account of the feeding of the 4000 (Matthew 15:37, 16:10).

[115] 2 Corinthians 11:33. One preacher, because of familiarity with modern customs in some Eastern cities, suggests that Paul was let down in a garbage basket. People put the garbage out in baskets like this,

7. Paul Again in Jerusalem

About three years after his conversion, *Paul returns to Jerusalem,* having just escaped death at Damascus.[116] Imagine the trip from Damascus to Jerusalem.

> Early in the night's journey he passed the spot where Jesus had appeared to him. We shall not attempt to depict his emotions when the walls of Jerusalem and the battlements of the temple came once more into view. As he approached the city, he saw the place of the crucifixion; and he may have passed near the spot where Stephen was stoned, and where he himself was consenting to his death. He was about to meet again, on the streets and in the synagogue, his old allies whom he had deserted, and some of the disciples whom he had persecuted. The tumult of his emotions we leave to the imagination of the reader, and their portrayal to the pages of the more voluminous writers (like Conybeare and Howson, or Farrar) while we follow Luke's account of his reception among the disciples at Jerusalem.[117]

Once he arrived in Jerusalem, Paul **was trying to associate with the disciples; and they were all afraid of him, not believing that he was a disciple.**[118] The verb "associate" is regularly used of close and intimate fellowship.[119] Paul wanted the Jerusalem Christians to accept him, and to have a sense of belonging with their group. The Christians, however, had misgivings for several reasons, but primarily because they remembered his former violence against Christians. He had been absent for three years. Had they heard of him during that time? Even if they had heard rumors about his conversion, might they not be suspicious? Paul's escape from Damascus had been too hurried, else he might have obtained letters of commendation from the brethren in Damascus to help make his introduction to the church at Jerusalem.

Having befriended Paul, *Barnabas introduced him to Peter and James* and told how he had been converted at Damascus.[120] Why should Barnabas be the one to take this special interest in Paul? Is there a possibility they knew each other from an earlier association together? Since Barnabas' home was on the island of Cyprus (and Cyprus was considered a part of the province of Cilicia), perhaps both had attended the university in Tarsus together in years gone by. Or perhaps Barnabas had affinities for Paul since both grew up in the same province outside of Palestine. Perhaps it is best to see the friendly actions of Barnabas as being part of his nature (since he was the son of consolation, Acts 4:36). Gala-

---

expecting it to be picked up the next morning; thus no one would be suspicious of a basket being lowered down the side of the wall. Then, when it was dark enough, Paul could make his way out of the basket and down the road.

[116] Galatians 1:18; Acts 9:26.

[117] McGarvey, *op. cit.*, p.187.

[118] Acts 9:26.

[119] Cf. Acts 10:28; Matthew 19:5; Luke 15:15, 1 Corinthians 6:16.

[120] Galatians 1:19; Acts 9:27.

tians 1:18-19 tell us that the only apostles in Jerusalem at the time were Peter and James, the brother of the Lord. The other apostles may have been away on preaching tours, of the kind like Peter and John had made earlier (Acts 8).

As he introduced Paul to the Christians, he **described to them how Paul had seen the Lord on the road, and that He had talked to him, and how at Damascus he had spoken out boldly in the name of Jesus.**[121] This seems to indicate that the apostles at Jerusalem had not yet heard of the conversion of Paul, or it may be that they had heard rumors and are now told the facts in the case. How Barnabas knew what had transpired, we are not told. Had he asked Paul for the particulars, and did he know by the gift of discerning of Spirits that what Paul told him was the truth?

Paul **stayed in Jerusalem for 15 days, becoming acquainted with Peter**, and also evangelizing with the apostles Peter and James.[122] Paul was admitted to their friendship and recognized as a fellow Christian and as an apostle (he had been called to be an apostle to the Gentiles). It would take no little amount of forgiveness on the part of many who had lost loved ones to his persecutions to welcome this one into their fellowship. On the expression "moving about freely" found in verse 28, which describes Paul's activities while in Jerusalem these fifteen days, see notes at Acts 1:21. It is a phrase that denotes constant companionship.

The ex-persecutor also **spoke out boldly in the name of Jesus**, and **disputed with the Hellenistic Jews** (in their synagogue?).[123] Paul appears to be right in the same synagogue where he before had debated with Stephen. Only a few years before, he had defended the same position his hearers are now in, and he had tried to refute the very same arguments he was now espousing. Paul is seeking to undo the evil that he had then done, by preaching to them the faith which he had then opposed, in an effort to win them to Christ.

The Hellenistic Jews now seek to kill Paul.[124] He could not preach Jesus as Messiah to these Jews without antagonizing them. Yet he did not shrink, but spoke boldly to them as did Stephen. And as they had done with Stephen, they resisted Paul's teaching and sought to kill him. Twice within a few weeks, first at Damascus and now at Jerusalem, Paul's life was in danger.

Now, at the same time the Jews are completing the details of their current plot against Paul's life, *Paul went up to the temple to pray, and there the Lord appeared to him, telling him to flee from Jerusalem.*[125] Paul himself words it this way, **"While I prayed in the temple, I fell into a trance."** A trance must have been something similar to a vision.[126] It

---

[121] Acts 9:27.

[122] Galatians 1:18-19; Acts 9:28. The verb used in Galatians for "get acquainted with" is in harmony with Paul's emphasis in that book that he received his gospel by revelation, rather than from men, for the verb means to become acquainted with, not to get information from.

[123] Acts 9:29. The word "disputed" is the same word commented on at Acts 6:9.

[124] Acts 9:29.

[125] Acts 22:17-21.

[126] See also comments at verse 10 and footnote #82 above, and compare comments at Acts 10:10,17. Barnes seems to be in error when he suggests that this is the time when Paul was caught up to the third

probably occurred during one of the Jewish hours of prayer when Paul was in the temple. He continues, **"I saw the Lord saying unto me, 'Make haste, and get out of Jerusalem quickly, because they will not accept your testimony about me.'"** Jesus is likely referring to the Hellenistic Jews in particular. Then Paul tries to argue with the Lord, **"Lord, they themselves understand that in one synagogue after another I used to imprison and beat those who believed in Thee. And when the blood of Thy witness Stephen was being shed, I also was standing by approving, and watching out for the cloaks of those who were slaying him."** Paul is saying that the decided change in his life should be evidence to the Jews that Jesus really is the Messiah, else he would not have changed so radically. Paul was convinced the Jews would listen if Jesus would just let him stay there and preach. But in the same way that the Lord Jesus would not hear the argument put forth by Ananias, so He now does not accept Paul's suggestion. **"And He said to me, 'Go! For I will send you far away to the Gentiles.'"** In effect, the Lord is saying, 'Depart, for your life is in danger here, and I have plans for you elsewhere.' In the years to come, Paul would travel far and wide in the lands where Gentiles lived. A large part of his ministry was spent in remote countries, and in the most distant regions then known.

8. Paul in Tarsus and Antioch

When they were told by Paul what had happened in the temple, **the brethren brought him down to Caesarea and sent away to Tarsus.**[127] Though the Jerusalem Christians were at first hesitant and apprehensive about Paul the Christian, thanks to the work of Barnabas, Paul has now been accepted as a brother by the Jerusalem church. This is evident from the fact that when he needs help to escape, they give him all the help they can. "Brought" means either that they accompanied him to Caesarea, or they gave him the provisions necessary for the trip. Caesarea was the chief seaport for the area since it had been built by Herod the Great. That Paul went to the seaport suggests he went by ship to Tarsus.[128] Subsequent events in Paul's life lead us to the conjecture that his parents did not accept him when he arrived home to Tarsus, but rather disinherited him when they found out he had become a Christian.[129]

Paul will next be seen at Antioch, where he is brought by Barnabas to help in the evangelistic work there.[130] If our chronology of Paul's life and the Acts record is correct:

---

heaven, an event that took place about 14 years before the writing of 2 Corinthians 12:1-5 (i.e., ~AD 44). If the being caught up to the third heaven took place ~AD 44, it was about the time of the beginning of the first missionary journey, or some seven years after these events of Acts 9.

[127] Acts 9:30.

[128] Some commentators have thought Paul came to Caesarea and then walked the Via Maris highway north toward Tarsus. They suggest this because of the order of words in Galatians 1:21, "Syria and Cilicia." That is the order you would come to the provinces if you were on foot going north from Caesarea.

[129] Philippians 3:8. Though he "suffered the loss of all things," it is still true he had a sister in Jerusalem who must have been friendly to him; at the very least, Paul's nephew was a friend to Paul (Acts 23:16). Perhaps it is saying too much to affirm that Paul was disinherited and to find proof of it in Philippians 3:8, yet that is the natural meaning the verse suggests.

[130] Acts 11:22-26; Galatians 1:21-24.

- Paul was converted about AD 34.
- About AD 37, he returned from Arabia to Damascus, only to have to flee for his life, whereupon he went to Jerusalem, from which he also has to flee.
- When next see Paul in Antioch of Syria, it is about AD 40 or 42.

We do not know much about these silent years between AD 37 and 42. Certainly, the writers are wrong who suggest that the time was spent in transition from one way of life to another – from Judaism to Christianity. We doubt that he had to hammer and shape his new theology, and that his theology was in the process of change and development through all these years. It would be more in harmony with the zeal and convictions of Paul to say that he met the hardest years of his life during this almost silent period. At a later time, Paul gives a short record of his sufferings, and few of these events are accounted for in the book of Acts.[131] Of the things recounted in that record, we know of only one shipwreck, but he had been in three others that we know nothing about. And when and where did he spend the night and day in the ocean before he was rescued? We know of one of the times he was scourged, but he speaks of five. Where and when did he almost drown in crossing rivers? Following the natural sequence of thought, it should be expected that his change from the years of his training to the preaching of Christ would have brought him his worst years of opposition and suffering. It should be expected that childhood friends, members of his family, and devout Jews of the hundreds of synagogues in the territory around Tarsus would have been bitter and caused him much suffering in the years he spent there. It would also have been normal for Paul to make Tarsus his headquarters for evangelizing in Cilicia and Syria. And there is evidence (e.g., Galatians 1:21) that Paul did use Tarsus as a center of evangelistic work. Importantly, Acts 15:41 mentions churches already organized in this area which had not been founded during what is called the "first missionary journey" of Paul and Barnabas; these must therefore have been planted by Paul during these "silent years." His call to the church at Antioch by Barnabas (Acts 11:25), where so many Gentiles had accepted Christ, would have been in line with the work he had already been doing.

D. Another Period of Peaceful Growth. 9:31-43

1. The Church Edified. 9:31

9:31 – ***So the church throughout all Judea and Galilee and Samaria enjoyed peace, being built up; and, going on in the fear of the Lord and in the comfort of the Holy Spirit, it continued to increase.***

So the church throughout all Judea and Galilee and Samaria enjoyed peace. Some versions read "churches" (see the KJV), and others read "church." In the better manuscripts, the Greek is singular. At this time there were congregations scattered all over Judea, Galilee, and Samaria, but all the churches together in a given geographical area make up the church, since all the congregations are but "members" of the body of Christ.

---

[131] See this record in 2 Corinthians 11:24-32, where what he suffered is listed.

These three provinces made up the land of Palestine. The planting of the church in Galilee has not been expressly mentioned by Luke before this, but there is no improbability in supposing that Christians had traveled there and preached the gospel as Acts 8:4 suggests.

They enjoyed peace because the persecutions against the church have ceased for the first time since the death of Stephen. There were likely two key reasons for this. First, the persecutors (at least their leader) were exhausted. Second, the unsettled political situation in Palestine may have lent greatly to the cessation of the opposition to the church. Caligula became emperor in AD 37. In AD 39 or 40, Petronius was appointed governor of Syria, and Caligula ordered him to set up a statue of the emperor in the temple at Jerusalem. Josephus tells us about it:

> Caligula ordered Petronius to go with an army to Jerusalem, to set up his statue in the temple there; enjoining him, if the Jews opposed it, to put to death all who made any resistance, and to make the rest of the nation slaves. Petronius therefore marched from Antioch into Judea with three legions and a large body of auxiliaries raised in Syria. All were hereupon filled with consternation, the army being come as far as Ptolemais. [The Jews were] abandoning their cities, villages, and open country, and going to Petronius in Phoenicia, both men and women, the old, the young, the middle-aged; and throwing themselves on the ground before Petronius with weeping and lamentation.[132]

The Jews had to use all their energies to prevent this form of idolatry, and so had little time to give any attention to the church. It was not till the emperor Caligula was assassinated in AD 41 that they were delivered from this threat. Then the persecution of the church will begin again (Acts 12:1).

Being built up. Some commentators believe this word is shorthand for the idea that more formal leadership like elders and deacons were elected and began to function. Perhaps it is, since we do find elders in the churches (Acts 11:30) even though no specific mention of them has been made earlier. But perhaps the word means no more than the church experienced orderly and continuous growth, both in numbers and in holiness of life.

And, going on in the fear of the Lord. "Going on" has the sense of "living." The word often is used to denote Christian conduct and manner of life. The word picture is of travelers who are going to a place and who are walking in the right path in order to get there. Christians are, in a sense, travelers to another country, a heavenly country. And the right path for them to walk is "in the fear of the Lord," i.e., reverence for Him and scrupulous obedience to His commandments.

And in the comfort of the Holy Spirit. The Holy Spirit, the Comforter, had been promised to the Church, and here we see Him at work. See notes at Acts 4:36, where it was noted that this word "comfort" includes also the ideas of counsel and exhortation. Thus, the meaning of this phrase is that the words of counsel and encouragement which came from the Holy Spirit as He spoke through the New Testament prophets were the chief agents in the expansion of the church.

---

[132] Josephus, *Antiquities*, XVIII 8.7-9.

It continued to increase. This seems to involve both an increase in the number of places to which the gospel was successfully carried, and a gain in the number of believers in the places where the gospel had previously been preached. Again, this growth came from the Christians walking in the fear of the Lord and from the comfort of the Holy Spirit!

2. Peter Cures Aeneas at Lydda. 9:32-35

9:32 – *Now it came about that as Peter was traveling through all those parts, he came down also to the saints who lived at Lydda.*

Now it came about that as Peter was traveling through all *those parts.* "Those parts" would be Galilee, Samaria, and Judea, the areas just named where the church had peace. Peter seems to have stayed at Jerusalem all through the times of persecution. Now he visits the churches all over the area, and in these visits he is fulfilling the charge Jesus gave him that morning on the shore of the sea of Galilee.[133]

He came down also to the saints who lived at Lydda. At verse 13, we learned that "saints" are ordinary Christians. Perhaps these people are Christians as a result of the evangelistic work done by Philip,[134] or perhaps they have come here as refugees.[135] The town of Lydda was located on the road that led from Jerusalem to Caesarea, about 20 miles northwest of Jerusalem and ten or twelve miles southeast of Joppa. In the Old Testament, the town was called Lod, as it is called in modern Israel. A church flourished here for years.[136]

9:33 – *And there he found a certain man named Aeneas, who had been bedridden eight years, for he was paralyzed.*

And there he found a certain man named Aeneas. This is a Greek name, and Aeneas was probably a Hellenist.[137]

Who had been bedridden eight years, for he was paralyzed. The word for "bed" was explained in notes at Acts 5:15 as referring to the little pallets used by the poorer people. A paralyzed man could have no way of earning a living and would likely be in great poverty, which would add to his suffering.

---

[133] John 21:15-17. See the instructions to feed His sheep and tend His lambs.

[134] Acts 8:40.

[135] Acts 8:4.

[136] A bishop of Lydda was present at the Council of Nicea in AD 325, and also one was at the Council of Constantinople in AD 451. For a time, the Romans renamed the town Diospolis (i.e., "City of Zeus"). A church council was held there in AD 415, at which Pelagius was acquitted of heresy, and thereupon Jerome spoke of "that miserable synod of Diospolis."

[137] The ability of a Greek name alone to tell us the ethnicity of a person has been discussed in footnote #27 in chapter 6.

9:34 – *And Peter said to him, "Aeneas, Jesus Christ heals you; arise, and make your bed." And immediately he arose.*

And Peter said to him, "Aeneas, Jesus Christ heals you. Peter claimed no power to perform the miracle himself. Compare Acts 3:6.

Arise, and make your bed." This would show his healing was complete. He was commanded to get up from the pallet, and take care of it in the manner in which beds were arranged when they were not in use during the daytime. He was commanded to do that which others had had to do for him for eight years. Did Peter remember the time when four men brought a paralyzed man to Jesus at Capernaum, and how Jesus had commanded the man to "Arise, take up thy bed, and go into thy house"?[138]

And immediately he arose. Be sure to see that here we have another example of an instantaneous healing. Healings in the Bible were regularly instantaneous.

9:35 – *And all who lived at Lydda and Sharon saw him, and they turned to the Lord.*

And all who lived at Lydda. "All" is probably not absolute, but instead speaks of the greater part of the population.

And Sharon. Sharon was the coastal plain, about 30 miles long extending from Mt. Carmel on the north to Joppa on the south.[139]

Saw him, and they turned to the Lord. The miracle would capture the people's attention and credential the message of salvation preached by Peter and the other Christians. Aeneas had been paralyzed long enough that the miracle would be much more impressive. In the word "turn" we hear Luke telling us they heard the gospel, repented of their sins, and were baptized into Christ, thus becoming part of the Church.[140]

3. Peter Raises Dorcas at Joppa. 9:36-43

9:36 – *Now in Joppa there was a certain disciple named Tabitha (which translated in Greek is called Dorcas); this woman was abounding with deeds of kindness and charity, which she continually did.*

Now in Joppa there was a certain disciple. Joppa was a seaport town situated on the Mediterranean Sea coast, about 30 miles south of Caesarea, and about 35 miles northwest

---

[138] Mark 2:1-11.

[139] Isaiah 33:9, 35:2.

[140] See Acts 3:19 for comments on the word "turn." "Turn to the Lord (Jesus)" is the language regularly used of converts from Judaism to Christianity (cp. 2 Corinthians 3:16; but see notes at Acts 11:21). "Turn to God" is the regular term for conversions from among the Gentiles (see Acts 15:19; 1 Thessalonians 1:9).

of Jerusalem. It served as the seaport for Jerusalem in Old Testament times,[141] until it was supplanted by Caesarea's harbor which Herod the Great had built. This is the first reference to Joppa in the Scriptures since Jonah 1:3. It was twice destroyed by the Romans, and rebuilt.[142] As was true with Lydda, there is evidence that the church continued in this town through the years, for a bishop from here was present at the council of Ephesus in AD 431.

Named Tabitha (which translated *in Greek* is called Dorcas). Tabitha is the Aramaic name, Dorcas the Greek. Both words mean "antelope, gazelle." It was not unusual in the East to give daughters the names of beautiful animals. "There is nothing said about a husband, and so it is inferred that she was unmarried," Boles writes.[143] Actually, no hint of her age or condition in life is given. Finding her among widows might imply she too was one. She is the first woman named in Acts since Sapphira (Acts 5:1ff).

This woman was abounding with deeds of kindness and charity. In a moment the women will show coats and garments to Peter which had been made by Dorcas. Perhaps she was a seamstress who made clothing for the poor and the widows as her Christian service. "Abounding with" tells us her life was characterized to a very high degree by these acts of kindness and charity to the poor.

Which she continually did. The verb tense is imperfect, implying that she was in the habit of doing these deeds of kindness. In many congregations there are thoughtful women like Dorcas who seem to have a knack for doing the beautifully helpful thing just at the right moment. What a blessing a woman like this is to the congregation, and what a loss is felt when such a woman dies.

9:37 – *And it came about at that time that she fell sick and died; and when they had washed her body, they laid it in an upper room.*

And it came about at that time that she fell sick and died. Dorcas fell sick and died about "that time" when Peter was in Lydda (verse 38). Luke does not tell us what the disease was with which she suffered and died. Perhaps (judging from the result, verse 42) this was one of those sicknesses for the glory of God.

And when they had washed her body. Among most people it has been customary to wash the body before it is buried or burned. Apparently, they did not finish whatever customary preparations would ordinarily have been made for burial, because they have something else come to mind rather than interment.

They laid it in an upper room. In the comments about the rapid burial of Ananias and Sapphira, we noted the reason for such hasty burials. Decomposition sets in rather rapidly in hot climates. That Dorcas is not quickly buried is evidence of a conviction that Peter could, by the help of God, raise her from the dead.

---

[141] 2 Chronicles 2:16.

[142] Josephus, *Wars*, II.18.10 and III.9.2.

[143] Boles, *op. cit.*, p.156.

9:38 – *And since Lydda was near Joppa, the disciples, having heard that Peter was there, sent two men to him, entreating him, "Do not delay to come to us."*

And since Lydda was near Joppa. See comments at verse 32. The towns were only ten or twelve miles apart. If Peter were sent for, he could be back before the body decomposed too much.

The disciples, having heard that Peter was there. Once more we ask the question about these disciples, as we have asked about disciples in other towns, are these the result of the evangelistic work of Philip?[144]

Sent two men to him. Why send men to Peter? Because they wanted Peter simply to come to comfort them? If so, what comfort were they expecting he could he give that was not already included in the gospel that had been preached to them? Apparently, they anticipated that Peter would raise her from the dead. Have other dead people been raised by Peter? If so, there is no record of such. But it is likely there have been some, else where did the conviction arise that he could help in Dorcas' case?

Entreating him, "Do not delay to come to us." They were very urgent in their request for Peter to come at once, as interment would have to be done, at the latest, on the following day.

9:39 – *And Peter arose and went with them. And when he had come, they brought him into the upper room; and all the widows stood beside him weeping, and showing all the tunics and garments that Dorcas used to make while she was with them.*

And Peter arose and went with them. We wonder how the apostles knew if they were going to be able to work a miracle in any given case? Did Peter know, when he started out with the messengers, that he was going to raise the dead woman?

And when he had come, they brought him into the upper room. Peter was with Jesus when He entered the room where the body of Jairus' daughter lay. We may think that Peter asked to be taken to where Dorcas' body had been laid.

And all the widows stood beside him weeping. Probably these widows had been aided by the kindnesses of Dorcas. Or perhaps they had been associated with her in the good works which marked her life. Luke's language here seems to imply some kind of regular charitable organization or administration similar to what was found at Jerusalem in Acts 6. Very likely we see the work of the evangelist Philip, who was one of those chosen to wait on the widows at Jerusalem. The widows are "weeping," yes, but there is none of the "great lamentation" that regularly characterized Jewish households at the time of a death in the family. Was Chrysostom right, when he suggested that death had come to be regarded more calmly in the light of Jesus' resurrection and the believer's blessed hope of being raised to be with Jesus? See 1 Thessalonians 4:13-18.

---

[144] Acts 8:4,40; 9:32.

And showing all the tunics and garments that Dorcas used to make while she was with them. The widows had lost a benefactor and associate, so it was natural that they should recall her deeds of kindness and charity, and express their gratitude by enumerating the proofs of her goodness. The scene Luke pictures is quite vivid: to see the prostrate body of Dorcas lying cold and stiff in death, and to hear the weeping widows sobbing in sorrow for the loss of their friend and sister. This must have made a very strong appeal to Peter. "Tunics" (*chitōnas*) are a "shirt-like undergarment," while "garments" (*himatia*) are the "outer garment, the mantle." Were these widows wearing the garments she had made (the verb "showing" is in the middle voice)? Or were they showing garments that together they had helped make for others while she was still alive?

9:40 – *But Peter sent them all out and knelt down and prayed, and turning to the body, he said, "Tabitha, arise." And she opened her eyes, and when she saw Peter, she sat up.*

But Peter sent them all out. As suggested in verse 39, we think Peter must have remembered what Jesus did as they came to Jairus' house to raise his daughter.[145] Why Peter sent the others out of the room is not explained. Perhaps it was because he did not wish to appear to be seeking publicity, or personal fame.

And knelt down and prayed. We find prayers offered from all different kinds of postures in the New Testament. As explained in comments at Acts 2:42, the posture is not the important thing; the attitude of heart is. For what was Peter praying? Was he praying that the Lord might give him the ability to work this miracle?

And turning to the body, he said, "Tabitha, arise." That is, after finishing his prayer, Peter turned and addressed the body in the words, "Tabitha, arise!" In Aramaic,[146] Peter said, *"Tabitha cumi!"* In a similar circumstance, Jesus had said, *"Talitha cumi!"* ("Little girl, get up!").[147] At Joppa, using almost exactly the words Jesus had used, Peter called Dorcas back to this life.

And she opened her eyes, and when she saw Peter, she sat up. Does she recognize him, or is Peter a stranger to her? We do not know. But she arose as one does when waking from sleep.

9:41 – *And he gave her his hand and raised her up; and calling the saints and widows, he presented her alive.*

And he gave her his hand and raised her up. Peter offers his hand to her to encourage her to make the effort to get out of the bed.

And calling the saints and widows, he presented her alive. It is almost as if Peter were introducing people who have never met. He has to present her to them, to overcome their

---

[145] Mark 5:40; Luke 8:54.

[146] Peter's use of her Aramaic name has been taken as an indication that he was speaking Aramaic.

[147] Mark 5:41.

hesitancy. She was living, where just a few moments before, she had been dead.

> Here the narration closes, as well it might; for not even Luke's graphic pen could describe the scene which followed. And if the restoration of one saint to the little band which she has left is indescribable, what shall we say or think of that hour when all the sainted dead shall rise in glory and greet one another on the shores of life?[148]

9:42 – *And it became known all over Joppa, and many believed in the Lord.*

And it became known all over Joppa, and many believed in the Lord. Throughout the book of Acts, Luke emphasizes over and over again that the purpose of miracle is to credential the message. And here, when the message is credentialed by the raising of Dorcas, there is a multitude of people who become believers. Time and again, Luke tells us about people becoming believers right after he tells us about one of the miracles that God performed through the apostles or the spiritually gifted believers.

9:43 – *And it came about that he stayed many days in Joppa with a certain tanner, Simon.*

And it came about that he stayed many days in Joppa. If "many days" in verse 23 was Luke's expression for the three years Paul spent in Arabia, perhaps we can picture Peter staying several years in Joppa. Was there such a number of prospective converts that Peter was needed this long in Joppa? Or had Philip won so many that it required this length of time for Peter to minister among them until they were built up in the faith? The close of the "many days" brings us to a time not far from AD 40, as the following chapter of Acts shows.

With a certain tanner, Simon. A tanner is a person who converts hides into leather. Because he worked with graves, carcasses, and hides of dead beasts, the tanner ran a high risk of being ceremonially defiled. It was an occupation that the stricter Jews would avoid. At Acts 10:6 we learn that Simon's house is by the sea shore. Tanners' workshops were required by law to be kept at a distance of 50 cubits from the walls of any town. If a tanner, about to marry, kept his trade a secret from his fiancée until after they were married, the contract of marriage was automatically voided. Since the house of a tanner was so repulsive to the strict Jew, it may be that Peter is already gradually getting away from old Jewish prejudices. His stay with Simon the tanner will help prepare him for the vision and experience that is about to be related in chapter 10.

---

[148] McGarvey, *op. cit.*, p.197.

A city of Judæa

E. The Conversion of the First Gentile (Cornelius) to Christianity. 10:1-11:18

1. Peter at Caesarea. 10:1-48

    a. Cornelius sends to Joppa for Peter. 10:1-8

10:1 – *Now there was a certain man at Caesarea named Cornelius, a centurion of what was called the Italian cohort,*

Now *there was*. Chapter 10 commences a very important part of the history of Christianity. Luke's estimate of the importance of the conversion of Cornelius is shown by the amount of space given to it; this account is given in greater length and more detail than the account of the conversion of thousands at Jerusalem. Before this, the gospel had been preached to the Jews only. And this was as God planned, for He had spent centuries preparing the chosen people for the coming Messiah. But the gospel of Christ was intended for all nations. The Old Testament prophets had predicted the inclusion of the Gentiles in a covenant relationship with God,[1] and Jesus had clearly taught that His good news was for Gentiles as well as Jews. The Great Commission spoke of preaching to every creature.[2] Just a few days before He ascended, Jesus spoke of the apostles' witness as being "to the uttermost parts of the world." God is now ready to fully reveal His purpose to include the Gentiles, and the case of Cornelius is the instance through which He does it.

It is noteworthy that God selected Peter for the purpose of preaching the gospel first to the Gentiles. This is in harmony with the events at Caesarea Philippi – where, after making the good confession of Christ, Peter was told that to him would be given the keys of the kingdom.[3] Peter used those keys for the Jews' benefit on the day of Pentecost. He is now about to use the keys to open the door of the church to the Gentiles.

From what follows in the next chapters of Acts, it is clear that the conversion of Cornelius opened the way of salvation to the Gentiles, enabling the apostle Paul to march across Europe with the gospel, converting scores of Gentiles. When the Lord ordered Paul away from Jerusalem, He said He would send him "far away to the Gentiles," but at the time Paul was given that charge no Gentiles had yet been admitted to the church.[4] Luke will now show how Peter opened the door of the kingdom for their admission.

A certain man at Caesarea named Cornelius. Caesarea at this time was the most prominent city in Palestine, and was virtually the capital.[5] It was built by Herod the Great

---

[1] Paul makes references to some of the prophetic announcements of the inclusion of the Gentiles in Romans 9:24ff.

[2] Mark 16:15.

[3] Matthew 16:18-19.

[4] Acts 22:21.

[5] Tacitus, *History*, II.29; Josephus, *Antiquities*, XIV.8.2. Caesarea had a very fine harbor, secured by a breakwater constructed at enormous cost by Herod. Extensive ruins today cover the greatest area of any city in Palestine visited by this commentator.

as a seaport, and was named in honor of Caesar Augustus. Caesarea was at this time the usual residence of the Roman governor of Judea, and consequently a garrison of troops was regularly found here. Cornelius is a Latin name, and shows that the man was probably a Roman. The population of Caesarea was mixed, some Jewish, but preponderantly Gentile. A massacre in the streets of 20,000 of the Jewish section was one of the first events of the war that led to the destruction of Jerusalem in AD 70.[6]

A centurion of what was called the Italian cohort. He was commander of a "century" in the Roman army, that is, he commanded 100 men. A "cohort" was composed of from six to ten centuries, and a Roman legion was made up of six cohorts plus 150 horsemen. He was not the commander of the whole cohort, but only of a small segment of the cohort.[7] The whole cohort was made up of soldiers from Italy.[8] This cohort was one of the best Rome had; and, since the soldiers were all Italians whose loyalty was above question, perhaps they were the governor's bodyguard.

10:2 – *a devout man, and one who feared God with all his household, and gave many alms to the* Jewish *people, and prayed to God continually.*

A devout man. The word translated "devout" (*eusebēs*) is not the same word Luke used at Acts 2:5 and 8:2. This word used here in verse 1 appears to have been a special designator for that special type of devotion to God which would be found in proselytes of the gate.[9]

And one who feared God. Many 1st century men were very thoroughly dissatisfied with their pagan religions and gods. Many were looking for something better than the idolatry they had learned from their parents. Perhaps that was what was back of Cornelius' becoming a proselyte of the gate. That he was such a proselyte is implied by the fact that he is keeping the Jewish hours of prayer.[10] While stationed in Palestine, we think of him as becoming interested in the Jewish religion and learning to have a reverence for Jehovah.

With all his household. It is implied that Cornelius had instructed and influenced his family and servants, and trained them in the fear of God. Not satisfied with having found a higher truth for himself, he sought to share it with those most under his influence.

And gave many alms to the *Jewish* people. This is the second time in recent verses in Acts that the NASB has the word "Jewish" in italics where the Greek has simply "people" (*laos*).[11] One of the primary meanings for the Greek word, however, is its use to designate

---

[6] Josephus, *Wars*, XX.18.1.

[7] Some have ventured the opinion that Cornelius was the centurion in charge of the crucifixion of Jesus, and who exclaimed, "Truly this was the Son of God"; but the opinion is incapable of proof.

[8] Other cohorts were composed of soldiers born and conscripted in the provinces.

[9] See comments at Acts 2:10 for an explanation of "proselyte of the gate" and "proselyte of righteousness."

[10] Cornelius is not a proselyte of righteousness, for Peter understood that he was a foreigner (verse 28), and the rest of the Jews knew that Cornelius was not considered to be one of them (Acts 11:3).

[11] See also Acts 26:17, which was reviewed in the comments on chapter 9 as part of the Harmony of the

the *Jewish* people, and so the translators have not gone beyond what the original suggests. To find a Roman soldier who was liberal in his charity toward the occupied peoples must have been a striking contrast to the usual practice of the legionnaires, for there was a special hatred and contempt for each other both by Jews and Romans.

And prayed to God continually. He was observing the Jewish hours of prayer, we learn from verses 3 and 30. A question that often requires an answer concerns what prayers of a sinner are heard by God. Maybe the prayers of Cornelius will help us learn the answer to the question. If what happened may be regarded as an answer to his prayers, then we may believe that he has been praying for guidance and help to know what to do to have his sins forgiven. What God did in Cornelius' case should serve as an encouragement to sinners today who would seek similar forgiveness.

> Let us not fail to observe that here is the prayer of a man not yet wholly converted to Christ, and that the prayer is answered. But how different is the answer from that which persons in similar spiritual condition are taught to expect in our own time. The angel does not bring him word that his sins are forgiven, nor does the angel leave him rejoicing in the forgiveness of sins because he is assured his prayers are heard. Instead of this, he is told to send for a man who will tell him what he must do to be saved. If similar prayers were answered now, who can doubt that the same God would answer them in the same way, by telling the inquirer to send for the preacher, or for some other disciple, who would rightly instruct him?[12]

10:3 – *About the ninth hour of the day he clearly saw in a vision an angel of God who had just come in to him, and said to him, "Cornelius!"*

About the ninth hour of the day. That is, 3:00 p.m., one of the regular hours of prayer.[13] This was the usual hour of the evening sacrifice among the Jews.

He clearly saw in a vision. Cornelius saw the vision while he was praying (verse 30).[14] A vision was but one of the different ways in which God revealed Himself to people. Lightfoot lists, in addition to visions, these different ways: dreams, apparitions while awake, visions while asleep, a voice from heaven, the Urim and Thummim, inspiration (auricular revelation), and a sort of rapture or ecstasy such as is spoken of in Genesis 2:21, 2 Corinthians 12:2 and Revelation 1:10.[15] The adverb "clearly" seems added to distinguish this vision from those given while one is asleep, and to distinguish it from a trance (e.g., compare Acts 10:10).

An angel of God who had *just* come in to him, and said to him, "Cornelius!" See Acts 1:10-11 for notes about angels. This angel showed himself in human form (verse 30).

Early Life of Paul.

[12] McGarvey, *op. cit.*, p.201.

[13] See notes at Acts 3:1 concerning the Jewish hours of prayer.

[14] At Acts 9:10 are notes concerning visions.

[15] Quoted by Dale, *op. cit.*, p.112.

10:4 – *And fixing his gaze upon him and being much alarmed, he said, "What is it, Lord?" And he said to him, "Your prayers and alms have ascended as a memorial before God.*

And fixing his gaze upon him. Cornelius gave such attention to the angel as was necessary to satisfy himself that he was simply seeing more than another human being standing before him.

And being much alarmed. The alarm was the result of the suddenness and unexpected nature of the vision. People have always shown alarm at the visit of angelic messengers.

He said, "What is it, Lord?" By these words, Cornelius gives expression to his feelings of surprise and alarm. *Kurios* (as at Acts 9:5) can be translated either "Lord" or "sir." Boles says "Lord" is correct. He writes, "It seems that Cornelius recognized the angel as a messenger from God; hence, he addressed the angel as 'Lord.'"[16] Others think that "sir" would be better, as there is no evidence that Cornelius regarded the personage as present from the Lord. In Greek thought, the word expresses respect, and this appears to be all that Cornelius means by it. In response to Cornelius' question, the angel reveals his mission.

And he said to him, "Your prayers and alms have ascended as a memorial before God. The word "memorial" was used in the Old Testament of a vegetable sacrifice which was burned on the altar together with frankincense and which produced a sweet, aromatic smoke which ascended toward heaven and, as it were, caught the attention of God and commended the worshiper's prayers to Him. Another meaning for "memorial" is "that by which the memory of any person or thing is preserved." This Roman soldier's prayers and alms had been observed by God, and God had not forgotten him. The angel is saying that Cornelius' prayers have been heard, and now an answer to them was on its way.

It should be observed from this paragraph of God's Word that morality does not save!

> At first glance it might appear strange that a man whose character is thus as has just been described should need conversion. There are many in the present day in whose favor not so much can be said – yet who flatter themselves that their prospects for final salvation are good. They are honest and honorable in their dealings with men, good spouses and parents, generous to their neighbors, and benevolent to the poor; what have they to fear at the hands of a merciful God? But Cornelius was all this, and beyond this he was a devout and prayerful man – yet it was necessary for him to hear words whereby he might be saved (Acts 11:14). Our present-day self-righteous men of the world must be deceiving themselves. They forget that while they are discharging in a creditable manner their obligations to their fellowmen, they are neglecting the much higher obligations to render direct service to God by observing His ordinances. The most inexcusable of all sins is a refusal to render to God, our Maker and Redeemer, the homage that is due to Him.[17]

Though the angel had spoken to Cornelius, and though God had heard his prayers, he must yet hear words from another person's lips before he will be saved. Watch Luke's nar-

---

[16] Boles, *op. cit.*, p.161.

[17] McGarvey, *op. cit.*, p.198.

rative as it continues, to see what words were spoken, and what they contained that was so necessary.

10:5 – *"And now dispatch* **some** *men to Joppa, and send for a man* **named** *Simon, who is also called Peter;*

And now dispatch *some* **men to Joppa, and send for a man** *named* **Simon, who is also called Peter.** See Acts 11:14 where we are told that the angel also explained to Cornelius that Peter would "speak words to you by which you will be saved." The doctrine of the direct operation of the Holy Spirit on a sinner's heart to save him is surely suspect in light of what was done in Cornelius' case. In his case, instead of direct operation, we see human agency involved. Someone must bring the Word (since faith comes by hearing the Word of God, Romans 10:17) so the sinner has something to believe.

Philip the evangelist was probably already living in Caesarea.[18] Why wasn't Cornelius told to get in touch with him? Why send for Peter? As has been indicated above, Peter has the "keys of the kingdom of heaven." Therefore, he is the one to first share the terms of pardon with the Gentiles, just as he had done with the Jews on the day of Pentecost. The "Simon" Cornelius is to contact is the one called Peter, not the one called "the tanner."

10:6 – *"he is staying with a certain tanner* **named** *Simon, whose house is by the sea."*

He is staying with a certain tanner *named* **Simon.** An angel may have something to do with a man's salvation. One did in Cornelius' case. See just what the angel did.

> It is interesting and instructive to observe that we here have another instance of the intervention of an angel in securing the conversion of a man. In comparing the angel's work in this case with that of the one who appeared in the case of the eunuch (Acts 8:26), we observe that though the latter appeared to the preacher, and the former to the person converted, both appeared for essentially the same purpose; that is, to bring the preacher and the subject for conversion face to face. Thus we learn that supernatural interventions never supersede the indispensable work of the human agent. Even when the Lord Himself, as in the case of Saul's conversion, appeared to the sinner, the human agency was still indispensable; and the Lord Himself directed Ananias to go to the still unforgiven Saul. These facts cannot be too urgently pressed upon the attention of an age like ours, in which they are totally ignored by the majority of religious teachers.[19]

Whose house is by the sea. The process of tanning hides requires a considerable amount of water to convey away the filth produced in the operation of dressing the hides, so they were often located by rivers or other large bodies of water.

10:7 – *And when the angel who was speaking to him had departed, he summoned two of his servants and a devout soldier of those who were in constant attendance upon him,*

And when the angel who was speaking to him had departed. The vision Cornelius was

---

[18] Acts 8:40.

[19] McGarvey, *op. cit.*, p.201.

having evidently ended with the angel departing, apparently walking away as a man would walk away, rather than just vanishing as Jesus sometimes did at the close of His resurrection appearances.

He summoned two of his servants and a devout soldier of those who were in constant attendance upon him. Officers in the army often have the services of men of lower rank, who may do cooking, cleaning, chauffeuring, or act as couriers. In addition to a devout soldier (note that military life does not preclude personal religion) to wait on him, Cornelius also had some slaves (marginal reading, "household slaves") provided for him from among the peoples that had been captured and were now dominated by the Romans. It may be that the soldier has been influenced toward the worship of the true and living God by the example of his commanding officer. On the word "devout" see notes at Acts 10:2.

10:8 – *and after he had explained everything to them, he sent them to Joppa.*

And after he had explained everything to them. Cornelius told them about what the angel had spoken to him.

He sent them to Joppa. "It has been remarked that from Joppa, Jonah was sent to preach to the Gentiles at Nineveh, and that from the same place Peter was sent to preach to the Gentiles at Caesarea."[20] It may have been late in the afternoon, but Cornelius is anxious to know more about how to be saved. He dispatches the messengers at once.

      b. Peter has a vision about clean and unclean things. 10:9-16

10:9 – *And on the next day, as they were on their way, and approaching the city, Peter went up on the housetop about the sixth hour to pray.*

And on the next day, as they were on their way, and approaching the city. The distance from Caesarea to Joppa is 30 miles, so the trip would take a full day's travel. In fact, in order to arrive at noon on the day after they left Caesarea, the messengers would have had to journey through most of the night.

Peter went up on the housetop. It is helpful to remember that houses in Palestine usually were built with flat roofs, with a stairway that led up to the roof. The roof served the same purposes in that country that porches and patios do in our country in the summer. Around the edge of the roof was a parapet (Deuteronomy 22:8), built for safety reasons. Once he was on his roof, a person could have a sense of privacy, for he was usually concealed from public view by a parapet.

About the sixth hour to pray. The time is about 12 noon, a regular time of prayer for a devout Jew.[21]

---

[20] Adam Clarke, *Commentary on the Whole Bible* (New York: W. and P.C. Smith, 1823) Vol. 5, p.771.

[21] See notes at Acts 3:1 concerning the regular Jewish hours of prayer.

10:10 – *And he became hungry, and was desiring to eat; but while they were making preparations, he fell into a trance;*

And he became hungry, and was desiring to eat. The Greek word translated "hungry" is *prospeinos*, and means "very hungry." The regular first meal of the day was about two hours late, and Peter is beginning to note his hunger. In Luke 14:12 we find the words "luncheon" and "dinner," which were the names of the two meals which regularly made up the diet of Jews, Greeks, and Romans in the 1st century world. The first of these was taken about 10 or 11 o'clock in the morning, and consisted of fruit, milk, cheese, etc. The principal meal was then eaten about 6 or 7 o'clock in the evening.

But while they were making preparations, he fell into a trance. The Greek says an ecstasy (*ekstasis*) fell on him. In classical Greek, *ekstasis* has the meaning of frenzy, often produced by artificial means, such as the concentration of the mind on some abstract idea or significant word, or by whirling, or by music and furious dancing. In this artificial sense, the intellectual activity is supposed to be heightened because the mind is dominated by emotional excitement and the control of the will is, for the moment, held in abeyance. Peter's trance was not artificially induced; he didn't try to self-manufacture such a state. Rather, the state came on him. His senses were partially suspended (for a time he forgot his hunger and all other things around him) while he concentrated his attention on the object coming down from the sky. Peter's senses are not so suspended that he no longer knows what is right or wrong (verse 14).

10:11 – *and he beheld the sky opened up, and a certain object like a great sheet coming down, lowered by four corners to the ground,*

And he beheld the sky opened up. Compare what is said at Acts 7:56. It is almost as if a sliding door up in the sky was shoved back, making a sort of trap-door opening through which the object can be lowered from above.

And a certain object like a great sheet coming down. It was not an actual sheet, but it appeared to be like a sheet.

Lowered by four corners to the ground. We picture that the "sheet" had "ropes" attached to the four corners, by which it seemed to Peter's gaze to be let down through the opening in the firmament above. The Greek word translated "corners" is the word usually translated "beginning." The word had a fluid meaning much like our own word "ends," and therefore the translation "corners" gives the proper idea.

10:12 – *and there were in it all* **kinds of** *four-footed animals and crawling creatures of the earth and birds of the air.*

And there were in it all *kinds of* **four-footed animals.** The particular point of the vision is that a law peculiar to the Law of Moses is going to be called into question. The vision is designed to teach Peter an important lesson in regard to the introduction to the gospel to all nations: certain distinctions that used to hold true are no longer true. "Four-footed" would include sheep, oxen, swine, rabbits, and wild animals of all kinds.

And crawling creatures of the earth. Snakes, lizards, etc.

And birds of the air. The sheet Peter saw contained a mixture of both clean and unclean animals. Leviticus 11 and Deuteronomy 14 give the Old Testament regulations used to distinguish between the two classes.

A general distinction between clean and unclean meats was made by various nations in antiquity. Some animals were recognized as fit for food and sacrifice, while others were not. When God gave the Law at Sinai, such a distinction was continued. Unclean animals were classified as follows:

1) Beasts that do not part the hoof entirely and chew the cud (Leviticus 11:3-4), including all that go on four paws (verse 27). This limitation accordingly admits only animals of the ox, sheep, and goat kind, and deer and gazelles (Deuteronomy 14:4-5) in the "clean" category. It excludes among other animals all carnivorous beasts because they eat blood and carrion, and were therefore intolerable to the Israelites.

2) Winged insects which, in addition to four legs, do not have two hind legs for leaping (Leviticus 11:20-23). All insects were unclean therefore except the locust (i.e., grasshopper).

3) Carnivorous birds, of which 20 or 21 are specially named (Leviticus 11:13-19; Deuteronomy 14:12-18). The enumeration included the bat as unclean, for it was classed as a bird.

4) Whatever in the water has not both fins and scales (Leviticus 11:9-10). This prohibition left for use the most wholesome varieties of fish found in the waters of Palestine. It excluded eels and water animals which are not fish, such as crabs.

Animals in the above categories were unclean under any circumstance. But the flesh of even clean animals might become unclean. For example, the Law forbade the eating of things sacrificed to idols, things strangled, or dead of themselves or killed by beast or bird of prey. Blood and fat of bird and beast were sacred to the Lord. None might eat the blood (Leviticus 17:10-14).

A person who offended the laws regarding unclean animals was unclean until evening (Leviticus 11:24,40; 17:15).

10:13 – *And a voice came to him, "Arise, Peter, kill and eat!"*

And a voice came to him, "Arise, Peter, kill and eat." Now Peter is reminded of the hunger he felt before he fell into the trance, for here is the means of satisfying his hunger. He is commanded to kill and eat any of the animals or birds he sees, without making any distinction between clean and unclean as he has done all his life. This would imply that the Law of Moses concerning the distinction between clean and unclean meats had been abrogated. Some think the word "arise" refers to getting up from a kneeling position (i.e., he had been praying), but this is not the only possible meaning for the word. It can imply simply moving into action from a state of inaction.

10:14 – *But Peter said, "By no means, Lord, for I have never eaten anything unholy and unclean."*

But Peter said, "By no means, Lord. Peter is always a man quick to act and quick to speak. He shows his usual characteristic here. Although he was in a trance, he still had his sense of right and wrong about him. He feels strongly enough about this subject that he is willing to contradict what the Lord has commanded!

For I have never eaten anything unholy and unclean." We have already explained the Jewish distinction between clean and unclean meats at verse 12. In defense of his hesitation to obey the command of the Lord, Peter pleads that he must continue to abide by the Old Testament Law, just as he has been accustomed to do all his days before this. "Unholy" was a term applied to things freely indulged in by the Gentiles. It is the opposite of "sacred," and denoted that which was in common use among the heathen. The same word is translated "impure" at Mark 7:2. "Unclean" has to do with things that would leave a man ceremonially defiled. Between the Law and the command which he just now had received in the vision, there seemed to him to be a contradiction. Peter may be in a trance; but he knows what the Law requires, and that he will do, he insists.

10:15 – *And again a voice* **came** *to him a second time, "What God has cleansed, no* **longer** *consider unholy."*

And again a voice *came* **to him a second time, "What God has cleansed, no** *longer* **consider unholy."** If God has commanded you to do a thing, that thing cannot be considered to be wrong. God "cleansed" all those meats by declaring them to be clean.[22]

Many things certainly must have begun to go through Peter's mind. For instance, if the distinction between clean and unclean meats is now abolished, how much more of the Law is abolished?[23]

10:16 – *And this happened three times; and immediately the object was taken up into the sky.*

And this happened three times. What was done three times? Does it mean that the whole vision and the dialogue between the Lord and Peter were all repeated three times? From the latter part of the verse, it seems that the vessel was let down only once, and then taken back up into the sky at the conclusion of the lesson to Peter. So we would suggest that the command to kill and eat is what was repeated the three times. Perhaps Peter became silent when the Lord spoke the second and third times.

And immediately the object was taken up into the sky. This is all still part of the vision Peter is seeing while in the trance. When the lesson had been sufficiently impressed upon Peter's mind, the vision is ended.

---

[22] 1 Timothy 4:4; Titus 1:15.

[23] Is this the first time it has been revealed to the apostles that the Old Testament is no longer binding as a codification of God's will for men to live by?

c. The delegation from Cornelius finds Peter in Joppa. 10:17-23a

10:17 – *Now while Peter was greatly perplexed in mind as to what the vision which he had seen might be, behold, the men who had been sent by Cornelius, having asked directions for Simon's house, appeared at the gate;*

Now while Peter was greatly perplexed in mind. When Peter came out of the trance, his mind was full of questions as to what was implied by the vision and the statement about God having cleansed all those meats.

As to what the vision which he had seen might be. God in His providence is working things out with perfect timing. The vision and the movements of the messengers who were dispatched by Cornelius show the same timing as did the call of Philip in relation to the travels of the Ethiopian (Acts 8:26-27).

Behold, the men who had been sent by Cornelius, having asked directions for Simon's house. When they arrived at Joppa, the messengers had to ask directions in order to get to the tanner's house where Peter was staying.

Appeared at the gate. The word rendered "gate" refers properly to the porch or principal entrance to an Eastern home. It speaks more of a door than a gate. The messengers from Cornelius arrive right when Peter is reflecting in his mind about the broader implications of the vision. Their inquiry will help solve his questions.

10:18 – *and calling out, they were asking whether Simon, who was also called Peter, was staying there.*

And calling out, they were asking whether Simon, who was also called Peter, was staying there. They probably called to the servant who was the doorkeeper. Compare Acts 12:13 and John 18:16, 17.

10:19 – *And while Peter was reflecting on the vision, the Spirit said to him, "Behold, three men are looking for you.*

And while Peter was reflecting on the vision. At the very time the men were knocking and inquiring at the door, the Holy Spirit was communicating a message to Peter.

The Spirit said to him, "Behold, three men are looking for you. "Spirit" here is the Holy Spirit.[24] Peter is no longer in the trance. Exactly how the Holy Spirit communicated with the apostles is nowhere stated or explained in Scripture. Peter had not heard what the messengers had called out as they made inquiry at the door.

---

[24] Compare also Acts 8:29 for a similar activity of the Holy Spirit.

10:20 – *"But arise, go downstairs, and accompany them without misgivings; for I have sent them Myself."*

"But arise, go downstairs. The Spirit instructs Peter to go downstairs off the roof, by means of the stairway that opened onto the porch.

And accompany them without misgivings. This command seems especially addressed to the perplexed questions of Peter. He has just been shown that things that used to be "unholy" are no longer unholy. Now, the Spirit instructs him, 'Accompanying Gentiles on a journey won't contaminate you, Peter.' Peter might not, for a time, know exactly where the destination to which he was going was, but he should just trust the Hand that was guiding him. The expression "without misgivings" is translated "without wavering" in Romans 4:20, 14:23, and "without doubting" in James 1:6.

For I have sent them Myself." The "I" is emphatic in the Greek. The Holy Spirit, through the angel's message to Cornelius, is the real reason the messengers are standing at the door.

10:21 – *And Peter went down to the men and said, "Behold, I am the one you are looking for; what is the reason for which you have come?"*

And Peter went down to the men and said, "Behold, I am the one you are looking for. Peter identifies himself and tells the visitors that he knows they are seeking him, before they have an opportunity to tell Peter that he is the one for whom they are looking.

What is the reason for which you have come?" He knows he is to go with them, but Peter is trying to find out what he is to do after he has accompanied them wherever they want him to go.

10:22 – *And they said, "Cornelius, a centurion, a righteous and God-fearing man well spoken of by the entire nation of the Jews, was* **divinely** *directed by a holy angel to send for you* **to come** *to his house and hear a message from you."*

And they said, "Cornelius a centurion, a righteous and God-fearing man. The word "righteous" tells us Cornelius was one who observed God's laws as found in the Old Testament; it does not indicate he was sinless perfect. The other designations (centurion, God-fearer) have been explained in notes earlier in chapter 10.

Well spoken of by the entire nation of the Jews. Cornelius was respected even by those who were the occupied peoples. This may have been said to help encourage Peter to make the visit, for Cornelius is the kind of man that even devout Jews will find respected.

Was *divinely* directed by a holy angel to send for you *to come* to his house and hear a message from you." Cornelius and his household are waiting to hear those "words whereby men can be saved" that the angel promised would be spoken by Peter. Peter had a message from God for Cornelius, for Peter had the gospel of God's power to save, and Cornelius was an unsaved man. Hence, he needed to hear the message Peter had for him.

10:23a[25] – *And so he invited them in and gave them lodging.*

And so he invited them in and gave them lodging. The messengers have traveled almost round the clock. After part of a day's and a full night's rest, they will be ready to make the return trip, with Peter accompanying them. If it is Simon the tanner's house, why is Peter taking care of a place for them to lodge? If we suppose that Simon the tanner was a Jew, we might suppose he would be hesitant to give Gentiles a place to stay; and we can without difficulty suppose all three of the messengers were Gentiles. Peter sees to it that they have a place to stay through the night.

      d.   Peter meets Cornelius. 10:23b-33

10:23b – *And on the next day he arose and went away with them, and some of the brethren from Joppa accompanied him.*

And on the next day he arose and went away with them. The journey will take this day and part of the next, before they all arrive back in Caesarea.

And some of the brethren from Joppa accompanied him. Christian brethren, they were. There were six of them.[26] Perhaps we should picture it as a usual thing for the early Christians to accompany the apostles when they traveled.[27] On the other hand, Peter may have asked these men to accompany him to Caesarea. After all, he is going to a Gentile's home, and he is going to deliver a message to them. Knowing the animosity that strict Jews have about such close association with Gentiles, Peter perhaps reasons it would be a good thing to take some witnesses along. If his actions are ever called in question, he will have adequate testimony to explain why he had acted as he did.[28] Peter probably informed the men from Joppa of the message which the servants of Cornelius had brought and of the vision that he had seen, as well as what the Holy Spirit had said to him.

10:24 – *And on the following day he entered Caesarea. Now Cornelius was waiting for them, and had called together his relatives and close friends.*

And on the following day he entered Caesarea. As noted earlier, the return trip seems to have taken the greater part of two days.

---

[25] According to the translators of the NASB, the paragraph break occurs in the middle of what is our verse 23. The New Testament was first divided into verses by Robert Stephen in AD 1551, and the divisions he made have been observed since that time. But, as when men previously divided the Bible into chapters earlier, there were some unfortunate choices made in the versification. In this place, it would have been better here to have included verse 23a with the paragraph material that precedes.

[26] Acts 11:12.

[27] For example, see Acts 9:30.

[28] Deuteronomy 17:6, 19:15.

Now Cornelius was waiting for them, and had called together his relatives and close friends. Cornelius would have known approximately how long it would take his messengers to get to Joppa and to return with Peter. He has an audience ready and waiting for the preacher. Included were some fellow Italians ("relatives") and some "close friends" (Italians? or Jews?). They were likely invited to be present because Cornelius knew of their interest in the same object for which he had sent for Peter (verse 33).

10:25 – *And when it came about that Peter entered, Cornelius met him, and fell at his feet and worshiped* him.

And when it came about that Peter entered, Cornelius met him, and fell at his feet and worshiped *him*. Does Cornelius meet Peter at the city limits, or are we to picture what Luke next records as taking place at the door of Cornelius' home? Probably the latter. Picture the commander of 100 men, in full dress uniform, bowing down to Peter. In Eastern countries, it was usual for persons to prostrate themselves on the ground before men of rank and honor. Cornelius first would have knelt, and then bowed forward until his forehead touched the ground. The word translated "worship" (*proskuneō*) is the one that tells us Cornelius bowed down before Peter in an act of extreme homage. It is possible, by such an act, to express worship to God,[29] but Cornelius' knowledge of the true God probably keeps us from thinking he looked on Peter as a deity.

10:26 – *But Peter raised him up, saying, "Stand up; I too am* just *a man."*

But Peter raised him up. That is, Peter reached down and helped Cornelius up to a standing position.

Saying, "Stand up; I too am *just* a man." Whatever was in Cornelius' mind as he prostrated himself before Peter, Peter looked on the act as expressing homage which ought to be reserved for God alone.[30]

10:27 – *And as he talked with him, he entered, and found many people assembled.*

And as he talked with him, he entered, and found many people assembled. Peter and Cornelius are entering into the interior of the house after Cornelius has met Peter at the door (verse 25). They are talking together as Cornelius ushers him in to where the relatives and close friends of Cornelius are gathered.

10:28 – *And he said to them, "You yourselves know how unlawful it is for a man who is a Jew to associate with a foreigner or to visit him; and* yet *God has shown me that I should not call any man unholy or unclean.*

---

[29] John 12:20; Act 8:27.

[30] How different the attitude of Peter than that of many modern popes, and religious leaders, and lesser men, too. Many men love to have their fellowmen bow down before them. Each of us must be careful of our inner wishes and motives! Only God and Jesus, the Son of God, are worthy of worship (see Revelation 22:8, 9).

And he said to them, "You yourselves know how unlawful it is. Peter is likely speaking Greek, which was familiar at Joppa and Caesarea and other seacoast towns in Palestine. "Unlawful" is a translation of *athemitos*, which means contrary to custom or law, a violation of an established way of doing things.

For a man who is a Jew to associate with a foreigner or to visit him. When Peter says "foreigner," he uses a word (*allophulos*) which is carefully and kindly selected to avoid the use of "Gentile." There is no such delicacy of feeling in Acts 10:45 or 11:3. Such social segregation as Peter here says is "unlawful" was not explicitly commanded by Moses, but it did seem to be implied in his law and was the common understanding of the Jews. Moses did forbid intermarriage with the pagan nations in the land of Canaan, and he did discourage participation in their idolatrous practices.[31] Such prohibitions the Jews (especially as the Pharisees interpreted the Old Testament) extended to social activities of all kinds, and understood they were to have no friendly relationships or commercial transactions with Gentiles. Strict Jews would not enter a Gentile's house, nor sit on the same couch, nor eat or drink out of the same vessel.[32] Although God Himself had not commanded such segregation as the Jews interpreted and practiced, because Peter had been so taught he feels a bit uncomfortable entering the strange surroundings he just has. So he goes on to explain why his conduct is different from what the ordinary Jew's would be.

And *yet* God has shown me that I should not call any man unholy or unclean. God showed this to Peter in the vision (verses 11-12). Peter had learned the lesson the vision was intended to teach. If God says it is proper to associate with people, then Peter will accept the Lord's instruction! Later Peter will learn there is more involved than association. He will learn that no man was to be regarded as excluded from the opportunity for salvation, whether bond or free, Jew or Gentile. Sin alone is what separates men from God and separates men from men. As the gospel is preached to all, the barriers between men and God and between men and men (such as between Jews and Gentiles) are removed.

10:29 – *"That is why I came without even raising any objection when I was sent for. And so I ask for what reason you have sent for me."*

"That is why I came without even raising any objection when I was sent for. God had told Peter to go with the messengers from Cornelius without having any misgivings (verse 20). And so without any hesitation or reluctance, without saying anything against such an idea (as he likely would have spoken against it had he not had the vision), Peter obeyed at once when the messengers arrived inviting him to Cornelius' home at Caesarea.

And so I ask for what reason you have sent for me." The main purpose for which Cornelius had sent for Peter had been told to Peter by the messengers (verse 22). They had said that Peter was to deliver a message to Cornelius. Just what message was it that Peter is supposed to preach? He asks Cornelius for a more particular statement of what the angel had instructed him to do as he gave Cornelius the order to send for Peter.

---

[31] Leviticus 18:24-30; Deuteronomy 7:3-12; Ezra 9:11-12.

[32] Compare Mark 7:3-4.

10:30 – *And Cornelius said, "Four days ago to this hour, I was praying in my house during the ninth hour; and behold, a man stood before me in shining garments,*

And Cornelius said, "Four days ago. Four days, or parts of four different days, have passed between the visit of the angel to Cornelius and Peter's arrival at Caesarea. On the first day the angel appeared to Cornelius, and the messengers were dispatched. On the second, the messengers arrived at Joppa, about noon. On the third, Peter and the rest started for the city of Caesarea. On the fourth, they arrived at the home of Cornelius.

To this hour. The ninth hour is 3:00 p.m.[33] Peter arrived at Cornelius' house at 3 p.m., the same hour it was when Cornelius had received the vision to send for Peter.

I was praying in my house during the ninth hour. See the comments at verse 3.

And behold, a man stood before me in shining garments. The angel had the appearance of a man. On the angel's dress, see notes at Acts 1:10-11.

10:31 – *and he said, 'Cornelius, your prayer has been heard and your alms have been remembered before God.*

"And he said, 'Cornelius, your prayer has been heard and your alms have been remembered before God. See notes at verse 4. The singular number here ("prayer") suggests that the one object of all his prayers has been the same. It must have been, in the nature of the case, a prayer for help to know the truth about God and salvation.

10:32 – *'Send therefore to Joppa and invite Simon, who is also called Peter, to come to you; he is staying at the house of Simon the tanner by the sea.'*

'Send therefore to Joppa and invite Simon, who is also called Peter, to come to you; he is staying at the house of Simon *the* tanner by the sea.' See Acts 11:14, where we are told that Peter would speak "words by which you shall be saved." We are still watching in Luke's narrative for those words to be spoken that would help save Cornelius. Simon had been given the name "Peter" the first time he met Jesus (John 1:41-42).

10:33 – *"And so I sent to you immediately, and you have been kind enough to come. Now then, we are all here present before God to hear all that you have been commanded by the Lord."*

"And so I sent to you immediately, and you have been kind enough to come. This is an expression, not of mere approval of Peter's actions, but of heartfelt gratitude.[34] Cornelius took no offense at Peter's attempted explanation of why his actions differed from those of most Jews with reference to association with Gentiles. He simply expresses his grateful feelings to Peter that Peter has taken the time and trouble to come.

---

[33] See comments about the hour of prayer at Acts 10:3.

[34] Paul, in Philippians 4:14, uses the same expression of heartfelt gratitude and thankfulness.

Now then, we are all here present before God. Cornelius expresses his belief that what they were doing God could see, and that it had His approval. Cornelius and his houseful of people have been wanting to do what was pleasing to God; and since they were convinced this had His approval, they were ready to listen to His instructions as given through the mouth of His spokesman Peter.

To hear all that you have been commanded by the Lord." In spite of being a good moral man, and in spite of having had a vision and visit from an angel, Cornelius was conscious he still had the burden of guilt and sin from which he had been seeking relief. Likewise, his relatives and close friends too were seeking salvation. He encourages Peter to proceed with the message whereby they would learn what they must do to be saved.

      e. Peter's sermon. 10:34-43

10:34 – *And opening his mouth, Peter said: "I most certainly understand* now *that God is not one to show partiality,*

And opening his month, Peter said. "Opening the mouth" has been explained in notes at Acts 8:35. Certain things about this sermon demand our attention. There is some reference to the Old Testament Scriptures, even if he is speaking to a Gentile audience,[35] though their familiarity with the Scriptures may have come only as they became proselytes of the gate. The sermon stresses the life of Jesus, His ministry, crucifixion, resurrection, appearances, and His command to His witnesses to proclaim the truth about Him. Jesus is presented not merely as the Messiah of the Jews, but as Lord of all,[36] and as Judge of all.[37]

I most certainly understand *now.* The verb is present tense, and might suggest the translation, "I am beginning to understand." If God has heard Cornelius' prayer, sent an angel to him and an object lesson to Peter, then it must be that God is no respecter of persons.

That God is not one to show partiality. A person who shows partiality does so on the basis of outward circumstances (such as rank, family, wealth) rather than judging a man on his intrinsic merits. The Jews supposed that because they were children of Abraham that they were especially favored by God. The Jews thought that when Messiah came, He would extend the offer of salvation to the Jews, but not to men of other nations. Peter here says that he is learning the error of the Jew's way of thinking, and has now come to realize that a man is not accepted just because he is a Jew, nor is he excluded just because he is a Gentile. This absence of partiality has been evident in Jesus, and was even acknowledged by His enemies.[38] In this, Jesus perfectly exemplified the Father. The same doctrine, that

---

[35] See the reference to "all the prophets" at verse 43.

[36] See verse 36.

[37] See verse 42.

[38] Matthew 22:16; Luke 20:21.

God does not show partiality, is elsewhere explicitly stated in the New Testament.[39] Jew and Gentile alike are equally admissible to the privileges and blessings of the New Covenant.

10:35 – *"but in every nation the man who fears Him and does what is right, is welcome to Him.*

But. Instead of what Peter used to think, it is now becoming clear that it is more important to God what a man believes and does, rather than who his ancestors were or where he was born.

In every nation. Among all people, whether Jewish or Gentile in background.

The man who fears Him. It appears from the account that Peter is still summarizing the things he is learning from Cornelius' case about who is welcome to learn more about salvation. Cornelius has been a "God-fearer" (verse 2), and this was a great plus in his favor when he was praying for more help to know what to do to be saved. Being descended from Abraham, or possessing external privileges such as the Law, are not the conditions which prepare a man to receive salvation through Christ as much as having a right attitude of heart. A reverence for God that leads a man to do his duty to God is the attitude that opens a man's heart to the message of salvation.[40]

And does what is right. Cornelius is still in the background, so that the word "right" appears to refer to man's conduct toward his fellow man. Remember from verse 2 the alms deeds he did for the captive peoples over which his soldiers were the occupation troops. Remember, too, that Cornelius has shared his limited knowledge of God with his relatives and close friends, and even some of his troops. A man who wants to do what is right will be receptive to the gospel when he is presented with the opportunity.

Is welcome to Him. That is, a person is capable of becoming a Christian when the opportunity is granted. "Welcome" does not say that the person has salvation without becoming a Christian. Cornelius didn't! Fearing God and doing what is right place a man in a state preparatory to receiving the salvation that is available through Christ. And since Cornelius is to that state, Peter will explain to him the message of salvation.

10:36 – *"The word which He sent to the sons of Israel, preaching peace through Jesus Christ (He is Lord of all) –*

The word which He sent to the sons of Israel. The structure of the sentence has proven to be difficult for the translator and the commentator to handle smoothly.

- Verses 35, 36, and 38 all begin with an accusative case (i.e., an object of a verb), and the only verb is "you know" in verse 37.

---

[39] Romans 2:11; Ephesians 6:9; Colossians 3:25.

[40] Peter is not saying, as some have supposed, that for the Gentile the way to salvation in Christ is first to become a proselyte (i.e., a God-fearer) to the Jewish religion.

- Some make the accusative here in verse 36 to be an object of the verb "I understand" back in verse 34.
- The NASB adds a dash as a break at the close of verse 36, so that Peter restarts his thought again in verse 37, as though verse 37 explains what the "word" is that Peter started to talk about in verse 36. This would be easier to accept if there were not different Greek words for "word" used in the two verses. Verse 36 uses *logos* ("word"), while verse 37 uses *hrēma* ("word," "thing").
- This commentator views verse 36 being an introduction to the "doctrine" Peter is going to preach. Peter is thus saying, "I'm going to tell you the word (i.e., the doctrine) that is necessary for you to believe if you would be saved."

The "He" who did the sending is God. The good news – the message, the doctrine, the word – was first sent by God to the Jews.

Preaching peace through Jesus Christ. Peter says God was preaching through the ministry of Jesus Christ. And what was God's message? The good news of peace!
- "Peace" sometimes has reference to the absence of hostility between men, and in Jesus the middle wall of partition between Jews and Gentiles was broken down.[41]
- The word also is used to designate the fact that there has been a reconciliation to God effected for us by Jesus Christ, and thus the hostility between man and God is removed.
- A third meaning of the word "peace" is to designate that serenity and calmness of feelings a redeemed man has, a tranquility of soul because he knows his sins are forgiven.

If we had to pick but one of the three meanings here, we would pick the second. However, the context does not require us to limit the meaning to just one of the possible meanings for "peace."

(He is Lord of all). This parenthetical statement tells Cornelius something about Jesus, that He is Lord of all men. Lest Cornelius think that Jesus was only a Jewish prophet or teacher, Peter shows He is sovereign and the ruler of all men, both Jews and Gentiles. Since He is Lord of all, Peter thought it proper to preach the gospel to one as well as to the other. Peace is available to all, for Christ is the Savior of all.

10:37 – *"you yourselves know the thing which took place throughout all Judea, starting from Galilee, after the baptism which John proclaimed.*

You yourselves know the thing. Peter says, 'You are familiar with the life of Christ, the message He preached, and the miracles He worked.' The word translated "thing" in the NASB is *hrēma*, a word which emphasizes the content or subject matter of the message.

Which took place throughout all Judea. The early ministry of Jesus is recorded only in John's Gospel (chapters 2-3), but Peter was there and so can speak of it first-hand. Jesus'

---

[41] See Ephesians 2:14.

early ministry was about eight months long, and His fame spread because of His miracles and preaching. It spread so much that Peter can allude to some knowledge of it being possessed even by this Roman soldier.

Starting from Galilee. Jesus began His ministry in Galilee after His baptism and temptation, and He worked His first miracle in Cana of Galilee. This ministry in Galilee lasted some days before he went up to Jerusalem for the first Passover and the first cleansing of the temple.[42] Galilee was not far from Caesarea, so Cornelius has likely heard of what happened there as well as what happened in Judea.

After the baptism which John proclaimed. Jesus began His public ministry after John the Baptist had done much of his preparatory work. By these words Peter reminds Cornelius of the ministry and message of John the baptizer.

Many early Christian writers say that Mark's Gospel is based on what Peter preached. It is interesting to note that Mark's Gospel follows the order of Peter's sermon at this place. Mark starts with the baptism of John, and takes us through the resurrection appearances of Jesus. This is exactly what Peter does here as he preaches to Cornelius.

10:38 – "You know of *Jesus of Nazareth, how God anointed Him with the Holy Spirit and with power, and* how *He went about doing good, and healing all who were oppressed by the devil; for God was with Him.*

You know of **Jesus of Nazareth.** This is the third of the accusative phrases that began in verse 35. The Italian cohort must have been stationed in Caesarea for some time if Peter is able to say, "You know about John the Baptist's preparatory ministry, and about the beginning of Jesus' ministry in Galilee and Judea." It was more than twelve years previous that these things had happened.

How God anointed Him with the Holy Spirit and with power. The reference is to the time of Jesus' baptism, when the Spirit of God descended on Him in the form of a dove.[43] By this Jesus was set apart to the work of the Messiah. The power God gave to Jesus at that time was the power to heal the sick, raise the dead, etc.[44]

And *how* **He went about doing good.** This is a good summary of Jesus' ministry. He looked for ways to be helpful to people, and then gave of Himself to be helpful.

And healing all who were oppressed by the devil. That is, He cast out demons. Those

---

[42] The early Judean ministry of Jesus is recorded in John 1-3.

[43] Luke 3:22; Matthew 3:16-17; John 3:34.

[44] Careful language is needed in the comments at this phrase, lest we introduce any of the wording associated with the "Adoptionist heresy."

who were demon possessed[45] were, in the language of this verse, oppressed by the devil.[46]

For God was with Him. This is given as the reason why Jesus was able to do good and help those who were demon oppressed. God approved of Him and graciously cooperated with Him.[47] Jesus' miracles were such that men could easily see that God was with Him and was giving evidence that He had sent Jesus. Dale causes us to go back and ponder what we've just read, when he reminds us that all three members of the Godhead have been introduced by Peter.

> Peter has presented here each of the members of the Godhead. God anointed or set Jesus apart for the work He was to do, and He imparted to Him the power of the Holy Spirit. Thus, in the work of redemption, the three are present – God the Father, God the Son, and God the Holy Spirit.[48]

10:39 – *"And we are witnesses of all the things He did both in the land of the Jews and in Jerusalem. And they also put Him to death by hanging Him on a cross.*

And we are witnesses of all the things He did. "We" refers to the apostles. Jesus had made His apostles His witnesses (Acts 1:8).

Both in the land of the Jews. Peter was speaking at Caesarea, so that by using this phrase he seems to be speaking of Jesus' Judean ministry. There was an early Judean ministry about which Peter spoke earlier (verse 37). Peter now makes reference to a later Judean ministry, which took place from October to December of AD 29.[49]

And in Jerusalem. This note reminds us of what has been called the climactic week of Jesus' earthly ministry. Sunday of that week was the triumphal entry, Monday was the second cleansing of the temple, Tuesday was the great day of questions, and Thursday witnessed the institution of the Lord's Supper and the agony in the garden.

And they also put Him to death by hanging Him on a cross. "They" is a reference to the Jews.[50] "Cross" represents the word *xulon*, or "tree." The word tells us the cross was

---

[45] "Oppressed" is *katadunasteuō*, which means to oppress, exploit, dominate, tyrannize. See James 2:6. It is a different word than is usually used to express demon possession. The usual word is *daimōnizomai*.

[46] Because an unusual word is used here by Luke, some commentators suppose that more than demon possession is intended. They believe that all disease is the work directly or indirectly of the great enemy, the devil. Luke 13:11 and 2 Corinthians 12:7 are further passages appealed to in order to prove this. These commentators believe Peter is speaking of healing sicknesses, rather than casting out demons. However this verse is understood, it must be emphasized again that the Bible makes a distinction between sickness and demon possession, and not all sickness can be healed simply by exorcising some demon.

[47] See notes at Acts 14:27 on the expression "with him," which in this case is *met' autou*.

[48] Dale, *op. cit.*, p.118.

[49] The later Judean ministry is recorded in John 7:11 through 10:39, and in Luke 10:1 through 13:21.

[50] Despite some modern attempts at denial, the New Testament insists that the Jews were guilty of and responsible for the death of Christ. The Jews were just as guilty as the Romans who did the actual crucifying. (The New Testament also teaches that, for each of us individually, our own personal sins are

made out of rough logs.

10:40 – *"God raised Him up on the third day, and granted that He should become visible,*

God raised Him up on the third day. As he did in the sermon recorded in Acts 3:13ff, Peter again contrasts what the people did to Jesus with what God did for Him. The people put Him to death on a cross. God raised Him from the dead.

And granted that He should become visible. Think of all the post-resurrection appearances of Jesus. Cf. Acts 1:3. From time to time through the 40 days between His resurrection and ascension, He became visible to their human eyes.

10:41 – *"not to all the people, but to witnesses who were chosen beforehand by God,* **that is, to us, who ate and drank with Him after He arose from the dead.**

Not to all the people. Jesus did not appear to all the Jewish people who had seen Him during His earthly ministry. It was not necessary that they all should see Him in order to establish the truth of His resurrection. He did show Himself to over 500 persons,[51] but basically the appearances were limited to the apostles. If even the apostles had to be convinced – i.e., had to touch Him and talk with Him – what would have happened if Jesus had appeared to huge multitudes? Accuracy of knowledge was the important thing, not a multitude of testings. And who was equipped to be more accurate than the twelve who had spent many intimate hours with Jesus?

But to witnesses who were chosen beforehand by God. Unbelievers have made this a ground of objection to Luke's narrative. Luke says that the apostles were chosen by God, when the Gospel narratives tell us that Jesus called His own apostles. But there is no contradiction, because in verse 36 we are specifically told that God was working through Jesus! Chosen "before" what? Before the death and resurrection of Jesus.

That is, **to us, who ate and drank with Him after He arose from the dead.** The chosen witnesses were not deceived about the resurrection. They ate and drank with the risen Lord.[52] Jesus, by eating and drinking with His disciples, furnished the clearest possible proof that He was truly risen. It was not a phantom or ghost or apparition that the disciples saw.

10:42 – *"And He ordered us to preach to the people, and solemnly to testify that this is the One who has been appointed by God as Judge of the living and the dead.*

And He ordered us to preach to the people. See the Great Commission for this order.[53] The apostles were to preach, not to Jews only, but to all the creation. 'And Cornelius, you

---

also a cause of Jesus' death, for His death proffered the necessary atonement for those individual sins.)

[51] 1 Corinthians 15:6.

[52] John 21:12-13; Luke 24:30,42.

[53] Matthew 28:18-20: Mark 16:15, 16.

are included in that commission. That is why I'm telling you about the good news of salvation to all men in Christ Jesus.'

And solemnly to testify that this is the One who has been appointed by God. Peter further explains that his commission is to bear witness that Christ has been appointed by God to be the final judge.

As Judge of the living and the dead. In a strikingly-similar statement, Paul also speaks of Jesus as being judge by virtue of His resurrection from the dead.[54] The future moment that Peter has in mind is the Great Judgment Day.[55] The Bible seems to present a picture of one universal judgment, where all men will stand before the Judge of the universe to receive the deeds done in the body, whether good or bad. All who have ever lived on this earth will be there – both those who are still living when He returns, and those who have died before He comes. Speaking particularly of the righteous (i.e., those "in Christ"), Paul shows that those who are still living on earth when Jesus returns will be caught up to meet their Lord in the air, without ever experiencing death. Instead, they will be transformed into their glorified bodies, and are then raptured to meet the Lord. This instantaneous change that will make them like those who have died but have been raised from the dead in their resurrection bodies.[56]

In their resurrection bodies, both saint and sinner will stand before Jesus to be judged. That Jesus is to be the future judge is a startling claim made for Him by Peter. Peter had lived on the closest of terms with Jesus during His ministry; he had seen many of his hopes crushed when Jesus was crucified, and now he affirms that Jesus had been appointed by God to be the Judge of all. Only if Jesus is risen from the dead, and only if He is Lord of all, can what Peter says be true. And the amazing change in Peter is evidence of the truth of the resurrection and coming judgment!

10:43 – *"Of Him all the prophets bear witness that through His name everyone who believes in Him receives forgiveness of sins."*

Of Him all the prophets bear witness. In Peter's sermons in both Acts 2 and 3, we were reminded of how Jesus explained the Old Testament prophecies that had reference to His suffering, death, and exaltation.[57] Peter's appeal to the prophets may imply that Cornelius and his guests were more or less acquainted with the Old Testament Scriptures.

That through His name every one who believes in Him. This is a good verse to show the fallacy of the modern premillennial (or dispensational) theory that the Old Testament prophets did not foresee the church age. The Old Testament not only gave prediction about Messiah and His atoning work, but also spoke about how believers in Him would be "justi-

---

[54] Acts 17:31.

[55] Revelation 20:11ff; Matthew 25:31ff; 2 Corinthians 5:10.

[56] 1 Thessalonians 4:16. 17. Concerning the new body, see Paul's discourse on it in 1 Corinthians 15:35ff.

[57] In Acts 3:24 there are extensive comments on the predictions about Messiah made by the Old Testament prophets.

fied by faith." Habakkuk 2:4 is an example. Neither Habakkuk nor Peter means "faith only." Bible belief includes an obedience to God's commands – a committal of the whole life. "Everyone who believes" includes Gentiles as well as Jews.[58]

Receives forgiveness of sins. The ASV reads "*shall* receive remission of sins." But the NASB is correct to translate the verb as a present tense, rather than the ASV's future tense. The verb tenses are such that the "believing" and the "receiving" are simultaneous.

Forgiveness of sins is conditioned on an obedient faith.[59] These words of Peter's are the words which Cornelius and his friends have been waiting anxiously to hear. Not by submitting themselves to the requirements of the Law of Moses, not by circumcision and all that implied, but by faith in Christ is the God-ordained way to remission of sins.[60]

f. The results. 10:44-48

10:44 – *While Peter was still speaking these words, the Holy Spirit fell upon all those who were listening to the message.*

While Peter was still speaking these words. Peter is apparently interrupted, and if we read correctly the situation, what happens next is for Peter's benefit. He has already expressed the fact that he is just learning that God is no respecter of persons. This was after he knew about God sending an angel to Cornelius, and after he himself had seen a vision on the rooftop at Joppa. The messengers told Peter he was to preach when he got to Cornelius' house; yet when he arrives he asks Cornelius for more specifics about what he is supposed to preach, as if he just can't believe what he is hearing. When Cornelius has explained his vision and his reason for sending for Peter, Peter realizes he has no option but to preach the gospel of peace to these Gentiles gathered in Cornelius' home.

What seems to have been going through Peter's mind at the time he was interrupted was this – 'I've told them what to do to have forgiveness of sins. What happens, though, if some of them want to obey the gospel? Do I encourage them? I don't know what to do. This is a spot.' You can see the conflict going on in his mind. He sees God is no respecter of persons. Anyone can have opportunity to believe and obey. Yet in the back of his mind

---

[58] Romans 10:11-13.

[59] Perhaps a word needs to be said concerning the expression "obedient faith." This expression is deliberately chosen to show that the faith that saves, in the Bible, is not a "faith only" thing, a mere mental assent. People in New Testament times knew this, but the idea has fallen upon hard times in recent years.

Two lines of thought will help the reader to see that the faith that saves is an obedient faith. (1) Peter will shortly insist that these listeners to his sermon be immersed. Just as in the Ethiopian's case, so here, preaching Jesus and a proper response to that preaching includes immersion for the forgiveness of sins. (2) The second line of argument is a bit more technical. Leon Morris has suggested that the fact the word "believe" is followed by two different constructions in the Greek is significant. When it is followed by a simple dative case, it speaks of what we call "mental assent." When it is followed by *eis* and the accusative case, it denotes what we have called "obedient faith." The construction here in Acts 10:43 is *eis* and the accusative; thus, an obedient faith is indicated. (Leon Morris, *The Gospel According to John* in the New International Critical Commentary (Grand Rapids: Eerdmans, 1971), p.335-337.)

[60] "Forgiveness of sins" was explained at Acts 2:38.

are those old Jewish reservations.

As God has been leading Peter along into this new truth, so again God helps his messenger at this juncture, too. The Holy Spirit is sent upon these Gentiles, and the question in Peter's mind is answered. If God gives this much evidence that He accepts these men, what reason is there to wait any longer to encourage them to accept the invitation to become Christians?

The Holy Spirit fell upon all those who were listening to the message. Those who are intended are Cornelius, his relatives and close friends (verse 27).

This is a second example in Acts where we are specifically told it is a case of baptism with the Holy Spirit.[61] This does *not* seem to be comparable to the Acts 2:38 "gift" of the Holy Spirit, for that comes when a penitent believer is immersed for the forgiveness of his sins, and these men at Caesarea in Cornelius' house have not yet been so immersed (verse 48). Nor does the Holy Spirit come, in this case, by the laying on of an apostle's hands, which suggests that this is not what we have called "spiritual gifts." In the case of Cornelius, Acts 11:15 tells us the Holy Spirit came as He did on the day of Pentecost.

In time Peter will have to explain his "association" with these Gentiles (i.e., Cornelius and his friends) to the Christians at Jerusalem. As recorded in Acts 11:3ff, Peter will base his whole defense on God's intervention and clear direction in the whole transaction. There was the vision of the sheet given to Peter, and the Spirit's words to go without misgivings. There was the angel's appearance to Cornelius. But Peter's ultimate and conclusive argument is based on the fact that the Holy Spirit came upon Cornelius and his friends.[62] Peter clearly shows that he viewed what happened from God's hand as clear proof that Gentiles were to be admitted to the same blessings of salvation that had been granted to the Jews.

10:45 – *And all the circumcised believers who had come with Peter were amazed, because the gift of the Holy Spirit had been poured out upon the Gentiles also.*

And all the circumcised believers who had come with Peter were amazed. The baptism with the Holy Spirit falling on any but the apostles of Christ was an exception to the norm. This is shown by the fact that this event was surprising to Peter and his Jewish companions.[63] But what was really surprising was that Gentiles (!) should be the recipients of such a gift. The "circumcised believers" were the Christians of Jewish background who had accompanied Peter from Joppa to Caesarea (verse 23).

> If Peter had finished his discourse, promising them the indwelling gift of the Holy Spirit on the terms which he had laid down on Pentecost, and had baptized them, these brethren would have taken it as a matter of course that they had received the indwelling gift of the Holy Spirit, Acts 2:38. And if, after this, Peter had laid hands on them and im-

---

[61] See Acts 10:47, 11:11-17, and 15:8. Especially note the Acts 11:15-17 passage, where it is made very plain that what happened was an example of the baptism with the Holy Spirit.

[62] Acts 11:17.

[63] For further information, consult Special Study #3, "The Person and Work of the Holy Spirit," at the close of chapter 2.

parted to them the miraculous gift of the Holy Spirit, as in the case of the Samaritans, they would not have been greatly surprised. The considerations which caused the amazement were: first, that the Holy Spirit was "poured out" upon them directly from God, as it had never before been on any but the apostles, and, secondly, that this unusual gift was bestowed on Gentiles.[64]

Because the gift of the Holy Spirit had been poured out upon the Gentiles also. Joel had predicted that God would "pour forth of his Spirit upon all flesh," and it has now been done.[65]

Several New Testament passages speak of "baptism" as having a place in a person's salvation, but those passages do not always specify that it is a baptism in water. Because of this, and in an effort to prove that baptism in water is not essential to salvation, some faith-only teachers have tried to use verse 45 to prove that the baptism that is essential is the "baptism with the Holy Spirit." McGarvey, long ago, effectively answered this evasion of clear Bible teaching:

> The baptism of Cornelius and his friends in the Holy Spirit previous to their baptism in water, has been urged as evidence that the remission of sins takes place before baptism in water. But in every other instance of a miraculous gift, remission of sins preceded the giving of the miraculous measure of the Spirit. This was true of the apostles on Pentecost, for they had long before been accepted as disciples of Christ. It was true of the Samaritans, for they had been baptized by Philip before the apostles sent Peter and John to them to impart the miraculous gift. It is true of the twelve disciples in Ephesus, to whom Paul imparted spiritual gifts after he had baptized them (Acts 19:1-7). It is true of all in the Corinthian church who had received similar [spiritual] gifts (1 Corinthians 1:4-7, 12:1-7). In none of these cases was the remission of sins connected with the giving of spiritual gifts, or with the baptism of the Holy Spirit – and it cannot be so assumed in the present instance ... This incident in the conversion of Cornelius cannot in any way be held as a precedent for subsequent ages; for it was certainly a miracle, and no miracles are now wrought [at least not like those read about in the Scriptures as coming from God].[66]

10:46 – *For they were hearing them speaking with tongues and exalting God. Then Peter answered,*

For they were hearing them speaking with tongues. This was one way that the circumcised believers with Peter could tell that the Holy Spirit had been poured out on the Gentiles. Just as on the day of Pentecost (Acts 2) when the apostles were baptized with the Holy Spirit and then spoke in foreign languages, so the same manifestation occurs in the case of Cornelius and his friends.[67]

---

[64] McGarvey, *op. cit.*, p.213.

[65] See comments on Joel's prophecy at Acts 2:17.

[66] McGarvey, *op. cit.*, p.215-216.

[67] Some modern interpreters have urged that the "tongues" in Cornelius' case were different than the tongues on Pentecost. Whereas in Acts 2 the tongues were foreign languages, it is urged that in Acts 10 Luke is describing "jubilant ecstatic praise." But Acts 10:47 and 11:17 tell us it was the same gift as at Pentecost, and this must imply that it was the same evidence. That is, it was foreign languages in both cases.

And exalting God. In their "tongues" they were extoling God, declaring how great and marvelous He is. What foreign language were Cornelius and his friends speaking? Perhaps these Romans were speaking Hebrew. That's how the men with Peter recognized the content of what the Gentiles were saying as they spoke in tongues.

A question often pondered is how long did the baptism with the Spirit and the tongues continue in Cornelius' life? Perhaps Dale gives as satisfactory an answer as any:

> There is no record that any of the house of Cornelius possessed miraculous powers after the purpose of the Spirit's coming upon them was completed. Once the purpose of the miracle (to convince Peter) was accomplished, it was not necessary that the Spirit's miraculous powers be continually demonstrated in them.[68]

Then Peter answered. Before he was interrupted, Peter had explained God's part in salvation (i.e., the atoning work of Jesus), and had just launched into an explanation of man's response (i.e., obedient faith). Once the initial surprise has passed, Peter continues his statement of what is involved in man's appropriate response, only the interruption has enabled him to speak with greater confidence to this audience than he would have otherwise.

10:47 – *"Surely no one can refuse the water for these to be baptized who have received the Holy Spirit just as we* **did,** *can he?"*

Surely no one can refuse the water for these to be baptized ... can he. The question seems to be addressed to the six Jewish Christians who had accompanied Peter. In effect, Peter asks, 'Is it not clear that the Gentiles are entitled to the privilege of being immersed into Christ for the remission of sins, and thus becoming a part of the Church?'

Those who practice sprinkling (as a substitute for the immersion Jesus commanded) try to find encouragement in these words of Peter. One author actually suggests that the preacher was calling for a small quantity (sufficient for sprinkling) of water to be brought into their presence! But Peter's question has no suggestion of sprinkling. He is talking about "*the* water" (i.e., the well-known water of baptism for the remission of sins), and is asking whether any will further oppose God's manifest will in this case by insisting that it would be wrong to immerse these Gentiles.

> Let us now recall the fact that Cornelius had been directed to send for Peter to hear words whereby he and all his house should be saved (11:14). Peter has come and spoken those words. He has told the company of the Christ, in whom they now believe. He has told them to be baptized, and in the next verse we shall see it done. What the pious, prayerful, and alms-giving Cornelius had lacked of being a Christian has now been supplied, and nothing has been required of him but to believe in Christ and be baptized.[69]

Today, a man who would hear words about the way of salvation should hear these same words!

---

[68] Dale, *op. cit.*, p.121.

[69] McGarvey, *op. cit.*, p.217-218.

Who have received the Holy Spirit just as we *did*. Peter recognizes that what has been poured out on Cornelius and his friends is the same thing that happened to the apostles at Pentecost.[70]

10:48 – *And he ordered them to be baptized in the name of Jesus Christ. Then they asked him to stay on for a few days.*

And he ordered them to be baptized. Why Peter did not himself baptize them is unknown. It might be for a similar reason that Paul did not personally baptize many at Corinth – i.e., to keep down future jealousy and party pride.[71] The six Jewish Christians who were present could baptize this group of Gentile believers in a short time. This appears to be a clear-cut case of unofficial members of the Church doing the baptizing.[72]

Underscore the word "commanded." Peter, the inspired apostle, *commanded* baptism. After Cornelius and his company have been baptized with the Holy Spirit, they are also, by apostolic command, to be baptized in water. There is, then, a necessary distinction between water baptism and Spirit baptism. Those who say that there is only one baptism that puts a man into the kingdom, and that is a Spirit baptism, are not presenting the Scripture in its proper terms; they have not harmonized all the passages that have a bearing on the subject.[73] Most people today who claim that it is a Spirit baptism that puts them into the body of Christ refuse to allow themselves to be immersed in water. They think they are already Christians, and so no water baptism is essential for their salvation. Indeed! Neither Cornelius, nor Peter, nor any other inspired preacher ever indicated that the immersion of a penitent believer was a non-essential, an optional extra, to their salvation! How different from today's "faith-only" preacher. If water baptism is necessary to obey what Jesus and the apostles commanded (and they did command immersion), then immersion is absolutely essential as one of the conditions of salvation.

---

[70] See Acts 11:15. Some Neo-Pentecostal writers in the 20th century attempted to use this verse to prove that every Christian receives the baptism with the Holy Spirit. The attempt is based on the explanation of the word "we" as being the *six Jewish Christians* rather than "we apostles." That Peter has in mind "we apostles" is clear from what is said in Acts 11:15, and if it means "we apostles," then the Neo-Pentecostal interpreters will have to look elsewhere for substantiation of their doctrine.

[71] 1 Corinthians 1:14-17.

[72] Denominational writers have trouble here with what is evidently a case of unofficial administration of the ordinance of baptism. Those who insist that only "official church leaders" are to administer the ordinances suggest that Philip the evangelist is the one commanded to baptize Cornelius, or that some of the leaders of the congregation of Jewish Christians already located in Caesarea are the ones who are commanded to baptize the first Gentile converts. This they must do, even though the record is such as to almost prohibit anyone else being present except Peter and the six brethren from Joppa, plus Cornelius, his relatives and close friends.

[73] 1 Corinthians 12:13a reads, "by one Spirit were you all baptized into one body." This verse must be harmonized with Scripture elsewhere that talks about baptism into the body of Christ. Those who insist it means that "Spirit baptism" puts a man into the church cannot make the verse harmonize with Peter's instructions and command of water baptism after Spirit baptism in the case of Cornelius. Only if we understand 1 Corinthians to mean "by the agency of the Spirit men are led (convicted of their sin) to the place where they seek baptism (in water) in order to enter the body of Christ" can we make it harmonize with Acts 10. And if such is the proper interpretation, there are no verses left that can be used to prove that there is a "Spirit baptism" that puts a man into the body of Christ.

In the name of Jesus Christ. In Matthew's record of the Great Commission, Jesus gave the baptismal formula as "in the name of the Father, and of the Son, and of the Holy Spirit." The question has been raised, Why is the formula here and elsewhere in Acts shortened to "in the name of Jesus"[74] only? Various explanations have been offered:

- Some suggest that to baptize in the name of one of the persons of the Godhead necessarily involves the other two.
- Some put forth the opinion that Luke here in Acts merely gives an abbreviation of the longer formula elsewhere used.
- Another suggestion that has some merit posits that the background of the person being instructed to be immersed makes the difference in the formula used. The words of Matthew 28 were to be used for the convert from paganism, who had been "without God in the world, knowing not the Father, Son, or Holy Spirit." For converts from Judaism, or those who had before been proselytes to Judaism, it was enough that there should be the distinctive profession of their faith in Jesus as the Christ, the Son of God, added to their previous belief in the Father and the Holy Spirit.
- Of course, the negative critics suggest that, "As the years went by, the formula got longer (growing from 'in the name of Jesus' to 'in the name of the Father, Son, and Holy Spirit')." However, this suggestion smacks of the evolutionary theory that the negative critics are seemingly forever trying to force on the inspired record. In fact, the words of Jesus as recorded by Matthew were spoken ten years *before* the words of Peter to Cornelius; that is, the longer formula was the one spoken first. Since Peter used the shorter formula within 15 days of the time Jesus spoke the longer formula (cp. Acts 2:38 with Matthew 28:19), surely we are to see that there can be no thought of a discrepancy between the two formulae, no matter how the difference be explained.

Then they asked him to stay on for a few days. Cornelius and his friends earnestly requested Peter to stay with them for a period of some days, and Peter consented. The days, we may suppose, were filled with teaching – teaching them to observe all the things that Christ had commanded of immersed disciples. Peter is living with Gentiles, sharing their food and drink, and sleeping there (Acts 11:3). The vision of the rooftop, which taught Peter that the distinction between clean and unclean meats was no longer binding, certainly aided Peter to live as the Gentiles lived. They were brothers in Christ. The middle wall of partition had been broken down. Jew and Gentile were one.

Now that God has taken great pains to make His will about preaching to Gentiles perfectly clear, the way is now prepared for Paul to begin his ministry as apostle to the Gentiles. Before the conversion of Cornelius, Paul would have faced almost insurmountable obstacles, not only from unbelieving Jews, but from his own fellow Christians of Jewish background. Even after God made it plain that He welcomed penitent believers from among the Gentiles, Paul still finds considerable obstacles to overcome as he takes the gospel to the western limits of the Roman empire. But now he will have some help in overcoming those obstacles, as Peter and James and John back him up in his evan-

---

[74] Acts 2:38, 19:5.

gelistic work among the Gentiles.[75]

Drawing by Horace Knowles
from the British and Foreign Bible Society

---

[75] Acts 15:1ff; Galatians 2:1ff.

2. Peter at Jerusalem Defends His Preaching to the Gentiles. 11:1-18

11:1 – *Now the apostles and the brethren who were throughout Judea heard that the Gentiles also had received the word of God.*

Now the apostles and the brethren who were throughout Judea. In Acts 8:1 Luke has told us that the apostles stayed in Jerusalem, even though the Church was scattered by the persecution that arose at the time of Stephen's death. The "brethren who were throughout Judea" would be many of those who were dispersed by that persecution. "Throughout Judea" is the correct translation, and we are apprised of the fact that news of what happened at Cornelius' house spread like wildfire across the length and breadth of Judea. It was a watershed event which the Christians were talking about.

Heard that the Gentiles also had received the word of God. "Gentiles also" – i.e., Gentiles as well as the Samaritans! Cornelius and his friends were representatives of Gentiles in general, and their baptism and welcome into the fellowship of the Church was a precedent. "Receiving the word" is equivalent to belief and obedience. We do not know how long after the conversion of Cornelius and his household it was until the news reached Jerusalem, but the context implies that the news reached Jerusalem while Peter was still staying at Cornelius' house in Caesarea.

11:2 – *And when Peter came up to Jerusalem, those who were circumcised took issue with him,*

And when Peter came up to Jerusalem. Was he summoned up by the Church, or did he come up of his own accord after the conclusion of his ministry in Caesarea?[1] The six brethren from Joppa accompanied Peter (see verse 12).

Those who were circumcised. We suppose that the people who took issue with Peter were converts made to Christianity in and around Jerusalem since the time six years earlier when the original congregation was scattered. They are converts from a Jewish background. It seems implied that some of the apostles who were still at Jerusalem also offered criticism. At the very least, had they expressed their approval of Peter's actions, there would have been less opposition from those circumcised believers who are making this complaint. Some commentators have suggested that these opponents of Peter are the ones who eventually develop into the extreme *Judaizing party* which will so bitterly oppose Paul's ministry among the Gentiles, as recorded in Acts 15, Galatians 2, and elsewhere. Even if it is not the very same people involved, these same principles will motivate the Judaizers' opposition to the gospel.

Took issue with him. These men separated themselves from Peter in a hostile spirit, and

---

[1] The Western text reads, "Peter therefore after a considerable time wished to journey to Jerusalem. He summoned the brethren to him and established them more firmly and then departed preaching many messages and teaching them throughout the regions. When he arrived [at Jerusalem], he announced to them the grace of God [in the case of Cornelius], but the brethren of the circumcision took issue with him ...."

opposed, disputed, contended, or charged Peter with being at fault. The verb tense implies continuous or repeated argument. It must be remembered that the Christians at Jerusalem who were challenging Peter were going through the same struggle which Peter had gone through, and they have not had any visions to help change and mold their attitudes and thinking as Peter had been granted.

Barnes points out the problem this passage causes for those who would like to picture Peter as being the first pope.

> This is one of the circumstances which shows conclusively that the apostles and early Christians did not regard Peter as having any particular *supremacy* over the church, or as being in any peculiar sense the *vicar* of Christ upon earth. If he had been regarded as having the authority which the Roman Catholics claim for him, they would have submitted at once to what he had thought proper to do. But the primitive Christians had no such idea of his authority. This claim for Peter is not only opposed in this place, but in every part of the New Testament.[2]

11:3 – *saying, "You went to uncircumcised men and ate with them."*

Saying, "You went to uncircumcised men and ate with them." The marginal note reads "you entered the house of uncircumcised men." The Jewish Christians did not complain so much about the instruction given to Cornelius, nor about his having been baptized, as they did about a violation of Jewish ceremonial rules by Peter. At Acts 10:28, it was noted that those rules were not based on the Law of Moses but on human tradition. The complaint about habitual eating with the Gentiles must be understood to be a complaint about Peter's eating "unclean" food."[3]

11:4 – *But Peter began* **speaking** *and* **proceeded** *to explain to them in orderly sequence, saying,*

But Peter began *speaking* **and** *proceeded* **to explain to them in orderly sequence, saying.** Peter is explaining to those in Jerusalem how he himself used to have prejudices based on human tradition just like they now have, and how these prejudices were overcome. He explains about the vision he received from the Lord and what God did for Cornelius. Just as Peter was led step by step into his new understanding, so now he is attempting to lead his objectors to the same understanding.

11:5 – *"I was in the city of Joppa praying; and in a trance I saw a vision, a certain object coming down like a great sheet lowered by four corners from the sky; and it came right down to me,*

I was in the city of Joppa praying; and in a trance I saw a vision, a certain object coming down like a great sheet lowered by four corners from the sky. For a detailed commentary on Acts 11:5-15, see notes at Acts 10:9-48. We shall confine ourselves here

---

[2] Barnes, *op. cit.*, p.180-183

[3] See Acts 10:13-14, and compare the attitude of the Pharisees toward Jesus when He broke their traditional rules (Luke 15:1-2).

to the few details not given already in chapter 10. Ellicott has a suggested explanation for the almost verbal repetition we find here in chapter 11. He suggests that Luke, as he examined eyewitnesses, got the information of chapter 10 from Peter and from people in Caesarea, and that the information in chapter 11 is from people in Jerusalem. The close agreement of the two sources is confirmation of the truth of the account.[4]

And it came right down to me. This is more vivid than the description in Acts 10:11. The sheet-like object came out of the sky right up to Peter.

11:6 – *"and when I had fixed my gaze upon it and was observing it I saw the four-footed animals of the earth and the wild beasts and the crawling creatures and the birds of the air.*

And when I had fixed my gaze upon it and was observing it. Peter here tells what was going on in his mind as he looked at the object coming toward him.

I saw the four-footed animals of the earth and the wild beasts and the crawling creatures and the birds of the air.

11:7 – *"And I also heard a voice saying to me, 'Arise, Peter; kill and eat.'*

11:8 – *"But I said, 'By no means, Lord, for nothing unholy or unclean has ever entered my mouth.'*

11:9 – *"But a voice from heaven answered a second time, 'What God has cleansed, no longer consider unholy.'*

11:10 – *"And this happened three times, and everything was drawn back up into the sky.*

And this happened three times, and everything was drawn back up into the sky. There is another touch of vividness here. "Drawn back up" expresses a rapid upward movement.

11:11 – *"And behold, at that moment three men appeared before the house in which we were staying, having been sent to me from Caesarea.*

11:12 – *"And the Spirit told me to go with them without misgivings. And these six brethren also went with me, and we entered the man's house.*

And the Spirit told me to go with them without misgivings. The verb translated "without misgivings" is the same verb translated "took issue" in verse 2. Peter, guided by the Holy Spirit, raised no such opposition as the Jewish Christians were now raising.

And these six brethren also went with me. Here we learn that the six who accompanied Peter from Joppa to Caesarea have also accompanied him to Jerusalem. Perhaps we have now learned the purpose for which Peter had these brethren accompany him to Caesarea. They were to be witnesses with him of what God had done.

---

[4] Ellicott, *op. cit.*, p.184.

And we entered the man's house. Not only Peter, but the six brethren too had broken traditional rules, because they had been instructed to do so, without any misgivings in their hearts about what they were doing. The six brethren have learned from Peter's instruction, it is implied. Can the brethren in Jerusalem also learn?

11:13 – *"And he reported to us how he had seen the angel standing in his house, and saying, 'Send to Joppa, and have Simon, who is also called Peter, brought here;*

And he reported to us how he had seen the angel standing in his house, and saying, 'Send to Joppa, and have Simon, who is also called Peter, brought here. The Greek reads *"the* angel," the one we learned about in Acts 10:3. The language used by Peter implies that the circumstances of the conversion of Cornelius were well known in Jerusalem (cp. also verse 1). Peter says "the angel" as though they were already acquainted with the appearance of the angel to Cornelius.

11:14 – *"and he shall speak words to you by which you will be saved, you and all your household.'*

And he shall speak words to you by which you will be saved, yon and all your household.' These words are not found in the account of the angel's speech in Acts 10, but they are implied. Cornelius has been praying for knowledge of how to be saved; and when the angel told him to send to Joppa for Peter, the implication is that Peter would share that knowledge when he arrived.

11:15 – *"And as I began to speak, the Holy Spirit fell upon them, just as* **He did** *upon us at the beginning.*

And as I began to speak. Peter already had spoken at length (Acts 10:34-44) when the Holy Spirit came upon Cornelius and his friends. This account shows that our suggestion that Peter was interrupted by the coming of the Spirit was correct, for Peter here says he had just opened his message and planned to say much more.

The Holy Spirit fell upon them. Just as *He did* **upon us at the beginning.** The reference in the word "beginning" is to the day of Pentecost (Acts 2), and the "us" is limited to the apostles.[5]

It is strongly implied that there had been no common reception of the baptism with the Holy Spirit since Pentecost, for if it were something that all Christians were expected to and did receive, Peter could have simply pointed to the numerous other incidents and not have had to go back to Pentecost for an example. The inference also can be drawn that the "baptism with the Holy Spirit" was not the thing that converted people, for Peter could have shown that the conversion of Cornelius was like the case of any other person who came to Christ to prove his point.

---

[5] Not many of those to whom Peter is explaining his actions would have been present at the day of Pentecost. for the original congregation at Jerusalem has been scattered. Therefore, the reference seems limited to the apostles.

11:16 – *"And I remembered the word of the Lord, how He used to say, 'John baptized with water, but you shall be baptized with the Holy Spirit.'*

And I remembered the word of the Lord, how He used to say, 'John baptized with water, but you shall be baptized with the Holy Spirit.' See Acts 1:5. Here is where we learn for certain that what happened at Cornelius' house was the baptism with the Holy Spirit just as at Pentecost, and not some other measure of the Spirit.

11:17 – *"If God therefore gave to them the same gift as* He gave *to us also after believing in the Lord Jesus Christ, who was I that I could stand in God's way?"*

If God therefore gave to them the same gift as *He gave* **to us also.** The "gift" is the baptism with the Holy Spirit. "Us" has reference to "us apostles."

After believing in the Lord Jesus Christ. The word "believed" is an aorist participle in the Greek, and probably implies that the believing preceded the giving of the Spirit to the apostles. But the real point is that in each case the Spirit was bestowed, not as a result of circumcision or uncircumcision, but in cases where there was belief!

Who was I. 'What right did I have to oppose the manifest will of God? For He was showing me that Gentiles should be welcomed into the fellowship of believers. I no longer hesitated to offer the invitation or to stay with them, even if they were Gentiles! Nor did I hesitate to eat and associate with them, for they had become brothers and sisters in Christ.' Peter has here reached the point of his explanation at which he has been building. He and other Jewish Christians could not refuse to "accept" those whom God had accepted.

That I could stand in God's way. Peter is saying that to take issue with what was done, as his opponents in Jerusalem were doing, was to attempt to oppose or resist God. [6] Who wants to do that? Peter's presentation causes the other apostles and Christians in Jerusalem to withdraw their opposition to Peter and to begin to commend him for what He did, and they rejoice with him in the conversion of the Gentiles.

11:18 – *And when they heard this, they quieted down, and glorified God, saying, "Well then, God has granted to the Gentiles also the repentance* **that leads** *to life."*

And when they heard this, they quieted down, and glorified God. The Jerusalem Christians were convinced, as Peter had been, by the manifest indications of the will of God. The difference of tenses in the two Greek verbs implies that they first quieted down (i.e., ceased taking issue with Peter), and then they began a continuous utterance of praise.

Saying, "Well then, God has granted to the Gentiles also the repentance *that leads* **to life."** As it did earlier in this passage, "Gentiles also" means to Gentiles as well as to Samaritans and Jews. "Repentance" has an article prefixed to it in the Greek, just as in the

---

[6] Several years later, in Ephesian 3:4-6, Paul will write, "You can understand my insight into the mystery of Christ, which ... has now been revealed to His holy apostles ... that the Gentiles are fellow heirs and fellow members of the body, and fellow partakers of the promise in Christ Jesus through the gospel."

NASB. Perhaps it is an article of previous reference, pointing back to the repentance which Jesus had commanded the Twelve to preach.[7] See also Acts 5:31 for an explanation of "granting repentance," where the same idea occurs. The brethren at Jerusalem have now come to see the truth that the door of salvation and intimate fellowship with God is open to the entire world. The facts rehearsed by Peter had the same effect on the minds of the objectors that they had on the mind of Peter.

Attention must be called to a significant statement in McGarvey's commentary concerning the way the Holy Spirit leads men into all truth. The way the church was led to an understanding of the acceptability of the Gentiles is a good example of how the Spirit leads.

> In this section of the history we have a striking example of one of the ways in which the apostles were led into all the truth, according to the Lord's promise (John 16:13). Peter did not know by virtue of his inspiration that the uncircumcised were to be admitted to baptism; neither did the other apostles, after Peter had baptized some uncircumcised persons, know by virtue of their inspiration that he had done right.
>
> As a matter of course, the Holy Spirit could have illuminated all of their minds internally on this, as on any other topic; but He chose, instead of this, to adopt a different method. By visions addressed to the eye, a voice adopted to his ear, a message sent to him through the command of the angel, reinforced by just one command from the Holy Spirit – and Peter was guided into this new truth; and by a verbal account of the same to his brethren, the latter were brought to the same light. The latter indeed were convinced by the same facts which had convinced Peter; the only difference being that the facts reached Peter through direct revelation, while they reached the others through the words in which Peter recounted them.
>
> In precisely this way the power of all Scripture facts reaches the minds and hearts of men at the present day, and thus the Holy Spirit operates on us through the Word.[8]

It will be important to remember this paragraph in chapter 11 when we come to chapter 15, which recounts Paul's troubles with the Judaizers. Not only did Peter take the first step in the admission of the Gentiles into full fellowship (without forcing them to keep the Law of Moses), but this action was under the direct guidance of the Holy Spirit. Further, the reception of the Gentiles received the approval of the apostles and the other members of the Jerusalem church, so much so that they gave praise to God for it. In chapter 15, as the Judaizers oppose Paul, they were acting against the very church from which they pretended to derive their authority, and against the very apostles they claimed had sent them.[9]

---

[7] Acts 24:47

[8] McGarvey, *op. cit.*, p.221.

[9] The Judaizers we meet later in Acts appear to be a new group, distinct from the one to whom Peter makes his defense. Paul will call them false brethren, who entered the church under false pretenses. It is doubtful that any of those present when Peter presented the Gentiles' conversion would be so styled. That entrance of false brethren into the congregation seems to be a later development.

A second matter must be given some brief attention. Some have urged that Peter began to lose his influence in the Jerusalem church after his association with the Gentiles, and this gave opportunity for James, the Lord's brother, to become the recognized leader of the Jewish element of the church. If anything caused Peter to lose influence, it was the fact that Peter is away from Jerusalem more and more on evangelistic trips, thus leaving the church there under the direction of others.

F. The Church Established in Antioch. 11:19-26

1. Beginning of the Work in Antioch. 11:19-21

11:19 – *So then those who were scattered because of the persecution that arose in connection with Stephen made their way to Phoenicia and Cyprus and Antioch, speaking the word to no one except to Jews alone.*

So then those who were scattered because of the persecution that arose in connection with Stephen. A new and important portion of the history of the church begins with these words. The conversion of Cornelius opens up to the gospel preachers the exciting possibilities of converting the whole Gentile world to Christ. Up to this time, Luke's record shows that the gospel was preached mainly to Jews and proselytes. From this point on, Acts is concerned with the efforts made to convert the Gentiles.

Concerning the scattering of the Church by the persecution that followed the death of Stephen, see notes at Acts 8:1ff. Luke the historian is here picking up another thread of the story which began at 8:1.[10] In some of the earlier chapters he has shown Philip going to Samaria, Saul to Damascus, and Peter to Joppa and Caesarea. Now, we shall see the disciples going to Antioch.

Made their way to Phoenicia and Cyprus. Phoenicia was the country, about 120 miles long and 15 miles wide, located north of Palestine between the shores of the Mediterranean Sea and the slopes of the Lebanon mountains. Its chief cities were Tyre, Sidon, and Tripolis. It formed part of the Roman province of Syria. The preaching in Phoenicia by these Christians (as they were being dispersed) suggests the origin of the churches which will be visited by Paul later in the book of Acts.[11] Cyprus is an island off the southern coast of Asia Minor, in the Mediterranean Sea.[12] It is likely that these people who evangelized in Cyprus prepared the way for the work of Paul and Barnabas (Acts 13:4).

And Antioch. There were as many as five different cities with this same name in the New Testament world, all built by the Seleucids and named in honor of Antiochus the Great. We meet two of them in the New Testament, one situated in Pisidia in Asia Minor,[13] and the other, referred to here, located in Syria on the banks of the river Orontes, near the junction of the Lebanon and Taurus mountain ranges.

To distinguish this city from the others of the same name, this one was called "Syrian Antioch" or "Antioch-on-the-Orontes." Before the Greeks conquered the world, Damascus was considered the capital of Syria, but the Greeks wanted to be nearer the Mediterranean and Asia Minor. Antioch was located about 15 or 16 miles inland from its seaport, Seleu-

---

[10] There is a manuscript variation here, some reading "at the time of Stephen" and the other being "against Stephen." The NASB nicely takes a position half-way between these two ideas with its reading "in connection with Stephen."

[11] Acts 15:3; 21:3,7; 27:3.

[12] See comments at Acts 4:36 for information about Cyprus.

[13] Acts 13:14.

cia. The city grew because of the commerce that passed through her. Josephus calls it the third largest city of the Roman empire.[14] All the varied elements of the life of an ancient city could be found in Antioch. The population was mixed, and the city was divided into "quarters," including Syrian, Greek, Roman, and Jewish.[15] A five-mile long paved highway led south from the city to the wicked suburb of Daphne, where groves, temples, fountains and baths beckoned to the people.[16] The city was renowned for its many public and private baths, its central heating, plumbing, and sanitary sewers, and especially for its lighting system. It was described as "a city where the brightness of the lights at night commonly equals the resplendence of the day."[17] Herod the Great had courted the favor of the Jews who lived there by building a marble colonnade the whole length of one of the main streets of the city.

Antioch was a free city; that is, all who were born there, even Jews, were considered Roman citizens. Years before the Romans, Seleucis Nicator had conferred on the people the right of citizenship, and the right to worship in their own way without molestation. When the Romans conquered the area, these privileges were continued. So this city, where possible influence upon and communication with Rome was greater than Jerusalem's,[18] and where heathenism's debasing and tempting influences were stronger than in Judea, is about to experience the life-changing power of the gospel. Syrian Antioch will become the center of evangelistic activity by the Christians for years to come.

Speaking the word to no one except to Jews alone. This verse apparently speaks of a time before the conversion of Cornelius, though after the persecution that arose about Stephen. These men who came to Antioch were following the custom of the apostles who for many years preached to Jews only. Luke is merely jumping back now and picking up what happened before the conversion of Cornelius. When the church was scattered (Acts 8:1), some went as far as Antioch on the Orontes; and they went preaching (Acts 8:4). In the course of the history of the church at Antioch, the conversion of Cornelius must be understood to come between 11:19 and 11:20.

11:20 – *But there were some of them, men of Cyprus and Cyrene, who came to Antioch and began speaking to the Greeks also, preaching the Lord Jesus.*

But there were some of them, men of Cyprus and Cyrene. "Some of them," i.e., the

---

[14] Josephus, *Wars*, III.2.4.

[15] Josephus, *Antiquities*, XII.3.1; *Wars*, VII.3.13.

[16] The groves of Daphne were infamous for gross sensuality, and the worship at the groves of Daphne in its main features was similar to the worship of Diana of the Ephesians, i.e., it had all the sensuality of witchcraft. An annual festival, known as Maiuma, was held, at which the harlot-priestesses, stripped of clothing, indulged in wanton activities in the waters of the lake.

[17] A. Marcellinus, *Constantius et Gallus*, XIV.1.9.

[18] Antioch had a line of influence and communication with Rome because the Prefect, or President, of the Roman province of Syria had his headquarters at Antioch. Men of arts and letters had carried the fame and vice of Antioch to Rome so that one Roman satirist complained that the Syrian Orontes had polluted the Tiber river with the tainted stream of luxury and vice. *Satire*, III.62-64.

ones who were scattered abroad. These people were natives of Cyprus and Cyrene.[19] The fact that the preachers who first spoke to the Greeks in Antioch were from Cyprus and Cyrene suggests the probability that they had first done some preaching in their own home places, before going upon a "missionary journey" to Antioch. Since this verse is five or six years after the death of Stephen, they have had an abundance of time to do this work.

Who came to Antioch. Antioch of Syria.

And *began* speaking to the Greeks also. It appears that there is a contrast here with those who preached the gospel to the "Jews only" (verse 19). Therefore, the meaning of "Greeks" must be "Gentiles" and not simply "Hellenistic Jews."[20] Why do these men have no prejudice against the Gentiles? Some think it is because of their Hellenistic backgrounds, for they were natives of lands other than Palestine. This commentator thinks it much more probable that the news of the conversion of Cornelius (the Gentile) by Peter, and the approval of those in Jerusalem, has reached the ears of these preachers.

> It appears that these men came to Antioch at a later period than did those who spoke only to Jews. It is clearly implied that something had taken place in the interval to cause the change. What else could that event be, save the conversion of Cornelius, which Luke has just related? So, while Peter's work opened the way, this work in Antioch was the first vigorous invasion of the Gentile world by the advance forces of the Lord's army.[21]

What is the probable date for the coming of these men to Antioch to preach to the Greeks?
- It is after the conversion of Cornelius, and sometime before the death of Herod (AD 44) which is related in chapter 12. But is it possible to date it with any more exactness?
- Per verse 26, Paul and Barnabas labored together for a whole year before Herod's death. Barnabas, then, must have brought Paul to Antioch in the year AD 43.
- Verses 22-25 show that Barnabas had not been in Antioch long before he went to seek for Paul to come help. We could infer that Barnabas was sent from Jerusalem perhaps late in AD 42.
- Since Barnabas was sent from Jerusalem as soon as the Jerusalem church had heard about the successful evangelistic work among the Greeks in Antioch (verse 22), we can conclude that the preaching to Greeks began in late AD 41 or early AD 42.
- Since the baptism of Cornelius occurred before the preaching to the Greeks in Antioch, the conversion of Cornelius must have occurred in AD 40 or 41.

---

[19] Concerning these places, see notes at Acts 2:10 and 4:36.

[20] There is a manuscript variation at this place. Some of the more recent manuscripts, followed by the KJV translation, read *hellēnistas*, which is translated "Hellenists" (see notes at Acts 6:1 for an explanation of this term). A few of the older manuscripts and many of the early Church Fathers have the reading *hellēnas*, which was followed by the ASV and NASB and is properly translated "Greeks," the reference being to Gentiles. This is one place where the context helps decide between the variant readings, and the context seems to require "Greeks."

[21] McGarvey, *op. cit.*, p.223.

Preaching the Lord Jesus. See Acts 8:35-36 for what "preaching Jesus" includes. The marginal reading is "preaching the good news of the Lord Jesus." The contents of the preaching had to do with the fact that Jesus is Lord. To Jews it has been preached that Jesus is Messiah. To these Greeks the emphasis is more on the lordship of Jesus.

11:21 – *And the hand of the Lord was with them, and a large number who believed turned to the Lord.*

And the hand of the Lord was with them. Does this mean that God blessed their work? Or does this mean that they were working miracles?[22]

And a large number who believed turned to the Lord. Note again that "turning to the Lord" is something that follows believing. The expression denotes the conversion of the people of Antioch from heathenism to Christianity.[23] Luke could just as well have said, "a large number that believed were baptized," for in Acts 3:19 we learned that baptism is the turning point at which a man comes into Christ. This turning to the Lord is the result of the preaching of the evangelists and the fact that the hand of the Lord was with them.

Per Luke's record, there is now a church in Antioch comprised of converts from both Jewish and Greek backgrounds. This church then becomes the springboard for the evangelistic efforts to the Gentile world at large.

2. The Jerusalem Church Sends Barnabas to Antioch. 11:22-24

11:22 – *And the news about them reached the ears of the church at Jerusalem, and they sent Barnabas off to Antioch.*

And the news about them reached the ears of the church at Jerusalem. "About them" includes news about both the preachers and the converts. The establishment of a congregation including both Jews and Greeks in such a large Gentile city as Syrian Antioch was a very great victory for the Lord. Naturally the good news would spread and the brethren in Jerusalem would hear of the progress of the gospel.

And they sent Barnabas off to Antioch. Barnabas was introduced at Acts 4:36-37. It is not difficult to suppose why Barnabas was the one picked. First, there was his particular ability of exhortation, just the thing needed by new Christians. Then there was the fact that he was from the same country as the preachers who were doing such a good work in Antioch; this common background would surely help them as they cooperated in the work of evangelism.

---

[22] The expression "hand of the Lord" can speak of God's blessing, or God's punishing, of whatever men are involved with. When "hand of the Lord" is followed by the Greek preposition *meta* (as it is here), the meaning is that God's hand is blessing. If the "hand of the Lord" is followed by *epi* (as it is in Acts 13:11). it means that God's hand is punishing.

[23] The expression "turn to the Lord" has already been explained in notes at Acts 3:19 and 9:35.

It is not hard, either, to figure out the reason why the Jerusalem church sent Barnabas to Antioch. Barnabas' trip was not some kind of investigation, as if the Jerusalem Christians were suspicious of what was happening in Antioch. If the church at Jerusalem can praise the Lord for Cornelius' conversion, they are to be pictured as seeking wholehearted cooperation with the work in Antioch. We should probably view this delegation of Barnabas to Antioch as an effort by the Jerusalem church to express their "fellowship" with the evangelistic work at Antioch.[24] This explanation is corroborated by the fact that the Greek reads "as far as Antioch." The language implies that, on his way, Barnabas was to visit most all the places where the gospel has been preached, and give what help he can.

Any idea that the Jerusalem church was trying (like an ecclesiastical hierarchy) to control all the other churches must be rejected.

> It should be noted that the church at Jerusalem did not send Barnabas to Antioch with orders to report back to the so-called "headquarters." There is no suggestion that they even told him what to do when he got to Antioch. They said that he should go as far as Antioch, but he went into Cilicia and found Saul for the work at Antioch. There was no effort to direct the work in other places from the city of Jerusalem [except as the apostles, who were the rulers of the whole church under Christ, might direct].[25]

11:23 – *Then when he had come and witnessed the grace of God, he rejoiced and* **began** *to encourage them all with resolute heart to remain* **true** *to the Lord;*

Then when he had come and witnessed the grace of God. What did Barnabas see? He saw that God had graciously been at work, drawing souls into the sphere of redemption in Christ. He saw people's lives changed because of the power of the gospel. "Grace" is a broad term in the Scriptures, and it expresses "all that God does to save a man." It can include the sending of the Savior into the world, the making of the way of salvation for people who didn't deserve it, the calling of men to be preachers of the gospel, the sending of preachers to prospects, the work of the Holy Spirit as He through the Word convicts people of their sin and need for a Savior, as well as all that God does to help the saint to persevere in the faith once he or she has accepted it. When all the shades of meaning are known, all the way from "favor" to "grace," the possibilities of what Barnabas witnessed are almost endless.

> In the light of the difficulties in getting Peter and the circumcision party to preach to the Gentiles, it appears that Luke uses "grace" to mean the opposite of the spirit of legalism that so pervaded the Jews, and also he included in the word "grace" a demonstration of the love of God in extending His mercy and salvation to those outside the realm of Judaism.[26]

---

[24] It is helpful to ponder the question, How do we show our "fellowship" when a revival is going on in a neighboring community? Is it done simply by visiting the services one night during the week of evangelistic services? Why not send some workers from our congregation to help them call and teach prospects about the way of salvation? Let Jerusalem's sending of Barnabas be an example we emulate.

[25] Dale, *op. cit.*, p.128.

[26] *Ibid.*, p.129.

He rejoiced. The grateful praise offered earlier at Jerusalem over the conversion of Cornelius now continues as Barnabas sees the results of preaching the gospel to the Gentiles in Antioch.

And *began* to encourage them all. The new converts at Antioch would be exposed to many temptations in the terrifically wicked city of Antioch. The verb tense implies continuing action over a period of time, and the verb in the Greek comes from the same root as that from which the Barnabas got his name "son of encouragement."[27] Luke is telling us that Barnabas was true to his name.

With resolute heart to remain *true* to the Lord. The Christian must have a resoluteness in heart, a fixed and settled determination. Barnabas urged them to make it their purpose in life to keep on remaining loyal to the Lord. The Greek has a definite article. It says "*the* resolute heart;" that is, *the* purposefulness that the Christian life requires. The word "remain true" speaks of "being glued to." The Christian must constantly aim in life to stick close to Christ. Only in this way can the temptations of a morally evil society be overcome.

11:24 – *for he was a good man, and full of the Holy Spirit and of faith. And considerable numbers were brought to the Lord.*

For he was a good man. Probably this verse is viewed as giving a reason why Barnabas was selected for the mission. He was a man who regularly went beyond just what was required of him.[28] There was a winsomeness and unselfishness, a sympathy and kindness, about the man that particularly suited him for the task he had to perform in this mixed congregation at Antioch. Words of praise like this are comparatively rare in the book of Acts, and we may, perhaps, think of them as expressing Luke's personal estimate of the man. This praise will help us to keep from forming a wrong opinion of Barnabas when we read in 15:39 of the sad contention between Paul and Barnabas.

And full of the Holy Spirit and of faith. The same language was used of Stephen.[29] "Full of the Holy Spirit" here would probably mean that his life was full of the fruit of the Spirit (Galatians 5:22ff), though some believe it means he had the power to work miracles and speak by inspiration.[30] "Full of faith" seems to mean that he was a man who had a good grasp of the doctrines of Christ, a man of settled convictions.[31]

---

[27] See notes at Acts 4:36.

[28] In Romans 5:7, Paul makes a distinction between a "righteous man" and a "good man." It is usually explained that the righteous man does what is required of him, whereas the good man goes beyond what is expected of him. This is the background of the comments in the text about Barnabas being "a good man."

[29] See notes at Acts 6:3,5.

[30] Barnabas did have such abilities, for he was an apostle (Acts 14:14), but this does not seem to be the right verse to demonstrate that he had such powers.

[31] "Faith" in the New Testament can refer either to a body of doctrine (as at Jude 3 and Acts 6:7). or to someone's personal convictions (as Acts 3:16 and 6:5). In places like this, when it is not easy to tell which is meant, the comments give both possibilities.

And considerable numbers were brought to the Lord. As the marginal reading shows, the Greek reads literally "great multitudes." "Brought to the Lord" (margin, "added to the Lord") means they became Christians. Because Barnabas continually exhorted them to be true to Christ, and because he was such a winsome man, the result was that multitudes became Christians.[32] Luke's note about the growth of the congregation means there was a large increase in numbers even in addition to what was already enumerated at verse 21. With God's blessing accompanying, the more workers there are, the more converts there will be.

3. Barnabas Brings Paul to Antioch. 11:25-26

11:25 – *And he left for Tarsus to look for Saul;*

And he left for Tarsus. See notes at Acts 9:30.

To look for Saul. The Greek, *anazētēsai,* indicates that Barnabas had some difficulty in locating Paul. He had to hunt for his man. Luke does not spell out the reason why Barnabas goes looking for Paul, but the reason is evident on the surface. Paul was needed because additional workers were needed to shepherd the "considerable numbers" (verse 24) who have been won. Barnabas was acquainted with Paul. He had already vouched for him and introduced him to the Jerusalem church after his conversion.[33] Barnabas must have known that Paul's future work was to be an apostle to the Gentiles. Paul is in the vicinity, there are Gentiles here in Antioch who need his attention, so why not get him? Paul's labors may have been limited to Jews before, but now it is time for him to enter upon his evangelistic work in the larger field of the "uttermost parts of the earth."

11:26 – *and when he had found him, he brought him to Antioch. And it came about that for an entire year they met with the church, and taught considerable numbers; and the disciples were first called Christians in Antioch.*

And when he had found him, he brought him to Antioch. How many things they must have had to talk about – all that had happened to each since they had parted five or six years before. The Western text indicates Barnabas had some difficulty talking Paul into joining the work at Antioch. Perhaps he did, but Paul does come and the work progresses.

And it came about that for an entire year. Antioch was a big city, and considerable numbers of them had become Christians, and needed further indoctrination. Here is an example of a "located ministry" as these men spend a year further instructing those who are already Christians. Later Paul will spend a year and a half in Corinth, and three years

---

[32] When people were added to the Lord, they were also added to the church. They were added when they heard the gospel, believed, repented of their sins, and were baptized into Christ. This is the regular way people are added to the Lord (Galatians 3:26-27; Ephesians 1:7; Romans 6:3ff).

[33] Acts 9:27 shows that Barnabas was acquainted with a number of the details of Paul's conversion as he introduces him to the brethren in Jerusalem.

at Ephesus.[34] New Testament evangelism was not limited to one or two weeks of effort by an itinerant evangelist.

They met with the church. "Met" is an aorist passive infinitive in the Greek, and this has caused some difficulty.

- The passive verb suggests "they (i.e., Paul and Barnabas) were brought together" (i.e., by someone else, perhaps the leading of the Holy Spirit?) in the "assembly" (i.e., the church).
- It probably speaks of coming together for worship, and says that these teachers, Paul and Barnabas, were hospitably welcomed by the congregation.

"With the church" (literally, "in the church" per the Greek) does not talk of church buildings. Such were not constructed until in the 2nd century AD.[35] The language pictures the Christians regularly meeting together as a congregation, an assembly, for worship and study.

And taught considerable numbers. This is an aorist active infinitive, and tells what Paul and Barnabas did. This teaching is done either during the "gathering" of the brethren or, if there is a contrast with the previous phrase which spoke of public assembly, then the teaching here would be the house- to-house teaching of those who are already converted. The same "considerable numbers" who were won earlier are now being grounded and settled in "whatsoever things Jesus has commanded."[36]

And the disciples were first called Christians in Antioch. Who is it that "called" the Antioch believers "Christians"? In fact, this phrase in verse 26 could just as well have been translated "and (they) called the disciples Christians first in Antioch."

- Up until this time, believers in Christ have been designated as "believers," "disciples," "saints," "brethren," "those of the way."
- The Greek verb *chrēmatizō* ("call") is almost always used in the New Testament to mean "divinely called."[37] In fact, the one time when it might have a meaning other than "divinely called," the context clearly indicates that this is the case.[38]
- It is important to note that the verb "called" is an aorist infinitive, and that it is *active* in voice.[39] The English translations (KJV, ASV, NASB, etc.) which translate it as if it were a *passive* voice infinitive (i.e., "were called") are not correct.
- One other technical note is needed. Both of the nouns in this phrase, "disciples" and "Christians," are in the accusative case. If the verb "called" was a *passive* voice infini-

---

[34] Acts 18:11, 20:31.

[35] The earliest known church buildings were in Edessa, Arbella, and the vicinity, about the year AD 200. Arbella is in Assyria, near Nineveh. Edessa is about 40 miles north of Haran in Mesopotamia.

[36] Matthew 28:20, Acts 2:42.

[37] Matthew 2:12; Luke 2:26; Acts 10:22; Hebrews 8:5, 11:7, and 12:25.

[38] Romans 7:3.

[39] *Harper's Analytical Greek Lexicon* (New York: Harper and Brothers, nd), p.438.

tive, the translations in the KJV, ASV, NASB, etc. would be defensible, for Greek grammar has a rule which states that in indirect statements (like we have here), "The subject of the infinitive is in the accusative." But since "called" is an *active* voice infinitive, the translation of the NASB is doubtful. Instead, we should understand that we have a "double accusative" here, and thus we translate it "they called the disciples Christians first in Antioch."

By and large, commentators who have ignored the Greek text and have instead based their comments upon the English translations, have made some conjectures as to the origin of the name "Christian."

- Some suggest that the Gentiles outside the church, with no evil intentions, gave the disciples this name to distinguish them from the Jews who still adhered to the Law. However, such an explanation does not agree with the idea of the verb, that this name is "divinely called."

- Others suggest that the enemies of Christ gave the name to His followers out of derision and vilification. But it is evident from the New Testament that it is not a term of reproach, at least not in the two other places it occurs in Scripture.[40] There is nothing dishonorable in the name Christian.[41] Further, this second suggestion likewise does not give *chrēmatizō* its regular meaning.

- A third suggestion for the origin of the name "Christian" is that the disciples took the name themselves because it is an appropriate title and description for all who faithfully follow Christ. However, this idea does not agree with the connotation regularly found in the word "call," which indicates a name divinely given.

The best and most likely understanding of this phrase is the suggestion made above, that the name was given by divine inspiration through Barnabas and Paul. As indicated above, the word "call" is an infinitive, and so must lean on the main verb of the sentence. In fact, the only finite verb in the sentence is the one translated "it came about." All the rest of the verb forms in this verse are infinitives: in the Greek, "met with" is an infinitive; "taught" is an infinitive; and "called" is an infinitive. The ones who are acting in all these infinitives are "they" (Paul and Barnabas). So, a good literal translation of the sentence would be, "And it happened to them also for a whole year to be assembled with the church and to teach a considerable crowd, and to call firstly in Antioch the disciples Christians." The idea that Paul and Barnabas are the ones who named the disciples Christians does justice to the "divinely given" meaning of the word "call," and it does justice to the verb as an active infinitive.[42]

---

[40] Acts 26:38; 1 Peter 4:16.

[41] Outside the New Testament we find the term "Christian" in Josephus (*Antiquities*, XVIII.3.3), in Pliny the Younger (*Letters*, 10.96), in Tacitus (*Annals*, XV.44), and in Suetonius (*Life of Nero*, XVI.2 and *Life of Claudius*, XVIII.2).

[42] It is probably not correct to appeal to Isaiah 62:2 as being a prediction of the name "Christian" being given to God's people. In Isaiah 62, there are six new names given. And so, in light of the context of Isaiah 62:2, we doubt that it is proper to appeal to it as being a prediction of the specific name "Christian."

At this point, it is probably appropriate to insert some thoughts in regard to the name for the church. Should it be "Christian Church" or "Church of Christ" or "Christ's church"? Here is another situation in which we must be careful not to build a doctrine on one particular translation, whether it be the KJV or ASV, or any other single version.

- In the Greek language, the most common way to denote ownership or possession was by using the genitive case ending of a noun. For example, to show Christ's ownership of something, in the Greek language "Christ" would be in the genitive case.

- In the English language, there are three ways to express the idea of ownership or possession. We may say "Plato's philosophy," or "the philosophy of Plato," or "the Platonian philosophy." In the one case we use an apostrophe and an "s," in one case we use "of," and in the other case we use "-ian." In all three we have expressed the same idea.

- Now, how shall we translate the Greek construction that shows ownership or possession? That is, how shall we translate *ekklēsia christou,* the *christou* being in the genitive case? In English, we could use an apostrophe and an "s" (Christ's church), or we could use "of" (church of Christ), or we may use "-ian" (Christian church). In each case, we have expressed precisely the same idea – that Christ owns the church, or that the church belongs wholly to Him.

To help us see that any one of these translations is proper, one has only to examine the versions at Romans 16:16. The ASV reads "churches of Christ." The NEB reads "Christ's congregations." The Authentic New Testament reads "the Christian communities." We must be very sure we are not guilty of splitting congregations (as has been done in the past in many places and countries) over the name to be worn, if the name being worn is Scriptural!

Surely it is lamentable that denominationalism has so divided and torn asunder the people of God that we must spend time talking about the "designation" by which we shall be called. God help us to work for the unity of believers for which Christ prayed. Let us speak of "the church" — and by such language let everyone know that we are speaking of the people for whom Christ died and rose again, a people "called out" of the world and into service for the Son.

G. The Judean Famine and Relief from Antioch. 11:27-30

11:27 – *Now at this time some prophets came down from Jerusalem to Antioch.*

Now at this time. That is, during the days when Barnabas and Paul were working at Antioch (verse 26).

Some prophets came down from Jerusalem to Antioch. The word "prophet" speaks of a man who preached by inspiration, no matter the content of the message he delivered."[43] This is Luke's first mention of the spiritual gift of prophecy among the Christians, but Aga-

---

[43] See Acts 2:17 for details about "prophet" and "prophecy."

bus and his companions seem to have been well-known already "as prophets." "Prophet" was one of the temporary offices in the early church.[44] The mission and purpose of these prophets was obviously to help the growing work at Antioch, and to show that the Jerusalem church heartily approved and wanted to help.

11:28 – *And one of them named Agabus stood up and* **began** *to indicate by the Spirit that there would certainly be a great famine all over the world. And this took place in the* **reign** *of Claudius.*

And one of them named Agabus stood up. This man is named in one other place in the New Testament. In Acts 21:10-11, he is the one who foretells that Paul would be delivered into the hands of the Gentiles when he gets to Jerusalem at the close of the third missionary journey. This current message Agabus speaks was probably delivered in a public assembly of the Christians. In fact, the Western text reads that Agabus came down from Jerusalem, "and when we had gathered around, he began to indicate ...."[45]

And *began* to indicate by the Spirit. He made his prediction about the coming famine by the revelation and inspiration of the Holy Spirit.[46]

That there would certainly be a great famine. A famine is a shortage of food, generally resulting either from lack of rain during the growing season so that the crops fail, or from the deliberate refusal of an attacking army to allow the entrance of food into a city it has under siege. The former was the cause of the famine Agabus predicts.

All over the world. The Greek word is *oikoumenē*, and it usually refers to "the whole inhabited world" – i.e., the whole Roman empire. Many commentators, however, try to limit the word here to just Palestine, since the next verse tells of sending an offering to Judea. If it were a world-wide famine, it is argued, wouldn't the Antiocheans themselves need help, rather than being able to send help? In reply, it could be that we have something similar to the case of Joseph, in which the people, having been forewarned, made preparation for the coming famine, not only for themselves, but for others.

And this took place in the *reign* of Claudius. This is a note by Luke, long after it happened, that the predicted thing came to pass. Luke is writing his history after the event predicted had happened, and it was natural to give passing notice to its fulfillment.

---

[44] See notes at Acts 15:32.

[45] Scholars whose life's work is an attempt to reproduce for us a Greek text of the New Testament similar to the autographs which have perished, usually divide the ancient copies of the New Testament into families. Often these are called the Alexandrian, the Eastern, and the Western families. The Greek texts used to create our English translations are more nearly like the readings of the first two, and the Western family is usually rejected whenever it differs materially from the other two. However, for Luke and Acts, some scholars believe that in many places the Western text is more nearly like the autographs. In this verse, if that were true, we would have some evidence that Luke was a native of Antioch, for observe that he writes "we" – i.e., "when we had gathered around." Compare notes at Acts 16:10.

[46] Concerning revelation and inspiration, see Special Study, "The Doctrine of Inspiration," at the close of chapter 2.

Claudius was the Roman emperor from AD 41-54.[47] His reign ended when he was poisoned by one of his wives, Agrippina, who wished for her son Nero to become emperor. During Claudius' reign, no less than four famines occurred. In AD 42 or 43, there was a severe famine in Rome.[48] In AD 50, there was a severe famine in Greece.[49] In AD 51, there was another famine at Rome.[50] A fourth famine is mentioned as having occurred in Judea, in AD 45, when Cuspius Fadus was governor.[51] Which of these famines is to be identified with the one Agabus predicts? Perhaps it is the same as the one mentioned by Josephus. If so, the famine relief comes as the famine is just about to begin. Some doubt that the famine Josephus tells of is to be identified with the one Agabus predicts, for it happened after the death of Herod Agrippa I, whereas in the following verses of Acts Herod Agrippa I is still alive when Paul and Barnabas arrive with the famine relief. Some authors believe that Luke's note about the date of the fulfillment of the prediction infers that the prediction was made in the last year of Caligula's emperorship, and then came true in Claudius' time.

11:29 – *And in the proportion that any of the disciples had means, each of them determined to send* **a** contribution *for the relief of the brethren living in Judea.*

And in the proportion that any of the disciples had means. The "disciples" are the Christians in Antioch, whether of Jewish or Gentile background. Here is a clear statement of the nature of Christian stewardship. Once the Christians have learned of the need (through Agabus), any of the disciples who could took part in contributing to the need. They are probably giving a proportionate offering; i.e., they are giving as they have been prospered. Now if a person was able, he gave much; if a person was not able, he gave as much as he could. They gave as they had means.[52]

Each of them determined to send *a contribution* **for the relief of the brethren.** Note that it is not something done by the few. "Each of them" is involved. This approaching famine gives the church at Antioch an opportunity to "fellowship" with the church at Jerusalem. Jerusalem has sent teachers and prophets to help the brethren in Antioch. Now the brethren in Antioch have an opportunity to help their fellow believers in Jerusalem. The obligation to relieve the temporal needs of those from whom important spiritual blessings are received is repeatedly enforced in the New Testament.[53]

---

[47] This chronological note given by Luke reinforces the correctness of the suggested dates given in the comments above at verse 20.

[48] Dio Cassius, LX.11; Suetonius, *Life of Claudius,* XVIII.

[49] Eusebius, *Chronicon,* p.204.

[50] Tacitus, *Annals,* XII.43.

[51] Josephus, *Antiquities,* XX.5. He writes, "A famine did oppress them at the time [in Claudius' reign], and many people died for want of what was necessary to procure food withal. Then Helena [queen of Adiabene] sent some of her servants to Alexandria with money to buy a great quantity of corn, and others of them to Cyprus to bring a cargo of dried figs."

[52] Here is another indication the community of goods (Acts 2:44-45; 4:32) was not absolute communism.

[53] Romans 15:25-27; 1 Corinthians 9:13, 14; 16:1, 2; 2 Corinthians 9:1, 2; Galatians 2:10.

Living in Judea. The reference seems to be to Jerusalem in particular. See Acts 12:25 where Jerusalem is specifically mentioned. Perhaps the congregations scattered throughout Judea were also beneficiaries of this demonstration of Christian love by the believers at Antioch.

11:30 – *And this they did, sending it in charge of Barnabas and Saul to the elders.*

And this they did, sending it ... to the elders. This is the first indication we have in the book of Acts that there are "elders" in the New Testament church.[54] In Acts 20:17,28 and Titus 1:5,7, we learn that "elders" and "bishops" were merely different titles for the same office. The elders were spiritual leaders in the congregation, and the benevolent offering from Antioch was turned over to them; and they in their turn were responsible for getting it to the Christians who were in need.

> The manner in which the elders of the churches in Judea are here mentioned, without previous notice of their having been appointed, shows the elliptical character of Luke's narrative, and results from the circumstance that he wrote after the churches had been fully organized, and all of the officials and their duties has become well known. The elders, being the rulers (overseers) of the congregations, were the proper persons to receive the gifts, and to see to the proper distribution of them to the needy.[55]

In charge of Barnabas and Saul. This visit of Paul to Jerusalem is not recounted in Galatians 1:18 and 2:1 because on this trip Paul did not meet any of the apostles.[56]

The order in which the names Barnabas and Saul here appear is noteworthy. Beyond any question of doubt, as far as the church at Antioch was concerned, Barnabas was by far the more prominent of the two men, in relation to the work that they are involved in now. The order of their names is the only thing such a statement is based on; but we must remember that it was Barnabas who came to Antioch first, nurtured the work, and then went to Tarsus to get Paul. He brings Paul back to Antioch to work there; and it is "Barnabas and Saul," not "Saul and Barnabas." Barnabas is the leader in this cooperative ministry at this time. These men have been trusted by the Antioch church to deliver all the relief money to the needy in Jerusalem and Judea.

---

[54] See also notes on "being built up" at Acts 9:31.

[55] McGarvey, *op. cit.*, p.230-231.

[56] See "The Relationship of Galatians 2:1-10 and Acts 15:1-35: Two Neglected Arguments," by Robert H. Stein, in *Journal of the Evangelical Theological Society*, Vol. XVII, No. 4 (Fall, 1974), p.17ff, for some other attempts at harmonizing the visits of Paul to Jerusalem. With Stein, we agree that the fewest problems are produced if we harmonize Galatians 2 with Acts 15, rather than if we try to harmonize Galatians 2 with Acts 11.

H. Persecution of the Church by the Civil Government. 12:1-25

1. James Beheaded and Peter Imprisoned. 12:1-11

12:1 – *Now about that time Herod the king laid hands on some who belonged to the church, in order to mistreat them.*

Now about that time. Perhaps the time referred to is the time of the famine predicted by Agabus. Perhaps the time is the time Paul and Barnabas went to Jerusalem. It is near the year AD 44.[1]

Herod the king. Herod Agrippa I is the man Luke is writing about. He appears only here in Acts 12 in the pages of the New Testament. He was born about 10 BC, the son of Aristobulus and Bernice, and thus was a grandson of Herod the Great and a brother of Herodias who asked for John the Baptist's head. He was named after the Roman statesman who was the chief minister of Caesar Augustus. When he was about four years old, his father was murdered by his grandfather; Herod the Great was suspicious that Aristobulus was plotting to take his throne. As a result, Herod Agrippa I was sent to Rome, partly perhaps as a hostage and partly to be out of the way of Palestine's intrigues. He was thus educated in Rome, and while there became a close friend of Gaius (the grandnephew of the emperor Tiberius), who afterwards is known in imperial history as the emperor Caligula.

After the marriage of his uncle Herod Antipas to his sister Herodias, Herod Agrippa I was made the ruler of the city of Tiberias, but he soon had a quarrel with the tetrarch and went back to Rome. There he soon fell under the displeasure of the emperor Tiberius because he one day foolishly spoke where others could hear his wish that his boyhood friend Caligula could quickly become emperor. Tiberius had him thrown into prison, where he remained until Tiberius died in AD 37. When Caligula came to the throne he loaded his friend Herod Agrippa I with honors, gave him the tetrarchies that had been ruled by both Philip and Lysanias, and conferred on him the title of King. His sister Herodias, out of jealous ambition, prompted her husband Antipas to go to Rome to claim a like honor for himself, but he fell under the displeasure of Caligula, and was banished to Lugdunum in Gaul (France), with his wife accompanying him. The tetrarchy that had been Antipas' was thereupon also given to Herod Agrippa I.

There came a time in Caligula's reign when he resolved to have a statue of himself set up in the Temple at Jerusalem. Agrippa I rendered an essential service to the Jewish people by using all his influence to deter the emperor from carrying his resolve into effect. When Caligula died, Herod Agrippa I supported the claims of Claudius to be the next emperor, and when Claudius became emperor he repaid Agrippa by confirming him in his kingdom. Claudius became emperor early in AD 41, and added Judea and Samaria to the lands that Agrippa I already ruled. The terms of Claudius' confirmation of Agrippa I made him an independent sovereign as far as any Roman provincial governor was concerned.

When Agrippa I, newly confirmed as king of Judea, arrived in Judea, he presented himself to the Jewish people as a devout worshiper, almost Pharisaic in his piety. He gained

---
[1] Compare Acts 11:20,25.

the favor of his new subjects by attaching himself to the companies of Nazarites when they came to the Temple to offer sacrifices on the completion of their vows.[2] The last three years of his life are covered by events in Acts 12.[3]

Perhaps the persecution of the church by Herod Agrippa I was part of his attempt to win the favor of his new subjects in Judea. We may suppose that when he arrived in Judea, he found much popular excitement against the Christians, perhaps caused by the new step which had recently been taken in the admission of the Gentiles to the church. (Remember, even the Christians were hesitant to accept this until Peter explained to them how God led in the matter.) Perhaps, too, the opposition to the Christians was spurred on by the Saducean aristocracy who Agrippa I would be anxious to please. It likely seemed advantageous to Agrippa to gain the favor of both Sadducees and Pharisees by making himself the instrument of their opposition to what the Christians were doing and believing.

Laid hands on some who belonged to the church, in order to mistreat them. "Laid hands on" is the same expression used in Acts 4:3 and 5:18 to signify an arrest in which the prisoners are roughly handled. Those earlier persecutions were of a religious nature, instigated by the Sadducees. This time the persecution is encouraged by a civil ruler. It has been over eight years since the death of Stephen and the last persecution, but the disciples were not popular with either the Sadducees or Pharisees. Now that the political situation is not one which demands that the Jews protect their interest from Rome, they can again encourage the opposition to the Christians. Two of the church members who were "mistreated" are immediately singled out by Luke, though it is probable that more than these two were involved.

12:2 – *And he had James the brother of John put to death with a sword.*

And he had James the brother of John put to death. This was the son of Zebedee, one of the twelve original apostles. He was the first of the apostles to be martyred.[4] Luke has told us nothing of James' work; but we may suppose he was doing significant evangelization, for otherwise it is hard to think of a reason for Herod or the Jews to make him a prime target of this persecution.

With a sword. When being executed by a sword, a man would either be beheaded or pierced through. Had this apostle been tried by the Sanhedrin on a charge of blasphemy and heresy, the sentence would have been death by stoning, as in the case of Stephen. Execution by means of a sword showed, as in the case of John the Baptist, that the sentence was pronounced by a civil ruler (adopting Roman modes of punishment). Execution by the

---

[2] Josephus, *Antiquities*, XIX.7.3.

[3] See the record of Herod Agrippa I's rule over the whole land of Judea in the brief paragraph about him in the Introductory Studies.

[4] In an early Christian calendar of martyrs, the deaths of James and his brother John are marked on the same day, December 27. This fact, plus the words of Jesus (Mark 10:37-39), have led some to conclude that John, too, died at the hands of Herod Agrippa I. But this is one early Christian tradition that is evidently in error. For example, seven years later when Paul visits Jerusalem for the Conference, John was still alive at that time (Acts 15:1ff; Galatians 2:1ff). The fact is that John lived the longest of any of the men Jesus chose to be His apostles, his life closing at the turn of the century in Ephesus.

sword was deemed by the Jews to be the most ignominious of the forms of capital punishment.

Eusebius, often called the Father of Church History, has a touching account of the death of James, as originally related by Clement of Alexandria. He tells how the soldier who led James to the judgment seat was so impressed by the testimony of James that he was moved and confessed that he himself was also a Christian. Both he and James were then led away to be executed at the same time. On the way to the execution, the soldier begged James to forgive him; and after James considered it for a moment, did so, kissed him, and said "Peace be to thee." Both were then beheaded at the same time.[5]

James is the only one of the Twelve of whose death there is any record in the New Testament, and how extremely brief is the record when compared with the details of Stephen's death.

> The death of James, the first apostle who suffered martyrdom, must have been a source of indescribable grief to the church in Jerusalem; and to an uninspired historian, it would have furnished matter for many pages of eloquent writing; what shall we think, then, of Luke as a writer, who disposes of it in a sentence of seven words in the Greek? Surely there is an indication here of some supernatural restraint upon the impulses of the writer, and it is accounted for only by his inspiration.[6]

12:3 – *And when he saw that it pleased the Jews, he proceeded to arrest Peter also. Now it was during the days of Unleavened Bread.*

And when he saw that it pleased the Jews. Luke is telling us that Agrippa I's motives were simply political expediency. It wasn't that he had any real anti-Christian fanaticism, nor was he particularly interested in justice or protecting the innocent. Whenever a civil official acts simply to promote his own popularity, he is not really discharging his duties in the proper manner; but such it ever was with the Herods. They held their appointment under the Roman emperor, and such foreign rule was not always popular with the Jews. In order, therefore, to secure as much cooperation as possible from the captive peoples it was necessary for them to court the favor of the Jews.

He proceeded to arrest Peter also. Peter was one of the apostles of Christ, just as was James. As a leader in the church, he would be a special target of this persecution if it were triggered by the church's acceptance of the Gentiles to fellowship without demanding of them all the old Jewish customs and taboos; in fact, he was the one who went to Cornelius' house and preached the gospel to them, and then he was the one who instructed all the Christians to do likewise as he defended his actions before the brethren in Jerusalem. Such actions would infuriate the fanatical Jews. When Peter was arrested, did he think that perhaps the time had come for Jesus' prediction about his manner of death to be fulfilled?[7]

---

[5] *Church History*, II.9.

[6] McGarvey, *op. cit.*, p.232.

[7] John 21:18.

Now it was during the days of Unleavened Bread. This speaks of the Feast of the Passover,[8] and of the seven days immediately following that feast, when the Jews were required to eat unleavened bread.[9] This particular time chosen to arrest Peter because, at the Passover, there would be a larger number of Jews than ordinary in Jerusalem; this meant more people would be able to see Agrippa I's "zeal for the Law," and it would help his popularity with the people over whom he has been appointed king.

12:4 – *And when he had seized him, he put him in prison, delivering him to four squads of soldiers to guard him, intending after the Passover to bring him out before the people.*

And when he had seized him, he put him in prison. After he was arrested, Peter was imprisoned, because during the time of the feast, it would have been deemed as improper to have taken time for a trial and execution of a supposed criminal. If Agrippa I is trying to show the Jews how devout he is, he must spend his time in the religious activities, rather than in such civil duties as would profane the feast. So Peter is to be kept in custody until the Passover week is ended. Did Peter, in jail during the Passover season, think of how Jesus had been taken into custody at the same season, some years before?

Delivering him to four squads of soldiers to guard him. Each "squad" consisted of four men. These sixteen soldiers were responsible for guarding the prisoner around the clock. The night was divided into four different watches, each three hours long.[10] Whether each squad of soldiers was on duty every twelve hours, or whether each squad was on duty for six hours before being relieved by the next one, we have no way of knowing. When each squad was on duty, two of the four were with Peter in the cell (verse 6), and two kept watch before the door of the prison. Why such strict security measures for this prisoner? Remember that this is the third time Peter has been in jail. The last time, he escaped through what must have appeared to the authorities to be mysterious circumstances.[11] This time the authorities are trying to make sure the prisoner doesn't escape.

Intending after the Passover. One problem a translator faces is choosing a word in the language of the translation that will help the reader to get a correct idea of what was said in the original. At this place, the KJV reads "after Easter." The Greek has simply, "after the Passover," and there was no need for the KJV translators to use "Easter" at this place when they had elsewhere translated the same Greek word "Passover" and expected the reader who was familiar with the Old Testament nomenclature to understand.

Why then this translation in the KJV? One of the instructions given to the translators by James, King of England, was that they were not to change any of the accepted terms found in the Bishops' Bible (which was more or less the basis for the KJV). Before that version, Tyndale and Coverdale had used the word "Easter" at this place; hence, it had become a customary rendering of this verse before it was ever incorporated in the KJV.

---

[8] "Passover" has been explained in comments at Acts 2:1.

[9] Exodus 12:15-18.

[10] The "watches" of the night are named at Mark 13:35.

[11] Acts 4:3, 5:18

The use of the word "Easter" in the KJV has led some to suppose the early church was already, in Herod Agrippa I's time, having special services of celebration at Easter time. In fact, however, no such festival as Easter was observed in the early church, and was not for several centuries.[12] During the New Testament times, the Christians did not celebrate with a special service in honor of the resurrection on one particular day of the year, as is the current custom in many places in our time. The early Christians celebrated His resurrection every Lord's Day by keeping the Lord's Supper and worshiping.[13]

To bring him out before the people. Agrippa I apparently is planning to have a public trial and execution. It is part of a carefully programmed and orchestrated effort to curry the favor of the people.

12:5 – *So Peter was kept in the prison, but prayer for him was being made fervently by the church to God.*

So Peter was kept in the prison. Things do not always work out the way men plan, especially when God is not included in the plans. Herod Agrippa I intended to execute Peter as soon as Passover week was ended. Instead, his own death was nearer than that of Peter's. Peter was kept in the prison, and the days of the week passed, until the last night of Passover week.

But prayer for him was being made fervently by the church to God. The adverb "fervently" implies both intensity and continuity.[14] The verb tense indicates that all the while Peter was being held, the church was continuing to pray for him. The picture is that the members of the congregation continued to meet, in spite of the persecution, perhaps in the home of Mary (verse 12), to send up prayers day and night to the throne of God.

12:6 – *And on the very night when Herod was about to bring him forward, Peter was sleeping between two soldiers, bound with two chains; and guards in front of the door were watching over the prison.*

---

[12] Dale. *op. cit.*, p.138, reminds us that the word Easter is Anglo-Saxon in origin. "The Anglo-Saxon races had a spring festival, celebrations at which they offered sacrifice to the Teutonic goddess Estera (or Eastre). She was the goddess of light and spring, so the sacrifice and festival was observed in April; and by coincidence the time of the festival corresponded roughly with the time of Christ's resurrection. Sometime about the 8th century AD, the name Easter was transferred to the Christian festival which had by then been observed some 300 years in honor of the resurrection of Christ."

[13] A word is in order about the observance of special days in the church calendar, including greatly promoted and programmed pre-Easter and pre-Christmas emphases. What must be examined is the *motive* behind having such special programs on these days and not on others. Certainly, there is nothing wrong with having our little children memorize parts and repeat them to the congregation. Certainly, there is no evil in preaching a good gospel sermon on the birth of Christ at the "Christmas" season, or on the resurrection of Christ at the "Easter" season. But why have special services only at these times of the year? Are we merely doing what the rest of the religious world is doing? (Remember, many of the special days have been inherited from the Roman Catholic church after years of evolutionary and traditional development.) Such methods as observance of special days do fall into the realm of opinion, so what this commentator is pleading for is that our motives and methods do not slowly lead us away from the simple New Testament practices and emphases.

[14] The same word is used in 1 Peter 4:8.

And on the very night when Herod was about to bring him forward. It is the night preceding the day when Peter was to be executed. It would be Saturday night, for the Passover week would end at 6:00 p.m. on Saturday. Peter could be executed on Sunday morning without profaning the services of the week of Unleavened Bread.

Peter was sleeping. It is difficult to sleep peacefully when the mind is filled with apprehension, or when the conscience is reproving because of some sin that is known and unconfessed. Some contemporary studies of death and dying have even suggested there are several stages through which a person goes as the time to die has come, stages varying all the way from rebellion to acceptance of the fact.[15] That Peter is able to sleep so calmly when tomorrow he will be executed suggests that he has no fear of dying since Jesus has transformed by His resurrection the meaning of death; it also suggests that his conscience is at peace because Peter is covered by the blood of Christ. Peter was prepared, if that is what the morrow brought, to enter into the intermediate state and be with Jesus again.

Between two soldiers, bound with two chains. Peter was chained to the two, one arm chained to one soldier's arm, and his other arm chained to the other soldier's arm. Is it implied that the two soldiers on either side of Peter were also sleeping, as was the prisoner? Is that why they give no alarm when the prisoner leaves?

And guards in front of the door were watching over the prison. Two soldiers of the four-man squad were stationed at the door of the cell in which Peter was bound, or perhaps one was at the door, and the other was at the beginning of the tunnel that led to the inner dungeon in which Peter was kept (verse 10). God is able to deliver Peter in spite of all the precautions of men – soldiers, prison, chains, iron gates. The wisdom of God so surpasses that of men, that He is able to overcome even the most ingenious man-made plans.

12:7 – *And behold, an angel of the Lord suddenly appeared, and a light shone in the cell; and he struck Peter's side and roused him, saying, "Get up quickly." And his chains fell off his hands.*

And behold, an angel of the Lord suddenly appeared. Either the angel is pictured as moving from the sky suddenly down into the room, or once in the room he suddenly becomes visible after having entered the cell in an invisible form. "Appeared" is Luke's regular word used for angelic appearances,[16] and is also used of our Lord's appearance to Paul.[17] Some information about angels has been given at Acts 1:10.[18]

And a light shone in the cell. This was not a flash of lightning. Light, splendor, and shining apparel are commonly represented as the accompaniments of heavenly beings when

---

[15] Elisabeth Kubler-Ross, *Questions on Death and Dying* (New York: Collier-Macmillan Co., 1974). p.1-38.

[16] Luke 2:9, 24:4.

[17] Acts 23:11.

[18] See also footnote #60 in chapter 7.

they visit the earth.[19] Whether or not the glow was seen only by Peter, or also by the soldiers, is not stated. The light did not awaken Peter, so the angel had to awaken him.

And he struck Peter's side and roused him, saying, "Get up quickly." It is often difficult to rouse a person from a sound sleep, and this is true for the angel who woke Peter. Are the guards chained to Peter stunned or asleep? At the resurrection of Jesus, the guards were stunned,[20] and some think a similar thing was done to the guards on either side of Peter and in the hall outside. In the absence of any specific word about their being stunned, some have urged that those inside with Peter were asleep along with Peter. It is true that guards at their posts – like those in the hall outside the door of the cell – could be put to death for sleeping at their posts. But those on the inside were in a little different situation.

And his chains fell off his hands. The removal of the chains was something miraculous. The suggestion that Manaen,[21] or some other human agent,[22] slipped in and freed Peter, is shown by this phrase to be too absurd to seriously consider. Further, this phrase shows that the suggestion that the "light" in the cell was lightning will not satisfy all the requirements of the text. It would have been strange lightning indeed that unchained Peter without disturbing the soldiers chained to him on either side, and at the same time made it possible for him to rise, put on his sandals and outer garments, and to walk from the prison.

12:8 – *And the angel said to him, "Gird yourself and put on your sandals." And he did so. And he said to him, "Wrap your cloak around you and follow me."*

And the angel said to him, "Gird yourself. When lying down to sleep, people of the 1st century laid aside their outer garments[23] (or used them for a cover), loosened the belt that bound the inner garment to the waist, and took off their sandals. Peter was directed by the angel to fasten his belt, and put on his outer garment, that is, to get dressed and get ready to go out. Peter now knew the time to be girded by another (John 21:18) had not yet arrived.

And put on your sandals." The Greek *sandalion* occurs only here and at Mark 6:9 in the New Testament. It regularly stands for shoes worn by the poor, a sole made of wood or leather, bound to the foot by thongs.

And he did so. Peter follows the angel's instructions explicitly.

And he said to him, "Wrap your cloak around you and follow me." Peter is now instructed to put his outer garment around his shoulders. The angel then leads the way toward freedom, with Peter following close behind.

---

[19] Luke 2:9, 24:4; Mark 9:3.

[20] Matthew 28:4.

[21] Acts 13:1

[22] *Aggelos*, the word translated "angel," can be translated "messenger" and thus speak of a human rather than angelic person.

[23] The outer garment was a large piece of cloth, nearly square

12:9 – *And he went out and continued to follow, and he did not know that what was being done by the angel was real, but thought he was seeing a vision.*

And he went out and continued to follow, and he did not know that what was being done by the angel was real, but thought he was seeing a vision. On "vision" see notes at Acts 9:10. It has been suggested that when Peter hit the cool night air, it really woke him up, and only then did he realize for the first time what was happening to him was more than a dream.

12:10 – *And when they had passed the first and second guard, they came to the iron gate that leads into the city, which opened for them by itself; and they went out and went along one street; and immediately the angel departed from him.*

And when they had passed the first and second guard. The soldiers outside the cell apparently were stationed at intervals in the entry way into the prison. These guards were passed silently. Probably something happened like was done to the two on the way to Emmaus, whose "eyes were prevented" (Luke 24:16), so that Peter's guards were unaware of what was happening.

They came to the iron gate that leads into the city. Perhaps the language means that the prison was outside the walls of the city, someplace like the Tower of Antonia. There would have been a door separating the barracks from the pavement and the door would have opened onto a raised platform above the pavement.[24]

Which opened for them by itself. The Greek word is *automatē*, i.e., automatically. There was no key used, nor force of any kind like a battering ram or a kick. As Peter and the angel approached the gate, it just swung open to allow them to pass through into the city. When we reflect on how such security gates would be barred for the night, that it opened of its own accord is miraculous indeed.

And they went out and went along one street. The angel accompanied Peter until he was one block away from the prison door. The word "street" is the one that speaks of the narrow streets of the city. Codex Beza tells us that after they went out through the opened gate, they "went down seven steps," and then through the city streets. This too would fit what we know of the Tower of Antonia, so that likely the prison in which Peter was held was inside that fortress.

And immediately the angel departed from him. The angel stayed with Peter until there was no further need of such supernatural aid as he had rendered to get Peter outside the prison. God's messenger had effected Peter's complete rescue; now Peter is able to make it on his own, in a natural human manner.

---

[24] See notes further on in verse 10 about the additional phrase found in Codex Beza regarding the "seven steps."

12:11 – *And when Peter came to himself, he said, "Now I know for sure that the Lord has sent forth His angel and rescued me from the hand of Herod and from all that the Jewish people were expecting."*

And when Peter came to himself. There is the tone of a personal remembrance in these words, as though Luke has learned these details from Peter himself. There he was, at night, free, standing in the open street. Peter thinks about it for a moment. He is not dreaming! It has actually happened, and he is on the outside of the prison, a free man.

He said, "Now I know for sure that the Lord has sent forth His angel. "Lord" is probably a reference to the Father rather than Christ. Just as in his previous prison stay (Acts 5:19), God has sent an angel to deliver Peter. Reflecting on all that happened, Peter is satisfied that what he saw was an angel, and that he was delivered by divine help.

And rescued me from the hand of Herod and from all that the Jewish people were expecting." Peter knew what the future held in store for him: he had been in prison awaiting execution. Peter had recognized that Herod's desire to be popular, and that the earnest desire of the unconverted Jews to exterminate Christianity, were the chief motivations behind his pending death. Those Jews who were present in great numbers at Jerusalem during the Passover week were talking about and anticipating Peter's death.

2. Peter Leaves the City and the Guards are Slain. 12:12-19

12:12 – *And when he realized this, he went to the house of Mary, the mother of John who was also called Mark, where many were gathered together and were praying.*

And when he realized *this.* The ASV's translation is probably better at this place when it uses the verb "consider," for the word seems to include a consideration of the future. Peter quickly surveys the situation as a whole, weighing the possibilities of what he should do. The apostle James was already dead. Many in the church were being harassed. He himself had been facing sentence and execution at the hands of Agrippa I. In a few hours, daylight would bring a change of guards, and then the alarm would sound when it was learned the prisoner had escaped. If he did not wish to be rearrested, he had to act promptly.

He went to the house of Mary, the mother of John. This house appears to be a regular meeting place for the Christians. It is very possible that it was in this home that Jesus instituted the Lord's Supper, and that it has been a center of Christian activity since Pentecost. If so, it appears that this is a family of Christians who stayed in Jerusalem in spite of the persecution that scattered many of the others (Acts 8:1ff).

Who was also called Mark. This is the young man who fled into the night, leaving the sheet which was his only outer covering, as Jesus was being arrested and led away to trial.[25] He is the one who later wrote the second Gospel, recording in that book what Peter used to

---

[25] Mark 14:51.

preach.[26] Mark is his Latin name; John is his Hebrew name. Peter calls Mark "my son,"[27] which likely means that Peter led him to Christ. Mark is frequently named later in the New Testament as he accompanies Paul, Barnabas, and Peter on their missionary journeys.[28] In Colossians 4:10, he is called a cousin of Barnabas.[29]

Where many were gathered together and were praying. The implication may be that this was but one of several prayer meetings being held in homes in and around Jerusalem. Verse 25 perhaps even implies that Paul and Barnabas were included in the group meeting in Mary's home for prayer.

We may picture it as being sometime after midnight when Peter arrives at the home of Mary. If he escaped before midnight, his absence would have been discovered before daylight given the timing of the changing of the guards. When he arrived at the house, the brethren have been praying. But for what were they praying? Verse 5 might seem, on first sight, to indicate that they were praying for Peter's release. But since Jesus taught his followers to pray believing they would have what they asked for, it is likely they have *not* been praying for Peter's release. Otherwise they would not have been amazed when Peter showed up at the door.

> One may safely assume the [topics and] burdens of their prayers. Each of them was in danger of losing his life at the hands of Herod [Agrippa I]. Sorrow bore down upon them at the loss of their beloved leader, James. Uncertainty and dread awaited them with Peter in prison awaiting death ... They were talking to the Father in heaven about their difficulties. Most likely they directed their prayers more to aid Peter's faith and courage in the hour of death than for his release. No doubt they asked for wisdom in trying to decide what they themselves should do, where they should go to escape, or if they should stand and die for their faith.[30]

12:13 – *When he knocked at the door of the gate, a servant-girl named Rhoda came to answer.*

When he knocked at the door of die gate. The floor plan of a house of a middle- or upper-class family, as this family certainly must have been, would be something like this:

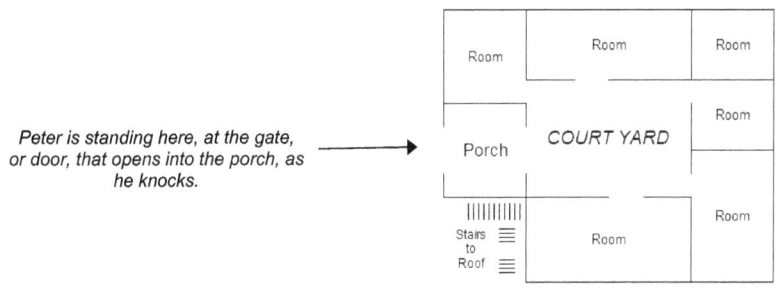

---

[26] Eusebius, *Church History*, III.39.

[27] 1 Peter 5:13.

[28] Acts 12:25, 13:5, 15:39; 2 Timothy 4:11; 1 Peter 5:13.

[29] The Greek word *anepsios* means "first cousin," not "sister's son" as the KJV reads.

[30] Dale, *op. cit.*, p.243.

Imagine what went through the minds of the brethren gathered inside when there is a knock at the door, at the outside passage way (porch) that leads from the inner court to the street! Have the persecutors come here to this well-known meeting place of Christians to take some more away to prison and death?

A servant-girl named Rhoda came to answer. We picture Rhoda as being 12 or 13 years old. The task of being doorkeeper was commonly assigned to a young female slave.[31] Visitors, upon arriving at the door, would call out. If the girl recognized the voice, she would unbolt the door and allow them to enter. If not, she would go and get one of the men of the house, who would come and admit or debar the visitor, as the case might require. "Rhoda" is a Greek name signifying "a rose." It was not out of the ordinary for girls to be named after flowers (thus Susanna, a lily; Tamar, palm tree). "Answer" is a Greek idiom meaning she came to answer the door.

12:14 – *And when she recognized Peter's voice, because of her joy she did not open the gate, but ran in and announced that Peter was standing in front of the gate.*

And when she recognized Peter's voice. Peter has been a visitor to this house before, if his voice was familiar to the servant girl. Peter must have been calling out, "Hurry, open the door!"

Because of her joy she did not open the gate. At this time of night, and in a situation where they feared what the Jews might do, the door would be locked and bolted. The Greek reads "the joy;" that is, the joy she felt at hearing the voice of Peter. She is so eager to share the good news she feels that she fails for the moment to have presence of mind to open the door to the one standing outside.

But ran in and announced that Peter was standing in front of the gate. Rhoda was aware of what the people gathered inside the house had been praying. Now here was Peter! In her joy she hastened through the porch to the interior of the house to tell them the latest news about the one they had been praying for.

12:15 – *And they said to her, "You are out of your mind!" But she kept insisting that it was so. And they kept saying, "It is his angel."*

And they said to her, "You are out of your mind." The expression should not be taken literally, but in a colloquial sense. They apparently have not been praying for Peter's release, for that was so unexpected that when Rhoda affirms he is outside, they accuse her of being out of her mind.

But she kept insisting that it was so. With a positive look on her face, and a confident tone to her voice, Rhoda insists over and over again that Peter is too at the door!

---

[31] Compare Matthew 26:69,71.

And they kept saying, "It is his angel." Jews held a common belief that every Israelite had a guardian angel.[32] Reflecting those Jewish ideas, the Christians assembled inside must have been assuming that Peter's guardian angel had appeared in human form (resembling Peter), and was speaking in Peter's voice (which he must also have assumed). It is not clear why they supposed Peter's angel had come to visit. Some suppose they would imagine the angel came to announce something respecting Peter, in order to motivate them to greater prayer on his behalf. Others suppose they thought the angel's presence at the gate meant Peter was already dead; having no longer any job as Peter's guardian angel, he was free to be standing at the gate. What we have here is evidently an old Jewish belief held by these Christians, just as people today often retain many of their old ideas long after they become Christians. Sometimes these old ideas are right, and sometimes they are very wrong.

    A brief word on the question of guardian angels is in order at this place. The following ideas are suggested in Scripture.

(1) *Angels care for the young in faith.* Our Lord's word about the angels and the young are admittedly capable of a double meaning.[33] Are young children, or babes in Christ, referred to? Could the verse be taken both ways? Did not Christ still have the young child in His arms whom He used to illustrate humility,[34] and to warn of offenses yet to come?[35] The Bible declares the definite and special guardianship of angels for young and old alike.[36] What is added in the Matthew passage is the fact that those who have the guardianship of the little ones assigned to them are among the most noble of the heavenly host, and are as the angels of the Presence, who, like Gabriel, stand before the face of God and rejoice in the beatific vision.[37] So the words in Matthew do refer to children. Yet, interpreted in the light of what follows later in Matthew 18,[38] the words of Christ appear to have a wider application and include the young in faith as well as the young in years. The pathway of those who are young in the faith is beset with trials and perils, but they have heavenly guards to protect them. The text also teaches heavenly representation of the redeemed while they are still living on the earth, and a divine warning is given not to despise such representation. What courtesy, care, and affection fellow saints should manifest toward those who are subjects of such continuous angelic interest and representation. How comforting is this daily and hourly promoted active agency of the most dignified angels, commissioned by the Savior to care for His own.

(2) Perhaps *angels assist in answering the prayers of the saints.* It is apparent that the angels exercise some particular function in presenting the prayers of believers, incen-

---

[32] Alfred Edenheim, *The Life and Times of Jesus the Messiah* (Grand Rapids: Eerdmans, 1947), Vol. II. p.748-55, especially p.752.

[33] Matthew 18:10.

[34] Matthew 18:1-6.

[35] Matthew 18:7-9.

[36] Psalm 34:7, 91:11; Hebrews 1:14.

[37] Luke 1:19.

[38] Matthew 18:11-14.

sed by (the one Mediator) Christ's merits, before God.[39] Angelic beings are also associated with the answering of prayers in the Old Testament. Daniel, perplexed by divine visions, prayed for understanding; and one of the ministering spirits assured him that wisdom would be granted to him.[40] King Hezekiah prays, and an angel destroys the Assyrians.[41] Angels have something to do with answers to prayers in the New Testament, too. Cornelius prays and an angel directs him to send for Peter.[42] This commentator believes the agency of angels is no less real today, just as John 1:51 implies was true in the case of one of the apostles before he ever met Jesus.

(3) What must be made clear is that *angels must not be prayed to,* for that is forbidden several times in the New Testament.[43] "When we send an offering to the king. the king's messenger must not appropriate the king's due." The angels themselves are worshipers, not beings to be prayed to.

(4) *One need not rush to extremes* in these matters where we are given but a glimpse into the activities in the unseen world. What we must be careful of is being influenced by the spirit of the age we live in, where it tends to be denied that heaven has any interest or active influence in the affairs of men. God does exercise an active presence in this world, and (the Bible says) so do God's angels!

12:16 – *But Peter continued knocking; and when they had opened* **the door,** *they saw him and were amazed.*

But Peter continued knocking. What must have been Peter's thoughts as he stood in the street for some minutes, continually knocking and calling out, while the people inside argued with Rhoda? What if a Roman soldier or someone else had come along? He might be right back in jail!

And when they had opened *the door***, they saw him and were amazed.** The people inside finally go to the door to see for themselves. Sure enough, it is Peter! Amazing! 'How did you get out of the prison, and how did you get here?!?' Excitement causes them all to ask questions at once.

12:17 – *But motioning to them with his hand to be silent, he described to them how the Lord had led him out of the prison. And he said, "Report these things to James and the brethren." And he departed and went to another place.*

But motioning to them with his hand to be silent. A speaker who wishes his audience to become quiet so that he can be heard often shakes his hand (palm toward the people) up and down, thus indicating his desire for silence. We can almost picture Peter also saying

---

[39] Revelation 8:3-4, 5:8.

[40] Daniel 10:12,14.

[41] Isaiah 37:36.

[42] Acts 10:2-3.

[43] Revelation 19:10, 22:8-9; Colossians 2:18.

"Shhh!" as he beckons for silence. A great noise at that time of night might excite neighboring Jews, who would call the authorities, and then it's right back in jail, not only for Peter, but maybe for the others also.

He described to them how the Lord had led him out of the prison. See verses 6 to 10 where it was all described.

And he said, "Report these things to James and the brethren." James and some of the other Christians are not at the house of Mary. The "James" of this verse is likely the one who later takes a leading part in the Jerusalem Conference, and seems to be a leader in the work of the congregation at Jerusalem. Paul identifies him as the Lord's brother, and as an "apostle."[44] Who were "the brethren?" Perhaps it is a reference to the apostles. Perhaps it is a reference to other members of the Jerusalem church who are not present in Mary's home, but who may have been meeting that night in prayer meetings all over the city.

And he departed and went to another place. Perhaps Mary's house being used as a meeting place for Christians was a fact too well known for Peter to remain there if he would escape from Agrippa I. Where Peter went is not known for sure, though the word translated "departed" seems to mean he "went out" of Jerusalem. Some think he went to Asia Minor (1 Peter 1:1) or Greece (1 Corinthians 9:5), and there gave the rest of his life in work for Christ. Peter did evangelize in both these places, but not this early, in this commentator's opinion. Another view is that Peter preached among the unconverted Jews in Palestine, just getting out of the city of Jerusalem for a short time in order to escape the persecution. He did eventually return to Jerusalem, for he was present for the Jerusalem Conference seven years after this escape.[45] A third view, held by some in the Roman Catholic Church, is that Peter went to Rome. See this view discussed in Special Study #14, "Was Peter Ever in Rome?" at the end of this chapter.

12:18 – *Now when day came, there was no small disturbance among the soldiers* as to *what could have become of Peter.*

Now when day came. The fact that Peter was not discovered as missing until dawn makes us believe the soldiers were on six-hour shifts, and that Peter's escape came after midnight; otherwise, he would have been discovered as missing before dawn.[46]

There was no small disturbance among the soldiers *as to* **what could have become of Peter.** It is hard to find an English word to convey the idea behind the word translated "disturbance." There was a scurrying around as they frantically searched for the missing

---

[44] Galatians 1:19. Writers who try to identify this man with James the son of Alphaeus (one of the original twelve apostles) are evidently mistaken. See this problem discussed in Special Study #2, "The Brothers of the Lord," at the close of chapter 1, and also in notes at Acts 1:14.

[45] Acts 15:7. The persecution will die down, and there will be less danger to Peter, once Herod Agrippa I has died, so Peter will be able to return to Jerusalem for the Conference.

[46] It is possible Peter did not escape until the fourth watch of the night; that is, between 3 and 6 a.m. If this is true, then we must envision a much longer prayer meeting before Peter's arrival interrupts it, and we must envision much more haste on Peter's part in order to escape from Jerusalem before dawn.

prisoner, a hundred questions flashing through their minds, and apprehension about what would soon happen to them. Roman law required that, if the prisoner escapes, the guards suffer the same penalty the prisoner would have received.[47] It is not quite possible to translate the last part of the verse smoothly, for it represents the perplexity of one of the soldiers who asks, "What then has become of him?"

12:19 – *And when Herod had searched for him and had not found him, he examined the guards and ordered that they be led away to execution. And he went down from Judea to Caesarea and was spending time there.*

And when Herod had searched for him and had not found him. Herod might have been moved (as Nebuchadnezzar and Darius were, by the miraculous preservation of God's men in the furnace and the den of lions) to become a worshiper of the true God. He might have remembered the failure of his grandfather's attempt to make the wisemen from the East instruments in discovering and destroying the Infant at Bethlehem. The information he learns as he searches for Peter should have pointed him to God, but it did not. Perhaps it was pride that kept Agrippa I in rebellion against God.

He examined the guards. The word "examine" is the regular word for a judicial investigation, a cross-examination. It is as though the squad of soldiers is subjected to a court martial in which they are thoroughly questioned about the escape of the prisoner. Following the examination, those conducting the inquiry, including Herod, must have known that it was another miracle of God that had freed Peter.

> When those standing in front of the gate were examined, we can see that the only answer they could give was, "We kept our post all night; we remained wide awake, and no one passed in or out of that gate!" When the man who kept the key of the iron gate was called, he truthfully said that it had not been out of his hand nor had it been placed in the lock. The two guards between the outer door and Peter's cell were positive that no one had passed by them during the night. And the two to whom Peter had been chained could only say, "When we went to sleep he was there with the chains all secure, and when we awoke he was gone, and that's all we know." Of course, none of these statements could be true unless a stupendous miracle had been wrought; and there was absolutely no alternative, but to admit the miracle, or to hold that all of the soldiers had conspired together to voluntarily release the prisoner. The last horn of the dilemma could not be accepted by any sane man, seeing that the soldiers knew perfectly well that their lives would pay the forfeit of such a release. It seems, then, impossible to believe that Herod doubted the reality of the miracle, or the truthfulness of the soldiers; but he was determined not to admit the miracle; and he deliberately chose in preference the murder of several innocent soldiers.[48]

And ordered that they be led away *to execution.* They were killed, as Roman law required, for having failed to keep Peter in prison. Some writers think that all sixteen were killed, others that only the squad of four on duty when the prisoner escaped were executed. It does not seem to be implied that any further search was made for Peter once the court

---

[47] *Cod. Just.*, IX.4.4.

[48] McGarvey, *op. cit.*, p.239.

martial of the soldiers was completed. Is this a tacit admission by Herod that he knew God's hand was in the deliverance of the man whose life he had planned to take?

And he went down from Judea to Caesarea. After Peter's escape, how soon Herod left Jerusalem is not known. These journeys of Herod are related by Josephus, who indicates it was after Herod had reigned over all Judea for three years. This would be in AD 44.[49]

And was spending time there. That is, until his death, which occurred during this visit to Caesarea. Apparently, Agrippa I caused no further persecution against Peter or against the Christian church.

3. The Death of Herod and the Return of Barnabas and Paul. 12:20-25

12:20 – *Now he was very angry with the people of Tyre and Sidon; and with one accord they came to him, and having won over Blastus the king's chamberlain, they were asking for peace, because their country was fed by the king's country.*

Now he was very angry with the people of Tyre and Sidon. The Greek word translated "very angry" means to be angry enough to plan war against them. Agrippa I planned a war against them to vent his anger, but we do not know the cause of the trouble. Tyre and Sidon were part of the Roman province of Syria, and therefore not in his own kingdom (as granted by Rome). To wage war against them would be very dangerous, and so his anger was extreme, to be willing to take such chances of infuriating Rome. Some have guessed that since Tyre and Sidon were seaports, they have just placed some economic sanctions on goods from Herod's lands that passed through the ports, and this is what angered Herod so. He has let the two ports know, in no uncertain terms, just how angry he is.

And with one accord they came to him. Fearing that he would do what he threatened to do, the two cities got together and sent ambassadors to Herod. The ambassadors spoke for both cities.

And having won over Blastus the king's chamberlain. "Blastus" is a Roman name, and it may imply that Herod, in his effort to copy Roman habits, has selected a Roman for his confidential aide. It is probable that the ambassadors from Tyre and Sidon used bribery to win Blastus as their friend. A "chamberlain" denotes an officer who was in charge of the king's bed chamber.

They were asking for peace. The ambassadors had likely bribed Blastus in order to get an audience with Herod. Herod granted the audience, and the ambassadors were asking that Herod abandon his plans to make war against their cities.

Because their country was fed by the king's country. Tyre and Sidon had large populations, and there was not enough farm land nearby to raise food for all the people.

---

[49] Josephus, *Antiquities*, XIX.8.2.

Therefore, the cities were dependent on Galilee for their food supply,[50] and Galilee was part of Herod's kingdom. If Herod carried out his threatened war, many people would starve to death. Tyre and Sidon are surrendering to Herod's demands.

12:21 – *And on an appointed day Herod, having put on his royal apparel, took his seat on the rostrum and* **began** *delivering an address to them.*

And on an appointed day. Josephus tells us this was the second day of the sports and games held in Caesarea, at Herod's insistence, in honor of Claudius Caesar.[51] The festival in honor of Claudius was held each year, beginning on August 1. The one in AD 44 could have involved special thanksgiving for Claudius' recent safe return from Britain.

Herod, having put on his royal apparel. Josephus tells us Agrippa I had put on a robe of silver tissue, such as Caligula used to wear at banquets and games in Rome. The garment glittered with a dazzling brightness as the rays of the morning sun reflected off of it.

Took his seat on the rostrum. The marginal note reads "on the judgment seat." Josephus tells us it was in the theater at Caesarea that Herod the Great had built. Agrippa I was in his special box at the theater, about half-way up, right in the midst of the crowd.

And *began* **delivering an address to them.** Neither Luke nor Josephus tells us what the subject of Herod's speech was. Some suggest from the context here in Acts that Agrippa I was announcing the agreement with Tyre and Sidon, which brought a great cheer from the crowd when they learned that harmony was restored between the two countries. But the truth is, we do not know what he said that should cause the people to respond as they did. Perhaps the people are copying the kind of cries usually given to Caesar when he dressed and appeared in public as Herod has done. Caesar was often hailed as a god.

12:22 – *And the people kept crying out, "The voice of a god and not of a man!"*

And the people kept crying out, "The voice of a god and not of a man!" It was a loud cheer because of what Herod had said. The verb tense shows the people kept it up. The glamor of the dress, and the address delivered, result in the people giving Herod the kind of flattery he longed to receive. We do not picture the Jews as joining in this acclamation; rather, it was made by the Gentiles who had come to a theater in honor of Caesar.[52]

12:23 – *And immediately an angel of the Lord struck him because he did not give God the glory, and he was eaten by worms and died.*

---

[50] 1 Kings 5:8-11; 2 Chronicles 2:10; Ezra 3:7; Ezekiel 27:17.

[51] Josephus, *Antiquities*, XIX.8.2. Actually, the occasion for this festival is uncertain. Some suggest it was a birthday celebration in honor of Claudius' birthday. Others have suggested it was a festival in honor of his return from Britain. Still others have called it the *Quinquennalia*, instituted by Herod the Great in honor of Caesar Augustus in 12 BC, and held every five years to honor whoever was the reigning Caesar.

[52] The Greek word translated people is *dēmos*, a different word than Luke uses when he means "Jewish people" (i.e., *laos*).

And immediately an angel of the Lord stuck him. Epidemics and even death which are intended as punishments on people because of their sins are often attributed to the action of an angel.[53] Such language is not simply the superstition of a benighted people. Rather, we might well believe that such things still happen in the unseen world! The sickness that led to Agrippa I's death was a divine judgment because he did not rebuke the crowd when they paid him their sacrilegious homage.[54]

Because he did not give God the glory. Josephus expressly says that the king did not rebuke the flattery or reject their flattery. Agrippa I was enough Jewish, and enough acquainted with the Law of Moses, that he knew better than to permit the people to do what they were doing. There may be more in the language than a suggestion Herod was at fault because he was willing to receive the kind of worship that only God should receive. In the Old Testament, "give glory to God" was often connected with the confession of sin.[55]

And he was eaten by worms. According to classical Greek lexicons, under the word *skōlēx*, these intestinal worms were similar in size and appearance to what we call earthworms (see Ascaris Lumbricoides in Webster's dictionary). Josephus tells how a terrible pain in the abdomen seized Herod as he addressed the crowd. He collapsed in his box at the theater, and was carried out a dying man. He lingered five days before he died.[56]

And died. The Greek phrase translated "died" is the same as was translated "breathed his last" at Acts 5:5. His soul left the body. Herod Agrippa I died, according to Josephus "in the 54th year of his life, being the seventh year of his reign."[57] The year is AD 44, and from this we can date the death of James at a time just prior to Passover (May 1, AD 44), and the release of Peter a week or so later.

Agrippa I's son, Herod Agrippa II, was only seventeen years of age at the time of his father's death, so Judea passed into the hands of a governor, Cuspius Fadus, whose unpopularity with the Jewish authorities gave the Christians a temporary respite from persecution.

---

[53] 2 Samuel 24:16 and 1 Chronicles 21:12ff; 2 Chronicles 32:21.

[54] Eusebius quotes both the passage from Acts and the one found in Josephus (*Church History*, II.10). Josephus tells us that while the people were crying out their words of flattery, that Herod looked up and saw an owl perched on a rope, and recognized it as an evil omen, fulfilling a prediction which had been made to him by a fellow-prisoner during his confinement at Rome. Eusebius speaks of "an angel sitting above his head," and for this he has been severely criticized. In addition to the possible explanations found in Schaff's footnote at this place in Eusebius, we would like to add this one: the word "angel" could be translated "messenger," and in that sense the owl would be looked upon by Herod as a "messenger" of evil, and there would be no contradiction at all.

[55] Compare Joshua 7:19 and John 9:24.

[56] Ever since men have tried to explain all of the Bible from a naturalistic standpoint (an impossible task!), natural explanations have been given to all of the Biblical miracles. In the case of the death of Herod, the suggestion has been advanced that he really suffered from a burst appendix. To this commentator, the accounts of Herod's death are more than a case of appendicitis! The particular sickness that struck Herod also was the cause of death of other men. Among those who could be listed are Pheretime of Cyrene (*Herod.*, IV.205), Antiochus the Great (2 Maccabees 9. 2), Herod the Great (Josephus, *Antiquities*, XVII.6.5), and Maximinus (Lactantius, *De mort. Persecut.*, c.33).

[57] *Antiquities*, XIX.8.2.

12:24 – *But the word of the Lord continued to grow and to be multiplied.*

But the word of the Lord continued to grow and to be multiplied. The verse begins with "but," marking a contrast. The persecution had been intended to slow or finish the church, *but* the persecutor is slowed and finished; and *instead* the church continues to grow. She grows in spite of all obstacles. The verb tenses imply continuous expansion. The preaching of the gospel results in numerous conversions. Perhaps too the providential death of Herod Agrippa I, so soon after his attempt to persecute the Church and his execution of James, would make a great impression on the mind of the people, which in turn caused them to take the gospel seriously.

As has been observed previously, Luke's use of such statements about the growth of the church is an indication that he is about to turn to another subject.

12:25 – *And Barnabas and Saul returned from Jerusalem when they had fulfilled their mission, taking along with them John, who was also called Mark.*

And Barnabas and Saul returned from Jerusalem. The names are still in this order because Barnabas is the more prominently recognized of the two. Because we read of the death of James, and the imprisonment and release of Peter, and the painful and loathsome death of Herod Agrippa I, between Luke's statements about the arrival and departure of Barnabas and Paul from Jerusalem, we take it that Luke is saying these events occurred in the interval between.

When they had fulfilled their mission. They had gone to Jerusalem to deliver the relief funds which had been contributed at Syrian Antioch. Now they are returning to Antioch from whence they had made the trip (Acts 11:30).

The word translated "mission" is *diakonos*, the same word translated "relief" at Acts 11:29. Because of the use of this particular word, Ramsay believes Barnabas and Paul stayed several years at Jerusalem. They arrived just about the time the famine was beginning (late AD 44 or early AD 45), and then stayed to administer the relief and care for the suffering people in any way they could when the famine became severe in late AD 46 and early AD 47. If this is true, we would have to move the dates of the first missionary journey from AD 44-48 (as given in the Chronology of the Apostolic Age in the Introductory Studies of this book) to a later date, say AD 48-50. But Ramsay may be putting too much weight on the word *diakonos*, for it does not necessarily involve the personal ministration he finds in it. In Romans 15:31, the offering Paul brought to Jerusalem on another occasion was called *diakonos*, and there was no personal ministration involved in the distribution of those funds.

Taking along with *them* John, who was also called Mark. "Taking along" is a word which indicates a certain subordination. The choice is probably explained partly by his relationship to Barnabas (see notes at verse 12).

We have outlined Acts under three major headings. The first two have now been completed. The Church has been established in Jerusalem, Judea, and Samaria, and in Antioch, too. Elders and deacons have been chosen to serve at the local level. Problems within and persecutions (both religious and civil) from without have tested her, only to result in greater growth. Thousands have accepted Christ, from among Jewish people, from among proselytes to the Jewish faith, and from among people of Gentile background.

Daniel had predicted that the church would start from small beginnings and grow until it filled the whole earth.[58] It has come time for the church to break out beyond the Roman province of Syria. There is Asia Minor, and Europe, and the capital city of Rome now to come! Pagan cities, teeming with souls, need to be won to Christ.

Part Three, which we are about to begin, and which covers the last half of the book of Acts, will tell the story of this conquest. The evangelization of the world will proceed now, not from Jerusalem, but from Antioch on the Orontes. The chief person about whom Luke tells in this section is the apostle Paul. Palestine and Jerusalem move into the background, except for a few brief visits made between missionary journeys to other places.

Street in a Roman City

Drawing by Horace Knowles
from the British and Foreign Bible Society

---

[58] Daniel 2:44.

SPECIAL STUDY #14

WAS PETER EVER IN ROME?

The Roman Church has taught that Peter was in Rome for upwards of 25 years, from AD 42-67, and that he became the first pope. The basis for those claims of a 25-year stay in Rome is found solely in tradition.

I. THE TRADITION STATED

Abbe Fouard, in his book *Saint Peter and the First Years of Christianity,* a work that has Cardinal Gibbons imprimatur, states:

> There is a very venerable tradition to the effect that during the same year in which Peter escaped from Herod's clutches, he arrived in Rome, and there established the Apostolic See, where it was to remain for ever after.[1]

In an "Appendix," Fouard confirms that this tradition is accepted as "trustworthy" by the Roman Catholic Church. He says;

> The tradition which states that Saint Peter arrived in Rome in the year [AD] 42 is handed down to us by trustworthy authorities, who are generally very exact; and furthermore it accords so well with what we know about the first years of the Church that we need not hesitate about adopting it.[2]

Fouard also says that the first church historian to mention Peter's coming to Rome is Eusebius,[3] who wrote about AD 325. Eusebius says simply that God in his providence led Peter to Rome during the reign of Claudius. Jerome, about AD 400, repeated the tradition, when he wrote:

> Simon Peter came to Rome in the second year of Claudius, and there he occupied the sacerdotal chair during twenty-five years, until the last year of Nero.[4]

Note, Eusebius does speak of Peter's coming to Rome in the reign of the emperor Claudius (and more about this in a moment), but it is not Eusebius who states that Peter was bishop of Rome for 25 years. William Cave, in his *Lives of the Apostles*, wrote:

---

[1] Henri Constant Fouard, *Saint Peter and the First Years of Christianity* (New York: Longmans, Green & Co., 1927), p.248.

[2] *Ibid.*, p.406-407.

[3] Eusebius, *Church History*, II.14.6.

[4] Jerome, *Lives of Illustrious Men*, chapter 1.

> It cannot be denied but that in St. Jerome's translation it is expressly said, that [Peter] continued five-and-twenty years bishop of [Rome]: but then it is as *evident* that this was *his own addition*, who probably set things down as the report went in his time, *no such thing being found in the Greek copy of Eusebius*.[5]

Cave's statement is important. Although Jerome acknowledges in the preface of his *Lives* a certain dependence on the writings of Eusebius, he did not find anything like his statement of a 25-year stay in Rome for Peter in Eusebius. It is Jerome's own addition, not the history of Eusebius, that is the basis the Roman Church has used for her doctrine for centuries!

Philip Schaff, in Volume I of the *Nicene and Post-Nicene Fathers,* has written a note concerning Eusebius' statement that Peter came to Rome as early as the reign of Claudius.

> Although we may accept it as certain that [Peter] did visit Rome, and that he met his death there, it is no less certain that he did not reach there until late in the reign of Nero. The tradition that he was for 25 years bishop of Rome is first recorded by Jerome, and since his time has been almost universally accepted in the Roman Catholic Church, though in recent years many more candid scholars of that communion acknowledge that so long an episcopate there is a fiction. The tradition undoubtedly took its rise from the statement of Justin Martyr (*Apology*, I.26) that Simon Magus came to Rome during the reign of Claudius. Tradition in Eusebius' time commonly connected the Roman visits of Simon [Magus] and Peter; and consequently Eusebius, accepting the earlier date for Simon's arrival in Rome, quite naturally assumed also the same date for Peter's arrival there, although Justin does not mention Peter in connection with Simon in the passage which Eusebius quotes. The assumption that Peter took up his residence in Rome during the reign of Claudius contradicts all that we know of Peter's later life from the New Testament and from other early writers ... As most of the accounts put Simon Magus' visit to Rome in the reign of Nero, so they make him follow Peter thither (as he had followed him everywhere, opposing and attacking him), instead of precede him, as Eusebius does. Eusebius follows Justin in giving the earlier date for Simon [Magus]'s visit to Rome; but he goes beyond Justin in recording his encounter there with Peter, which neither Justin nor Irenaeus mentions. The earlier date for Simon's visit is undoubtedly that given by the oldest tradition. Afterward, when Peter and Paul were so prominently connected with the reign of Nero, the visit of Simon [Magus] was postponed to synchronize with the presence of the two apostles in Rome. A report of Simon [Magus]'s meeting with Peter in Rome is given first by Hippolytus (VI. 15); afterward by Arnobius (II.12), who does not describe the meeting, by the *Ap. Const.*, the Clementine *Recognitions* and *Homilies*, and the *Acts of the Apostles Peter and Paul*. It is impossible to tell from what source Eusebius drew his information. Neither Justin, Irenaeus, nor Tertullian mentions it. Hippolytus and Arnobius and the *Ap. Const.* give too much, as they give accounts of his death, which Eusebius does not follow. As to this, it might, however, be said that these accounts are so conflicting that Eusebius may have omitted them entirely, while yet recording the meeting. Still, if he had read Hippolytus, he could hardly have omitted entirely his interesting account. Arnobius and Tertullian, who wrote in Latin, he did not read, and the Clementines were probably too late for him; at any rate, they cannot have been the source of his account, which differs entirely from theirs. It is highly probable, therefore, that [Eusebius] followed Justin and Irenaeus as far as they go, and that he recorded the meeting with Peter in Rome as a fact commonly accepted in his time, for which he needed no written authority ....[6]

---

[5] William Cave, *Lives of the Apostles* (London: Oxford University Press, 1840), p.170.

[6] Philip Schaff and Henry Wace, *A Select Library of Nicene and Post-Nicene Fathers of the Christian Church*, Second Series (Grand Rapids: Eerdmans), Vol.1, p.115.

A study of the pertinent literature of the first several centuries leads us to this conclusion: **the tradition which puts Peter in Rome as early as AD 42 rests on a very shaky foundation,** in spite of the assurances of "trustworthiness" which some advocates assert for this tradition.

II. THE CATHOLIC VERSIONS OF THE BIBLE

What do the various Roman Catholic versions of the Bible imply on the matter of whether or not Peter was in Rome for 25 years?

The Douay Version of AD 1609 has a footnote on 1 Peter which reads, "He wrote it from Rome ... about 15 years after the Lord's ascension," (i.e., AD 45-48). This particular introductory note would agree with the idea that Peter came to Rome in AD 42. However, a note in the index of the Douay Version would tend to deny an uninterrupted 25-year stay in Rome for Peter. The note in the index reads, "AD 68. St. Peter about this time wrote his second Epistle. About this time St. Peter and St. Paul came to Rome. Not long after they were both put in prison, and suffered martyrdom." This note must be understood to imply that Peter was away from Rome for some years after he wrote 1 Peter, and then returned before he wrote 2 Peter.

The Confraternity edition of the Challoner Rheims (an official Catholic translation published in 1950) offers a more recent pronouncement on the subject. This edition's note on 1 Peter reads, "It appears very likely that it was written in the latter part of AD 63 or in the early part of AD 64." Certainly, we must be careful how much we read into the difference between the introductory notes in the two versions. But at the very least, could it not be said that the change in wording and the date of writing assigned to 1 Peter is evidence that there is not absolute certainty, even among Catholic scholars, that Peter lived in Rome for 25 years?

III. THE NEW TESTAMENT'S EVIDENCE

What does the New Testament imply on the matter of whether or not Peter, upon fleeing from Jerusalem (Acts 12:17), went to Rome, and then stayed there for 25 years? Remember, the date assigned by the Roman Church to Peter's arrival in Rome is AD 42.

- First, it is doubtful that we are to date Peter's flight from Herod Agrippa I as early as AD 42. Agrippa I died in AD 44, and it is unlikely that Barnabas and Saul were absent from Syrian Antioch for two years or more as they carried the famine relief offering to Jerusalem. An AD 42 date would seem to place Peter in Rome two years before he left Jerusalem.
- As noted above, the Douay Version's note has Peter writing his first letter from Rome in AD 45-48. According to Acts 15, Peter was in Jerusalem for the Conference in AD 51. Acts provides little corroboration of the idea that Peter had been in Rome prior to the Jerusalem Conference.
- Somewhere between AD 50 and AD 52, we find Peter at Antioch (Galatians 2:11ff).

- Paul wrote 1 Corinthians in AD 57 or 58, and indication is given in this letter that Peter has held an evangelistic crusade in Corinth (see 1 Corinthians 1:12; 9:5). Peter's work in Corinth would have to have been after the church was begun in c. AD 52.

- Paul wrote Romans in the spring of AD 58 from Corinth. If Peter was then in Rome with the rest of the saints, why did not Paul list his name with those disciples to whom he sends greetings in chapters 15 and 16? The absence of Peter's name from these greetings to the Roman church most likely reflects the fact that Peter has not yet ever been to Rome, nor was he there when the letter to the Roman church was written.

- As importantly, Paul wanted to come to Rome. Yet he states that he never built on another apostle's work (Romans 15:20). The clear implication of Paul's statement is that, as of AD 58 when Paul wrote Romans, Peter had not been to or worked in Rome.

- Paul arrived in Rome in AD 61 as a prisoner. Acts 28:30 tells us he stayed there two years. Because his accusers did not come, he was released from prison about AD 63. During this first Roman imprisonment, Paul wrote four or five epistles (Philippians, Ephesians, Colossians, Philemon, and perhaps Hebrews). Peter is not mentioned in any of these, even though Paul is writing from Rome. In Colossians 4:11 Paul refers to several of his friends at Rome, and concludes the list by stating, "These are my only fellow workers in the kingdom of God." Peter is not mentioned in Paul's reference because Peter is not in Rome in AD 63.

- Upon his release from the first Roman imprisonment, Paul visited the churches of Asia again. 1 Timothy and Titus were written during this time. In AD 66 or 67, Paul was imprisoned again. During this second Roman imprisonment, he wrote 2 Timothy, probably in the fall of AD 67. 2 Timothy 4:11 reads, "Only Luke is with me." The conclusion drawn from this reference is that as of AD 67 Peter was not yet in Rome.

Certainly, then, the New Testament gives considerable evidence that Peter did not live in Rome on an uninterrupted basis for 25 years beginning in AD 42.

IV. THE TRADITION CONCERNING PETER'S DEATH IN ROME

The tradition that Peter suffered martyrdom in Rome is as old and as universal as that in regard to Paul. However, owing to a great amount of falsehood which became mixed with the original tradition by the end of the 2nd century AD, the whole has been rejected as untrue by some modern critics, who even go so far as to deny that Peter was ever at Rome at all. Especially is this denial to be found in those authors who go to extremes in their attempts to show that Peter couldn't possibly have been pope (for, they argue, he never even got to Rome at all).

Yet the tradition is too strong to be entirely set aside, and there is absolutely no trace of any alternate tradition regarding the location of Peter's death. We may therefore assume it as overwhelmingly probable that Peter suffered martyrdom in Rome. His martyrdom is plainly referred to in John 21:18, though the place of it is not specified.

The first extra-biblical witness to Peter's martyrdom is Clement of Rome.[7] Though

---

[7] Clement of Rome, *Ad Cor.* 5.

Clement leaves the place of the martyrdom unspecified, he evidently assumes the place was well known; indeed, it is almost impossible to believe that the early Church could have known of the death of Peter and Paul without knowing where they died. In neither man's case is there a single opposing tradition other than that their deaths occurred in Rome.

- Ignatius connects Paul and Peter in an especial way with the Roman church, which seems plainly to imply that Peter had been in Rome.[8]
- Papias, writing c. AD 120, gives witness to the apostles' stay in Rome.[9]
- Dionysius of Corinth, writing c. AD 170, speaks of Peter and Paul being together in Rome, and gives Gaius of Rome (c. AD 120) as a witness for it. He also tells of Peter's suffering martyrdom there.[10]
- Irenaeus (c. AD 180) speaks of Peter and Paul conjointly founding (the Greek is *themelioō*, "to establish, to strengthen") the church in Rome.[11]
- Clement of Alexandria (AD 190) tells that Peter publicly preached the word at Rome.[12]
- Origen, writing c. AD 200, relates that "Peter appears to have preached through Pontus, Galatia, Bithynia, Cappadocia, and Asia, to the Jews of the dispersion; who also finally coming to Rome was crucified with his head downward, having requested of himself to suffer in this way."[13]
- Eusebius, writing c. AD 325, tells us that Peter and Paul had a common martyrdom at Rome, Peter being crucified.[14] He also specifies the fourteenth year of Nero's reign (i.e., October AD 67 to October AD 68) as the year of the apostles' death.[15]
- Tertullian (c. AD 200) wrote about Rome, "How happy its church, whose entire doctrine the apostles promulgated at the expense of their lives; where Peter's sufferings resembled those of our Lord; where Paul wins his crown in a death like John's."[16]
- Lactantius (AD 300) has the same testimony. "When Nero was emperor, Peter came to Rome ... Nero ... first of all having persecuted the servants of God, crucified Peter, and slew Paul."[17]
- Eusebius, in his *Demonstration* (Lib. III) writes, "Peter was crucified at Rome with his head downward; and Paul beheaded."

---

[8] Ignatius, *Ad Rom.*, chapter 4.

[9] Eusebius, *op. cit.*, III.39.15-16; II.15.2.

[10] Dionysius is quoted by Eusebius, *op. cit.*, II.25.8

[11] Irenaeus, *Against Heresies*, III.1.1.

[12] Eusebius, *op. cit.*, VI.14.6.

[13] Origen is quoted by Eusebius, *op. cit.*, III.1. To Origen, also, has been attributed the beginnings of the "Quo Vadis, Domine?" tradition. This legend is found in detail in a Gnostic "Acts of Peter." For details, see F.H. Chase's article "Peter (Simon)" in Vol. III of *Hastings' Dictionary of the Bible,* p.773-774. Chase's article shows how flimsy is the claim that the legend is based on Origen's writings.

[14] Eusebius, *Church History*, II.25.5.

[15] Eusebius, *Chronicon*; Jerome, *Lives of Illustrious Men*, chapter 1.

[16] Tertullian, *The Prescription Against Heretics*, chapter 36.

[17] Lactantius, *On the Manner in which the Persecutors Died*, chapter 2.

The witnesses need not be followed farther. Jerome, Sulpicius Severus, Athanasius, Chrysostom, and others, attest the same thing.

It will be noted that all ancient writers speak of the fact of Peter's martyrdom. And if he died that death, it most likely was at Rome. No other place is ever hinted at, though churches were most eager to claim for themselves illustrious martyrs. The accounts too in favor of Rome reach back to an early date, even to very early in the 2nd century AD. It was never doubted that Peter suffered at Rome until the time of the Waldenses, when the pretensions of the Roman Catholic Church caused the Protestants to be carried away to extreme views.

CONCLUSION

Peter did come to Rome late in his life. About AD 67, after 2 Timothy had been written, it would seem that Peter arrived in Rome.

During his short stay in Rome, we believe he wrote the two New Testament letters which bear his name.

And while he was in Rome, he was arrested by the soldiers of Nero, and martyred in AD 68.

**Drawing by Horace Knowles
from the British and Foreign Bible Society**

III. THE CHURCH IN THE UTTERMOST PART OF THE EARTH – Acts 13:1-28:31

A. The First Missionary Journey. 13:1-14:28

1. At Antioch of Syria. 13:1-3

13:1 – *Now there were at Antioch, in the church that was* **there,** *prophets and teachers: Barnabas, and Simeon who was called Niger, and Lucius of Cyrene, and Manaen who had been brought up with Herod the tetrarch, and Saul.*

Now there were at Antioch. Here begins Part Three of this history, and the main topic is the labors of Paul. Antioch becomes the center from which the gospel spreads. It was situated geographically on some of the main travel routes, by land and sea. In respect to Paul's missionary journeys, having a knowledge of the towns visited, of which companions accompanied Paul, of what happened in each town, and the Scriptural references which bookend each journey will be of great help when it comes time to determine the time and place of writing of many of the New Testament epistles.

In the church that was *there.* Were there several congregations in this city of one-half million people, or just one large congregation? The singular "church" could mean either. See notes at Acts 11:19ff for the beginnings and progress of the church in Antioch. Remember that "large numbers" were converted before Barnabas came, and "considerable numbers" were added after he came.

Prophets and teachers. Luke has introduced his readers to the office of "prophet" before.[1] Perhaps some of the prophets who came to Antioch from Jerusalem (of which Agabus was one) are named here in this verse. Which of the men named are prophets, and which are teachers, is not known. It may be that all held both offices or, more likely, those who are afterwards named apostles held both offices, and the other spiritually gifted men held but one office.

"Teachers" are several times mentioned in the New Testament.[2] It evidently was one of the temporary offices in the New Testament church, just as apostle and prophet were temporary offices. "Prophets" and "teachers" were not necessarily identical, as some distinction is made both here in Acts 13 and at Ephesians 4:11. Perhaps all prophets were teachers, but not all teachers were prophets, for it seems that the prophet had a higher and greater measure of the Spirit. However, it must be remembered that "teacher" was indeed one of the spiritual gifts, too.[3]

---

[1] See comments at Acts 2:17, 11:27, and 15:32.

[2] 1 Corinthians 12:28-29; Ephesians 4:11; 2 Peter 2:1. In the Ephesian passage, the elders are designated by the double term "pastors and teachers," as is evident from the Greek construction where the two terms connected by "and" have but one article.

[3] 1 Corinthians 12:28.

Barnabas. This man has already been a prominent figure in Luke's history. See Acts 4:35-36 and 11:22ff.

And Simeon who was called Niger. Niger is a Latin name meaning black, and the title evidently had some allusion to his skin color. Nothing more is known of him than what is here given by Luke. Some have attempted to identify him with Simon the Cyrene who carried the cross for Jesus,[4] but it is more in harmony with ancient ways to say that this title was given to Simon to distinguish him from the other Simons in the New Testament.

And Lucius of Cyrene. Cyrene was a place in North Africa.[5] Lucius is not to be confused with Luke, the one who later becomes the companion of Paul and the author of the book of Acts and the third Gospel.[6] Lucius, who seems to be the same person who afterwards is a companion of Paul when the epistle to the Romans is written,[7] is a Jew, whereas Luke was a Gentile.[8] Since men from Cyrene were some of the original evangelists in Antioch, it has been suggested that Lucius may have been one of those evangelists.

And Manaen who had been brought up with Herod the tetrarch. "Manaen" is the Greek way of spelling the Jewish name Menahem,[9] and indicates he may have been a Jewish boy who became intimately connected with the Herod household. Herod the tetrarch is Herod Antipas, tetrarch of Galilee and Perea, who by this time in church history had been banished to Gaul.[10] The word *suntrophos* (here translated "brought up with," "foster brother" in the ASV) is a word whose meaning is still rather indefinite as far as our knowledge goes. It may mean to grow up together, or it may even be a court title. Manaen was connected with the Herodian family, and being nearly the same age as Herod Antipas, had been educated in Rome along with him and Archelaus.[11] We wonder, as Luke researched the facts he recorded in his Gospel, if it was from Manaen that Luke learned about Herod's thoughts and words concerning John the Baptist and Jesus which are recorded in Luke 9:7-9. What a commentary on the mysterious methods of God's workings

---

[4] Mark 15:21.

[5] Acts 2:10, 11:20.

[6] The reasons some advance for identifying Lucius and Luke are these: (1) There was a flourishing medical school at Cyrene and Luke was a physician. (2) The fulness of the details given here in Acts 13 suggests the writer of Acts himself was present in Antioch at this period.

[7] Romans 16:21.

[8] In Colossians 4:10-14, Luke is plainly distinguished from "those of the circumcision."

[9] Do not confuse "Manaen" with the Menahem of Old Testament fame (2 Kings 15:14-22). Josephus tells us that when Herod the Great was but a youth, his future greatness was predicted by an Essene prophet by the name of Menahem, or Manaen. When the prediction came true, Herod the Great sought to honor that prophet. It may be this Manaen of verse 1, who grew up with Herod's children, was a son or grandson and a namesake of the Essene prophet, and that the boy had been taken into the Herodian household as part of that honor to the old prophet. (Josephus, *Antiquities*, XV.10.5).

[10] Do not confuse the Herod the tetrarch with Herod Agrippa I, whose death has just been recorded in Acts 12. Compare notes at Acts 12:1 and under Herod the tetrarch in the Introductory Studies, concerning the banishment to Gaul.

[11] Josephus. *Antiquities*, XVII.1.3.

– that one of these boys should attain divine honor as a Christian leader, while the other should be known for his shameful behavior in the killing of John the Baptist and in the trial of Jesus.

And Saul. This one who becomes the major figure in the rest of the book of Acts may be named last here because the others were all older members of the church in Antioch.

13:2 – *And while they were ministering to the Lord and fasting, the Holy Spirit said, "Set apart for Me Barnabas and Saul for the work to which I have called them."*

And while they were ministering to the Lord and fasting. "They" seems to refer to the prophets and teachers, rather than to the whole congregation, since prophets and teachers is the nearest antecedent.

Both Catholic and Protestant commentators offer considerable comments on the word "ministering." The Greek word is *leitourgeō*, a word regularly used in the Old Testament (LXX) and the New Testament for the work of the priests and Levites in the Temple.[12] The Catholic church is interested in the word as a proof text for their priesthood;[13] some protestants are interested in it as a proof text that only ordained clergymen may officiate at the worship services. How shall we untangle such a knotty problem? First, note that the word is not limited, either in the New Testament or in early Christian literature, to worship services.[14] Second, although it is true that our word "liturgy" (which has special reference to the communion service) comes from this Greek word, remember that such a usage belongs not to New Testament times, but to later ecclesiastical practices. Even if Acts 13 does speak of a worship service, there is still a long way to go to demonstrate that only ordained clergymen can celebrate the Lord's Supper since "liturgy" was not made to refer exclusively to the Lord's Supper till a much later time. Third, since Paul uses the word "ministry" to refer to supplying the needs of someone,[15] it may be that what Luke is telling us is that there was a relief ministry to the poor at Antioch similar to the one at Jerusalem (Acts 6), but at Antioch was administered this time by the prophets and teachers.[16] The conclusion of this reasoning is this: *leitourgeō* in verse 2 may refer either to leading the public worship services or to an everyday supplying of the needs of the saints, whether by prayer, or instruction concerning the way of salvation, or by edifying the saints, or helping relieve the widows and orphans.

"Fasting" is also a present participle, speaking of continual fasting over a period of time. Some have advanced the suggestion that the Christians were keeping the twice-weekly fasts of the Jews,[17] but if the Antioch brethren were mostly from Gentile back-

---

[12] Deuteronomy 10:8; Exodus 29:30; Numbers 16:19; Hebrews 10:11.

[13] Romans 15:16 is another text used by the Catholic church to justify the idea of a priesthood from the New Testament. However, such a use of Romans 15:16 is patently misusing what Paul wrote.

[14] Arndt-Gingrich, *Greek-English Lexicon of the New Testament* (Chicago: University of Chicago Press, 1957), p.471,472.

[15] Philippians 2:30.

[16] The verb Luke uses in verse 2 is a present participle, indicating continuing action over a period of time.

[17] Luke 18:12.

ground (Acts 11:20, 24), that is not likely. Some have appealed to the *Didache* for an explanation, where it is taught that Christians should observe two fasts a week, on Wednesday and on Friday (i.e., the days of the Betrayal and Crucifixion), and that before baptism both candidate and baptizer should fast.[18] Some, who see a reference to the Lord's Supper in the word *leitourgeō*, immediately speak of a "fasting communion" in this place.[19] Others suggest the prophets and teachers are so busy that they simply ate on the run or did not get a chance to eat at all, as they go about instructing, edifying, and doing charitable work.

The Holy Spirit said. This seems to have been a direct revelation. Perhaps the message was communicated through one of the prophets and/or teachers.

"Set apart for Me Barnabas and Saul. The Greek text includes the particle *de* that is untranslated in our versions. That particle may either indicate that the command to set apart these men came as an answer to a special prayer, or it may signify the urgency and importance of the command. The command is to be acted upon at once. The missionaries are to be set apart by a formal act, in one of their public services. It will be done by the laying on of hands.

Observe that Barnabas is still mentioned before Paul, showing that he is still regarded as the leader. And when Barnabas and Paul have departed from Antioch, the church there will still be under the capable leadership of the remaining prophets and teachers, just as it must have been while the two were gone on their relief mission to Jerusalem.[20]

For the work to which I have called them." This passage does not conflict with the idea that Paul has already been called to be an apostle. In fact, it is in harmony with it. He earlier has been called, the Spirit says; now he is to embark on that work. We do not know when Barnabas was called to be an apostle (and he is called an apostle in Acts 14:4,14), but Paul was called about ten years before this.[21]

13:3 – *Then, when they had fasted and prayed and laid their hands on them, they sent them away.*

Then, when they had fasted. "Then" seems to indicate a new and special act of fasting and prayer. Fasting in the New Testament is voluntary in nature. What is the subject of this sentence? Is it the whole church, or only the prophets and teachers who are involved?

---

[18] *Didache*, VIII.1; VII.14.

[19] Matthew 26:26-28 has considerable bearing on the question of a fasting or non-fasting communion.

[20] Perhaps there is also a missionary principle suggested — pick the best preachers available to be the missionaries. Why not let a person gain experience in teaching and dealing with people; and then if the Spirit leads that person to work on the mission field, the churches can support him with confidence.

[21] Acts 26:16-18. Lightfoot has shown in his commentary on *Galatians* (Grand Rapids: Zondervan, 1957), p.95ff, that in the New Testament the term "apostle" is never applied to anyone who may not very well have satisfied the qualifications for apostle, as given in Acts 1:22. Barnabas has been called to be an apostle of Christ sometime previous to this command to set him apart to the work. That call may have been years before, as in Paul's case, or simply some weeks before.

It seems the whole congregation is involved in a voluntary fast as they solemnly prepare for this new mission to the uttermost parts of the earth.

And prayed. They probably are praying for further guidance from the Lord, and a blessing for Paul and Barnabas as they go forth into the field.

And laid their hands on them. Who laid hands on Barnabas and Paul? Perhaps it was the other three prophets and teachers mentioned in verse 1. Perhaps the whole congregation was present, and the leaders, as representatives of the church, laid their hands on the two being separated.

What was imparted by this laying on of hands? Certainly not spiritual gifts, for both Barnabas and Paul as apostles had spiritual gifts previous to this time. Further, the men who lay hands on Barnabas and Paul are not apostles, so it would not be spiritual gifts being passed on. Others think this was the official ordination of Barnabas and Paul to the ministry, but both have been engaged in this type of work before. The purpose of the fasting and prayer and laying on of hands is clearly indicated in the context: these actions were the means by which Barnabas and Paul were "set apart" for the work they were called to do. This would be a solemn way of impressing upon the church the serious and important duties that were to be performed. By sharing in the service, the church was imploring the blessings of God to attend the missionaries, and was also indicating its own support and encouragement of the proposed missionary work.[22]

They sent them away — The church, represented by their leaders, under the direction of the Holy Spirit, sent them forth.

In the 5th century AD, John of Antioch (also known as Chrysostom), wrote "Many do not know the Book of Acts is in existence."[23] A little over 100 years ago, another John – this one from Lexington, Kentucky, and also known as J.W. McGarvey – wrote about the book of Acts, also expressing regret that the book was not better known than it was. If another John in this century would write a commentary on the book of Acts, he would be justified in saying the same thing, that the book is not well known. Certainly, the Christian churches have emphasized a distinctive message from the book of Acts, namely, what one must do to be saved – and this message of salvation is not to be neglected. But the book of Acts includes another distinctive message that should also be emphasized – the missionary emphasis. The book of Acts not only answers the question, "What must I do to be saved?" but it has been called an INSPIRED MISSIONARY MANUAL, for it gives both the message of the Christian missionary and the methods to be used. Both the message and the methods were inspired by the Holy Spirit.

Interestingly, notice who is involved in this missionary program in Acts 13. Here is an evangelistic tour about to begin, and who are the ones who decide this business? Who

---

[22] Is what the Antioch church did a precedent for ordination services today? That is, are fasting, prayer, and the laying on of hands to be essential features of an ordination service for preachers and other church officers still today? In Special Study #12, "A Method of Selection of Elders and Deacons," this question has already been discussed. Each of these elements has a value and a place today, if voluntarily done by both candidate and the church doing the setting apart.

[23] Chrysostom, *Homily on Acts*, I.

is behind these missionaries, or evangelists, as they go forth? The church at Antioch is the only church which is involved in this missionary activity. The apostles at Jerusalem had nothing to do with it, as far as we can tell; they are not the instigators of it. Luke's record mentions the local church, the prophets, and teachers, and the words of the Holy Spirit. If there is any person behind the missionary effort at all, then God is the one, as He through His Spirit guides the Church.

Thus, Acts has now presented two methods of New Testament evangelism.

- The first was illustrated in the life of Philip, in the fact that he simply went out to preach the gospel when he went to Samaria. No one sent him; no missionary society was behind him; no mission board gave him an official stamp of approval; Philip simply went out to Samaria to proclaim the gospel because he saw a need. Likewise, today, individual Christians may take it upon themselves to evangelize wherever they see a need they can fill.

- The second method, presented here in the chapter 13, is a church, as directed by the Holy Spirit, sending the missionaries out. Luke shows us a church in a certain city sending forth two of its own number as missionaries. Likewise, today, a local congregation may choose to support its own living-link missionary.[24]

2. At Seleucia. 13:4

13:4 – *So, being sent out by the Holy Spirit, they went down to Seleucia and from there they sailed to Cyprus.*

So, being sent out by the Holy Spirit. "The journeys now entered upon by Saul and Barnabas are the most momentous ever undertaken."[25] They have shaped the history of the world. Too much stress could not be laid upon the fact that the Holy Spirit Himself is the one who said this ought to be done.[26] The first work of the church is evangelism.[27]

---

[24] There is some question whether the Antioch church gave financial support to the missionary work of Barnabas and Paul. (Compare Philippians 4:15, which shows that on the second missionary journey, only Philippi supported Paul while he was in Macedonia.) Still, there was a vital interest in the missionary work Barnabas and Paul were going forth to do, and the missionaries regularly return to Antioch and report when their journeys draw to a close.

[25] McGarvey, *op. cit.*, p.5. (McGarvey's work on Acts is divided into two parts. Beginning with Acts 13, his book's page numbers restart at 1.)

[26] No doubt, many of us have been raised in communities where some church members say, "We ought not to undertake missionary work until we have converted the United States (and our own town)." Upon this same principle, the gospel would never have gotten outside the city walls of Jerusalem. Upon this same principle, you and I likely would not be His disciples; rather, we would be bowing down to some stick or stone and calling that our god! We should be glad that the New Testament church did not follow such fallacious reasoning. Surely "the gospel must be preached first at Jerusalem" (Acts 1:8), but there are always those in a given locale who will not accept the gospel even when given the opportunity; and when this is the case, it is time to go elsewhere with the gospel, as we are directed by the Holy Spirit.

[27] The task of a preacher in a given congregation is not ended when he has evangelized the community in which he serves. He must get the brethren to realize that Jesus said, "Preach the gospel to all nations." To help the brethren accomplish this work, the preacher may have to take the lead in presenting the work of missions, in praying for his church and the missionaries, and in inviting missionaries to speak in the

"Sent out by the Holy Spirit," Luke says. These words may be only a summary of what has been said earlier, but the verb used, *ekpempō*, is a word that often denotes personal conduct, and just may mean that the Holy Spirit is conducting the apostles on their way. If so, we must think of a fresh revelation being given to them, directing them where to serve,[28] with this revelation coming after their being "set apart" by the congregation.

They went down to Seleucia. Seleucia was founded in 300 BC by Seleucis I Nicator, to provide a seaport for Syrian Antioch. This city was located near the mouth of the river Orontes, where it falls into the Mediterranean. The distance from Antioch to Seleucia by water was 41 miles, while overland it was 16 miles.[29] It was often called "Seleucia by the Sea" to distinguish it from other towns bearing the same name, and served as a naval base in Roman imperial times.

And from there they sailed to Cyprus. Since Caesar Augustus had farmed out the copper mines of Cyprus to Herod the Great, considerable numbers of Jews had moved to Cyprus to work there. Barnabas was a native of the island, and acquainted with conditions there. Some evangelistic work has already been done there.[30] The church at Antioch was originally planted, in part, by men from Cyprus.[31] We can see in these facts several reasons why the Spirit selected Cyprus as a place for missionary work.

3. In Salamis. 13:5

13:5 – *And when they reached Salamis, they* **began** *to proclaim the word of God in the synagogues of the Jews; and they also had John as their helper.*

And when they reached Salamis. This was the largest city on the island of Cyprus, for it was the old Greek capital of the island. Located on the southeast part of the island, a few hours of sailing in favorable weather would bring the missionaries from the port of Seleucia to the port of Salamis, which was a splendid harbor in New Testament times. The people of Salamis needed the salvation offered in the gospel, whether Jews or native Cypriots. The locals were mostly worshipers of Aphrodite, whose worship included human sacrifice.[32]

They *began* to proclaim the word of God in the synagogues of the Jews. The Jewish

---

church where he serves. No congregation should ever be found apologizing to a visiting missionary, saying, "We haven't begun a missionary program yet; our people are not ready for it." If a congregation is not ready for that, it will be hard for them to be ready for anything!

[28] Compare how the Holy Spirit led the missionaries in Acts 16:6-7.

[29] The river was not navigable by ocean-going boats because of its many rapids.

[30] Acts 11:19.

[31] Acts 11:20.

[32] According to Lactantius, human sacrifices were offered there periodically until the time of Hadrian. *Div. Instit.*, I.21.

colony at Salamis must have been large since Luke mentions "synagogues" (plural).[33] Apparently, Barnabas and Saul were in this city for some weeks, visiting different synagogues every week or so. The apostles uniformly preached first to the Jews before going to the Gentiles, for so God had so ordered it.[34] Luke is silent in regard to the success of the preaching in Salamis, and from this McGarvey concludes that it was not great.

And they also had John as their helper. This is the John Mark who was introduced at Acts 12:12. The word translated "helper" is the word commonly rendered "deacon" or "minister," and either of these words would give some suggestion as to what Mark's duties were. He may have helped in such tasks as carrying the luggage, baptizing the converts, making needful arrangements for the apostles' comforts, anything that would free the apostles more for their work of evangelizing. Another attractive suggestion is that Mark's task was to train the converts after they had been won, for Luke uses the same word of Mark that he uses in Luke 1:2 of those whose job it was to give their eyewitness accounts of the life of Jesus. (Mark had seen some of the earthly ministry of Jesus, but not all.)

4. At Paphos. 13:6-12

13:6 – *And when they had gone through the whole island as far as Paphos, they found a certain magician, a Jewish false prophet whose name was Bar-Jesus,*

And when they had gone through the whole island as far as Paphos. Cyprus' length was nearly 150 miles, but it would be only about 100 miles from Salamis to Paphos. Did the apostles evangelize as they went? Conybeare and Howson think they did not, for if Paul followed his later custom, they may have evangelized only the larger populated centers, and then allowed those centers to evangelize the other surrounding areas. On the other hand, Ramsay thinks the verb "gone through" is a technical term in Acts for "going over a country as a missionary."[35]

Paphos was a city at the western end of the island, and served as the Roman capital of the island. It had a small harbor, which at times offered no shelter from the prevailing winds. There was a celebrated temple there in which Aphrodite (Venus) was worshiped. The worship was notorious for the licentiousness of the harlot-priestesses who served in the temple. They needed the gospel, too!

They found a certain magician. Concerning "magician" or "wizard," see the comments at Acts 8:9. The word is *magos*, the same word translated "wise man" at Matthew 2:1, but it is obviously used here in its bad sense.[36]

---

[33] See also notes at verse 15 and Special Study #15, "The Synagogue and Its Services," at the close of this chapter.

[34] See Romans 1:16, Acts 13:46.

[35] William Ramsay, *St. Paul the Traveller and Roman Citizen* (Grand Rapids: Baker Book House. 1960), p.72,384.

[36] The word had a bad sense attached to it as early as the days of Sophocles *(Oed. Rex.*, 387).

It is a fact that neither in the Old Testament nor in the New Testament is a magician or soothsayer approved. In the Old Testament, the Israelites were commanded to put all witches and wizards out of the land, by death! Certainly, that ought to suggest to us that a Christian has no business whatever in patronizing a spiritualistic medium, a fortuneteller, or any star gazer, or person of that sort. If any one does, that would seem to reveal a loss of faith in the Lord Jesus Christ, and in His Word as all sufficient to govern and direct one's life. Christians ought not to succumb to the temptation to sin by going to a fortuneteller and having their fortune told. Underscore the word "sin" in that statement because sin is exactly what it is when a Christian engages in such activities.[37]

A Jewish false prophet. Like many present-day occultists, this servant of the devil pretended to be a prophet of God. Luke says his claims were false! Likewise would be the claims of magicians today, if they claim to be a prophet of God.

Whose name was Bar-Jesus. This name is patronymic. "Bar" means "son of" in the Syriac. "Jesus" or "Joshua" was a common name among the Jews. In addition to sacred books from Jehovah, certain Jewish people claimed that some books (supposedly having come down from Solomon) had information about charms and spells and how to cast them. Perhaps Bar-Jesus has some of these in his library.

13:7 – *who was with the proconsul, Sergius Paulus, a man of intelligence. This man summoned Barnabas and Saul and sought to hear the word of God.*

Who was with the proconsul, Sergius Paulus. The island of Cyprus swung back and forth between government by a proconsul and government by a governor.[38] Strabo tells us the island was originally an imperial province, but in 22 BC it was transferred by Augustus to the Senate.[39] Under Hadrian it was under a governor, and again under a proconsul in Severus' time.

For a long time, skeptics argued that there was a mistake in the Bible when Luke calls Sergius a proconsul; the skeptics contended that Luke should have called him a governor. However, in the years since the skeptics first assailed the historicity of Luke, coins and inscriptions from the time of Claudius have been found at Curium and Citium, in which the title of proconsul is given to Cominius Proclus, Julius Corduo, and L. Annus Bassus, who must have been the immediate successors of Sergius Paulus. Still later, at Soli, a coin with the inscription "Paulus the proconsul" was found. Thus, Luke's historical accuracy was again affirmed.[40]

Some have suggested that the proconsul of Cyprus is the same man known as Lucius Sergius Paulus, a commissioner in charge of Roman streets during the reign of Claudius.

---

[37] For further information on the subject, see Special Study #17, "The World of the Occult," at the close of chapter 19.

[38] On page *xiv-xv* in the Introductory Studies, we have explained the nature of the offices of proconsul and governor.

[39] *Dio Cassius*, LIII.12, LIV.4.

[40] Luigi Palma DeCesnola, *Cyprus, Its Ancient Cities, Tombs & Temples* (London, 1877), p.425.

A man of intelligence. The Greek word is difficult to translate, for it carries the multiple ideas of "judicious, cultured, desirous of ascertaining the truth." It may even imply that Paulus was dissatisfied with his natural religion. While we might not call him very wise when he has a false prophet accompanying him, we should remember ...

> ... that statesmen and generals in that age were in the habit of consulting oracles and auguries about all important matters, and of keeping about them someone who was credited with interpreting the signs of approaching good or evil. [Since there had been true prophets among the Jews,] Paulus showed some sense in trusting to a so-called prophet of that nation, rather than of some pagan nation. And when the two Jews came to Paphos, claiming to bring fresh revelations from the God of Israel, the same good sense prompted him to send for Barnabas and Saul.[41]

This man summoned Barnabas and Saul. It is probable that they have preached in Paphos, and that intelligence of what they were preaching had reached the ears of the proconsul, who of necessity would need to have knowledge of what was going on in the land he was responsible for governing.

And sought to hear the word of God. The verb *epizēteō*, in the classical Greek, means to "put questions to" someone. Did Sergius Paulus ask a number of questions of the two apostles, in order to learn the context of the message they were preaching? Is he simply superstitious, thinking that these men may be able to tell him his future (similar to what he might learn from any fortuneteller), or does Luke's description that he was "a man of intelligence" preclude such an idea? If the word "intelligence" does include dissatisfaction with his own pagan religions, then what Paulus really wanted was to hear something more lasting and satisfying than he knew. He really was anxious about his own salvation.

13:8 – *But Elymas the magician (for thus his name is translated) was opposing them, seeking to turn the proconsul away from the faith.*

But Elymas the magician (for thus his name is translated). Elymas is the Greek spelling of an Arabic word, either *ulema* ("strong") or *'alim* ("wise"). The name gives us some idea of the claims Bar-Jesus was making for himself.[42]

Was opposing them. Elymas resisted the messengers of God. Did he try some spell or hex, or did he simply utter half-truths about the Christian message?[43] Whichever he did, he certainly was motivated by the knowledge that if the influence of Barnabas and Paul should be extended over the proconsul, he would be out of a job. The devil always finds a way to get his servants to oppose the gospel. Often the motive he appeals to is self-interest, as was the case with Elymas.

---

[41] McGarvey, *op. cit.*, p.8.

[42] Observe that "Elymas" is a translation of the word "magician," not a translation of the name Bar-Jesus.

[43] The same word is used in 2 Timothy 3:8 of the magicians who "withstood" Moses. What they did may give some idea of what Elymas was doing in his attempt to influence Sergius Paulus.

Seeking to turn the proconsul away from the faith. He was trying to keep Sergius Paulus from becoming a Christian. "Faith" here stands either for the Christian religion, or the body of doctrine that Christians believe, which not only points in the right direction, but also points out the error of magic and witchcraft.

13:9 – *But Saul, who was also* **known as** *Paul, filled with the Holy Spirit, fixed his gaze upon him,*

But Saul, who was also *known as* **Paul.** This is the last time in Acts that Luke calls the apostle by the name of "Saul" (save when reference is made to his previous life at Acts 22:1 and 26:14). We do not know much about the reasons for or the date of the change of name. All we can do is summarize some of the suggestions.

When was Saul's name changed to Paul? (1) Perhaps his parents gave him two names, one a Hebrew name (after King Saul in the Old Testament), and the other a Gentile name (Paulus, in Latin signifies "little, dwarfish"). (2) Perhaps Paul himself assumed the Latin name as being appropriate of his own estimate of himself, for he often called himself less than the other apostles and other saints.[44] (3) Perhaps his physical size caused others to give him this nickname that stuck, though such a suggestion that he was runty in stature does not seem to harmonize with what is said of him at Acts 14:12. (4) Perhaps the name of his first illustrious convert, Sergius Paulus, is given to Saul to commemorate what happened on the island of Cyprus.[45]

Why was Saul's name changed to Paul? (1) Foakes-Jackson suggests that the reason for the change is that this is the beginning of the "Pauline source" of the Acts narrative.[46] (2) Jerome and Augustine advanced the idea that members of the missionary party changed Paul's name because of the exceptionally bold and startling way in which Elymas was silenced and Sergius Paulus was convinced of the truth of the Gospel. Supposedly, the change was easily made, since there was but one letter to change to make "Paul" out of "Saul." Then, as a matter of course, since everyone had put on him this new name, Paul was compelled to adopt it, as he does in all his epistles. (3) Perhaps the best suggestion is that Paul himself adopted the Gentile name (probably one his parents had given him) because he is now working among Greek and Roman people. The name change is part of his "becoming all things to all men in order to win more" of them.[47]

Filled with the Holy Spirit. "Filled" is an aorist participle, which indicates an action prior to the action of the main verb. Two explanations have been offered for this participle.

---

[44] 1 Corinthians 15:9; 2 Corinthians 12:11; Ephesians 3:8; 1 Timothy 1:15.

[45] Several points lead us to reject this suggestion. (a) Luke presents the name "Paul" as one the man also had, an indication that he has had it for a long time. (b) If the name-change was made to commemorate the *conversion* of Sergius Paulus, the name-change comment should have been included by Luke at the close of verse 12 rather here in verse 9. (c) There were certainly converts to Paul's preaching before this one. If Paul were going to be named after his first illustrious convert, that would have been done a long time before.

[46] F.J. Foakes-Jackson. and Kirsopp Lake, *The Beginnings of Christianity* (Grand Rapids: Baker Book House. 1965). Vol. IV, p.145. We reject this conclusion of modern negative criticism. There is no indication that Acts is merely a compilation of the works of different authors.

[47] 1 Corinthians 9:22.

- The word "filled" is sometimes used to signify the baptism with the Holy Spirit, as at Acts 2:1ff. Verse 9, therefore, might be saying, "Before these events of Acts 13:9ff, Paul had been filled (baptized) with the Holy Spirit. As a result of this previous empowering, he was able to afflict Elymas in that manner that Luke will now describe."
- The aorist tense, even in participle form, indicates a one-time act. The participle is therefore said to imply a sudden coming of spiritual power just especially for what will be done to Elymas. From this explanation it is also suggested that these gifts were not permanently abiding things, but that the apostles and spiritually gifted men received the powers just when they were needed.

It is just possible that both explanations of this verse are true. That is, a man who had been baptized with the Holy Spirit was endowed from time to time as need required. In this case, the Spirit enabled Paul to detect the sin of Elymas, to pronounce the divine judgment, and to inflict the punishment.

Fixed his gaze upon him. Luke has used this phrase before, at Acts 1:10, 3:4, and 6:15, Some think this word is one of the indications in the New Testament that Paul had eye trouble, and had difficulty seeing; that is, he had to strain to see Elymas. However, there is very little evidence Paul had such a physical defect.[48] Surely the use of this Greek word is no proof, for it just as well expresses the fixed gaze of men who suffered no eye infirmity.

13:10 – *and said, "You who are full of all deceit and fraud, you son of the devil, you enemy of all righteousness, will you not cease to make crooked the straight ways of the Lord?*

And said, "You who are full of all deceit and fraud. "Deceit" is the rendering of *dolos*, a word which means "bait," like that used to catch fish or trap animals. The word suggests that Elymas was using his magic to catch or trap the proconsul, and Elymas knew it. "Fraud" represents the word *hradiourgia*, a word which literally means "ease of working," doing something adroitly. It says that the actions of the magician (levitation, telekinesis, etc.) were done in a slick, cunning manner, in order to trick and deceive the proconsul.

You son of the devil. By this accusation, Paul tells Elymas that he is under the influence of the devil. By parity of reasoning, a man today who is involved in magic, like Elymas was, would also be a tool of the devil because he would be promoting the devil's desires and purposes. Some have thought there may be an intentional contrast between the meaning of the man's Hebrew name "son of Jesus (Bar-Jesus)" and "son of the devil."

You enemy of all righteousness. "Righteousness" is a word regularly used in the Bible of God's way of saving people; when accepted, God's righteousness results in right living by the man. Elymas' activities, by the design and prompting of the devil, are opposed to both a man's becoming saved and then living rightly.

Will you not cease to make crooked the straight ways of the Lord? Still today, magi-

---

[48] In the comments on Acts 9:17, we noted one suggestion that Paul had bad eyesight and rejected it. Other verses used to support this theory are Paul's "thorn in the flesh" (2 Corinthians 12.7) and the passage in Galatians 4:15, both of which can be explained as something very much other than chronic ophthalmia.

cians, who in fact are practicing their occult arts by the power of the devil, will insist what they do is done by the power of God. They will even point to Biblical examples which they claim are similar to what they are doing. (E.g., Philip's being caught away from the Ethiopian is said to be an example of apport, and the sudden appearances of angels is said to be simply an example of materialization.)[49] Let it be carefully observed that Paul, filled with the Holy Spirit, says such claims are false. The magicians are instead giving a perverse twist ("making crooked") to the ways of the Lord; they are employing the devil's methods of counterfeiting the truth!

13:11 – *"And now, behold, the hand of the Lord is upon you, and you will be blind and not see the sun for a time." And immediately a mist and a darkness fell upon him, and he went about seeking those who would lead him by the hand.*

"And now, behold, the hand of the Lord is upon you. This expression has already been shown, in the footnote at Acts 11:21, to be an expression indicating divine punishment.[50] That the apostles could inflict punishment through the power of God is apparent from 1 Timothy 1:20 and Acts 5:1-11.

And you will be blind. By this sudden and miraculous punishment, Elymas would be awed and humbled, and perhaps encouraged to repent. Bystanders, such as the proconsul, would be convinced that he was a fraud and that the gospel was true.

And not see the sun for a time." One who cannot see the sun is stone blind. Why this particular punishment was picked, we don't know, but we wonder if Paul remembered the time when a blindness he suffered enabled him to be able to see much better with his spiritual eyes? "For a time" suggests that the punishment would cease when his opposition to Christ ceased. In mercy it was ordained that his blindness should not be permanent and final, but was intended not only as a punishment but as a means of leading him to repentance.[51]

And immediately a mist and a darkness fell upon him. "Immediately" is Luke's characteristic word meaning "forthwith, on the spot." The word "mist" is one of the regular medical words used to describe a disease of the eye. Hippocrates (the father of medicine) used the word to denote an extinction of sight by the drying up of, or a disturbance of the fluids in the eyeball.[52] "Darkness" indicates that everything went black. In the same ancient medical works it denotes the final stage of blindness. Elymas no longer could see and distinguish colors and light and darkness. He is totally blind!

---

[49] More will be said on this matter in Special Study #17, "The World of the Occult," at the close of chapter 19.

[50] Exodus 9:3; Judges 2:15; 1 Kings 18:46; 1 Samuel 5:6ff; Psalm 32:4; Job 19:21; Ezekiel 1:3; Hebrews 10:31.

[51] Barnes, *op. cit.*, p.202. There is a tradition in the early church that Elymas did become a Christian. Origen wrote, "Paul, by a word striking him blind, by anguish converted him to godliness." Adam Clarke. *Commentary on the Holy Bible* (New York: W. and P.C. Smith, 1823) Vol. 5. p.794.

[52] Barnes, *op. cit.*, p.202.

And he went about seeking those who would lead him by the hand. Here is another of those graphic touches, as Luke pictures the man suddenly blind, then stumbling around the room, begging for someone to help him. And the tense of the verb ("he was seeking") seems to imply that no one would offer to help. The miracle is so astounding, that the bystanders are thoroughly frightened; and none has the courage even to offer to take him by the hand to help him wherever he wished to go.

> As he groped about, calling on one and then another of the frightened bystanders to lead him by the hand, the falsity and iniquity of his pretensions stood practically confessed; and the divine mission of the apostles was demonstrated.[53]

13:12 – *Then the proconsul believed when he saw what had happened, being amazed at the teaching of the Lord.*

Then the proconsul believed when he saw what had happened. Miracles in the Bible were to credential the message, and the same is true here. It has been said that "the blindness of Elymas opened the eyes of the proconsul." "Believed" is Luke's way of saying that he became a Christian; he repented and was baptized.[54]

Being amazed at the teaching of the Lord. The conversion of the proconsul is not presented as the result of the miracle alone. There also, as in all cases of conversion, is the hearing of the Word, through which faith comes. The genitive is probably an objective genitive, and the phrase means "the teaching about the Lord," or the teaching which had the Lord Jesus as its main theme. The amazement may stem from the fact that they are surprised to find out that the Lord actually objects to the occult, and directs men away from it.

5. In Perga. 13:13

13:13 – *Now Paul and his companions put out to sea from Paphos and came to Perga in Pamphylia; and John left them and returned to Jerusalem.*

Now Paul and his companions put out to sea from Paphos. "Put out to sea" is a verb used here in its technical sense, meaning to "set sail." "His companions" speaks of Barnabas, John Mark, and perhaps some converts recently made during their missionary work on Cyprus, for it was a common thing for some of the converts to Christianity to travel with their teachers in a sort of apprenticeship. In this way men studied for the ministry in the early church. Paul from this point on is looked on as the leader of the missionary party, and henceforth is named first (with two significant exceptions[55]). It is significant of how much Paul has become the leader that the others are simply called "his companions."

---

[53] McGarvey, *op. cit.*, p.9.

[54] Compare notes at Acts 8:12 and 11:21.

[55] Acts 14:12, 15:12 and 25.

And came to Perga in Pamphylia. Pamphylia was one of the provinces of Asia Minor, which is the land we now call Turkey. It was north of Cyprus about 100 miles, and had Cilicia on its eastern border, Lycia on its western, and Pisidia on the north, with the waters of the Mediterranean forming its southern boundary. Perga, the capital city of the province, was located, not on the seacoast, but about seven miles inland on the banks of the river Cestus. There was on a mountain near the city a celebrated temple of Diana. There are extensive Greek and Roman ruins at Perga.

And John left them and returned to Jerusalem. It is plain from Acts 15:37-39 that Mark's reason for returning to Jerusalem was something that Paul deemed unworthy – enough so that Paul was unwilling to have him as a companion on another journey. Various reasons have been suggested for John Mark's conduct, though in truth we can only guess his motives.

- Some suggest he was unhappy now that Barnabas is no longer the leader of the missionary party, but rather Paul is.
- Some suggest that he refused to go on in the journey because he was afraid of the dangers in the future. Howson suggests that he was moved by fear of the robbers they were likely to meet in the mountains which they would have to cross as they passed into the interior toward Pisidia. He writes:

> No population through the midst of which Paul ever travelled abounded more in those "perils of robbers" of which he himself speaks, than the wild and lawless clans of the Pisidian highlands.[56]

- Some suggest disease (e.g., malaria) was the danger John Mark feared. Ramsay suggests that Paul contracted malaria in the lowlands of Pamphylia and decided to go into the higher altitudes to try to shake it, so that when the missionary journey now turned out to be longer than first anticipated, John heads for Jerusalem. In favor of Ramsay's theory is the fact that in Galatians 4:13-15 Paul reminds the Galatians that he came to Galatia the first time because he was sick.
- Some suggest Mark became homesick and thus returned home.
- Yet others have suggested the hardships of the journey as the reason.

Whatever the cause, Mark later proved his worth and value as a minister of Jesus Christ, not only to Barnabas, but also to Paul.[57]

6. In Antioch of Pisidia. 13:14-52

13:14 – *But going on from Perga, they arrived at Pisidian Antioch, and on the Sabbath day they went into the synagogue and sat down.*

---

[56] W.J. Conybeare and J.S. Howson, *The Life and Epistles of St. Paul* (London: Longmans, Green, and Co., 1873), p.130.

[57] Colossians 4:10; 2 Timothy 4:11.

But going on from Perga. The missionaries do not seem to have remained long in Perga. If indeed Paul did become stricken with malaria as Ramsay suggests, they would have left in haste looking for relief for Paul's fever.

They arrived at Pisidian Antioch. Leaving Perga, they traveled north about 100 miles to Pisidian Antioch, more than likely following one of the ancient trade roads. Luke does not recount the dangers and hardships of the journey across the mountains, but certainly they faced some of the perils to which Paul later refers.[58] There are extensive ruins in the spot today, testifying that Pisidian Antioch was a great city on the main route between Ephesus and Cilicia. It was called Pisidian Antioch to distinguish it from Antioch of Syria and a number of other towns which also were called Antioch (like Antioch on the Meander, or Carian Antioch), all of which were originally built by Seleucis I Nicator and named after his father Antiochus. The plateau on which Antioch stood commands the chief east-west road across the land we now call Turkey, and was typical of the locations where Seleucis regularly founded cities. He planted one wherever it would strengthen his hold on the native tribes. In Roman times, which means since 39 BC for this area, Pisidian Antioch was the capital of the Roman province of South Galatia. In 6 BC it was made a Roman colony by Augustus, and citizens born there from then on had Roman citizenship and certain other rights. In earlier years Jews were trusted supporters of the Seleucids, and found a home in many of the cities they founded. Thus, there was a considerable Jewish population in Pisidian Antioch when the apostles arrived.

And on the Sabbath day they went into the synagogue. Though Paul and Barnabas were on a special mission to the Gentiles, yet they availed themselves of every opportunity to offer the gospel to the Jews first. They were, in today's language, working with the "best prospects" first. Luke's language "*the* synagogue" leads us to believe there was but one in the city, yet there was a large Jewish community there, for 2000 families had been moved there by Antiochus the Great.[59] "On the day of the Sabbath" does not necessarily mean that it was the first sabbath after their arrival. Perhaps they have spent some time previously in evangelistic work in the city before this critical event took place.

And sat down. This likely means they "sat down" as any worshiper would, though some have ventured the idea that they sat down in one of the front seats where the rabbis would usually sit (thus intimating that they expected to be called on to speak).

13:15 – *And after the reading of the Law and the Prophets the synagogue officials sent to them, saying, "Brethren, if you have any word of exhortation for the people, say it."*

And after the reading of the Law and the Prophets. See the Special Study #15, "The Synagogue and Its Services" at the close of this chapter, plus the notes at Acts 6:9 and 9:20, concerning the synagogue, and the reading of the Law of Moses and the Prophets during the Saturday worship services.

---

[58] 2 Corinthians 11:26.

[59] William M. Ramsay, *A Historical Commentary on St. Paul's Epistle to the Galatians* (Grand Rapids: Baker Book House, 1965), p.191.

The synagogue officials sent to them, saying. Their office ("rulers of the synagogue") gave them authority to guard against anything unfitting from taking place during the services, and also to conduct the services, choosing someone to read the lessons, someone to have the prayers, and someone to deliver the sermon. Usually there was only one such officer, but in large synagogues there might be several (compare Mark 5:22).

"Brethren, if you have any word of exhortation for the people, say it." Paul and Barnabas may have asked permission to speak, or since they were visitors they were invited to speak. It may be the two were already known as having come to town with a message to deliver if this is not their first sabbath in town.

13:16 – *And Paul stood up, and motioning with his hand, he said, "Men of Israel, and you who fear God, listen:*

And Paul stood up, and motioning with his hand, he said. Luke 4:20 expresses the custom of the Jews in Palestine to sit while speaking to an audience. It was a custom among the Greeks and Romans to stand when so speaking (Acts 17:22). Even though in a Jewish synagogue, Paul uses the Roman method as he stands to address the worshipers. He makes his customary gesture to get the attention of the audience.

Men of Israel. "Jews, listen!" The next few verses of Acts recount Paul's first recorded sermon. He begins by reciting many of the events in the Jews' past history. This perhaps was suggested by the Scriptures that have just been read from the Law and the Prophets, as we shall show in comments on verse 17.

And you who fear God. This was the word used in Acts 10:2 to designate proselytes of the gate. Paul's audience was made up both of descendants of Abraham and of converts to the Jewish religion.

Listen. The usual direction a sermon to Jews took was to drive home the point that the Nazarene Jesus was the long-awaited Messiah. Paul will shortly come to this doctrine in his sermon in the synagogue at Antioch. However, to commence with such a statement, without first laying a suitable foundation, would have accomplished no purpose at all. Knowing that the Jews loved to hear their history recounted, and that such a procedure would make them more receptive to the rest of the message he intended to deliver, Paul likely starts with the Scripture lesson for the day, and goes over that history, especially emphasizing God's plan to bring a Savior into the world.

The main truths of Paul's sermon are as follows: (1) Jesus is the fulfillment of the history of God's dealings with Israel. (2) The Jews in Jerusalem rejected Jesus, but in crucifying Him they fulfilled God's purpose. (3) God fulfilled His promise to the Patriarchs by raising Jesus from the dead. (4) The blessings of forgiveness and justification, which the Law could not provide, are now offered in Jesus' name to all who believe.

13:17 – *"The God of this people Israel chose our fathers, and made the people great during their stay in the land of Egypt, and with an uplifted arm He led them out from it.*

The God of this people Israel. Here begins the section about God's dealings with Israel. Paul's opening words "Men of Israel" and now "this people Israel" would appeal to the national pride and sense of being someone special in God's plan. God had a special purpose in mind for Israel when He dealt with them and protected them as He did.

Chose our fathers. This phrase recalls to mind the call of Abraham, Isaac, and Jacob, and through them the calling of this nation to be a chosen and peculiar people to Himself (Deuteronomy 7:6-7).

And made the people great during their stay in the land of Egypt. During the Jewish sojourn in Egypt, Israel was "made great." Think of the honors conferred on Joseph, the miracles wrought on their behalf, and the extraordinary multiplication of their numbers.

The word "made great" is found in the Greek of Isaiah 1:2 (where our English version of Isaiah reads "I have brought up children"), and it may be that this opening statement of Paul's message is an echo from the lesson of the day just read from the Law and the Prophets. That Paul's words are an echo of the day's scripture lesson is based on two facts: (1) There are three very peculiar Greek words in Acts 13:17-19 which also occur in Isaiah 1 and Deuteronomy 1-3.[60] (2) Those two Old Testament passages make up the lesson read in the synagogue on the 44th sabbath of the year, sometime in July or August.[61]

And with an uplifted arm He led them out from it. The expression "uplifted arm" is symbolic of great power. The historical reference is to the plagues inflicted on Egypt, the passage through the Red Sea, and the victories over their enemies (e.g., Jericho, etc.).

13:18 – *"And for a period of about forty years He put up with them in the wilderness.*

And for about a period of forty years. The Israelites were about forty years going from Egypt to the land of Canaan.[62]

He put up with them in the wilderness. The marginal reading here is "He bore them up in His arms as a nurse in the wilderness." There is a manuscript variation here, some reading *etropophorēsin* (represented by "put up with") and some reading *etrophophorēsin* (represented by "bore up as a nurse"). The former is the better supported reading, but the latter fits the context because of its conciliatory connotation.[63] "To put up with" implies that the conduct of the Israelites in the wilderness was such as to exasperate God, yet He fed them manna and cared for them through the wilderness wanderings.

---

[60] The three words are "exalted," "bore up as a nurse," and "distributed as an inheritance." The first occurs in Isaiah 1:2, and the second and third in Deuteronomy 1:21 and 3:28.

[61] The current calendar of lectionaries (i.e., scripture readings for the various sabbaths) was written down several hundred years after Paul's time. How accurately the current written calendar represents the actual practice in Paul's time cannot be determined. However, it is conceivable that the current written calendar was simply an attempt to make permanent what had long been remembered as the practice.

[62] Exodus 16:35; Numbers 33:38; and see comments at Acts 7:42.

[63] R.J. Knowling, "Acts" in the *Expositors Greek Testament* (Grand Rapids: Eerdmans, 1967), Vol. 11, p.292, has a good discussion of the textual problem here involved.

13:19 – *"And when He had destroyed seven nations in the land of Canaan, He distributed their land as an inheritance* – all of which took *about four hundred and fifty years.*

And when He had destroyed seven nations in the land of Canaan. "Destroyed" equals subdued, finished them as nations, cast them out of their sovereignty. As the Old Testament account of the capture of the promised land shows, the Israelites did not put every individual of these seven nations to death, for many of them were left in the land. The seven nations were the Hittites, the Girgashites, the Amorites, the Canaanites, the Perizzites, the Hivites, and the Jebusites.[64] The whole land of Canaan was called by the name of one of the principal nations.

He distributed their land as an inheritance. The manuscripts behind the KJV speak of the "dividing of the land by lot," as recorded in Joshua 14-15. However, the better manuscripts behind the ASV do not speak of "dividing the land by lot," but that "He distributed the land as an inheritance." As noted in the footnote at verse 17, this is the third of the words that Paul may have picked up as he made use of the Scripture reading for the day in the opening of his sermon.

All of which took **about four hundred and fifty years.** This passage has caused much trouble for the commentators, especially those who are commenting on the text of the KJV. The difficulty has been to reconcile verse 19 (as the KJV has it) with 1 Kings 6:1. Briefly, the problem is this: according to 1 Kings, Solomon began building the temple *480 years after the exodus* from Egypt, but Paul's sermon (as verse 20 reads in the KJV) would have him beginning it *573 years after the exodus.*[65]

- One solution to this alleged Biblical discrepancy that has been acceptable to many is to say that Paul has adopted a chronological system completely different than that of the Old Testament, but which was generally adopted by the learned Jews of his day. Josephus, for example, gives 592 years from the Exodus to the building of the temple.[66] But this solution is somewhat unsatisfactory since it leaves the discrepancy with 1 Kings 6:1 unexplained. Of course, were it not for this discrepancy, there would be nothing strange in Paul's following the same traditional chronology as Josephus, even when it differed from that of the present Hebrew Text of the Old Testament.

- The NASB (as in most modern Greek texts and in Codices *Aleph,* A, B, C, and numerous ancient versions) has the words "about 450 years" as part of verse 19, not verse 20 as in the KJV. Thus, per the NASB, Paul has said (not that the period of the Judges was 450 years long) that the interval between the choice of "our fathers" (often dated from the birth of Isaac) and the distribution of the land in Joshua's day was 450 years.

---

[64] Deuteronomy 7:1; Joshua 3:10; Nehemiah 9:8.

[65] The total of 573 years = 40 years in the wilderness + 450 years under the judges + 40 years for Saul's reign + 40 years for David's reign + 3 years of Solomon's reign before the Temple was begun.

[66] *Antiquities,* VII.3.1. 65 years were involved in the wilderness wanderings and the conquest under Joshua + 83 years for the reigns of Saul, David, and the first three years of Solomon. This leaves 444 years for the period of the judges, which would be reasonably close to Paul's "about 450 years" here in Acts 13.

This second explanation appears to be best for several reasons. It correctly treats the dative case (*hōs etesi*, a dative of time, specifying within which). It makes Paul agree in all of his statements about the length of the captivity in Egypt.[67] Finally, the statement of 1 Kings 6:1 – that it was 480 years from the Exodus to the building of the Temple – is not contradicted by what Paul says in verse 19.

13:20 – *"And after these things He gave them judges until Samuel the prophet.*

And after these things. The things mentioned in verses 17-19.

He gave *them* judges. The judges were raised up in an extraordinary manner to administer the affairs of the nation, to defend it from enemies, to settle civil disputes, etc.

Until Samuel the prophet. Samuel was the last of the judges and the first of the prophets.

13:21 – *"And then they asked for a king, and God gave them Saul the son of Kish, a man of the tribe of Benjamin, for forty years.*

And then they asked for a king. In the process of asking for a king like the nations around them, the Israelites were rebelling against God's order of government.[68] Still, God had foreseen this, and it had been predicted that they would have a king.[69]

And God gave them Saul the son of Kish. See 1 Samuel 9:1ff.

A man of the tribe of Benjamin. This was Paul's own tribe.[70] The only other references to tribal background in the New Testament are in the cases of Anna[71] and Barnabas.[72]

For forty years. The length of Saul's reign is not given in the Old Testament, but there are several lines of thought that show Paul's statement here to be reasonable. Ish-bosheth, his youngest son[73] was 40 years old at the time of Saul's death.[74] Saul himself had been a "young man" (i.e., under 40) when chosen as king.[75] A more definite corroboration of this statement of Paul's is given by Josephus who states that Saul reigned 18 years before Samu-

---

[67] See notes at Acts 7:6 and Special Study #13, "Difficulties in Acts 7," both of which discuss the length of the captivity in Egypt Stephen references in his speech.

[68] 1 Samuel 8:5; Hosea 13:10.

[69] Deuteronomy 17:14-15.

[70] Romans 11:1; Philippians 3:5.

[71] Luke 2:36.

[72] Acts 4:36.

[73] 1 Chronicles 8:33.

[74] 2 Samuel 2:10.

[75] 1 Samuel 9:2.

el's death and 22 years after it.[76]

13:22 – *"And after He had removed him, He raised up David to be their king, concerning whom He also testified and said, 'I HAVE FOUND DAVID the son of Jesse, A MAN AFTER MY HEART, who will do all My will.'*

And after He had removed him. Saul was removed as king because he rebelled against God in sparing the sheep and oxen and valuable property of Amalek, together with Agag the king, when he had been commanded to utterly destroy it all.[77] Saul eventually was killed in a battle with the Philistines.[78] Some writers have advanced the idea that "removed him" refers to Saul's death. However, David was anointed king before Saul's death, so it seems more likely that Paul had reference to Saul's being rejected as king.

He raised up David to be their king. This is recorded in 1 Samuel 16:1ff.

Concerning whom He also testified and said. As Paul's words are here quoted, they are a combination of two passages, Psalm 89:20 and 1 Samuel 13:14. Some of the words quoted were originally pronounced by God himself, and some of them by Samuel His prophet to King Saul.

'I HAVE FOUND DAVID the son of Jesse, A MAN AFTER MY HEART, who will do all My will.' "A man after my heart" means simply a man who would not be rebellious and disobedient as Saul had been.[79] David would do the Lord's will, in contrast to Saul who had not done the will of God. Saul had disobeyed God in a case where he had received a specific and clear command. The characteristic of David – that he obeyed the express commands of God by maintaining the worship of God, opposing idolatry, and seeking to promote universal obedience to God among his subjects – is specifically recorded of him in 1 Kings 14:8-9.

13:23 – *"From the offspring of this man, according to promise, God has brought to Israel a Savior, Jesus,*

From the offspring of this man. Out of David's descendants, one of his great-great-grandchildren (some centuries later), is the idea.

According to promise. Compare what Peter said in Acts 2:30. The promise of the coming Messiah was frequently repeated in the Old Testament era.[80] The expectation of a coming

---

[76] *Antiquities*, VI.14.9. There is a manuscript variation in Josephus at this place, with some reading that Saul reigned only two years after Samuel's death. Those who accept that two years is the true reading believe Paul's 40-year reference includes the time Samuel was judge over Israel as well as the time that Saul was king.

[77] 1 Samuel 15:8-23.

[78] 1 Samuel 31:1-6.

[79] 1 Samuel 13:13-14, 15:28. When David sinned, he repented – something Saul refused to do.

[80] 2 Samuel 7:12; Psalm 132:11; Isaiah 11:1,10; Jeremiah 23:5-6; Zechariah 3:8; Ezekiel 34:23, 37:24.

King in the Davidic line was a live hope among the Jews of the 1st century.[81] However, the promised son of David, when he appeared, came as a Savior rather than as the earthly king that many had been expecting the Messiah to be.

God has brought to Israel a Savior, Jesus. Paul opened his sermon by appealing to the Scripture lesson for the day. Using it as a springboard to rehearse the history of the Jews, he quickly comes to David. He then passes immediately from David to the appearance and work of David's promised Son, which all along was the main theme Paul had in mind. Paul affirms that God has fulfilled the promise He made to David, and that the Messiah has already come. He was a Savior, not an earthly king, and His name is Jesus. Note how "Jesus" is put at the end of the sentence in the Greek in order to emphasize it. Along with Plumptre, we agree that it is probable that the names of Jesus and of John the Baptist (in verse 24) were not utterly unknown, even to these Jews in this region of Pisidia. No Jew could have gone up to keep a feast at Jerusalem for some years past without having heard something of the one or the other. Paul's tone of voice is clearly that of one who assumes that their story is already vaguely known, and he comes to offer knowledge of greater clearness.

13:24 – *"after John had proclaimed before His coming a baptism of repentance to all the people of Israel.*

After John had proclaimed before His coming. The promised Savior, Jesus, came after John had preached and prepared the way, Paul tells his audience.[82] Paul pointed to the close of John the Baptist's ministry as the time of Jesus' "coming"[83] (i.e., entering His public ministry). A Jew, familiar with the Messianic promises of the Old Testament, would have been reminded of Malachi 3:1 by the word "come" used here by Paul.

A baptism of repentance to all the people of Israel. Paul uses the very terms found in the Gospel accounts of the Baptist's preaching.

13:25 – *"And while John was completing his course, he kept saying, 'What do you suppose that I am? I am not* He. *But behold, one is coming after me the sandals of whose feet I am not worthy to untie.'*

And while John was completing his course. As John was coming toward the close of his ministry, he more and more pointed men's attention away from himself to the Messiah. John's ministry is called a "course" or a race, that which was to be run or completed. The verb tense "was completing" implies continuous action. This phrase is one of the little notes outside of the Gospels that suggests a chronological outline of the life Jesus which has part of His ministry overlapping John's is indeed the correct way to harmonize and integrate the various Gospel accounts.

---

[81] See, for example, the pseudepigraphical Psalms of Solomon 17:23ff.

[82] Compare Matthew 3:1-22. Paul's almost verbatim quotation of John's words show that he was familiar with the details of John's ministry.

[83] Matthew 3:11; Mark 1:4; Luke 3:3. Compare comments at Acts 1:5.

He kept saying, 'What do you suppose that I am? I am not *He*. See John 1:21 and Matthew 3:11. Some of those who came out to the Jordan to hear John supposed that he was the Messiah. But John corrected their false impressions, and pointed them to Jesus.

But behold, one is coming after me the sandals of whose feet I am not worthy to untie.' It was the job of the lowest slave in the house to untie the sandals and look after them when guests came. If such an honored guest came that John was not worthy to untie them, who could that guest be but the Messiah?

> The purport of the quotation as used by Paul is that John bore formal testimony that one was coming after him so much more exalted than himself that he was not worthy to perform for him the menial service of untying his sandals – and who could this be but the Christ, the Son of David? No other conclusion could appear possible to Paul's hearers, and thus the words of John furnished proof of the two affirmations contained in the proposition which Paul had announced: first, that the Savior had appeared; and second, that he appeared after John the Baptist had preached repentance to all the people of Israel.[84]

13:26 – *"Brethren, sons of Abraham's family, and those among you who fear God, to us the word of this salvation is sent out.*

Brethren, sons of Abraham's family. Paul now exhorts his audience to embrace the Lord Jesus as the Messiah. "Sons of Abraham's family" are Jews who can trace their family trees back to Abraham, through Isaac, the child of promise.

> At this point in his discourse, moved, perhaps, by some favorable expression in the countenances of his hearers, or possibly by some apparent lack of attention, the speaker interrupts the course of his argument momentarily, and vehemently urges upon his hearers their personal interest in the matters of which he is speaking.[85]

And those among you who fear God. Paul speaks to the proselytes present. As he did at the opening of his sermon (verse 16), Paul addresses both groups in his audience.

To us the word of this salvation is sent out. The demonstrative "this" implies that the salvation being preached rested on the work of Jesus. The salvation promised through David has come to pass, Paul is saying. And he goes on to show how this Jesus became the savior of the world – by His dying in Jerusalem to atone for sins.

13:27 – *"For those who live in Jerusalem, and their rulers, recognizing neither Him nor the utterances of the prophets which are read every Sabbath, fulfilled these by condemning Him.*

For those who live in Jerusalem, and their rulers. "For" means "Let me explain in greater detail what I've just introduced." If we are correct in suggesting that Paul's listeners were familiar, at least in bold outline, with the facts of Jesus' life, then we can understand why Paul introduces the crucifixion of Jesus as he does. He has asserted that Jesus was the

---

[84] McGarvey, *op. cit.*, p.18.

[85] *Ibid.*

Messiah, authenticated by the testimony of the forerunner himself. Now then, if He really was the Messiah, why was He put to death in Jerusalem? "And" may be ascensive here, better translated "even." "Those who live in Jerusalem, *even* their rulers ...."

Recognizing neither Him. The ignorance of those who cried for the crucifixion of Jesus is a point Peter also made in his preaching.[86] That they did not recognize Jesus as the Messiah did not remove their guilt, but it did mitigate the degree of their guilt. The Jews did not "recognize" Jesus as the Messiah because He did not jibe with their preconceived idea of what Messiah would be. They had emphasized the Old Testament prophecies that pictured Jesus as a conquering king, and dismissed those which pictured Him as a suffering servant. This is why Jesus didn't match what they expected Messiah to be.

Nor the utterances of the prophets which are read every Sabbath. The verb "read" is the one which means "read out loud." The prophets were read in the synagogues during the weekly sabbath services (see, for example, verse 15). Paul began his sermon by appealing to the very Scriptures themselves as bearing witness to the kind of Messiah he was preaching, namely, a Savior (not an earthly king). The popular Jewish notion resulted from having missed the import of the prophets' predictions respecting the coming Messiah.

Fulfilled *these* by condemning *Him*. The prophets had predicted that Messiah would be rejected, a man of sorrows and acquainted with grief. The Jesus whom John the Baptist introduced matches what was predicted of Messiah. The people and the rulers, by crucifying Him, did just as the Old Testament prophets predicted people would do to Messiah.

13:28 – *"And though they found no ground for* **putting Him to** *death, they asked Pilate that He be executed.*

And though they found no ground for *putting Him to* **death.** It was not because they didn't try that the Jewish religious leaders could find no crime which deserved the death penalty. They employed Judas to be a traitor, they bribed false witnesses, and they held a preliminary trial in hopes that Jesus would utter some unguarded word that they could use against Him. They tried to make it look as though Jesus were guilty of blasphemy, but they were unable to prove the charge by any adequate evidence. Finally, the High Priest put Jesus under oath and asked Him if He were the Son of God, and Jesus answered "I am!"[87] When they went to Pilate, they first accused Jesus of being a man who did criminal deeds everywhere He went; but because they gave no specific instances of any such crimes, Pilate threatened to dismiss the case.[88] They accused Him of inciting revolt against Rome, but neither Pilate nor Herod found that charge true.[89] They accused Him of being a King, and Pilate found nothing in this charge that Rome was interested in.[90] They finally settled

---

[86] Acts 3:17.

[87] Matthew 26:59-66.

[88] John 18:30-31.

[89] Luke 23:14-15.

[90] John 18:33ff.

on the charge of blasphemy, yet not even this charge could be substantiated.[91]

At the time Paul was speaking, no part of the New Testament had been written. Paul shows great familiarity with the details of the trials of Jesus, but his hearers may have been hearing these facts for the first time. That Jesus had been condemned, the hearers probably knew – but the details Paul here shares with them, perhaps, they did not know.

They asked Pilate that He be executed. Pilate several times during the trials of Jesus stated that he found no fault in Him, so Paul in effect is saying that the Jewish religious leaders had asked for the execution of an innocent man. They chose that Barabbas, a murderer and revolutionary, be freed so that Jesus be crucified.[92]

13:29 – *"And when they had carried out all that was written concerning Him, they took Him down from the cross and laid Him in a tomb.*

And when they had carried out all that was written concerning Him. Jesus suffered and died just as the Old Testament had predicted that Messiah would. Not a bone of His was broken, they gambled over His garments, the sayings from the cross – all had been foreseen and told in the Old Testament.

They took Him down from the cross and laid Him in a tomb. Paul now shows that he was also well acquainted with the details of the crucifixion, death, and burial. Joseph of Arimathea and Nicodemus were the ones who took the lead in asking for the body to be granted to them; when it was, they took it down from the cross and placed it in Joseph's new tomb.[93]

> In this account of the death and burial of Jesus, the mention of their taking him down from the cross, without previous mention of their hanging Him on the cross, implies either that Paul's hearers were familiar with the fact of the crucifixion, or that Luke, in abbreviating, has omitted much of what Paul said.[94]

13:30 – *"But God raised Him from the dead;*

But God raised Him from the dead. Again and again in Acts we have seen the preachers emphasize the resurrection of Jesus from the dead. That God raised Him is evidence that God approved of Jesus' sacrifice for sins, and is setting Him out in a conspicuous way for all people to consider and obey.[95]

13:31 – *"and for many days He appeared to those who came up with Him from Galilee to Jerusalem, the very ones who are now His witnesses to the people.*

---

[91] John 19:7ff.

[92] John 19:14-16.

[93] Matthew 27:58-60; John 19:38, 39. On the use of the word "tree" for the cross, see notes at Acts 10:39.

[94] McGarvey, *op. cit.*, p.20.

[95] Compare comments at Acts 2:23-24.

And for many days He appeared to those. See comments at Acts 1:3. Jesus made His post-resurrection appearances over a period of forty days.

Who came up with Him from Galilee to Jerusalem. Those to whom the bulk of the post-resurrection appearances were made were the original apostles and the women who ministered to them out of their substance.[96] A large group came as a caravan to the last Passover of Jesus' ministry, and so were present in Jerusalem during His suffering and death.

The very ones who are now His witnesses to the people. Even while Paul is preaching in Pisidian Antioch, the original apostles are even then still witnessing in Jerusalem (and to Jewish people[97] living elsewhere) the announcement that Jesus is the Messiah. Such preaching as Paul was doing in Antioch was not some new doctrine just recently made up by Paul. It is the same message the Twelve were still preaching.

13:32 – *"And we preach to you the good news of the promise made to the fathers,*

And we preach to you the good news. "We" might be a reference to all the apostles, whether Paul or the Twelve; or it might be a reference to Paul and Barnabas in particular.

Of the promise made to the fathers. "The promise" means "the thing promised," namely, the coming Messiah, as promised in the Old Testament. Paul is saying, 'We are here to tell you that the promise God made to the fathers has been fulfilled, and that's good news!' Jesus, Paul declared, was the fulfillment of the Old Testament promise. The Messianic hope given to the fathers and nourished and cherished by them has been fulfilled in Him.

13:33 – *"that God has fulfilled this* **promise** *to our children in that He raised up Jesus, as it is also written in the second Psalm, 'THOU ART MY SON; TODAY I HAVE BEGOTTEN THEE.'*

That God has fulfilled this *promise* **to our children.** The Greek word translated "fulfilled" in this sentence is a stronger word (because it is a compound verb) than the word translated "fulfilled" in verse 27. The implication of "fulfilled" here in verse 33 is that the fulfillment by God is complete; there is nothing further to be expected. The chief emphasis of all the promises made centered in this, the coming of the Savior through David's lineage. That promise has been fulfilled to the utmost, insists Paul.

In that He raised up Jesus. As noted previously in this commentary,[98] "raised" does not always mean "raised from the dead". The word here probably speaks of Jesus' appearance in history, rather than to His resurrection from the dead. It is the next verse that speaks of His resurrection, not this one.

---

[96] John 19:25. Compare notes at Acts 10:41 concerning the ones to whom His appearances were limited.

[97] "People" here is *laos* in the Greek. This word is regularly used of *Jewish* people, unless the context demands a broader interpretation.

[98] See Acts 3:22, 7:37.

As it is also written in the second Psalm. The verse about to be quoted is Psalm 2:7. The reading "in the first Psalm," as some manuscripts have it, is interesting. It shows that in some copies of the Old Testament, what we call Psalm 1 was treated as a kind of introduction or prelude to the whole book, and the numeration began with what is now Psalm 2. Our second Psalm was understood by the Jews as being a Messianic Psalm, and that is how Paul, by Holy Spirit inspiration, interprets it, too.

THOU ART MY SON; TODAY I HAVE BEGOTTEN THEE. The New Testament applied this expression to two different events. (1) In Luke 1:35, it is applied to Jesus' incarnation – a special reference to the virgin birth. Jesus was begotten by God. (2) In Romans 1:4, the Psalm is quoted as being a prediction of Jesus' resurrection from the dead. It would seem Paul's usage here in Acts 13 is similar to Luke's, and that the entrance of Jesus into the world is one way that God fulfilled the promise made to the fathers.

It is contrary to all other Scripture to use this language ("begotten") as proof that Jesus is not an eternal being, but was conceived somewhere back in eternity previous to the creation of the world. Such an idea, often called "eternal generation," is foreign to the doctrine taught in John 1:1, that Jesus has existed just as long as the Father has.

13:34 – *"And as for the fact that He raised Him up from the dead, no more to return to decay, He has spoken in this way: 'I WILL GIVE YOU THE HOLY and SURE blessings OF DAVID.'*

And as for the fact **that He raised Him up from the dead.** This time the verb "raised up" does refer to Jesus' resurrection from the dead, as the verse and the quotations introduced from the Old Testament plainly show.

No more to return to decay. Compare Peter's sermon at Acts 2:27. The words do not, of course, mean that Jesus had already seen corruption.

He has spoken in this way. The quotation is made from Isaiah 55:3 from the LXX.

I WILL GIVE YOU THE HOLY *and* SURE *blessings* OF DAVID. The key word in this quotation from Isaiah, which helps us understand the point of the quotation, is the word that must be added by the translators, the word "blessings." In the Greek, the words "holy" and "sure" are neuter plural adjectives, and a plural noun must be supplied. In addition to the resurrection which the near context has spoken of, the far context has spoken of the promise made to David that one of his descendants would sit on his throne forever.[99] The resurrection was absolutely necessary to the fulfillment of this promise made by God.

The added word is a good choice because involved in the word "blessings" is forgiveness of sins (verse 38). "Blessings" are connected with the resurrection of Jesus because only in His resurrection and exaltation are such blessings ratified and assured. Although the words of Isaiah, at first sight, might not seem to have any reference to the resurrection of Jesus from the dead, when we remember that the resurrection was vitally necessary if "blessings" would come to sinful men, we can easily see the connection Paul makes.

---

[99] 2 Samuel 7:16; Psalm 59:4-5, 132:11-12.

The blessings are called "holy" because they have to do with making men "holy," and they are called "sure" because they would surely be accomplished, just as sure as He who promised is faithful!

13:35 – *"Therefore He also says in another* **Psalm,** *'THOU WILT NOT ALLOW THY HOLY ONE TO UNDERGO DECAY.'*

Therefore He also says in another *Psalm.* "Therefore" represents *dioti*, and in this case the word seems to be inferential. The holy and sure blessings of David have been promised. For these to be realized there must be a resurrection of Messiah after His death for sin. *Therefore,* that is exactly what is predicted, in Psalm 16:10, for example.

THOU WILT NOT ALLOW THY HOLY ONE TO UNDERGO DECAY. See Acts 2:27. Paul is quoting the same Psalm that Peter used on the day of Pentecost, and to prove the same thing, namely, the predicted resurrection of Jesus from the dead.

13:36 – *"For David, after he had served the purpose of God in his own generation, fell asleep, and was laid among his fathers, and underwent decay;*

For David. This verse seems to be a further explanation of the passage in Psalm 16, showing that it did not have reference to David, and must therefore be a prediction about some other person. Verse 37 will affirm that this could refer to no one, in fact, but to the Lord Jesus.

After he had served the purpose of God in his own generation. One of the contrasts between David and Christ is stated in this verse. David's service lasted only for a generation, whereas the service of Christ lasts through all generations continually. David, years ago, carried out God's will in serving the people, so the Psalm cannot refer to him, Paul is saying.

Fell asleep. He died.[100] In 1 Kings 2:10 this very expression is used of David's death.

And was laid among his fathers. "He was buried" is what some believe this phrase means, but there is more than "buried" indicated here. It is instructive to observe that in some cases in the Old Testament, "being gathered unto his people" is something distinct from the burial of the body.[101] The Greek of verse 36 is exactly the same as that used in the LXX which is translated "gathered to his people." Therefore, the passage in Acts says this – "David died. His soul, in going to the place of the departed spirits (i.e., Sheol/Hades), was 'gathered to his people.' His physical body saw corruption."[102]

---

[100] See this expression explained in notes at Act 7:60.

[101] Compare Genesis 49:33 and 50:13. Jacob died, was gathered to this people, and then long after was buried. See also 2 Kings 22:20. Note also that *God* gathered, but *man* did the burying.

[102] That "gathered to his people" has reference to the soul, not the body, can be clearly seen in the case of Moses, whose body was not laid to rest in a family grave plot somewhere. See Deuteronomy 32:50.

And underwent decay. David's body remained in the grave and returned to the dust it was.[103] This is the second point of the contrast between David and Christ. David's body decayed as it laid in the tomb. Jesus' body was not in the tomb long enough to decay.

13:37 – *"but He whom God raised did not undergo decay.*

But He whom God raised. Namely, the Lord Jesus.

Did not undergo decay. Jesus' body was raised before it experienced any decay. As David's body did decay, and the body of the Lord Jesus did not, it follows, Paul says, that Psalm 16 must be a prediction about Jesus, not David.

13:38 – *"Therefore let it be known to you, brethren, that through Him forgiveness of sins is proclaimed to you,*

Therefore let it be known to you, brethren. Paul now draws a conclusion from the previous facts – the promise of the sure and holy blessings of David being ratified by the resurrection. Paul will specifically state the benefits that were the result of the death and resurrection of Jesus.

That through Him forgiveness of sins is proclaimed to you. The Greek here is very pointed. "Through this man," it reads. Salvation is through the agency of Christ, and through Him alone. "Forgiveness of sins" is the keynote of New Testament preaching. It was what Peter preached,[104] and what Paul was instructed to preach.[105] The force of the verb tense ("*is* proclaimed") emphasizes the fact that the forgiveness of sins was, at that very moment, in the act of being proclaimed. Paul will, in his next breath, share with his listeners the conditions of that forgiveness.

13:39 – *and through Him everyone who believes is freed from all things, from which you could not be freed through the Law of Moses.*

And through Him. Note that in both verses 38 and 39 we have the phrase "through Him." In the Greek, the *genitive* case in verse 38 expresses intermediate agency. It was through the agency of Jesus that forgiveness of sins is available. In verse 39, the Greek is in the *dative* case, and is likely a dative of sphere. The thought is that the man who is "in Christ" is justified in the sense of enjoying forgiveness of his sins, a blessing a man could not enjoy if he tried to find it "by means of the Law."

> The remission of sins is here proclaimed to the believer who is "in Christ;" and as we learn by another characteristic expression of Paul, the believer is "baptized into Christ," "baptized into His body," Romans 6:3, Galatians 3:27, 1 Corinthians 12:13. Thus, the connection of the remission of sins with baptism, which was plainly stated in Peter's first

---

[103] See the point argued more at length in Acts 2:29-31.

[104] Acts 2:38, 5:31, 10:43.

[105] Acts 26:18.

sermon (Acts 2:38) is implied in this, the first recorded sermon by Paul.[106]

Everyone who believes is freed. Instead of "freed," the margin reads "justified." "Justified" means to be regarded and treated as if they are "not guilty." The word often has a forensic sense, meaning that the judge (God in this case) pronounces a verdict of acquittal. They are treated as if they had not offended.

Some scholars say verse 39 is the book of Galatians and Romans in a nut shell. See Romans 1:17, 3:24-25, and 4:1-8 where "justification by faith" is worked out in detail. It is interesting that the only occurrence in Acts of this verb *dikaioō* is found in the first recorded example of Paul's preaching. As time passed, the word "justify" came to be almost identified with him and his work.

From all things. The "all things" from which a person is justified, if he or she is in Christ, includes the guilt and penalty of all sins.

From which you could not be freed through the Law of Moses. Paul's argument here, that the Law of Moses had nothing to do with a man's justification, is the same argument found in detail in Romans 3-4 and in the book of Galatians. What Paul preached at Pisidian Antioch and what he later wrote to these very people in Galatians is essentially the same: justification is found only in Christ, and there is no hope of forgiveness or salvation in attempting to earn salvation by perfect obedience to the Mosaic Law. The Law of Moses had a very high standard of righteousness and demanded entire obedience.[107] There were sacrifices commanded, but those sacrifices did not take away sin, or justify the disobedience of the people who offered the sacrifices.[108] It was the purpose of the Law to prepare the people for Christ.[109] Even the Law itself indicates that salvation is not in Law keeping, but in a life of faith, as Habakkuk 2:4, etc. says, "The righteous shall live by faith." At this point, it must be added that just a moment before, Paul has used the words "everyone who believes" – this faith is a condition open to all, Jew or Gentile. Everyone who has an obedient faith in Jesus is justified.

13:40 – *"Take heed therefore, so that the thing spoken of in the Prophets may not come upon you:*

Take heed therefore. The change of tone in Paul's message is best explained by saying that Paul observed, at this point in his message, a disapproving expression in the faces and actions of many of his Jewish hearers.

---

[106] McGarvey, *op. cit.*, p.24-25.

[107] Romans 7:12; James 2:10.

[108] Hebrews 9:7-14, 10:1-4, 10:11.

[109] Galatians 3:24.

> The reason Paul did not, like Peter, urge his hearers to repent and be baptized, that they might be in Christ and enjoy the remission of their sins, was because, as we shall see below, he saw that they were not prepared for such an exhortation.[110]

After driving home one truth from the Old Testament prophets, that the blessing of forgiveness of sins was available to obedient believers through the atoning work of Christ, Paul drives home another point, also by using the words of the prophets. Those same prophets spoke of a severe punishment in store for those who failed to become obedient believers. 'Take care that punishment doesn't come to you,' is Paul's exhortation.

So that the thing spoken of in the Prophets may not come upon *you*. The Jews divided the Old Testament into three parts, called the Law, the Prophets, and the Hagiographa (Holy Writings).[111] Paul is about to cite Habakkuk 1:5, and the point Habakkuk emphasized is this – if people scoff and refuse to obey when God visits them, they will certainly perish!

13:41 – 'BEHOLD, YOU SCOFFERS, AND MARVEL, AND PERISH; FOR I AM ACCOMPLISHING A WORK IN YOUR DAYS, A WORK WHICH YOU WILL NEVER BELIEVE, THOUGH SOMEONE SHOULD DESCRIBE IT TO YOU.'

BEHOLD, YOU SCOFFERS, AND MARVEL, AND PERISH. Where Paul has "you scoffers," the Hebrew has "You among the heathen [nations]." The change from one expression to the other was made by the LXX translators, and represents a very slight alteration in the Hebrew word.[112] That change also leads to a difference in the next phrase between Paul's "and marvel, and perish" and the Hebrew's "wonder marvelously."

"Perish" (*aphanizō*) is not the word which is commonly translated "perish" (*apollumi*), which has reference to eternal punishment. This has led to several explanations of Paul's statement about the scoffing Jews' "perishing."

- When Habakkuk originally spoke the words, he was referring to temporal judgments following an invasion by the Chaldeans. Thus, some writers think the punishment that will come on the Jewish nation at the hand of the Romans in AD 70 was in Paul's thought,[113] a punishment that was coming because, as a nation, they rejected Christ.
- Some writers think of the difficulties that would befall the Jews through the centuries as a result of their being cut off and the Gentiles grafted in.[114]
- Still others insist such temporal applications were rather far removed from the specific situation Paul was addressing. Thus, Paul must have been threatening eternal punishment in Hell to those who persisted in rejecting the gospel. That is, these listeners in

---

[110] McGarvey, *op. cit.*, p.25.

[111] See notes at Acts 7:42, where it is explained what books were included in "The Prophets" division of the Hebrew Old Testament.

[112] There is one letter difference between *baggoim* ("among the heathen") and *bogedim* ("scoffers"), a change of a vaw to a daleth.

[113] Compare Matthew 24:2-28, where Jesus himself predicted such a fate for the Jews who rejected him.

[114] Romans 11:7ff.

Antioch would see the work of God and be amazed by it, yet because they did nothing about it but be amazed, they would perish.

FOR I AM ACCOMPLISHING A WORK IN YOUR DAYS. The thing about which Habakkuk spoke was the invasion by the Chaldeans. God has a hand in history, and used the Chaldeans as an instrument of judgment and punishment upon the rebellious Jews. Paul implies that similar calamities, both temporal and eternal, will come upon those who reject the Messiah. The entrance of Messiah into the world, His being raised from the dead and exalted to the right hand of the Father, all were the activities of God. God was working a work, even as Paul preached, in that forgiveness of sins was being made available to the listeners to whom Paul was speaking.

A WORK WHICH YOU WILL NEVER BELIEVE, THOUGH SOMEONE SHOULD DESCRIBE IT TO YOU. "You will never believe" equals 'you never supposed such a thing would happen.' "Though someone describe it" equals 'even though a *prophet* of God predicted it, you will not believe it.' There is an implication that the declaration would contain such evidence as to make its rejection inexcusable.[115]

13:42 – *And as Paul and Barnabas were going out, the people kept begging that these things might be spoken to them the next Sabbath.*

And as Paul and Barnabas were going out. There is a notable manuscript variation at this place. Beginning with verse 40, Luke's narrative indicates that at least some in the audience appear to be rejecting Paul's message, which is why he closed his sermon with a warning. This phrase seems to say that Paul and Barnabas are in the process of leaving the meeting place before the service is finished. And as they are in the process of leaving, some of the listeners make a request of the preachers.

The people kept begging that these things might be spoken to them the next Sabbath. The Greek of the better manuscripts reads, "they kept begging;" i.e., there is no word for "people" in the original.

- Some manuscripts read "the Gentiles kept begging ...." If this be the true reading, then the meaning is that the Jews as a whole rejected the gospel; but the proselytes present ("the Gentiles") asked to hear the gospel again.
- The NASB reads as do the better manuscripts, and the verse then means that as Paul and Barnabas were leaving, the congregation – both Jews and proselytes – begged that they would return and preach again.

"The next Sabbath" (and not the marginal reading in the 1960 version of the NASB, "in the week between Sabbaths") is the true meaning of the Greek words, though they admit, literally, of the other meaning.[116]

---

[115] Those who think the coming destruction of Jerusalem is in the back of Paul's mind as he utters this warning are careful to point out that, only a few years after Paul spoke these words in the synagogue at Antioch, the Romans captured and destroyed Jerusalem (AD 70). This effectively brought an end to Temple worship and also brought on the complete dispersion of the Jewish nation.

[116] There is some evidence that the Jews also had a meeting at the synagogue on Mondays and Thursdays,

13:43 – *Now when the meeting of the synagogue had broken up, many of the Jews and of the God-fearing proselytes followed Paul and Barnabas, who, speaking to them, were urging them to continue in the grace of God.*

Now when *the meeting of* the synagogue had broken up. Paul and Barnabas had left the meeting before it was dismissed. Once it had been dismissed and the crowd begins to disperse, there follows the action now described.

Many of the Jews and of the God-fearing proselytes followed Paul and Barnabas. The two apostles were on their way to their place of lodging. Many of those who had begged them to preach again the next week now follow Paul and Barnabas to their lodging, in order to continue their earnest appeals to the preachers. "God-fearing proselytes" would be what are elsewhere called proselytes of the gate.[117] Based on the order in which the names of the missionaries appear Paul is now the leader of the missionary party.[118]

Who, speaking to them. The apostles, Paul and Barnabas, are the ones who are speaking to the worshipers who have followed them home.

Were urging them to continue in the grace of God. The verb tense indicates the "urging" was done over a period of time, perhaps all through the next week. This is the third time the word "grace" has appeared in the book of Acts.[119] If this use of the word is intended to draw a contrast with how a typical Jew tried to save himself by works of the Law, then "grace" stands for the doctrine that forgiveness of sins is attainable by faith, not by legal works. On the other hand, if the word is intended to draw a contrast with the unbelief exhibited by some in the synagogue, then "grace" stands for the favor of God, and Paul is encouraging them to keep on believing, that they may remain in the sphere of God's favor.

One outline of Paul's first recorded sermon has been given as follows:

JESUS IS THE MESSIAH

I. PROOF FROM HISTORY
    a. God chose and exalted a people, v.17
    b. He delivered them from Egypt, v.17
    c. He gave them a country, v.18,19
    d. He provided judges for them, v.20
    e. At their request he gave them a king, v.21
    f. He removed Saul and raised up David, v.22
    g. From David's seed came Jesus, v.23

---

the two days each week on which the Pharisees fasted (Luke 18:12).

[117] See notes at Acts 2:10 where the two types of proselytes are explained.

[118] Compare Acts 11:30 and 12:13,25.

[119] See also Acts 4:33 and 11:23.

- II. JESUS PROVEN TO BE THE SAVIOR
  - a. By the testimony of John, v.24,25
  - b. By His rejection, which prophecy foretold, v.26-29
  - c. By His resurrection – a fact attested:
    1) By eyewitnesses, v.30-32
    2) By Scripture, v.33-37

- III. PAUL'S APPEAL AND WARNING
  - a. Encouragement to believe, v.38-39
  - b. Warning from the prophets, v.40-41

13:44 – *And the next Sabbath nearly the whole city assembled to hear the word of God.*

And the next Sabbath. It may be (as noted above under "were urging") that Paul and Barnabas have spent a busy week in Antioch, teaching and evangelizing. The news of what the apostles preached has been circulated by many of the crowd who were present the first Sabbath to hear them, as well as by those who heard during the week.

Nearly the whole city assembled to hear the word of God. The words "nearly the whole city" are probably not to be taken absolutely literally, for such a crowd would not be able to get into the synagogue building. It is, however, metaphorical language signifying that a very large crowd was on hand. Further, verse 48 ("the Gentiles") seems to indicate people are present besides the Jews and proselytes who usually would assemble at the synagogue. How would the apostles go about speaking to such a crowd (in an age before the invention of public address systems)? One suggestion is that Paul spoke to those on the inside of the building, and Barnabas spoke to those assembled on the outside. Another suggestion is that Paul stood in the doorway of the synagogue and was thus able to speak both to those without and within. Synagogues often did not have pews as do our worship buildings. In such cases the people sat on mats laid on the floor, and thus could easily turn their face toward the door, while those outside sat in the same way on the ground. The gospel is here designated "the word of God."

13:45 – *But when the Jews saw the crowds, they were filled with jealousy, and* **began** *contradicting the things spoken by Paul, and were blaspheming.*

But when the Jews saw the crowds, they were filled with jealousy. No such overflow crowds came to the synagogue when the Jewish teachers were the speakers. Hence, they were jealous of these new preachers. Especially if the crowds included Gentiles, we can better understand the source of the religious leaders' bitter feelings.

And *began* contradicting the things spoken by Paul. The Jewish opposition did not precede Paul's preaching on this day. Rather, the mental picture we should have includes a sermon delivered by Paul, the content of which was very similar to that taught the previous Sabbath. Then, during the course of his preaching, Paul was interrupted over and over again by the Jewish religious leaders. Part of the time, they were simply contradicting the things spoken by Paul. That is, they seem to have been opposing the doctrine that Jesus was the Messiah, and that salvation was available to all who believe (rather than through the keeping of the Law).

And were blaspheming. The Greek verb could also be translated by the less intense English word "reviling" (see the marginal reading). Thus, we do not know if the Jews were attacking the apostles (reviling) or vilifying Jesus of Nazareth (blaspheming). Since Paul and Barnabas spoke by inspiration, it should be remembered that, when the Jews contradicted and blasphemed, they were opposing the Holy Spirit.

13:46 – *And Paul and Barnabas spoke out boldly and said, "It was necessary that the word of God should be spoken to you first; since you repudiate it, and judge yourselves unworthy of eternal life, behold, we are turning to the Gentiles.*

And Paul and Barnabas spoke out boldly and said. To speak "boldly" is to speak fearlessly, to express oneself openly and freely.[120] Rather than being intimidated into silence by the outspoken contempt and scorn of the Jewish religious leaders, the apostles speak all the more boldly. There are times when it takes courage to declare the truth. Such was the case with the announcement about to be made.

It was necessary that the word of God should be spoken to you first. Paul earlier spoke of the "purpose" of God (verse 36). The necessity to preach to the Jews first was part of that purpose also.[121] It was part of the divine order that the gospel should be offered to the Jews first that they might accept it and in turn evangelize the Gentiles. However, since the Jews rejected the word of God and thereby judged themselves unworthy of the life of the age to come, Paul must himself turn to the Gentiles.

Since you repudiate it. 'Because you reject the gospel.' The same doctrine is taught in detail in Romans 9-11.

And judge yourselves unworthy of eternal life. By their conduct the Jews at Pisidian Antioch had condemned themselves. Paul had thought them "worthy" to share in the great blessing of forgiveness of sins and eternal life. Instead, by their jealousy, their ill-mannered interruptions of his preaching, and their blasphemy, they have demonstrated that they really were "unworthy" of the opportunity of having the offer of salvation made any further to them.

Behold, we are turning to the Gentiles. 'We shall offer the gospel to the Gentiles here in Antioch. As long as we remain in this city, we shall work primarily with the Gentiles. They will receive Christ!'[122]

---

[120] Paul had exhibited the same kind of speech in the synagogues at Damascus (Acts 9:27).

[121] Compare Romans 1:16.

[122] This verse is not properly explained by those dispensational Bible teachers who find here the "final repudiation" of the Jews by God. See Acts 17:2, 18:5-6, 18:19, and 28:23.

13:47 – *"For thus the Lord has commanded us, 'I HAVE PLACED YOU AS A LIGHT FOR THE GENTILES, THAT YOU SHOULD BRING SALVATION TO THE END OF THE EARTH.'"*

For thus the Lord has commanded us. Paul is giving a reason for his going to the Gentiles; his actions were not arbitrary. "Lord" here is a reference to the Father. Because the Jews might recognize the authority of their own Scriptures, whereas they would have turned in scorn from a command of Jesus of Nazareth, Paul appeals to the Old Testament. Isaiah 49:6 is the prophecy Paul appeals to. Originally, the prophecy referred to the Servant of the Lord, but in this case, Paul says it was a command made to the apostles ("the Lord has commanded *us*," he says). The prophecy predicted what would occur in the Gospel age, and if God said the gospel would go to the Gentiles, then Paul considers that a command to go to the Gentiles!

I HAVE PLACED YOU AS A LIGHT FOR THE GENTILES. The aged Simeon, who had been promised he would see the Messiah before he died, also quoted Isaiah 49 as he held the infant Jesus in his arms.[123] Jesus only spoke as the Father gave Him to speak, and before His ascension He made it clear that His disciples were to be witnesses to the uttermost part of the earth. That command included Gentiles as well as Jews.

THAT YOU SHOULD BRING SALVATION TO THE END OF THE EARTH. "Salvation" includes forgiveness of sins, the indwelling gift of the Holy Spirit to help people live the Christian life, and also preservation in the future state from the woes that will overwhelm the disobedient. "The end of the earth" here represents the same Greek translated "remotest part of the earth" in Acts 1:8. We could have wished the NASB had been consistent, for "end of the earth" at times has a connotation involving the close of the age, or the end of time, which is probably not the right idea here.

13:48 – *And when the Gentiles heard this, they* **began** *rejoicing and glorifying the word of the Lord; and as many as had been appointed to eternal life believed.*

And when the Gentiles heard this. It seems there were people visiting the Jewish synagogue that day who were neither Jews nor proselytes. They are hearing Paul's statement that the gospel was to be preached to them, and that God had long ago predicted it!

They *began* rejoicing and glorifying the word of the Lord. Both verbs imply continuing action; it was more than a momentary outburst of emotion. The Jews had long taught that salvation was for the Jews only, so part of the rejoicing by the Gentiles must have been over the fact that they are hearing from the mouth of Jews a different doctrine. "Word of the Lord" (if this is the correct reading; note the marginal note "word of God") probably means the teaching about the Lord Jesus. "Glorifying" that teaching means the Gentiles are expressing the thought, "That's amazingly wonderful news! The possibility of salva-

---

[123] Luke 2:25-32. This passage is notable as showing that Paul identified the "Servant of Jehovah" as being Christ. See other discussion about the identity of the Servant in notes at Acts 8:34.

tion through Jesus to everyone who believes is a message worthy of our highest praise!"

And as many as had been appointed to eternal life believed. This verse has been called upon as being prime evidence for the correctness of the Calvinistic doctrine of absolute predestination. Calvin taught that certain ones were appointed to be saved, and certain appointed to be lost, no matter what they did. God had simply decreed it to be thus, and men were saved or lost simply because God had so decreed it.[124]

The Greek word translated "appointed" is *tetagmenoi*, from the root *tassō*. That word had a primary meaning of "set in order, to place in a certain order." It would be used of arranging a body of soldiers in order for a march.

There are several ways of determining what a word means in any given passage. One is to see how the word is used elsewhere in the Bible, and the other is to examine the current context for a clue to the word's connotation within the particular passage that is in doubt.

- How is the word used elsewhere in the New Testament? (1) *Diatassō* is translated "set in order" (ASV) or "arrange" (NASB) at 1 Corinthians 11:34. (2) At Romans 13:1, the NASB, NIV, etc. render *tassō* according to its primary meaning: "The authorities that exist are established (i.e., arranged, appointed, set in order) by God." The KJV uses the word "ordained," as it does in only one other of its eight occurrences in the New Testament. In this Romans verse, *tassō* can easily and understandably be rendered by its primary meaning. (3) The word is several times rendered "appoint" or "designate," as to appoint a place (Matthew 28:16), to appoint something to be done (Acts 22:10), and to appoint (set) a day (Acts 28:23). By making appointments, order is brought of preceding confusion, or lack of order, so that the primary meaning of the word is not lost sight of even in this use of it. The same is true when the word is used of a mental act. When the mind has been in confusion on a subject, not knowing what to think, and finally reaches a definite conclusion or purpose, the thoughts are brought out of confusion into order; and this term properly expresses the change (cp. Acts 15:2).

  We have found several different connotations included in the word, but in each there is the idea of order where before there was a disorder of some kind.

- How is the word used in the current context? Calvinistic writers attempt to make the passage teach the doctrine of unconditional election and predestination. One writer, for example, comments, "as many as were appointed (by God) to eternal life, or to whom God had decreed eternal life, believed."[125] However, to help show that such a Calvinistic interpretation does not fit the context, it has been rightly pointed out that if as many as were foreordained to eternal life believed on that day, then all the rest were reprobates, doomed to everlasting punishment. Therefore, any further preaching by Paul to them would have been useless. Yet, on the contrary, verse 49 clearly indicates that such further preaching was not useless.

- We are thus led to one of two possible explanations for this difficult phrase. *Tetagmenoi*, which the NASB translated "appointed," may be treated as either a middle

---

[124] There is a good discussion of this problem in McGarvey, *op. cit.*, p.29-33.

[125] Joseph H. Thayer, *Thayer's Greek-English Lexicon of the New Testament* (Grand Rapids: Zondervan Publishing House, 1976), p.615.

or passive voice verb.[126] (1) If we take it as a passive verb, it speaks of *something God did*. The verse is explained in this manner by Knowling:

> There is no countenance here for the *absolutum decretum* of the Calvinists, since verse 46 had already shown that the Jews had acted through their own choice. The words are really nothing more than a corollary of St. Paul's *anagkaion* ["necessity"]: the Jews as a nation had been ordained to eternal life – they had rejected this election: but those who believed amongst the Gentiles were equally ordained by God to eternal life, and it was in accordance with His divine appointment that the Apostles had turned to them.[127]

(2) If we take it as a middle voice verb, it speaks of *something the people did for their own benefit*. We would translate it, "Those who were *determined* to have eternal life believed." In the passage before us, the context presents no allusion to something done by God for one part of the audience and not done for the other. Rather, it speaks of two contrasted states of mind among the people, and two consequent courses of conduct. Of the Jews in Paul's audience it is said, first, that they were filled with jealousy; second, they contradicted the things which were spoken by Paul; third, that they judged themselves unworthy of eternal life. In contrast with these, the Gentiles, first, were glad; second, they glorified the word of the Lord; third, they were *tetagmenoi* to eternal life. (If we read "determined, disposed" that they would have eternal life, if at all possible, then the contrast with the mental state of the Jews is clear.)

Let it be noted that being determined to have eternal life, and the consequent believing, stand here as cause and effect, or at least as antecedent and consequent. This is not at all unnatural or uncommon. A person who has learned that eternal life may be obtained, and has made up his or her mind to obtain it if within his power, is the very person to readily accept the true way of obtaining it when that way is clearly pointed out. Conversely, the person who is so much absorbed in worldly matters as to be indifferent to eternal life is the very person to allow the testimony concerning the way of obtaining it to pass in at one ear and out at the other.

The latter interpretation – of treating *tetagmenoi* as a middle voice verb – appears to be the correct one, for it leaves the responsibility for belief and unbelief, with their eternal consequences, on the individual, and not on God. "Believed" equals "made a public confession of their faith."[128]

13:49 – *And the word of the Lord was being spread through the whole region.*

And the word of the Lord was being spread through the whole region. The message about the Lord Jesus was preached by the apostles and also, we may assume, by small groups of converts in other towns. The gospel is being received by the Gentiles, even though the Jews rejected it.

---

[126] The verb we are studying is used in the middle voice at Acts 20:13, and in Josephus repeatedly.

[127] Knowling, *op. cit.*, p.300.

[128] Acts 8:13, 11:21; Romans 13:11.

The verse clearly indicates that Paul and Barnabas remained for some time in the "region" of Antioch. This word "region" introduces us to another important fact of Roman imperial administration. Each *province* was subdivided into *regions*. Here in southern Galatia there were several regions, one of which had Pisidian Antioch as its administrative center.[129] Not only in Antioch, but in all the towns and villages round about, the gospel was preached. We shall see that this is one of Paul's methods of evangelism. He went to large cities, and worked there to establish a Christian congregation. Then, as people were trained, they went out to the neighboring villages; and the citizens of these towns had the opportunity to hear the gospel and be saved, and be built together into new congregations. Shortly, in each of these towns, there would be people who no longer sacrificed to their ancestral gods, or who were no longer content to worship after the manner of the Jews. They were new creatures in Christ Jesus, and He was the object of their worship. This was the beginning of the churches of Galatia.

13:50 – *But the Jews aroused the devout women of prominence and the leading men of the city, and instigated a persecution against Paul and Barnabas, and drove them out of their district.*

But the Jews aroused the devout women of prominence. "Devout women" are likely proselytes to the Jewish religion. That they were women of prominence means either that their husbands were the local authorities, or that the women themselves held high administrative positions.[130] The fact that the Jewish religious leaders could arouse these women to opposition to the two apostles brings before us another feature of the 1st century world. The Pharisees "compassed land and sea to make one proselyte."[131] They found it easiest to make proselytes of women, for in many places there was a real longing for a higher and purer life than was assigned to woman in the debased Greek and Roman society. But there was a bad side to such proselyting. It was found in the absolute trust in the leadership of their new teachers. Thus, when the religious leaders speak to the prominent women about these two preachers who have spoken against the religion they had recently adopted, the women are quickly willing to oppose the gospel.

And the leading men of the city. The leading men would be the officials of the Roman government, and the administrators of the region's affairs. Perhaps the Jewish leaders were able to contact and influence the city leaders through the prominent women.

And instigated a persecution against Paul and Barnabas. Toward the close of his life, Paul will recall to mind the persecution he faced in Antioch. It was something never to be forgotten.[132] It may be too that the preachers were not the only ones to suffer in this persecution. Some days later, Paul will return to Antioch and, in the midst of giving encouragement to the brethren, he will teach them the lesson that they must "through much

---

[129] Ramsay, *St. Paul the Traveller and Roman Citizen,* p.102-104, 109, 110-112.

[130] *Ibid.*, p.102; Conybeare and Howson, *op. cit.,* p.144.

[131] Matthew 23:15.

[132] 2 Timothy 3:11.

tribulation enter into the kingdom of God."[133] Perhaps we are to understand that after the apostles are driven from town, their newly won converts become the target of the Jewish opposition.

And drove them out of their district. This word is synonymous with the word "region" of verse 49. The expulsion was a tumultuous thing, a near-riot, not a legal proceeding.

13:51 – *But they shook off the dust of their feet* **in protest** *against them and went to Iconium.*

But they shook off the dust of their feet *in protest* **against them.** This action by Paul and Barnabas as they left the city was in literal obedience to one of Jesus' commands when He sent His apostles out on their limited commission.[134] The two would have stooped down, pulled off their sandals, and held them up for all to see, and then shook off the dust from them. It would be very dramatic! This act by the departing apostles, witnessed no doubt by those who had just thrown them out of town, was not an idle or childish act of resentment, but would have had grave meaning to the Jews who had been urging the persecutors on. The dust of heathen lands, as compared to the land of Israel, was regarded as polluted and unholy.[135] The Jew, therefore, considered himself defiled by such dust. For the apostles to shake off the dust of any city from their clothes or feet was to place that city on a level with the cities of the heathen, and to renounce all further dealings with the people against whom they shook off the dust. The Jews who were watching would understand that Paul and Barnabas were calling them worse than the heathen.

And went to Iconium. This city, called Konya on modern maps, was in the region of Phrygia, and was located near the border between Phrygia and Lycaonia. In Acts 14:6 Paul and Barnabas are represented as fleeing from Iconium to the cities of Lycaonia, which implies the border of Phrygia and Lycaonia was crossed somewhere between Iconium and Lystra. Iconium was about 60 miles southeast of Pisidian Antioch. Several Roman roads met at this point, and Iconium was therefore an important center for missionary labors. This Phrygian region, with Iconium as its administrative capital, was part of the Roman province of Galatia in New Testament times.

13:52 – *And the disciples were continually filled with joy and with the Holy Spirit.*

And the disciples were continually filled with joy. "The disciples" were the new Christians left behind in Antioch of Pisidia. They had "joy" because of forgiven sin, and because of newfound peace with God. A heart full of joy is almost a normal sequence following conversion.[136]

---

[133] Acts 14:22.

[134] Luke 9:5; Matthew 10:14. Evidently the command had become known to Paul and Barnabas, even though they were not numbered in the group to whom it was originally given. More and more we are learning how many facts about Jesus' ministry Paul received by revelation. Compare comments on Acts 13:33-38 about Paul's knowledge of the earthly ministry of Jesus.

[135] Amos 7:17; Ezekiel 14:11.

[136] Acts 8:8,39.

And [were continually filled] with the Holy Spirit. This reference seems to be to the measure of the Spirit called spiritual gifts. It is highly probable that before departing from these new Christians, Paul and Barnabas laid their hands upon them, and bestowed upon them the special gifts of the Holy Spirit, such as prophecy, speaking in tongues, supernatural knowledge, and the power to heal the sick. These spiritual gifts would guide them into the necessary truth until the New Testament could be written, and also support the truth which they would preach, now that the two missionaries were gone.

Interior of a Synagogue

**Drawing by Horace Knowles
from the British and Foreign Bible Society**

SPECIAL STUDY #15

THE SYNAGOGUE AND ITS SERVICES[1]

An understanding of the origin, the organization, and the order of services in the Jewish synagogue is helpful to the understanding of many verses in the Bible where we find ourselves "attending the Sabbath services."

I. ITS ORIGIN

The only reference to the synagogue in the Old Testament is Psalm 74:8, which leads scholars to the conclusion that the synagogue is something that grew up during the Babylonian Captivity.

The Babylonians had destroyed the city of Jerusalem and had taken much of the Jewish population into exile, moving them over 1,000 miles from the Holy City. It is assumed that the people in Exile, wishing a place to worship, established synagogues as places of assembly in their midst.

The Jews worshiped each Saturday in the synagogue. During the week, children went there to school to learn to read and write. The chief textbook was the Old Testament.

Anywhere there were ten family heads, a synagogue established.

II. THE BUILDING ITSELF

It seems that the synagogues often consisted of two compartments – one for prayer, preaching, and the offices of public worship; and the other for the meetings of the learned men, for discussions concerning questions of religion and discipline, and for purposes of education. The place where the Jews met for worship was called *Bet-ha-Cneset,* and the place where the lectures were given was called *Bet-ha-Midrash*.

Synagogues in prosperous communities were often fine edifices according to the taste of time and place; the community did not spare money on the decoration and furnishings.

There were several pieces of essential furniture in a synagogue. The rolls of the Scriptures were kept in a chest, or press, which was usually standing in an alcove or recess shut off by a curtain from the body of the synagogue. The roll of the Pentateuch or the Prophets was laid for the reading of the lessons on a *bema,* or platform that contained a reading desk. Lamps and candelabra also belonged to the furnishings of the synagogue.

---

[1] Adapted from Paul Levertoff, "Synagogue" in the *International Standard Bible Encyclopedia*, Vol.5, p.2878-2879.

III. THE OFFICIALS OF THE SYNAGOGUE

The elders.[2] These officials formed the local tribunal, and in purely Jewish localities acted as a Committee of Management of the affairs of the synagogue. To them belonged the power of excommunication. The elders were usually Pharisees by belief and training.

The ruler. In some synagogues there were several rulers.[3] They were most probably chosen from among the elders. It was the ruler's business to control the synagogue services, as for instance who was to be called upon to read from the Law and the Prophets, and to preach. The ruler looked after the discussions and generally kept order.

The minister (or servant) (or servants). The synagogue attendant,[4] or minister, was a salaried officer. In his charge were the synagogue building and its furniture, especially the rolls of the Scriptures. The minister saw to the lighting of the synagogue and kept the building clean. Sometimes he had his dwelling under the same roof. From the roof of the building he gave the signal to the people to stop work on the approach of the Sabbath by a triple blast of a trumpet, and similarly gave notice of the close of the holy day. During the synagogue services, the attendant brought the roll of Scripture from the press and then delivered it to the reader; when the reading was concluded, he received it back, rolled it up, and after holding it up to the view of the congregation, returned it to the press. He also indicated to the priest the point at which the benediction should be pronounced, and at the fasts he told the priests when to blow the trumpets. When punishment had to be meted out to anyone in the synagogue, he wielded the scourge.[5] In smaller communities, the minister often had to fill a variety of other offices. When there were not readers enough at the service, he had to fill out the number, or even read the whole lesson himself; he might also have to lead in prayer.

The delegate of the congregation. This office was not permanent. Rather, at each meeting the ruler chose a congregational delegate, a man of good character, to conduct the prayers. The same person who was asked to read the Scriptures was also expected to read the prayers.

The Interpreter translated into Aramaic the passages of the Law and the Prophets which were read in Hebrew. This also was probably not a permanent office, but was filled at each meeting by someone chosen by the ruler.

The Almoners. Alms for the poor were collected in the synagogue.[6] The collecting was done by at least two persons, and the distributing of the alms was done by at least three persons.

---

[2] See, for example, Luke 7:3.

[3] See, for example, Mark 5:22 and Acts 13:15.

[4] Luke 4:20.

[5] See, for example, Matthew 10:17, 23:34; Mark 13:9; Acts 22:19

[6] See, for example, Matthew 6:2

IV. THE ORDER OF SERVICE

The synagogue service varied little from one Sabbath to the next, and was on this order:

The Recitation of the Shema. This was a confession of God's unity, consisting of passages from Deuteronomy 6:4-9, 11:13-21, and Numbers 15:37-41. Before and after the recitation of these passages, blessings were said in connection with the passages.

Prayers. The most important prayers were the *Shemoneh esreh,* "eighteen eulogies," a cycle of 18 prayers. The following is the first of the eighteen:

> Blessed art Thou, the Lord our God, the God of our Fathers, the God of Abraham, the God of Isaac, and the God of Jacob: the great, the mighty, and the terrible God, the Most High God who showest mercy and kindness. Who createst all things. Who remembrest the pious deeds of the patriarchs, and wilt in love bring a redeemer to their children's children for Thy name's sake; O King, Helper, Savior, and Shield! Blessed art Thou, O Lord, the Shield of Abraham.

The prayers of the delegate were met with a response of "Amen" from the congregation.

The reading of the Law and the Prophets.[7] After the prayers, the *parasaah,* i.e., the pericope from the Law for that Sabbath, was read, and the interpreter translated verse by verse into Aramaic (or into whatever was the native language of the worshipers). The whole Pentateuch was divided into 154 pericopes, so that in the course of three years it was read through in order. After the reading of the Law came the *haphtara,* the pericope from the Prophets for that Sabbath, which the interpreter did not necessarily translate verse by verse, but in paragraphs of three verses.

The sermon. After the reading from the Law and the Prophets, the sermon followed, which was originally an exposition of the Law that focused on ethical principles and morality, but which in process of time assumed a more devotional character. Anyone in the congregation might be asked by the ruler to preach, or might ask the ruler for permission to preach.

The Benediction. After the sermon a benediction was pronounced by one of the elders or the ruler, and the congregation answered "Amen." With this, the crowd dispersed and went to their homes.

---

[7] The Law was first read in the synagogue until 163 BC, when it was prohibited by Antiochus Epiphanes; the reading of the Prophets was thus substituted for the reading of the Law. However, the Maccabees restored the reading of the Law, and after this, the reading of both Law and the Prophets was continued.

7. At Iconium. 14:1-6

14:1 – *And it came about that in Iconium they entered the synagogue of the Jews together, and spoke in such a manner that a great multitude believed, both of Jews and of Greeks.*

And it came about that in Iconium they entered the synagogue of the Jews together. On Iconium, see notes at Acts 13:51. "Together" represents the Greek *kata to auto*, and might mean "at the same time" or "after the same fashion."[1] Taking the latter as a possible meaning here, we could say that Paul's evangelistic methods have taken on a pattern, and he will use that same method almost everywhere he goes. First, he would seek out the local Jewish population – perhaps in a synagogue, if there was one – and preach the Gospel to them. Some Jews would become believers, and so would some Gentiles. Then, the unbelieving Jews would stir up opposition, and in time Paul would be forced to move on. By going to the synagogue at Iconium, the missionaries could reach the Jews, and the proselytes there would put them in contact with other Gentiles. Importantly, the two apostles have not been deterred from their practice by the memorable persecution they've just experienced at Pisidian Antioch.

And spoke in such a manner that a great multitude believed. This phrase reminds us that Paul knew the Scriptures, had received revelations from Christ, and was speaking by the inspiration of the Holy Spirit. This phrase is another example of the doctrine taught in Romans 10:17, that "faith comes by hearing the Word of Christ."

Both of Jews and of Greeks. "Greeks" here probably means proselytes of the gate, who were in the habit of attending the Sabbath services in the synagogue. If they had shown no interest in Judaism, they would not have been welcome to the synagogue. If they had been circumcised, they would not have been called "Greeks." Further, in verse 2, Luke will make reference to "Gentiles," which must signify the non-Jews who had no involvement at all with Judaism. Therefore, the word "Greeks" in verse 1 likely refers to proselytes.

14:2 – *But the Jews who disbelieved stirred up the minds of the Gentiles, and embittered them against the brethren.*

But the Jews who disbelieved. "Disbelieved" comes from the Greek verb *apeitheō*, which is properly translated "disobey" (see the NASB margin).[2] It might be said that the Jews

---

[1] Our comments about a set evangelistic method are questioned by some who urge that the Greek for "the same fashion" (sec Acts 17:2) is different than the expression used here in verse 1.

[2] Arndt-Gingrich state in their lexical notes on *apeitheō* that the simple meaning "disbelieve" (rather than the stronger "disobey") is a disputed meaning since not all scholars agree that "disbelieve" is a proper rendering. The argument is based on the fact that the simple meaning "disbelieve" is not found outside certain passages in the Bible and once in early Christine literature, and even in these cases, the simple meaning is not at all proven to be the right one. It is this commentator's contention that this is one place where the NASB translators' theology ("faith-only") has colored their choice. It should also be noted that the NASB (which was translated under the auspices of a Baptist foundation, and would therefore tend to be faith-only) is not consistent in its rendering of *apeitheō*. At times it uses "disbelieve," and at times it uses "disobey." See John 3:36, Hebrews 3:18, Romans 11:30-32. A consistent translation would better help readers to understand what the Bible means when it speaks of "faith" and "disobedience."

have shown a stubborn refusal to be persuaded by the truth preached by Paul and Barnabas. The word is stronger than simply "unbelieving" (*apistos*), and pictures their unbelief as breaking forth into rebellion. In verses 1 and 2, Luke says that, on the one hand, a great number of Jews and Greeks believed; by contrast, on the other hand, Luke says, "the Jews were disobedient." By using this contrast, Luke is indicating that those who *believed* were those who were *obedient*; this is not surprising since it is an obedient faith that saves! That is, the only way "belief" and "disobedience" can be contrasted as they are in these verses is if the belief that saves is an obedient faith.[3]

Stirred up the minds of the Gentiles. It is the distinguishing feature of nearly all the persecutions recorded in Acts that they were instigated by the unbelieving Jews. Perhaps there was the same racial prejudice then as there is now, and the unbelieving Jews took advantage of it. We do not know what charges were made against the apostles. We do know that the Jews sometimes accused Christians of sedition, sometimes of teaching an illegal religion. Perhaps they used one of these charges here.

And embittered them against the brethren. The word might be translated "exasperated." Some think that "brethren" is a reference to Paul and Barnabas. Others think the word, which was one of the titles by which the early Christians were known, implies that a congregation had been formed in Iconium.

14:3 – *Therefore they spent a long time* **there** *speaking boldly* **with reliance** *upon the Lord, who was bearing witness to the word of His grace, granting that signs and wonders be done by their hands.*

Therefore they spent a long time *there.* "Therefore" points back to both verse 1 and verse 2 – i.e., because multitudes were being converted, and because there was opposition, they stayed a long time. "Long time" is a relative term. We do not know whether it was a month, three months, or longer.

Speaking boldly *with reliance* **upon the Lord.** The apostles bravely continued to declare the gospel of the grace of God, even in the face of the opposition. Probably they are no longer speaking in the synagogue, though we have no definite statement about that. When the missionaries ran into opposition in the synagogue in Pisidian Antioch, they left off worshiping there, and found other places from which to preach to the Greeks about Jesus. We may assume something similar happened in Iconium. There is opposition, but there have been no forcible measures as yet to expel them from the town as there had been at Antioch. The NASB addition of the words "with reliance" is a happy rendering, for the Greek suggests that the Lord was the support of their preaching. Relying on Him, they took courage and continued to preach.

Who was bearing witness to the word of His grace. It is hard to decide if "Lord" in the previous phrase was a reference to Jesus or to the Father. Arguments can be marshalled for

---

[3] This same contrast between "belief" and "disobedience" is also noted in John 3:36.

either view.[4] "The word of grace" is a message that offers salvation by grace rather than by works of Law, the message boldly preached by Paul and Barnabas. Involved in grace[5] is the death of Christ for sin and the justifying of the sinner who believes.

Granting that signs and wonders be done by their hands. Here is how the Lord "bore witness" to the preaching of the apostles: He granted (in answer to prayer?) that the apostles could work miracles to credential the message they preached.[6]

14:4 – *But the multitude of the city was divided; and some sided with the Jews, and some with the apostles.*

But the multitude of the city was divided. The gospel has always been like this. When the gospel is preached, it makes a division. Jesus said, "I have not come to bring peace but a sword,"[7] and He predicted that He was going to make division between members of one household,[8] setting a son against father, daughter against mother, etc. This is the result of the gospel when it is faithfully proclaimed. "Multitude" evidently speaks of those outside either the church or the synagogue – i.e., the city's pagan population. Unchurched people in a community often know what is going on within a congregation, and they do take sides.

And some sided with the Jews, and some with the apostles. When a community does take sides, many things influence their choices. Perhaps they take the same side that some of their respected friends have taken, even though they personally have never learned the truth in the matter. Perhaps the opposition has tried to make it look like the ones telling the truth (i.e., the missionaries) were the ones at fault; deceivers often do this, even today. Perhaps some had actually studied the matter for themselves and had arrived at informed decisions. Note that Paul and Barnabas are designated as "apostles" here for the first time in Acts.[9]

---

[4] At times in Acts, miracles are called the works of Christ (Acts 3:16, 4:30). Thus, "Lord" might refer to Christ. On the other hand, "Lord" might be the Father, as seen by comparing Acts 4:24 and 20:32.

[5] See notes at Acts 11:23 on "grace."

[6] See Acts 2:22 where these different names for miracle are explained. See also Mark 16:17-20, where it plainly says that miracles were intended to credential the message. Also compare John 20:30-31 and Hebrews 2:3-4.

[7] Matthew 10:34.

[8] Luke 12:53. Division is still likely to result today if and as the gospel is faithfully proclaimed. Within many congregations, there are at times unconverted persons in positions of leadership who do not want the gospel, who have never been touched by its power, who do not want others to be, and who will oppose the faithful preaching of the gospel. Likewise, there will be people outside the church who will be in opposition.

Still, this commentator believes that the words of Jesus need to be heard – "Woe be unto you when all manner of men speak well of you" (Luke 6:26). If all do speak well of the preacher, it just might be an indication that he has not been faithful to his calling to preach the Word with boldness.

A caution, however, is needed. Not all opposition arises from unbelievers who are opposed to the gospel. The preacher must be careful that he is not himself (rather than his message) the cause of the opposition. Opposition because he has been thoughtless or unloving or careless in his dealings with people is a completely different matter than the opposition we read about directed against Paul and Barnabas.

[9] See more extended comments at verse 14 on the term "apostle."

14:5 – *And when an attempt was made by both the Gentiles and the Jews with their rulers, to mistreat and to stone them,*

And when an attempt was made. It is difficult to find an English word that conveys the idea involved in the Greek word *hormē* ("attempt"). The KJV rendering "assault" is perhaps too strong, though in intertestamental writings it does have the idea of attack, violence.[10] If we think of a hostile plan being formed, a plot being developed, we may be closer to the idea.

By both the Gentiles and the Jews with their rulers. "Gentiles" from among those who took sides with the Jews were included in on the plot. The "Jews" included would be those who have actively rebelled against the gospel from the first (verse 2). "Their rulers"[11] evidently means "Jewish rulers," rather than city officials, since the form of punishment selected (stoning) was a Jewish method of execution. We picture these religious leaders as staying in the background as much as possible, yet all the time urging on those who were opposed to the apostles.

To mistreat and to stone them. "Mistreat" (*hubridzō*) speaks of doing bodily harm, violence, to someone. "Torture" is too strong, but some sort of physical abuse prior to the stoning was what was planned. The violence was to end in death by stoning, probably on the charge of blasphemy. The crowd either was about to start moving through the streets, or perhaps they already were when the apostles became aware of the plan.

14:6 – *they became aware of it and fled to the cities of Lycaonia, Lystra and Derbe, and the surrounding region;*

They became aware of it. Shortly before the hostile crowd is able to execute their plan, the apostles become aware of it. Perhaps some friend ran ahead of the mob to warn the apostles. Perhaps one of the plotters was talking about the plot before it came time to execute it, and was overheard; and thus the danger was made known to the preachers. The same word here translated "became aware" is translated "considered" at Acts 12:12. It may be that the apostles thought over what was the best course to follow in the light of the intelligence they have just received, and determined that it was best to flee.

And fled to the cities of Lycaonia. Luke has, in times past, been accused of another mistake here, for his language seems to imply that Iconium from which the preachers are fleeing is not in the region of Lycaonia. However, Ramsay has shown that Luke is exactly right in his use of terms in that period of time, for Iconium was a Phrygian city when Paul visited it.[12]

The actions of Paul and Barnabas bring up the question, When should a preacher run, and when should he stay to fight? In verse 2, when the opposition increased, the bold-

---

[10] 3 Maccabees 1:16,23; 4:5.

[11] See Special Study #15, "The Synagogue and Its Services," for further information about these synagogue officials called "rulers."

[12] Ramsay, *St. Paul the Traveller and Roman Citizen*, p.111-112.

ness of Paul and Barnabas increased and caused them to continue there a long time. Now we are told that they fled. It is not wrong to flee when your life is in danger, and when by staying you can do no more good. One of the first laws of human life is self-preservation. God expects us to preserve ourselves unless truth, honesty, and integrity are involved. Certainly, if the time ever comes when one is forced either to deny Jesus or die, his line of duty is clear. But under such circumstances as here in Iconium, when the apostles can see that there is no more possibility of doing good, and that there is evidence that their lives are at stake, then it is time to get out.

Lycaonia was one of the ethnic provinces of Asia Minor in pre-Roman times. In Roman times, it was incorporated into the area called southern Galatia. In pre-Roman times it was a wilder and less civilized area than Phrygia,[13] but with the coming of the Romans, and the colonizing of the area, it may no longer have been so wild and uncivilized.

Lystra and Derbe. Lystra was about 40 miles to the southeast of Iconium. and Derbe was about 20 miles farther to the east. The location of Lystra was tentatively identified by archaeologists in 1820, and then conformed when an inscription was found in 1885 by Sterrett. Lystra had been made a Roman Colony by Augustus in AD 6. Derbe was in the extreme southeast corner of the Lycaonian plain, almost on the border between Lycaonia and Cilicia. It was the first city a traveler came to after passing through the mountain pass called "The Cilician Gates" as he traveled from the east toward southern Galatia. The site of Derbe was identified in 1956 by Michael Ballance.[14] Both these cities would have been commercial centers for the whole region; and at Derbe, there would have been a customs house where customs on goods entering the country would have been collected.

And the surrounding region. Luke used the term "region" at Acts 13:49. This verse might mean exactly what that one did, that while Paul worked in the larger cities, his helpers and converts took the gospel to the nearby villages and towns. The language might also indicate that Lystra and Derbe were smaller cities than Paul usually worked in, and that he himself evangelized the neighboring villages, and thus was departing (when the occasion called for it) from his usual method of evangelizing by going to the big cities.

8. In Lystra. 14:7-20

14:7 – *and there they continued to preach the gospel.*

And there they continued to preach the gospel. Though persecuted, the apostles still preached; when driven from one city, they went to another. They were doing just as Jesus had commanded as He gave instructions for an earlier missionary journey.[15] The Greek for "preached" is an imperfect tense, indicating continuing action.

---

[13] Ovid, *Metamorphoses*, VIII.621.

[14] Michael Ballance, "The Site of Derbe, A New Inscription," *Anatolian Studies,* Vol. 7 (1957), p.147-151.

[15] Matthew 10:23.

Jewish people lived in this area, but there seem not to have been enough Jews to form a synagogue or even have much influence. For example, Timothy's mother and grandmother lived here. But even though he was the son of a Jewish mother, Timothy had reached his teens without even being circumcised. We therefore can picture Paul and Barnabas, for the first time, so far as we know, beginning their evangelistic work by preaching mostly to the Gentiles since there apparently was no ready-made Jewish group here with which to begin.

14:8 – *And at Lystra there was sitting a certain man, without strength in his feet, lame from his mother's womb, who had never walked.*

And at Lystra. As in other towns and villages of this area, we must picture the two apostles preaching in the forums and the areas of public assembly.

> Finding at Lystra no Jewish synagogue to afford them an assembly of devout hearers, the missionaries were constrained to preach in the open air. The narrow streets universal in the cities of that age were unsuited to gatherings of people; but in every city there was a more or less unoccupied space about the gates, both inside and outside, and these were always favorite places for crowds to gather. It seems from the context (verse 13) that Paul was addressing a crowd at the principal gate when the following incident took place.[16]

There was sitting a certain man, without strength in his feet. The word translated "sitting" might be rendered "lived,"[17] but what Luke is telling us is evidently that the man used to sit in the forum. Maybe he was a beggar, for such people often sat in such public places to beg alms.[18] Luke the physician uses the medical term for the man's physical problem. He didn't have enough strength in his feet to be able to walk.

Lame from his mother's womb. This case is very much like the lame man that Peter and John healed.[19] Like that man at the Gate Beautiful, this man at Lystra was one whose history from infancy was well known.

Who had never walked. The miracle, therefore, would be more remarkable since the man was well-known. Some writers have commented on Doctor Luke's characteristic care to record the duration of the infirmities that were miraculously healed.[20]

---

[16] McGarvey, *op. cit.*, p.39.

[17] Acts 18:11; Luke 21:35; Revelation 14:6.

[18] Mark 10:46.

[19] See Acts 3:1-11. Negative critics have made attacks on Luke's book from two sides at this passage. (1) They have tried to disprove Luke's authorship of this section from the fact that "Lystra" in verse 8 is neuter, whereas in verses 6 and 21 it is feminine. But the same grammar occurs in 16:1-2, and that passage is not questioned. (2) Because this miracle is so similar to the one in chapter 3, it is said Luke simply made up the story. But in the Introductory Studies where "assurances of trustworthiness" were studied, it has been noted that such a parallel account was the accepted way to write a history in Luke's day. Such parallelism is not evidence that the story was made up.

[20] Compare Acts 3:2, 9:33.

14:9 – *This man was listening to Paul as he spoke, who, when he had fixed his gaze upon him, and had seen that he had faith to be made well,*

This man was listening to Paul as he spoke. As there was no synagogue in Lystra, and as the sequel takes place at the gate of the city, we conclude that Paul was speaking in an open-air meeting, and the crippled man was in the audience listening. The imperfect verb tense (in Nestle's Greek Text) indicates that he was a habitual hearer of Paul's preaching. He used to listen, or he was listening continually, to Paul's preaching. We picture that Paul has been preaching some days in the market place by the gate, and each day the lame man was there. He has heard the gospel of the death and resurrection of Jesus, and of the salvation that is available in Him.

Who, when he had fixed his gaze upon him. That is, Paul looked at the man, perhaps also reading his heart. See notes at 1:10 and 13:9 for this verb "fixed his gaze."

And had seen that he had faith to be made well. Notes at Acts 3:8-10 discuss the question of whether or not the one about to be healed had to have faith in order to be healed. This passage clearly does speak of faith on the part of the one about to be healed.[21] Matthew 9:21-29 may tell what is involved in this faith: a belief that it was possible to be healed, and that Paul (by the Lord's help) could do it. Since "faith comes by hearing," the source of this man's belief must have been something Paul said. Perhaps Paul had spoken of the miraculous ministry of Jesus, or of the power given by Jesus to His apostles to work similar cures in proof of their divine mission. Exactly what Paul saw as he gazed at this lame man is not stated. Perhaps he saw an expression on the cripple's face that told Paul he had faith. Or, by the gift of discerning of spirits, perhaps Paul read the man's heart.

14:10 – *said with a loud voice, "Stand upright on your feet." And he leaped up and* **began to walk.**

Said with a loud voice. Paul raised his voice so that the attention of all the people in the market place would be called to the miraculous cure.

"Stand upright on your feet." Hitherto his feet had been too weak to support him. "Upright" (if he were to so stand) would indicate that he was entirely whole. Without the man's faith to encourage his will to make the effort, the command would have been cruel.

And he leaped up and *began* to walk. The man obeyed immediately. As the different verb tenses indicate, the man leaped up at once with a single bound, and then began and continued to walk around. Observe that this miracle is another example of the instantaneous nature of Bible miracles. It was not that the lame man just gradually began to get well. Rather, the miracle was entire and complete in a moment. One who has never learned to walk, walking immediately, is a very striking miracle.

---

[21] In notes at Acts 4:9,12, we have explained how the same word can be translated either healed or "saved"; it depends on the context which is correct. Here "healed" (i.e., made whole) is the better idea.

14:11 – *And when the multitudes saw what Paul had done, they raised their voice, saying in the Lycaonian language, "The gods have become like men and have come down to us."*

And when the multitudes saw what Paul had done, they raised their voice. When people are excited, their speech naturally comes out with more volume. All over the marketplace the Lystrians cry out to anyone who will listen, that the gods have come to visit! The verb tense here indicates a sudden outburst of excited speech.

Saying in the Lycaonian language. What this language was has much perplexed the commentators. It was a local dialect of some kind, is about all we can say. The fact that the natives were speaking the local dialect is given by Luke for some reason – perhaps to explain why Paul and Barnabas make no objection until they see the preparations for a sacrifice to be made to them. Paul and Barnabas apparently preached in Greek, and the people would have understood them, for most people were bi-lingual, knowing enough Greek to carry on business with strangers who might come to town. It was perfectly natural for the people, in their excitement, to revert to their native language.

That Paul did not understand the Lycaonian dialect helps in our understanding of the "gift of tongues." Though Paul could speak ever so many languages (1 Corinthians 14:18), he evidently did not immediately nor automatically understand every language and dialect with which he came in contact.[22]

"The gods have become like men and have come down to us." The region surrounding Lystra was idolatrous. The various gods worshiped in Lystra would be the same gods worshiped over the whole heathen world. "Become like men" means "in human form." Paul's miracle led the Lystrians to suppose that the missionaries were gods. It was obviously beyond mere human ability to heal a man, so they could fathom no other explanation to account for the healing.

Barnes tells us that the poems of Homer and Virgil are filled with accounts of how the gods took on human form and then were supposed to learn about human affairs and aid the men they came to visit.[23] There was also a fable among the inhabitants of Lycaonia about Jupiter (Zeus) and Mercury (Hermes).[24] According to mythology, Jupiter and Mercury one day took the forms of men and came to Lystra to visit. They walked up and down the streets, knocking on all the doors, but no one invited them in to visit. Finally, they came to the last house in town, a tumbledown shack, at the edge of the city dump, the home of Philemon and Baucis. Philemon (not the Philemon of the New Testament) and Baucis invited Jupiter and Mercury to visit a while in the shade of an old tree. Then the mythological gods were invited to stay for a feast. Late at night, the gods left the city, taking with them Philemon and Baucis. When they were at a safe distance, Jupiter called down fire on the town; and all those who had refused Jupiter and Mercury were put to death. Philemon and Baucis were made priests. A new city was built by the gods, and a magnificent temple was built. In this temple, Philemon and Baucis served. Ever after, when

---

[22] See Special Study #4, "Speaking in Tongues," after chapter 2 for additional information on this gift.

[23] Barnes, *op. cit.*, p.218.

[24] Ovid, *op. cit.*, VIII.611-724.

a stranger came to town, he was well received. This is perhaps one of the reasons the Lystrians made ready to sacrifice to Paul and Barnabas. Perhaps they were thinking that the gods had come to town again.[25]

14:12 – *And they began calling Barnabas, Zeus, and Paul, Hermes, because he was the chief speaker.*

And they *began* calling Barnabas, Zeus. The verb tense here indicates that after their initial outburst of excited speech (verse 11) they went on to devise names for the two preachers. Luke gives us the Greek names for the gods; this same one was known as Jupiter by the Romans.

> Jupiter was the most powerful of all the gods of the ancients. He was represented as the son of Saturn and Ops, and was educated in a cave on Mount Ida, in the island of Crete. The worship of Jupiter was almost universal. He was the Ammon of Africa, the Belus of Babylon, the Osiris of Egypt. He was commonly called The Father of gods and men. He was usually represented as sitting upon a golden or an ivory throne, holding in one hand a thunderbolt, and in the other a sceptre of cypress. His power was supposed to extend over other gods; and everything was subservient to his will except the Fates.[26]

Chrysostom made the conjecture that Barnabas was a man of large stature, and hence the Lystrians were reminded of Zeus.

And Paul, Hermes, because he was the chief speaker. Hermes, called Mercury by the Romans, was one of the celebrated gods of classical mythology.

> He was the messenger of the gods, and of Jupiter in particular; he was the patron of travellers and shepherds; he conducted the souls of the dead into the infernal regions; he *presided over orators, and declaimers*, and merchants; and he was also the god of thieves, pickpockets, and all dishonest persons. He was regarded as *the god of eloquence*: and was light, rapid, and quick in his movements.[27]

Paul has been pictured by some as a runt, and is said by some to have had sore eyes, perhaps was hunch-backed, had epilepsy, was bald and had a hooked nose.[28] But given Paul's extensive and physically demanding travels all around the Roman empire, it is difficult to imagine that he was a runty, scrawny, epileptic, sore-eyed, undernourished man. Furthermore, it is not easy to believe Paul could have been thought of as being a Greek god,

---

[25] The study of comparative religions has become popular. Because of some remote parallels between Bible records and the wild stories of mythology, liberal arts professors like to equate the God of the Bible with the gods of mythology. It is hard to understand why such teachers are harder on Christianity than on Buddhism or Hinduism. Why do they go out of their way to discredit Christianity? For instance, they say little unfavorable regarding Krishna (i.e., one of the chief gods of Hinduism) even though he is pictured as a drunken god who wildly rides his chariot around the heavens. The God of the Bible is good and kind, not like the gods of the heathen, yet the God of the Bible is belittled. Why is this?

[26] Barnes, *ibid.*

[27] *Ibid.*

[28] These physical features are included in the description of Paul in the dubious *Acts of Paul and Thecla*.

knowing the people's concept of a god (as seen in the sculpture of the age), if he had been that sort of a physical specimen.

Hermes was called the "ruler of speech" by the ancients, and the same words translated "ruler of speech" are the words Luke uses here (i.e., "chief speaker") to describe why the Lystrians began calling Paul "Hermes." It seems that Paul has been doing the bulk of the preaching; and since it was the office of Hermes to deliver the messages of the gods, they think of him as being Hermes.

> Their excitement caused them very naturally to break forth in their native tongue, instead of the Greek in which Paul had addressed them and which they spoke as an acquired language. Their shouts necessarily silenced Paul for the time being; and perhaps, while he was waiting for silence to be restored so that he could continue his sermon, he failed to notice that a part of the crowd darted away, some to bring two or more fat bulls which were in readiness for a sacrifice to Jupiter, and some to bring garlands of flowers with which to decorate the horns of the victims.[29]

14:13 – *And the priest of Zeus, whose* **temple** *was just outside the city, brought oxen and garlands to the gates, and wanted to offer sacrifice with the crowds.*

And the priest of Zeus. Codex Beza reads "priests." At each of the great temples in Asia Minor a number of priests would be in regular service. It was the job of the priest to conduct the worship of Zeus by offering sacrifices in the near-by temple of Zeus.

Whose *temple* **was just outside the city.** Each of the ancient cities had one mythological chief deity they worshiped and who, they supposed, guarded and protected the people who lived in that city. Zeus was that deity at Lystra. The temple where he was worshiped was just outside the main gates of the city. Perhaps there was a statue of Zeus inside the temple.

Brought oxen and garlands to the gates. The Greek has "bulls" (*taurous*), and probably there were two bulls brought, one to be sacrificed to each "god." "Garlands" were wreaths of flowers which were draped over the horns of the victim, just before it was sacrificed. Priests and worshipers were also decked with these flowers. The animals were being led to the place where Paul and Barnabas were. The same word "gate" was used at Acts 10:17 and 12:13 of the entrance to a house. It is because it is plural here that some have spoken of the gates of the temple of Zeus, or the gates of the city, rather than the outer porch of the house where the apostles were staying. It seems most likely that "gates" speak of the entrance to the city, the place where the missionaries have been doing their preaching.

And wanted to offer sacrifice with the crowds. The crowds who had seen the miracle must have been eager to follow the priest and participate in the worship of the two gods. The sacrifice, had they been allowed to complete it, would have been on this fashion. The throats of the bulls would have been cut, and the blood received in a vessel. The blood and the tail of the animal sacrificed to Zeus would have been burned on the altar; and the blood, tail, and tongue of the animal offered to Hermes likewise burned on the altar in the nearby

---

[29] McGarvey, *op. cit.*, p.41.

idol's temple. The rest of the animals would have been roasted, and then the people would have had a feast in honor of the gods.

14:14 – *But when the apostles, Barnabas and Paul, heard of it, they tore their robes and rushed out into the crowd, crying out*

But when the apostles, Barnabas and Paul. This is one of the few places after the beginning of the first missionary journey that the name of Barnabas appears first. It likely indicates that on this occasion Barnabas received the chief honors from the people, since he was thought to be Zeus. Hence, Luke puts his name first.

Was Barnabas an "apostle"? The word apostle is used in several senses in the New Testament.

- It is used of Christ, the apostle of God."[30] The word "apostle" means one sent, and Christ is called an apostle in the sense that He had been sent by God on a mission.
- The word apostle is most often used of men specially commissioned by Christ, such men as the Twelve,[31] Paul,[32] and perhaps others.[33]
- The term is found in 2 Corinthians 8:23, where the messengers chosen by the churches to carry the offering to the saints in Jerusalem are called "apostles."

So the question remains: is Barnabas called an apostle in the sense that he has been sent on a mission by the church at Antioch, or is he called an apostle in the same sense the Twelve were, i.e., an apostle of Christ, an equal with Paul and Peter and John et al.? Since Paul claimed to be an apostle, and equal to the Twelve,[34] and the word here evidently is used in the limited sense of an apostle *of Christ*, we incline to believe Barnabas was also an apostle *of Christ*, and not just called an apostle in the sense that he was an apostle of the Antioch church.[35]

Heard of it. Just how the apostles came to understand that the sacrifice was about to be made in their honor, we are not told. Did someone come up to put garlands around their necks, and request of them to take part in the activities?

They tore their robes. Usually the garments torn were the *under*garments; the hems of the garments were torn at the neck as an expression of abhorrence at what was being done or said. In this case, however, the apostles tore their *outer* garments, as the use of the word *himatia* (rather than *chiton*) shows. The practice of tearing the clothing when suddenly and

---

[30] Hebrews 3:1.

[31] Matthew 10:2.

[32] 1 Corinthians 4:9, 9:2.

[33] Romans 16:7.

[34] Galatians 1:1; 1 Corinthians 4:9, 9:1-2, etc.

[35] The chief objection to calling Barnabas an apostle *of Christ* (rather than an apostle *of the church*) is the qualification (Acts 1:22) of having witnessed the earthly ministry of Christ. We just are not told one way or the other. Perhaps he, like Matthias, did witness much of Jesus' ministry, and perhaps he did see the risen Lord, and thus, like Matthias (Acts 1:15-26), became an apostle of Christ.

violently agitated, is as old as the time of Jacob.[36] This is the last time in the New Testament that we read of such a practice. Why did it fall into disuse? Perhaps the "self-control" that Christianity teaches caused men to cease such acts. Perhaps, since garment-rending seems to have been a Jewish custom, and as much of the New Testament deals with the gospel among the Gentiles, that is why we do not again hear of the custom. How far such an act would have been understood by the heathen population at Lystra may be a question, but its very strangeness might arrest the attention of the people.

And rushed out into the crowd, crying out. The crowd of Lystrians around the gates of the city are in a festive mood. One can picture Paul and Barnabas running from one excited Lystrian to another, urging them to cease their preparations for a sacrifice to Zeus and Hermes.

14:15 – *and saying, "Men, why are you doing these things? We are also men of the same nature as you, and preach the gospel to you in order that you should turn from these vain things to a living God, WHO MADE THE HEAVEN AND THE EARTH AND THE SEA, AND ALL THAT IS IN THEM.*

And saying, "Men, why are you doing these things? Compared with the opening address of other speeches in Acts, "Men" is rather brief, but the moment called for haste if the apostles were going to stop the sacrifice from being made. The message that follows is Paul's first recorded sermon preached to a wholly Gentile audience.[37]

We are also men of the same nature as you. Paul is saying, 'We are not gods to be worshiped! We are mere men, just like you.' The word translated "same nature" may have either of several implications. The mythological gods were not subject to many of the feelings that humans experience, so Paul may be saying that he and Barnabas can't be gods, because they do have such human feelings. Again, the gods were thought of as powerful beings, so Paul may be saying that he and Barnabas were prone to human weakness, and therefore they could not be the gods the people thought they were. Or, the gods were thought of as being immortal, so Paul may be saying that they were mortals, liable to suffering and death, and therefore could not be gods worthy of worship.

And preach the gospel to you. 'This is why we have come – not to be worshiped, but to preach the gospel of the living God to you. We've come to get you to stop such idol worship, not to encourage it.' Codex Beza reads "preach the gospel of the God to you," and Ramsay has made the suggestion that just as Paul introduced his message at Athens by referring to an "Unknown God" whom they had been worshiping, so he may have used a term "*the* God" (a familiar term for the Great God that the Lystrians regularly used) as a starting point for this message about the "living God."[38]

In order that you should turn from these vain things. Idols are often called "vanities"

---

[36] Genesis 37:29-34.

[37] Acts 17 will record another of Paul's sermons to a wholly Gentile audience.

[38] Ramsay, *St. Paul the Traveller and Roman Citizen*, p.118.

or "vain things."³⁹ *Mataios* means empty, fruitless, useless, powerless, lacking truth. Idols are powerless to truly help. When Paul said "*these* vain things," he may have gestured toward the animals and the temple and the flowers. When a person becomes a Christian, he or she gives up the worship of idols. The same word "turn" is found at Acts 3:19, and the notes there have a discussion of what is included in "turning." Just like Peter did when he used the word, Paul has in mind a definite purpose in the turning. We are often prone to forget that purpose in turning, that we are to turn from "these vain things" to a living God!

To a living God. In 1 Thessalonians, Paul says those converts had turned from their idols to serve a living God. Jehovah is called the "living" God in order to contrast Him from those dumb, powerless idols. The God Paul is preaching about truly lives and acts, whether it is as the God of nature or as the God of redemption.

Notice, Paul is rightly implying that there is no such thing as a spiritual vacuum! A person's life will be occupied with something. When a person has spent his life in the service of sin and then becomes a Christian, the only way to guarantee that he will not return to the service of sin is for that person to fill his life with service for Christ. Remember the story in Luke 11:24-26 about the man who had a demon. The demon went out and while he was gone, the house was swept and cleaned. However, when the demon came back, he found it still empty. How many more demons he brought with him when he returned! And then it is said that the last condition of the man was worse than he was to begin with. This is a correct picture of many who become Christians, but never do fill their lives with service; their lives are empty as far as Christian fruit and service are concerned. They then are entangled in the affairs of this world and in the service of the devil more than they were even to begin with. When we turn from sin, we must turn to something new ... to the living God, so that we let Him and our service for Him fill us.

WHO MADE THE HEAVEN AND THE EARTH AND THE SEA, AND ALL THAT IS IN THEM. What a contrast between the God who created all things, and the gods these pagans worshiped. On the one hand was a God who was the maker of all things and who was all-powerful. On the other hand were the gods who had been made by the hands of men, and who were powerless.

The ideas about the origin of the universe differed among the pagans. Some worshipers of Zeus believed he was the creator.⁴⁰ The idea that matter was eternal was also a doctrine very widely believed. Either one of these doctrines would have been contradicted by Paul's claim that the living God was the creator of all.

In passing, it is important to contrast Paul's preaching to the Jews with Paul's preaching to the Gentiles:

---

[39] See Deuteronomy 32:21; 2 Kings 17:15; 1 Kings 16:13, 26; Jeremiah 2:5, 8:18; Isaiah 44:12ff.

[40] See notes at Acts 17:18, where the beliefs of the Stoics are enumerated.

JEWISH AUDIENCE GENTILE AUDIENCE

INTRODUCTION: All the openings of Paul's sermons are dependent on the audience to whom he is speaking. Whether he was before a Roman governor, or before the Athenians who were ignorant of the living God, or in a synagogue, Paul's introductions were appropriate to the moment and the audience. If Paul must defend himself or give his credentials, these would be in the introduction. Following the introduction, the main points emphasized to his respective audiences would usually be:

1. God's dealings with the Jews	• The creative activity of God
2. Reference to the Law and the Prophets	• Man's relationship to the Creator (sometimes shown by a reference to the poets)
3. Jesus is the Messiah (telling of His death, burial, and resurrection)	• Repentance is now required of all men. These are no longer days of ignorance which God previously overlooked
4. Forgiveness through Christ	• Coming judgment and need for Jesus as a personal Savior
5. Universal salvation (the Gospel is for the Gentiles also)	• Resurrection of Jesus is proof He can save

This is not saying that Paul had only two sermons. Rather, there were certain topics that Paul emphasized in each sermon, depending on his hearers' needs.

More is to be learned about Paul's preaching to Gentile audiences from a comparison of his messages to such audiences. From them we may learn what needs to be emphasized as we preach to similar peoples.

> Howson notes the coincidence between the exhortation to the Lystrians, that they should "turn from these vain things to the living God," and Paul's remark to the Thessalonians, that they had "turned from idols to serve the living and true God;" between the remark that "in generations past God had suffered the Gentiles to go in their own ways," and his statement to the Athenians that "the times of ignorance God has overlooked;" and finally, between the argument to prove that God had not left Himself without witness among the heathen, and that in Romans 1:20 where he says, "The invisible things of Him since the creation of the world are clearly seen, being perceived through the things which are made, even his everlasting power and divinity; that they may be without excuse."[41]

14:16 – *"And in the generations gone by He permitted all the nations to go their own ways;*

And in the generations gone by. In ages previous to the Gospel age.

He permitted all the nations to go their own ways. God allowed the Gentiles ("nations") to conduct themselves without the restraints and instructions of a written law like the one He gave to the Jews. The Gentiles were permitted to live through the centuries with only

---

[41] McGarvey, *op. cit.*, p.43.

oral tradition to guide them, and through the years the Gentiles went farther and farther away from the original truth revealed to the forefathers. But God gave them no *written* laws and sent them few messengers.

Why did not God send the Redeemer immediately after man fell from his close relationship with God? Several reasons have been suggested why God should have followed such a course of action.

- If the Savior had come immediately to the Garden of Eden to offer Himself, Adam and Eve would not have appreciated Him. Man had to learn what sin is and had to know something of the consequences of sin – consequences to himself and to his fellowman.
- Man had to learn that he could not save himself from sin, but that he needed a Savior.
- Since God permitted men to see what they could do and would do, they were better prepared to receive the newer light of the gospel.
- God chose to wait for the opportune time to arise. God had to have time to prepare the Jewish nation, the Greek nation (language), and the Roman nation (government) to get the world prepared for the entrance of the Savior. In Galatians, Paul writes that in the fullness of time God sent forth his Son.

God's dealings with the Gentiles were all part of His grand plan of redemption where all were "shut up in disobedience so that He might show mercy to all" (Romans 11:32).

14:17 – *"and yet He did not leave Himself without witness, in that He did good and gave you rains from heaven and fruitful seasons, satisfying your hearts with food and gladness."*

And yet He did not leave Himself without witness. Paul is still telling the Lystrians what the "living God" was continually doing. Not only was He creator, but He is active in history. There are three present tense participles here in verse 17 and they mark the continuous activity and goodness of God, and tell us about the "witness" that God gives of Himself.[42] Even though God gave the Gentiles no written revelation like He did to the Jews, still He did give plenty of demonstrations of His existence and of His moral character.

In that He did good. By doing good, God gave evidence of Himself. The present tense participle implies God was always doing good. In what particular ways He did good will be specified in the next two phrases.

And gave you rains from heaven and fruitful seasons. "Rains" (it is plural in the Greek)

---

[42] The study of apologetics is divided into two fields. One is the study of Natural Theology, and the other is the field of Evidences of the Christian Religion. (1) Natural Theology studies the evidences for the existence of God apart from the testimony of the Word of God. One of its key arguments is the argument of design. There seems to be a purpose in this world about us, and the sending of the rains and the fruitful seasons reveal God's purpose to care for us and to supply our needs. (2) Christian Evidences examines the reasons for believing that God's special revelation (in Scripture, in the Incarnation, and in the Resurrection) is trustworthy. Care must be exercised that the proper weight is given to both of God's revelations of Himself. Natural Theology tells us of God's wisdom, power, and providential care, but it does not tell us of His redemptive purpose or of God's will to save. Only in His revealed Word, and especially in Jesus, do we learn of His redeeming love.

is possibly a reference to the earlier and latter rains.[43] Zeus, the one specially worshiped by the Lystrians, was called "the one who sends rain," and "the giver of all the products of the earth." Paul says it is not Zeus but the living God who is the real giver of rains and the products of the earth. Rains to help the crops grow is one of the evidences of the good constantly done by God. "Fruitful seasons" are seasons when the harvest is abundant. It is part of the evidence that God is actively doing good in His world that so few seasons are unfruitful. After the flood, God promised seed time and harvest as long as the earth stands.[44] God keeps His word, but man sometimes forgets his Great Benefactor.

Satisfying your hearts with food and gladness. "Hearts" may be a Hebraism denoting the persons themselves. In other words, we would say, "filling you with food." "Gladness" equals "joy, comfort" – the comfort that arises when man's constantly returning wants and needs are supplied.

14:18 – *And even saying these things, they with difficulty restrained the crowds from offering sacrifice to them.*

And *even* saying these things. With the arguments just recorded in verses 15-17.

They with difficulty restrained the crowds from offering sacrifice to them. The Lystrians were so fully convinced by the miracle that the gods had appeared (verses 9-11), and were so anxious to do them the proper honor, that Paul and Barnabas barely could keep them from going ahead with the sacrifice of the animals.

14:19 – *But Jews came from Antioch and Iconium, and having won over the multitudes, they stoned Paul and dragged him out of the city, supposing him to be dead.*

But Jews came from Antioch and Iconium. We must suppose an interval of time passes between verses 18 and 19. Likely, Paul and Barnabas carry on their evangelistic labors day by day, and in due time a congregation is planted. Meanwhile, news of that strange scene in Lystra where men were about to be worshiped as gods spreads to other cities until it reaches the ears of Paul's enemies in Iconium and Pisidian Antioch. Not satisfied with having driven Paul and Barnabas from their region, a number of the Jews, urged on by hatred for Paul's message, made a swift journey to Lystra. These enemies of the gospel came a distance of over 100 miles in order to continue their active opposition to Paul and Barnabas, and to keep the Lycaonians from becoming involved in this new religion.

And having won over the multitudes. The Greek word here is "persuaded." In order to persuade the populace, the Jews may have argued that Paul and Barnabas were imposters. McGarvey has written:

> It is not so difficult to imagine the representations by which they won the Lystrians to their side. They would say, "We understand that you have taken these two countrymen of

---

[43] James 5:7

[44] Genesis 8:22

ours for gods in human form. We can tell you who they are. They are Jews who came to Antioch and acted so base a part as to disgust all of their fellow Jews in the city, and to cause the honorable women and chief men of the city to rise up and drive them away. Then they went to Iconium and made themselves such pests that the city rulers, with the aid of the Jews and Gentiles acting together, prepared to stone them, whence they fled like thieves and came to Lystra. We are not willing for them to disgrace our name and nation any longer, and with your permission we will put an end to their sorcery; for it is by the power of evil spirits that they work wonders among the people." [They could easily attribute the miracle to sorcery, and then lead the Lycaonians to believe the apostles declined worship out of fear of the gods.] On hearing such representations from the countrymen of Paul and Barnabas, the Lystrians readily consented to let them have their own way.[45]

What a striking instance of the fickleness and instability of popular feeling![46] A few days or weeks before the Lystrians were ready to worship the two apostles; now, they give permission to let them be stoned.

They stoned Paul. The visiting Jews from Pisidian Antioch and Iconium did the stoning, satisfied that they were punishing a blasphemer. Paul had come preaching that men were saved by grace rather than deeds of Law. This sounded to the Jew like blasphemy against the Law, and they were merely carrying out the requirements of the Law when they put such a teacher to death.[47] McGarvey has given a vivid suggestion of how it happened:

> Knowing from the past experience how certainly Paul would escape their hands if he should learn what was afoot, they waited till he came forth as usual to preach near the gateway, at which time they made a rush with stones already prepared, and pelted him to death in a moment. He fell inside the city gate.[48]

And dragged him out of the city. As a last indignity, two or three of the crowd removed Paul's body. Seizing it by the hands and perhaps by the feet, they dragged him to a place outside the city walls, where his body was left, like the carcass of a dead beast, to any fate which might await it.[49] Since Lystra was not a Jewish city, the Jews seem to have had no conscience against doing the actual stoning within its walls (compare Acts 7:58), but they would not leave the body there.

Supposing him to be dead. No one, including Paul himself, seems to know just how close to death's door, or on which side of it, he actually was.[50] Four theories have been advanced as to Paul's condition at the conclusion of the stoning, as his battered body lay there in a heap outside the city gates.

---

[45] McGarvey, *op. cit.*, p.45.

[46] There is a similar instance of fickleness in Acts 28:4-6. There is one, too, in the closing days of Jesus' earthly ministry, when the shouts of "Hosanna!" quickly change to "Crucify Him!"

[47] Deuteronomy 13:10, 17:5.

[48] McGarvey, *ibid.*

[49] Compare notes at Acts 8:2 concerning no burial after a stoning.

[50] 2 Corinthians 12:2-3.

(1) Some, like Barnes, say that Paul was not dead, but that he was just knocked unconscious. This commentator believes it is not defensible for Barnes to state, as he does, "The probability is that he was stunned by a blow – perhaps a single blow – and after a short time recovered from it."[51] This explanation seems to minimize the severity of this stoning, a thing that Paul in later years, as he looked back over his life, considered to be one of his greatest persecutions.[52]

(2) Pricaeus and Wetstein suppose that Paul feigned himself to be dead, and when out of danger rose and returned to the city.[53] But this is wholly improbable.

(3) Others feel that Paul was badly hurt, but that Lois and Eunice quickly administered first-aid and revived him. However, this theory appears to be contradicted by verse 20.

(4) Others understand that Paul may actually have been dead, and that his soul went out of his body and went up into what he calls the third heaven, where he heard words that were "unlawful" for a man to speak.[54]

Some doubt that the 2 Corinthian 12:1ff passage refers to Paul's stoning at Lystra. And it is true that according to the chronology in the Introductory Studies, 2 Corinthians would be dated in the fall of AD 57. The "14 years before" of 2 Corinthians 12:2 would thus be AD 43, which is before the first missionary journey began. However, the time is reasonably approximate and the problems of New Testament chronology are many, so not a few commentators are convinced that 2 Corinthians 12:3-5 and Acts 14:19 speak of the same event, even if 2 Corinthians 12:2 speaks of some other time than at Lystra.

How Barnabas escaped stoning can only be conjectured. Perhaps the persecutors intended to stone both, but for some reason Barnabas was not present when they attacked Paul. Or perhaps they singled out Paul because he was the leader and chief speaker in the missionary party. It is implied that the murderers started homeward the same hour as they supposed Paul was finally no longer among the living. They could have searched and found Barnabas and executed him had they been of a mind to stay around Lystra any length of time after the stoning of Paul. Perhaps they feared what the Roman authorities, higher in authority than the city rulers, might do to them if they ever were called to account.

14:20 – But while the disciples stood around him, he arose and entered the city. And the next day he went away with Barnabas to Derbe.

But while the disciples stood around him. This verse is the first indication of the evangelistic success in Lystra. This group of sorrowing disciples almost certainly included Timothy who was from Lystra,[55] for this event seems to be reflected in Paul's later refer-

---

[51] Barnes, *op. cit.*, p.221.

[52] 2 Corinthians 11:25; 2 Timothy 3:11.

[53] Quoted by Barnes, *ibid.*

[54] Concerning the terminology "third heaven," see notes in Special Study #7, "Hades and the Intermediate Place of the Dead."

[55] Acts 16:1.

ence to Timothy's tears,[56] and in the fact that Timothy had observed Paul's sufferings and persecutions in this area.[57] Since the date of the stoning of Paul occurred about the year AD 47; and since Timothy was still a "youth" (i.e., under 40 years of age) at the date of Paul's first epistle to him;[58] and since 1 Timothy was written about AD 65, Timothy could not have been much older than 15 or 18 when Paul came to Lystra the first time. Paul calls Timothy his "son,"[59] which probably means Timothy was converted to Christianity by Paul. One wonders if it was after Paul's stoning that Timothy was baptized; or was he already a Christian before the stoning and miraculous recovery of Paul?

The Lystrian Christians are apparently also convinced that Paul was dead, or they would have been nursing his wounds rather than just standing about. There evidently was no way they could prevent the attack on Paul; but now that it is over, they have come, it would seem, with the purpose of giving Paul's body a decent burial.

He arose and entered the city. His swift recovery from apparent death required something more than the recuperative powers of a clean and energetic body dominated by a courageous spirit. Some sort of miracle is indicated, though not named. Some writers speak of his being cared for in the home of Timothy's family in the ensuing hours, but such talk is all unnecessary. The record shows that his recovery was complete and instantaneous! At first thought, it is surprising that he should have entered again into the same city. But the Jews who were behind the attack apparently have left.

And the next day he went away with Barnabas to Derbe. The violent opposition at Lystra rendered it vain to attempt to preach there longer. A meeting with the Christians, however, after Paul's supposed death, would have helped confirm them in their faith. Once this was done, the two departed to preach in another place.

Derbe was a town about 20 miles away to the southeast.[60] It would have been a journey of some hours and not free from risk. Several commentators speak of how difficult the journey must have been for one like Paul who was bruised and sore from the stoning. But again, we urge that the healing was complete and instantaneous, with no lingering after-effects. That Paul makes the journey on the very next day indicates instead how wonderfully complete was the miracle.

9. At Derbe, Then Back to Lystra, Iconium, and Antioch. 14:21-23

14:21 – *And after they had preached the gospel to that city and had made many disciples, they returned to Lystra and to Iconium and to Antioch,*

---

[56] 2 Timothy 1:4.

[57] 2 Timothy 3:10-11.

[58] 1 Timothy 4:12.

[59] 1 Corinthians 4:17; 2 Timothy 1:2.

[60] See notes at verse 6 on the identification of the site of Derbe.

And after they had preached the gospel to that city. We suppose Paul used the same methods he had used at Lystra as he preached the gospel at Derbe over a period of time. Since the beginning and end of this first missionary journey are voyages at sea, and as those would not be made during the winter, we can conclude that one and most likely two winters were spent in the highlands of Galatia, perhaps one at Iconium and another here at Derbe. It seems that the two apostles were not disturbed by the Jews at Derbe as they had been in earlier locales.

And had made many disciples. Gaius of Derbe, who was one who later accompanied Paul carrying the offering from the Gentile churches to Jerusalem,[61] was probably one of the converts on this first missionary tour. The congregation that is now planted took part in that benevolent offering nearly a decade later.

They returned to Lystra and to Iconium and to Antioch. Derbe was just across the border from Cilicia. The missionaries could have chosen to travel east, passed through the Cilician Gates (i.e., the pass through the Taurus mountains), visited Tarsus, Paul's native city, and shortly completed their return to Antioch of Syria. Instead, they determined to retrace their route in order to visit the new congregations they have just started in Lystra, Iconium, and Pisidian Antioch. This choice would take no little courage for the apostles to return to the very cities where they have been persecuted and stoned. Yet in the face of danger, they return.

Why would Paul and Barnabas choose the more dangerous path? One of the most important points of Paul's missionary method comes into view at this time. Not only are people to be won to Christ, but the converts must be conserved and strengthened! The welfare of the infant churches was considered to be more important than their own physical safety.

Some ask, How could the apostles re-enter the cities where they had been expelled without arousing a new wave of persecution? Perhaps there was more persecution to be faced! Perhaps there has been a change of government in this area, and thus the persons who had been expelled might return. Perhaps Paul confined his efforts to strengthening the brethren, rather than trying to gain new converts, so his presence was tolerated. But again, the events of a considerable time are compressed into a very few words by Luke.

14:22 – *strengthening the souls of the disciples, encouraging them to continue in the faith, and saying, "Through many tribulations we must enter the kingdom of God."*

Strengthening the souls of the disciples. Some of the older translations read "confirming the souls of the disciples." Various denominations have an ordinance of "confirmation." According to Roman Catholic theology, for example, sanctifying grace is increased in the soul and a special sacramental grace consisting of the seven gifts of the Holy Spirit is conferred upon the recipient at the time of confirmation. In the Lutheran Church, for example, confirmation is a rite rather than a sacrament, and the recipient offers it as a confirmation in his own heart of those baptismal vows which his parents assumed on his or

---

[61] Acts 20:4.

her behalf. However, Paul was by no means holding "confirmation" services of these types. These modern ideas of confirmation are completely forward of what is taught in the New Testament. In fact, these present-day concepts are based on false premises – the Roman Catholic doctrine on a "second work of grace," and the Lutheran doctrine on infant sprinkling. Indeed, the Greek word translated "strengthen (confirm)" in verse 22 is not even the same word used by later ecclesiastical writers when they spoke of the "ordinance of confirmation."

In this verse, "strengthening" has nothing to do with getting people to be full-fledged members of the church. As we read on in verse 22, we find these people were already "in the faith." They were in Christ; they were in the church; and they were in fellowship with God and His people. There is not the slightest evidence that they had not previously been admitted to the full privileges of church membership, or that any ceremony was now performed to confirm them, or receive them into the church as full members.

In this context, "strengthening" – as explained by the participles following, namely, "encouraging" and "appointing" – means simply that the Christians were established, strengthened in the faith: by the presentation of the truth, by the examples of the apostles, and by the selecting of men to spiritual leaders in the congregations. These Christians were young converts. They were surrounded by both unbelieving Jews and outright idolaters. They lived in the midst of many temptations and dangers. Family ties had been broken in some cases. Social ties had been broken in others. Thus, they needed encouragement, which is what they received from the returning missionaries.

Encouraging them to continue in the faith. Here is another place in Acts where we must choose between "faith" as a personal belief, or as a body of doctrine.[62] Perhaps the latter is the correct idea here. They are already Christians, and the preachers are encouraging them to stay that way.[63]

And *saying,* **"Through many tribulations.** We have the exact words of the preachers recorded here. They are warning the brethren of impending persecutions that will be inflicted. This is the first mention in Acts of the "tribulations" that believers must be prepared to face.[64]

We must enter the kingdom of God." "Must" is a translation of *dei*, "it is necessary." God has so willed that His children enter the eternal kingdom after suffering much affliction. The Scriptures elsewhere abundantly teach that we must suffer with Christ if we would reign with Him.[65]

---

[62] Compare Acts 3:16, 6:5, 6:7, or 13:8.

[63] At Acts 13:43 there is another phrase that may be similar. There, the preachers encouraged the believers to continue in the grace of God.

[64] Luke 14:27; Matthew 5:11.

[65] 2 Timothy 2:11-12, 3:12. Most of us do not want any tribulation; we do not want the hard or tight or difficult places. We prefer an easier path, with few difficulties and little or no opposition. But if we would reign with Him, we must first suffer with Him.

The use of the first-person personal pronoun ("we") is suggestive. Is Luke merely reporting the exact words of the preachers, or was Luke himself one of the listeners? If he is giving their exact words, then the use of "we" by the preachers shows how they included themselves with their hearers as they spoke. On the other hand, many insist that Paul and Luke clearly had met before we find them both at Troas on the second missionary journey. Maybe the "we" here has a similar meaning to what it has in 16:10ff.

It might seem surprising to notice that we "must enter the Kingdom of God," as though it were still something future.

- There is clearly a sense in which the Church and kingdom are synonymous.[66] The immersion of a penitent believer translates him or her into the kingdom of the Son. Becoming a Christian – getting into the faith and into fellowship with God – puts one into the kingdom of God. Paul says that he had translated people out of the dominion of the power of darkness into the kingdom of the Son.

- If individuals who are in the Church are already in the kingdom, how can it be said to them that they "must enter the kingdom"? We are led to this conclusion, that the phraseology "kingdom of God" has different meanings in the Scriptures. (a) The Jews of Old Testament times in a sense enjoyed, possessed, and were in the (Theocratic) kingdom of God on earth. (b) Yet the Scriptures also teach that the church is the present manifestation of the kingdom on earth. (c) And there is a sense yet to be fulfilled, in which you and I will enter into the eternal and perfect kingdom of God.

It is this latter sense – the eternal, heavenly kingdom – about which Paul is talking as he returns to the churches, to encourage them to be faithful unto death. The Christians at Lystra, Iconium, and Pisidian Antioch were made to realize that the prize of the upward call in Christ Jesus is worth all the suffering and hardships along the way. With this hope, they were made strong to endure whatever tribulation came their way.

We might learn from this passage two things that are necessary for every Christian to do: to grow in the faith, and to recognize the fact that we must needs have trials and tribulations to help us grow.

14:23 – *And when they had appointed elders for them in every church, having prayed with fasting, they commended them to the Lord in whom they had believed.*

And when they had appointed elders for them in every church. Various interpretations have been given to the word "appointed." Very often the kind of church government favored by the commentator will color the comments offered on this verse. In the present age, there are three forms of church government recognized by the courts – Episcopal, Presbyterian, and Congregational.

- Writers who favor the Episcopal form (such as in the Roman Catholic church, etc.), where there is a belief in apostolic succession, explain verse 23 to mean that the apostles laid hands on certain candidates in an ordination service, a service by which the candidates are officially put in office.

---

[66] See notes at Acts 1:3, and Special Study #1, "Diverse Opinions About the "Kingdom of God."

- Writers who favor the Presbyterian form of government, where presbyters (as representatives of the people) give orders and directions, see the apostles as giving directions to the church as to who were to be chosen as elders.
- Writers who favor the Congregational form of church government, where the congregation has a voice in the affairs of the congregation, have held that this passage implies a selection of elders by the members of the congregations – the election being under the oversight of the apostles.

Which, if any, of these is right?

The meaning underlying the word "appoint" (*cheirotonēsantes*) is helpful to understand. The word is a compound of two words, "hand" and "to stretch," and so the word literally means "to stretch the hands." From this literal meaning, the word came to signify to "choose or appoint by a show of hands," and finally "to elect or appoint by any means." The word occurs in but one other place in the New Testament, at 2 Corinthians 8:19, where it is applied to Luke (the common interpretation) and translated, "who was *chosen* by the churches (i.e., who was elected by the suffrage of the churches) to travel with us."[67]

The New Testament gives little detail as to how *elders* were selected – there is this passage in Acts and there is Titus 1:5, where the evangelist is given instruction to "ordain (*kathistēmi*) elders in every church."[68] We also have several passages which show how other leaders were selected. There is Acts 1, where the people have an opportunity to nominate someone to take the place of Judas. There is Acts 6, where the selection of the deacons was made by the congregation under the direction of the apostles,[69] and then the selection was followed by an "ordination" (*kathistēmi*) service conducted by the apostles. In view of all these examples, perhaps it can be safely said that Luke does not feel that it is necessary here in Acts 14 to repeat details as to the method of choosing men to the eldership since he has already given details twice before. We may be reasonably sure that the selection of the elders here in Acts 14 was made by the congregation under the direction of the apostles who set forth the qualifications.

Verse 23 does plainly say that Paul and Barnabas did the "stretching of hands" in this case.[70] Probably what we should see is an ordination service following the congregational vote, an ordination service in which Paul and Barnabas stretched forth their hands as they laid hands on each of the men who had been chosen to be elders.

The phrase "elders in every church" is of interest because of the word "church." In connection with the first missionary journey, prior to this point nothing definite has been said about churches (i.e., congregations). But since Luke now refers to them in the plural, we can reasonably infer that at least in every city where the missionaries preached, one or more congregations had been founded. As far as the New Testament teaches, there is abso-

---

[67] A compound form of the same verb appears at Acts 10:41 and is translated "chosen."

[68] *Kathistēmi* seems to refer to an ordination service following a selection by the congregation, and does not at all exclude a voice by the people in the selection.

[69] See Special Study #12, "A Method of Selection for Elders and Deacons," for further details.

[70] "Appoint" is a nominative plural participle and Paul and Barnabas are the subject of this participle. Therefore, it can be said that Paul and Barnabas do the "stretching of the hands."

lutely no concept of salvation outside of the church.[71] The Christians made on the first missionary journey were not just left to go it alone, but were brought together into local congregations because there is a purpose for assembling regularly with the body.[72] Hebrews 10:23-25 indicates that purpose is so that we can encourage each other to love and good works. Ephesians 4 indicates the body is to build itself up in love. Congregational life is vitally important.

The phrase "elders in every church" is also of interest because of the word "elders." Luke records that there were elders (plural) in every church (singular). In each congregation there is to be more than one elder.[73] The New Testament knows nothing of a ruling elder (singular) in any congregation, such as we find in many churches today.

In 1 Timothy 3:6, Paul gives the qualifications for the office of elder. As part of those qualifications, Paul says the man appointed is not to be a "new convert, lest he become conceited." Since these men here in Acts 14 who were chosen to the office of elder could not have been Christians for more than eight months or a year, did Paul violate his own instruction? McGarvey's opinion is that Paul did not:

> It must be remembered that, although these disciples had been but a comparatively short time in the church, many of them were in character and knowledge of the Scriptures the ripest fruits of the Jewish synagogue; and they needed only the additional knowledge which the Gospel brought in order to be models of wisdom and piety for the churches.[74]

Perhaps the men chosen were men who just months previously had been the elected rulers of the synagogues. Also consider that, by laying on hands, the apostles could pass on spiritual gifts, which would help make leaders for the infant congregations.[75]

---

[71] The church is the body of Christ and a person cannot be a Christian without being a member of His body. A man can no more be a Christian without being a member of a local congregation than a fish can live outside water. Before God created the living things in the beginning, He already had an environment for each. Before God created you as a new creature, He had an environment ready for you, the church. The first converts on the day of Pentecost were immediately joined together into a congregation (Acts 2:41). Everything God creates must fit in with and correspond to the environment and atmosphere God made for it. Put a man under water, and he dies. Take a fish out of the water, and it dies. Pull up a tree, and when the roots break contact with the ground, the tree dies. When you become a new creature in Christ, your environment and atmosphere is the local church in your home community. Get away from that environment, and you die. A branch separated from the vine dies.

[72] Of what church (congregation) today should we be a member? (a) If a given congregation is not teaching the gospel and is not preaching New Testament Christianity, and is determined not to do it, then why sojourn among them? The Scripture says, "Come ye out and be ye separated." (b) It does not take a lot of people to make up a congregation. "Where two or three are gathered together in My name, there am I in the midst of them," said Jesus. Where as many as two people agree to live as the New Testament teaches, there you have a church. (c) Some Christians, having moved to such and such a place, find no New Testament church there. They often, therefore, elect to worship with a denomination. Why? Instead – and unless you are able to convert the whole denominational church – why not start a Church in your own home? That is the way the church began in the New Testament, as you can read in book of Acts.

[73] See also Titus 1:5; Acts 20:17.

[74] McGarvey, *op. cit.*, p.50.

[75] As this appears to be the first appointment of elders in theses Galatian churches, it would seem to follow that the Christians had in the meantime met, and taught, and baptized, and had broken bread without elders. Appointment of elders like Paul and Barnabas are doing is important for the permanence of the life

Concerning the position these "elders" held, see notes at Acts 11:30. They are elsewhere in the New Testament called presbyters and overseers (i.e., bishops). Their job was to oversee the work of the church;[76] New Testament elders are the rulers, the overseers. Paul and Barnabas could not stay with the churches indefinitely. If the churches were to continue, thrive, and grow, they needed to have responsible leadership of their own. Hence, the two apostles "appointed elders in every church."[77]

Having prayed with fasting. It is not easy to tell just when the praying and fasting occurred. It may be that it was done in conjunction with the selection of men to be elders, just as there was prayer and fasting when the two apostles were set apart back at Antioch.[78] It may be that the fasting and prayer came after the appointment of the elders, at the time the apostles were about to resume their journey back to Antioch of Syria. Paul and Barnabas have suffered greatly in an effort to plant these new congregations, and now they are about to leave Asia Minor for a time. The churches are being turned over to local leadership. It was a solemn and fearsome moment, and so there was prayer and fasting. We can hear their prayers as they asked God to lead the new churches and their newly elected leaders, and also that He would guide and protect the apostles on their journey.

They commended them to the Lord in whom they had believed. Paul and Barnabas committed these newly planted congregations to the care and guardianship of the Lord Jesus. The word "commend" is the word regularly used when one entrusts his money or property to someone else's care. Jesus had promised to be with the church always, even to the end of the age.[79] The believers, the missionaries are confident, will be watched over and helped by the Christ in whom they have come to believe.

10. Through the Provinces of Pisidia and Pamphylia. 14:24

14:24 – *And they passed through Pisidia and came into Pamphylia.*

And they passed through Pisidia. This might mean that they made a missionary journey through Pisidia. Or it might simply be a summary of their activities since they started retracing their steps. If so, we would translate it, "and after they passed through Pisidia ...."

---

of the church, but it is evidently possible for there to be a congregation without having such leaders in place from the beginning. In this commentator's judgment, in newly planted congregations, it is better not to select men to be elders or deacons than to select men who are not qualified. It is better to function without elders and deacons until some grow enough spiritually to meet the qualifications.

[76] The New Testament knows nothing of an "official board" which oversees the work of the church.

[77] At times, the present-day church can be slow to appreciate the divine wisdom of making each congregation a locally self-sustaining unit. For example, for many centuries missionaries in foreign lands have at times been reluctant to let the natives shepherd and oversee their own churches. The missionaries have kept the converts dependent on foreign help, both for leadership and for finances, with the result that when, for any cause, the missionary was removed from the scene, the church dwindled and often died. How much better for us to learn from and follow Paul's example.

[78] Acts 13:2-3.

[79] Matthew 28:20.

And came into Pamphylia. Retracing the route by which they had come,[80] Paul and Barnabas made their way toward the seacoast, till they came to the province of Pamphylia.[81]

11. At Perga and Attalia. 14:25

14:25 – *And when they had spoken the word in Perga, they went down to Attalia;*

And when they had spoken the word in Perga. Did Paul and Barnabas preach here on their way inland (Acts 13:13)? Perhaps they did; perhaps they did not; we are not told one way or the other. Those who believe Paul contracted malaria while preaching in the lowlands of Pamphylia, and that that was the cause of John Mark's going home, might be inclined to believe that some preaching had taken place here before they went on up into the highlands. McGarvey suggests it is probable that the preaching done here now was actuated by the desire to usefully occupy the time while waiting for a ship bound for Antioch of Syria.

They went down to Attalia. Attalia[82] was a town on the seacoast, about 16 miles from Perga. It was named after its founder, Attalus II Philadelphus, king of Pergamus from 159-138 BC. He desired to have a port as convenient for trade with Syria and Egypt as Troas was for commercial activities across the Aegean. Its modern name is Antalya. Apparently finding no ship bound for Syria in the port of Perga, the missionaries decide to go down to the sea- coast, where they might have a better possibility of finding a ship on which they could book passage.

12. In Antioch of Syria. 14:26-28

14:26 – *and from there they sailed to Antioch, from which they had been commended to the grace of God for the work that they had accomplished.*

And from there they sailed to Antioch. Antioch of Syria, that is. Actually, they would have landed at Seleucia, the port which served Antioch of Syria. Apparently, the voyage was direct from Attalia, between Cyprus and Cilicia.

From which they had been commended to the grace of God. The church at Antioch had sent Paul and Barnabas on this missionary tour,[83] and they are now coming home. They had been "commended to the grace of God." That is, the church had committed these

---

[80] Acts 13:14.

[81] Compare notes at Acts 13:13.

[82] It is pronounced "Att-a-LYE-a." On the inland trip they had sailed right up the Cestrus river to Perga, thus bypassing Attalia.

[83] Acts 12:1-4.

men to God's favor and protection during their perilous tour. As Paul and Barnabas were beginning their tour, the church had prayed that God would care for them, and it is entirely probable the church continued to pray for them while they were gone. And God's grace was found to be sufficient.[84]

For the work that they had accomplished. These men had done all that the Holy Spirit had intended for them to do. They had accomplished ("fulfilled" the margin reads) the missionary task to which the Holy Spirit had called them.

14:27 – *And when they had arrived and gathered the church together, they* **began** *to report all things that God had done with them and how He had opened a door of faith to the Gentiles.*

And when they had arrived. It has been several years since the two apostles had left this city to begin their journey. Now they have come back home.

> It is doubtful whether the church in Antioch had heard from Paul and Barnabas since the missionaries first left Perga. John Mark, on his return, may have brought them news of the journey to that point. When, therefore, they appeared unheralded in the streets of the city, after an absence of three or four years, we may well suppose that they were met with hearty greetings and much questioning.[85]

And gathered the church together. Paul and Barnabas had gone on the first mission ever sent out to the pagan world, and they were as eager to tell their story as the disciples were to hear it. This gathering involved the Christians of the city of Antioch, those brethren who had a vital concern in the work that had been done (see 13:3).

They *began* **to report ail things that God had done with them.** The two told all about their journey. They would speak of the miracles and other evidences of divine intervention in the accomplishment of the journey. "With them" is *met' auton* (not *sun autois*) and it speaks of God's gracious cooperation with the apostles (compare Acts 10:38, 15:4).

> "With them" ... is an interesting expression; it loses some of its force in English. I can drive a nail "with" a hammer – but in Greek that would take a different preposition. Or I can spend an evening "with" my family. This is the word used here. They had gone on the mission and God had gone with them. While He was with them, He performed His wonderful and gracious acts – acts of saving, of healing, of watching over His own, of advancing His redemptive purpose in this world.[86]

God had protected and guided them during the journey. They could speak of the dangers

---

[84] In this verse we have a new connotation for the word "grace" in addition to those already suggested in comments at Acts 4:33 and Acts 11:23.

[85] McGarvey, *op. cit.*, p.52.

[86] William Sanford LaSor, *Church Alive* (Glendale, CA: Gospel Light Publications. 1972), p.222. Be careful in the use of the words "acts of saving," for some use those words to indicate their belief that man is wholly passive in salvation, a doctrine that is not taught in the New Testament.

and successes, the numbers of people converted, and the congregations established.

And how He had opened a door of faith to the Gentiles. God had furnished an opportunity of preaching the gospel to the Gentiles, and that preaching had met with success beyond any heretofore made in the conversion of the Gentiles. "Open doors" is a characteristic expression of Paul's;[87] it speaks of abundant opportunities and great progress. And note, the door that God opened was a door of "faith," not a door of "Law." The religion from God for the Gentiles excludes the Law of Moses; it was a door of faith. Some have said, "Prayer is the key that opens Heaven's door." That may be true in a sense, but it is also true that "*Faith* is the key that opens Heaven's door."

14:28 – *And they spent a long time with the disciples.*

And they spent a long time with the disciples. It is not possible to say with any certainty how long Paul and Barnabas stayed in Antioch, and expressions like this make a chronology of Acts extremely difficult. We hear no more about these two until the Jerusalem Conference in the next chapter.

- The first missionary journey started, probably, in AD 45; that is, per Acts 12, it began just after the death of Herod Agrippa I in AD 44. The first missionary journey probably lasted through AD 47 or 48, or perhaps as long as AD 49.
- The Jerusalem Conference was held in AD 50 or 51.
- Thus, there is a period of 2-4 years passing in the words of this verse.

As to what Paul and Barnabas were doing during this time, we have no information. It is doubtful that Barnes is correct when he places a trip to Illyricum in this interval.[88] The time would be spent profitably in sharing with others what they had learned in their labors, helping and teaching the church, and recuperating from the strenuous labors of the intervening years.

SUMMARY AND REVIEW OF THE FIRST MISSIONARY JOURNEY

Boles has figured the distance the missionaries traveled on this first journey. "Paul and Barnabas traveled over 1,200 miles, and established more than half a dozen churches in the few years they were gone on this journey."[89]

The Holy Spirit is the author of the first Christian missionary enterprise among the Gentiles. We find no organization or fellowship telling the missionaries where to go, or,

---

[87] See 1 Corinthians 16:9; 2 Corinthians 2:12; Colossians 4:3.

[88] Barnes. *op. cit.,* p.224. Whether or not Paul ever made a trip *into* the province of Illyricum (see Romans 15;19) is a disputed point, on which see further discussion at Acts 20:2.

[89] Boles, *op. cit.,* p.231.

for that matter, telling the church what missionaries are qualified to go. One looks in vain to find even a first cousin to that sort of organization in the New Testament.

In his *Declaration and Address*, Thomas Campbell suggested there are three kinds, or types, of Biblical authority: an express command of God, approved apostolic precedent, and necessary inference.[90] Only the first – an express command of God – can be made binding on all people today. The *methods* used by the apostles (i.e., apostolic precedent) may or may not be examples for us today, depending on the circumstances and the leading of the Holy Spirit.

It is important to preach the same *message* the early preachers did, for it comes from the heart of God; it is His revelation for this whole dispensation. In terms of the *method*, we hope to see the time when congregations see their responsibility for sending out their own missionaries, supporting them in every way. Instead of a dozen congregations with a few pennies for this, a few pennies for that, a few pennies for the other, it would be better for each congregation to be send out two, three, five, even dozens of missionaries. Perhaps this is an ideal, but if we never set up an ideal, we shall never approximate it with reality.

The apostles went to the large cities because the population was there, because they were on the main roads, and also because there were Jewish synagogues there which gave them an opening. They preached Jesus as the Christ, established churches, appointed elders in each church, and revisited the churches in order that they might be strengthened in the faith. After this, they wrote letters to the churches, and at a later time revisited them again. At intervals, the missionaries presented a report of their work to the church that sent them, and to other interested congregations.

Such is the pattern of the missionary work carried on under the Holy Spirit's guidance.

---

[90] Thomas Campbell, "Declaration and Address" in *Historical Documents Advocating Christian Union* (Chicago: The Christian Century Company, 1904), p.77ff.

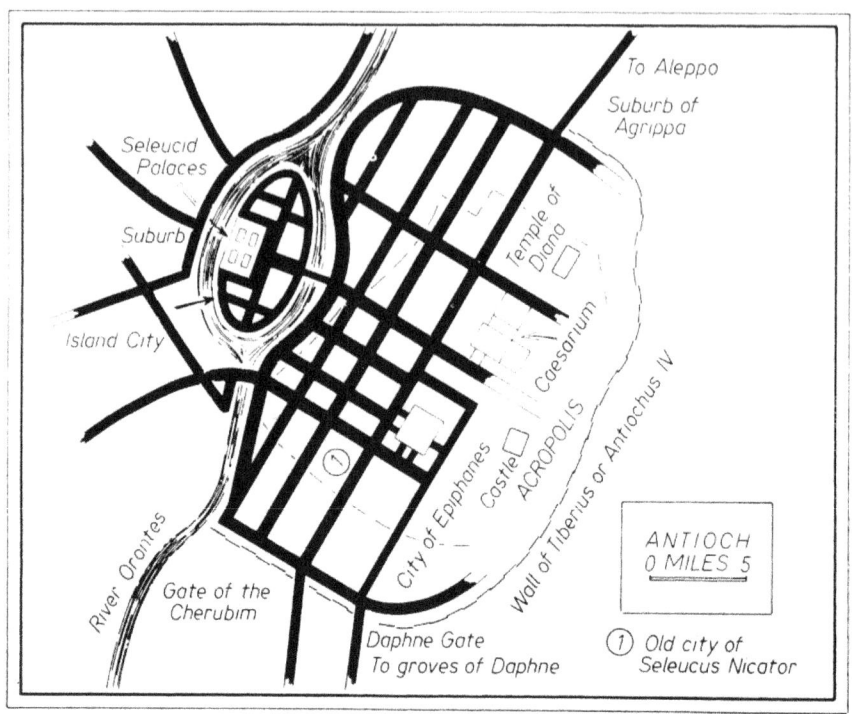

B. The Conference in Jerusalem. 15:1-35

15:1 – *And some men came down from Judea and* **began** *teaching the brethren, "Unless you are circumcised according to the custom of Moses, you cannot be saved."*

And some men came down from Judea. These were men who had been Jews of the sect of the Pharisees (verse 5), but who were converted –only superficially – to Christianity.[1] The fact that they were willing to refer their dispute to the apostles and elders (verse 2) shows they had professedly embraced the Christian religion. However, in Galatians 2:4 they are styled "false brethren who had sneaked in to spy out our liberty."[2] They came from Jerusalem to Antioch of Syria, and incorrectly claimed to have been sent from Jerusalem by the apostles.[3] Perhaps they built their doctrines on statements like the one written in James 2:10, which, if taken out of context, might sound as if keeping the Law of Moses was necessary to salvation.[4]

And *began* **teaching the brethren.** Whether this teaching was publicly in the worship services or whether it was via private audiences with those willing to listen, we do not know. The verb tense is imperfect, and suggests their continual efforts to force their teaching on the Christians at Antioch. Enough of the brethren listened to their teaching so that a greater part of the church there was disturbed.

Unless you are circumcised. It is evident from their argument that Paul and Barnabas had dispensed with this rite as far as the Gentile converts were concerned. The missionaries had founded the Christian church among the Gentiles on the principle that the Jewish ceremonies had ceased to be obligatory on the people of God. Circumcision was the litmus test of whether or not one would be obedient to the Law of Moses, but we may also suppose that the Judaizers' demands also included the keeping of the Old Testament distinctions between clean and unclean meats and drinks, and the other peculiarly Jewish customs.[5]

According to the custom of Moses. *Ethos* ("custom") is a word that often implies a national custom. Moses had commanded it to be done and so the Jewish nation had prac-

---

[1] For further information about these "false brethren," see notes below at verse 5.

[2] We accept the idea that the trip to Jerusalem described in Acts 15 and the one in Galatians 2 are the same trip. However, since other commentators equate the Galatians 2 with either Acts 11:30 or 18:22, it is helpful to list some of the reasons why we accept that Acts 15 = Galatians 2: (1) The early Church identified Acts 15 and Galatians 2. (See Irenaeus, *Against Heresies*, III.3.3 and Tertullian, *Against Marcion*, V.2.) (2) It is not easy to place the 14 years specified in Galatians 2:1 between the visit of Acts 9:27 and that of Acts 11:30. (3) If the decision referred to in Galatians 2:9 had already been reached at Acts 11:30, it surely would have been appealed to during the course of the debate in Acts 15. (See also footnote #56 in chapter 11.)

[3] Acts 15:24.

[4] In fact, this commentator posits that the epistle of James was written about AD 51, after the Jerusalem Conference, and was the apostle's reply to the Judaizers who had misappropriated his name and distorted his teachings.

[5] Compare Galatians 2:1-9, 4:10, 5:2. For a description of what it means to be a "Judaizer," see comments at Acts 11:3.

ticed circumcision through the centuries. The Judaizers were appealing to Moses as their authority in demanding that the rite be continued. Circumcision, they may have argued, was given as an everlasting covenant,[6] and therefore it must still be kept. Or they may have used an analogy: if circumcision was an absolutely necessary condition for admission to the Passover,[7] it must also be necessary for the forgiveness of sins, they may have argued.

You cannot be saved. These Judaizers regarded circumcision (and the keeping of the whole Law) as indispensable to salvation. They wished to force the keeping of the Law on the Gentile converts, and they falsely claimed that the church at Jerusalem had authorized them to so teach (verse 24).

It seems surprising, after the conversion of Cornelius and Peter's explanation of how it was God's will to include the Gentiles, that members of the Jerusalem church should teach the doctrines these Judaizers have taught. About ten years separates the events of Acts 11 and Acts 15. However, in that interval, there have been new converts who were not present at that memorable meeting in Jerusalem, and who therefore would have had no opportunity to have been convinced first-hand by Peter's compelling arguments. Further, since Paul calls them "false brethren who sneaked in to spy out our liberty," there is a good possibility they didn't want to be convinced by Peter's or anybody's arguments. Peter had been criticized before this time for not observing Jewish customs ("you entered the house of uncircumcised men and did eat with them!", Acts 11:3), and the same criticism of Paul's missionary work is now raised by these Judaizers. The demand is that Gentile Christians must keep the Old Testament rules and regulations – just as many of the Jewish Christians in Jerusalem have apparently been doing.

15:2 – *And when Paul and Barnabas had great dissension and debate with them,* **the brethren** *determined that Paul and Barnabas and certain others of them should go up to Jerusalem to the apostles and elders concerning this issue.*

And when Paul and Barnabas. The apostles at Antioch opposed these Judaizing teachers who have come from Jerusalem and who are troubling the brethren there at Antioch. Paul had received the gospel he preached through a direct revelation from Christ,[8] and so had a correct knowledge of the will of God for this age. He knew perfectly well that this teaching about circumcision and the observing of the Law of Moses as a condition necessary for salvation was a false teaching. Barnabas had learned the same truth, either from Paul or by revelation just as Paul had. So the two united with all their might in opposing the doctrines taught by the Judaizers.

Had great dissension and debate with them. The word "dissension" was used by classical Greek writers to express the greatest evil of all political societies – the discord

---

[6] Genesis 17:3. However, the word "everlasting" must be understood in light of whatever limitations are placed on it by its context.

[7] Exodus 12:43-48.

[8] Galatians 1:11-12.

and faction that opposite sides of a question often generate.[9] It is the same word used of the "insurrection" in which Barabbas had been involved.[10] "Debate" comes from *zēteseōs*, and speaks of a "questioning," an "examining together," and the word regularly has a depreciatory sense. We probably should picture all this taking place in a public meeting, with each side trying to put the other down. Doctrines had been advanced by the Judaizers which were false, and Paul and Barnabas stood up for the faith. Is it wrong to debate and discuss? Not when the truth is in the balance![11] It is Christlike to stand for the truth (John 8). Evidently, Paul and Barnabas were displaying the spirit of Christ as they opposed the Judaizers.

The brethren **determined that Paul and Barnabas.** Galatians 2:2 tells us the two went up to Jerusalem because of a revelation, but this does not contradict what Luke here tells us. Harmonizing Luke's and Paul's accounts, the order of events might have occurred in this fashion: The two apostles were unable to convince the Gentile believers at Antioch that the Judaizers were wrong. But because of the revelation they had received, they conducted the debate so that the brethren accepted the suggestion, "If you don't believe us, go to Jerusalem and ask the Twelve!" The Judaizing teachers from Jerusalem had claimed to be contending for the rite of circumcision (and compliance with all of Moses' Law) because they had learned it from the original apostles and because it was so practiced by the church at Jerusalem. Paul knew that such was not the case, that the Twelve had not been teaching such doctrines. Thus, it was best to go to Jerusalem to settle the matter, not for himself, but for those who did not know any better.

> If the brethren at Antioch had properly estimated the authority of an inspired apostle, they would have accepted implicitly Paul's decision without this mission to Jerusalem. But their familiarity with the person of the apostle, like that of the Nazarenes with Jesus, made them slow to realize that he spoke with Divine authority. Perhaps also the fact that he was not one of the original twelve caused them to think of his utterances as being less authoritative than theirs. But we dare say that they learned, as a result of this mission, what they should have realized at first; and it is never again recorded that they ever doubted Paul's teaching after this.[12]

The church at Antioch determined that they should send a delegation up to Jerusalem to find out for themselves the truth in this issue. Paul and Barnabas are part of that delegation.

And certain others of them. Barnes suggests that there may have been some from each side in this debate[13] – those who sided with the Judaizers and those who believed with Paul. Galatians 2:1 tells us that Titus was one of the ones whom Paul took along. Titus is not named or mentioned in the book of Acts.

---

[9] Thucydides, *History of the Peloponnesian War*, III.82; Aristotle, *Politics*, V.2.

[10] Mark 15:7; Luke 23:19.

[11] Jude 3 and Philippians 1:17 are other passages often appealed to, for they teach Christians to resist error with all the arguments from the Word that they can muster.

[12] McGarvey, *op. cit.*, p.55.

[13] Barnes, *op. cit.*, p.226.

Should go up to Jerusalem. Why go to Jerusalem? Because that is where the majority of the original apostles of Jesus were. The Judaizers might not acknowledge the authority of Paul as an apostle (in fact, there is some evidence in Galatians 2:6-9 that they did not value him as highly as the Twelve), but they would recognize the authority of the apostles at Jerusalem. In the Introductory Studies, we have dated this trip to Jerusalem and the Jerusalem Conference in AD 51.

To the apostles and elders. We do not know how many of the original twelve apostles were in Jerusalem at this time, save that from Galatians 2 we learn that Peter and John are there, as is James the Lord's brother (who is called an apostle,[14] but who was not one of the original twelve). We can understand why they would go to the apostles for information about the issue being disputed. Claims have been made by the Judaizers that the Twelve are teaching that circumcision is essential to salvation. The authority of the apostles in Jerusalem would be acknowledged by all, for they had been instructed by the Savior personally, and had been promised the supernatural guidance of the Holy Spirit, so that their teaching must be right![15] But why are the "elders" included? Why is it necessary to send to them to ask information? Not, it seems, because they are on an equal with the apostles, for they were not.[16] But if we have assumed correctly that the Judaizers were claiming the example of the members of the Jerusalem church as living proof of the correctness of their doctrine of the necessity of circumcision, then the elders – whose job it is to oversee the spiritual life of the brethren – would be the ones to ask about the practices of the members of the church in Jerusalem.

Concerning this issue. The question is whether the Law of Moses – and in particular circumcision, which was the litmus test of a man's intention to keep the Law – was binding and necessary for salvation. Paul and Barnabas had been proclaiming salvation through *faith* in Christ,[17] with no mention of the need of keeping the Law of Moses. Their converts have now been told by the Judaizers that Paul and Barnabas had been teaching a soul-destroying falsehood. Were the Judaizers right in their charges, or were Paul and Barnabas correct? This is the issue that must be settled in the people's minds.

15:3 – *Therefore, being sent on their way by the church, they were passing through both Phoenicia and Samaria, describing in detail the conversion of the Gentiles, and were bringing great joy to all the brethren.*

Therefore, being sent on their way by the church. The word can indicate either that they were provisioned for the journey (i.e., assisted in paying the expenses, and encouraged by prayers for a safe journey) by the brethren at Antioch, or that some of the brethren actually accompanied them on the journey.[18] Such an act is a mark of love and respect; it

---

[14] Galatians 1:19.

[15] John 14:26; Matthew 18:18.

[16] Ephesians 4:11; 1 Corinthians 12:18.

[17] Acts 14:27.

[18] The same idea of conducting a beloved friend on a journey is found in Acts 21:5.

shows that the sympathy of the church at Antioch was with the apostles, not the Judaizers.

They were passing through both Phoenicia and Samaria. See Acts 11:19 and 8:5 for the record of the evangelization of these two countries which were directly on the route from Antioch of Syria to Jerusalem. The group would have traveled along the coast as far south as Ptolemais, and then crossed the plain of Esdraelon into Samaria.[19]

Describing in detail the conversion of the Gentiles. As they journey through the various towns where there are congregations, the two apostles told of the results of the first missionary tour, how the Gentiles in Asia Minor had responded to the preaching of the gospel.[20]

And were bringing great joy to all the brethren. The "great joy" was the result of the news of the extensive spread of the gospel. Phoenicia and Samaria were not bound by Jewish prejudices, as Judea would have been. For that reason, we can understand why they rejoiced when they learned that God had opened the door of faith to the Gentile world. See it again! It was a door of faith, not a door for the Law of Moses, that God opened (Acts 14:27). Where Christians themselves are vibrant in their witness for Christ, they rejoice at the news of the conversion of sinners. The verb tense suggests a continuing joy. Whenever the two apostles spoke, the account of the Gentiles' conversion was received with a gladness which presented the strongest possible contrast to the narrowness and bitterness of the Judaizers.

15:4 – *And when they arrived at Jerusalem, they were received by the church and the apostles and the elders, and they reported all that God had done with them.*

And when they arrived at Jerusalem. It was a journey of some 300 miles from Antioch to Jerusalem. This was Paul's third visit to Jerusalem since his conversion.[21]

They were received by the church. The Greek word "received" carries the connotation "welcomed." Both were acknowledged as Christian brethren and received in a friendly, hospitable manner, with Christian kindness. Barnabas was welcomed because he had been so useful in the infancy of the Jerusalem church. Paul was welcomed as a fellow-apostle and a brother. There is no reason for Paul to have been received otherwise at the Jerusalem church, for when he last left Jerusalem he was in good standing with the brethren.[22]

---

[19] They could have gone by ship, landed at Caesarea or Joppa, and bypassed both Phoenicia and Samaria. The very route they chose, therefore, was an assertion of the principle for which they were contending.

[20] Herein is another indication of 1st century missionary methods. Not only did Paul report to the church that had committed him to the missionary tour (Acts 14:27), but he shared the good news with other congregations, too. It would be well for present-day missionaries to follow this example, by visiting congregations other than the ones which have been the source of living-link support. Not only may it help the missionary in his enterprise, but he ought to count it a privilege that he has the opportunity of helping those churches at which he preaches to become more missionary-minded.

[21] See Acts 9:26 and 11:30 for the two earlier visits. The second visit to Jerusalem, the famine visit recorded in Acts 11, is not mentioned by Paul in the Galatian letter, evidently because he did not meet with any of the apostles long enough that he was ever accused of learning his doctrine from them during that visit.

[22] Acts 9:30, 12:25.

And [they were received by] the apostles and the elders. We know not how many of the apostles were present. Galatians 2:9 indicates that at least Peter and John and James the Lord's brother were there. Nor do we know how many elders were in the church at Jerusalem. This verse would seem to imply that even though the apostles were there with all their apostolic authority over the church, still the elders of each congregation were also looked on as leaders in those congregations – men whose function was not superseded or impinged upon even by an apostle.

And they reported all that God had done with them. This was the first of several meetings that together made up the Jerusalem Conference.[23] As this meeting begins, Paul and Barnabas, in a presentation of some length, told those assembled at Jerusalem of the thrilling journey they had made among the Gentiles. Observe that the two apostles state in their rehearsal of what they had done that it was really God working "with them."[24] If God was so working, then it must follow that God had accepted the Gentiles without circumcision; and the Jewish brethren ought to so accept them, too.

15:5 – *But certain ones of the sect of the Pharisees who had believed, stood up, saying, "It is necessary to circumcise them, and to direct them to observe the Law of Moses."*

But certain ones of the sect of the Pharisees. There is a contrast between verses 3 and 5. Phoenicia and Samaria on the one hand had been filled with joy at the news of the conversion of the Gentiles. On the other hand, some at Jerusalem have only criticism for what had been done.

There is a manuscript variation at this place, making it difficult to be sure whose words these are, or exactly who is identified as involved at this part of the Conference.

- Perhaps these are the words of Paul and Barnabas, telling what had happened at Antioch when the Judaizers came there.
- Perhaps these are Luke's words explaining what happened next at the Conference.
- And who are the "certain ones"? Are they the Judaizers who went up to Antioch and then returned to Jerusalem? Or are they sympathizers from among the brethren still in Jerusalem, so that the Judaizers who went to Antioch could indeed say they were sent by people at Jerusalem?

Out of these various possibilities, we suppose they are the words of Luke, and the Judaizers are some of the very ones who went to Antioch. If so, it appears that the Judaizers, immediately upon the conclusion of the wonderful account of the first missionary journey, take an opportunity to point out what they regard to be a serious defect in the ministry of Paul and Barnabas among the Gentiles.

Who had believed. These Pharisees indeed believed; they were members of the Jerusalem church, having been converted from "the sect of the Pharisees" to Christianity. But there is considerable evidence that they did not leave all their old Jewish beliefs behind as they

---

[23] See notes below at verse 6 concerning the various meetings during this Conference.

[24] See comments on these same words "with them" at Acts 14:27.

came into the Church. They may believe that Jesus is indeed the Messiah; but they picture him as the Messiah only for a glorified Judaism from which Gentiles are to be excluded, unless they conform rigidly to the Law of Moses.

> After reading so much in the earlier chapters of Acts respecting the hostility of the sect of the Pharisees to the church (and to Jesus), it is a surprise to meet here with some of that party inside the church, occupying a position of some influence. But it is not a surprise to find them on the wrong side of this important question. They found it no longer possible to resist the evidence in favor of Jesus, and had therefore been baptized into His name; but they still clung tenaciously to some of their former ideas. Long after this meeting, when Paul had come to fully understand the motives of the Judaizing party [if indeed he did not understand them at the time of the Jerusalem Conference], he writes, styling them as "false brethren privily brought in, who came in to spy out our liberty[25] which we have in Christ Jesus, that they might bring us into bondage" (Galatians 2:4). From this judicial sentence in Galatians upon these Judaizers, we ascertain that when they despaired of destroying the church by persecution from without, they deliberately confessed Christ and came into the church for the purpose of controlling it from within.[26]

It was the purpose of these Judaizers to keep the church under the bondage of the Law, and thus prevent it from very seriously modifying the state of things among the Jews in which the Pharisees were the predominant party. Partisan zeal, the bane of their former life, was still their controlling motive.

Stood up, saying, "It is necessary to circumcise them. See this discussed under verse 1.

And to direct them to observe the Law of Moses." "Them" speaks of the Gentile converts to Christianity in general, not just men like Titus who (being Gentiles) accompanied Paul and Barnabas to this Conference. The essential issue at the Jerusalem Conference is the relationship between the Law and the Gospel. McGarvey has a fine note on this matter:

> The essential issue between Paul and the Pharisees had reference to the perpetuation of the Law of Moses in the church of God: and the same issue has been in debate under different phases from that day to this.
>
> Paul defeated the attempt to fasten circumcision on the church, but later Judaizers succeeded in perpetuating it under the form of infant sprinkling. That which the Pharisees failed to accomplish openly was thus accomplished under a thin disguise.
>
> The Pharisees failed to consolidate the Law and the Gospel, but their imitators have largely succeeded in teaching men that the church of Christ originated in the family of Abraham, and that the Jewish tribes and the Christian congregations constitute one identical church.
>
> The Roman [Church] perpetuates the daily sacrifice and pompous ritual of the Temple; religious zealots have slaughtered Canaanites in the persons of modern heretics; professed Christians go to war under the old battle-cry of the "sword of the Lord and of Gideon"; the "Latter-day Saints" emulate Solomon in the multiplication of wives; and for all these corruptions authority is found in the laws and customs of ancient Israel.

---

[25] Concerning this "liberty in Christ," see notes below at verse 31

[26] McGarvey, *op. cit.*, p.58-59.

The intelligent reader of the New Testament knows scarcely which of these errors is farthest from the truth; and he feels bound to struggle with untiring energy and ceaseless vigilance to uproot them from the minds of men.[27]

For further information concerning the distinction between the Law and the Gospel, see Alexander Campbell's "Sermon on the Law."

15:6 – *And the apostles and the elders came together to look into this matter.*

And the apostles and the elders came together to look into this matter. Comparing the language of verse 6 with that of verse 4, we are led to see that verse 6ff speaks of a different meeting than verses 4 and 5 did. In the first meeting, Paul and Barnabas had declared in detail the conversion of the Gentiles. Then the Judaizers stated their position, distinctly insisting that the Gentile converts must be circumcised and required to keep the Law. At this point, that first meeting seems to have been dismissed without further discussion or debate. Verse 6 then introduces us to a second public meeting, and the narrative related to this second meeting continues through verse 29.

Both meetings recorded by Luke were *public* meetings, meetings where the whole church at Jerusalem was present. There was also, however, a *private* meeting which Luke does not record – involving Paul, Barnabas, and Titus on the one hand, and Peter, John, and James the Lord's brother on the other, which was held between the two public meetings. This we learn from Galatians 2, in which Paul both states the fact and gives the reason for seeking the meeting with the three apostles who were in Jerusalem:

> Then after an interval of fourteen years I went up again to Jerusalem with Barnabas, taking Titus along also. And it was because of a revelation that I went up; and I submitted to them the gospel which I preach among the Gentiles, but I did so in private to those who were of reputation, for fear that I might be running, or had run, in vain.[28]

In these words Paul has given the reason for the interview. If he found that any of the original apostles were on the side of the Judaizers, their influence would have overborne his, and the brethren all would have begun observing the Law of Moses as one of the requirements for salvation. And if this had happened, all of his work would have been overthrown. Some have misunderstood Paul's words in Galatians. Several commentators think his language shows that at this period in Paul's life he had not arrived at a definite theology, and they say that "for fear that I might be running ... in vain" means he wasn't quite sure if he was right or not. But such an idea is totally inconsistent with Paul's repeated declarations in Galatians 1 that he had received his knowledge of the gospel by direct revelation; his preaching wasn't something that he himself slowly forged and developed as the years passed. Since he received his gospel by revelation, and preached it by inspiration, he could not have had any doubts concerning its content.[29]

---

[27] McGarvey, *op. cit.*, p.59-60.

[28] Galatians 2:1-2.

[29] However, like Peter (Acts 2 and 10) and the Old Testament prophets (1 Peter 1:10-11), Paul may have had questions as to the whole meaning of what he preached by inspiration.

The results of the private meeting between the six men is stated in the following words from Galatians:

> Well, those who were of reputation contributed nothing to me. But on the contrary, seeing that I had been entrusted with the gospel to the uncircumcised, just as Peter with the gospel to the circumcised (for He who effectually worked for Peter in his apostleship to the circumcised effectually worked for me also to the Gentiles), and recognizing the grace that had been given to me, James and Cephas and John, who were reputed to be pillars, gave to me and Barnabas the right hand of fellowship, that we might go to the Gentiles, and they to the circumcised. They only asked us to remember the poor – the very thing I also was eager to do.[30]

From this account of the private meeting, it appears that as soon as the three older apostles heard Paul's statement of the case, they heartily approved it and indicated their approval by extending their right hands to him and Barnabas. The words "contributed nothing to me" are also important, for the question was whether or not the Gentiles had been taught their whole duty; if not, the older apostles would have "contributed something" to Paul and Barnabas. They would have urged (had it been obligatory on Christians) that Paul and Barnabas teach men to keep the Law.

From Galatians 2:3, it appears that in this private meeting the general issue was debated on an individual case. Titus was a Gentile convert to the Christian religion, and he was taken down to Jerusalem as a test case. 'Now what about this man? Is he a saved man or a lost man? He is an immersed believer; but he is not circumcised, and he does not observe the Law. What more, if anything, is necessary in his case?' Now observe what Paul says in Galatians! Titus was not compelled to be circumcised. Had the keeping of the Law been necessary in order to remain in good standing as a follower of Christ, they would have compelled Titus to submit to this requirement of the Law.

One other thing must be noticed before we leave this private meeting related in Galatians 2. With the information about the perfect understanding and agreement between the apostles in mind, we can understand the purpose of the second public meeting. It was not to figure out what they were going to believe: that had already been determined for them by revelation! The purpose of the second public meeting was to *enable the apostles to bring the whole church into agreement with themselves!* If we do not keep this thought in mind as we study the proceedings, we shall totally misunderstand them.

Returning then to verse 6 and the report of the second public meeting, we see the apostles taking the lead in the discussion, attempting to show all the people exactly what the true answer to the issue was.

15:7 – *And after there had been much debate, Peter stood up and said to them, "Brethren, you know that in the early days God made a choice among you, that by my mouth the Gentiles should hear the word of the gospel and believe.*

And after there had been much debate. The Greek word here is the same as was translated "debate" in verse 2; and though it is not the usual word for "debate" (that word

---

[30] Galatians 2:6-10.

is *suzētēsis*), still it is unusual to find "questioning" (as per the ASV) in the middle of a sentence. This is why the NASB uses "debate" as a translation.[31] It seems that as the second public meeting opens, both sides are again heard presenting the points at issue.

> Men who are in error can never be convinced that they are wrong by denying them freedom of speech. Not until they have been allowed to express themselves to the last word are they capable of listening dispassionately to the other side. The apostles, knowing this, or at least acting on it, permitted the Judaizers in the church to say all they wished to say before any reply was made to their position and arguments.[32]

When the Judaizers have run out of arguments, then the apostles, one by one, and in an order that was perhaps prearranged during their private meeting, rise to explain God's will in such a way as to bring the church into agreement with their divinely-inspired conclusion.

Peter stood up and said to them. Peter had been the first of the apostles to go to the Gentiles and offer salvation to them (Acts 10-11). He was the logical one to introduce the apostolic doctrine in this issue.[33]

Brethren, you know that in the early days. If "early days" (literally "of ancient days") refers to the conversion of Cornelius, it has been ten years since God made the choice of Peter. It could be, however, that Peter is thinking back over twenty years, to the time when Jesus spoke to Peter at Caesarea Philippi about the keys to the kingdom.[34]

God made a choice among you. "Made a choice" is in the middle voice: God did it for His own benefit. What God chose to do is specifically stated by the two infinitives that follow – (1) the Gentiles are to "hear" and "believe," and (2) it was God's choice that Peter be the human instrument in the initial conversion of the Gentiles.

That by my mouth the Gentiles should hear the word of the gospel and believe. Cornelius and his relatives were the first Gentiles to be invited to become Christians, and it was done by God's choice. Remember how He sent His angel to Cornelius and a vision and a message from the Spirit to Peter to make His directions and will very plain in the matter! It was God's choice that the Gentiles "*believe*" – not keep the Law – Peter tells the Conference attendees. "Hear ... and believe" reminds us of Romans 10. Faith comes how? By hearing the Word! "Faith comes by hearing" has thus far been a theme in Acts, and we will continue to find it thus throughout the remainder of the book.[35]

---

[31] If we retain the translation "questioning" (ASV), then we might picture the opening of the second meeting as a time each side tried to present its position chiefly by asking questions — which is a very common way of putting an adversary at a disadvantage.

[32] McGarvey, *op. cit.*, p.62.

[33] In passing, it might be noted that Peter's position is that of any other apostle at this meeting. He is not pre-eminent; he neither called the meeting to order, nor dismissed it. If any apostle is pre-eminent, it is James, not Peter.

[34] Matthew 16:13-20.

[35] See Romans 10:17.

15:8 – *"And God, who knows the heart, bore witness to them, giving them the Holy Spirit, just as He also did to us;*

And God, who knows the heart, bore witness to them. Since God is able to read men's hearts,[36] He knew whether Cornelius and those with him were true believers or not. The coming of the Spirit, after God examined their hearts, was evidence that He approved of what Peter was doing – even though Peter was not demanding observance of the Law from these Gentiles.

Giving them the Holy Spirit. See Acts 10:45-46.

Just as He also did to us. See Acts 2:2-4, where the apostles ("us") received the baptism with the Holy Spirit.

15:9 – *"and He made no distinction between us and them, cleansing their hearts by faith.*

And He made no distinction between us and them. Though Cornelius and those other Gentiles at Caesarea had not been circumcised, and though they did not conform to all the requirements of the Law, still God accepted them.

Cleansing their hearts by faith. Perhaps Peter's choice of the word "cleansing" is because the Conference was disputing the question of purity, which the Pharisees insisted came through observance of the ceremonial law and circumcision. The real uncleanness of the Gentiles was not so much in externals, as the Jews thought, but in the heart; and for that, faith, not circumcision, was the remedy. There was no distinction between Jew and Gentile as far as the terms of forgiveness of sins was concerned; neither was "cleansed" by keeping the Law. Both Jew and Gentile alike had to hear the same gospel, believe the same gospel, repent of their sins, and be immersed into Christ for the forgiveness of their sins.

15:10 – *"Now therefore why do you put God to the test by placing upon the neck of the disciples a yoke which neither our fathers nor we have been able to bear?*

Now therefore why do you put God to the test. A child puts his parents to the test when he tries to get by with contradicting the expressed will of the parents. Will the parents let him get by, or not? Peter's question has this implication: 'Why are you acting as though God made a mistake when He gave the Holy Spirit to the household of Cornelius and accepted them without circumcision? God has expressed His will. You don't think you can get by with contradicting that, do you? If you continue to argue for the necessity of circumcision, you will only be going against His manifest will. And in that opposition you will bring on yourselves His displeasure.'

By placing upon the neck of the disciples a yoke. A "yoke" is a figurative expression, in this case, for something burdensome and oppressive – something which would greatly

---

[36] The expression "knower of hearts" was used by Peter earlier in Acts. See comments at Acts 1:24.

infringe upon the freedom that a person who is in Christ has.[37] Peter seems to have the Law in view, more than the traditions of the Pharisees, when he speaks of a yoke.

Which neither our fathers nor we have been able to bear. "Our fathers" would not be Abraham, Isaac, and Jacob, who were not under the Law, but would be those Israelites, after Moses, who lived under the Mosaic code. Peter's words are an appeal to the consciences of the Jews. They knew the Law couldn't be kept faithfully, so why demand that the Gentiles be forced to try?

If people could not keep the Law,[38] of what value was it, some might ask. Elsewhere in the New Testament this question is answered. The Law was given in order that men would better know what things were sin. The Law defined sin. The Law helped men come to see the exceeding sinfulness of sin. It demanded conformity with the will of God, but gave men no help for living according to His will. The Law's real purpose was to help prepare men for the salvation that Jesus offered, because they would be keenly conscious of their sins and the need for forgiveness.

Peter had now made several points in his portion of the apostolic presentation. He had been directed by God to offer the gospel to the Gentiles. It was God's choice that the condition be "belief" rather than Law-keeping. God even gave evidence of His endorsement by giving the Gentiles at Cornelius' house the baptism with the Holy Spirit. Throughout this Christian dispensation, all people (Jew or Gentile) are saved by faith, and to insist otherwise is to put God to the test. Now we come to Peter's conclusion.

15:11 – *"But we believe that we are saved through the grace of the Lord Jesus, in the same way as they also are."*

But we believe. "We apostles." This is our settled belief, says Peter, speaking for all the apostles, whom he perhaps includes with a sweep of his arm as he speaks. Peter is merely reiterating what had already been preached, and reaffirmed in the private meeting.

That we are saved through the grace of the Lord Jesus. Salvation was not to come through circumcision or keeping the Law for even the Jews (whom Peter here calls "we"). The Jew's hope (and the Gentile's, too) of salvation was found in the death and resurrection of Christ,[39] not in their own efforts to earn or merit salvation by works of Law.

In the same way as they also are. Peter is saying, 'We Jews, in fact, are saved in the same way as the Gentiles. Not even we Jews are saved by the keeping of the Law. Instead, we

---

[37] See verse 31. See also Galatians 2:4, 5:1.

[38] Only one person ever kept the Law perfectly: Jesus alone fulfilled it, and all its responsibilities. Not only that, but He fulfilled all its types and prophecies. "I have not come to destroy, but to fulfill," said Jesus (Matthew 5:17). Peter is not speaking of Jesus, but of men, when he says no Jew ever kept the Law of Moses perfectly.

[39] "Through grace" (*dia* and the genitive case) here is a slightly different expression than "by grace" (a dative case) in Ephesians 2:8. The expression here in Acts speaks of all that Jesus did to save mankind. Neither passage should be understood to mean that a "first work of grace" is involved in the preparing of any individual heart so that it may be receptive to the gospel. This latter idea, made popular by Calvin s theology, is foreign to the New Testament teaching on salvation.

are saved through the grace of the Lord Jesus, just as the Gentiles are.'

"Saved through Grace" – these are the last recorded words of Peter in the book of Acts.[40] These words should have been enough to end the whole controversy, but it was wisely planned among the apostles that the evidence on the subject should be multiplied in such a way as to leave no room for more controversy or more questions.

15:12 – *And all the multitude kept silent, and they were listening to Barnabas and Paul as they were relating what signs and wonders God had done through them among the Gentiles.*

And all the multitude kept silent. The whole assembly became silent after Peter's speech. The silence is testimony to the effect of Peter's presentation. He had presented such clear and forcible arguments that there was nothing that could be said against them.

And they were listening to Barnabas and Paul. After Peter sat down, Barnabas spoke next, and then Paul, each setting forth other evidences of God's will on the question at issue. They are repeating in public what they had already shared in the private meeting. The verb "were listening" is in the imperfect tense, indicating sustained hearing. Both made a lengthy presentation of their missionary activities, Barnabas speaking first because he was the more familiar and accepted figure at Jerusalem.

As they were relating what signs and wonders. The two apostles set forth in detail all the miracles worked on the first missionary journey. Such an appeal to miracles was exactly the kind of appeal that would convince Jews.[41]

God had done through them among the Gentiles. Just as Peter had done, so Barnabas and Paul now do. They appeal to what *God* had done! Peter had appealed to what God did to show His approval of Cornelius, even though Cornelius was uncircumcised. Barnabas and Paul continue the same idea, showing how God indicated His approval of the Gentile converts in Asia Minor. The miracles that God wrought through Barnabas and Paul among the Gentiles there were evidence that God approved their ministry among those Gentiles. Churches had been organized without circumcision being required, and without requiring them to keep the Law. Since God approved the Gentiles without circumcision, it therefore followed that it was not needful to command Gentiles anywhere to begin now to keep the Law of Moses.

15:13 – *And after they had stopped speaking, James answered, saying, "Brethren, listen to me.*

And after they had stopped speaking. "Stopped speaking" is the same verb in the Greek as was translated "kept silent" in the previous verse. So far on this day's agenda there has been a general debate in which all who wished took part; then Peter told of the beginning

---

[40] Other sources relate some of Peter's subsequent work and words – his visit to Antioch (Galatians 2:11), the two letters that bear his name, and his death in Rome.

[41] Compare notes at Acts 2:22 on the words "signs and wonders." See also Matthew 12:38, 16:1; John 3:2; 1 Corinthians 1:22.

of the gospel's spread among the Gentiles; then Barnabas and Paul have spoken of what God did for the Gentiles through them. The clear conclusion of all this is that God does not require a man to be circumcised or to keep the Law in order to be saved. Now James will make the final presentation of the apostles' doctrine.

James answered, saying. This is James, the Lord's brother.[42] If this were a present-day meeting, we would say that James was acting as chairman of the meeting, and it was left to him to summarize the whole presentation. There is no evidence that he alone made the final decision – a decision which all the others were duty-bound to accept. The decision which he here presents is the one which all the Holy Spirit-inspired apostles had been led to agree upon, in the private meeting. In fact, they had agreed to this even before the Conference, as they went where the Spirit led and preached what He led them to preach.

Brethren, listen to me. What James says can be summarized under two points: (1) what the Old Testament prophets said about the reception of the Gentiles, and (2) his judgment about the conditions to be met by the Gentile converts if they wished to remain in God's favor.[43]

15:14 – *"Simeon has related how God first concerned Himself about taking from among the Gentiles a people for His name.*

Simeon has related how God first concerned Himself about taking from among the Gentiles a people for His name. "Simeon" is the Hebrew spelling of Peter's name. It is very natural that James should use the Hebrew form, for he shows himself to be thoroughly Jewish in many of his words and actions.[44] The only other place we find the Hebrew spelling of Peter's name is his own use of it in the signature of 2 Peter. James uses a title for these Gentile converts that the Jews had always reserved for themselves exclusively. They alone were the "people;" the rest of mankind were the "nations" – the Gentiles. By using this title, James is implying that the Gentile converts were no less the people of God than Israel used to be.[45] "For His name" may mean that these people bear His name as a people of God, or it may mean that they are considered His special people.

---

[42] See Galatians 1:19; and Special Study #2, "The Brothers of the Lord," where the problem of the identification of "James, the brother of the Lord" is explained. Concerning the position held by James in the Jerusalem church, see notes at Acts 21:18. It is likely that this James is the author of the epistle of James. See also footnote # 4.

[43] Barnes (*op. cit.*, p.229) drives home the suggestion that the action of this Conference shows that Peter had no such authority as the Roman Catholic Church contends, for otherwise his opinion would have been law without further talk.

[44] James was not one to compromise the articles of the Christian faith, yet his personal practices were Jewish enough that people from Jerusalem could claim his example as a precedent for their own strict adherence to Jewish customs (Galatians 2:12). See also James' effort to conciliate the Jewish Christians in later years (Acts 21:18ff).

[45] Compare Romans 9:24-26; 1 Peter 2:9-10 (where even the descriptive phrases that used to be applied exclusively to Israel, are now applied to spiritual Israel, the Church).

15:15 – *"And with this the words of the Prophets agree, just as it is written,*

And with this the words of the Prophets agree. It was very important with the Jews to appeal to the Old Testament Scriptures for evidence of any claims being making. James quotes only one prophet, Amos. His use of the plural "prophets" may be another example of quoting from the book of the prophets.[46] Other Old Testament prophets had also foretold the acceptance of the Gentiles: see Isaiah 2:2-4, 49:6; Micah 4:1-4. A list of Old Testament prophecies about the Gentiles becoming God's people is found in Romans 15:9-11.

Just as it is written. The following quotation, from Amos 9:11-12, is an exact quotation of neither the Hebrew nor the Septuagint, yet the main point from the passage that James is stressing rests on a clause found in the LXX and not the Hebrew. It is from the LXX reading of Amos that James is able to find proof that, according to the prophets, it was predicted that the Gentiles should be accepted into God's favor.

A brief review of Amos' predictions may be helpful here, for it may help us to see what a Jew who was familiar with Amos would be thinking as he hears James' appeal to this Old Testament passage. Amos, in the verses just prior to the ones James quotes, predicted the fall of the Jewish nation, including the overthrow of the house (tabernacle) of David whose descendants were reigning as kings at the time Amos made his prediction. Then in the verses James quotes, Amos predicts the rebuilding of the house of David; that is, that one of David's descendants would again reign as king. The fall of the Jewish nation came as Amos predicted; yet between the time of that fall and the time when James was speaking, none of David's descendants had become king. When Jesus was enthroned in heaven at the time of His ascension, He began to fulfill Amos' prophecy. Jesus reigns on David's throne as Lord; and once He reigns as Lord, the Gentiles are pictured as seeking the Lord's favor. That is exactly what Gentiles have been doing, ever since Peter's visit to Cornelius' house. What the prophet Amos predicted, James says, is coming true in the conversion of the Gentiles by the gospel.

15:16 – *'AFTER THESE THINGS I will return, AND I WILL REBUILD THE TABERNACLE OF DAVID WHICH HAS FALLEN, AND I WILL REBUILD ITS RUINS, AND I WILL RESTORE IT,*

AFTER THESE THINGS I will return. In Amos, "after these things" means after the predicted chastisement of Israel by the Babylonians. "I will return" is an addition to the prophecy by James; there is nothing in the Hebrew or LXX answering to it, though it may be affirmed that the Hebrew implies it.

AND I WILL REBUILD THE TABERNACLE OF DAVID WHICH HAS FALLEN. "Tabernacle" is not a reference to the temple which was the work of Solomon, nor to the "tabernacle of testimony" which was the work of Moses. The reference is apparently to the Davidic monarchy,[47] which figuratively was no palatial thing in Amos' day, but simply the equivalent of a hut or a "tent." (The Hebrew word speaks of a temporary structure made

---

[46] See this phrase explained at Acts 13:40.

[47] The Davidic *monarchy* – the throne of David – is poetically spoken of as a "tabernacle" in 2 Samuel 7:12.

of boughs and branches.) The monarchy had fallen onto very hard times because of the Babylonian captivity. Amos predicted that the time would come when God would restore one of David's offspring to a position of reigning monarch.

AND I WILL REBUILD ITS RUINS. The Hebrew reads, "I will close up the breaches thereof." When the Babylonians captured Jerusalem, buildings were destroyed, and great gaping holes were left in the walls the city. These words of Amos predict those holes will be patched and closed up. Perhaps Amos was making a veiled reference to the Divided Kingdom, and the suggestion that God would "wall-up the breaches thereof."

AND I WILL RESTORE IT. We have Messianic prophecy in Mosaic terminology in this passage. It is not that the literal city of Jerusalem in Palestine was to be rebuilt and restored. Rather, it is a prophecy that in the Messianic age God would erect a kingdom, and then the Gentiles would be gathered into it. This Messianic kingdom began on the day of Pentecost (Acts 2).

15:17 – 'IN ORDER THAT THE REST OF MANKIND MAY SEEK THE LORD, AND ALL THE GENTILES WHO ARE CALLED BY MY NAME,'

IN ORDER THAT THE REST OF MANKIND MAY SEEK THE LORD. Here is the phrase from the LXX on which James' argument hinges.[48] The Hebrew text reads, "that they may possess the remnant of Edom," but it takes only a slight change of spelling to get to the word "mankind" (*adam*) used in the LXX instead of "Edom." The translators of the LXX, and James, too, understand that Amos was referring to others than the Jews – i.e., to the Gentiles, the rest of the world. Amos was predicting that many of those who were not Jews would seek the Lord after God's Messianic kingdom was set up and one of David's descendants (i.e., the Christ) sat on the throne of David.

AND ALL THE GENTILES WHO ARE CALLED BY MY NAME. The marginal reading "upon whom My name is called" is easier to understand. It means that Gentiles would be called "God's people." This phrase in the LXX lacks a verb, but we would naturally supply "seek the Lord" from the previous phrase. Amos is thus saying, "The Gentiles who are called God's people *shall seek the Lord*." This was a clear prediction that other nations besides Israel would be blessed by God, and that blessing was given without any mention of their conforming to the Law of Moses.

15:18 – "SAYS THE LORD, WHO MAKES THESE THINGS KNOWN FROM OF OLD.

SAYS THE LORD, WHO MAKES THESE THINGS KNOWN FROM OF OLD. The margin gives a variant reading, "who does these things which were known from of old." According to the marginal reading, the admission of the Gentiles was not an innovation, but was in harmony with the plans and purposes God formed back in eternity before creation, and so is part of the work He carries on now. Reading as does the text, James'

---

[48] James may be very Jewish in many of his personal practices (see footnote #44), but he is not so Jewish in his personal habits that he won't use the Greek language Septuagint translation.

argument (in the words of Amos) is this: 'Since God has foretold a long time ago that the Gentiles would be a part of the kingdom, without circumcision, it should not be opposed and resisted by us. We rather should get our ideas in harmony with God's revealed will!'

15:19 – *"Therefore it is my judgment that we do not trouble those who are turning to God from among the Gentiles,*

Therefore it is my judgment. That is, James say, 'In the light of the harmony among the inspired apostles (as evidenced in the private meeting), and in the light of what Peter and the others have shown today about God's own action and will in this case, and in the light of the very clear predictions of the Old Testament, my inspired judgment is ....' The Greek here is emphatic. James is speaking as the president of the meeting, and in harmony with this his name is listed first in Galatians 2:9.

That we do not trouble those who are turning to God from among the Gentiles. Our word "harass" rather catches the idea of the word "trouble." To demand of the Gentile Christians more than the things about to be listed would cause unnecessary difficulty for them. "Turning" is a present participle, and suggests that even as the council is meeting Gentiles are being converted to Christ.[49] The "turning" is a process constantly going that began before the Jerusalem Conference met and would continue long after. None of these converts must be "troubled," says James. It would be a trouble if the burdensome restrictions of the Law of Moses were required for salvation.

15:20 – *"but that we write to them that they abstain from things contaminated by idols and from fornication and from what is strangled and from blood.*

But that we write to them. James urges that the leaders of the church (verse 23) write a letter to the new congregations of Gentile believers, and explain to them in writing exactly what the inspired apostles teach. This will leave no opportunity for the Judaizers to again misrepresent what Gentiles have to do to be saved, for the Gentiles will have a specific word from the Lord on the matter.

That they abstain. "Abstain" is a present middle infinitive, which indicates that they are to continue to abstain from these things for their own benefit. They have been abstaining, and let them continue to abstain!

When we ask the question, "Why does James think the Gentile Christians should abstain?" we have raised one of the most difficult problems to answer that there is in all of the book of Acts. Several answers that have been proposed for this question.

1) *James is offering a compromise solution to the issue being discussed.* In favor of this it may be said: (a) The four conditions about to be given were the same required by the Pharisees of a Gentile who would become a proselyte of the gate. Surely the Pharisaic Judaizers could accept Gentiles into fellowship in the church on these conditions, if for years they have been accepting people into Judaism who met the very same conditions. (b) One way disputes are often settled is to give both sides a part of

---

[49] See notes at Acts 8:35 on the phrase "turn to God."

what they ask, and to refuse both sides a part of what they ask. The Gentile Christians had asked for freedom from all the Law of Moses. The Judaizers had demanded adherence to all the Law. In the compromise solution, each got a part of what they asked.[50] Against the idea that James' "judgment" was a compromise solution, it may be said: (i) The whole tone of the decree is that the claims of the Judaizers were rejected *in toto*. The Judaizers were just wrong in the matter.[51] (ii) We cannot picture James as appealing to certain provisions in the Law of Moses, and insisting that Christians must keep these. The Law of Moses never was and never will be binding on Christians; it has been abrogated, being nailed to the cross. Any explanation of James' reason for demanding abstention from certain things because the Law of Moses requires such abstention is clearly based on a false premise.

2) *The abstention James demands is nothing more than the Noahic Commandments required of all Gentiles.* According to rabbinic interpretation of Genesis, the whole race was commanded to observe seven basic moral laws: obey civil authorities, no idolatry, no profaning God's name, no fornication, no murder, no theft, no eating of meat with blood in it.[52] Although the Noahic Covenant is still binding even in the Christian age, it was given so long ago, and only passed down among the Gentiles from generation to generation by oral tradition, that in the intervening years it came to be forgotten, ignored, and even willfully changed by men who were plunging deeper into sin. Because James recognizes that these moral laws are still binding on mankind, whether Jew or Gentile, he urges that the Gentiles, who have never had a written revelation in which they were embodied, now be given one.[53]

3) *James urges abstention in four areas where temptations were particularly strong for these new Christians from among the Gentiles who were living in the midst of an idolatrous, immoral society.* These were areas where the Gentile Christians needed special warning, especially since their background did not give them much warning that these temptations could be particularly deceptive and ruinous. Indeed, the early Christians did have trouble with these particular temptations, as shall be shown in the notes on the following phrases.

Perhaps the full reason why James, by inspiration (verse 28), insists on abstention from the four things, lies somewhere in a combination of (2) and (3) above. There are moral laws binding on all mankind, and there are temptations that must be particularly guarded against. James would have the new converts to be especially aware of both of these.

---

[50] Some New Testament scholars affirm that the Jerusalem decree was never appealed to by Christian preachers once it was delivered to the Gentile churches planted before and during the first missionary journey. These scholars affirm that it proved to be only a temporary solution because it satisfied no one. However, this reasoning is hard to accept when we remember it was a Holy Spirit-inspired decree (Acts 15:28). And, in fact, there are places where the teachings of the decree are in the background as Paul and John write their letters — e.g., 1 Corinthians 8-10 and Revelation 2:14-24.

[51] See verses 24 and 25. See also Galatians 2:4.

[52] Noachide Laws, *Universal Jewish Encyclopedia* (New York: Universal Jewish Encyclopedia Inc., 1942), Vol. VIII, p.227-228. See also *Tractate Sanhedrin*, 56 (Talmud).

[53] Against the suggestion that James has the Noahic Commandments in mind, it has been urged that the four things specified in the Jerusalem decree are hard to match with any but two of the Noahic prohibitions.

From things contaminated by idols. The marginal reading ("from the pollutions of idols") actually represents the Greek in this verse better than the text of the NASB. The word "pollutions" here is actually a wider term than is finally written into the decree (verse 29). *Alisgēma* not only speaks of pollution from the flesh used in heathen idol sacrifices, but also would require getting rid of the busts and statues of the gods that used to be found in the houses and gardens of these converts.

"Pollutions of idols" is further clarified in verse 29 as being "things sacrificed to idols." What was a "thing sacrificed to an idol"? A heathen decides he will worship his favorite deity. He selects an animal for the sacrifice, usually an ox. The ox was taken to the heathen temple, where the tail was cut off, and the tail would be burned on a sacrificial altar. The rest of the animal was then roasted and used for a feast. All the worshiper's friends were invited. What this group would not eat was given to the priests in charge of the idol's temple. If there were several parties coming to the temple to sacrifice on any given day, the priests could not possibly eat all that was left of the several sacrificial animals. So the priests sold the remains to the local butcher. In fact, some idol's temples had a butcher shop right next door, operated as an adjunct of the temple. The butcher would in turn offer the meat for sale to the townspeople, with the profit going to the temple where the meat was originally offered in sacrifice to the idol.

What is meant, then, by "abstaining from things contaminated by idols"? Paul tells us what is meant in 1 Corinthians 10:14-33. He there tells the Corinthians not to go to the idol's temple to eat (see especially 10:20-22). However, the meat that a person might purchase in the marketplace, he was allowed to eat, with no worry about it (see 10:25). Abstaining from the contamination of idols means, "Do not go to the idol's temple and participate in the feasts held there!"

The early Christians had difficulty, in some places, living by this restriction. Some Christians at Corinth claimed the right to eat what they chose, because the idol was nothing.[54] At Pergamum and Thyatira, about 45 years later, some actually argued that it was perfectly proper to go to the idol's temple, that it even helped one be a better Christian![55] Jesus' condemnation of such arguments (Revelation 2.14ff) shows He considered the Jerusalem Conference decree to be still binding.

And from fornication. The word used here is applied (depending on the context) to any one of several forms of illicit sexual intercourse, sometimes adultery, sometimes incest, sometimes marriage within forbidden degrees, and sometimes prostitution. Really, it is a general term including both premarital and extra-marital relations – and it forbids both! Among Christians there is to be no sexual license!

Bible scholars have struggled to explain exactly what James had in mind when he introduced this prohibition into the list. Each of the above specific forms of the sin have been made the topic thought to be in James' mind, but it seems to this commentator to be best simply to leave the prohibition stand in its general form as noted above. The term is very broad, and none of the violations of this prohibition are actually innocent (as some in our time would maintain).

---

[54] 1 Corinthians 8-10.

[55] Revelation 2:14,20,24.

There are specific reasons why it was very fitting for James to include this particular sin in the decree. Fornication is named in the list immediately following idolatry, and some use this fact as a key to explain the verse. Idolatry does degrade a person's morals. Thus, often included in the "worship" of the pagan deities was a visit to one of the harlot priestesses at the temple. It was believed that the man, by entering into relations with the priestess, was identified with or came into union with the god in whose service she was employed. In many of the cults, every woman was expected, once a year, as part of her devotion to the god, to go up to the idol's temple and offer herself to any man who might also be coming to the temple. No wonder the women in the ancient world had difficulty having any sense of self-respecting purity, and no wonder the men had little reverence for womanhood! Finally, remember that many pagans look upon fornication in any of its forms as no more wrong than getting a drink when one is thirsty, or eating when one is hungry. So the Gentile Christians are being asked to take a stand in an effort to purify the morals of mankind. Since there were few outcries against this very debasing sin in the Gentile world, the Christians needed a special word, lest their morals soon cause them to lose their new-found salvation in Christ.

And from what is strangled. That is, animals or fowl that have not been properly bled when being butchered are not to be used for food. However, as with "and from fornication," as commentators have looked at the practices of the ancient world in an effort to find the particular thing that is prohibited, they have been hard pressed to determine an exact meaning for this phrase.

- Because it has not been easy to distinguish between this and the next prohibition ("and from blood"), many commentators have agreed with the Western text and omitted this phrase. Indeed, the Western text is consistent, for the phrase is omitted here, in verse 29, and at Acts 21:25. In the place of this prohibition that is omitted, the Western text adds the "Golden Rule" as a command the Gentile Christians are to live by.

- Some commentators think this rule would require Christians to buy meat and poultry from a market where the meat was *kosher* because it had been killed according to the prescriptions taught in the Old Testament. Yet this does not seem to be a right interpretation. In 1 Corinthians 10, as he expounds the decree of the Jewish Conference, Paul teaches that while Christians are prohibited from attending feasts at the idol's temple, they are permitted to purchase meat at any market, even those affiliated with the idol's temple.

- Another idea that has gained some following is that all four of these prohibitions are made against a background of idolatrous worship, including witchcraft and the occult. More and more, as this ancient "religion" sweeps across America, there is evidence that the worship involves cutting the heart out of the sacrificial victim and eating it while it is still beating. Whether or not such practices were in James' mind when he uttered this third prohibition, the practices would be unthinkable for the Christian in the light of his command to abstain from flesh with blood in it.

And from blood. Several interpretations have been put on this prohibition, especially as scholars try to distinguish it from the previous one.

- Some think it refers to abstaining from shedding blood (i.e., not to commit murder).[56]
- A better idea is that men are not to eat or drink blood, as was common among the Greeks and Romans. They often drank it in their sacrificial feasts in toasts to the god, or when making covenants or compacts. This injunction would, of course, rule out such dishes as blood pudding.
- Again, it has been noted that one of the practices in many occult circles is to drain the blood from the mutilated carcasses of the sacrificial victim and to drink it as part of the worship. This explains why little blood is found near the mutilated victims. Perhaps this is what James has in mind as he urges the propriety of this prohibition.

Once more we must pay attention to the matter of the Law and the Gospel. When it is affirmed that the Law is no longer binding, it must be remembered that there are covenants in the Old Testament which precede the Mosaic, and which are still binding. Among these that are still-binding covenants would be the one made with Adam, the one with Abraham, and the one with Noah.

> The four things, from which James proposed that the Gentiles should be required to abstain, had been made unlawful, not by the Mosaic Law, but by the revelations of the Patriarchal Age. From the beginning it had been known to the Patriarchs that it was sinful to have any responsible connection with idols, or to indulge in fornication; and from the time of the law given to the race in the family of Noah (Genesis 9:4), eating blood and consequently eating things strangled which retained their blood within them had been wrong; and so will continue to the end of the world.[57]

15:21 – *"For Moses from ancient generations has in every city those who preach him, since he is read in the synagogues every Sabbath."*

For Moses from ancient generations. How far back "ancient generations" takes us is disputed, but it is at least as far back as the time when the captivities caused the Jews to be scattered among the pagan nations.

Notice, this verse begins with "for," which means either that James is further explaining something just said, or is giving a reason for something just said. Different views are given for why James appealed to what Moses' Law taught. (1) Some affirm that James is answering an objection the Judaizers had advanced; namely, that if such freedom were granted to the Gentiles, the Law of Moses would decline in authority. James is thus assuring them that the Law would not fall into disrepute since it was read every week in the synagogue services. However, this explanation fails to take into account that the Law had been nailed to the cross, and was indeed no longer binding. (2) Others conjecture that these words were spoken in an effort to promote peace and harmony between the Gentile and Jewish Christians. If the Gentiles did not keep at least these four prohibitions, it would only tend to keep alive the antagonism between the Jewish Christians and their uncircumcised brethren who had complete freedom from the Law of Moses. James is thought to be

---

[56] This interpretation of "abstaining from blood" is tied up with the Western text, which omits the third prohibition. If we reject the Western text, we will probably reject the interpretation that the thing to be abstained from is murdering.

[57] McGarvey, *op. cit.*, p.67.

saying that Jews are to be found everywhere and their scruples are to be respected. There may be some truth in this suggestion, for Christians are taught to beware of being a stumbling block to others. (3) The best explanation, and the one with which this commentator tends to agree, is that James is giving a reason why there was need to write only to the Gentiles (verse 19 and 23), and not also to the Jewish Christians. James says that the Jewish Christians have the writings of Moses, and so do not need such instructions as these. But the Gentiles, who are without written revelation, need to be given these prohibitions.[58]

Has in every city those who preach him, since he is read in the synagogues every Sabbath. See notes at Acts 13:15 and Special Study #15 concerning the reading of the Law and the Prophets during the Sabbath services in the synagogues. In addition to reading the Law, it was customary to offer an explanation and application of the passages read. Thus Moses has those who "preach" him.

Do these words imply that James assumes the Christians from Jewish background will continue to be worshiping in the synagogue long after their conversion? Probably so! We picture these new Christians not only as meeting on the Sabbath with the Jews (what an opportunity to teach and witness to the unconverted Jews!), but as also breaking bread on the first day of the week.[59]

15:22 – *Then it seemed good to the apostles and the elders, with the whole church, to choose men from among them to send to Antioch with Paul and Barnabas – Judas called Barsabbas, and Silas, leading men among the brethren,*

Then it seemed good to the apostles and the elders. The presentation by James brought the Jerusalem Conference to a close. The combined force of the four speeches made the will of God so clear that the opposition was totally silenced, and the only remaining question was how best to carry out the proposal submitted by James. That the "elders" are here named right after the apostles does not mean they were equal in authority, but rather expresses their concurrence in the decision to which the apostles have led the brethren.

With the whole church. The intent of this second public meeting was to bring the church into agreement with the apostles. Here is evidence that this goal has been reached. A unanimous decision it was – including even the wishes of the members of the Jerusalem congregation – that men be sent to accompany Paul and Barnabas to Antioch, and there repeat the decision held by the Jerusalem church after the teaching by the apostles.

We are not told how the congregation expressed its concurrence with the apostolic teaching. Perhaps it was by some method of voting. However, even if the congregation formally voted their approval, that was not what gave the decree its authority. The decree had authority since it was given by the Holy Spirit-directed apostles (verse 28) – the ones who have always been recognized as the universal, God-approved leaders of the church.

---

[58] This explanation of verse 21 does not contradict the idea that the Law of Moses is no longer binding. The Adamic, Abrahamic, and Noahic covenants are all recorded in Moses' writings, and these are still valid even to Jews.

[59] Watch throughout the rest of Acts to see the early Christians' practices as far as the day of worship is concerned.

To choose men from among them to send to Antioch with Paul and Barnabas. This was a wise move on the part of the brethren at Jerusalem, for it would guard against suspicion. Had Paul and Barnabas alone returned to Antioch, even with the letter, the Judaizers could have said, "They just forged the letter in order to deceive you." But when leading men from the Jerusalem church accompany the letter, and they say "This indeed is the true conclusion of the Conference, and the practice of the Jerusalem church," there is no way the Judaizers can explain that away. Note, too, that the sending of these men along with the letter was one of the things that seemed good to the entire church.

Judas called Barsabbas. Many are of the opinion that this is the same man who was nominated to fill the vacant place in the apostleship (Acts 1:23). But since one is called Joseph Barsabbas and one is called Judas Barsabbas, if there is any relation at all, perhaps the idea that they were brothers is the right idea. If so, if the natural inference is that the two were brothers, the disciple now named was also one of the personal followers of Jesus, just as was the one nominated to be an apostle.

And Silas. This is the man who will afterward accompany Paul on his second missionary journey.[60] He is also certainly to be identified with Silvanus who is included with Paul in the opening sentence of the Thessalonian letters[61] – letters written during the second missionary journey. Silas is also named as the one whom Peter used in the writing of 1 Peter.[62] He traveled with Paul as far as Corinth on the second missionary journey. If Peter came to Corinth after that (and 1 Corinthians 1:12 and 9:5 indicate he did), perhaps that is when Silas became associated with Peter.

Leading men among the brethren. Exactly what position in the church a "leading man" had, has been difficult to determine. In verse 32, these same men are called "prophets." The same word translated "leading men" in this verse is rendered "leaders" in Hebrews 13:7,17,24, and "*chief* speaker" in Acts 14:12. If we consider the possibility that these men may also have been among the personal witnesses of Jesus' earthly ministry, then we have some idea of the respect in which they were held in the early church. They would have been working as leaders in the church at Jerusalem, and would have been recognized as preachers whose messages were inspired ("prophets"), and as men who should be given a special attention because they had personally heard Jesus.

15:23 – *and they sent this letter by them, "The apostles and the brethren who are elders, to the brethren in Antioch and Syria and Cilicia who are from the Gentiles, greetings.*

And they sent this letter by them. That is, the letter was carried by Silas and Judas. Since the document incorporates several expressions found elsewhere in the New Testament only in the epistle of James, we may conclude that the letter was drawn up chiefly by him, yet with the approval of the others who are included in the signature. This is one of the earliest documents, so far as we know, that was written by any apostle. It may be that Matthew's

---

[60] Acts 15:40, 16:25, 16:29, 17:4, 17:10, 17:15; 2 Corinthians 1:19.

[61] 1 Thessalonians 1:1; 2 Thessalonians 1:1.

[62] 1 Peter 5:12.

Gospel has been written by this time; but other than that, this letter antedated all the Gospels and Epistles in the New Testament. Copies of it would have circulated among the churches until it was incorporated into Acts, after which those copies would likely be allowed to perish. That copies of it were circulated is indicated by the note about the decrees of the Jerusalem Conference being shared with all the churches (Acts 16:4).

The apostles and the brethren who are elders. The proper form for a letter in the 1st century was this: signature first, address second, and then a word of greeting, followed by the body of the letter. This letter composed at the close of the Jerusalem Conference follows the formal style of the day.

There is a manuscript variation in this verse, with the better ones omitting the conjunction and the article before the noun "brethren." This reading has both the apostles and elders calling themselves "brethren" of the readers in Syrian Antioch. The issue brought to Jerusalem seriously questioned whether the Gentiles were brethren. The opening of the letter already intimates what the rest of the letter will say.

To the brethren in Antioch and Syria and Cilicia who are from the Gentiles. The decision inculcated by the apostles during the second public meeting at Jerusalem affected all Gentile Christians in every country, but only Syria and Cilicia are addressed by name in the letter. Perhaps the address includes all the areas that had been thus far affected by Judaizing teachers. The city of Antioch is named first because it was there where the difficulty first came out into the open.

When were the churches established in Cilicia? Luke's record in Acts does not specifically say. Perhaps they were planted by Paul before he came to Antioch (Galatians 1:21; Acts 11:24ff). Or it may be that missionaries from Syrian Antioch had gone to Cilicia to evangelize, just as Paul and Barnabas had gone to Cyprus and Asia Minor. Whoever planted the churches there, Gentile converts were members of these congregations, and thus the letters are addressed to them.

Greetings. Literally the word expresses a wish on the sender's part for joy and happiness to the persons addressed. This particular word occurs only here, at Acts 23:26, and at James 1:1 in the New Testament. This is one of the things said to point to James as being the one who drew up this letter.

15:24 – *"Since we have heard that some of our number to whom we gave no instruction have disturbed you with their words, unsettling your souls,*

Since we have heard. The brethren at Jerusalem first heard about the Judaizers at Antioch when the delegation arrived in Jerusalem from Antioch.

That some of our number. The Judaizers were members (see verse 1) of the Jerusalem congregation before they undertook their trip to Antioch.

To whom we gave no instruction. The Judaizers had no authority from the Jerusalem church, though they evidently had claimed to have come from the mother church, sent by them on an official mission to Antioch. This opening paragraph of the letter sent to Antioch is an official denial that the Judaizers had ever been authorized or sent by the church at Jerusalem. We cannot help but wonder if the Judaizers were present in the assembly at Antioch when this epistle was read to the congregation, and if so, what their reaction was.

Have disturbed you with *their* words. The word "disturbed" has a number of connotations. Literally, it is used of waters that are "troubled." In a figurative sense the word means to stir up, disturb, throw into confusion, be agitated, or intimidated. "Words" here might have the connotation that they were mere words, words without true doctrine. They were just words; they weren't the truth. Nevertheless, such words can have a very serious, unsettling effect on men's minds.

Unsettling your souls. This verb occurs nowhere else in the New Testament. In classical Greek it meant "to collect together the vessels used in a house – the household furniture and silver – for the purpose of carrying it off." Then it meant to dismantle, to overthrow. Metaphorically, it can mean "to *break* a treaty" or "to *destroy* an opponent's arguments." Whenever a man's salvation is called in question, and it appears that the one who has asked the questions just might be right, it has a very unsettling effect on the mind. Interestingly, the verb is present tense – indicating that the Judaizers might still be at it. The Judaizers have been teaching doctrines which unsettled the minds of the Christians, and left them disturbed and anxious.

15:25 – *"it seemed good to us, having become of one mind, to select men to send to you with our beloved Barnabas and Paul,*

It seemed good to us, having become of one mind. This tells again that the apostles have brought all the members of the church in Jerusalem to the judgment in which they themselves had previously united as they met in the private meeting held between the two public meetings. The thing that seemed to be a good thing to do is stated in verses 26-29.

To select men to send to you with our beloved Barnabas and Paul. The names of the men selected will be introduced in verse 27. The word "beloved," plus the words of praise in verse 26, are intended to confirm and exalt Barnabas and Paul in the eyes of those who heard and read the letter. Perhaps the word "beloved" reflects what is stated in Galatians 2:9. The order in which the missionaries are named likely represents the estimate of the Jerusalem church, to whom Barnabas was still the more conspicuous of the two.

15:26 – *"men who have risked their lives for the name of our Lord Jesus Christ.*

Men who have risked their lives. It is clear from this that the suffering and narrow escapes during the first missionary journey were well-known in Jerusalem. We remember that the missionaries told the conference in detail about the first journey. That they risked their lives is called to the attention of the readers in order to secure more sympathy and respect for the two apostles.

For the name of our Lord Jesus Christ. In the cause of Christ, the two risked their lives.[63]

15:27 – *"Therefore we have sent Judas and Silas, who themselves will also report the same things by word of mouth.*

Therefore we have sent Judas and Silas. See verse 22. The verb "sent" is aorist tense, and is an example of what is called an "epistolary aorist." That is, the verb tense reflects the perspective of the readers of the letter, not the writers. The sending was past when the letter was finally delivered to the readers, even though as the letter is being penned Judas and Silas had in fact not yet made the trip.

Who themselves will also report the same things by the word *of mouth*. They, by word of mouth, would speak the same things as were contained in the letter. The verb "report" is present tense, suggesting that the writers actually think of Judas and Silas reporting right at the time the letter was received.

15:28 – *"For it seemed good to the Holy Spirit and to us to lay upon you no greater burden than these essentials:*

For it seemed good to the Holy Spirit and to us. This is a claim that the decision agreed upon by the Jerusalem Conference was inspired. The "one accord" to which they came (verse 25), and which they were passing on to the brethren at Antioch, was not merely men's opinion, but was the inspired will of God. "To us" seems to indicate that before the Jerusalem Conference, there were many in Jerusalem who would have been narrow in their attitudes toward the Gentile converts, but now they have been so taught that they too will admit the Gentiles.

To lay upon you no greater burden. "Burden" seems to be used in the sense of "restraints," of "rules by which to pattern one's behavior." To demand that the Gentiles keep all the restrictions of the Law of Moses would have been excessively burdensome, and likely would have driven people away from the gospel.

Than these essentials. The four restrictions about to be written were (1) "essential" to preserve the purity of the church, (2) "essential" to the circumstances of the Gentile converts who have just come out of heathenism, wherein a knowledge of God's will was greatly obscured, and (3) "essential" for their continuing salvation.

Some contend that these four restrictions were "essential" only for the time in which they were written, and are not at all standards of conduct demanded of present-day Christians. However, at verse 20, we have shown the abiding validity of these prohibitions. See also the comments given at verse 31.

---

[63] This is likely a good text for a sermon. It is doubtful if the church will ever amount to much until the people in it are willing to do as Paul and Barnabas did. Nor will the preachers ever sufficiently and efficiently carry the message until they come to the place where they are willing to hazard their lives for the cause of Christ.

15:29 – *"that you abstain from things sacrificed to idols and from blood and from things strangled and from fornication; if you keep yourselves free from such things, you will do well. Farewell."*

That you abstain from things sacrificed to idols. The wording here is much more specific than the wording ("the pollutions of idols") of verse 20. Abstaining from things sacrificed to idols would be accomplished if the Christians did not attend feasts in the idols' temples.

And from blood and from things strangled and from fornication. See these words explained in the comments on verse 20.

If you keep yourselves free from such things, you will do well. That is, you will be doing all that is necessary to remain in Christ. No circumcision nor a minute observance of the Mosaic regulations is required as a condition of your continuing salvation.

Farewell. This comes from the Latin, *valete* (the word used in the Vulgate to translate the Greek). The Greek word is a form of the verb *hronnumi* which means primarily "to be strong," and then "may things be well with you." This closing salutation (like the word used in the opening of the letter) was the regular Greek salutation. It is exactly what we would expect in a letter addressed to Greeks. This word likely is more than the perfunctory "Yours truly" used in modern letter. It likely involves a prayer for peace and harmony in the church wherever this letter is read.

15:30 – *So, when they were sent away, they went down to Antioch; and having gathered the congregation together, they delivered the letter.*

So, when they were sent away, they went down to Antioch. It seems that there was some formal dismissal or sending away of the ones who will go to Antioch – Barnabas, Paul, Titus, Judas, Silas, and perhaps others. The Western text includes the additional phrase "in a few days." If we accept that reading, it might express their eagerness to bring the good news to Antioch. The group made the 300-mile trip in a few days. We may well imagine the return trip passed through Samaria and Phoenicia and that the disciples there were gladdened by the contents of the decree.

And having gathered the congregation together. The church at Syrian Antioch is the one assembled.

They delivered the letter. If any of those who had raised the issue at first were still in the city, doubtless they were crestfallen, but their mouths were stopped. Whether they acquiesced in the decision, or were just silenced for the moment, is a matter that cannot be determined with certainty. Churches in other places will be troubled by Judaizers for more than twenty years after this, but whether they were the same men who had unsettled the brethren in Antioch, or a wholly different group, we have no data for determining.

15:31 – *And when they had read it, they rejoiced because of its encouragement.*

And when they had read it. Does this say that the apostles read the letter to the congregation? Apparently so.

They rejoiced because of its encouragement. These Christians at Antioch are rejoicing. Their salvation was complete, and the Judaizers who had been saying they were lost because of lack of circumcision had been mistaken. They are rejoicing because they are not to be subjected to the burdensome rites and ceremonies of the Law of Moses.

The fact that men no longer have to keep the Law of Moses immediately suggests to us the principle of "Christian Liberty." Instead of having to keep the Law of Moses, we have a liberty in Christ. This liberty is not freedom to do as one pleases, for the Christian is under law to Christ.[64] The following chart helps to explain this matter of liberty in Christ.

THE TWO KINDS OF LAW IN THE NEW TESTAMENT

I. MANDATORY LAWS (commands and requirements).

   A. Some of these are *Precepts*

      (These are the "thou shalts" in the New Testament – certain things Christ requires that His people do).

   B. Some of these are *Prohibitions*

      (These are the "thou shalt nots" – not in the Law of Moses –found in the New Testament. E.g., Galatians 5:19ff; Ephesians 5:3-5; the four restrictions in the Jerusalem decree).

II. PERMISSIVE LAWS (the realm of Christian Liberty).

What Christians are permitted to do in those areas where Christ has neither commanded nor prohibited – the realm of Christian Liberty – has some limitations which help serve as guidelines for determining acceptable conduct.

   A. Limited by the law of *expediency* (1 Corinthians 6:12a)

      (If what I propose to do will cause my brother to stumble, I have no liberty in Christ to do that thing. Compare also 1 Corinthians 10 and Romans 14.)

   B. Limited by the law of *self-control* (1 Corinthians 6:12b)

      (Some things, used in certain ways or degrees, will destroy the liberty which claims the right to use them. For example, the Scriptures nowhere prohibit or command drinking coffee, so the Christian has a "liberty" to drink coffee. But if drinking coffee becomes a binding habit, we no longer have a freedom to drink coffee. We have lost our liberty, and have become slaves to coffee; and at this point it is a sin to drink coffee.)

---

[64] 1 Corinthians 9:20-21.

C. Limited by the law of *self-preservation* (1 Corinthians 6:19)

(Our bodies are temples of the Holy Spirit. We have no liberty to take anything into our bodies, or do anything with our bodies that would tend to destroy our bodies and make them unfit as a dwelling place for the Spirit. Under this limitation, smoking or the consumption of alcoholic beverages seem to be prohibited to the Christian, although both, to begin with, fall in the realm of liberty.)

D. Limited by the law of *duty to God* (1 Corinthians 6:20)

(We are to do everything to bring glory to God. Anything that would tend to shame Him, we have no liberty to do.)

CONCLUSION: Instead of looking at Christianity as something that restricts us, it is proper to view Christianity as giving us a freedom to find ways to be helpful to others.

The idea of liberty in Christ is a fundamental principle of Christianity. The way for a Christian to determine questions of conduct and activities is to check the proposed activity in the light of the two kinds of law in the New Testament. For example, may a Christian drive an automobile? To find the answer to this question, first check the Mandatory Laws in the New Testament. Is there any passage that either commands it or prohibits it? If not, then the Christian has a right, a liberty, to drive an car – providing he does not violate any of the limitations to the liberty that is in Christ. If your driving will neither cause a brother to stumble, nor cause you to lose your self-control, etc., then in the light of the coming Judgment you have a freedom to drive. The right of the Christian to enter into any activity must be determined in the light of the laws of the New Testament *before* he acts, for "we all must stand before the judgment seat of Christ to receive the things done in the body."[65]

This Jerusalem Council (Acts 15) has been appealed to as a precedent, or as a proof, that church councils may meet all through the church age to control and regulate the life and doctrine of the church.

- There is not the slightest intimation that this council was a permanent, or even a self-perpetuating, body, or that it would be periodically repeated.

- The conclusion reached by the Jerusalem Conference was a Holy Spirit-inspired decree handed down through the apostles. It would not be possible to duplicate such a thing today.

- While this Jerusalem Conference is referred to by Roman Catholics as the first general council, it was no *general* council at all. It was nothing like the Vatican II ecumenical council convened by Pope John XXIII in 1963. The Jerusalem Conference was not composed even of the representatives of a region or a province. There was a small delegation from Antioch, and the church at Jerusalem with its leaders. It certainly cannot be called a *general* council.

---

[65] 2 Corinthians 5:10.

- The Jerusalem Conference decided a question of doctrine concerning the conditions of salvation. Such a matter no group of men, save the apostles speaking on behalf of Christ, ever has the right to determine. The terms of salvation are a matter God has already decided and men have no authority to alter or amend His new covenant. Acts 15 cannot be used to prove that a particular denomination has a right to have *delegate* conferences or conventions which meet to settle points of doctrine or to regulate the church.

Christians today may indeed settle their problems just as they were settled in the early church. While it is not possible to duplicate the gathering at Jerusalem, for there are no longer any living apostles, we are able to go to the apostles (i.e., their writings) to find the solutions to present-day problems of doctrine and polity. And this we must do if we would keep the church today like the church the apostles established.

15:32 – *And Judas and Silas, also being prophets themselves, encouraged and strengthened the brethren with a lengthy message.*

And Judas and Silas, also being prophets themselves. Judas and Silas were both introduced at verse 22. A "prophet" is one who, under the influence of the Holy Spirit, speaks the words and thoughts of God, whether they relate to the past, to the present, or to the future.[66] Some of the different functions of the prophetic office include:

a) To predict future events. Acts 11:27-28, 21:10-11, 20:23
b) To distinguish between the inspired Word of God and the uninspired teachings of men. 1 Corinthians 14:37; 1 John 2:20,27
c) To reveal the counsels and purposes of God. Ephesians 3:4,5
d) To unfold the meaning of the Holy Scriptures, or the spoken oracles of God. 1 Corinthians 14:1-4; Exodus 7:1
e) To exhort, comfort, confirm, and edify the church. 1 Corinthians 14:31; Acts 15:32

In rank and dignity, the prophets were next in authority to the apostles.[67] The prophetic office, like the apostolic, was only temporary.[68]

Encouraged and strengthened the brethren with a lengthy message. The time the two prophets spent teaching and preaching to the congregation at Antioch shows they were the very opposite of the Judaizers. These men took a personal interest in the brethren, encouraging and strengthening them,[69] just the opposite effect that the Judaizers had, who "unsettled the souls of the disciples" (verse 24)

---

[66] Acts 2:17, 11:27.

[67] Ephesians 4:11; 1 Corinthians 12:18.

[68] 1 Corinthians 13:8; Ephesians 2:20.

[69] Compare notes at Acts 14:22 on "strengthened" and at Acts 4:36 on "encouraged."

15:33 – *And after they had spent time there, they were sent away from the brethren in peace to those who had sent them out.*

And after they had spent time *there*. A couple of months? Some think the Galatian letter was written during this interval, but it appears that this is too early for the Galatian letter. Galatians 4:13 indicates Paul had visited the Galatians at least twice, and at the time of the close of the Jerusalem Conference, Paul had visited the Galatians but once.[70]

They were sent away from the brethren in peace. "In peace" is an expression which means that when their stay was finished, and there was a special meeting to bid them goodbye, Judas and Silas had the affectionate regard of the saints to whom they had ministered. The emissaries from Jerusalem had the congregations' highest wishes for Godspeed on the journey.

To those who had sent them out. Judas and Silas returned to the brethren in Jerusalem.[71]

15:34 – *[But it seemed good to Silas to remain there.]*

[But it seemed good to Silas to remain there.] Many of the ancient manuscripts and ancient versions do not carry this verse. Those that do carry it have many variations – some reading as it appears in the ASV, and others reading as the Vulgate, "It seemed good to Silas to remain, but Judas went alone to Jerusalem." It is probably a marginal gloss, introduced by some early scribe, who judged it necessary to explain how Silas conveniently is at hand (verse 40) for Paul to choose as a companion for the second missionary journey. Because the verse is of questionable authority, many commentators feel that Judas and Silas both returned to Jerusalem to give an account to the church there, but that Silas soon returned to Antioch, where he and Paul soon became fellow workers.[72]

15:35 – *But Paul and Barnabas stayed in Antioch, teaching and preaching, with many others also, the word of the Lord.*

But Paul and Barnabas stayed in Antioch. How long a time is not known. It is probably at this time that the unhappy incident occurred between Paul and Peter which is recorded in Galatians 2:11-14.[73] Peter, when he came to Antioch, acted in direct conflict with the

---

[70] The Galatians passage appears to imply more than the two visits that some of the Galatian churches had from Paul during the first missionary journey, one when the church was founded, and one when Paul returned from Derbe to "strengthen the brethren" (Acts 14:22). It is much more likely that Galatians was written from the third missionary journey, at the same time as the Corinthian letters and Romans, since the contents of these four epistles are so similar, and since Paul has visited Galatia, by that time, on two different missionary journeys.

[71] KJV reads "to the apostles." but there is a manuscript variation here. The better-supported reading is as the NASB reads.

[72] It is no more difficult to explain how Silas is present to go with Paul than it is to explain how Mark is there to go with Barnabas, when the last mention of him was "in Jerusalem" (Acts 13:13).

[73] There is no way to be certain just when Peter dissimulated at Antioch. (1) Though the account in Galatians seems to be chronological, some insist Galatians 2:11-14 must have occurred before the Jerusalem Conference since they cannot conceive of Peter so acting once the Conference has been held.

decision of the Jerusalem Conference and with the directions of the letter which he and others wrote to the Antioch church.[74] That Jerusalem decree had reference to imposing the Law of Moses upon the Gentiles, and the kind of social contacts which should be maintained between Christians of different backgrounds. Peter's conduct during his visit to Antioch tended to put a stumbling block in the path of the brethren there. The liberty he had in Christ gave him freedom to live either as a Jew, or as a Gentile, and Peter has been continuing his old Jewish customs. Indeed, he had lived like a Gentile in the house of Cornelius, and he did the same for a time at Antioch; but after certain Jews came from Jerusalem, he refused to live with the Gentiles in Antioch any longer. His example gave the wrong impression. By his withdrawal he was virtually saying to the Gentiles, 'You must live like the Jews if you wish to have fellowship with me.' Peter was being hypocritical and Paul rebuked him before them all; that is, Peter was rebuked in an assembly of the congregation. Paul, in effect, said to Peter in that church meeting, "By your actions you are saying (in direct contradiction to the decree from Jerusalem) to the Gentiles, 'If you wish to be saved, you must live like the Jews.'" Even Barnabas, for a while, was "carried away by their hypocrisy."[75]

Teaching and preaching with many others also the word of the Lord. Though no firm distinction between the words can be pressed, the former word perhaps speaks of giving additional instruction to those who were already Christians, while the latter speaks of sharing the gospel with those who have not yet obeyed it. The former might often be done privately in the home, and the latter publicly, though even this distinction cannot be pressed. Luke tells us that in addition to Paul and Barnabas there were many other teachers and preachers in Antioch, too.

---

(2) Others insist Galatians 2:11-14 should be inserted at the close of the second missionary journey, at Acts 18:22,23. They also believe the presentation in Galatians is chronological; but they find it hard to think of Peter being on the wrong side so soon after the Conference, as it would be if we locate the event between the Conference and the beginning of the second missionary journey. At that later date, the Judaizers would have had time to regroup so that their influence was such that Peter would be swayed by it, it is affirmed.

If the later date for Peter's dissimulation is correct, several things would follow. (a) There would be a record that Paul and Barnabas got together after their separation at the beginning of the second journey, for in the Galatian's account they are together in Antioch. (b) We would certainly have to date Galatians from the third missionary journey, if Peter's dissimulation did not occur till the close of the second journey.

Given the various possibilities for locating the time of Peter's dissimulation, we still incline to put it here, just shortly after the Jerusalem Conference, and to suggest that Peter's actions stem from a desire to be popular with the Jewish portion of the church, with which he is especially working. Barnabas, too. who has recently been displaced by Paul as the leader in the eyes of the Gentile churches, may have been moved by the same motive, since he was still held in high esteem among the Jewish Christians.

[74] Galatians 2:11.

[75] Galatians 2:13.

C. The Second Missionary Journey. 15:36-18:22

   1. In Antioch of Syria. 15:36-40

15:36 – *And after some days Paul said to Barnabas, "Let us return and visit the brethren in every city in which we proclaimed the word of the Lord,* **and see** *how they are."*

And after some days Paul said to Barnabas. Paul takes the lead in this new missionary activity among the Gentiles. Per the Introductory Studies, the second missionary journey has been dated AD 51-54.

Let us return and visit the brethren in every city in which we proclaimed the word of the Lord. "Visit" includes the idea of "helping" or "looking after" as its use in Acts 7:23 and James 1:27 indicates. Paul suggests that they revisit the churches which they had established in Asia Minor on the first missionary journey (Acts 13-14). In fact, as the next chapters of Acts will relate, this second tour extended far beyond the remotest churches which the two had previously planted. It will introduce the gospel to Europe.

And see **how they are.** Paul was anxious to see how the young churches were getting along, and to give them whatever further instruction they might need. It has been suggested that Paul was interested not only in the general condition of the churches, but also in the spiritual growth of each individual member.[76]

15:37 – *And Barnabas was desirous of taking John, called Mark, along with them also.*

And Barnabas was desirous of taking John, called Mark, along with them also. Some manuscripts here have an aorist tense, indicating that Barnabas had already made up his mind to take Mark on the tour. Others have an imperfect tense, and would indicate only a continual wish on Barnabas' part, rather than a fixed determination. The latter is the correct reading. May we not see in Barnabas' actions in behalf of Mark the thing that reclaimed him for the ministry, just as earlier Barnabas' intercession on behalf of Paul had greatly helped his relationship with the brethren whom he shortly before had been persecuting? Barnabas and Mark were related (Colossians 4:10), but there must have been more to Barnabas' desire for taking Mark than simple kinship.

15:38 – *But Paul kept insisting that they should not take him along who had deserted them in Pamphylia and had not gone with them to the work.*

But Paul kept insisting that they should not take him along. This was a difference of judgment. We are not to understand that the Holy Spirit guided either one of these men; it was a difference in human judgment as to what was expedient in the matter. Just as best friends can sometimes differ on questions of expediency and personal preference, we now learn that on such questions even inspired individuals are liable to differences. The word "desirous" used of Barnabas' wishes is a much milder word than Paul's "insisting." Note

---

[76] Plumptre, *op. cit.*, p.250.

also the contrast between "Take him along!" (verse 37) and "We'll not take him along!" (verse 38).

Who had deserted them in Pamphylia. See Acts 13:13 on Mark's leaving the two apostles during the first missionary journey. Paul here uses "apostasy" to describe Mark's leaving the missionary group, while in Acts 13:13 Luke uses a much milder word. It wasn't apostasy to Christ, but it was apostasy from the mission.

And had not gone with them to the work. The "work" was the preaching of the gospel in the interior of Asia Minor, in particular to the towns of Antioch, Iconium, Lystra, and Derbe. The only reason Paul gives for not at all wishing to take John Mark on this second journey was that he turned back and went home before the first journey was completed. Boles suggests there could have been more in the background.

> Some think that the incident between Paul and Peter (Galatians 2:11-21) was known to Mark, and that Mark took sides with Peter; hence, Paul was not kindly disposed to take Mark with them; he would have been a hindrance to the gospel among the Gentiles had he gone with them and held that the Gentiles ought to be circumcised. However, we do not know more than is recorded here.[77]

15:39 – *And there arose such a sharp disagreement that they separated from one another, and Barnabas took Mark with him and sailed away to Cyprus.*

And there arose such a sharp disagreement. It may be that the "son of consolation" lost his temper in this dispute over his cousin, and Paul used sharp words toward his benefactor and friend. Involved in the words "sharp disagreement" is the idea of irritation of mind. It was not a permanent falling out between the two men, but was serious at the moment. Barnes has made several interesting observations concerning this contention and separation between Paul and Barnabas.[78]

1) No apology or vindication of it is offered by Luke, the sacred writer. It undoubtedly was not a proper thing for Christians to engage in, but no apology is given.

2) In this contention, [Barnes suggests that] perhaps Paul was right. It is clear that Paul and Silas had the prayers of the church in their favor (verse 40), and it may be intimated that Barnabas departed without any such commendation.

---

[77] Boles, *op. cit.*, p.249. Perhaps this is the place where a word should be said about the alleged Petrine-Pauline split in the early church. The private meeting at the Jerusalem Conference allows no such split between these apostles. The apostles were in perfect agreement about the Gentiles and the doctrine being preached to both Jews and Gentiles; there was not one doctrine preached to one, and a different doctrine preached to the other. And the close of the episode at Antioch, when Paul withstood Peter to his face, allows for no continuing division between the two apostles. The whole theory of a Petrine-Pauline split, though ingenious, falls for lack of evidence. Furthermore, the idea that Mark ruined his testimony among Gentiles by being Judaistic in his views is hard to accept, too. With no evidence of a continuing difference of doctrine between Peter and Paul in which Mark could take sides, and with evidence that Mark's ministry was acceptable to the Gentiles (from references in Colossians, Philemon, Timothy, 1 Peter, and early Christian literature), the whole idea of an alleged Petrine-Pauline split becomes unacceptable.

[78] Barnes, *op. cit.*, p.237.

3) This contention, in the directing providence of God, turned out for the furtherance of the gospel. We now have two evangelistic teams, rather than one.

4) Later in Paul's life, these differences have been reconciled. Barnabas is spoken of with words of praise (1 Corinthians 9:6). There is also evidence that Paul became reconciled to John Mark (Colossians 4:10, 2 Timothy 4:11, Philemon 24).

5) In this account there is evidence of the truthfulness and historicity of Luke's record. What forger or imposter would have thought of including this unhappy incident showing differences between the early saints?

That they separated from one another. As noted, Barnes feels Paul was correct. McGarvey demurs when he writes, "Which of the two acted the more wisely we are not now able to determine, for lack of acquaintance with the motives which actuated Mark in turning back."[79]

And Barnabas took Mark with him and sailed away to Cyprus. Perhaps Paul's refusal to take Mark along is the event that made Mark determine to overcome his faults. The traditions for Barnabas' later life are rather untrustworthy, but there is a tradition to the effect that Barnabas ministered to the island of Cyprus until his death.[80]

> Notwithstanding their disagreement and separation, they did not allow the good cause to suffer, nor did they fail to accomplish separately that which Paul proposed that they should accomplish together; for Barnabas, in revisiting Cyprus, saw a portion of the brethren to whom he and Paul had preached, while Paul by a different route, visited others. The separation of Barnabas from Paul is our separation from Barnabas, for his name is not mentioned again in Acts. But as we bid him a final farewell, the sails are spread which are to bear him over the sea, that he may make the islands glad with the knowledge of salvation; and the later incidents of his life will be made known to us when we sit down with him in the everlasting kingdom.[81]

15:40 – *But Paul chose Silas and departed, being committed by the brethren to the grace of the Lord.*

But Paul chose Silas and departed. Has Silas returned from Jerusalem (verse 33), maybe even accompanied by Mark?[82] Perhaps both Mark and Silas have been summoned from Jerusalem in order to join Barnabas and Paul respectively on these missionary trips.

---

[79] McGarvey, *op. cit.*, p.76.

[80] The tradition about Barnabas' death is found in the rather late *Periodi Barnabae*.

[81] McGarvey, *ibid.*

[82] See verses 33 and 34 above concerning the travels of Silas since the Jerusalem Conference. Silas was in harmony with the mission to the Gentiles, he was a Roman citizen (Acts 16:37), and his ministry in Antioch must have been the place where Paul's attention to him was stirred.

Being committed by the brethren to the grace of the Lord. See Acts 13:3 and 14:26 for similar language. The church had a prayer meeting, praying that God will guide and care for Paul and Silas.

   2. In Syria and Cilicia. 15:41

15:41 – *And he was traveling through Syria and Cilicia, strengthening the churches.*

And he was traveling through Syria and Cilicia. Paul is traveling overland from Antioch to Cilicia. Little has been said about churches in these areas thus far in Acts. Either Paul planted them during the interval between his departure from Jerusalem to Tarsus (Acts 9:30) and the time Barnabas brought him to Antioch (Acts 11:25-26), or they were planted by missionaries going out from Antioch just as Paul and Barnabas had.

Strengthening the churches. This is the third time we've had this word "strengthening." As before, it was done by instruction and exhortation.[83] Paul must have been sharing with all these brethren, just as he does later (Acts 16:4), the decrees from the Jerusalem Conference.

The Sea of Galilee

Drawing by Horace Knowles
from the British and Foreign Bible Society

---

[83] See Acts 14:22, 15:32. Even if the "strengthening" done in these Acts passages includes the laying on of hands in order to pass on spiritual gifts, this is still rather far removed from the Episcopal rite of confirmation where it is supposed that the indwelling gift of the Spirit is given by the laying on of hands.

3. At Derbe and Lystra. 16:1-3

16:1 – *And he came also to Derbe and to Lystra. And behold, a certain disciple was there, named Timothy, the son of a Jewish woman who was a believer, but his father was a Greek,*

And he came also to Derbe and to Lystra. Actually, Paul and Silas both came to these cities, but Paul only is mentioned, being the dominant personality. "Came" is a word used by Luke not only of arriving at a place but of staying there for a time. The order in which the towns are mentioned is in the reverse of what they were named in Acts 14:6, but this is because the missionary party is coming from Cilicia rather than from Pisidian Antioch. The route traveled seems to have been overland from Syrian Antioch to Tarsus; and from there, passing through the mountain pass called the Cilician Gates, they would have come to Derbe first, and then to Lystra.[1] Between two and four years have passed since Paul had preached in these cities during the first missionary tour.

And behold, a certain disciple was there, named Timothy. "Behold" may indicate that it was surprising that someone to take Mark's place was found so quickly. It was providential, too. In comments at 14:20, we have indicated that Timothy's home was probably at Lystra, and that Timothy, at the time of this second missionary journey, was about twenty years old. The name "Timothy" means "one who honors God." This young man was to become one of Paul's dearest and closest co-laborers through the rest of Paul's earthly life.[2]

The son of a Jewish woman who was a believer. 2 Timothy 1:5 tells us the mother's name was Eunice. She was a convert to Christianity (a "believer"). In comments at 14:20, the suggestion was made that mother and son were converted during the first missionary journey.[3]

But his father was a Greek. Luke's account of the marriage of a devout Jewess to a Greek has been the occasion for some surprise. Ezra 9:12 shows that such marriages were not lawful. A Jew was neither to marry a woman of another nation, nor to give his daughter in marriage to a Gentile. What may have happened is that Eunice's father, living a long way from Palestine where the Law would have been strictly enforced, had relaxed the careful observance of this (and perhaps others?) precept under the constant pressure of the Greek world around him. Evidently the father was not even a full proselyte to the Jewish religion, for had he been, he would have had his son circumcised.[4]

---

[1] See notes at Acts 14:6 concerning the towns of Derbe and Lystra. Ramsay has given details of the difficulty of such a trip as this verse describes in his *Pauline and Other Studies in Early Christian History* (Grand Rapids: Baker Book House, 1970), p.273ff.

[2] 1 Corinthians 4:17; 2 Timothy 1:2. See the terms of love and affection Paul uses for Timothy.

[3] Some would have Timothy converted during Paul's absence from Lystra. But since Paul calls Timothy "my son" (1 Timothy 1:18, 2 Timothy 2:1), it is best to think of Timothy as being converted by Paul during Paul's visit to Lystra on the first missionary tour.

[4] See notes below at verse 3. Timothy's father, who was a Greek, must have acquiesced in his wife's continual devotion to the Jewish religion.

16:2 – *and he was well spoken of by the brethren who were in Lystra and Iconium.*

And he was well spoken of. "He" is Timothy, not the father. In the years since Paul's first missionary tour and the conversion of Timothy, Timothy has been conspicuous for his devotion and "unfeigned faith." His religious education while still living at home – well versing him in the Old Testament Scriptures[5] – would have been one reason for his right living which had led to his good reputation.

By the brethren who were In Lystra and Iconium. The fact that he was known as a fine Christian, not only in his home town but in the distant city of Iconium, suggests the fact that he had already been active as a preacher or leader of young people. His good reputation was certainly one of the things that called him to Paul's attention, and led to his being invited to join the missionary party.

16:3 – *Paul wanted this man to go with him; and he took him and circumcised him because of the Jews who were in those parts, for they all knew that his father was a Greek.*

Paul wanted this man to go with him. Maybe this is an instance where Paul had received some divine directions concerning Timothy's mission.[6] On the other hand, maybe this is an instance where Paul selected a young man of promise in order that he might be further trained for the ministry. The apostles did keep on the lookout for such young men who could be trained, and who then would carry on the work after they had passed from the scene.[7] As the missionary journey moves from city to city, these young men, when trained, were often left to help the just-planted congregations.

And he took him and circumcised him because of the Jews who were in those parts, for they all knew that his father was a Greek. Circumcision might be performed by any Israelite, and this verse says Paul performed the act himself. Just a few weeks ago, Paul adamantly refused to circumcise Titus.[8] Now he himself circumcises Timothy! How is this seeming inconsistency explained, especially in light of the decree of the Jerusalem Conference against the necessity of circumcision for salvation? Further, Paul's course of action with Timothy seems to conflict with statements Paul himself makes in several of his epistles, especially that in Galatians 5:2-4. The difference lies in the interpretation that other people would put on the act.

- To have circumcised Titus would have led people to think that Paul himself believed circumcision was indeed necessary for salvation. Paul refused so that people would not be misled.

- To have failed to circumcise Timothy would have led many Jewish people to recoil from

---

[5] 2 Timothy 3:15.

[6] 1 Timothy 1:18.

[7] Similarly, elders and older ones in the church today should train young men to carry on the work of the Lord (2 Timothy 2:2).

[8] Galatians 2:3.

either Paul or Timothy,⁹ thus greatly limiting Paul's opportunities to tell them about Jesus. Since no one would look upon what was done to Timothy as evidence circumcision was necessary to salvation, Paul could do it, and not be the least bit inconsistent.

All of this fits with the idea that, in the Christian age, circumcision is one of the things falling into the realm of Christian liberty; whether or not it is done depends on whether or not one of the limitations on liberty would be violated.¹⁰ The Jerusalem Conference had made it clear that circumcision had nothing to do with salvation. Gentiles did not have to begin practicing it, nor did Jews have to cease practicing it, in order to be saved. In the case of Timothy, Paul was acting in harmony with a principle of conduct that he observed all his Christian life; namely, falling in with the customs of the people among whom he was living, doing all he could to win them, short of compromising the gospel.¹¹

"All knew that his father was a Greek' is the reason given why Paul circumcised Timothy. The people of the whole area knew of Timothy's parentage, and the high likelihood that because he had a Greek father he was not circumcised. It is this phrase, too, that has been appealed to as evidence that Timothy's father was dead, though the verb tense "was" doesn't absolutely demand such an interpretation.

At some time or other, perhaps at this time when Timothy was about to join the missionary party, the elders of the church laid their hands on him,¹² and so did Paul.¹³

4. Through Iconium and Pisidian Antioch. 16:4-5

16:4 – *Now while they were passing through the cities, they were delivering the decrees, which had been decided upon by the apostles and elders who were in Jerusalem, for them to observe.*

Now while they were passing through the cities. "Through the cities" of Syria and Cilicia, says Barnes. Through Pisidian Antioch and Iconium, say other writers. It is likely best to combine both ideas.

They were delivering the decrees, which had been decided upon by the apostles and elders who were in Jerusalem, for them to observe. Paul and Silas tell the Christians in all the churches they visit about the decrees ordained by the Jerusalem Conference.¹⁴ Some

---

⁹ Jews would have regarded with horror an uncircumcised Israelite, even if he were born of half-descent. They would have considered Paul unclean in consequence of companionship with such as Timothy, had he not been circumcised. The people of the whole area knew of Timothy's parentage and the high likelihood that because he had a Greek father he was not circumcised.

¹⁰ See extensive notes on Christian liberty at Acts 15:31. Compare also Romans 4:10ff, Galatians 3:17.

¹¹ 1 Corinthians 9:19-23.

¹² 1 Timothy 4:4.

¹³ 2 Timothy 1:6.

¹⁴ "Decrees" refers to the letter drawn up at the close of the Jerusalem Conference, which contained four things from which Christians are to abstain (Acts 15:23-29).

commentators claim the word "deliver" implies that Paul left copies of the "decree" wherever he went. A copy left with each congregation would give the brethren something to appeal to if Judaizers ever came and tried to force their doctrines on the brethren. The particular word translated "decrees" (*dogma*) is often used in the Old Testament with reference to commands that are God-given.[15] The use of this word shows the divine authority behind the decision of the Jerusalem Conference, just as did the statement in Acts 15:28. This verse also indicates that the decrees were not intended for Syria and Cilicia alone, even though they were addressed to them in particular (Acts 15:23).

16:5 – *So the churches were being strengthened in the faith, and were increasing in number daily.*

So the churches were being strengthened in the faith, and were increasing in number daily. Luke has used the word "strengthened" for what happened to the lame man at the gate Beautiful.[16] Perhaps there is an implication that the years between visits by the apostle have seen a decline in the life and witness of some of these churches that is now remedied by preaching and teaching. In Acts 6:7 and 9:31, Luke gave a note about the growth of the churches. Is Christianity more attractive and acceptable to prospective converts from among the Gentiles now that the Jerusalem Conference has made it clear that the minute regulations of Moses do not have to be adhered to? People today often hesitate to obey Jesus and become involved in the church because they think there are things they will have to quit, i.e., the church has a lot of rules that limit freedom. Let it be known that there is bondage in continuing in sin, and genuine freedom in obedience to Christ. And let it also be known that God will change a man's desires so that he will no longer desire to do some of the things he does before his surrender to Jesus.

5. Through Phrygia and Galatia Toward Troas. 16:6-8

16:6 – *And they passed through the Phrygian and Galatian region, having been forbidden by the Holy Spirit to speak the word in Asia;*

And they passed through the Phrygian and Galatian region. On maps of Paul's journeys, the reader will note that some maps have Paul's second journey as a straight line from Pisidian Antioch to Troas, while others have the line going northeast out of Pisidian Antioch up into northern Galatia – through Ancyra, Tavium, Pessinus, etc. Why is this? Why do not the maps agree? During the 1st century, the term "Galatia" was used in two different senses. Map makers who take it in its old *Hellenistic* sense draw Paul's journey through northern Galatia. Those who take it in its *Roman provincial* sense draw Paul's journey through southern Galatia.

On the various maps, it is also notable that the area called Galatia is larger on some than on others. Why is this? In our time, wars between nations change boundary lines between nations; consequently, maps have to be changed. So it was in Bible times. About

---

[15] Compare Colossians 2:14.

[16] Acts 3:7,16.

300 BC, great hordes of Gauls left France and Germany and moved toward Asia Minor. After some years they were invited by the king of Bithynia to cross the Hellespont and help him in a war. After the war was over, they refused to go home, and settled instead in the hill country of central Asia Minor. This area in which they settled became known as Galatia (i.e., the northern Galatia spoken of earlier). As the years passed, the area was conquered by the Romans (189 BC) and finally became a Roman province in the time of Augustus (25 BC). A map of this area before 25 BC is titled "Asia Minor in Hellenistic Times" and shows many small countries in this area. When the area became a Roman province, the map was changed. Following 25 BC, the map would be called "A Roman Provincial Map," and shows fewer and larger countries in Asia Minor. Many of the smaller countries of Hellenistic times were consolidated into fewer and larger provinces by the Romans. Thus, the two different meanings for the word "Galatia" were these: (1) It might speak of the Galatia of Hellenistic times, often called "North Galatia" or "Geographical Galatia" or "Ethnographical Galatia." (2) It might refer to the whole Roman province, including what in earlier times was known as Pisidia, Lycaonia, and a part of Phrygia, as well as northern Galatia.

The next question is, How do the New Testament writers use the geographical designations in their writings? Paul appears to have regularly used the Roman provincial titles, as did Peter.[17] Luke, however, generally used the Hellenistic names of geographical locations. To see this, check the names in this verse against a Hellenistic map and against a Roman provincial map of Asia Minor; notice that there was no Phrygia or Mysia on a Roman provincial map. But here is an exception: Luke also speaks of "Asia" in this verse, and an examination of the maps will show that there was no "Asia" on most Hellenistic maps.[18]

Having established this background, we are ready to attempt to determine where Paul went on the journey indicated in Acts 16:6-8.

- Some commentators hold that Paul visited northern Galatia – in particular the cities of Ancyra, Pessinus, and Tavium. Many commentators also speak of the fact that Paul had not intended at first to preach among these ethnic Galatians, but because of sickness he was constrained to tarry there.[19] Most of those commentators who think Paul visited northern Galatia also believe that Paul's epistle to the Galatians was addressed to the churches of northern Galatia.

- Other commentators (with whom we agree) deny that Paul visited northern Galatia (in the sense that he preached in the cities of Ancyra, Tavium, etc.). These commentators reconstruct the second missionary tour in the following fashion. (i) As Paul, Silas, and Timothy leave Lystra, they crossed the regional boundary between Galactic Lycaonia

---

[17] Note how the geographical names are used in the addresses of Paul's letters, and also compare 1 Peter 1:1.

[18] "Asia" does appear on some Hellenistic maps. Before the Roman provincial changes, the name "Asia" was sometimes applied to the land named "Lydia" on most of the Hellenistic maps. "Lydia" was the area bounded on the north by Mysia and on the south by Caria.

[19] Galatians 4:13. Luke does not mention Paul's sickness, so we are not able to place it with certainty in his Acts record. Some would say the sickness of Galatians 4:13 happened during the second journey (e.g., at Acts 16). This commentator agrees with those who say the sickness happened on the *first* missionary journey (Acts 13-14). See notes at Acts 13:13.

and Galactic Phrygia and visited the brethren in Iconium and in Pisidian Antioch. (ii) Paul then planned to go to Asia, but he was forbidden by the Spirit to go there. (iii) Since they were forbidden to go on toward the west, they turned north, going through the region that was both Phrygian and Galatian.[20] Soon they arrived at Dorylaeum (or perhaps Cotyaeum), having followed the Roman highway west from Pisidian Antioch until it turned northward. (iv) Then, if we take "over against Mysia" (verse 7) to mean something like "the eastern border of Mysia," verse 7 suggests that when they reached Dorylaeum (or Cotyaeum, both of which were on the eastern border of Mysia), they tried to continue in a northerly direction, only to be hindered by the Spirit again. (v) So they followed the Roman highway west until they reached the sea at Troas.

This commentator is also of the opinion that the Galatian letter was addressed to the churches of southern Galatia (i.e., Pisidian Antioch, Iconium, Lystra and Derbe). According to Galatians 2:5, Paul had already visited those addressed in the Galatian letter *before* the Jerusalem Conference. This fact eliminates northern Galatia from consideration as being the ones addressed in the Galatian letter.[21]

Having been forbidden by the Holy Spirit. We naturally infer from the aorist participle that they had received this prohibition before they journeyed through the Phrygian-Galatian region. How did the Spirit do this forbidding? Some suggest it was an inward monition, an urge prompted by the Spirit.[22] Some suggest that this was a providential turning created by setting up a natural barrier – e.g., a river up, an avalanche in the mountains, etc. Yet others suggest that a prophet in the church at Antioch delivered this message to the missionary party.[23] Still others suggest that God spoke directly to Paul, giving him the instructions not to go into Ephesus at this time.

To speak the word in Asia. As suggested above, their original plan probably had been to go on to Asia with its teeming cities of Ephesus, Smyrna, and Sardis. There were large Jewish quarters in these cities, and the province was full of centers of idolatrous worship. Indeed, it was an area that needed the gospel. According to Luke's usage of geographical terms, the reference apparently is to the area in which Ephesus was the principal city, the area called "Lydia" on most Hellenistic maps. This restraint on preaching there was only

---

[20] Sharp's rule of grammar is the reason for the expression "the region that is both Phrygian and Galatian." Sharp's rule shows that the words (according to the Nestle text) "Phrygia and Galatia" do not refer to two different areas, but the word "Galatian" is a further description of the region already called Phrygian. Both names are adjectives in the Greek, describing an area that was both Phrygian (by ethnic standards) and Galatian (by Roman provincial standards).

[21] There is no place in the first missionary journey where a visit to northern Galatia can be fitted in. If Paul ever went there, it has to be after he leaves Pisidian Antioch on the second journey. Even if we were to admit Paul did visit northern Galatia, in the light of Galatians 2:5, we must still have Galatians addressed to the churches of southern Galatia.

[22] The Spirit does seem to have the ability to plant thoughts in men's minds. However, when some commentators speak of this being an inward monition, some of them are using such language in a naturalistic sense, denying the objective reality of a personal being such as the Holy Spirit. A reader must therefore observe carefully how each commentator defines the terms used; otherwise, he may be severely misled by the euphemistic language of the naturalistic theologians.

[23] Acts 21:4 records a case of a prophet passing on a message to other inspired men of God.

temporary, for at the close of this second journey and at the beginning of the third Paul will preach in Asia.

16:7 – *and when they had come to Mysia, they were trying to go into Bithynia, and the Spirit of Jesus did not permit them;*

And when they had come to Mysia. The language seems to speak of their being on the eastern border of this region.

They were trying to go into Bithynia. Bithynia was a province of Asia Minor located north and east of Mysia, bordering on the Black Sea. As far as we know, Paul never preached in Bithynia; but the gospel was early preached there, for one of Peter's letters is addressed to brethren in this province.[24] This province, too, had a large Jewish population which would have served Paul's usual method of going to the Jew first before he went to the Greek.

And the Spirit of Jesus did not permit them. In saying that this second prohibition was imposed by the "Spirit of Jesus," whereas the former one is ascribed to the "Holy Spirit" (verse 6), Luke poses an interesting theological question. One and the same Spirit is intended, of course; but is there any significance to the change in phraseology?

> Possibly the methods used to communicate the Spirit's will on the two occasions were different. It may be that on the second occasion the communication took a form closely associated with the exalted Christ.[25]

Or it may be that the Spirit was specifically sent by Christ to communicate this message to Paul.[26] The introduction of the gospel to Europe was to be delayed no longer. Jesus wanted Europe to hear!

16:8 – *and passing by Mysia, they came down to Troas.*

And passing by Mysia. Either this means that they passed through the region without stopping in any of the cities to preach, or they passed around the province by traveling along its southern borders till they came to Troas.

They came down to Troas. This city bears the name of ancient Troy (of Trojan horse fame), but was actually about four miles south of the site of that famous town. This Troas, called Alexandria Troas (in honor of Alexander the Great), had been built by Antigonus, one of the successors of Alexander. It was a Roman colony and a free city. "Came down" suggests they have come down out of the highlands to the seacoast. As the missionaries travel westward, they would be looking out over the waters of the Aegean Sea.

---

[24] 1 Peter 1:1.

[25] Bruce, *op. cit.*, p.327.

[26] This title, "Spirit of Jesus," for the Holy Spirit has considerable bearing on the disputed problem of the procession of the Holy Spirit. He proceeds not only from God, but also from Jesus (John 16:7).

6. At Troas. 16:9-10

16:9 – *And a vision appeared to Paul in the night: a certain man of Macedonia was standing and appealing to him, and saying, "Come over to Macedonia and help us."*

And a vision appeared to Paul in the night. Try to imagine the thoughts of these men, since they must be wondering where God wants them to serve. They had thought of Asia, and were hindered. They had thought of Bithynia, and were hindered. Now they have come to Troas without difficulty, but where to now? Preach here, or elsewhere? Perhaps Paul went to the Lord in prayer, and the vision granted was in answer to that prayer. The vision on which Paul looked explained to him all the varied promptings and hindrances during this journey from Pisidian Antioch. This was the door that was to be opened to him, for the Christian faith was to pass from Asia to Europe.[27] As subsequent history has shown, the cry "Come over and help us!" was a cry from the whole Western world.

A certain man of Macedonia was standing and appealing to him. In the vision the appearance of the man, his dress and language, led Paul to know he was a Macedonian. Some suggest the person seen by Paul was none other than Luke, whose home was allegedly in Philippi (according to the suggestion),[28] but there is no evidence that Luke's home was Philippi.[29] Macedonia was an extensive country, the northern part of what to us is modern day Greece. In New Testament times, modern day Greece was actually two Roman provinces: Macedonia in the north and Achaia in the south.[30] Macedonia came to prominence during the reign of Philip and his son, Alexander the Great (c. 300 BC).

And saying, "Come over to Macedonia and help us." "Help us," that is by preaching the gospel to them.[31] To fulfill this call, Paul and his team will labor for much of the second missionary journey to plant churches in some of the principal cities of the province.

16:10 – *And when he had seen the vision, immediately we sought to go into Macedonia, concluding that God had called us to preach the gospel to them.*

And when he had seen the vision, immediately we sought to go into Macedonia. The "we" is significant because this is the first instance in which Luke refers to himself as being a member of the missionary party. From here on, as long as Luke is with the party, there is a vigor and freshness to the account that is possible only from an eyewitness.

How did Luke and Paul come to be together at Troas? Has Paul sought the services

---

[27] We view the move to Macedonia as taking the gospel to another continent, but the missionaries themselves probably looked on it as no more than going from one Roman province to another.

[28] Ramsey, *St. Paul the Traveller and Roman Citizen*, p.202.

[29] See notes on verse 10, where Luke's hometown and previous history are discussed.

[30] See 1 Thessalonians 1:7 where both Roman provinces are named.

[31] From all portions of the earth, a similar call for "help" is now coming to the churches. Openings of a similar character for the introduction of the gospel are presented on all hands. Appeals come from every quarter. In our time, we must do all in our power to see that the gospel is spread.

of the "beloved physician"?[32] Luke is evidently already a Christian (for there is no mention of his conversion), and a logical assumption is that Paul and Luke were already acquainted with each other before Luke joins the party. Had they met when both were students at the university in Tarsus? Perhaps they met in Syrian Antioch, for early Christian writers tell us that Luke's home was in Antioch.[33]

In Luke's words, "God called *us* to preach." This implies that Luke, too, is a preacher of the gospel, just as Paul and Silas were, and also that he was involved in preaching before he joined the missionary party. Interestingly, there is no record of any missionary work done at this time in Troas by Paul, yet the language of 2 Corinthians 2:12 and of Acts 20:6 indicates the existence of a congregation of Christians in Troas. Perhaps Luke was the founder of the church in Troas since the church had been planted before Paul ever arrived in the city. Likely, Paul was impressed by the evangelistic work Luke has done; he speaks of Luke as being "famous for the gospel" as he writes 2 Corinthians.[34]

Luke's travels might be tentatively reconstructed in this manner: He leaves Syrian Antioch sometime after the first missionary journey began, and is in the midst of Asia Minor as the first journey draws to a close. In the three or four years since, he has come to Troas to evangelize there. He now joins Paul's missionary party.

The "immediately we sought" pictures a hurried trip to the dock the next morning, with inquiry made as to what ships might be sailing, bound for any port of Macedonia.

Concluding that God had called us to preach the gospel to them. McGarvey says these words imply that Luke was one of those who had been turned aside from the places in which they had intended to preach (verses 6-7), and that therefore he joined the group of missionaries in the interior of Asia Minor.[35] But it could as well be that Luke joins them at Troas before the vision was granted to Paul. "Concluding" is the same verb translated "proving" at Acts 9:22. Paul must have shared with his companions the content of the vi-

---

[32] Colossians 4:14. Perhaps Luke's work with Paul suggests an apostolic example for having a doctor along as the gospel is taken to a new field. A physician can do much to keep the other workers in condition for efficient service, and can secure a hearing for the Word in places where people realize their physical needs better than they realize their spiritual needs.

However, as a general order of evangelization, take care of the spiritual needs first, then take care of the physical. Since religious Liberalism has invaded the ranks of the Restoration Movement, there has been some contention as to the proper method of doing missionary work. Liberals have tended to ridicule and ignore any attempt to "save men's souls," opting instead for some merely humanitarian effort, and called that "missionary work."

In the 20th century, four different methods of missionary work were widely used: educational, medical, agricultural, and evangelistic. Each has a certain Scriptural precedent, and may be used depending on the place and the need. We must be careful that our opposition to any but the evangelistic method is not just a carry-over from our opposition to religious Liberalism and all that it stands for.

[33] See Eusebius, *Church History*, III.4; and Jerome, *Lives of Illustrious Men*, ch.7. Remember also the "we" reading in Codex Beza at Acts 11:27, and the "we" at Acts 14:22. If both those passages indicate the presence of Luke, he would have been in Syrian Antioch at the time Paul and Barnabas founded that church, and then would have been somewhere in southern Galatia as Paul was retracing his steps while winding up the first missionary journey.

[34] 2 Corinthians 8:18. A different, but hardly plausible, suggestion as to the origin of the church in Troas is briefly introduced in notes at Acts 20:7.

[35] McGarvey, *op. cit.*, p.86.

sion, and used it to prove they should head for Macedonia to preach.

7. Through Samothrace and Neapolis. 16:11

16:11 – *Therefore putting out to sea from Troas, we ran a straight course to Samothrace, and on the day following to Neapolis;*

Therefore putting out to sea from Troas, we ran a straight course to Samothrace. Samothrace is an island in the Aegean Sea, about half-way between Troas and Neapolis. It is about eight miles long, and six across, very mountainous, with some of its peaks being 5000 feet above sea level. The island can be seen from both continents, both from Troas and from the hills between Neapolis and Philippi. This little island was the chief seat of the Cabirian mystery religions (second in reputation only to the Eleusinian mysteries), initiation into which carried with it the right of asylum; thus, many of the people living here were fugitives and criminals who had come here seeking asylum.

The direction they were sailing was to the northwest, and the nautical word "straight course" implies that they had the wind in their favor. They would be sailing against the current. A subsequent voyage (Acts 20:6) in the opposite direction and with the current took five days; it must have been a stiff wind they had behind them on this trip. After the manner of navigation of the time, the missionary party put into harbor each night until the destination was finally reached. Thus, Samothrace is the end of the first day's voyage.

And on the day following to Neapolis. Another day's sailing northwest from Samothrace, and they come to Neapolis, modern day Kavalla, a seaport with two harbors. The Greek name means "new city." (Several miles to the west of Neapolis archaeologists have uncovered the ruins of Palaeopolis, "old city.") Neapolis served as the seaport for Philippi, which was some twelve miles inland. Archeological remains of Neapolis are still visible – ruins of an aqueduct, columns, and Greek and Latin inscriptions – all attesting to the former importance of this Roman city. It was the regular landing place for those who proposed to travel by the Egnatian Way, the great Roman military highway stretching some 490 miles across Macedonia, linking the Adriatic with the Aegean Sea. The road was built after the Roman conquest of Macedonia in 146 BC. Toward the western end of the road, it branched, with one branch terminating at Dyrrhachium and the other at Valona in the land we call Albania. Just across the sea from Valona, at Brundisium, in the heel of the boot of Italy, the road continued toward Rome, only it was called the Appian Way in Italy. Portions of the Egnatian Way are still visible between Neapolis and Philippi.

8. In Philippi. 16:12-40

16:12 – *and from there to Philippi, which is a leading city of the district of Macedonia, a Roman colony; and we were staying in this city for some days.*

And from there to Philippi. The city of Philippi had been repaired and adorned by Philip of Macedon, the father of Alexander the Great, and the name was changed by Philip from Krenides ("wells" or "fountains") to Philippi. In former years, Philippi was a "gold rush" town whose silver and gold mines were found on nearby Mt. Pangaeus. Near here, during the civil wars of the Romans, the decisive battle between Brutus and Antony was fought. Fifteen years after his first visit, while he was in Rome during his first Roman imprisonment, Paul wrote the New Testament book of Philippians, to the church located in this city.

Which is a leading city of the district of Macedonia. The whole region of Macedonia had been conquered by the Romans under Paulus Aemilius about 150 BC. What had been in Greek times four different countries were joined together by the Romans into the province called Macedonia; so, in New Testament times, the Roman province was made up of four districts.

The word "leading city" gives some difficulty, and has been alleged by negative critics as being an instance of Luke's inaccuracy.

- The KJV reads "the *chief* city of the district," which gives the impression that it was the largest city of the district in which it stood. But this is not true, for Amphipolis was the largest city in the district.

- Others have suggested that "chief" meant it was the capital city of the district, but again this honor belonged to Amphipolis.[36]

- The ASV reads "*first* of the district," by which the translators meant that Philippi was the first town entered when crossing the border from Trace and entering Macedonia.

- The NASB, noting the fact that there is no definite article in the Greek, translates "a *leading* city of the district." *Prōtē polis* frequently appears on coins of cities which enjoyed certain privileges, such as we shall note shortly that Philippi enjoyed. To say that Philippi was a "leading city of the district" is exactly right, and Luke cannot be charged with making a mistake here.

A *Roman* colony. The Greeks had two words for "colony." One designated a Greek colony, and one designated a Roman colony.[37] The latter is used here, so the NASB rightly adds the word "Roman" to the text. A Roman "colony" differed from the modern idea of a colony (like the 13 colonies which were the beginning of the United States). A Roman colony was essentially a military position for the defense of the frontiers, or for keeping the more hostile provincials in order. Philippi was designated as a "colony" after the battle between Brutus and Antony.[38] A Roman colony enjoyed three privileges: (1) *libertas*, or self-government, (2) *immunitas*, or freedom from paying tribute to the Emperor, and (3) *jus Italicum*, or the rights of those who lived in Italy – including Roman dress, language, coinage, and holidays. The Philippians were proud of their Roman citizenship, and in the Philippian letter there are several references to that pride.[39]

---

[36] The other district capitals were Thessalonica, Pella, and Pelagonia.

[37] *Apoikia* is the word for a Greek colony. *Kolōnia* is the word for a Roman colony.

[38] Six Roman colonies are named in Acts, but only Philippi is designated as such by Luke. The others are Pisidian Antioch, Lystra, Troas, Corinth, and Ptolemais.

[39] Philippians 1:17, 3:20.

And we were staying in this city for some days. Some of the events that happened during these days are recorded in the following verses.

16:13 – *And on the Sabbath day we went outside the gate to a riverside, where we were supposing that there would be a place of prayer; and we sat down and began speaking to the women who had assembled.*

And on the Sabbath day. Apparently several days passed before Saturday, the first Sabbath after their arrival.

We went outside the gate to a river side. Cities in that day were walled for protection; traffic entered and departed through gates in the walls. The missionaries exited through one of these gates, heading for the river side. The river Gangites (sometimes spelled Gargites) was one mile west of the town.[40]

Where we were supposing that there would be a place of prayer. There had to be at least ten family heads in a community to have a synagogue.[41] Where fewer Jews than this lived, they often had a meeting place near any body of water suitable for their many ceremonial washings.[42] Such "places of prayer" might be no more than a simple circle of stones in a grove of trees.[43] The English translation "would be" is more indefinite than is actually true in the Greek.[44] The Greek expresses sufficient definiteness about a place of prayer being found there that we may suppose the missionaries have inquired around town and were told that if any Jews were worshiping, they could be found out by the river.[45]

And we sat down and began speaking. Note that Luke includes himself, along with Paul, Silas, and Timothy, as one of the preachers. Perhaps the picture is of the men taking turns from Sabbath to Sabbath. Jewish teachers habitually sat down to teach.[46]

---

[40] Barnes is in error when he says, "What river this was is not known" (Barnes, *op. cit.*, p.240). On the plain just west of this river, in 42 BC, the armies of Brutus and Cassius met the armies of Octavian and Antony in the battle which decided the fate of the Roman Republic. Brutus and Cassius, who were responsible for the assassination of Julius Caesar, took their own lives as the armies of Octavian and Antony won the battle. Octavian was later known as the Emperor Augustus.

[41] *Pirke Aboth*, III.7.

[42] While in the Babylonian captivity, Jews sat down "by the rivers of Babylon" (Psalm 137:1; Ezra 8:15,21). Juvenal (*Sat.* III.11-13) lamented how the Jews had succeeded in buying up many pieces of ground for use as places of prayer.

[43] The word *proseuchē* was the Greek equivalent for the Hebrew "house of prayer." It can refer to a building (Matthew 21:13; Josephus, *Life*. 54) as well as a place by a river side such as we have described.

[44] In technical terms, the Greek grammar is a case of indirect discourse after the verb *nomidzō* (to think). "We were thinking there *was* a place of prayer" would be a good translation.

[45] In the background of this verse may be the historical fact that Claudius had commanded all Jews to depart from Rome (see Acts 18:2). Since Philippi was a colony, that expulsion order would likely have been honored there, too. When the missionaries made inquiry, they would have been told, "There aren't many Jews here anymore, but you might find some meeting out by the river side." Still, we must be careful in our reconstruction here, because the laws made for the city of Rome were not always carried out in the colonies. What was done in the colonies often depended on the local conditions.

[46] Matthew 5:1; Luke 4:20-21.

To the women who had assembled. Was it that Lydia and several of her servants and friends were all the people in Philippi who worshiped Jehovah God? It is possible that the edict of Claudius against the Jews had been enforced in Philippi. Some commentators, noting that Lydia was a proselyte of the gate, suggest that she and a few others like her have attempted to remain true to their new faith, even though the male Jewish leadership has been expelled from the town. Others suggest the missionaries spoke before the regular worship service, and that there were other men present also. It is entirely within the range of probability that among these women who had assembled were Euodia and Syntyche,[47] who Paul tells us labored with him in the gospel, and whose alienation from each other about the time Paul wrote to the Philippians was such a cause of concern to the apostle.

16:14 – *And a certain woman named Lydia, from the city of Thyatira, a seller of purple fabrics, a worshiper of God, was listening; and the Lord opened her heart to respond to the things spoken by Paul.*

And a certain woman named Lydia. The fact that she, and not her husband, is named as the purple-seller is at least presumptive evidence that she was carrying on the business by herself. Whether or not this woman was ever married, or if she had been and her husband is now dead, is not indicated anywhere in the text. Lydia was a popular name for women.

A seller of purple fabrics. Purple was a most valuable color, obtained usually from shellfish. One tiny drop of dye was obtained from each fish. Whether Lydia sold the dye, or the fabric already dyed, is not certain. Fabric dyed with this purple dye was in great demand among the rich, for it was used as the official toga at Rome and in the colonies. The term "royal purple" is still used.[48]

From the city of Thyatira. Its modern name is Akhisar, and it was in the Roman province of Asia.[49] Homer indicated that the art of dyeing had long been one of the things Thyatira was noted for.[50] Inscriptions found at Thyatira bear witness to the existence of a guild (or labor union) of purple-sellers there, and perhaps Lydia belonged to it. She would likely have been a woman who possessed a considerable amount of wealth to be able to carry on her business so far from her native city. It may be that the home office of her business was located in Thyatira, and she had a branch office in the city of Philippi.

A worshiper of God. She apparently was a proselyte of the gate, for the Greek word *sebomenē* means "God-fearer" or a proselyte of the gate.[51] She could have gained her knowledge of the Jewish religion at Thyatira, for there was a Jewish population there. Or she may have become interested in a better religion than heathenism while living in Phil-

---

[47] Philippians 4:2-3.

[48] The rich man in the story Jesus told wore such purple garments (Luke 16:19).

[49] Revelation 2:18 shows there eventually came to be a church at Thyatira, but it was probably not planted until the third missionary journey, when "all Asia" heard the word of the Lord (Acts 19:10).

[50] *Iliad*, IV.141.

[51] See comments at Acts 13:50 on "the devout women."

ippi. One wonders why she is not mentioned in the letter Paul later addresses to the Philippians, since she was the first convert to Christ there. Has she moved on with her business to another city, or (as one commentator suggests) has she died in the interval?

Was listening [to us]. The verb tense indicates that she has been listening to the preaching of Paul, Luke, and the others over a period of time.

And the Lord opened her heart to respond. Whatever this difficult verse means, it does not appear that it is an example of what has been called "a first work of grace."[52] According to that Calvinistic doctrine, man is so totally depraved as a result of inheritance from Adam, that he cannot even want to do right (e.g., respond to the gospel in this case) until God's Spirit first, by an immediate and direct action on the heart of the sinner, makes the man capable or able to believe. This direct operation on the heart is known as a "first work of grace."[53] Special Study #3, "The Person and Work of the Holy Spirit," showed that in conversion God's Spirit works through the Word to bring about conviction in the heart of the sinner. The Spirit's work in conversion is not something done directly upon the heart apart from the preached Word.

It must be insisted that in Lydia's case God worked the same way He did in any other case of conversion. This affirmation does not rule out the idea that God had something to do with the conversion of this woman. In fact, He did.[54] He many years before had given a revelation to Moses, intended to point people to Christ; and Lydia had become a proselyte to that religion. He had brought the preachers to Philippi right at the proper time (instead of permitting them to go into Asia or Bithynia). There may even have been circumstances in her life (e.g., has her husband just recently died?) which in the providence of God made her more receptive at this time than she might have been at other times. And there was the convicting work of the Spirit as the preachers presented the gospel. A person's heart is said to be closed when that person is unwilling to hear and obey God's message. The heart is open when the message is received.[55]

To the things spoken by Paul. All the missionaries had been involved in the teaching as

---

[52] Compare notes at Acts 15:11 on "grace," including footnote #39. The reader will quickly see that in this passage we have met another of the five points of Calvinism. Compare footnote #42 in chapter 8. The verse we are now commenting on is one in which part of the doctrine of "Irresistible Grace" is thought to be found. The whole Calvinistic system is based on a preconceived view of man that was learned from Augustine, rather than from the Bible, and this is one reason it is to be rejected. One of the contributions made by Restoration Movement theologians to 20th century religious thought was the dislodging of Calvinism's doctrines from their well-nigh stranglehold on theological thinking. This battle must yet be continued by the heirs of the Restoration Movement.

[53] The doctrine of prevenient, or first work of, grace is objectionable because it tends to make God a respecter of persons, which the Bible plainly says He is not! For if God gives some individuals this prevenient grace, and withholds it from others, it is hard to see anything but partiality towards some.

[54] We might use the language "God's initiative" in salvation, were it not that we might be misunderstood as teaching prevenient grace. God has always taken the initiative in providing the opportunity for salvation to sinful men. What we are objecting to is the idea of a special work of the Spirit directly on the heart, apart from the Word.

[55] See notes at Acts 8:6 on the phrase "were giving attention to," where Luke uses the same Greek verb which is here translated "respond."

the weeks passed, but it was to one of Paul's messages that Lydia finally responded. Luke has so often shared with us the topics and emphases which Paul was speaking that he does not need to repeat them here. Involved in Paul's preaching was not only the facts about Jesus, but what was needed to respond to the invitation. Prospects were always directed to believe the gospel, to repent of their sins, and to be immersed for the forgiveness of their sins. Baptism was one of the things the missionaries spoke about, as can be seen from the way in which Luke tells us of Lydia's observance of that ordinance. He says, "And when she had been baptized," implying that this was one of the things she had been taught to do.

16:15 – *And when she and her household had been baptized, she urged us, saying, "If you have judged me to be faithful to the Lord, come into my house and stay." And she prevailed upon us.*

And when she ... had been baptized. She was baptized without any delay.[56] It was usual to be baptized immediately upon believing. She perhaps was baptized in the river beside which the group has been meeting.[57] Lydia has sometimes been called the first convert to Christianity in Europe. She seems to be Paul's first convert in Europe, but we have already noted the possibility that there were Christians in Rome several years before this.[58]

And her household. The word seems to have reference to her *familia*, servants and others who were employed by her in her business. That these household members were present at the place of prayer implies either that they were proselytes like Lydia, or that she has been bringing them specially to hear the preachers.

Those who practice infant sprinkling often attempt to appeal to such passages as this to "prove" that infant sprinkling was practiced in Bible times, but it certainly is reading a great deal between the lines to find such proof in this passage. There are four cases of household baptism mentioned in the New Testament, and there is positive proof that in three of these there were no infants baptized.

- In the case of Cornelius, all who were baptized had previously spoken in tongues and believed.[59]
- In the case of the Philippian jailer, all those who were baptized rejoiced in the Lord and believed.[60]
- In the case of Stephanas, "they devoted themselves to the ministry to the saints" after they were baptized.[61]

In these three cases there is an absence of infants. We are therefore justified (no evidence

---

[56] Compare Acts 2:41 and 8:38. It is rather anomalous to preach baptism for the remission of sins, but then put off baptizing the penitent believer for several days or even weeks — as has been practiced in some places recently.

[57] See notes at verse 13.

[58] See Introductory Studies, p.*xiv*, under comments on "The Edict of Claudius."

[59] Acts 10:46, 15:9.

[60] Acts 16:34.

[61] 1 Corinthians 1:16, 16:15.

to the contrary appearing) in holding that it was similar in the case of Lydia's household, i.e., no infants were baptized.[62]

She urged us, saying, "If you have judged me to be faithful to the Lord, come into my house and stay." And she prevailed upon us. It appears that she several times invited the missionaries to stay in her home while they were working in Philippi, and that they several times refused. Finally, she said, "If my faith was sufficient to be baptized on, why is it not good enough for me to be your hostess?" When she said this, there was nothing more that Paul could do to object, and so they went to Lydia's home to stay. Again, here is evidence that she was rather wealthy, for it would cost some money to provide room and board for the four missionaries.

It was rare for Paul to accept aid from his converts while he was still in their town.[63] He did not want any of his opponents to be able to say that he was just preaching because of the money it made for him. Up to this time the missionaries must have been providing their own lodging (was Paul earning the money by tent-making, or Luke by practicing his medicine?). Now Lydia will take care of these expenses. The hospitality Peter received in the house of Cornelius and the hospitality extended by Lydia are two examples of the hospitality which early in the life of the church came to characterize the brethren, and which many of the writers of the New Testament were to encourage.[64] Ever after this, the Philippian church keeps sending missionary offerings to help Paul in his evangelistic work, and we do not doubt that Lydia was one of the generous contributors to these offerings (cp. Philippians 4:2,3,15).

16:16 – *And it happened that as we were going to the place of prayer, a certain slave-girl having a spirit of divination met us, who was bringing her masters much profit by fortunetelling.*

And it happened that. It appears that some days have passed since Lydia's conversion.

As we were going to the place of prayer. They are still using the spot by the riverside as a schoolroom to teach people about Christ. Most modern translations take the article before "prayer" (the Greek reads "unto *the* prayer") as meaning "the place of prayer."

A certain slave-girl having a spirit of divination met us. The following phrases indicate that this slave girl was demon possessed.[65] Literally translated, the Greek says that it was a "Python spirit" by which the girl was possessed. In Greek mythology, Python was a monstrous dragon who lived in a cave on Mt. Parnassus just north of the town of Delphi in Greece. In the town of Delphi was a temple where people could get their fortunes told. The place had long been a center of pagan worship, whose priests had developed an elaborate ritual, centered about a chief priestess whose title was Pythia. Kings and public

---

[62] Further, baptism (i.e., immersion) and sprinkling are very different things.

[63] Act 20:33; 2 Corinthians 12:17.

[64] 1 Peter 4:9; Romans 12:13; 1 Timothy 5:10; 3 John 5.

[65] See notes regarding demon possession in Special Study #11, "Demons and Demon Possession."

officials would come to get their fortunes told and to get advice on matters of national policy, and private citizens would come to seek information about marriage or business ventures. The Python was supposed to give them the advice they sought. It worked in this fashion. In the center of the temple at Delphi was a small opening in the ground from whence mind-bending fumes arose. The priestess breathed these, sat down on a three-legged stool located over the opening, and thence delivered the "oracles." Having breathed the fumes, the priestess became violently agitated, and spoke in tongues (frenzied, ecstatic syllabication) whatever the Python prompted her to say.[66] A poet or priest standing by would then "translate" what the Pythoness had said and give the "prophecy" to the worshiper who had come to inquire of the Oracle at Delphi.

Connecting all this mythology with the slave girl who has been following Paul, she had the same kind of "spirit" that characterized the priestess at Delphi. She was demon possessed, and the demon seemed to speak from inside her body when she was giving out her "fortunes."[67] How she became involved in this type of thing, Luke does not say. Perhaps she at one time was one of the women who told fortunes in one of the temples of Apollo.[68] Luke's language is entirely in harmony with the idea that demons took over and controlled these priestesses, enabling them to tell the fortunes of the inquirers.

Who was bringing her masters much profit by fortunetelling. There were at least two men who had joint ownership of this girl (perhaps they bought her at a slave market), and who used her powers as a source of revenue. It appears that they made large sums of money from her unfortunate condition. "Fortunetelling" (*manteuomai*) appears only here in the New Testament, and it is significant that in the Septuagint it is always used of lying prophets or of divination contrary to the Law.[69] The Greeks themselves distinguished between fortunetelling and prophecy (*propheteuō*), and recognized the superior dignity of the latter.[70]

16:17 – *Following after Paul and us, she kept crying out, saying, "These men are bond-servants of the Most High God, who are proclaiming to you the way of salvation."*

Following after Paul and us. Why should she continually follow the missionaries? Some suggest she was trying to gain advertising for herself or her masters, that their business might prosper. Another suggests that down deep in her heart (when not under the influence of the demon) she knew that she was in bondage, and hoped by following the apostles to have the spirit rebuked. Another suggests that she followed because of the overwhelming power of the evil spirit, forcing her to follow and cry out as the demon attempted to get at

---

[66] According to Greek mythology, Apollo, Zeus' son, had long ago slain the dragon, and himself took over giving these revelations. But the priestesses were still commonly said to be possessed by a Python spirit.

[67] From Plutarch (*De Defectu Orac.*, IX) it appears that "Python" is synonymous with *eggastrimuthos* ("ventriloquist"), the word regularly used to translate the Hebrew '*ob*. All these words refer to the voice that seems to come from inside the chest cavity of the medium through whom the familiar spirit (demon) speaks. See further details on this in Special Study #17, "The World of the Occult."

[68] Apollo had temples at places other than Delphi, namely, in Thebes, Delos, Claros, and at Patara in Lycia.

[69] Deuteronomy 18:10; 1 Samuel 28:9; Ezekiel 13:6; Micah 3:11.

[70] R.C. Trench, *Synonyms of the New Testament* (Grand Rapids: Eerdmans. 1953), p.19ff.

these Godly men through the possessed girl. Before this incident in Philippi, there seemed to be unusual opportunities for the spread of the gospel. The Jews were making no effort to persecute the missionaries, nor were the civil authorities taking any unfavorable actions toward the preachers.

She kept crying out, saying, "These men are bond-servants of the Most High God. "Crying out" is a word regularly used of the loud outcries of men who were demon possessed. "Most High God" is also a title regularly used of God by the demons.[71]

Who are proclaiming to you the way of salvation." The Greek reads "*A* way of salvation," and this is the way it must be translated if the verse is to make any real sense. One of the doctrines of the occult is that Christianity is just one of many ways of salvation. It is "*a* way" of salvation, no better or no worse than others, like Buddhism, Islam, or Zoroastrianism. Since he knew that Christ is the *only* way of access to God (Acts 4:12), no wonder Paul was troubled by her speech and took action!

16:18 – *And she continued doing this for many days. But Paul was greatly annoyed, and turned and said to the spirit, "I command you in the name of Jesus Christ to come out of her!" And it came out at that very moment.*

And she continued doing this for many days. That the slave girl followed the preachers to the place of prayer for many days before the demon was expelled indicates that the place of prayer had been chosen as their daily place of meeting. It may be that they could find no suitable place inside the city. Day by day, as the missionaries went to the place of prayer, she followed them through the streets of Philippi, crying out in a loud voice that these men were servants of the Most High God, who were proclaiming a way of salvation.

But Paul was greatly annoyed. The word can include at once the different ideas of grief, pain, and anger. At times Paul felt sorrow for the girl. At times he was angered by the demon's actions. It is obvious that the constant repetition of these clamorous cries must have been a hindrance to the apostle's work, disturbing him as he talked to the people assembled at the place of prayer. God's messengers have never needed the demons to testify and witness for them. If Paul had continued permitting her to tell about the missionary party, people would have begun to think, "They're all alike! Birds of a feather flock together, you know."

And turned and said to the spirit, "I command you in the name of Jesus Christ to come out of her." Suddenly, Paul turned and ordered the demon out of the girl. The same strong word for command was used by Jesus when He cast out a demon.[72] What Paul did is an example of a miraculous casting out of a demon, an example of the spiritual gift of casting out demons.[73]

---

[71] Luke 4:41, 8:28; Mark 5:7.

[72] Luke 8:29. See notes at Acts 3:6 on the phrase "in the name of" as signifying nothing less than Jesus' personal power and existence.

[73] Mark 16:17ff; Acts 5:16.

And it came out at that very moment. The compound verb "came out" gives the idea that the demon not only came out, but departed, too. The expulsion of the evil spirit would be a signal evidence of the fact that the missionaries were really from God – a far better proof than her clamorous cries had been. Luke doesn't tell us what became of the girl out of whom the demon was cast.

> What became of the maid thus miraculously relieved of demon possession we are not informed; but gratitude for so great a deliverance should have thrown her under the influence of Paul and of the good women who were now actively cooperating with him and who would naturally be interested in her welfare.[74]

16:19 – *But when her masters saw that their hope of profit was gone, they seized Paul and Silas and dragged them into the market place before the authorities,*

But when her masters saw that their hope of profit was gone. This is the thing that troubled and enraged her owners – loss of profit. Instead of being happy that an afflicted person is made well, instead of being aware of divine power being present, they were intent only on their profits. No small part of the opposition to the gospel arises from the fact that, if embraced, it would strike at so much of the dishonorable employments of men and make them honest and conscientious. The only two times Luke records a Gentile persecution of the missionaries, the attack arises from a threat to the pocketbooks of the persecutors.[75] By repeating the Greek word "gone," Luke makes a play on words, which is lost to the English reader. He says that when the evil spirit "went out" (*exēlthen*), the masters saw that their hope of profit "went out" (*exēlthen*).

They seized Paul and Silas. In that day men could do their own arresting; they did not have to call the police, as is our practice today. It was a sort of "citizen's arrest." Luke and Timothy are not arrested for some reason. Either they are not as conspicuous as Paul and Silas, or they were not present at the time of the arrest.

And dragged them into the market place before the authorities. The market place in Philippi would have been similar to the Roman forum, since this was a colony. The judgment seat, on which the authorities sat to administer justice, and from which orators made speeches, would have been located there. There would have been some similarity to the courthouse square in many of our county seat towns. The forum was the center of social and commercial life. If the "authorities" named in this phrase are different men than the magistrates spoken of in the next verse, then the idea is this: the two missionaries were first brought before rulers of a lower rank (e.g., city officials), and then these authorities sent them to a higher court (i.e., the magistrates).

This is the first Gentile persecution recorded by Luke. All the persecutions that had preceded this one had been instigated by the Jews.

---

[74] McGarvey, *op. cit.*, p.97.

[75] See Acts 16:19 and 19:23ff.

16:20 – *and when they had brought them to the chief magistrates, they said, "These men are throwing our city into confusion, being Jews,*

And when they had brought them to the chief magistrates. "Magistrates represents the Greek word *stratēgois*, and was the regular title for the leader of an army, a general. Outside the army, the term was given to the highest office holders in the colonies. Their Latin title was *duumviri* ("two men"). These men had the power to administer justice in all but the most important cases (which went either to the governor or proconsul, or to Caesar himself). Since Philippi was a Roman colony, there is a good possibility that the magistrates had in their earlier days been officers in the army, and now that they have retired from the army they have become the civic rulers of the city.

They said, "These men are throwing our city into confusion, being Jews. Noting that the missionaries were "Jews" appears to be an attempt to prejudice the court before any evidence was given. Romans and Greeks all over the empire already had an antipathy for the Jews, and if the decree of Claudius expelling the Jews from Rome was just a recent thing, this identification of the missionaries as Jews would have more influence on the judges. In addition to the aspersion that they were Jews, the owners of the slave girl charge the missionaries with disturbing the peace. An additional charge will be given in verse 21.

> Roman magistrates would not pass sentence on abstract theological questions (Acts 18:15); but if the peace was disturbed or a secret sect was organized, the magistrates would pass sentence on these things.[76]

16:21 – *and are proclaiming customs which it is not lawful for us to accept or to observe, being Romans."*

And are proclaiming customs which it is not lawful for us to accept or to observe, being Romans." The word "customs" refers to religious rites or forms of worship.[77] The owners of the slave girl are charging the missionaries with introducing a new religion which was unauthorized by Roman laws. When Rome conquered a land, they allowed the people to keep all the religions they had. Such were called *religio licita*. Thus, the Jews were allowed to continue to practice their ancient religion, provided they did not attempt to proselytize Roman citizens. Roman law forbade the introduction of any new religion. Such religions were called *religio illicita*. Cicero wrote, "No person shall have any separate gods, or new ones; nor shall he privately worship any strange gods, unless they be publicly allowed."[78] Virgil wrote, "Care was taken among the Athenians and the Romans that no one should introduce new religions."[79] The Christian religion was permitted in the Empire since it was thought of, in the first years, as being just another sect of Judaism.

---

[76] Boles, *op. cit.*, p.260.

[77] See Acts 6:14 where the word "customs" was used before.

[78] *De Legibus*, II.8.

[79] *Aeneid*, VIII.187.

"Being Romans" reflects the pride of the Philippians in their Roman citizenship. "We are Roman citizens," these slave owners claimed, "and these Jews have broken the law by teaching the religion they do." It is likely that the slave owners cared little either for the Jewish religion or any of the Roman religions, but it was a cunning charge they have brought against the missionaries.

16:22 – *And the crowd rose up together against them, and the chief magistrates tore their robes off them, and proceeded to order* **them** *to be beaten with rods.*

And the crowd rose up together against them. There would have been many people in the forum on business, and these are the ones who join in the attack on the missionaries. Perhaps the crowd has been inflamed by the contemptuous use of the name "Jews." As they stand around the judgment seat, they demand a verdict against Paul and Silas.

And the chief magistrates tore their robes off them. This was normal when the prisoner was about to be beaten with rods. In a Roman court, the criminal was usually stripped entirely naked. Usually the lictors would be the ones to tear the robes off the prisoner, rather than the magistrates doing it. However, in this case, perhaps because of the rising furor of the crowd, the magistrates themselves begin the punishment by violently tearing all the clothes off the missionaries.

And proceeded to order *them* **to be beaten with rods.** The beating was done by the lictors, whose job it was to administer the punishment ordered by the court.[80] Apparently there was no serious investigation of the charges against the missionaries. This beating was one of three that Paul suffered during his lifetime of service for Christ.[81] Paul was very humiliated by the treatment, for he tells us in 1 Thessalonians 2:2 about how he was "shamefully treated" at Philippi.

16:23 – *And when they had inflicted many blows upon them, they threw them into prison, commanding the jailer to guard them securely;*

And when they had inflicted many blows upon them. Luke seems to be telling us that the punishment was more severe than usual. A word needs to be said here about the difference between Roman and Jewish beatings. The Jews used a leather whip and were not allowed to inflict more than 40 stripes.[82] The Romans used a rod, similar in size to a present-day broom stick or hoe handle, and there was no limit to the number of blows that could be struck. Such treatment would leave a man lacerated and bleeding.

They threw them into prison. Barnes gives several reasons for throwing Paul and Silas into prison: it was partly as a punishment, and partly with a view of later taking further vengeance on them more according to forms of law.[83]

---

[80] Concerning "lictors," see the additional comments at verse 35.

[81] 2 Corinthians 11:25.

[82] 2 Corinthians 11:24.

[83] Barnes, *op. cit.*, p.244.

Commanding the jailer to guard them securely. See verse 27 for information concerning the responsibility of the Roman jailer.

16:24 – *and he, having received such a command, threw them into the inner prison, and fastened their feet in the stocks.*

And he, having received such a command, threw them into the inner prison. In a Roman prison, there were usually three distinct sections: (1) the *communiora*, a room where the prisoners had light and fresh air; (2) the *interiora*, a room where the prisoners were made secure by strong iron gates with bars and locks, and (3) the *tullianium*, or dungeon, a room where there would be little air or light, sometimes an underground dungeon like the Mamertine prison at Rome, sometimes above ground, but a place of maximum security. It was into this *tullianium* part of the jail at Philippi where the jailer threw the missionaries. While prisoners who were kept in the inner prison often were executed there, or kept there awaiting execution, it is not necessary to suppose the missionaries are close to being executed. It is just a case of the jailer making sure he doesn't fail to do as he was commanded.

And fastened their feet in the stocks. The Greek reads, "He made their feet secure into the wood." Stocks, as with us, speaks of a wooden frame with holes in it for arms or legs or head. Such an instrument of punishment is as old as Jeremiah's day.[84] Some criminals were fastened hand, head, and foot, but the language here indicates that only their legs were fastened in this case. The two heavy pieces of timber would be opened, the legs of the prisoners stretched widely apart till their muscles began to hurt, and the timbers clamped shut. Clamped in such a spread-legged position they would be unable to walk, and they would be forced to lie with their backs or faces on the ground. Their wounds have been unattended since the beating with rods. McGarvey has an understanding note at this place. "These men's faith would have been heroic indeed if some painful questioning did not intrude as to why God allowed them to receive such a reward for their faithful service."[85]

16:25 – *But about midnight Paul and Silas were praying and singing hymns of praise to God, and the prisoners were listening to them;*

But about midnight. Probably their painful posture and the soreness from the beating combined to prevent their being able to go to sleep. What are these two thinking when they are unable to go to sleep at night? "At midnight, I will rise up to give thanks unto you, O God, because of your righteous judgments," wrote the Psalmist.[86]

Paul and Silas were praying and singing hymns of praise to God. The Greek grammar expresses one act rather than two. "Paul and Silas were singing while praying." Whether they were singing some of the prayer-psalms written by David, or whether they were singing some of the new songs of the church that offered adoration to Jesus, they turn their

---

[84] Jeremiah 29:26.

[85] McGarvey, *op. cit.*, p.100.

[86] Psalm 119:62.

thoughts heavenward and seek the sustaining grace of God.

And the prisoners were listening to them. The Greek verb "listen" used here is an unusual one, and tells us they "were listening eagerly." It was the kind of listening which men give to music that thrills the soul. Paul and Silas were singing a prayer to the God in whose service they had been led to this city. And the prisoners were listening, because this was different, greatly different, from the sounds they usually heard echoing through the halls and rooms of this prison! Instead of wild curses and foul jests, these men are hearing what amounts to a sermon in song as Paul and Silas call to God.

16:26 – *and suddenly there came a great earthquake, so that the foundations of the prison house were shaken; and immediately all the doors were opened, and everyone's chains were unfastened.*

And suddenly there came a great earthquake. "Suddenly" indicates these events happened while Paul and Silas were in the midst of singing their prayers to God. The area around Philippi was known for its recurring earthquakes, but this is no natural, chance happening. This is God taking a hand in the proceedings, just as in chapter 4:31.

So that the foundations of the prison-house were shaken. It takes a considerable tremor to cause movement and shaking of the foundations of buildings.

And immediately all the doors were opened. This effect gives evidence of the magnitude of the event God caused. The earthquake was violent enough to shift the walls and leave the doors torn off hinges.

And everyone's chains were unfastened. This effect is evidence that something more than a natural earthquake is involved. The tremor apparently cracked the walls, allowing the chains by which the prisoners were shackled to detach; that is, the rings and staples slipped free from the mortar and stones which held them. But it also seems apparent that the stocks in which Paul and Silas were fastened were opened, and this is hardly possible from the effects of an earthquake alone. That these men's stocks were loosed appears from verse 29, where Paul and Silas are apparently standing as the jailer falls down before them.

16:27 – *When the jailer had been roused out of sleep and had seen the prison doors opened, he drew his sword and was about to kill himself, supposing that the prisoners had escaped.*

When the jailer had been roused out of sleep and had seen the prison doors were opened, he drew his sword. The Greek language has several words for "sword." There is the big *romphaia* which often had to be held with both hands as it was swung at an opponent. There was also the small straight sword, *xiphos*, used for thrusting in close hand-to-hand combat. Then there was the *machaira*, the word used here. Sometimes *machaira* speaks of a large knife, the kind that would be used for killing animals and cutting up the flesh. Other times it speaks of a small, curved, and at times double-edged sword, that would be wielded with one hand during fighting.

And was about to kill himself, supposing that the prisoners had escaped. It was customary to hold a jailer responsible for the safe keeping of prisoners, and to subject him to the punishment the prisoners would have received if he permitted them to escape.[87] It was a very common thing, even considered to be an honorable thing, among the Greeks and Romans, for a man to commit suicide when he was encompassed with dangers from which he seemed to be unable to escape.

16:28 – *But Paul cried out with a loud voice, saying, "Do yourself no harm, for we are all here!"*

But Paul cried out with a load voice, saying. How did Paul know what the jailer was about to do? Some have questioned the accuracy of the record here, saying that Paul could not have seen what the jailer was about to do when the jailer could not see well enough to know that the prisoners had not escaped. However, there are a host of satisfactory answers to this question without doubting Luke's record.

- There is a good possibility Paul *could* see what was happening. There was enough light in the outer area of the prison that the jailer could see the doors were open. From the darkness of the inner prison Paul could see what was happening in the more lighted area without difficulty, whereas the jailer could not see into the inner prison for it would be lost in darkness.

- Perhaps the jailer may have uttered a mortal cry as he drew the sword. Perhaps also, given that the sword was typically in a metal sheath, Paul heard a rattle as the sword was being drawn. The Greek word for "draw" is one from which comes our word "spasm," so it suggests something more than a simple drawing of the sword.

- Perhaps Paul, being a Roman citizen, knowing the penalty for a jailer whose prisoners escaped, and knowing the "honorable way" out, may have been anticipating what any jailer would be thinking in a time like this.

Do yourself no harm, for we are all here. Here is the evidence that Paul knew what the jailer was thinking about the prisoners having escaped.[88] Paul quickly assures him that the

---

[87] See Acts 12:18-19.

[88] Is "Do yourself no harm!" a prooftext against suicide? Barnes says it is (*op. cit.*, p.246), but it likely is stretching Paul's statement somewhat to find in it a general principle against suicide.

- There is no explicit prohibition of suicide in the Old Testament. Cases of suicide in the Old Testament include Ahithophel, Zimri, Samson, Saul, and Abimelech.

- There is no explicit prohibition of suicide in the New Testament, though some draw prohibitory implications from Romans 14:7-9, 1 Corinthians 6:19, Ephesians 5:29, and Acts 1:25 (where the actions of Judas are called "iniquity").

- The early church fathers allowed the taking of one's own life under very stringent circumstances. However, Augustine, in the *City of God*, denied its legitimacy no matter what the situation, arguing that it precluded the possibility of repentance, and that, as a species of murder, it violated the sixth commandment.

- Thomas Aquinas held that it was a usurpation of God's power "to kill or make alive." (*Summa Theologica*, II.II, Q.64, article 5.)

- Present-day attitudes toward suicide vary. (1) Many churchmen find no sin in suicide if it is a case of mental illness or insanity. (2) Others posit that when a man becomes so depressed that he commits

prisoners have not fled.

"We are all here." Why did the other prisoners not leave the prison when they had been freed by the earthquake? Some suggest the prisoners were too terrified by the violent tremors of the quake to think of escaping. Some suggest that they did not have time to escape before the jailer was roused from sleep (although the jailer seemed to think they had had time – else why the thought of suicide?). Luke does not state the exact reason, but it is likely that God's hand was in it. Perhaps the impression which the two missionaries' behavior had produced on the other prisoners (verse 25) kept them from escaping after the sudden earthquake had loosed them.

What happened to the prisoners who listened to Paul and Silas in that midnight service of prayer? We can only make a speculate. We should like to think some were led to hear and obey the gospel. Some, undoubtedly, merely wondered, and continued their way of life, unchanged.

16:29 – *And he called for lights and rushed in and, trembling with fear, he fell down before Paul and Silas,*

And he called for lights. The lights would be torches, rags on a stick, soaked in a flammable liquid such olive oil. The jailer's subordinates would quickly have come running with some burning torches.

And rushed in. Perhaps seizing a torch in his own hand, the jailer leaps into the darkness of the inner prison, to see for himself that all were there, just as Paul had said. We can see him making a hasty investigation, only to learn that Paul had spoken the truth.

And trembling with fear. Barnes explains the fear in these words, "Alarmed at the earthquake; amazed that the prisoners were still there; confounded at the calmness of Paul and Silas; and overwhelmed at the proof of the presence of God."[89] The Western text tells that the jailer first secured the others before he came trembling to where Paul and Silas were. We can agree with the idea expressed there, for his life was at stake and he would see to the security of the prisoners before he did much else.

He fell down before Paul and Silas. This was an act of reverence and respect. Did he remember the cries of the slave girl about how these were servants of the Most High God? By this act he places himself at the mercy of these men, who just a few hours before he had roughly handled as he threw them into the inner prison and put them in stocks. Neither

---

suicide, he more often than not brought himself to that state of mind because of sin in his life, and therefore God will hold him accountable. A Christian will never commit suicide, this second group should argue. (3) Voluntary euthanasia (also called "mercy killing") is a form of suicide and finds many supporters among preachers and theologians today. A vigorous defense of voluntary euthanasia is made by Joseph Fletcher in his book, *Morals and Medicine* (Boston: Beacon, 1960), but his views are based more on current philosophy than on Scripture. The moral issues at stake are discussed by Willard L. Sperry in his book, *The Ethical Basis of Medical Practice* (New York: Harper, 1950). See also *Who Shall Live?* edited by Kenneth Vaux (Philadelphia: Fortress Press, 1970).

[89] Barnes, *op. cit.*, p.246.

Paul nor Silas rebuked the jailer.[90] If the homage was in excess of what should be paid to a man, the missionaries evidently made allowance for the terror of the moment, and gently encouraged the jailer to rise.

16:30 – *and after he brought them out, he said, "Sirs, what must I do to be saved?"*

And after he brought them out. The jailer brings the two out from the inner prison.

He said, "Sirs, what must I do to be saved?" It is not likely that the jailer is speaking here of his own personal safety. He could scarcely now consider himself to be in danger of punishment from the Romans, for none of the prisoners in his charge had escaped. Nor did the missionaries understand his question to refer to his own physical safety. They immediately begin telling him about how to find salvation from guilt and punishment for sin. The evidence is that the jailer was concerned about his eternal, spiritual salvation. How would a pagan Roman know about such salvation? He could not but know that the slave girl had been crying "These men show you a way of salvation." He must have known that the crime these men were charged with had to do with religion (Christianity). He must now have been conscious (after the expulsion of the slave girl's demon and after the earthquake) that these men were under the protection of God Almighty, and that, perhaps, he was in danger of feeling the wrath of that God. If there was a mortal cry as he drew his sword, was that indicative of the fact that he was not ready to die, because his gods were powerless to save him or to help him after he was dead? All the events of the last few hours were fitted to show him his need of knowing the message these men had come to town preaching. "Sirs (*kurioi*)," he says, "help me!"

16:31 – *And they said, "Believe in the Lord Jesus, and you shall be saved, you and your household."*

And they said. The plural is not without significance. Paul was not the only teacher. Silas also took part in the explanation of what God required for salvation.

Believe in the Lord Jesus, and you shall be saved. There is a contrast in the Greek which the English reader misses. The jailer had addressed the preachers as "lords (*kurioi*)." They answer, 'There is just one Lord (*kurios*). Believe in Him, and salvation is yours!'

"Faith-only" adherents rely on this verse as a chief prooftext. All a person has to do to be saved is believe on the Lord Jesus, they tell us. Just believe – faith only! In a Special Study at the close of this chapter we examine this whole matter in detail. In the meantime, McGarvey's note will suffice.

> Those who catch at these words of Paul to the jailer, and draw the conclusion that salvation is by faith alone, leave the jail too soon. They should remain till they hear all – till they hear Paul tell the man to repent and be baptized, till the design of baptism is explained to him, till he is baptized, till he is found rejoicing greatly immediately after his baptism.[91]

---

[90] Compare Peter's response to the homage offered by Cornelius at Acts 10:26.

[91] McGarvey, *op. cit.*, p.103.

The salvation promised included deliverance from slavery to sin, deliverance from the guilt of sin, and deliverance from the penalty of sin, both in this world and the one to come.

You and your household. The household here includes those who are able to believe; the household of the jailer, therefore, cannot be appealed to as a prooftext for infant sprinkling.[92] The missionaries are telling the jailer that the same way to salvation was open to the members of his household as was open to him.[93]

16:32 – *And they spoke the word of the Lord to him together with all who were in his house.*

And they spoke the word of the Lord to him. How does faith come? It comes by hearing (Romans 10:17). Paul preached so that they might have something to believe. The jailer and his household cannot believe on Jesus as the Savior without evidence.

Together with all who were in his house. Paul and Silas instructed them in the fundamental doctrines of Christianity, which would include the ordinances (else how and why would they have known to be baptized?). Again, we have evidence that a person is not speaking the Word of the Lord if he omits baptism for the forgiveness of sins.

It is clear that belief in the Lord Jesus requires an explanation. The very title "Lord" indicates something about Jesus' exalted position, from which He directs God's creation. How did He come to have the position "Lord"? That requires an explanation about His life, death, and resurrection. The missionaries must have told how Christ Jesus came into the world to save sinners, and how people could meet the conditions upon which such salvation was granted. All this would have been included in "the word of the Lord" which was preached to that household providentially assembled between the hours of midnight and dawn.

16:33 – *And he took them that very hour of the night and washed their wounds, and immediately he was baptized, he and all his* **household.**

And he took them that *very* hour of the night. Again, there is a change of location. First, they were brought out of the inner prison (verse 30). Now, the prisoners are taken elsewhere in order that their wounds might be tended to.

And washed their wounds. The wounds were caused by the beating which they had received the evening before. It appears from this that though the apostles had the gift of miracles (including healing), they did not use the gift to alleviate their own sufferings or heal their own wounds. They restored others to health, but not themselves. It also has been properly pointed out that this action by the jailer indicates repentance. He was sorry for his sins and was willing to do what he could for the comfort and ease of Paul and Silas, to

---

[92] Compare notes on infant sprinkling at verse 15.

[93] There is no salvation by proxy in the New Testament. Salvation is an individual and personal matter. The words "and your house" cannot mean that all the other people in the house would be saved automatically if just the jailer believed. They must believe too if they would be saved. This understanding is reinforced by the activities of verse 33, where the missionaries "spoke the word of the Lord to ... all who were in his house."

whose hurt he had contributed.

And immediately he was baptized, he and all his *household*. Note again, there was no waiting several days to immerse this believer. Having heard the gospel, having believed it, having become repentant, now he and his household are immersed.[94] Having met these conditions, the jailer now had the salvation he had asked about (verse 30).

16:34 – *And he brought them into his house and set food before them, and rejoiced greatly, having believed in God with his whole household.*

And he brought them into his house. The Greek says "He brought them *up* into his house." Were his living quarters on the floor above the cells? He is not shirking his duty as a jailer by these kindnesses. He had been charged to keep them securely. How he did it was his own choice. He can share with the prisoners in this fashion, for if they didn't flee when they had the chance right after the earthquake, he need not worry about them trying to escape now.

And set food before them. Perhaps the prisoners have had nothing to eat for more than half a day, having been cast into the prison, evidently without any food. Here is another evidence of the jailer's thankfulness to the preachers.

And rejoiced greatly. This is the same word Luke used in 2:46 to describe the gladness of the early Christians. They found joy in doing things together. So at the table in the jailer's house, there was deep joy as they ate together. Perhaps one of the reasons for the joy in the jailer's heart is that it is one of the emotions produced by the indwelling Holy Spirit.[95] In addition, there was the joy that comes from a sense of sins being forgiven, that comes from having been obedient to the Lord. Observe that the emotion comes after obedience, not before.

Having believed in God with his whole household. Again, let the point be driven home that there was no infant baptism here in this household. This passage plainly states that each of these who were baptized were believers. The household became believers because the head of the household saw to it that they were present in order to hear and believe.

16:35 – *Now when day came, the chief magistrates sent their policemen, saying, "Release those men."*

Now when day came, the chief magistrates sent their policemen. The word translated "policemen" means, literally, "those having rods," i.e., the lictors. The magistrates are evi-

---

[94] Barnes (*op. cit.*, p.248), still trying to defend sprinkling, states that there was not enough water in the prison for this to be an immersion. However, verse 13 indicated there was a river near the town. And there is evidence in both verses 30 and 33 that the group is no longer in the inner prison. Verse 34 will say they went up into the jailer's house. The washing of the prisoners' wounds, and the washing away of the jailer's sins (i.e., his baptism) took place neither in the prison nor in the house. There is nothing in the passage that militates against immersion.

[95] Romans 14:17.

dently copying what was done in Rome, where the high public officials always had in their attendance such men who would carry out the sentences that the officials assessed. They carried as symbols of their office bundles of rods, with an axe inserted among them, denoting the magistrates' right to inflict corporal and capital punishment.[96] By these men the missionaries had been beaten the day before. Now they are sent to the jailer with a message about the prisoners.

Saying, "Release those men." The account of verses 22-24, when the magistrates first had the missionaries thrown in prison, seems to imply that the magistrates had not intended to let the prisoners go so soon. Luke does not tell us what caused them to change their minds. Perhaps they were influenced by the earthquake.[97] Perhaps during the night they have had time to reflect on how the prisoners had been the victims of mob action rather than receiving justice. In some towns, when undesirable characters are jailed on some insignificant charge, they are only too happy to move on and get away once released. Perhaps the magistrates, with an uneasy conscience about the whole affair, and hoping to be done with it as quietly as possible, send word to release the prisoners, thinking they would be glad to escape from the city.

16:36 – *And the jailer reported these words to Paul, saying, "The chief magistrates have sent to release you. Now therefore, come out and go in peace."*

And the jailer reported these words to Paul, *saying,* **"The chief magistrates have sent to release you. Now therefore come out and go in peace."** After the baptismal service, and the meal and the rejoicing, have Paul and Silas gone quietly back to jail? It seems to be so implied. We can imagine that the jailer was delighted to receive the message from the lictors, and supposes that the prisoners will be delighted, too. "Go in peace" indicates the same affectionate regard for the missionaries as the language did when it was used of the prophets from Jerusalem.[98]

16:37 – *But Paul said to them, "They have beaten us in public without trial, men who are Romans, and have thrown us into prison; and now are they sending us away secretly? No indeed! But let them come themselves and bring us out."*

But Paul said to them, "They have beaten us in public without trial. A public beating was a great disgrace. Worse, the judges had not even made any effort to investigate the case or question the prisoners, or permit them to speak in their own defense. This was a flagrant violation of the Roman law of which the magistrates were the dispensers.

---

[96] See the illustration of what a fasces (a bundle of rods around an axe) looked like on the front cover of this book.

[97] The Western text and Syriac H both read, "The magistrates who were alarmed by the earthquake, sent ...."

[98] See comments at Acts 15:33 on "go in peace."

Men who are Romans. Paul and Silas were born of Jewish parents; but they are here claiming that they were Roman citizens, and had a right to the privileges that such citizenship extended.[99] Paul includes Silas as being a Roman citizen, and it is possible, for the Latin form of his name, Silvanus, suggests some kind of Roman background. By the Valerian and Porcian laws, enacted between 500 and 200 BC, it was expressly forbidden that a Roman citizen should be beaten.[100] Roman citizenship brought with it certain personal privileges and exemptions from many of the more degrading forms of punishment meted out to criminals.

Why had not the missionaries claimed their citizenship to keep from being beaten in the first place? Whenever on trial, a Roman citizen could claim his legal rights by saying, "I am a Roman citizen." Those words acted almost like a charm in stopping violence from the judges in the provinces. To claim citizenship falsely was punishable by death.[101] We are not informed if there was any documentary evidence which had to be produced on the spot in confirmation of the claim. Perhaps Paul and Silas did claim their rights, but the clamors of the mob kept the plea from being heard. Maybe they did claim their citizenship, but the magistrates ignored it. Cicero relates, as one of the greatest crimes by Verres, governor of Sicily, that he ordered a Roman citizen publicly beaten in the market place of Messina, in spite of the fact that the cry of the prisoner, "I am a Roman citizen," was the only voice speaking at the time.[102] More than likely, though, in the light of the word "without trial," the missionaries were not even given a chance to defend themselves or claim their citizenship.

There is irony in the Paul's claim, "we are men who are Roman citizens." It is an echo of the speech of the two slave-masters the day before (verse 21) as they sought to inflame the court and the crowd against the preachers. Paul, too, could stand on his rights as a citizen.

And have thrown us into prison. Paul has now charged the magistrates with four violations of justice: (1) beating them publicly, (2) not even giving them an opportunity to defend themselves, (3) disregarding their rights as Roman citizens, and (4) after beating them, throwing them into prison.

And now are they sending us away secretly? Paul asks. 'After doing so much to us publicly and unjustly, are they trying to release us privately?' Paul rather demands that the magistrates acknowledge their mistakes and correct them as far as possible.

No indeed! But let them come themselves and bring us out." Paul argues that the release should be as public as the unjust acts of the day before. The acquittal should be just as public as the condemnation. Paul's motive is not that he is trying to urge the magistrates to do a better job of administering justice. Paul must have had the Philippian church in mind. The public disgrace to which they had been subjected could have a serious

---

[99] In Acts 9, in the study of Paul's youth, we learned how a person could become a Roman citizen.

[100] Livy, *History of Rome*, IV.9.

[101] Suetonius, *Claudius*, XXV.

[102] Cicero, *Orations*, II.5.161.

effect on the congregation, and on others' willingness to accept the gospel. It might even start a persecution against the Philippian converts. To ensure that no dishonor was reflected on the gospel, Paul demands that the magistrates themselves come and publicly declare the missionaries' innocence by escorting them out of prison personally.

16:38 – *And the policemen reported these words to the chief magistrates. And they were afraid when they heard that they were Romans,*

And the policemen reported these words to the chief magistrates. The lictors departed from the jail to report to the magistrates, and they report in detail each of the charges Paul had made. One of the violations of the prisoner's rights left the judges particularly dismayed.

And they were afraid when they heard that they were Romans. To subject a Roman citizen to an unlawful punishment was a serious offense, and was severely punished by the law. If the prisoners pressed charges, the magistrates could be stripped of their office, and would never be allowed to hold office again.[103] In AD 44, by order of the emperor Claudius, the people of Rhodes lost their own privileges of citizenship because they did not regard the fact that some prisoners they executed by crucifixion were Roman citizens who by law were exempt from such a mode of punishment.[104] The punishment could even be more severe. Dionysius of Halicarnassus wrote, "The punishment appointed for those who abrogated or transgressed the Valerian law was death, and the confiscation of his property."[105]

16:39 – *and they came and appealed to them, and when they had brought them out, they kept begging them to leave the city.*

And they came and appealed to them. The Western text indicates that the magistrates brought a great number of people with them as they came to attempt to right the wrongs of the previous day. Before such a group of people it would have been a very humiliating thing for the Roman magistrates to fawn and make over the prisoners; but in this case it was unavoidable, unless they wished to face the higher authorities to whom the prisoners might appeal. The Western text has the magistrates pleading ignorance, "We did not know the truth about you, that you were righteous men." Such a plea, however, would not have stood up in a Roman court. So the magistrates "kept appealing" (apologizing, RSV) to the prisoners in the hope that charges will not be pressed.

And when they had brought them out, they kept begging them to leave the city. The Greek, with its tenses indicating continuing action, vividly points out the change in the whole situation. Yesterday, as they tore the clothes off the "Jews," they were showing everyone what authority they had! Today, over and over again, they keep begging them to leave the city, perhaps out of fear of further trouble. A Roman citizen could not be expelled

---

[103] Cicero, *In Verrem*, V.66; *De Republic*, II.31.

[104] Dio Cassius, *Romaika*, Book 60.

[105] Dionysius, *Roman Antiquities*, II.

from a Roman city when he had been convicted of no crime, so the magistrates cannot demand that Paul and Silas leave. But cities in this part of the Roman world were notoriously weak in their ability to control the populace, and if Paul and Silas were as unpopular as yesterday's crowd had made it seem, then the officials could not guarantee their safety.

The two missionaries see fit to comply with the advice of the officials, and shortly will leave Philippi. They had accomplished their main purpose for coming to Philippi: they have preached the gospel to a large cross-section of the Roman world – to Jews and proselytes, to a fortunetelling slave-girl, to a Roman jailer, and to others. They had laid the foundation for a flourishing congregation that will become one of Paul's favorite churches.[106]

16:40 – *And they went out of the prison and entered* **the house of** *Lydia, and when they saw the brethren, they encouraged them and departed.*

And they went out of the prison and entered *the house of* **Lydia.** We can see in our mind's eye how the magistrates and other citizens of Philippi make every attempt to treat Paul and Silas as some great dignitaries, as they escort them out of the prison. Lydia's house appears to have been a meeting place for the brethren (congregations of Christians did meet in homes in those early days), as well as the place where the missionaries were living while in Philippi.

And when they saw the brethren, they encouraged them. "Brethren" suggests there are more members in the Philippian church than just the families of Lydia and the jailer. Some would be apprehensive of treatment similar to what the preachers received on the previous day, and could be giving some consideration to quitting the church. Paul and the other preachers encourage them to persevere in the Christian faith, no matter what opposition and persecution they might meet.

And departed. Paul and Silas are the ones who departed, heading westward along the Egnatian way. It would appear that Luke stayed in Philippi (perhaps as their preacher?), for here the "we" sections cease and do not return to the narrative until Acts 20:4-5. In the intervening sections, the narrative is in the third person.

Under Luke's influence, the Philippian church grew and became a missionary-minded church.[107] Luke stays here five years, from AD 52 (verse 40) through AD 57 or 58 (Acts 20:4-5).[108] Timothy, it appears, also stayed in Philippi for a short time after Paul and Silas left.[109]

---

[106] See this idea developed in A.T. Robertson, *Paul's Joy in Christ* (Nashville, TN: Broadman Press, 1959).

[107] Compare Philippians 4:14-15; 2 Corinthians 11:9.

[108] Luke's 5-year stay in Philippi has considerable bearing on the question of "the located ministry." Further notes about the located ministry are included at Acts 11:26.

[109] See notes at Acts 17:15.

Antioch in Syria

Drawing by Horace Knowles
from the British and Foreign Bible Society

SPECIAL STUDY #16

THE FAITH THAT SAVES

One of the fundamental differences separating the various bodies of the Christian world arises from the way they each explain and define what is involved in the "faith" that is a condition of salvation. Catholic, Protestant, and Christian each has a different explanation of what faith is.

Some passages in the Bible attribute salvation to "faith" (or belief),[1] while others specifically exclude works.[2] What does the Bible mean when it uses "faith" (belief) in passages such as "we are justified by faith" and "whosoever believes in me shall ... have eternal life"?[3]

Our proposition is that the faith that saves is composed of four constituent parts: knowledge, assent, confidence, and obedience.

I. HISTORY OF THE PROBLEM

A. Early Church

The early church understood the four constituent parts to faith, but controversies that raged caused each of the parts to fall into disuse or to be ignored. Origen's assertion that knowledge was greater than faith and the long battle with Gnosticism led to a loss of emphasis on the knowledge element of faith. In many circles, Stoic morality's emphasis on self-reliance led to a decline of emphasis on confidence (trust, dependence on another). Then the idea of a mystical approach to God (as Neo-Platonism was assimilated into the theology of the church) brought on a de-emphasis of the element of obedience. "Faith" had been reduced merely to "assent."

B. Roman Catholicism

By the time of Thomas Aquinas, Rome had given its own definition to faith. All the elements but "assent" had been canceled, and then "assent" had been redefined as being (not assent to what one knows of Christ and His will, but rather) blanket assent to whatever Rome might say about Christ and the Word. Further, mere "assent" was not enough to procure salvation. Mere assent was the Roman *fides informata* (i.e., faith with no shape or

---

[1] Some passages which speak of "belief" as a condition of salvation are John 1:12; 3:14-16, 18, 36; 5:24; 6:40, 47; Acts 10:43, 13:39, 16:30-31.

[2] Some passages which exclude "works" as a condition of salvation are Titus 3:5; Galatians 3:11; and Romans 4:5.

[3] Romans 3:28; John 3:16.

form). In order to procure justification, in Roman thinking, it had to become *fides formata*. And what gave the *fides* its *forma*? Works of love (Galatians 5:6). But Rome also constantly redefined what constituted a "work of love" or a "work of charity." If Rome said that the giving of an offering to help build St. Peter's Cathedral would result in the forgiveness of a certain number of sins, then such an offering was one of the "works of charity" which gave faith its form so that it was looked on as being saving faith.

C. The Reformers

The Reformers restored one or more of the Biblical perspectives to the word "faith."

- Luther urged that instead of being assent to Rome, it had to be assent to the Bible. If it could be found in the Bible, he'd believe it!
- The Reformers also restored the element of confidence. They insisted that faith was not *fides* merely, but *fiducia* (trust). It was at Romans 3:28 that Luther added the word *sola* ("only"), when he insisted that a man is justified by *fides sola* (by "faith only").[4]
- John Calvin's contribution to Protestant thought came from his emphasis on the knowledge element of faith.

Protestants who have inherited their theology from Luther and the other Reformers define the faith that saves as being made up of three parts: knowledge, assent, and confidence (*fiducia*).[5]

D. Religious Liberalism and Neo-Orthodoxy

During the time when a newly developing interest in science was growing, and when corresponding doubts about the literal accuracy of the Bible were also growing (especially where it claims to be supernatural), "faith" was redefined as being one's religious feelings that had been put into words. Instead of being knowledge learned by testimony, and assented to, and acted upon, faith was viewed as something entirely subjective. Though the more contemporary theologians (the Neo-orthodox) use language that sounds almost orthodox, they mean something entirely different than orthodox theologians do when they speak of faith. To Neo-orthodox theologians, the Bible becomes the Word of God only when one of its passages makes an impression on the reader. Then if some kind of response is made to that impression, that is "faith."[6]

---

[4] So that Luther is not unjustly criticized, it should be pointed out that the cause for which he was contending was correct. His *sola* was opposed to the Roman system of giving *fides* its *forma* by works of charity (indulgences). Luther was right in denying the Roman doctrine, but it is a dangerous thing to add a word to the text in order to prove a point.

[5] Charles H. Spurgeon, "Saving Faith: What is it?" in *Sword of the Lord*, Vol. 34, No. 8 (February 23, 1968), says faith is made up of three things: knowledge, belief, and trust. For Wesley's view, see "Saving Faith as Wesley Saw It" by John Lawson, in *Christianity Today*, Vol. VIII, No. II (April 24, 1964), p.673.

[6] For a more detailed explanation of "faith" as defined in Liberal and Neo-orthodox circles, see "faith" in the following sources: *Baker Dictionary of Theology* (Grand Rapids: Baker Book House, 1960); Van A. Harvey, *A Handbook of Theological Terms* (New York: Macmillan, 1964); and Bernard Ramm, *A Handbook of Contemporary Theology* (Grand Rapids: Eerdmans, 1966).

II. DEFINITIONS AND AUTHORITIES

In English we have two words, "faith" and "belief," and they have different connotations. "Belief" is assent to testimony, whereas "faith" includes both assent and trust. The Bible translator has a problem, then, when he finds the words for faith/belief in the Scriptures. Which English word shall he use? He must decide if the original writer had emphasis on the earlier stages of faith – the *belief* element – or to the later stages of faith – the *trust* and *obedience* elements.

Lightfoot has shown that the translator does get some help from both the original languages and from the Latin translations.[7]

- The Hebrew did have the verb *aman* for "believe," but had no corresponding noun for "faith." *'Emunah* was sometimes used as a noun, but it meant something more like "truth, genuineness" (i.e., it was more nearly akin to "faith" than to "belief").
- The Greek verb *pisteuō* and the corresponding noun *pistis*, depending on the context, can have either connotation (i.e., it can emphasize either the *assent* element or the *trust/obedience* element).
- So, in the LXX, since there was no Hebrew equivalent for "belief" (i.e., assent), *pistis* always has the connotation of "faith" (i.e., trust and obedience).[8]
- In the New Testament, however, *pisteuō* and *pistis* are found in both senses.[9]
- When the Bible was translated into Latin, the translators faced an old problem. The Latin had a verb for "belief" (i.e., assent), *credo*, but this verb had no word that would express "faith" (i.e., trust and obedience) since *credulus* had a bad connotation. So the Latin scholars used *fides* or *fidelis* for this latter idea.

These words of background give the English translators some help, though even in English there is no verb corresponding to the noun "faith," like there is a verb ("believe") corresponding to the noun "belief."

These words of background also prepare us for what we find in the Greek lexicons as we attempt to discover exactly what is the "faith" that saves.

Thayer's *Greek English Lexicon of the New Testament* gives this definition of *pisteuō* when used of the faith by which a man embraces Jesus:

> A conviction, full of joyful trust, that Jesus is the Messiah – the divinely appointed author of eternal salvation in the kingdom of God, conjoined with obedience to Christ.[10]

James M. Whiton abridged Liddell and Scott's *Greek-English Lexicon,* and under *pisteuō* gives these possible meanings:

> 1. To believe, trust in, put faith in, confide in, rely on a person or thing. —2. to believe,

---

[7] J.B. Lightfoot, *The Epistle of St. Paul to the Galatians* (Grand Rapids: Zondervan, 1957) p.154ff.

[8] Even Habakkuk 2:4 is an example of "faith" (i.e., trust and obedience) rather than "belief" (i.e., assent).

[9] The different connotations to "belief" in the New Testament will be documented in the next section of this Special Study.

[10] Joseph H. Thayer, *A Greek-English Lexicon of the New Testament* (New York: American Book Company, 1889), p.511,

comply, obey.[11]

Bultmann has the article on *pisteuō* in Kittel's *Theological Dictionary of the New Testament*. After giving a history of the use of the word in the Old Testament, he outlines its use in the New Testament.

> II. General Christian Usage: 1. The Continuation of the Old Testament and Jewish Tradition: a. *pisteuo* as to Believe; b. as to Obey; c. as to Trust; d. as to Hope; e. as Faithfulness ....[12]

Thus, the Lexicons reflect the idea advanced earlier in this study that any of the elements of *pisteuō* (i.e., knowledge, assent, confidence, obedience) may be emphasized, and that the context or the Greek grammatical construction (for example, certain prepositional phrases) in which *pisteuō* appears will often determine the exact meaning.

III. KINDS OF FAITH IN THE NEW TESTAMENT

A. Miraculous Faith

"Miraculous faith" was a faith in addition to the "faith" that every Christian possesses, and was received as a gift of the Spirit by the laying on of an apostle's hands.[13] It was the kind of "faith" that could move mountains and sycamore trees.[14] This was one of the temporary spiritual gifts that graced the early church.[15]

At this juncture, it should also be noted that there is, according to Calvinistic theology, a "faith" that is *given* to every Christian. "Faith is a saving grace miraculously wrought in the soul by the Spirit, whereby we receive Christ and rely upon Him and His righteousness alone for justification and salvation," is a good summary of Calvinistic beliefs. According to Calvinism, a person is entirely passive in conversion, and is utterly unable to make a single response toward God because of total depravity. He has no ability to believe or repent because he is dead in sin, and must therefore wait until God in some miraculous way gives him "saving faith." A misinterpretation of Ephesians 2:8, which makes "faith" to be the "it" which is a gift of God, is one of the key verses used to prove that the faith that saves is a gift given to individuals by God. E.V. Zollars, in *The Great Salvation*, has shown that the faith that saves (as distinguished from miraculous faith) comes by hearing the Word of God, and is not a gift from God wrought in the heart by the direct operation of the Spirit (as Calvin taught it).[16] George Stevens has shown that there is no Scriptural justification for the theory of total depravity, and clearly brings out that

---

[11] James M. Whiton, arranger, *A Lexicon Abridged from Liddell and Scott's Greek-English Lexicon* (New York: American Book Company, 1871), p.561.

[12] G. Friedrich, *Theological Dictionary of the New Testament* (Grand Rapids: Eerdmans, 1968), Vol. VI, p.174-175.

[13] Acts 8:17-18, 9:17, 19:6; 1 Timothy 4:14.

[14] Matthew 21:21; 1 Corinthians 13:2; Luke 17:6.

[15] 1 Corinthians 12:9, 13:2. See Special Study #3, "The Person and Work of the Holy Spirit," and Special Study #4, "Speaking in Tongues" for evidence that the spiritual gifts were of a temporary nature.

[16] E.V. Zollars, *The Great Salvation* (Cincinnati: Standard Publishing Co., 1895), p.93ff.

Paul did not teach Calvinism as John Calvin proclaimed it.[17]

There was a "faith" that was given by God in the New Testament times. It was one of the "spiritual gifts" and should be clearly distinguished from the faith that saves.

B. "The Faith" – A Body of Doctrine

Paul calls Titus his son according to "the common faith."[18] The gospel is referred to as many as thirty times as "the faith." (For example, see Jude 3, Acts 13:8, Acts 14:22.)

"Faith" used in this sense is in accord with the dictionary definition: "A system of religious belief of any kind, as the Jewish faith; and especially the system of truth taught by Christ, as the Christian faith."

At times, the New Testament uses the word "faith" for the body of doctrine that is believed. Again, the context and the special construction in the Greek ("*the* faith") is the clue that it is a body of doctrine that is in the writer's mind, rather than the act of believing.

C. Saving Faith

We now examine the word "faith" as it is found in verses which have to do with salvation. As set forth in the proposition earlier, the word can have a number of shades of meaning, ranging from mere mental assent to faith in the highest and fullest meaning.

1. Saving "faith" includes *knowledge.*

Romans 10:17 and Hebrews 11:6 suggest that something must be heard in order for faith to exist. That is, there are objective facts to be believed. This is another way of saying that there is a certain amount of knowledge involved in faith.

However, if a person's "faith" includes no more than knowledge of certain facts, this faith is not sufficient for salvation. A man can say he believes there is a God, and even that Christ lived on earth about 2000 years ago. However, if by his daily life he shows that he pays no allegiance to either, the knowledge that there is a God has no relevance to his daily habits and thoughts. Because he makes no further response to his "knowledge," he is lost forever. This illustration helps us to see that a faith which is mere intellectual knowledge is not the faith that saves.

2. Saving "faith" includes *mental assent.*

Sometimes the idea of mental assent is indicated by the verb *pisteuō* followed by the simple dative case in the Greek. Acts 8:12-13 is an example, where the Samaritans "believed" Philip (and their obedience followed). Acts 26:27 is another example, where Agrippa II "believes" the prophets (though there is no obedience). These are clear-cut cases

---

[17] George B. Stevens, *The Theology of the New Testament* (New York: Scribners, 1953), p. 2ff, 349ff.

[18] Titus 1:4.

where "believe" means only mental assent, and does not involve trust or obedience.[19]

At times, the verb "believe" standing alone (without any dative case following) also implies only mental assent. Acts 11:21 is an example, where those in Antioch "believed" and then "turned" to the Lord. Acts 18:8 is another example, where Luke says the people heard, believed, and were baptized. "Belief" in these cases indicates mental assent.[20] Just as saving faith includes "knowledge" but must include more than mere knowledge, so saving faith includes "mental assent," but it also must include more.

If a person's "faith" includes no more than mental assent, he does not have the faith to be saved. James 2:19 tells us the demons "believe," but they certainly are not saved thereby. Acts 26:27 indicates Agrippa II believed the prophets, yet he was not saved. John 12:42 says that many of the rulers of the Jews believed on Jesus, but did not confess Him for fear of being put out of the synagogue. That is, they gave assent to Jesus' claims, and wished to confess Him, but didn't.[21] Mental assent alone is not the kind of faith that saves.

Sometimes an attempt is made to show that all that is necessary to salvation is mental assent, and appeal is made to Romans 4:3-5, which includes a quote of Genesis 15:6. We are told that "Abraham believed God (*pisteuō* followed by the dative case) and it was reckoned to him as righteousness." This would seem to teach that all the verses where the Greek has "believe" followed by a word in the dative case are examples that must mean the person was saved just by faith (mental assent). However, remember that James also quotes Genesis 15:6, and argues that Abraham's *obedience* was the thing that completed his faith so that it was counted for righteousness.[22] In order to harmonize James with Romans, it must be insisted that the faith that saves, while it includes mental assent, must include more elements than knowledge and assent if it is to be "perfected" as far as righteousness is concerned.

    3. Saving "faith" includes *confidence* (trust).

The Greek construction which has *pisteuō* followed by the preposition *epi* and the

---

[19] Other passages which have been interpreted as meaning "mental assent" are Acts 5:14 and 13:39 (depending on how you translate the passages). See also Acts 24:14 and 27:25.

[20] "Believe" appears in other passages in which the context indicates that mental assent is the thing intended. See Romans 10:17 and Mark 16:16. See also John 2:11, where the belief of the disciples is noted, but subsequent passages show it was a growing thing.

[21] John 12:42 has given much trouble to faith-only advocates who believe in an instantaneous conversion the moment one has faith. To be consistent, they must admit that these Jewish rulers were saved even though they did not confess Jesus. In fact, some faith-only advocates attempt to do just this. That is, they indeed affirm that these Jewish religious rulers were saved people even without confession of Jesus! J.B. Moody, in the "Harding-Moody Debate" unhesitatingly said that the rulers were saved. J.N. Hall, in the "Fleming-Hall Debate," as reported by David Lipscomb, said, "Hall said either the chief rulers who refused to confess Him had only a pretense of faith, which is no faith, or that they were saved notwithstanding their refusal to confess Him, as many are now saved." Jacob Ditzler, in the "Wilkes-Ditzler Debate," said that these rulers probably exercised a true faith, and then, like Simon Magus, immediately backslid.
    Instead of forcing ourselves into such a tenuous position, if we will just recognize that "believe" sometimes means no more than mental assent, and that mental assent alone is not sufficient for salvation, we'll be able to harmonize the Scriptures much more easily.

[22] James 2:22-23. More will be said on this matter of justification by faith in the final section of this study.

dative case seems to be the way that this idea of confidence was particularly expressed. 1 Timothy 1:16 speaks of relying on Christ for salvation. Romans 9:33 and 1 Peter 2:6 both quote Isaiah 28:16, and use this particular grammatical construction. Luke 24:25 is an encouragement to rely implicitly on all the prophets have spoken. See also Romans 10:11.

Just as saving faith must include knowledge and assent, so it must include confidence. However, the Romans 10 reference is part of a context that shows that confession and calling on the name of the Lord are also necessary to salvation. Hence, it must be that in order for "faith" to be saving faith, it must include more than confidence.

4. Saving "faith" includes *obedience*.

The Greek-English lexicons quoted above consistently include obedience in the "faith" that saves. The following evidences point in the same direction:

(a) The fact that *pisteuō* is followed by one or another of three different prepositional phrases, all of which indicate obedience. First, there is the phrase *eis* and the accusative, which is used some 49 times. Acts 10:43 and 24:24 are two examples of this use, the latter of which shows by the context that righteousness, self-control, and awareness of the judgment to come are included in "faith in Christ."[23] Second, there is the phrase *en* and the dative. John 3:15 and 16 are verses that must be studied in this place. In 3:15, "believe in Him" is *en* and the dative, but in verse 16, "believe in Him" is *eis* and the accusative. The two phrases must be synonymous in order to be used interchangeably by John.[24] Third, there is the prepositional phrase *epi* and the accusative. Every place this construction appears it speaks of an obedient faith.[25] Consider Romans 4:5,25 where Abraham's obedient faith in the Lord, rather than trusting his own meritorious works, was the way of salvation for the father of the faithful.

(b) The fact that there are passages where belief and obedience are synonymous (or belief and disobedience are antonyms). If the belief that saves includes only three elements (knowledge, assent, confidence), then it is hard to explain how *pisteuō* (believe) and *apeithō* (disobey) can be antonyms. There are at least two places in the New Testament where "belief" and "disobedience" are contrasted,[26] and these convincingly show that the faith that saves includes obedience as one of its constituent elements. And there is one passage where "unbelief" and "disobedience" are synonymous,[27] so that the faith that saves (the opposite of "unbelief") must include obedience (the opposite of disobedience).

(c) The passages that speak of the "obedience of faith" show that there is an obedience

---

[23] Other passages where this same *eis* and the accusative construction is used are Acts 20:21 and Galatians 2:16.

[24] Other passages where it is plain that *en* and the dative speaks of obedience are Ephesians 1:13 and Mark 1:15.

[25] See Acts 16:31, 22:19, 9:42, 11:17; Matthew 27:42.

[26] John 3:36 and Acts 14:1-2. The NASB does not show the reader that different Greek words are involved in John 3:36, though it does in Acts 14. One wonders if this was done purposely by translators who were of faith-only persuasion?

[27] Hebrews 3:18-19.

within the very essence of faith. This phrase has been met in Acts 6:7, and also appears in Romans 1:5 and 16:26. This phrase provides us solid help to know what kind of faith is the condition by which a person is justified. Peter too talks about how his readers have purified their souls by obedience to the truth,[28] and throughout his letters shows the close connection between obedience and forgiveness.[29] If there is an obedience that belongs to the very essence of faith, the faith that saves must involve obedience to what God requires.

(d) Passages in which baptism is a constituent part of believing indicate that the faith that saves is an obedient faith. In Acts 19:1ff, as Paul speaks to the followers of John the Baptist, his language clearly shows that he assumed baptism is part of believing. See how he asks them about the time when they believed, and immediately asks about their baptism, indicating that the two were part and parcel of the same thing. In Acts 16:31-34, after the jailer showed his repentance and was immersed, Luke summarizes it all by stating that he "had believed." Galatians 3:26-27 show that baptism is involved in the faith on which God justifies. See how verse 27 begins with "for," which means that verse 27 is a further explanation of how they are sons of God through "faith." Many other passages, especially in Acts, show that "believed" includes everything that was done (i.e., repentance, confession, baptism) in order to become a Christian.[30]

(e) Saving faith must include obedience because many times *pistis* may be properly translated "faithfulness."[31] Justification is a thing that happens over and over in a person's life. God reckons a person as just because of his faithfulness, just as was true in the case of Abraham (Romans 4:24). John 3:36 teaches this same principle.[32] It says that if a man is not faithful, he will lose eternal life.

These evidences converge to strongly indicate that the faith that saves includes all four elements – knowledge, assent, confidence, and obedience.

IV. A QUESTION ASKED THREE TIMES IN THE NEW TESTAMENT

In the New Testament, different answers are given to the question, "What must I do to be saved?" How shall we account for the fact that different answers were given to different people?

If a person wanted to know what to do to be saved, there could be no plainer, no wiser, no surer way to answer the question than to turn to the New Testament and find the answer given there. If the question is found 100 times, then read the answer given to each of the 100 questions; what is found would be the Scriptural and right answer. Furthermore, it would present the whole truth of the New Testament on the subject.

---

[28] 1 Peter 1:22.

[29] See 1 Peter 1:2, 3:1, 4:17; 2 Peter 1:1. (See also 1 Thessalonians 1:8 and Romans 10:5 for other evidences that obedience is involved in a person's faith.)

[30] Acts 2:44; 4:5; 5:14; 13:12,39,48; 14:23; 15:7; 16:1,34; 17:12,34; 19:18; 21:21; 1 Timothy 4:12.

[31] Examples include Revelation 2:10, 13:10; James 5:15, 1:6.

[32] See references to the teaching implicit in John 3:36 in footnote #26 of this Special Study, and in footnotes #1 and #2 related to the comments given at Acts 14:1-2.

But we do not find the question 100 times. We find it, substantially, only four times in the New Testament; and one of those was under the Mosaic dispensation.

The question was first put forth by the rich young ruler who came to Jesus.[33] Jesus referred him to the Ten Commandments, for the Mosaic Law was still in force at the time Jesus spoke to this man since Christ had not yet died and nailed the Law to the cross.[34] It was the Jew's duty, therefore, to keep the Commandments. When the young man replied that he had kept the Law from his youth up, Jesus said, "One thing you lack; go, and sell all you possess, and give it to the poor, and you shall have treasure in heaven; and come, follow Me."[35] This answer would not be given today, because Jesus was speaking before the New Testament became effective.[36]

The question "What must I do to be saved?" is recorded and answered three times in the book of Acts. Interestingly, three different answers are given to the question. Each answer was given by the authority of the Holy Spirit.

In Acts 2:38, the answer is given, "Repent and be baptized every one of you for the forgiveness of sins." Review the comments at Acts 2:37,38. Those Jews who believed the message that Peter had been preaching – they were pricked in their hearts – asked what to do to be saved. Peter, by inspiration, told them what to do. Note, also that, according to Peter's answer, salvation requires more than belief. The Jerusalem Jews believed the message that Peter had preached to them. Was this kind of "faith" (mental assent and confidence) all that was necessary to save those Jews? No! Peter told them to repent and be baptized for the forgiveness of their sins.

After Paul's experience on the Damascus road, when he saw the risen Lord, Jesus told him to "rise and enter into the city, and it shall be told to you what you must do."[37] Obviously, there was something that Paul had to do for he yet lacked something. It was not faith that he lacked, for he was convinced he had seen Jesus, and that sight caused him to believe in the deity and lordship of Jesus. It was not repentance that Paul lacked, for he was so penitent that he spent three days fasting and praying. What was it he lacked? Christ had said he would be told what to do. Ananias came and said, "Arise and be baptized and wash away your sins."[38] This is the second answer to the question. It is somewhat different than the answer given on the day of Pentecost by Peter. However, it is plain from Ananias' instructions that something more than "faith" (mental assent and confidence) and repentance are needed to save a person!

In the case of the Philippian jailer, we have the third case in Acts where the question "What must I do to be saved?" is asked; a still different answer is given. The jailer is told

---

[33] Mark 10:17.

[34] Colossians 2:14.

[35] Mark 10:21. The Law of Moses had not yet been abrogated, so the young man was to keep it. Also, he needed to free himself from his riches that were a stumbling block to him. And in addition, he was directed to follow Christ, as the disciples did, so that he would be better trained for work in the coming Kingdom.

[36] Hebrews 9:16-17.

[37] Acts 9:6.

[38] Acts 22:16.

to "Believe (*pisteuō*) on the Lord Jesus."[39]

We have read three different answers to the very same question. How are these different answers to be explained?

- The jailer was an unbeliever. He was told to believe. The missionaries preached to him for the purpose of producing faith. He then repented and was baptized.
- The people on Pentecost already believed, so they were told to repent and be baptized for the forgiveness of their sins.
- Paul was a believing, penitent man. He therefore was told to be baptized.

In each case, a different answer was given because the individuals were at different places on the road to salvation. But in total, they eventually all did the same things and traveled over the same road.

Consider an illustration. A man asks how far it is to the next town, and is told 30 miles. He drives 10 miles and asks again. He is then told 20 miles. He travels up the road another 10 miles, and he is now told he has 10 miles to go. He has been given a different answer each time he asked; in fact, he was given three different answers to the same question. Yet all the answers were correct. The same is true of the question, "What must I do to be saved?" The *unbeliever* has not begun to travel the road to pardon. He is told to believe, repent, and be baptized. The believers are not told to believe, but to repent and be baptized. The *penitent believer* was not told to believe and repent, but was told to be baptized and wash away his sins. All traveled over the same road; all were converted alike.

Furthermore, all three answers are correct only if the faith that saves includes obedience to commands such as repentance and baptism for the remission of sins. If the faith that saves is composed of less than all four elements, it is not possible to explain the different answers satisfactorily.

V. JUSTIFICATION BY FAITH[40]

There are two conditions necessary to an accurate and complete statement of any Bible doctrine. First, it must harmonize with every other statement in the Bible on the same subject. This is necessary to accuracy. Second, it must provide for a reconciliation of all Bible statements on the subject with each other. This is necessary to completeness.

These two conditions will suggest the true method of ascertaining the teaching of the Bible on any given subject. Too often, however, instead of using this method, men have formed their doctrines as a result of opposing some error, or by deducing them from some preconceived notion. Thus, the doctrine of the miraculous operation of the Spirit in conversion is derived, not from any plain statement in the Bible, but from the previously held theory of total depravity. The popularly taught idea that baptism is merely an outward sign of an inward grace, and therefore has nothing to do with salvation, is the result of ex-

---

[39] Acts 16:31.

[40] The following material is condensed from J. W. McGarvey's treatment found in *Lards Quarterly*, Vol. III, No. 2 (January 1866).

treme opposition to the Catholic doctrine of "baptismal regeneration." The theory of justification by faith-only arose from opposition to the Catholic doctrine of meritorious works. Such a route to a doctrine is always a dangerous one, and usually leads to incorrect conclusions, conclusions which have just enough truth in them to give the appearance of being Biblical.

The point of this section of the Special Study is to round out our study of the "faith" that saves, while at the same time putting the theory of "faith-only" to the test, and likewise answering a few of the popular objections to the position set forth earlier in this study, that the faith that saves is an obedient faith.

To get a clear perspective of the problem, let us put side by side the statements of Paul and James on the subject.

> For we maintain that a man is justified by faith apart from works of the Law. (Romans 3:28)

> You see, then, how that by works a man is justified, and not by faith only. (James 2:24, ASV)

At first sight there is a striking contradiction between these two statements. They both admit that man is justified by faith; but Paul adds "without works of law," and James adds "not without works." If the terms "justified," "faith," and "works" are used alike in both propositions, then there is a real and irreconcilable contradiction. But if any of these leading terms is used in a different sense, then the statements may both be true. Because both books are inspired, we cannot do as Luther did, and discard the book of James simply because it contradicted his doctrine of "faith-only." What we must do is find out which of the terms is ambiguous and used in a different sense.

- Some suggest the ambiguity is in the word "faith." The faith of which James speaks requires accompanying works, while that of Paul does not.
- Some suggest the ambiguity may be in the term "justified." Perhaps one speaks of initial salvation, and the other speaks of continuing justification after one is first saved.
- Some suggest the ambiguity is in the word "works." The works of which James speaks are necessary to justification, while those of Paul are not.

The first alternative gets faith-only advocates in deep trouble. The moment they admit that James teaches there is a faith (an obedient faith) that justifies, they have lost their whole case for salvation by faith-only (knowledge, assent, and trust).

An elaborate argument is given by some faith-only advocates to show that the word "justification" is used in two different senses. They contend that Paul uses the word in regard to Abraham's initial salvation, while James uses it of a justification that happened many years later, at the time he offered his son Isaac. This is true; and if it were all James says on the matter of justification, the argument could be substantiated.[41] But notice that James uses two examples of people who were justified by works, and Rahab's in no way can be anything other than initial salvation (justification). Thus, it is evident that Paul and James are using "justified" in the same sense.

---

[41] We write "*could* be substantiated" rather than "*would* be" since it would be difficult in light of what we learn about Abraham in Genesis 11 and 12 to affirm that his initial justification was not till Genesis 15:6.

The third alternative is resorted to by many commentators as they seek to explain this apparent contradiction between Paul and James. That is, Paul and James must use "works" in two different senses. The works that Paul speaks of are works that "make faith void" (Romans 4:14). The works that James speaks about are works that "make faith perfect" (James 2:21-22). Actually, Paul and James are saying the same thing. Paul is arguing against the "meritorious works" system.[42] James is arguing against the "faith-only" idea. In the Romans passage, the contrast is between an "obedient faith" and meritorious works. In the James passage, the contrast is between an "obedient faith" and "faith-only." Both insist that an obedient faith is the condition of justification, rather than meritorious works being the condition, or faith-only being the condition.

As it was in Abraham's life, so it is in ours – justification was a continuing thing. Abraham was justified several times, as a harmony of all the passages that speak of his justification clearly show. The condition of this justification is an obedient faith. For sinners, immersion is one of the acts of obedience that is required for forgiveness. For the erring saint, confession of sin is one of the acts of obedience that is required.[43] As James and Paul both insist, the faith that saves, whether it be initial or continuing justification, is an obedient faith!

CONCLUSION

The faith that saves is made up of four constituent elements – knowledge, assent, confidence, and obedience. Only if "faith" is so defined is it possible to harmonize all the passages in the Word that have to do with salvation.

Paul's own conversion is a perfect illustration of this conclusion. Writing in Romans 5, he says, "Therefore, being justified by faith, we have peace with God through our Lord Jesus Christ." Notice, Paul includes himself in this statement. Now, remember the record of his conversion. His trip to Damascus to persecute the Christians was interrupted by the risen Lord appearing to him. He came to see himself as the chief of sinners, desperately in need of forgiveness and peace with God. In submission to Jesus, he says, "Lord, what will you have me to do?" He then passes the next three days in prayer and fasting. It would be idle to search for an example of more undoubting faith and heart-broken repentance than praying, fasting Paul. If saving faith includes but three elements (as faith-only advocates affirm), Paul ought to already be justified and have peace with God. But he doesn't! Can there be found a clearer demonstration of the impotency of "faith-only" to secure justification and peace? Not until after Ananias the preacher comes and explains to him about the need for immersion and having his sins washed away, and he complies with this command, does he find peace with God! Only when Paul's faith became an obedient faith was he justified!

This is saving faith through the whole book of Acts, and through the whole Christian dispensation.

---

[42] Romans 4:4 shows that Paul has "meritorious works" in mind in the closing words of chapter 3. Meritorious works are deeds done by which one hopes to earn salvation as a matter of debt.

[43] 1 John 1:9 shows that a Christian must confess his sins if he wishes a faithful God to forgive them.

BIBLIOGRAPHY

Archer, Knowles Shaw, "A Study of Faith," *Christian Standard*, LXIX (March 10, 1934), p.161ff.

Lightfoot, J.B., *The Epistle of St. Paul to the Galatians* (Grand Rapids: Zondervan), 1957, p.154ff.

McGarvey, J.W., "Justification by Faith" in *Lard's Quarterly*, III (January 1866), p.113ff.

Sanday, William, "The Epistle to the Romans" in *Ellicott's Layman's Handy Commentary on the Bible* (Grand Rapids: Zondervan), 1957, p.175.

Sanday, William, and Headlam, A.C., "Romans" in *International Critical Commentary* (Edinburgh: T&T Clark), 1895, p.31.

Stevens, George B., *The Theology of the New Testament* (New York: Scribners), 1953.

Warfield, B.B., "Faith" in *Hastings' Dictionary of the Bible* (New York: Scribners), 1908, Vol. I, p.827-838.

9. Through Amphipolis and Apollonia. 17:1a

17:1a – *Now when they had traveled through Amphipolis and Apollonia,*

Now when they had traveled through Amphipolis and Apollonia. Both of these cities were on the Egnatian Way between Philippi and Thessalonica.[1] Amphipolis was the capital of the eastern district of the province of Macedonia, and was about 33 miles west of Philippi. Amphipolis ("around the city") got its name from the fact that the river Strymon flowed almost around it. Prior to the time the Romans conquered this area, it was called "Nine Ways," indicative of its strategic location on several major roads.[2] Apollonia was another 30 miles farther west of Amphipolis, and Thessalonica was another 37 miles beyond that. These distances were evidently such as might be traveled each in one day. We may conjecture that Paul and Silas rested one night at each of these intermediate places, and thus our notice of the journey is divided into three parts. A thirty-some mile journey would have been a hard trip in a day for men who had so recently been beaten with rods.

10. At Thessalonica. 17:1b-9

17:1b – *they came to Thessalonica, where there was a synagogue of the Jews.*

They came to Thessalonica. A seaport for the second district of Macedonia, Thessalonica served as the capital not only for the district but also for the whole Roman province of Macedonia. It was the largest city in Macedonia, and because of its location it has always been an important city. The city was formerly called Therma. But when a daughter was born to Philip of Macedon on the day he won a victory over Thessaly, he celebrated by naming his daughter Thessaly. She married Cassander, who changed the city's name from Therma to Thessalonica in honor of his wife.

Where there was a synagogue of the Jews. The Greek construction might imply that things were different at Thessalonica than the missionaries had found at Amphipolis and Apollonia.[3] Finding a Jewish synagogue at Thessalonica would give Paul a place to begin his evangelistic work among people who had been brought to a readiness for Christ by the "tutor" – i.e., the Old Testament Law.[4]

17:2 – *And according to Paul's custom, he went to them, and for three Sabbaths reasoned with them from the Scriptures,*

And according to Paul's custom, he went to them. Paul's regular method of evangelism

---

[1] See information at Acts 16:12 about the Egnatian Way. The Appolonia named here is different from the one at the west end of the highway.

[2] Thucidides, I.100; Herodotus, VII.114.

[3] There is a manuscript variation here, some reading "*the* synagogue." Luke's use of *hopou* ("where") is the basis for implying that Thessalonica differed from the other cities in that it had a synagogue.

[4] Galatians 3:24.

was to preach the gospel to the Jews first.[5]

And for three Sabbaths. This may be the exact length of his work within the synagogue. In the intervals between the Sabbaths, the apostle worked, as usual, for his livelihood, probably as a tent-maker.[6] From reading the Thessalonian epistles (written shortly after Paul left Thessalonica), it is obvious that Paul stayed in the city much longer than the three weeks he spoke in the synagogue.[7] Luke does not need to tell us that Paul finally had to withdraw from the synagogue and begin preaching at another location; nor does he need to tell us that this subsequent audience then would have been predominantly Greek. Paul's work among the Greeks (which we can fit into Acts between verses 3 and 4) was largely successful, for he later speaks of the church at Thessalonica as being made up, for the greater part, of Gentiles.[8]

Reasoned with them from the Scriptures. This is the first time we have had the word *dialegomai* ("reasoned") in the book of Acts.[9] Followed here as it is by a dative case, it may imply a conversational interchange between rabbi and worshipers as often took place in the synagogue.[10] "From the Scriptures" suggests that Paul was drawing his proofs from the Scriptures, or perhaps used the Scripture lessons for the day as his starting point. He was attempting to convince the worshipers that Jesus of Nazareth was the Messiah by comparing His life with the Old Testament predictions concerning Messiah.

17:3 – *explaining and giving evidence that the Christ had to suffer and rise again from the dead, and saying, "This Jesus whom I am proclaiming to you is the Christ."*

Explaining and giving evidence that the Christ had to suffer. What Paul was doing as he "explained" was to unfold the meaning of the Scriptures to his audience; he was making the passages plain and understandable for the worshipers. "Giving evidence" (*paratithēmi*) conveys the idea that he was bringing forward passages from the Old Testament and using them for proof. Paul was pointing to all the passages where it was predicted that Messiah would suffer and rise from the dead.

---

[5] Acts 13:14-15; Romans 1:16. Again, notice that the rejection of the Jews recorded in Acts 13:46 applied only to those in Antioch of Pisidia, and not to Jewish people generally.

Perhaps we might learn from Paul some methods for present-day evangelism. The evangelist, whether at home or abroad, should develop a prospect list, indicating what people are the nearest ready to accept the gospel. These are approached first, using their present level of understanding to build Christian teaching and commitment. He will seldom win all of these, and in the process he will probably win some whom he did not expect to be receptive. But somewhere in the process he will probably reach a point where the responsiveness of this initial group will wane, and opposition might perhaps even set in. The wise worker will then shift his approach to take advantage of greater responsiveness in others, and will go on to reap and glean the greatest possible harvest.

[6] 1 Thessalonians 2:9; 2 Thessalonians 3:7-8.

[7] 1 Thessalonians 1:5,9.

[8] 1 Thessalonians 1:19, 2:14.

[9] *Suzēteō* was used at Acts 6:9 and 9:29.

[10] John 6:25-26; Matthew 12:9.

That Messiah would suffer was a side of the Messianic prophecies that the Jews had missed or ignored. They saw only the verses that spoke of Messiah being a glorious king like David or Solomon, and could not harmonize with this idea the verses that spoke of a suffering servant. Verses about the suffering of Messiah were a stumbling block to the Jews.[11]

And rise again from the dead. Old Testament prophecies of the resurrection include Psalm 16:10, the book of Jonah,[12] etc. Paul also worked miracles in Thessalonica as proof of what he said about the resurrection.[13] If preaching today is to be apostolic in its content, it must include instruction that Jesus is the Messiah, a fact proven by His bodily resurrection from the dead.

And *saying*, "This Jesus whom I am proclaiming to you is the Christ." Paul called attention to the relevant predictions about Messiah in the Old Testament, and then affirmed that Jesus of Nazareth must be the One predicted, for He exactly fulfilled what was predicted of the Messiah.

17:4 – *And some of them were persuaded and joined Paul and Silas, along with a great multitude of the God-fearing Greeks and a number of the leading women.*

And some of them were persuaded. It seems that but few Jews out of the synagogue were converted, few in comparison with the "great multitude" of Greek proselytes.

And joined Paul and Silas. Literally, "they threw in their lot with Paul and Silas." They became followers of the Christ the missionaries preached, and began meeting regularly as a congregation with the missionaries as teachers. They, too, left the synagogue.

Along with a great multitude of the God-fearing Greeks. The "God-fearing Greeks" were proselytes of the gate.[14] Whether these are the Gentiles to whom reference is made in 1 Thessalonians 1:9 and 2:14, or whether such converts came after Paul left preaching in the synagogue, it is not possible to tell, though the latter explanation is perhaps preferable. Aristarchus and Secundus are likely two of these Greek converts.[15]

And a number of the leading women. For a definition of leading women, see notes at Acts 13:50. In the Macedonian towns of Philippi, Thessalonica, and Berea, there is a specific mention of women among the converts. Women were freer to take part in public activities in Macedonia than in many parts of the Roman empire.

---

[11] See notes at Acts 3:17,18

[12] Matthew 12:40 indicates Jonah's experience was a type for which Jesus' own death and resurrection was the antitype.

[13] 1 Thessalonians 1:5.

[14] See notes on "God-fearing" at Acts 16:14.

[15] Acts 20:4.

17:5 – *But the Jews, becoming jealous and taking along some wicked men from the market place, formed a mob and set the city in an uproar; and coming upon the house of Jason, they were seeking to bring them out to the people.*

But the Jews, becoming jealous. The Jews – perhaps the synagogue leaders – who were not persuaded by the gospel, are the ones who become jealous. Their jealousy seems to have been over the fact that Paul and Silas had taken away some of the families who used to worship in the synagogue, plus the fact that many of the converts were of Greek background. See 1 Thessalonians 2:14ff, where the hostility of the Jews toward the early Thessalonian Christians is alluded to.

And taking along some wicked men from the market place. "Wicked" is a translation of *ponēros*, a word that implies a delight in doing harm to others. They would be men who had no steady jobs and who just loafed around the forum. Such men are always ready to earn a quick dollar, and "take along" might indicate that the Jewish leaders have bribed these loafers to be a part of the mob.

Formed a mob and set the city in an uproar. The same thing had happened in Galatia on the first missionary journey.[16] Here the rabble began a parade through the streets, raising loud outcries against the missionaries.

And coming upon the house of Jason, they were seeking to bring them out to the people. Jason's house was where the missionaries were staying.[17] We don't know much about Jason. He is called a "kinsman" of Paul in Romans 16:21, but this probably means no more than that he was a Jew, rather than that he was actually a blood relative of Paul's. It cannot now be determined whether he was a Jew by birth, and changed his Hebrew name Joshua (Jesus) into the Greek form "Jason,"[18] or whether he was born to Hellenized parents who gave their son a Greek name.[19] The mob that was collected by the Jewish leaders has assembled before Jason's house, intending to seize the two missionaries and bring them out to the people. "Out to the people" might mean no more than that the crowd would begin then and there to do violence to their intended victims. More likely, it has reference to the regular town meeting where the government of the city was administered. Thessalonica was a free city and would have had its own assembly of the people.[20]

17:6 – *And when they did not find them, they began dragging Jason and some brethren before the city authorities, shouting, "These men who have upset the world have come here also;*

And when they did not find them. Whether Paul and Silas had been warned, or were ab-

---

[16] Acts 13:50.

[17] See verse 7.

[18] See the example of the brother of the high priest Onias III, 2 Maccabees 4:7.

[19] Among the Greeks, an ancient hero was Jason who made an expedition with the Argonauts.

[20] See notes at Acts 19:30 concerning such an "assembly." Government in free cities was different than government in Roman colonies such as Philippi (Acts 16:20).

sent on an evangelistic call, or were at the place of work, Luke does not say. Someone usually suffers the wrath of a mob like this, and since the mob did not find the two missionaries, they turned on Jason and some of the Christians who happened to be there when the mob arrived.

They *began* dragging Jason and some brethren before the city authorities. The verb "drag" indicates violence or force. Jason and the other believers are being manhandled as they are taken downtown to the forum for trial before the city authorities.

The Greek term Luke uses, *politarchs* ("city authorities"), is very unusual, occurring nowhere else in the New Testament, nor indeed, in any classical writer. Aristotle, whose *Politics* well-nigh exhausts the list of all known official titles in Greek cities, does not even mention it. On this evidence (or lack of it), the negative critics used to say that Luke made a mistake in this place in Acts; therefore, his record is not trustworthy (thus also implying that the doctrine of inspiration is suspect). But at the western edge of the city, an archway dating to the time of Vespasian has been found on which is chiseled the name "politarchs" and underneath are the names of seven men. Other inscriptions too have been found in Macedonia, five of them from Thessalonica, which show that "politarchs" was the regular title for the political leaders of the city, and that Luke was exactly right and his critics exactly wrong.[21]

Shouting, "These men who have upset the world have come here also. "Shouting" has the connotation, "Yelling like the house is on fire." Paul and Silas have been disturbers of the peace in other places, they charge, and now they have come to our city.[22] "World" probably has reference to the Roman empire.

17:7 – and Jason has welcomed them, and they all act contrary to the decrees of Caesar, saying that there is another king, Jesus."

And Jason has welcomed them. The mob charges Jason with aiding and abetting the crime of which Paul and Silas are accused by receiving them hospitably into his house. Perhaps this also indicates that the church regularly assembled in Jason's home.

And they all act contrary to the decrees of Caesar. "All" means Jason and all the brethren who were arrested and were standing before the politarchs. The Jews who led the mob (verse 5) probably pointed to them as they spoke. The plural "decrees" has caused some question among the commentators. Some appeal to the decree of Claudius as being in the mind of the accusers.[23] Others appeal to a series of decrees against treason. Still others are reminded of the Roman law that prohibited the introduction of a new religion.[24]

---

[21] Conybeare and Howson, *op. cit.*, p.258. F.F. Bruce, *op. cit.*, p.344.

[22] Some preachers take this term and turn it to its true light, saying that the missionary turns the world right-side up; it was the devil who turned it upside down.

[23] Acts 18:1-3. Compare notes at Acts 16:20.

[24] See notes at Acts 16:21.

Saying that there is another king, Jesus." Only by permission from Rome could the name "king" be used in any of the vanquished provinces.[25] This was a charge to which the politarchs would have to pay attention. The religious leaders who clamored for Jesus' death urged a similar charge against Him,[26] and the Jews in Thessalonica are likely following that template as they make charges against Paul and Silas. They could deliberately twist some things the preachers had said, and then such a charge would have just enough truth in it to be believable. It is clear from the two epistles to the Thessalonian that the kingdom of Christ, and especially His second coming as King, had been very prominent in Paul's preaching while in Thessalonica.[27] Such statements could easily have furnished materials for this accusation that the preachers say there is another "king."

17:8 – *And they stirred up the crowd and the city authorities who heard these things.*

And they stirred up the crowd and the city authorities who heard these things. The "crowd" would be those who gathered in the market place to see what all this commotion and yelling was about as the mob dragged the brethren into court. When they heard the charges, they too became inflamed against the Christians. Even though the Jews had actually caused more disturbance when they dragged Jason and the other Christians before the court than Paul and Silas had caused, the citizens of Thessalonica would be worried about what the Romans might do when they heard that treasonable plots had been set forth in the city against Caesar. The authorities were worried what the Romans would do to them for not defending the honor of Caesar better.

17:9 – *And when they had received a pledge from Jason and the others, they released them.*

And when they had received a pledge from Jason and the others. The Greek says "they received the sufficient (amount?)" and seems to be a technical term for putting up a bond or surety. Jason and the other Christians who had been dragged to the forum had to put up money or other securities. We can only infer from what happens next what the exact nature of the "pledge" was. Perhaps we are to understand that the bond would be forfeited if Paul and Silas continue to preach in the city.[28] Jason and the brethren were made responsible for seeing that the men who were the cause of the disturbance no longer taught their doctrines in Thessalonica. While Paul and Silas might go back to preaching after a stoning or a beating that they received personally, it is a different thing when their converts would be the ones suffering for the boldness of the missionaries.

They released them. The only charges against Jason and the brethren were that they had aided the preachers. They themselves were not charged with treason, or the authorities could not have let them go so easily.

---

[25] John 19:15; 1 Peter 2:13,17.

[26] Luke 23:2; John 19:12.

[27] 1 Thessalonians 4:14; 5:2,23; 2 Thessalonians 1:7-8; 2:1-12.

[28] Chrysostom understood the passage to mean that Jason and the brethren gave pledge to produce the apostles in court, and that they took a risk in helping them instead to escape.

11. At Berea. 17:10-14

17:10 – *And the brethren immediately sent Paul and Silas away by night to Berea; and when they arrived, they went into the synagogue of the Jews.*

And the brethren immediately sent Paul and Silas away by night. The leaving by night was to safely escape their enemies who would still have dragged them to the politarchs if they could only have found them and captured them. It is probable that Paul had spent upwards of six months in Thessalonica.[29] A new congregation of Christians has been planted,[30] and he had been in the city long enough that on at least two different occasions the church at Philippi had sent missionary offerings to him.[31]

To Berea. Berea was about 50 miles southwest of Thessalonica. To reach it they could have traveled the Egnatian Way westward until, about daylight, they would come to the side road leading off in a more southerly direction toward Berea (i.e., modern Voeria). We do not know if Timothy is traveling with Paul and Silas or not. It may be that Timothy is still with Luke in Philippi.[32]

And when they arrived, they went into the synagogue of the Jews. Following his God-directed pattern of evangelism, Paul begins his work in the new town among the Jews first. Berea may have been a secluded town, but there were enough Jews here to have a synagogue.

17:11 – *Now these were more noble-minded than those in Thessalonica, for they received the word with great eagerness, examining the Scriptures daily, to see whether these things were so.*

Now these were more noble-minded than those in Thessalonica. "These" are the Jews of Berea, who evidently listened to Paul's preaching for longer than the three weeks that he was allowed to speak in the synagogue at Thessalonica. "Noble" is a word that often means "well born, of noble birth,"[33] but here the word seems to apply more to attitude. Two reasons are given for this good word about the Jews in Berea: (1) they received the word (i.e., the gospel), and (2) they studied the Scriptures daily. This is one of very few occasions when Paul was received well by his Jewish kinsmen for whose salvation he yearned so much.[34]

For they received the word with great eagerness. These Berean Jews listened attentively

---

[29] 1 Thessalonians 4:13-5:5; 2 Thessalonians 3:7-8.

[30] 1 Thessalonians 1:7, 2:13, 2:20.

[31] Philippians 4:15-16.

[32] See upcoming notes at verses 14 and 15 concerning Timothy's travels.

[33] Compare 1 Corinthians 1:26 where the word is used of noble birth. Rackham interprets the word in this same manner here as well.

[34] Romans 9:3.

and eagerly to the Gospel. They were open-minded and ready to hear more and more of what God had to say to them.

Examining the Scriptures daily. The Scriptures they studied were the Old Testament books. Either these people had copies of the books in their homes where they could examine the prophecies to which Paul appealed, or else they came to the synagogue to study the rolls of Scripture kept in the presses there. That this was done daily implies that Paul spent some time there.

To see **whether these things were so.** They were comparing the things preached by Paul and Silas to the Scriptures. At Thessalonica Paul and Silas urged that the Old Testament taught that the Messiah must suffer and be raised from the dead. Likely these same doctrines are now shared with the Jews at Berea, and the Bereans then began their own personal investigation of the Scriptures. Philosophers and theologians have struggled over the right relation between Faith and Reason. The Bereans give a good example to follow.[35]

17:12 – *Many of them therefore believed, along with a number of prominent Greek women and men.*

Many of them therefore believed. As a result of hearing the gospel and of studying the Scriptures, they are led to become converts to the Christian religion. In many cities, the majority of converts were of Gentile background. At Berea it is different. "Many" Jewish people became Christians.

Along with a number of prominent Greek women and men. "Prominent" likely modifies both women and men. The evangelistic work of the apostles included more than people who attended the synagogue. Here are Greeks who are converted, including some city leaders.[36] Among all of these Jewish and Greek converts, we know the name of only one, Sopater,[37] and he was Jewish.

17:13 – *But when the Jews of Thessalonica found out that the word of God had been proclaimed by Paul in Berea also, they came there likewise, agitating and stirring up the crowds.*

But when the Jews of Thessalonica found out that the word of God had been proclaimed by Paul in Berea also. The missionaries had left Thessalonica by night in order to elude their persecutors, but the persecutors have not forgotten them. And when they are brought intelligence that many Jews at Berea have become Christians, their anger is kindled. They badly want to silence the Christian preachers if they are willing to travel 50 miles to do it. Paul apparently refers to these Jewish religious leaders of Thessalonica in 1 Thessalonians 2:15 when he writes, "they are not pleasing to God, and are hostile to all men, even hindering us from speaking to the Gentiles so that they might be saved."

---

[35] Bible school classes and churches have long chosen for themselves the name "Berean" to indicate that they wish to follow the worthy example set by the Jews of Berea.

[36] Compare notes at Acts 13:50 on "prominent women."

[37] Acts 20:4.

They came there likewise. There is no way to determine how long Paul had been in Berea before the Jews of Thessalonica learned his whereabouts, but he had been there long enough to establish a congregation. The same evil zeal which characterized the Jews of Galatia during Paul's first missionary journey, he meets now during this second tour.[38] Jews who caused him trouble earlier will harass him from town to town.

Agitating and stirring up the crowds. The word translated "agitating" is quite picturesque – it denotes the boiling of the waves of the sea when blown by a gale. We are not told what charges the Jews made against Paul, or even who listened to the charges. It often has been surmised that Berea had an influential Jewish population, and it was through these that the Jewish leaders from Thessalonica were able to arouse popular feeling against Paul. If charges ever were made against Paul to the Gentile population, perhaps they mirrored the charges raised at Thessalonica.[39] Per verse 14, the Jews are particularly after Paul. Is this because he has become so evidently the dominant member of the missionary party?

17:14 – *And then immediately the brethren sent Paul out to go as far as the sea; and Silas and Timothy remained there.*

And then immediately the brethren sent Paul out. The "brethren" are the Christians in Berea. In order to protect Paul from bodily harm and perhaps death, they get him out of town quickly. According to verse 15, some of the Berean believers accompanied Paul on the journey.

To go as far as the sea. One who would make a map of Paul's journeys finds he must make a choice here. Some manuscripts read as though Paul pretended to go toward the sea, but actually went overland toward Athens. The feigned movement was to elude the Jews who might be pursuing, it is thought. Other manuscripts read as though Paul actually did go to the nearest seaport at Dium, and went by ship to Athens. According to this latter reading, "to go as far as the sea" means that when Paul was hurriedly leaving town, he had had opportunity to do no more than plan that far ahead. He simply told those who stayed behind that he was heading toward the seaport. While on the journey to that seaport, some 20 miles away, he formulated his plans to make Athens his next stop.

And Silas and Timothy remained there. The last time Timothy was referenced, he was in Philippi.[40] This verse now has him in Berea, so at some point Timothy has joined Paul during the ministry in Berea. This verse also says that Timothy and Silas remained behind at Berea as Paul fled toward the sea. It was Paul's custom to leave a helper behind to edify the infant churches. In Paul's absence, these two preachers would be involved in that type of ministry, as well as winning more to Christ.

---

[38] Acts 14:19

[39] See comments at verses 5 and 7.

[40] Compare Acts 16:3,12,40.

12. At Athens. 17:15-34

17:15 – *Now those who conducted Paul brought him as far as Athens; and receiving a command for Silas and Timothy to come to him as soon as possible, they departed.*

Now those who conducted Paul brought him as far as Athens. The distance between Berea and Athens by land was 250 Roman miles, or about 12 days' journey, but only about 3 days by sea. Some of the Berean brethren accompanied Paul, not only to show their affection for him, but also perhaps for guidance and protection. If he arrived by ship, Paul would have docked at the port of Piraeus, and then walked the new highway, called Hamaxitos, northeastward toward the city. At intervals along this highway were raised altars to the unknown gods. Peddlers and merchants would have had their booths set up around the gateways of the city, offering fruit, olives, and fish for sale. Pushing his way past these he would enter the forum, surrounded on several sides by *stoas*, or porches, painted by the brush of famous artists and adorned with the noblest statues. Located there also was the tower and waterclock of Andronicus. South of the forum rose Mars Hill and the Acropolis with the Parthenon. On the south side of the Acropolis was the theater of Dionysius. We can picture Paul climbing the steps of the Propylaea and entering onto the platform of the Acropolis, where all around him were buildings housing statues of the gods. Since the time of Alexander the Great and the capture by the Romans, Athens was no longer the politically powerful city she used to be; but she was still the cultural, philosophical, and intellectual capital of the world.[41] Evidences of this were all around; but as he stood on the Acropolis looking out over the city, what he really saw were people in need of Christ.

And receiving a command for Silas and Timothy to come to him as soon as possible. The Christians from Berea who accompanied Paul to Athens served as messengers to deliver this command to Silas and Timothy who were still at Berea. Paul wants the two to join him as quickly as possible. Timothy indeed came to Paul while Paul was still in the city of Athens, but Silas apparently did not catch up with Paul until Paul got to Corinth (where Paul went after he left Athens). According to 1 Thessalonians 3:1-2, Paul deemed his time at Athens to be an opportune time to be left alone, so Timothy was sent to Thessalonica to establish the brethren. From this we reconstruct Timothy's travels. He must have come to Paul before Paul left Athens. Apparently, too, he had never yet been to Thessalonica, so his coming would not endanger Jason (or cause him to forfeit his bond) as would the coming of Paul or Silas. When Paul leaves Athens and goes on to Corinth, both Timothy and Silas will join him there.[42]

They departed. With the Bereans returning home, Paul is left alone in Athens for a time, and he will evangelize alone for a time.

17:16 – *Now while Paul was waiting for them at Athens, his spirit was being provoked within him as he was beholding the city full of idols.*

---

[41] Rome was the political center and Corinth was the commercial center of the Roman world.

[42] Acts 18:5.

Now while Paul was waiting for them at Athens. The length of Paul's stay in Athens is not given. Some time would be required for trips to and from Berea to be made, and for Timothy to wind up his work so that he was free to head for Athens to join Paul. In the meantime, Paul had ample time to observe the idolatrous condition of the city.

His spirit was being provoked within him. The same Greek word was translated "sharp disagreement" at Acts 15:39. "Provoked" does carry the connotation of burning with anger, and the imperfect tense here indicates the continuance of Paul's feelings about the idolatry, the more he saw of it.

As he was beholding the city full of idols. That the city was full of idols is a fact abundantly testified to by ancient secular writers. Pausanius writes, "the Athenians greatly surpassed others in their zeal for religion."[43] Lucian wrote, "on every side there were altars, victims, temples, and festivals."[44] Petronius says, somewhat in humor, "It is easier to find a god than a man there."[45] Busts of Hermes at every corner, statues and altars in the courtyard of every home, temples and porches and colonnades, all reminded Paul of the idolatry in which these people were steeped. He looked on the Theseus and the Ilissus, and the friezes of the Centaurs and Lapithae on the Parthenon, with horror that men should bow down and worship what their hands had made. The artistic beauty we admire in the Apollo, or the Aphrodite, or the Mercury, or the Faun, would be to Paul a thing to shudder at since they were objects of worship, behind which were demons.[46] Where we are used to seeing lamp poles, street name markers, fire plugs, and post office mail boxes on every corner, Paul saw idols and altars. And in these, he saw evidences of the degradation men sink into when they try any of the devil's substitutes for the real, God-revealed, way of worship.

17:17 – *So he was reasoning in the synagogue with the Jews and the God-fearing* **Gentiles,** *and in the market place every day with those who happened to be present.*

So. Note the connection. Paul saw the great amount of idolatry in Athens. His spirit was provoked. So he began to speak up. What they really need is Christ!

He was reasoning in the synagogue with the Jews and the God-fearing *Gentiles*. Even at Athens, Paul went to the Jews first, even after the attempts on his life by Jews in the last several towns. He used the same method ("reasoned"[47]) in Athens that he did in Thessalonica. He is trying, week after week, to help the Jews and proselytes to see that Jesus was the Messiah predicted by the Old Testament prophets.

And in the market place every day with those who happened to be present. See the map of the Agora at the close of this book, showing its location north of the Areopagus.

---

[43] Pausanias, *in Attic.* (which is a part of his *Hellados Periegesis*), I.24.

[44] Lucian, *The Literary Promethius*, p.180.

[45] Petronius Arbiter, *Petronii Arbitri Satyricon*, XVII.

[46] 1 Corinthians 10:20.

[47] Compare verse 2.

This forum was a large area, rectangular, with covered walks (i.e., porches) along the sides.[48] Temples, public buildings, statues, fountains, and monuments filled the area. Each day, for several hours in the early forenoon, the place swarmed with people who came to buy and sell. The rest of the day, the philosophers and teachers would find a raised stone or dais from which to teach, or they might be found walking along the porches with their pupils. Paul took his place daily in the market place, likely competing with other teachers. It certainly is not a new method of evangelism for Paul to speak in the market place. He had done so at Lystra on the first missionary journey. Paul is working hard to convert the Jews and pagans of Athens to Christianity.

17:18 – *And also some of the Epicurean and Stoic philosophers were conversing with him. And some were saying, "What would this idle babbler wish to say?" Others, "He seems to be a proclaimer of strange deities," – because he was preaching Jesus and the resurrection.*

And also some of the Epicurean ... philosophers. The Epicureans were one of the two great schools of Greek thought in the 1st century. Men who embraced the doctrines of the philosopher Epicurus (342-270 BC) were called Epicureans.

Some of the major tenets of the Epicureans were: (1) Pleasure is the highest end in living. "Eat, drink and be merry" has come to be a popular summary of this philosophy, though it may be a not-quite-proper summary. By pleasure, Epicurus meant good pleasure (and it pleased him to be generous, kindly, and patriotic). But his followers formed their own standards of pleasure, and too often they lived lives indulging the pleasures of the flesh. (2) Matter is eternal, and therefore they denied that the world was created by some deity. (3) A denial of the immortality of the soul. (4) A denial of any idea of future retribution after death for deeds done in this life. (5) A denial of the idea that the gods exercised any providential control over human affairs.

And Stoic philosophers. Stoics were advocates of the theory originally taught by Zeno of Cyprus (d. 264 BC, after living to the age of 96). Because he regularly held his classes on one of the porches in the market place, Zeno's followers were called "Stoics" (from the Greek word *stoa*, which means "porch"). Stoicism was well known in Tarsus, Paul's hometown; at least six famous Stoic philosophers came from Tarsus.

Doctrines of the Stoics included: (1) The world was created by Zeus. (2) All things were governed by the "Fates," to whom Zeus himself was subject. (3) Self-denial was thought to contribute to the highest end in life. Passions and affections were to be suppressed and restrained ("Grin and bear it!"). Apathy or indifference to either pleasure or pain, and mastery over all desires and lusts, so that none gained control of the man, were what the Stoic aimed for.[49] (4) They denied the immortality of the soul, some holding that the soul would exist only until the destruction of the universe, and others that it would finally be absorbed into the divine essence and become a part of deity (i.e., they believed in

---

[48] On the east side of the forum was the "painted porch" where Zeno used to teach. This porch was adorned with frescoes of the battle of Marathon, and from these paintings the porch got its name.

[49] Stoics have been called the Pharisees of the world of philosophy, for in their apathy they lost any feeling of sympathy (much like the Pharisees who, in their legalism, also had little sympathy for their fellow men). Josephus. *Life,* C.2.

the transmigration of souls).

Both systems of thought, Epicurean and Stoic, were two different attempts by pre-Christian pagans to explain the great questions of life.[50]

Were conversing with him. At Acts 4:15 this same word was translated "confer." As Paul would address the people in the market place each day, some would stop to discuss his teaching with him.

And some were saying, "What would this idle babbler wish to say?" "Babbler" comes from a word which means, literally, "seed picker." It was applied by the Greeks to the poor people who after a harvest would collect the seeds that were left in the fields, and then to the men who hung around the shops and the markets, picking up scraps which fell from the loads of food, and living off them. It was also a name given to a little bird who hopped here and there picking up the scattered kernels of grain. The word then came to be applied to men who picked up scraps of information here and there and then tried to palm them off as their own. Perhaps it was the Stoics who leveled this contemptuous criticism at Paul, for the word had been used by Zeno, their founder, of one of his disciples.[51] Some of the Greek philosophers who conversed with Paul dismissed him as a man who had picked up bits of philosophy here and there, and was proclaiming merely a syncretistic philosophy.[52] There is a broken sentence here in the Greek. We might complete it on this fashion. "What would this idle babbler wish to say, if he could express his thoughts clearly?"

Others (were saying), "He seems to be a proclaimer of strange deities." These hearers pictured Paul as setting forth new deities to be added to their pantheon – gods whose existence Paul is now making known to them. The word translated "deities" denotes properly "demons" – i.e., those beings in Greek mythology who were superior to men, but inferior to the gods. In Greek mythology, demons had been exalted to this superior place after being heroes or distinguished men in this life. The word "strange" is used here in the sense of "foreign," i.e., gods from another country. The Greeks worshiped many gods themselves, and they believed that every country had its own peculiar divinities. They supposed that Paul had come to announce the existence of some such foreign, and to them heretofore unknown, gods.[53]

Because he was preaching Jesus and the resurrection. Luke here gives us the reason some of the Greeks thought Paul was setting forth multiple, strange deities. The tense of the verb "preaching" shows this was the ever-recurring theme of Paul's sermons to the audiences in the market place.

---

[50] Post-Christian philosophers who ignore God's revelation will not do appreciably better in formulating a world-view than Epicureans and Stoics did. In fact, they have not, though a number have tried.

[51] Diogenes Laertius, *Zeno*, C.19.

[52] Paul, of course, denies that his teaching was a syncretistic conglomeration. He says his message was revealed to him by God (Galatians 1:11ff).

[53] This was the precise charge on which Socrates had been condemned; namely, that he proclaimed "strange deities." Xenophon, *Memorabilia*, I.1.1.

It seems that the Athenians supposed Paul was talking about two different deities, Jesus and Resurrection (the latter as a female deity, *Anastasis*[54]). There doesn't seem to be any other satisfactory explanation of the plural "deities" in the previous phrase, except to say that they supposed that *anastasis* was the name of some goddess (just as they had Pity, Piety, Modesty, and Harmony as goddesses, and had erected altars to them, as well as to Shame, Famine, and Desire). Some deny this interpretation, urging as proof the assertion that Paul would hardly have expressed himself so obscurely as to be thus misunderstood. Such a denial, however, ignores the problem of "verbalisms" that is always present when a speaker addresses an audience. Audiences tend to put their own interpretation on a speaker's words, rather than listening to the definition the speaker himself gives.

Whatever the Greeks may have understood, Luke informs us about the content of Paul's preaching to the various listeners in the forum. He emphasized Jesus (i.e., God's savior for the world) and the resurrection (i.e., not so much an emphasis on Christ's own resurrection, but upon the resurrection of the dead bodies of all men – an idea foreign to Greek thinking, but a truth guaranteed by the resurrection of Jesus).

17:19 – *And they took him and brought him to the Areopagus, saying, "May we know what this new teaching is which you are proclaiming?*

And they took him and brought him to the Areopagus, saying. It seems that Paul is brought to the hill where the celebrated court, the supreme court of Athens, often held its meetings.[55] This hill was almost in the middle of the city, but little remains on its summit to help us determine what it looked like in Paul's day. There are benches cut in the rock on which the judges sat. Sixteen worn steps lead to the summit from a plateau between the Areopagus and the Acropolis. Two stones in the midst of where the judges sat were for the accuser and accused to sit on as murder cases were being tried. Though the words "the Areopagus" can either mean the place where the court met, or the court itself, we probably are to picture Paul as being surrounded by the judges ("the council of the Areopagus"), since at the close of the message one of the Areopagites is named as a convert.[56]

The exact purpose the philosophers had in mind when they brought Paul to the Areopagus (also called Mars Hill) must be inferred from the context. Some suggest the Areopagites (judges) merely wanted a quiet place, away from the crowd and noise of the forum, where they could listen undisturbed to what Paul was saying. Others think this is a preliminary hearing, and that if Paul didn't satisfy the judges who looked harshly at men who came teaching about "strange deities," he would be bound over for trial.

"May we know what this new teaching is which you are proclaiming? Whether this was the opening of a formal trial has been argued. It has some of the forms of a trial, for verse 20 might be looked on as an accusation. Yet there does not seem to be an accuser

---

[54] They seemed to be personifying the word "resurrection." This was easily done since all ancient names had a meaning.

[55] The "council of the Areopagus" also held meetings on the Royal Porch on the west side of the forum of Athens, as Demosthenes informs us in *Phillipic* I.

[56] See verse 34.

sitting on the rock opposite Paul. The question put to Paul might be a courteous question, or it might be full of irony and sarcasm.[57] Perhaps we should picture what is happening to Paul as a preliminary investigation to see if there was any reason to lodge formal charges against him since in Athens the introduction of "strange deities" could be a capital offence.[58] That there was no formal indictment of Paul at this time seems to be implied by the parenthetical note (verse 21) which Luke inserts below.

17:20 – *"For you are bringing some strange things to our ears; we want to know therefore what these things mean."*

"For you are bringing some strange things to our ears. The word "strange" again carries the idea of "pertaining to a foreign country."[59] It is not the exact same word that Luke used in verse 18 (for here there is the connotation of startling, bewildering, strange), but it seems that this is an explanation of why they wanted to know more about his teaching.

We want to know therefore what these things mean." Give us more information so we may understand more clearly what is affirmed respecting Jesus and the resurrection.

17:21 – *(Now all the Athenians and the strangers visiting there used to spend their time in nothing other than telling or hearing something new.)*

(Now all the Athenians and the strangers visiting there. This is Luke's parenthetical explanation about the people of Athens, explaining why they were eager to hear what Paul had to say. The Greek reads "Now all Athenians," without any article, thus speaking of a characteristic of the whole population. 400 years earlier Demosthenes had rebuked the Athenians for idling away their time in the forum, asking about the latest news concerning the movements of Philip of Macedon who was then rising to power, when instead they should have been preparing for battle. Athens was a center of art, philosophy, architecture, science, and literature. Young students from all over the empire came there to finish their education. These would be included in the "strangers visiting there," as would sightseers and tourists.

Used to spend their time in nothing other than telling or hearing something new.) Luke's explanation shows how the Athenians sacrificed the more important interests of life to this restless inquisitiveness to know about the latest thing.[60] They even had an expression "What's news?" in which the adjective was in the comparative degree; literally, "What's newer?" Such an attitude leads men to regard anything old as obsolete and worth

---

[57] The Greek could be translated "We are able to know ..." or it could be rendered "Are we able to know ...?"

[58] Josephus (*Against Apion*, II.38) tells us how a certain priestess had been condemned in Athens because she initiated people into the worship of strange deities.

[59] See above at verse 18.

[60] The adjective here translated "new" is in the comparative degree in the Greek, "newer." What the Athenians wanted to hear was the thing newer than the latest thing that heretofore was new. Many of the ancient writers bear witness to the insatiable curiosity of the Athenians to hear something newer. See Thucydides. *History*, III.38 or Aelian, *Various Histories*, V.13.

little. It drives a person to try the latest fads and pleasures, but it never leaves him satisfied and content. People with such a philosophy will have a difficult time being interested in the everlasting gospel for any length of time. Luke's parenthetical note helps to explain that this was no formal trial, but it does not rule out the idea that this may have been a preliminary examination into Paul's doctrines; and it also prepares us for the fact that the response to the invitation was not as great as in other cities.

17:22 – *And Paul stood in the midst of the Areopagus and said, "Men of Athens, I observe that you are very religious in all respects.*

And Paul stood in the midst of the Areopagus. It is evident that Luke has recorded but a mere summary or outline of the discourse; but it is enough to enable us to see clearly Paul's course of thought, and the manner in which he met the Epicurean and Stoic philosophers.[61] The benches on which the judges sat formed three sides of a quadrangle, and in the midst of these men Paul stands as he speaks.[62]

And said, "Men of Athens. This was the usual way of beginning a speech to the Areopagites. Paul is perfectly respectful in his language, even though his heart had been deeply affected by their idolatry.

I observe that you are very religious in all respects. Wherever he looked (verse 23) he saw evidence of the "religiousness" of the Athenians.[63] Instead of "very religious," it is possible to translate *deisidaimōn* as "very superstitious."[64] This word was either a compliment or a rebuke depending on what else the speaker said. It served as an attention-getter. The hearer would think, "Did he just compliment us, or did he take a slap at us?" It is not easy to express the exact force of the Greek word because there is no exact English equivalent. "Superstitious" is, perhaps, too strong on the side of blame; "religious" is too strong on the side of praise.

17:23 – *"For while I was passing through and examining the objects of your worship, I also found an altar with this inscription, 'TO AN UNKNOWN GOD.' What therefore you worship in ignorance, this I proclaim to you.*

For while I was passing through and examining the objects of your worship. "Passing

---

[61] Opposing views have been expressed on the question of whether or not Paul did or could make such a speech as here given. Luke has been accused of making up the speech and putting it in Paul's mouth. On the other hand, those who are at home in the classics have been the staunchest defenders of the authenticity of this speech. See the matter discussed in F.F. Bruce, *op. cit.*, p.354. A recent writer on Acts, Ernst Haenchen, has asserted that all the speeches in Acts are compositions made up later, and uses the Areopagus speech as one of the strongest proofs of his theory. However, Haenchen's whole theory fails if it can be shown that Acts was written before the AD 90 date to which he assigns the book.

[62] See also comments at verse 19 for additional descriptions of the setting.

[63] Testimonies to the "religiousness" of the Athenians, similar to Luke's, can be found in Josephus, *Against Apion*, II.11; Pausanias, *op. cit.*, I.17.1; and Thucydides, *op. cit.*, II.40.

[64] It should also be noted in passing that *deisidaimōn* could be rendered "worshiper of many demons," an expression exactly suited to a pagan people like the Athenians who lived in fear of evil spirits and who went out of their way to keep from offending the spirits.

through" likely means "walking along the streets." "Examining" is a present participle which implies that he attentively considered them again and again. The "objects of worship" would be the temples, altars, shrines, and statues connected with the worship of the gods. It does not mean that Paul saw the people while they were engaged in the act of worship (as some English translations might be understood), but that he saw the objects and places of worship. Some suggest there were from 2000-3000 notable idols in the city.

I also found an altar with this inscription, 'TO AN UNKNOWN GOD.' An altar is a place on which to offer a sacrifice. Where this altar was located, or on what occasion it was built, has been the subject of much debate among commentators, and they have searched secular literature to find the historical event at which this altar was erected. For example, many appeal to the time when Epimenides of Crete, who, as a great prophet, was invited to Athens at a time when the city was suffering from an epidemic, as affording a probable explanation of its origin.[65] It is said that Epimenides turned sheep loose into the city, and wherever the sheep happened to stop, there they were sacrificed. If no altar was near, the Athenians sacrificed to the unknown god who should be worshiped there, and who, they thought, had the power to stop the plague if he would just get over being angry with the Athenians. However, there are so many causes which could have led to this altar that it is impossible to fix upon any one with much assurance. Instead, it is sufficient that such existed,[66] and answered Paul's purpose in proving that the Athenians were very demon-fearing, and also served as an introduction and a point of contact for the presentation of the only true and living God.

What therefore you worship in ignorance. Paul is going to speak of Jehovah as a God that they already worshiped, only they did not know His name. Paul can point to the yearning to worship that he found in men, a yearning which they had tried to express in their idols and temples, as evidence of a dim and imperfect knowledge of the true God. "What" (neuter) indicates they were as yet ignorant of the personality of God.

This I proclaim to you. In these words there is an answer to the slander that he was just a seed-picker. If he is explaining something that they admitted they didn't know, he could hardly have picked up his information from them, could he? Paul is saying, "You have a dim and imperfect understanding of the God I've come to tell you about. You admit that with your altar to 'an unknown God.' I know Him! I'll tell you about His name, His attributes, and His efforts to save men." As Paul tells them about the Living God, notice how he attacks the major ideas of both the Epicurean and Stoic philosophers.[67]

17:24 – *"The God who made the world and all things in it, since He is Lord of heaven and earth, does not dwell in temples made with hands;*

The God who made the world and all things in it. In a city so full of idolatry and false

---

[65] Diogenes Laertius, *Epimenides*, C.3.

[66] Pausanius, *op. cit.*, I.4; Philostratus, *Life of Apollonius*, VI.3.5.

[67] It will be helpful at this point to review the major tenets taught by each school of philosophy (see verse 18 above), and then to see how Paul meets each of these in his speech.

ideas of what deity is really like, it could be said that the main object of Paul's sermon is to convince them of the folly of idolatry (verse 29), and thus lead them to repentance. "God" (singular) would be a word that would oppose their opinions that there were many "gods." When he speaks of "God" as being creator, he would be opposing both Epicurean and Stoic thinking, for they either thought of matter as eternal, or that Zeus was the creator. Paul uses the word *kosmos* for world in the same sense the philosophers used it for the ordered universe.

Since He is Lord of heaven and earth. The verb translated "is" has the connotation that God is the *natural* Lord of heaven and earth. Involved in the expression "Lord of heaven and earth" is the idea of God's providence, that He is actively controlling this universe. This assertion would have been contrary to Stoic beliefs (who held that the Fates governed everything) and to Epicurean beliefs (who held that the gods weren't interested in the every-day affairs of men and nations).

Does not dwell in temples made with hands. If He is the maker of all things and the Lord of heaven and earth, He is infinitely above the gods whose dwelling was in a little temple made with hands and who were limited to a small space. Not even the Jerusalem temple could contain God, as Solomon well recognized when that structure was dedicated.[68] As Paul spoke about temples made with hands, he could have pointed to the Parthenon just to the east, and also to the temples of Apollo, Vulcan (Hephaestus), Theseus, and Ares. God does not live in buildings like these, Paul affirms.[69]

17:25 – *"neither is He served by human hands, as though He needed anything, since He Himself gives to all life and breath and all things;*

Neither is He served by human hands, as though He needed anything. Worshipers used to set offerings of food before the idols of the gods. When the feasts held in the idol's temples were finished, the worshipers would leave food and offerings on the raised platforms overnight with the thought that the gods would come and eat to their satisfaction. Jehovah God does not need the assistance of men to exist!

In his last two statements, Paul has struck at the false theory of the value of temples and at a false theory of religion. All the pagan religions emphasize what the worshiper must do for the god. Christianity is distinctive in that it emphasizes what God has done, and continues to do, for the worshiper.[70]

Since He Himself gives to all life and breath and all things. Jehovah is the source of life and therefore cannot be dependent on that life which He has Himself imparted. Commentators have struggled to explain the difference between "life" and "breath." Per-

---

[68] 2 Chronicles 2:6.

[69] It is obvious that this truth places the "sacredness" of church buildings on an entirely different ground from that which influenced the mind of the Jew or Greek in regard to their respective temples. Church buildings are holy, not because God lives in them, but because they are set apart for the highest acts of the congregation that uses them.

[70] Compare Paul's statement of God's activities for men in Acts 14:16ff.

haps the best distinction is to suppose that the first term speaks of life itself (i.e., existence), while the second refers to the continuance of that life (i.e., God provides the oxygen which men must have to breathe, etc.). God is preserver and sustainer as well as creator; He provides all things necessary for the preservation of life and breath.

17:26 – *"and He made from one, every nation of mankind to live on all the face of the earth, having determined their appointed times, and the boundaries of their habitation,*

And He made from one every nation of mankind. The Genesis record says that God created Adam and then formed Eve out of a part of Adam, and from this pair have come all the nations of the earth. This statement of the origin of the human race was in direct opposition to the Athenians' notion of their own origin as being different from that of other peoples.[71] The national pride held by various races (e.g., that their gods were better than others; that their origins were superior to other men's) tended to make the races alien to each other, and led to a haughty attitude toward foreigners and cruelty toward slaves. Paul here tears at the roots of that whole idea, stating that all have descended from Adam.[72]

This God who cannot be housed in buildings made by men's hands and who is Lord of heaven and earth, instead of being the god of some single nation over whose destiny He presides and which He defends from all other nations, actually created every nation, made them all from one man, and He guides the destinies of all.

This verse accords with the Mosaic history. And beyond Genesis, throughout all of God's Word, the assertion is made many times that God created the earth and those who dwell therein. To deny the Creation is not just to deny the Genesis record only; rather, it is to deny all the Scripture. To deny that God is the creator of all, out of one man, because we find some difficulty in reconciling it with the present diversities in the types of men, is to deny an assertion of the Scriptures not because of what we know, but because of what we do not know. If we knew the whole history of the races of men, we would doubtless know the causes of the varieties, and the time or times in which they came into existence.

To live on all the face of the earth. According to the record in Genesis, the earth was created and made livable before man was put on it. Then man was given a command to have children and fill up the earth.[73] God has so ordered it by His providence that the descendants of Adam have found their way to all the lands that are habitable on the face of the earth.

Having determined *their* appointed times. God has, in His plan, fixed the times when each nation should be settled, and the rise, the prosperity, and the fall of each. The different continents and islands have not, therefore, been settled by chance. Nations have risen and waned not because of chance, or because of survival of the fittest, but because God's hand was in it! From verses like this we can formulate a divine philosophy of history.

---

[71] Aristotle, *Vespasian*, 1076; Cicero, *Pro Flacco*, XXVI.

[72] See the same point made in Romans 5:15-19, and notice how important it is to a correct worldview. A denial of the creation of all through Adam leads directly to a denial of the value of Christ's work of atonement.

[73] Genesis 1:28.

And the boundaries of their habitation. God has had a hand in determining how much territory a given nation should include. Paul's doctrine is in accord with the accounts in the Old Testament where it is taught that the Most High had given to nations their inheritance.[74] More is involved than geographical features (mountains, rivers, and seas) that might serve as barriers to expansion. Paul insists that God's providence overrules all such natural barriers, as well as war and migration, when He determines how far a nation's boundaries shall spread. The ideas presented in these last few phrases would have been opposed to both Epicurean and Stoic ideas of history.

17:27 – *"that they should seek God, if perhaps they might grope for Him and find Him, though He is not far from each one of us;*

That they should seek God. The reason why God did what was affirmed of Him in verse 26 (i.e., placing men on earth, determining when nations rise and fall) was that men might seek after God. What is the greatest good? It is not *pleasure* (as the Epicureans taught) nor *apathy* (as the Stoics taught). Instead, it is to be found in seeking God! God planned it all so that men's longings for God might be awakened, so that men would long for more knowledge of His existence and character. All nations, though living in different regions and climates, have a constant evidence before them of God's eternal power and divine nature.[75] This passage shows that man can come to a knowledge of God (though not a saving knowledge) by studying nature and God's dealings with men. It must also be remembered that a man can reject the evidence long enough that sooner or later he will no longer be able to find God.[76]

If perhaps they might grope for Him and find Him. "Perhaps" implies that it is possible to find God through natural theology, but that it might be attended with some difficulty. Even when He is finally recognized via the path of natural theology, the knowledge will be only a partial knowledge since the only way to fully know God is through His revelation of Himself in Jesus and in the Word. The verb "grope for" pictures one groping in the dark (which is the way it is for men without the revelation in Jesus and the Word to aid them). The Greek particles that open the sentence and the optative mood verb all suggest (a fourth class condition) a vague hope of its being fulfilled. Men may have their longings for Him aroused as they contemplate His works, but it will not be a saving knowledge of God to which they come.

Though He is not far from each one of us. This seems to be said in order to guard against the idea that by natural theology one can arrive at a full knowledge of God. Even though God is not far from each one of us, it is still like groping in the dark if one tries to learn about Him fully only through study of the creation. At the same time there is encouragement in the words, so that one without a verbal revelation need not despair of ever becoming acquainted with His existence and perfections.

---

[74] Deuteronomy 32:8; Job 12:23: Psalm 115:16; Daniel 2:21.

[75] Romans 1:19-20.

[76] Romans 1:21ff, 2:11-15; Acts 10:34-35.

The Epicureans would be more and more repelled by this attack on one of the central propositions of their system. Epicurus had taught that the gods, in their eternal tranquility, were too far off from man to trouble themselves about his needs, sorrows, or sins.

17:28 – *"for in Him we live and move and exist, as even some of your own poets have said, 'For we also are His offspring.'*

For in Him we live and move and exist. Here is evidence that God is not far from each of us. He has not gone off somewhere a great distance away from His creation. Instead, He is intimately concerned about each individual person in His world. "In Him" probably has reference to His providential sustenance and provision. An explanation of the three verbs in this phrase has proven a difficult thing for the commentators. Some think it is merely a repetition of the "life and breath and all things" expressed in verse 25, i.e., the idea of absolute dependence on God. Others think each of the verbs had a definite philosophical significance for the audience to whom Paul was speaking.[77] A third suggestion is that the three verbs speak of past, present, and future. That we live at all is His gift; that we have the power to move now is His gift; that we continue to live is His gift also. The Stoics, who were pantheists, could have accepted what Paul says here.[78] But Paul was no pantheist, for pantheism is a corruption of the ideas of God's omnipresence and His providence.

As even some of your own poets have said. The precise expression is found in the writings of Aratus (270 BC),[79] who was a native of Cilicia, the same country Paul was from. Though not the exact words, the general idea is also found in the writings of Cleanthes (300-220 BC).[80] Cleanthes was a Stoic philosopher, and the sentiment here quoted was directly at variance with Epicurean beliefs. This quotation of the heathen poets would at once quicken the attention of the hearers. This was not an illiterate Jew, but a man of culture, acquainted with the thoughts of their own great poets.[81]

'For we also are His offspring.' We might think this quotation was just happily introduced at this time; but the fact that Paul quotes it from memory shows that it had been impressed on his mind, it may be, some years before. This verse is often used to show that

---

[77] According to this suggestion, "live" speaks of our animal life; "move" speaks of our emotions like fear, love. hate, and the like — rather than moving through space; and "exist" speaks of our intellectual and volitional elements.

[78] This first part of verse 28 might also be a quotation of a Greek poet. A four-line poem, that is sometimes attributed to Epimenides of Crete, has Minos saying to Zeus,

> They fashioned a tomb for thee, O Holy and high one —
> The Cretans, always liars, evil beasts, idle bellies!
> But thou art not dead; thou livest and abidest forever;
> For in thee we live and move and have our being.

There is considerable doubt about the authenticity of the fourth line of the poem, however. See the problem discussed in Bruce, *op. cit.*, p.359.

[79] Aratus, *Phaenomena*, V.5.

[80] Cleanthes, *Hymn to Zeus*, V.

[81] For other quotations of the Greek poets by Paul, see 1 Corinthians 15:33 and Titus 1:12.

Paul had a Greek as well as a Jewish education when he was a younger man. The truth that Paul intends to draw from this quotation follows in the next verse.[82]

17:29 – *"Being then the offspring of God, we ought not to think that the Divine Nature is like gold or silver or stone, an image formed by the art and thought of man.*

Being then the offspring of God. One consequence from the thought of us being the offspring of deity is pressed home at once.

We ought not to think that the Divine Nature is like. Reworded, Paul's argument is that "Children resemble their parents. Since we are God's children, it is absurd to think that God is a stick or stone. You are not a stick or stone, or gold, are you? So where did you ever get the idea that God (your Father) is a stick or a stone?" "Divine nature" is neuter in the Greek, and Paul may use this expression in order to get behind all the Athenian various gods to the real nature of God.[83]

Gold or silver or stone, an image formed by the art and thought of man. All these materials were used in making images or statues or temples for the gods at Athens. Phidias had made a lavish use of gold for his colossal statue of Zeus. The silver mines at Laurium (east of Athens) and the marble quarries at Mt. Pentelicus (north of Athens) supplied the materials used in the idols and temples.

It is absurd to think that God – who is the source of all life and intelligence, and even of man himself, too – resembles a lifeless block of wood or stone or precious metal. The latter part of this phrase may be Paul's criticism of the way in which pagan societies allow human thought to become the measure of the gods, so that eventually the gods simply resemble men. Like Xenophanes, some 600 years before, Paul has seen how the gods are made in the likeness of men. The Thracians represented their gods as having blue eyes and fair complexions; the Ethiopians represented their gods as flat-nosed and swarthy. "Image formed by art" speaks of something sculptured.

17:30 – *"Therefore having overlooked the times of ignorance, God is now declaring to men that all everywhere should repent,*

Therefore having overlooked the times of ignorance. The "times of ignorance" was that long period, before the preaching of the gospel, when people were ignorant of the true God because they had no written revelation.[84] Instead of "overlooked" the KJV reads "winked at." That expression now carries a connotation of conniving, of concurring in some improper act, and God certainly does not thus condone sin! Paul will elsewhere say to other

---

[82] Since the words quoted by Paul are all, in their original form, addressed to Zeus, some have questioned how valid and forceful Paul's quotation of them would be in the midst of a sermon that rejects Zeus and all other pagan gods in favor of Jehovah. Paul is only drawing one thought from the quotation, not endorsing the whole context in which the quotation originally appeared.

[83] The Greek here could be translated either "we ought not think …," which would be criticism; or as "we are not obligated to think …," which would be an appeal by Paul to the listeners to give thought to the new ideas that he was presenting to them.

[84] Compare what Acts 14:16 said about God's dealings with the Gentiles in prior times.

readers, "All have sinned and come short of the glory of God."[85] "Overlooked" equals "looked beyond." God, when He was giving a partial revelation (i.e., the Old Testament) to the Jews only, *looked beyond* to the time when the revelation of His will would be complete (i.e., the New Testament) and would be made to all, Gentiles as well as Jews.

When Paul, whether here or in Romans 3:25, says God "passed over the sins" of the Gentiles, he is not saying that God inflicted no punishment on the sins of the ignorant Gentiles. Romans 1:19 is a decided statement to the contrary. What Paul says is similar to what Jesus once said, "The servant who knew *not* his Lord's will, and committed deeds worthy of a flogging, *will be beaten* with few stripes."[86] Instead of immediately coming and wiping out the sinners, God patiently worked toward the time when there would be a full revelation of His will. That time has now come, Paul insists.

God is now declaring to men that all everywhere should repent. If ignorance mitigated their sins before, their sins are far less excusable now. Not just the Jews, who had been favored with special privileges, but all men, even Epicureans and Stoics, have it demanded of them that they repent.[87] Perhaps the Epicurean might later regret some of the ways he had sought for pleasure (e.g., think of indigestion after too much food, or a hangover after too much drink), but repentance? The Epicurean had little time for sorrow or loathing for the past, or for a change of mind about his future conduct. The Stoic was ready to accept the consequences of his actions with a serene apathy; each was his own master, and therefore did nothing to be sorry about or to repent of. Neither school of philosophy had much room for any idea that they needed repentance.

17:31 – *"because He has fixed a day in which He will judge the world in righteousness through a Man whom He has appointed, having furnished proof to all men by raising Him from the dead."*

Because He has fixed a day in which He will judge the world in righteousness. This is given as a reason why God declares that men need to repent. They are going to be judged, and if they are not penitent and pardoned, they must be condemned. Neither the Epicurean nor the Stoic had any place in their systems for a final judgment such as Paul here announces. But the Creator has said there *is* going to be such a day, and the agent has already been appointed! "Fixed a day" may mean no more than that God has absolutely determined that there will be a consummation of history, including a judgment day. In light of 2 Peter 3:12, whether the actual day has been set or whether it is flexible, is a moot point. However, the whole world, Jews and Gentiles, and among them even Epicureans and Stoics, will be judged according to the principles of God's own righteousness.

The thought that each of them would one day stand in judgment before a just and righteous God must have come as a tremendous shock to the Athenians, who had no such idea in their religion. Not only did they not have an idea of a coming judgment, they did not even have an idea of a righteous God. The mythological deities were thought to share

---

[85] Romans 3:23.

[86] Luke 12:48.

[87] See Special Study #8, "What is Repentance?"

every human sin and foible found among men, only to a greater degree. The idea of a God with standards that were righteous would have been a new idea to these pagans.

Through a Man whom He has appointed. God has already appointed one to be the Judge. Who the Man was (we know Him to be Jesus!) either was a topic saved for another address (since perhaps Paul was interrupted so that he never finished his speech), or Luke's brief outline assumes that his readers already know who the Man is. Christ is the one so appointed by the Father to be the judge of all.[88]

Having furnished proof to all men. God has given proof and evidence that Jesus is to be the judge. The Greek phrase here was used in classical Greek in the sense of a "guarantee."

By raising Him from the dead. Just as sure as Jesus was raised from the dead, there will be a universal judgment. Whether Paul listed evidences for the resurrection, or whether he was interrupted and so got no opportunity to share them, we cannot tell for sure. Yet Paul has preached the gospel to these people. In this short address he has taken note of human philosophy's failure to answer the deepest questions of the human heart; he has taken note of men's faulty knowledge about God when that knowledge is unaided by special revelation; and he has been too loving to forget that all men have sinned and that a judgment is to be faced. He has preached Jesus and the resurrection, and has called them to repentance.

Paul's sermon has been outlined in this fashion, even adding a conclusion that causes us to pause and consider.

THE UNKNOWN GOD

Introduction: The observance of idols. Verses 22b, 23
Proposition: Characteristics of the Unknown God

I. Creator of All. Verses 24-26
   a. Made all things
   b. Lord of heaven and earth
   c. Dwells not in any one place
   d. Not served by men's hands
   e. The maker of nations

II. Within the reach of all. Verses 27-29
   a. In Him we live, move, and have our being
   b. We are His offspring or creation
   c. Cast away then these idols and worship the true God

III. Gives Salvation to All. Verses 30-31
   a. The days of ignorance are over
   b. Men now are to repent and turn to Christ
   c. The final judgment

---

[88] Matthew 25:31ff.

Conclusion: Will a person's response today be different from the response that day? Verse 32

    a. Some rejected
    b. Some procrastinated
    c. Some believed

17:32 – *Now when they heard of the resurrection of the dead, some* **began** *to sneer, but others said, "We shall hear you again concerning this."*

Now when they heard of the resurrection of the dead, some *began* **to sneer.** Some Greeks believed in the existence of the soul after the death of the body. But among the Epicureans and Stoics, many of their greatest representatives denied any immortality to the soul, and certainly both would have rejected the idea of a bodily resurrection. To the Greeks, the body was a prison house for the soul, and they looked forward to getting rid of the body. A resurrection in which men got bodies back just didn't fit their thinking at all.

Who the "some" are that mocked has been debated since the verse gives a contrast between "some" who mocked and "others" who wanted to hear more. It has usually been said that the Epicureans were the ones who "sneered;" that is, they mocked both by look and gesture as well as by words of derision. Other possibilities are that it was the Areopagites who sneered, or perhaps even bystanders visiting this meeting.

But others said, "We shall hear you again concerning this." It has often been affirmed that those who wanted to hear more were the Stoics, since some of what Paul had said was similar to Stoic beliefs. Some commentators view these words as a polite way of rejecting Paul's appeal to repentance. People have a way of saying, "I know I ought to obey Christ, and one of these days I'll do it." For some it is an honest intention to one day do it, but for others it is a courteous way to get rid of the preacher. In this particular case at Athens, it's conceivable this group truly was moved by Paul's teaching. He has offered a way for the pagans to get out of the grip of fear of the "many demons" they were in bondage to. Neither philosophy, nor their mythological deities, nor astrology, nor the newer mystery religions, had been able to get them out of their bondage. Hungry for help, they want to hear more of what Paul has to say about Jesus and the resurrection.

17:33 – *So Paul went out of their midst.*

So Paul went out of their midst. When this hearing began, Paul was standing in the midst of the Areopagus (verse 22). The Areopagites are satisfied that Paul is not teaching about "strange deities" as some had supposed (verses 19,20), so there is no need for him to be bound over for trial. Paul is free to leave, and he walks away from the assembly on the Areopagus.

17:34 – *But some men joined him and believed, among whom also were Dionysius the Areopagite and a woman named Damaris and others with them.*

But some men joined him and believed. There is a contrast here with the unfavorable responses of some who sneered. The verb "joined" has been explained at Acts 5:13. The verb pictures a time of close companionship and then later they are converted. We are to understand that there was more teaching involved, which eventually led these individuals to the faith. How long Paul stayed in Athens after his address on the Areopagus is not known, but it was long enough to win several converts.

Among whom also was Dionysius the Areopagite. Nothing more is certainly known of this man than is here stated. The language can mean nothing less than that he was one of the judges. In order to become an Areopagite, one had to serve in a high magisterial function, such as that of Archon, and then upon retiring, had to be elected to serve as a judge. Another qualification was age. To be eligible, one had to have passed his 60th birthday. There are some traditions about this man, which may or may not be true. Eusebius ascribes to Dionysius of Corinth the statement that the Areopagite (also named Dionysius) became bishop of Athens.[89]

And a woman named Damaris. The presence of this woman along with others referred to in the next phrase is taken as evidence that there were bystanders at the meeting on the Areopagus. Some suppose she was one of what Luke has elsewhere called "prominent women,"[90] but the manuscript evidence of this is scant. Chrysostom suggested that she was the wife of Dionysius, but the Greek is not quite right for this to be true.[91] Ramsay suggests that she may have been the mistress (*hetairai*, such women were called) of one of the leaders of the city or the court, for no woman of respectable position would have been present in a public meeting like this in Athens. It is usually surmised that Luke names only these two converts because they are likely the only ones who would have been known to the original readers of Acts.

And others with them. Perhaps Stephanas and his household were included in these "others" since he is named as among the first converts in Achaia.[92]

Some writers affirm that here in Athens Paul attempted to try his hand at Greek philosophy, and that he found this method failed to win men from sin. These writers say that Paul waxed strong, displaying his knowledge to these learned Athenians, and that as a result his ministry in Athens was a failure. Evidence for this view is based on a possible interpretation of 1 Corinthians 2:1-2. Just a short while later on this same missionary journey, Paul will say that he determined at Corinth to know nothing among them but Jesus Christ and Him crucified. Supposedly, Paul is contrasting the preaching approach he used at Corinth with the approach he had attempted to use in Athens.

This commentator rejects this method of interpreting the Corinthian passage, and he rejects the idea that Paul tried to awe the Athenians with his learning. (1) There is no evidence that Paul was trying to be eloquent. His message in Athens follows the general

---

[89] Eusebius, *Church History*, III.4; IV.23.

[90] See Acts 13:50, 17:4, and 17:12.

[91] If Luke had connected an article or a possessive pronoun with the word *gunē* ("wife" or "woman"), this might be the right idea

[92] 1 Corinthians 16:15.

outline of Paul's sermons to Gentile audiences.[93] (2) Some of Paul's hearers did believe. Only the gospel is the power of God unto salvation. (3) Anytime a sermon results in converts (and there were at least six), it cannot be said to have been a failure!

Other writers contend that Paul founded no church at Athens. While it is true that Paul did not stay in Athens as many months as he stayed in some other cities where Luke explicitly records that churches were founded during this missionary journey, the six Athenian believers identified in the New Testament would have provided the nucleus for a congregation. Paul never allowed new believers to go it alone; they always were formed into congregations for mutual edification and encouragement in the faith. True, there are no letters addressed to "the church at Athens," but Paul did not write letters to every church he planted.[94] And do not forget, 2 Corinthians 1:1 has that letter addressed to "the saints throughout Achaia," which must have included Athens.

---

[93] See this general outline presented in comments at Acts 14:15.

[94] For example, there is no "Epistle to the Bereans" either.

13. At Corinth. 18:1-17

18:1 – *After these things he left Athens and went to Corinth.*

After these things he left Athens. After what occurred at Athens, as was recorded in the chapter 17. The journey may have been either by land along the Isthmus of Corinth, or by sea from Piraeus to Cenchrea.

And went to Corinth. This city was about 50 miles southwest of Athens, and was located on the narrow Isthmus which divided the Peloponnesus from Attica. It was the capital of the Roman province of Achaia, and for years had been the most important commercial center of the ancient world. It had two seaports – Lechaeum on the west in the Gulf of Corinth, and Cenchrea on the east in the Saronic Gulf. Because of the dangers of sailing around the Peloponnesus (especially Cape Malea), it was customary to haul ships and cargoes across the Isthmus over a route called the Diolkos. While slaves were doing this work, the sailors had shore-leave in Corinth, so along with the commerce that went through the two seaports had come luxury and vice.[1] In 146 BC, the city had revolted against Rome, and the Romans levelled the city. 100 years later, Julius Caesar had the city rebuilt, and shortly she regained her old commercial prosperity. Into this city, whose population was part Roman, part Greek, and part of mixed nationality, came Paul in about the year AD 52.[2] It was typical of the locations he picked to preach the gospel, for it was a crossroads of the ancient world.

18:2 – *And he found a certain Jew named Aquila, a native of Pontus, having recently come from Italy with his wife Priscilla, because Claudius had commanded all the Jews to leave Rome. He came to them,*

And he found a certain Jew named Aquila. Though he was a Jew by birth, it seems evident that Aquila[3] was already a convert to Christianity. While there is no general agreement regarding when Aquila became a Christian, this commentator believes he was already a believer *before* Paul joined him in the work of tent-making. (1) There is no mention of Priscilla's and Aquila's listening to Paul, of believing, of being obedient to Christ through baptism – as there is in the case of Lydia, etc. If Aquila was one of Paul's first converts in

---

[1] Because of the notorious immorality at Corinth, there was already in classical Greek a word *korinthiazō* ("to live or act like a Corinthian") which was a euphemistic way of referring to the practice of fornication. And over the empire, women who were promiscuous or of loose morals were often called "Corinthian girls." The reason for this is that at the temple of Aphrodite on the Acropolis at Corinth there were 1000 "Corinthian girls" employed as prostitutes. The worship of Aphrodite at Corinth involved having sexual relations with one of these harlots. This worship formed a great temptation, even to the new Christians at Corinth, as evidenced from Paul's exhortations against it in 1 Corinthians 5:1ff and 6:9-19.

[2] See Introductory Studies on p.*xiv-xv*, where we discuss the date of the Edict of Claudius and the Proconsulship of Gallio in Achaia.

[3] *Akylas* is the Greek spelling; *Aquila* is the Latin spelling; and *Onkelos* is the Hebrew spelling of this same name, which means "eagle." There was an Onkelos who perhaps had something to do with a Targum (i.e., a paraphrase into Aramaic) on the Old Testament. Also, about AD 130, there was another, different Aquila from Sinope in Pontus who made a translation of the Old Testament into Greek that proved to be very popular with the Jewish people, even more popular than the earlier LXX translation.

Achaia, should there not be reference to his conversion in the list of early converts found in 1 Corinthians 1:14ff?[4] (2) An unbelieving Jew was not likely to have admitted Paul into partnership in his business, yet that is exactly what Aquila did. In light of these thoughts, we believe that when Paul joined Aquila and his wife, he was able to share with this family lately come from Rome his thoughts and hopes, even before he begins preaching in the synagogue.

If Aquila is already a Christian, why is he here called a "Jew"? Perhaps Luke notes his ethnicity in order to prepare us for Claudius' edict which he is about to introduce. It is Luke's way of telling us that that edict did indeed affect Aquila and Priscilla.

A native of Pontus. Aquila had been born in the province of Pontus. After the Dispersion, Pontus was one place where the Jews became quite numerous.[5]

Having recently come from Italy. How did Aquila get to Italy? Since the Romans often deported people with special skills to Rome to serve the upper classes there, many suppose that he was taken there as a slave. A further supposition is that after a time Aquila has become a freedman. Now, because of the decree of Claudius (see below) he has left Rome and Italy and settled for the time being in Corinth.

With his wife Priscilla. The wife's name is spelled, both here and elsewhere in the manuscripts, two different ways. There is "Prisca" and the diminutive form found here, "Priscilla."[6] The name Prisca probably indicates there was some connection with the *gens* of the *Prisci*[7] who appear in the earliest stages of Roman history. The gens of the Prisci had supplied a long line of praetors and consuls to the Roman government. If Priscilla was of the Prisci gens, then the marriage to the Jew Aquila would be another example of the influence gained by the educated Jews over the higher classes among Roman society.[8]

In many of the verses where this family appears, her name is listed first.[9] It has long been a subject of conjecture as to why she should be named first, especially in a world where women did not usually have such prominence. Chrysostom defended her being named first because she was the stronger of the two personalities. Another idea is that she

---

[4] In reply to this question it has often been answered that Paul only mentions by name those of his converts who were still living in Corinth at the time he wrote 1 Corinthians. Aquila and Priscilla had left Corinth and were with Paul in Ephesus (1 Corinthians 16:19) so, of course, they were not named, it is affirmed. Yet this same verse also shows that the Corinthian church knew Aquila and Priscilla; otherwise, they would not be named in the letter as sending greetings. Not only did the Corinthian church know them, they must have known them as members of long-standing, which would tend to suggest they were some of the first of the brethren to be found in Corinth.

[5] See notes at Acts 2:9 on the location of the province of Pontus.

[6] Such diminutives were commonly used. In like manner we find Lucilla from Lucia, Domitilla from Dimitia, Atticilla from Attica, etc.

[7] In ancient Rome, a *gens* (pronounced *jĕnz*) was a clan united by a descent through the male line from a common ancestor. The family had the same name and also a religious observance in common.

[8] See Josephus, *Antiquities*, XVIII.3.5.

[9] See verse 18 and 26, and regularly in Paul's writings (e.g., Romans 16:3; 2 Timothy 4:13; but not 1 Corinthians 16.19).

was converted first. A third explanation is based on the fact that, if she were of higher social position than her husband, she would consequently be regularly named first.

Because Claudius had commanded all the Jews to leave Rome. Claudius was the Roman emperor who reigned from AD 41-54. At what exact date this command was given is not certainly known. It has been variously dated from AD 48-52, and was likely after a disturbance between Jews over the question of whether Jesus was the Messiah.[10]

He came to them. Paul began living with this couple (as verse 3 shows) and working for them. A Jew could easily meet people with a similar trade at the regular synagogue services, and even be invited to stay with people who already are residents of the town.

18:3 – *and because he was of the same trade, he stayed with them and they were working; for by trade they were tent-makers.*

And because he was of the same trade, he stayed with them and they were working. "Trade" equals "occupation." Aquila and Priscilla have a private business, and Paul is taken in to live with them and to share in the work. Luke does not tell us why Paul was working, but likely it was for the same reason we learn from Paul's own writings: he wanted to keep himself free from the suspicion of self-interest in his work as a teacher.[11] Paul often worked to support himself and the whole missionary party since missionary offerings were few, save from Philippi.[12]

For by trade they were tent-makers. It was a regular custom among the Jews to teach their sons some useful trade so that they would always have a way to earn an honest living.[13] The fact that Paul had learned a trade is not, then, inconsistent with the comparative opulence suggested by the expensive education he received both in boyhood and in Jerusalem at the feet of Gamaliel.

The word "tent-maker" has been the subject of various opinions. Recent attempts have been made to show that Paul was an artist (i.e., a landscape painter) or a weaver of tapestry. In earlier days, Chrysostom called him a "worker in leather."[14] But there seems to be no reason for departing from the usual connotation of the word, that he worked with the cloth from which the huge tents and sails were made. The trade of "tent-maker" was one Paul could have learned in his native land of Cilicia, which was noted then, as now, for the rough goats' hair fabrics used in tents and sails. The fabric was a dark color.[15]

---

[10] See the Introductory Studies concerning the date of Claudius' edict, as well as a detailed explanation of Suetonius' account of the expulsion because of riots over one "Chrestus."

[11] 1 Corinthians 9:15-19; 2 Corinthians 11:7-13; Acts 20:34; 2 Thessalonians 3:9-10.

[12] Philippians 4:15. There is no shame in a preacher or missionary working to support himself. But where the church is large enough, the preacher should be supported by the people who benefit from his spiritual leadership. (See 1 Corinthians 9:14; 1 Timothy 5:17; Galatians 6:6.)

[13] See comments at Acts 9:1 under the study of Paul's youth.

[14] Chrysostom, *Homilies*, IV.5.3.

[15] Song of Solomon 1:5; Revelation 6:12.

18:4 – *And he was reasoning in the synagogue every Sabbath and trying to persuade Jews and Greeks.*

And he was reasoning in the synagogue every Sabbath. See notes at Acts 17:2 on the word "reasoning." This was Paul's invariable rule: he preached the gospel "to the Jew first" and then to the Gentiles. He went to the synagogue Sabbath after Sabbath in order to teach the Jews who met there for worship.[16]

And trying to persuade Jews and Greeks. Paul is trying to persuade them to believe his message and to become Christians. Since the verb tense is imperfect, the translators' rendering, "trying to persuade," seems to be the right idea. The "Greeks" included with the Jews in the synagogue should be understood to be proselytes of the gate.[17]

To be under the necessity of laboring as a tent-maker, when he was aiming to evangelize this key city in Roman empire, might seem to Paul to be anything but encouraging. From the calm and straightforward style of Luke's narrative, we might imagine that Paul was callous to such feelings. But when writing to the Corinthians several years later, Paul tells us his feelings. He says, "I was with you in weakness, and in fear, and in much trembling."[18]

18:5 – *But when Silas and Timothy came down from Macedonia, Paul* **began** *devoting himself completely to the word, solemnly testifying to the Jews that Jesus was the Christ.*

But when Silas and Timothy came down from Macedonia. Earlier, when Paul arrived at Athens, he had directed the Berean brethren who had accompanied him to send Silas and Timothy to him from Macedonia as soon as possible (Acts 17:15). We learned, in notes on that passage, that Timothy had come to Paul while Paul was at Athens, but was almost immediately sent back to Thessalonica to bring further news to Paul about the converts there. Timothy now returns from Thessalonica, and Silas comes from Berea. It is at this point, when Timothy and Silas are both with Paul in Corinth, that 1 and 2 Thessalonians were written.[19] It is likely that Timothy carried 1 Thessalonians back to Thessalonica, and then returned to Paul with a report and many questions, to which Paul replied in 2 Thessalonians. We suppose that Timothy then carried that second letter to Thessalonica, and remained there. This is the last time that Silas is mentioned in Acts, though he continues to travel with Paul, until at some later time he becomes associated with Peter.[20]

Paul *began* **devoting himself completely to the word.** The coming of Silas and Timothy

---

[16] Such a practice undertaken by Paul in order to evangelize the Jews is in no sense an endorsement of the Jewish Sabbath as the day to be observed for worship by Christians.

[17] See notes at Acts 14:1 and 17:4.

[18] 1 Corinthians 2:3.

[19] Both Silas and Timothy were with Paul when the Thessalonian letters were penned, as the first verse of each letter shows. In fact, both participated with Paul in the actual writing of both of those epistles.

[20] 1 Peter 5:13. Did Silas stay at Corinth when Paul left it at the close of the second journey, and then join Peter when the latter came to Corinth on an evangelistic crusade (as language about Peter in 1 Corinthians 1 and 9 implies)?

greatly encouraged Paul.[21] It is likely that they brought gifts of money from Macedonia to Paul which relieved him for a while from having to work at tent-making for his living.[22] Instead, he can give all of his time to preaching the gospel.[23] Up to this time he is still working among the Jews, urging upon them the fact that Jesus is the promised Messiah.

Solemnly testifying to the Jews that Jesus was the Christ. How Paul went about testifying this fact to the Jews and proselytes in the synagogue has already been set forth at Acts 17:3, for we suppose Paul's methods were the same in the synagogue at Corinth as they had been at Thessalonica.

18:6 – And when they resisted and blasphemed, he shook out his garments and said to them, "Your blood be upon your own heads! I am clean. From now on I shall go to the Gentiles."

And when they resisted and blasphemed. Some older translations read as though they were "opposing themselves" (and the commentaries talk of how they were really hurting themselves more than Paul by their rejection of the gospel). However, the grammatical construction here is evidently what is called a genitive absolute, and the NASB treats it properly. "Resisted" is a military term, implying an organized and systematic resistance. On "blasphemed," see notes at Acts 13:45. Luke does not specify whether they blasphemed Paul, or whether they blasphemed Christ, though some have supposed that "Anathema be Jesus" (1 Corinthians 12:3) reflects what some in Corinth had been saying.

He shook out his garments and said to them. Was it at the close of one of the Sabbath services that Paul took off his outer garment and began shaking the dust off it? It would be an act that the Jews would remember long after the service was over, for it was the type of thing a man would do when he found that his appeals to their reason and conscience made no impression. As did the shaking off of the dust from their feet, so this would signify to the Jews in a dramatic fashion the same thing that Paul next speaks by word of mouth.[24] He had an obligation to share the message of Christ with them, and had gone beyond what was reasonably expected of a man in carrying out that obligation. He would go further if there was any kind of positive response, but since there was only active opposition, he was renouncing any further association with them.

"Your blood *be* upon your own heads, I am clean. This was not a curse (an imprecation on them), but a solemn disclaimer of responsibility should they be lost.[25] Paul was not re-

---

[21] For the effect of Timothy's coming on Paul's feelings, see 1 Thessalonians 3:5-8.

[22] The KJV and the NASB read differently at this place because of a manuscript variation. The Greek text behind the KJV reads, "Paul was pressed in spirit." But the better supported reading is the one translated "devoted to the Word," as in the NASB.

[23] 2 Corinthians 1:19 and 11:9; Philippians 4:15. Some commentators urge that 1 Corinthians 9:1ff is proof that Paul never did quit working at tent-making all during his Corinthian stay. But all the verses actually demand is that Paul did not ever take money from the Corinthians while he was in Corinth. The verses would not preclude his taking offerings from other churches while he was working at Corinth.

[24] Compare notes at Acts 13:51.

[25] Ezekiel 3:18ff and 33:4-8; and Acts 20:26 all teach the same doctrine. Perhaps Paul had the Ezekiel passages in mind when he speaks as he does to these rebellious Jews.

sponsible any further. He had preached the gospel to them, and they had opportunity to accept Jesus, but had rejected it. Paul is saying, 'If you people are lost in Hell, and you likely will be, the guilt for your destruction is yours alone.' "I am clean" means, 'I am not to blame for your destruction, as I would be if I had not faithfully tried to persuade you. I have done my duty.'

From now on I shall go to the Gentiles." This statement of any further effort to try to win the Jews has a limited and local application, just as similar words did at Acts 13:46. Later on, Paul will work with his Jewish countrymen in other places as he tries to win them.[26] But this is the end of his direct, Jewish-focused evangelism in Corinth.

18:7 – *And he departed from there and went to the house of a certain man named Titius Justus, a worshiper of God, whose house was next to the synagogue.*

He departed from there. We may picture Paul, having shaken out his garments and put them back on, striding purposefully out of the synagogue building. He will now cease teaching there. If Jews wish to hear, they will have to come to where Paul is teaching. He is no longer going to go to them.

And went to the house of a certain man named Titius Justus. We wish we knew more about this man who offered his house to Paul. Several likely guesses have been advanced. He likely was a Roman citizen (since his name is Roman), and perhaps was a second or third generation member of one of the families who settled there when Julius Caesar was rebuilding the city. Ramsay has put forth the attractive suggestion that his whole name was Gaius Titius Justus,[27] that he was one of Paul's first converts at Corinth,[28] and that on his later trip to Corinth, Paul again was shown hospitality by this man.[29] He was evidently not the same man as the Titus who was taken along to the Jerusalem Conference by Paul, and who also was one of Paul's traveling companions and co-workers.[30] The names are spelled differently, and this man in Corinth seems to have become acquainted with Paul while he was teaching in the synagogue at Corinth, as the next phrase suggests.

A worshiper of God. It is probable that Titius Justus had been attending the synagogue as a proselyte of the gate, and was converted to Christianity by Paul.[31] Some of the efforts of Paul to persuade the Jews and Greeks (verse 4) bore fruit.

---

[26] Acts 19:8, 28:17ff.

[27] William Ramsay, *Pictures of the Apostolic Church* (Grand Rapids: Baker, 1959), p.205. Romans usually had three names. The first was called *prenomen*, and distinguished the person from others in the same family. The second was called *nomen*, and was the name of the gens. The third was the *cognomen*, and was the family name. Some had fourth and fifth names, called *agnomen*, which usually reflected some personal characteristic or achievement.

[28] 1 Corinthians 1:14.

[29] Romans 16:23.

[30] Galatians 2:3; Titus 1:1; 2 Corinthians 2:12, 7:14, 8:16, and 8:23.

[31] See notes at Acts 17:4 on "God-fearer."

Whose house was next to the synagogue. The house of a proselyte of the gate would offer greater access to the apostle, whether the inquirer was Jew or Greek, than would any other. We picture Paul as still staying with Aquila and Priscilla, but as using Justus' house for his place of teaching and preaching.[32] If Justus was a descendant of Roman colonists, Paul would gain access through him to many of the Romans in the city.

18:8 – *And Crispus, the leader of the synagogue, believed in the Lord with all his household, and many of the Corinthians when they heard were believing and being baptized.*

And Crispus, the leader of the synagogue, believed in the Lord. Crispus is named in 1 Corinthians 1:14 as one of the few whom Paul personally baptized.[33] When Paul left the synagogue, so did the ruler of the synagogue and his family. Verse 17 refers to a new ruler of the synagogue, the one evidently chosen to replace Crispus after he became a Christian.

With all his household. Crispus' family became Christians also.[34] This is the first recorded instance of the conversion of an entire Jewish family.

And many of the Corinthians when they heard were believing and being baptized. Not only were there some converts from the Jewish quarter of the city, but here we are told there were converts from among the Gentile population as well. The tense of the two verbs "believing" and "being baptized" implies a process going on daily, over a long period of time. The growth of the church was gradual but continuous.

> This was the order and steps of the conversion of all men. First, the gospel is preached; people hear the gospel, believe it, repent of their sins [since repentance follows belief per Acts 2:38], and are baptized; they are then in Christ and are called Christians.[35]

Among the converts we may count the household of Chloe,[36] Quartus and Erastus, the treasurer of the city,[37] and many of the lower and middle classes of society.[38]

18:9 – *And the Lord said to Paul in the night by a vision, "Do not be afraid any longer, but go on speaking and do not be silent;*

And the Lord said to Paul in the night by a vision. "Lord" is evidently a reference to Jesus. Note the recurrence of these visions[39] at each great crisis in the apostle's life. Paul

---

[32] The Western text has Paul leaving Aquila's house at this point, too, as well as leaving the synagogue.

[33] Paul did the baptizing himself only when he had no helpers present, lest the converts be filled with pride over being baptized by the great apostle to the Gentiles. See 1 Corinthians 1:15.

[34] Compare notes at Acts 10:2 and 16:15 on household baptisms.

[35] Boles, *op. cit.*, p.289.

[36] 1 Corinthians 1:11.

[37] Romans 16:23.

[38] 1 Corinthians 1:26.

[39] On "vision," see notes at Acts 9:10.

had seen the Lord on the Damascus road,[40] and in the temple after his escape from Damascus.[41] Now he sees Jesus once more. Other such visions are yet to come in Acts.

"Do not be afraid *any longer*, but go on speaking and do not be silent. The Greek prohibits the continuance of something already going on. "Stop being afraid," Jesus says to Paul. We've already noted that 1 Corinthians 2:3 tells us of Paul's feelings during his early work at Corinth. Almost everywhere he has gone prior to Corinth, he has been beset and often physically harmed by the unbelieving Jews. Especially was this true when he began ministering to the Gentiles. Evidently, he was expecting the same thing to happen in Corinth. Perhaps Jesus' words of encouragement even intimate that Paul had given thought to speaking out less and less. Many of God's greatest heroes have experienced moments of discouragement and despondency. Just as Paul is "low" at this juncture in Corinth, we are reminded of the discouragement at one time in Elijah's life, and of the times when Jeremiah was likewise depressed.[42]

18:10 – *for I am with you, and no man will attack you in order to harm you, for I have many people in this city."*

For I am with you. Jesus speaks these words to give Paul a foundation for confidence. Jesus is promising to be close by Paul, to protect and bless him. For a time, the wrath of men would be restrained so that Paul would have relative peace.

And no man will attack you in order to harm you. This implies that Paul was afraid someone was seeking or threatening to harm him. The resistance by the Jews might at any moment burst into furious violence or deliberate plots of assassination. Jesus here promises that He would providentially preserve Paul from harm. Some might form plans to harm him, and might even try, but they would not succeed. Paul was to be kept safe from harm here in Corinth.

For I have many people in this city." This was another reason why Paul should speak the gospel boldly, rather than becoming silent out of fear. Jesus' statement is to be taken in the potential sense – there were many people in the sinful streets of Corinth who would obey the gospel if they had opportunity. Their souls were yearning for deliverance from the sin into which they had plunged; what they needed to hear was a call to repentance.[43] There is a sense in which it may be said that God takes the initiative in the salvation of men since by various means God helps prepare men to receive the gospel. One thing a preacher does is to find those prepared by God and lead them to full obedience. This is what Paul

---

[40] Acts 9:4-18.

[41] Acts 22:17.

[42] 1 Kings 19:4-14; Jeremiah 1:6-8, 15:15-21.

[43] Footnote #42 in chapter 8 introduced the five points of Calvinism, one of what is unconditional election. Calvin used the language of this verse ("I have much people in this city") to help prove his idea that God's people are a definite and select number, selected from eternity past. Luke's language might agree with Calvin's doctrine, but it does not prove it. Luke's language equally accords with the explanation given in the notes that it is simply potential.

will do for the next several months in Corinth. He will win some. In others, he will plant a seed, and someone else will win them later.⁴⁴

18:11 – *And he settled* **there** *a year and six months, teaching the word of God among them.*

And he settled *there* **a year and six months.** Supported by the assurance given in the vision, and full of fresh confidence, Paul settles down to evangelize the city. "Settled" is not the usual word for "dwelling" in a town. It has been translated "he took his seat," i.e., as a teacher. We do not know how long Paul was in Corinth altogether. He was there sometime before the encouragement was given to him in the vision. After the vision, he was able to teach undisturbed for a year and a half. There was then an attempt by the Jews to silence Paul by dragging him before Gallio's court. After this trouble caused by the Jews was past, Paul then remained many days. Altogether, perhaps Paul was in Corinth as long as two years.⁴⁵

Teaching the word of God among them. This may mean, "teaching from house to house." Or the right understanding of this phrase may be McGarvey's.

> The word "teaching," which describes his work, shows that during this long period he was executing chiefly the second part of the Great Commission, "teaching them to observe all things whatsoever I have commanded you" (Matthew 28:20).⁴⁶

Paul's evangelism went beyond the city limits during this period of time. At a subsequent time, we find churches in many of the neighboring districts, such as the port of Cenchrea.⁴⁷ Note also that 2 Corinthians was addressed "to the church that is in Corinth, and *to all the saints that are in all Achaia*"⁴⁸ – which clearly indicates an extension of evangelistic work beyond the limits of the city of Corinth.

18:12 – *But while Gallio was proconsul of Achaia, the Jews with one accord rose up against Paul and brought him before the judgment seat,*

But while Gallio was proconsul of Achaia. Gallio and his brother Seneca were born in Cordova, Spain, and their father brought them to Rome in the reign of Tiberius Caesar. Gallio's real name was Marcus Annaeus Novatus; after his arrival in Rome he was adopted

---

⁴⁴ 1 Corinthians 3:6ff.

⁴⁵ In notes at Acts 11:26 and 16:40, we have introduced the matter of the located ministry. Let us consider this issue one more time. Paul stayed two years at Corinth, and three years at Ephesus. Luke had a five-year ministry at Philippi (Acts 16:40). Philip had a 20-year ministry at Caesarea. How then can anyone object to an evangelist staying on a field for a period of time, supported by those to whom he ministers? In some places, Paul stayed just long enough to plant a congregation, and then moved on. In other instances, unbelieving Jews harassed him so that he had to move before the work of planting was anywhere near finished, so that others had to be left to carry on the work. Here in Corinth and later in Ephesus, Paul stays long beyond the time it took merely to plant the congregation.

⁴⁶ McGarvey, *op. cit.*, p.138.

⁴⁷ Romans 16:1.

⁴⁸ 2 Corinthians 1:1.

by the rhetorician Lucius Junius Gallio, and so took the *agnomen* Gallio from his adoptive father. Several ancient writers note the fact that he had a remarkably mild and easy-going disposition, and he evidently was a man of personal charm.[49] An inscription found at Delphi places him in office at Corinth in the year AD 52.[50] The nature of the office of proconsul has been explained at pages *xiv* and *xv* of the Introductory Studies.

Luke shows once again his characteristic accuracy in the use of official titles. Achaia became a province in 27 BC, when it was separated from Macedonia. At first, as a senatorial province, it was governed by a proconsul. In AD 15, responding to complaints of corruption within the provincial government, Tiberius converted Achaia to an imperial province, and it was then ruled by a legate.[51] Another change in government took place in the same year as the expulsion of the Jews from Rome by Claudius, when the emperor restored the control of the province of Achaia to the Senate. Thus, at the time of Paul's trial, Achaia was again ruled by a "proconsul" rather than by a governor or a legate.[52]

The Jews with one accord rose up against Paul. This is the first time this particular word translated "rose up" is used in Acts. The word speaks of hostile intentions and perhaps a rush at their victim once he has been surrounded. We may picture Paul as being captured by the hostile Jews after they blocked the usual path by which he walked from Aquila's house to his place of teaching at Justus' house next door to the synagogue. In the vision (verses 9-10), Jesus had promised Paul he would not be harmed; He did not promise that no attack would come.

And brought him before the judgment seat. On certain days each week, the Roman officials held court sessions in the market place, presiding from a raised platform, called *bema* in the Greek. This raised platform is still visible among the ruins of ancient Corinth.[53] A portable chair, called a *curule*, was carried to the platform and covered with a purple cloth. When Gallio the proconsul had seated himself on the chair, court was in session.

On the days of these court sessions, any one might appeal to the judge to have his grievance heard. The Jews, having made their plans, took advantage of the opportunity. This is the most serious of the trials Paul has yet faced. If the politarchs at Thessalonica found him guilty, it would have limited his activities only within their jurisdiction (i.e., in and around Thessalonica). But if a Roman proconsul found Paul guilty, that might serve as a precedent for the governors and proconsuls of other provinces. The Jews could then use this as a means of silencing Paul wherever he might go with the gospel.

---

[49] Seneca, *Natural Questions*, IV, Preface; Statius, *Silvae*, II.7.32; Seneca, *Epitstolae Morales*, CIV.

[50] See the Introductory Studies, p.*xv*. Kirsopp Lake, *Christian Beginnings*, Vol. 5, p.490ff, shows how the inscription is datable by its reference to Claudius as having been acclaimed as emperor for the 26th time just before the letter is written to Gallio.

[51] Tacitus, *Annals*, I.76.

[52] Suetonius, *Claudius*, c.25.

[53] See the map of Corinth at the close of this book, and notice where the *bema* is located. Acts 19:38 references the courts being in session on a regularly scheduled basis.

18:13 – *saying, "This man persuades men to worship God contrary to the law."*

Saying, "This man persuades men to worship God contrary to the law." What law? Some commentators think that the Jews are referring to the Law of Moses. Others think the Jews are referring to Roman law. It is most likely that the Jews deliberately word the charge they make against Paul so that it could be taken with a double meaning. Josephus tells us that the Jews had been granted permission by the Romans to worship according to their own Law.[54] The Jews were saying, 'Paul is preaching a new religion – not like the Jewish religion. His religion is not recognized by the laws of Rome.'[55] Verse 15 will show that Gallio understood them to be more interested in defending their own Law than Roman law.

18:14 – *But when Paul was about to open his mouth, Gallio said to the Jews, "If it were a matter of wrong or of vicious crime, O Jews, it would be reasonable for me to put up with you;*

But when Paul was about to open his month. As noted at Acts 8:35, this phrase often implies the beginning of a set discourse. From speeches recorded later in Acts, we might surmise that Paul would have argued that the gospel he preached was not an innovation, but was exactly what the Jewish prophets had looked forward to.[56] However, on this occasion, Paul does not get the opportunity to speak in his own self-defense.

Gallio said to the Jews, "If it were a matter of wrong or of vicious crime, O Jews. "Wrong" speaks of injustice, acts of open wrong, such as robbery or assault or crimes of violence. The word rendered "crime" is the same one translated "fraud" in Acts 13:10. A "vicious crime" would be one where you were deliberately trying to harm the person by your fraud.

It would be reasonable for me to put up with you. We can feel the intense impatience that Gallio had with the Jews. Augustine tells us that both Gallio and his brother Seneca considered the Jews to be a "most polluted race."[57] If it were a type of crime that demanded his attention as a Roman judge, he would tolerate having to hear the case because he had been appointed to guard the peace and to punish criminals.

18:15 – *but if there are questions about words and names and your own law, look after it yourselves; I am unwilling to be a judge of these matters."*

But if there are questions about words and names. The noun translated "words" in English is actually singular in the Greek. Paul was known as a teacher, one who preached the Word of God. If this dispute was about teaching, and not about deeds, Gallio wasn't interested. By using the word "names," Gallio shows that he apparently understood the

---

[54] Josephus, *Antiquities*, XIV.10.2ff.

[55] See comments at Acts 16:21 concerning legal and illegal religions in the Roman empire.

[56] Acts 24:10ff and 26:2ff are examples of what such a set discourse might have been like.

[57] Augustine, *City of God*, VI. 10.

controversy to be over whether or not Jesus of Nazareth was entitled to wear the name Messiah. Having come to Corinth from Rome, Gallio would have been acquainted with the "Chrestus" over which the Jews at Rome were fighting. In the charges against Paul, Gallio is hearing some of the same things he had heard before in Rome. If the Jews in Corinth were trying to take advantage of the new proconsul, Gallio shows that he is not as naïve as the Jews might have supposed.

And your own law. Gallio understands this to be a question, basically, respecting a proper interpretation of the Law of Moses, and the rites and ceremonies which it commanded. The thing that really motivated the Jews, as Gallio realized, was Jewish law, not Roman law. Gallio, an executor of Roman law, was not interested in the religious law of a subjugated people which had been superseded by Roman law.

Look after it yourselves. That is, 'Settle this difficulty among yourselves. Don t ask me to get involved in this religious matter.'

I am unwilling to be a judge of these matters." There is a strong emphasis on the personal pronoun in the Greek, "I, for my part, have no wish to be a judge of these things." Gallio did not regard questions of Jewish law as being within the realm of matters his office called on him to judge. This is one of the few instances in all of Paul's experiences in which his accusers were dealt with justly and summarily.

Gallio's decision was a landmark decision. It could be pointed to as a precedent for other Roman courts for the next ten or twelve years. Christianity was allowed by the Romans as a *religio licita* – a permitted religion – until the official attitude changes after the burning of Rome in AD 64.

18:16 – *And he drove them away from the judgment seat.*

And he drove them away from the judgment seat. These words probably imply that Gallio gave an order to his lictors to clear the court. Any of the Jews who did not immediately retreat would expose themselves to blows from the lictors' rods.

18:17 – *And they all took hold of Sosthenes, the leader of the synagogue, and began beating him in front of the judgment seat. And Gallio was not concerned about any of these things.*

And they all took hold of Sosthenes. Some think this Sosthenes is the same one mentioned in 1 Corinthians 1:1, as one of Paul's associates in preaching the gospel. Since 1 Corinthians was written about five years after this court scene, it is entirely possible that this beating started Sosthenes on the way to becoming a Christian and a fellow-minister with Paul. On the other hand, Sosthenes was a rather common name, so we cannot be absolutely sure of the identification.

The leader of the synagogue. In verse 8, Crispus was named as "the leader of the synagogue." Either Sosthenes became the ruler when Crispus was converted, or Sosthenes and Crispus were rulers together at the same time. (Some of the large synagogues did have several men who were called "rulers.")

And *began* beating him in front of the judgment seat. "Beating" is in the imperfect tense, suggesting that Sosthenes received a thorough beating. Just why would he receive a beating? That depends on who laid hold of Sosthenes and gave him the beating.

- There is a manuscript variation here, with some reading as does the KJV, that "the Greeks" beat Sosthenes. If we think that the crowds of Greeks around the open-air judgment seat are the ones who administered the beating, then we can see them encouraged to vent some of their anti-Jewish feelings by Gallio's handling of the Jews in the court.
- The nearest antecedent is the Jews. If we suppose that the Jews gave their own leader the beating, then we must suppose they were angry because he, acting as their spokesman, had presented the case so poorly that it was thrown out of court. Some commentators, supposing that Sosthenes was already showing tendencies toward becoming a Christian (as 1 Corinthians 1:1 indicates he later did), think the Jews suspected him of only half-heartedly presenting the case against Paul.
- A third suggestion is that the lictors, implied in the narrative as the ones who cleared the court, were the ones who beat Sosthenes. Perhaps Sosthenes was slow to leave the court; perhaps he even attempted to advance his case in more forceful and convincing terms. If so, the lictors use force on him to quiet him and get him to leave the court.

That the lictors are the ones who administer Sosthenes' beating seems the most satisfactory explanation of the verse.

And Gallio was not concerned about any of these things. These words should not be interpreted as meaning that Gallio was indifferent about religion, but that "he is commended [by Luke] for his impartiality."[58]

14. At Cenchrea. 18:18

18:18 – *And Paul, having remained many days longer, took leave of the brethren and put out to sea for Syria, and with him were Priscilla and Aquila. In Cenchrea he had his hair cut, for he was keeping a vow.*

And Paul, having remained many days longer. Thanks to the favorable decision by Gallio, Paul's opportunities to evangelize in Corinth were not injured by the attack on him by the Jews. Corinth is one of the few places where Paul was able to remain as long as he wished. The Greek says he stayed "sufficient days."[59]

---

[58] F.F. Bruce, *The Acts of the Apostles* (Grand Rapids: Wm. B. Eerdmans Publishing Co., 1953), p.348. In another of his books (*The Book of Acts*, p.375), Bruce suggests that this expression means that Gallio turned a blind eye to this violent activity against Sosthenes. If this were so, then what happened was not really legal, and someone other than the lictors were the ones who administered the beating. However, as noted in the comments on verse 12, ancient writers spoke of Gallio as being a most mild and amiable man, an upright and just judge. Thus, the latter explanation by Bruce, of the events of verse 17 being extra-legal, seems out of character for Gallio. Such extra-legal actions would repel a man of such character.

[59] Some commentators place the writing of 2 Thessalonians in this period after the arraignment before

Took leave of the brethren. The Latin has "he made his goodbyes." Perhaps we might picture Paul spending time with each of his dear friends, making the rounds till all are visited. There was no reason for haste in leaving, yet Paul usually left a town and the infant congregation after a crisis of the kind as he had just passed through.

And put out to sea for Syria. It appears from verse 22 that Syrian Antioch, the home church, the one that sent Paul on the missionary journey, was his destination. Paul was returning in order to report to the home church. The time of this voyage was probably, as in the third missionary journey, after the Passover and before Pentecost,[60] i.e., in the spring of AD 54. This was the most favorable time of the year for traveling.[61]

And with him were Priscilla and Aquila. Concerning the priority given the name of the wife, see notes at 18:2.[62]

In Cenchrea he had his hair cut, for he was keeping a vow. A "vow" is a solemn, voluntary promise made to God, to perform some service or to do something pleasing to Him, in return for some hoped-for benefit. A man might devote himself or his children to the Lord. He might devote any part of his time or property to the Lord's service. Among the Jews, vows were not something that the Law commanded a man to do; but once a vow was undertaken, it was to be sacredly observed. Only in certain specified cases could the maker of the vow redeem that which had been thus devoted.[63]

Four questions must be answered about this vow:

1) *Who made the vow?* Paul or Aquila? The Greek grammar is such that it is not possible to affirm absolutely that it was Paul and not Aquila.

    - Perhaps it was Aquila who made the vow. (a) The Vulgate reads in this manner. (b) The naming of Priscilla before Aquila is contrary to Luke's regular order.[64]
    - On the other hand, several arguments support the idea that it was Paul who made the vow: (a) The Syriac reads in this manner.[65] (b) The other participles in this

---

Gallio, but we think it best to have both 1 and 2 Thessalonians written during the 18-month period before the arraignment. (See the comments at verse 5 related to Timothy's travels.) The indications of time and place in the second epistle are similar to 1 Thessalonians, and we conclude that there were about six months of time that elapsed between the writing of the two letters.

[60] Acts 20:3,6.

[61] See notes at Acts 27:9 concerning the sailing season on the Mediterranean. At Acts 18:21, in the KJV, there is a mention of a feast that Paul wished to attend at Jerusalem, but that reading does not enjoy integrity. See this discussed in notes at verse 21.

[62] Since Luke names Priscilla first here, but not in verses 2 and 26 (according to some manuscripts), an argument has been urged from this change that Luke deviated from his usual way of naming this couple in order to make it clear that it was *Aquila* who had the vow. See comments on the next phrase of this verse.

[63] Deuteronomy 23:21-23; Judges 11:35; Ecclesiastes 5:4; Psalm 66:13.

[64] In verses 2 and 26, Luke names Aquila first, as noted in footnote #62. Meyer, *op. cit.*, p.352ff, appeals to the order of names as proof that Aquila was the one who had a private vow. Other writers who have interpreted it of Aquila have been Grotius, Howson, and Wieseler.

[65] The Syriac is an older translation than the Latin Vulgate, and some would therefore trust it to be more

passage all have Paul as their subject, so why not this one too?[66] (c) It is urged that it would be quite irrelevant to Luke's purpose to narrate such a fact about one of Paul's companions. (d) It is further argued that nobody would ever have thought of making Aquila the subject of "had his hair cut" if it were not for the thought that there is an incongruity with Paul's New Testament Christianity were he keeping a vow of this kind.[67]

So far there has been nothing in our study of this matter that would cause us to reject the idea that it was *Paul* who made the vow.

2) *What kind of vow was it?* (a) Most commentators think that it was a Nazarite vow. In such a vow, in addition to whatever was promised to God, the person taking the vow also undertook certain self-imposed restraints. Included were abstinence from wine, allowing the hair and beard to grow, and not coming in contact with any dead body.[68] The length of such a vow could vary anywhere from eight days to a month or longer, even for the rest of the man's life. If it were a temporary Nazarite vow, when the time of the vow expired, the hair was to be shaved off by a priest at the temple in Jerusalem and burned on the altar of burnt offering, along with a sacrifice of a male lamb for a burnt offering, a female lamb for an expiatory sacrifice, or a ram for a peace-offering. (b) A number of commentaries refer to a passage in the Mishna that deals with those cases in which the one who took the vow could not be at Jerusalem at the time the vow expired. Such a man was allowed to cut his hair short (not shave it with a razor) and take it with him the next time he went to Jerusalem, and there offer it at the same time that he offered his sacrifices and had his head shaved by the priest.[69]

3) *What motive might Paul have for making such a vow?* When he takes a scissors to his hair, Paul has come to the end of the days of his vow, which means that something earlier in Corinth had led him to make the vow. (a) Some believe Paul made a promise to God, if God would only deliver him from his troubles in the hands of the Jews. God answered (e.g., Gallio threw the case out of court), Paul kept his promise, and the days of the vow have now expired. (b) A second suggestion is that Paul loved the Jews so much that even after they tried to ruin his testimony, he did something that Jews recog-

---

nearly what the original intended. Augustine, Erasmus, most of the Reformers, Bengel, Alford, Hackett, Ramsay. Hort, and perhaps the majority of commentators have understood it was Paul who had the vow.

[66] In the consecutive narrative from verses 18-25, there are nine aorist participles, of which eight apply to Paul, who is the subject of this whole section, making it doubtful that this one in verse 18 refers to anyone but Paul also.

[67] Some feel that Paul is here too involved in keeping Old Testament ceremonies. Time and again, Paul says that the Old Testament is over and done with, that the New has taken the place of the Old. How then is he being consistent if he is keeping a vow taught in the Old? See this same problem discussed further in notes at Acts 21:23ff.

[68] Numbers 6:1-21.

[69] Mishna, tractate *Nazir*. All the arguments against this being a Nazarite vow are based on the supposition that the passages in the Mishna are post-apostolic, and would not therefore have been what was practiced in the 1st century. To see that there is a difference between the verbs "shaved" and "shorn" (i.e., had his hair cut), see notes at 1 Corinthians 11:6. Normally, in countries where it was customary to wear a turban, the men shaved their heads, or had very short hair. Only when a Nazarite vow was taken did they allow their hair to grow.

nized as a most sacred act. That is, Paul took a Nazarite vow in order that he might win the Jews. This would be another example of Paul living as he describes in 1 Corinthians 9:14. Apparently, his actions led to successful results, at least in the case of Sosthenes, the ruler of the synagogue, who is won to Christ. (c) A third suggestion is that it was not so much a vow of promise as it was a vow of gratitude that he had been delivered by God from such a dangerous situation.

4) *Why would Paul take a vow?* Certainly it was not out of deference to the Old Testament, as though the Law of Moses were still in force. Vows are in the realm of Christian Liberty.[70] There is nothing contrary to New Testament teaching in a Christian's making such solemn promises to God.

"In Cenchrea" tells us that Paul and Aquila and Priscilla have walked the eight or nine miles to the eastern seaport that served Corinth. Five years later, when Paul writes his epistle to the Romans, he tells how Phoebe, a member of the church in Cenchrea, had been a great help to Paul and many other brethren.[71] Perhaps some of that help was extended to Paul and his friends during this visit to Cenchrea, while they were waiting for a ship.

15. At Ephesus. 18:19-21

18:19 – *And they came to Ephesus, and he left them there. Now he himself entered the synagogue and reasoned with the Jews.*

And they came to Ephesus. Ephesus was just across the Aegean Sea, nearly due east from Cenchrea, and was a celebrated city in Asia Minor. It was chiefly famous for the Temple of Artemis, usually accounted as one of the seven wonders of the ancient world. Ephesus was the capital of the Roman province of Asia.[72] The city could have been reached in a week or less by ship.

And he left them there. That is, Aquila and Priscilla were left at Ephesus.[73] They perhaps moved their business to Ephesus, and having established it, would also have been making acquaintances in the synagogue. They evidently served as preliminary workers, laying the groundwork for Paul's coming and lengthy work at Ephesus.[74] Paul no longer continues working with them at tent-making.

Now he himself entered the synagogue and reasoned with the Jews. There had been a colony of Jews living in Ephesus for more than 100 years, for already in Julius Caesar's time they receive special treatment from the Roman government.[75] "He reasoned with the

---

[70] See the explanation of "Christian Liberty" at Acts 15:31.

[71] Romans 16:1,2.

[72] See notes at Acts 19:1ff and a map at the close of this book for more information about Ephesus.

[73] Acts 18:18,24-26.

[74] Acts 19:1ff.

[75] Josephus, *Antiquities*, XIV.10.12,25 and XVI.6.2,4,7.

Jews" seems to be Luke's favorite expression for Paul's sermons in the synagogues.[76] The aorist verb tense shows it was a one-time preaching. Paul still yearns for the conversion of as many Jews as he can.

18:20 – *And when they asked him to stay for a longer time, he did not consent,*

And when they asked him to stay for a longer time. Of all the synagogues visited by Paul, only Berea had ever shown Paul this kind of receptivity to the gospel. This request was obviously a hopeful sign, an earnest of fruitful labors here, if only he has opportunity to work the area. However, he cannot stay now; perhaps he can return later.

He did not consent. Paul must have had a compelling reason for temporarily refusing such an invitation to continue preaching in the synagogue, though Luke does not tell us what it was.[77] Probably the best suggestion is that Paul feels it was time for him to report to the church at Syrian Antioch before he begins evangelizing a new area.

18:21 – *but taking leave of them and saying, "I will return to you again if God wills," he set sail from Ephesus.*

But taking leave of them. "Taking leave" was also used at verse 18.

And saying, "I will return to you again if God wills." Paul does return to Ephesus (Acts 19:1ff) and remains there three years (Acts 20:31). Paul saw his travels as only possible if God willed them and aided them. In resting his future on the will of God, who was seen as ordering all things by His providential control, we find another point of agreement between Paul and James.[78]

He set sail from Ephesus. Ephesus, though inland, had a harbor which required constant dredging to keep the silt carried down by the Cayster River from closing the channel. It would require about a month to sail from Ephesus to Caesarea.[79]

---

[76] Compare Acts 17:2,17; 18:4; 19:8,9.

[77] Those reading the KJV, which follows a variant reading at verse 21, think there was something about a coming feast at Jerusalem which compelled Paul to want to be there in time for it, and thus causing him to refuse the request of the synagogue to say longer at Ephesus.
- Some manuscripts, including the Western text and the Byzantine text, read, "he took his leave of them, saying, 'I must keep the feast that is coming in Jerusalem.'"
- Although the phrase does not have enough manuscript support to enjoy integrity, the feast intended would be the Feast of Pentecost. (Passover could not be the feast intended since there was no sailing on the Mediterranean until after Passover. See notes about the sailing season at Acts 27:9.)
- Verse 22 will indicate that Paul did indeed visit Jerusalem, but in the best-supported Greek text Luke simply does not give us enough information to determine that there was something about this Feast of Pentecost that Paul felt compelled to attend.

[78] James 4:15. Another agreement with James was studied in Special Study #16, "The Faith that Saves." Both teach that it is an obedient faith which God requires in order to reckon us righteous.

[79] In chapters 20 and 21, it is a seven weeks' voyage, but several sojourns of a week's duration were made on that particular trip.

16. At Caesarea and Jerusalem, and to Syrian Antioch. 18:22

18:22 – *And when he had landed at Caesarea, he went up and greeted the church, and went down to Antioch.*

And when he had landed at Caesarea. This is the Caesarea where Philip has settled, and where Cornelius lived.[80] It is on the eastern end of the Mediterranean and on the western border of the land of Palestine.

He went up and greeted the church. Luke's language is geographically correct since the elevation of Jerusalem was much higher than that of Caesarea.

Some think the church Paul visits is the church at Caesarea. McGarvey is one who opts for the church at Caesarea, and he writes about how Paul would have greeted the church that had been planted there when Cornelius and his friends were baptized. McGarvey expresses his opinion in this fashion:

> The commentators in general, misled by the interpolated clause in the Textus Receptus, and the Old English versions, "I must by all means keep this feast that cometh in Jerusalem" (verse 21), assume that the church which Paul went up and saluted was the Jerusalem church; but in the absence of that clause there is nothing to justify the conclusion. Paul had doubtless landed at Caesarea because the ship in which he sailed was bound for that harbor, and he had been contented to sail in that ship rather than lose time waiting for another, because it was but a short sail from Caesarea to Antioch, and coasting vessels for the voyage could be found daily.[81]

However, it appears to this commentator that there is little doubt that the words "went up and saluted the church" refer to the Jerusalem church. The words "went up" and "went down" certainly do not fit what one would do if he were traveling simply from Caesarea to Antioch, but they do make sense if Jerusalem is in between. If it be true that Paul's vow was a Nazarite vow (verse 18), he would go to Jerusalem to complete it.

"Greeted" implies that Paul expressed for them his affections and regards as there was a round of holy kisses between Paul and the men at Jerusalem. In this way the brethren at Jerusalem, including James and the elders, would express a friendly welcome for Paul. This would be Paul's fourth visit to Jerusalem since his conversion.[82]

And went down to Antioch. "Down" is geographically correct, for the elevation of Syrian Antioch is less than that of Jerusalem. Paul probably traveled by land to Antioch. He is returning there to report, a thing similar to what was done at the close of the first missionary

---

[80] See notes at Acts 8:40 and 10:1.

[81] McGarvey, *op. cit.*, p.144-145.

[82] See Acts 9:26, 11:30, and 15:4 for the first three trips. If verse 22 does in fact record a visit by Paul to the Jerusalem church, and we see no reason to doubt that it is, it would be a second trip to Jerusalem that is not reported in the Galatian letter, an epistle which (in our opinion) has yet to be written. But there is no more problem with the omission of the fourth visit to Jerusalem than there was with the omission in that letter of his second visit.

tour.[83] On reaching Antioch, we cannot doubt that he once more gladdened the hearts of the brethren who had commended him and Silas to the favor of the Lord, by rehearsing to them all that God had done with him, and how He had opened still wider the "door of faith to the Gentiles."

We do not know whether or not Silas accompanied Paul back to Antioch. If he were not along, Paul would have reported the place where Silas remained behind, and the reasons why.[84]

As noted previously in this commentary, some theologians place the dissimulation of Peter, and Paul's having to correct him in a public assembly, at this point in the Acts narrative.[85] It is this commentator's opinion that the unhappy incident recorded in Galatians 2 happened before the second missionary journey began, rather than here at its close.

When Paul arrives at Syrian Antioch, his second missionary journey has been completed. It had extended over a three-year period of time, AD 51-54. During this time, Paul revisited the churches in southern Galatia, and with the help of some new workers (Silas, Luke, and Timothy) he has planted and nurtured new congregations in the cities of Philippi, Thessalonica, Berea, Athens and Corinth. Some helpers (Aquila and Priscilla) have been left at Ephesus in anticipation of a coming evangelistic effort there.

During this second missionary journey, the Jews have made repeated efforts to block the progress of the gospel in most of these cities. But their efforts, though personally distressing and often physically and emotionally painful to Paul, have been in vain. The newly established churches in those cities were flourishing even in his absence.

---

[83] See notes at Acts 14:27.

[84] Compare notes at verse 5 concerning Silas' later life and work.

[85] See notes at Acts 15:38. If the affair with Peter were to be placed here at the close of the second missionary tour, a rather imaginative reconstruction can be made. (a) Paul has been absent from the city for three years, during which time the Judaizers could have regained some of their strength. (b) Peter arrives in the city while Paul is there, and the events recorded in Galatians 2:11 occur. (c) Shortly after that, the Judaizers trouble the churches of Galatia, too. This will lead directly to the need for Paul's epistle to those brethren. Such a theory, however, creates difficulties in an attempted reconstruction of Peter's evangelistic travels, for this theory requires Peter to still be in Syria when 1 Corinthians seems to have him in Greece.

D. The Third Missionary Journey. 18:23-21:16

1. In Antioch of Syria and Through the Provinces of Galatia and Phrygia. 18:23

18:23 – *And having spent some time* **there,** *he departed and passed successively through the Galatian region and Phrygia, strengthening all the disciples.*

And having spent some time *there.* "There" is Antioch of Syria. We cannot tell how long Paul stayed with the church there, but if he begins the third missionary journey the same year he finished the second one, he did not stay long at Antioch. The following verses will show Paul hurrying through several countries in order to take advantage of the traveling season in the highlands.

He departed. This is the beginning of the third missionary journey. It is now probably AD 54. As far as we know, this was Paul's last visit to Antioch of Syria, even though it was the center of his apostolic work for so many years. Slowly, the center of world-wide evangelism moves westward toward Ephesus and Rome.

And passed successively through the Galatian region and Phrygia. The verb "passed through" was used in Acts 13:6 to speak of a trip involving missionary activity. The trip begins with Paul taking the overland route from Antioch, north to Tarsus, and from thence by way of the Cilician Gates into the elevated tablelands of Lycaonia and Pisidia, passing through Derbe, Lystra, Iconium, and Pisidian Antioch.

On this visit he found few traces (or none at all) of the work of the Judaizers among these churches,[86] but soon after he passed through this area, the Judaizers came and disturbed the churches. When news of their activities reaches Paul, he will write to them the letter we call Galatians. In that letter, he warns of some falling away from their first love and of some relapsing into old national vices,[87] both of which he may have noticed during this visit.

What churches in Phrygia were visited we are unable to say. A possible interpretation of Colossians 2:1 might lead us to think that Paul at this time visited the congregations in the Lycus River valley – Colossae, Hierapolis, and Laodicea. But the usually accepted interpretation of Colossians 2:1 is that Paul never had visited those places before writing "Colossians" to them. If that is true, they cannot be the churches in Phrygia that Paul visited at the beginning of this third missionary journey.

Strengthening all the disciples. This speaks of strengthening their faith by means of exhortation and counsel.[88] It is amazing how Paul systematically revisited congregations

---

[86] Galatians 1:6 shows that only recently the Galatians had begun deviating from the truth. Their defection had been sudden.

[87] Galatians 5:21.

[88] The same word was used at Acts 14:22.

which he started. This repeated labor is a part of his settled method of evangelism.[89] Paul was not trying to officially supervise their every action and thought; rather, it was a teaching and building program to strengthen their faith. Given the content of the epistles Paul wrote, he certainly believed that if a person's doctrines are right, his lifestyle practices and actions likely will be right, too!

Luke, when he is not personally traveling with Paul, covers a journey of several months, and some 500 or 600 miles, in but a few brief words. With Paul now on his way back to Ephesus, the record of events there is brought up to date (Acts 18:24ff) before we are told of Paul's return to that city (Acts 19:1).

2. Apollos in Ephesus and Corinth. 18:24-28

18:24 – *Now a certain Jew named Apollos, an Alexandrian by birth, an eloquent man, came to Ephesus; and he was mighty in the Scriptures.*

Now a certain Jew named Apollos. Some think this name is short for Apollonius (which is the reading of Codex Beza), or for Apollodorus. The name is spelled "Apelles" in Codex Sinaiticus, and "Apollo" in the Latin Vulgate.

An Alexandrian by birth. Alexandria was a famous city and seaport of Egypt, twelve miles inland from the mouth of the Nile River. It had been named Alexandria in honor of Alexander the Great, who founded it in 332 BC. A large part of the population of Alexandria was Jewish, and one of the leading Hebrew colleges was located there, as was one of the most famous libraries in all the world.[90] The construction here is the same that was translated "a native of" in regard to Aquila in verse 2. Apollos not only was born in Alexandria, but his ancestry had been native to that city for some generations.

An eloquent man. The word translated "eloquent" carries a double meaning. The Greek can mean either a man skilled in the use of words (an eloquent speaker), or a man eloquent in ideas and thinking (learned). Alexandria was famous for its schools, and it is probable that Apollos had received training in them. We doubt, however, that Apollos made use of the allegorical method of Scripture interpretation for which Alexandria was famous.

Came to Ephesus. Apollos came to Ephesus while Paul was staying in Syrian Antioch, or while he was traveling through the areas of Galatia and Phrygia.

And he was mighty in the Scriptures. When we reflect that knowledge of the Scriptures had to be learned from manuscripts and that these were often available only in the synagogues, and when we remember that the ability to read was learned by only a few, we begin to appreciate what an accomplishment it was for Apollos to be so familiar with the

---

[89] One famous missionary used to insist that "No man has the right to hear the gospel twice until every man has heard it once." It appears that Paul did not ascribe to such an idea, for this is the fourth time he has visited some of these areas.

[90] See other notes concerning Alexandria at Acts 6:9.

Scriptures. It likely means that he had great portions of the Old Testament memorized.

Without falling into the error of Fundamentalism where college education is depreciated, and at the same time avoiding the error of worshiping at the altar of advanced education, it is well to hear Dale's words about modern education:

> This was the secret of his power and ability. He knew the Scriptures. Modern education manifests a sad and even tragic lack of learning in any phase of the Scriptures. The weakest spot in modern training falls at this very point where Apollos was "mighty." Today, the power of preaching has been confused with the expedient externals of politeness, polish, personality, and position. But Apollos was an efficient preacher because he had an understanding of the Scriptures, purity of heart and motives, and ability to proclaim the message. Too often congregations select their teachers for the Bible School on the basis of manners, personality, or degrees from some university. These expedients should not be scorned nor overlooked, but the essential thing is to select men and women who are wise in the Scriptures. Many a modern tent-maker in the congregation can and will serve much better as a teacher of the Word than the so-called well-educated person who knows science but has never met nor surrendered to the Savior.[91]

18:25 – *This man had been instructed in the way of the Lord; and being fervent in spirit, he was speaking and teaching accurately the things concerning Jesus, being acquainted only with the baptism of John;*

This man had been instructed in the way of the Lord. "Instructed" is the regular word for oral instruction.[92] By whom Apollos had been instructed we have no sure information. Perhaps it was by John the Baptist, or by one of the Baptist's disciples. The phrase, "the way of the Lord," is from Isaiah 40:3 and was applied to John's ministry as forerunner of the Messiah.[93] This phrase gives insight into the content of what Apollos had been taught – he was acquainted with John's role in God's acts of redemption.

And being fervent in spirit. He was "boiling over in spirit," i.e., full of enthusiasm. It speaks of zealousness and arduousness. Our translators have correctly left the word "spirit" uncapitalized.[94] The reference is not to the Holy Spirit, for the Holy Spirit and His gifts are the seal of the Christian faith which Apollos had not yet embraced.[95]

He was speaking and teaching accurately the things concerning Jesus. Both verbs are in the imperfect tense, which implies continuous action. Some have explained "speaking" to refer to private conversations, and "teaching" to the public speaking in the synagogue.

---

[91] Dale, *op. cit.*, p.287.

[92] Luke 1:4 indicates Theophilus had also been orally instructed in the truths about Jesus.

[93] See the prophecy from Isaiah applied to the Baptist in Matthew 3:3 and Mark 1.3.

[94] Another example of the use of "spirit" for a man's spirit is Romans 12:11.

[95] See the chart in the comments on Acts 1:5, "Five Different Baptisms in the New Testament," and Special Study #3, "The Person and Work of the Holy Spirit," where it was documented that the baptism of the Great Commission has a promise of the Spirit that John's baptism did not.

The phrase "things concerning Jesus"[96] gives another intimation of the content of Apollos' beliefs. He knew something about the fact that *Jesus* was the Messiah for whom John was the forerunner. This verse might suggest that Apollos' information was limited to such information about Jesus as John the Baptist would have known. When John was beheaded, his followers were scattered; perhaps one of them went as far as Alexandria, and from him Apollos learned what he was now teaching.[97] Apollos' teachings were "accurate;" that is, they were correct as far as they went, but his knowledge was incomplete.

Being acquainted only with the baptism of John. These words are quite interesting, for they show a much wider extent to the Baptist's influence as the forerunner of Jesus than is indicated in the Gospels. Even among the Alexandrians, there were those who had come under his influence. Did some Jews from Alexandria, having come to Jerusalem for one of the feasts, hear of this powerful preacher out at the Jordan River, go to hear John, and then return to Alexandria and spread there what they had heard? Or did some of John's disciples travel as far as Alexandria, just as some (Acts 19:1ff) came as far as Ephesus?[98]

Again we must look into the question of the content of Apollos' beliefs. This passage indicates that he was not acquainted with the baptism of the Great Commission, and therefore not acquainted with the gift of the Holy Spirit. May we understand this phrase as implying that Apollos knew something of Jesus' life and teachings, but did not know of His death, burial, resurrection, or ascension? Nor did he know that repentance and remission of sins were now being proclaimed in His name to all nations.[99] Apollos would not have learned as yet that "circumcision [was] nothing,"[100] and that the temple and all its ordinances were decaying and growing old, and ready to vanish away.[101]

18:26 – *and he began to speak out boldly in the synagogue. But when Priscilla and Aquila heard him, they took him aside and explained to him the way of God more accurately.*

And he began to speak out boldly in the synagogue. Whatever the exact content of Apollos' beliefs, he had the courage of his convictions. Luke does not tell us why Apollos came to Ephesus. Was it to preach what he knew, or was he on a business trip? In any case, on the Sabbath, he found his way to the synagogue and, like Paul had done in other communities, either would have requested permission to speak or would have been requested by the elders to speak since he was a visitor.

---

[96] The better manuscripts read "Jesus" and not "Lord" in this verse.

[97] Mark 6:17ff, and especially verse 34 ("sheep without a shepherd"), implies that John's disciples were scattered when he was beheaded, which was about one year before Jesus was crucified.

[98] Some modern writers have supposed that short, written accounts of Jesus' ministry (such as referred to in Luke 1:1-4) have circulated in Egypt, and from these Apollos learned his doctrine about Jesus. Without denying that such were already circulating, it seems that the word "instructed" at the beginning of verse 25 directs us to look for some oral teaching as the source of Apollos' doctrine.

[99] If this reconstruction is correct, then we must accept the idea that little knowledge of Pentecost (Acts 2) has come to Alexandria (at least to Apollos), even though men from Egypt were present on that occasion (Acts 2:10).

[100] 1 Corinthians 7:19; Galatians 5:6.

[101] Hebrews 8:13.

But when Priscilla and Aquila heard him. Here we learn that Priscilla and Aquila continued to attend the services of the synagogue. Undoubtedly, they were doing this as part of their foundation work for the coming of Paul, and the following verses will indicate they have won some converts.[102]

They took him aside. They took Apollos into their house, and into their hearts, in order to teach him privately. How much better to correct a person privately than to denounce him publicly.

And explained to him the way of God more accurately. Aquila and Priscilla filled in the gaps in Apollos' knowledge about Jesus and about God's way of saving men. If our reconstruction of the content of Apollos' doctrine was correct, then Aquila and Priscilla would have acquainted Apollos with the events of the closing year of Jesus' ministry, including the climactic week of His ministry, His death, burial, resurrection, and ascension. He would have learned about the doctrine of justification by faith, and about the institution and observance of the Lord's Supper. He would have learned about the indwelling of the Holy Spirit to help a person to live the Christian life.

Implied in the earlier statement about Apollos that he "knew only the baptism of John" is the truth that something has taken the place of John's baptism. Priscilla and Aquila were not so ignorant on this subject as to suppose, as do some present-day teachers, that there is no difference between the two baptisms. Nor were they so indifferent to the ordinance (thinking of it as a "mere external rite" as some moderns do) that they considered the difference to be of no great importance.

> Apollos learned that, while John's baptism had attached to it no promise of the Holy Spirit, this was one of the distinctive features of Christian baptism; and that while John baptized into no name, the apostles were taught to baptize into the name of the Father, Son, and Holy Spirit.[103]

After learning all these facts, who can doubt that Apollos was baptized into Christ – just like the followers of the Baptist whom Paul teaches are baptized (Acts 19:5)?

Take note of the fact that Priscilla's name is listed first at this place in the better manuscripts. The very least that this means is that Priscilla took part with her husband in giving instruction to Apollos. It speaks something to us about her understanding of the Scripture, that she is able to help this man who was "mighty in the Scriptures" to understand them better than he had understood them before. Her sharing in the teaching of Apollos also throws some light on the prohibitions against a woman's teaching recorded in 1 Timothy 2:12 and 1 Corinthians 14:34. Certainly, the Priscilla's activities make it difficult to take those prohibitions as meaning that a woman may never teach a man. However,

> It should be observed that Priscilla took part with her husband in giving more perfect instruction to Apollos, and this illustrates the manner in which certain faithful women were

---

[102] Verse 27 speaks of a congregation of Christians already in Ephesus before Paul arrives there on his third missionary journey.

[103] McGarvey, *op. cit.*, p.148.

eminent helpers of the apostles and evangelists in the spreading of the gospel. This should not, however, and cannot, without a deceitful handling of the Scriptures, be urged as proof that even the most eminent of the female helpers took part in public preaching.[104]

18:27 – *And when he wanted to go across to Achaia, the brethren encouraged him and wrote to the disciples to welcome him; and when he had arrived, he helped greatly those who had believed through grace;*

And when he wanted to go across to Achaia. Luke does not name a city in this verse. But Corinth was the capital of Achaia, 1 Corinthians 1:12 indicates Apollos had been to that city, and Acts 19:1 has Apollos in Corinth. Thus, Corinth was likely his destination.

Why he wanted to go to Corinth, Luke does not expressly inform us. Two reasons, though, have been offered: (1) Codex Beza has an addition at this place which says that some people from Corinth were visiting at Ephesus, heard Apollos preach, and invited him to Corinth. Though not a part of Luke's original manuscript, such a reason does have a ring of truth about it.[105] (2) Perhaps it was Apollos' own desire and decision to go to Corinth because he had heard from Aquila and Priscilla of the work Paul began there, and of the great opportunity to render a worthy service.

The brethren encouraged him. The Christians at Ephesus seem to be the ones called "brethren" here. This apparently indicates a congregation of Christians already are meeting in Ephesus, no doubt brought together by the work of Aquila and Priscilla. Since Apollos was mighty in the Scriptures and an eloquent speaker, the Christians at Ephesus see he would meet some of the needs that the brethren at Corinth had. Especially if the Corinthian Christians are still meeting next door to the synagogue, someone who knew the Scriptures and could therefore effectively speak to the Jews would be especially suited.

And wrote to the disciples to welcome him. This is the first recorded instance of what were afterwards known technically as "letters of commendation," written by one church to another, and intended to introduce the bearer.[106] The congregation at Corinth knew Aquila and Priscilla, and their recommendation of Apollos would have been well received.[107]

And when he had arrived. When Apollos arrived at Corinth, he immediately entered into the work with enthusiasm and vigor.

---

[104] *Ibid.*

[105] The matter of searching for a suitable preacher for an already established congregation or community is introduced by this explanation. More is needed in the selection process than simply inviting a man to come for a trial sermon. More attention should be given to delineating the church's needs – so that the church knows its own needs, and so that the church will also know whether or not the prospective preacher will complement those special needs. Once the leaders of a congregation have a good idea of their own peculiar needs, they may visit another congregation (as Codex Beza suggests was done by men from Corinth) in order to hear and interview a prospective preacher. When they have found a man whose abilities they believe are suited to their needs, they may extend a call to him.

[106] See 2 Corinthians 3:1; Romans 16:1.

[107] Such letters, if granted today, should be scrupulously truthful. It is no help to the bearer's spiritual welfare to describe him as "a member in good standing" if in truth he is anything but.

It is significant that as he received more light from Aquila and Priscilla, his zeal did not diminish. We then wonder why a great increase in the knowledge of modern learning has quenched the zeal of many of the learned leaders of the Christian faith. It is equally important to ask, Why do cults and sects with half-truths and self-evident limitations in true knowledge manifest such overwhelming zeal in the work of Christ?[108]

He helped greatly those who had believed through grace. He helped the Corinthians who evidently were the objects of Jewish antagonism now that Paul was gone. Has there been persecution of the new church in Corinth, or pressure to return to the Jewish faith? The extent of Apollos' influence at Corinth may be gauged from the references to him in 1 Corinthians, for some of the Corinthians after Apollos' ministry there declare themselves to be his special followers.[109] But this partisanship was certainly without Apollos' approval or encouragement, else Paul would hardly have encouraged that eloquent preacher to return to Corinth when he did.[110] Paul, instead of criticizing Apollos' work (as would have been done if Apollos had knowingly contributed to the schism in the church at Corinth), thought of Apollos as continuing the work which he himself had begun at Corinth.[111]

The words "through grace," in both the Greek and the English, could modify either the verb "helped" or the verb "believed."

- It may mean that because God helped Apollos (i.e., Apollos is the recipient of the grace), he was able to help the Corinthians.
- It may mean that because God helped the Corinthians (i.e., the Corinthians were the recipients of the grace), Apollos was able to help them, too. This explanation would mean that the grace of God had something to do with the Corinthians first becoming believers.[112]

18:28 – *for he powerfully refuted the Jews in public, demonstrating by the Scriptures that Jesus was the Christ.*

For he powerfully refuted the Jews in public. The Greek is a compound verb, indicating he thoroughly, completely refuted them. The word does not mean that he convinced them, but only that he argued them down. By strong arguments he bore down all opposition and effectually silenced the Jews. And it was done in public – either in the synagogue or in public debate. Apollos entered into a public discussion with the Jewish leaders concerning whether Jesus of Nazareth was the Christ. Apollos, before he came to know Christ, was already "an eloquent speaker" and "mighty in the Scriptures." Now that he had been taught the way of God more accurately, he was that much more powerful in argument. The Jews were no match for this preacher from Alexandria.

---

[108] Dale, *op. cit.*, p.288.

[109] 1 Corinthians 1:12ff.

[110] 1 Corinthians 16:12.

[111] 1 Corinthians 3:6.

[112] This language should not be explained as being part of Calvinism's doctrine of "Irresistible grace," or a first work of grace." See footnote #42 in chapter 8, or comments at Acts 16:14.

Demonstrating by the Scriptures. Apollos was proving his arguments from the Old Testament. If, as suggested earlier, he had the Scriptures memorized, he would be able to recall just the exact passage needed to meet the counter-arguments that the unbelieving Jews might raise against the Messiahship of Jesus.

That Jesus was the Christ. Apollos is insisting that Jesus of Nazareth corresponded with the account of the Messiah as predicted by the Old Testament prophets, and therefore must be the Messiah.

Someone has given the following outline of the paragraph we have just studied. It is entitled, "The Conversion of a Preacher."

I. Who he was — Verses 24-26
   a. An eloquent or learned man
   b. Mighty in the Scriptures
   c. He had been instructed in the way of the Lord
   d. He was fervent
   e. He taught accurately the things of Jesus
   f. He was bold

II. What he lacked — Verse 25b
   a. He lacked the Holy Spirit
   b. He lacked the forgiveness of sins
   c. He lacked the baptism of Jesus

III. What he did — Verses 26b-28
   a. He did not get angry
   b. He listened to further instruction
   c. He was probably rebaptized as were the other "Baptists"
   d. He then preached the whole truth
   e. He was sent with a letter of recommendation from the church in Ephesus to the church in Corinth
   f. He helped the church in Achaia

This is the last mention of Apollos in Acts, but we learn from other sources some of what happened to him later. According to this verse, Apollos went to Corinth and worked there, about AD 54. While Paul was at Ephesus (where he stayed for over two years), Apollos returned and took up a ministry in the vicinity of Ephesus.[113] Since there is no further notice of him in Acts, we lose sight of him for some years. We would like to believe that these years were filled with the sort of evangelistic activity he undertook at Ephesus and Corinth. Toward the close of Paul's ministry, we get our last glimpse of Apollos.[114] He and another man who had a profound knowledge of the Mosaic Law, Zenas, the lawyer, were together on a missionary tour.[115]

---

[113] 1 Corinthians 16:12.

[114] Titus 3:13.

[115] Some modern commentators attribute to Apollos the authorship of the letter we call Hebrews, but there is no solid evidence that Apollos was in fact its author.

Philippi

Drawing by Horace Knowles
from the British and Foreign Bible Society

3. Paul's Ministry in Ephesus. 19:1-41

   a. Paul corrects some on the baptism of John. 1-7

19:1 – *And it came about that while Apollos was at Corinth, Paul having passed through the upper country came to Ephesus, and found some disciples,*

And it came about that while Apollos was at Corinth. Luke has interrupted his account of the beginning of the third missionary journey to tell us about the conversion of Apollos and his call to Corinth (Acts 18:24-28). Now he resumes the account of Paul's travels.

Paul having passed through the upper country. The last geographical note about Paul's travels had him in Galatia and Phrygia.[1] Now Luke has him passing through some "highlands." Some commentators locate Paul up in northern Galatia again, just as they tried in Acts 16:6 to get him there. But the first impression one gets from this language is that, having left Pisidian Antioch, Paul is traveling westward toward Ephesus, not north east from Antioch. There were two routes by which a traveler might journey from Pisidian Antioch to Ephesus. One was through the *low* country, along the Lycus and Meander River valleys, passing through Colossae, Hierapolis, and Laodicea.[2] The other route was called the *upper* route because it took the traveler across the high tablelands of the interior of Asia Minor. Taking the northern route through the highlands, Paul would have approached Ephesus from around the north side of Mt. Messogis, a long range of mountains between the Meander and Cayster rivers.

Came to Ephesus. Paul has returned to Ephesus just as he conditionally promised he would when he left Aquila and Priscilla there about a year before.[3] Ephesus was one of the great cities of the world during New Testament times. There were political (it was the provincial capital), economic (much commerce with the interior of Asia Minor flowed through the harbor of Ephesus), and religious (the Temple of Artemis) reasons for her importance. Ephesus was located four miles from the Aegean Sea, and possessed an inland harbor connected with the Cayster River. As noted in comments on Acts 18:21, it took constant dredging to keep the harbor open; and in the 3rd century AD, when the city could no longer afford the dredging, the harbor silted up and the city died.

Archaeologists have located some of the major features of the ancient city. A marble street, 1735 feet long, connected the harbor to the west with the 25,000-seat theater on the east end of this main thoroughfare. The old forum, including the shops of the silversmiths, was located just to the south of this street. A new forum, built between Paul's time and the apostle John's time, lay to the north of this marble street. A town hall, a stadium (about a half-mile north of the theater), and the Magnesian Gate (about three-fourths of a mile south-

---

[1] Acts 18:23.

[2] See this same problem discussed at Acts 18:23. The fact that Paul is acquainted with Philemon, who is an inhabitant of the Lycus valley, has often been urged against the conclusion that Paul never visited the churches in this valley. But Paul might easily have met Philemon when the latter came to Ephesus during Paul's ministry there.

[3] Acts 18:21.

east of the theater) have been excavated. The Temple of Artemis was located about a mile northeast of the stadium.[4]

And found some disciples. By the time Paul reached Ephesus, Apollos had crossed the Aegean Sea to Corinth. But shortly after his arrival in Ephesus, Paul met a dozen men whose knowledge of Christianity was in much the same incomplete condition as Apollos' knowledge had been before he met Priscilla and Aquila.

What is the right understanding of the word "disciples"?

- At times, Luke has used the term as a name for Christians.[5] Thus, some commentators call these twelve "Christians."[6] But that is hardly possible if these twelve do not have the indwelling gift of the Holy Spirit.[7] The word "disciple" means "learner," so the words "disciple" and "Christian" are not necessarily synonymous.[8]
- Another, better explanation is that they were disciples of Apollos, taught by him before he received his further instruction from Aquila and Priscilla.[9]
- Perhaps the best suggestion is that they were disciples of John the Baptist, just as Apollos had been. These disciples were persons who had been baptized into John's baptism, and who had embraced John's doctrine that the Messiah was soon to appear.[10]

Where are Aquila and Priscilla? According to Romans 16:3-4, this couple is back in Rome when Paul writes that epistle late in this third missionary journey. When did they leave Ephesus? Before Paul returned at the beginning of the third journey? Or were they still present in Ephesus even at the time of the riot of Demetrius and the silversmiths? Romans 16:4 is often harmonized with what happened at that riot, the supposition being that Aquila and Priscilla risked their lives to keep Paul from going into the theater.[11]

19:2 – *and he said to them, "Did you receive the Holy Spirit when you believed?" And they said to him, "No, we have not even heard whether there is a Holy Spirit."*

And he said to them, "Did you receive the Holy Spirit when you believed?" "When you believed," i.e., at the time you were baptized, as verse 3 shows. In fact, when Paul's language in these verses is harmonized, it is seen that "believing" and "being baptized" and "receiving the Holy Spirit" are all regarded as part of the same transaction.

---

[4] See a map of Ephesus at the back of this book.

[5] Compare Acts 6:1, 9:25, 11:26.

[6] McGarvey is one who thinks these "disciples" are to be identified with the "brethren" who gave the letter of recommendation to Apollos (Acts 18:27). But this hardly seems probable, else would not Apollos or Aquila and Priscilla have taught them the way of the Lord more accurately?

[7] Romans 8:9.

[8] Note Matthew 28:19-20. A disciple is not necessarily a Christian, but may become one.

[9] Acts 18:25-26. The beliefs of these twelve are so similar to Apollos' that a case could easily be made that they were pupils of Apollos before his conversion.

[10] See verses 3 and 4 of this chapter.

[11] Acts 19:30.

"Did you receive the Holy Spirit?" This is a much-disputed phrase, and at least three major opinions have been advanced in an attempt to explain it.

1) Some think Paul has in mind the baptism with the Holy Spirit. Most commentators who so explain this verse evidently are confused about the nature of the baptism with the Holy Spirit.[12] Since only apostles received the baptism of the Holy Spirit (the sole exception being the household of Cornelius), it is not reasonable to think that Paul is asking non-apostles if they had been baptized of the Holy Spirit. While the standard Pentecostal or Charismatic interpretation of this passage leaves much to be desired, so does Boles' when he suggests that Paul's question means, "Do you know of the events of Pentecost, when the Spirit came and when the gospel of Christ was made known in its completeness?" But this is not the question Paul asked. His question was, "Did *you* receive the Holy Spirit?" and not "Did you ever hear about the coming of the Spirit?"

2) Others explain that the verse is a reference to miraculous, spiritual gifts; in fact, this might be the majority opinion. Exegetes defend this interpretation by noting that such gifts are in the context (see verse 6). It is explained that Paul was intending to bestow such gifts on these "disciples" if they had none, and that Paul was surprised to learn that they knew so little about the Holy Spirit. Against this interpretation are the following key points: (a) Would Paul have had to ask if they had such powers? Only an apostle could grant such spiritual gifts. Had these men ever been in the company of another apostle?[13] (b) Paul's question was not about a reception of the Holy Spirit during the period *since* their baptism (i.e., when they believed), but about a reception simultaneous with their original belief. The Greek is "*when* you believed," not "*since* you believed." The Greek translated "received" and "believed" are both aorist tense verbs, showing that the receiving and the believing were something that took place at the same time. Miraculous, spiritual gifts were not regularly given simultaneously with baptism for the remission of sins, so it is doubtful that "Did you receive the Holy Spirit *when* you believed" has reference to spiritual gifts.

3) The explanation that is most likely correct is that Paul is asking if they had received the indwelling gift of the Holy Spirit. Several lines of thought are offered in support of this interpretation. (a) It accords with the affirmation that the believing and the receiving are simultaneous, and is an event occurring when a person is immersed into Christ. That's the indwelling gift of the Holy Spirit! (b) Perhaps Paul noticed in them, as they attended the meetings of the church (or the synagogue), a lack of the peace and joy and brightness that was evident in the lives of the other "brethren" (of 18:27). These twelve had been baptized with the baptism of repentance, and were leading a life of fasting and prayers and alms as the Baptist taught, but they had not passed on to "righteousness and peace and joy in the Holy Spirit."[14] Paul thus set about to teach them the way of God more accurately – just as Priscilla and Aquila did with Apollos. (c) In the latter part of verse 2, the sentence construction is parallel to John 7:39, which was a prediction of the indwelling of the Holy Spirit.

---

[12] See Special Study #3, "The Person and Work of the Holy Spirit," about the baptism with the Holy Spirit.

[13] Paul may not have known if they had ever been with other apostles, but they evidently had not, or they would have been baptized into Christ already.

[14] Romans 14:17.

Some object to this third explanation. McGarvey, for example, has written:

> Paul's question "Did ye receive the Holy Spirit when ye believed" had reference not to the ordinary indwelling of the Spirit; for this all receive who repent and are baptized (Acts 2:38), and therefore, Paul could have no ground for doubting that they received this.[15]

However, in his comments, McGarvey is assuming the point to be proved. It is more likely that Paul is doing one of two things by asking this question. (a) He might be trying to stir the twelve to interest and action by showing them that their obedience was imperfect. (b) Or he might have been asking this question, much as Philip asked a question of the Ethiopian in Acts 8, in order to learn the spiritual condition of these twelve men.

And they *said* to him, "No, we have not even heard whether there is a Holy Spirit." Note the marginal reading, "whether the Holy Spirit has been *given*." In this place, the marginal reading is to be preferred to the one the NASB translators have put in the text.

- This sentence is the same construction found in John 7:39 – where there is no word in the Greek for "given," just the use of the linking verb "is." And John 7:39 was a prediction of the indwelling of the Holy Spirit.
- It would be hard to believe the twelve have never even heard of the Holy Spirit, as the NASB seems to say. They would have met Him if they had read the Old Testament. They would have heard John the Baptist refer to Him.[16]

When such facts are considered, the translators of the ASV – which point the twelve's answer toward the *giving* of the Holy Spirit, rather than the Holy Spirit's *existence* – have provided the superior translation. The twelve were not aware that the indwelling gift of the Holy Spirit was being given.

19:3 – *And he said, "Into what then were you baptized?" And they said, "Into John's baptism."*

And he said, "Into what then were you baptized?" "Then" (*oun*) presupposes that if they had been baptized into the name of Jesus, they would have received the Spirit at baptism. The neuter "what" has caused some difficulty.

- Barnes explains it as meaning "into what doctrine? What did you profess to believe when you were baptized?"[17]
- McGarvey thinks it means "into what name were you baptized."[18]

---

[15] McGarvey, *op. cit.*, p.151. Remember, McGarvey held that these twelve were already Christians (see discussion under "disciples" at verse 1). If his assumption about the meaning of that word is incorrect, and we think it is, then his notes explaining Paul's question would likewise be incorrect.

[16] Matthew 3:11; John 1:33.

[17] Barnes, *op. cit.*, p.275.

[18] McGarvey, *ibid.* This explanation is consistent with Luke's words in verse 5. However, his notes here are not consistent with his affirmation in verses 1 and 2 that the twelve were already Christians. How could

- When we remember that at Acts 3:19 we learned that baptism is recognized as the point of exit from one state into another, this question asked by Paul makes sense. By baptism he pictured them (if it were John's baptism) as moving out of a life characterized by impenitence into a life where repentance was a pattern of life, or (if it were the baptism of the Great Commission) moving out of a life outside the body of Christ into a sphere where one was a part of the body of Christ.

Notice again Paul's evident belief in the necessity of baptism for salvation. His questions ("Did you receive the Holy Spirit when you believed?" and "Into what then were you baptized?") demonstrate that he had no concept of believers (i.e., people justified by faith) who had not been immersed. For Paul, there was no such thing as "unimmersed believers" in the fellowship. In another place, Paul wrote, "For as many of you as were baptized into Christ have clothed yourselves with Christ."[19] Paul's questions in verses 2 and 3 are evidence that, for Paul, belief in Jesus is made effective and vital by obedience in baptism.

And they said, "Into John's baptism." Concerning John's baptism, see notes at Acts 1:5 and 18:25. "We believed what John preached, and submitted to his baptism to show that we so believed." John's baptism, of course, as is here clearly implied, had no promise of the gift of the Holy Spirit, as does the baptism of the Great Commission (Acts 2:38). John's baptism was valid during John's ministry, and for perhaps a year after his death, during which time the disciples of Jesus continued to baptize with John's baptism.[20]

19:4 – *And Paul said, "John baptized with the baptism of repentance, telling the people to believe in Him who was coming after him, that is, in Jesus."*

And Paul said, "John baptized with the baptism of repentance. The design of John's preaching was to turn the people from their sins and to prepare them for the coming of the Messiah – to not only get them to change their lives, but to get them to change their minds about the type of coming kingdom it was to be.

Telling the people to believe in Him who was coming after him. Paul here summarizes the thrust of John's preaching. John told of One coming after him who was mightier by far.[21] John did not want to make disciples for himself; he wanted men to believe on Jesus.[22] It seems to be clearly implied that these twelve disciples of John at Ephesus had not accepted Jesus because they did not know of Him, for in accepting John's baptism, they had pledged themselves to receive the Messiah when He came.

---

they already be Christians and yet need to be baptized in the name of Jesus?

[19] Galatians 3:27.

[20] John's baptism would continue to be valid for a man who submitted to it, and then who never heard the gospel, just as the Law was valid for the man who never heard the gospel (Romans 2:12). But once a man heard the gospel, he was required to submit to the baptism of the Great Commission to be saved.

[21] Matthew 3:11; Mark 1:7-8; Luke 3:16; John 1:15,26.

[22] John 3:25ff, especially verse 36, where the Baptist said, "He who believes in the Son has eternal life; but he who disbelieves the Son shall not see life, but the wrath of God abides on him."

That is, in Jesus." These are the words of Paul, explaining what John meant. John taught his followers to believe in the Messiah if they wanted eternal life. Paul now shows these twelve that Jesus of Nazareth was the Coming One to whom John had been directing them.

These words in verse 3 may fairly be regarded as giving but a summary of what was actually a fuller teaching. The distinctive point Paul makes is that by his own testimony, John had indicated that his baptism was provisional and preparatory, and that after Messiah came, something more would be expected of men.

19:5 – *And when they heard this, they were baptized in the name of the Lord Jesus.*

And when they heard this. They heard what Paul said about the temporary nature of John's baptism, and about the necessity of believing on Jesus if one would have eternal life.[23]

They were baptized in the name of the Lord Jesus. On the use of this formula in connection with the baptism of Jewish converts, see notes at Acts 10:48. The baptism of the Great Commission takes the place of John's baptism. Barnes is correct in his conclusion here:

> The disciples of John were re-baptized, not because baptism is designed to be repeated, but because they never had been, in fact, baptized in the manner prescribed by the Lord Jesus [in the Great Commission].[24]

F.F. Bruce and J.W. McGarvey have given an entirely different explanation of the reason why Paul demanded these twelve to be baptized in the name of Jesus.[25] It involves these points: (a) Those baptized by John the Baptist personally, or who submitted to John's baptism, *before* Jesus died were not required to submit to the baptism of the Great Commission. (b) Those who received John's baptism *after* the death of Christ (as is assumed for the twelve here in Acts 19) were required to obey Jesus' command since John's baptism (being an Old Testament rite) was no longer valid. (c) Evidence for this view is thought to be found in Acts 2:41 where it is said the 3000 baptized on Pentecost were "added unto them." The baptism of John, *before* Christ's death, is conceived of as already putting people into the body of Christ, to which the 3000 were then added.

There are several weighty objections to this explanation of why Paul commanded the twelve to be baptized into the name of Jesus. (1) If people already baptized by John's baptism did not need to submit to Christ's command, why didn't Peter, on Pentecost, say, "Repent and be baptized every one of you who haven't been baptized of John's baptism"? Almost certainly, some of the 3000 baptized had been disciples of John, who then obeyed

---

[23] Once more, let us drive home what is here implied as we compare Paul's statements about John's ministry with the record of the Baptist's preaching as found in John 3. John 3:36 is the only passage where it is specifically recorded that John told his disciples they should "believe" on Jesus if they wanted eternal life. Paul interprets that "believing" as including baptism and receiving the gift of the Holy Spirit. How is it that some say baptism is not necessary to having eternal life?

[24] Barnes, *op. cit.*, p.276.

[25] McGarvey. *op. cit.*, p.152-153; Bruce, *op. cit.*, p.386.

Peter's commands. (2) It appears to be contradictory to many passages to say that John's baptism put a person into the body of Christ, and that it did so even *before* Christ died. (3) Consult the notes at Acts 2:41 for a better explanation of "added unto them." (4) While the Bruce-McGarvey suggestion addresses a standard objection to the doctrine that immersion is necessary to salvation (i.e., "If immersion is so necessary to salvation, why weren't the apostles baptized?"),[26] it must be rejected since it raises more problems than it answers.

It seems best, therefore, to understand that since John the Baptist lived under the dispensation of the Law of Moses (and therefore what he commanded would pass with the cross, just as did all those things which Moses commanded), all who had been baptized of his baptism were immersed into Christ (if they ever came into contact with the full gospel).

What about rebaptism today? Dale has written a fine paragraph in answer to this question.

> Often young people who study for the ministry feel that their increased knowledge of the meaning of baptism may require another baptism. But if one should be baptized every time his knowledge increased concerning baptism, he would constantly have to be rebaptized. However, there must be a scriptural basis for a valid baptism; and any person who has accepted Christ without the basic understanding of what he was doing may well have reason to question and to be concerned about this matter. It seems clear that if one comes into the church of Christ upon the basis of a baptism which was understood and accepted as unnecessary to salvation, his baptism would be invalid. If a boy or a girl accepted Christ on his own faith, he has no cause to question; but if it was on the basis of his parent's desires with little or no will of his own being exercised, he should be gravely concerned. If he was baptized "in the name of Jesus only," and understood this to be a denial of the Godhead, his baptism would be invalid. Reduced to its simplest terms, a valid baptism necessarily includes the basic belief that Jesus is the Christ, the Son of the living God, the only Savior; that Christ has commanded true repentance to sin and obedience to the command of Christian baptism, which is by immersion; and that the person baptizing should so baptize in the name of the Father, the Son, and the Holy Spirit. What is miscalled "re-baptism" becomes a rare thing when a proper investigation has been made in each individual case.[27]

19:6 – *And when Paul had laid his hands upon them, the Holy Spirit came on them, and they began* **speaking with tongues and prophesying.**

And when Paul had laid his hands upon them, the Holy Spirit came on them. There can be little doubt that the same thing is happening to these twelve disciples at Ephesus as happened to the brethren in Samaria (Acts 8:17).[28] What we have here are spiritual gifts being given by the laying on of an apostle's hands.[29]

---

[26] If McGarvey and Bruce are correct, it could be answered when this old objection is raised, "They were baptized (with John's baptism), and it was for the remission of sins, too!" (Mark 1:4).

[27] Dale, *op. cit.*, p.292.

[28] See notes at Acts 8:17-18.

[29] See Special Study #3, "The Person and Work of the Holy Spirit," particularly the section on spiritual gifts.

And they *began* speaking with tongues and prophesying. Both these activities were listed among the miraculous spiritual gifts.[30] The verbs are imperfect in tense, implying continuous exercise of the gifts.

19:7 – *And there were in all about twelve men.*

And there were in all about twelve men. There has been no end of speculation as to why an inspired historian like Luke should use the word "about."[31] None of these speculations are very satisfying. Since the incident with these twelve men is mentioned before anything else, it seems probable that Paul found them and taught them, before he visited the synagogue (as mentioned in the next verse).

      b. Paul preaches in the synagogue and school of Tyrannus. 8-10

19:8 – *And he entered the synagogue and continued speaking out boldly for three months, reasoning and persuading* **them** *about the kingdom of God.*

And he entered the synagogue. Having corrected what he found deficient in the twelve disciples of John, Paul next turns to the needs of the Jews and the pagans in the city. Athens, Corinth, and Ephesus each presented a typical problem for a preacher of the gospel. Athens was a place where men were proud of their ancient past, their culture and intellectual attainments. Corinth was a city where men who did not know God tried to satisfy their spiritual hungers by fleshly indulgence. Ephesus, on the other hand, looked to Oriental religions for something to satisfy their hungers.[32]

    The Jews met in the synagogue for worship on the Sabbath. As was his custom, Paul begins his work in this city by first turning to those who by the Old Testament had been prepared for the gospel. He had paid this synagogue an earlier visit; now, as he had promised, he returns.[33]

And continued speaking out boldly for three months. He may have preached only on the Sabbath days, but there are those who think that he taught daily those who might assemble there. According to Acts 20:34, Paul also worked at his trade of tent-making during this time. He was permitted to speak for a longer period of time in the synagogue here than perhaps any other place, unless it be Corinth. As we have followed Paul's journeys from city to city, one to three Sabbaths was about the limit of the Jews' toleration of having the gospel preached in their synagogues.

Reasoning and persuading *them.* These two verbs have been used regularly of Paul's ac-

---

[30] See Special Study #4, "Speaking in Tongues," and see comments on prophesying at Acts 2:17.

[31] The Syriac, Arabic, and Ethiopic versions read "twelve" without the addition of the word "about."

[32] Each of these devilish substitutes is still tried today. As was true for the ancients, people who are trying these substitutes instead need Christ. He's the only one who can satisfy.

[33] See Acts 18:19.

tivities as he opens the Scriptures to show that Jesus is the Messiah and as he urges them to surrender their lives to Him. Not everyone was reasonable, or was persuaded, as the next verse shows. Paul had the same experience here in Ephesus that he had at other places: some believed and some disbelieved.

About the kingdom of God. Earlier in Acts Luke has told us that Paul was persuading men about Jesus being the Messiah. Now it is persuasion "about the kingdom of God."[34] There is little difference, for the ascended, glorified Lord is now sitting as king on David's throne,[35] and the church which was purchased with the precious blood of Christ[36] is the present manifestation of the kingdom of God on earth. Paul understood and taught that the kingdom had already been established.

19:9 – *But when some were becoming hardened and disobedient, speaking evil of the Way before the multitude, he withdrew from them and took away the disciples, reasoning daily in the school of Tyrannus.*

But when some were becoming hardened and disobedient. Both these verbs imply actions that were continuous, gradual, progressive. As the Jews resisted the truth, they gradually became more and more callous to it; and the more they were hardened, the more they were disobedient. The only way a person can refuse to believe in the face of evidence is by hardening his heart. From the example of Pharaoh in the Old Testament we can see how a person's heart becomes hardened. In Exodus 8:15,32, we are told that Pharaoh hardened his own heart. In Exodus 8:19, we are told that his heart was hardened. In Exodus 7:3 and 10:1, we are told that God hardened Pharaoh's heart. Through Moses, God presented His message to Pharaoh, and worked miracles as proof, offering Pharaoh the opportunity of repentance. Pharaoh rejected what God had to say, with the result that he was hardened to the place where he could not respond. Another illustration of how God's appeals work on a man's heart can be learned from the operation of the sun on various substances. The same sun will melt wax but it will harden clay; it depends on the substance it strikes. So it is with the gospel. God has so arranged it that the same gospel will melt some hearts and harden others, depending on the substance it strikes. A person who allows himself to be persuaded will be softened and molded into God's image. A person who steels himself to refuse the invitation will find himself hardened, and it will be more difficult, next time, for him to surrender to the invitation to repent and obey. Here in Ephesus, hearts were hardened by the gospel because the Jews deliberately refused to believe the evidence presented by Paul.

Speaking evil of the Way before the multitude. They spoke evil of the gospel, the way in which God saves men.[37] The "multitude" apparently refers to non-Jews in the community of Ephesus. That is, the unbelieving Jews of Ephesus are trying the same thing

---

[34] See Special Study #1, "Diverse Opinions About the Kingdom of God."

[35] Acts 2:33.

[36] Acts 20:28.

[37] See Acts 9:2 for comments on the expression "the Way."

the Jews at Thessalonica did. They are trying to vent their hatred against Paul by stirring up suspicion among the Gentiles.

He withdrew from them. Paul no longer attends the synagogue services, nor attempts to preach the gospel to them.

And took away the disciples. Paul encourages the Christians to meet no longer with the Jews in their synagogue. He is removing the brethren from the influence and society of those who were resisting the faith and speaking evil of the Way. This is often the best way to prevent the evil influence of others. Paul had done a similar thing at least once before, at Corinth.[38] At Corinth, the Christians used the house of Justus for their continued assembling together. Here in Ephesus, Paul will use a school room.

Reasoning daily in the school of Tyrannus. "School" here likely speaks of a lecture room, which it would appear was either loaned or rented to Paul for use as a place to preach and teach. Teachers and sophists would use such rooms to lecture on medicine, philosophy, or rhetoric, and would give their lectures in the early morning. The Western text at this place has Paul teaching between the hours of 11 a.m. and 4 p.m., and this may reflect accurately the life in a 1st century city.[39] Since Paul tells us he worked at tent-making while in Ephesus, Paul likely worked from daybreak till late in the morning at his trade. Then, when the regular morning classes in the lecture hall were finished, he would come to this school to begin his day's teaching.

Who Tyrannus was is not known. One view is that the room was simply named after its original owner or user. It would also be believable to assert that he was a Christian, for an unconverted teacher of philosophy or rhetoric would not likely have loaned or rented his classroom to a preacher of the new faith. Plumptre makes a further suggestion that Tyrannus may have been a physician, since a physician by the name of Tyrannus is listed as among those buried in the Columbarium of the household of Livia on the Appian way. He urges further that since the name Tyrannus was often a name given to a slave or a freedman, the man mentioned in Acts could have been among the Jews whom the decree of Claudius had driven from Rome, and could even have shared the faith that Aquila and Priscilla did. Thus, Tyrannus would happily make his lecture hall available to Paul.

Christians at that time had no church buildings, and so were obliged to assemble any place where it might be convenient to conduct public worship. Since Paul was reasoning "daily," he would be teaching even on days when services were held in the synagogue. This would help make permanent the separation that had taken place.

19:10 – *And this took place for two years, so that all who lived in Asia heard the word of the Lord, both Jews and Greeks.*

And this took place for two years. "This" was the public instruction in the school of Ty-

---

[38] Acts 18:17.

[39] Ramsay, *St. Paul the Traveller and Roman Citizen*, p.271, has documented the fact that the schools opened at daybreak, and that by eleven o'clock the students would be dismissed.

rannus. Where our translation reads "for two years," we would tend to say, "two whole years." In Acts 20:31, Paul speaks of being about three years in Ephesus. The "two years" of this verse are added to the "three months" of verse 8, and there would be some time besides this (after the riot of Demetrius). Paul's stay in Ephesus is dated from the fall of AD 54 to the spring of AD 57.

The comments of several writers must be rejected at this point. Boles speaks of a previous letter written by Paul to Corinth at this point in time, a letter which is now lost to us.[40] Paul's language in 1 Corinthians 5:9, on which the idea of a previous letter is wholly dependent, most likely does not refer to a letter previous to 1 Corinthians, a letter now wholly or in part lost. Rather, it refers rather to the first eight verses of 1 Corinthians 5. The verb in 1 Corinthians 5:9 is what is called an epistolary aorist.[41]

Some negative critics suggest that the Prison Epistles were written by Paul from Ephesus at this time.[42] We reject this hypothesis, and believe that the Prison Epistles were written from Rome during Paul's first Roman imprisonment.[43]

So that all who lived in Asia heard the word of the Lord. "Asia" is the Roman province of Asia, of which Ephesus was the principal city. Ephesus was on the major route from Rome to the eastern part of the empire, and a number of major highways from the interior of Asia had their terminus here. In addition, the famous Temple of Artemis would regularly be visited by thousands of strangers. Many of these would hear the gospel and then take it home with them. The word of the Lord is the teaching respecting the Lord Jesus Christ.

Both Jews and Greeks. The wording of this verse reflects a gap in Luke's narrative which can only be partially filled up by inference or conjecture. Ephesus, probably, became the center of Paul's evangelistic activities, from which his helpers would journey to the neighboring cities in order to plant churches there. In the years after the events Luke records here in Acts, there are churches at Ephesus, Laodicea, Colossae, Hierapolis, Pergamum, Smyrna, Thyatira, Sardis, Philadelphia, and the other towns and cities of this province of Asia. Asia became a center of Christian activity for centuries.

No better illustration of settled, located evangelism can be found in the New Testament, unless it is Luke's five-year ministry in Philippi or Philip's 20-year ministry in Caesarea. The growth of Christianity among both sections of the population ("Jews and Greeks") began to tell upon the pilgrims who brought their offerings to the Temple of Artemis, and carried away souvenirs from it (see verse 23ff).

---

[40] Boles, *op. cit.*, p.301. By "previous letter" is meant a supposed letter written by Paul to Corinth previous to the letter called 1 Corinthians in our New Testament, which would be a letter now lost to us.

[41] Gareth L. Reese, "The Communication Between Paul and the Corinthian Christians" in *1 Corinthians* (Moberly, MO: Scripture Exposition Books, 2013), p.17ff.

[42] The "Prison Epistles" are Ephesians, Philippians. Colossians, and Philemon. They are called "prison epistles" because in each letter Paul speaks about how he is in prison as he writes.

[43] Gareth L. Reese, "The Place of Writing" in *Paul's Prison Epistles* (Moberly, MO: Scripture Exposition Books, 2017), p.7ff.

c. Miracles worked. 19:11-20

19:11 – *And God was performing extraordinary miracles by the hands of Paul,*

And God was performing extraordinary miracles by the hands of Paul. The Greek phrase is negative, "no common works of power." This is a litotes. All miracles are extraordinary (that lies in the definition of "miracle"), but these were extra-special, extraordinary miracles. They were "extraordinary" in the sense that they were wrought without personal contact with the patient, possibly without even consciousness on the part of Paul (see verse 12). The tense of the verb "was performing" shows that these special miracles continued for some time. That Luke should pick this particular item to comment on, out of all the possible things from a three-year ministry, must have been because these extraordinary miracles were intended to offset the magical practices so common among the Ephesians. In a city where demonic "miracles" were commonplace, it would take extraordinary miracles to credential the true message from God that Paul was delivering.[44]

19:12 – *so that handkerchiefs or aprons were even carried from his body to the sick, and the diseases left them and the evil spirits went out.*

So that handkerchiefs or aprons were even carried from his body to the sick. These two nouns are of Latin origin and are transliterated from the Latin into the Greek. The word translated "handkerchief" speaks of the towel used to wipe sweat from the brow or face. We might call it a hand towel, or shop towel, or even a sweatband. The word "apron" speaks of the short apron worn around the waist by the craftsmen as they worked, worn to preserve the clothes from wear and tear and soil. As Paul was working at his trade of tent-making it would have been common to use both items.

The picture behind the words "carried away from his body to the sick" is of Christians coming to Paul as he was working and carrying away with them the very towels and aprons which he had been wearing. Of course, the power to heal was not in the cloth. Never forget that God is the source of power behind genuine miracles. The efficacy of such media stands on the same footing as that of the hem of Jesus' garment,[45] Peter's shadow,[46] or the clay used in the healing of the blind man.[47]

And the diseases left them and the evil spirits went out. Observe that doctor Luke distinguishes between diseases and demon possession, just as in Acts 5:16. The evil spirits are called "pernicious" (*ponēros*); that is, they were trying to harm the persons in whom

---

[44] Once again, we contend that miracles in New Testament times were wrought to credential messengers. Some modern-day so-called faith-healers, on radio and TV, urge their listeners to send in for cloths that have been blessed – apparently taking their example from this text. Since modern so-called miracle workers do not even preach the New Testament message, their works are either fake or wrought by a power other than the Divine.

[45] Matthew 9:20-21.

[46] Acts 5:15.

[47] John 9:6.

they were living.[48] The bringing of the towels and aprons led to the healing of the sick, and the casting out of demons. This is what Luke termed "extraordinary" (verse 11).

19:13 – *But also some of the Jewish exorcists, who went from place to place, attempted to name over those who had the evil spirits the name of the Lord Jesus, saying, "I adjure you by Jesus whom Paul preaches."*

But also some of the Jewish exorcists. The word translated "exorcist" is derived from *orkizō*, which means "to bind with an oath." Such a person, in the process of exorcizing (i.e., casting out) a demon, would say, "I adjure you by Jesus" or "by Jehovah," or by some other person (e.g., Abraham, Raphael, Michael) – and this meant, "I bind you; come out! You are under His power!" These words were repeated over and over as the exorcist recited the whole magical formula (or charm, or spell, or incantation) by which he obtained control over the demon being cast out.[49] Observe, too, that these exorcists were Jewish. A person does not have to be a "Christian" in order to be able to exorcize demons! Notice the word "also." It contrasts these Jewish exorcists with what Paul was doing. Paul's power was of God; the Jews' powers were counterfeit.

Who went from place to place. Between the years AD 50 and 100, there were numerous such Jews in the Roman empire who went around hoodwinking people by magic. They traveled wherever there was any prospect of gaining monetary advantage by their exorcisms. It was a regular thing for the Jews to be exorcists;[50] there seemed to be a special power in the use of the specially-sacred Divine Name that only the Jews would know. Josephus[51] and Justin Martyr[52] both speak of Jewish exorcisms.

Attempted to name over those who had the evil spirits the name of the Lord Jesus. In the name of Jesus, Paul had cast out demons and wrought extraordinary miracles. Perhaps these Jews supposed there was the same kind of magical charm or spell in this name as in the names they had been using, only the name of Jesus was a more powerful spell as was obvious when they observed Paul's genuine miracles. So they substituted the name they heard Paul use for the old names they had been using in their incantations.

Saying, "I adjure you by Jesus whom Paul preaches." "I bind you. You are under the power of that Jesus whom Paul preaches." The name Joshua (i.e., Jesus) was so common that some further specification was necessary.

---

[48] See notes at Acts 8:7 concerning demons (i.e., evil spirits).

[49] See an example of such an incantation in the article "Exorcism" in *Hastings' Dictionary of the Bible*, Vol. I, p.812.

[50] Matthew 12:27.

[51] Josephus, *Antiquities*, VIII.2.5.

[52] Justin Martyr, *Dialogue with Trypho*, 85; *Apology*, II.6. While acknowledging that a Jew might exorcise an evil spirit by the name of the God of Abraham, Justin complains that as a class the Jewish exorcists used the same superstitions and magical aids the unconverted heathen did.

19:14 – *And seven sons of one Sceva, a Jewish chief priest, were doing this.*

And seven sons of one Sceva, a Jewish chief priest, were doing this. The derivation of the father's name is disputed. Some think it is a Greek name, some a Latin name, and some a Hebrew name. This being true, commentators have attempted to learn more about him by working with the word "chief priest." It might mean that he actually was a "high priest" of the Jews at some earlier time. However, in the lists of Jewish high priests that we know about, there is no such name. Therefore, others suggest that this title means he had been or was one of the heads of the 24 courses of priests,[53] and this seems the most likely idea. A third suggestion is that he was merely of priestly descent.[54] A fourth idea is that it was an assumed title, part of his deliberate effort to deceive the people. Many tried to use the name of Jesus as part of an oath over the demons, among whom were these seven boys. It didn't turn out for them like it did when Paul spoke these words as he cast out demons.

19:15 – *And the evil spirit answered and said to them, "I recognize Jesus, and I know about Paul, but who are you?"*

And the evil spirit answered and said to them. The seven exorcists, even more confident of success now than before since they have a new magical name in their incantation, stand face to face with the man who was demon possessed. The possessed man is physically stronger (by the power of the demon) than ordinary men, similar to the Gadarene demoniac.[55] The demon speaks to the would-be exorcists, either using the man's vocal cords, or speaking from within the chest cavity of the possessed man.

I recognize Jesus, and I know about Paul. "Jesus I recognize (*ginōskō*)" means "I acknowledge Jesus' authority and His power to cast out demons." *Ginōskō* denotes that the spirit was familiar with this fact by personal experience. "Paul I know (*epistamai*)" means "I am acquainted with Paul; his power to cast out demons is known to me."

But who are you? The Greek reads, "But *you* (emphatic, and with a tone of contempt), who are you?" The demon had an awe of Jesus, and a respect for Paul, but only contempt for these seven would-be exorcists. It may be learned from what happens next that when a person attempts to exorcize a demon by power other than Divine, it might backfire to his own hurt, especially if the demons become angered by the attempt to control them.

19:16 – *And the man, in whom was the evil spirit, leaped on them and subdued all of them and overpowered them, so that they fled out of that house naked and wounded.*

And the man in whom was the evil spirit leaped on them. The demon gave abnormal strength to this man whom the seven were attempting to heal. The reality of demon possession is surely assumed in the language of this phrase and in the previous verse where the evil spirit did the answering.

---

[53] See notes at Acts 4:5.

[54] Acts 4:6.

[55] Matthew 8:28; Mark 5:3-4.

And subdued all of them and overpowered them. The ASV reads "both of them," which seems to imply that only two of the seven were attempting to practice upon this evil spirit. However, the Greek word *amphoterōn* may mean "all of them;" hence, all seven evidently are included. Most of the modern versions (e.g., NASB, NIV, ESV, RSV, NEB, Phillips, etc.) render it, "He mastered all of them."

So that they fled out of that house naked and wounded. Luke has in mind a certain house (he says "that house") but no other identification is given; it likely is the house in which the possessed man lived. "Naked" may mean either that they lost all their clothes, or that they simply lost their outer garments in the ensuing struggle, leaving them with nothing but their short tunics. The sight of seven naked, wounded men, running through the streets of Ephesus, would have attracted attention, and the next verse shows it did.[56]

19:17 – *And this became known to all, both Jews and Greeks, who lived in Ephesus; and fear fell upon them all and the name of the Lord Jesus was being magnified.*

And this became known to all, both Jews and Greeks, who lived in Ephesus. The news of what happened to the seven sons of Sceva spread quickly through the community.

And fear fell upon them all. The occult is fascinating to many in our day, and so are attempts at exorcisms. But the evil spirit world is not something to play with; it's deadly serious. The Ephesians learned to have a healthy respect for the dangers of the occult when they heard what the demon had done to the sons of Sceva.

And the name of the Lord Jesus was being magnified. The Ephesians also learned that the name of the Lord Jesus stood on a very different level from the names the exorcists liked to employ in their charms. "Magnified" is an imperfect tense verb; it suggests a continuous growth of profound respect for the name of the Lord. Men would also be more and more aware that the miracles performed in the name of the Lord Jesus by Paul were genuine, and were worked to accredit the truth of the doctrine he taught. Occultists and spiritists came to see that the counterfeit miracles they worked were second rate, and that those who practiced such arts only exposed themselves to the rage of the evil spirits.

19:18 – *Many also of those who had believed kept coming, confessing and disclosing their practices.*

Many also of those who had believed. The word "believed" is probably used for the whole process of conversion, including baptism.[57] The perfect tense verb indicates they had been believers for some time before they came confessing.

---

[56] In passing, this paragraph is often referred to when defenders of the Bible's truthfulness speak of the "unaccountable brevity" of the Biblical narratives. A human writer, who was making up such a story and inventing miracles, would no doubt have crowned the story by having Paul come into the house where the demoniac lived, and healing him in conspicuous contrast to the failure of the seven sons of Sceva. The inspired Scriptures simply have a different feel and flavor than a merely human writer would create.

[57] See Special Study #16, "The Faith That Saves."

Kept coming, confessing. People who have become Christians often find that, even though the slavery to sin has been broken, they still have very strong temptations in the same areas where they used to sin. This is why, for example, Paul must exhort the Christians to "put to death the deeds of the flesh,"[58] and "stop letting sin reign in your mortal bodies" and "stop presenting your bodily members to unrighteousness."[59] Therefore, it is likely that this passage teaches that many of the early converts in Ephesus continued to practice many of the occultic arts they had been involved in before their conversion. But now, since fear had come upon them, they were ready to renounce everything that pertained to this sorcery and magic.[60]

Exactly what is meant by "confessing" is disputed, particularly whether it was public or private confession. The words do not state definitely whether the confession was made privately to Paul or to some other Christian, or publicly in the presence of the congregation. The confession made to John the Baptist is appealed to as an example of the latter,[61] while James 5:16 is appealed to as evidence for the former. One of the steps in renouncing Satan and all he stands for is vocal confession, to a fellow believer in Christ or to the whole congregation, of the past involvement in the occult.

And disclosing their practices. Another step in breaking away from the occult is for the former occultist to disclose, one-by-one, all his occultic practices. Deissmann has shown that in such a context, "practices" has the technical sense of "magic spells."[62] Bruce helps us understand the value of such a disclosure when he reminds us that "according to magical theory, the potency of a spell is bound up with its secrecy; if it becomes divulged, it becomes ineffective."[63]

19:19 – *And many of those who practiced magic brought their books together and* **began** *burning them in the sight of all; and they counted up the price of them and found it fifty thousand pieces of silver.*

And many of those. In the Greek, the word that opens this verse seems to imply a smaller number than the word that opened verse 18. "Many" confessed; "several" burned their books. Perhaps verse 19 speaks of the "priests" of the occultic world, whereas verse 18 spoke of their followers.

Who practiced magic. "Magic" (*perierga*) denotes such things as telekinesis, levitation, apports, and such mantic and magic practices as would be practiced by a person who was trying to get special knowledge or power from the spirit world. These magic arts were almost, so to speak, the specialty of Ephesus. Astrologers and magicians swarmed in her

---

[58] Colossians 3:5.

[59] Romans 6:12-14.

[60] Other commentators interpret this passage differently. They think the people who confessed were declaring the secret things which they did *before* they became Christians.

[61] Matthew 3:6.

[62] Adolf Deissmann, *Biblical Studies* (Edinburgh: T&T Clark, 1923), p.232.

[63] Bruce, *The Book of Acts*, p.391.

streets; there was a brisk trade in the charms, incantations, books of divination, rules for interpreting dreams, and the like.

Among the things bought and sold would have been the "Ephesian Letters," which were well known among the ancients, and some of which have survived even down to the present.[64] These Letters seem to have consisted of certain combinations of letters or words which, by being pronounced with certain intonations of voice, were believed to be effectual in expelling diseases or evil spirits; or which, by being written on parchment and worn (like an article of jewelry) were supposed to operate as amulets or charms to guard the wearer from evil spirits or from danger. Plutarch wrote of them, "The magicians compel those who are possessed with a demon to recite and pronounce the *Ephesian Letters,* in a certain order, by themselves."[65] Clement of Alexandria said, "Androcydes, the Pythagorean, says that the Ephesian Letters, which are so celebrated, are of the class of symbols."[66]

Brought their books together. These books would be those, for example, which explained the magical arts, or which contained the magical forms and incantations, recipes for love philters, and formulas for casting out evil spirits. Included too would have been the "Bibles" used in the occultic practices; similar to today's "Book of Shadows," or "The Book of the Dead," or "The Book of Venus," or the so-called "6th and 7th Book of Moses."

And *began* burning them in the sight of all. The tense of the verb implies that the "burning" was continuous; book after book was thrown into the burning fire. This act points us to another step in breaking off all involvement with the occult. Not only must there be confession and disclosure, but there must be a renunciation – a complete break – a destruction of the charms and books and paraphernalia of the occult. This not only guards against a relapse on the part of the one doing the renouncing, but also guards against the abandoned items becoming a stumbling block to others.

And they counted up the price of them. Whether this counting was by those who used to be in the business or by the bystanders is not told. As folk threw their books into the fire, they shared what had been spent to purchase the books in the first place.

And found it fifty thousand pieces of silver. What coin the word here translated "piece of silver" denotes is impossible to tell; consequently, the precise value of this conflagration in unknown. In order to make the figure meaningful to any place or time, let it be noted that a "piece of silver" was an ordinary day's wages for a workingman. The value of the books burned was equivalent of 50,000 day's wages – an enormous sum of money. Such books commanded what might be called "fancy" prices, according to their supposed rareness, or the value of the secrets which they professed to include.[67] The example of the

---

[64] Adolf Deissmann, *Light from the Ancient East* (Grand Rapids: Baker, 1965), p.254ff. Bruce M. Metzger, "St. Paul and the Magicians" in *Princeton Seminary Bulletin*, XXXVIII (1944), p.27ff.

[65] Plutarch, *Symposiaca*, VII.5.4.

[66] Clement of Alexandria, *Stromata*, V.8.

[67] A sign of the sickness of the times in which we live is the booming interest in witchcraft and occultism. Magazines and books are flooding the market, and astrology columns find their way into more and more newspapers. Greater detail is given in Special Study #17, "The World of the Occult."

Ephesian Christians, who destroyed their magic articles so that the word of the Lord might grow, is one for Christians of all ages to emulate.

19:20 – *So the word of the Lord was growing mightily and prevailing.*

So the word of the Lord was growing mightily and prevailing. There is no such thing as a spiritual vacuum – people will seek something to fill their hearts. In this case, the truth as preached by Paul, and as accredited by the miracles God worked through him, found a home in their hearts. The more they give up their old magical practices, the more they were ready to accept the word of the Lord. This was a day of triumph for Christ and His word in Ephesus.

This verse is one of Luke's typical summary statements, and an indication that he is about to introduce a new phase of Paul's evangelistic work.[68]

  d. Paul's future plans and the two sent to Corinth. 19:21-22

19:21 – *Now after these things were finished, Paul purposed in the spirit to go to Jerusalem after he had passed through Macedonia and Achaia, saying, "After I have been there, I must also see Rome."*

Now after these things were finished. After the gospel was firmly established at Ephesus and in Asia, Paul's presence there was no longer so necessary. The young churches could be left in the hands of Paul's helpers and to the care of the Holy Spirit.

Paul purposed in the spirit. Notice that the text reads "spirit" and the margin "Spirit." On a previous missionary journey, it was the Holy Spirit who had a hand in directing Paul's steps,[69] so some commentators believe the Holy Spirit prompted Paul to make his plans to go to Rome.[70] On the other hand, Luke has also used the word "spirit" for Paul's mind,[71] so some commentators think this means that Paul "resolved in his mind to go to Rome."[72] McGarvey combines the two ideas and supposes that Paul formed this purpose subject to the approval of the Holy Spirit.[73]

To go to Jerusalem. The epistles Paul wrote about this time indicate that he wanted to carry an offering from the Gentile churches to Jerusalem for the poor Christians in Judea.[74]

---

[68] Compare notes at Acts 12:24.

[69] Acts 13:4, and compare Acts 16:6-7.

[70] For example, W.R. Walker, *Studies in Acts* (Joplin, MO: College Press, nd), Part II, p.56.

[71] Acts 17:6.

[72] For example, Barnes, *op. cit.,* p.280.

[73] McGarvey, *op. cit.*, p.159.

[74] Romans 15:25; 1 Corinthians 16:1-3; 2 Corinthians 8,9.

After he had passed through Macedonia and Achaia. "Passed through" is Luke's word for a missionary or evangelistic tour.[75] On an earlier missionary journey, Paul had planted churches in these two provinces that were now needing further attention and encouragement. Remember, it was Paul's method of evangelism to return to strengthen and encourage the brethren. There were some disorders which were disturbing several of the congregations, and Paul wanted to correct these. In addition, he was trying to bring the collection for the poor saints at Jerusalem to a close. This offering was intended by Paul not only to benefit the Christians at Jerusalem in their need, but also to help develop a higher sense of unity between the Jewish and Gentile brethren.[76]

Saying, "After I have been there, I must also see Rome." From this point on, Rome is the goal towards which the Acts account moves, until at last, in chapter 28, Luke writes, "and so we came to Rome."

Why did Paul want to go to Rome? Paul tells us in his letter to the Romans that he had cherished the idea of going to Rome for many years, but his evangelistic work in the areas between Jerusalem and Rome had prevented him from making the trip before this.[77] That same passage also tells us that Paul's future plans included having the brethren in Rome help him on his way for a missionary journey to Spain.[78] Further, Paul's old friends, Aquila and Priscilla, have by now returned to Rome, and many of Paul's acquaintances also had moved there (see the long list of names in the closing chapters of the epistle to the Romans). Paul had a longing to preach in Rome, too. He eventually will arrive in Rome, but in a way far different from how he expected.

19:22 – *And having sent into Macedonia two of those who ministered to him, Timothy and Erastus, he himself stayed in Asia for a while.*

And having sent into Macedonia two of those who ministered to him. These two were helpers like John Mark had been on the first journey.[79] They were sent to Macedonia to make the needful arrangements for the offering for Jerusalem.

Timothy. He was a delightful selection for the task Paul had in mind. He had been to many of these churches with Paul when the churches were planted.[80] We have not heard of Timothy since his arrival in Corinth from Macedonia, and his return to Thessalonica carrying the Thessalonian correspondence.[81] He may have accompanied Paul to Ephesus, or more likely, he joined him during Paul's three-year ministry there.

---

[75] See notes at Acts 13:6 for comments on the verb "passed through."

[76] 2 Corinthians 9:12-14. Compare notes at Acts 21:20.

[77] Romans 1:15, 15:23.

[78] See the *Epilogue* at the close of this commentary for a summary of Paul's later travels.

[79] Acts 13:5; 16:1-3. Most newer English translations render the phrase as "two of those who assisted him" or as "two of his helpers," indicating that Timothy and Erastus ministered *with* Paul.

[80] Acts 16:3, 17:14.

[81] Acts 18:5.

And Erastus. Erastus is probably the man who was treasurer of the city of Corinth,[82] even though the name Erastus was common in the ancient world. He was a very useful person to be sent with Timothy for the purpose of making the collection for the poor at Jerusalem. Paul was wise to employ a man accustomed to monetary transactions as a helper and adviser to the churches involved in this financial campaign.

He himself stayed in Asia for a while. How long he stayed here after sending Timothy and Erastus away on their mission is not certain.

- 1 Corinthians was written from Ephesus after Timothy and Erastus had been sent.[83] After the two had departed on their journey, very disturbing news came from Corinth. People from Chloe's household brought a letter and news by word of mouth.[84] Since one of the places where Timothy was to go on this mission was to Corinth, now that Paul has learned of the lack of harmony in the congregation there, and knowing how easy it would be for them to ruin the young preacher, Paul admonishes the Corinthian church to treat him with kindness when he arrives.[85]

- Paul also expected Timothy to return to Ephesus and report. When Timothy did finally arrive back and report to Paul, the news that the 1 Corinthian letter was not well received caused Paul to make his intermediate trip to Corinth.[86]

- When that mission failed, Paul returned to Ephesus, and then sent Titus to Corinth in the hope that he could accomplish what both he and Timothy had not quite succeeded in doing. Titus also had instructions to meet Paul in Troas when he had finished with his effort to correct the problems at Corinth.[87]

According to 1 Corinthians 5:6-8, Paul wrote 1 Corinthians about Passover time, and then intended to stay in Ephesus till Pentecost.[88] Having returned from the intermediate trip to Corinth and having dispatched Titus to Corinth, Paul now waits till it is time for his own departure for Troas and Macedonia. 1 Corinthians 16:9 tells of a great door that was opened for evangelistic work at Ephesus, but there were many adversaries, too.

    e. The riot of Demetrius and the silversmiths. 19:23-41

19:23 – *And about that time there arose no small disturbance concerning the Way.*

And about that time. It is in the spring of AD 57, some weeks after 1 Corinthians was written, that the riot of Demetrius occurs. While Paul is waiting in Ephesus for Pentecost,

---

[82] Romans 16:23; 2 Timothy 4:20.

[83] 1 Corinthians 4:17.

[84] 1 Corinthians 1:11, 7:1.

[85] 1 Corinthians 16:10-11.

[86] Evidence of this trip is found in 2 Corinthians 12:14 and 13:1 in the words "third trip."

[87] See notes at Acts 20:1 for the continuation of this story.

[88] 1 Corinthians 16:8.

it comes time for the regular yearly festival in honor of Artemis. Between our months of March and May, the Ephesian calendar had a month called Artemision, during which a special pilgrimage was made by worshipers of Artemis to her temple in Ephesus. Ordinarily a great multitude would come to the city. It is possible this riot followed a sparsely attended festival.

There arose no small disturbance. "Disturbance" is the same word used in Acts 12:18, only here it seems to have more the idea of tumult or riot than simply excitement. The actual events are detailed in the following verses. There had continually been opposition to Christianity in Ephesus. Paul speaks of "adversaries" in 1 Corinthians 16:9. Also, there is the statement about fighting with wild beasts at Ephesus at 1 Corinthians 15:32.[89] Now the opposition breaks forth again as Demetrius inflames the craftsmen by his speech.

Concerning the Way. "The Way" is one of Luke's regular names for Christianity.[90]

19:24 – *For a certain man named Demetrius, a silversmith, who made silver shrines of Artemis, was bringing no little business to the craftsmen;*

For a certain man named Demetrius. With the word "for" at the beginning of the verse, this begins Luke's explanation of the "disturbance." We do not know whether the Demetrius introduced here is the same man spoken of in 3 John 12. It was a common name, yet the Demetrius named by John was from the neighborhood of Ephesus.

A silversmith. A silversmith is one who works in silver in any way, either in making coins or jewelry, or making silver utensils or religious artifacts.

Who made silver shrines of Artemis. The word "shrine" is *naos*, the word often translated sanctuary, meaning the place where a deity dwells. What Demetrius made most likely were small models of the shrine with the statue of the goddess in it. Examples of these shrines made of terra-cotta or marble have been found around the site of Ephesus by archaeologists. While no silver shrines have yet been unearthed, reference is made to such in extra-Biblical literature.[91] Such miniature models would be purchased by worshipers of Artemis, or by visitors to Ephesus, and once they had been blessed in the temple at Ephesus, would be taken home and either placed reverently in their homes or worn as amulets.

---

[89] Whatever that "fight with the wild beasts" was, it was something that happened before 1 Corinthians was written, and is therefore different from the riot of Demetrius. Paul was a Roman citizen, and if Roman law was observed, he could not be made to fight with actual four-legged, wild beasts. Therefore, most commentators take the language of 1 Corinthians 15:32 as being figurative, symbolizing the violent opponents of Christ. Ignatius (*Ep. ad. Rom.*, c.3) speaks of himself as "fighting with wild beasts" – the very word Paul used – and describes the soldiers who kept guard over him on his journey from Antioch to Rome as the "ten leopards" who were his companions. Compare also 2 Corinthians 1:8-10.

[90] See notes at Acts 9:2 and 19:9 regarding "the Way."

[91] See "Diana" in *Hastings' Dictionary of the Bible*, Vol. I, p.605; Deissmann, *Light*, p.112ff.

Pagans commonly carry with them small images of their gods as a good-luck charm. The Romans regularly kept such images (called *penates*, or household gods) in their homes.[92] The huge number of worshipers who regularly came to Ephesus to worship would constitute a lucrative market for such shrines and make their manufacture a profitable employment.

Ephesian Artemis should not be confused with Diana of the Romans or Artemis of Greek mythology.

- The Greek Artemis was thought of as the daughter of Zeus and the sister of Apollo.[93] In the heavens she was Luna, the goddess of the moon. On earth she was Artemis, the goddess of the hunt, with a bow in her hand and a hunting habit for dress. In Hades, she was Proserpine.
- Artemis of the Ephesians was a very different goddess. She was the same as Cybele, the mother-goddess, the nurse of all, a fertility goddess.[94] A statue of the goddess represents her as a many-breasted female figure with arms extended in a gesture of welcome or invitation. From the waist down her legs are wrapped in cloth much like an Egyptian mummy, and this is covered with tier under tier of heads of lions, stags, oxen, bees, flowers, and corn. At Ephesus, her worship was presided over by a chief priest called *Megabyzos* and a body of priests called *Essenes* (king bees). The priestesses were even more numerous and were called *Melissai* (honey bees), and these were divided into three classes: *Mellierai* (those about to become priestesses), *Hierai* (priestesses), and *Parierai* (ex-priestesses). The worship was orgiastic, accompanied by frenzied dancing and ceremonial prostitution, and other abominations among which often was human sacrifice.

Was bringing no little business to the craftsmen. The silver shrines were sold to worshipers, and at most Artemision festivals there would be huge profits for the craftsmen who made the shrines. But not this year, it seems. The term "craftsmen" speaks of the higher class of workmen, what we might call "skilled labor." Barnes thinks that these were the laborers employed by Demetrius in the manufacture of the shrines.[95] Another possibility is that they were the leaders of the trade guilds mentioned in the next verse.

19:25 – *these he gathered together with the workmen of similar* **trades,** *and said, "Men, you know that our prosperity depends upon this business.*

These he gathered together. That is, Demetrius called a meeting of the men who worked at this trade.

---

[92] A similar thing is mentioned as early as the time of Laban, whose images Rachel had stolen and taken with her (Genesis 31:19).

[93] Compare also related notes and footnotes at Acts 16:16.

[94] The same deity was worshiped by the name of Astarte in Phrygia, and as Ashtoreth in Canaan. "Witchcraft" (see Special Study #17, "The World of the Occult," at the close of chapter 19) is the modern form of this same worship.

[95] Barnes, *op. cit.*, p.281.

With the workmen of similar *trades*. As already noted, shrines were made of clay and marble, as well as silver. The makers of these non-silver shrines are the ones spoken of. "Demetrius was organizing every branch of the guild in a concerted effort to put pressure on Paul and his preaching."[96] This was a meeting of one of the ancient labor unions (i.e., trade guilds), which were found among almost every kind of trade in the Roman empire.

And said, "Men, you know that our prosperity depends upon this business. The word translated "business" is the same one that was translated "profit" at Acts 16:19. 'We are dependent on this craft for a living,' Demetrius reminded them.

19:26 – *"And you see and hear that not only in Ephesus, but in almost all of Asia, this Paul has persuaded and turned away a considerable number of people, saying that gods made with hands are no gods at all.*

And you see and hear that not only in Ephesus, but in almost all of Asia. The Roman province of Asia, of which Ephesus was the capital, is intended. It is the area which Paul has been evangelizing for the past three years.

This Paul has persuaded and turned away a considerable number of people. Demetrius' assertion, though perhaps betraying a certain alarm and exaggeration, nevertheless is an assessment of Paul's labors from the standpoint of an outsider, similar to what Luke's comment (verse 10) was. A half century later, Pliny in his letter to the emperor Trajan uses language which is hardly less strong. He speaks of "deserted temples," "worship neglected," "hardly a single purchaser" found for sacrificial victims, because the Christians have so converted the whole area."[97]

Saying that gods made with hands are no gods *at all.* See notes at Acts 7:48 and 17:24 on the expression "made with hands." Demetrius correctly represented Paul's teaching when he said that Paul preached against their idolatrous worship.

19:27 – *"And not only is there danger that this trade of ours fall into disrepute, but also that the temple of the great goddess Artemis be regarded as worthless and that she whom all of Asia and the world worship should even be dethroned from her magnificence."*

And not only is there danger that this trade of ours fall into disrepute. "Trade" is not the same Greek word used in verse 25, but the English gives the right idea, speaking of the business in which they were engaged. The danger was that the "shrine making" part of their work would "come to be held in contempt" and they would have no further employment.

But also that the temple of the great goddess Artemis be regarded as worthless. In verse 1, the temple's location northeast of downtown Ephesus has been noted. The temple, which was built to house the image of Artemis, was several times built and rebuilt.[98]

---

[96] Dale, *op. cit.*, p.91.

[97] Pliny, *Epistle*, X.96.

[98] As noted previously, the Temple of Artemis in Ephesus was one of the wonders of the ancient world.

- One building was completed in the reign of Servius Tullus, c. 570 BC.
- Another building was designed by Ctesiphon, 540 BC, and was completed by Daphnis of Miletus and a citizen of Ephesus. This second building was partially destroyed by fire on the very day on which Socrates was poisoned in 400 BC. It was more completely destroyed in 356 BC by the philosopher Herostratus, who confessed, on being put to torture, that his only motive was to immortalize his name.
- The next structure on this site took 220 years to complete, and was the one standing in Paul's day. Pliny tells us much about the building.[99] The building was 377 feet in length, 180 in breadth, and was supported by 117 pillars of Parian marble, each of which was 60 feet high. 36 of these pillars were variously carved; the rest were finely polished. Each pillar, it is supposed, with its base contained 150 tons of marble. The whole building was built on layers of charcoal and hides stuffed with wool as a protection against earthquakes. The doors and paneling were made of cypress wood and the roof of cedar. The interior was decorated with gold and with the finest statues the ancient artists could produce. There were paintings and sculptures by the great masters of Greek art: Phidias, Polycletus, Calliphron, and Apelles. So magnificent was the building that it was said, "The temple of Artemis in Ephesus alone is a house suitable for gods," and the sun, so the saying ran, "saw nothing in his course more magnificent than the temple of the Ephesian Artemis."[100]
- Almost as many years were consumed in the destruction of the temple as in its building. Nero robbed this temple (as he also robbed the temples of Delphi, Pergamum, and Athens) of many of its art-treasures for the adornment of his Golden House at Rome.[101] Trajan sent its beautifully sculptured doors as an offering to the temple at Byzantium. The ruins furnished materials for the church building erected by Justinian. (In fact, the building is now called the Mosque of St. Sophia.) The remains of the temple were burned by the Goths in AD 263. What Demetrius feared actually came to pass because of the preaching of the gospel of Christ.

Luke seems to have reproduced the precise title of the goddess in the words "the great goddess Artemis." The temple was not looked on as being Artemis' home, but rather the chief place where she was worshiped. She could also be worshiped anyplace where one of the little shrines might be located.

And that she whom all of Asia and the world worship. Again, "Asia" is a reference to the Roman province of Asia. The "world" was the Roman empire, the known world at that time. Bruce has given a note that there were at least 33 temples in different parts of the world where Ephesian Artemis was worshiped, in addition to all the places where the little shrines had been carried.[102] The kind of worship of which Artemis was a form was one of the oldest substitutes for Divinely revealed religion, so it could truthfully be said that the

---

[99] Pliny, *Natural History*, XXXVI.95.

[100] Philo Byz., *Spect. Mund.*, 7.

[101] Tacitus, *Annals*, XV.45.

[102] Bruce, *op. cit.*, p.399.

whole world worshiped Artemis.[103]

Should even be dethroned from her magnificence. There is a play on words in the Greek – "The *great* goddess was in danger of being robbed of her *greatness*." Demetrius is anticipating that unless Paul and the other preachers are stopped, this wonder of the ancient world would lose all her beauty and awe-inspiring majesty. There would be no one to keep up the maintenance of the building, or to bring the costly gifts that were needed to support the priests and priestesses, or to educate the children employed in the temple services, or to pay the retirement pensions to the priests and priestesses who lived past their 60th birthdays.

Boles sums up Demetrius' arguments. "He made two points: (1) Their trade would be injured. (2) Their religion would be in danger."[104] Notice that in both cases where Paul confronts the world of the occult, the cultists are worried about the profit they make from the people they take advantage of.[105]

19:28 – *And when they heard* **this** *and were filled with rage, they* **began** *crying out, saying, "Great is Artemis of the Ephesians!"*

And when they heard *this*. Demetrius' speech evidently was quite effective. He probably made his speech in some open place near the shop where the shrines were manufactured.

And were filled with rage. They were greatly enraged, particularly at the prospect of losing their livelihood.

They *began* crying out, saying. "They went on crying out," the verb tense implying continuous action.

"Great is Artemis of the Ephesians!" "Great" was often applied by the worshipers to Artemis. Thus in Xenophon, "I adjure you by your own goddess, the great Artemis of the Ephesians ...."[106] The same adjective appears on many of the coins and medals of the city. The cry was probably the usual prayer offered to Artemis by the worshipers in the temple at the edge of the city.[107] "Great Artemis of the Ephesians," they kept chanting over and over, praying to her for help and reaffirming their devotion to her. The result of such a continuous prayer is that their emotions would be raised, and soon they would look for a way to vent their emotions.

19:29 – *And the city was filled with the confusion, and they rushed with one accord into the theater, dragging along Gaius and Aristarchus, Paul's traveling companions from Macedonia.*

---

[103] Pausanias, *op. cit.*, IV.31.8; Xenophon, *Anabasis*, V.3.4.

[104] Boles, *op. cit.*, p.308.

[105] Compare Acts 16:19.

[106] Xenophon, *Ephes.* I

[107] William Ramsay, *Historical Geography of Asia Minor* (Amsterdam: Adolf M. Hakkert, 1962), p.410.

And the city was filled with the confusion. The shouts from the craftsmen's meeting place were heard elsewhere in the forum. There was a feeling of confusion, of something disturbing, that raced like electricity from person to person. There was something in the air, but they did not know quite what it was (verse 32). The craftsmen, still shouting their prayers, started down the marble street. Others joined the mob, not quite knowing what was happening, save that the leaders were disturbed about something.

And they rushed with one accord into the theater. "One accord" speaks of having one purpose in mind. The fact that they dragged along some of Paul's helpers indicates that their purpose was to vent their fury on what they thought was the cause of their reduced wages and lack of employment. The theaters of the Greeks were not only places for presenting dramas and plays, but also for political gatherings, and for public assemblies to transact the public business of the community.[108] The theater at Ephesus, next to the temple of Artemis, was its chief glory, being the largest such theater in the world.[109]

Dragging along Gaius and Aristarchus. Gaius was one of the most common of Latin names, and three or four different persons in the New Testament were known by this name: (1) the Macedonian named here,[110] (2) Gaius of Derbe,[111] (3) Gaius of Corinth, the host of Paul, the one Paul baptized with his own hands,[112] (4) Gaius to whom John addressed his third epistle.[113] The Gaius named here in Luke's history is evidently not mentioned anywhere else in the New Testament. Aristarchus was a Thessalonian[114] and is named in the epistle to Philemon as one of Paul's fellow-laborers.[115] He will travel with Paul on the trip toward Rome,[116] and was there a prisoner with Paul.[117] We wonder if the crowd rushing along the marble street happened to meet Gaius and Aristarchus by chance and seized them, or whether they searched for Paul at his place of lodging and, disappointed at not finding him, seized these two companions of his instead.

Paul's traveling companions from Macedonia. Did these men travel with Paul since the time he was last in Macedonia, or did they join Paul at Ephesus? Perhaps the church at Thessalonica sent them to help Paul evangelize Asia. The description given of them as "Paul's traveling companions" implies that they had traveled and helped Paul with missionary work beyond Ephesus.

---

[108] Josephus, *Wars*, VII.3.3; Tacitus, *History*, II.80.

[109] See notes at verse 1 for more information about the theater.

[110] A few minuscule manuscripts make only Aristarchus a Macedonian, which would allow us to identify this Gaius with Gaius of Derbe.

[111] Acts 20:4.

[112] Romans 16:23; 1 Corinthians 1:14.

[113] 3 John 1. Some believe the Gaius addressed by John is Gaius of Corinth.

[114] Acts 20:4.

[115] Philemon 24.

[116] Acts 27:2.

[117] Colossians 4:10.

19:30 – *And when Paul wanted to go into the assembly, the disciples would not let him.*

And when Paul wanted to go in to the assembly. He probably intended to address the crowd, and defend his own cause. Too, since his traveling companions, Gaius and Aristarchus, had been seized by the crowd, Paul was not one to leave them to suffer alone. He was no coward; he was ready to help his brethren, even if it might mean his own harm.

The disciples would not let him. The members of the Ephesian church would not permit him to risk his life with the mob in the theater. It has been observed in notes at verse 21 that when Romans is written (6 to 8 months after this riot) Aquila and Priscilla are in the city of Rome. At what time they left Ephesus, we are not told, so it is not possible to be sure if it was during this riot or at some other time that Aquila and Priscilla "laid down their own necks" (risked their lives) on behalf of Paul.[118] The Christians who restrained Paul very likely saved the lives of all three men. Paul, the famous preacher, by showing up in the theater would have incited the mob to drastic action. 2 Corinthians 1:8-9 seems to reflect the danger Paul knew he was getting into, if he ventured into the theater.

19:31 – *And also some of the Asiarchs who were friends of his sent to him and repeatedly urged him not to venture into the theater.*

And also some of the Asiarchs. In the Introductory Studies it has been noted that the Asiarchs were men from all over the province, elected to superintend the games and festivals in honor of Rome and the emperor.[119] Their duties would take them now to one city, now to another, according as festivals or games were held, now at Ephesus, now at Colophon, now at Smyrna. The fact they are in Ephesus lends strength to the suggestion that this riot took place during Artemision.

Who were friends of his. Though apparently not Christians, these Asiarchs had a respect for Paul. Their high regard for him stemmed from the fact that Paul always attempted to see that Christianity had a good reputation in the cities where he worked. Such a reputation greatly helps church growth, and can be earned without compromising the gospel.

Sent to him and repeatedly urged him not to venture into the theater. The very way the emissaries from the Asiarchs worded their plea expresses the feeling of danger they had for Paul's life. The Greek reads, "not to give himself into the theater;" that is, 'Don t throw away your life by going into the theater.'

19:32 – *So then, some were shouting one thing and some another, for the assembly was in confusion, and the majority did not know for what cause they had come together.*

So then. The two conjunctions translated "so then" seem to carry the account back to what was happening in the theater, after the explanatory note of what had been going on between the apostle, the disciples, and the Asiarchs, outside of it.

---

[118] Romans 16:4.

[119] See Introductory Studies, p.*xxx-xxxii* for more information concerning the Asiarchs.

Some were shouting one thing and some another, for the assembly was in confusion. The verb tense says they "kept on shouting." This account is graphic enough to lead commentators to suggest the details were learned from one of the two who had been dragged into the theater by the craftsmen. Aristarchus will accompany Paul and Luke to Jerusalem and then toward Rome, and Luke could have gotten this information from him. The confusion that had been observed outside the theater (verse 29) continues to reign inside the theater. The word translated "assembly" is *ekklēsia*, the word sometimes used for "church." But here, as in verse 39, it has reference to the public gathering in the theater.

And the majority did not know for what cause they had come together. It was not a lawful assembly (as the town clerk is careful to point out, verse 39), for if it had been, someone would have been presiding and there would not have been all this confusion as to why they had come together. This note seems to imply that as the craftsmen passed down the marble street toward the theater, many of the people in the forum joined them, only to be left in confusion when they arrived at the theater, wondering what the hubbub was all about. Perhaps some thought that a town-meeting had been called, only to learn from the town clerk's speech that no such meeting had been called at all.

19:33 – *And some of the crowd concluded it was Alexander, since the Jews had put him forward; and having motioned with his hand, Alexander was intending to make a defense to the assembly.*

And some of the crowd concluded *it was* **Alexander.** The reason Alexander was put forth is at best conjecture. The general thread running through the paragraph seems to be that the silversmiths were angered by someone who had threatened Artemis, but who it was, or what was said, no one in the crowd seemed to know. When Alexander was put forward, some in the crowd concluded he was the one the craftsmen were unhappy with.

Who this Alexander was is not known.[120] Some have tried to identify him with "Alexander the coppersmith" who had in some way done much harm to Paul, and whom, with Philetus, Paul had excommunicated.[121] Others suggest that he was one of the leading Jews in the community, perhaps a ruler of the synagogue.

Since the Jews had put him forward. They apparently rushed him up onto a raised platform, perhaps the stage in the theater, where he could be seen and heard. What motive the Jews had in putting him forward is hard to determine.

- Meyer, following the reading of the KJV, suggests he was a Jewish Christian who was put forward by the Jews maliciously, in the hope that he would be sacrificed to the popular tumult.[122]

---

[120] There is also a manuscript variation here which causes some ambiguity of meaning.

[121] 2 Timothy 4:14. It is doubtful if the two men named Alexander are the same. Only their names, and a possible connection of both with Ephesus, is in favor of identifying the two. Against the identification is the fact that the crafts of each are different (silversmith v. coppersmith), and the one excommunicated by Paul was a Christian, where the one in the theater seems to have been Jewish (verse 34).

[122] Meyer, *op. cit.*, p.375. Use is made of the word "defense" (*apologeomai*) to support this interpretation.

- Another suggestion is that the Jews were anxious to guard against the suspicion that they were at all to be identified with Paul or his companions. Though the Old Testament taught Jews to be opposed to idolatry, Romans 2:22 indicates the Jews could ignore the abhorrence for idols they were supposed to show if it was to their benefit. Supposedly, Alexander gets up to tell the crowd in the theater not to confuse all Jews with Paul and the Christians.

And having motioned with his hand. He raised his hand, motioning for the crowd to become silent, so that he could speak to them and be heard.

Alexander was intending to make a defense to the assembly. If Alexander was about to defend the Jews, the general content of his speech would have been, "The Jews have had nothing to do with the diminution of Demetrius' profits, so please do not concentrate your anger on us. Concentrate it on the Christians!"

19:34 – *But when they recognized that he was a Jew, a* **single** *outcry arose from them all as they shouted for about two hours, "Great is Artemis of the Ephesians!"*

But when they recognized that he was a Jew. By his dress and his features they would recognize him as a Jew. There was not much distinction being made between Jews and Christians in this early period of the church, as the remainder of chapter 19 confirms. Both were opposed to the idolatrous practices of the pagans

A *single* outcry arose from them all as they shouted for about two hours, "Great is Artemis of the Ephesians!" This they shouted, at first, to prevent Alexander from speaking. The shouting then continued in order to show their devotion to Artemis. Remember, this was the exact language they used in order to invoke the help of Artemis when worshiping in her temple precincts.[123]

19:35 – *And after quieting the multitude, the town clerk said, "Men of Ephesus, what man is there after all who does not know that the city of the Ephesians is guardian of the temple of the great Artemis, and of the* **image** *which fell down from heaven?*

And after quieting the multitude the town clerk said. The conduct of the crowd especially worried the town clerk, so he set about to calm the people's emotions and quiet the crowd. He finally succeeded, and then made an address to the assembly.

The Greek word translated "town clerk" is the same word translated "scribe" in the gospels. The English word "town clerk" probably expresses, as well as any English word could, the function of this man. He was the most important city official in Ephesus,[124] one who was in contact both with the Roman proconsul and also with the lawful assembly of the Ephesian citizens. He would express the wishes and decisions of the Romans to the assembly, and the decisions of the assembly back to the Roman officials. Among his duties

---

[123] See comments at verse 28.

[124] Only the proconsul, who was a Roman government official, held a more important position in Ephesus.

were the drafting of official decrees, the guardianship and tabulation of state papers, keeping the citizenship lists, and acting as bursar for all the city funds.

Men of Ephesus. As we read this speech, we find that, like the Asiarchs, the town clerk obviously looks on Paul and the Christians with respect. He has no feeling of fanaticism and does not wish to be a part of a persecution against them. Yet he dares not oppose the multitude; instead he tries to soothe them with a loud profession of his devotion to the religion of the city. He will appeal to their superstition and to their civic pride.

> An interesting inscription of the date of Trajan, from an aqueduct at Ephesus, gives nearly all the technical terms that occur in the town clerk's speech, and so far confirms the accuracy of St. Luke's report: "This has been dedicated by the loyal and devoted Council of the Ephesians, and the people that serve the temple (*neōkoros*) Peducaeus Priscinus being proconsul, by the decree of Tiberius Claudius Italicus, the town clerk of the people."[125]

What man is there after all who does not know that the city of the Ephesians is guardian of the temple of the great Artemis. The word translated "guardian of the temple" (*neōkoros*) does not appear elsewhere in the New Testament, though it has been found on inscriptions and on several Asiatic coins, one of which bears the name of Nero and could be nearly contemporary to Paul's time in Ephesus.[126] The word is derived from *naos* (temple) and *koreō* (to sweep), but it was regarded as an honor among the ancients to have charge of the temples of the gods and to keep them in order. Ephesus could boast of being the guardian of the temple of Artemis, just as other cities could boast the same title in relation to other deities.

And of the *image* which fell down from heaven. The marginal reading, "fell down from Zeus," is an interchangeable or equivalent expression.[127] Anything that fell from the sky, like a meteorite, was considered to have been sent from Zeus whose home was thought to be in the sky. Two explanations have been given to this expression. (a) Some think it means that the image was so old that no one knew for certain about its origin. (b) Others think the original image worshiped at Ephesus was a meteorite (which of course actually would have fallen from the sky) of such a configuration that to some it resembled a many-breasted female.[128]

19:36 – *"Since then these are undeniable facts, you ought to keep calm and to do nothing rash.*

Since then these are undeniable facts. The language of the town clerk has the ring of an

---

[125] Plumptre, *op. cit.*, p.328.

[126] A picture of this coin can be seen in Conybeare and Howson, *op. cit.*, p.433.

[127] Herodotus, *History*, I.11, gives "fallen from heaven" as an equivalent to "fallen from Zeus."

[128] See notes at verse 24 on the shape of the statues of Artemis which have been found by archaeologists. Meteorites had become objects of worship at Troy (the Palladium), in Sicily (Ceres), and at other places. Cicero, *in Verr.*, V.187; Bruce, *op. cit.*, note 53, p.398.

official acceptance of the established system of worship in the area, rather than of any strong personal devotion. Such language has often been heard from the defenders of institutions which were almost on the verge of decay and ruin.

You ought to keep calm. The town clerk's *first argument* emphasizes that the popular tumult was useless (verses 35-36) because no one was about to forget the fact that Ephesus was the guardian of the temple of Artemis. Such knowledge was not going to become more widespread because they filled the forum and theater with shouts of devotion to their goddess.

And to do nothing rash. Actions such as the inciting of the silversmiths, which resulted in this parade to the theater, were really more emotion than the result of careful thought. It would be rash to continue in the same pattern that started the day, and the results might be other than they had intended.

19:37 – *"For you have brought these men* **here** *who are neither robbers of temples nor blasphemers of our goddess.*

For you have brought these men *here*. Either the town clerk accuses Demetrius and his fellow craftsmen of bringing Gaius and Aristarchus to the theater, or he accuses the whole crowd. Note that the verse begins with "for"; the town clerk is explaining that something rash has already been done. Perhaps at the place in his speech the town clerk gestures toward the prisoners, who have been held near the platform all this time.

Who are neither robbers of temples. There is emphasis in the Greek, which reads *"these men are not robbers of temples."* [129] The wording creates an implied contrast, perhaps between Gaius and Aristarchus on the one hand, and the Jews who tried to put forward Alexander on the other. "Robbing temples" is found in inscriptions as denoting a crime to which the severest penalties were attached.[130] At the very least, the town clerk is saying that the two men who were dragged into the theater are not guilty of any crime that Ephesian law is interested in.

Nor blasphemers of our goddess. Paul and his preacher friends had not used harsh, reproachful, or scurrilous language as they spoke of the folly of religions such as Ephesian Artemis. They indeed opposed idolatry; they had reasoned against it; they had performed miracles which showed it to be second rate when compared to Christianity; they had endeavored to turn the people from it. But instead of naming names and ridiculing by name, Paul drove home principles ("gods made with hands are no gods at all") which undermined the very foundations of such pagan religions.[131] The town clerk's *second ar-*

---

[129] A word of explanation may be useful for the KJV's rendering, "robbers of churches." In the 1600s, "church" was a word used of pagan temples, just as often as we use it for Christian buildings.

[130] John T. Wood, *Discoveries at Ephesus* (London: Longmans, Green & Co., 1877), Vol. VI, 1 (page 14).

[131] There is a great need for positive preaching, preaching which will encourage and uplift the hearers, even as sin is also denounced and pointed out. Care must be taken that as sin is denounced, the hearers are not left with a feeling of having been beaten and driven down. As Paul pointed his hearers to a better way after he pointed out their sins, so our preaching and teaching must point people in the right direction,

gument is that the popular tumult was unjustifiable (verse 37), for the "defendants" were not guilty of any crime.

19:38 – *"So then, if Demetrius and the craftsmen who are with him have a complaint against any man, the courts are in session and proconsuls are* **available;** *let them bring charges against one another.*

So then, if Demetrius and the craftsmen who are with him have a complaint against any man. The town clerk's *third argument* is that the popular tumult was unnecessary (verses 38-39). He calls attention to the proper channels through which Demetrius and the craftsmen could go, if they had any grievance. 'You should be law-abiding citizens, and let the proper authorities handle any violations of the law,' the town clerk counsels.

The courts are in session. Legal matters properly should be brought to the attention of the courts. These courts were customarily held in the forum.[132]

And proconsuls are *available.* If the courts that met in the forum were not able to handle the complaints, they could be appealed to a higher court. Strictly speaking, there was only one proconsul in each province.[133] Though the Syriac version has a singular "proconsul" here, the reading is not well supported, and the plural is apparently what the town clerk spoke. Several explanations have been given for the plural:

- Perhaps it is a colloquial way of saying "there are courts and there are judges."
- The proconsul might have several subordinates who heard cases on his behalf, and these are described as "proconsuls" since they spoke with the authority of the proconsul when they made decisions.
- By a strange combination of circumstances, perhaps there were actually two persons at this time at Ephesus who were invested with proconsular authority. Marcus Junius Silanus, a great-grandson of Augustus, was proconsul of Asia when Paul arrived in Ephesus in AD 54. Nero, the emperor, was also a great-grandson of Augustus. Shortly after his accession and with the urging of his mother Agrippina, Nero had Silanus poisoned. Two men, Celer and Helius, carried on the functions of government in the province until a new proconsul arrived. So the plural "proconsuls" may have referred to them.[134]

The town clerk is arguing that the complaint that Demetrius had might be brought before these judges with the certainty that it would be heard and decided.

Let them bring charges against one another. 'Let them accuse each other in the court. The laws are equal and impartial. Justice will be done.' Demetrius and his followers were to lodge any formal complaint they might have against the accused, whereupon the accused

---

and leave them with a feeling of positive hope and anticipation of a more abundant life.

[132] See notes at Acts 18:12 concerning the "courts" held in the forum.

[133] See the Introductory Studies, p.*xiv-xv*, for a description of the position of a proconsul.

[134] Tacitus, *Annals*, XIII.1.

would, in turn, put in a rejoinder. Thus, it could be said they were "bringing charges against one another."

19:39 – *"But if you want anything beyond this, it shall be settled in the lawful assembly.*

But if you want anything beyond this. The town clerk is recognizing that these citizens might have a matter of public rather than personal interest, in which case the public assembly (rather than the courts or the proconsuls) was the place to handle it.

It shall be settled in the lawful assembly. "Lawful assembly" has been preferred as a translation rather than "regular assembly." The latter seems to suggest that such town meetings could only be held on stated customary days, whereas (with permission from the Roman authorities) meetings could be called[135] to pass on some special business. Chrysostom tells us that the lawful assembly was regularly scheduled to meet on three different days each month.[136] Deissmann tells us that the lawful assemblies of the citizens met in the theater, and resolutions could be introduced and voted upon, and action taken on various civic and community problems.

19:40 – *"For indeed we are in danger of being accused of a riot in connection with today's affair, since there is no* **real** *cause for it; and in this connection we shall be unable to account for this disorderly gathering."*

For indeed we are in danger of being accused of a riot in connection with today's affair. "Accused" means to have the city's affairs called in question by the Roman government. There was a Roman law which made it a capital offense for anyone to be engaged in promoting a riot. "He who raises a mob, let him be punished with death."[137] If the Romans were to demand an accounting for the day's disorderly conduct, it might involve consequences far more serious than the loss Demetrius has attributed to Paul's preaching.

Since there is no *real* **cause** *for it.* The assembly had not been summoned in the lawful fashion, nor was what they were doing the proper way to handle such grievances as they had.

And in this connection we shall be unable to account for this disorderly gathering. The town clerk uses the most contemptuous word he can to describe the gathering. It was not a lawful assembly. It was a mob meeting to try to take the law into its own hands. If the Romans were to ask them to explain their actions, they would be unable to give a satisfactory reason, and they might lose their status and privilege of being a free city. The *fourth argument* advanced by the town clerk is that the popular tumult was dangerous.

---

[135] The word translated "assembly" is the same word elsewhere in the New Testament translated "church." The word means "called out." The "lawful assemblies" were "called out" by the town clerk. The "church" is "called out" by the Lord.

[136] Chrysostom, *Homily*, XLII.2.

[137] Barnes, *op. cit.*, p.287.

19:41 – *And after saying this he dismissed the assembly.*

And after saying this he dismissed the assembly. The town clerk's four arguments have quieted the crowd, and now he attempts to give an appearance of a lawful assembly to the gathering by dismissing it in the regular manner. Such an official dismissal would help to shield this disorderly gathering from any evil report that might get to the Romans.

McGarvey has noted that this is evidently the speech of a man well-skilled in the management of excited crowds, which, indeed, the town clerk would need to be.

> His assertion that no man could be ignorant of the devotion of Ephesus to the worship of Diana, or of the fact that the image was heaven-descended, was an open espousal of their cause. The remark that the unquestionable certainty of these facts ought to make them feel quiet, even though someone should contradict them, was the very remark to bring about the composure at which he aimed. Advancing then to the cause of the disturbance, like a trained advocate, he ignores the real charge against the disciples – that of denying that images made with hands are gods – and declares that the men are neither temple robbers or blasphemers of the goddess. Clearing them of this charge appeared to the majority, who "knew not wherefore they had come together," to be a complete vindication of the prisoners. Then, as for the men who had disturbed the multitude with private matters of their own, their proper recourse was to the proconsular court. This was calculated to turn the feeling of the people against the silversmiths, as having made tools of their neighbors for the benefit of their craft. Finally, the remark about the unlawfulness of the assembly and their inability to account for the riot was a hint of danger from the Roman authorities in the way of fines which might be imposed on the whole community. It made every man of property feel anxious to get away. The formal dismissal, as if the assembly had gotten through with its business and a motion to adjourn had been adopted, was the last skillful device of the clerk, and it sent the people down the streets toward home in perfect quiet.[138]

Idols

Jupiter and Mercury

---

[138] McGarvey, *op. cit.*, p.167-168.

The Acropolis, Athens

Drawing by Horace Knowles
from the British and Foreign Bible Society

SPECIAL STUDY #17

THE WORLD OF THE OCCULT

Just a few years ago, the Western mind found it difficult to believe in demons and satanic powers. Rationalism and Determinism were philosophies that made belief in the supernatural difficult, if not impossible. Now, with the rise of the "church of Satan" and with the increasing popularity of occult practices and witchcraft, the Western man is more and more willing to believe some of the truths the Bible has taught all along. There is still considerable skepticism, but it should be noted that many verses in the Bible only make sense when the reality of the world of the occult is granted; these same verses do not make sense when interpreted from a purely naturalistic standpoint.

Important terms need to be defined at the outset.

- "Occult" is derived from the Latin *occultus*, which means hidden or secret or mysterious. It almost always has to do with the spiritual, unseen world, the world where the devil and demons hold sway and bear influence.
- We shall examine four areas: mantic, magic, spiritism, and doctrines of demons. All of these have connection with the world of the occult.
- "Demon" is understood to be a created spiritual being, one of the angels that rebelled against God prior to the creation of the world.[1]

Of the dozens of verses that speak of the world of the occult, several are notable for the illumination they provide to this topic. (1) *Mark 5:1-20*. Note the superhuman strength because of the demons who possessed the Gadarene, and the number of demons in the man. As the demons are being exorcised, one of the last places they wish to go is into swine. (2) *Luke 11:14ff*. When the demon was cast out, the house was left empty, and the demon came back to fill the spiritual vacuum. So it can likewise be with men today. Note the number of demons in this person at the end. (3) *Acts 16:16ff*. Divination may be done by the power of demons. Also, the possessed girl gave out a false message, "Jesus is *a* way of salvation." Paul cast out the demon "in the name of Jesus." (4) *Acts 19:16ff*. Here were Christians involved in magic, who confess it publicly and repudiate it. Following the Lord Jesus Christ is absolutely opposed to magic practices, else why would the Ephesian Christians reject their former way of life so completely? (5) *Colossians 1:13*. When a person becomes a Christian, he is delivered from the kingdom of darkness and translated into the kingdom of Christ. He is freed from one person's sphere of dominion, and introduced to another's. (6) *Ephesians 6:10-18*. The "beings" against whom the Christian is wrestling are of different orders (i.e., different grades of authority) in the world of demons. Those demons motivate men, who in turn harass the Christians. The passage gives information about how to be prepared to meet these enemies when they attack.

---

[1] See Special Study #11, "Demons and Demon Possession," for more detail concerning the identity of demons.

Interest in the occult is exploding. In some countries, it has become the fastest growing religion. Millions of people are involved. In the United States, where involvement in Christianity is declining, there are evidences that people are accepting one of the devil's substitutes: astrology, witchcraft, spiritism, and several kinds of Eastern religion are winning great numbers of devotees. Perhaps it is time for the church to become reacquainted with some of these ancient religious practices in order to be able to recognize the warnings and prohibitions about them found in the pages of the Bible.

The basic assumptions behind each of the four areas of the world of the occult are these: the spirits possess knowledge or power desired by men, and the spirits are willing to impart it to men under certain conditions. Often, this knowledge or power is desired either for the person's protection from evil, or for his own well-being.

I. MANTICS[2]

This area of occult practice has to do with obtaining *knowledge* from the occult powers. It is the area of the occult sometimes called "divination"[3] or "soothsaying."

A. Examples

The division of this area of occultic practices into two major headings – Impersonal v. Personal – is somewhat artificial, but it aids in outlining the topic. Each of these separate examples is a means by which people have tried to, and in fact do, make contact with the demons for purposes of gaining "knowledge" – either of the past, the present, or the future.

1. Impersonal Methods of Divination

   a. Astrology

Astrology is an ancient belief that a person's destiny is determined by his horoscope, and that the plan for his life is to be found in the pattern of the stars at the time of his birth.

- *Zodiac* – The heavens are divided into twelve sections ("houses"), each with a title appropriate to the star formations (i.e., "signs" – Libra, Aries, Aquarius,[4] etc.) in that house.

---

[2] Many of the technical words in this section end in the letters -*mancy* (e.g., cheiromancy, rhabdomancy), which represents the Greek word *mantis*, which speaks of "inspiration from a god."

[3] "Divination" comes either from *deus* (god) or from *divus* (pertaining to gods).

[4] Astrologers divide history into 2000-year-long periods. The age of Aries, symbolized by a ram, thought to suggest God the creator, ended about the time Christ was born. The age of Pisces followed. Pisces is symbolized by a fish, is considered a sorrowful age (as represented by the death of Christ), and is marked by tears and dissolution. Now, so the theory goes, the age of Aquarius is dawning. This age, symbolized by air, is to be a sort of new spiritual beginning, marked by the promise of universal brotherhood, wide learning, and the shedding of our hurtful inhibitions. Imbibing ideas advanced in media such as the musical "Hair," this generation rejects the standards and mores of the prior generation because, the theory goes, we are in the grip of newly operative celestial powers, so of course we will have new rules and standards.

- *Horoscope* – A diagram of the position of the stars and planets at the time of one's birth, asserted by astrologers to reveal an individual's personality and destiny, and which also predict national events.[5] The Tower of Babel in Genesis 11 may have been an ancient attempt at worship of the "gods" who inhabit the houses in the heavens.[6]
- *Acupuncture,* the ancient Chinese method of healing, is connected with astrology. The gold and silver needles represent the sun and moon. If the sun and moon are right, the cure is definite. If the patient is a believer in astrology, there is more possibility he will be cured.

b. Crystallomancy

This method of divination uses a crystal ball, or a pond of still water, or a mirror, into which the diviner gazes in order to "see" the events, either national or personal, about which he wishes to know. *Nostradamus* was a famous 16th century soothsayer. *Jeane Dixon*, who got her information from a crystal ball and a talking snake, was a renowned prophetess in the 20th century. *Edgar Cayce*, called the "sleeping prophet," made medical diagnoses and prescriptions while in a trance. *Sirhan Sirhan*, in the months before he fatally wounded Robert F. Kennedy, steeped himself in the lore of occultism, primarily that of a mirror mantic. Sirhan studied Sirhan in a mirror hour after silent hour, day after day. It was during one of his self-induced trances that he scribbled over and over, "Kennedy must die!"[7]

Note again: the power is not in the mirrors, the crystal balls, or any other of these impersonal objects. By means of these the medium clears his mind to make it a vehicle to which the demons can communicate. The medium is making himself wide-open and receptive to messages from the occult world. What the demons predict, they then try to make come true, and much of the time they are successful. This is why Jeane Dixon's predictions are right about 70% of the time. Sometimes, however, the demons are overruled by a higher power.

c. Bibliomancy

This method of divination is the study of "secret messages" found in books, especially the Bible.

d. Numerology

Numerology is the analysis of the hidden – supposedly prophetic – meaning of numbers. The letters of your name and your birthdate provide the numerical value used to predict your future. "Why were your parents so anxious to select a suitable name for you

---

[5] One of the problems with horoscopes is that if a person has a horoscope cast by two different astrologers, the horoscopes most likely are different, though presumably cast for the same person and based on the same raw material.

[6] Wm. J. Peterson, *Those Curious New Cults* (New Canaan, CT: Keats, 1973), p.15.

[7] *Time Magazine*, April 4, 1969, p.28.

at the time of your birth?" asks a modern numerologist. "Because your name signifies your destiny and is the medium through which your character is expressed. It is the sign board or blueprint along your road to success. Your parents sensed this and unconsciously named you for the particular character you were destined by birth to express."

e. Cartomancy

Cartomancy is divination by card-laying. A popular modern form is found in the *Tarot Cards*, a deck of 78 cards which can supposedly reveal the secrets of people and the universe. A common deck of playing cards can be used by the diviner and accomplish the same objective.

f. Palmistry / Cheiromancy

The Greek for hand is *cheir*. The addition of *mantis* suggests the idea of divination (i.e., gaining knowledge) by reading the hand. According to this occult belief, there are inbred characteristics reflected on the left hand, and acquired characteristics reflected on the right. There are four main lines (heart, head, fate, and life) as well as seven planet mounds on each person's palm. The presence of the mounds indicates the presence of certain personality traits; the absence of these mounds indicates the absence of those traits.[8]

g. Tea Leaves

Similar use for purposes of divination are made of coffee grounds, beetle crawlings, plant growth, and bones (i.e., the ancient Viking method of divination, called Runes). A well-known example is a scene from the novel *Moby Dick*, in which the black sailor saw his own death predicted after he cast the bones, and then sat stoically and waited for it to come.

h. Lots

The casting of lots (including sortilege) is another method of divination. As is the case with several of these methods of divination, there is a genuine, God-approved method talked about in the Bible, as well as an illicit, counterfeit, and prohibited method.

The *Urim and Thummim* in the Bible was a legitimate form of divination. Proverbs 16:33 gives some idea of how the method worked. Urim, if it was cast into the lap, brought to light the guilt of the subject. Thummim established his innocence. 1 Samuel 14:37 also gives an idea of the method. Only one question, with two alternative answers, could be asked. It was the priest's prerogative to handle the casting of the lots. By means of Urim

---

[8] The seven mounds and supposedly what they signify are: (1) Jupiter denotes honor and a happy disposition; (2) Saturn, prudence and therefore success; (3) Apollo, appreciation of beauty; (4) Mercury, scientific, industrial, and commercial interests; (5) Mars, courage; (6) Moon, dreamy disposition; (7) Venus, amorous nature. We wonder why, since new planets have been discovered by the astronomers, the astrologers still base their practice on the old belief of a universe with but seven planets?

and Thummim, criminal cases were settled,[9] men were appointed to office,[10] the promised land was divided up,[11] the scape goat was chosen,[12] men were chosen for the army,[13] priests were chosen to serve,[14] and men could inquire of Jehovah.[15] The use of this means of divination began to decline after the time of David and the rise of the prophetic office. The Talmud says the Urim and Thummim were missing from the second temple.[16] Josephus says it was obsolete 200 years before his time.[17] Yet Matthias was selected to the office of apostle by the casting of lots.[18]

There are some illegitimate methods of divination by lots also found in the Bible. *Bellomancy* (interpretation of the future by throwing arrows)[19] and *rhabdomancy* (using a divining rod or a pendulum)[20] are examples. A *dowser* is one who searches for lost, hidden, or uncovered objects with the use of a "divining rod" or a "pendulum." Far from being "fun," or a party game, a simple and harmless practice, dowsing and pendulum use often result in serious mental and psychic disturbances.[21]

I Ching remains a popular book with college age young people. It is the Chinese Book of Changes, containing methods and explanations of prophecies, and utilizing a method of coin tossing and then consulting the book to guide in the decision making.

    i.   Hepatoscopy and Haruspicy

Hepatoscopy is divination by cutting an animal open and inspecting the liver. Each of the various parts of the liver, its lobes, the gall bladder, the ducts and so forth, had a special significance allotted to it. Haruspicy is the study of the entrails of the animal.

    j.   Ornithomancy

This is the study of the activity of birds in an effort to arrive at knowledge of the future.

---

[9] See Achan (Joshua 7:14) and Jonathan (1 Samuel 14:22). Jonah 1:7 also is an example of "casting lots," but it was not the Urim and Thummim, which only a priest cast.

[10] 1 Samuel 10:20ff.

[11] Numbers 26:56ff; Joshua 18-19.

[12] Leviticus 16:7-10.

[13] Judges 1:1-3, 20:9

[14] 1 Chronicles 24:5,7; 1 Samuel 26:13ff; Nehemiah 10:34ff.

[15] 1 Samuel 30:7ff; Joshua 7:14-18; Judges 20:27ff; 2 Samuel 2:1, 5:19, 5:23.

[16] Mishna, *Sotah*, IX.10; *Yoma*, XXI.b.

[17] Josephus, *Antiquities*, III.8,9.

[18] Acts 1:26. As in the case in Jonah, this was not via the use of the Urim & Thummim.

[19] Ezekiel 21:21 has Nebuchadnezzar determining which way to march by casting arrows.

[20] Hosea 4:12; Ezekiel 8:17. The rod and pendulum have been used by men to gain a knowledge of the future since the reign of the Chinese emperor Yu of the H-Sia Dynasty (2205 BC).

[21] Kurt Koch, *Christian Counseling and Occultism* (Grand Rapids: Kregel, 1972), p.81-93.

k. Graphology

This word speaks of character analysis based on handwriting. A person's character, disposition, and aptitudes are judged, or discerned, from his handwriting.

l. Pyromancy

The diviner gazes into the flames of a fire (rather than at tea leaves or a crystal ball) in an effort to blank his mind, so the spirits can communicate with him.

m. Omens

The idea of augury through reading of signs or omens has a legitimate side, as illustrated by the fleece of Gideon,[22] and by Jonathan deciding whether or not to attack the Philistines by the words he hears them speak.[23]

There is also an illicit or foolish side to omens. Such omens are divided into three classes: (1) those concerned with days and heavenly bodies (e.g., an eclipse on a certain day of the month); (2) those concerned with the features of human or animal birth (e.g., a child born with a left ear missing portended distress entering the land); and (3) omens seen in the movements of animals (e.g., a dog coming up on the right side was a good omen; a dog coming up on the left was an evil omen; a raven flying over was a portent of death).

2. Personal Methods of Divination

a. Oneiromancy

This is a form of divination in which through dreams one can learn the will of the gods. Some dreams are involuntary, are unsought by the person, and are legitimate. Some such unsought dreams have been used of God to communicate His will to men.[24] It is the dreams which are deliberately sought, often by incubation,[25] in order to receive a message from the spirits, that the dreams are illegitimate and prohibited. Other methods of inducing dreams are fasting and drugs.

b. Necromancy

This allegedly is contact with the souls of the dead for purposes of learning about the future. More will be said about this area of the occult world under the "Spiritism" topic.

---

[22] Judges 6:36-40.

[23] 1 Samuel 14:8-13.

[24] At Genesis 20:3 and 6; 31:10,11, and 24; 37:6; Daniel 2:9 and 7:1; Judges 7:9-14; Matthew 1:20 and 2:12; Acts 23:11 and 27:23 God gave revelations through dreams. See also His promise at Acts 2:17.

[25] "Incubation" is the technical term for sleeping in a sacred place, with the intent of having a dream (i.e., a visit from the god). Homer, *Iliad*, XXII.209; Cicero, *De Div.* I.34; Herodotus, IV.72 and I.181.

c. Clairaudience

Some mediums, after long involvement in the occult, "hear voices" which give them information about the future, or even the present, but a long distance removed from where the medium is at the moment.

d. Clairvoyance

Some mediums, after long involvement in the occult, are able to "see" and know about objects or events that are taking place a long distance away, and can tell about them before they happen, or even as they are happening. The spirits help the person to know what is happening.

B. The Bible Has Something to Say About Mantics

- *ASTROLOGY* (Heb., *ashshaph*) is plainly prohibited, as is Moloch worship, Saturn worship, the worship of the Golden Calf, and the worship of the "Host of Heaven."

    Deuteronomy 18:10,11; 4:19; 17:2-7; 2 Kings 21:6; 2 Chronicles 33:6; Isaiah 47:13; Jeremiah 8:1-3; 10:2; 19:13; Daniel 1:20; 2:2,10,27; 5:7,11,15; Zephaniah 1:4-6; 2 Kings 17:16; 2 Kings 23:4; Acts 7:42,43.

- *SOOTHSAYING* (Heb., *'anan*, "to observe the clouds"; and *gezar*, "seer") is prohibited. *'anan* is said by some to mean "augury," "observing the movements of animals and birds," while *gezar* literally means "cutter," i.e., dividing the heavens, or cutting animals open to examine the liver and entrails.

    Jeremiah 27:9; Isaiah 57:3 ("sorceress"); Isaiah 2:6; Micah 5:12; Daniel 2:27; 4:7; 5:7,11; Leviticus 19:26; Deuteronomy 18:10-14; 2 Kings 21:6; 2 Chronicles 33:6.

- *DIVINATION* (Heb., *qesem;* Greek, *puthen*), which is knowledge by direct interrogation of the spirits, is forbidden. This would prohibit cartomancy, ornithomancy, studying the arrangement of dregs in a cup, the interpretation of dreams, rhabdomancy, and crystallomancy.

    Deuteronomy 18:10-14; Numbers 22:9; 23:23; 2 Kings 17:17; Jeremiah 14:14; Ezekiel 12:24; 13:6-9; 21:22-29; 22:38; 1 Samuel 6:2; 15:23; Isaiah 44:25; Jeremiah 27:9; 29:8; Zechariah 10:2; Micah 3:6-11; Acts 16:16ff, and Genesis 44:1-5.

- *ENCHANTMENT* (Heb., *nachash*) sometimes seems to have the idea of divination, and is protested against by God's men. The Hebrew word is closely akin to "snake," and perhaps signifies a "snake-charmer" or "one who fascinates like a snake," e.g., a mesmerist or hypnotist. The word is used in connection with Joseph's divining cup (Genesis 44:1-4), and its use is akin to the more modern crystal-gazing with the hypnotic state induced by prolonged staring.

    Genesis 30:27 (Laban's superior knowledge is attributed to *nachash*); Deuteronomy 18:10-14; Acts 19:19; 2 Kings 17:17; 21:6; 2 Chronicles 33:6; Numbers 23:23, 24:1 (Balaam found enchantment and divination impotent against the people of God); 1 Kings 21:30.

- *HEPATOSCOPY* (Heb., *qesem*, "to divide") is referred to in Ezekiel 21:21.

- *RHABDOMANCY* is spoken of in Hosea 4:12 and Ezekiel 8:17.

- *TERAPHIM* (Heb., *teraphim*) were household idols, sometimes nearly life-size (1 Samuel 19:13,16) and sometimes miniature (Genesis 31:34,35), shaped like human bodies or simply human heads or busts. Involved was either ancestor worship (*necromancy*), or they were used as crystal balls today are used, either use being a method of divination.

   Samuel 15:23 (Samuel disapproved of them); Ezekiel 21:21; Zechariah 10:2 (Zechariah disapproved of them); 2 Kings 23:24; Genesis 31:19-35; 1 Samuel 19:13-19 ("images"); Judges 17:5; 18:14-20; Hosea 3:4.

- *OMENS* were looked for by the servants of Ben-Hadad the Syrian, 1 Kings 20:33.

- *PASSING THROUGH THE FIRE* was another means of divination, involving the sacrifice of children. Moloch, the fire-god, and other deities were worshiped by certain Canaanitish and other tribes with human sacrifices, and this seems to have been a method of obtaining an oracle. (See Porphyry, *Apud Euseb. Praep. Ev.* IV. 64.4; and *Diod. Sic.* XX.14).

   2 Kings 3:27; Deuteronomy 18:10, 11; 2 Kings 21:6; 17:17; 2 Chronicles 33:6.

- *DREAMS* (Heb., *halom*; Greek, *onar*) of the false prophets are warned against in the Bible, and incubation is clearly designated as evil (Isaiah 65:4).

   Jeremiah 23:28,32; 29:8; Zechariah 10:2. (Also see Sirach 34:1, 2, 5, 7).

   C. Divination is a Substitute for God's Providence.

All this desire for knowledge basically stems from a loss of awareness of God's providential control of our universe and lives.[26] Not being confident that a loving God is caring for us, people try to find comfort in the knowledge about the future than can be gained from demonic sources. Also lost is an awareness of the lordship of Jesus. Unless it is realized that our confession of Jesus as "Lord" means that we believe He is on the throne of the universe, actively causing things to happen in our world and in the everyday lives of God's children for their benefit, we will soon be searching for something to fill the vacuum. Thus, many people try to find satisfaction in the world of the mantic.

---

[26] Providence is that care, preservation, and control exercised by God over His creation so that it accomplishes the purposes for which it was created.

II. MAGIC

This area of occult practice has to do with gaining *power* from the spirit world. It is the area of the occult sometimes called "sorcery" or "witchcraft."

A. Preliminaries

It is difficult to find a good English word to express the idea involved in this part of the world of the occult. "Magic" sometimes has the connotation of pulling rabbits out of a hat, or sleight-of-hand tricks, or "sawing ladies in two." The idea of calling on occult powers never occurs to many who hear the word "magic." "Witch" or "witchcraft" has sometimes been used, but it too has come upon a questionable connotation. The witch is often caricatured as an old hag who rides a broomstick through the air, so that the concept of calling on occult powers does not readily come to mind in such a connection. "Sorcerer" and "sorcery" are probably the best words, for they have the connotation of seeking power through the help of demons.

For the sake of an orderly presentation, we make a distinction between two different forms of magic: white magic and black magic. There are two problems involved in this distinction. First, the meanings of the terms are fluid. Black magic used to mean invoking evil on one's enemies by the aid of evil spirits, curses, and spells. Now it has come to be Satanism, the worship of the devil. Second, the distinction could be misleading if it left the impression that some magic is good and some bad. Anton LaVey, a high priest of the First Church of Satan, researched witchcraft in the United States and England. "There is no such thing as a 'white witch,'" he said. "White witchcraft is pure mythology. All witches are drawing on occultic power, and that power does not originate with God!"[27]

Before introducing the specific information about white and black magic, it must be stated that some of the terms listed under the one could be and are involved in the other. For example, incantations are listed under black magic, but they are very much a part of the regular practices among the so-called white witches, too.

B. Examples

1. White Magic

a. Witch

A witch is a male or female who uses occultic powers for what he considers to be good or evil ends. In some versions of the Bible, such people are sometimes called "wizards" or "magicians" or "sorcerers."

---

[27] Walter R. Marlin, "Witchcraft and Satanism" in *The Kingdom of the Occult* (Costa Mesa, CA: One Way Library, 1972), Volume I.

b. Coven

Coven is analogous to a "brotherhood" or "congregation," being an assembly of thirteen or less witches, meeting often in someone's home. The meeting is led by the Head Witch, either male or female, who is often called a high priest or priestess. Traditional witches work robed, but modern witches, the Gardnarian and Alexandrian, work in the nude.

c. Book of Shadows

This is the "Bible" used by the coven. It contains charms, chants, spells, and incantations. It is read at every Esbat or Sabbat meeting. This traditional book of rituals is copied by hand by each new head witch after his initiation.

d. Esbat

This is the name given to meetings of the coven other than on one of the Sabbats. These once or twice weekly meetings are a more or less local affair. Meetings may include reports on accomplishments since the last meeting (did the charms and spells work?), laying plans for next week, and joining together in working magic and spells for the benefit of the other members of the coven.

e. Sabbat (Witches' Sabbath)

There are four (some books add four more – at the beginning of each season) main holidays in the witchcraft religion, and these are more of a regional affair than Esbats. The four are: May Eve (April 30),[28] Lammas (July 31),[29] Halloween (October 31),[30] and Candlemas (or Brigid's Day, February 2).[31] The Sabbats include initiation ceremonies for new members, and general "worship" which usually ends in a sex orgy.

f. Magic Circle, Altar, and Tools

A table stands at the north side of the Circle, on which are laid various items of the craft. The witch's black-handled knife, Athame, with engravings on it, is a ritual tool, used in casting and banishing the Circle. A white-handled knife is used within the Circle for fashioning other tools. Candles at each point of the compass around the Circle are variously designated as Earth, Air, Fire, and Water. Also appearing on the table are the Witches' Ladder, a string of forty beads, or a cord with forty knots; a Sistrum, a larger equivalent of a child's rattle, used for ritual purposes; a chalice; and a bowl for burning incense.

---

[28] This Sabbat introduces spring. The festival of Ephesian Artemis, called Artemision, was a witchcraft festival (Acts 19).

[29] This Sabbat introduces summer.

[30] This is the last day of the year for the witches. Predictions for the new year are made, since this night is the most propitious for contacting the spirits for purposes of divination.

[31] This festival introduces winter.

g. Thaumaturgy ("Lying Wonders")

Since the main idea in "magic" is power, there are various kinds of "supernatural" wonders that can be observed. *Telekinesis* is the movement or rearrangement of objects by spirit beings. *Levitation* is the capacity of solid objects to defy the laws of gravity and to be moved from the earth with no visible means of support. Chairs are made to rise from the floor. A cigarette lighter rises off the table. No one is touching the table, yet it rises off the floor.[32] Other examples of "lying wonders" will be listed under "Spiritism" below.

h. Amulets

An amulet is a charm, worn like jewelry, said to possess certain powers that will protect the wearer from harm, disease, witchcraft, snake bite, poison, and other perils, both bodily and spiritual. The *Ankh*, the Egyptian cross of life, is one example. The *Pentacle*, a disc shaped talisman which represents the earth element among the witch's working tools, and the crescent shaped metal "moon" are others.

i. Talisman

A talisman is thought to bring positive benefits to the wearer.

j. Charms

Grimoire is the name for books of spells and magical procedures. The classic grimoires are medieval,[33] the best-known being the *Key of Solomon* (whose whole title is *The Greater Key of Solomon the King*) and *Abra-Melin* (whose whole title is *The Book of the Sacred Magic of Abra-Melin the Mage*). Included are remedies to ward off evil spirits and the sickness and disease they cause, recipes for turning a bad omen into a good one, incantations to be whispered over the ear of the patient to be healed, and magical names (e.g., the sacred tetragrammaton, the names of angels like Raphael and Michael, etc.) that were thought to be specially powerful when chanted or recited as part of magical formulae.

k. Cabala

This Jewish mystery lore is based on an occult interpretation of the Old Testament, and is said to have been given by God to Adam, or Abraham, or Moses, and then handed down over the generations. This ancient Hebrew system centers on the "Tree of Life" (Sephiroth – ten inter-linked spheres), and its basic concept involves the theory of the soul's descent or ascent through these ten "spheres" to ultimate union with God (i.e., reincarnation).

---

[32] Merrill F. Unger, *Demons in the World Today* (Wheaton, IL: Tyndale House Publishers, 1971), p.39,40.

[33] Tradition attributes the compilation of *Key of Solomon* to King Solomon himself, but there is no evidence corroborating this attribution.

l. Hexagram

The six-pointed star known as the Seal of Solomon (it is called the "Star of David" in non-occultic circles) consists of two interlaced triangles, standing for the occult principle of "as above, so below."

m. Pentagram

The five-pointed star. With one point up, it represents a human being, and is sometimes used for invoking and banishing. In black magic rituals, two points of the star are up. The head of a goat is usually found in the center, with two horns defiantly pointed heavenward and three points of the star point downward representing the Trinity denied.

2. Black Magic

Black magic is the religion of Satan-worship. The devil is given higher standing than God and is worshiped through hideous ritual and sacrifice (animal and human). It means praying to the devil, seeking things from him, bargaining with him, and following the practices prescribed in Satanic worship.

a. Black Mass

The black magic antithesis of the Roman Catholic mass, it is a perverted sacrilege. The communion wafer and wine are contemptuously treated; all references to God or Christ are omitted or desecrated; hymns are sung (sometimes backwards); crosses are inverted, etc. The Satanic Bible is read at these services. The First Church of Satan, founded by Anton LaVey, San Francisco, 1966, worships with a nude woman on the altar, and the high part of the mass is when the high priest violates her.[34]

b. Esbath

Satanist covens usually hold their celebrations in parks or forests during the nights of the full moon. Nude participants follow ritual ceremonies akin to the old religion of Ephesian Artemis. At times the female victim involved is an innocent young woman kidnapped off the street.[35] Drugs are often used to produce hallucinations.

c. Hex

Satanists cast a spell or an evil wish upon their enemies. Hexing, or cursing, usually involves the invocation of demonic powers. A whole ritual, kept track of by counting the knots in the Witches' Ladder, may be involved as the curse is gradually accomplished.

---

[34] Martin, *ibid.*

[35] Although verifiable eyewitness accounts of Esbaths are rare or nonexistent, there is considerable anecdotal or secondhand information on this subject.

d. Incantation

A chant or a song is used in pagan rituals to invoke the blessing or curse of the gods. This is a part of the ceremony for both black and white magic rituals.

e. Voodoo

This is the West Indian and West African brand of black magic and includes charms, conjuring, snake worship, and witchcraft. Worship is at night, including prayers made to the snake, hysterical manifestations of priest and priestess, a dance for the initiation of novices, wild debauchery and indecency, cannibalism and human sacrifice.

C. Ways to Become Involved in Magic

There are four common ways to become involved in white or black magic.

1. Heredity

Magical powers are passed on by families that practice these rituals. The movie *Rosemary's Baby* describes this. Often the attempt to pass on the "ability" ends in death-bed tragedies if members of the family do not want to accept the gift the dying person wants to pass down, for the person cannot rest until it is passed. This is also referred to as diabolical succession.

2. Devil's Subscription

This is a blood ritual counterpart to Christian baptism, whereby one sells his soul to the devil in a black magical ritual.

3. Occult Experimentation

With the bookstores full of "how to do it" books, such as *Guide to the Supernatural*, many people are browsing through these, taking them home, trying their own experiments, and finding themselves slowly submerging. Occult games are available in stores, online, through catalogs and magazines, etc.

4. Occult Transference

Occult transference is the black magical equivalent of the Christian "laying on of hands," in which the power is passed from one person to another.

D. **Witchcraft is Dangerous!**

A little booklet, available in drugstores and supermarkets, titled *Everyday Witchcraft*, is a do-it-yourself booklet of magic for the masses. The cover blurb reads "Love, magic, charms, spells, fortune-telling – everything you need to know to enjoy occult power."[36]

Some of the statements in this booklet need to be listened to, for they come from a secular source, not from some religious fanatic hung up on the Bible:

- On page 4 is this sentence, "Though you needn't be a witch to practice witchcraft, there are some witchy things you must do, if you are to summon occult powers." Then it goes on to tell you the basic rules. *And what are you doing?* Summoning demonic forces to do your bidding!

- Another statement reads:

   Various malign influences are always loose in the atmosphere. No matter what you do or don't do, one day these forces may decide to focus on you, or your family. However, when you start practicing witchcraft, the chances of drawing the attention of these mischief-makers increases greatly.[37]

Again, what are you doing? Open the door, turn the knob – and what comes through are malign influences! You are inviting demons into your house!

Which of us can afford to carelessly, thoughtlessly, or intentionally become involved with such diabolical powers? The risks are simply too great! Consider the case of Charles Manson and his "family," who received wide publicity when Sharon Tate and a houseful of guests were found sadistically murdered.[38] An ex-convict, a self-styled prophet, calling himself God, Jesus, and Satan, drawing around him his community which he called Satan's slaves or "the family," Manson had a mentality very close to the Medieval "man in black" who reportedly ordered sacrificial killings and rewarded his followers with sex. When asked by a reporter why he did it, he said, "I'm the Devil, and all my women are witches." In fact, the various influences behind him show the logical terminus of so many of the fringe trends of this generation. Lawlessness, the use of drugs, the Eastern notion that he was beyond good and evil, the involvement in Satanist worship – all were fatally combined in this man. And it led to a horror which so shook society. Witchcraft *is* dangerous!

E. The Bible Has Something to Say About Magic

The KJV reads "Thou shalt not permit a witch (Heb., *kashshaph*) to live," (Exodus 22:18). The word would better be translated "sorceress" (see the ASV).[39]

---

[36] Delphine C. Lyons, *Everyday Witchcraft* (New York: Dell Publishing Co., 1972).

[37] *Ibid.*, p.31.

[38] *Time Magazine*, June 19, 1972, p.66.

[39] See below under "The Bible has Something to Say about Spiritism" for an explanation of the word "sorcerer."

- *WIZARD* (Heb., *yidh'oni*, "one who knows") is a male or female magician or sorcerer; one acquainted with the secrets of the unseen world; one who can interpret the ravings of a medium. At times this word shades off toward the divining function of the evil spirit that inhabits a necromancer (see below on "Spiritism"). Wizards are uniformly spoken of with scorn in the Scriptures.

    Leviticus 19:31; 20:6,27; Deuteronomy 18:10,11; 1 Samuel 28:3,9; 2 Kings 21:6; 23:24-26; 2 Chronicles 33:6; Isaiah 8:19; 19:3.

- *CHARMER* (Heb., *chabar*, "One who inflicts a spell, one who binds with magical knots") is a word which covers the chanting or recitation of certain magical formulae while keeping track of the process by use of the Witches' Ladder. It is a forbidden practice.

    Acts 19:13-20 (the "Ephesian Letters" were likely the magical formulae used to "charm"); Isaiah 19:3; 47:9, 12; Deuteronomy 18:11 ("spells"); Psalm 58:5.

- *AMULETS* (Heb., *kemia'*, "something tied to a person"; *lehashim*, "something whispered or muttered over") were objects that had been "blessed" and then were worn as a good-luck charm. Gems, rings, herbs, seeds, and bracelets have been so used. The Bible's attitude toward such amulets is negative.

    Isaiah 3:16-26 (amulets worn by women, moonlets and sunlets, like are still seen on Arab girls); 3:20 (the LXX has *peridexia*, armlets for the right arm); Proverbs 17:8; Ecclesiastes 10:11; 2 Maccabees 12:40 (the leader of the army was appalled to find amulets on the bodies of the dead soldiers); Genesis 35:4 (Jacob burned amulets at Bethel).

- *INCANTATIONS* (Heb., *lahash*, to whisper, to mutter, in imitation of the hiss of snakes) are formulas for charming. These are named in the Bible with disapproval.

    Ecclesiastes 10:11; Isaiah 3:3; Jeremiah 8:17; Psalm 58:4-5.

- *ELEMENTS* (Greek, *stoicheia*). In a context of Colossians 2:8, in which Eastern religious practices are being condemned as part of the Colossian heresy, "elements" likely describe what Hesychius writes about as he defines *stoicheia* as "earth, air, fire, and water, of which bodies are formed."

- *BOOKS* used in the magical rites were burned at Ephesus (Acts 19:19). These must have been the books of magical formulae, the "bibles" used in the magical rites at Ephesus.

- *MAGICIANS* (Heb., *chartom*) were men who used occult rituals and processes designed to control or influence the course of nature or to dominate men by the aid of supernatural powers. It is uniformly condemned. (Attention should be given to the verses under "Sorcery" below, for the word is closely allied.)

    Genesis 41:8,24 (Pharaoh called magicians to interpret his dreams); Exodus 7:11,24 (magicians of Egypt opposed God, and couldn't work a genuine miracle); Exodus 8:18 (the word in Exodus translated magician is *lehatim,* to wrap up, muffle – there was some hidden element or trickery to their deeds of magic); 8:7,19; 9:11; Daniel 1:20 (the king found Daniel [with the Holy Spirit] to be ten times better in every matter of wisdom and understanding than all the magicians and conjurers in his realm); 2:2,10,17; 4:7,9; 5:11.

- *IMPOSTERS* (Greek, *goētes*) may involve the exorcism of demons by magic, or by incantations. The word appears in 2 Timothy 3:13 ("seducers" in KJV), and the idea appears in Revelation 19:20. The word indicates that it is a trick, a deception; it is something done to take advantage of the people.

F. Magic is a Substitute for Holy Spirit Power

Just as divination (i.e., Mantic practice) is a substitute for genuine religion, so it appears that magic is one of the devil's substitutes, too. God's Holy Spirit gives individuals the power to live the Christian life, the power to master Satan and evil in their lives, and the power to accomplish worthwhile things for others in this life. But where people are not aware of the divine power that is available to them, they seek and hunger for help, and in blindness and folly they turn to the devil's counterfeit methods.

III. SPIRITISM

This area of occult practice has to do with gaining both *knowledge* and *power* from the spirit beings. Spiritism, sometimes called spiritualism, has been defined as "a spiritual activity, grounded in the persuasion that people can by means of certain mediums make contact with the deceased, and so acquire revelations and help from beyond."

A. Examples

1. Seances (Necromancy)

Seances are meetings at which communication with the "other side" is attempted through a medium, usually held around a circular table in a dimly lit room. Some common terms need identification.

- *MEDIUM* – The male or female who is in charge of the seance. He or she serves as a sort of relay station between the seen and unseen world. Spirits (demons) seem to want a body (medium) to work through.
- *CONTROL SPIRIT* – The spirit which is the first one with whom the medium always makes contact. The control spirit is usually named and reappears to one particular medium throughout his or her life. The medium will share with the control spirit who it is that is being called up from the other side.
- *FAMILIAR SPIRIT* – A term used by spiritualists to designate the spirit of a deceased person which manifests itself at a seance. This is actually an evil spirit which is impersonating the deceased (i.e., a spirit "familiar" with the dead person). Both the Hebrew term *obh* and the Greek *engastrimuthos* carry the idea that the demon speaks

through the medium who has been taken control of by the spirits.[40] Many spiritists really believe they are talking to the dead person's soul – not to demons who impersonate. This is part of the devil's deception.

- *TRANCE* – A state of semi-consciousness into which a genuine medium lapses during the seance; at times, the mind is made void of any conscious thought and becomes a vehicle for spirit communication. Mediums go into trances to invite (or let) the spirits in.

  2. Phenomena Produced by Spiritists

There are physical manifestations including telekinesis, materializations, apport and spirit writing.

Materializations are the forms in which the spirit beings make themselves visible to human beings. Usually the form is recognizable as the likeness of the deceased individual. What convinced Ben Alexander of the reality of the spirit world is ectoplasm (that out of which the materializations are made). In London, Alexander came into contact with a trumpet medium. Before engaging in a seance with him, he examined the room in which the seance was to be held. There was nothing but bare walls, no trap doors, only a red light at the ceiling. They sat around the room and the seance began. The medium went into a trance. A cool breeze went through the room though the doors and windows were closed. Energy waves began to go out through the medium's fingers or out of his abdomen, or out of his nose and mouth. The spirits would take these energy waves and fashion them into forms of people or animals or objects.[41] The same form appeared at meeting after meeting – the ectoplasm, that is, was shaped by the spirits into the same shape at each meeting; those who regularly attended the seances recognized him and called him by name.[42] During the seance the trumpet[43] began to rise from the floor where the medium had placed it. The spirits often spoke to those assembled at the seance. At times in this meeting room, they used the Bible and prayed over it, in hopes of bringing forth a greater phenomenon. One time the Bible began to rise, and slammed against the wall. Spiritualists think that an evil spirit has tried to come into the meeting, and that a good spirit has tried to expel it by throwing the Bible at it. The good spirits (?) promised it wouldn't happen again, but it did, over and over. (Demons were hurling the Bible across the room.)

Apport is the phenomena of objects being fetched over great distances and through solid walls by the power of demons. Walter Martin has given numerous examples of documented apports. One man, hands and feet tied, is sitting in a chair, in a room that is 85 feet above ground level. He rises off the chair, goes out through one window, across six

---

[40] A woman in a trance may speak in a man's voice if the dead person to be contacted was a man. It is the demons who are speaking out of the medium.

[41] Ben Alexander has handled and touched the materialized forms and has photographs of them; there is something there. Further information may be obtained by contacting Ben Alexander, Exposing Satan's Power Ministries, Inc., PO Box 11029, St. Petersburg, FL 33733-1029.

[42] The shape the control spirit took was always the same, and reminded Alexander of the cowled figure that appears on the Ouija boards.

[43] A trumpet is a cone-shaped implement through which the spirits speak.

feet of space, back in the next window, and floats back down into the chair. There is no ledge between the windows, nor was he ever untied during the whole apport. Another example is of a medium at a railroad station. At a given moment he disappears from the crowd that is standing around him, only to reappear immediately in the midst of a crowd at another station 100 miles away. There has been no train, but telegraph confirmation comes from the second station to the first that he has appeared there.[44]

Spirit writing is writing done unconsciously by a medium while in a trance. Once the trance is past, the medium cannot remember doing the writing. Spirit painting is another trance phenomenon done in similar fashion. The history textbooks used in a leading university in Brazil were written by a functionally illiterate Brazilian while in such a trance. In another case, classical music in the style of Beethoven, Chopin, and Shubert were composed and played by a woman who knows little music. It too was done while in a trance. The record made of her work, called "A Musical Seance," can be purchased.[45]

In addition to the physical phenomena, there are also what are called psychic phenomena involved in spiritism. Among these are clairvoyance, clairaudience, psychometry, hyperesthesia, and xenoglossy.

3. Ouija Boards

This ancient device for discerning the will of the spirits might have been included in one of the earlier sections of this Special Study, but it is presented here since it is a method of contacting spirits and its use is often accompanied by physical and psychic phenomena. It is a flat wooden board with each letter of the alphabet as well as ancient symbols and a "yes" and "no" area. Seekers place fingertips on a triangle which then moves (uncontrolled by the seeker) as it spells out its message. What actually happens is that an unseen intelligence takes control of the hand and moves the pointer. It doesn't always take two persons to "work" the Ouija board; it is possible to lift your fingers three inches off the pointer, and it will still follow the fingers to the letters. The ease with which the Ouija board can be procured, coupled with an inherent fascination to the novice, makes it one of the most deadly of all the spiritualist "devices." The operator of the board is easy prey for evil spirits. A substantial percentage of young people, even those who have grown up in the church, have "played" with this board. Those who have will testify that something unseen moves the pointer. It is dangerous to invite evil spirits to pay attention to you!

Several things happen when a person uses the Ouija board with some regularity. (1) He or she is committing divination, against which the Bible speaks in no uncertain terms. (2) He is inviting demons to pay attention to him. She calls on demon forces when she operates the board, and temporary possession can lead to permanent obsession. (3) He or she finds himself involved in the devil's compensation.

---

[44] Walter R. Martin, "Psychic Phenomena – Biblical and Otherwise" in *The Kingdom of the Occult*, Vol. 2. J. Stafford Wright, *Man, Mind, and the Spirit* (Grand Rapids: Zondervan Publishing House, 1972) lists other documented cases.

[45] Walter R. Martin, "Hypnotism – Medical and Occultic," in *The Kingdom of the Occult*, Vol. 2.

B. The Devil's Compensation

In much the same way that a drunkard experiences a "hangover" the morning after, the person who participates in seances and Ouija board activities will experience certain after-effects, called "the Devil's compensation." There are several stages, each more severe than the previous: (1) Mental depression. (2) Thoughts planted in the mind encouraging the person to commit suicide. (3) Clairaudience – i.e., many hear voices imparting "secret" information to them about the future. (4) Clairvoyance – i.e., seeing things over a distance as they happen or before they happen.

Each of these stages is a step toward demonization. Each of these stages brings on more bondage, and more compensation.

C. The Bible Has Something to Say About Spiritism

- *CONSULTERS OF FAMILIAR SPIRITS* (Heb., *obh*; Greek, *engastrimuthos*) are everywhere condemned.

  Leviticus 19:31; 20:6,27 (the spirit dwelt in the medium); Deuteronomy 18:11; 1 Samuel 28:3,7-9; 2 Kings 21:6; 23:24-26; 2 Chronicles 33:6; Isaiah 8;19ff; 19:3; 29:4.

- *NECROMANCY* (Heb., *darash 'el ha-methim*, "to call up spirits of the dead") is likewise prohibited. The word means to converse with the "dead" for purposes of consultation or divination.

  Deuteronomy 18:11; 1 Samuel 15:23; Ezekiel 21:21; Zechariah 10:2 Isaiah 8:19; 1 Samuel 28:7; Leviticus 19:31; 1 Chronicles 10:13 (the passage affirms that King Saul died because he consulted a medium!).

- *SORCERY* (Greek, *pharmakeia*, "drugs") would have to be included either under this category of spiritism, or under the previous one dealing with magic.

  Galatians 5:20; Revelation 9:21; 18:23; 21:8; 22:15.

- *SORCERY* (Heb., *kashshaph;* Greek, *magike*) would involve what we today have come to call levitation, apports, materializations, psychokinesis, and the like. God's attitude toward those who seek supernatural power and knowledge from the spirits is clearly delineated in these verses:

  Exodus 7:11, 22:18; Isaiah 47:9,12; Jeremiah 27:9; 2 Kings 9:22 (Jezebel is condemned as a sorceress); 2 Chronicles 33:6; Deuteronomy 18:10,11; Micah 5:12; Nahum 3:4; Malachi 3:5; Acts 8:9-13 (Simon the sorcerer could see that Satan's miracles were second rate!), 13:8-11, 19:19 (where the Greek is *periergeia*).

D. Spiritism is a Substitute for God's Resurrection Power

Having lost any idea of what the Bible says about death and the hereafter, people turn to spiritism to escape their fear of death, and to find out if there is something beyond. But what God promises is not mere shadowy survival after death – or reincarnation – but resurrection to a full and rich dimension of living (1 Corinthians 15:35ff; Philippians 3:21).

For ourselves, and for all our loved ones who have gone beyond, we can know that all those who trust in Christ are gone to be with Him forever, and that the joy and bliss they share are beyond our imaginations. What folly to substitute spiritism for awareness of God's resurrection power!

IV. DOCTRINES OF DEMONS

A. Basic Assumption

The thing that all cults have in common is that their founders were individuals who were in contact with demons. As a result, certain key false ideas tend to appear in each of the cults and religions.

B. Some Typical Religions

1. Theosophy

This cult is the mother of the modern occultic revolution. It is the result of the teachings of Madam Blavatsky and Col. Henry S. Olcott, in the 1850's. Some of their key doctrines are: (1) Gnosticism is true Christianity; (2) Man is a god in the making, a "spark of the divine fire"; and (3) reincarnation.

2. Scientology

L. Ron Hubbard is the personality behind this new cult. It is a mixture of occultism and do-it-yourself psychoanalysis. Reincarnation is a key doctrine. "Engrams" are thought to foul-up your present life; they are prenatal and previous life influences. Converts to this religion are taught how to clear their life of these, and thus "cross the bridge to total freedom and total power."

3. Eckankar

This is the name for the teachings of Paul Twitchell, by which men can enjoy "all-inclusiveness with God." One of the features taught and encouraged is soul travel (astral projection) – the idea that a person's soul may leave his body, observe, and then relay incidents and happenings hundreds of miles away.

4. Zen Buddhism

This Japanese form of Buddhism emphasizes meditation as a means of contact with deity. The worshiper meditates on a paradoxical problem called a *koan*, of which there are some 1700 (e.g., "meditate on the sound of one hand clapping"). By means of meditation the worshiper may reach Satori, a flash of consciousness that helps you get the most out of now. One of the elements that makes Zen popular among the young people is its emphasis

5. Hinduism

This Eastern religion has many offshoots found in our Western society.

Krishna consciousness is an offshoot of Hinduism. The teachers of this religion are called *gurus*. The aim of the movement is to achieve a state of *santadhi* – a permanent condition of ecstatic god-consciousness (without use of drugs). Sankirtan (i.e., reciting the name of Lord Krishna, the supreme Godhead) over and over again, is the means of reaching *santadhi*.[46] Reincarnation is a primary doctrine of Krishna consciousness.

Yoga is an offshoot of Hinduism. Yoga means "union," and the goal of this religion is to be in union with Brahman, the supreme spirit. Again, there is mental discipline involved, which consists of directing attention exclusively upon any object, abstract or concrete, with a view to the identification of consciousness with the object. Attainment of this end is *samadhi*. The chief yogas are *bhakti* (devotional) yoga, *dhyana* (contemplation) yoga, and *hatha* (physical) yoga. There are three stages of a yoga trance: *dharana* (fixed attention), *dhyana* (contemplation), and *samadhi* (concentration). By exercise or concentration, a person gets into position to invite the spirits. When he becomes subconscious, he can have knives stuck through his cheeks, or lie on a bed of spikes. The next stage is cosmic influence, in which he can practice levitation, materializations, and other feats of magic.

Transcendental meditation is an offshoot of Hinduism. Maharishi Mahesh Yogi has popularized this type of Hinduism. In it the worshiper meditates on the ring of one word (a mantra) given to him alone, until he reaches *samadhi*. Transcendental Meditation is becoming a popular relaxer and escape mechanism in Western societies. According to its teachers, it requires no faith or belief and does not involve intense concentration or control of the content of consciousness. If other thoughts enter the mind while he is concentrating on his mantra, he simply examines them and discards them, and goes back to the mantra. Soon he enters the pleasant, relaxed state of *samadhi*.

6. Rosicrucianism

Rosicrucianism is an international fraternity (said to be of Egyptian origin) operated on the lodge system and devoted to the practical application of the arts and sciences to human relationships. Some of the doctrines include the espousal of evolution, reincarnation, and the idea that men will one day become gods.

7. Unity School of Christianity

Reincarnation is a major tenet of this religion which aims at health, well-being, and prosperity. Devotees travel to the Lee's Summit, Missouri, headquarters of this cult for

---

[46] George Harrison, formerly a member of the "The Beatles" rock group, made popular a song titled "My Sweet Lord." It is a song, not about Jesus, but about Krishna, as can be determined by carefully listening to the chant that serves as background music through the latter part of the song.

seances in order to contact and communicate with dead friends and loved ones.

8. Baha'i Faith

The Baha'i religion is an offshoot of Islam. Jesus is considered to be a prophet but not greater than Moses or Mohammed, or Baha'ullah. It is a syncretistic religion which combines some of the major tenets of nine different world religions.

C. Summary of the Major Doctrines

From these examples it is possible to summarize the doctrines of demons that keep appearing in these (and other) religions. Almost all of these doctrines were found in ancient Gnosticism. (1) God is impersonal. He is a great fire, a cosmic consciousness, who has no personal interest in man. (2) Jesus is a created being. God created angels; angels created Jesus; Jesus created the Devil; the Devil created the world. (3) Dualism. (4) Auto-salvation. Men save themselves by living better this time than they did the last time. (5) Reincarnation. The best of men, Jesus, had to make at least thirty different cycles through life on this earth, so the rest of us will have to make even more, before we reach union with the divine fire.

D. The Bible Has Something to Say About Doctrines of Demons

God is presented as a personal God, Who is interested in each of His creatures. He knows the number of the hairs of men's heads (Matthew 10:30), and Peter tells us that people matter to Him (1 Peter 5:7). There's something personal, too, in the concept of men's "names" being written in Heaven (Luke 10:17-22).

Jesus is not a created being; instead, in Him dwells all the fullness of the Godhead bodily (John 1:1ff; Philippians 2:6ff; Colossians 1:16). Hebrews 1:2 indicates that Jesus Himself did the creating; He did not turn that task over to the devil.

As far as the doctrine of dualism is concerned, the devil is neither coequal nor co-eternal with the Father (Luke 11:14ff; Revelation 20:1ff).

The Bible holds out the hope of resurrection, not reincarnation. Reincarnation denies:

- The personality of God.
- It has a perverted doctrine of sin, denying that Jesus "has by one sacrifice forever perfected them that are sanctified," (Hebrew 10:14).
- It denies the record of the New Testament which has John the Baptist and Jesus alive at the same time (i.e., reincarnationists teach that the same person was John and Jesus), and which has Moses and Elijah appearing to Jesus on the Mount of Transfiguration (i.e., if the same person had been Moses, then Elijah, then John the Baptist, then Jesus, how could this appearance of Moses and Elijah to Jesus be possible?).

E. Demonic Doctrines are a Substitute for God's Revealed Religion

As the other areas of the World of the Occult were substitutions for the genuine thing, so it is with all the doctrines of demons. People are religious by nature, it seems, and however much they wish to be religious, the devil is ready with a counterfeit of the real thing. If it is knowledge of the future, he has divination. If it is power, he has sorcery. If it is knowledge and power and information about the future, he has spiritism. If a person wants to be even more religious and devoted, there are the complete religious systems that originated as doctrines of demons.

V. DELIVERANCE FROM THE OCCULT

Deliverance from occult enslavement challenges both the local church and the occult-oppressed person. Each has a function to perform, and each has a responsibility in the matter.

A. The Responsibility of the Church

The church must expose the craft and power of demonic spirits and point the way to deliverance.

- The church cannot afford to think, "There is no personal devil, nor demons!"
- Church members should be taught that occultists will attempt to defend their demonic practices by appealing to Bible passages for examples of their arts. The ascension of Jesus is said to be an example of levitation; the catching away of Philip from the Ethiopian is said to be an example of apport; the appearances of angels are said to be materializations; and prayer is nothing but telepathy, the occultist will argue.
- Christian parents should watch carefully the games and toys their children have. Watch their parties for seances. Watch for evidences of interest in meditation. Adult members too must beware of astrology, ESP, seances, and other forms of occult practices.
- The church has a responsibility to furnish a ministry, spiritually and intellectually competent, to minister to those oppressed of the devil and his demons. John's letters and Colossians will have to be taught to the brethren, so they will be able to meet the doctrines of demons.
- Church members must beware of thinking "We're Christians, and we are knowledgeable. It won't hurt us to dabble in the occult." That is exactly the attitude Paul condemns in 1 Corinthians 8-10.
- The responsibility of the church also includes leading unsaved men to a saving relationship with Christ. This is the only genuine way to break the bondage the devil has over men (Colossians 1:13).

B. The Responsibility of the Occult-Oppressed Person

If the occult-oppressed person is not a Christian, he needs to surrender to Christ. Until he does, his slavery to the spirits in the occult world will become more and more oppressing. But "if the Son shall make you free, you shall be free indeed" (John 8:36). Confession of Christ as Savior is the starting point to be free of condemnation (Romans 8:1ff).

If the occult-oppressed person is a Christian, there are several steps he must take if he would be free of his bondage to the prince of darkness, and Acts 19:18 is the passage that gives directions here. He must confess his sins of occult involvement. He must declare (to a Christian brother or to the congregation) his occult practices. He must renounce the devil and all he stands for. And he must destroy all his occult paraphernalia as the Ephesians burned their books. Repentance and prayer may also be needed, as in the case of Simon the magician (Acts 8). Then the person liberated from the occult bondage must realize that deliverance is an every-day walk as well as an initial experience. Ephesians 6:10ff gives instructions about the armor needed if you would be still standing when the "evil day" is over.

CONCLUSION

The devil is deadly serious in his efforts to defeat the purposes of the Creator and His Son, Christ Jesus. The Book of Acts chronicles ways people oppose the gospel, whether they be religious men (like the Jewish people who would not be obedient), or whether they be pagan (like Elymas, or the owners of the girl at Philippi who was possessed, or Demetrius).

Acts also shows how the gospel is so much superior to all the occultic practices, for it not only delivers men from their terrible bondage, but leaves them wholesome and pure in their relationships to each other.

BIBLIOGRAPHY

Edersheim, Alfred, *Life and Times of Jesus the Messiah*. Grand Rapids: Eerdmans, 1947, Vol. II, Appendices XIII and XVI.

Godwin, John, *Occult America*. New York: Doubleday.

Koch, Kurt, *Christian Counseling and Occultism*. Grand Rapids: Kregel, 1972.

---------------, *Occult Bondage and Deliverance*. Grand Rapids: Kregel, 1972.

Martin, Walter R., *The Kingdom of the Occult*. Costa Mesa, CA: One Way Library, 1972. (This work is a series of cassette tapes.)

Neff, H. Richard, *Psychic Phenomena and Religion*. Philadelphia: Westminster.

Peterson, William J., *Those Curious New Cults*. New Canaan, CT: Keats Publishing Co., 1973.

Unger, Merrill F., *Demons in the World Today*. Wheaton, IL: Tyndale Publishing House, 1971.

Wilson, Colin, *The Occult, A History*. New York: Random House, 1971.

Wright, J. Stafford, *Mind, Man and Spirits*. Grand Rapids: Zondervan, 1972.

Gardiner, M.H., "Egyptian Magic" in *Hastings' Encyclopedia of Religion and Ethics*, VIII, p.262-69.

Gaster, M., "Jewish Magic" in *Hastings' Encyclopedia of Religion and Ethics*, VIII, p.300-305.

See, too, the articles on various areas of magic and divination in *International Standard Bible Encyclopedia* and *Hastings' Dictionary of the Bible*.

4. From Ephesus to Troas to Macedonia. 20:1,2

20:1 – *And after the uproar had ceased, Paul sent for the disciples and when he had exhorted them and taken his leave of them, he departed to go to Macedonia.*

And after the uproar had ceased. Paul had already planned to not remain at Ephesus beyond Pentecost.[1] Perhaps the riot of Demetrius caused Paul to leave Ephesus a few weeks before he had planned to, for it was usually Paul's custom to leave a community after such an event. His helpers could remain and carry on the work without the terrific opposition all the Christians would have faced if Paul had continued in their midst. Those helpers can continue to go through the "great and effectual door" even if for him it was closing.

Paul sent for the disciples and when he had exhorted them and taken his leave of them. There were parting words of exhortation and blessing, and a holy kiss all around (implied in the word "taken leave of them"). Compare the departure events at Miletus later on this same third journey (verses 36-38).

He departed to go to Macedonia. Luke again is very brief as he passes over a very important period in Paul's life in just a few words. Paul's own epistles fill in some of the details. At Acts 19:22, Paul's intermediate trip to Corinth and subsequent return to Ephesus were noted; Titus was then tasked with a mission to Corinth and given instructions to report to Paul at Troas. It seems that Paul left Ephesus by land and went to Troas, and there waited anxiously for Titus, and waited, and waited some more.[2] Titus was working to lead the Corinthians to repentance in some areas where repentance was needed, and also was encouraging the Corinthians' participation in the offering that was being received for the poor in Judea.[3] For some reason, perhaps because the Corinthians were slow to respond to his preaching and the correction of their errors, Titus was delayed in his return to Paul. So Paul left Troas to go into Macedonia, being greatly troubled, hoping to meet Titus all the sooner. Because of the Corinthians' stubbornness, Paul made a slight change of plans concerning his itinerary about this time. His original plan had been to go first to Corinth when he left Ephesus, then go to Macedonia, and then return to Corinth, before sailing for Judea with the offering.[4] Because he did not wish to be hurt and rejected in Corinth a second time, and in order to spare the Corinthians, Paul revised his plans and went first into Macedonia, planning next to arrive at Corinth on his way to Judea. Plummer has suggested (correctly, we think) that Paul's enemies brought a charge of fickleness against Paul for thus changing his plans (see 2 Corinthians 1:15ff).[5]

---

[1] 1 Corinthians 16:8-9. Compare notes at Acts 19:21.

[2] 2 Corinthians 2:12-13.

[3] See information about the offering for Jerusalem in the comments at Acts 19:20-21.

[4] For Paul's original plans, see 1 Corinthians 16:5-6.

[5] Alfred Plummer, "Second Corinthians" in *International Critical Commentary* (Edinburgh: T&T Clark, 1915), p.31ff.

20:2 – *And when he had gone through those districts and had given them much exhortation, he came to Greece.*

And when he had gone through those districts. "Gone through" speaks of an evangelistic, or missionary, tour through an area.[6] As was noted at Acts 17:1, Macedonia was divided into "districts." We picture Paul as revisiting the churches in this area – Philippi, Thessalonica, and Berea. Again, Paul's own epistles, especially 2 Corinthians, fill in some of the details. Paul's feelings at this time are given at 2 Corinthians 7:5. "When we came into Macedonia, our flesh had no relief, but we were afflicted on every side; without were fightings, within were fears." Finally, the long-looked-for Titus came, meeting Paul either at Thessalonica or, more probably, at Philippi, and he came bringing tidings that partly cheered Paul and partly roused his indignation. There had been repentance in the area where Paul most wanted to see them repent, and this brought cheer.[7] But someone at Corinth had said some bitter things about him, made fun of the impression he left when dealing with people personally,[8] and held him up to contempt because he did not have letters of recommendation like the false teachers who had recently come to town and presented.[9] Hearing about the disruption this had caused filled him with indignation. So with these mixed feelings (which plainly show in the letter as it changes tone quickly several times) Paul sat down and dictated the letter known as Second Corinthians, and sent it along with Titus and two other brethren (probably Luke and Tychicus, or Timothy) back to Corinth.[10] Paul then resolved to delay his intended visit to Corinth even longer to give them time to bring matters into better order, and to give them opportunity to lay up a much larger offering for Jerusalem.[11] We date the writing of 2 Corinthians in the fall (or maybe late summer) of AD 57.

No sooner did Paul find some relief for his anxieties about the Corinthians from the report of Titus and the subsequent letter of encouragement and correction, than disquieting news came from another region. Judging from the numerous parallels of thought between it and the letters of 2 Corinthians and Romans, we date the letter to the Galatians from this same period of Paul's life. It is most likely that, shortly after Titus and the two brethren left for Corinth, news came from Galatia that the Judaizers had been through the churches in that province, and had been only too successful. So Paul sits down and hurriedly writes the Galatian letter to attempt to correct that situation. We date Galatians in the fall of AD 57.

A few months later than his journey through Macedonia, Paul writes Romans from Corinth. In Romans 15:19ff, he says he has preached the gospel "as far around as Illyricum," which was at the eastern end of the Egnatian Way. Some commentators place a missionary journey to Illyricum into this period, when Paul is waiting for the opportune

---

[6] See notes at Acts 13:6.

[7] See 2 Corinthians 2:5ff, 6:6-12.

[8] 2 Corinthians 10:10.

[9] 2 Corinthians 3:1

[10] 2 Corinthians 8:18-19.

[11] 2 Corinthians 9:5.

time to travel to Corinth. However, it seems better to believe that Paul's work in Macedonia (which bordered on Illyricum) is all that Paul referred to in Romans 15:19ff. We picture Paul as traveling overland through Macedonia, stopping to preach messages of encouragement to the brethren along the way.

And had given them much exhortation. Paul is again following his usual custom of revisiting the churches he has planted, to give them further instruction in the gospel.[12] His exhortation would include directions for the completion of the offering which was being gathered for the relief of the poverty-stricken Jewish Christians at Jerusalem. A three- to six-month period of time may be indicated.

He came to Greece. The word *hellas* ("Greece") seems used as synonymous with Achaia. Perhaps he visited the brethren at Athens and at Cenchrea. But the chief town visited was Corinth. This was Paul's third trip to Corinth.[13] The first trip was when the church was planted; the second was the "intermediate trip."[14]

5. At Corinth. 20:3

20:3 – *And* **there** *he spent three months, and when a plot was formed against him by the Jews as he was about to set sail for Syria, he determined to return through Macedonia.*

And *there* he spent three months. The three months he spent in Greece were the winter months (January to March) of AD 58. During this time, he wrote the epistle to the Romans, in which he prepared that church for the visit which he hoped to make to their city quite soon, and to warn them about the Judaizers. As he writes to them he is enjoying the hospitality of Gaius.[15] According to Romans 15:24-25, Paul's plans were to go to Jerusalem with the offering, and then to visit the church in Rome, and then to go on to Spain. It will not work out quite as Paul anticipated.

And when a plot was formed against him by the Jews as he was about to set sail for Syria. The unbelieving Jews seem to have been looking for an opportunity to assassinate Paul. It seems they must have heard of his plans to continue on to Jerusalem, so they began looking for a way to carry out their plot where it would most likely not fail. McGarvey thought the plot would have been carried out on the eight-mile stretch of highway between Corinth and Cenchrea; the Jews could have notified some highwaymen to lie in wait to rob Paul and his friends of the money they were bearing to Jerusalem.[16] Since Luke tells us that the plot was at the time Paul "was about to set sail," most think the attempt on Paul's life would have come either in Cenchrea, or later on shipboard out in the Mediterranean Sea. In a crowded harbor like Cenchrea, there would have been many opportunities to carry

---

[12] Compare Acts 15:41; 18:23; 14:22 for other examples of this practice.

[13] 2 Corinthians 13:1.

[14] See notes at Acts 19:22.

[15] Romans 15:22. Compare Acts 18:7, where it is suggested the man's whole name is Gaius Titius Justus.

[16] McGarvey, *op. cit.*, p.176.

out such a plot. Or on a ship filled with Jewish pilgrims headed for one of the feasts, many of them openly hostile to Paul, he could have been pushed overboard to drown some night; by the time he was found missing, it would have been too late to go back to look for him.

He determined to return through Macedonia. Luke leaves us to wonder how Paul learned of the plot against him. Before he learned about the plot, Paul had planned to sail directly from Cenchrea to Jerusalem. We suppose that the sailing season is just opening on the Mediterranean, which would cause an extra flurry of activity as ships which had wintered in the port would be anxious to be underway. Paul changes his plans in order to frustrate the plot against him: he goes overland back toward Macedonia while his friends take a ship bound for Troas. We can further imagine his enemies taking the ship they thought Paul would be on, heading out of the port toward Judea, only to find out after they were at sea that their intended victim wasn't even on board.

When Paul was writing 1 Corinthians (about a year before this), he had indicated he would go along with the offering to Judea only if it was "fitting" (i.e., a large enough offering), so that he would not be ashamed.[17] By the time they were to leave with the offering, Paul could see that it was "fitting" for him to accompany the messengers from each of the churches on their way to Judea.

6. From Corinth to Philippi to Troas. 20:4-6

20:4 – *And he was accompanied by Sopater of Berea,* **the son** *of Pyrrhus; and by Aristarchus and Secundus of the Thessalonians; and Gaius of Derbe, and Timothy; and Tychicus and Trophimus of Asia.*

And he was accompanied by. Each congregation which shared in the collecting of the offering chose some of its own men to bear that offering to Jerusalem. These men had already joined Paul in Achaia so that they might go together to Jerusalem, where Paul intended to introduce each one and allow them to present their church's part of the offering. By having each church choose a man out of their own number, Paul sought to avoid even the suspicion that he was only collecting the money to put it in his own pocket.[18] Too, there were no such things as checks or paper currency, so the money had to be carried in gold or silver coin on the persons of the messengers. It was important that no one be so loaded as to indicate the fact to the sharp eyes of would-be robbers.

Taking this offering to the Christians in Jerusalem was a vital thing for Paul, for he hoped it would help show the unity between the brethren, whether of Jewish or Gentile background. In his letter to the Romans, we see Paul's fears that the Jews at Jerusalem would not accept "charity" after he had worked so long and hard to collect it.[19] He therefore asked for the prayers of the brethren in Rome that the mission to Jerusalem would be successful and would help heal the breach between Jews and Gentiles in the church.

---

[17] 1 Corinthians 16:3-4. He said to the church, "Whomever you may approve, I shall send them with letters to carry your gift to Jerusalem; and if it is fitting for me to go also, they may go with me."

[18] 2 Corinthians 8:20-21.

[19] Romans 15:30-32.

Sopater of Berea, *the son* of Pyrrhus. Sopater was likely an abbreviation of Sosipater. As has been suggested in notes at Acts 17:12, he was likely one of Paul's converts at Berea. He is included in the list of men who were with Paul and who sent greetings to the brethren in Rome.[20]

And by Aristarchus and Secundus of the Thessalonians. Aristarchus is certainly to be identified with the Macedonian who was seized by the mob in Ephesus.[21] Of Secundus we know little more than what is here given. McGarvey has an interesting conjecture.

> Secundus (second) was probably so named because he was his father's second son; as were Tertius and Quartus (third and fourth) because they were the third and fourth sons of their respective fathers, Romans 16:22,23. As all three had been with Paul in Corinth, it is possible they were brothers.[22]

Such names were commonly given to slaves who had no family names. Further, the Latin form of their names suggests they had been slaves in Rome. Putting all of this information together, it is possible these men were Jews who were now freedmen.[23] Such an inference might also help explain why they would want to send greetings to their brethren in Rome.[24]

While the churches of Berea and Thessalonica are represented by messengers carrying their offerings, no one is named as being from Philippi, a church that through the years has been very missionary-minded. Rather than believing they did not take part in the offering for Jerusalem, it is better to suppose that Luke carried the Philippian portion of the offering since the "we" passages begin again in verse 5ff.

And Gaius of Derbe, and Timothy. "Of Derbe" is added in order to distinguish between this bearer of the offering and the Gaius of Acts 19:29 who was a Macedonian.[25] Timothy was from Lystra, and these two were carrying the offering from the churches of Galatia.

And Tychicus and Trophimus of Asia. Tychicus is a name that means "fortunate" (the Greek equivalent of "Felix"), and was a very common name among slaves and freedmen. The Tychicus here mentioned seems to have been an Ephesian. In the Prison Epistles he is shown to be with Paul in Rome during the first Roman imprisonment.[26] He is mentioned again in Titus 3:12 as being on the verge of being sent to Crete, and at a later time he was with Paul again during the latter's second Roman imprisonment.[27] Trophimus means "fos-

---

[20] Romans 16:21.

[21] Acts 19:29.

[22] McGarvey, *op cit.*, p.177. The first son would have been named Primus or Primativus.

[23] See notes at Acts 6:9 for an explanation of the term "freedman."

[24] Romans 16:22-23.

[25] The Western text calls Gaius a "Doberian"* (which is a slight difference in spelling), and thus makes him a Macedonian, a native of Doberus, a town about 26 miles from Philippi. This seems to be a deliberate effort to harmonize this verse with Acts 19:29.

[26] Ephesians 6:21; Colossians 4:7.

[27] 2 Timothy 4:12.

ter-child" or "nursling," and was also a common name of slaves and freedmen. Trophimus appears again in Acts 21:29, and is described definitely as a Gentile from Ephesus. He will be the indirect cause of Paul's arrest at the close of this trip to Jerusalem. His name appears again toward the close of Paul's life, having been left at Miletus, sick.[28] These two men were carrying the offering that had been contributed by the churches of Asia.

Who carried the Corinthian part of the offering? Perhaps Titus did, or even Paul, but this is only a guess. Titus is not mentioned in the book of Acts, and could have been traveling with the messengers, just as he did in Acts 15:2ff. Ramsay has suggested the reason why Titus is not named is because he was a brother to Luke.[29] Titus was last seen being sent back to Corinth carrying the epistle of 2 Corinthians.[30] It would not be beyond reason that he now carries the Corinthian portion of the offering.

20:5 – *But these had gone on ahead and were waiting for us at Troas.*

But these had gone on ahead and were waiting for us at Troas. There is a manuscript variation at the beginning of verse 4 which has led commentators to make quite diverse explanations of this passage.[31]

- Some have only two of the messengers going ahead to Troas.[32]
- Others have all seven going by ship to Troas while Paul travels alone overland toward Macedonia.
- Still others suppose that all the messengers had to be told of a change of plans. That is, instead of meeting in Asia, the meeting of messengers was to be at Troas, from whence they would go together to Jerusalem.

When it is recognized that the phrase in verse 4 does not enjoy integrity, then it is easier to reconstruct the elements of this journey. The seven go by ship from Cenchrea to Troas. Paul, accompanied by Luke and Titus, goes overland from Corinth toward Macedonia, and thence to Troas. This is how the "waiting for *us*" is to be explained.[33] By going to Troas, the seven would avoid those among their enemies who knew they had money on their persons. The visit to the brethren in Philippi (verse 6) will give opportunity to pick up their offering for Jerusalem, too.

---

[28] 2 Timothy 4:20.

[29] Ramsay. *St. Paul the Traveller and Roman Citizen*, p.390.

[30] Compare notes at verse 2.

[31] See the KJV, which reads "accompanied him as far as Asia." The phrase "as far as Asia" is omitted in Codices Sinaiticus and Vaticanus, and in the excellent minuscule 33, and several ancient versions.

[32] Boles, *op. cit.*, p.317; Barnes, *op. cit.*, p,288.

[33] As indicated in previous notes, the messengers had already joined Paul in Corinth in anticipation of the departure for Judea. Luke and Titus also were there. The "us" is explicable only if Luke (and probably Titus, too) has traveled with Paul from Corinth. The introduction of "us" here, right after Timothy s name has been listed, is fatal to the idea that the "we" sections were authored by Timothy. (See Introductory Studies under "Attacks on the Lucan Authorship.")

20:6 – *And we sailed from Philippi after the days of Unleavened Bread, and came to them at Troas within five days; and there we stayed seven days.*

And we sailed from Philippi. The "we" again denotes that somewhere along the way Luke has joined Paul's party again. Since the Philippian church was planted nearly 5 years earlier, Luke has been working in that city, save for a trip to Corinth a few months earlier.[34] Having accompanied Paul from Corinth, and having been appointed by the Philippians to carry their part of the offering, he now travels with Paul on toward Jerusalem. They would have gone down to Neapolis to catch a ship bound for Troas.

After the days of Unleavened Bread. This was the Passover. The Passover proper lasted only one day, the 14th day of the month called Nisan, but there followed the seven days of unleavened bread, which is referred to here in the word "days." Luke seems to use this expression as a chronological note of time, since it was about this time in the spring that the Mediterranean was opened again to shipping.[35] This note about Passover time also helps us to realize that nearly a whole year had passed since Paul left Ephesus (verse 1), for he left there some time after Passover (see notes at Acts 19:22) and it is once again after Passover when he sails away from Philippi.

And came to them at Troas within five days. That is, the voyage lasted until the fifth day. They must have encountered some rough weather. It was not long after the spring equinox, and at that season of the year there are storms, and the prevailing winds (the Etesian winds, they are called) are from the northeast. Coupled with the strong currents flowing out of the Dardanelles toward the southwest, these made sailing toward Troas a slow process.

And there we stayed seven days. Troas has been visited before.[36] Since the last of these seven days was a Sunday (the first day of the week, verse 7), Paul must have arrived in Troas on the preceding Monday, and left Neapolis (i.e., the seaport of Philippi) on the preceding Thursday.

Why did they stay here a whole week? Was it because their ship was laying over this long? Or was it deliberate, in order to spend a Lord's Day with the brethren in Troas? The supposition that they were using this time to plant a congregation in Troas seems to founder on the fact that there was already a congregation there.[37] A suggestion that would be more defensible is that they were holding a "revival" of an already flourishing congrega-

---

[34] 2 Corinthians 8:18-19. See also notes at verse 2 for information about Luke's travels.

[35] See Acts 27:9 for information about the sailing season on the Mediterranean. Some suppose Paul was observing the feast of Passover as a Jew away from Palestine would have (it was in the realm of liberty, it is asserted), and that is why he delayed at Philippi. While this cannot be categorically denied, it seems doubtful. Instead, we think of Paul as remaining in Philippi until he could find a means of sailing to Troas.

[36] See Acts 16:8-10, plus comments at Acts 19:22 and 20:1.

[37] Verse 7 indicates there were already "brethren" in Troas before this visit. At Acts 16:10 we have developed the thesis that Luke planted the church in Troas before joining the second missionary journey. A year earlier (2 Corinthians 2:12-13) Paul had come to work with the church at Troas, so it was not the purpose of this seven-day stay to plant a congregation here for the first time.

tion. Paul came to Troas a year earlier "for the gospel," but his anxiety over the situation at Corinth and the tardy appearance of Titus with news from there severely curtailed his missionary activity at that time.[38] Paul and the nine other men (the seven named in verse 4, plus Titus and Luke) could greatly encourage and help a congregation in a week's time.

7. In Troas. 20:7-13

20:7 – *And on the first day of the week, when we were gathered together to break bread, Paul* **began** *talking to them, intending to depart the next day, and he prolonged his message until midnight.*

And on the first day of the week. The phrase translated "first day of the week" is the regular Greek way of designating the day we call "Sunday."

> The expression "first day of the week" was used because the Jews did not have names for the days of the week [except that they used "Preparation" as a name for the day we call Friday]. They had to refer to the days before or after the Sabbath. The same expression [found here in Acts 20:7] occurs elsewhere in the New Testament, and always has reference to Sunday. Matthew 28:1; Luke 24:1; Mark 16:2,9; John 20:1,19; 1 Corinthians 16:2.[39]

Having established that the day is "Sunday," there remains the question of whether Luke is using Jewish or Roman time. The Jews counted time from sunset to sunset; the Romans counted from midnight to midnight. This fact has caused much dispute as to whether this meeting of the Troas church was on Saturday night (per our calendars), or on Sunday (either a day-time or an evening service).

- Some formulate arguments to show that Luke used Jewish time, and that therefore the meeting began on Saturday night, after 6 p.m. (a) One such argument is that it seems probable that in churches which were so largely organized after the pattern of the Jewish synagogue, and which contained so many Jews and proselytes who had been familiar with the synagogue practices, that the Jewish mode of counting time would still be kept. Since the Jewish Sabbath ended at sunset, the first day of the week would begin at sunset on the day we call Saturday. (b) Another argument is based on the reasoning that the inconvenience of such a protracted service as the all-night meeting described here in verse 7ff led to the transfer of the Lord's Supper from the evening of Saturday to the early morning of Sunday.[40]

- It is surely possible that Luke is using Roman time, and that this meeting in Troas was held during the daytime on Sunday, or that it began early Sunday evening. Troas was located in Gentile territory, and would schedule things according to Roman time. Dale's note at this place is helpful:

---

[38] 2 Corinthians 2:12-13.

[39] Dale, *op. cit.*, p.303.

[40] This second argument presumes all the churches originally held services on Saturday night, and so Troas must have also followed this practice. However, this is begging the question; it is this very presumption that we are seeking to prove or disprove.

> Either let it be an all-day meeting beginning on Sunday morning, or a Sunday night meeting ... Since all knew it was the last time Paul planned to be with them, they would naturally plan for a long meeting.[41]

This commentator is convinced that Luke is using Roman time, and that this meeting recorded in verse 7ff was on the day we call Sunday.

This is the first reference in Acts to services "on the first day of the week." There is evidence, however, that meeting for worship and fellowship on Sunday has long been the Christians' practice.

- When this passage is compared with the counsel given in 1 Corinthians 16:2, that contributions should be laid by in store on the first day of the week, the conclusion is properly drawn that the church had already begun to observe the weekly festival of the Resurrection in place of, or, where the disciples were Jews, in addition to, the weekly Sabbath.
- The same instructions given to the Corinthians had also been given to the Galatian churches (1 Corinthians 16:1). Thus, it can be affirmed that the Galatian churches also were in the habit of meeting each week for services.
- From late in the 1st century comes the unusual expression "Lord's Day" which, without doubt, is a reference to Sunday.[42]
- Writings still extant from the early 2nd century and onwards force one to accept the fact that the day of worship for the early Christians was Sunday, and that, too, long before Constantine officially changed the day for the whole empire.[43]

When we were gathered together to break bread. If we accept the idea that this was a night meeting, there is a ready explanation for the time of services. Slaves in the service of non-Christian masters would have to meet for worship either very early in the morning, before their day's labors began, or else very late in the day, after their labors were finished. Sunday was not officially made a holiday on which working-men were freed from their labors until Constantine so decreed in AD 321.

"To break bread" parallels the expression we found in Acts 2:42; it speaks of the Lord's Supper. Hence, this verse indicates the purpose of the Christians gathering together on the first day of the week was to observe the Lord's Supper.[44] Barnes has noted, "It is probable that the apostles and early Christians celebrated the Lord's Supper on every Lord's Day."[45] When Christians recognize the fact that salvation is grounded in the death and exaltation of Christ, then they will come to understand that one of the most important

---

[41] Dale, *op. cit.*, p.305.

[42] Revelation 1:10.

[43] See "Communion in the Apostolic Church" in Special Study #18, "The Lord's Supper."

[44] Compare notes at Acts 2:42 on the important of participating in a communion service at least weekly. Christians who do not have the Lord's Supper weekly deprive themselves of one of the very purposes for meeting together on the first day of the week.

[45] Barnes, *op. cit.*, p.288. Barnes, a Presbyterian writer, would be more correct if he omitted the word "probable."

reasons for worship together is to commemorate those redemptive acts by participating in the breaking of bread.[46]

Paul *began* talking to them. Did this teaching session precede or follow the Lord's Supper? We are not told of the exact time of the observance of the Lord's Supper at this meeting.[47] The word translated "talking" is the same word translated "reasoned" at Acts 17:2. Paul answered questions, explained difficulties, and satisfied doubts in the minds of the brethren.

This passage is of interest for it shows some of the elements of an early worship service. It also gives us an example of how the injunction of Hebrews 10:23-25 was practiced in real life. By these "reasonings" Paul is encouraging the Christians to love and good works.

Intending to depart the next day. Some suggest the ship on which he was riding was scheduled to leave at dawn. Others, who believe Paul has chartered a coasting vessel to take them as far as Patara (Acts 21:1-2), suggest he had set the next dawn as the time of departure. There are times in the following verses when it seems as though Paul had complete control of the ship's movements.

Those who believe this was a Saturday night meeting of necessity have Paul traveling on Sunday – and there would be little wrong with that, since they were about the Lord's business on the Lord's Day. There is no evidence that Paul ever applied the Jewish Sabbath restrictions to Sunday during the Christian age.[48] If it is correct that it was a Sunday meeting (and we think it is), then Paul and his party intend to depart on Monday morning.

And prolonged his message until midnight. We learn further on (verse 38) that he expected never to see these disciples again; hence, his desire was to give them all possible instruction and admonition while he was with them. Bruce has written, "Church meetings were not regulated by the clock in those days, and the opportunity of listening to Paul was not to be cut short; what did it matter if he went on preaching until midnight."[49]

20:8 – *And there were many lamps in the upper room where we were gathered together.*

And there were many lamps. The Greek word can mean either "lamps" or "torches." The majority of writers speak here of the little hand lamps like are mentioned at Matthew 25:1. The presence of "sufficient lamps" is one of the little touches that not only suggest an eyewitness is describing the event just as he remembered it, but that it was a meeting that had been planned for, even down to who was responsible for bringing the lamps.

---

[46] See Special Study #18, "The Lord's Supper." Most congregations receive an offering each Lord's Day because of examples given in Scripture. If the few passages dealing with the offering are sufficient to warrant a weekly place for it in worship services today, then we ought also to keep the Lord's Supper each week as a vital part of the worship service. There are as many Scriptures teaching the weekly communion as there are teaching the weekly offering.

[47] See notes at verse 11 for further discussion of this matter.

[48] Galatians 4:10; Colossians 2:16.

[49] Bruce, *op. cit.*, p.408.

Commentaries have assigned reasons why they think Luke tells about the lamps.

- One idea is that already the early Christians were accused of meeting in secret and of their practicing all kinds of wickedness. By mentioning the lamps, Luke refutes such a charge.[50]
- Some later writers attach a distinctive ritual or symbolic character to the presence of the lamps, as though out of respect, two would be set near the apostles and elders, and two or more were set near the loaf and the cup on the Lord's table. However, there seems to be little reason to assume that the use of lamps held such a significance at this early period in church history.
- A third suggestion is that the sufficient light was spoken of to guard against any charge that there was deception with regard to the miracle of raising Eutychus.

In the upper room where we were gathered together. Verse 9 further indicates that it was on the third floor of a home where the meeting was being held. The upper rooms were often larger than those on lower floors, and would be much more suitable for holding a large crowd. These rooms also would be further removed from the noise of the street which would tend to interrupt the services if it became too noticeable.

20:9 – *And there was a certain young man named Eutychus sitting on the window sill, sinking into a deep sleep; and as Paul kept on talking, he was overcome by sleep and fell down from the third floor, and was picked up dead.*

And there was a certain young man named Eutychus sitting on the windowsill. The room was evidently crowded. With all the other places filled, Eutychus was sitting in the opening in the wall that served as a window.[51] Glass was not used in windows of that time period, though the windows did have shutters; evidently the shutters were open. The word "young man" speaks of a person between 24 and 40 years of age.

Sinking into a deep sleep. "Perhaps he had put in a hard day's work from dawn to sunset, and now in the stuffy atmosphere not even the words of the apostle could keep him from falling fast asleep."[52] The crowd of bodies in the room would soon raise the room temperature, and the odor from the burning lamps would contribute to his feeling of drowsiness. The verb tense indicates he was gradually becoming more and more sleepy.

And as Paul kept on talking, he was overcome by sleep. The verb tense here changes, and the two verbs taken together vividly present to us Eutychus' struggle to keep awake, and then all of a sudden (aorist tense) dropping off to sleep. "Talking" is the same verb used in verse 7 above.

---

[50] See such charges given in Tertullian, *Apol.*, c.8.

[51] The Greek is *"the* window," that is, the only one in the room.

[52] Bruce, *ibid.* "It is an instance of sleeping in public worship that has some apology. The late hour of the night, and the length of the services, were the excuse. But though the thing is often done now, yet how seldom is a sleeper in a church furnished with an excuse for it. No practice is more shameful, disrespectful, and abominable than that so common as sleeping in the house of God." (Barnes, *op. cit.*, p.289.)

And fell down from the third floor. As he fell asleep, Eutychus lost his balance and fell off the windowsill through the opening to the ground below, falling three stories.

And was picked up dead. Because of Paul's statement in verse 10 about "his life being in him," some have supposed that Eutychus was merely stunned by the fall, and that he was still alive. But the obvious meaning is that he was actually killed by the fall.[53] Luke does not tell us that he was taken up "*as* dead." Luke says he was dead. We might picture Luke the physician as making an examination, and then pronouncing the young man dead.

20:10 – *But Paul went down and fell upon him and after embracing him, he said, "Do not be troubled, for his life is in him."*

But Paul went down. We have to think of the cries of alarm, the rush of people down the staircase from the third floor, with lamps in their hands, and the wail of sorrow on finding the young man dead.

And fell upon him. What Paul did in this case is very similar to what is recorded of Elijah and Elisha when they raised the dead.[54] Paul would have stretched his body across the chest of the body of Eutychus, and accompanied this action with prayer.

And after embracing him, he said, "Do not be troubled, for his life is in him." The word "embracing" is a further description of "falling on him."[55] The word translated "Do not be troubled" prohibits weeping and wailing and carrying on as was common of mourners in the East,[56] for there was no need to weep and loudly lament as though he were permanently dead. "His life is in him" evidently does not mean that Eutychus had not been dead, but rather that he had returned to life as a result of Paul's efforts. By the time Paul said this, he evidently had been assured of a miraculous restoration in answer to his prayer. The language clearly implies that Paul has raised Eutychus from the dead.

20:11 – *And when he had gone back up, and had broken the bread and eaten, he talked with them a long while, until daybreak, and so departed.*

And when he had gone *back* up, and had broken the bread. Just as the phrase "breaking bread" gives commentators difficulty the second time it appears in Acts 2:42ff, so it gives difficulty the second time it appears here in chapter 20. And the question is the same, Is it the Lord's Supper that is signified, or a common meal?

- *Is it the Lord's Supper?* Initially, the problem involved must be clarified. If this was the Lord's Supper, and if the meeting began on Sunday night, then the Lord's Supper

---

[53] See also the comments in verse 12, where Eutychus being "alive" is the cause of joy. The death of Ahaziah, king of Israel, was occasioned by a similar fall (2 Kings 1:2,17).

[54] 1 Kings 17:21; 2 Kings 4:34.

[55] The suggestion offered in recent years that Paul applied artificial resuscitation does not explain all the details of the record.

[56] The same word is used in Mark 5:38, 39 and at Acts 9:39.

was being celebrated on a Monday.[57] What are the arguments that this phrase speaks of the Lord's Supper? (1) In some verses, this language does signify the Lord's Supper.[58] But in other verses, it is also true that the same language signifies a common meal.[59] So although the language alone is indeterminate, the language is perhaps one point of the argument pointing towards the Lord's Supper. (2) There is an article with "breaking of bread" in verse 11. Grammatically, in the Greek, this would be treated as an article of previous reference, pointing back to some place previous where the same topic was discussed. In this case, "breaking of bread" is found in verse 7, and refers to the Lord's Supper.[60] (3) If verse 11 signifies the Lord's Supper, it can be said that the whole night was spent in religious conversation and worship, interrupted at midnight by a death and a resurrection, which was followed by the commemoration of the Lord's death which brings hope of a resurrection to a life which is very far better.

- *Is it a common meal (perhaps even a "Love Feast")?* Again, it is needful to clarify the problem. If this phrase is not a reference to the Lord's Supper, then Luke's account of the meeting never specifically records the observance of the Lord's Supper, even though according to verse 7 this was the purpose of the meeting. What are the arguments that this phrase speaks of a common meal? (1) It should pose no problem to affirm that the actual observance of the Lord's Supper is not specifically mentioned, for neither are the other elements of the worship service. Where is it recorded they prayed, sang, or took an offering? It must simply be assumed that all these elements were present in the service, and so it must likewise be assumed they partook of the Lord's Supper before the message by Paul. (2) That verse 11 speaks of just a common meal of refreshment seems to be shown by the fact that it was something done by Paul himself. The verb says, "*He* broke the bread." If this is something Paul himself did, it is evidently distinguished from the celebration of the Lord's Supper, which was a congregational matter.[61] (3) That verse 11 speaks of a common meal, or the Love Feast, is indicated by the use of the verb "tasted" (*geusamenos*).[62]

Clearly, either explanation of this phrase contains difficulties. The use of the article before "bread" makes it difficult to say it is a common meal. But the use of the verb "tasted" and the fact it was something done by Paul himself (rather than them all) makes it difficult to say it is the Lord's Supper. This commentator inclines toward the idea that Luke is recording the eating of a common meal.[63]

---

[57] To some degree, this means the congregation did not do what they met to do on the first day of the week. Perhaps this is why some commentators treat this as a Saturday night meeting (verse 7). That would allow the Lord's Supper to fall on Sunday. Accordingly, Luke would be using a Jewish method of counting time.

[58] Acts 2:42; 1 Corinthians 10:16.

[59] Acts 2:46.

[60] The difficulty with making this a reference to the Lord's Supper is that verse 11 is something Paul himself did, not something that all the members of the congregation did. Can this mean that Paul alone partook of the Lord's Supper? Not if the Lord's Supper was celebrated here as in other congregations.

[61] Can the language be stretched to mean that Paul presided at the celebration of the Lord's Supper at Troas? Not easily, we presume.

[62] See notes on the next phrase, "And eaten."

[63] Even if this phrase does signify the Lord's Supper, and even if it were observed on Monday, the day of

And eaten. Literally, the verb means "tasted." Commentators are again divided over what it was that Paul "tasted," and the interpretations are bound up with the previous question about Lord's Supper v. common meal. (1) Those who believe it is the Lord's Supper struggle to explain the use of the word "tasted" here, for it is a word not used elsewhere of the Lord's Supper.[64] Attention is often called to the fact that the loaf was not the round wafer found in the Roman Catholic Church of today, nor the cubed loaf found in Protestant churches of today, but one large loaf from which each communicant broke a small piece. It would only be, as it were, a "taste." (2) Those who believe it is a Love Feast wrestle less with the verb "tasted." However, although it was customary to keep the Love Feast in connection with the Lord's Supper,[65] this does not relieve many of the difficulties this passage raises. The Lord's Supper customarily *followed* the Love Feast, and if that were true in Troas, then it was not held till after midnight. Or, if the explanation be given that at Troas the Lord's Supper was observed before midnight, and the Love Feast after, it must then be explained why the order at Troas was different than, say, at Corinth.[66] (3) Those who believe it is simply a common meal think "tasted" refers to the refreshments Paul ate after raising Eutychus.

He talked with them a long while. "Talked" is a word that implies a more relaxed, familiar conversation than the word used in verses 7 and 9. Having taken some refreshments after his "reasoning" was interrupted by Eutychus' fall, it is now past midnight when Paul resumes his conversation with the congregation.

Until daybreak. The whole service must have lasted some seven or eight hours, sunrise at that time of the year being between 5 and 6 a.m. Maybe this meeting at Troas is an example of the "watchings often" (KJV), or "sleepless nights" (NASB) that Paul wrote of in an earlier epistle.[67]

And so departed. Verse 13 describes the actual departure. As dawn breaks, the apostle and his friends say farewell and prepare to go from the upper room to the ship.

20:12 – *And they took away the boy alive, and were greatly comforted.*

And they took away the boy alive. The ASV reads, "they *brought* the lad." McGarvey thinks it means they *took* the boy to his own home from the place of meeting.[68] However, it is better to think of the expression as speaking of the young man's being brought into the

---

observance matters little, for there is no command to observe the Lord's Supper *only* on Sunday.

[64] The word regularly used for "eating" the Lord's Supper is some form of *esthiō* – either *esthein,* as at 1 Corinthians 11:26-29, or *phagein,* as at 1 Corinthians 11:20, 24.

[65] See section 5 of Special Study #18, "The Lord's Supper," for more information about the connection of the Love Feast with communion.

[66] Some attempt to explain this change of order in the service by suggesting that at Troas the Lord's Supper and Love Feast were deliberately separated in order to avoid the excesses that occurred at Corinth, where the one was observed immediately at the conclusion of the other.

[67] 2 Corinthians 11:27.

[68] McGarvey, *op. cit.*, p.182.

assembly room in a normal, healthy condition.[69] "It is clear that the young man[70] had remained away from the services after the accident. His loved ones brought him to the services, and rejoice with Paul and the other Christians over his recovered condition."[71]

And were greatly comforted. The congregation was encouraged by the fact that Eutychus was alive. Perhaps also they were strengthened by the fact that a miracle had been wrought among them, thus confirming the message of Paul.

20:13 – *But we, going ahead to the ship, set sail for Assos, intending from there to take Paul on board; for thus he had arranged it, intending himself to go by land.*

But we, going ahead to the ship, set sail for Assos, intending from there to take Paul on board. "We" in this place excludes Paul. Shortly after dawn, the ship on which they were traveling was due to sail, so the messengers from the churches went on board. Why did Paul stay behind, while the others set sail? The idea advanced by Bruce is weak – i.e., that Paul needed to "be assured that Eutychus was completely restored to health."[72] Miracles do not take time to become effective in the New Testament. Verse 13 itself explains that Paul wished to walk overland; that's why he stayed behind when the rest boarded the ship.

For thus he had arranged it. This is one of the expressions that has been used to show that Paul had chartered the ship on which they were sailing toward Jerusalem. See more discussion of this matter at verse 7 and at verse 16.

Intending himself to go by land. Why did Paul choose, after spending a sleepless night in preaching and teaching, to still further tax his power of endurance by this walk of 20 miles? It is hard to think of any very satisfactory reason, unless this long walk was Paul's way of "unwinding" after an emotionally exhausting time. Perhaps Paul spent time in prayer as he walked along the highway in solitude.

8. At Assos and at Mitylene. 20:14

20:14 – *And when he met us at Assos, we took him on board and came to Mitylene.*

And when he met us at Assos. Troas and Assos are on the opposite sides of a peninsula

---

[69] The word "living" here is pointless if the fall was not fatal. This is but one of the indicators in the passage that Paul raised Eutychus from the dead.

[70] Few commentators deal with the issue created by the translation "boy" in comparison with the use of "young man" in verse 9. Both Rackham and Jacobsen suggest that "boy" shows Eutychus was less than 24 years old. It would also be plausible to take "boy" in a secondary sense, thus taking "young man" in its primary sense.

[71] Dale, *op. cit.*, p.314. Since miracles in the Bible were instantaneous, it seems doubtful that it took the lad four or five hours to completely recover consciousness.

[72] Bruce, *op. cit.*, p.409.

which terminates at Cape Lectum. The two towns, about 20 miles apart, were connected by a Roman road. While the ship was covering the 40 miles around the coastline, Paul could walk the highway to Assos. The remains of Assos are on the northern shore of the Gulf of Adramyttium, opposite the island of Lesbos. Some of the most important examples of ancient Greek art were found here.

We took him on board. Paul joins them at Assos on Monday, late in the day.

And came to Mitylene. Mitylene was the capital of the island of Lesbos, and was located on the eastern shore of the island. It could be reached from Assos in a few hours sailing time. According to Ramsay and McGarvey, they cast anchor in the harbor of Mitylene on Monday night.[73]

9. A Voyage Past the Islands of Chios and Samos to Miletus. 20:15

20:15 – *And sailing from there, we arrived the following day opposite Chios; and the next day we crossed over to Samos; and the day following we came to Miletus.*

And sailing from there. It was usual on the Mediterranean, when sailing in a coasting vessel, to put into a harbor and drop anchor each evening if at all possible.

We arrived the following day opposite Chios. The island of Chios is separated from the mainland by a picturesque channel about 5 miles wide. It is Tuesday night now as they found anchorage at a point near the mainland opposite Chios.

And the next day we crossed over to Samos. Samos is an island about 50 miles southeast of Chios. There are ruins of a town by the same name on the southeast shore of the island. Either they stayed Wednesday night at Samos or, if the Western Text is correct, at Trogyllium. Trogyllium is the name of the peninsula which juts out from the mainland toward the island of Samos, leaving a channel only about a mile wide.

And the day following we came to Miletus. A short voyage on the fourth day, Thursday, brought them to Miletus, an important seaport in the ancient world. More and more as the harbor at Ephesus silted up, the harbor at Miletus gained in commercial importance. Ephesus lay about 28 miles north of Miletus. Miletus was about four miles inland on the Meander River. Ruins of an enormous theater, traces of an aqueduct, and sites of several temples have been found here by archaeologists.

10. In Miletus. 20:16-38

20:16 – *For Paul had decided to sail past Ephesus in order that he might not have to spend time in Asia; for he was hurrying to be in Jerusalem, if possible, on the day of Pentecost.*

---

[73] McGarvey, *op. cit.*, p.184.

For Paul had decided to sail past Ephesus. This expression has been pointed to as being further evidence that the ship was chartered. (See additional comments at verses 7 and 13.) It appears Paul is directing where it is to sail. On the other hand, it might be affirmed that back at Troas, Paul had the choice of two ships, one sailing to Ephesus and one to Miletus, and picked the second for the reason about to be stated.

In order that he might not have to spend time in Asia. Several considerations might contribute to a sojourn in Ephesus longer than Paul wished to stay. If he showed up there, Demetrius and his colleagues might again become inflamed, and this time Paul might not get away. Paul's long ministry in Ephesus had led to making many friends, both in the city and in the regions all about Ephesus. By the time he visited with all these who would want to see the apostle, too much time would be involved to permit him to get to Jerusalem by the date he hoped to be there.

For he was hurrying to be in Jerusalem, if possible, on the day of Pentecost. The imperfect tense verb "hurrying" expresses the desire for speed during this whole voyage. Why he wanted to be in Jerusalem for Pentecost is rather easy to suggest. In chapter 2, it was suggested that Pentecost was the feast that attracted the most pilgrims to Jerusalem during any one year, and this would give Paul a great opportunity to witness for Christ. He was contemplating a journey from Judea to Rome after his visit to Jerusalem, and that would hardly have been feasible had he waited until later in the year than Pentecost to go to Jerusalem. There were only a few months of navigation on the Mediterranean after Pentecost, until it was closed for the winter season.[74]

20:17 – *And from Miletus he sent to Ephesus and called to him the elders of the church.*

And from Miletus he sent to Ephesus. The ship evidently was to lie at anchor at Miletus for 3 or 4 days, so Paul used this time to satisfy his desire to communicate once more with the brethren of Ephesus.[75] It would take a day for the messenger to get to Ephesus, and a day for the return trip of the elders to Miletus, so the meeting would not take place until the third day. If the earlier notes about the different days sailing have been correct, they landed at Ephesus on Thursday (or even Friday), so this meeting with the elders probably took place on Sunday.

And called to him the elders of the church. Luke has not previously indicated that the church at Ephesus had elders appointed to serve, but neither did he tell of the appointment of the elders at Jerusalem.[76]

> Paul did not send for the evangelist nor the deacons. He sent for the spiritual overseers of the church. If the minister had been the one to see, Paul would have sent for him. How different from the modern professional ministry! Today it is the minister who is expected

---

[74] See notes at Acts 27:9.

[75] "Some think that if the ship had been entirely at Paul's disposal, he would have asked the Ephesian elders to meet him at Trogyllium, a place very near to Ephesus." Boles, *op. cit.*, p.322.

[76] Acts 11:30. See notes there and at Acts 14:23 concerning the office and function of elders.

to be the spokesman for the congregation. Although this is not always true, it is still too often true. It can and should be corrected both by the elders and the minister in each congregation.[77]

By comparing verses 17 and 28, it is evident that "elder" and "bishop" are two names for the same office in the New Testament church.

20:18 – *And when they had come to him, he said to them, "You yourselves know, from the first day that I set foot in Asia, how I was with you the whole time,*

And when they had come to him. Paul's speech is difficult to analyze or outline because it was an occasion filled with intense emotion. However, the following is a rough summary of the major thoughts.

   I. PAUL'S EXAMPLE. Verses 18-27
      a. Serving with humility and industriousness. 18,19
      b. Teaching publicly and privately the essentials of the Faith. 20,21
      c. His plans for the future. 22-25
      d. His claim to be free from the blood of all men. 26,27

   II. PAUL'S EXHORTATION. Verses 28-35
      a. To accept the responsibilities of oversight. 28
      b. To be aware of coming dangers. 29-31
      c. To depend on prayer and the Word of God. 32
      d. To support the work by their own labor. 33-35

He said to them, "You yourselves know. There is emphasis on "You" as though someone somewhere had attacked Paul, and so Paul appeals to these men's own personal experience of Paul if they would know the truth.

> This speech is quite distinctive among all the speeches reported in Acts. It is the only Pauline speech delivered to Christians which Luke has recorded ... Just as the sermon in the synagogue at Pisidian Antioch (13:16ff) is a sample of Paul's approach to synagogue audiences, and his speeches at Lystra (14:15ff) and Athens (17:22ff) are samples of his approach to pagan audiences, so we may say that his Milesian speech is a sample of his ministry to Christian [leaders].[78]

From the first day that I set foot in Asia. To know about all of Paul's ministry in Asia,

---

[77] Dale, *op. cit.*, p.315.

[78] Bruce, *op. cit.*, p.412-413. At most places in the book of Acts where negative critics find material to use in their attacks against the genuineness and trustworthiness of the book, we have not taken time to refute each specific argument. Since the account of Paul's speech to the Ephesian elders is especially attacked by those who think Luke composed Paul's speeches, or that a redactor, perhaps even an anti-Jewish redactor, has reworked the little material in the book that can actually be attributed to Luke, it seems appropriate at this place to share the information that Knowling's commentary on Acts in *Expositor's Greek Testament* (though highly scholarly and therefore hard for the reader just being introduced to such critical matters) is excellent in its refutation of the standard critical approaches to Acts. Also, F.F. Bruce has some excellent paragraphs from time to time.

from its earliest days in the synagogue, these men who are now elders must have been among the first fruits of the gospel in Ephesus. Is it possible that among this group are some of the men won by Aquila and Priscilla, or even some of the twelve disciples of John whom Paul baptized?

How I was with you the whole time. The word translated "with" here is *meta*, and suggests an intimate association while he was with them in Ephesus. That association had begun about four years prior. All the while he worked in Ephesus and the surrounding area, these men had been able to observe Paul's actions and hear his words first-hand. If anyone knew Paul's manner of life well enough to vindicate his conduct against any derogatory report that might be circulated, these men did!

20:19 – *"serving the Lord with all humility and with tears and with trials which came upon me through the plots of the Jews;*

Serving the Lord with all humility. "Serving the Lord" speaks of Paul's discharge of the duties of his apostolic office. As he went about these tasks, Paul did so in a spirit of humility. He did not exhibit a puffed-up conceit, or boast of what he had done. "Humility" is one of Paul's favorite words.[79] Not until Jesus had shown what a virtue this characteristic could be, and not until Christians began following His example, did men come to know that "humility" was anything other than a lowly, vile characteristic that should be avoided.

And with tears. Tears of urgency for the acceptance of the Word (Acts 20:31), and of sorrow for the rejection of the gospel by some, and because of the backsliding of others. Paul was emotionally involved with the people to whom he was speaking about Jesus.[80]

And with trials which came upon me through the plots of the Jews. The earlier record of the Ephesian ministry mentioned only the Jewish plot to set forward Alexander, apparently to testify against Paul before the mob in the theater.[81] The reference to the "plots of the Jews" is something altogether distinct from Demetrius' tumult, and implies unrecorded sufferings. Paul wrote in 2 Corinthians 11:26 (just shortly after the close of his Ephesian ministry) about "perils from his own countrymen." 1 Corinthians 15:32 and 2 Corinthians 1:8-10 also speak of Paul's troubles in Asia. It appears that Paul's life was never safe, that plots against him were numerous.

20:20 – *"how I did not shrink from declaring to you anything that was profitable, and teaching you publicly and from house to house,*

How I did not shrink from declaring to you anything that was profitable. Some have noted that "shrink not" is language that Paul would hear while traveling on a ship, for it was the regular term for reefing or lowering a sail. Paul affirms that he did not become si-

---

[79] Ephesians 4:2; Philippians 2:3; Colossians 2:18,23; 3:12. Elsewhere in the New Testament "humility" appears only at 1 Peter 5:5.

[80] See Acts 20:31; 2 Corinthians 2:4; Philippians 3:18.

[81] See Acts 19:23ff. The part instigated by the Jews via Alexander is related at 19:33-34.

lent out of fear on any occasion when to do so would have caused the truth of the gospel to slow down in its forward progress.

> This statement presents Paul in striking contrast with the time-servers so abundant in our modern pulpits, who never rebuke sin except at a long distance; who speak none but smooth words about corruption in the church; and whose whole study is personal popularity.[82]

Holding back truth, out of considerations of personal popularity or advantage, that would be profitable for the salvation of the listeners is as wrong as proclaiming a false doctrine!

And teaching you publicly. This points to teaching in the synagogue and in the lecture room of Tyrannus (Acts 19:9).

And from house to house. This may speak of personal evangelism from house to house,[83] or it may speak of Paul's teaching in the different house churches in the area.

20:21 – *"solemnly testifying to both Jews and Greeks of repentance toward God and faith in our Lord Jesus Christ.*

Solemnly testifying. The same word was used at Acts 2:40. It includes not only testifying for something, but also speaking against the false views held by the listeners.

To both Jews and Greeks. The same gospel was available to both groups, and required of both the same response, if they wished to become God's children by adoption.

Of repentance toward God. The Greek reads "*the* repentance;" that is, the repentance required of people ever since John the Baptist and Jesus had begun proclaiming it.[84] The Jews had to repent because their lives were full of sin, and because they did not have right ideas about the kingdom of God, nor did they believe in Jesus Christ. The Gentiles too needed repentance. Preaching to the intellectual Gentiles at Athens, Paul spoke that God commanded all men everywhere to repent.[85]

And faith in our Lord Jesus Christ. "Faith" includes and involves active commitment and obedience, both of which distinguish living faith from dead faith.[86]

---

[82] McGarvey, *op. cit.*, p.186.

[83] Taking the passage to speak of personal evangelism from house to house, Dale shared his perspective: "There has never been a substitute for this method that will work as well. It should be observed that these were not mere social calls. Although contact and get acquainted visits are necessary, the real teaching must be done by appointment. The most effective personal work being done today is carried out in this fashion. An hour each week spent in systematic teaching of the Bible in homes will win more people to the Christ than the weekly sermons. A revival of personal evangelism by all Christians will do more to save the world than all other methods and means of soul-saving." Dale, *op. cit.*, p.327.

[84] Luke 3:3; Mark 1:15.

[85] Acts 17:29-31. Also consult Special Study #8, "What is Repentance?"

[86] James 2:17. See also Special Study #16, "The Faith that Saves."

The order in which Paul here mentions repentance toward God and faith in the Lord Jesus Christ has been an occasion of confusion to some minds, and has furnished a proof text to some who have espoused the position that in the sinner's conversion to Christ, repentance precedes faith. It is true that Paul preached repentance toward God before faith in Jesus Christ, and that his aim was to induce men to repent as a preparation for faith in Christ ... The two themes were not presented in this order because it was impossible for men to believe in Christ before repenting toward God; but because, if they are brought to repentance toward God in whom they already believe, they are in a better frame of mind for hearing the Gospel of Christ and believing in Him ... This is very far from supporting the idea that repentance precedes faith in the sense usually attached to that proposition; for this would require men to repent toward God before they believe in God, and toward Christ before they believe in Christ – an obvious absurdity.[87]

20:22 – *"And now, behold, bound in spirit, I am on my way to Jerusalem, not knowing what will happen to me there,*

And now, behold, bound in spirit, I am on my way to Jerusalem. Compare notes at Acts 19:21 about "purposing in spirit." Though this expression is stronger than the one there, neither of them seems to be a reference to the Holy Spirit. It was because of his own personal conviction that Paul was going to Jerusalem; the Holy Spirit was not forcing him to make this trip. There was, however, the constraint of an overpowering sense of duty, in spite of the dangers he was everywhere being apprised were inherently connected with this trip.[88] There is further evidence in Acts 21:14 that it was within Paul's will to choose, and not that the Holy Spirit was deciding for Paul apart from Paul's own will in the matter.

Not knowing what will happen to me there. He knew that some very difficult trials would be experienced in Jerusalem (verse 23), but he did not know whether the bonds would be any different than, say, at Philippi, nor did he know their final outcome, whether it would be life or death.

20:23 – *"except that the Holy Spirit solemnly testifies to me in every city, saying that bonds and afflictions await me.*

Except that the Holy Spirit solemnly testifies to me in every city. This speaks of predictions made by prophets in the churches, such as those spoken later by Agabus (Acts 21:11). Apparently, though Luke does not record the specifics, prophets in every city – Corinth, Berea, Thessalonica, Philippi, Troas –made utterances similar to Agabus' words.

Saying that bonds and afflictions await me. One of these predictions was likely made before Paul left Corinth, and gave rise to the request he made in Romans 15:31, that the brethren in Rome pray for his deliverance from the disobedient Jews in Judea. These verses provide important insight into the nature of miraculous spirituals gifts in New Testament times. Just as Paul apparently could not use the gift of healing to heal his own thorn in the flesh, neither could Paul use his gift of prophecy to foresee his own future.

---

[87] McGarvey, *op. cit.*, p.187.

[88] See verse 23.

20:24 – *"But I do not consider my life of any account as dear to myself, in order that I may finish my course, and the ministry which I received from the Lord Jesus, to testify solemnly of the gospel of the grace of God.*

But I do not consider my life of any account as dear to myself. Paul had given his life to Christ; now he was willing to die, if necessary, in order to further the cause of Christ. He did not consider his life so valuable that he would turn away from bonds and persecutions, thereby sacrificing duty, just to preserve himself alive.

In order that I may finish my course. Paul plainly tells the Ephesian elders that finishing the activity that Jesus had given him to do was of greater importance to him than preserving his own life. Jesus, when He appeared to Paul on the Damascus Road, called Paul to his life's work, and sent him as an apostle to the Gentiles.[89] And by the grace of the Lord, Paul was going to complete the task that had been given to him.[90]

And the ministry which I received from the Lord Jesus. See Acts 9:15-17 concerning the "ministry" (i.e., the apostleship) he received.

To testify solemnly of the gospel of the grace of God. Paul was called to bear witness to the good news that God's grace was available in Jesus Christ, to bear witness to a dying world of the good news that God is merciful toward repentant sinners.

20:25 – *"And now, behold, I know that all of you, among whom I went about preaching the kingdom, will see my face no more.*

And now, behold, I know that all of you, among whom I went about preaching the kingdom. "Know" (*oida*) here is a conviction based on personal observation and on his own plans to work in another area other than the central Mediterranean and Aegean Seas.[91] Barnes has expressed it, "I have no expectation of seeing you again; I have every reason to suppose that this is my final interview with you."[92]

See notes at Acts 1:6 and 14:22 concerning the "kingdom." There can be little doubt that Paul emphasized that the kingdom was present in the world, and had been since Peter used the keys of the kingdom on the day of Pentecost, some 28 years earlier. Paul would have spoken of how Christians are presently citizens of the kingdom, and that "through much tribulation" they could enter the kingdom in its future perfect realization.[93]

Will see my face no more. At this point, it looked to Paul very much as if his missionary

---

[89] See notes at Acts 26:16ff.

[90] Compare Paul's statement at the close of his life (2 Timothy 4:7).

[91] It had long been Paul's plan to first visit Jerusalem, and then to go to Rome and Spain (Acts 19:21; Romans 1:15).

[92] Barnes, *op. cit.*, p.294.

[93] A comparison of this phrase about the "kingdom" with the previous phrase about "grace" (verse 24) suggests that the two are synonymous. This is another place that Acts suggests that the doctrine of Dispensationalism is wrong. See Acts 3:24.

activities would take him to other areas of the world so that he would not see the brethren from Ephesus again. However, when God eventually worked out His plans, Paul was in fact able to visit these brethren again at the close of the first Roman imprisonment. He will visit Ephesus, and Troas, and Miletus, and Macedonia again.[94]

20:26 – *"Therefore I testify to you this day, that I am innocent of the blood of all men.*

Therefore I testify to you this day. "Therefore"[95] sums up all he has just said about his past ministry and labors among them. The Greek word here translated "testify" is spelled a bit differently than the one in verse 24. This one means "I call you to witness." That is, Paul is saying, 'You know how hard I labored in an effort to reach men with the gospel. If men are lost, or if they prove unfaithful and so become lost again, I appeal to your own experience of me that the fault is not mine.' "This day" is the very day of his departure (he thought for good) from this area of service.

That I am innocent of the blood of all men. If some individuals should die the second death, if they should be lost forever, Paul would not be to blame. He had discharged his duty in faithfully warning and teaching them.

> Paul had taught them the will of God and had warned them of the doom of those who would not obey the gospel. As a watchman standing on the wall, he had warned all; hence, he was not chargeable with their destruction; his skirts were clear from the blood of all, as he had faithfully warned all of their duty and of the coming wrath (Ezekiel 3:18-21). Paul had declared the whole counsel of God here as he had at Corinth (Acts 18:6).[96]

20:27 – *"For I did not shrink from declaring to you the whole purpose of God.*

For I did not shrink from declaring to you. Since the verse begins with "for" it must be understood as giving a reason for what was just said in the previous verse.[97] It explains why Paul regarded himself as innocent if some should be lost. We've already had the verb "shrink" in verse 20. Again, Paul is saying, "I have not kept back; I have not been deterred by fear or by desire of popularity, or by the fact that the doctrine of the gospel is often unpalatable to people, from declaring to you the complete message." Comparing this verse with what he says about "profitable" in verse 20, we are led to see that whatever might con-

---

[94] 1 Timothy 1:3, 3:4, 4:13; 2 Timothy 4:13,20.

[95] The word translated "therefore" is *dioti*, a word found only in Luke's writings (it is used of Paul at Acts 13:35; 18:10; 20:26; 22:18) and in Paul's writings in the New Testament. All through this speech of Paul's there are similar words and phrases that are peculiar to Paul, which should be viewed as evidences that this is not a discourse that was made up later and attributed to Paul.

[96] Boles, *op. cit.*, p.325. If this is a reference to Ezekiel 3, it is noteworthy as being one of the few places where Ezekiel is quoted in the New Testament.

[97] Verses beginning with "wherefore" or "therefore" give a conclusion that is based on things that have just been said in the previous verses. Verses beginning with "for" give a reason for, or an explanation of, something just stated in a previous verse.

tribute to their salvation was what was included in Paul's teaching.[98]

The whole purpose of God. The epistle to the Ephesians, even if we consider it to be a circular letter that ended up at Ephesus, has a striking parallel to what Paul affirms here. In chapter 1 of that letter, Paul speaks about the divine purpose of God that has been running through all the ages, he talks about the church as the body of Christ, and he encourages believers, whether Jew or Gentile, to endeavor to keep the unity of the Spirit, lest men frustrate what God planned for them back in eternity before creation. God had revealed all this to Paul, and Paul had in turn shared with the people of Ephesus about Jesus, salvation, the kingdom of God, and how God is working through the Church to unite all things unto Himself.

20:28 – *"Be on guard for yourselves and for all the flock, among which the Holy Spirit has made you overseers, to shepherd the church of God which He purchased with His own blood.*

Be on guard for yourselves. The verb translated "be on guard" was also used in Acts 5:35 ("take care") and 8:6 ("give attention to"). Paul is exhorting the elders to be careful or cautious, to give attention first of all to their own life and faith. Any leader has temptations peculiar to his position, and connected with the duties of his office. The faithful ministry of any elder must grow out of a faithful life. Hence, their first concern must be to establish their own faith (see 1 Timothy 4:16).

And for all the flock. The relationship of the elder to the church (here called "the flock") is like that of the shepherd to the flock (1 Peter 5:1-5). Each believer is in need of an elder's shepherding ministry.

Among which the Holy Spirit has made you overseers. Observe that the elders are "among" the flock; that is, they are themselves part of the flock. The word translated "overseers" (note the marginal reading, "bishops") literally means to "look upon, to look at, to take care of," and hence to oversee, superintend, to be a guardian of. This is one of the indications in the New Testament that elders are the overseers, or governors, or guardians of the church.[99]

In what sense could it be said that the Holy Spirit *made* them bishops?

- Some find in this verb "made" evidence for a group of men who were unordained by the apostles, but simply had been appointed by the Holy Spirit. While the doctrine of apostolic succession"[100] is unfounded, we doubt this verse is a proof text that there were officers in the early church who were unordained.

- "Made" likely includes the ideas that the Holy Spirit provided the pattern for the church

---

[98] Some treat "you" in this sentence as emphatic, implying that Paul could teach the Ephesians things he was unable to share with others, because the Ephesians were more receptive.

[99] Elders are the leaders (overseers). The New Testament knows nothing of a church board where the deacons can outvote the elders and thereby govern the church.

[100] See the paragraph on "Ordination" in Special Study #12, "A Method of Selection of Elders and Deacons."

by which men were chosen as elders (i.e., shepherds, bishops),[101] and the Spirit had also provided the spiritual gifts which had qualified these men for the work.

To shepherd the church of God. "Shepherding" includes more than the act of feeding, though that is certainly involved. There is also the matter of governing and protecting.

The correct reading of this passage, along with 1 Timothy 3:16, has long been a source of controversy among scholars, and that controversy has not yet been absolutely settled. That is, what did Luke write in his autograph copy? If Luke wrote "God," then this is a New Testament passage which affirms that Jesus is God, for the verse goes on to speak of how He (and the reference must be to Jesus) purchased the Church with His own blood. However, there are three different readings found in the manuscripts at this place.

1) Some manuscripts read "the church of God." Among the manuscripts which have this reading are Codices Vaticanus and Sinaiticus. Typically, textual critics hold that when these two important manuscripts agree on a reading, more than 99% of the time it can be considered to be what was in the original. Other evidences for this reading are the Vulgate and Harkleian Syriac versions, and a number of the early church fathers. The fact that Paul elsewhere speaks regularly of "the church of God"[102] and never of "the church of the Lord" may also be an argument that "church of God" was what Paul said when speaking to the Ephesian elders.

2) Some ancient manuscripts read "the church of the Lord," among which are Codices Alexandrinus, Ephraemi, and Claromontanus. In addition, this is the reading found in the Egyptian versions of the New Testament, in the margin of the Harkleian Syriac, and in a number of early church fathers as well, among them Irenaeus, Chrysostom, and Jerome. Some have even advanced an idea how the wording may have changed from the original "Lord" to the reading "God." It is affirmed that in the ancient manuscripts the words were often abbreviated. Thus, the name Christ (*christos*) is abbreviated CHOS; the name God (*theos*) is abbreviated THOS; the name Lord (*kurios*) was abbreviated KOS. Hence, a mistake of a single letter by a copyist would lead to the variations observable in the manuscripts.

3) Another variant reading has "the church of the Lord and God." Codices Mutinensis, Angelicus, and Porfirianus, along with most minuscules have this reading. However, since all these latter come from the 8th and 9th centuries and later, we probably can reduce our options to one of the first two as being representative of Luke's autograph.

At this writing, there seems to be no reason to object to the reading found in the NASB. And there certainly is no reason to object to the idea that Paul spoke of Jesus, the one whose blood was shed, as being God, for he certainly so speaks of Him in Romans 9:5 and Titus 2:13.

---

[101] "Elder" and "bishop" are titles for the same office, and the terms were used interchangeably through the whole 1st century and into the early part of the 2nd century. In Clement of Rome (*Cor.* XLII.4; XLIV.1,4,5) the terms are still synonymous, and the same is true by implication in the *Didache*, XV.1. It is in Ignatius, at the beginning of the 2nd century, that the two terms begin to be given different meanings than they had in the New Testament.

[102] 1 Corinthians 1:2; 2 Corinthians 1:1; Galatians 1:13; 1 Thessalonians 2:14.

Which He purchased with His own blood. This word "purchased" occurs but one other place in the New Testament, at 1 Timothy 3:13 where it is translated "obtain." It properly means "to acquire or gain anything." In this place it means that Christ acquired, gained, or procured the church for Himself, and the price was His own blood.[103]

20:29 – *"I know that after my departure savage wolves will come in among you, not sparing the flock;*

I know that after my departure savage wolves will come in among you. The opposition of false teachers was already evident among some of the churches Paul had planted, but they had so far been held in check by the apostle's presence. When he was no longer in their midst, the false teachers would have an easier time.

Paul keeps up the same figure he has been using of a shepherd and a flock as he now talks of ferocious wolves[104] destroying the flock. These savage wolves might come disguised in sheep's clothing (Matthew 7:15), but still their teachings would tear and divide the church. Just what group of false teachers Paul had in mind, we cannot say. He may have been speaking of the Judaizers who were already entering into the churches from the outside and causing divisions, as they had at Galatia. He might have had in mind the teachers of false and destructive doctrines, such as those of the Nicolaitans (Revelation 2:6) and the Gnostics (against whom John particularly argues in his Gospel and in 1 John). These wolves did scatter the church into divided fragments, and brought spiritual death to many of their victims.

In the present day, such a title as "savage wolves" could be properly given to the modernists, the Neo-orthodox, and the Neo-liberals, who deny the teachings of Scripture and bind burdensome disbeliefs on Christ's disciples. Such a term, too, could properly be applied to those who compromise God's Word in order to seek ecumenicity at any price, whether it is in harmony with God's Word or not. And Paul would not hesitate to apply the title to troublemakers who selfishly and ambitiously seek to use the church for personal gain and glory. An elder has a tremendous task to be on guard against such persons, whether men or women.

Not sparing the flock. This expression is probably a *litotes* for "seeking to destroy the church." What Paul predicted did happen. The Pastoral Epistles, two of which were written to Ephesus about eight years after this message to the Ephesian elders was delivered, contain references to the fact that many have defected from the faith.[105] And a generation later, Christ will direct a letter to the Ephesian church, reproaching the Christians at Ephesus for having left their first love.[106] 2 Peter, which was written about the same time as the Pastoral Epistles were, is addressed partly to this same area, and also speaks of false prophets who bring in heresies that when embraced lead to damnation, and

---

[103] F.J.A. Hort in *Christian Ecclesia* (London: Macmillan, 1900), p.14 and 102, suggests Paul's language had Psalm 74:2 in mind, and was pouring new content into that passage as he applied it to the Church.

[104] Jesus had spoken of false teachers as wolves in the Sermon on the Good Shepherd (John 10:1ff).

[105] 1 Timothy 1:19ff, 4:1ff; 2 Timothy 3:1ff.

[106] Revelation 2:1ff.

who deny even the Lord who bought them (2 Peter 2:1).

20:30 – *"and from among your own selves men will arise, speaking perverse things, to draw away the disciples after them.*

And from among your own selves men will arise. Not only from the outside, but from among the membership, and even from the very eldership here listening to Paul speak, would come those who would disturb the church.

Speaking perverse things. The Pastoral Epistles again supply abundant evidence of the rightness of Paul's prediction. In a few years, the Ephesians will have witnessed Hymenaeus, Alexander, and Philetus saying that the resurrection was past already,[107] Phygelus and Hermogenes will have turned away,[108] and evil men and seducers would become worse and worse,[109] resisting the faith, as Jannes and Jambres had resisted Moses.[110] Some suggest that Hymenaeus and some of the other men named in 1 and 2 Timothy were actually present, listening to this warning by Paul, only to be warned in vain.

To draw away the disciples after them. Men who had previously been disciples of Christ will become apostate because of the influence of the leaders who went astray, Paul declares. And if what happens in our day also happened then, we could say that the influence of these teachers would leave homes divided and congregations split. Numerous men, babes in Christ, would become disgusted and leave the church altogether.

Paul has spoken of two sources of potential trouble for the Ephesian elders: false teachers from the outside, and defections from within their own ranks. It would be considerably easier to victoriously oppose those from without, if there were no foes arising within. All the power of the persecutors is not so much to be feared as the secret plans, the party strife, the character assassination, and the contentions which are produced by those who love and seek power among the professed friends of Christ. In his comments on this verse, Dale has suggested the following principle:

> No congregation, or Bible college, or human agency can be assured of faithfulness beyond one generation. Not even a church founded by an apostle was so assured. Such congregations and arms of the congregations fall from inward decay, deception, or departure from the faith. Faithful leaders must not allow this fact to discourage them. Men of faith always arise to defend and to develop the opportunities for service and salvation in every generation. Each generation has to save itself. Each individual is responsible for the institutions he supports by his own life and service. It is the faith of our Lord that we must constantly be concerned about. Attachments to persons or property must not weaken nor destroy our faithfulness to Christ and His Word. Men go bad and friends disappoint us, but Christ will never fail us or forsake us.[111]

---

[107] 1 Timothy 1:20, 2 Timothy 2:17.

[108] 2 Timothy 1:15.

[109] 2 Timothy 3:13.

[110] 2 Timothy 3:8.

[111] Dale, *op. cit.*, p.331.

20:31 – *"Therefore be on the alert, remembering that night and day for a period of three years I did not cease to admonish each one with tears.*

Therefore be on the alert. The men who were the shepherds, the guardians, the overseers of the flock, ought, above all others, to set an example of vigilance. In view of the dangers which were peculiar to the men in places of leadership (verse 28), the danger posed by false teachers outside the church (verse 29), and the danger which defections from among their own number would raise (verse 30), they needed to be on their guard.

Remembering that night and day for a period of three years. Calling to mind Paul's own efforts at "being on the alert" might well spur them to similar vigilance. "Night" may be listed first in order to emphasize how ceaselessly and tirelessly Paul had acted as a watchful shepherd over them. "Three years" is probably a round number, including the three months in the synagogue (Acts 19:8), the two years in the school of Tyrannus (Acts 19:10), and some time in Ephesus after closing his ministry from the school of Tyrannus.

I did not cease to admonish each one. "Admonish" is a word that appears only here and in Paul's writings in the New Testament. It speaks of giving another a loving warning. There is a difference between teaching and admonishing. Teaching is inculcating the truth as given by God. Admonishing has to do with correcting, warning, disciplining, and encouraging for the purpose of getting the listener to do as he had been instructed.

With tears. Compare notes at verse 19. The salvation offered in the gospel was a matter of life and death, for eternity as well as time. Paul felt such urgency that men and women believe it and obey it, that it left him in tears when people rejected the Savior.

20:32 – *"And now I commend you to God and to the word of His grace, which is able to build you* up *and to give* you *the inheritance among all those who are sanctified.*

And now I commend you to God. About to leave them, and thinking he would not again be able to shepherd them personally, he commits them to the care and keeping of a faithful God.[112] "Commend," as explained at Acts 14:23, carries a connotation of "trust," like is involved when one commits his money to another for safe-keeping.

And to the word of His grace. This expression seems to be synonymous with the gospel preaching (and writing), which, for several years yet, would be passed along mostly by oral tradition. Only Matthew of the Gospels has been published at this time, and a few of Paul's epistles. The rest of the "Word of His grace"[113] was still in oral form. That gospel, with

---

[112] Instead of "God," Codex Sinaiticus, a few minuscules (including 33 and 68), the Egyptian versions, and some other manuscripts read "Lord," which Wescott and Hort adopted as the reading in their text. Because of this and the use of the expression "Word of His grace" in the next phrase, some have argued that Paul is telling these elders to study the Gospel of John, which speaks about Word and grace in its early verses. However, there is precious little evidence that John's Gospel had yet been written. In fact, it may be another 25 or 30 years till that Gospel is published at Ephesus.

[113] "Word of His grace" probably includes the ideas that the gospel proclaims God's grace in redeeming man, and His grace in sanctifying them, too.

its facts to be believed, its commands to be obeyed, its warnings to be heeded, and its promises to be enjoyed, would give these elders the direction and guidance they needed as they did their shepherding of the flock. In time, there would be a collection of New Testament books which would serve the same purpose

Which is able to build *you* up. There is a technical problem here that cannot be settled from the Greek. It is not possible to be certain whether it is God who is able to build them up, or whether it is the Word which does the building. The NASB translation is based on the practice of referring back to the nearest antecedent, unless such an interpretation would cause a contradiction. "Which is able" has the connotation of "has the inherent power." The gospel has power to build a man up to salvation.[114] The figure in the word "build up" is that of a house which is being raised and completed by slow degrees. According to the NASB reading, Paul says that the gospel was the powerful tool used by God to confirm and establish men. It helps them to grow spiritually. A person just cannot spend time studying and meditating on the Word of grace without very quickly becoming different than he was.

And to give *you* the inheritance. The "inheritance" is eternal life in heaven, plus the anticipation of a resurrection body.[115]

Among all those who are sanctified. Paul is looking forward to the time when all redeemed, in their glorified resurrection bodies, are sharing the joys of heaven. Those redeemed people he here calls "sanctified ones." A person who is in Christ is sanctified, a saint; he has been sanctified by the truth (the Word of God),[116] and "by faith in Christ Jesus."[117] The participle here is in the perfect tense, indicating that the sanctification was an act completed in the time past (long before their entrance upon the inheritance) but with present continuing results.

20:33 – *"I have coveted no one's silver or gold or clothes.*

I have coveted no one's silver or gold or clothes. These three words were the terms listed when a man talked about riches in the ancient world.[118] Paul not only did not take riches from his students, he did not even covet them! As the suggested outline of Paul's address to the Ephesian elders shows, we consider this to be another area where Paul appeals to his own example as a model for them to imitate. The point is this: a man who shepherds and leads the people of God must do so without thought of how much material reward he will receive. Of course, it is proper for preachers of the gospel to be supported by those who

---

[114] Romans 1:16; Hebrews 4:12; Isaiah 49:2; Jeremiah 23:29.

[115] Ephesians 1:14.

[116] John 17:17.

[117] Acts 26:18. Comments on this verse are located earlier in this book under the section titled "Paul's trip to Damascus" (see p.351ff).

[118] Genesis 24:53; 2 Kings 5:5; Psalm 45:13ff.

are taught by them,[119] and elders who rule well are worthy of a double honor.[120] But, considering the following verses, the thing Paul is warning against is the desire to be ministered to, for that would be a wrong motive. The proper motive for the Christian is how to be helpful to others. Paul himself has given us the example to follow. He did not preach for the love of money, nor to display his talent, nor to satisfy any selfish ambition; he had only a simple and sincere desire to serve his Lord and His church.

20:34 – *"You yourselves know that these hands ministered to my* **own** *needs and to the men who were with me.*

You yourselves know that these hands ministered to my *own* **needs.** "You yourselves" is emphatic. Others might not know it, but they did! We can see Paul hold his hands out for the elders to see as he spoke about how he had worked with "these hands" to support himself while at Ephesus. Paul had come to Ephesus with Aquila and Priscilla, with whom he had worked at tent-making in Corinth (Acts 18:3). He makes it clear, both here and in 1 Corinthians 4:12, that he had continued to earn his living by working at tent-making while in Ephesus. Some appeal to Philemon 17 as evidence that Philemon also was a partner in the same trade, along with Aquila and Paul.

And to the men who were with me. Paul had worked not only to support himself, but he helped to support those who were with him in the missionary party.[121]

20:35 – *"In everything I showed you that by working hard in this manner you must help the weak and remember the words of the Lord Jesus, that He Himself said, 'It is more blessed to give than to receive.'"*

In everything I showed you. Whether it be in spiritual labor or manual labor, Paul's example was one the elders could emulate. Paul's example was that by his own work he not only supported himself, he also helped to support others who needed it. Paul's words to the elders will be repeated later in Ephesians 4:28, where he sets forth the Christian work ethic. It takes the monotony out of a person's everyday labor, if, while he works, he anticipates and prayerfully plans how he will help others with the money he is earning!

That by working hard in this manner you must help the weak. "Working" may speak of spiritual or manual labors, as the context may require. "Working *hard*" is suggested by the particular Greek word Paul used, a word that has a connotation of the weariness that accompanies hard work. "Help" pictures "taking another man's part," to hold him up when he is too weak to stand. "Weak" (*asthenēs*) is a word which may speak of physical sickness, moral weakness, or financial weakness, depending on the context. We may take it of bodily sickness (which would cause a man to be unable to work, and thus to be without income to support himself or his family), or just of general poverty in this passage. In al-

---

[119] 1 Corinthians 9:13-14.

[120] 1 Timothy 5:17.

[121] 1 Corinthians 9:12,15.

most all of Paul's letters he has something to say about the "weak."[122] He is himself on his way to Jerusalem with a large offering for the poor saints there.

And remember the words of the Lord Jesus. The words that follow are not found in the Gospels of Matthew, Mark, Luke, or John, nor indeed even in any of the Apocryphal Gospels. The command to "remember" these words implies, however, that they were well-known and familiar. This passage, then, furnishes an evidence of how widespread was the oral teaching about the acts and words of Christ, of which the four Gospels are but partial representatives.

That He Himself said, "It is more blessed to give than to receive." This is not the only place where Paul quotes the very words of the Lord Himself.[123] The word Jesus used was "blessed" – it is something much higher and deeper and fuller than mere happiness. There is a deep sense of blessedness that is experienced by the one who gives! There is a more lasting satisfaction resulting from being one who gives than there is in being one who simply gets.

With this memorable quotation from Jesus, Paul closes his address. Long after he has left the area, these elders will be able to recall this meeting at Miletus, and most of all, they will remember his closing statement from the lips of Jesus.

20:36 – *And when he had said these things, he knelt down and prayed with them all.*

And when he had said these things, he knelt down and prayed with them all. The message is finished. Together they all kneel for prayer.[124] While Luke does not record the words of the prayer, there have been many parallels between this message to the elders and the letter Paul wrote to the Ephesians. Perhaps some of the prayer thoughts expressed in Ephesians 3:14-21 were also part of this prayer.

20:37 – *And they began to weep aloud and embraced Paul, and repeatedly kissed him,*

And they *began* to weep aloud. When Christ and His love have welded souls together, a time of parting is a time of open crying.

And embraced Paul. The elders embraced him, as is still the custom among the peoples of the Middle East, as token of affection.

And repeatedly kissed him. "Kissed" is a translation of *katephiloun,* an imperfect tense verb, which speaks of a repetition of the act. Either they kept on kissing him, or one after another the elders embraced him and kissed him farewell.[125]

---

[122] Admonitions about helping the weak are found in Romans 15:1; Galatians 6:2, 5:14; 2 Thessalonians 3:10ff.

[123] 1 Corinthians 7:10-12 is another example of where Paul quoted Jesus' own words.

[124] Concerning the posture while praying, see notes at Acts 2:42.

[125] Such a means of greeting or bidding farewell was as customary with them as shaking hands is with us when we meet or say good-bye to a close friend.

20:38 – *grieving especially over the word which he had spoken, that they should see his face no more. And they were accompanying him to the ship.*

Grieving especially over the word which he had spoken, that they should see his face no more. The thing that most grieved them and filled them with sadness was the thought that they would probably see Paul no more this side of Heaven.

And they were accompanying him to the ship. The harbor was a short distance from the place where they had met. The ship was about to weigh anchor and sail away from Miletus. The Ephesian elders escorted Paul to the dock, and, comparing notes on this same expression at Acts 15:3, they perhaps even gave him some provisions for his continuing trip. They then returned home to Ephesus.

Ships of the Period

Drawing by Horace Knowles
from the British and Foreign Bible Society

SPECIAL STUDY #18

THE LORD'S SUPPER

There are few things more tragic in the history of Christ's followers than the fact that they have fought and argued over the Lord's Supper. Some who sincerely thought they were following Christ have cruelly persecuted and even put to death others who thought they too were following Christ, and the reason for the persecutions was that the victims did not hold certain doctrines respecting the Lord's Supper, doctrines which could not be proved, and which possibly are not even true. Let each reader who begins this Special Study do so with the prayer that he not be guilty of further adding to the distress that Christ must feel as He watches men struggle over the ordinance He left to help men "proclaim His death till He comes."[1]

Points of special interest in this study will be the names applied to the Lord's Supper; the original institution of the Lord's Supper; the elements used in that original institution and the elements used today; the observance of the Supper in the church during the days of the apostles, in the post-apostolic church, in the Roman Catholic church, in Luther's theology, in Zwingli's, Calvin's, in the Church of the Brethren, and in the Restoration Movement.[2]

I. THE PERTINENT PASSAGES

The passages dealing with the Lord's Supper, in the order that they were written, are Matthew 26:26-30; 1 Corinthians 10:16-17 and 11:23-32; Luke 22:14-20; Acts 2:42 and 20:7; Mark 14:22-25; and John 6:52-58.[3]

II. THE NAMES APPLIED TO THE LORD'S SUPPER

In the Scriptures, various terms are used to refer to the Lord's Supper – Lord's Supper (1 Corinthians 11:20); Lord's Table (1 Corinthians 10:21);[4] Communion (1 Corinthians 10:16); and breaking of bread (Acts 2:42). The cup is called the cup of blessing (1 Corinthians 10:16), the cup of the Lord (1 Corinthians 10:21), and the fruit of the vine (Matthew 26:29).

---

[1] 1 Corinthians 11:26.

[2] Some of the following materials are adapted from the article on the Lord s Supper in the *International Standard Bible Encyclopedia* (Grand Rapids: Eerdmans, 1949), Vol. III. p.1921ff.

[3] The relevance of John 6 to the Lord's Supper has been disputed for ages, and still is today.

[4] The expression "Lord's Table" has been taken to mean that at Corinth there was a raised platform on which the loaf and cup rested during the service, until it was time to celebrate the Lord s Supper.

Following the days of the apostles, other terms have been introduced to speak of the Lord's Supper.

In many groups, the Lord's Supper is called the "Eucharist." This term comes from the Greek word *eucharisteō*, meaning "to give thanks" (Matthew 26:27; 1 Corinthians 11:24). This term is incomplete since it speaks not of the Lord's Supper itself, but merely of one feature in the institution of the Supper, namely, the giving of thanks.

In post-apostolic days, Communion also became known as the "liturgy,"[5] and as the "sacrifice" and as the "mystery."

The Roman Church calls it "the Mass." The word "mass" is a reapplication of the Latin word *missa*, which is found in the phrase *congregation missa est,* meaning "the congregation is sent away." In post-apostolic times, the first part of the worship services, known as the *missa catechumenorum* (that is, the service for the catechumens, at the end of which the catechumens were dismissed), was closed. The second part of the worship, known as the *missa fidelium* (that is, the service for believers) included the Lord's Supper. Since the Lord's Supper was observed in the latter part of the meeting, and since its observance was the chief purpose of this assembly, and since after its observance the congregation was dismissed and sent away, through an unusual transition and corruption of the word *missa*, the Lord's Supper came, in time, to be called "the mass."[6]

Also in the Roman Church, the "bread" is regularly called the "Host." This word comes from the Latin *hostia*, meaning "a sacrifice, a victim." This idea is closely connected with that of transubstantiation, which will be discussed later. The word is applied to the wafer, or bread, only; it does not refer to the cup.[7] Just before the wafer is presented to the people, the priest holds it up before the people for their adoration, in an act is called "the elevation of the host."

Many groups also call the Lord's Supper a "Sacrament." This word comes from the Latin *sacramentum*, and means, according to Webster, "an oath, a sacred thing, a mystery." According to the *Catholic Faith Based on the Catholic Catechism* (A Roman Catholic study guide), "a sacrament is an outward sign instituted by Jesus Christ to bring grace to our souls."[8] "Grace is a supernatural gift which God gives us through the merits of Jesus Christ[9] ... God gives us two kinds of grace: Sanctifying grace, i.e., that supernatural gift of God which makes us ... pleasing to him;[10] and Actual grace, i.e., the supernatural help

---

[5] "Liturgy" is a transliteration of the Greek work *leitourgeō*, meaning a "sacred ministration." The application to Communion comes perhaps from a misinterpretation of Romans 15:16

[6] In passing, the Roman Catholic Church has developed three kinds of masses. (1) The low mass, in which the ritual is spoken by the priest in a low tone, without any response by the choir or instrument. (2) The high mass, in which the ritual is spoken by the priest in an ordinary tone, with responses, at intervals, by the choir and instrument. (3) The solemn high mass, which is the same as the high mass, with the addition that the priest is now attended by a deacon and a subdeacon.

[7] Prior to the Second Vatican Council, the members of the congregation in a Roman Catholic Church did not partake of the cup; the congregation partook of the bread only. The priest partook of the cup for all.

[8] Gasparri, Peter Cardinal, *Catholic Faith Based on the Catholic Catechism* (Washington DC: Catholic University of America Press, 1938), p.192.

[9] *Op. cit.*, p.164.

[10] *Op. cit.*, p.166.

which God gives us to know, to will, and to do what is right."[11] The *Shorter Catechism of the Westminster Standards* says that "A sacrament is a holy ordinance instituted by Christ; wherein by sensible signs, Christ and the benefits of the new covenant are represented, sealed, and applied to believers" (Answer 92).[12] The use of the word "sacrament" for the Lord's Supper seems to be related to Jesus' statement, "This cup is the new covenant in my blood."

To conclude this section on "Names," a question is in order. Should we not be content with Bible names for Bible things?

III. THE ORIGINAL INSTITUTION OF THE LORD'S SUPPER

In each of the four accounts of the institution of the Lord's Supper in the New Testament (Matthew 26; Mark 14; Luke 22; 1 Corinthians 11), there is a general agreement as to the main features included. The accounts of Matthew and Mark have close affinities. So have those of Paul and Luke. The main differences between the two groups is that Matthew-Mark omit the words "This do in remembrance of Me" which Luke-Paul have. Matthew-Mark include the words "shed for many unto remission of sins" after reference to the blood of the covenant, which Luke-Paul do not have. The Synoptic Gospels also have the Lord's statement about His reunion with the disciples in the Kingdom, while Paul alone has "For as often as you eat this bread and drink this cup, you proclaim the Lord's death until He comes" (1 Corinthians 11:26).

The Lord's Supper was instituted at the close of the Passover meal, the night before Jesus was crucified (Luke 22:20). Both groups record Jesus giving thanks over the bread, breaking it, and giving it to His disciples to eat. Matthew-Mark mention Jesus' giving of thanks over the cup, which Paul omits in 1 Corinthians 11, but alludes to in "cup of blessing" (1 Corinthians 10:16). Matthew relates that Jesus urged the apostles to "Drink from it, all of you," and Mark tells us "They all drank of it." By the words "Do this (Greek, "Continue to do this!") in remembrance of Me," Jesus commanded His followers to observe the Lord's Supper regularly.

The institution of the Lord's Supper by Jesus has been entirely called into question by radical German critics.[13] They point to the absence of the whole matter in John (according to their interpretation of John 6), and to the omission of the words "Do this in remembrance of Me" in Matthew-Mark. From this, they argue that Jesus never commanded the Supper as an ordinance.[14] The negative critics further allege that the words "Do this in remembrance of Me" are found in Luke's Gospel only because Paul exerted an undue in-

---

[11] *Op. cit.*, p.170.

[12] Westminster Shorter Catechism, Question 92, in *The Creeds of Christendom,* by Philip Schaff (Grand Rapids: Baker Book House, 1966), Vol. III, p.696.

[13] Some of the critics and the names of their writings are given in the article on "The Lord's Supper" in Schaff-Herzog's *Encyclopedia of Religious Knowledge* (Grand Rapids: Baker Book House, 1956), Vol. 7, p.24.

[14] In general, negative critics assign primacy to Mark's Gospel, and then contend that all the other Gospel writers copied from Mark. Thus, if an event is not found in Mark, it is of doubtful authority.

fluence over Luke's narrative. Thus, the German critics would have us believe the Lord's Supper is something Paul thought up. However, the fact that the Lord's Supper was a fixed part of the worship in the pre-Pauline church (Acts 2:42) denies this German theory. It is small wonder that the Lord's Supper should be so attacked by the radicals. The doctrine of Christ's vicarious suffering is nowhere so clearly enunciated as in the words of the institution of the Lord's Supper, "This is My body which is given for you." For the negative critics to maintain their doctrine that the death of Christ was not vicarious, the testimony of the Lord's Supper regarding the vicariousness of His death had to be destroyed.

We conclude that the Lord's Supper was given to the Church by a command of Jesus, being first instituted just after the Passover meal, the night before Jesus was crucified.

IV. ELEMENTS USED IN THE ORIGINAL INSTITUTION, AND TODAY

THE BREAD. The bread used by Jesus would have been the unleavened bread of the Passover (Exodus 12:19). In fact, Matthew refers to the Passover as "The feast of unleavened bread" (Matthew 26:17.) "Unleavened bread" is *adzumos* in the Greek. However, in all the New Testament passages which speak of the early church's observance of the Lord's Supper, the word translated bread or loaf is *artos*, a word which can mean either leavened or unleavened bread.

The bread used today varies among religious bodies. The Eastern Church (Greek Catholic), perhaps influenced by the bitter Ebionite spirit of the Judaizers, later adopted the use of common bread (*kainos artos*), just to be different from the Jews. The Western Church (Roman Catholic) has regularly used unleavened bread. Protestants have generally left the matter among the *adiaphora* ("matters of indifference").[15]

It cannot be categorically said that unleavened bread must be used in the observance today. However, the weight of evidence is that unleavened bread was used by Jesus when the Supper was originally instituted.

THE CUP. It has been a matter of dispute from the beginning as to what "wine" was used in the institution of the Lord's Supper. Disputed has been not only whether the "wine" was fermented or unfermented, but also the raw materials out of which the "wine" was made.

At the beginning, this fact should be noted. Nowhere in the New Testament is the word "wine" (*oinos*) used in connection with the Lord's Supper. The terms used in the New Testament are "fruit of the vine" and "the cup." The Greek word for "wine" (*oinos*) can mean either fermented or unfermented wine. And neither does the word by itself determine the raw materials out of which the drink was made; *oinos* was used of the liquids made from the juices not only of the grape, but also from apples, pears, and palms.[16] Still, might it be possible that the words "the fruit of the vine" are deliberately used to limit the kind of liquid used in the Lord's Supper to the juice of the grape? This commentator tends to think so.

---

[15] ISBE, *op. cit.*, p.1925.

[16] Herodotus, I.193, II.86. See also Josephus, *Antiquities*, II.5.2.

What "wine" was used in the celebration of the Passover? Was the cup Jesus used to institute the Lord's Supper fermented or unfermented? Ancient Jews, we are told, used a thick boiled wine at Passover, mixed with water.[17] According to the command of God (Leviticus 10:9) and the teaching of the Mishna, Jewish religious leaders were not allowed to drink intoxicating wine when serving before the Lord. It is therefore very doubtful that the wine used in the Passover by the ancients would be intoxicating (i.e., fermented). If the Mishna is true, which tells us that a total of three pints would be consumed during the Passover, were it intoxicating, the majority of celebrants would be drunk by the close of the meal. Modern Jews quite generally use raisin wine, made by steeping (soaking) raisins overnight in water, and expressing the juice the next day for use at the Passover meal. How ancient this practice is, is not known. Even if the Jews of Jesus' day used this type of "wine" in the Passover, it would be the "fruit of the vine," for raisins are dried grapes. It is generally believed that the early church used mixed wine (wine and water) just as was the Jewish Passover custom.[18] Whether the contents of the cup were fermented or unfermented would likely have reflected Jewish Passover customs prevailing at the time.

Because of the uncertainty related to the fermented or unfermented question, the practice among churches in regard to the wine used in the celebration of the Lord's Supper has varied. The Roman Church through the years has used fermented red wine. The word "new" (Matthew 26:29) is believed by many to indicate the character of the wine used by Christ as being the juice of fresh grapes pressed out.[19] That unfermented grape juice was called "wine" is demonstrated by the fact that Josephus so speaks of grape juice when writing of the story of Joseph interpreting the cupbearer's dream.[20] On the other hand, the Third Council of Braga, c. AD 675, explicitly forbade the use of unfermented grape juice as heretical. Some ancient sects substituted an entirely different element – such as water or milk. (The same Council of Braga also condemned these alternate practices.) As late as the 16th century, the Nestorian Christians celebrated Communion with raisin wine, which was made in the same way as modern Jews make their Passover wine.

This commentator believes the "fruit of the vine" used by Jesus in the institution of the Lord's Supper, and therefore, the suitable element to be used today, is unfermented grape juice. Jesus' use of unfermented "juice" would reflect God's having prohibited the presence of ferment or leaven during the feast of unleavened bread. Ferment was not even to be found in the houses or the land (Exodus 12:15,19; 13:7; Deuteronomy 16:4). At the time of our Lord, it is highly improbable that any intoxicating beverage could have been found that did not contain ferment or leaven. And unfermented juice is suitable for us today since the color of grape juice reminds the communicant of the blood of the covenant.

---

[17] Mishna, *Terumoth*, XI.

[18] Wine for the Passover was weakened with water (2 Maccabees 15:39; Mishna, *Pesachim*, VII.13, X.2,4,7). In the 2nd century church, it was the custom to mix the communion wine with water (Justin Martyr, *Apology*, I.67.5). See Robert H. Stein's article on "Wine-drinking in the New Testament" in *Christianity Today*, XIX.19, p.923 (June 20, 1975).

[19] "The Greek *oinos* (wine) means the fermented juice of the grape, except when it is qualified by the word 'new' ... New wine is [called] *must*; i.e., it is juice that flows out either spontaneously before treading begins, or just freshly trodden out of the grapes. [*Must*] only becomes wine by fermentation." See the article on "Wine" in *Westminster Dictionary of the Bible* (Philadelphia: Westminster Press, 1944), p.641.

[20] Josephus, *ibid*. Josephus, speaking of the juice freshly squeezed into Pharaoh's cup, called it *gleukos*.

V. COMMUNION IN THE APOSTOLIC CHURCH

The *International Standard Bible Encyclopedia* asserts that "originally, the apostolic church celebrated communion at every meeting for worship."[21] ISBE is implying that this was a daily occurrence, and Acts 2:42 and 2:46 are cited as support. The article goes on to say, "Soon, however, its administration was confined to the meeting on the first day of the week."[22] Admittedly, the observance of daily communion in the early church is a real possibility (see notes at Acts 2:42, 46). However, it still appears best to treat Acts 2:46 as a reference to the frequent sharing of common meals, not the Lord's Supper.

Acts 20:7 is recognized by most reputable scholars as indicating that the early church celebrated the Lord's Supper every Lord's Day. And such a weekly observance was not an isolated event in the city of Troas. A comparison of 1 Corinthians 16:2 (which speaks of weekly assemblies on the first day of the week) and 1 Corinthians 11:20ff (which speaks of the abuse of the Love Feast and the Lord's Supper at those assemblies) shows that weekly communion was the practice in Corinth also.

There is testimony in early Christian literature to the weekly observance of the Lord's Supper. Justin Martyr, writing about AD 150, says:

> And on the day called Sunday, all who live in cities or in the country gather together to one place and the Memoirs of the Apostles or the writings of the prophets are read, as long as time permits; then when the reader has ceased, the president verbally instructs, and exhorts to the imitation of these good things. Then we all rise together and pray, and as we before said, when our prayer is ended, bread and wine and water are brought and the president in like manner offers prayers and thanksgiving, according to his ability, and the people assent, saying "Amen"; and there is a distribution to each, and a participation of that over which thanks has been given, and to those who are absent a portion is sent by the deacons.[23]

In like manner read Pliny, *Epistles,* Book 10, and Tertullian, *De Oratione,* p.135.

In the 4th century, the practice of weekly communion began to decline (cf. John Erskine, *Dissertations*, p.271; Canon 28 of the Council of Illiberis, Spain, AD 324; and Canon 2 of the Council of Antioch, AD 341). By the 6th century, Christianity had so deteriorated from what Christ intended that it was decreed at the Council of Agatha (AD 506) that "none should be esteemed good Christians who did not commune at least three times a year – Christmas, Easter, and Whitsunday (Pentecost)."[24] The ideas of having the Lord's Supper at other times than each Lord's Day have been promulgated at various times since this council at Agatha.

Bible scholars of all religious bodies agree that in the early church the Christians met every Lord's Day for the Lord's Supper. John Calvin, a Presbyterian, in his *Institutes*, writes, "And that custom which enjoins believers to communicate only once a year, is un-

---

[21] ISBE, *op. cit.*, p.1925.

[22] *Ibid.*

[23] Justin Martyr, *Apology*, I.67.

[24] C.J. Sharp, *The Communion* (Cincinnati: Standard Publishing Co., 1930), p.63.

questionably an invention of the devil, whoever were the persons by whom it was introduced."[25] And Calvin went on, "A very different practice ought to have been pursued. At least once in every week the table of the Lord ought to have been spread before each congregation of Christians ...." John Wesley, a Methodist, in his *Letter to America* of 1784, said, "I also advise the elders to administer the supper of the Lord every Lord's Day."[26] Thomas Scott, an Anglican, in his commentary on Acts 20:7, wrote, "breaking of bread, or commemorating the death of Christ in the Eucharist, was one of the chief ends of their assembling; this ordinance seems to have been constantly administered every Lord's Day."[27]

Since the covenant ratified by the blood of Christ is in force until the end of time, we find it proper and right to have regular weekly observance of the Lord's Supper, just as was done in the early church.

The Love Feast (*agapē*) regularly preceded the Lord's Supper in most congregations of the apostolic church. See 1 Corinthians 11:17ff; 2 Peter 2:13; and Jude 12.

By a slow transition, not complete till after the apostolic age, the practice of having a "supper" (i.e., celebrating the communion in the evening) was changed so that the Lord's Table was spread in the morning.

VI. THE LORD'S SUPPER IN THE POST-APOSTOLIC CHURCH

The records in early Christian literature have been listed already, to the effect that the table of the Lord was spread every Lord's Day. It was during the 2nd and 3rd centuries that the practice began whereby the non-Christians were dismissed, and only the Christians stayed for the Communion service. Bread and "wine" from the Love Feast were solemnly set apart by the person officiating with a consecrating prayer (*eucharistia*). The bread and "wine" (along with the other foods for the Love Feast) were furnished by the free-will offerings of the believers. Gradually, these gifts of bread and wine came to be called "oblations" (*prosphorai*), or "sacrifices" (*thusiai*).

The **SACRIFICIAL CONCEPT** of the Supper was thus gradually developed, but was in place by the time of Ignatius,[28] Justin,[29] and Irenaeus[30] – i.e., AD 120-180. Once the Supper was conceived of as a "sacrifice," the corollary idea of the officiating bishop being a "priest" logically followed. The *Apostolic Constitutions* (53:4) provides a fair idea of church worship at the close of the 3rd century. Well-developed ritual replaced the simplicity of worship of apostolic days. In the African and Eastern churches, baptized children

---

[25] John Calvin, *Institutes of the Christian Religion* (Philadelphia: Westminster Press, 1967), vol. 2, Book 4, chapter 17, section 46, p.1424.

[26] Quoted by V.E. Howard, *What is the Church of Christ?* (Greenville, TX: published by the author, 1956), p.198.

[27] *Ibid.*

[28] Ignatius, *Philadelphians*, IV.1; *Smyrna*, VII.1 and VIII.2.

[29] Justin Martyr, *Apology*, I.66; *Dialogue with Trypho*, XII.70.

[30] Irenaeus, *Against Heretics*, IV.18.5.

were allowed to partake of communion through the fear engendered by John 6:53.[31]

By the close of the 4th century, several doctrinal concepts of the Lord's Supper had developed.

- There was the dynamic view of Origen, Eusebius, Basil, and Gregory Nazianzen. Under this doctrine, Christ is understood as being present in the emblems only in a spiritual or symbolic sense.
- There was the realistic view of Cyril, Gregory of Nyssa, Chrysostom, and John Damascenus. The idea is that Christ is really present in the emblems.
- Some held the *Diophysitic* opinion (consubstantiation).
- Others held *the Monophysitic* theory (transubstantiation).[32]

VII. THE ROMAN CATHOLIC CHURCH AND THE LORD'S SUPPER

The Roman Catholic Church has come to her present doctrinal position with reference to the Lord's Supper gradually.[33]

- Augustine knew nothing of the theory of transubstantiation as now taught by the Roman Church. He taught that Communion carries a blessing only for believers, while to the unbelieving it is a curse, and that the true eating of the body of Christ (John 6) consists in believing.[34]
- Pope Gelasius I was the first to teach that the substance of the bread and wine did not cease to exist, but that the elements pass over (*transeant*) into a divine substance. This process, he believed, was done by the work of the Holy Spirit.[35]
- Before he died in AD 865, Paschasius Radbertus, a monk, was the first to attempt to systematically formulate the realistic view of the Lord's Supper as now taught by the Roman Church. He argued that our omnipotent God does what He wishes; hence, there is a miracle of divine omnipotence which occurs at the Lord's Supper when the prayer of thanks is offered by the officiating priest. He taught that a creative act takes place

---

[31] ISBE, *ibid.*

[32] See Schaff-Herzog *Encyclopedia of Religious Knowledge*, p.31, for details. Basically, the Eastern church held a symbolic-spiritual doctrine of the Lord's Supper, in which the term "transmutation" (Greek, *metapoiēsis*) point to the idea that a person who continually communed on the loaf and cup could look forward to a resurrection body like the one Christ now has.

The Western church started out holding a symbolic-spiritual doctrine until Ambrose led the way to the doctrine of transubstantiation (Greek, *metousiōsis*). Augustine slowed this development, but by the 9th century the Western church fully held to the doctrine of transubstantiation.

The Western church then in turn influenced the Eastern church, so that it too came to hold the doctrine of transubstantiation by the AD 1200's.

[33] Schaff-Herzog *Encyclopedia of Religious Knowledge*, p.32ff.

[34] Augustine, "Homilies on the Gospel of John" in *Nicene and Post Nicene Fathers* (Grand Rapids: Eerdmans, 1956), First Series, Vol. 7, Tractate XXVI.18, p.173. See also Augustine, *City of God*, X.6 and XX.10.

[35] Philip Schaff, *History of the Christian Church* (Grand Rapids: Eerdmans, 1968), Vol. III, p.498.

at communion just as when Jesus was brought into His physical creation in the womb of the virgin Mary. In this creative act, the body of Christ, as it was in His flesh on earth, is present in the bread and wine. Radbertus was saying that there are both symbolism and reality in the Lord's Supper. We see the symbol in the outward forms of the substance; but the body of Christ, which we do not see, is present, and only those who possess faith to believe this actually receive His body.[36]

- After Radbertus, the dynamic view of the Lord's Supper triumphed for a time in the Roman Catholic Church. But the condemnation of Berengarius of Tours (in AD 1088), who held the dynamic view, proved that by the mid-11th century the realistic view of the Lord's Supper had become a generally accepted doctrine in the Roman Church.[37]

The Roman Church today teaches **transubstantiation**, which means the conversion of the substance of the elements used in the Supper into the actual body and blood of Christ. The word was first used by Hildebert of Tours (c. AD 1134) in a sermon. This doctrine of the Supper was finally fixed, together with the new term, by Pope Innocent III, at the Lateran Council, AD 1215.[38] This doctrine is that the loaf and the cup, upon being blessed by the priest, become, respectively, the actual flesh and actual blood of our Lord, and this change is made by divine power. The doctrine is based chiefly upon two passages – Mark 14:22-24 (and similar passages in the other Gospels and in 1 Corinthians 11) where Jesus said, "This is My body" and "This is My blood"; and John 6:53,54 where Jesus spoke about eating His flesh and drinking His blood.

These objections are rightly raised against a literal understanding of Jesus' words:

1) If, when Jesus said, "This is my body," He meant that the loaf had actually become His body, then at that moment He had two bodies, and one was passing the other around.

2) This doctrine involves Christ's continual suffering, for if His actual flesh is broken and His actual blood is poured. He must suffer again every time transubstantiation takes place. But the Scriptures say He suffered "once for all" and "for by one offering He has perfected forever them that are sanctified" (Hebrews 10:10,14).

3) This doctrine makes it possible for His body to be mutilated, eaten by mice, widely scattered, or for other things no less absurd to happen.[39]

If the statements of Jesus at the Supper and in His Sermon on the Bread of Life are taken figuratively, then all fits into a beautiful, harmonious whole. The verb "be" is often used in English in the sense of "represent." For example, we say of a photograph, "This is my mother," meaning "This represents my mother." The same is true of the Greek verb

---

[36] Radbertus, *De corpore et sanguine Domini* in J.P Migne, *Patrology* (Latin Series), Vol. CXXI, p.125. This, of course, leaves the doctrine of the real presence a matter of subjective faith and personal spiritual understanding on the part of the one participating.

[37] The four chief men who opposed Berengarius, and who therefore have formulated the doctrine of transubstantiation as it is held today, were Hugo, Durand of Thoarn, Lanfranc, and Guitmund. Their contributions to the controversy may be seen in the summary given in the article on "Transubstantiation" in *Schaff-Herzog Encyclopedia of Religious Knowledge* (Grand Rapids: Baker Book House, 1956), Vol. 12, p.495.

[38] Loraine Boettner, *Roman Catholicism* (Philadelphia: Presbyterian and Reformed Publishing Co., 1962), p.187.

[39] Boettner, *op. cit.,* p.175ff, has further arguments against the doctrine of transubstantiation.

eimi ("to be"). See Galatians 4:25, "Hagar is Mount Sinai ...." Jesus, therefore, no doubt meant, "This represents My body," and "This represents My blood."

A few other items need to be noted for the sake of accuracy when one speaks of the beliefs and practices of the Roman Church.

- It is taught that by the institution of the Supper, Christ made His disciples priests, wherefore the Supper may be administered only by an ordained priest.
- It is taught that in the miracle of the sacrament (i.e., the changing of the elements) the "accidents" (their size, shape, weight, color, and taste) of the elements remain but they are no longer what they were before the prayer of consecration (i.e., they look the same, but they are actually of different substance).[40] This new substance is the body and blood of Christ, which is hidden from physical observation under the appearance of the elements.[41]
- It is taught that the real presence of Christ remains long after communion, until the accidents (species) are altered by corruption or fermentation.
- It is asserted that the entire body of Christ is present in each of the consecrated elements, being present from the very moment the prayer of the priest has ended. Since the whole Christ is present in each of the elements, it is not necessary for the worshiper to commune under both forms (*sub utraque*). Hence, only the wafer is given to the worshiper; the cup is given to the priests only.[42]
- In the Romish concept of the Supper, communion with Christ is a secondary idea. The important thing is the transubstantiation itself. The Supper becomes an actual sacrifice for sin.[43]
- It is further alleged that the Lord's Supper feeds faith, keeps from mortal sin, wards off temporal punishment due for sin, unites believers, and has a potency even for the dead in purgatory. (I.e., masses said for the dead supposedly help them eventually to have all their sins forgiven.)

VIII. LUTHER AND THE LORD'S SUPPER

"The Reformers rejected the doctrine of transubstantiation, the idea that the Eucharist was a sacrifice, the adoration of the 'host,' the withholding of the cup from the laity, and the belief in the efficacy of the mass (Lord's Supper) on behalf of the dead – i.e., the entire Romish concept of the Supper."[44] The original position of Luther, that the elements

---

[40] Alger of Liege (d.1132) clearly states this doctrine of the difference between accidents and substance in his *De sacramentis corporis et sanguinis Dominici*, in Migne's *Patrology* (Latin Series), Vol. CLXXX, p.743ff.

[41] The Protestant argument long-used against transubstantiation – i.e., "Why won't they let us examine and chemically analyze the elements after the priest's prayer?" – doesn't carry much force.

[42] Withholding either one of the elements from the worshiper is contrary to 1 Corinthians 11:26.

[43] Cardinal Gasparri, *op. cit.*, p.215ff.

[44] ISBE, *op. cit.*, p.1926.

of the Supper were signs and seals of the remission of sins, was soon replaced by the doctrine of **consubstantiation**. The bitter controversy with Carlstadt, and especially the failure of the Marburg Conference, drove Luther forever into the camp of the realists.[45]

Concisely, the doctrine of Consubstantiation is this: (1) The elements of the Supper are of two kinds – bread and wine are *materia terrena,* earthly material; the body and blood are *materia coelestis,* heavenly material. (2) The two elements are related one to another. In offering the earthly material to the disciples, Jesus is said to have employed the *locutio exhibitiva*, thereby offering them the heavenly material at the same time. *Locutio exhibitiva* means, "He names that which is seen, while giving that which is not seen." (For example, when the grocer says, "Here is your sugar," he hands you the *box* that contains the sugar). According to this doctrine, when Jesus said, "This is My body," the disciples saw unleavened bread, but the body of Jesus was really present in the bread.

The theory differs only slightly from transubstantiation. Transubstantiation says the bread *becomes* the body, while consubstantiation denies that any change takes place, and says the bread *is* the body and the wine *is* the blood.[46] Evidence that the body and blood of Christ are actually present is allegedly found in 1 Corinthians 10:16-17, in the word "communion," which means "participation in." Therefore, they say, in the loaf there is a participation in the body of Christ, and in the cup, a participation in the blood of Christ.

It is impossible to define the mode and manner of this communion of the earthly and heavenly elements. Such terms as "consubstantiation" and "invination" are faulty attempts to define the undefinable. All we can believe is that in a manner incomprehensible to us, the body and blood of the Lord are in a sacramental union with the eucharistic bread and wine. There is neither a mixture of the real presence with the substance of the emblems, nor are we to think of the body's being enclosed in the bread, but rather in, with, and under the bread, the communicant (even the unbelieving one) receives Christ's true body and blood. When the elements – i.e., the bread and cup – are passed, it is actually the body and blood of Christ being passed. They are passed together.

The reformed wing of the Lutheran movement argues that there is no real presence of Christ's body in the Lord's Supper. They teach a symbolic and figurative interpretation, in contrast to the Lutheran doctrine of the real presence of Christ in the elements.

IX. ZWINGLI AND THE LORD'S SUPPER

Zwingli's doctrine of the Lord's Supper might be called **commemoration**. He interpreted the words of the institution – "this is" – to mean "this stands for," "this signifies," "this represents."

Zwingli's concept of the Lord's Supper is that of a symbolic memorial of the suffer-

---

[45] *Ibid.*

[46] Bread and wine remain bread and wine, though after the consecration, the real flesh and blood of Christ coexist in and with the natural elements, just as a heated iron bar still remains an iron bar, though a new element, heat, has come to coexist in and with it. This was an illustration which Luther himself used in a letter to Henry VIII. (See article on "Consubstantiation" in Schaff-Herzog *Encyclopedia of Religious Knowledge.*)

ing and death of Christ, although Zwingli did not deny that Christ is present to the eye of faith. On the contrary, he taught that Christ was enjoyed through the Word and through faith, i.e., in a spiritual way. In the Supper we confess our faith, we express what that faith means to us, and we do it in memory of Christ's death.[47]

The Zwinglian view has been consciously or unconsciously adopted by a very large portion of the Protestant churches, and is regularly taught in the Christian churches, whose communion tables often bear the words "This Do in Remembrance of Me."

X. CALVIN AND THE LORD'S SUPPER

Calvin's position was somewhat between Luther and Zwingli, and is called **impanation**. The word comes from the Latin *in* and *panis* (bread). Jesus is thought to be spiritually present "in the bread."

Calvin's doctrine attempted to explain just how there is a union between the elements and the body and blood of Christ. Remember, Roman Catholics said that the union took place at the consecration. The Lutherans said that the union is a mystery (unexplainable). Impanation says that the body of Christ is in the bread after the consecration (and apparently the blood of Christ is in the cup after the consecration prayer). Impanation says that Christ's body and blood are present with the elements and the believing communicant actually receives the body and blood of Christ. Christ communicates Himself to the spirits of those who take part in the communion service. That is, the material bread and wine become digested and absorbed into the body; the body and blood of Christ are unabsorbed, and remain to strengthen and comfort the spirit of the believer. Those who do not believe but partake receive only material bread and wine, not the body and blood of Christ.

To Calvin, the Supper is more than a sign (as per Zwingli); it is both a sign and a seal. The Supper is far more than a memorial service; it is a means of grace.

Luther, Zwingli, and Calvin differed in regard to: (1) The mode of Christ's presence (whether corporeal or spiritual); (2) The organ receiving His body and blood (whether by mouth or by faith); (3) The extent of this reception (whether by all, or only by believers).

XI. THE CHURCH OF THE BRETHREN AND THE LORD'S SUPPER

This group teaches the necessity of repeating today all of the acts done by Jesus with the apostles in the upper room the night the Supper was originally instituted – i.e., foot-washing, a meal (the Love Feast), and the Lord's Supper.

The Love Feast, in their belief, takes the place of the Passover meal which Jesus shared with His disciples. Among the Brethren, the Lord's Supper is held once or twice a year, always in the evening, at the discretion of the local congregation. Preparatory services of "self-examination" (1 Corinthians 11:28) precede the ordinances.[48] The church

---

[47] ISBE, *ibid.*

[48] The Brethren believe that foot-washing and the Lord's Supper itself are both ordinances.

pews are converted into tables. The Love Feast is made ready beforehand by the deacons and deaconesses, as are the loaf and cup to be used in the Lord's Supper. The evening's activities begin with devotional exercises aimed to special consecration, confession, and reconciliation. John 13:1-17 is read and explained, whereupon the brethren proceed to wash one another's feet, and the sisters likewise by themselves. All wait for one another until all are ready for the Love Feast (1 Corinthians 11:33). The person officiating then calls upon someone to offer prayer for the meal, which is then eaten together. Another prayer of thanksgiving is offered at the close of the meal. After the meal, the officiating elder calls upon one to read the story of Christ's sufferings (Isaiah 53 or John 19). After a short explanation of the meaning of the symbols, the communicants rise while the officiating elder gives thanks for the bread. He then turns to his brother on his right and breaks a piece of the unleavened bread for him with the words, "My beloved brother, the bread which we break is the communion of the body of Christ" (1 Corinthians 10:16). The brethren then break the bread one to another with these words. Likewise, the sisters partake with one another in the same manner. Again, the congregation rises while the officiating elder gives thanks for the cup, which is then passed by one to the other with these words, "Beloved brother (or sister), the cup of the New Testament is the communion of the blood of Christ" (1 Corinthians 10:16). This is followed by prayers of praise and thanksgiving, then a hymn (Matthew 26:30), and a benediction.[49]

XII. THE RESTORATION MOVEMENT AND THE LORD'S SUPPER

The Lord's Supper is usually considered to be a memorial, or a commemoration – the loaf and the cup *representing* the broken body and shed blood of Christ. Luke 22:19, "This do in remembrance of Me," seems to indicate that the Supper is a memorial.[50] The bread and the cup are emblematic of His body and His blood, and in these emblems we are to discern His body and blood. It is, therefore, a most practical way by which He would keep us spiritually alive.

Alexander Campbell has a beautiful word here:

> Upon the loaf and upon the cup of the Lord, in letters which speak not to the eye, but to the heart of every disciple is inscribed, "When this you see, remember Me." Indeed, the Lord says to each disciple when he receives the symbols in his hand, "This is My body broken for *you*. This is My blood shed for *you*." The loaf is thus constituted a representation of His body – first whole, then wounded for our sins. The cup is thus instituted a representation of His blood – once His life, but now poured out to cleanse us from our sins. To every disciple He says, "For *you* My body was wounded; for *you* My life was taken." In receiving it the disciple says, "Lord, I believe it. My life springs from Your suffering; my joy from Your sorrows; and my hope of glory everlasting from Your humiliation and abasement unto death." Each disciple, in handing the symbols to his fellow-disciple, says, "You my brother, once an alien, are now a citizen of heaven; once a stranger, are now brought home to the family of God. You have owned My Lord as your Lord, my people as your people. Under Jesus the Messiah we are one. Mutually embraced

---

[49] ISBE, *op. cit.*, p.1929.

[50] Compare also 1 Corinthians 11:23-26.

in the everlasting arms, I embrace you in mine: thy sorrows shall be my sorrows, and thy joys my joys. Joint debtors to the favor of God and the love of Jesus, we shall jointly suffer with Him, that we may also jointly reign with Him. Let us then renew our strength, remember our King, and hold fast our boasted hope unshaken to the end."

> Blest be the tie that binds
> Our hearts in Christian love:
> The fellowship of kindred minds
> Is like to that above.

Here he knows no man after the flesh. Ties that spring from eternal love revealed in blood and addressed to his senses, draw forth all that is within him of complaisant affection and feeling toward those joint heirs with him of the grace of eternal life. It represents to him the "bread of life" – all the salvation of the Lord – it is the strength of his faith, the joy of his hope, and the life of his love.[51]

XIII. FURTHER PROBLEMS AND QUESTIONS

A. "United" by Participating Together in the Lord's Supper (1 Corinthians 10:16-17)[52]

These verses are manifestly difficult, but they will not bear an interpretation which would be in diametric opposition to the plain teaching the Scriptures give elsewhere.

There are many who say these verses mean that when people partake of the Lord's Supper, that makes them members of Christ's body – even if they are unimmersed. Verse 17 – "We who are many are ... one body, for we all partake of the one bread" – is alleged to show this. To see the fallacy of such an interpretation, consider the following:

(1) *The emblems must not be detached from that which makes possible real communion.* Consider this illustration. At the end of World War I, Lawrence of Arabia brought an Arab emir with him to the Paris Peace Conference, and then on to visit London. The emir and his staff were amazed at many things, but nothing astonished them so much as the running water in their hotel rooms. They knew of the scarcity of water, and its value; yet here it was, to be had by the turning of a tap, free and exhaustless. So they expressed a desire to take these faucets back with them to Arabia, so that in their native deserts they might have water. Lawrence had to explain that behind the flowing water were huge reservoirs, and that without this supply the faucets were useless.[53] The faucets were no good without being attached. In like manner, the realistic view of the Lord's Supper cannot be maintained. That is, the eating of the bread will not, merely by eating, make a person a part of the body of Christ. The emblems must not be detached from that which makes possible real communion.

---

[51] Alexander Campbell, *Millennial Harbinger*, Extra #2, December 1830, p.68 of an article titled "The Breaking of the Loaf." Printed and published by the editor, at Bethany, VA.

[52] These materials are adapted from George Mark Elliott, "United Around the Lord's Table" in *Christian Standard*, XCIII.14, p.209 (April 6, 1957).

[53] Lowell Thomas, *With Lawrence in Arabia* (New York: The Century Co., 1924), Chapter XXIX, "Lawrence Narrowly Escapes Death; Adventures of Feisal and Hussein."

(2) *There can be a Communion Service without there being any real communion.* A young man wrote to George Mark Elliott from a county jail, "It is very lonely here in the jail, and a boy of my age can sure think of a lot of things ... I had gone to church every Sunday for three years straight and just sat there ... I used to sit there thinking about something that had nothing whatever to do with church." This is a perfect example of breaking Jesus' injunction to worship "in spirit." What did brother "x" do last Sunday? He put a little piece of unleavened bread in his mouth, then chewed and swallowed it. He also swallowed a little bit of grape juice. But there was no communion with the body and blood of Christ; there was no real fellowship with his brethren. He was not worshiping in spirit and in truth. Just as there could be animals sacrificed without there being a sacrifice for sins (Hosea 8:13), so there can be a Communion Service without there being any real communion.

(3) *A Scriptural whole cannot be conjured up out of anti-scriptural units.* Even if those from various denominational bodies participating in the World Council of Churches should assemble around a Communion table and partake together from the same loaf, this would not be Christian unity. The Lord's Supper is not a talisman that, in some magical way, dispenses with the necessity of compliance with Divine Revelation. In spite of the report from "The Commission on Restudy of the Disciples of Christ" – which urges that between infidels and believers in "the brotherhood" there should exist "the spirit of mutual consideration, respect, and brotherly trust ... an exceeding precious fellowship" – if an infidel and a believer both break bread at the same table, that does not make them Scripturally one. Because of the factions, parties, and dissensions at Corinth, it was not possible for the Corinthians to properly eat the Lord's Supper (1 Corinthians 11:20). Do the different factions in the World Council eat properly the Lord's Supper, if the factions at Corinth could not?

A proper interpretation of 1 Corinthians 10:16-17 shows that the above use of these verses is completely aside from what the passage was intended to teach.

- In Corinth, "one bread" (one loaf) was apparently passed from hand to hand, and each would break off a piece and eat of it. The fact that a man partook of the Lord's Supper indicated to the world that he claimed to be a part of the body of Christ.

- In the context, Paul is speaking of what people believe about you, judging from the places you go and the things you do. Paul says that the Christians could not go to the idol's temple because they would be thought to be worshipers of the idol. And he illustrates this by showing that when the Christians met together to observe the Lord's Supper, those who partook of the emblems were thought to be worshipers of the Christ.

- Our communion is with Christ, yet when properly observed, there is also involved in the Lord's Supper a relation between the communicants.

If we follow the teaching of the Scriptures and accept the redemption that is in Christ Jesus, we must also embrace His plan for the church – including its law of admission, organization, regulation, and exclusion. In the Lord's Supper, we renew our allegiance to Christ under the new covenant in His blood. And Campbell (see above) was right when he said that by passing the elements to the next person, we are necessarily sustaining a corresponding relationship to that brother. But we cannot sustain by this Supper alone a relationship which never existed before.

B. Who May Partake of the Lord's Supper?

When our Lord instituted the Lord's Supper, it was given only to those who were His disciples since Judas had already gone to get the soldiers before the Supper was instituted. When the early church observed the Supper, no one thought of including any but Christians in the service (Acts 2:42-43; 1 Corinthians 1:1-2 compared with 11:23-26).

Perhaps, then, the question is not "Who may partake of the Lord's Supper?" All agree that it is exclusively given for Christians.[54] The question would better be put, "Who is a Christian?" Is an unimmersed person a Christian? Is he in the kingdom of God? If those commentators are correct (and they constitute the great majority) who believe that Jesus was referring to Christian baptism in John 3:5, and if Christian baptism involves an immersion (a burial, a dipping), then unimmersed persons are not in the kingdom.[55] If in fact unimmersed persons are not in the kingdom, the conclusion seems inevitable that they are not eligible to the Lord's Supper. If immersion only is Scriptural, and Christian baptism is a condition of pardon, all unimmersed persons are still in their sins, in spite of the fact that they are trying to serve Jesus. If these statements are true, then when the unimmersed meet together quarterly on "Worldwide Communion Sunday" around the communion table, it would follow that they only seem to commune. Indeed, they break bread and drink the cup, but is this a genuine communion?[56]

We must, at this point, be careful of denigrating those in the denominations. For example, it is often said, "The Catholics are not consistent. They go to Mass and take the Eucharist, and then go out and commit the same sins. I can't see it." But do we do any differently? Should persons who are not trying to live the Christian life partake?

That said, who is to decide who shall partake? The Holy Spirit teaches that the Supper is the Lord's; it is not any man's, but the Lord's. If a person thinks he is an invited guest, it is not mine to say to him, "Yea" or "Nay." That is a matter to be decided between him and his Host (Christ). But since that Host is not here in person, but has spoken in His Word, the supposed guest should examine that Word and decide his eligibility in the light of that examination. Paul taught this when he said, "Everyone ought to examine themselves before they eat of the bread and drink from the cup" (1 Corinthians 11:28, NIV).

C. Self-Examination

"But let a man examine (ASV, "prove") himself, and so let him eat of the bread and drink of the cup" (1 Corinthians 11:28).

---

[54] A person who has not accepted Christ as Savior should not partake, nor should such persons expect or desire to partake.

[55] This is said in all kindness. Indeed, it is spoken with regret. But we must endeavor to be true to the Scriptures. Jesus has laid down definitely the conditions of entrance into the kingdom of God, and we dare not change them. It is ours to proclaim them to the world. Again, we must adhere to the guidance of the Word. Those unimmersed of whom we speak need to be "taught the word of the Lord more accurately." This should be done with great kindness and love, but with absolute fidelity to the Scriptures.

[56] Would not this be similar to a case where a man is put under water but who has not repented of his sins? In such a case, we would not say he was "baptized," at least not in the Scriptural sense of the term.

When a young man prepares himself to call on his sweetheart, he examines himself to see if he is properly dressed, his hair combed, his hands and face clean – in a word, to see if he is presentable. This is altogether normal and proper. Indeed, it is even necessary to obtain the best results.

If such care and examination of one's outward appearance is proper and necessary in matters pertaining to worldly things, how much more is the self-examination of one's spiritual condition proper and necessary in regard to spiritual things? It is only by such self-examination that we avoid partaking "in an unworthy manner" (1 Corinthians 11:27). One should never approach the Lord's table carelessly. We should have our minds occupied, not with thoughts of business, of social duties, of journeys to be made, of pleasure, but with those things that pertain directly to the Savior's death. We must come examining ourselves, being aware of our sins; we must come repenting; we must come pledging anew our allegiance to Christ.

D. Who May Preside and Serve at the Table?

The only detailed example given in the Scripture is the one in which the Lord Himself presided and served. Beyond this the Scripture gives no command or example as to who is to preside and serve. (Not even the "we" of 1 Corinthians 10:16 limits the one doing the blessing to the apostles and their successors, as one group teaches.) There is no Biblical authority for limiting this privilege strictly to the elders and deacons. Thus, it is proper for any Christian to preside at the table or to serve the emblems.

E. Is Communion a Means of Grace?

What about the idea that the Lord's Supper has something to do with the forgiveness of the Christian's sins?

- Many theologians believe that there is nothing more in communion than a means of remembering Christ's sacrifice for our sins.
- Others believe that baptism takes care of a person's sins committed up to the time he was baptized. After that point in time, the Lord's Supper is the place where the blood of Christ is applied to the sins the Christian committed the past week, so that they may be forgiven. 1 Corinthians 10:16 reads, "Is not the cup of blessing ... a sharing in the blood of Christ? Is not the bread ... a sharing in the body of Christ?" John 6:53 indicates that eating the flesh and drinking the blood of Christ results in the spiritual life being sustained. And at Matthew 26:28, Jesus explains the significance of the cup by saying, "This is My blood of the covenant, which is shed for many for the forgiveness of sins."
- While 1 Corinthians 10:16 is indeed a deep and complex verse, this commentator does teach that Paul is in fact indicating that participating in communion (with the proper self-examination preceding) has something to do with the forgiveness of sins. This does not mean that there is something in the loaf and cup themselves that magically takes away sin, any more than there is something in the water of the baptistry that magi-

cally washes away sin. But as baptism is a condition on which God forgives sins to a penitent believer, so communion may be conceived as being one condition on which God forgives the sins of a penitent Christian.[57]

Since it can be shown that the Lord's Supper is a *proclamation* and a *commemoration* as well as a condition of forgiven sin, it is this commentator's practice to carefully share *each* of these idea as he preaches and teaches, lest he contribute to the very problem he lamented in the introductory paragraph of this Special Study.

CONCLUSION: HOW IMPORTANT IS THE LORD'S SUPPER?

Since this institution is the memorial of our Savior's suffering and death on the cross, it seems that the question can be decided by determining the importance of the death of Jesus in the plan of redemption. How important was it, then, for Jesus to die? It is by His death that men are drawn to Him (John 12:32-33). It is by His death that reconciliation is effected (Romans 5:10). The death of Jesus was the topic of conversation at one of the most important meetings ever held in the universe (Luke 9:30-31).

In view of the importance of the death of Jesus, what place should the memorial of that death have in divine worship? From a logical standpoint, it should occupy first place. And that is exactly the place the Word of God gives it. According to Acts 20:7, the Church met for the purpose of breaking bread. They did not gather together fundamentally to pray, although prayer is important, and we do not doubt that they did pray. Neither, first of all, did they gather together to sing, though singing is important, and they probably did sing. Nor yet was their purpose in gathering together to bring their offerings, though that was important, and there is no doubt that they brought their offerings. In fact, the purpose of their gathering was not even to hear Paul preach, though Paul was a very great preacher, and he did preach. None of these was the primary purpose of the gathering. Their explicit and expressed purpose was to break bread, that is, to observe the Lord's Supper.

At our own worship services, not everyone present may be able to sing. Not everyone may offer an audible prayer. Not everyone may be able to preach. But all can reverently, prayerfully, thoughtfully "break bread," and thus strengthen their own souls, "proclaim the Lord's death till he come," and keep the church of Christ alive to give its burning message of love to a wayward world.

---

[57] If one were of a legalistic bent, this latter statement, that the Lord's Supper is a means of grace, might quickly lead a person to slip into the practice of extreme unction (i.e., the giving of communion to a dying person, lest he enter eternity with some unforgiven sin). A healthy concept of salvation by grace rather than by sinless perfection will guard against this error.

BIBLIOGRAPHY

Blakely, Fred O., "The Weekly Communion" in *The Apostles' Doctrine*. Highland, IN: published by the author, 1959, p.8-63.

Campbell, Alexander, *Christian System*. Cincinnati: Standard Publishing Co., nd, p.265-293.

---------------, *Millennial Harbinger*. Bethany, VA: published by the author, 1830, Extra #2.

Dale, L. Edsil, *Acts Comments*. Lansing, MI: published by the author, 1960, p.303-313.

DeWelt, Don, "The Table of Remembrance" in *The Church in the Bible*. Joplin, MO: College Press, 1958, p.372ff.

Dungan, D.R., "The Lord's Supper" in *The Old Faith Restated*, edited by J.H. Garrison. St. Louis: Christian Publishing Co., 1891.

Dunn, Chester V., "Ten Talks on the Lord's Supper" in *Christian Standard*, LXX, 27, (July 20, 1935), p.692ff.

Nash, Donald, "The Beverage was Grape Juice" in *Christian Standard*, LXXXIX, 24, (June 13, 1953), p.376.

Orr, James, ed., *The International Standard Bible Encyclopedia*, Vol. III. Grand Rapids, MI: Wm. B. Eerdmans Publishing Co., 1949.

Schaff, Philip, ed., Schaff-Herzog Encyclopedia of Religious Knowledge. Grand Rapids, MI: Baker Book House, 1956.

Sharp, C.J., *The Communion*. Cincinnati: Standard Publishing Co., 1930.

Drawing by Horace Knowles
from the British and Foreign Bible Society

11. At Cos, Rhodes, and Patara. 21:1-2

21:1 – *And when it came about that we had parted from them and had set sail, we ran a straight course to Cos and the next day to Rhodes and from there to Patara;*

And when it came about that we had parted from them. The Ephesian elders had escorted Paul and his friends to the ship, and now they have parted to go their separate ways. "Parted" is a strong word in the Greek, and might almost be rendered "When we had torn ourselves away from them." There was a strong reluctance to leave the elders.

And had set sail. At this time of year in the Aegean Sea, the wind regularly comes up between midnight and dawn, blowing from the north, and continues until the next afternoon. We wonder if Paul's party boarded the ship in the early morning hours.

We ran a straight course to Cos. Paul and the men carrying the offering are still aboard the coasting vessel they have been sailing on since they left Troas. "Straight course" indicates they had excellent sailing weather.[1] Cos was the chief city on the island of Cos, which was about 40 miles south of Miletus. Cos was famous both for its wines and its silk fabrics, and for the great medical school that had flourished there for many years.

And the next day to Rhodes. Rhodes is an island about 50 miles southeast of Cos. On the north end of the island of Rhodes is the city of Rhodes, and there the ship cast anchor for the night. The harbor's mouth had once been ornamented by the Colossus of Rhodes.

> For 56 years the brazen Colossus of Helios stood across the mouth of the harbor. It was so large, being 105 feet high, that ships sailed between its legs. It was considered one of the seven wonders of the ancient world. The brazen Colossus represented the sun which shown almost every day on the island. About 224 BC, an earthquake threw the [statue] down, [though its fragments were still on the spot at the time of Paul's visit.] In AD 600, its remains were sold to a Jew by the conquering Saracens. It took 900 camels to carry the brass away.[2]

The island was named "Rhodes" because of the beautiful roses that grow there.

And from there to Patara. Patara was a harbor on the coast of Lycia, and served as the seaport for Xanthus, the capital of Lycia. Although both cities are now in ruins, those of Patara show it was a commodious harbor based on the silt build up and the remaining marsh.

According to the Western text, the coasting ship on which they were passengers put in at Myra on the next day after their stop at Patara. Such a reading might be plausible, since Myra was the harbor where ships that sailed across the Mediterranean to Syria and Egypt put into port. However, this reading in the Western text is disputed.

---

[1] Compare notes at 16:11 where the same expression "straight course" appears.

[2] Dale, *op. cit.*, p.333.

- Some believe Luke's autograph included the words, and that Paul and the messengers changed ships here (verse 2) on their way to Jerusalem. That the words were dropped and are thus not found in other textual traditions is explained as an instance of *homoeoteleuton*.[3]
- Others affirm that Luke's autograph did not have "and Myra" in it, and that it was probably interpolated into the Western text by a scribe who remembered that Myra was the port where Paul changed ships on a later voyage.[4]

21:2 – *and having found a ship crossing over to Phoenicia, we went aboard and set sail.*

And having found a ship crossing over to Phoenicia, we went aboard and set sail. They change ships, leaving behind their coasting vessel and boarding a large, ocean-going vessel for the 400-mile trip across the open sea toward Jerusalem. Remembering that Paul is hurrying to be at Jerusalem by Pentecost, we can conjecture on the reason for the change of ships. Either the coasting vessel was chartered only to come this far and so they must now find other transportation, or the coasting vessel is going to continue a slow journey from port to port, while the ocean-going vessel promises a speedier trip toward their destination.

12. Sail by Cyprus and Stay at Tyre. 21:3-6

21:3 – *And when we had come in sight of Cyprus, leaving it on the left, we kept sailing to Syria and landed at Tyre; for there the ship was to unload its cargo.*

And when we had come in sight of Cyprus, leaving it on the left. Their ship was headed in a southeasterly direction, and Cyprus passed by on the left side. "Come in sight of" is the correct nautical term, characteristic of Luke's account. As they were sailing toward Syria, they came near enough to the island that it seemed to rise above the horizon. They would have passed close to Paphos, and Paul must have had memories of the first missionary journey, when he and Barnabas had evangelized the island, even having opportunity to preach to the proconsul there.[5]

We kept sailing to Syria. "Syria" was the name given to the whole eastern coast of the Mediterranean Sea from Cilicia in the north to Egypt in the south. It included Phoenicia and Palestine.

And landed at Tyre; for there the ship was to unload its cargo. Tyre was a main port for commerce on the eastern end of the Mediterranean in ancient times. It was the chief city of Phoenicia, and though about 400 miles from Patara, could be reached under favorable

---

[3] *Homoeoteleuton* occurs when two separate phrases or lines have identical endings and the copyist's eye slips from one to the other and omits the intervening words.

[4] Acts 27:5.

[5] Acts 13:4,12.

sailing conditions in four or five days.[6] Commentators have conjectured that the "cargo" was either grain or wine. "Unload" is a present tense verb, indicating that the job took some days, during which time Paul and the messengers from the churches visited the Christians in Tyre.

> The ship's run from Patara to Tyre was one of several days and nights on the open sea, without casting anchor as they had done every night since leaving Troas. Such a run the ships of that day seldom made, except when they could hope for the light of the moon or stars at night, and such light they could have had on this trip. Paul left Philippi seven days after the full moon; and he was five days in reaching Troas, where he spent seven days (20:6). This makes 19 days after the full moon. Leaving Troas, they reached Miletus in four days, and from Miletus they sailed to Patara in three days of sailing (20:13-15, 21:1). These seven days added to the 19 make 26 days. If they spent three or four days in Miletus, these would make the aggregate 29 or 30 since the last full moon. It would be a full moon again as they are sailing [toward Syria]. Any traveler who has sailed by moonlight in the summer time on the Mediterranean Sea, where the water was smooth, remembers it as a delightful experience; and it must have helped to soothe the troubled spirits of Paul and his companions.[7]

21:4 – *And after looking up the disciples, we stayed there seven days; and they kept telling Paul through the Spirit not to set foot in Jerusalem.*

And after looking up the disciples, we stayed there seven days. "Looking up the disciples" indicates that they had to inquire, after they landed, from people on the streets of the port city, whether any Christians were to be found there. After some time and trouble, they located the disciples. This is the first mention of a congregation of Christians in Tyre, though we learned at Acts 11:19 that there was evangelizing done in Phoenicia, and at Acts 15:3 that Paul visited churches in Phoenicia. The church may have been small, for the Greek reads "*the* disciples," as involving all that were resident there. At Tyre it took seven days to unload and, perhaps, to reload the ship. The week's delay in the trip toward Jerusalem gave Paul and the messengers an opportunity to visit with the church there and encourage the brethren. There would have been one, and possibly two Lord's days included in this period of time.

And they kept telling Paul through the Spirit. These repeated utterances (the verb tense indicates continuing action) likely were the exercise of the gift of prophecy, as was also implied in the similar statement recorded in Acts 20:23. At a Lord's day meeting and during the week, the Spirit over and over gave such messages to the prophets to deliver.

Not to set foot in Jerusalem. It is difficult to determine whether or not Paul is disobeying a command of the Holy Spirit at this point. What has been told to Paul by revelation and inspiration earlier in this trip is part of the material out of which to help decide this question.[8] What then are the possibilities?

---

[6] Chrysostom (*Homily*, XLV.2) speaks of a trip from Patara to Tyre as taking five days.

[7] McGarvey, *op. cit.*, p.196-197.

[8] Compare notes at 19:21 ("Paul purposed in spirit to go to Jerusalem") and 20:22-23 (Paul says, "I am

1) Perhaps this is a command by the Spirit that Paul should not go to Jerusalem, and Paul deliberately disobeys, with the result that he is imprisoned and confined for several years as punishment for disobeying the Holy Spirit.[9]
2) Perhaps this verse does actually contradict 19:21 and 20:22-23, but Luke did not write both. In fact, some commentators present these verses as contradictory in order to prove that a redactor worked over what Luke wrote, inserting some materials, but unaware that he was contradicting what had earlier been included.[10]
3) Perhaps this passage means that the Spirit revealed to some of the Christians at Tyre, as he had done in other cities, what awaited Paul in Jerusalem. After becoming aware of the contents of the revelation about Paul's future, they of their own accord kept pleading with him not to go to Jerusalem.[11]

21:5 – *And when it came about that our days there were ended, we departed and started on our journey, while they all, with wives and children, escorted us until* **we were** *out of the city. And after kneeling down on the beach and praying, we said farewell to one another.*

And when it came about that our days there were ended. The word translated "ended" means "completely equipped or furnished" as well as "finished." Some have suggested that not only did the missionaries outfit themselves for the rest of the voyage, but that the ship was "furnished" (reloaded) and ready to sail at the end of the seven days. All the preparations for the rest of the voyage were completed.

We departed and started on our journey. The verb tenses picture something of a procession wending its way from the city to the shore.

While they all, with wives and children, escorted us until *we were* **out of the city.** When it was time for the ship to sail, all the Christians of Tyre, with their families, went with Paul and the messengers of the churches to the shore. This is the first specific mention of children in connection with the early church,[12] and in the group we see some young parents whose children are brought along as their parents join in the group escorting the missionaries to the ship.

---

bound in spirit to go to Jerusalem ... although the Holy Spirit solemnly testifies to me in every city, saying that bonds and afflictions await me."). Having understood both these passages to have reference to Paul's own human spirit, we do not find that the Holy Spirit is contradicting Himself. If those passages had spoken of the Holy Spirit, then it might be said that He indeed did contradict Himself, having said to go in those passages, and now is saying not to go.

[9] If this is the correct understanding, it should not to be extrapolated and taken as proof that all calamities are punishment for sin, though some, indeed, are.

[10] See this method of interpreting Acts denied in Knowling, *op. cit.*, p.443. This commentator also rejects the redactor theory as a valid interpretation of this verse.

[11] The Greek in this verse is not "*by* the Spirit" but "*through* the Spirit," so this last option is a possible explanation of the intent of the passage.

[12] "Households" might have included young people of accountable age, but, as we have shown, no infants. Acts 2:39 uses "children" in a figurative sense, meaning "descendants." And Eutychus was called a "boy," but whether or not he was a Christian is not said.

And after kneeling down on the beach. Compare Acts 20:36. There is a beach on both sides of the site of ancient Tyre.

And praying. The Greek says "*We* prayed." In this instance, it seems that several of the Christians from Tyre, as well as several of the missionary party, joined in reciprocal intercession.

We said farewell to one another. This has many of the appearances of another painful parting like the one which occurred at Miletus. The Christians at Tyre may not have known Paul for as long as the Ephesian elders had, but where people are bound together because of a common relationship to Christ, a week together can make them as firm in their friendship as if they had known each other all their lives.

21:6 – *Then we went on board the ship, and they returned home again.*

Then we went on board the ship. The article, "*the* ship," here, whereas in verse 2 there was no article, seems to make this what is called the article of previous reference. It indicates that it was *the* same ship that had brought them, and which, after finishing the unloading and loading of cargo, was now ready to weigh anchor to sail to the next port.

And they returned home again. As the sailors weigh anchor, and sails are raised to the wind, the Christians from Tyre are making their way back to their homes.

13. In Ptolemais. 21:7

21:7 – *And when we had finished the voyage from Tyre, we arrived at Ptolemais; and after greeting the brethren, we stayed with them for a day.*

And when we had finished the voyage from Tyre, we arrived at Ptolemais. Ptolemais was about 30 miles south of Tyre. The Bay of Acre forms a half circle, about 9 miles across from north to south. On the south side of this bay is Mount Carmel and the modern port of Haifa. Ptolemais is located on the north side of this bay.

In Old Testament times, this Mediterranean sea port was named Accho.[13] When Alexander the Great's kingdom was divided, this city was given to Ptolemy Soter (Ptolemy I), king of Egypt, who rebuilt it, and after whom it may have derived its name.[14] When it passed under the dominion of Rome, it was called *Colonia Claudii Caesaris* in honor of the Emperor Claudius. Today it is known as Acre (or St. John of Acre, a name that reminds us of the importance of the city during the Crusades, when a magnificent church was built here and dedicated to the Apostle John). The tell, or mound, which was Biblical Ptolemais is located several thousand yards inland from the fortifications that were called Acre in Crusader times and later.

---

[13] Judges 1:31. The city is also so named in the Tell el Amarna letter.

[14] Others would attribute the name to Ptolemy II (Phildelphus), 285-246 BC.

And after greeting the brethren. Each of the cities that lined the coast of the Mediterranean seems to have been evangelized, for in almost every one we find notice of a congregation of Christians. Perhaps Philip the evangelist planted the church here in Ptolemais, or perhaps some of the Christians scattered after the persecution of Stephen were responsible for planting the churches.[15] The "greeting" would include an embrace and a holy kiss.[16]

We stayed with them for a day. Either this is how long the ship they were sailing on would be in port, or this is all the time they can stay if they are to be in Jerusalem by Pentecost. We suppose Paul and his friends are seeking to avail themselves of the hospitality of the brethren in Ptolemais, as well as seeking opportunity to preach to them by way of admonition and encouragement.

14. At Caesarea. 21:8-14

21:8 – *And on the next day we departed and came to Caesarea; and entering the house of Philip the evangelist, who was one of the seven, we stayed with him.*

And on the next day we departed.[17] Whether they went by land or by sea is not known. If by land, they traveled the road that leads around the Bay of Acre, along a smooth beach, to the sea-end of Mt. Carmel, from whence it leads in a direct line almost due south along the Mediterranean shore to Caesarea. The distance is about 35 miles, and if they went by land, the trip would take upwards of two days.

And came to Caesarea. For information about the city, see notes at Acts 8:40 and 10:1.

And entering the house of Philip. This was Paul's third visit to Caesarea.[18] Philip has lived here for upwards of 20 years, so it is possible to suppose that Paul is simply renewing a previous acquaintance. It may be the first time that Luke has met Philip, and perhaps during the following years, as Luke did research for the third Gospel and Acts, that he learned some of his information from Philip.

The evangelist. The word evangelist is a translation of a compound Greek word made up of *eu* ("well") + *angelos* ("a messenger"). The word seems to imply that an evangelist was one who proclaimed by word of mouth the glad tidings, the good news, of the gospel. The office or function of evangelist is mentioned but two other places in the New Testament, at Ephesians 4:11 and 2 Timothy 4:5. From these limited sources, the following implications have been drawn:

---

[15] Acts 11:19.

[16] For the meaning of "greet," see notes at Acts 18:22.

[17] The KJV reads, "We that were of Paul's company departed," but this additional language, present in some manuscripts, is evidently a later addition.

[18] Acts 9:30 and 18:22 record the first two visits.

1) It is not easy in every case to distinguish between the activities of an apostle and an evangelist.[19]

2) Perhaps the title was given to Philip because of the type of missionary work he did.[20]

3) What about the rank of the office of evangelist? This immediately raises the question of whether the listing of offices in Ephesians 4:11 is one of descending authority. (a) If so, the office of evangelist is next in order to that of apostle and prophet. This in turn raises the question of the evangelist's position in relation to that of elder (i.e., pastoring teacher). Even if Ephesians 4:11 lists the offices in the order of descending authority, the placing of evangelist before elder cannot give the evangelist absolute, dictatorial powers in a congregation, for not even an apostle exercised that kind of powers. Furthermore, it is still the elders who are called the "rulers," or "overseers," of the local congregation. Not even Titus (who likely was an evangelist, though he is not specifically so called in the New Testament), who was to appoint elders in every congregation,[21] did so in an autocratic fashion. (b) If not, then we may say that the listing is of a "geographical" nature. Apostles and prophets were limited in their work to no one individual church, whereas the elders were attached to a particular congregation. In between these two stood the evangelists, whose job was to preach the Word. Evidently, evangelists sometimes did this preaching in several different locations, and sometimes, like Philip, settled in one place for upwards of twenty years. (c) A question that is certainly left open in the New Testament is whether or not the evangelist is to be under the oversight of the elders, or an "outside advisor to the elders," when he is serving with any given congregation.

4) How were evangelists appointed? From the beginning, evangelists received their commission from the churches, and not directly from Christ, as did the apostles of Christ.[22] This can be shown from the case of Timothy, in which the hands of the eldership were laid on him for the purpose of setting him aside for the work on which he was embarking.[23]

5) Was the office of evangelist temporary, like that of apostle and prophet? Or was it permanent, like that of elder and deacon? Timothy was told to commit the gospel to faithful men, who in turn would be able to commit it to others,[24] and this has properly been taken as a prerogative for setting aside evangelists all during the church age.[25]

---

[19] "Evangelist" was the name given to the writers of the four Gospels. Two of those were apostles, too. The distinction between apostle and evangelist then might be this: all apostles are evangelists, but not all evangelists are apostles.

[20] Some suggest the title was given to distinguish Philip from the apostles, but the next phrase "one of the seven" would then be redundant.

[21] Titus 1:5.

[22] Remember that there were "apostles of churches," too (Acts 14:14).

[23] Acts 16:1-3; 1 Timothy 4:14. Paul also laid hands on Timothy (2 Timothy 1:6), evidently to impart to him those spiritual gifts which in that age were necessary in order to enable him to fulfill the commission which he had received from the church through the hands of the elders.

[24] 2 Timothy 2:2.

[25] Concerning the qualifications of an evangelist, see Don DeWelt's *The Church in the Bible*, p.94-95.

Who was one of the seven. This designation reminds the reader of the seven men chosen to serve tables in Acts 6:5. Philip was one of these, the same person who led in the evangelism of Samaria and baptized the Ethiopian alongside the road to Gaza.[26] He is evidently called "one of the seven" to distinguish him from Philip the apostle.[27]

We stayed with him. He must have had a large home to enable him to extend his hospitality to Paul and the nine men who were with him. Bruce and others have found in this present paragraph what they think are evidences of the unity and integrity of the book of Acts. Not only is there mention of the "seven" in both "parts" of the book, but Philip is connected with Caesarea in both the earlier chapters and now here.[28]

21:9 – *Now this man had four virgin daughters who were prophetesses.*

Now this man had four virgin daughters. This family most likely was among those whom Luke interviewed as he did his research for his two books of history.[29] Luke was here in Caesarea on this trip, and also during the two years during which Paul was imprisoned here.[30] This latter time especially would have given Luke excellent opportunity for the questioning of eye-witnesses to the ministry of Jesus, and to the history of the church before he himself became involved. Eusebius, who lived in Caesarea years later, quotes Papias (of Asian Hierapolis) as saying that these daughters were among Luke's informants on the early history of the church.[31]

The designation "virgin" probably indicates not merely the simple fact that they were not yet married, but it may also indicate that they had devoted themselves to the single life in order that they could devote their whole time to the service of Christ.[32] However, neither the example of Philip's daughters nor Paul's instructions in 1 Corinthians 7:25ff are to be interpreted as if the virgin life were more holy or more acceptable to God than the married state. In 1 Corinthians, Paul plainly says that his instructions about "remaining as they are" were for "the present distress."[33]

Eventually, there came to be an order of "virgins" in the church, and is still evidenced in the Roman Catholic sisterhoods. There is also evidence from the catacombs of the early

---

[26] Acts 8:12-13,26-40.

[27] In spite of such precautions, the two Philips were confused by later Christian writers. Polycrates (bishop of Ephesus, AD 190) and Gaius of Rome (AD 200) are interpreted by Eusebius of Caesarea (AD 325) as saying that the tombs of Philip the evangelist and some of his daughters were to be seen in Asia Minor near Hierapolis, and yet this same Philip is called "Philip the apostle" in these same sources. This problem is discussed, and references given for research into the problem, in F.F. Bruce, *op. cit.*, p.423.

[28] The "seven" are referenced here and at Acts 6:3ff. Philip's connection with Caesarea is found here and at Acts 8:40.

[29] Luke 1:3 speaks of the research Luke did before writing his Gospel. It is assumed he did similar research for his history called Acts.

[30] Acts 24:47.

[31] Eusesbius, *Church History*, III.18.

[32] Compare 1 Corinthians 7:32-34. Jesus also spoke of those who chose the celibate life for the Kingdom's sake (Matthew 19:12).

[33] 1 Corinthians 7:26.

existence of "virgins" as an order in the church.[34] It is probably reading back into the account here a practice of later origin if it is affirmed that Philip's daughters already were a separate order, or living in a place apart from the home of their father.[35]

Who were prophetesses. This phrase translates a present participle, which indicates the daughters exercised this gift over a period of time.[36] The question, "When and where did they prophesy?" has far-reaching implications in regard to the Biblical role of women in the church. Did they prophesy in the assemblies of the church? If so, is this a Biblical precedent for women preachers today?

Yet it is also true that Paul had forbidden women to prophesy at Corinth,[37] and later forbids them to teach at Ephesus.[38] How then are we to harmonize the passages which forbid women prophesying with those which indicate they were indeed prophesying (i.e., speaking by inspiration)? Did the Holy Spirit lead women to do in one place what He forbade them to do in another? Or is there another underlying theme running all through these passages that allows us to harmonize them?

- The historic Christian answer is that there is a principle articulated in these verses, that women are not to assume a teaching position in the church that would usurp the divine order of authority – God, Christ, man, woman. It is perfectly possible that Philip's daughters confined their ministrations to those of their own sex. Especially would they be able to speak and teach among the women of both Jew and Gentile backgrounds, to whom in the East men would have had no access. Or, if the four daughters did exercise their gift in the public assemblies, it might be that they held the function, but not the office, of prophet in the early church.[39]

- Certainly, there is no proof from this case that women are to be ordained today to the office of evangelist, or to some other position of authority and leadership in the church.[40] Theologians today often appeal to Galatians 3:28 ("there is neither male nor female ...") in their efforts to support the ordination of women into leadership offices, as though the verse indicated one was just as eligible as the other for such tasks. However, such a use of Galatians 3 takes that verse from its context. The context speaks of classes of people to whom the gospel invitation is offered (i.e., there is no limitation in the New Testament; all people are equally acceptable to God if they come in faith and obedience). The verse does *not* give one of the qualifications necessary for

---

[34] Plumptre, *op. cit.*, p.350.

[35] Jerome, *Epistles*, V.8, XVIII.8.

[36] On the meaning of the word "prophet," see Acts 2:17.

[37] 1 Corinthians 14:34.

[38] 1 Timothy 2:12.

[39] The distinction between function and office is best illustrated from the case of Daniel, whose book appears in the Hebrew canon as part of the Holy Writings rather than among the Prophets. This i most likely because he held the function, but not the office, of prophet.

[40] A succinct presentation of current liberal and new evangelical positions, as well as a solid statement of the traditional view, is given by George W. Knight, "The New Testament Teaching on the Role Relationship of Male and Female with Special Reference to the Teaching/Ruling Functions in the Church" in *Journal of the Evangelical Theological Society*, XVIII, No. 2 (Spring 1975), p.81ff.

a person who would be ordained to some office in the New Testament church.

21:10 – *And as we were staying there for some days, a certain prophet named Agabus came down from Judea.*

And as we were staying there for some days. We shall learn below that it may have been as many as six or seven days. The adjective "many" is in the comparative degree, and implies, accordingly, a longer time than had been expected. The messengers and Paul have been hurrying to be at Jerusalem by Pentecost,[41] and that purpose has not been abandoned. Perhaps they arrived in Judea sooner than they had anticipated, and so can spend more days at Caesarea than originally had been supposed. There was, at any rate, time for the news of Paul's arrival to reach Jerusalem, and for Agabus to come to Caesarea.

A certain prophet named Agabus came down from Judea. This is most likely the same prophet[42] spoken of at Acts 11:28, though from the way Luke introduces him some suppose he is a different man of the same name. Since the name is somewhat unusual, he is likely the same man.

21:11 – *And coming to us, he took Paul's belt and bound his own feet and hands, and said, "This is what the Holy Spirit says: 'In this way the Jews at Jerusalem will bind the man who owns this belt and deliver him into the hands of the Gentiles.'"*

And coming to us, he took Paul's belt. The outer garments worn in the 1st century were loose and flowing robes, and the belt was used to bind them to the body at the waist. It also often served as a money-belt.

And bound his own feet and hands. The manuscripts vary between "his hands" (i.e., Paul's) and "his own hands" (i.e., Agabus'), though the latter is by far the better-supported reading. Agabus is using an object lesson to vividly present his prophecy. Old Testament prophets had often employed such vivid object lessons to impress the message they had to deliver.[43]

And said, "This is what the Holy Spirit says. Agabus was quoting directly the words of the Holy Spirit as they had been revealed to him.

'In this way the Jews at Jerusalem will bind the man who owns this belt and deliver him into the hands of the Gentiles.'" Paul s hands were indeed pinned by the Jewish mob that swirled around him, and he was delivered into the hands of the Roman soldiers as they rushed down out of the tower of Antonia to rescue him.[44]

---

[41] Acts 20:16.

[42] See notes at Acts 15:32 on the office of prophet in the New Testament.

[43] 1 Kings 21:11; Jeremiah 13:1-11, 27:2; Ezekiel 4:1-6, 5:1-4; Isaiah 20:3-4.

[44] Acts 21:23 and 24:1ff will show how many of these predictions were fulfilled.

21:12 – *And when we had heard this, we as well as the local residents* **began** *begging him not to go up to Jerusalem.*

And when we had heard this, we as well as the local residents *began* **begging him not to go up to Jerusalem.** Hearing the prediction, Paul's traveling companions and the Caesarean Christians[45] urged Paul not to go to Jerusalem. Even Luke joined in this protest against Paul's resolution to accompany the offering to Jerusalem. Their protests likely were made in this fashion: 'Could not we, who are less known and therefore in less danger, go up to Jerusalem with the offering, deliver it to the leaders there, and return to Caesarea to report how it had been received?' Paul at times was moved by the entreaties of his friends,[46] but it was not to be so this time.

21:13 – *Then Paul answered, "What are you doing, weeping and breaking my heart? For I am ready not only to be bound, but even to die at Jerusalem for the name of the Lord Jesus."*

Then Paul answered, "What are you doing, weeping and breaking my heart? Paul's companions and the Caesarean Christians were so moved in their entreaties to Paul that tears accompanied their pleas. The verb "breaking" is picturesque, being used of the pounding a washerwoman would give clothes to get them to yield to her efforts to clean them. Paul's determination to go to Jerusalem weakened before the forceful pleadings of the brethren.[47] He respected their judgment, knew they had his best interests at heart, and knew as well as they (since he also would remember the predictions from city to city all along this journey) the dangers and persecution that awaited him at Jerusalem. He was not stoically hard as he resisted their pleadings; they almost talked him out of going on with the trip.

For I am ready not only to be bound, but even to die at Jerusalem for the name of the Lord Jesus." "I" is emphatic in the Greek. "I for my part" am ready, whatever others may think or feel. Although Paul knew about the possibility of being bound and imprisoned, nothing previously recorded has spoken about the possibility of his dying at Jerusalem. Thus, Paul is saying that he is ready to go beyond the sufferings that have been predicted for him if it will further the cause of Christ. Clearly, he is convinced that in this particular case, his presence with the offering is exactly the thing that is needed, whatever may be the cost to him personally.

21:14 – *And since he would not be persuaded, we fell silent, remarking, "The will of the Lord be done!"*

And since he would not be persuaded, we fell silent. They all ceased pleading with him not to go to Jerusalem when it became evident that Paul had his mind made up to go, and

---

[45] The "local residents" would have included Philip and his daughters, and if they were still there, Cornelius and his friends, and others.

[46] Acts 9:25, 19:30.

[47] At Acts 19:21 we noted the reason why Paul had a sense of obligation about personally accompanying the offering to Jerusalem.

that he had continued in his resolution fully aware of the dangers to himself.

Remarking, "The will of the Lord be done!" This evidently does not mean, "We now see that it is the Lord's will that Paul go to Jerusalem," though this is the way the majority of the writers interpret. Rather, it is an expression of resignation. They resigned themselves to the fact that Paul is going on with his plans. By these words they are commending their friend to the protection of God, confident that whatever should occur would ultimately result in the advancement of His cause, even if it cost His servants much suffering and trials.

15. To Jerusalem. 21:15-16

21:15 – *And after these days we got ready and started on our way up to Jerusalem.*

And after these days. "These days" indicate their stay at Caesarea (verse 10ff), including the visit of Agabus, his prediction, and the entreaties by Paul's friends.

We got ready. The word *aposkeuazō* speaks either of packing knapsacks or packing animals for the trip.[48] If, as the Western text suggests, they made the trip to Jerusalem in but two days, they must have ridden horses rather than walked.

And started on our way up to Jerusalem. Caesarea is about 65 miles northwest of Jerusalem. Jerusalem was situated on a higher elevation than Caesarea, so the language "went up" is correct.[49] The NASB has translated the imperfect tense verb "started on our way," and this is probably the right way to treat the verb.

21:16 – *And some of the disciples from Caesarea also came with us, taking us to Mnason of Cyprus, a disciple of long standing with whom we were to lodge.*

And *some* of the disciples from Caesarea also came with us. When the brethren at Caesarea could not dissuade Paul from going to Jerusalem, some of them prepare to accompany him. Or perhaps they too were going up to Jerusalem for the feast of Pentecost; multitudes of Jews would be traveling in these last days before the feast began.

Taking us to Mnason of Cyprus. Some older versions read as though Mnason accompanied them from Caesarea. The Western text reads as though the travelers stayed with Mnason the first night out, somewhere between Caesarea and Jerusalem. Probably the right idea is that Paul and the others were conducted to the house of Mnason in Jerusalem. Some have thought it incongruous that Paul would stay with someone to whom he would have to be introduced by the Christians from Caesarea, if that person lived in Jerusalem. These prefer the reading of the Western text, supposing that the Christians of

---

[48] The KJV has "carriages" rather than "baggage" as the ASV has. 400 years ago the word "carriages" spoke of something carried, like baggage or luggage. Today it has the connotation of coach, wagon, or buggy, which is not the idea of the Greek at all.

[49] Compare notes at Acts 18:22.

Caesarea would introduce Paul to one of the brethren at some intermediate place between Caesarea and Jerusalem. However, rather than being incongruous, perhaps Luke names Mnason as he does because it was from Mnason that he himself learned about much of the early history of the church.

A disciple of long standing. Opinions have varied as to when this man was converted. Some think he was converted during the first missionary journey (which included Cyprus[50]). Others suppose he was one of the converts on the day of Pentecost. It is interesting to speculate too on whether Mnason and Barnabas are old friends, since both were from Cyprus.

With whom we were to lodge. Like Philip, this man too must have had a large dwelling in Jerusalem in order to be able to extend hospitality to all the people in Paul's party. The language used by Luke seems to imply that the Caesarean Christians have prearranged the hospitality in Jerusalem, perhaps during the days that Paul and his companions spent at Caesarea. Reading between the lines, it may be true that not everyone at Jerusalem would be willing to keep Paul. Perhaps the arrangement to stay with Mnason was made as the best course that could be taken to minimize the danger which had been predicted for Paul. In that house, at least, Paul might be sure of personal safety. In addition, the party from Caesarea would form a kind of personal escort as Paul went here and there in the city.

There is no reason to doubt that the journey from Corinth had indeed been accomplished in time for Pentecost. In verse 3 we learned that 29 or 30 days were spent between Passover and the arrival at Patara. To these we may add three or four days for the voyage from Patara to Tyre, seven days at Tyre, and three more until they arrive at Caesarea, which make between 43 and 45 out of the 50 days between Passover and Pentecost. Thus, about six days were left for the stay in Caesarea and the trip to Jerusalem. It is a legitimate inference from their tarrying at Caesarea that they were early for the feast. The presence of the Asian Jews in Jerusalem, the ones who will trigger the difficulties for Paul in the temple,[51] also seems to be accounted for best if it is the feast of Pentecost to which they have come as pilgrims.

Paul's arrival at Jerusalem ends the third missionary journey. New churches have been established in Asia Minor.[52] Congregations established on previous journeys have been revisited and strengthened. Letters, too, have been written to help and strengthen the Christians. An offering for the Jerusalem church has been received among the Gentiles as an attempt to bridge the chasm between the Jewish and Gentile elements in the church, a chasm caused by old Jewish prejudices.

---

[50] Acts 13:5ff.

[51] See notes beginning at verse 27.

[52] Acts 19:10; 1 Corinthians 16:19.

E. The Last Years of the Apostle Paul. 21:17-28:31

1. Paul's Last Visit to Jerusalem. 21:17-23:30

    a. His reception by the church. 21:17-26

21:17 – *And when we had come to Jerusalem, the brethren received us gladly.*

And when we had come to Jerusalem. Paul and the bearers of the offering made the journey from Caesarea to Jerusalem in about two days.

The brethren received us gladly. This was, perhaps, an informal welcome, given in Mnason's house, by those who came there to greet the expected guests.

21:18 – *And now the following day Paul went in with us to James, and all the elders were present.*

And now the following day Paul went in with us to James. Looking to Paul's wish, stated in Acts 20:16, and noting Luke's counting of the passing days as they sail toward Jerusalem, it seems natural to infer that this visit to James was on or near the day of Pentecost. Luke classes himself as one of the people present in this meeting, and it already has been suggested he was a bearer of part of the offering.[53]

"James" seems to be the same one called "the Lord's brother," who has been introduced before in Luke's narrative. But what leadership position did he hold in the church?

- Already in the early AD 40's he was a leader of some kind.[54] He presided at the Jerusalem Conference in AD 51, and worded the letter sent out after that Conference.[55]
- Since elders are overseers of the local congregations, some have proposed that James was an elder at Jerusalem. However, he is nowhere in the New Testament called an elder; in fact, in this verse he is distinguished from the elders. So he was something other than an elder when it comes to the position of leadership that he held.
- Some suggest that James was bishop of Jerusalem.

    In a later age, when the organization of the church had been changed by uninspired men, it became customary, and still is among Episcopalian bodies, to call him bishop of the church in Jerusalem, because he seems to have had precedence over the elders. But nowhere in the New Testament is the title bishop thus used; and consequently, this custom reads into the inspired record most improperly an unauthorized concept of a later age.[56]

---

[53] See notes at Acts 20:6.

[54] That James was a leader of some kind is implied in the instructions at Acts 12:17 that James is to be told of Peter's escape from Herod's hand.

[55] Acts 15:13 compared with Galatians 2:9,12 shows his leadership during the Jerusalem Conference, and even after.

[56] McGarvey, *op. cit.*, p.205. The New Testament knows nothing of a monarchical episcopate. Acts 20:17ff shows that elder and bishop were synonymous terms (see notes there). McGarvey was of the conviction

Since it was not till the 2nd century that there were "bishops" in the modern sense of the term, it does not seem right to speak of James as bishop of Jerusalem.

- Others suggest James was given a distinguished place in the church because of his relationship to Jesus. However, it is rather difficult to find places of leadership being assigned in the New Testament simply on the basis of family relationship.
- Perhaps the simplest solution to the question is found in Galatians 1:19, where James is called an "apostle." The office of an apostle of Christ was not limited to the original Twelve, and so there is no reason why it cannot be said that James was an apostle. If so, he was equal in rank to the Twelve, Paul, and Barnabas.[57]

Because only James is named, it has regularly been deduced that the other apostles were all absent from Jerusalem on evangelistic missions. Comparing what is here stated with Luke's account in chapter 15, it is regularly said that the apostles began leaving Jerusalem about the time of the Jerusalem Conference, leaving James alone to direct the affairs of the Hebrew Christians in Judea.

And all the elders were present. Their presence seems to imply that a special meeting had been arranged with James and all these leaders from the various congregations in Jerusalem. Once before, when alms were brought to Jerusalem, they were entrusted to the elders for distribution among the needy.[58]

21:19 – *And after he had greeted them, he* **began** *to relate one by one the things which God had done among the Gentiles through his ministry.*

And after he had greeted them. What is involved in such a "greeting" is explained in notes at Acts 18:22 and 21:7.

He *began* **to relate one by one.** Paul is giving his report in detail, reporting about place after place, and the acceptance of the gospel in each.

> Paul's minute rehearsal of the things which God had wrought through his ministry probably went back no farther than the time of the Jerusalem Conference (Acts 15), for at that time he had rehearsed to James and the others all that preceded that date (Acts 15:4).[59]

The things which God had done among the Gentiles. Paul emphasized that God had done the work. God was working through Paul.

Through his ministry. It is not difficult to imagine some of the things Paul would have

---

that James was a sort of sub-apostle, one of a secondary class of apostles, which is said to account for his being given a place of eminence in the congregation. However, there does not appear to be any significant difference between McGarvey's conclusion and the idea that he was a monarchical bishop.

[57] See notes at Acts 14:14. James met the qualifications to be an apostle as outlined in Acts 1:22, for he had seen the risen Lord (1 Corinthians 15:7).

[58] Acts 11:30.

[59] McGarvey, *ibid.* Some affirm that Paul's rehearsal included only the events of the third missionary journey, on the supposition that he had reported the second journey during the visit recorded at Acts 18:22.

said in his report. He would have told how many Gentiles had forsaken idols and were living faithful to God, even to the point where attendance at idols' temples had greatly fallen off. He would have explained about how the gratitude of those Gentiles led them to undertake a generous contribution for the brethren at Jerusalem. He would have introduced the messengers of the churches who had carried the offering, perhaps telling about the individual congregations they represented as he introduced each man. And it's likely that he referenced the admonition he was given at the close of the Jerusalem Conference, that he should remember the poor.[60] The offering, he would say, was just one example that he had made every effort to practice his care for others. Perhaps as he spoke, Paul experienced some of the anxiety he had spoken about in the letter to the Romans, an anxiety about how the offering would be received.[61] Now he was at the moment of finding out!

21:20 – *And when they heard it they* **began** *glorifying God; and they said to him, "You see, brother, how many thousands there are among the Jews of those who have believed, and they are all zealous for the Law;*

And when they heard It they *began* **glorifying God.** The tense of the verb "glorifying" implies continued action, and its meaning would be satisfied by assuming there were continued, heartfelt expressions of wonder and praise. It is also probable that there were more formal thanksgivings to the messengers from the churches. Luke does not at this place speak of the offering,[62] but we imply from their glorification of God that they gratefully received the gifts. Their praises to God also show that they were in full accord with Paul and his teaching and practice among the Gentiles, and keeps us from putting a wrong connotation on the suggestion about to be made by James and the others.[63]

And they said to him. As was explained at Acts 19:21, the offering was an attempt by Paul to heal the breach between the Jewish and Gentile Christians.[64] There was an animosity toward Jews that Christian faith and love had helped the Gentile Christians to overcome. But there was also a deep-seated animosity toward any Gentile on the part of the Jews, and they too needed to practice some Christian faith and love. The Jerusalem leaders graciously received the offering, but they tell Paul that it will take more to heal the breach than the offering, for there were many old prejudices and some vicious rumors that had to be overcome.

You see, brother, how many thousands there are among the Jews of those who have believed. Paul is recognized as a "brother," which will also help us to keep from putting

---

[60] Galatians 2:10.

[61] See this anxiety explained in notes at Acts 20:4.

[62] Luke does make a definite reference to the offering at Acts 24:17.

[63] The reception of Paul by the leaders of the Jerusalem church flatly contradicts the liberals' reconstruction of early church history wherein they have proposed there was a split in doctrine and practice between Paul and the leading Jewish Christians.

[64] The book of Ephesians was Paul's great gesture to the Gentile part of the church on behalf of unity. See notes at Acts 19:21, where it is documented that the offering to Jerusalem was partly a unity measure as well as a means of relief.

a wrong connotation on this suggestion by James and the elders. The leaders of the Jerusalem Christians are not going against the spirit of the agreement discovered at the time of the Jerusalem Conference.[65] "You see" implies that this fact of the large numbers of Jewish people who had become Christians was something that Paul already was cognizant of from his own observations. Literally, the passage says "how many myriads," i.e., tens of thousands. This might seem to be too large a total if we think of the population of Jerusalem only, but if there are crowds of Jews present from all over the world for the feast of Pentecost, then the statement is easily justifiable. Evidently, the majority of Jewish Christians continued to come to the feasts, and they continued keeping other regulations prescribed by Moses.

And they are all zealous for the Law. The Jewish Christians still were observing the Law of Moses – in particular, the sacrifices, the distinctions of meats and days, the hours of prayer, and the feasts. It may seem surprising that these Christians should continue to observe the Mosaic rites since the Law was abolished, having been nailed to the cross (Colossians 2:14). But remember: (1) The Mosaic Law was ordained by God, and the Jews had been trained all their lives, before becoming Christians, in the observance of its statutes; and even still there was nothing sinful in them. (2) The apostles conformed to much, if not the greater part, of the Law while they remained in Jerusalem, thus setting an example for the converts from Judaism.[66] (3) The decision of the Jerusalem Conference related only to the *Gentile* converts. Though that Conference did make clear that the works of the Law were not necessary to salvation, it did not touch the question whether the Law was or was not to be observed by the *Jewish* converts. In their religious practices, people often observe many things not absolutely necessary to justification, yet which are not wrong in themselves. (4) They have had to rely on the Old Testament for their written words from God since only a few New Testament books had been written by this time. (5) In the arrangement of God's providence, the time was drawing near when the temple would be destroyed by the Romans, and this would bring an effective end to the observance of the Mosaic rites.

Yet it does seem, as one reads the epistles of Paul and the sermons in Acts, that the people should have begun by this time to lose some of their over-zealous attachment to Moses. But people can be slow to give up the old, traditional way of doing things, even when they know a better way. Zealousness for the Law had become almost a national characteristic among the Jews.

21:21 – *"and they have been told about you, that you are teaching all the Jews who are among the Gentiles to forsake Moses, telling them not to circumcise their children nor to walk according to the customs.*

And they have been told about you. The Greek word translated "told" is used of the formal instruction given to catechumens; it speaks of something sounded down into the ears, and thus comes to mean "rumor." Someone has deliberately been spreading false teach-

---

[65] See notes at Acts 15:6.

[66] James was well respected not only by the Christians, but also by the Jewish part of the population at Jerusalem. He was known as "James the Just" (Eusebius, *Church History*, II.23).

ings about Paul among the Jewish community of believers. Gossip and rumor are still favorite ways to destroy those who take a stand for truth and right. And it does not speak well of the people who have ears open to rumors and prefer to believe rumor and gossip, rather than trying to ascertain facts and truth for themselves. It is not certain who started these deliberate slanders against Paul. Some say it was the Judaizers who had been defeated but not converted by the Jerusalem Conference. Others say it was Paul's enemies from Asia Minor. A comparison of the charges against Paul (verses 21,28) with what Paul said, did, and wrote while in Asia makes it seem the latter suggestion is correct.

That you are teaching all the Jews who are among the Gentiles to forsake Moses, telling them not to circumcise their children nor to walk according to the customs. There was just enough element of truth to these misrepresentations of Paul's teaching to give them an air of believability. "Who are among the Gentiles" equals "who live in the countries outside Palestine." We've learned how the Jews first came to be thus dispersed in notes at Acts 2:5.

- Perhaps the point of the slander against Paul in the first charge is to be found in the word "forsake" (or *apostatize*). The same word is used in 1 Maccabees 2:15 of what the officers of Antiochus Epiphanes wanted the Jews at Modin to do as he ordered them to make a sacrifice on a pagan altar. The charge made against Paul is a half-truth. Paul has not been urging an abandonment of the Law, but an obedience to the Christ to whom the Law everywhere pointed.[67]

- The second charge is also a half-truth. Paul did not circumcise Titus, but Timothy he did. He did teach that in Christ neither circumcision nor uncircumcision availed anything,[68] but there is a vast difference between saying "it is not necessary" (which he did say), and saying "You must not do it" (which his enemies accused him of saying).

- It is hard to determine if walking "according to the customs" has reference to the precepts of the Law, or the traditions of the elders.[69] Again, this is a half-truth. In the Corinthian, Galatian, and Roman letters, Paul had made it plain that keeping the Mosaic Law was not essential to man's justification now that Christ has come. Paul taught that the Law had been "our tutor to bring us to Christ," and that since faith is come "we are no longer under a tutor."[70] His letters were directed at the Judaizers who tried to force the keeping of the Law on the Gentile converts. Paul would never stand for a matter of liberty being made a test of faith.

To understand Paul's teaching, and to avoid misrepresenting him as the Jews did, we must observe the distinction which Paul never lost sight of – between that which we are at liberty to do for the sake of others, and that which we are bound to do in order to obey God.[71]

---

[67] Compare Acts 19:4, which speaks of John the Baptist's similar testimony.

[68] Galatians 5:6; 6:15; 1 Corinthians 7:19.

[69] See Acts 6:14 and 15:1.

[70] Galatians 3:24-25.

[71] See chart at Acts 15:31.

21:22 – *"What, then, is to be done? They will certainly hear that you have come.*

What, then, is *to be done*? "This offering is a wonderful argument against the charges spread about you, but something more is needed to counteract the rumors. Is there something more that could be done that would help negate the effects of the evil report which has been circulated?" is the gist of James' question to Paul.

They will certainly hear that you have come. This is given as a reason why more needed to be done. The report of Paul's arrival at Jerusalem was sure to spread, and those who heard it would be eager to see how he acted. They would be curious to see if he would reproduce at Jerusalem that anti-Mosaic teaching and living which they heard was his manner at Corinth and Ephesus. James' tone suggests that neither he nor the elders believed the rumors, but it would take more than a verbal assurance to convince those brethren who were zealous for the Law that they had been misinformed. James and the elders now suggest that a visual act of some kind, which all could observe, was needed.

21:23 – *"Therefore do this that we tell you. We have four men who are under a vow;*

Therefore do this that we tell you. It is very difficult to reach everyone who has heard and believed a rumor in an effort to correct them. The Jerusalem leaders therefore suggest to Paul a course that the whole brotherhood would observe, or hear about, and which would show to them that Paul had not abandoned all the customs of Moses. It also seems that the plan which they supposed would have the best effect was arrived at after some deliberation by the elders. Perhaps Paul's own conduct on his previous visit to Jerusalem furnished a precedent for the line of action now recommended. Paul evidently had then come as a Nazarite.[72] Why not repeat the process now, the elders suggest.

We have four men who are under a vow. The four men are evidently Jewish Christians. Comparing what is said of these men here with the law of the Nazarite, these four were under a Nazarite vow.

There is a manuscript variation associated with the preposition "under." Some read *epi* (which would emphasize the unfulfilled obligation), and some read *apo* (which would emphasize that the vow had been voluntarily undertaken).[73] The indication given here in Acts is that these men had become unclean (for example, by accidentally touching a dead body) before the termination of the time included in the vow. Such ceremonial uncleanness meant the men had to purify themselves and begin their vow all over again.

21:24 – *"take them and purify yourself along with them, and pay their expenses in order that they may shave their heads; and all will know that there is nothing to the things which they have been told about you, but that you yourself also walk orderly, keeping the Law.*

Take them and purify yourself along with them. Nazarite vows usually were for a period of thirty days. Such a long period would present a difficulty for Paul if he intended

---

[72] See Acts 18:18. The notes there also explain the Nazarite vow and its background.

[73] Codices Vaticanus and Sinaiticus read *apo,* and this might be the correct reading.

(as Acts 19:21 suggests) to leave Jerusalem shortly for Rome; he likely would not wish to stay for the whole thirty days. Jewish practices, however, offered another course of action. A man might associate himself with a Nazarite or a company of them, go through the purification process, offer sacrifices with them, and pay for their sacrifices.[74] This was considered a devout act. Agrippa I, for instance, had in this way gained acceptance with the Jews, as showing his reverence for the Law.[75]

And pay their expenses in order that they may shave their heads. The expenses would involve payment to the priest or Levite who shaved the head, and payment for the animals sacrificed.[76]

And all will know that there is nothing to the things which they have been told about you, but that you yourself also walk orderly, keeping the Law. James and the elders hoped such a devout act would overtly and evidently contradict the rumors that had been spread about Paul. "Walk" is used in its figurative sense, meaning "living," a "pattern of conduct." "You yourself" is emphasized, meaning "you as well as the other Jewish Christians."

21:25 – *"But concerning the Gentiles who have believed, we wrote, having decided that they should abstain from meat sacrificed to idols and from blood and from what is strangled and from fornication."*

But concerning the Gentiles who have believed. James and the elders assure Paul further that they are not suggesting something contradictory to the conclusion of the Jerusalem Conference. They are not attempting to impose legal requirements on Gentile converts.

We wrote, having decided that they should abstain from meat sacrificed to idols and from blood and from what is strangled and from fornication. The four points of the Jerusalem decree have already been explained.[77] James affirms that the Jewish leaders are quite prepared to adhere to the plan presented to the church (Acts 15). At the same time, Paul can exercise his Christian liberty towards the Jewish brethren in whose midst he temporarily is.[78] If the Jewish brethren have decided to take advantage of the liberty they have in Christ and continue some of their Jewish practices, there is no reason why Paul cannot do the same.

---

[74] At the end of the seven days of purification, the devotees' heads would be shaved at the altar of burnt offering, and the animal sacrifices offered as a burnt offering for each of them. Thus would begin again the time of the vow.

[75] Josephus, *Wars*, II.15.1.

[76] Numbers 6:9-12. The sacrifice was two doves or pigeons, and a lamb. It is doubtful that the other animals (a he-lamb, a ewe lamb, a ram) and offering (a basket of unleavened bread, a meal offering, and a drink offering) were included in the things for which Paul would have to pay. These were offered only when the thirty days were completed.

[77] See comments at Acts 15:20-29.

[78] Some writers, because they fail to rightly harmonize the advice here given to Paul with Acts 15, have used this passage to deny what is there affirmed. If we consider Paul to be practicing his Christian liberty, there is no contradiction between these two passages.

21:26 – *Then Paul took the men, and the next day, purifying himself along with them, went into the temple, giving notice of the completion of the days of purification, until the sacrifice was offered for each one of them.*

Then Paul took the men, and the next day purifying himself along with them. The entire purification process took seven days. On the first day of the seven, the men would wash their clothes, bathe, and then go to the temple to notify the priests about the process.[79]

Went into the temple, giving notice of the completion of the days of purification. This phrase does not mean that the seven days had already been completed (see verse 27). Rather, Paul is announcing to the priests in the temple his intentions to observe the vow with these four men, and also is notifying the priests when their seven days of purification would be completed so that a priest might be prepared to sacrifice their offerings. The four men themselves could not go into the temple and notify the priests because the Law shut them out of the Jewish court during their uncleanness. But since Paul was not ceremonially unclean, he could enter and speak for them.[80]

Until the sacrifice was offered for each one of them. At verse 24, the sacrifices that would be offered at the close of the week's purification process were noted. Paul thus enters into one of the ceremonies prescribed by the Law of Moses.

It is incorrect to charge Paul with inconsistency, or double-dealing, or compromising the gospel.[81] However, commentators are not in agreement on how to harmonize Paul's actions here with his teaching elsewhere concerning the Law of Moses.

- Some say Paul does not, at this time, have a full understanding of the relationship of the Law to the gospel, and that a few years later, when he had come to a fuller understanding, he would not have acted as he does here in Acts. McGarvey writes,

> I think it must be admitted that subsequent to the writing of the epistle to the Ephesians, and more especially that to the Hebrews, [Paul] could not consistently have done this; for in those epistles it is clearly taught that the death of Christ has broken down and abolished the law ... and priesthood ... and sacrifices. Ephesians 2:13-15, Hebrews 7-10. But in Paul's earlier epistles, though some things had been written which, carried to their logical conclusion, involved all this, these points had not yet been clearly revealed to his mind.[82]

Just as Peter on Pentecost (Acts 2) uttered words whose full import he did not apprehend until later revelations made them plain (e.g., Acts 10), so it may have been that the Holy Spirit guided Paul into all the truth, not at one bound, but step by step.

---

[79] Leviticus 15:1-30.

[80] This phrase is not to be interpreted to mean that Paul spent the whole week living in the temple area. On the contrary, he has been walking through the streets with Trophimus (verse 29) on some occasion during this interval.

[81] See also notes at Acts 16:3, 18:18, and 21:33,35.

[82] McGarvey, *op. cit.*, p.208.

- The better way to harmonize Paul's teachings in his epistles with his actions here in Acts is to say that he is merely exercising his rights in a matter of expediency (Christian liberty).

> We do not believe Paul was as yet ignorant of what was later revealed in Ephesians and Hebrews. He exercised his rights on matters of expediency as he did in Acts 16:3. He did not offer an animal sacrifice for his own sins. He merely shared in the poverty of the Jerusalem Christians who still practiced some of the Mosaic customs.[83]

That is, in subscribing to this Nazarite vow, Paul is acting in full accordance with his own stated practice, "To the Jews I became as a Jew, that I might win Jews ... I have become all things to all men, that I may by all means save some."[84]

Certainly, Paul's concession to Judaism raises various important questions:

- *How much concession should be made to pagan religious customs on the mission field?* As we urge upon the nationals the doctrines and practices of Christianity, how many of their pagan religious practices do we permit them to keep? In part, the answer is that there is a difference between Jewish and pagan religious practices. Jewish religious practices were God-revealed; pagan religious practices are devil-inspired. In part, the answer is also that it is fully acceptable to allow them to keep those customs that are indifferent, where there is no compromise of the gospel.

- *What concessions to tradition and prejudice ought a Christian make today? And, what is likely to be the result of these concessions?* Christians must always take care to avoid anything that is plainly contrary to the letter or spirit of Scripture. If we expect to win over other people by participating in religious rites that are doctrinally wrong, or by doing so to change an implacable enmity into warm friendship, we might well learn from Paul's experience in Jerusalem not to expect too much.

    b.   Paul is arrested. 21:27-36

21:27 – *And when the seven days were almost over, the Jews from Asia, upon seeing him in the temple,* **began** *to stir up all the multitude and laid hands on him,*

And when the seven days were almost over. The seven days refer to the interval between the notification and the actual acts completing the purification. Literally it reads "were on the point of completion." Since Acts 24:18 suggests Paul was actually in the process of offering the sacrifices, we may suppose that the whole week has passed without incident, and that it seemed for a time that the plan of the elders would succeed.

The Jews from Asia. These are Jews who likely had come to Jerusalem to keep the feast of Pentecost. Some surely are from Ephesus, for they recognize Trophimus the Ephesian

---

[83] Dale, *op. cit.*, p.339.

[84] 1 Corinthians 9:20ff.

(see verse 29). It is entirely likely some of these same Jews had been the moving force behind the plots that Paul had to face during his Ephesian ministry.[85] They are continuing their hostility to Paul here in Jerusalem.

Upon seeing him in the temple. Paul had preached for an extended period in the synagogue at Ephesus, and had then spent two years among the Gentiles in Ephesus, so he was well known to the Jews from that area.

***Began* to stir up all the multitude and laid hands on him.** They stirred up the crowds of Jewish worshipers in the temple area by the charges recorded in verse 28. We doubt that Jewish Christians were in the multitude that vented their displeasure on Paul; rather, unconverted Jews are the ones inflamed by the cries of the Jews from Asia.

21:28 – crying out, "Men of Israel, come to our aid! This is the man who preaches to all men everywhere against our people, and the Law, and this place; and besides he has even brought Greeks into the temple and has defiled this holy place."

Crying out, "Men of Israel, come to our aid. This anguished outcry, like an injured, innocent person pleading for help against a wicked invader, was calculated to stir the passions of the crowd and prevent any real investigation of the charges.

This is the man who preaches to all men everywhere against our people, and the Law, and this place. Here is the implication that it was the Asian Jews who had started the vicious rumor (verse 21) against Paul. They have already been telling that there was such a man, and now they are claiming to have captured him, and need the help of others to give him his just deserts. The charges brought against Paul by these Jews are very similar to the charges brought years before against Stephen.[86]

And besides he has even brought Greeks into the temple. Paul is charged with not only teaching against the Holy Place, he is charged with proceeding to pollute it by his actions. The court of Israel is the part of the temple into which he is charged with taking a Greek.

Around the court of Israel was a wall beyond which the Gentiles (even proselytes) were not to go.[87] There were inscriptions over the gates in this wall which read, "No man of alien race is to enter within the barricade which surrounds the temple. Anyone who is caught doing so will have himself to blame for the penalty of death that follows." Two such "Thanatos Inscription Stones" have been found by archaeologists,[88] a composite of which would look like this (one is complete; the other is imposed in heavier lines):

---

[85] See also Acts 19:39 and 20:19 concerning the Jews' activities against Paul.

[86] Acts 6:11-13.

[87] See the diagram of the temple on page 151, which clearly shows the walls that divided the various courts of the temple area.

[88] One of these inscriptions was found in 1871 by C.S. Oermont-Ganneau and is now in the Turkish State Museum in Istanbul. The other was found in 1935 and is now in the Palestine Museum.

Even though the Romans had taken away from the Jews the right of capital punishment, violation of the temple was one area where they permitted the death sentence even when it was passed against Roman citizens.[89] The charges they are making against Paul put the apostle in a serious situation, one that could mean his death; and the Romans would have permitted it, if the charges were true.

And has defiled this holy place." The Asian Jews were seeking the death penalty for Paul as they charge him with polluting the temple.[90]

21:29 – *For they had previously seen Trophimus the Ephesian in the city with him, and they supposed that Paul had brought him into the temple.*

For they had previously seen Trophimus the Ephesian in the city with him. Luke here explains the last charge made against Paul, that he had profaned the temple. Trophimus, a fellow townsman of some of these Asian Jews, had accompanied Paul to carry the offering from the Ephesian church to the Jewish Christians.[91] Some of them knew Trophimus on sight, and knew he was a Gentile.

And they supposed that Paul had brought him into the temple. Trophimus had accompanied Paul as he passed along the streets of Jerusalem, but it was a conclusion which they erroneously drew that he also had accompanied Paul into the court of Israel. "Evil minds and wicked hearts possess fertile imaginations and easily draw circumstantial conclusions."[92] They had not actually seen Trophimus in the temple, but they had seen him with Paul. They see one thing, and infer another.[93]

---

[89] Josephus, *Wars*, VI.2.4.

[90] Given Jesus' teachings in the Sermon on the Mount, it might be well to ask what was really polluting the temple, Paul or the Jews' hatred for Paul?

[91] Acts 20:4.

[92] Dale, *op. cit.*, p.340.

[93] Slanderous accusations often begin from this same kind of inferential evidence. If people would only state the facts just as they are, rather than as they suppose them to be, no small part of church problems between people could be avoided.

21:30 – *And all the city was aroused, and the people rushed together; and taking hold of Paul, they dragged him out of the temple; and immediately the doors were shut.*

And all the city was aroused, and the people rushed together. A mob scene, similar to the one in Ephesus, was repeated,[94] as excited Jews come running from every direction to see what the disturbance was. The "Jews from Asia" have been successful in stirring up a riot against Paul.

And taking hold of Paul, they dragged him out of the temple. The mob was treating Paul as they would have treated an intruding Gentile. To avoid defiling the sacred pavement with the blood of the polluter they intended to kill, the mob hustled their victim out of the court of Israel into the spacious court of the Gentiles.

And immediately the doors were shut. The gates leading from the outer courts to the court of Israel are the ones which are shut,[95] probably by the Levite gatekeepers, as if to seal the area against further pollution.

21:31 – *And while they were seeking to kill him, a report came up to the commander of the Roman cohort that all Jerusalem was in confusion.*

And while they were seeking to kill him. The mob's intention was to beat Paul to death, and if they had not been hindered, they would have done so. Having dragged him outside the gates to the court of Israel, they were already pummeling Paul. Once they out in the court of the Gentiles, their furious activity can be seen from the tower of Antonia.

A report came up to the commander of the *Roman* Cohort that all Jerusalem was in confusion. John Hyrcanus (c. 125 BC) had built a fortress at the northwest corner of the temple enclosure, on a rock rise that is about 20 feet higher than the level of the floor of the temple area. This fortress was rebuilt by Herod the Great, and called Antonia in honor of his friend, Mark Antony. There were four towers to the fortress, one of which overlooked the temple area. The fortress was connected to the temple area by two flights of stairs, one of which entered the temple area on the north side, the other on the west side.[96] During the Jewish feasts the garrison of soldiers in the fortress remained under arms in constant readiness to suppress any tumults that might arise. Watchmen on the towers would be quick to notice and report the swift spreading tumult that swirled around Paul.

"Commander" (*chiliarchos*) denotes one who commanded a thousand men (plus 120 horsemen), i.e., one-sixth of a legion. Under him would be ten centuries and their centurions. In present-day language we would call him a military tribune. This tribune's name was Claudius Lysias (Acts 23:26). Had the procurator Felix been in Jerusalem rather than Caesarea at this time, he would have been in command of the garrison.

---

[94] Acts 19:23-32. Luke used this word "aroused" at Acts 6:12 ("stirred"). Perhaps these Asian Jews were deliberately imitating the methods they had seen Demetrius use in stirring the mob against Paul in Ephesus.

[95] A description of one or two of these gates was given at Acts 3:2.

[96] Josephus, *Wars*, V.5.8 describes the tower in detail. Additional information is given at Acts 12:10.

21:32 – *And at once he took along some soldiers and centurions, and ran down to them; and when they saw the commander and the soldiers, they stopped beating Paul.*

And at once he took along *some* soldiers and centurions. Since each centurion was at the head of a hundred soldiers, the force included several hundred, enough to deal quickly and effectively with the riot.

And ran down to them; and when they saw the commander and the soldiers, they stopped beating Paul. The Roman soldiers came down the stairways from the fortress on the dead run, right into the midst of the mob in the court of the Gentiles. The sight of several hundred armed men paralyzed the mob for a moment, so that they were more worried about defending themselves than in finishing the beating of their victim. Paul's "beating" would seem to have been rough treatment with the fists and perhaps clubs.

Was Paul wise in following the path that James and the elders suggested? That question cannot be answered without knowing whether or not he would have been subjected to "bonds and imprisonment" in some other fashion if he had not been caught in the temple area by the Asian Jews. Only if it be affirmed that Paul's suffering and imprisonment are the direct result of a foolish choice could we say he was unwise in practicing his liberty in an effort to overcome misunderstanding and misrepresentation.

And what effect did Paul's actions produce on those Jewish Christians whom James has described as "zealous for the Law"? Did they ever come to Paul's aid after his arrest in the temple, or during his subsequent imprisonment? There is no statement by Luke that they did, but we must be careful not to press too much such an argument from silence. Perhaps Paul's actions and teachings helped them begin to be prepared for the day a dozen years hence when they themselves will have to flee Jerusalem and their beloved temple in order to escape the desolation wrought on the city by the Romans.

21:33 – *Then the commander came up and took hold of him, and ordered him to be bound with two chains; and he began asking who he was and what he had done.*

Then the commander came up and took hold of him. Arresting the central figure in the melee would be the quickest way to stop the uproar. Lysias might even suspect that a man being subjected to such violent action could well be a dangerous criminal.

And ordered him to be bound with two chains. This action would show the rioters that he did not intend to rescue anyone from justice, but was merely interested in restoring public order. That he ordered such a binding indicates Lysias' snap judgment that his prisoner must be a dangerous criminal against whose escape secure precautions must be taken. If Paul was treated with usual Roman practice, he would have been bound by his arms to the arm of a soldier on either side of himself. Or perhaps one chain was used on his hands, and another on his feet.

And he *began* asking who he was and what he had done. It was the commander's responsibility to try to find out what was going on and who was responsible, so it seems he asked Paul his name, and asked the crowd what the prisoner had done. It is doubtful that

Lysias would ask Paul what he had done, for not many criminals will state accurately their own crimes.

21:34 – *But among the crowd some were shouting one thing* and *some another, and when he could not find out the facts on account of the uproar, he ordered him to be brought into the barracks.*

But among the crowd some were shouting one thing *and* some another. Again, there is a parallel to the confused shouts at Ephesus (Acts 19:32). It seems some shouted one charge, and some another, and that they continued shouting out confused and conflicting replies. Lysias could make little sense out of what the mob was shouting.

And when he could not find out the facts on account of the uproar, he ordered him to be brought into the barracks. The tribune soon saw that if he were to learn the facts, it would have to be by other means than asking the Jews. So he commanded the soldiers to take Paul into the tower of Antonia.[97]

21:35 – *And when he got to the stairs, it so happened that he was carried by the soldiers because of the violence of the mob;*

And when he got to the stairs. As explained at verse 31, this was one of the flights of stairs that led from the courtyard up into the fortress.

It so happened that he was carried by the soldiers because of the violence of the mob. Luke indicates the situation was perilous at that moment. The Jews make an increasingly violent effort to get at the prisoner, so some soldiers pick Paul up bodily while others form a protective shield to defend those who were carrying the prisoner. As a body, the soldiers began to move up the stairs into the fortress.

21:36 – *for the multitude of the people kept following behind, crying out, "Away with him!"*

For the multitude of the people kept following behind, crying out, "Away with him!" As it becomes evident the soldiers were going to prevent them from tearing the prisoner away so that they can finish killing him, the mob presses as closely as the protective shield will permit, all the while crying out for Paul's execution. Their cry reminds us of the same words that were raised in this same city about 30 years earlier, as the Jews on that day bayed for the blood of Jesus.[98] Their cries left no doubt as to what would happen if they could get their hands on Paul again.

---

[97] The word translated "barracks" literally means "encampment," and so came to mean anyplace an army was quartered. One of the towers of the fortress served as the barracks for the Roman soldiers stationed in Jerusalem.

[98] Luke 23:18; John 19:15.

c. Paul obtains permission to address the mob. 21:37-40

21:37 – *And as Paul was about to be brought into the barracks, he said to the commander, "May I say something to you?" And he said, "Do you know Greek?*

And as Paul was about to be brought into the barracks, he said to the commander, "May I say something to you?" Paul hoped to clear up the matter, and perhaps even to win his freedom, before the closing of the iron gate made him a prisoner indefinitely. Any appeal would need be addressed to the commander. The modesty of the request, from a supposed brigand, must have astonished the tribune as much as the language Paul spoke.

And he said, "Do you know Greek? The commander, as he had tried to size up the situation, had jumped to a conclusion about the identity of the prisoner. He supposed him to be an Egyptian revolutionary, who about three or four years earlier had deceived the people by claiming to be a prophet. Josephus gives a figure of 30,000 who were the man's followers, and who were assembled on the Mount of Olives, having been told that when he gave the command the walls would fall down (like ancient Jericho) and they could march in and defeat the Roman garrison. Felix sent out a body of troops, killed 400 and wounded another 200, and the band of Jews was scattered, while the Egyptian himself escaped.[99] The feelings of those who had been made fools of by this Egyptian would not be friendly. The tribune thought Paul was this Egyptian, who had come back to the city, had been detected by the people in the temple, and was now being shown what they really thought of him. Lysias was surprised, then, as Paul spoke to him in Greek, a language the Egyptian was not likely to speak as fluently as this prisoner did.

21:38 – *"Then you are not the Egyptian who some time ago stirred up a revolt and led the four thousand men of the Assassins out into the wilderness?"*

"Then you are not the Egyptian who some time ago stirred up a revolt. In the Introductory Studies, page *xv,* the revolt that Lysias speaks of as being "some time ago" was dated.

And led the 4000 men of the Assassins out into the wilderness?" There is a discrepancy between the number given by Lysias and the number given by Josephus.
- While Josephus is often accused of exaggerating his figures, this difference is so great that Luke has been the one accused of making a mistake here.[100]
- Since Luke is simply recording Lysias' statement, it is quite possible no mistake at all. Lysias may simply have been counting only a part of the followers of the Egyptian, the part who were armed.

The word rendered "assassins" is *sikarioi*, which passed into Greek from the Latin *sicarii*. The *sicarii*, or "dagger-men" (from the Latin *sica,* dagger), became a force to be reckoned

---

[99] Josephus tells about the Egyptian both in both *Wars*, II.13.5 and *Antiquities*, XX.8.6.

[100] Given Luke's proven trustworthiness as a historian, it is indeed curious that Luke is singled out as being in error. If indeed it is an error, it could well be Josephus making the mistake.

with early in the governorship of Felix, who was in power from AD 52-60. They were terrorists who were bitter enemies of the Romans and the Roman sympathizers in Palestine. They would mingle with the crowds at the feasts, for example, pull their daggers from beneath their robes and stab a man, return the dagger to its hiding place, and then join in the outcry against such violence that the bystanders would raise.

21:39 – *But Paul said, "I am a Jew of Tarsus in Cilicia, a citizen of no insignificant city; and I beg you, allow me to speak to the people."*

But Paul said, "I am a Jew of Tarsus in Cilicia. Paul's answer to the tribune served several purposes. It denied he was the Egyptian. It denied he was a Gentile who had defiled the temple. It gave the tribune some idea as to Paul's identity.

A citizen of no insignificant city. The tribune does not interpret this to mean "Roman citizen," for he is later surprised to find out that Paul is a Roman citizen.[101] It may be that the tribune thinks of Paul as having full rights to vote in the assembly that governed Tarsus when he hears this statement, "a citizen of no insignificant city." If this is what the tribune understood, it would immediately have raised Paul in his estimation, because citizenship in Tarsus was limited to a select few inhabitants who had rank and fortune. On the importance of Tarsus compared to other cities of the empire, see notes at Acts 9:1.

And I beg you, allow me to speak to the people." Not content with mere denial of mistaken identity, Paul wasted no time in making his request to speak to the people. He has just given the tribune a reason why his request should be granted: a man of such status as to be a citizen of Tarsus would hardly make a dangerous or seditious address.

We can imagine that Lysias expected Paul to address himself to the charges that the Jews had raised against him. Instead, Paul sought to speak of his faith. Actually, the two subjects were closely related. If the unbelieving Jews could only be persuaded about the Messiahship of Jesus, their opposition to Paul would disappear. Because he himself used to be an opponent of Christianity, he will now tell how he came to be converted, in the hopes that his testimony will get them to see and accept the truth.

21:40 – *And when he had given him permission, Paul, standing on the stairs, motioned to the people with his hand; and when there was a great hush, he spoke to them in the Hebrew dialect, saying,*

And when he had given him permission, Paul, standing on the stairs. The picture of Paul – beaten, bruised, and perhaps bloody – standing on the stairs to the tower of Antonia, about to address the mob below in the courtyard, is one to view with wonder and amazement. Off to the side is Lysias, preparing to listen. All around are soldiers, with their weapons ready, in case the mob should attempt to seize the prisoner.

Why did Paul want to talk to these persecutors? The content of his message answers that. He loved these people; they were his people. He had once been as they now are – with a zeal for God, but not according to knowledge. He longed to win them to Christ!

---

[101] Acts 22:27ff.

There is nothing strange or incongruent in the fact that Lysias granted Paul's request to address the crowd. It would give him opportunity to learn more about this prisoner he now had on his hands.

Motioned to the people with his hand. This seems to be a gesture used by speakers the world over, who, upon rising to speak, raise their hands in an effort to get the people to quiet down so that they can be heard. We probably may suppose that the chains were removed from Paul while he addresses the people.

And when there was a great hush, he spoke to them in the Hebrew dialect, saying. The word translated "Hebrew" can also be translated "Aramaic." However, this commenta-tor believes that Paul used the pure Hebrew in addressing this multitude – the language the people would hear in the synagogue as the Law was read. Aramaic was the language of the street, and Greek was the language which might be expected by one who was a friend of Greeks. By speaking pure Hebrew, Paul would cause them to become quieter yet and to listen more carefully to what he was saying, in order that they might understand him completely.

d. Paul's defense in the Hebrew language. 22:1-21

22:1 – *"Brethren and fathers, hear my defense which I now offer to you."*

Brethren and fathers. Paul begins his defense with the same formula as did Stephen.[1] It was, perhaps, the regular formula used in opening an address to an assembly which included the scribes and elders (i.e., the members of the Sanhedrin), here called "fathers."

Hear my defense which I now *offer* to you. As we enter the study of chapter 22 and following, we come upon a series of pleas which Paul made in his self-defense. His first plea is a vindication of himself before his own people.

22:2 – *And when they heard that he was addressing them in the Hebrew dialect, they became even more quiet; and he said,*

And when they heard that he was addressing them in the Hebrew dialect, they became even more quiet. Paul's opening words did what they were intended to do. His audience presumed that one speaking in Hebrew was not likely to blaspheme the temple or the Law, so extending him a temporary good will, they became more silent than they had been when he gestured for silence so he could speak.

And he said. Several charges had been made against Paul (Acts 21:28). In order to meet these charges, Paul: (1) Stated that he was a Jew by birth, with a close association with Jerusalem, enjoying even an education under the respected Gamaliel (verse 3).[2] (2) Recounted how he, too, once had been a fanatical opponent of Christianity, just as they were that day (verse 4). (3) Shared the circumstances of his conversion, and the reason why he was now preaching the gospel (verses 5-16).[3] (4) Began explaining his reasons for doing evangelistic work among the Gentiles, evidently intending to vindicate his conduct there (verses 17-21).[4] But at this point, when he mentioned the word *Gentiles*, his defense

---

[1] Acts 7:2.

[2] Paul's opening words were intended to build a rapport with the audience. He identifies himself with them as far as he can. Gamaliel, his teacher, had been dead about six years as Paul is speaking, but his memory was still held in reverence.

[3] In verse 5, when Paul calls the high priest as a witness of his truthfulness, there is an implication that Caiaphas, who had given Paul his commission to go to Damascus, is still living. He was no longer in office; instead Ananias, son of Nebedaeus (Acts 23:2) was serving as high priest. On the word "elders" in verse 5, see comments on "senate" at Acts 5:21. At the close of this section, in verse 15, Paul uses language that shows he had the same call to witness that the original apostles had (Acts 1:8). His obedience to Jesus is the reason Paul has been living as he did.

[4] In verse 17 Paul speaks of returning to Jerusalem. This would be Paul's first trip to Jerusalem after his conversion, not his second, as Ramsay (*St. Paul the Traveller and Roman Citizen*, p.60) tries to show. Paul tells how he used the temple as a place of prayer during that visit, with the implication that he still looks on the temple as a place where prayers may be suitably offered. Paul's mention of a trance coming upon him (he didn't seek it or attempt to artificially induce it), in verse 17, would have signified to the hearers that this was a revelation from on high, and one therefore that should be heeded. Then, in verse 18ff, as he talks with Jesus, Paul argues that testimony from a former enemy ought to be impressive to similar enemies. That idea fits the present case, in which Paul is defending himself to his enemies.

Much has already been written at Acts 2:38 and in Special Study #16 concerning the place of baptism

was interrupted by the cries of the Jews in the courtyard below, and he was not able to continue. (5) Most likely would have offered an invitation had he been permitted to finish.

For a commentary on verses 3-21, see notes in chapter 9, beginning on p.345.

    e.   The response of the mob, and Paul imprisoned. 22:22-30

22:22 – *And they listened to him up to this statement, and* **then** *they raised their voices and said, "Away with such a fellow from the earth, for he should not be allowed to live!"*

And they listened to him up to this statement. The Jews listened to Paul's defense until he spoke the word "Gentiles." Their contemptuous hatred for Gentiles[5] coupled with the announcement by Paul that he had been commissioned by God to go to the Gentiles caused the unbelieving Jews to quit thinking clearly. They became again an unreasoning mob.

> What the rest of his speech would have been, but for this interruption, we can only judge by what had already been said. It certainly would have been a still further attempt to convince his hearers of the divine authority under which he ever acted; for he sought no vindication for himself that did not involve the vindication of the cause to which he had committed his life.[6]

And *then* **they raised their voices and said, "Away with such a fellow from the earth.** That is, "Put him to death!" The scene is very much like the one when Stephen ended his speech. Immediate execution without the formality of a trial, based on an eager craving for the blood of this temple polluter and betrayer of Moses' Law – this was what their wild cries demanded and expressed.

For he should not be allowed to live!" The verb here is in the imperfect tense, implying that Paul should have been put to death a long time ago. The source of their indignation was two-fold: (1) Based on hearsay, the mob still believed that Paul taught apostasy from the Mosaic covenant; and (2) Paul's rehearsal of his conversation with the Lord before leaving Jerusalem (verses 17-19) implied that the Jews were more hardened than the Gentiles, and that Paul felt he had a greater prospect of success in bringing Gentiles to God than he had of bringing the Jews to God.

---

in the plan of salvation. But a particular comment is needed here in regard to Acts 22:16, to make sure some modern religious language is clearly understood. It is common for faith-only teachers to speak of baptism as "an outward sign of an inward grace," i.e., baptism supposedly is a picture of a change that has already taken place before baptism. In the light of Romans 6:1ff, it is not Biblically correct to separate the outward act of obedience from the inward cleansing. Paul there insists that the inward cleansing is simultaneous with the baptism. Acts 22:16, "wash away your sins," agrees perfectly with Romans 6:1ff.

[5] Compare 2 Esdras 6:55.

[6] McGarvey, *op. cit.*, p.220.

22:23 – *And as they were crying out and throwing off their cloaks and tossing dust into the air,*

And as they were crying out and throwing off their cloaks. It is not easy to tell what this act signified. Perhaps it speaks of anger, or disgust, signified by throwing their garments violently to the ground. Or it may be acting as if they were preparing to stone him (compare Acts 7:58). The fact that they shortly will be throwing dust into the air tends to favor this latter interpretation of their action.

And tossing dust into the air. Those who see the throwing of the cloaks as a sign of uncontrollable rage also see this act as a further expression of that same uncontrolled passion. It may be, however, that the handfuls of dust were aimed at the apostle, that they would have pelted him with rocks if there had been any handy. Compare 2 Samuel 16:13 where Shimei's behavior to David is recorded. This act would demonstrate their loathing for what they had just heard.

22:24 – *the commander ordered him to be brought into the barracks, stating that he should be examined by scourging so that he might find out the reason why they were shouting against him that way.*

The commander ordered him to be brought into the barracks. We cannot tell whether the commander understood Paul's speech in Hebrew (one might suppose he at least would have had an interpreter) or not; but he could see that Paul's words had infuriated the mob again, and the permission earlier granted to Paul to speak is now withdrawn. The mob had been somewhat quieted by the Roman rescue of Paul, but now they were inflamed again, and threatening violence. In order to help control the mob, he commanded his soldiers to get the prisoner out of the people's sight.

Stating that he should be examined by scourging. If he had hoped to learn from Paul's defense what the Jews' complaint against him was, he was disappointed. He therefore orders that Paul be tortured until he should confess his crime. The Roman scourge (Latin, *flagellum*) was a fearful instrument of torture, consisting of three to nine strands of leather thongs, weighted with rough pieces of metal and attached to a stout wooden handle. The person to be scourged was stripped to the waist, and then tied with leather thongs, either in a stooping position over a short post or suspended by the hands above the ground. During the brutal lashing, men were known to have had their eyeballs gouged out by the metal ends of the thongs, or to have their abdomens torn open. Tacitus tells us that in such beatings seven out of ten men died, literally beaten to death; the other three were carried out in a stretcher, and most remained cripples for life.[7] Paul had been beaten with rods on several occasions by Roman lictors, and five times he had been subjected to the Jewish lashings (which were intended to be disciplinary, rather than fatal),[8] but neither of these penalties had the murderous quality of the scourging.

---

[7] Tacitus, *History*, IV.27. See also Eusebius, *Church History*, IV.15.

[8] 2 Corinthians 11:24ff.

So that he might find out the reason why they were shouting against him that way. The actual scourging was turned over to a centurion to supervise, and we suppose that Lysias remained on the platform above the courtyard to direct whatever measures were needed to get the mob under control. He could see from the Jews' action that they thought Paul to have committed some offense worthy of death, but he as yet was not aware of what it was. He could not learn what it was from the confused and conflicting cries of the mob and he had not learned it from Paul's defense, so he proposed to torture the prisoner till he broke down and told the truth.

22:25 – *And when they stretched him out with thongs, Paul said to the centurion who was standing by, "Is it lawful for you to scourge a man who is a Roman and uncondemned?"*

And when they stretched him out with thongs. The verb tense here might be an ingressive aorist, signifying that they were beginning to tie Paul's hands. Or it might mean that he was completely stretched out and tied, and things were ready for the scourging to begin when Paul appeals to his Roman citizenship.

Paul said to the centurion who was standing by. Centurions usually presided over the punishment and interrogation of prisoners. It was true in Jesus' case,[9] and in Paul's case.

"Is it lawful for you to scourge a man who is a Roman and uncondemned?" As explained in the notes at Acts 16:37, it was directly contrary to Roman law to bind and scourge a Roman citizen. The centurion who was presiding over the punishment would have been shocked to learn that Paul was a Roman citizen, especially since he already had "bound" him preparatory for scourging.

22:26 – *And when the centurion heard* this, *he went to the commander and told him, saying, "What are you about to do? For this man is a Roman."*

And when the centurion heard *this,* **he went to the commander and told him, saying, "What are you about to do? For this man is a Roman."** Now it was the commander's turn to be shocked. As noted in Acts 16, the soldiers, by breaking the Roman laws, were themselves subject to similar punishment if the prisoner wished to press charges.

22:27 – *And the commander came and said to him, "Tell me, are you a Roman?" And he said, "Yes."*

And the commander came. Alarmed by the report the centurion brought, the tribune came quickly to the place of the scourging. We wonder if Paul has been tied to the same post Jesus had been when he was scourged. If so, it was on the lower floor of the barracks, if the post shown today to visitors to Jerusalem is indeed the place of scourging.

And said to him, "Tell me, are you a Roman?" The pronoun is emphatic in the Greek. "*You*, the Jew of Tarsus, speaking both Greek and Hebrew, are *you* a Roman citizen?" Paul

---

[9] Matthew 27:54; Mark 15:39; Luke 23:47.

probably was bedraggled after being set upon by the Jews and dragged out of the court of Israel. His body would have shown welts and bruises from the attempts to kill him before the Romans intervened. He surely didn't look the part of a Roman citizen at the moment. There were so many discordant elements as to make such a claim of citizenship almost incredible to the tribune.

And he said, "Yes." Each city had a citizenship list, and it would not be too difficult to find out whether a prisoner was making a false claim to being a Roman citizen. The punishment for making such a false claim was death.[10]

22:28 – *And the commander answered, "I acquired this citizenship with a large sum of money." And Paul said, "But I was actually born a citizen."*

And the commander answered, "I acquired this citizenship with a large sum of money." The commander was finding it difficult to believe that Paul could be a Roman citizen. He appears to be thinking, "It cost me a huge sum of money to purchase citizenship; how would such a sorry-looking figure as you ever be able to become a citizen?" That the commander had "bought" his citizenship fits in with what we know of some of the activities in the court of Claudius. Claudius' wife Messalina had an on-going affair with the Censor, and the two were selling "citizenships" as a means of lining their own pockets, without Claudius' knowledge.[11] Bruce conjectured that Lysias bought his citizenship during Claudius' reign, and that's why he now went by the name *Claudius Lysias*. Bruce also suggests that it was both by wealth and influence that Lysias had become a superior officer in the Roman army.[12]

And Paul said, "But I was actually born *a citizen*." In Acts 9:1 we learned that there were three ways a person might become a Roman citizen, one of which was by birth. Paul's birth in Tarsus, and his citizenship in that city, did not make him a Roman citizen; if it had, his statement to Lysias earlier this day[13] would have been sufficient to make him immune to being bound and scourged. If Tarsus had been a Roman *colony*, birth there would have carried with it Roman citizenship; but Tarsus was a *free city*.[14] In the Roman empire, free cities were permitted to make their own laws, keep their own customs, and name their own magistrates, and they were free from having Roman occupation troops quartered there. Such cities were only required to acknowledge the supremacy and authority of the Roman people, and to aid Rome in her wars.

---

[10] Suetonius, *Claudius*, XXV.

[11] Dio Cassius, *History*, LX.17.5.

[12] Bruce, *op. cit.*, p.416.

[13] Acts 21:39.

[14] Tarsus was first honored and favorably treated by Julius Caesar for help rendered to him during his march on Egypt. Cassius, on the other hand, harshly treated Tarsus for their help to Caesar. Mark Antony granted Tarsus the status of "free city," and he himself lived there for a while, and was visited by Cleopatra who sailed up to Tarsus in 38 BC in extraordinary magnificence and luxury. When Augustus triumphed over Antony, he continued to recognize Tarsus' privilege as a free city.

Since birth in a free city did not necessarily bestow citizenship, we must look in another direction to figure out how Paul could be *born* a citizen of Rome. We must affirm that one of Paul's ancestors had received the honor of citizenship for some service (perhaps military) to the Roman state, or that one of Paul's ancestors had purchased his Roman citizenship. In either case, all of that person's natural descendants were automatically citizens when they were born. Thus Paul, by descent, is a born citizen. Hence, he stood in a more honorable position to the Roman government than did the commander. To be a citizen by birth was more honorable than to be a citizen via purchase.

22:29 – *Therefore those who were about to examine him immediately let go of him; and the commander also was afraid when he found out that he was a Roman, and because he had put him in chains.*

Therefore those who were about to examine him immediately let go of him. Binding or scourging a Roman citizen carried with it a severe penalty of which the centurion and his men wanted no part. Paul is quickly loosed from the position in which he had been stretched with leather thongs, and the soldiers retreated to their quarters.

And the commander also was afraid when he found out that he was a Roman. The commander shuddered when he realized how near he had come to breaking a law which would have subjected him to the same penalty as he had ordered meted out to Paul.

And because he had put him in chains. These words seem to refer to the binding preparatory to the scourging (verse 25), and not to the binding with chains (21:33).[15] The chains fastened to the arms were not something against Roman law, nor were the chains incompatible with the respect due to a Roman citizen. But the binding preparatory to scourging was something only slaves and criminals had to submit to, and that was quite another matter. It was this latter action that worried the commander.

22:30 – *But on the next day, wishing to know for certain why he had been accused by the Jews, he released him and ordered the chief priests and all the Council to assemble, and brought Paul down and set him before them.*

But on the next day. Paul spent the night in the barracks, or more likely in some part of the same prison in which Peter had been held some years earlier.[16]

Wishing to know for certain why he had been accused by the Jews. The tribune seems to have been anxious to treat the prisoner fairly and justly, but he was having difficulty finding out what his duty was. He still thought that Paul was a criminal of some sort, but he could not learn of what crime he had been guilty, and so he could not properly continue to hold him if there was no sufficient charge. On the other hand, to release him would seriously endanger Paul's own life if the Jews got hold of him again. Rome would not look

---

[15] Some have argued that the binding with chains of 21:33 is referred to, since the verb both there and here is *deō*, whereas the verb "stretched" is *proteinō*.

[16] Acts 12:5ff.

with favor on any such breach of the peace as an assassination of a Roman citizen.

So far, Lysias' attempts to establish a charge against Paul had been blocked at every turn. He had asked questions of the mob that attacked Paul, but had met with nothing but noise and confusion. He had hoped to learn something from Paul's address to the people, but that had been given in the Hebrew dialect and provided him with little information helpful in determining the charge. He had started to wring a confession from Paul using torture, but quickly abandoned that approach on learning that Paul was a Roman citizen. Finally, he determined to assemble the Jews' own high court, the Sanhedrin, in order to learn the charge against the prisoner.

He released him. Either they took the chains off Paul, or they released him from a cell.

And ordered the chief priests and all the Council to assemble. Lysias summoned a meeting of the Sanhedrin.[17] "Chief priests," here distinguished from the other members of the council, must have reference to the high priest (and his immediate predecessors),[18] who would have been Ananias, son of Nebedaeus (Acts 23:2).

Where was this meeting held? Some believe it was held in the regular council chamber called Gazith, or "Hall of Hewn Stones." The hall Gazith was located on the western slope of the temple hill, just outside the western wall of the temple area, at the east end of the bridge across the Tyropean valley.[19] Others believe the meeting was held in the court of the Gentiles, just below the tower of Antonia. A third possibility is that this session was held inside the fortress of Antonia, in the open area called the Pavement.

And brought Paul down and set him before them. Paul was brought down the stairs out of the tower of Antonia.[20] Paul is stood in the midst of the judges, with Roman soldiers nearby to prevent any violence to the prisoner.

---

[17] Concerning the "Sanhedrin," see notes at Acts 4:5.

[18] Compare Acts 4:6.

[19] Mishna, *Middoth*, V.4.

[20] Compare notes at Acts 12:10.

f. Paul's defense before the Sanhedrin. 23:1-10

23:1 – *And Paul, looking intently at the Council, said, "Brethren, I have lived my life with a perfectly good conscience before God up to this day."*

And Paul, looking intently at the Council, said. Luke once more uses the word for a piercing look that has become characteristic of Paul.[1] Paul is looking over the Sanhedrin. He had not seen it since he had stood there among Stephen's accusers, nearly a quarter of a century ago. Many changes had likely come about in the interval, but some of the faces were probably the same. Does Paul begin speaking before he has been asked any questions, or is Luke's account abbreviated, omitting the preliminaries that led up to Paul's statement?

"Brethren, I have lived my life with a perfectly good conscience before God up to this day." Paul's self-defense begins along this line, "I have considered myself a citizen of God's theocracy, and have always conducted myself so as to maintain a good conscience."

- The first idea comes from the word translated "lived my life," which in the Greek is "I have conducted myself as a citizen."[2] Paul recognized himself as a member of God's kingdom, His theocracy, and insists that he has so carried out his duties and responsibilities that he can claim a pure conscience before God his king. "Until this day" suggests that even since he left the Jewish religion to be an apostle for Christ, he was still operating by the same principle, namely, to carry out the commands of his King.

- "Conscience" comes from *suneidēsis* – *sun* ("with") + *oida* ("to know"). Hence, it means a co-knowledge with oneself. The conscience is a faculty with which every person is born. Its main function is *prompting* – prompting the person to do what his mind thinks is right and to avoid what his mind thinks is wrong. Note, the conscience prompts to do what is *thought* right. It is not a standard of judgment as to what is right or wrong. In addition to prompting, the conscience also *condemns* a person after he has done what his mind thinks is wrong, and *approves* a person after he has done what his mind thinks is right. The one who fails to abide by the promptings of his conscience will sear it, until it will no longer function; he then will have one less God-given obstacle to keep him from being eternally lost.

Paul makes a bold declaration, and yet there is no reason why it cannot have been true. His persecution of Christians had been conducted conscientiously (Acts 26:9). Of his conscientiousness and fidelity in their service, the Sanhedrin could bear witness. Paul meant to say that as he had been doing what he thought right when persecuting Christians, so he had been conscientious in his conversion and in his subsequent course of life. The mere fact that a man is conscientious does not prove that he is right or innocent; having a clear conscience and being honest did not make Paul right in his actions when he murdered Christians. Paul may have been able to claim a clear conscience, but he could not affirm that he was without guilt. In fact, he called himself the chief of sinners.[3]

---

[1] Acts 13:9.

[2] The same word is used in Philippians 1:27 in its technical sense, and in that technical sense it equals "to carry out the duties incumbent on one who is a citizen."

[3] 1 Timothy 1:13-16.

This point is worth re-emphasizing. A person may have a clear conscience and still be lost! Conscientiousness alone will not save any person. All that a clear conscience means is that one is acting upon the knowledge he has obtained. The conscience will prompt the doing of what the mind thinks is right, but the mind may or may not have been instructed in what God has declared right.[4]

Paul's defense was, "I have lived in such obedience to what I understood to be God's demands on me, that I have always had a clear conscience." He was not allowed to carry this line of defense very far.

23:2 – *And the high priest Ananias commanded those standing beside him to strike him on the mouth.*

And the high priest Ananias. See pages *xv* and *xvi* for information concerning this man.[5]

Commanded those standing beside him to strike him on the mouth. Perhaps Ananias could not conceive of a man living his whole life "with a perfectly clear conscience." Perhaps he thought this assertion was intended to be a personal insult, for he at least pretended to regard Paul's words as an insult to the Council. Imagine a man who was arraigned before them as a criminal of the worst sorts proudly declaring that he had lived in all good conscience before God! "The smiting on the mouth was a judicial and symbolic mode of silencing the speaker from saying what was deemed improper or false."[6]

23:3 – *Then Paul said to him, "God is going to strike you, you whitewashed wall! And do you sit to try me according to the Law, and in violation of the Law order me to be struck?"*

Then Paul said to him, "God is going to strike you, you white-washed wall! "White-washed wall" was a blunt way of calling Ananias a hypocrite. Whitewash was used to cover the real and often precarious condition of buildings and other structures, so there was a close similarity to men who disguised their real character by hypocrisy. Jesus had used a similar figure of speech when speaking to the Pharisees one day,[7] and Paul may have been familiar with that interchange. This may also have been a customary Jewish proverb.

This statement is seen by some as merely a prediction of what would happen to any man such as Ananias; others view it as an imprecation of evil on this particular man. Ananias' command was such an unexpected and exasperating interruption that it evoked from Paul a burst of indignation similar to the one he spoke years before to Elymas the sorcerer in the presence of Sergius Paulus.[8] Some appeal to Ananias' removal from office shortly, and his cowardly death in the siege of Jerusalem some years later, as a partial ful-

---

[4] Still, even though the mind may not be properly instructed, one is never to go against his conscience (Romans 14:23).

[5] This Ananias is not to be confused with Annas (Acts 4:6), with the Ananias of Acts 5:1, or with the Ananias of Acts 9:10.

[6] Boles, *op. cit.*, p.362.

[7] Matthew 23:27; Luke 11:44.

[8] Acts 13:10.

fillment of Paul's words.

And do you sit to try me according to the Law. Paul here gives the reason for his strong rebuke. Herein was Ananias' hypocrisy: he pretended to be doing one thing (judging according to the Law), but was actually doing another (violating the Law). His years of training in Jerusalem, under Gamaliel, would have left Paul very familiar with the statutes and legal requirements and rights of the accused. There is emphasis on "you" in the Greek. "*You*, you are sitting to judge me?"

And in violation of the Law order me to be struck?" The rights of defendants were carefully safeguarded in the Jewish law in such passages as "You shall do no unrighteousness in judgment" (Leviticus 19:35). Such efforts at intimidation of the defendant were no part of a fair trial. Paul is asking these judges, "Would you apply the Law to others, but not to yourselves?"

23:4 – *But the bystanders said, "Do you revile God's high priest?"*

But the bystanders said. These by-standers might be servants or deputies in service of the court.

"Do you revile God's high priest?" The bystanders were shocked at the way Paul spoke to the high priest, and they rebuke Paul for his outburst. The high priest while sitting on the judgment seat was God's representative in spite of his bad character (Deuteronomy 17:8ff).

23:5 – *And Paul said, "I was not aware, brethren, that he was high priest; for it is written, 'YOU SHALL NOT SPEAK EVIL OF A RULER OF YOUR PEOPLE.'"*

And Paul said, "I was not aware, brethren, that he was high priest. These words have been given several interpretations.

1) Some suppose that Paul spoke with *irony*, as if he were saying, "Pardon me, brethren, I did not consider that this was the high priest. It did not occur to me that a man who would conduct himself thusly could be God's high priest."

2) Some suggest that Paul is admitting that he *spoke hastily*. His meaning then would be, "I acknowledge my error and my haste. I did not for the moment consider that I was addressing the high priest, him whom God has commanded me to respect."

3) Another suggestion is that Paul, having been away from Jerusalem, was not aware of the *changes in the high priesthood*. No fewer than twenty-eight different high priests are enumerated in the years between AD 37 and 70. Paul's long absences from the city would have made it difficult for him to know, by sight, the man currently in office.

4) Others suppose that Ananias was *not wearing his usual white robe*, and was not sitting in his usual place. It is suggested that, since this was a meeting summoned by the tribune, they were not meeting in their usual place of meeting, and Ananias was not officially dressed for the occasion, nor was he in the middle of the semi-circle of Sanhedrin members. Some have further tried to excuse Paul's actions by suggesting

they were in a room that was dimly lit, or that Paul had bad eyesight which caused him difficulty in identifying at a distance the person who spoke the command that he should be struck on the mouth, but there is little foundation for either of these suggestions.

5) Still others suggest that *Ananias had usurped the office*, and was therefore not properly the high priest. Paul's words would, in this case, be somewhat ironical, as if he said, "I was not aware that this usurper should be granted the honor the word of God accords to the office of high priest."

6) The most likely suggestion is that Paul's words are an *apology*, that he is saying, "I didn't bear in mind for the moment that I was addressing the high priest. I lost my temper."

For it is written. Paul will quote Exodus 22:28. This passage had no specific reference to the high priest, but it inculcates a general spirit of respect for those in office, whatever that office might be. The passage is also interesting as one of those in which the Hebrew word *elohim*, commonly translated "God," is used of earthly rulers.

'YOU SHALL NOT SPEAK EVIL OF A RULER OF YOUR PEOPLE.'" Paul appeals to this Old Testament passage to show that it was his purpose to observe the Law, that he would not intentionally violate the Law, and that, if he had known Ananias to be high priest, he would have been restrained by his regard for the Law from using the language he had. Just a few months before he had written the same principle of conduct – about submission to government authorities – to the Romans.[9]

23:6 – *But perceiving that one part were Sadducees and the other Pharisees, Paul began crying out in the Council, "Brethren, I am a Pharisee, a son of Pharisees; I am on trial for the hope and resurrection of the dead!"*

But perceiving that one party were Sadducees and the other Pharisees. The change of tone from that of apology to this espousal of the Pharisees' position in regards to the resurrection seems abrupt, as if Luke records only a condensed account of all Paul said that day. Verse 9 may also be an intimation that much more was said by Paul. In any case, there comes a time in the hearing when it became evident that the whole procedure was not going to change the general attitude of the Sanhedrin toward Paul and his message. They had come to the meeting with preconceived notions, and nothing Paul has said so far has changed those notions. Then it dawned on Paul's awareness that the same parties were still members of the Sanhedrin as had been in it twenty-five years before.[10] Whether the different parties sat in groups on different sides, or whether Paul recognized the faces of individual members of each sect, men with whom he had formerly been acquainted, we have no data for deciding.

Paul *began* crying out in the Council, "Brethren, I am a Pharisee, a son of Pharisees. See notes at Acts 9:1 for the meaning of "a Pharisee, a son of Pharisees." Was there such

---

[9] Romans 13:1-7.

[10] See Acts 4:1ff.

an undercurrent of comment among the members of the Sanhedrin that Paul had to shout to make himself heard? As a result of some of the presentations made by Paul, have the Pharisees begun to show some sympathy, only to be badgered by the Sadducees; and when they replied back in kind, had a confusion begun to arise in the assembly?

Paul has been criticized by commentators for the methods he used.

> Paul's declaration that he was a Pharisee has been treated by some writers as being deceptive. The charge that Paul was being deceptive is unfounded; for while it is true that he was not in every particular a Pharisee, he was one in the sense attached to his remark by his hearers. All present knew that he was a Christian, and consequently, they knew that he claimed to be a Pharisee only in the sense of agreeing with that party in their points of antagonism with the Sadducees [with the matter of the resurrection being especially prominent].[11]

Another commentator thinks Paul was acting on the principle of "divide and conquer." But Acts 24:20,21 clearly shows that Paul did not regard his conduct in the Council as unworthy or tricky. Hence, Paul ought not be charged with any suppression or bending of the truth. His claim to be a "Pharisee" involved no tacit disclaimer of his faith in Christ; rather, it is as though he said, "I am one with you Pharisees in all that is truest in your creed."[12]

I am on trial for the hope and resurrection of the dead!" That is, concerning the hope that the dead will be raised, as well as the fact of the resurrection of Jesus. The "resurrection" has much been emphasized in Acts; almost every sermon has an appeal to it. The reason Paul gave up Judaism for Christianity was that the resurrection of Jesus proves Christianity to be a superior religion. And the hope inspired by anticipation of the resurrection of all men at the close of the age was a truth untaught by any pagan religion. The resurrection of Jesus and all that His resurrection implied was the real fact and substance that was behind all of Paul s life and teaching.

23:7 – *And as he said this, there arose a dissension between the Pharisees and Sadducees; and the assembly was divided.*

And as he said this, there arose a dissension between the Pharisees and Sadducees. As an act of strategy, Paul's words immediately had the result which he anticipated: they prevented a unanimous vote which might otherwise have united the two parties, as they had been united in the case of Stephen. Concurrence by the Council in a criminal charge against the defendant became immediately impossible as the two parties began arguing amongst themselves about their distinctive doctrines. The picture is of the two parties standing and yelling their arguments back and forth while Paul and the soldiers watched.

And the assembly was divided. The Pharisees would immediately begin to look at Paul

---

[11] McGarvey, *op. cit.*, p.225.

[12] The Pharisees had found the doctrine of the resurrection taught in the Old Testament, but they were never able to convince the Sadducees of their interpretation of the pertinent passages. Now, Paul is saying that the thing that convinced him – namely, the resurrection of Jesus – was the very proof they needed, and was the crown and completion of all their hopes and yearnings.

with more favor. A man so sound in his doctrine of the resurrection, in harmony with their own beliefs, could not be so bad after all. The Sadducees would become more adamant in their hatred of him for daring to speak in public what, in their eyes, was a great heresy. So instead of debating Paul's case, which was the actual issue on the docket before them, the group immediately began debating the merits of the question of the resurrection.

23:8 – *For the Sadducees say that there is no resurrection, nor an angel, nor a spirit; but the Pharisees acknowledge them all.*

For the Sadducees say that there is no resurrection. Luke, in this verse, is giving an explanation to his readers who might not be knowledgeable of the theological distinctions held by the different Jewish sects.[13] The Sadducees, perhaps influenced by Greek philosophy, denied the doctrine of the bodily resurrection. The Sadducees, says Josephus, "take away the belief of the immortal duration of the soul, and the punishments and rewards in Hades."[14] "The doctrine of the Sadducees is this, that the souls die with the bodies."[15] Of course, if the soul doesn't survive death, there would be no need to have a resurrection of the body.

Nor an angel, nor a spirit. There is not a consensus on how to understand Luke's explanation.

- Some think "angels" includes a rejection of both angels and demons, especially the developed doctrine of two kingdoms (one of good and the other evil) with their hierarchies of more or less authoritative angels.[16] The Sadducees would have explained away the appearances of angels in the Pentateuch as beings created for a particular task and therefore only transient in nature. By their rejection of "spirit" the Sadducees may have been saying no more than that there was no intermediate state to which the souls of men go.

- On the other hand, noting that the Pharisees held to the doctrine of reincarnation, some have understood that the Sadducees argued against this doctrine of reincarnation by affirming that there was no "spirit" (soul). Since there was nothing to transmigrate to another body, how could the doctrine of transmigration be true? The Sadducees would thus have been materialists, saying there is nothing but matter.

But the Pharisees acknowledge them all. "Them all" is the same word *amphoteroi* used at Acts 19:16. The beliefs of the party of the Pharisees have been detailed Special Study #9. They held to the idea of a resurrection of the body, of an immaterial world with angels intermediate between God and man, and with souls disembodied awaiting the resurrection and final judgment.

---

[13] See Special Study #9, "The Sects of the Jews," for an introduction to these parties and their beliefs.

[14] Josephus, *Wars*, II.8.14.

[15] Josephus, *Antiquities*, XVIII.1.4.

[16] This is the most probable explanation, and the one given in Special Study #9, "The Sects of the Jews."

23:9 – *And there arose a great uproar; and some of the scribes of the Pharisaic party stood up and* **began** *to argue heatedly, saying, "We find nothing wrong with this man; suppose a spirit or an angel has spoken to him?"*

And there arose a great uproar. The argument immediately became too heated for orderly debate. Each time someone new expressed his beliefs, he raised his voice more than the one who had just finished speaking. Soon, partisans from both sides were all talking at the same time, shouting to make their points, refusing to even listen to what the other side said. The Council quickly began to resemble the recent mob in the temple court.

And some of the scribes of the Pharisaic party stood up and *began* **to argue heatedly.** Concerning "scribes," see notes at Acts 4:5. "Argue heatedly" is a very strong word in the Greek (*diamachomai*) and means "to fight it out," "to fight back and forth fiercely." The yelling match has degenerated into fistfights.

Saying, "We find nothing wrong with this man. This was the acquittal that, if it could have been concurred in, would have won Paul's freedom. But this was not said as a vote by a judge. It was said in the heat of argument, and perhaps with a tone of delight in the voice similar to that with which "certain of the scribes" had rejoiced in Jesus' devastating answer to a Sadducee's argument on the Great Day of Questions.[17]

Suppose a spirit or an angel has spoken to him?" Because nothing is recorded in this chapter about an angel or spirit speaking to Paul, some deduce that the scribes must be referring to statements Paul had made in his speech from the steps the day before,[18] about how he had gone among the Gentiles in obedience to a command he received in a vision in the temple. Others suggest that Luke records only an abbreviated account of the day's proceedings, so that in this speech Paul has also spoken of the risen Lord's appearance to him on the Damascus road, as well as subsequent visions. The scribes would then be referring to what has been said in this very meeting.

Since the Pharisees believed in angels and spirits, and since they believed that God often delivered His will to men by the agency of angels, they are willing to admit (if it will help their argument against the Sadducees) that what Paul called the risen Lord was at least an angel or spirit of some kind. This was a direct and deliberate cut at the Sadducees, who denied the very existence of such beings.

Some manuscripts, like the KJV, close verse 9 with the words, "Let us not fight against God." If these words were part of the original text, they would be an almost exact reproduction of the advice given years before by Gamaliel (Acts 5:39). However, the textual evidence is against their inclusion. These words are lacking in the best manuscripts and were apparently added in order to complete the broken sentence, because the copyist did not appreciate the emphasis that the unfinished statement gives to the argument advanced by the scribes.

---

[17] Luke 20:39.

[18] Acts 22:17-18.

23:10 – *And as a great dissension was developing, the commander was afraid Paul would be torn to pieces by them and ordered the troops to go down and take him away from them by force, and bring him into the barracks.*

And as a great dissension was developing. With yelling matches among some of the Sanhedrin members, and physical scuffling among others, it was becoming a dangerous place for the prisoner. Some were defending Paul, and others would want him dead more today than they did yesterday. It must have quickly become clear to the commander that he was not going to learn much more about the charges against Paul this day.

The commander was afraid Paul would be torn to pieces by them. "Torn to pieces" is a word used when a wild beast tears its prey to pieces. The tribune's fear suggests that the Sadducees have tried to seize Paul to kill him, while the Pharisees attempted to rescue and defend him. Some were pulling him one way; some the other. Just as he had saved Paul from the mob on the previous day, he is again obliged to send in soldiers, this time to rescue one whom he knew to be a Roman citizen for whose life and safety he was responsible.

And ordered the troops to go down and take him away from them by force, and bring him into the barracks. If the Council was assembled either in the courtyard below the tower of Antonia or on the Pavement inside the walls of fortress, this language is easily understandable. The tribune has been observing the procedures from one of the towers above, and when the court scene begins to sour and become violent, and Paul's life is endangered, he orders the soldiers down the stairs and to the rescue. Once Paul was back in the barracks of the fortress, he would be safe from the violence of the Jews.

Lysias seems to have been at a loss to know what disposition to make of the case. He keeps Paul in custody, though such custody may have been only for the prisoner's own protection.

      g.   The Lord encourages Paul. 23:11

23:11 – *But on the night immediately following, the Lord stood at his side and said, "Take courage; for as you have solemnly witnessed to My cause at Jerusalem, so you must witness at Rome also."*

But on the night *immediately* following. Paul's words from the Lord came on the night following the trial before the Sanhedrin.

The Lord stood at his side. The reference is to Jesus, as the context shows. The appearances of Jesus to Paul, fulfilling the promise made on the Damascus road,[19] came at those times when they were most needed, when danger and reason for despondency were greatest, and when human companionship was most lacking.[20]

---

[19] The promise, made years earlier, is recorded in Acts 26:16.

[20] Jesus appeared to Paul at Jerusalem (Acts 22:18-21), at Corinth (Acts 18:9), and will do so again later on the way to Rome (Acts 27:23).

And said, "Take courage. This word was a familiar one on Jesus' lips during His earthly ministry.[21] Paul needed this word, for there was little enough in Paul's surroundings to encourage optimism. There is no record that Paul was singing hymns in prison the night following his session with the Sanhedrin. No Silas was present to join in the singing, and it was hard to find anything to sing about. Having brought a huge offering to his brethren in Jerusalem, he had been attacked and almost murdered in the temple by some of his old enemies from Asia. Rescued by the Roman soldiers, his defense from the steps up to the tower of Antonia had been rejected, and his rescue turned into a near flogging and an indefinite imprisonment. Making a defense before the Sanhedrin, he had been cuffed at the command of the high priest and had been set upon like a carcass contested for by vultures. Now uncounted dreary days in prison stretched before him. The predictions of Agabus and the others had come true, and no friend was near to weep with him now. Was his work to be cut short? Was he to fall victim to the malice of the Jews? Was the desire, which he had cherished for so many years, to preach the gospel in Rome,[22] to be frustrated? These problems and questions pressed upon him in the wakeful night that followed his day in court. Perhaps he prayed, and this appearance of Jesus was in answer to that prayer.

For as you have solemnly witnessed to My cause at Jerusalem. Paul's address to the people (22:1-21) had been far more a presentation of Christ than a defense of himself.

So you must witness at Rome also." The promise Jesus makes to Paul is not that he will be delivered from the imprisonment, only that he eventually will get to Rome and have opportunity to witness there also. There might be delay and suffering, and days of inactivity in several different prisons that would try his patience, but in the end he would reach the goal at Rome. Henceforth, Paul was confident that he would live to preach in the capital of the Roman empire, and laid his plans in that direction.

    h.   The plot to kill Paul. 23:12-30

23:12 – *And when it was day, the Jews formed a conspiracy and bound themselves under an oath, saying that they would neither eat nor drink until they had killed Paul.*

And when it was day. It was not long after Jesus promised Paul that he would get to Rome that a series of events were set in motion, events which ultimately led to Paul's voyage from Caesarea to Rome.

The Jews formed a conspiracy. There is a good possibility that it was the Asian Jews, who led the original attack on Paul in the temple, who were behind this plot. Or, if they have already left town because the feast of Pentecost is past, perhaps the plot was instigated by the Sadducees who, angry at what happened on the day before, sought a way to get even.

---

[21] Jesus spoke this word of cheer to the physically sick (Matthew 9:2, 27); to men who were filled with fear because of a storm on the sea (Matthew 14:27); and to the apostles who were troubled about the future (John 16:33).

[22] Romans 1:13, 15:23; Acts 19:21.

The Jews who joined in this conspiracy could have been members of the fanatical party of assassins,[23] for they were active at this time in Jewish politics; in later years, they played a dreadful part in connection with the destruction of Jerusalem.[24] This present conspiracy was intended to result in the assassination of Paul.

And bound themselves under an oath. Literally, the passage says "they placed themselves under an anathema." They were praying that they themselves would suffer direct punishments from God unless they carried out their plot. The person or thing on which an anathema was pronounced was regarded as subject to the wrath of God, either in this life or the next.[25]

Saying that they would neither eat nor drink until they had killed Paul. The inclusion of the words about eating and drinking in their oath to kill Paul does not imply so much a desire for haste as it does the idea that nothing else in their life was more important than the death of Paul. Every thought and moment were to be concentrated on that one end. There had been such assassination plots before, against others. Matthias, the founder of the Maccabean dynasty, was slain by an apostate Jew who offered sacrifice at the altar of Modin.[26] Ten zealots at Jerusalem conspired to assassinate Herod the Great because he had built an amphitheater and held gladiatorial games in the Holy City.[27]

23:13 – *And there were more than forty who formed this plot.*

And there were more than forty who formed this plot. The large number of fanatical men, giving every waking moment to planning and preparation, could very likely be expected to be successful in their plot (judging from a purely human standpoint). Paul's life was in great danger.

23:14 – *And they came to the chief priests and the elders, and said, "We have bound ourselves under a solemn oath to taste nothing until we have killed Paul.*

And they came to the chief priests and the elders. Probably only two or three of the forty are delegated to visit the religious leaders.[28] It speaks volumes about the chief priests that the conspirators felt quite sure of a hearty concurrence when they presented the assassination plot to them for approval.

---

[23] Acts 21:38.

[24] The assassins were especially active in Felix' time, and he sent troops against them. Later they took a leading part in the Jewish War and in the disturbances which led to it, being always among the most violent of the combatants. They held Masada, using it as a base from whence to pillage the country. Eventually they were dispersed to Egypt and Africa where they continued their terrorism.

[25] Compare Romans 9:3; 1 Corinthians 16:22; Galatians 1:8-9.

[26] 1 Maccabees 2:24.

[27] Josephus, *Antiquities*, XII.6,12; XV.8.3-4.

[28] On "chief priests," see notes at Acts 4:5. "Elders" may refer to the "senate" (see notes at Acts 5:21), or to the Sadducean members of the Sanhedrin. The choice made on this identification has some bearing on comments in this paragraph, especially with reference to who instigated the conspiracy.

And said, "We have bound ourselves under a solemn oath to taste nothing until we have killed Paul. Literally, "We have anathematized ourselves with an anathema." In this place, the Greek, like Hebrew idioms, expresses intensity by duplicating the leading word.

23:15 – *"Now, therefore, you and the Council notify the commander to bring him down to you, as though you were going to determine his case by a more thorough investigation; and we for our part are ready to slay him before he comes near the place."*

Now, therefore, you and the Council notify the commander. "Notify" is a legal term for giving official notice of a formal investigation. "The Council" likely means "the whole Council." The Pharisees could hardly decline to take part in such a proceeding, even if it were suggested by the Sadducean members.

To bring him down to you. They are asking for a meeting at the high priest's house or at the hall Gazith. It was only by such a request that they had any hope that the tribune would remove Paul far enough away from the tower of Antonia so as to make him vulnerable to an ambush. Specially if by "to you" they meant to the house of the high priest, the distance between Antonia and that residence would afford more location choices for the ambush.

As though you were going to determine his case by a more thorough investigation. This request appeared so reasonable that they did not doubt that the tribune would grant it to the Council, especially since his efforts the previous day were disappointing.

And we for our part are ready to slay him before he comes near *the place.***"** The plotters have suggested the part the religious leaders should have in the plan; then they say, "You can be sure we'll carry out our part. Rely on us!" If Paul were slain before he got near to the place where the Sanhedrin was to meet, there would be less suspicion that they themselves had a part in the deed.

It was a well-conceived plot; if it had not been overheard and exposed, it would almost certainly have resulted in Paul's death. Lysias would have complied with their request in order to gain more information about Paul's case. As the prisoner was escorted along the streets to the meeting place, these assassins, having chosen the spot for the ambush attempt in advance, would have rushed in among the unsuspecting soldiers to slay Paul almost before any blow could have been struck in his defense. Some of the assassins might be killed in the following retaliation by the soldiers, but it was a price they were willing to pay if they could rid the earth of Paul.

It is hard to know if the assassins were assured the religious leaders would listen to the plot because it was a justifiable thing to assassinate apostates, or because justice had fallen so low that such iniquitous requests could be made with a reasonable prospect that Ananias and his co-leaders would listen and join in.

23:16 – *But the son of Paul's sister heard of their ambush, and he came and entered the barracks and told Paul.*

But the son of Paul's sister. This verse raises many tantalizing questions about Paul's family relationships, and is, in fact, one of the few passages in the New Testament that gives any information at all.[29] The verse indicates a friendliness towards Paul, yet it also tends to raise more questions than it answers. Did the sister live in Jerusalem? If so, why did Paul stay with Mnason rather than with his own relatives? Or did only Paul's nephew live in Jerusalem? If only the nephew lives there, was he there as a rabbinical student as Paul himself had been a generation before (Acts 22:3)? Or may we assume that he has come up to Jerusalem for the feast of Pentecost? Is it possible that the son is friendly to Paul even though the sister wasn't? Paul says in Philippians 3:8 that he has "suffered the loss of all things for the sake of the excellency of the knowledge of Christ Jesus." This is usually interpreted to mean that Paul was disinherited by his family after he became a Christian; perhaps they even held a funeral for him as Jews do today for a family member who becomes a Christian. If Paul were disinherited, did Paul's sister act as though he no longer existed? Or at this point, has she too become a Christian, and thus would be friendly toward Paul with a friendliness that influences her son to attempt to help Paul?

Heard of their ambush. How did he hear of the ambush? Did he accidentally stumble onto the meeting where it was being conceived? Verse 16 might be rendered, "But Paul's sister's son heard the plotting having come upon *them*, and he entered the fortress and told Paul." Another idea is that an old Pharisee friend of Paul's tipped off his nephew regarding the secret plot to kill Paul, and the young man was sent to warn Paul. Or perhaps the nephew overheard one of the conspirators talking, after the plot was hatched.

And he came and entered the barracks and told Paul. There is no need, as some have done, to suppose on the basis of this boy's access to the prisoner that the whole story is fabricated. Paul was a Roman citizen; no firm charges were laid against him; he was in protective custody, but not necessarily solitary confinement. It is probable that he would be allowed to have visitors. One might even suggest that the tribune would permit Paul to have visitors with a witness present in hopes of gaining more information about the prisoner from their conversations.

23:17 – *And Paul called one of the centurions to him and said, "Lead this young man to the commander, for he has something to report to him."*

And Paul called one of the centurions to him. This centurion is possibly the one in charge of the soldiers guarding Paul. He was one of the ten under the tribune Lysias.

And said, "Lead this young man to the commander. How old was Paul's nephew, here styled a "young man"? If he had come up to the feast, he would have been over 20. The Greek word is the same one used of Paul when he was about 35,[30] and of Eutychus, who is

---

[29] Attempts have been made to find other passages that might tell something about Paul's family relationships. Appeal has been made to Romans 16:7,11 where Paul speaks of "kinsmen" in Rome, as though these were other of his family members, but it is probable that the reference there is to men who were kinsmen only in the sense that they were Jews.

[30] Acts 7:58.

also called a "boy."[31] If Paul's nephew were one of the rabbinical students, he would be in his late teens or early twenties. Yet many appeal to the fact that the commander took him by the hand (verse 19) as evidence he was a mere boy, full of fear.

For he has something to report to him." Passages like this and Acts 27:22ff play an important and consequential role in helping us understand the nature of God's promises. Paul had the most positive assurance from Jesus that his life would be spared, and that he would witness in Rome (verse 11). Such a promise, however, did not rule out care and effort on Paul's own part toward securing his own safety. Likewise, during the voyage to Rome, when the angel declared there would be no loss of life, there still had to be human effort. In chapter 27, the sailors' efforts and activities and work in the process of abandoning the ship was not needless nor superfluous. Instead of thinking the Lord would do it all, Paul looked on the promise made to him as an encouragement to put forth his own efforts for security and salvation.

23:18 – *So he took him and led him to the commander and said, "Paul the prisoner called me to him and asked me to lead this young man to you since he has something to tell you."*

So he took him and led him to the commander and said, "Paul the prisoner called me to him. "Paul the prisoner" is a term that will become familiar. It is the first time such a title is used in Acts, and it is doubtful that at this time Paul had any awareness of how long he was going to be "the prisoner." Some years later, it has become a title of honor and the basis of making pleas to the churches he founded, when he wrote to them.[32]

And asked me to lead this young man to you since he has something to tell you." The fact that Paul did not tell the centurion the message, but sent the young man, would indicate to the tribune that the message was somewhat confidential.

23:19 – *And the commander took him by the hand and stepping aside,* **began** *to inquire of him privately, "What is it that you have to report to me?"*

And the commander took him by the hand. This was an understanding gesture, designed to encourage a young, courageous, but thoroughly frightened messenger.

And stepping aside, *began* **to inquire of him privately, "What is it that you have to report to me?"** The tribune caught the hint that the message was confidential. Hearing the report from the boy would be more believable than if Paul had told the centurion and he had delivered it third or fourth hand.

23:20 – *And he said, "The Jews have agreed to ask you to bring Paul down tomorrow to the Council, as though they were going to inquire somewhat more thoroughly about him.*

And he said, "The Jews have agreed to ask you to bring Paul down tomorrow to the

---

[31] Acts 20:9.

[32] Ephesians 3:1, 4:1; Philemon 1:9.

Council. Not all the Jews, but their influential leaders.[33] After what Lysias had seen in the temple court and in the trial the day before, the term would be specific enough for him.

As though you were going to inquire somewhat more thoroughly about him. How shall we explain the "you" when it is the Council making the request?[34] It is possible that when the messengers came from the Sanhedrin, they would say, "If you wish to know more about Paul, bring him down, and we'll do our best to be more orderly than yesterday."

23:21 – *"So do not listen to them, for more than forty of them are lying in wait for him who have bound themselves under a curse not to eat or drink until they slay him; and now they are ready and waiting for the promise from you."*

So do not listen to them. Paul's nephew pleaded with Lysias not to heed the request from the Jews when it came.

For more than forty of them are lying in wait for him who have bound themselves under a curse not to eat or drink until they slay him. Here he gives Lysias a reason for not heeding the request.

And now they are ready and waiting for the promise from you. Already they are done with their planning, and were but waiting for Lysias' consent to bring Paul down, before taking up their places of ambush.[35]

23:22 – *Therefore the commander let the young man go, instructing him, "Tell no one that you have notified me of these things."*

Therefore the commander let the young man go, instructing him, "Tell no one that you have notified me of these things." The tribune made no promises and revealed no plans to the young man that might possibly have gotten back to the conspirators. The young man's own safety, as well as the successful frustration of the plot, depended on the utmost secrecy. Lysias had three alternatives from which to choose a course of action: (1) He could accede to the Jews' request and lose his citizen prisoner. (2) He could resist the Jews' request, with the resultant loss of favor with the Jewish authorities, and with probable bloodshed. (3) He could avoid any more trouble by removing Paul from the city before the request was made of him. He quickly chose the latter course.

---

[33] "The Jews" is used here, as the phrase often is in John's Gospel, of the authorities, the religious leaders (John 1:19, 5:15-16).

[34] In fact, there is a manuscript variation here, some reading "as though *they* would inquire" (see the KJV). The plural is not well supported at all, so the singular "you" must be explained. We think it is more than merely deference on the youth's part that he says "you."

[35] Once their conspiracy had no more chance of being carried out, the conspirators would have been released from their hunger vows. The Talmud (*Nedarim*, III.1.3) says that those who took a vow were released from it if it was impossible to carry out. These forty conspirators most likely would have considered themselves absolved from their vow as soon as they heard of the prisoner's removal to Caesarea. Thus, their fast may have lasted no longer than eighteen or twenty hours.

23:23 – *And he called to him two of the centurions, and said, "Get two hundred soldiers ready by the third hour of the night to proceed to Caesarea, with seventy horsemen and two hundred spearmen."*

And he called to him two of the centurions, and said. The Greek says, "a certain two centurions," and probably speaks of those who specially could be trusted. Each of them would have 100 soldiers under his authority.[36]

"Get two hundred soldiers ready by the third hour of the night to proceed to Caesarea. The 200 soldiers will not go all the way to Caesarea, but some of the force that Lysias is ordering to prepare to march will accompany Paul the whole way.[37] Assuming that Lysias is using the Jewish method of counting time, the "third hour" would be about 9 p.m. This hour was picked in order that the escape might be made in as much secrecy as possible, under the cover of darkness, in order to elude the band of assassins who had resolved to murder Paul.

With seventy horsemen and two hundred spearmen." Lysias is ordering over half of his cavalry out in this detachment.[38] The exact meaning of the Greek word translated "spearmen" is disputed. It might refer to slingers (users of slingshots), or javelin-throwers, or to light-armed spearmen (those who handled the spear in their right hand, as contrasted with those spears that required both hands to wield). The force totaled 470 soldiers, with light and heavy arms. This escort seems to be large for just one prisoner, but the tumults of the previous days and the information just received about the conspiracy gave Lysias good reason to anticipate a formidable attack should they encounter one.

23:24 – They were *also to provide mounts to put Paul on and bring him safely to Felix the governor.*

They were **also to provide mounts to put Paul on.** The order was for mounts for Paul in particular. The word translated "mounts" (*ktēnē*) is a general word which in this context could speak of horses, mules, or even camels. Commentators differ as to the reason for the plural. Some suppose there was to be an animal for every member of the force. Others suggest that more than one would be needed for Paul's use; since he was chained to a soldier, the soldier would have to be mounted, too. Others suggest that Luke and some others are to accompany Paul and a mount is provided for each.[39] Or perhaps the plural signifies some changes of mounts so that they can travel as quickly as possible, stopping only to change animals, and then continuing on.

---

[36] See notes at Acts 10:1 on the position in the Roman army held by centurions.

[37] See verses 32-33.

[38] Comments at Acts 21:31 included the explanation that the force under Lysias would include 120 horsemen, plus a thousand soldiers.

[39] Luke's account has been narrated in the third person (rather than "we") for a number of verses now. This probably means that Luke and Paul's other associates did not know of his removal to Caesarea until after it happened. They, too, had to catch up with him there.

And bring him safely to Felix the governor. In addition to the brief sketch about Felix in the Introductory Studies,[40] there are some important notes that will help give background and context for the events that happen to Paul the next several months.

- At Rome in the household of Antonia, who was the mother of the emperor Claudius, there were two brothers who were first slaves before becoming freedmen. These brothers were Antonius Felix and Pallas.
- When Claudius became emperor, Pallas was one of his favorite companions and advisers. Through Pallas' influence, Felix obtained the position as governor of Judea. There he governed as one who thought, in reliance on his brother's power and influence with the emperor, he could commit any crime with impunity. Tacitus describes Felix as one who wielded "the power of a king in the mind of a slave."[41]
- Suetonius, another historian, tells us Felix married three different queens over the course of the years.[42] His first wife was Drusilla, and she was the granddaughter of Antony and Cleopatra.[43] Suetonius does not name his second wife, but calls her a princess. His third wife was also named Drusilla, and she was the youngest daughter of Herod Agrippa I, and therefore was a sister of Agrippa II.
- At the time of Paul's trial, the second Drusilla was about 20 years old. As a small girl, she had been betrothed to the crown prince of Commagne, in eastern Asia Minor; but the marriage did not take place because the prospective bridegroom (Epiphanes, the son of Antiochus) would not embrace Judaism. When she was 15 years old, her brother, Agrippa II, then gave her in marriage to king Azizus of Emesa, a petty state in Syria. Azizus did embrace the Jewish religion in order to marry her, in the year AD 52. When she was but 16, Felix, with the help of a Cypriot magician called Atmos, persuaded her to leave her husband and marry him. She thus became Felix's third wife, and bore him a son named Agrippa, who met his death in the eruption of Vesuvius in AD 79. Drusilla also perished at Pompeii in the eruption.[44] She is said to have been a very beautiful woman.
- Felix became governor of Judea about the year AD 52, after reigning over Samaria from AD 48 on. He governs the province until Festus is appointed in his place.[45] Felix was residing in the governor's quarters at Caesarea, the capital of the province of Judea.

23:25 – *And he wrote a letter having this form:*

And he wrote a letter having this form. It was a requirement of Roman jurisprudence to send a written statement (technically called an *elogium*) along with the prisoner regarding

---

[40] See p.*xvi*.

[41] Tacitus, *Annals*, XII.54; *History*, V.9.

[42] Suetonius, *Life of Claudius*, c.28.

[43] Drusilla was the daughter of Juba (the king of Mauritania) and Selene (the daughter of Mark Antony and Cleopatra).

[44] Josephus, *Antiquities*, XX.7.2. See more notes at Acts 24:24 about this Drusilla.

[45] See notes at Acts 24:27.

the case involved. In this case it was an official explanation of why Paul had been sent for trial to a higher court.

There is much speculation about how Luke became acquainted with the contents of this letter. Perhaps it was read out loud when Paul was presented to Felix, and Luke learned the contents either firsthand or from Paul at a later time. Perhaps a copy of it was sent along with Paul after he appealed to Caesar, and Luke saw this copy. In any case, Luke is not giving a verbatim reproduction of the letter as the phrase "having this form" indicates. Luke is providing only the general contents indicated.

23:26 – *"Claudius Lysias, to the most excellent governor Felix, greetings.*

Claudius Lysias, to the most excellent governor Felix. Compare notes at Acts 1:1 on this title "most excellent." Its use here shows that the title was given to provincial governors as well as to members of the Roman equestrian order (i.e., the order of "knights" who ranked next after senators in Roman society, an order to which Felix did not belong).

Greetings. This letter follows the regular format for 1st century letters.[46]

23:27 – *"When this man was arrested by the Jews and was about to be slain by them, I came upon them with the troops and rescued him, having learned that he was a Roman.*

When this man was arrested by the Jews and was about to be slain by them. Lysias uses the term for "man" (*andra*) which shows a certain respect for the prisoner. See notes at Acts 21:30ff regarding Paul's capture and the attempt to kill him after dragging him out of the temple.

I came upon them with the troops and rescued him, having learned that he was a Roman. The tribune here deliberately slants his statement so as to claim credit for having rescued a Roman citizen when, as a matter of fact, he did not know Paul was a Roman until he was about to scourge him without a trial. Lysias passes over this fact because he was subject to censure and punishment for his poor handling of the case in those early hours. The letter does state the facts, but not in the order of their occurrence, nor is anything said about the erroneous opinion under which Lysias labored for a while (21:37ff).

23:28 – *"And wanting to ascertain the charge for which they were accusing him, I brought him down to their Council;*

And wanting to ascertain the charge for which they were accusing him, I brought him down to their Council. Certain negative critics have affirmed that verses 28 and 29 were not in the original letter sent by Lysias to Felix; however, without the information these verses contain, Lysias' presentation to Felix would be greatly lacking. The account of Paul before the Council is given in detail in the notes at Acts 22:30ff.

---

[46] See notes at Acts 15:23.

23:29 – *"and I found him to be accused over questions about their Law, but under no accusation deserving death or imprisonment.*

And I found him to be accused over questions about their Law. Lysias has listened to Paul's speech from the stairs and his defense before the Sanhedrin. Out of these he has been able to discern two things: (1) It was a typical Jewish dispute, and (2) the prisoner has done nothing Rome would be interested in.

Lysias would have been able to list several topics that were, to his mind, "Jewish": (a) The prisoner was accused of breaking the rules of the temple; (b) the prisoner affirmed and the Jews denied that a teacher named Jesus had risen from the dead; and (c) the prisoner affirmed and the Jews denied that that teacher was entitled to the name Messiah.

But under no accusation deserving death or imprisonment. The tribune affirms here that his investigation has turned up no instance where Paul has broken a Roman law that would deserve being sentenced to death or imprisonment.[47] About all Paul could have been accused of was contributing to the disturbance of the peace, something that Roman soldiers found an almost daily occurrence.

23:30 – *"And when I was informed that there would be a plot against the man, I sent him to you at once, also instructing his accusers to bring charges against him before you."*

And when I was informed that there would be a plot against the man. See notes at verses 16ff concerning the conspiracy. Lysias has just said Paul was innocent as far as Roman law was concerned. Why should Lysias then send him to Felix? That question the tribune now answers. Lysias presents himself as the protector of a fellow Roman citizen.

I sent him to you at once, also instructing his accusers to bring charges against him before you. This statement that he had commanded Paul's accusers to appear before Felix, though not strictly true at the time when the letter was written, was true by the time the letter was read to Felix. Implied is the idea that when the Sanhedrin members, on the morrow, appear to suggest another investigation of Paul's case, Lysias intends to say something like, "I found out about your plot against the prisoner's life, and I have moved him to Caesarea where he is safe from your intrigues. Furthermore, I order you to appear there and press charges against him. If you do not, I shall be forced to make a more thorough investigation of your complicity in the plot against my prisoner's life!"[48]

In some manuscripts, Lysias' letter closes with the word "Farewell." Codices *Aleph* and 31, and the Byzantine text in general, carry this closing word. Such a closing formula, like the opening one, would agree with the usual form for letters in the 1st century.

---

[47] If Acts was originally written as a brief for Paul's trial (see Introductory Studies, p.*xxiii*), it is interesting to note how time and again no Roman court before which Paul appeared ever found him guilty of anything Rome would be interested in, whether it be Gallio, Lysias, Felix, Festus, or whoever.

[48] Perhaps we have been too strong in our representation, but it is clear that there was some kind of threat held by Lysias over the Jews to get them to comply and to take a lawyer (Acts 24:1ff) along with them.

2. At Antipatris. 23:31-32

23:31 – *So the soldiers, in accordance with their orders, took Paul and brought him by night to Antipatris.*

So the soldiers, in accordance with their orders. Luke inserted the contents of the letter composed by Lysias, which broke the continuity of the narrative of historical events. With these words, Luke takes up again where he left off at verse 24.

Took Paul and brought him by night to Antipatris. They arrived at Antipatris sometime after daybreak, having marched "through the night." Since Antipatris was over 30 miles from Jerusalem,[49] it must have been something of a forced march for the infantry. Further, the route took them through mountainous country. At one time the place was known as Caphar-Saba,[50] but it was rebuilt by Herod the Great about 35 BC, and renamed in honor of his father, Antipater.

23:32 – *But the next day, leaving the horsemen to go on with him, they returned to the barracks.*

But the next day. This would be after dawn of the day following their all-night march.

Leaving the horsemen to go on with him. Only the seventy cavalrymen travel the 35 miles from Antipatris to Caesarea with Paul. Now that they are out of the mountains and on the plain, there is less danger of surprise attack or ambush.

They returned to the barracks. The 200 soldiers and the 200 spearmen turn back immediately to return to Jerusalem. Since they were practically beyond all danger of pursuit or attack, the 400 foot soldiers are no longer needed to guard Paul. Because they may be needed in Jerusalem (should the Jews decide to riot over the tribune's spiriting away of Paul), they turn right around after an all-night march and return to the fortress of Antonia.

---

[49] The scholarly sources have long struggled over the location and identity of Antipatris.
- Current maps of Israel show Antipatris located at the mound (tell) called Tell Aphek, northeast of Joppa Tel Aviv about 10 miles.
- About a mile to the east of Tell Aphek is Rosh Ha'Ayin (the fountain head), which until 1948 was the source of much of the water supply for Jerusalem, and whose waters are now piped into the Negev.
- Complicating the identification is the fact that 5 miles north of Tell Aphek is a town called Kefar Sava. Josephus identifies Antipatris with Caphar-Saba, and says it was different than Aphek (*Wars*, II.19.1).

Thus, all three locations (Tell Aphek, Rosh Ha'Ayin. and Kefar Sava) have at times been affirmed to be Antipatris, and the different locations account for the different distances the commentaries affirm Antipatris to be from Jerusalem or from Caesarea.

The detachment of soldiers escorting Paul could have traveled north up the Way of the Patriarchs to the road that branches off west through Emmaus (Qubeiba), then on through the valley of Beth Horon, and then on to Antipatris. Or they could have traveled the Way of the Patriarchs as far north as Gophna (Jifna), and thence turned westward to Antipatris. There are ruins of Roman roads along either of these routes.

[50] Josephus, *Antiquities*, XIII.15.1; *Wars*, IV.8.1.

3. Paul's Two-Year Imprisonment at Caesarea. 23:33-26:32

    a. Paul is presented to Felix. 23:33-35

23:33 – *And when these had come to Caesarea and delivered the letter to the governor, they also presented Paul to him.*

And when these had come to Caesarea and delivered the letter to the governor. It would be a half-day journey from Antipatris to Caesarea. They entered Caesarea, we suppose, late in the day, and a parade of seventy horsemen plus the prisoner would have attracted many curious eyes. Perhaps Philip and some of the other Christians at Caesarea were surprised to see Paul in the midst of this group, which would cause them to reflect on how quickly the prophecy of Paul's being bound at Jerusalem had been fulfilled.

They also presented Paul to him. Paul is turned over to the custody of Felix.

23:34 – *And when he had read it, he asked from what province he was; and when he learned that he was from Cilicia,*

And when he had read it, he asked from what province he was. Felix was seeking to learn what his own duties were in the case,[51] to learn if Paul properly belonged to his jurisdiction. Would he need to consult the ruler of another province before trying Paul, or did he already have jurisdiction? Since Cilicia, Judea and Phoenicia were all part of the Roman province of Syria, Felix already did have jurisdiction in Paul's case.

And when he learned that he was from Cilicia. Tarsus, the birthplace of Paul, was in the province of Cilicia (Acts 21:39).

23:35 – *he said, "I will give you a hearing after your accusers arrive also," giving orders for him to be kept in Herod's Praetorium.*

He said, "I will give you a hearing after your accusers arrive also." The Greek verb expresses the idea of a thorough hearing, a full investigation. It was a practice of Roman law that whenever a prisoner was sent from one court to another with a written statement (*elogium*) of the charges against him, he was given a fresh hearing.

Giving orders for him to be kept in Herod's Praetorium. The Greek word *praetorium* was somewhat elastic in its application; it could speak of a palace where a king lived or it could mean a barracks for soldiers. It came to signify any building where an imperial representative lived.[52] This building in Caesarea was probably built by Herod the Great for use as a royal residence; it had been appropriated by the Romans for use by the governor and his troops. As was common with most such official headquarters, it contained a guard-room for confining prisoners. Paul is now locked up, awaiting his trial before Felix.

---

[51] Compare Pilate's question recorded in Luke 23:6.

[52] Compare Matthew 27:27; Philippians 1:13, 4:22.

b. Paul's trial before Felix. 24:1-23

24:1 – *And after five days the high priest Ananias came down with some elders, with a certain attorney* named *Tertullus; and they brought charges to the governor against Paul.*

And after five days. On the day following Paul's being escorted out of Jerusalem, the Jews arrived at the tower of Antonia to request another investigation of Paul's case, only to be disappointed to find that their plot had failed. The tribune then orders them to appear in court at Caesarea. "After five days" can mean either five days from Paul's departure from Jerusalem, or five days after his arrival in Caesarea. Part of the time was needed for the priests and elders to make preparations for the journey, and part of the time was spent engaging the professional services of Tertullus. The rest of the time would have been taken up making the trip from Jerusalem to Caesarea.

The high priest Ananias came down. Perhaps Ananias[1] was specifically ordered by Lysias to be one of the prosecutors in the case, or perhaps Ananias was so anxious to get Paul out of the way that he deliberately lent his prestige to the case for the prosecution, just as he had earlier welcomed and entered into the assassination plot against Paul.[2]

With some elders. These are very likely the same elders who were party to the assassination attempt with the forty fanatical Jews.

With a certain attorney *named* **Tertullus.** The word "attorney" is translated "orator" in the marginal note. There was a class of men, representatives of whom could be found in most every province in the empire, who for a fee would present the case of a plaintiff or a defendant by bringing to bear on the court their knowledge of Roman law and especially by using their eloquence in an attempt to influence the judge. Based on the way he speaks, Tertullus himself was likely not a Jew; it is more likely that he was a Greek or a Roman. One would assume that the Jews, when ordered by Lysias to appear in Felix's court, recognized that they were in some serious difficulty, else they would not have had to resort to hiring an attorney like Tertullus.

> There is not the slightest ground for supposing, as some have done, that the proceedings were conducted in Latin, and that while the chief priests were obliged to employ an advocate to speak in that language, Paul, because of the ability to speak in tongues, did not need a Roman lawyer. Proceedings before a procurator of Judea and the provincials under him were almost of necessity (as in the case of our Lord and Pilate) in Greek. Had Paul spoken in Latin, Luke, who records when [Paul] spoke in Hebrew (21:40) and when he spoke in Greek (21:37), would have told us.[3]

And they brought charges to the governor against Paul. "Brought charges" is a techni-

---

[1] Information about Ananias, son of Nebedaeus, is given at Acts 23:2 and on p.*xv-xvi* of the Introductory Studies.

[2] Acts 23:14.

[3] Plumptre, *op. cit.*, p.378.

cal word, and implies something of the nature of an indictment. Even though Lysias' letter had said he could find nothing of which Paul was guilty, Felix had said he would give Paul's case a full investigation when his accusers arrived. This verse says that those accusers formally presented themselves to Felix, and so he prepares to have the hearing.

24:2 – *And after* **Paul** *had been summoned,* **Tertullus** *began to accuse him, saying* to the governor, *"Since we have through you attained much peace, and since by your providence reforms are being carried out for this nation,*

And after *Paul* **had been summoned.** Paul was being held in custody elsewhere in the Praetorium, so a messenger was sent to summon him to the trial. Paul is expected to appear on a moment's notice.

Tertullus began to accuse him, saying *to the governor.* The orator begins by offering exaggerated flattery of Felix the judge. In the orator's trade, such flattery was called an *exordium,* instructions and rules for which can be found in Cicero.[4] Such a beginning to a speech was intended to win a case by getting into the good graces of the judge before he even heard any of the evidence.

"Since we have through you attained much peace. "We" have attained, says Tertullus, and in verse 6 the use of "we" designates the Jews. By contrast, when later in verse 2 he says "this nation," he apparently does so to differentiate between the Jews and the Roman governor, Felix.

The flattery offered to Felix was indeed somewhat exaggerated, for there was little about his administration that could be praised. The "peace" that Tertullus speaks of was one of the few positive contributions Felix made to Palestine; he had broken up the bands of robbers, and had by force put down the organized assassins (*sicarii*).[5] But in fact, Felix was guilty of much corruption in his administration of affairs, including the assassination of Jonathan the high priest, who had dared to urge Felix to be more worthy of his office. Opposition to Rome's rule, which used to be isolated and sporadic, became a more fixed and widespread rebellion during Felix's tenure. A decade after Felix's governorship, this opposition flamed into the open, leading eventually the destruction of Jerusalem. It was his corruption and cruelty while in office that finally caused the attitude of rebellion to jell in the hearts of the average Jew.[6]

And since by your providence reforms are being carried out for this nation. In the 1st century, the Greek word rendered "providence" had almost the connotation of "divine action." Men spoke then, as now, of the "providence" of God, and already in the empire there was a tendency to attribute such divine actions to the emperor himself. In time, because men had spoken so often about the "providence of Caesar," those words will appear on the coins and medals struck in Caesar's honor.

---

[4] Cicero, *Orations,* II.78-79.

[5] Acts 21:37-38; Josephus, *Antiquities,* XX.8.5; *Wars,* II.13.2.

[6] Josephus, *Antiquities,* XX.8.6; *Wars,* II.13.6.

Tertullus goes one step further, and extends to the procurator of Judea a phrase that had been used only of Caesar. Tertullus is almost saying, "Crimes are being eradicated because of your 'divine actions.'" The "reforms" of which Tertullus speaks were few, as far as Felix's own government was concerned. Within two years of these events in Acts 24, Felix will be removed from office and summoned to trial in Rome, where he escaped punishment only because of his brother's influence in the court there.[7]

24:3 – *"we acknowledge this in every way and everywhere, most excellent Felix, with all thankfulness.*

We acknowledge *this* **in every way and everywhere.** "Not merely in your presence as I am now, but we always acknowledge that it is due to your vigilance that our land is secure."

Most excellent Felix. Compare notes at Acts 1:1 and 23:26 on the title "most excellent."

With all thankfulness. "We admit that the reforms we have (e.g., fewer robbers to worry about when we travel) are because of you; and we accept your attempts to promote peace with gratitude." Perhaps there was some sincerity in this statement of gratitude for relief from the crime wave that had bothered travelers in the hill country of Palestine.

24:4 – *"But, that I may not weary you any further, I beg you to grant us, by your kindness, a brief hearing.*

But, that I may not weary you any further. "Weary you" is a possible translation; it is also possible to translate it as "in order that I not detain you too long." Note again the flattering approach taken by the orator. Felix is so busy keeping the peace, that it would be a shame to keep him away from his duties much longer! Tertullus speaks as if he had to restrain himself from uttering the further words of praise that his feelings naturally prompted him toward.

I beg you to grant us, by your kindness, a brief hearing. The word translated "kindness" (*epieikeia*) means mildness, gentleness, sweet reasonableness. The "kindness" of Felix was an invention of Tertullus' flattery. Felix was well-known as a cruel, severe, avaricious man, who allowed himself indulgence in every license and excess. Luke may be giving only an abbreviated summary of all that Tertullus said, but, if the time spent by way of flattery as compared to the time spent giving the charges against Paul is in proportion to the actual speech, there is some indication of the weakness of the charges against Paul.

24:5 – *"For we have found this man a real pest and a fellow who stirs up dissension among all the Jews throughout the world, and a ringleader of the sect of the Nazarenes.*

For we have found this man a real pest. The Greek word is more emphatic than "pest." Tertullus labels Paul a pestilence, a plague, an epidemic. The lawyer passes from flattering the judge to hurling invectives against the defendant, and in doing so puts strong emphasis

---

[7] See notes at Acts 24:27.

on charges against Paul which would have him doing the very thing Felix has been trying to reform! That Paul was a pest, a plague, is a general charge. Everywhere Paul goes, there have been extensive disturbances of the peace. In the following phrases we shall have three specific cases by which Tertullus tries to prove this general accusation.

And a fellow who stirs up dissension among all the Jews throughout the world. "World" in a Roman court would be a reference to the Roman empire. This is the first charge against Paul – that he is the cause of disturbing the peace all over the empire, at least among the Jewish communities. Recall the difficulties Paul encountered at Pisidian Antioch and Iconium,[8] at Thessalonica,[9] and at Ephesus.[10] By only slightly twisting what actually happened in those towns, each event could be portrayed as Paul's fault, rather than being the fault of the unbelieving Jews who fomented the agitations against Paul.

And a ringleader of the sect of the Nazarenes. The word translated "ringleader" occurs nowhere else in the New Testament. It is a military word denoting one who stands first in an army, a standard bearer, a leader, a commander. Paul is accused of being so prominent in preaching the gospel that he is the leader, or principal person, behind the spread of the sect of the Nazarenes.[11]

Perhaps the words "sect" and "Nazarenes" contain the substance of the second charge against Paul in this trial. This is the first instance of the use of the term "Nazarene," expressive of contempt, as a designation for the followers of Jesus.[12] Tertullus, evidently, is accusing Paul of founding a religion that is an offshoot of Judaism, and which was therefore unlawful in the Roman empire. Tertullus claims that the religion Paul advocates is not Judaism, so it is a religion not licensed by the state.[13] Paul, Tertullus says, is teaching heresy! If he were not trying to introduce an unlawful religion, there wouldn't be the disturbance of the peace that he has incited.

24:6a – *"And he even tried to desecrate the temple; and then we arrested him.*

And he even tried to desecrate the temple. This third charge against Paul in the case before Felix has been modified slightly from the original charges levied in Jerusalem.[14] In Jerusalem, the Jews had asserted that Paul had actually taken Trophimus into the court of

---

[8] Acts 13:50ff, 14:5ff, 14:19ff.

[9] Acts 18:6.

[10] Acts 21:28. Behind this charge about dissensions all over the empire must be the fact that intelligence has come to the religious leaders at Jerusalem about the spread of Christianity in communities as far away as Asia Minor and Greece. Did the Jews from Asia share this news with the religious leaders in Jerusalem, or was there some other source of information?

[11] The Greek word behind "sect" has been commented on at Acts 5:17 and 15:5.

[12] This pejorative was also cast at Jesus Himself (John 1:46; Acts 6:14). Peter also uses the term as an identifier for Jesus (Acts 2:22), but not with contempt.

[13] For information about illicit religions, see Acts 16:4. This interpretation of the specific charge being made against Paul is better than the explanation that it involved a matter of political Messianism.

[14] Acts 21:28. The Asian Jews' activities and claims as they grabbed Paul in the temple lie in the background of this current charge against Paul.

Israel; now they are content with accusing him of only attempting to take Trophimus in. The idea behind Tertullus' charge is that it's another example of how Paul causes trouble everywhere he goes.

And then we arrested him. As in verse 2, the lawyer identifies himself with his clients. "We arrested" intentionally downplays what was a near lynching. Lysias in his letter to Felix was not the only one who spun the details of this incident in his own interests.

24:6b-8a – *"[And we wanted to judge him according to our own Law. But Lysias the commander came along, and with much violence took him out of our hands, ordering his accusers to come before you.]"*

The Western text, the Syriac and Vulgate versions, and the Byzantine text (and thus the KJV) carry these verses. However, they may or may not be genuine.[15]

If these words were part of the attorney's speech, observe these key points: (a) In Tertullus' recounting, the tumult in the temple becomes a legal arrest by the proper officers. As would have been the case for any breach of the law of Israel, this arrest would have been followed in due course by a legal trial. (b) However, the uncalled-for interruption by Lysias thwarted the whole orderly procedure. Note that Lysias is also charged with "much violence" (i.e., police brutality) as he interferes with the Jewish legal process.[16]

Tertullus again spins the facts to his clients' benefit, to make it look as if the Jews were going to give Paul a fair trial in accordance with Jewish law. In truth, without regard to law or justice, they would have murdered Paul on the spot had not Lysias intervened.

24:8b – *"And by examining him yourself concerning all these matters, you will be able to ascertain the things of which we accuse him."*

And by examining him yourself concerning all these matters, you will be able to ascertain the things of which we accuse him." "Examining" is from the Greek *anakrinō* (a different word than was used in 22:24), a word often used in a legal context of a preliminary investigation.[17] But who is the "him" who is to be examined?

- If verses 6b-8a are accepted as genuine, it is Lysias (the nearest antecedent) whom Tertullus suggests Felix examine. If the verses are omitted, then it is Paul whom Felix

---

[15] Some of the arguments for and against the integrity of these verses include:
  a. *Arguments for its integrity:*
   1. Felix makes mention of questioning Lysias (verse 22), which might presuppose the accusation made against him by Tertullus.
   2. If the words are omitted, Tertullus suggests that Felix ask the prisoner to testify against himself.
  b. *Arguments against its integrity:*
   1. Manuscript evidence is heavily in favor of its omission.
   2. If the words were part of the original, why and how did they come to be omitted?
   3. Would the attorney truly try to throw blame on Lysias, a Roman tribune?

[16] According to Acts 21:32, there was little if any violence at the time of Paul's rescue. The actual violence came later as the Jews tried to prevent Paul's being taken into the tower of Antonia (Acts 21:35).

[17] It is doubtful that *anakrinō* includes the idea of torture.

is to question.

- As footnote #15 suggests, this phrase is one reason to believe verses 6b-8a enjoy integrity. Without them, it is *Paul* who is to be asked about the truth of the charges against *Paul*.
- Yet if we understand this as a suggestion that Felix question Lysias (as if Tertullus and the Jews are alleging that Lysias was the real troublemaker), then the Jews' arguments immediately become somewhat thin. In effect, the Jews would be saying, "It is the other fellow (always) who is the cause of the disturbance. It's Paul! It's Lysias! We are the law abiding citizens!"

Notice also that Tertullus employs another oratorical device as he attempts to sway the judge. He seeks to prejudice Felix by saying, before Paul has even had a chance to defend himself, that he would find things to be just as the Jewish prosecution had presented them.

24:9 – *And the Jews also joined in the attack, asserting that these things were so.*

And the Jews also joined in the attack. Ananias and the elders are here guilty of endorsing the misrepresentations made by Tertullus against Paul and Lysias. We picture them as being called as witnesses for the prosecution,[18] and then as swearing falsely that the accusations against Paul were true in every detail.

Asserting that these things were so. In summary form, here is the case made by Tertullus: (1) He made a general charge against Paul – "This fellow is a troublemaker, a pestilence, a plague, wherever he goes." (2) He gave three specific examples to support the general charge – he had excited the Jews in many places to riot; he was charged with being the chief promoter of a religion not licensed by the Roman government; and he had attempted to profane the temple. Any of these examples, if sustained to the judge's satisfaction, would put the defendant in a difficult spot, and perhaps could even have led to a sentence of death in Felix's court.

The Jews so much wanted Paul out of circulation that they are willing to solemnly affirm the truth of a lie (something prohibited in their Law, "You shall not bear false witness …," Exodus 20:16) in order to get him convicted.

24:10 – *And when the governor had nodded for him to speak, Paul responded: "Knowing that for many years you have been a judge to this nation, I cheerfully make my defense,*

And when the governor had nodded for him to speak. The word translated "nodded" can speak of beckoning either by a nod or by the hand.

Paul responded. If not for the promise of Jesus that it would be given to his disciples what to say when they were hauled into court,[19] Paul would have been at a distinct disadvantage.

---

[18] To picture the religious leaders testifying for the prosecution seems better than explaining that "joining in the attack" is merely nodding approval, or cheering Tertullus on from the sidelines with shouts of approval.

[19] Luke 12:11-12.

Paul was now required, without previous notification of the charges, and without a moment for premeditation, to make his defense against an accusation which, if sustained in the judgment of the court, could have cost him his life. Without a single witness to support his representations, he could rely only upon the self-evident truthfulness of what he might have to say. But Paul also had the support of the promise of Jesus, "Settle it therefore in your hearts, not to meditate beforehand how to answer; for I will give you a mouth and wisdom, which all your adversaries shall not be able to withstand or gainsay" (Luke 21:15).[20]

"Knowing that for many years you have been a judge to this nation. There is a wide difference in tone between Paul's opening statement and the flattering words of the attorney. Paul's tone was one of frankness and truthfulness, not of flattery and distorted facts. He was content to appeal to the "many years"[21] during which Felix had been a judge. In almost all circumstances, all the deep ramifications of a quarrel betwixt Jews could only be understood by one who had long lived among Jews. Paul implies that the years Felix had administered the law in Samaria, and after that in Judea, would help him to understand Paul's defense.

I cheerfully make my defense. "Since you have had long experience with the customs and habits of the Jews, I the more readily submit the case to your disposal." Paul had three specific charges against which he needed to defend himself. His answer to the charge of disturbing the peace is given in verses 11-13; the matter of heading the sect of the Nazarenes is replied to in verses 14-16; and the charge of profaning the temple is dealt with in verses 17-19.

24:11 – *"since you can take note of the fact that no more than twelve days ago I went up to Jerusalem to worship.*

Since you can take note of the fact. "By a little investigation, you can learn the truth that it has been not more than twelve days ago that I went up to Jerusalem." When a long period of time intervenes between an event and an investigation of it, it can be difficult to reconstruct what happened. But in this case, the time is short enough that Felix can learn, with little difficulty, what really happened.

That no more than twelve days ago. Commentators have struggled to explain how Paul figured his "twelve days," for almost a day-to-day account of Paul's activities has been given, beginning at Acts 21:17. On the surface, it would seem that the seven days of 21:27 plus the five days of 24:1 make up the twelve, and leave no time for any of the other days Luke has reported. Thus, different methods of figuring the time have been suggested.

---

[20] McGarvey, *op. cit.*, p.235.

[21] "Many years" has been variously explained. Both Tacitus and Josephus combine to inform us that Felix became governor in AD 52 (*Annals*, XII.54; *Antiquities*, XX.7.1). This would be six years before Paul s trial. This was "many years" when compared with the average length of a governor's stay in any province. In addition, as early as AD 48, Felix was in power with the previous governor Cumanus in Samaria (*Annals, ibid.*), before he became sole governor of the whole area. These years too might be included in Paul's "many years," for he used the word "judge" either in the sense of a magistrate or of one appointed to administer the affairs of government.

- Boles gives this one:

    These "twelve days" may be reckoned as follows: first day, Paul arrived at Jerusalem and met with James (21:15); second day, he made his first visit to the temple as a Nazarite; third to seventh days, he performed the Nazarite ceremonies and was arrested by Claudius Lysias; eighth day, he was brought before the Sanhedrin; ninth day, he was informed of the assassination plot and left that night for Caesarea; tenth day, he arrived at Antipatris; eleventh day, he was delivered over to Felix in Caesarea; twelfth day, he was in the palace (praetorium) of Herod; and the thirteenth day he appeared before Felix.'[22]

- Beza reckoned the twelve days in a different manner:

    The first was that on which he came to Jerusalem, 21:15. The second he spent with James and the elders, 21:18. Six days were spent in fulfilling the vow, 21:21,26. On the ninth day the tumult arose, being the seventh day of his vow, and on this day he was rescued by Lysias, 21:27, 22:29. The tenth day he was before the Sanhedrin. On the eleventh the plot was laid to take his life, and on the same day, at evening, he was removed to Caesarea, arriving there on the twelfth day.[23]

Of the two, Beza's reckoning is to be preferred. The days on which Paul was confined at Caesarea (24:1) are not enumerated since he was out of circulation and had no opportunity for stirring up disturbances among the Jews from his place of imprisonment.

I went up to Jerusalem to worship. His trip to Jerusalem had not been for the purpose of stirring up a riot. On the contrary, he had gone to Jerusalem "to worship." Actually, this sentence could be used as a defense against all three of the charges against him. Instead of "heresy," he was worshiping as the Law taught; instead of profaning the temple, he had come to worship.

24:12 – *"And neither in the temple, nor in the synagogues, nor in the city* **itself** *did they find me carrying on a discussion with anyone or causing a riot.*

And neither in the temple, nor in the synagogues, nor in the city *itself* **did they find me carrying on a discussion with anyone.** Paul is developing his defense against the charge that he was a troublemaker, a disturber of the peace. He affirms the charge is incapable of being proved, either in Jerusalem (verse 12), or anywhere else (verse 13). Not in the temple, nor in any of the synagogues, nor even up and down the streets of the city, had he even been in discussions about anything that might be construed as inflammatory or tumultuous.

Or causing a riot. There was not one activity they could point to that any way could be called "causing a riot." He had gone quietly and peacefully about his business in Jerusalem.

---

[22] Boles, *op. cit.*, p.380-381. This method of calculating the twelve days is typical of those which exclude the day of Paul's arrival in Jerusalem in figuring the twelve.

[23] Quoted by Barnes, *op. cit.*, p.331. This method of calculating the twelve days is typical of those which exclude the five days of Acts 24:1.

He had not gathered a crowd around him in any part of the city before the time he was falsely accused and set upon by the Jews from Asia.

24:13 – *"Nor can they prove to you the charges of which they now accuse me.*

Nor can they prove to you *the charges* of which they now accuse me. Paul denied being a troublemaker in Jerusalem; he now denies the charge of having caused trouble among the Jews all over the empire. The record of Acts is clear with reference to the disturbances in the other cities: it was the unbelieving Jews, not Paul, who agitated and stirred the people. Paul challenges his accusers to bring any adequate evidence – i.e., two or three witnesses, independent and agreeing – in proof of their charges.

24:14 – *"But this I admit to you, that according to the Way which they call a sect I do serve the God of our fathers, believing everything that is in accordance with the Law, and that is written in the Prophets;*

But this I admit to you. Paul now takes up the second of the specific charges against him, that he has been preaching an illegal religion.

That according to the Way which they call a sect. Tertullus has used "sect" in a derogatory way (verse 5), a fact of which Paul here takes notice, as he speaks of "the Way"[24] which was his religion. Paul is saying, "Although they call it a heresy and sect, what I have been preaching and living is the way to serve the living God. The religion called Christianity is exactly what is anticipated by the Law and the Prophets."

I do serve the God of our fathers. "Fathers" is *patrōos*, a word which puts emphasis on descent from father to son, and that denotes descent occurring over and over through a long period of time. This emphasis was intentionally directed to Felix; Paul wanted him to hear that the God he serves was the ancestral God of the Israelites, and under Roman law he had every right to do that. Paul affirms he serves the same God, Jehovah, that his ancestors had served for generations.[25] The word translated "serve" (*latreuō*) implies complete devotion, whether in worship or service. Paul has denied doing those things his opponents have charged him with, but he has no hesitation in telling Felix that did serve God.

Believing everything that is in accordance with the Law, and that is written in the Prophets. The "Way" Paul "serves" the ancestral God may indeed be different from the way the Pharisees and Sadducees "serve" Him, but Paul insists that his way was far more in harmony with everything the sacred Scriptures contained. Paul affirms that he found in

---

[24] See notes on "the Way" at Acts 9:2.

[25] In proposition #2 of the *Campbell-Rice Debate*, Rice used language like this verse to show that Christianity is a continuation of the Jewish church, and therefore that the baptism of infants has come into the place of circumcision of infants. Rice's approach is a patent misuse of the passage, for Paul is saying, "I only do and teach what my old religion predicted and directed me to do." There has been a change of covenants, and any doctrine which fails to recognize this is liable to be in great error. Jeremiah 31:31 is but one Old Testament passage which predicts the coming of a new covenant to take the place of the old. Paul himself makes a distinction between the Jews' religion and his own Christianity.

Christianity the culmination of the Law and the fulfillment of the Prophets; Christianity was predicted and typified both by the Law and the Prophets. By this means Paul denies that his religion was an illegal religion. Christianity was not a sect, a split, a heresy off Judaism. Christianity was that for which Judaism prepared the world.

24:15 – *"having a hope in God, which these men cherish themselves, that there shall certainly be a resurrection of both the righteous and the wicked.*

Having a hope in God. By these words Paul insists he is already in possession of the thing (i.e., hope) that the fathers and prophets had only in prospect. God had promised to them that He would work out His plans in history, plans which included the sending of His Messiah into the world, and of bringing history to its consummation in the resurrection. Whereas the unbelieving Jews were still looking for that Messiah to come, Paul points out that Messiah had already come, and by His resurrection from the dead provided the assurance of the resurrection of all men. What the Jews only hoped for was already being realized in Christianity.

Which these men cherish themselves, that there shall certainly be a resurrection of both the righteous and the wicked. This is one of many passages in the Word that plainly teaches there is to be a resurrection of all the dead. Both the righteous and the wicked will be raised.[26]

By the words "these men themselves" Paul certainly takes in his accusers, the chief priest and the elders who came down to Caesarea from Jerusalem. Because the chief priest was usually a Sadducee, who would not have cherished a belief in the resurrection,[27] some have wondered at this statement by Paul. Some explain it by saying that some of the elders present would have been Pharisees who did believe in the resurrection. Others attempt to solve the difficulty by saying that Paul is referring to the great majority of the Jewish people as holding a belief in the resurrection.[28]

24:16 – *"In view of this, I also do my best to maintain always a blameless conscience* **both before God and before men.**

In view of this. Paul has presented several ideas to show that his way of serving was not a sect or a "heresy": he served the same ancestral God that had been served for centuries, and he had the same hope in God that the great majority of Jews did, a hope that included a belief in the resurrection. "In view of this" seems to sum up all he's said since verse 14. 'It is not a heresy; it is *the* way to serve the living God. Since this is true, you'd expect me to put forth the kind of effort that would leave some calling me a "ringleader."'

---

[26] Other passages teaching the resurrection include 1 Corinthians 15:1-58; Luke 14:14, 20:34ff; Daniel 12:1-2; John 5:28ff; Revelation 20:12ff; 1 Thessalonians 4:13ff.

[27] Acts 23:8.

[28] If the Sadducees hold a different doctrine than the one taught everywhere in the Old Testament, they are the ones, not Paul, who has deviated from the ancestral beliefs.

I also do my best to maintain always a blameless conscience *both* before God and before men. This explains what drove Paul on his missionary journeys. He made it his constant aim to so live that his conscience would be clear.[29] Paul affirms that his whole life's conduct was aimed at being free even from the suspicion of such charges as have been lodged against him. The only way to have that freedom is to carry out everything he knew that God required of him, and at the same time to so live as not to cast a stumbling block before men. It was Paul's aim to do whatever was needed to help men come to a knowledge of salvation, living so that he could look back on his life with the reflection that he had done all he ought to have done, all he could to promote their spiritual welfare.

24:17 – *"Now after several years I came to bring alms to my nation and to present offerings;*

Now after several years. Paul now commences his reply to the third charge made by Tertullus, that he had attempted to profane the temple. He begins by telling the court the purpose he had for going to Jerusalem in the first place, namely, to bring to his countrymen (who were brethren in Christ) needed aid in a time of distress. The "several years" were at least four, for it had been that long since his previous visit to Jerusalem (Acts 18:22).[30]

I came to bring alms to my nation. Paul uses *ethnē* ("nation") rather than *laos* ("people") because the latter term, to many Gentiles, would have included a certain assumption of superiority to the judge (and any other Gentiles) before whom he stood. The alms were, of course, the large sums of money which Paul, all during his third missionary journey, had been urging the Gentile churches to give for the benefit of the poor Christians who were in Judea and around Jerusalem.[31]

And to present offerings. The "offerings" were the sacrifices which the apostle was about to offer upon the completion of the Nazarite vow with which he had associated himself.[32]

24:18 – *"in which they found me* occupied *in the temple, having been purified, without* any *crowd or uproar. But* there were *certain Jews from Asia* –

In which they found me *occupied* **in the temple, having been purified, without** *any* **crowd or uproar.** "In which" refers to the "offerings" he's just spoken of. At the very time when the Jews from Asia found him, Paul was in the midst of offering the sacrifices needful to begin the time of a Nazarite vow.[33] Far from being there to profane the temple, he had gone through all the process of purification required for such vows as he had attached himself to.

---

[29] "Conscience" has been commented upon at Acts 23:1.

[30] If in fact Jerusalem was not visited at Acts 18:22, then it has been eight years since Paul had been to Jerusalem, his last trip being the Jerusalem Conference (Acts 15).

[31] This is the only direct notice in Acts of this offering which features so prominently in the epistles Paul wrote during the third missionary journey. See Romans 15:25; 1 Corinthians 16:1-4; 2 Corinthians 8-9; Galatians 6:6-10. Compare also notes at Acts 21:20 concerning the importance of this offering to Paul.

[32] Acts 21:23-24.

[33] Acts 21:26.

But *there were* certain Jews from Asia –. There is a broken sentence here; Paul evidently does not complete his thought. Perhaps Paul was going to say it was not the accusers here in this court who had found him in the temple, but certain Jews from Asia had found him.[34]

24:19 – *"who ought to have been present before you, and to make accusation, if they should have anything against me.*

Who ought to have been present before you. The originators of the disturbance in the temple shrank from the consequences of their actions, and either remained at Jerusalem (rather than coming to the court session), or else had started on their journey homeward as soon as the feast of Pentecost was over.

And to make accusation, if they should have anything against me. This was a key point in Paul's defense against the charge of profaning the temple. The men who were in court did not have any firsthand evidence that he either had profaned it or even attempted to do so. All they had was hearsay evidence. Those people who had claimed to witness his profanation of the court of Israel had not even troubled to appear in Felix's court. It is not difficult to suppose why they did not appear; it would not take many questions either from Felix or during a cross-examination to reveal who the real authors of the disturbances were.

24:20 – *"Or else let these men themselves tell what misdeed they found when I stood before the Council,*

Or else let these men themselves. The real eyewitnesses of what was done in the temple are not here to tell what they saw, so Paul suggests, "Let these leaders share the verdict of the trial they already conducted." Lysias mentioned the trial before the Sanhedrin in his letter to Felix, so Paul is not bringing up a subject of which Felix was unacquainted.

Tell what misdeed they found when I stood before the Council. He challenges the high priest and the elders to state any charges that were proved against him in his trial before them.[35] This is a reminder to his present accusers that they heard no charges against him like the ones they've presented to Felix's court when he stood before the Sanhedrin.

24:21 – *"other than for this one statement which I shouted out while standing among them, 'For the resurrection of the dead I am on trial before you today.'"*

Other than for this one statement which I shouted out while standing among them. At Acts 23:6, it was suggested that Paul had to shout in order to make himself heard. That is, he was not the cause of the disturbance even in the Sanhedrin; the pitch amongst the Council members had already become loud, making it necessary for him to shout above the din.

---

[34] Acts 21:27.

[35] Acts 23:1-10. Paul had no apprehension of being censored for rebuking Ananias, or for his statement that divided the Sanhedrin.

'For the resurrection of the dead I am on trial before you today.'" 'The only place,' Paul says, 'at which I have been at variance with these accusers of mine was on a point on which they themselves do not even agree.' Some commentators treat this statement by Paul to mean that there was one time when his words had been the occasion of a disturbance, an occasion which he is sorry about now that he looks back on it. However, such an interpretation is inconsistent with Paul's own stated aim to always have a conscience void of offence before God or men.

Paul's self-defense before Felix is now concluded, and he has directly replied to each of the three specific charges that Tertullus had made against him.[36] Had Felix not been motivated by greed and a desire to conciliate the Jews, Paul certainly would have been acquitted immediately and set free.

24:22 – *But Felix, having a more exact knowledge about the Way, put them off, saying, "When Lysias the commander comes down, I will decide your case."*

But Felix, having a more exact knowledge about the Way. Felix had a better knowledge about Christianity ("the Way") than some (i.e., the Jewish accusers) gave him credit for.[37] He knew enough about the life and doctrines of the Christians to know that Paul was guilty of no crime such as his accusers were alleging. Felix knew the Jews were not presenting things as they really were.

It is interesting to conjecture just where Felix obtained his knowledge about Christianity. The Romans had an excellent spy system to keep abreast of developments among the people. Was this the source of his information? Has Philip the evangelist, who has lived at Caesarea for years, made an evangelistic call on the governor, and thus Felix learned about Christianity? Did he learn some of the details from his present wife, Drusilla, who was a member of the Herod family, a family whose fortunes have been intertwined with Christianity for over half a century? Felix himself has been in Samaria and Judea for ten years, and in both of those areas the church was growing and becoming more and more influential. He would have had frequent opportunities to learn what Christians taught and how they lived.

Put them off, saying. "Put them off" is the technical legal term for postponing the hearing until another date. Felix continued the case indefinitely, not because he had some question about Paul's innocence (his knowledge of Christianity was "more accurate" than that[38]), but because he had some selfish interests (as Luke will explain in verse 26).

---

[36] (1) His visit to Jerusalem was a short enough time ago that it would be easy to ascertain whether or not he had even been in the midst of any crowds discussing or agitating anywhere in Jerusalem, or anywhere else for that matter. (2) The Way called Christianity was not an illegal religion, but was indeed what was predicted in the Law and the Prophets. (3) Rather than profaning the temple, he was using it as it was intended to be used, a place to make sacrifices and promises to God. Then he calls upon the Sanhedrin members who were present to state any crime on his part that they had personally witnessed.

[37] The Greek simply contains a comparative adjective. It doesn't actually say whose knowledge of the Way was less accurate than Felix's.

[38] The circumstantial participle in the Greek says it was *because* he had a more accurate knowledge of the way that Felix recognized Paul's testimony to be the truth.

"**When Lysias the commander comes down, I will decide your case.**" The reason he gave for postponing any decision in the case was a mere subterfuge, but he gave it an air of reasonableness by saying he wished to hear Lysias' side of the story. Either Tertullus had made the tribune's actions in the case a part of his argument for prosecution, or Felix wants more information than was given in the brief letter Lysias had sent along with the prisoner. He did not wish to condemn the prisoner when the evidence was all against such a course, but the Jews could get rather fanatical and bothersome if they didn't get their way. To save himself considerable time and trouble, Felix determines to keep Paul a prisoner indefinitely. This way neither side wins the case. We do not know that Lysias ever came to tell his side of the story. We hear no more of him, nor did Felix ever make any final determination of the case as he here promised he would do.

24:23 – *And he gave orders to the centurion for him to be kept in custody and yet have some freedom, and not to prevent any of his friends from ministering to him.*

And he gave orders to the centurion for him to be kept in custody. The Greek reads "the centurion" (there is an article in the original), indicating either the centurion into whose custody Paul had been placed by Lysias,[39] or the one who had special charge of the prisoners awaiting trial here at Caesarea. "Kept in custody" might be intended to limit his sphere of movement to inside the Praetorium, or it might mean that Paul is kept in chains.[40]

And *yet* have *some* freedom. Luke used the word *anesis*, meaning "to loose, relax, or to moderate restrictions" upon Paul.[41] Paul's confinement was to be the least irksome consistent with safekeeping.

And not to prevent any of his friends from ministering to him. The ministry would include providing food and clothing, and visiting. In the Greek, "his friends" is "his own (people)," i.e., his brethren, the fellow Christians. The Christians of Caesarea would be carrying out Jesus' instructions about visiting their brethren in prison during Paul's two years in Caesarea.[42]

It is likely that Luke now arrives in Caesarea and is one of those who visits Paul during his confinement. We can imagine that when Paul failed to return to Mnason's house that day in Jerusalem (remember, Paul left to go to the temple to offer sacrifices with the men who had taken the Nazarite vow), Luke and the others began to look for him. They may have been with him while he was still held in the tower of Antonia, but they would not have learned about his removal from Jerusalem by night until some time later, at which time some of them would go down to Caesarea to be near him and be of help if possible.

---

[39] Acts 22:26.

[40] Josephus (*Antiquities*, XVIII, 6.7.10) has an example of such "relaxed" custody where the prisoner was indeed kept in chains.

[41] Some versions read "indulgence" where the NASB reads "some freedom." The word has no relationship to the doctrine of indulgences held by some religious bodies. At Colossians 2:23 there is a phrase that speaks of "indulgence (*plēsmonē*) of the flesh," but that is a different Greek word entirely from what Luke used, and should not be confused with what is granted to Paul by Felix.

[42] Matthew 25:36.

c. Paul before Felix and Drusilla. 24:24-27

24:24 – *But some days later, Felix arrived with Drusilla, his wife who was a Jewess, and sent for Paul, and heard him* **speak** *about* **[the]** *faith in Christ Jesus.*

But some days later, Felix arrived with Drusilla, his wife who was a Jewess. It is not possible to tell how long the "some days" were. The word "arrived" indicates that the two have been away from Caesarea for a time and had now returned to it.

Drusilla was introduced in comments at Acts 23:24. A few additional notes will be helpful as well.

- Her name is the diminutive of Drusus, which was the name of a sister of Caligula's. Thus, in her name, we trace the early connection of her father, Herod Agrippa I, with the emperor Caligula.
- Drusilla had been six years old when her father died his horrible death, shortly after murdering the apostle James, and imprisoning Peter.[43] Her own and her family's history had long overlapped with the Way.
- Drusilla was noted for her great beauty, and because of her beauty she was constantly persecuted by her older sister Bernice, who was rather plain in appearance. One of the reasons Drusilla decided to be unfaithful to Azizus and to marry Felix was in order to be in a more important position than her sister Bernice. It was partly in an effort to get even with Bernice for all the petty things she had suffered that she was now living in adultery with Felix.

And sent for Paul. Attempts to assign a motive to Felix and Drusilla's wish to hear Paul have not altogether proven satisfactory. Some appeal to the statement in the Western text which says that Drusilla asked to see Paul and hear him speak, and Felix so ordered it to satisfy her. Some have appealed to her memory of her father's death here at Caesarea years before, supposing she may have connected it somehow with Christianity. Now that one of Christianity s eminent preachers is in custody, it gave her opportunity to satisfy her curiosity to see if there was any connection between this religion and her father's death. Others suggest that Felix and Drusilla intended this audience with Paul to be nothing more than a matter of entertainment or amusement. Still a fourth suggestion is that having this preacher in custody gave Felix a suitable opportunity to improve his already fairly accurate knowledge of "the Way." The next phrase in Luke's narrative likely gives the motive that led to Paul's being summoned before the governor and his wife.

And heard him *speak* **about [the] faith in Christ Jesus.** Felix and Drusilla evidently wanted to know more about "the faith" (note there is an article here in the Greek) that puts a man "into (the preposition is *eis*) Christ Jesus." Luke's language here seems to say that Felix and his wife for a time were willing to listen to the gospel, and even gave some thought to becoming Christians.

Paul's example in this case is worthy of imitation. He took advantage of the opportunity to preach the gospel to these people, though he might have complained about

---

[43] Acts 12:1ff.

the lack of justice, the prolonged delays, and the seemingly interminable imprisonment. Not only did he take advantage of the opportunity to preach, but he was as bold in his presentation as at other times, even though he was dependent upon Felix's good will if he was ever going to be released. Many preachers might have been tempted in such circumstances to speak on such innocuous subjects in order to win the favor of the judge, in hopes of hurrying the date of release. Perhaps Paul was tempted in this way, too; but what he did preach was not for his benefit, but what Felix and Drusilla needed to hear if they were going to be convicted of their sins and led to repentance and obedience.

24:25 – *And as he was discussing righteousness, self-control and the judgment to come, Felix became frightened and said, "Go away for the present, and when I find time, I will summon you."*

And as he was discussing. This verse lists some of the things included in "the faith into Christ Jesus" – namely, righteousness, self-control, and an anticipation of the final judgment. "Discussing," as explained earlier in Acts,[44] may imply a conversational interchange, or it may signify "preach." In earlier passages, Paul "discussed" with the prospects by presenting Scripture to them, allowing the gospel message (which is the power of God unto salvation) to do its effective work.[45]

Righteousness, self-control and the judgment to come. Given the lives and characters of Felix and Drusilla, it is no surprise that Paul spoke of these three subjects as he discussed "the faith into Jesus" with them. He had been invited to speak concerning faith in Christ, so he chose the special topics that were directly related to the spiritual needs of his hearers.

- "Righteousness." This word covers two different topics in the New Testament, one flowing naturally out of the other. At times, it speaks of the "righteousness of God" – not so much God's characteristic or standard of being right and holy in Himself, but that which in Romans is explained as God's way of saving men, justifying men, imputing righteousness to those who have faith in Christ. Flowing out of this comes a second idea, which is men's relationship to other men. Once men are right with God, they are much more likely to have right relationships with their fellowmen. Such right relationships Felix had often violated, and so had his wife.

- "Self-control" is from the Greek *egkrateia* ("controlled power"), and it means to con-

---

[44] The same word is used at Acts 17:2, 18:4, 18:19; 19:8-9, and 24:12.

[45] Even today, Scripture must be presented to the potential convert, for it is through the Word that the Holy Spirit convicts of sin, righteousness, and the judgment to come. A personal evangelist must exercise care at this point. In his desire for the prospect to respond to the gospel, he may employ some well-known, high-pressure methods to get the response he seeks. Sociologists and psychologists have learned methods of controlling human behavior. The gospel preacher must beware of using such methods rather than allowing the Spirit to work through the gospel on the heart of the sinner to win him. Those won by emotional appeals and high-pressure methods are likely to fall away quickly in the face of temptations, whereas those who have been won by God's power will in times of temptation find their faith resting in God rather than in the wisdom of men.

See John 16:8, and also Special Study #3, "The Person and Work of the Holy Spirit," for the work of the Holy Spirit in conversion.

trol or master the passions and desires of the body.[46] Once a person becomes a Christian, he has help from the indwelling Spirit to control the house he lives in.[47] This matter, too, was something the governor and his wife needed to hear.

- "The judgment to come" speaks of the final judgment that is coming upon all men.[48] Paul points out that there is a final judgment in which each person is going to stand before the God of the universe and answer for the deeds done in the body. A person's moral principles and behavior are greatly influenced by the idea that he will have to face condemnation and punishment for continuing in wickedness, as well as by the idea that there is praise and reward from the Creator promised to the one who practices well doing.[49] "It is appointed unto men to die once, and after this comes judgment."[50] "For we must all appear before the judgment-seat of Christ, that each one may be recompensed for his deeds in the body, according to what he has done, whether good or bad."[51]

He became frightened. Any time a person thinks seriously about standing in judgment before Him with whom we have to do, unless his sins are covered by the blood of Christ, he becomes alarmed.[52] The emotions and intellect and conscience are all involved in this alarm, and there are but two ways to quiet it: one is by surrender to Christ, the other is by hardening the heart through an act of the will. Paul's presentation of the gospel caused Felix to see himself as he really was; he saw not only his life in comparison to what God demands of His creatures, but also the judgment he had to face.

> As he glanced back over the stained and guilty past, he was afraid. He had been a slave in the vilest of all positions, and the vilest of all epochs, in the vilest of all cities. He had crept with his brother Pallas into the position of a courtier at the most morally degraded of all courts. He had been an officer of those auxiliaries who were the worst of all troops. What secrets of lust and blood lay hidden in his earlier life we do not know; but ample and indisputable testimony, Jewish and pagan, sacred and secular, reveals to us what he had been – how greedy, how savage, how treacherous, how unjust, how steeped in the blood of private murder and public massacre – during the eight years he had spent in the government, first of Samaria, then of Palestine.[53]

As to the effects of Paul's message on Drusilla, the record is silent. Was she as moved as

---

[46] The KJV renders *egkrateia* as "temperance." This translation is fine, providing one remembers that in 1611 the word "temperance" meant more than "control of the body's desires for alcoholic beverages."

[47] The indwelling Holy Spirit's help to the Christian to live the Christian life has been studied under "The purpose of the indwelling Holy Spirit" in Special Study #3.

[48] See notes at Acts 17:31.

[49] Romans 2:5-10

[50] Hebrews 9:27.

[51] 2 Corinthians 5:10.

[52] "Frightened" is the same Greek word translated "alarmed" at Acts 10:4. The KJV renders it "trembled," but the Greek does not denote that his body was shaking, only that Felix was alarmed or terrified.

[53] F.W. Farrar, *The Life and Work of St. Paul* (New York: E.P. Dutton, 1879), p.550.

Felix, or was she unaffected? Two members of the same family do sometimes arrive at the same spiritual conviction at the same time, and respond to the invitation together. On other occasions one member of the family will be slower than another, and may even discourage the one who has come under some conviction.

And said, "Go away for the present. Felix's response to his alarm over his spiritual condition was considerably different than the Philippian jailer's when he was alarmed in a similar manner. The jailer asked, "What must I do to be saved?" and was directed to Him in whom he found peace from a troubled conscience.[54] Felix quiets his alarm by an exertion of his will and by convincing himself that he will pay attention to this matter later.[55] It may have been ambition, or lust (some men put off salvation simply because they are not ready to quit their sinning), or greed, or even some other vice, that made him decide to postpone taking God's way of quieting a guilty conscience.

And when I find time, I will summon you." It has often been preached that Felix never found another time to listen to the gospel. It is true that he probably never became a Christian, but the very next verse tells us that he did hear Paul often.

24:26 – *At the same time too, he was hoping that money would be given him by Paul; therefore he also used to send for him quite often and converse with him.*

At the same time too, he was hoping that money would be given him by Paul. Felix had put off a definitive decision when Paul's trial was held (verse 22), and he had put off a positive decision when offered the gospel invitation (verse 25). One of the reasons for this procrastination is now explained by Luke. Felix had caught at the word "alms" in verse 17. Paul, then, was not without resources.[56] Felix hoped by detaining Paul in custody that the prisoner would become tired of his confinement and would offer to purchase his freedom with a bribe. He thought that by giving Paul access to his friends, and by often meeting him himself and showing kindness, that Paul would be induced to attempt a bribe. Paul, of course, did not do so.

Therefore he also used to send for him quite often. It is not difficult to picture what happened at these meetings. On Felix's part there were the suggested hints, the half-promises, the half-threats, having to do with Paul's freedom or being turned over to the Jews. On Paul's part there was steadfast refusal to purchase the freedom which was his because he had proved his innocence, and there were the fruitless attempts to win Felix to Christ. But for Felix, there apparently was never again was the degree of alarm kindled as on that first discussion with Paul; there never again was the real, heart-felt interest in be-

---

[54] Acts 16:30-31.

[55] See Acts 19:9 on "hardening." Those who procrastinate by putting off doing what they know to be right in the matter of salvation should learn from the example of Felix. He postponed acting upon the message only by hardening his heart. Once he did this, it became harder for the gospel to prick his conscience and stir his emotions. A continual hardening of the heart will bring the time when the Holy Spirit will no longer strive within, even though the message of God is being preached in all its power.

[56] Philippians, in our opinion, cannot be said to be written from the Caesarean imprisonment, and therefore we cannot appeal to an offering from Philippi as being part of Paul's resources.

coming a Christian and having the guilt and penalty of sin taken care of.

And converse with him. The imperfect tense implies that this took place repeatedly. It may seem unusual that he would put himself in a place where that old alarm about facing the judge of the universe would be kindled again. But his hope for money and his continual hardening of his own heart overcame all that. Having once resisted the invitation offered in the gospel and the strivings of the Spirit of God, he could again hear the same man and the same message, and remain quite unaffected.

24:27 – *But after two years had passed, Felix was succeeded by Porcius Festus; and wishing to do the Jews a favor, Felix left Paul imprisoned.*

But after two years had passed. The two years are reckoned from the commencement of Paul's imprisonment at Caesarea.[57] We can only conjecture on how these years were spent by Paul. Some writers who maintain the Pauline authorship of the epistle to the Hebrews assign its date of writing to this period.[58] Another group of writers suppose that the Prison Epistles[59] were written from the Caesarean imprisonment, but there is no adequate evidence to support this.[60] Some of Paul's time would have been spent in visits with Philip and other members of the church at Caesarea who would come to comfort and refresh him. Did he ever wonder how the promise about preaching at Rome[61] would be fulfilled?

The years may have proved a tedious period for Paul, but Luke apparently was making full use of the time. In all likelihood, in Caesarea and elsewhere in Palestine, Luke was collecting materials for his Gospel by examining people who had been eyewitnesses of Jesus' ministry.[62] In fact, it is possible that Luke's Gospel was published at this time, being the second of the Gospels to be written.[63] There is also a strong likelihood that Luke was collecting material for Acts, too, during this two-year period of time.

Felix was succeeded by Porcius Festus. Festus became governor in about the year AD 60.[64] He made a valiant attempt to correct many of Felix's abuses, but died in office after

---

[57] Acts 23:33.

[58] This commentator holds to the Pauline authorship of Hebrews, but would assign its date of writing to the first Roman imprisonment.

[59] See notes at Acts 19:10 concerning the Prison Epistles.

[60] This commentator also dates the Prison Epistles from the first Roman imprisonment.

[61] Acts 23:11.

[62] Luke 1:3.

[63] Matthew's Gospel was likely published about AD 50. In passing, in light of the contents of the books and the statements found in early Christian literature. we date Mark's Gospel about AD 67 or 68, and John's Gospel about AD 80.

[64] The date assigned to the recall of Felix varies from AD 55 to as late as AD 61. Those who date it as early as AD 55 do so because of Josephus' statement that Pallas interceded on Felix's behalf before Nero. However, since Nero came to the throne in October of AD 54. and Pallas fell from favor before February of AD 55, it is hard to have the recall of Felix this early in Nero's reign. A recall for Felix at such an early date would require us to suppose that the order went out and Felix traveled to Rome during the winter months when the Mediterranean was closed to shipping. Albinus, the successor of Festus. was in office

serving a little less than two years.⁶⁵ The change of governors was caused by complaints levied by the Jews against Felix. There was racial strife in Caesarea between the Jewish and Gentile factions, and every time Felix could capture the leaders of either side, they were beaten (i.e., scourged). But these methods did not quell the strife over equal citizenship rights. During one riot, Felix sent in troops who were friends of the Gentile faction; there was much bloodshed among the Jews, and the soldiers plundered many Jewish homes for their riches. As the strife continued, Felix ordered leaders from both sides to Rome to argue their case before Nero, to let Nero decide. At this point Nero recalled Felix, and some of the principal Jewish leaders of Caesarea went to Rome to accuse Felix. Felix's brother Pallas interceded on Felix's behalf, and thus Felix barely escaped execution.⁶⁶ He was banished to Gaul, where he died. Drusilla stayed with him despite his failing fortunes.

And wishing to do the Jews a favor, Felix left Paul imprisoned. The word translated "favor" speaks of a "deposit for which a due return might be expected." His object in keeping Paul in jail was to conciliate the Jews. He sought to secure their favor and to prevent them, if possible, from accusing him for the evils of his administration during his examination before Nero, the emperor who had recalled him. However, his plan failed.

The Western text gives an additional reason for leaving Paul in custody; it says Drusilla asked Felix to leave Paul in bonds.

"Imprisoned" is thought by some to mean that Paul's confinement is now a severer form of custody than the "some freedom" (verse 23) he had had for the past two years.

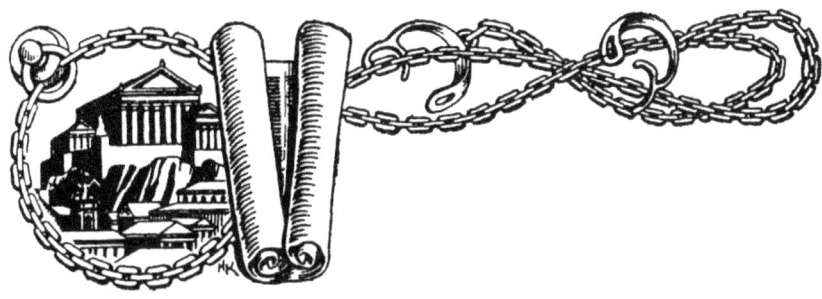

Drawing by Horace Knowles
from the British and Foreign Bible Society

---

by the year AD 62. Since it would be difficult to squeeze the events from Festus' reign that Josephus does tell us about (*Antiquities*, XX, 8.9ff; *Wars*, II.14.1ff) into much less than two years, we choose AD 60 for Festus' accession to office.

⁶⁵ More information is given about Festus in notes at Acts 25:1.

⁶⁶ The statement from Josephus that Pallas helped Felix after the latter's recall, plus the fact that Pallas himself fell from favor in AD 55, has produced problems for those attempting to make a chronology of the book of Acts. Either Josephus was in error, or else Pallas still exercised considerable influence even though he had been removed from the treasury. The latter idea accords with Tacitus' history, who indicates that, even while being removed, Pallas was in a position to stipulate certain conditions relative to his removal (*Annals*, XIII.14). Thus, it is possible to suppose that Pallas would have still been influential enough to aid Felix as Josephus says he did.

d. Paul's trial before Festus. 25:1-12

25:1 – *Festus therefore, having arrived in the province, three days later went up to Jerusalem from Caesarea.*

Festus therefore, having arrived in the province. See notes at Acts 24:27 concerning Festus' becoming governor of Palestine in place of Felix. During his governorship, Porcius Festus endeavored to correct the excesses of his predecessor. One of the unresolved matters left to him was the prisoner Paul, and the Jews will urge Festus to do something about this as one of his first official acts after entering upon his duties in the province.

Strictly speaking, the title "province" did not apply to Judea inasmuch as it was subordinate to Syria. Judea was more like a district within a province, save that the "governor" of Judea was more or less independent of the legate of Syria.

Three days later went up to Jerusalem from Caesarea. The "three days" have been variously figured. According to Jewish methods of counting time, it could be one whole day and parts of two others (e.g., he arrived in Caesarea one day, rested the next, and started for Jerusalem on the third); or it could be three whole days after he arrived that he remained in Caesarea, and then started to Jerusalem on the fourth. The new governor would want to make a trip to Jerusalem in order to meet the leading local government officials, namely, the Sanhedrin members and the other leading Jews. It has even been proposed that it was feast time when Festus visited Jerusalem, perhaps the feast of Tabernacles.[1]

25:2 – *And the chief priests and the leading men of the Jews brought charges against Paul; and they were urging him,*

And the chief priests and the leading men of the Jews brought charges against Paul. "Chief priests" here might be the heads of the twenty-four courses, as at Acts 4:23. As far as the high priest is concerned, Ananias had been put out of office in AD 59. It is probable that he was still influential, though there is evidence that by this time Ismael, the son of Fabi, had become high priest.[2] Though Paul has spent two years in prison at Caesarea (Acts 24:27), the hatred of his enemies still burns. Perhaps their hopes of being permanently rid of their old enemy had been raised by Felix's leaving Paul in prison as a favor to the Jews. Felix must have told them why he was leaving Paul in custody. When the new governor comes to get acquainted, one of the first things they ask for is Paul's extermination, hoping to take advantage of Festus' desire to get his new administration off on the right foot. "Brought charges" is the same word used in Acts 24:1, and indicates that it was a formal accusation the Jews made against Paul.

And they were urging him. May we imagine all the religious leaders standing in a group (as their spokesmen present their case) expressing their displeasure against Paul, and attempting by constant chanting of slogans against Paul to show the new governor he could have instant popularity if he would just deliver Paul into their hands?

---

[1] See notes at Acts 2:1 concerning "Tabernacles."

[2] See page *xiv* for Agrippa's installation of Ismael into the high priesthood.

25:3 – *requesting a concession against Paul, that he might have him brought to Jerusalem (*at the same time, *setting an ambush to kill him on the way).*

Requesting a concession against Paul. It would take a certain amount of boldness to ask such a favor of the new governor as they were asking.[3] They are asking Festus to acquiesce in the murder of a prisoner (see verse 15).

That he might have him brought to Jerusalem. The Sanhedrin must have told Festus that when Paul arrived in Jerusalem he would be tried by their court, or perhaps they wished Festus to hear the case there and to decide it while he was still in Jerusalem. Are these Jews trying to take advantage of the newness of Festus to his office like the Jews at Corinth tried to take advantage of Gallio?[4] He was likely enough, they thought, to accept their statements of Paul's guilt and yield to their pressure; remember, they had shown themselves powerful enough to bring about his predecessor's recall. These religious leaders, under the guise of seeking justice, were plotting to commit murder.

(*At the same time,* **setting an ambush to kill him on the way).** The religious leaders have adopted as their own the plot of assassination that others first suggested years before.[5] They likely would employ a band of Sicarii to take Paul's life. At an opportune spot along the way they would ambush Paul and the soldiers guarding him. Festus was not aware of this part of the plot against Paul, though he did understand they planned to kill Paul.

25:4 – *Festus then answered that Paul was being kept in custody at Caesarea and that he himself was about to leave shortly.*

Festus then answered that Paul was being kept in custody at Caesarea. We do not know why Festus refused the Jews' request. Possibly Festus had heard from Felix, or Lysias, or others, of the former plot, and he took care to be on his guard against this. Some have thought that Festus did not plan to stay in Jerusalem long enough to get Paul there and tried, but this is hard to square with the "eight or ten days" (verse 6) that he actually did stay there. "Kept in custody[6] in Caesarea" is Festus' way of saying there will be no abuses during his administration (as there were during the previous one), either against prisoners or against innocent citizens.

And that he himself was about to leave shortly. With these words Festus softens the refusal. He would not bring him to Jerusalem, but that did not mean there was to be no hearing of Paul's case. There could be one at Caesarea, if they wished.

25:5 – *"Therefore," he said, "let the influential men among you go there with me, and if there is anything wrong about the man, let them prosecute him."*

---

[3] See notes at verse 15 as to the exact nature of the "favor" (concession) they asked.

[4] Compare Acts 18:2.

[5] Acts 23:12-15.

[6] On the word "kept in custody" and the nature of the custody, see notes at Acts 24:23,27.

"Therefore," he said, "let the influential men among you go there with me. As has previously been the case in Acts,[7] it is not easy to carefully define all the different terms used of the Jewish leaders. "Chief priests" for example can refer to the president of the Sanhedrin, or to men who were former presidents of the Sanhedrin, or to the heads of the twenty-four courses of priests. "Elders" can mean either the older men who made up a portion of the Sanhedrin, or it may speak of the body called the "Senate." The fact that we have such difficulty determining who is intended serves as an introduction to the problem raised by Festus' expression, "influential men." Perhaps being new to the area, he did not know the technical terms for the Jewish officials, and so he used this rather general expression. Others have tried to show that "influential men" and "chief priests" are synonymous terms even among the Jews. Or perhaps it possible that Festus is asking that the charges against Paul, whatever they may be, be supported by the leaders and representatives of the people, and not by a hired attorney like Tertullus.

And if there is anything wrong about the man, let them prosecute him." Festus also told them (verse 16) that it was contrary to Roman law to condemn a man before he had an opportunity for defense, face to face, with his accusers. The extra-Biblical record about Festus is that he was a man who tried to run a just and equitable administration, and his handling of Paul's case, so far, shows that he is trying to be fair to both sides.

25:6 – *And after he had spent not more than eight or ten days among them, he went down to Caesarea; and on the next day he took his seat on the tribunal and ordered Paul to be brought.*

And after he had spent not more than eight or ten days among them. The time would have been spent getting acquainted with some of the peculiar problems and pressing duties of his office among the Jews. The indefinite "eight or ten days" is thought to be figured from Luke's standpoint, since in Caesarea he wouldn't know how many days were spent in Jerusalem and how many in travel between the cities.

He went down to Caesarea; and on the next day he took his seat on the tribunal. Festus has been in office only about two weeks on the day of Paul's hearing. If he had not taken his seat on the tribunal[8] the decision rendered would have been of no legal effect. The Jews, as Festus suggested, have accompanied him on his return from Jerusalem to Caesarea (verse 7).

And ordered Paul to be brought. Again, on a moment's notice, Paul is brought up from his room in the Praetorium for trial.

25:7 – *And after he had arrived, the Jews who had come down from Jerusalem stood around him, bringing many and serious charges against him which they could not prove;*

And after he had arrived, the Jews who had come down from Jerusalem stood around

---

[7] For example, see the words "Council" v. "Senate" used in Acts 5:21.

[8] See the explanation at Acts 18:12ff concerning the "judgment-seat."

him. Whether they "stood around him" in a semi-circular court, or whether they surrounded Paul while they brought their charges, pointing to him and gesturing all the while in an attempt to intimidate him, is not clear.

Bringing many and serious charges against him which they could not prove. It is clear from Paul's self-defense (verse 8) that the current slate of charges against Paul were similar to the charges made by Tertullus.[9] They accused him of breaking the Law of Israel, of profaning the temple, and of being a disturber of the peace (i.e., probably charging him with political Messianism, teaching there was another king besides Nero).

25:8 – *while Paul said in his own defense, "I have committed no offense either against the Law of the Jews or against the temple or against Caesar."*

While Paul said in his own defense, "I have committed no offense. Paul categorically denied the charges against him. His defense this time was very likely similar to the one he made against the charges brought by Tertullus.[10]

Either against the Law of the Jews or against the temple or against Caesar." See also Stephen's defense in Acts 7, where he had to answer two of these same charges. Jesus, when on trial, was charged with the other, namely, of being inimical to Caesar's interests.

25:9 – *But Festus, wishing to do the Jews a favor, answered Paul and said, "Are you willing to go up to Jerusalem and stand trial before me on these* **charges?"**

But Festus, wishing to do the Jews a favor, answered Paul and said. Since the Jews were not able to prove their accusations (verse 7), and since the defendant had pleaded "not guilty" to every one of them, we might have expected Festus at this point to release Paul from custody. But that is to ignore the pressure the Jews could put on a man. LaSor has written succinctly at this point:

> Unless we have steeped ourselves in the history of the Jews from the days of the Maccabees to the First Revolt, we probably cannot understand how a Roman governor could set aside justice in order to placate the people. In the days of the Maccabees, zealous Jews had defeated a powerful Gentile ruler. The Romans knew this. Rome was well aware of the fact that the Jewish people had to be handled in a special way. A Roman procurator, such as Pontius Pilate or Antonius Felix or Porcius Festus, knew when he took over his post in Judea that he was sitting on a "powder keg."
>
> Pilate bent Roman justice in the case of Jesus rather than antagonize the Jews. Felix did the same, in the case of Paul. Josephus, who was a Jew but also a loyal Roman, records that other governors did the same thing in other cases. Festus had just taken office. He "had to live with these people." He certainly didn't want to get off to a bad start.[11]

---

[9] Acts 24:5-6.

[10] Acts 24:10-21.

[11] LaSor, *op. cit.*, p.348.

"Are you willing to go up to Jerusalem and stand trial before me on these *charges*?" As he attempts to placate the Jews, Festus makes the same proposal to Paul that the Jews had made to Festus a week or so earlier at Jerusalem. Festus' proposal seems to be an invitation to Paul to waive his rights as a Roman citizen and consent to being tried before the Jewish Sanhedrin, perhaps with Festus as an official observer and a check against violence or injustice. This appears to be how Paul understood Festus' query (verse 10).[12]

25:10 – *But Paul said, "I am standing before Caesar's tribunal, where I ought to be tried. I have done no wrong to* **the** *Jews, as you also very well know.*

But Paul said, "I am standing before Caesar's tribunal, where I ought to be tried. If Festus was making the proposal to go to Jerusalem in order to do the Jews a favor, what would keep him from making another concession to them after the trial by the Sanhedrin? Paul seems to be saying to Festus, "There is no reason that I should be dragged back to Jerusalem. Doesn't Roman law and justice operate in Caesarea?"[13]

I have done no wrong to *the* **Jews, as you also very well know.** With these words, Paul affirms that Festus has no reason to expect him to go back to Jerusalem for a trial. What need is there for a trial when the would-be defendant is already known to be innocent? And Festus did already know that Paul was innocent. Paul had not injured the Jews' persons, property, or character. Festus knew that the Jews had asked Paul to be delivered into their hands as a favor. He had refused this request, and had suggested a trial instead at Caesarea. He had given Paul that trial and had called upon the Jews to send their influential men to accuse Paul. In spite of all this, no charges were proved against Paul. Festus knew, therefore, that Paul was innocent. That Festus knew this is also abundantly clear from his own confession (verses 18-19).

25:11 – *"If then I am a wrongdoer, and have committed anything worthy of death, I do not refuse to die; but if none of those things is* true *of which these men accuse me, no one can hand me over to them. I appeal to Caesar."*

If then I am a wrongdoer, and have committed anything worthy of death, I do not refuse to die. In these words, Paul is saying that his refusal to permit Festus to return him to Jerusalem is not motivated by a wish to evade justice or to take advantage of his circumstances to shield himself from punishment he actually deserved.

But if none of those things is *true* **of which these men accuse me, no one can hand me over to them.** One of the readings in the ASV is "No man can grant me as a favor to them." That is, Paul saw through the feigned fairness of the governor, and did not shrink

---

[12] Another way of explaining Festus' suggestion is to suppose that the Sanhedrin would try Paul, and if they found him guilty, the verdict would still have to be ratified by Festus. This would be similar to Jesus appearing before Pilate after the Sanhedrin had found Him guilty.

[13] This paraphrased interpretation is more satisfactory than the one which paraphrases Paul's words in this fashion: "In my mind and purpose, I already stand before the emperor's court in Rome, for God has shown me by a special revelation that I am to preach the gospel in Rome (Acts 23:11). Your suggestion that I go to Jerusalem would be taking me in the wrong direction since I am supposed to go to Rome."

from showing that he did. "Since you very well know I am innocent, but you seem either unwilling or unable to do in my case what is the right thing, you leave me only one course of action."

I appeal to Caesar." The right of appeal to Caesar had taken the place of the earlier right of appeal to the sovereign people of Rome, which Roman citizens had enjoyed since 509 BC. As the years went by, and power became more and more centralized in the emperor, the appeal to the people became an appeal to Caesar.

Once a prisoner had made an appeal to Caesar, the judge to whom the appeal was made was obliged to stop all proceedings in the case immediately, and to send the prisoner, together with his accusers, to Rome to be tried there with Caesar himself sitting as judge. Paul's appeal to Caesar took the case out of Festus' hands from that moment on.

> To us who know Nero's record in relation to Christianity, it may seem strange that Paul should have appealed with such confidence to him. But whatever Nero's personal character might be, the first five years of his reign (AD 54-59), when the imperial administration was carried on under the influence of his tutor Seneca, the Stoic philosopher, and Afranius Burrus, the honest prefect of the Praetorian guard, were looked back upon as a miniature Golden Age. There was little in AD 59 or AD 60 that gave warning of the events of AD 64 and after.[14]

25:12 – *Then when Festus had conferred with his council, he answered, "You have appealed to Caesar, to Caesar you shall go."*

Then when Festus had conferred with his council. The word "council" does not refer to the Sanhedrin (*sunedrion*), but to the assembly of counsellors (*sumboulion*) who acted as advisers of the governor. Such local advisers were necessary and helped judges or governors who, as in the case of Festus, often needed their experience and advice. Their chief function seems to have been to advise the governor on matters of Roman law, in this case, what an "appeal to Caesar" entailed for him and for the defendant.

He answered, "You have appealed to Caesar, to Caesar you shall go." The advisers would have told him that he had no choice but to send Paul and his accusers to Rome once the defendant had appealed to Caesar.

> The answer of Festus betrays some bitterness of feeling, the natural effect of the reproach implied in the appeal; and at the same time it hints of the inconvenience to which Paul would himself be subjected by it. It subjected him to being sent to Rome as a prisoner under a military guard, and to all the delay which might attend the coming of the witnesses to testify against him, as well as that often resulting from the dilatoriness of the imperial court itself.[15]

McGarvey may be correct in this comment on Festus' reply to Paul's appeal. After all, had not Festus just come from Rome? He would know what Paul was getting himself into.

---

[14] Bruce, *op. cit.*, p.479.

[15] McGarvey, *op. cit.*, p.245.

e. Paul's defense before Herod Agrippa II. 25:13-26:32

1) Herod Agrippa II visits Festus. 25:13-22

25:13 – *Now when several days had elapsed, King Agrippa and Bernice arrived at Caesarea, and paid their respects to Festus.*

Now when several days had elapsed, King Agrippa and Bernice arrived at Caesarea. See pages *xvii-xviii* of the Introductory Studies for historical background on this brother and sister. Four or five years prior to the events of Acts 25, Herod Agrippa II became king of Galilee and Perea (plus some other small areas), and since AD 52 he has been, for all intents and purposes, the one who controlled the temple and who appointed and deposed high priests, all of this for Rome's interest. Herod Agrippa II would thus be looked upon by Festus as an authority in matters respecting the Jewish religion.

And paid their respects to Festus. From their capital city of Caesarea Philippi they have come to Caesarea on the coast of the Mediterranean Sea, the capital city of the district that was on the border of their kingdom. They have come in order to extend congratulations and a formal recognition to the new governor.

25:14 – *And while they were spending many days there, Festus laid Paul's case before the king, saying, "There is a certain man left a prisoner by Felix;*

And while they were spending many days there, Festus laid Paul's case before the king, saying. The subject seems to have come up in the course of conversation between the two. Agrippa II had the reputation of being an authority in the Jewish religion, and Festus probably thought that Agrippa could shed light on the problem case he had on his hands. Why was Paul, a Jew professing the greatest reverence for the Law and the temple, being so violently accused and denounced by the Jewish religious leaders?

"There is a certain man left a prisoner by Felix. See Acts 24:27.

25:15 – *"and when I was at Jerusalem, the chief priests and the elders of the Jews brought charges against him, asking for a sentence of condemnation upon him.*

And when I was at Jerusalem. See verses 1-5.

The chief priests and the elders of the Jews brought charges against him, asking for a sentence of condemnation upon him. This conversation reveals that the religious leaders had asked for a death sentence to be pronounced against Paul without a fair trial. Harmonizing this statement with verse 3, it must be that when Festus first went to Jerusalem, the Jews made two proposals: (1) that he should condemn and execute Paul without trial, and that being denied this, (2) that he should bring Paul to Jerusalem for trial there, secretly planning all the while to have him assassinated on the road.

25:16 – *"And I answered them that it is not the custom of the Romans to hand over any man before the accused meets his accusers face to face, and has an opportunity to make his defense against the charges.*

And I answered them that it is not the custom of the Romans. Festus stated the facts of the case to Agrippa II with fair accuracy, but there is a ring of superiority and disdain for the Jews when he invokes "the custom of the Romans." Several Roman authors may be quoted to show that the Romans did require a fair trial.[16] Appian in his *Roman History* says, "It is not their custom to condemn men before they are heard,"[17] and in his *Civil War* he says, "The law requires, members of the council, that a man who is on trial should hear the accusation and speak in his own defense before judgment is passed on him."[18] Tacitus asserts, "A defendant is not to be prohibited from adducing all things by which his innocence may be established."[19]

To hand over any man[20] **before the accused meets his accusers face to face, and has an opportunity to make his defense against the charges.** "To hand over" is the same verb Paul used in verse 11, which the ASV translated "granting a favor." Perhaps Paul had touched a nerve as he stated his reason for appealing to Caesar, so that Festus was taking pains now to affirm that he never intended to hand Paul over to the Jews. Maybe he didn't, but Paul perceived there was a chance Festus would do so. It may also be that Festus is now trying to conceal his actual intents as he speaks to Agrippa II.

25:17 – *"And so after they had assembled here, I made no delay, but on the next day took my seat on the tribunal, and ordered the man to be brought.*

And so after they had assembled here. See verse 6.

I made no delay. This seems to imply some disgust with reference to his predecessor's actions in the case. If Felix hadn't let two years pass with the apostle's case still undecided, Festus wouldn't have the problem he now has.

But on the next day took my seat on the tribunal, and ordered the man to be brought. Festus here again accurately states the facts. The impression is that Festus was trying to justly administer his office; had he not been trying so hard to please his new subjects, he would have been exactly fair to Paul in the earlier trial.

---

[16] Many of the Western world's judicial practices are inherited from Roman practices. Barnes suggests such a system of justice is a cause for expression of gratitude to God. "We may remark that it is a subject of sincere gratitude to God that in our nation the privilege is enjoyed ... It is a right which every man has, to be heard; to know the charges against him; to be confronted with the witnesses; to make his defense; and to be tried by the laws, and not by the passions and caprices of men." (Barnes, *op. cit.*, p.343)

[17] Quoted by Barnes, *ibid.*

[18] Appian, *Civil War*, III.54.

[19] Tacitus, *Annals*, II.

[20] In the KJV the words "to die" are added at this place, but these are not found in the better manuscripts and seem to have been added by some scribe by way of explanation.

25:18 – *"And when the accusers stood up, they* **began** *bringing charges against him not of such crimes as I was expecting;*

And when the accusers stood up, they *began* **bringing charges against him not of such crimes as I was expecting.** Festus seems to have expected charges of sedition and breach of the peace like the bloody conflict in Caesarea that had figured directly in the recall of Felix his predecessor.[21] Or he may have been expecting them to accuse Paul of atrocious crimes against other men's persons or property.

25:19 – *"but they* **simply** *had some points of disagreement with him about their own religion and about a certain dead man, Jesus, whom Paul asserted to be alive.*

But they *simply* **had some points of disagreement with him about their own religion.** Notice that Festus tells Agrippa II something that was not specifically stated in Luke's earlier account of the trial; namely, that during the trial itself he learned the real charges against Paul were disagreements over the Jewish religion.

"Religion" is the same word (*deisidaimonias*) Paul used as he began his speech on Mars Hill. As explained at Acts 17:22, the word can either be a compliment or an insult.

- The NASB translation, which adds the word "simply," suggests Festus used the word with a certain disdain or contempt for the content of the charges the Jewish religious leaders brought up when they finally had their day in court.
- However, there are reasons to believe Festus used the word in its good sense. It was the regular word by which a Roman would designate his own worship. If Festus was not familiar with any technical Jewish words for worship, he would naturally use the same word for their religion as he did for his own. Further, Agrippa II professed a certain deference for the Jewish religion. Festus would not likely speak of the religion of his royal guest in a derogatory sense.

And about a certain dead man, Jesus. Here is another detail of the trial that was not specified before. The earlier account has no mention of Jesus. If Festus is lumping together into one the ideas "about their own religion" and "about a certain … Jesus," we can truly say that the governor, just new to the area, has much to learn about the local people and their beliefs. Paul would insist that Jesus was the culmination and fulfillment of all that the Jewish religion looked forward to, but the unconverted Jew would not put the two together. It may also be that Festus' words indicate that he was ignorant of Jesus (whom he calls a "certain dead man") before he came to Judea. Was Festus like many politicians in that he never made a study of religious questions?

Whom Paul asserted to be alive. Paul not only taught that Jesus had died, but he affirmed that Jesus was alive again from the dead. Throughout the book of Acts, the presentations of the gospel Luke records confirm the constant and recurring emphasis on the resurrection of Jesus. Note also another detail of the trial that was not specified before, but which Festus includes in his rehearsal of the events: not only had Paul spoken about Jesus' crucifixion,

---

[21] Acts 24:27.

he had also emphasized His resurrection, and it had made an impression on the mind of the governor.

25:20 – *"And being at a loss how to investigate such matters, I asked whether he was willing to go to Jerusalem and there stand trial on these matters.*

And being at a loss how to investigate such matters. Festus was "at a loss" how to conduct a trial about such matters of religion. He just didn't know which way to turn. He tells Agrippa II that the thought that perhaps at Jerusalem witnesses could be found who would help in the determination of the matter. Remember, though, that Paul viewed the whole suggestion about going to Jerusalem as evidence that Festus was being partial to the Jews, at the expense even of the defendant's life.

I asked whether he was willing to go to Jerusalem and there stand trial on these matters. See notes at verse 9.

25:21 – *"But when Paul appealed to be held in custody for the Emperor's decision, I ordered him to be kept in custody until I send him to Caesar."*

But when Paul appealed to be held in custody for the Emperor's decision. Here and in verse 25, Festus refers to Nero by his title. (Note the marginal reading, "the Augustus.") A contemporary equivalent to this title would be "his majesty." The title "Augustus" was first conferred on Octavian in 27 BC, and thereafter he was called Caesar Augustus, the name which Luke uses in the narrative about the birth of Jesus.[22] After Octavian's death, the title was given to his successors in office, and so Festus uses it of Nero. The title included a connotation of divinity (i.e., venerable, worthy of reverence). Tiberius did not like having "Augustus" applied to him; but the other emperors seemed to have no scruples about being attributed with divinity.

I ordered him to be kept in custody until I send him to Caesar." Paul was even now being held in custody at Caesarea until arrangements could be made for sending him to Rome. "Caesar" originally was a name of the Julian family. Octavian used it as an official title since it was less repugnant to his subjects than "king." After the death of Gaius, the last of the Julian line, the emperors assumed the title Caesar as a designation of their office (similar to "president" or "king" in our culture).

25:22 – *And Agrippa said to Festus, "I also would like to hear the man myself." "Tomorrow," he said, "you shall hear him."*

And Agrippa said to Festus. After hearing all these details about Paul's case from Festus, Agrippa II revealed that also had an interest in the case.

"I also would like to hear the man myself." The imperfect tense verb is better translated "I also was myself wishing." That is, the phrase implies that the wish was not now formed

---

[22] Luke 2:1

for the first time. Just why he hadn't asked before to hear Paul we can only guess. Perhaps he felt his official position in relationship to the temple and the appointment of Jewish religious officials would be jeopardized if he showed too great an interest in Paul and his message. Perhaps he felt that Festus would have been insulted were he to find out that Agrippa II had come to Caesarea with any other purpose than to welcome the new governor. Perhaps he thought it was too great a favor to ask.

But Agrippa's words show that this is not the first time he has heard of Paul, and likely not the first time he has heard of Jesus. This king who was the last of the Herodian line surely would have been acquainted with some of the incidents where Christianity had crossed his family's history. It was his great-grandfather who had attempted to kill Jesus in the cradle at Bethlehem. It was his uncle who had killed John the Baptist and sat as judge in a trial of Jesus on the day He was crucified. It was his own father who had tried to suppress Christianity and thereby please the Jews by killing the apostle James and imprisoning Peter with the intention of killing him. The names of Jesus and the apostles would have been familiar in the household of Agrippa II, but he could not lower himself to go hear one of the apostles preach. Now, though, he could satisfy his long-cherished desire to hear one of these men preach by being part of Festus' invited audience on such an occasion, without diminishing his influence among the Jews.

"Tomorrow," he said, "you shall hear him." If indeed Festus deliberately brought up Paul's case in an effort to get Agrippa II involved in it, there would be a tone of delight and satisfaction as he announces, "I'll arrange it for you to hear him!" Given the words of verse 23, the rest of the day would include making arrangements, sending out invitations, and getting everything in readiness for the morrow.

2) Paul appears before Herod Agrippa II. 25:23-27

25:23 – *And so, on the next day when Agrippa had come together with Bernice, amid great pomp, and had entered the auditorium accompanied by the commanders and the prominent men of the city, at the command of Festus, Paul was brought in.*

And so, on the next day when Agrippa had come together with Bernice, amid great pomp. The description begins to sound as if it were recorded by an eyewitness to the pomp. The Greek word for pomp (*phantasia*, literally "show, pageantry") is not found elsewhere in the New Testament, though it is found in secular writers to describe a great display or parade. All these people would have been dressed in their finest royal garments or official robes. There would have been a procession in which rigid protocol would have been followed, with entrances made in the proper sequence and the right amount of time between each. Perhaps there were ruffles and flourishes of horns and drums.[23] Bernice accompanied Agrippa II, as was her custom whenever they traveled.[24] They were so much

---

[23] In America, we rarely have an opportunity to see such pomp and display. Even those who watched the funeral of President John F. Kennedy, with kings and presidents from all over the earth in attendance, saw only subdued pomp.

[24] Josephus, *Wars*, II.16.3.

together that letters of state were addressed to Agrippa and her conjointly.[25]

And had entered the auditorium accompanied by the commanders and the prominent men of the city. The "auditorium" probably was the audience room in the Praetorium where the governor would receive visitors of state. That the tribunes[26] and prominent men were present suggests that they have been given a special invitation. The "prominent men" are likely civil officers of the Jewish and Gentile local government of Caesarea.

At the command of Festus, Paul was brought in. After the procession of kings and dignitaries had entered the audience room and were seated in their places, Paul the prisoner was brought in. Jesus one day had promised His disciples that they would be "brought before governors and kings ... as a testimony to them and to the Gentiles."[27] On another occasion, as He was instructing Ananias to go to Paul and tell him what to do to be saved, Jesus had indicated that Paul would "bear my name before the Gentiles and kings and the children of Israel."[28] Paul's appearance in the audience chamber of Festus is a partial fulfillment of those predictions.

25:24 – *And Festus said, "King Agrippa, and all you gentlemen here present with us, you behold this man about whom all the people of the Jews appealed to me, both at Jerusalem and here, loudly declaring that he ought not to live any longer.*

And Festus said. Festus, as recorded in verses 24-27, uses great oratorical flourish to introduce the case to those who were assembled.[29]

King Agrippa, and all you gentlemen here present with us. Luke very carefully notes that Agrippa II did have the title "king," but he is not called "king of Judea." He was the last man in Roman times to bear the title "king" in Palestine.

You behold this man about whom all the people of the Jews appealed to me, both at Jerusalem and here. The Jews have done a good selling job on Festus, for when he says

---

[25] Josephus, *Life*, c.11.

[26] Josephus (*Antiquities*, XIX.9.2) indicates there were five cohorts stationed at Caesarea, so there would have been five cohort commanders present.

[27] Matthew 10:18.

[28] Acts 9.15.

[29] Christians must be careful how they introduce other speakers. Dale (*op. cit.*, p.361) offers these words:
> Usually little men in big offices love the pomp and display which dignify, they think, their small souls. And again undue pomp and display are usually signs of a weak or disintegrating power. True power needs no display. The higher the office is, the less display. This may be seen when one introduces the President of the United States. The fewest possible words are spoken in the introduction ["Ladies and Gentlemen, the President of the United States"]. Preachers and politicians fall prey to much flattery and display. It is well to remember that our lives and our messages speak for themselves. It is also right and desirable that honor be given where honor is due (Romans 13:7). It would be difficult to picture Jesus and the apostles parading in the pomp of modern preachers. Likewise it would be foreign to their ears to hear the oft repeated jokes and jesting found so necessary today in the introductions of [preachers and] sermons."

"all the people of the Jews appealed to me," he speaks as though the feeling against Paul among the Jews was well-nigh universal. Of course, to date, he had come in contact only with Paul's enemies during his brief stay in the province. The word translated "appealed to me" is rendered "complain against" and "accused" in 1 Maccabees 8:32 and 10:61.

Some have understood the words "and here" to mean that the Jews who lived at Caesarea, and who were very antagonistic to Gentiles because of the racial strife in the city, had gone to Festus and demanded the death of the apostle who was so friendly to Gentiles. But it is also possible, in the light of previous verses, that the language means no more than that both in Jerusalem and later at Caesarea the Jerusalem Jews demanded Paul's death.

Loudly declaring that he ought not to live any longer. The same cry that had been raised against Paul the day he was arrested some two years earlier (Acts 21:36) is still being raised against him.

25:25 – *"But I found that he had committed nothing worthy of death; and since he himself appealed to the Emperor, I decided to send him.*

But I found that he had committed nothing worthy of death. Here is an emphatic declaration by Festus that he found no evidence that would sustain the Jews' accusations against Paul. What was but implied in the narrative in verses 9ff is here clearly stated. Interestingly, even when he was asking Paul if he were willing to go to Jerusalem to be tried there, he already knew Paul was innocent.

And since he himself appealed to the Emperor, I determined to send him. These words may imply that Festus was giving thought to setting Paul at liberty at the close of that first trial. He hesitated doing it immediately because of the persistent clamor of the Jews against Paul. But then Paul appealed to Caesar, and after conferring with his counselors, Festus arrived at the determination that there was nothing to do but send him.

25:26 – *"Yet I have nothing definite about him to write to my lord. Therefore I have brought him before you* **all** *and especially before you, King Agrippa, so that after the investigation has taken place, I may have something to write.*

Yet I have nothing definite about him to write to my lord. Roman law seemed to require that when a case was appealed to Caesar, the lower courts were to send along a full report of the legal proceedings which had preceded the appeal. This requirement put Festus into difficulties. He couldn't very well write that Paul could not get justice in the lower courts, and therefore had to appeal to Caesar. But what was he going to write to Nero? Thus, he is asking for help as he introduces Paul.

The title "lord" is a reference to Nero, the emperor. This title had even more of a connotation of divinity than did "Augustus,"[30] so that both Octavian and Tiberius refused to let anyone address them with this particular title.[31] But Caligula and Nero permitted the

---

[30] See notes at verse 21.

[31] Suetonius, *Augustus*, 53; *Tiberius*, 27; Tacitus, *Annals*, II.87. Octavian so objected to the title "lord" that he did not allow it to be used even by his children or grandchildren, either seriously or at play. The name

use of the term, and even gloried in it.³²

Therefore I have brought him before you all, and especially before you, King Agrippa, so that after the investigation has taken place, I may have something to write. The choice of "investigation" to translate the Greek word here is a good one, since it conveys the idea that this is not a formal trial. Indeed, it could not be a formal trial, for Paul's appeal to Caesar had stopped all legal proceedings except those at Rome. Festus is carefully explaining that this was not a formal hearing, but only an attempt to gather further information. Festus' inclusion of all the officials and dignitaries would be looked on as an act of courtesy. It would do something else. It would include them, and especially Agrippa, in the letter to the emperor. If Nero reads between the lines that Paul had not gotten justice in Judea, many men besides Festus were involved in the miscarriage of justice. In some respects, Festus is protecting himself. And if he can obtain some bit of help formulating a letter to Caesar that will sound reasonable, he'll be out of the case without much harm to his position or reputation.

25:27 – *"For it seems absurd to me in sending a prisoner, not to indicate also the charges against him."*

For it seems absurd to me in sending a prisoner. Festus admits that he felt he was in an embarrassing position. He was about to send a prisoner to Rome who had been tried in his own court, and who had appealed from his jurisdiction, and yet he, the judge, as yet cannot clearly state the nature of the charges against the man, if indeed any crime at all had been committed.³³ And not only would it be absurd to send a prisoner without clearly stating the charges against him, but Festus also risked arousing Nero's displeasure if a case came to the supreme court and there were no charges of any Roman law having been violated.

Not to indicate also the charges against him. Festus hopes that this present attempt to gather additional information will bring out some fresh facts which he had not before been able to grasp. Someone as conversant with Jewish politics and religion as Agrippa II would surely be able to help him understand what the case was all about, and could help him put down in writing something that would be a satisfactory introduction of the case to Caesar.

"Augustus" had enough connotations of divinity for him.

³² Some early Christians refused to utter the word "lord" with reference to Caesar, or any other human government official. They preferred to save it for speaking of Jesus only. Tertullian, *Apology*, 34; Polycarp, *Martyrdom*, VIII.2, IX.2.

³³ This whole introductory speech by Festus has been attacked as being not genuine because of a supposed repetition (verse 25 compared with verse 21), and because of a supposed contradiction (verse 27 compared with verse 19). However, these criticisms are without merit; both statements made by Festus are natural enough within the context. The statement of verse 25 was needful because many of the people present in the audience room would be unaware of Festus' personal judgment in the matter until Festus informs them. As for the supposed contradiction, even if Festus recognizes that he is being asked to litigate a religious dispute, that was not something Rome was interested in. He'll have to find something more substantial than that to write about as he forwards Paul's case to Rome.

Drawing by Horace Knowles
from the British and Foreign Bible Society

3) Paul's sermon to Herod Agrippa II. 26:1-23

26:1 – *And Agrippa said to Paul, "You are permitted to speak for yourself." Then Paul stretched out his hand and* proceeded *to make his defense:*

And Agrippa said to Paul, "You are permitted to speak for yourself." This investigation was held in Festus' audience room, but chapter 26 gives every appearance that Festus has turned over the investigation to Agrippa II. Many of Paul's expressions are addressed directly to Agrippa, and when Agrippa rises (verse 30) that signals the end of the proceedings.

Then Paul stretched out his hand and *proceeded* **to make his defense.** The Greek behind "stretched out his hand" is not the same as in Acts 13:16 or 21:40, where the word signifies a gesture inviting silence and attention so he could speak. The word here speaks of a hand raised in salutation, or in a gesture to emphasize his message. It is indicative that Paul is preaching with power as he asserts the dignity of his call to the apostleship by Jesus, and at the same time makes as clear an explanation of his own conduct as he can.

It can further be affirmed that Paul is preaching. It cannot be supposed that he expected by his speech to win his release from confinement; he was being held in custody until his transfer to Rome could be arranged.[1] Lenski has it right when he affirms that "Paul converted this great hall into a church, and acted as a preacher."[2]

Chapter 26 is the third account in Acts of Paul's conversion. This one is from Paul himself, so it contains more vivid details than do the other two. As we go from one account to another, supplemental details are provided.[3] Rather than being evidence that one or all are simply fabrications, the additional facts are exactly what we might expect when we consider the differences in audiences to whom the accounts are originally addressed.

A suggested outline of the different points that Paul emphasized is:[4]

1. A complimentary introduction. Verses 2,3
2. Paul speaks of his Pharisaic heritage. Verses 4-8
3. Then he speaks of his former persecuting zeal. Verses 9-11
4. Then of his vision on the Damascus road. Verses 12-18
5. Then of his lifelong obedience to the vision. Verses 19,20
6. Then of his arrest. Verse 21
7. And finally of the doctrine he teaches. Verses 22,23

---

[1] Acts 15:11.

[2] Lenski, *op. cit.*, p.1020. Further information is given in the next verse about the word "defense," and the word "defense" does not nullify what has been said about Paul's "preaching" to this auditorium full of people.

[3] The accounts found in chapters 9 and 22 speak of Ananias; chapter 26 does not. Chapters 9 and 22 contain an account of Paul's blindness; chapter 26 does not. Chapter 26 contains a fuller account of Paul's commission (verses 15-18). These are examples of the variations in the accounts that negative critics have appealed to in order to deny the truthfulness of much in all the accounts.

[4] The outline is adopted from Bruce, *op. cit.*, p.488.

26:2 – *"In regard to all the things of which I am accused by the Jews, I consider myself fortunate, King Agrippa, that I am about to make my defense before you today;*

In regard to all the things of which I am accused by *the* Jews. The main points which the Jews had raised in accusation during the past two years are that Paul is a cause of disturbances among Jews wherever he goes; that he is a ringleader of the Christians; that he is a profaner of the temple; and that he is one who teaches men to ignore the Law of Moses.[5] Four times the phrase "the Jews" is repeated in verses 2-7, as though Paul is, on this occasion, seeking to separate himself from his unbelieving countrymen. Since on other occasions he attempted to identify himself with them, this part of Paul's defense has seemed strange to some. But it must be remembered that already in Romans 9-11, written several years before this date, Paul has already indicated that such a division did indeed exist between Christians and unbelieving Jews.

I consider myself fortunate, King Agrippa, that I am about to make my defense before you today. Just as there was frankness and courtesy in Paul's defense before Felix, so again we see it in this defense before Agrippa II. He gives a truthful explanation of his feelings, and the reason for them, but he does not flatter the king whose character, he must have known, did not deserve unmitigated praise. Paul does tell how fortunate he feels it is to have opportunity to speak to one like Agrippa who had some understanding of all the intricacies of Jewish life and thought. This is not a "defense" in the strict sense of the term; it is not a defense made in court.

The word translated "defense" is *apologeia*, a word that meant something quite different then than it means today.[6] Paul was not apologizing for being wrong. Quite the opposite; his statement was set forth intending to prove that he was right! He is explaining his actions and motives so that Festus, Agrippa II, and the others could better understand why he acted as he did.

26:3 – *"especially because you are an expert in all customs and questions among the Jews; therefore I beg you to listen to me patiently.*

Especially because you are an expert in all customs and questions among the Jews. In the notes at Acts 25:13 it has been noted that Agrippa II not only professed the Jewish religion, but also had been given certain administrative functions in connection with the temple and priesthood by the Roman government. He was an expert in the Jewish religion. Customs, as it has several times before in Acts,[7] has reference to the particular practices found in the Law of Moses. "Questions" would speak of the subjects of debate between the Pharisees and Sadducees.[8] With all these Agrippa II was conversant.

Therefore I beg you to listen to me patiently. By this request, Paul is letting Agrippa II

---

[5] See Acts 24:4,6; 25:8.

[6] Compare the explanation of "apology" at Acts 7:1.

[7] For the meaning of "customs" and "questions" in greater detail. see notes at Acts 6:4; 16:21; 21:21,35.

[8] Acts 23:8.

know that this would be a rather lengthy presentation. It would need a bit of patience to hear it to its conclusion. A person who did not know the peculiarities of the Jewish religion (e.g., the disputes between Pharisee and Sadducee, the expectations of a Messiah, the devotion to Moses and the temple) might find it hard to follow Paul's arguments, and could grow tired before the message was finished. But Paul expected Agrippa II to have no difficulty following the presentation.

26:4 – *"So then, all Jews know my manner of life from my youth up, which from the beginning was spent among my* **own** *nation and at Jerusalem;*

So then, all Jews know my manner of life from my youth up. From the time Paul came to Jerusalem as a rabbinical student, Jewish people were acquainted with him. "Youth" here likely means a "teenager."[9]

Which from the beginning was spent among my *own* nation and at Jerusalem. Paul here stresses his Jewish heritage, and notes especially that his training was at Jerusalem. Paul is referring to the time when he first came up to Jerusalem to study the Law and the traditions of the elders with Gamaliel as his teacher.[10]

26:5 – *"since they have known about me for a long time previously, if they are willing to testify, that I lived* **as** *a Pharisee according to the strictest sect of our religion.*

Since they have known about me for a long time previously, if they are willing to testify. If Jewish people in Jerusalem and Judea have known Paul even during his days as a student, he must have done something to call their attention to him. As he himself says, "I advanced beyond many of my own age in the Jews' religion."[11] The fact that he was early entrusted with a commission against Christians (chapter 9) shows that he had distinguished himself in his earlier days, enough so people knew about him. Paul insists that the Jews could testify to the truth of what he was now saying, since they have known him for a long time previous to his arrest two years ago.

That I lived as a Pharisee according to the strictest sect of our religion. The Jews who knew Paul in those days more than a quarter of a century earlier could also testify that he was a member of the sect of the Pharisees, the one out of all the sects that was most exact and rigorous when it came to interpreting the Law and enforcing ceremonial observances. Paul knew all the rules of discipline that the Pharisees laid down, and he lived rigidly according to these rules. The word "religion" (*threskeias*) is the old word for religious worship or discipline, and has special emphasis on the external, ceremonial observances.[12] Paul has emphasized his training and his beliefs before his conversion in this opening part

---

[9] See "Paul in Jerusalem," at Acts 9:1ff concerning Paul's probable age when he came to Jerusalem as a student.

[10] See notes on Acts 22:3.

[11] Galatians 1:14.

[12] The word also appears in James 1:26,27 and Colossians 2:18. On the word "sect" see notes at Acts 24:5,14.

of his message. He was a jealous adherent of all the tenets of faith taught in the Old Testament.

26:6 – *"And now I am standing trial for the hope of the promise made by God to our fathers;*

And now I am standing trial for the hope. Paul's doctrine and preaching since his conversion, he insists, are in full accord with his whole past life. He has been led to the very place that the Law was intended to lead a man, to Jesus as the Messiah.[13]

Of the promise made by God to our fathers. The one promise that was made over and over through the Old Testament age was that Messiah was coming, and when He did arrive, all the nations of the earth would be blessed (a term which involves the forgiveness of sins).[14] Included too was the promise of a future state, and a resurrection of the dead. "Unto *our* fathers," Paul said.[15] The NASB reading is very much in harmony with Paul's usual manner of identifying himself with those to whom he speaks. There is a sense in which he will claim even Agrippa II as a descendant of Abraham.

26:7 – "the promise *to which our twelve tribes hope to attain, as they earnestly serve* **God** *night and day. And for this hope, O King, I am being accused by Jews.*

The promise **to which our twelve tribes hope to attain.** Paul uses the "twelve tribes"[16] to designate the Jews of all the tribes, generation after generation, as hoping to see the fulfillment of that which God promised to the fathers.

As they earnestly serve *God* night and day. "Serving" (*latreuō*) is serving with worship, prayers, sacrifices, and the like. "Earnestly," (or "with intense devotion") was used at Acts 12:5. "Night and day" may be an allusion to the temple services, some of which were at night as well as during the day;[17] or it may be an allusion to the incessant personal devotions of the conscientious Jew's religious life.

---

[13] Galatians 3:23ff. Compare Paul's affirmation at Acts 23:6 and 24:14-15.

[14] Genesis 12:1ff; Romans 4; et al. See also notes at Acts 3:25,26.

[15] Some manuscripts read "to the fathers," but the better ones read "our fathers."

[16] Neither Paul nor any other New Testament writer can be found to support the fiction sometimes heard in our day that Britain and America are the "ten lost tribes of Israel." The legend is that the ten northern tribes (Israel), after they had been carried away to captivity by Shalmaneser and the Assyrians, never returned to Palestine after the captivity. Instead, they wandered far away and were to be found, under some strange disguise, in a far-off land (i.e., Britain and America). The theory even has it that in order to understand Old Testament prophecy, every time there is a reference to some future event for "Israel," it must be interpreted as if it were true of Britain and the United States. This whole scheme of eschatology is often called "British Israelism," and is a doctrine everywhere contradicted in the Bible. (E.g., see Matthew 19:28; Luke 22:30; James 1:1; Revelation 7:4ff, 21:12.) The earliest appearance of this fable is in the apocryphal II Esdras 13:40-46, where the ten tribes are said to have gone to "a country where never mankind dwelt, that they might there keep the statutes which they never kept in their land." But that fable is nowhere taught in the canonical books. Ezra 2 and 1 Chronicles 9:3 indicate that exiles from "all Israel" were among the returnees who resettled Palestine. Thus, Paul, speaking of the Jews in Palestine, can refer to "twelve tribes" and mean by it the whole body of Jews.

[17] Compare Psalm 134:1 and 1 Chronicles 9:33.

And for this hope, O King, I am being accused by Jews. The position of "by Jews"[18] in the Greek is at the end of the sentence for emphasis. It is an utterly amazing thing that the Jews, who have the hope which the Old Testament Scriptures promised, should persecute Paul for entertaining the very same hope! The key difference between Paul and the unbelieving Jews was that they still looked forward to the fulfillment of those promises, whereas Paul affirms the thing hoped for has already been realized in the person of Jesus. The whole dispute boiled down to a question of evidence: was Jesus the promised Messiah and the fulfillment of Israel's hopes? To that evidence Paul now turns.

26:8 – *"Why is it considered incredible among you* **people** *if God does raise the dead?*

Why is it considered incredible among you *people.* Paul adduces three evidences in this and the following verses to show that Jesus indeed is the Messiah. The first of these appears in this verse: namely, the resurrection of Jesus from the dead. By this question Paul expresses his continuing surprise that the members of his audience are still unconvinced as far as the fact of the resurrection is concerned. "You" is plural in the Greek, and this plural shows that Paul is not, at this moment, addressing Agrippa II in particular, but has turned to the whole audience.[19]

If God does raise the dead? The Greek reads "If God raises dead *people*." That is, there is no article in the Greek, and "dead" is a plural adjective. A similar construction in Romans 1:4 certainly includes the resurrection of Jesus (and that as involving the resurrection of all men), and that would seem to be Paul's point here, too. The great truth to which Paul has been building is that Jesus, although crucified, was at that moment living and seated at the right hand of God. His resurrection proves Him to be the Messiah, the very one the Jews were looking for to fulfill their hope. Jews might believe in the idea of resurrection as part of their doctrine. If so, then why could they not accept the well-authenticated resurrection of Jesus?

26:9-18 – *"So then, I thought to myself that I had to do many things hostile to the name of Jesus ...."*[20]

So then, I thought to myself. Paul now turns to the second evidence he adduces to prove that Jesus is the Messiah: namely, his own conversion.

That I had to do many things hostile to the name of Jesus .... Verses 9 through 18 tell of Paul's persecuting the church, the appearance of the risen Christ to him on the Damascus road, and Christ's apostolic commission to Paul to preach the gospel. Paul is explaining how he came to associate the fulfillment of Israel's hope with Jesus of Nazareth. He had

---

[18] The construction of the phrase is anarthrous; that is, there is no article in the Greek. Thus, it should be rendered "by Jews" (rather than "by *the* Jews").

[19] There was indeed an audience in the audience room (see Acts 25:23ff). That Paul is addressing this entire audience, and is arguing for the validity of Jesus' resurrection in particular, is much superior interpretation to the one that has Paul's words being an appeal to the Sadducean part of the audience only.

[20] Verses 9-18 have already been explained in notes under chapter 9. Consult that harmony of portions of chapters 9, 22, and 26 to understand the details which Paul recalls from those extraordinary events.

not always been of this persuasion. There was a time in his life, only about 25 years ago, when he thought he should oppose Jesus. Some of those present would remember! Paul is saying he understands the unbelief of many in the audience, and their opposition to Jesus, because he himself once felt like they do. However, if Paul was telling the truth (and there is no reason to doubt it), then his statements were evidence of the resurrection and glorification of Jesus, enough to convince Agrippa II and the other listeners.

26:19 – *"Consequently, King Agrippa, I did not prove disobedient to the heavenly vision,*

Consequently, O King Agrippa. "Consequently" points back to everything from verses 12-18. Paul affirms that since the proof of Jesus being the Messiah, and of His resurrection, and of His calling of Paul to the work of an apostle were so unmistakably plain, he deemed it his duty to become involved without delay in spreading the news that Jesus was Messiah.

I did not prove disobedient to the heavenly vision. The language "heavenly vision" would convey to Agrippa II the idea that the commission to Paul had come from God Himself.[21] The Sadducees would have scoffed at the story of Christ's appearance to Paul, but King Agrippa II, a Pharisee in his sympathies, would respect it, and he would also respect Paul's emphasis on obedience.

Literally, the Greek says, "I did not become disobedient." This is significant for its bearing on the relationship between God's grace and a person's freedom. Paul may have been a "vessel of election,"[22] marked out beforehand for the ministry to the Gentiles, and even constrained by the love of Christ,[23] but even for him there was the possibility of disobedience. Paul could have become disobedient! Grace is not irresistible! There was an act of the will involved in passing from his previous state of rebellion to that of obedience. "From the time that he heard the words 'I am Jesus whom you are persecuting,' Paul knew but one Master. For him henceforth to receive a commandment from that Master was to set about obeying it."[24]

26:20 – *"but* **kept** *declaring both to those of Damascus first, and* **also** *at Jerusalem and* **then** *throughout all the region of Judea, and* **even** *to the Gentiles, that they should repent and turn to God, performing deeds appropriate to repentance.*

But *kept* **declaring both to those of Damascus first, and** *also* **at Jerusalem.** Paul emphasized the fact that his labors had been in obedience to the divine commission from the risen Lord. Acts 9:19ff tell of his labor in Damascus. Acts 9:28-29 speak of his first visit to Jerusalem after his conversion, and his preaching there. The verb "kept declaring" is in the tense which speaks of a long-continued activity.

---

[21] Compare Luke 1:22 and 2 Corinthians 12:1. The Greek word "vision" carries the idea that there was an objectivity to the thing seen.

[22] Acts 9:15.

[23] 2 Corinthians 5:14.

[24] Bruce, *op. cit.*, p.492.

And *then* throughout all the region of Judea, and *even* to the Gentiles. Since we know of no preaching by Paul in Judea during the time of his first visit to Jerusalem after his conversion, and because at Galatians 1:22 Paul writes of this timeframe, "And I was *still* unknown by sight to the churches of Judea which were in Christ," several solutions have been suggested for this difficult phrase.

- McGarvey suggests that Paul is following an order of place rather than an order of time, and that at some time or another, Paul did preach in Judea, though not at the time of his first visit to Jerusalem after his conversion.[25]
- *Pulpit Commentary* also places this Judean work subsequent to the time recorded in Galatians 1, and suggests that sandwiched between his missionary journeys to Gentile areas he did preach in Judea.[26] For instance, the language of Acts 11:29 clearly suggests that such an opportunity may have arisen when Paul and Barnabas carried up to Jerusalem the alms from the Christians at Antioch. Other such opportunities occurred as he passed with Barnabas through Phoenicia and Samaria to Jerusalem (Acts 15:3), and when he went from Caesarea to Jerusalem (Acts 18:22).
- A third explanation for this difficult phrase is that of Blass, who made a conjectural emendation of the text so that it reads "in every land to both Jews and Gentiles."[27]

Paul's brief summary of his work would suggest to Agrippa II that he began with his own people, and then went to the Gentiles.[28]

That they should repent and turn to God, performing deeds appropriate to repentance. Three states of a person's spiritual life are here noted: repentance for past sins; turning to God (which is probably a reference to baptism, cf. Acts 3:19); and then performing deeds appropriate to the repentance professed (i.e., one of the elements in the progressive sanctification of the Christian life). Why had Paul undertaken all those extensive missionary travels? Because the Lord Jesus from heaven had commanded him to do this, and he had to obey the Lord's command, especially since he had evidence that the Lord was Messiah and deity, the fulfillment of Israel's hopes.

26:21 – *"For this reason some Jews seized me in the temple and tried to put me to death.*

For this reason *some* Jews seized me in the temple. Paul here tells Agrippa II why he was arrested in the first place.[29] "For this reason" likely includes the fact that he preached the gospel, rather than conformity to the Law, and especially because he delivered the message to the Gentiles.

This is a most telling statement. Paul declares, "I have spent my life trying to persuade all men to repent and turn to God, and for doing so the Jews tried to kill me." Paul

---

[25] McGarvey, *op. cit.*, p.254. That is, McGarvey limits the application of Galatians 1:22 to Paul's first visit to Jerusalem after his conversion.

[26] Hervey, *op. cit.*, p.267.

[27] Quoted by Knowling, *op. cit.*, p.508.

[28] "Gentiles" refers to the missionary journeys after the conversion of Cornelius.

[29] For details about the Asian Jews' seizure of Paul, see notes at Acts 21:27ff.

is affirming that his one unpardonable sin in the eyes of those Jews was not that he profaned the temple, but that he taught the Gentiles that they too might claim every gift and grace which had once been looked on as the exclusive privilege and prerogative of Israel.

And tried to put me to death. Several attempts were made on Paul's life, one when he was first seized (Acts 21:31ff) and again when he stood before the Sanhedrin (Acts 23:10). Festus had found himself at a loss to understand why Paul had been arrested in the first place, and why the Jews were so bitterly opposed to him. Yet he had to have something to write Nero to send along with Paul. He indicated that he wanted Agrippa's help to better understand this matter. Now Agrippa has learned why the Jews mobbed Paul and nearly executed him on the spot in the temple. Involved is Paul's belief that Jesus is the Messiah, and the Savior of all men, Gentiles as well as Jews.

26:22 – *"And so, having obtained help from God, I stand to this day testifying both to small and great, stating nothing but what the Prophets and Moses said was going to take place;*

And so, having obtained the help from God. Paul saw and felt the danger he had been in during his 20+ years of evangelistic work. In town after town, he had known the determined malice of the Jews and their efforts to take his life. There had been the persecution at Pisidian Antioch, the stoning at Lystra, the persecutions at Philippi, Thessalonica, and Corinth, and the deadly perils at Jerusalem, all because of unbelieving Jews. There had been troubles from Gentiles, too, like the riot at Ephesus. He may have been restrained by Asiarchs at Ephesus, and rescued at Jerusalem by Lysias, and even made every effort himself to avoid danger and prolong his ministry, but at the end of it all, he traced his safety entirely to the help of God.

I stand to this day testifying both to small and great. "Small" are those in humble positions in life; the poor, the ignorant, the obscure. "Great" are the rich and noble, the kings, princes and governors. Paul was right at this very moment speaking to both "small and great" as he spoke to the assembled audience and the rulers, Festus and Agrippa. On "testifying," see notes at Acts 9:7ff (which include the harmonization with Acts 26:17).

Stating nothing but what the Prophets and Moses said was going to take place. As part of the logical arguments begun at verse 8, Paul now turns to the third evidence he adduces to prove that Jesus is the Messiah, and thus the fulfillment of Jewish hopes: namely, the magnificent way the Old Testament prophecies and the life and ministry of Jesus match in every detail. Paul insists that his preaching embodied nothing except that which the prophets and Moses had foretold. Far from flouting the Law of Moses, as the Jews accused him of doing, Paul was proclaiming its perfect fulfillment in Jesus as the Messiah.

The Greek word order, "Which the prophets said should come, and Moses," suggests the thought that Paul was going to stop his sentence with the word "come," and that the name of Moses was added as an afterthought to meet the beliefs of those who, like the Sadducees, placed the Pentateuch on a higher level of authority than the Old Testament Prophets. Verses 23-24 infer that at this point Paul introduced passage after passage from the Old Testament writings, only to show how they were fulfilled in the life, death, resurrection, and exaltation of Jesus.

26:23 – *"that the Christ was to suffer,* **and** *that by reason of* **His** *resurrection from the dead He should be the first to proclaim light both to the* **Jewish** *people and to the Gentiles."*

That the Christ was to suffer. Paul's point here is that the Old Testament writings everywhere had foretold the suffering and resurrection of Messiah, and that good news of salvation through Him would be preached to the Gentiles as well as to the Jews.

The marginal note at this place shows that this clause and the next one begin with an interrogative conjunction meaning "whether?" So we translate, "Whether the Messiah is to suffer?" Having observed the presence of the interrogatives, the commentaries undertake to explain the significance of the question.

- Knowling suggests that nothing more is stated than the question at issue between Paul and the Jews.[30]
- F.F. Bruce suggests that in this verse we have the headings from a collection of Messianic proof texts (called "Testimonies").

    At an early period in the course of Christian preaching, these Old Testament passages appear to have been grouped together under appropriate headings, which sometimes took the form of questions. Here Luke does not give us Paul's citations of Messianic "testimonies" *in extenso*, but indicates them briefly by quoting the interrogative captions under which they were grouped. "Must the Messiah Suffer?" "Must He rise from the dead?" "Must He bring the light of salvation to the people of Israel and to the Gentile nations?" (See J.R. Harris, *Testimonies*, V.1, [Cambridge, 1916], p.19f; and C.H. Dodd, *According to the Scriptures* [London, 1952], p.16f; and Justin, *Dial.* 89).[31]

- Eberhard Nestle and James Moffatt, trying to make the verse read smoothly while doing justice to the questions as they appear in the Greek, without adequate warrant, transfer verse 8 to a place between verses 22 and 23, and use it to introduce the *ei* (how, whether) clauses. Transposed in this manner, the passage reads, "Why should you consider it incredible that God raises the dead, that the Christ is capable of suffering, and that he should be the first to rise from the dead and bring the message of light to the Jewish people and to the Gentiles?" Though this is one way to provide the "if-clauses" of verse 23 with a corresponding conclusion clause, there is no manuscript justification for making this transposition, nor is it necessary since either of the prior two explanations of the *ei* clauses is satisfactory.

- A fourth attempt to explain the significance of the questions in this verse differs only slightly from the one suggested by Bruce.[32] It puts together the immediately preceding statement about what was predicted in Moses and the Prophets, and understands the questions to have this significance: whether it is possible, in the light of what was predicted in the Old Testament writings, that the Messiah should be expected to suffer, or rise from the dead, or whether the gospel would go to the Gentiles?

---

[30] Knowling, *op. cit.*, p.510.

[31] Bruce, *op. cit.*, p.493-494.

[32] Bruce says Paul is using "Testimonies" already collected. This fourth suggestion suggests that such collections were made only after this and only as a result of Paul s presentation to Agrippa II.

The great body of the Jews had fixed their thoughts only on the prophetic visions of the glories of the Messiah's kingdom. Even the disciples of Jesus were slow to receive any other thought than that of conquest and triumph. Peter's "far be it from Thee, Lord" (Matthew 16:22) expressed the horror with which the thought of a suffering Christ first struck him. It is not until they were led, after the crucifixion and the resurrection, into our Lord's own school of prophetic interpretation (Luke 24:25,26,44), and taught to recognize the undercurrent of types and prophecies that pointed to a righteous Sufferer, as well as to a righteous King, that they were able to receive the truth.[33]

And that by reason of *His* resurrection from the dead. When Mary and Joseph had brought the infant Jesus to the temple, the aged Simeon spoke of how this One would become a light to the Gentiles and a glory to the people of Israel.[34] Here Paul affirms that it is only because He rose from the dead that what Simeon (and other Old Testament prophets) predicted had any chance of being fulfilled.

If the Bible teaches that the righteous are raised from the dead before the wicked, then this passage harmonizes beautifully with that doctrine, for it speaks of an "out resurrection of the dead," as though Jesus was the first to be raised (leaving others behind), and that as the consummation begins, others (the righteous) will be raised, leaving others (the wicked) behind temporarily.

He should be the first to proclaim light both to the *Jewish* people and to the Gentiles. On "light" compare notes at Acts 13:47. The Old Testament predicted the forgiveness of sins and the final resurrection. Vitally and inseparably intertwined with these promised blessings was the resurrection of Jesus from the dead, as Romans 4:24-25 and 1 Corinthians 15:20ff clearly show. The long-cherished Jewish hope of resurrection had now taken a new turn because of the resurrection of Jesus. His resurrection was not an isolated event; instead, Messiah's resurrection was the beginning of the resurrection itself – Christ was the first fruits of them that sleep,[35] the firstborn from the dead.[36]

The word "Jewish" is in italics, but the NASB translators were right to add it, as both the context and the particular word (*laos*) used here show. In spite of clear prophecies, like the one at Isaiah 60:3, the Jews had difficulty accepting the idea that Messiah would come to save the Gentiles equally with the "people" – i.e., the children of Israel.

4) Interchange between Paul, Festus, and Herod Agrippa II. 26:24-29

26:24 – *And while* **Paul** *was saying this in his defense, Festus said in a loud voice, "Paul, you are out of your mind! Your great learning is driving you mad."*

---

[33] Plumptre, *op. cit.*, p.401.

[34] Luke 2:32.

[35] 1 Corinthians 15:20.

[36] Colossians 1:18.

And while *Paul* was saying this in his defense. The present participle here indicates that Festus broke in and interrupted Paul's defense. Up to this point, Paul has shown to Agrippa II and the others why he and the unbelieving Jews differed. They looked for a Messiah yet to come; he (because of several lines of evidence) looked upon Jesus as the Messiah who had already come and fulfilled God's promises to Israel. In the verses following are several of those vivid touches which may just indicate that Luke was present in the audience room as a personal witness of what he here describes.

Festus said in a loud voice. He cried out loud enough to interrupt while Paul was preaching. As Paul's defense stretches to some length, just as he had suggested to Agrippa II that it would,[37] Festus finds himself increasingly unable to follow the course of the argument. He concluded that if it made no sense to him, it simply made no sense.

"Paul, you are out of your mind. The statement means that Paul's enthusiasm (in Festus' opinion) has overcome his better judgment. Festus had earlier described Jesus simply "as one who was dead,"[38] yet Paul says He has risen from the dead! Indeed, who ever heard of such things? And Paul talks about bringing "light" to Gentiles, and that, of course, included Romans like Festus. Festus' interjection appears to be some combination of irritation, bemusement, indignation, and dismissal. To Festus, the Romans were superior to the conquered peoples. They didn't need any light! Festus' only conclusion is that Paul is confused in his thinking. He even has already assigned a reason for that confusion.

***Your* great learning is driving you mad.** The Greek reads, "Your many writings are turning you to madness." Festus speaks of "writings," the very word used by the Jews for their collected body of sacred books.[39] He has been listening to a long quotation of passages from those writings as Paul adduces passage after passage and compares what it says to what Jesus did. This constant study of the Old Testament, Festus concludes, is the real source of Paul's madness;[40] those writings must be clouding Paul's better judgment.

26:25 – *But Paul said, "I am not out of my mind, most excellent Festus, but I utter words of sober truth.*

But Paul said, "I am not out of my mind. With the courtesy and respect due to rulers, Paul calmly rejects the conclusion to which Festus has come. During this whole defense, as far as the record goes, this is the only word addressed directly to Festus. Paul had been addressing himself to Agrippa II who was presiding over this inquiry, who was well acquainted with Jewish thought and life, and whom Paul fervently hoped he might win to faith in Christ.

---

[37] See verse 3.

[38] Acts 25:10.

[39] Compare John 7:15 and 2 Timothy 3:15.

[40] It may be that during his years in prison at Caesarea Paul had with him books and parchments. 2 Timothy 4:13, though written several years later, implies that he took these along with him when he traveled. Included in these "books and parchments" are certainly copies of the Old Testament scrolls.

Most excellent Festus. "Most excellent" was the usual title given to the Roman governor. Compare Acts 24:3.

But I utter words of sober truth. It is not the man whose world view is based on the clear teachings of God's Word who is "mad" (i.e., not using good judgment). In fact, it denotes just the opposite. "Sober" (*sōphrosunē*) was a favorite term used by the Greek ethical writers. It had a higher meaning than "temperance," and was used to express the perfect harmony of impulses and reason.[41] The word was the exact opposite of the "madness" of which Festus had just spoken. In harmony with the predictions of Moses and the prophets, and the facts which have occurred in the death and resurrection of Jesus, Paul could say his words were "words of truth." Not only that, they were "words of sober truth." Far from denoting madness, the words he uttered gave true evidence of clear, right, sound thinking.

26:26 – *"For the king knows about these matters, and I speak to him also with confidence, since I am persuaded that none of these things escape his notice; for this has not been done in a corner.*

For the king knows about these matters, and I speak to him also with confidence. After stating that he himself was quite sane and spoke the sober truth, Paul appealed to Agrippa II to vouch for the truth of what he had just said. "Know" (*epistamai*) means knowledge gained by proximity to the thing known. Agrippa II was close enough to the matters Paul had been talking about to have knowledge of them. By personal experience he could testify to the truthfulness of Paul's presentation of the Old Testament, and the facts about Jesus' life and death. "Also" in the second phrase means "because of his knowledge, I am speaking with the boldness you hear." Paul may have been a prisoner in chains (verse 29), but the Word of God in his mouth was not bound; he continues to boldly and freely present the message of the gospel.

Since I am persuaded that none of these things escape his notice. As a member of a Jewish family involved, even as persecutors, in the affairs of Christ and the apostles, Agrippa II was familiar with the Prophets and Moses, with the Messianic hopes of Israel, with the death and resurrection of Christ, and with the spread of Christianity after the resurrection of Christ. It would have been difficult for any normally intelligent man to have been unaware of these things.

For this has not been done in a corner. The ministry of Christ and his crucifixion did not occur secretly and obscurely, but was public, some of it in the chief city of Palestine with thousands of witnesses. It was of such a character as to attract attention, and the ministry and death of Jesus were matters of common knowledge. There was ample proof, too, of His resurrection from the dead, since He had been seen after His resurrection by hundreds of people. For thirty years now, the gospel had been openly and fearlessly preached in His name, and all over the Roman empire were congregations of believers who had experienced the power of the risen Lord to change their lives. If a person believed the Prophets, and compared the facts of the life and ministry of Jesus of Nazareth with those Prophets' pre-

---

[41] Aristotle, *Nicomachean Ethics*, III.10.

dictions, he must acknowledge the truth of Christianity.

Paul now takes up the thread of his presentation from the spot where he was when he was interrupted by Festus.

26:27 – *"King Agrippa, do you believe the Prophets? I know that you do."*

King Agrippa, do you believe the prophets. Having pointed to the historical facts of Jesus' ministry and compared them with the predictions in the Old Testament, Paul now makes his appeal to Agrippa II. Has Paul seen some response in Agrippa? Some look or gesture, a slight nod of the head in the affirmative, which led him to make this bold appeal for a commitment to Jesus? With Paul, to believe the Prophets was the logical step toward believing in the One of whom they spoke.

I know that you do." Paul is following the same course with Agrippa II that has been followed in thousands upon thousands of conversions. Tell about what Christ has done for you, tell about His life and ministry, His death and resurrection, and appeal to the Scriptures for the truth of what you are asking the person to believe. Then appeal for a response. Once Agrippa II admits his belief in what has been said up to this point, the next step would be to ask him for a surrender of his life to Jesus. Paul is about to ask for that surrender when Agrippa II interrupts.

26:28 – *And Agrippa* replied *to Paul, "In a short time you will persuade me to become a Christian."*

And Agrippa *replied* **to Paul.** Paul's appeal had placed Agrippa II in an uncomfortable dilemma. As a representative of Rome and a colleague of Festus in the administration of government, he did not wish to appear to Festus to share Paul's insanity; therefore, it would have been unpleasant to agree with Paul and admit that he believed the Prophets. He knew what Paul's next question would be: it would have something to do with believing in Jesus. On the other hand, to deny that he believed the Prophets would have seriously impaired his influence with the Jews. Agrippa II, therefore, parried Paul's appeal.

"In a short time you will persuade me to become a Christian." At the cost of giving up a familiar and impressive text, it must be admitted that the presently-accepted Greek text cannot possibly be translated as the KJV has it, "almost thou persuadest me to be a Christian."[42] The Greek phrase is very difficult, and, literally translated, says, "In a little[43] you are persuading me to make a Christian." If we had been there and heard Agrippa II's tone of voice, and seen the expression on his face, we could better understand his reply.

- It is possible that he was being sarcastic and ironical, and is rejecting in disdain Paul's appeal that he become a Christian. If so, the translation of the RSV would be correct,

---

[42] The accepted Greek text used by the KJV might be so translated. It had "become" rather than "made" as the verb in this verse, and in the next verse that text had a different word for "much" than does the present, improved Nestle Greek text.

[43] Literally, the Greek words are "in a little," and might mean "in a few (more) words," or "with a little (more) effort," or "in a little more time." The word supplied after "little" depends on the context.

"In a short time, you think to make me a Christian!"[44]

- It is possible, on the other hand, that Agrippa was sincere and serious. If so, the ASV translators are correct, "With but a little (more) persuasion, you would make me a Christian."

"Christian," the name first used at Antioch,[45] had come to be widely accepted. Agrippa II was familiar with it. It is difficult, however, to determine how he was using the word. If he is rejecting Paul's appeal, then he likely used the term in a contemptuous way. If he is serious, he would have been using the name with respect and reverence.

26:29 – *And Paul said, "I would to God, that whether in a short or long time, not only you, but also all who hear me this day, might become such as I am, except for these chains."*

And Paul *said*, "I would to God. In this last appeal the fervency of Paul's yearning for Agrippa II's conversion spent its force. "I would to God" means "I pray to God ...."

That whether in a short or long time. This was a direct answer to Agrippa II's words "in a little." Paul is saying, "With one sermon or a hundred, with little effort or great,[46] it is my prayer that I might win you to Christ." Many commentators have expressed their opinion that Paul's answer to Agrippa II is evidence that he was serious in the reply he made to Paul (verse 28).

Not only you, but also all who hear me this day, might become such as I am. Paul would have Agrippa II and all the others, whether tribunes or city officials, governor or commoner, to be Christians – but he would have them to be free of the persecution and bonds which he had had to endure. "Such as I am" – that is, pardoned and at peace with God and man, with a hope stretching beyond the grave, and an actual present participation in the powers of the eternal world. This is what Paul was desiring for them!

Except for these chains." Paul probably held up his shackled wrist at this point. The words show that all the time Paul has been preaching (since 26:1), his wrists have been manacled. He was brought into the court chained, perhaps after Roman fashion, to a soldier or soldiers who kept guard over him. Paul wanted these men to be Christians just like he was, except for the chains.

---

[44] This seems to be the way the NASB translators understood Agrippa II's response, too.

[45] Acts 11:26.

[46] If we read "great" (*megalō*) rather than "much" (*poliō*), it is probably not a reference to time as the NASB has it.

5) Agreement about Paul's innocence. 26:30-32

26:30 – *And the king arose and the governor and Bernice, and those who were sitting with them,*

And the king arose. With this gesture Agrippa II closed the interview. He had decided two things: Paul was innocent, and that he did not wish to face further appeals to his own responsibilities before God and Christ. Paul had sought to vindicate the gospel rather than himself. He had succeeded in winning a verdict for himself, but not for the gospel.

And the governor and Bernice, and those who were sitting with them. The king's action led the others to follow his example, which also signaled the end of the hearing.

26:31 – *and when they had drawn aside, they* **began** *talking to one another, saying, "This man is not doing anything worthy of death or imprisonment."*

And when they had drawn aside, they *began* **talking to one another, saying.** By retreating from the audience room, they may escape the appeal to their souls which Paul is making. But they cannot get his case out of their minds, for they continue talking about it later.

"This man is not doing anything worthy of death or imprisonment." It is clear to Festus, Agrippa II, and Bernice that Paul was completely innocent in the eyes of Roman law. Since Paul's arrest at the close of his third missionary journey, Luke has given the testimony of Lysias,[47] Felix,[48] Festus,[49] and now Agrippa. All concurred that Paul was innocent. Luke is obviously emphasizing this additional witness given to Paul's innocence. The others were Romans; this new statement of Paul's innocence is given by a Jewish king, an authority on Jewish affairs. Such testimony would come in handy when, and if ever, they presented their case in Nero's supreme court. No one will be able to sustain the charge that Paul is a lawless man, a revolutionary dangerous to Rome, in the light of all these testimonies to his innocence.

26:32 – *And Agrippa said to Festus, "This man might have been set free if he had not appealed to Caesar."*

And Agrippa said to Festus, "This man might have been set free. It was obvious that Paul had violated no law and deserved neither death nor imprisonment. If there were no other circumstances involved, he certainly could have been set free then and there. But instead of going free, as the royal party lead leaves the audience room, the soldiers led Paul back to jail. Perhaps if he had gone free his life would have been exposed to new assassination attempts by the Jews, and he may never have reached Rome. As it is, he soon will be on his way.

---

[47] Acts 23:29

[48] Acts 24:1ff.

[49] Acts 25:26-27.

If he had not appealed to Caesar." Paul had appealed, and the appeal had been accepted; the legal processes had to be carried out and the appeal carried through. No one but Caesar could convict or acquit him now. Both Festus and Agrippa II know that, but both have declared their belief in his innocence.

We may suppose that Festus, with the aid of Agrippa II, composed the letter to the emperor explaining the charges the Jews made against the prisoner, and also perhaps included a recommendation that Paul be dismissed. If there was such a statement, it makes it easier to explain the mildness of Paul's treatment when he finally reached Rome this first time.[50]

> It is not without interest to note the subsequent relations between Festus and Agrippa, during the short government of the former, as showing a continuance of the same *entente cordiale* as that which we have seen in this chapter.
>
> Agrippa took up his abode at Jerusalem in the old palace of the Hasmonean (Maccabean) princes. It commanded a view of the city, and, from the banquet hall which he had erected on its roof, he could look down upon the courts of the Temple and see the priests sacrificing as he sat at meat. The Jews looked upon this as a profanation, and built a wall which blocked the view both from the king's palace and from the tower where the Roman soldiers used to stand guard during the festivals. This was regarded by Festus as an insult, and he ordered the wall to be pulled down. The people of Jerusalem, however, obtained leave to send an embassy to Rome. They secured the support of Poppaea, already half a proselyte, after the fashion of the times among the women of the higher class at Rome, and by the strange irony of history, the Temple of Jehovah was rescued from profanation by the concubine of Nero (Josephs, *Ant.* XX.8.11).
>
> Agrippa continued to display the taste for building which was the hereditary characteristic of his house. Caesarea Philippi [his capital city] was enlarged and named Neronias, in honor of the emperor. A vast theater was erected at Berytus (Beyrout) and adorned with statues. The Temple [at Jerusalem] was at last finished, and the 18,000 workmen who were thus thrown out of work were employed in re-paving the city with marble. The stateliness of the Temple ritual was enhanced by the permission which the king gave to the Levites of the choir, in spite of the remonstrance of the priests, that they should wear a linen ephod. Once again we note the irony of history. The king who thus had the glory of completing what the founder of his dynasty had begun, bringing both structure and ritual to a perfection never before attained, saw, within ten years, the capture and destruction of the Temple (Josephus, *Ant.* XX.8.7).[51]

When Festus died after a short, approximately 2-year term in office, Albinus was sent to succeed him,[52] and then Gessius Florus followed Albinus into the governorship of Judea. Both these successors to Festus were extremely cruel and ruthless, and during their administrations Jewish attitudes hardened until, in AD 66, the Jews revolted. It was this revolt that resulted in the destruction of Jerusalem in AD 70

---

[50] Acts 28:16,30,31.

[51] Plumptre, *op. cit.*, p.405.

[52] It was under the governorship of Albinus that James, the brother of the Lord, was executed.

Drawing by Horace Knowles
from the British and Foreign Bible Society

4. The Voyage to Rome. 27:1-28:15

a. From Caesarea to Sidon. 27:1-3

27:1 – *And when it was decided that we should sail for Italy, they proceeded to deliver Paul and some other prisoners to a centurion of the Augustan cohort named Julius.*

And when it was decided. The deciding was done by Festus, in consequence of Paul's appeal to Caesar. When chapter 27 begins, all the plans and arrangements for the voyage to Rome had been completed and the time for sailing had been fixed. We have no way of determining how long Paul was a prisoner in Caesarea after his appeal, but the time was probably not long. Paul had long wanted to go to Rome to preach. Jesus had appeared to Paul at night back during Paul's imprisonment in Jerusalem and told him he would testify at Rome. He now begins his long-anticipated trip to the capital of the empire, though not, perhaps, as he had imagined, some years before, that he would make the trip.

That we should sail for Italy. Thus begins the longest "we" section in the book of Acts. Paul's arrest at the close of the third missionary journey had kept him somewhat apart from Luke through the intervening years, but now they are together again. At Acts 24:27, we suggested that Paul's two-year imprisonment in Caesarea was when Luke was doing research for his history books, and perhaps even publishing volume one, his Gospel.[1]

Whether Luke went along with Paul on this voyage to Rome at his own expense, or whether he went at the expense of the Roman government, is not told. Some think Luke was allowed to go as an attendant or slave of Paul, which was a common practice in those days. Ramsay's note is to the effect that both Luke and Aristarchus (verse 2) traveled as Paul's slaves:

> [Luke and Aristarchus were] not merely performing the duties of slaves ... but actually passing as slaves. In this way not merely had Paul faithful friends always beside him; his importance in the eyes of the centurion was much enhanced, and that was of great importance. The narrative clearly implies that Paul enjoyed much respect during this voyage, such as a penniless traveler without a servant would never receive either in the first century or the nineteenth.[2]

Dale thinks Luke, as a physician, would have been a welcome passenger regardless:

> The officers and crew would have been glad to have such a man aboard. The amazing notations of ancient seafaring by the historian and physician Luke may indicate that he had been a physician who had sailed in that capacity [as ship's physician] upon many an occasion. Some have suggested that this was his life work at one time (before he became a preacher of the gospel and a companion of Paul).[3]

---

[1] There are those who believe that Luke did not publish his Gospel until after he reached Rome, even though the research was completed before Paul's Caesarean imprisonment was over.

[2] Ramsay, *St. Paul the Traveller and Roman Citizen*, p.316.

[3] Dale, *op. cit.*, p.368.

The account of Paul's voyage to Rome is like no other story in all the Bible. The reader's attention is directed, not to spiritual truths or acts of devotion, but rather to such mundane things as ships and seas, winds and waves, islands, towns, and harbors. Altogether Luke gives a description of 1st century ships and seamanship surpassing anything else in extant Greek and Roman literature. A fascinating story of adventure, it stands also as a descriptive masterpiece. Its nautical descriptions are authentic to the last detail.

We are glad Luke wrote as he did. Elsewhere in Acts he had presented the apostles as men devoted to a single, high, and holy purpose – saints in the truest sense of the word. Saints, however, are often thought to be impractical dreamers, helpless in the face of hard facts and physical emergencies. Whether or not it was Luke's original intent to do so, this chapter answers the challenge that "saints are sissies" finally and firmly. It tells of a man who began a voyage as a prisoner among other prisoners, but who gradually assumed a position of respect and even command. And Paul's cool courage, common sense, and resourcefulness set him apart again and again under increasingly dangerous circumstances. That he acknowledged God as the source of every virtue, and that he completed the journey still a prisoner, diminishes his stature as a hero not one iota, but rather emphasizes the fact that a saint of this kind is the best possible man to have at hand in any emergency.

The chain of circumstances by which God accomplished His purpose of having Paul preach the gospel at Rome was nearly complete. The plots of the unbelieving Jews had resulted in Paul's arrest; the quick thinking and acting of the Roman officer, Claudius Lysias, had prevented Paul's death. The avarice of Felix, the indecision of Festus, the prudence of Paul, and the provision made by the empire for the protection of its citizens had all operated together to keep Paul in custody and bring him to the sea voyage that was to end in Italy.

Several reference books are helpful to understanding chapter 27. One of these is James Smith's *The Voyage and Shipwreck of St. Paul*.[4] The other is William Ramsay's *St. Paul the Traveller and Roman Citizen*.[5]

They proceeded to deliver Paul and some other prisoners. The exact position of these "other prisoners" is disputed. Some suggest they were men who, like Paul, had appealed to Caesar and were being sent to Rome for trial before the emperor.[6] Because the word "other" is *heteros* (i.e., others of a different kind), in some fashion these other prisoners are of a different class than Paul. The difference may have been that Paul was a Christian whereas the others were not, or the difference may have been that they were already condemned men, being sent to fight in the arena.

To a centurion of the Augustan cohort named Julius. Howson, with some degree of probability, considers that Julius may be identified with Julius Priscus, who in later years

---

[4] James Smith, *The Voyage and Shipwreck of St. Paul* (London: Longmans, Green & Co., 1880).

[5] William Ramsay, *St. Paul the Traveller and Roman Citizen* (Grand Rapids: Baker Book House, 1960).

[6] It was common to send prisoners from Judea and other provinces to Rome, either for trial or for fighting in the arena. See Nathaniel Lardner's *The Credibility of The Gospel History* (London, 1727-57), Part 1, X.10.248-249; and Josephus, *Life*, III.

was prefect of the Praetorian Guard under the emperor Vitellius.[7] However, it must be remembered that Julius was a common name. Centurions – i.e., officers over a hundred soldiers – receive uniformly favorable treatment in Scripture.[8]

According to Luke's narrative, Julius had a body of men under his command on this voyage to Rome. Whether the whole 100 were with him, or only a detail or two, the record does not make plain. A cohort has been explained in notes at Acts 10:1 as being a subdivision of a Roman legion. Several different attempts have been made to explain the term translated "Augustan" (*sebastēs*). (1) The cohort may have consisted of soldiers recruited in Sebaste (i.e., Samaria). Josephus speaks of a detachment of Sebastene cavalry, and there may have been a corresponding band of foot soldiers.[9] Against this view is the fact that the word translated "Augustan" and the word translated "Sebastene" are different words. (2) The Praetorian Guard, which was the emperor's special bodyguard, might have been called the "Augustan cohort" since the emperor had the title "Augustus." (3) "The Augustan cohort" might refer to a cohort of officer-couriers (Latin, *frumentarii*[10]) whom the emperor detailed to various governors and provincial army leaders with personal messages and instructions. At some time, perhaps as early as Octavian's time, perhaps as late as Hadrian's, these officer-couriers came to be called Peregrini.[11] (4) The title "Augustan" might be given to any legion, cohort, or battalion "for valor." If this suggestion is correct, none of the first three suggestions would necessarily be true.

Having studied through the various options, this commentator inclines to (3) as being most likely correct. Perhaps Julius, as the emperor's personal escort, had accompanied Festus as the new governor came into the province. Since Festus has been installed, Julius is now returning to Rome.

27:2 – *And embarking in an Adramyttian ship, which was about to sail to the regions along the coast of Asia, we put out to sea, accompanied by Aristarchus, a Macedonian of Thessalonica.*

And embarking in an Adramyttian ship. "Embarking" means to go on board. The port from which they sailed is not specified, but it was likely from Caesarea itself. Adramyttium (the modern name is Edremit) was a harbor city on the coast of Mysia, opposite the island of Lesbos. It was an important ship-building center in the 1st century, and probably was the ship's home port. Very likely this vessel was en route to some final stop before the long winter ahead set in and made sailing impossible. The reader will benefit from having a map of the Mediterranean for reference in order to follow this thrilling account of Paul's voyage to Rome.

Which was about to sail to the regions along the coast of Asia. This language indicates

---

[7] Tacitus, *History*, II.92, IV.11.

[8] Matthew 8:5, 27:54; Acts 10:1, 23:17.

[9] Josephus, *Antiquities*, XX.6.1; XIX.9.2

[10] The name *frumentarii* ("pertaining to grain") came from their original work of administering the grain supply for the empire. As time passed, their sphere of duties was enlarged.

[11] See additional notes on the Peregrini at Acts 28:16.

the ship was a coasting vessel, which would stop at various ports along its way back home and north towards Adramyttium. There would have been little direct commerce between Caesarea and Rome, and the voyage had therefore to be made, now in one ship, then in another. Julius likely anticipated that he would find a ship bound for Rome in one of these ports. And if it didn't work out as Julius anticipated, and they had to stay with the Adramyttian ship until it arrived at its home port, they could always go overland on the great Egnatian Way toward Rome.

We put out to sea, accompanied by Aristarchus, a Macedonian of Thessalonica. Aristarchus, like Luke, had journeyed with Paul to Jerusalem as they brought the offering for the Jerusalem Christians.[12] He is now with them as they start for Rome.[13] In Colossians 4:10, written from the first Roman imprisonment, Aristarchus is called a "fellow-prisoner." If this description is taken literally, then we understand that for some cause not mentioned in the Scriptures, Aristarchus had also been arrested in Judea and is now being sent to Rome as a prisoner, perhaps also on appeal to Caesar. If we take the designation "fellow-prisoner" in a figurative sense (and this is the preference of this commentator), then we understand that Aristarchus is traveling home to Thessalonica, and that he leaves the party after it reaches Myra, crossing the province of Asia until he can travel the Egnatian Way to Thessalonica. After arriving in Thessalonica, Aristarchus will later go on to Rome, where he will join Paul during the latter's first Roman imprisonment.[14]

27:3 – *And the next day we put in at Sidon; and Julius treated Paul with consideration and allowed him to go to his friends and receive care.*

And the next day we put in at Sidon. Sidon[15] was about 70 miles north of Caesarea, and the voyage could easily be accomplished under favorable sailing weather in twenty-four hours. The coasting vessel possibly put in here to load or unload some cargo.

And Julius treated Paul with consideration. The word translated "consideration" is *philanthrōpos*, and speaks of "love for man;" that is, Paul was treated humanely and kindly. Julius' attitude was, "Can I make you comfortable?" Why Paul, a prisoner, was given such consideration and courtesy is a matter of conjecture. If Luke and Aristarchus who are traveling with Paul are passed as slaves, then he is given respect as a gentleman. Or perhaps Julius had received orders from Festus or Agrippa II to treat Paul courteously. At any rate, it seems that Paul received favors from Julius that the other prisoners did not receive.

---

[12] Acts 20:4.

[13] Because Aristarchus seems not to accompany Paul all the way to Rome on this voyage, some suggest he was simply an independent passenger who paid his fare and traveled on this ship to be with Paul and Luke.

[14] "Fellow-prisoner" is used figuratively at times. In Romans 16:7 Paul calls Andronicus and Junius his "fellow-prisoners," and this may be an example of a figurative use, though some have insisted that at some time before Romans was written they and Paul had been imprisoned together. In the epistle to Philemon, verses 23-24, Epaphras is called a "fellow-prisoner," yet in the same letter he does not describe Aristarchus in that same way, even though Philemon is written from the first Roman imprisonment, just as is Colossians.

[15] Sidon was named in connection with Herod Agrippa I in Acts 12:20.

And allowed him to go to his friends. The "friends" at Sidon were probably Christians who had seen him when he passed through Phoenicia, as in Acts 15:3, or on other journeys. When the church at Sidon was founded, or by whom, the book of Acts does not say. Christians fleeing the persecution that followed the death of Stephen may have been responsible.[16] If Paul is chained to a soldier during this voyage, he would have accompanied Paul ashore.

And receive care. Literally, "to avail himself of their care." The Greek suggests the idea of provision of personal needs, clothing and the like, for the voyage. After spending two years in confinement, we can imagine that such provision would be both necessary and acceptable. Some suppose, since the word was commonly used among medical writers for the care and attention required by the sick, that Paul needed medical attention, and that Julius gave Paul liberty to go ashore where this could best be administered by Luke. It is well to note, as in other instances, the favorable impression that Paul's conduct made on official persons who came in contact with him.[17]

    b.   Under the lee of Cyprus to Myra. 27:4-6

27:4 – *And from there we put out to sea and sailed under the shelter of Cyprus because the winds were contrary.*

And from there we put out to sea. The ship remained at anchor in the port of Sidon long enough to transact her business.

And sailed under the shelter of Cyprus because the winds were contrary. The ship headed north after leaving the harbor at Sidon. At some other time of year, when the prevailing winds blew from a different direction, they might have sailed directly from Sidon to Mysia, leaving Cyprus on the right.[18] However, during this time of year when it was getting late in the sailing season,[19] the prevailing winds, called Etesian winds, blow from the west and northwest.[20] As the ship sails northward, it would sail past the east side of Cyprus, and while near Cyprus they would be sheltered from the prevailing winds making sailing somewhat easier.

27:5 – *And when we had sailed through the sea along the coast of Cilicia and Pamphylia, we landed at Myra in Lycia.*

And when we had sailed through the sea along the coast of Cilicia and Pamphylia.

---

[16] Acts 11:19.

[17] Compare Acts 18:14, 19:31, 19:37.

[18] In fact, this is just what Paul had done on an earlier voyage from Patara to Tyre. See Acts 21:1.

[19] Acts 27:9.

[20] Smith, *op. cit.*, p.66,74, quotes Admiral De Saumarez as writing from near Cyprus, "The westerly winds invariably prevail at this season," and M. DePages, a French navigator, as saying, "The winds from the west which prevail in these places [i.e., Cyprus] forced us to run to the north."

Once they have passed the island of Cyprus, there was a stretch of open sea to be crossed between Cyprus and the southern coast of Cilicia. Once they came near to the coast of Cilicia, they would have begun working slowly westward, just offshore first of the country of Cilicia, and then of Pamphylia. The voyage would have been helped by local land breezes and by the steady westward current which runs along the southern coast of Asia Minor. Ramsay writes, "The Adramyttian ship crept from point to point up the coast, taking advantage of every opportunity to make a few miles, and lying at anchor when the westerly wind made progress impossible."[21]

We landed at Myra in Lycia. Lycia was a province in the southwestern part of Asia Minor. Pamphylia was on its eastern boundary, and Caria (Asia) was on its western side. Phrygia and Pisidia lay to the north. The city of Myra, situated on the river Andriacus, lay some two miles inland from its harbor Andriaca. The city stood on a hill where two valleys met, and its harbor grew in importance once Roman grain ships started sailing across the Mediterranean. The ruins found here, including an elaborately decorated theater and rock-hewn tombs with many bas-reliefs and inscriptions, are among the most impressive in that part of Asia Minor.

The Western text gives fifteen days as the time spent in sailing across the open sea from Cyprus to Myra, a reasonable estimate if the ship had to hug the south coast of Asia Minor for a good part of the voyage.

27:6 – *And there the centurion found an Alexandrian ship sailing for Italy, and he put us aboard it.*

And there the centurion found an Alexandrian ship sailing for Italy. The first part of Paul's voyage to Rome was completed at Myra. About 300 years earlier, Egypt had become the bread basket of Rome, but the grain grown in Egypt had to be shipped to Rome. A whole fleet of ships was devoted to this trade, the fleet being organized under the department of state and thus directly responsible to the Roman government. It is clear from verse 38 that this Alexandrian ship was one of these grain ships on her way to Rome. The ships sailed out of Alexandria, and when the prevailing winds in the Mediterranean were westerly (as they are late in the sailing season), they would sail north, passing the west end of the island of Cyprus, and put into harbor at Myra. The voyage from Alexandria took a week or ten days unless they were forced by adverse westerly winds to sail around the southern and eastern ends of Cyprus, and along the shore of Asia, just as Paul's ship had been doing. The grain ship was in port at Myra, and once her sailors offered prayers to the deity that protected their voyage on towards Rome, they would weigh anchor and sail past Cnidus, and if possible take advantage of the shelter of numerous islands in the Aegean Sea south of Greece until they could reach Sicily, and then sail to Puteoli.

These Alexandrian ships were very large and were steered by two broad oars, one on each side of the stern, and one large mast with the huge sail fastened to an enormous yard arm. Another sail was often seen in the forepart of the ship.[22] One consequence of such a design is that in storms the strain was concentrated in a relatively small area, and the ships

---

[21] Ramsay, *St. Paul the Traveller and Roman Citizen*, p.317.

[22] See a picture of one of these boats on the cover of this book.

tended to spring leaks rather quickly. From the descriptions of such ships found in ancient literature, it has been estimated they could carry between ten and eleven hundred tons. The design was especially suitable for running with the wind, but they could sail almost into the wind, perhaps coming within even seven points of the wind's direction. Fully loaded, with a good breeze favoring, they could make about seven knots an hour.[23]

And he put us aboard it. If Julius was one of the Peregrini, he would have immediate authority to commandeer a part of the grain ship for transporting the prisoners he was escorting to Rome. It was a common to have such passengers aboard the grain ships.

        c. To Cnidus and under the lee of Crete. 27:7

27:7 – *And when we had sailed slowly for a good many days, and with difficulty had arrived off Cnidus, since the wind did not permit us* **to go** *farther, we sailed under the shelter of Crete, off Salmone;*

And when we had sailed slowly for a good many days. The shoreline of Asia Minor from Myra westward tends in a more northwesterly direction, and so the sailing was slow because they would have less shelter from the northwest wind than they had from the coastline on their voyage from off the coast of Cilicia to Myra. The "many days" may have been two or even three weeks.

And with difficulty had arrived off Cnidus. Cnidus was a harbor on the Carian peninsula called Triopium. To reach this place they have coasted along Lycia and gone through the straits between Rhodes and the mainland. It was a distance of about 130 miles from Myra to Cnidus, and with a good wind they could have made it in twenty-four hours. It must have been slow sailing indeed.

Since the wind did not permit us *to go* **farther.** At Cnidus the coast of Asia Minor trends away to the north. Once a ship passed Cnidus, all shelter from the land is gone; now, the ship would be exposed to the full force of the Etesian winds. Facing such adverse conditions, the ship's captain had to choose between alternatives.

- Cnidus had two harbors, so the ship could put into one of them and spend the winter.
- If there were still a few days left in the sailing season, they might wait in one of the harbors for a wind that would allow them to sail through the islands until they arrived off Cythera, an island off the southern end of Greece. From there, they could sail on toward Sicily and Rome.
- They could attempt to continue the voyage by sailing south until they came under the shelter of the island of Crete. Then by sailing along the southern shore of that island, they could gain another hundred miles toward Rome, with the possibility that by that time the winds will have changed and will be blowing from a direction that would permit the rest of the voyage to Rome. This is the choice made by the sailors.

---

[23] I.e., 8-9 miles per hour. Greater details about the Alexandrian grain ships are given in Conybeare and Howson, *op. cit.*, p.623ff.

We sailed under the shelter of Crete, off Salmone. Salmone was a cape on the eastern end of Crete. After rounding this cape, the ship began sailing in a westerly direction. By this route they have avoided the open sea west of Cnidus, but even after they have tried this tack in hopes the wind would change, they find that it had not.

      d. At Fair Havens. 27:8-15

27:8 – *and with difficulty sailing past it we came to a certain place called Fair Havens, near which was the city of Lasea.*

And with difficulty sailing past it. The difficulty arose from being in the shelter of the island. While they were sheltered from the northwest wind, that same shelter left them with little wind by which to move their ship. Along the south side of Crete, they would have had the same difficult sailing conditions they had had along the coast of Asia Minor.

We came to a certain place called Fair Havens, near which was the city of Lasea. Fair Havens was nothing more than a small bay. In fact, the nearest town was two hours' walk to the east, called Lasea. The comparative obscurity of the town has led to a variety of readings at this place in the manuscripts – Lassoea, Alassa, Thalassa, and other forms. Pliny speaks of a town in Crete named Lasos, which some think is an alternate spelling for the same town.[24] In 1856, archaeologists found remains of buildings, columns, and the walls and foundations of temples[25] at a place still known as Lasea by the natives on the island. After the ship rounded Cape Salmone, it managed to cover several miles, but Fair Havens was the last convenient shelter before they came to Cape Matala. So, having gone as far west as they can go against a northwest wind, they put in and waited for the wind to change directions.

27:9 – *And when considerable time had passed and the voyage was now dangerous, since even the fast was already over,* **Paul** *began to admonish them,*

And when considerable time had passed. About five miles west of Fair Havens[26] lies Cape Matala, beyond which the south coast of Crete trends away suddenly to the north, thus removing all protection from the northwest wind. This is why the ship waited at Fair Havens for the wind to change. The "considerable time," measured by the common experience of sailing vessels waiting for a favorable wind, may mean one or two weeks.[27]

And the voyage was now dangerous. Sailors on the Mediterranean called the days between September 14 and November 11 the "dangerous season;" it was a "sail-at-your-own-

---

[24] Pliny, *Natural History*, IV.59.

[25] Smith, *op. cit.*, p.82, and Appendix III on p.268.

[26] The name "Fair Havens" still survives under the modern name Kali Limniones.

[27] It is more natural to apply the phrase "time passed" to only the time spent at Fair Havens rather than to the whole time elapsed since they had sailed away from Caesarea.

risk" period.[28] Then, from November 11 until about March 10, all navigation on the Mediterranean ceased.[29] The voyage has taken so long that they are now in the "dangerous season" for sailing, and every day they have to wait makes it more apparent that they are not going to complete the voyage to Italy this sailing season.

Since even the fast was already over. The "fast" was another name for the Jewish Day of Atonement. As fixed by the Law of Moses, the Day of Atonement fell on the tenth day of Tishri.[30] In the year AD 59, Atonement fell on October 5; in AD 60 it would have been September 23.[31] It is already October as they wait in the bay of Fair Havens for a change of wind, meaning that they are right in the middle of the dangerous season for sailing.

Paul *began* to admonish them. Ramsay suggests that a ship's council was held.[32] What is a prisoner doing speaking out at a ship's council? Perhaps he speaks as an experienced sailor,[33] or perhaps it is indicative of the respect in which he is held. "Admonish" is used in medical writers of the advice that a doctor gives his patient.

27:10 – *and said to them, "Men, I perceive that the voyage will certainly be* **attended** *with damage and great loss, not only of the cargo and the ship, but also of our lives."*

And said to them. The voyage thus far had been so slow that weeks had passed since they left Myra. They were nearing the time when the Mediterranean was closed to sailing. They are going to have to spend the winter on this island, but the question was where? Should they plan to stay where they were, or try to reach a more sheltered harbor? Paul's advice (found by comparing the language here with verse 21) was to remain here at Fair Havens.

"Men, I perceive that the voyage will certainly be *attended* with damage and great loss. Here is the reason for his advice to stay where they were. Any further sailing will cost them injury inflicted by the elements, and loss of cargo, maybe the ship, and even lives of the men on board. "I perceive" represents the result of experience and observation, not revelation, but the words came very near being fulfilled to the letter.

As we study the last few chapters of Acts, we are left with the impression that God is turning the direction of Paul, more and more, over to general providence. In earlier chap-

---

[28] They did not sail unless absolutely necessary during the dangerous season. According to Philo in his *Life of Moses*, no prudent man went to sea after the Fast.

[29] Vegetius, *On Military Affairs*, IV.39.

[30] Leviticus 16:29, 23:27; Numbers 29:7; Josephus, *Antiquities*, XIV.16.4. The Jewish month of Tishri is roughly comparable to our September or October.

[31] It should be noted that Paul is using Jewish time here (as he does in Acts 20:16; 1 Corinthians 16:8; and Acts 18-21 KJV). Or perhaps Luke uses Jewish time in his account of what Paul said. Rather than speaking of sailing being dangerous from the Ides of November to the Ides of March, Luke uses the Jewish means of reckoning. In Jewish language, the sailing season was reckoned from the feast of Passover until the feast of Tabernacles (i.e., five days after the Day of Atonement). This language should not be construed to necessarily mean that Paul still observed the rituals and ceremonies of the Day of Atonement, especially not in the light of the epistle to the Hebrews.

[32] Ramsay, *St. Paul the Traveller and Roman Citizen*, p.322.

[33] 2 Corinthians 11:25.

ters, Paul was often led by the Spirit and by visions. Now, more and more, it seems that Paul is left to exercise his own good judgment.[34]

Not only of the cargo and the ship, but also of our lives." The ship's "cargo" was wheat (verse 38). Paul had assurance that he was to preach at Rome (Acts 23:11), but he had not yet been assured of the safety of his fellow-voyagers; hence, he is concerned for their safety. The harbor they are in may have had drawbacks (verse 12), but they had best remain there, is his advice. When all is said and done, no lives were actually lost (verse 44), but everything else Paul warned them about came true. He was not far wrong in his opinion.

27:11 – *But the centurion was more persuaded by the pilot and the captain of the ship, than by what was being said by Paul.*

But the centurion was more persuaded by the pilot and the captain of the ship. The "pilot" was the helmsman, or steersman, who occupied a conspicuous place on the stern of ancient ships; he steered it and gave directions to the crew. Some versions translate the other term as "captain" on the supposition that if this were one of the grain ships, it belonged to the state, not to some private owner. But there is nothing to keep us from translating it "owner" on the supposition that the ship was merely leased to the state. The "owner" would own both the ship and the cargo. He would have paid for it in Egypt, and would not be repaid (with profit) until he delivered the wheat in Puteoli. He had the general command of the ship since it was his property, but he had employed "the pilot" to direct and manage it and the crew.

This verse harmonizes with the idea that the centurion is the ranking Roman official on board. Perhaps he is presiding at the ship's council, but he does not make the final decision. It is a case of majority rule, as the next verse shows.

Than by what was being said by Paul. The centurion's conduct was understable. Perhaps he gave thought to what would be said of him in Rome if it was learned that he followed the advice of a prisoner rather than the judgment of the pilot and owner of the vessel. And he naturally tended to weigh more heavily the advice of those who had been sailors for years rather than the advice of a prisoner who may or may not have had any real sailing experience.

27:12 – *And because the harbor was not suitable for wintering, the majority reached a decision to put out to sea from there, if somehow they could reach Phoenix, a harbor of Crete, facing southwest and northwest, and spend the winter there.*

And because the harbor was not suitable for wintering. The Fair Havens bay, while it gave immediate shelter from the northwest gales, was open to all the southern points of the

---

[34] Note these parallels: (1) In the same way, the church was established and led by a miracle. As the years pass, God seems to employ the overtly miraculous less and less; consequently, the church must depend more and more on the natural guidance of divine providence. (2) Compare also the instructions which were given early in the church's history (Matthew 10:17-20) concerning how one would answer if hauled into court with the later instructions about giving thought beforehand to what would be said (1 Peter 3:15). It seems that little by little the miraculous is diminishing.

compass.[35] It would put a strain on Lasea, too, to show hospitality to 276 people through the winter.

The majority reached a decision to put out to sea from there. It appears they took a vote. Since further sailing would be at the risk of all their lives, it is reasonable to think all on board were allowed a part in reaching the decision. The majority voted to try to make it to a more suitable harbor for the winter.

If somehow they could reach Phoenix. The risk was admittedly great, as the Greek, "on the chance that somehow they could reach Phoenix," shows; the majority was by no means sure they would reach the harbor farther up the coast. There was no thought of attempting to continue on to Italy this sailing season, only of making a more suitable Cretan port.

A harbor of Crete, facing northeast and southeast. The harbor which they wished to reach is regularly identified with the modern harbor of Lutro, but the identification is somewhat disputed. The Greek (as the margin shows) reads, "looking down the southwest wind and down the northwest."

- If Lutro is the place intended, it is described from the standpoint of the sailors as they come into the harbor. The harbor opens to the east, and you are almost facing the wind as you enter it. Entering the harbor, you are sailing in a westerly direction, with either a southwest or a northwest wind blowing at you.[36]
- A second choice for the location of the harbor is on the west side of the same Muros peninsula, where there is a harbor that opens to the west. It even has the name Phinika (which is rather close to the Biblical Phoenix), and a sailor would be facing in an easterly direction as he entered the harbor. "Looking down the southwest wind and down the northwest" would be a description of the harbor from the standpoint of a man on land, as he looked out into the harbor, since he would be facing west.[37]

This commentator favors the Lutro choice. Phinika opens to the west, and consequently is exposed to the most furious winter storms. That is, Phinika would not seem to provide the winter-related safety and security that the sailors were seeking. Lutro is the only secure harbor from winter winds on the south coast of Crete.

And spend the winter *there*. The harbor at Phoenix was more sheltered than the one at Fair Havens, and the nearby town would better be able to handle such a large number of people through the winter months.

27:13 – *And when a moderate south wind came up, supposing that they had gained their purpose, they weighed anchor and* **began** *sailing along Crete,* **close** *inshore.*

---

[35] Smith, *op. cit.*, p.84.

[36] Readers wishing to do further research will find arguments favoring Lutro as the harbor in Ramsay, *St. Paul the Traveller*, Alford's *Greek Testament*, Smith (*op. cit.*, p.87-88), the article "Fair Havens" in *Hastings' Dictionary of the Bible*, and Plumptre, *op. cit.*

[37] Arguments defending Phinika as the harbor may be seen in Hackett, *op. cit.*, the article on "Crete" in *Hastings' Dictionary of the Bible,* and Bruce, *op. cit.*

And when a moderate south wind came up. Fair Havens was east of Cape Matala, and Phoenix lay to the west of the cape. Once the cape had been passed, the ship would have no chance of making Phoenix in the face of a west or northwest wind. As they waited in Fair Havens, the stormy northwest wind ceased, and a gentle breeze came up from the south.

Supposing that they had gained their purpose. A south wind would be quite favorable for sailing west or northwest from Fair Havens toward Phoenix. "The words 'thinking they had obtained their purpose' express the thought that they were 'as good as there' when they started running this soft wind from the south."[38]

They weighed anchor and *began* sailing along Crete, close *inshore*. It was about five miles from Fair Havens to Cape Matala, and about 35 miles from there to Phoenix. If the south wind lasted just three or four hours, they could sail the distance and put the ship in the harbor for the winter. The tense of the Greek verb "sailing" implies that they were in the act of doing this when the storm (verse 14) burst upon them. The adverb "close inshore" is a comparative degree adverb, and tells us they were closer to the shore than usual for sailing this stretch of water.

27:14 – *But before very long there rushed down from the land a violent wind, called Euraquilo;*

But before very long there rushed down from the land a violent wind. After they rounded Cape Matala, suddenly the wind changed. Such sudden changes of wind seem to be a common occurrence in this area. A violent wind (the Greek says, "a typhoon wind") out of the northeast, sprang up, and blew down upon them from Mount Ida.[39] There was no way to go back to Fair Havens because of the direction of the wind, and there was no way to continue their voyage toward Phoenix because of the violence of the storm.

Called Euraquilo. That Luke uses the word "called" suggests he is using a word he heard from the sailors. They recognized this type of storm as an old enemy, and they had a name for it. Euraquilo is an "east-north-east" wind,[40] the name being a combination of the Greek *euros* ("east wind") and the Latin *aquilo* ("north wind").

27:15 – *and when the ship was caught in it, and could not face the wind, we gave way to it, and let ourselves be driven along.*

And when the ship was caught *in it*, and could not face the wind. The Greek here is vivid: the ship was not able to "look the wind eye to eye." As the ship tried to sail in a northwesterly direction, this wind would have caught it almost broadside, blowing so violently that the ship was being blown sideways. The pilot could not manage to steer the

---

[38] McGarvey, op. cit., p.265.

[39] "Rush down from Mt. Ida" is exactly right, for the mountains of Crete are over 7000 feet high.

[40] The KJV has "Euroclydon" (a word that means "blown wave" or "wind (blown) wave"), but that reading is not well attested in the manuscripts. The spelling of the NASB is much to be preferred.

ship in the direction they wanted to go.

We gave way *to it*, and let ourselves be driven along. They turned the big paddles that served as rudders, so that the ship changes course. They are now running with the wind in a south or southwesterly direction.

       e.   Under the lee of Clauda. 27:16-17

27:16 – *And running under the shelter of a small island called Clauda, we were scarcely able to get the **ship's** boat under control.*

And running under the shelter of a small island called Clauda. This small island (whose modern name is Gavdho) is about 23 miles southwest of Crete. The sheltered side from this storm would have been the southwest side of the island. It is probable that they first passed the eastern side of the island as they were being driven along by the storm, and then when the shelter of the island permitted, they sailed in a more westerly direction. Once they were in the shelter of the island, they would have had relatively smooth water for ten or fifteen miles, and in this stretch of smooth water they make what preparations they can for riding out the storm. Three different precautions are taken.

We were scarcely able to get the *ship's* boat under control. The Greek says, "we barely had strength enough." They would have secured the ship's boat by hoisting it up onto the deck of the ship. This ship's boat had been towed astern, as was normal practice during good sailing weather. But this storm had come upon them so suddenly that they did not have time to secure the boat. Now, having been dragged across twenty or thirty miles of storm-tossed sea, it must have been nearly full of water. Luke says "we," indicating that this was one of the jobs that it didn't take a trained seaman to do, and so he and Paul (and the other prisoners and passengers?) were assigned the task of hauling on the rope attached to the boat until they had dragged it alongside the ship. The sailors had jobs to do that required trained men to look after. "Scarcely," says Luke. He evidently remembered his aching hands and sore muscles when the task was finally finished.

27:17 – *And after they had hoisted it up, they used supporting cables in undergirding the ship; and fearing that they might run aground on **the shallows** of Syrtis, they let down the sea anchor, and so let themselves be driven along.*

And after they had hoisted it up, they used supporting cables in undergirding the ship. After the ship's boat was hauled aboard and secured on deck, the next thing to do was to undergird the ship. The ship's one huge mast put a great strain on the hull of such wooden ships, and in a storm like this the timbers would begin to part and the ship would start leaking badly. In 1837, archaeologists found marble tablets at Piraeus containing a list of Athenian ships and an inventory of their tackle and rigging, and it is there shown that a part of their tackle was "hanging gear" (the same word here translated "supporting cables"). To undergird the ship, these cables were passed around the hull of the vessel and drawn tight by the capstan.[41] The British call this "frapping." Dr. Luke says they "bandaged" the ship! This precaution would help the hull stand the strain and reduce the danger of leaking so badly that they would founder. These operations were likely made with desperate haste and straining efforts.

And fearing that they might run aground on *the shallows* of Syrtis. Now that they have taken precautions against their immediate dangers, they begin to anticipate future dangers. There were two celebrated *syrtes* along the Mediterranean shores of North Africa called the greater and lesser. The former lay just to the west of Cyrene, and the latter was further west, near Carthage. They were vast beds of sand driven up by the sea, and were constantly shifting their position so that it could not be known with certainty where the sandbars were under the surface of the shallow water. These constantly changing sands were a terror of all Mediterranean sailors.[42] Since the Greek here is singular, Luke probably is thinking of the greater Syrtis. The greater Syrtis was almost exactly southwest of Crete, so they could not allow themselves to continue in their southwesterly course indefinitely. The shallows were still a great distance away, but the violent wind is driving them in the very direction of the shallows. They are going to have to do something to change their course.

They let down the sea anchor. This is the third precautionary measure, but the exact nature of the measure is not quite clear because the Greek translated "sea anchor" is itself not quite clear.

- Some explain that they took down the main sail and lowered that huge yard arm in an effort to reduce the strain on the hull of the ship. This was what the translators of the KJV understood, for they rendered it, "they strake sail." But others object. They contend that lowering sail would be the wrong thing to do, as it would rob the ship of the necessary means of sailing away from the danger they were trying to avoid. However, since these ships also had a foresail, which was likely sufficient to keep the ship's bow pointed in the direction they wished to go, it may be that they did lower the main yard arm.

- Barnes suggests that they even took down the mast. He writes, "The most probable [explanation] is that they took down the mast, by cutting or otherwise, as is now done in storms at sea, to save the ship."[43]

- A third suggestion, and the one adopted by the NASB translators, has the sailors letting down weights and great stones by ropes into the sea for the purpose of slowing the progress of the vessel. These sea anchors would serve as a sort of brake. But others object, contending that this latter explanation has nothing to do with altering the ship's course, which seems to have been the main intent of the sailors.

---

[41] There is some dispute as to whether these cables were stretched crossways around the ship, or whether they were stretched from stem to stern. On sailing vessels of the 1800's they would have been stretched crossways, and perhaps so they would have been on this grain ship from Alexandria. On the other hand, knowing the design of the ancient ships, many have argued that the only way to keep the timbers from parting was to undergird it lengthways.

[42] Josephus, *Wars*, II.16.4.

[43] Barnes, *op. cit.*, p.364. Barnes wrote in the 1800's, and so had a proximity and familiarity with the practices of sailing ships.

All things considered, the first is likely the better explanation. The heavy main yard arm on ancient ships was nearly as long as the ship itself. Lowering it in a gale would tend to reduce the ship's top-heaviness and reduce the great strain on the hull.[44]

And so let themselves be driven along. With storm sail set, and with the steering paddles set at eight points (the strongest rudder possible, when trying to turn the ship toward the wind and keep it off the shallows of Syrtis), they were carried along by the storm. The ship aimed at sailing as close as possible into the storm, making for the northwest in order to avoid the Syrtis.

      f.   Storm and shipwreck. 27:18-44

27:18 – *The next day as we were being violently storm-tossed, they began to jettison the cargo;*

The next day as we were being violently storm-tossed. Does Luke's use of "we" indicate the passengers have been out on deck where they had to hang on for dear life? Or were they below decks finding themselves pitched about as another violent wave hit? The ship was still taking too much punishment from the storm. Some more precautions were going to have to be taken if they were going to weather the storm.

They began to jettison the cargo. Through the night and into the next day the violent wind kept blowing, the rain pelted down, and the huge waves continued to batter the ship. The efforts to lighten the ship noted in this verse and the next imply that, in spite of the efforts at undergirding, the ship was leaking and getting heavier with water, in danger of going down. Luke uses the proper technical phrases for throwing cargo overboard. The very same language appears in the LXX of Jonah 1:5. Whether they threw out part of their cargo of grain (cp. verse 38), or whether there was cargo in the holds other than grain and this is what is jettisoned, is not clear. Being lighter, the vessel would draw less water, and the waves would strike the sides with less force. The ship would tend to ride more on top of the waves, rather than wallowing through them.

27:19 – *and on the third day they threw the ship's tackle overboard with their own hands.*

And on the third day. This is the third day out of Fair Havens, the third day since the commencement of the storm.

They threw the ship's tackle overboard with their own hands. "Tackle" has been variously explained. Smith suggests that the "main yard arm is meant," and this immense spar would require the united efforts of many men to launch it overboard.[45] Howson, on the other hand, thinks it unlikely they would have thrown away a great timber which would

---

[44] Not only was the great yard arm an enormously heavy thing, but the sail, too, strengthened by bands of rope sewn into it crossways and lengthways, would hardly have been left up in the face of such a violent storm as Euraquilo.

[45] Smith, *op. cit.*, p.116.

have supported 20 or 30 men in the water if they had to abandon ship.[46] Barnes suggest that it was "the anchors, sails, cables, baggage, etc., that is, everything that was not indispensable to its preservation."[47] Alford thinks that it means all the furniture, beds, and moveable items of all kinds.[48] Wetstein explains it of the passengers' baggage.[49] McGarvey speaks of the spars, planks, cordage, and so forth which were carried for the purpose of making repairs.[50] It is likely the "tackle" included the furniture and the yard arm and the huge wet canvas sails – all of which that would be useless in a storm.[51]

27:20 – *And since neither sun nor stars appeared for many days, and no small storm was assailing us, from then on all hope of our being saved was gradually abandoned.*

And since neither son nor stars appeared for many days. Eleven days and nights of wind, and rain, and waves threatening their lives, followed (verse 27). Because of the low, dark clouds they could not see the sun by day nor the stars by night. In those days before the invention of the compass, sighting the sun or the stars was the only way the sailors had to determine their position. After so many days without a reckoning the sailors had no idea where they were.

And no small storm was assailing *us*. Luke uses understatement here to describe the storm. In fact, it was a great storm. From verse 15, it might appear that the only problem was high wind. But from this verse we learn that the skies were leaden, that it was pouring rain, and that the storm continued day and night without letting up. "Assailing us" indicates the very great violence of the storm.

From then on all hope of our being saved was gradually abandoned. The ship's crew had taken precaution after precaution to keep the ship afloat, all the time hoping that the storm would let up. But it does not, and the fact that they are gradually losing hope implies that the ship is leaking badly. When a ship is beginning to founder, the usual course of action is to head for the nearest land, run the ship aground, and make for shore. But without sun or stars for a reckoning, they do not even know which way to head for the nearest land. They are gradually accepting the fact that they are going to drown at sea. One by one the people on board lost hope.

27:21 – *And when they had gone a long time without food, then Paul stood up in their midst and said, "Men, you ought to have followed my advice and not to have set sail from Crete, and incurred this damage and loss.*

---

[46] Conybeare and Howson, *op. cit.*, p.649.

[47] Barnes, *ibid.*

[48] Alford, *op. cit.*, p.294.

[49] Hervey, *op. cit.*, p.296, quotes Wetstein.

[50] McGarvey, *op. cit.*, p.266.

[51] This verse has a manuscript variation that bears on who threw the tackle overboard. Some MSS read "we threw" and some read "they threw." The evidence marginally favors the third person verb form "they threw," but the NASB's "own hands" uses the first person reading. It is difficult to decide which is correct.

And when they had gone a long time without food. "Without food" (*asitia*) is the common medical term for "loss of appetite." The storm had deprived them of the means, the time, and the inclination to prepare or to eat any regular meals. If the ship is leaking badly, many of the food stores would have been water soaked. The pitching and rolling would make food preparation a difficult chore and could induce seasickness. And about the time they sat down to eat, there would be a call for all hands on deck to meet some new emergency. Verses 35-38 indicate there was still a fair supply of food on board, so this verse must mean they just weren't interested in eating.

Then Paul stood up in their midst and said. About the time the last man on board has lost hope, Paul stands up one morning with a message of encouragement for his companions in distress. Now we will begin to see the value of a saint, even in the midst of emergency circumstances. He had free access to all the ship, even though he was a prisoner, and had labored with the rest to meet the emergencies (verse 16). The following narrative implies that, while others may have burst into wailing cries of despair and calling,[52] Paul has been addressing his prayers to the only One who could help. He now comes forward with the assurance that his prayers were heard.

"Men, you ought to have followed my advice. Paul opens this word of encouragement and counsel with a firm warning not to dismiss his advice again like they had back at Fair Havens. At that ship's council, he had urged them not to try to sail on toward Phoenix. He had been in the minority when a vote was taken, yet as he had predicted (verse 10), their decision had already cost them much damage and loss. This opening comment is more than "I told you so!" Rather, it is a reminder to them that his advice was good. And this time his advice was based not just on personal experience and observation, but on a message directly from God.

And not to have set sail from Crete, and incurred this damage and loss. Some English translations read as if they were ironical, but the Greek is not. The pilot and captain of the ship, and the centurion Julius, we suppose, by this time have formed a much more respected opinion of Paul; they are prepared to listen to his suggestions this time.

27:22 – *"And* **yet** *now I urge you to keep up your courage, for there shall be no loss of life among you, but* **only** *of the ship.*

And *yet* **now I urge you to keep up your courage.** The morale of the whole company of people on the ship was at a dangerously low level. Paul had news designed to lift their morale and to restore their hope of living through the storm, rather than being lost at sea.[53]

For there shall be no loss of life among you. Paul's former warning had indicated fear for the lives of those on the ship (verse 10). But on that occasion, he spoke only as an experienced traveler of sound judgment. This present assurance contains more than personal experience and judgment. His calm assurance as he spoke must have been as cheering

---

[52] Compare the sailors' actions in Jonah 1:5, "every man calling unto his god."

[53] The word "urged" is the same as used in verse 9, translated "admonished."

as the news itself that he had to share with those who had given up all hope.

But *only* of the ship. No amount of experience or judgment based on the best available information could have enabled Paul make this prediction regarding the loss of the ship, but without the loss of a single life. In verse 23 he explains the source of the statements that he is making.

This is one of the places in the New Testament where the miraculous is woven right into the warp and woof of the historical events, the supernatural right alongside the natural. There is no way to remove the appearance of the angel from the account, and leave an account whose elements are still coherent and fully explainable.

27:23 – *"For this very night an angel of the God to whom I belong and whom I serve stood before me,*

For this very night an angel of the God to whom I belong ... stood before me. Again, note that this time Paul claims direct revelation from heaven for this message, which he did not claim when he spoke in the conference at Fair Havens. It was now the twelfth or thirteenth night they had been at sea in the storm. Paul here gives the authority behind his specific prediction about no loss of life but loss of the ship. "The God to whom I belong to," said Paul. He had to specifically identify the source of his message, or the sailors might have thought of a messenger like Mercury was intended. Paul identifies the source of his revelation as Jehovah, the One Creator worshiped by Paul and the other Christians. The being who brought the message to Paul was not Christ himself, who had on some other occasions appeared to Paul,[54] but an angel whose message was similar to the ones Jesus had given to Paul on those occasions.

And whom I serve. Paul's life of devotion and service would explain why the angel appeared to him and not to others on the ship. The word "serve" is similar to Romans 1:9, and suggests that some on board have seen Paul at regular devotions. Observe also Paul's open confession of God before the heathen crew.

27:24 – *"saying, 'Do not be afraid, Paul; you must stand before Caesar; and behold, God has granted you all those who are sailing with you.'*

Saying, "Do not be afraid, Paul; you must stand before Caesar. The angel urges Paul to cease being afraid. The appearance of the angel, and his message, are obviously an answer to prayer, prompted by fear, not of death or danger itself, but lest the cherished purpose of his heart (preaching in Rome) should now fail to be attained. As the angel's next words show, Paul's prayer was not limited to his own interests; he had been interceding for those who, like him, were on board that ship in that raging storm. The angel repeats the substance of the promise formerly given to Paul by Jesus (Acts 23:11). "Stand" is the proper word for standing before a judge. Since Paul is promised that he will be tried before Caesar, it must be that he will not perish at sea.

---

[54] Acts 18:9, 22:17-18, 23:11.

And behold, God has granted you all those who are sailing with you." Not only would Paul himself live through this peril on the sea to stand before Caesar, but the lives of all those on board the ship were to be spared for his sake.[55] This does not mean that they would all be converted to Christ, but that their lives would be preserved. The world has no idea how much it owes, in the mercy of God, to the presence of righteous men in its midst. For ten righteous men, Sodom would have been spared.[56] Now, for the sake of an apostle whom God needed to bear His testimony before Caesar, 276 soldiers, sailors, and passengers were to be spared. But for this grant they would likely all have perished at sea.

27:25 – *"Therefore, keep up your courage, men, for I believe God, that it will turn out exactly as I have been told.*

Therefore, keep up your courage, men. Note how the messenger of God has exactly the needed message of light and hope, and that too when things seemed darkest.[57]

For I believe God, that it will turn out exactly as I have been told. Having received a revelation from God through the angel, Paul was completely assured that it would happen just as he had been told. He had complete confidence that God could do what He promised He would do. Paul had long ago learned that when God makes a prophecy, it is matched by its fulfillment.

27:26 – *"But we must run aground on a certain island."*

But we must run aground on a certain island. "Must" because that's the way God has appointed it to be. "Run aground" is the same word used in verse 17. This statement clearly was part of the message the angel had spoken to Paul, though in Paul's report it is separated from the other things the angel said by Paul's affirmation of belief that God would do as He promised. The ship would go down, the angel had said, but the men would be saved, washed ashore on some island or another. No easy escape was promised. This element of the prediction must have been part of the angel's message, for there was no way the men had any idea of where they were. The last they knew, they were headed toward the north coast of Africa. As events transpire, the island will be Malta.[58]

27:27 – *But when the fourteenth night had come, as we were being driven about in the Adriatic Sea, about midnight the sailors* **began** *to surmise that they were approaching some land.*

But when the fourteenth night had come. The time is reckoned from their leaving Fair Havens (verses 18-19).

---

[55] "Granted" is something given as a favor because it has been asked for, and is thus one of the indications we find in the text that Paul has been in prayer. Compare Acts 3:14 where this same word appears.

[56] Genesis 18:23-32.

[57] Psalms 112:4,7; 46:1-3.

[58] Acts 28:1.

As we were being driven about in the Adriatic Sea. The "Adriatic Sea" here spoken of is the central Mediterranean. This is learned from several sources in extant ancient literature. Ptolemy speaks of the Adria as washing the south coast of the Peloponnesus (Greece) and the east coast of Sicily.[59] Josephus, who himself was shipwrecked just two years after Paul, was on a voyage from Judea to Puteoli and states that he was picked up in the "middle of Adria" by another ship sailing from Cyrene to the same port of Puteoli.[60] The intersection of the lines the two vessels took would fall right in the region now mentioned by Luke under the same name.

A better translation than "Adriatic Sea" would be "the Sea of Adria." To modern readers, the "Adriatic Sea" speaks of the gulf between Italy and Yugoslavia, and some have even attempted to show that this is where the ship had drifted,[61] as if a storm blowing from the northeast could have blown them in that direction from the south coast of Crete. The body of water we call "the Adriatic Sea" was known then as "the *gulfoi* Adria," in distinction from the central Mediterranean which was called "the *sea* of Adria."

A number of commentators insist that "driven about" means no more than "driven through (or across)" the space of water. If so, with storm sail set, and rudders lashed in a fixed position, they were being driven in a rather straight course from Clauda toward Malta. "Driven about" implies anything but a straight course across the sea of Adria.

About midnight the sailors *began* to surmise that they were approaching some land. The sound of breakers was the thing that gave rise to this impression.[62] The ears of the sailors were alive to the sound of the breakers before the passengers were aware.[63] If it had been during the daylight hours, they may have seen the flying spray from the breakers as well as heard them. As Smith tells us, no ship can enter St. Paul's Bay from the east without passing within a quarter of a mile of point Koura, and once the ship is at this distance the breakers can be seen, for they are especially violent in a northeast wind.[64]

The tradition that they finally came ashore at what today is called St. Paul's Bay is substantiated by the facts about to be related by Luke concerning the "soundings" compared with the present-day soundings around the island of Malta. A ship passing Koura in a northwesterly direction would be in 20 fathoms of water close to the spot where the breakers can first be heard.[65]

It is one of the striking proofs of the truth of Luke's record that at the rate at which it is calculated that a large ship laying to in a gale would drift in 24 hours, viz., 36 miles, multiplied by 14 days (the number of days occupied by the voyage) gives 504 miles – and

---

[59] Ptolemy, *Geographical Outline*, III.4,14-16.

[60] Josephus, *Life*, III. Some Greek texts have the name aspirated, so their translation would be "Hadria."

[61] W. Falconer, *Dissertation of St. Paul's Voyage*, quoted in the article on "Adria" in *Hastings' Dictionary of the Bible*, Vol. I, p.43-44. See further discussion of this subject in notes at Acts 18:1.

[62] In fact, there is an alternate reading in the manuscripts to the effect that "some land was resounding."

[63] If they threw out a sea anchor as the left Clauda (verse 17), it may have struck bottom, which would have given the sailors a warning that they were nearing land.

[64] Smith, *op. cit.*, p.126.

[65] Smith, *op. cit.*, p.127.

it is 476 miles in a straight line from Crete to Malta. Had the ship been driven at a uniform rate and in a straight line, it would have covered the distance in slightly over 13 days.[66] As it was, after they headed the ship toward the north-northwest in an effort to keep from being driven from Crete onto the Syrtis, they were driven across that stretch of open sea by the northeast winds in 14 days.

27:28 – *And they took soundings, and found* it to be *twenty fathoms; and a little farther on they took another sounding and found* it to be *fifteen fathoms.*

And they took soundings, and found *it to be* **twenty fathoms.** To take a "sounding" they made use of a line with a lead weight on the end of it. They would have heaved the leaded end of the rope into the depths to learn how much water was underneath them. Usually, there were knots on the rope, each a fathom apart. They learned there was 120 feet of water where they were.[67]

And a little farther on. Smith has estimated that the time between the two soundings was about half an hour.

They took another sounding and found *it to be* **fifteen fathoms.** Now, the water is about 90 feet deep. The water getting shallower indicates they were drawing near to some shore.

27:29 – *And fearing that we might run aground somewhere on the rocks, they cast four anchors from the stern and wished for daybreak.*

And fearing that we might run aground somewhere on the rocks. The soundings were proof that a shore was near, and the sound of the breakers indicated the area was rocky. There was danger they would go aground, perhaps on some hidden reef of rock.

They cast four anchors from the stern. They feared danger if they permitted the ship to drift any farther, so they dropped the anchors to keep them in current depth of water until daylight came and they could better ascertain their situation. Smith tells us that the ground on the bottom of the bay is such that anchors will not slip, if they catch. As long as the cables hold, there is no danger the ship will move, even though it is being buffeted by a gale.

Ancient ships were usually anchored from the bow, but occasion often demanded they be anchored as well from the stern. Thus, ships were built with "hawse-holes aft to fit them for anchoring from the stern."[68] Had they anchored from the bow, there was danger they would swing around and get crosswise of the waves. Ancient anchors were much smaller than those now used, and therefore ships carried many; some accounts of ancient

---

[66] Smith, *op. cit.*, p.122-124.

[67] The Greek noun rendered "fathoms" (*orguias*) literally means the distance from fingertip to fingertip when the arms are outstretched, including the chest, or about six feet. Before knots were tied on the rope and counted to determine the number of fathoms, the leadsman would measure the line as he took it in by grasping it and pulling it to arms' length, grasping again and pulling another arms' length of rope up from the depths, and so on, until the whole length was retrieved.

[68] Hervey, *op. cit.*, p.298.

ships speak of eight iron anchors.[69] Casting the anchors from the stern, as they did, will also make it easier in the morning to make the run for the beach.

And wished for daybreak. One can imagine sailors' feeling after they have been at the mercy of the storm on the high seas for fourteen days. They are near land. They can hear the waves crashing onto the rocks, and they are afraid they will be driven onto the rocks. What would it be like to be thrown into the ocean in the blackness of the night in the midst of a storm! No wonder they "prayed" (*euchomai*) daylight would hurry and come.

27:30 – *And as the sailors were trying to escape from the ship, and had let down the* **ship's** *boat into the sea, on the pretense of intending to lay out anchors from the bow,*

And as the sailors were trying to escape from the ship, and had let down the *ship's* **boat into the sea.** The sailors' fears aroused by the breakers and perhaps by the leaky condition of the ship also aroused their instincts for self-preservation. Some of the sailors devised a way to save themselves, perhaps at the expense of the other people on the ship. They are going to get into the ship's boat and row toward the sound of the breakers. That way they will avoid drowning in the deeper water. They were already lowering the boat (the one they had earlier hoisted aboard, verse 16), and were preparing to board it, when Paul stopped them.

On the pretense of intending to lay out anchors from the bow. Such a maneuver, the sailors might have plausibly argued, was necessary to keep the ship from swinging around too much into the wind. The boat, they could argue, was necessary to their purpose, as they intended to run the anchors out to the end of their cables before they dropped them into the sea. Perhaps they supposed that no one on board would know better than to suppose such anchors from the bow were needed. Actually, they had no intentions of coming back to the ship, even if they did actually drop the anchors at cable's end.

27:31 – *Paul said to the centurion and to the soldiers, "Unless these men remain in the ship, you yourselves cannot be saved."*

Paul said to the centurion and to the soldiers. How Paul detected the intention of the sailors to escape, we are not told. Perhaps he had enough experience at sea to know that there could be no possible value in the present circumstances of anchoring from the bow. Paul went to the centurion Julius, the highest-ranking authority on the ship, and warned him that if the sailors were successful in their plan to escape, then his promise of safety to all would no longer be true.

"Unless these men remain in the ship, you yourselves cannot be saved." The presence of the able seamen was necessary to the safety of all aboard for skilled hands would be needed when it came time to drive the ship onto the beach. Landsmen like the soldiers and prisoners would be quite unequal to the task of handling so large a ship under such critical conditions.

---

[69] Julius Caesar, *Civil Wars*, I.25.

Here is another time in Paul's life when he refuses to be presumptuous. He had been promised by the angel that no lives would be lost, but he did not simply sit back and permit the Lord to do it all for him from that moment on. Instead, he made use of all the proper means at his disposal to ensure that, with God's help, their lives would be safe.[70] The centurion immediately responds to Paul's suggestion.

> By this time the centurion has learned that it was unwise to disregard Paul's advice, though it is not certain that his advice was correctly interpreted when the soldiers cut the hawsers and let the dinghy fall into the water, to drift away.[71]

27:32 – *Then the soldiers cut away the ropes of the* **ship's** *boat, and let it fall away.*

Then the soldiers cut away the ropes of the *ship's* **boat.** In an instant the soldiers draw their swords and cut the ropes by which the boat was being lowered. On first thought the act may have seemed foolish, for the boat might have offered a good way to get the passengers ashore once the ship was beached. But history is full of accounts of the terrible scene which accompanies frantic men's attempts to take what seems the last means of escape from a disaster. Furthermore, if the boat were still available through the rest of the night, what is to keep the sailors from trying to escape again later?

And let it fall away. By cutting the ropes which fastened the boat to the ship and letting it go, all possibility of their fleeing from the ship was taken away. They will still be on board when daylight comes, to help sail the ship. We can picture the feelings of mortification, and then anger, on the sailors' part now that their selfish plan to escape has been detected and frustrated. And in these hard feelings, not only on the sailors' parts, but hard feelings toward the sailors by those who would have been left behind to perish, there was a new danger. Tempers were worn thin by the fourteen emotion-sapping days of storm. Something must be done to keep the situation from developing into an ugly fight between the people on the ship.

27:33 – *And until the day was about to dawn, Paul was encouraging them all to take some food, saying, "Today is the fourteenth day that you have been constantly watching and going without eating, having taken nothing.*

And until the day was about to dawn, Paul was encouraging them all to take some food. One way to break the tension was the means Paul used. Soldiers and sailors needed something that would draw them together after the incident narrated in verses 30-32. So Paul advises them to sit down together and eat some food. The verb tense indicates Paul made continual entreaties through the last few hours until dawn. Again we see the apostle's practical insight. The food will not only serve as source of energy for the task of the next

---

[70] Compare notes at Acts 23:17. When God makes a promise, the realization of which can in part be promoted by the responses and activities of the individual people involved, such responses are an understood condition to the fulfillment of the promise. To look for the end without using the means is not to trust God, but to tempt Him.

[71] Bruce, *op. cit.*, p.516.

morning, but it would get their minds on something besides the treachery of the sailors.

Saying, "Today is the fourteenth day that you have been constantly watching and going without eating, having taken nothing. The words "constantly watching" suggest that most of the nights were sleepless, as they all anxiously awaited the dawn to see what the new day might bring. "Without eating, having taken nothing" seems to suggest they have missed their regular meals. It has been proposed that on an ancient ship, they did not have a mess hall or dining room in which they ate; instead, each person who wanted food had to go to the galley and get it for himself. This latter action is the very thing they have not done during the fourteen days. What they needed physically was some food; what they needed morally was the sense of restored companionship. These are exactly what Paul's advice would lead them to. There was hard work ahead when daylight came, and if they were all to come through safely to land, they would need all the energy and enthusiasm and cooperation they could muster.

27:34 – *"Therefore I encourage you to take some food, for this is for your preservation; for not a hair from the head of any of you shall perish."*

Therefore I encourage you to take some food. Paul continues to encourage them to eat. Paul had promised them that all of them would live through this ordeal, but they must work and cooperate with him if the promise were to be realized.

For this is for your preservation. Paul indicates that the preservation of their lives depended on their keeping up their strength. The word rendered "preservation" is the one that is also rendered "salvation," but since the context speaks of physical life being preserved, rather than salvation from sins, the NASB has chosen a helpful rendering for the word in this phrase.

For not a hair from the head of any of you shall perish. Paul uses this proverbial expression[72] to reassure them that not one would perish. These words may have been aimed particularly at the sailors whose attempt to save themselves had been foiled. Paul assures them they will get safely to land yet.

27:35 – *And having said this, he took bread and gave thanks to God in the presence of all; and he broke it and began to eat.*

And having said this, he took bread and gave thanks to God in the presence of all. We picture Paul himself going to the galley and getting some food to distribute to those who refuse to follow his suggestion to go get some for themselves. Before he passed it out, he paused to offer thanks to God for the food. In another place, Paul teaches that prayers of thanksgiving are to be offered at meal time.[73] We observe again Paul's unhesitating confession of the Living God in the presence of unbelieving men (cp. verses 23,24). "Paul was among [people] who were not Christians; but he was not ashamed of the proper acknow-

---

[72] 1 Samuel 14:45; 2 Samuel 14:11; 1 Kings 1:52; Luke 21:18.

[73] 1 Timothy 4:5-6. Jewish people too were accustomed to give thanks at their meals (Matthew 14:9).

ledgment of God, and was not afraid to avow his dependence on Him, and to express his gratitude for His mercy."[74] Paul asked the soldiers and sailors to listen to the prayer of thanks for food to strengthen their bodies.

And he broke it and began to eat. Paul encouraged them by example as well as by word.[75]

27:36 – *And all of them were encouraged, and they themselves also took food.*

And all of them were encouraged, and they themselves also took food. The words present a striking contrast to the growing abandonment of hope in verse 20. Paul's hearty cheerfulness, his words of encouragement, and his own example has begun to communicate itself to the others on board the ship. What moments before had been an explosive situation has been effectively defused.

27:37 – *And all of us in the ship were two hundred and seventy-six persons.*

And all of us in the ship were two hundred and seventy-six persons. We presume that Luke has helped distribute the food that Paul has offered thanks over. We also presume that it had to be rationed out to make sure everyone on board would get a fair share. That, we suppose, is why Luke has the number of people on board at this point rather than at the close where he says "we all got safely to land."[76]

Instead of "276" some manuscripts read "76," but those manuscripts are not of sufficient weight to change the reading here. There is nothing unbelievable or improbable in the larger and better attested number. Josephus tells us there were 600 people on board the ship on which he set sail for Italy, and which, too, went down in the sea of Adria in the year AD 63.[77]

27:38 – *And when they had eaten enough, they* **began** *to lighten the ship by throwing out the wheat into the sea.*

And when they had eaten enough. "Eaten" is from the Greek *koresthentes*, and suggests they were "satisfied, satiated, filled."

They *began* to lighten the ship by throwing out the wheat into the sea. One of the results of eating and taking courage was that they began the preparations for running the ship ashore once it becomes daylight.

---

[74] Barnes, *op. cit.*, p.367.

[75] Because of the juxtaposition of three words, "bread," "break," and "give thanks" (*eucharisteō*), some have tried to show this was an observance of the Lord's Supper, for those terms were used of the breaking of bread and the giving of thanks at the Lord's Supper. However, the same words are expressly applied to an ordinary meal in Luke 24:30, and we see no way to understand this eating aboard the ship as anything but a common meal.

[76] Acts 27:44.

[77] Josephus, *Life*, III.

There is a difference of opinion as to what Luke means by *ton siton*, translated "the wheat."

- Meyer and others think it was the rest of the ship's food rations which, since this large number of people have not been eating, would have been considerable, for it was enough for a fortnight's provision.[78] In support of their theory, they argue it must have been the food rations, for the cargo had already been thrown overboard (verse 18).

- Meyer's suggestion is rejected by Howson and Smith and others, on the supposition that it would not have been enough to significantly lighten the ship even if they had thrown all the rest of the food rations overboard. They argue it was the rest of the ship's cargo, only a part of which was jettisoned at verse 18.[79] As long as there was hope of saving the ship, they had tried to preserve a portion of the cargo, too. But as is done in all cases where it becomes necessary to choose between saving the people on board, or saving the ship, they now are preparing to run the ship aground in order to save the people. That required getting it as light as possible, so that it drew as little water as possible.

The verb tense in "throwing out" is one that implies a process of some continuance. It was no easy task to raise the sacks of grain from the hold of the ship (perhaps many of which were waterlogged) and dump them overboard, for the storm is still raging, and the ship must have been pitching and tossing.

27:39 – *And when day came, they could not recognize the land; but they did observe a certain bay with a beach, and they resolved to drive the ship onto it if they could.*

And when day came, they could not recognize the land. When daylight came, the sailors looked for familiar landmarks, but there were none by which they could identify the land off which they had anchored. St. Paul's Bay, the traditional site of the shipwreck,[80] has no marked features by which even a native coming upon it suddenly can recognize it.[81]

But they did observe a certain bay with a beach. After looking for a place to beach the ship, their attention was attracted to a little bay, with a level, sandy beach. The word translated "beach" means a level or pebbly or sandy beach,[82] as opposed to *aktē*, a "high rugged coast."

---

[78] Meyer, *op. cit.*, p.488.

[79] Conybeare and Howson, *op. cit.*, p.656.

[80] Valetta is the main harbor on the island of Malta, and lies about 10 miles east of St. Paul's Bay. Valetta does have some landmarks by which some of the sailors might have recognized it.

[81] Smith, *op cit.*, p.136,143. We have followed James Smith's account in the above notes. Recently, however, W. Burridge in *Seeking the Site of St. Paul's Shipwreck* (Valetta, 1952), has argued, on the basis of local observation, that the shipwreck took place not in St. Paul s Bay but in Melliha Bay farther west. Perhaps we may never know with absolute certainty the exact spot. When speaking of St Paul s Bay as the place, we do so with the same mental reservation used when pointing to other Biblical places that are supported by no more than tradition as to their exact geographical location.

[82] Matthew 12:2; Acts 21:5,40.

And they resolved to drive the ship onto it if they could. Again there seems to have been a consultation among the sailors as they pick the most likely spot to run the ship aground. As they talked about it, there was some doubt whether or not they could maneuver the ship toward that sandy beach, but they decided to try. The word "drive" is a quasi-technical one, answering to our "to run the ship aground." Their object was no longer to save the ship from being destroyed, but to save the crew from drowning.

27:40 – *And casting off the anchors, they left them in the sea while at the same time they were loosening the ropes of the rudders, and hoisting the foresail to the wind, they were heading for the beach.*

And casting off the anchors, they left them in the sea. The four anchors which had been dropped to stop the ship's progress during the middle of the night are left behind in the sea. All the sailors had to do was cut the cables which were attached to the anchors since the anchors were of no further value. Even if they could have been recovered in spite of the continuing storm, they would only have added weight, the very thing they have spent the early morning hours getting rid of as they emptied the grain into the sea.

While at the same time they were loosening the ropes of the rudders. When they had put out the anchors, the two big paddle-rudders had been hoisted up and lashed fast, lest they should foul the anchor-lines at the stem. But now when their use was absolutely necessary to steer the ship toward the beach, the lashings by which they had been held up out of the water were loosened, and the paddles fell back into the water.

And hoisting the foresail to the wind, they were heading for the beach. At the same time the anchor ropes were cut and the rudders dropped, they hoisted up the foresail on the smaller mast at the front of the boat. "Foresail" is a better translation of the Greek *artemōna* than "mainsail" as found in the KJV.[83] A sailing ship has to be moving through the water before the rudders will be of any use in steering the ship. A small foresail would give it enough movement that they could guide it. The word for "wind" here is strictly the participle, "the (breeze) that was blowing." Perhaps the change in words implies that there was a lull in the fury of the gale.

27:41 – *But striking a reef where two seas met, they ran the vessel aground; and the prow stuck fast and remained immovable, but the stern* **began** *to be broken up by the force* **of the waves.**

But striking a reef where two seas met, they ran the vessel aground. Instead of running the ship aground on the smooth, sandy beach they had seen, the ship unexpectedly ran aground on a mudbank out in the bay while they were still some distance from the shore. As the ship stood at anchor in the bay's mouth, it would have had the Koura point on its left and the little island of Salmonetta on the right. From the mouth of the bay, the little

---

[83] Many have been the translations and explanations for *artemōna*. Some make it the main sail, though that sail seems to have been unusable since verse 17. Some make it a top sail, though those were not introduced until the 16th century. Some make it a stern-sail. Ancient ships did have small foresails (Juvenal, XII.68), and we think that is what is intended, though *artemōna* is not the usual word for foresail.

island looks to be a part of the island of Malta, but actually it is separated by a narrow channel about 100 yards in width. The waters coming through this narrow channel meet the waters flowing into St. Paul's Bay from the mouth of the bay, and where these "two seas" meet, there is an underwater sandbar (mudbank). In endeavoring to make the beach, the ship struck this underwater sand bar. The word translated "vessel" here is a different word than Luke has used all the way through his narration; perhaps what used to be a fine sailing ship is now just a hulk.

And the prow stuck fast and remained immovable. Smith says that this bar is mud and tenacious clay.[84]

But the stern *began* to be broken up by the force *of the waves*. The front part of the ship was stuck in the mudbank, while the stern was still afloat in deeper water and exposed to the force of the currents and the waves rolled up by the storm. As the ship began to break apart, the entire crew and passengers would have crowded toward the bow. The verb tense in "break up" is one that indicates continuous action. Each time a wave hit, the hulk that remained of the ship would break up some more.

27:42 – *And the soldiers' plan was to kill the prisoners, that none* of them *should swim away and escape;*

And the soldiers' plan was to kill the prisoners, that none *of them* should swim away and escape. According to traditional Roman discipline, the soldiers would have to pay the same penalty their prisoners would have received if the prisoners escaped.[85] As the men stood on the forepart of the ship, deciding what to do next, the soldiers suggested that the thing to do with the prisoners was to kill them lest they escape. In the general confusion of abandoning ship, surely some of the prisoners would escape; and then the soldiers themselves would be liable to a death sentence, or fighting in the arena. In putting the prisoners to death, the soldiers saw what looked to them like the only chance of escaping death themselves. Included among the prisoners slated for death was Paul. It seems unbelievable that the soldiers could plan to kill Paul along with the others after he had been instrumental in saving their lives. The soldiers are being as selfish and unfeeling at this moment as the sailors had been during the night.

27:43 – *but the centurion, wanting to bring Paul safely through, kept them from their intention, and commanded that those who could swim should jump overboard first and get to land,*

But the centurion, wanting to bring Paul safely through, kept them from their intention. The centurion commanded the soldiers to do no such thing as kill the prisoners; he felt too grateful to Paul to expose him to such a fate. Again, we see that for the sake of one righteous man, the lives of all the prisoners were spared.

---

[84] Smith, *op. cit.*, p.139.

[85] Acts 12:18-19, 16:27.

And commanded that those who could swim should jump overboard first. The centurion has a plan which will prevent any of the prisoners from swimming away and escaping. He orders any of the soldiers who can swim to dive in and make for shore. Once they are ashore, they can stand watch and round up the prisoners as they in turn made for shore. Once the prisoners made shore, they could be clamped back into custody. Also, once the swimmers had gotten to the beach, they would be in readiness to help their comrades who could not swim and might therefore need help. The centurion was just as anxious as the soldiers that none of the prisoners should escape, and his plan was intended to keep that very thing from happening.

And get to land. They would have to swim from one-fourth to one-half mile from the sand bar to shore.

27:44 – *and the rest* **should follow,** *some on planks, and others on various things from the ship. And thus it happened that they all were brought safely to land.*

And the rest *should follow*, **some on planks, and others on various things from the ship.** The words of the centurion's command are continued in this phrase. Whether this was addressed also to the soldiers, or whether it included all the others on board, is not certain. Even if his words include only the soldiers, the others on board would follow the example of the soldiers once the order was given to them to jump overboard and start for the shore. The ship was breaking up, and floating planks and other large timbers offered a means of getting ashore for those who could not swim. Bruce suggests that the last phrase might be translated "and some on some of the (people) from the ship," as though some of the non-swimmers might be helped ashore by clinging to the backs of the crew and others who could swim.[86]

And thus it happened that they all were brought safely to land. This was exactly what Paul had promised (verses 22-24). Ship and cargo were lost, but every person on board lived through the shipwreck. The soldiers would have perished if the sailors had gotten away with their selfishness; the prisoners would have died if the soldiers had not been stayed in their plan. Instead, all came through the shipwreck because God heard the prayers of the apostle.

> It was a remarkable instance of divine interposition to save so many through so long-continued dangers; and it shows that God can defend in any peril, and can accomplish all His purposes. On the ocean or the land we are safe in His keeping; and He can devise ways that shall fulfill all His purposes, even though His people pass through all kinds of danger. Indeed, we have seen that God's men are good men to have around in any event![87]

---

[86] Bruce, *op. cit.*, p.519.

[87] Barnes, *op. cit.*, p.369.

g. At Malta. 28:1-10

28:1 – *And when they had been brought safely through, then we found out that the island was called Malta.*

And when they had been brought safely through. In Acts 27:43 this same expression "safely through" appeared. It was the regular way of stating the idea of passing through extreme danger and still being alive. Prior to their shipwreck, they had drifted for two weeks without any reckoning where they were; the storm was so violent they have had to take precaution after precaution just to keep their ship afloat. It was likely little more than a hulk when they made final efforts to run her aground. After it was stuck on the mudbar and was beginning to break up, they had to swim the last several hundred yards to safety. But they made it, with all 276 still alive!

Then we found out that the island was called Malta. While still aboard the ship, they had tried to distinguish what land it was they were anchored off, but they couldn't tell.[1] Now they learned that the island was called Malta. It reads as if it was the answer to their question to the natives, "What is this land called?" The name in Greek is *Melita*.

In the 19th century there was some dispute over the identification of this island. Some supposed that the island was Melita Illyrica (modern Meleda, or Mljet, off the coast of Yugoslavia) rather than Sicula Melita (Malta near Sicily). This supposition was based on a misinterpretation of the "sea of Adria" (27:27) and a misunderstanding of the meaning of "barbarian" (native) in verse 2 below. This view was first mentioned by Constantine Porphyrogenitus (a 10th century emperor),[2] was revived in the 1700's by Padre Georgi (a Dalmatian monk and a native of the island of Meleda), and then was espoused by Falconer.[3] Against the idea that the island was Meleda are these facts: (1) It would almost have required a miracle to get the ship, with a northeast gale blowing strongly, up to the Dalmatian coast from Crete. (2) A grain ship would not naturally have wintered at Meleda on its way from Alexandria to Puteoli.[4] (3) There has been no local tradition that Meleda was the place, as there has been at Malta. (4) From the place of his shipwreck, Paul went directly to Syracuse, Rhegium, and Puteoli, thus sailing in a direct course toward Rome. If sailing from Meleda, a different course, through Dyrrachium and Brundisium, would have been taken toward the city of Rome. (5) If a direction toward Meleda has been the course, there would have been no reason to fear going aground on the Syrtis.[5] (6) The time spent drifting (Acts 27:27) fits the distance from Crete to Malta, but not from Crete to Meleda, which is 780 miles, not through open sea but amidst many islands.

But there is no longer any reason to question the identification of Malta as the place. The island of Malta was originally a Phoenician colony. It is about 20 miles long from east

---

[1] Acts 27:39.

[2] Constantine, *De Admin. Imper.*, 36

[3] See footnote #61 in chapter 27.

[4] Acts 28:11.

[5] Acts 27:17.

to west, and about 10 or 12 miles wide from north to south. The island is an immense rock of white sandstone, with a covering of earth about one foot in depth, which had been brought from the island of Sicily. The name Melita was first given to the place by Phoenician sailors, though the derivation is uncertain. It might come from a word meaning "clay" and be a reference to the clay which forms the bottom of the sea around the island, which makes for such a safe anchorage. It might come from a word which means "refuge" and be a reference to the shelter that the Phoenician sailors found at this island as they sailed back and forth between Phoenicia and the straits of Gibraltar. If the latter derivation is true, then Luke, looking back on the experience, is saying Malta was named well, for he and Paul and the others found it was a refuge indeed.

28:2 – *And the natives showed us extraordinary kindness; for because of the rain that had set in and because of the cold, they kindled a fire and received us all.*

And the natives showed us extraordinary kindness. Along a seashore, whenever dawn reveals a foundering vessel off the shore, everyone who lives close to the place hurries to the site of the wreck in order to help rescue survivors. The Maltese may even have watched the desperate run for the shore that this ship made. In any case, they are at the place in crowds by the time the people from the ship are wading ashore.

"Natives" is a happy translation of the Greek word *barbaroi* (sometimes translated "barbarians"), a word which indicates only that the people of Malta did not speak Greek, Latin, or Hebrew.[6] The Greeks regarded all as barbarians who did not speak their language, and the Egyptians likewise regarded all as barbarians who did not speak their language. *Barbaroi* is onomatopoetic, indicating the confused sound which a strange language has in a man's ears.[7] Luke is therefore saying that the language of Malta was different than those on the boat were used to speaking. "Barbarian" does not indicate, as the word sometimes does with us, that the people were savage, uncultured, and of cruel habits.

The Maltese and the people who just suffered shipwreck may have had difficulty communicating with each other, but the natives received the shipwrecked people with warm hospitality. There may not have been enough houses nearby to take care of that many people, but they did their best to make the 276 shivering refugees comfortable.[8]

For because of the rain that had let in and because of the cold. Some have understood this to mean that it just started raining that morning. Rather, the language pictures a heavy rain that had accompanied the whole storm. It was one of those chilling October or November rains (remember it is several weeks after the Day of Atonement[9]). The plight of the shipwrecked people must have been lamentable, soaked to the skin, without a thing in the world but what they were wearing, and a chill wind blowing.

---

[6] Being African or Asiatic in descent, they would have spoken the Punic dialect. Linguists have noted that Modern Maltese is an Arabic dialect, but there are inscriptions from Malta which have Phoenician on them.

[7] *Barbaroi* says no more than that the speech is unintelligible. Compare Romans 1:14 and 1 Corinthians 14:11.

[8] The word translated "kindness" is the same word (*philanthrōpia*) used at Acts 27:3.

[9] Acts 27:9.

They kindled a fire. It would take considerable work to kindle a fire out of the rain-soaked wood and brush they could find nearby, and it would have to be a huge fire if 276 men are to get near it. Too, it would take some work to keep it going. These men were soaked during their swim ashore, and the rain that was falling would prevent their clothes from drying out. The large fire would provide some warmth against the cold wind, and would give opportunity for drying their clothes.

And received us all. The word implies both shelter and hospitality. They "received us all" means the Maltese made no distinction between the different classes (slave, prisoner, free, sailor) represented among the shipwrecked people.

28:3 – *But when Paul had gathered a bundle of sticks and laid them on the fire, a viper came out because of the heat, and fastened on his hand.*

But when Paul had gathered a bundle of sticks and laid them on the fire. It would take considerable help to gather enough wood to keep a large fire like this from going out. Paul had been helpful on board the ship; it would be natural for him to join the local people as they spread out over the area in search of more fuel for the fire.[10]

The fact of gathering a bundle of fuel has been dwelt on by the negative critics as militating against the truth of Luke's narrative, since no wood is now found on the island of Malta. However, the word "bundle of sticks," which occurs only here in the New Testament, can means "dry sticks," "kindlers," or any combustible material. In other Greek literature, it is applied to the straw or stubble of herbaceous plants, as well as the branches of trees, and, as such, exactly describes the stout, thorny heather that still grows near St. Paul's Bay. Lewin writes as follows.

> When in Malta in 1853, I went to St. Paul's Bay at the same season of the year as the wreck occurred ... We noticed eight or nine stacks of small faggots ... They consisted of a kind of thorny heather, and evidently had been cut for firewood.[11]

And over the years, when an area becomes more thickly populated, stands of timber (if the bundle of sticks were tree limbs) are commonly depleted.

A viper came out because of the heat. The snake had been torpid. The viper was likely in a bundle of sticks which someone had brought to the fire. When the bundle was laid on the fire, the viper became warmed by the heat, and ran out and fastened on the hand of Paul, just as he was throwing the bundle of sticks he had collected onto the fire.

What kind of snake was it? The Greek *echidna* is the regular word for "viper," i.e., a very poisonous snake. The poison of the viper that lives in the Mediterranean area is one

---

[10] "Paul was not a preacher after the style of many modern 'clergymen,' who are particular not to soil their hands with menial labor, and who expect everybody to be ready to serve them, while they preserve their dignity and look on. He did not stand by the fire which others had kindled, and allow others without his help to keep it burning. He took his turn bringing the wood along with the barbarians and the sailors." McGarvey, *op. cit.*, p.275.

[11] Thomas Lewin, *The Life & Epistles of St. Paul* (London: Bell, 1890). Vol. 2, p.208.

of the deadliest known among the snake family. The viper, however, usually only strikes, fixing the poison-fangs in the flesh for a moment, and withdraws its head instantly. It does not regularly hang on, like Luke pictures this one doing. Since this snake had to be removed from Paul's hand by force, and since it did not prove to be fatal, some have attempted to show that it was not a poisonous snake at all that bit Paul.

> There is one species, *Coronella Leopardinus*, that looks like a viper, and that hangs on when it strikes, but is not poisonous. Another species, *Coronella Austriaca*, is a little snake that when it strikes requires some force to pull it off, but its teeth are too short to do much injury, and it too is not poisonous.[12]

But such an attempt misses the fact that Luke uses the regular word for poisonous snake in verse 4, and it misses the fact that Luke calls it a "viper" here in verse 3. Due weight must be given to Luke's identification of the snake, for as Ramsay has well said, "A trained medical man in ancient times was usually a good authority about serpents, to which great respect was paid in ancient medicine and custom."[13]

Just as Luke's record has been attacked concerning the "bundle of sticks," so it is attacked concerning the presence of a poisonous snake on Malta, since there are no poisonous snakes on Malta today. The fact there is no timber on Malta now did not cause us to doubt the truthfulness of Luke's record, nor does the fact there are no poisonous snakes on Malta now cause us to doubt it. The island now has a denser population than at any previous time, and such animals are driven away and destroyed by man as the population increases. In our own country, there were areas which were infested by dangerous animals and poisonous snakes at one time, but the growing population has driven them away and caused some species to even become extinct in some localities. In this connection there is an interesting note in Lewin suggesting that as recent as 1853 he believed he did see a viper in a bundle of sticks near St. Paul's Bay.[14] Perhaps just a bit over 100 years ago, there were still a few poisonous snakes left on Malta.

And fastened on his hand. The snake fastened its fangs in Paul's hand. Lenski suggests that this was God's way of turning all eyes on Paul right from the first moment on Malta.[15]

28:4 – *And when the natives saw the creature hanging from his hand, they began saying to one another, "Undoubtedly this man is a murderer, and though he has been saved from the sea, Justice has not allowed him to live."*

And when the natives saw the creature hanging from his hand. Luke uses the regular word *thērion* ("creature") used in medical writers for venomous snakes. Compound words made from *thērion* are used for "bitten by a viper" (*thēriodektoi*) and for an antidote made from the flesh of vipers (*thēriake*). Some older translations at this place have "*venomous* creature," though there is no word in the Greek corresponding to "venomous." Still the idea

---

[12] William Ramsay, *Luke the Physician* (Grand Rapids: Baker Book House, 1956), p.63ff.

[13] *Ibid.*

[14] Lewin, *ibid.*

[15] Lenski, *op. cit.*, p.1102.

conveyed by "venomous" is correct given the names Luke used for this snake and the expectations of the onlookers as to what would result from the bite (verse 6).

They *began* saying to one another, "Undoubtedly this man is a murderer. A number of the Maltese saw the snake hanging by its fangs from Paul's hand, and they have an explanation ready for what has happened. They knew, evidently, that he was a prisoner from the fact that he was constantly guarded by a soldier.[16] And so the Maltese, seeing that he was one of the prisoners, but not knowing why he was a prisoner, in harmony with their pagan and mythological notions of the divine government of the world, rushed to the conclusion that they were looking at another example of the work of Justice, a mythological goddess whose responsibility it was to see that men got what was coming to them. The fact that the viper had fastened on Paul and that, as they supposed, he must now certainly die, was the proof from which they inferred his guilt.

> Why they thought he was a *murderer* rather than guilty of some other crime is not known. It might have been that they inferred that he must be guilty of some atrocious crime, and as murder was one of the most terrible crimes one could commit, they inferred that he had been guilty of this. It might have been that they had an opinion that when divine vengeance overtook a man, he would be punished in a manner similar to the offence; and as murder is usually committed with the hand, and as the viper had fastened on the hand of Paul, they inferred that he was guilty of taking a life [with that very hand]. It was supposed by the ancients that persons were often punished in the part of the body which had been the instrument of the sin.
>
> [The Maltese] reasoned from great original principles, written on the hearts of all men by nature, that there is a God of justice, and that the guilty will be punished. They reasoned incorrectly, as many do, only because they supposed that *every* calamity is a judgment for some particular sin. Men often draw this conclusion, and suppose that suffering is to be traced to some particular crime, and to be regarded as a direct judgment from heaven. Compare John 9:1-3. The general proposition that all sin will be punished at some time is true, but we are not qualified to affirm of particular calamities always that they are direct judgments for sin.[17]

Calamity besetting a person in this life does not necessarily mean he or she is guilty of some sin,[18] nor is it true that justice is always meted out here in this life.

And though he has been saved from the sea. The Maltese are thinking it was useless for the criminal to have escaped death by drowning, for vengeance and justice followed the guilty till they received proper retribution. Paul may have escaped one form of punishment, but the gods were not so easily baffled; a more terrible death was awaiting him.

---

[16] It seems unlikely that Paul would still have had chains on after having to swim from the ship to shore (unless the chains were left on, thereby necessitating the prisoners to hang on to a plank and make for shore by kicking their feet). Considering the concerns which the soldiers had shown for maintaining proper custody of the prisoners (Acts 27:42), surely they soon would have rounded up the prisoners once they were on shore, and would keep them well guarded.

[17] Barnes, *op. cit.*, p.370.

[18] Compare notes at Acts 12:23 and 14:22.

Justice has not allowed him to live." In pagan mythology, "Justice" was a goddess, the daughter of Jupiter. It was her duty to take vengeance and to inflict punishment for crimes. "Allowed" is a past tense in the Greek and indicates that the Maltese regarded Paul as already a dead man. A bite from a viper was so certainly fatal that they could speak of him as already dead.

28:5 – *However he shook the creature off into the fire and suffered no harm.*

However he shook the creature off into the fire. This was a natural enough reaction. The snake will not be able to bite another person around this fire.

And suffered no harm. Ordinarily, after a snakebite, there are certain first-aid precautions that are taken to counteract the venom. None was taken in Paul's case, nor did he begin to swell up, nor did any red streaks begin to show running up his arm. Jesus had promised His apostles that they would take up serpents, and the serpents would not harm them.[19] The event that happened to Paul on Malta is often pointed to as one fulfillment of that promise.

28:6 – *But they were expecting that he was about to swell up or suddenly fall down dead. But after they had waited a long time and had seen nothing unusual happen to him, they changed their minds and* **began** *to say that he was a god.*

But they were expecting that he was about to swell up or suddenly fall down dead. They knew that the bite of a viper would soon produce death. They expected Paul's hand to first become inflamed, and swell up. This was the usual effect of a viper bite. This swelling came quickly as the blood stream carried the venom to other parts of the body. And then almost as suddenly they expected Paul to collapse, already dead, for in their experience the poison of the viper was very rapid in its effects.

But after they had waited a long time and had seen nothing unusual happen to him. The Maltese looked on quietly and waited for Paul to begin showing the usual signs of approaching death after a viper bite, but nothing they had reasoned to themselves would happen did. There was no swelling, no inflammation, no nothing. The word translated "nothing unusual" was used by medical writers in two senses: of "unusual symptoms," or of "fatal consequences." Hobart quotes a remarkable parallel to this phrase from Damocrites. He says that whosoever, having been bitten by a mad dog, drinks a certain antidote, "shall suffer no harm" – using the same Greek word as the one here translated "nothing unusual."[20]

They changed their minds and *began* **to say that he was a god.** The word "change their minds" is *metaballō*;[21] clearly their original conclusion had been wrong. If Paul does not suffer the usual results of a viper's bite like all mortal men do, then he must be other than

---

[19] Mark 16:18.

[20] Quoted in Hervey, *op. cit.*, p.319.

[21] It is a different word than the ones used for repentance (*metamellomai* and *metanoeō*), which are sometimes rendered "change the mind."

mortal! He cannot be a murderer pursued by divine justice; instead, he must be a divine person who is immune to things that would prove fatal to mortal men.

Clearly, the reason Paul suffered no harm is that God did something miraculous for Paul, and this produced a strong impression on the natives of Malta. At another time, Paul had been thought of as a god because he worked a miracle; he was thought to be Mercury, the messenger of the gods.[22] Perhaps this time the Maltese think of one of the mythological gods who was famous for subduing serpents, namely, Apollo or Aesculapius, quickly jumping to the conclusion that that is who Paul really is. We must suppose that as Paul had to teach the people at Lystra that he was not a god, so he had to instruct the Maltese. Still, what happened there on the shore of St. Paul's Bay made a lasting impression on these people, and connected with Paul's further instructions, it would not be many days until they have a true concept of his person and office.

28:7 – *Now in the neighborhood of that place were lands belonging to the leading man of the island, named Publius, who welcomed us and entertained us courteously three days.*

Now in the neighborhood of that place. This is near to the place where the shipwreck had occurred. Tradition locates the lands belonging to Publius at Civita Vecchia, the old capital city of Malta, located about five miles southeast of St. Paul's Bay.

Were lands belonging to the leading man of the island, named Publius. The island of Malta was a part of the province of Sicily. Since Sicily was ruled by a procurator (governor), Publius was the legate under the Sicilian governor. "Leading man" was an official title,[23] technically correct for Malta, to designate the "legate." It is likely that Publius had been appointed to the position of "leading man" on Malta, and that he lived on an estate near the capital city of the island.

Who welcomed us and entertained us courteously three days. We can hardly think of the hospitality of Publius as extended to the whole 276 who had been on board, and the omission of the word "all" from verse 2 probably indicates a limitation to a chosen few – perhaps the centurion Julius, Paul, Luke, the ship's pilot and captain, and perhaps a few others. There is a good possibility that Publius would have been officially responsible to care for the Roman soldiers and the prisoners, but "courteously" indicates the duty was performed in an attitude of gracious generosity. It is also likely that Publius made arrangements with the inhabitants of the island for lodging for the refugees for the winter months. McGarvey suggests that many found accommodations in the homes of those on the island whose sick were healed by Paul and Luke during their three-day stay at the home of Publius.[24]

---

[22] Acts 14:1ff.

[23] This term has been found in both Greek and Latin inscriptions at Malta, from which it has been determined that it was on official title. *Inscriptions Graecae XIV* (Berlin, 1891), p. 601; *Corpus Inscriptionum Latinarum X* (Berlin, 1883), p.7495.

[24] McGarvey, *op. cit.*, p.277.

28:8 – *And it came about that the father of Publius was lying* in bed *afflicted with recurrent fever and dysentery; and Paul went in* to see *him and after he had prayed, he laid his hands on him and healed him.*

And it came about that the father of Publius was lying *in bed* **afflicted with** *recurrent fever and dysentery.* The Greek word translated "fever" is plural, and the NASB translators have happily rendered it "recurrent fever." *Dusenteria* (Greek) is the regular technical term for dysentery and is found frequently in medical writers. A combination of recurring fever and dysentery would make the case more than usually critical, according to Hippocrates.[25] "Malta has long had a peculiarly unpleasant fever of its own – 'Malta Fever' – due to a microbe in goat's milk."[26]

And Paul went in *to see* **him.** As Paul works this miracle we see him following the same general course of action as Peter did in the case of Dorcas.[27] Compare, too, the comments at Acts 20:10 on Paul's actions in the raising of Eutychus.

And after he had prayed, he laid his hands on him. As was suggested before, the prayer evidently concerned whether or not a special healing was to be performed in this particular case. Having received the affirmative answer, the miracle is done as Paul lays his hands on the sick man. A number of writers are reminded of the instructions given in James 5:14.

And healed him. Paul was given miraculous power on this occasion to heal Publius' father. That is Luke's plain intent, and here is another case where the account of the miraculous is part of the warp and woof of the narrative; it is impossible to strip the miraculous away and have anything left of the historic facts which Luke is narrating. The miracle has been called a suitable return for the courteous hospitality of Publius, and it had considerable to do with winning the favor of the people on the island. It also no doubt opened the way for Paul to preach to the people, too.

Such healing was in accordance with the promise made by Jesus (Mark 16:18). Some writers attempt to show that Luke had seen Mark's Gospel before he wrote Acts; others insist Mark saw Acts before he wrote his Gospel. The former idea is very much in doubt since it appears Mark is not written until some four or five years after Acts was published. The latter idea might be true, but that is hardly why Mark wrote as he did. Both Luke and Mark are simply relating facts, which just happened to be similar. We cannot accuse one of copying the other.

28:9 – *And after this had happened, the rest of the people on the island who had diseases were coming to him and getting cured.*

And after this had happened. The news that Paul, the one whom viper bites did not harm, had miraculously cured Publius' father of a very serious illness soon spread over the island.

---

[25] Hippocrates, *Aphorismi*, VI.3.

[26] Bruce, *op. cit.*, p.523.

[27] Acts 9:36ff.

The rest of the people on the island who had diseases were coming to him and getting cured. Notice, the Greek has an article, "*the* rest." That is, everyone on Malta who was suffering from any physical ailment came to receive suitable treatment. "Were coming" pictures a continuous stream of people, from all over the island, coming to Publius' estate to profit from the apostle's gift of healing. Most writers suggest at this point that doctor Luke was able to help, too, because of his medical skills. Two reasons are given for supposing that Luke as well as Paul was involved.

- There is a change of verbs. The word "heal" in verse 8 is *iaomai*, while the word "cure" here in verse 9 is *therapeuō*, the regular word for a physician's work of helping the sick.
- Verse 10 indicates that both Paul and Luke were "honored" by the people of the island. If Paul is being honored for his healing, may we not suppose that Luke is being honored for his medical work, too?

If it is true that we have both miracles (by Paul) and medicine (by Luke), it is but one more example of the truth that gradually the dependence on miracles is ceasing, and divine providence is allowed to take over, where possible.[28]

> We cannot suppose that Paul healed diseases among the islanders generally, without also mentioning the name of Jesus. Though Luke makes no mention of it, we must think that from the palace of the *legate* to the remotest hamlet on the island, the name and power of Jesus [and the good news of salvation to believers in Him] were fully made known during the three months of [Paul's] stay.[29]

It is likely correct to picture the gospel being preached and souls being won. Perhaps the tradition is true that Publius became an early leader of the church on Malta.[30]

28:10 – *And they also honored us with many marks of respect; and when we were setting sail, they supplied us with all we needed.*

And they also honored us with many marks of respect. It would seem correct to say that the "marks of respect" took the form of gifts. The word used here was the regular word used of the fee (i.e., *honorarium*) paid to a physician for his services, and it is likely that doctor Luke used the word to describe what the people of the island gave out of gratitude.[31] Of course, we are not to picture Paul as charging people before he would work miracles; such an idea is contrary to all the New Testament teaches. But the islanders, noting that Paul and Luke had lost all their possessions in the shipwreck, must have presented some needed and acceptable gifts to these men, so that their wardrobes and pocketbooks were replenished quickly.

---

[28] See comments at Acts 27:10.

[29] McGarvey, *op. cit.*, p.278.

[30] There is another group of people on the island we wonder about. Notice that in Luke's narrative he speaks no more about the prisoners who were aboard the ship en route to Rome. Did Paul baptize many of them, too?

[31] Compare Ecclus. 38:1. The same word translated "marks of respect" is used of the pay an elder was to receive (1 Timothy 5:17).

And when we were setting sail, they supplied *us* with all we needed. In addition to gifts of clothing and for other personal needs, when it came time to sail the Maltese supplied all the provisions that would be necessary for the rest of the voyage.[32] The thoughtfulness of the Maltese seems to stem from more than their sick having been healed. We suppose there is also gratitude to God for the salvation brought to the island by the preachers of the gospel.

      h.   At Syracuse. 28:11-12

28:11 – *And at the end of three months we set sail on an Alexandrian ship which had wintered at the island, and which had the Twin Brothers for its figurehead.*

And at the end of three months. It is now late February or early March of AD 61.[33] The three months after the shipwreck would have been the winter months during which the Mediterranean was closed to shipping.[34] It might actually be several weeks before the opening of the regular sailing season (if we follow the commonly accepted statement of Vegetius as we have done in these notes at 27:9); however, there is a statement in Pliny the Elder to the effect that navigation in this part of the Mediterranean began about February 8, at which time the west winds start to blow regularly.[35] If it is earlier than the regular opening of the sailing season, perhaps the officers and crew of the Alexandrian ship were anxious to take the earliest opportunity for pressing on to Puteoli.

We set sail on an Alexandrian ship which had wintered at the island. This ship apparently was part of the grain fleet, just as was the one which had wrecked.[36] Perhaps this ship was forced to seek refuge in Valetta's harbor by the same storm which had wrecked the ship Paul had been on. Something had caused them to stop short of their destination of Puteoli, when only three or four more days would be needed to complete the voyage.

And which had the Twin Brothers for its figurehead. It was the practice of the age to put an image of the person or thing after which the ship was named on the prow (and sometimes also on the stern). Luke indicates this Alexandrian ship had the name *Dioscuri* ("twin brothers").[37]

---

[32] These notes suggest that it was especially Paul and Luke for whom the Maltese showed such thoughtfulness. Other commentators understand that all 276 souls are now continuing their voyage to Rome, and all have provision made for them as they are about to leave.

[33] The Fast (dated September 23 of AD 60) had already passed while the ship was still at Fair Havens (27:9), although we are not told how much time had elapsed since its passing. Then came the 14 days of Acts 27:27, which would be the end of October or the beginning of November. Sometime after three months had been spent on Malta, they sailed for Rome, which would be late February or early March of AD 61 for the date of the sailing from Malta.

[34] See notes at Acts 27:9.

[35] Pliny, *Natural History*, II.122. Several attempts have been made to harmonize Vegetius and Pliny. Perhaps the former spoke of sailing across the sea, whereas Pliny spoke of coasting vessels.

[36] See notes at Acts 27:6.

[37] *Dioscuri* is the Greek name; *Gemini* is the Latin. Here is another place in Acts where we encounter the mythological ideas of the time. According to mythology, Zeus and Leda, the wife of Tyndarus, king of

28:12 – *And after we put in at Syracuse, we stayed there for three days.*

And after we put in at Syracuse. The ship left the island of Malta and sailed nearly due north to Syracuse, the capital city of the isle of Sicily. The distance was about 80 miles, and would have been a day's journey. Ships bound from Alexandria to Puteoli commonly put in at this port.

We stayed there for three days. The three days may have been spent in transacting ship's business, or more probably, in waiting for favorable winds to continue the journey.

    i.   At Rhegium and Puteoli. 28:13-14

28:13 – *And from there we sailed around and arrived at Rhegium, and a day later a south wind sprang up, and on the second day we came to Puteoli.*

And from there we sailed around. Codices Sinaiticus and Vaticanus read "weighing anchor," and if this is the true reading, we understand that they sailed in a rather straight line from Syracuse to Rhegium. The other manuscript readings indicate that they took a circuitous route ("sailed around"); that is, the voyage was in the form of a half-circle from Syracuse to Rhegium. The NASB seems to imply that the wind was in the northwest, and that the ship sailed east from Syracuse, then north till they were in the shelter of the toe of Italy, and then took advantage of the coastline to work its way windward till it came to Rhegium. Since the northwest wind was still blowing, they could not proceed through the straits of Messina, and were forced to put into the port of Rhegium.

And arrived at Rhegium. This town, now Reggio, is located on the toe of the boot of Italy, and was on the southern end of the straits of Messina. They had to wait at Rhegium for a suitable wind to take them through the three-mile-wide straits. Ships from Alexandria to Italy commonly put in at Rhegium to wait for such winds, considering the danger posed by the straits.

And a day later a south wind sprang up. They did not have to wait long, for a favorable wind sprang up the next day. The form of the Greek verb implies a change of wind, and such a south wind was what they needed if they were to sail without undue danger between the famous rocks of Scylla and the whirlpool of Charybdis.[38]

And on the second day we came to Puteoli. Since the distance from Rhegium to Puteoli

---

Sparta, had twin sons, whose names were Castor (he was a horse-tamer) and Pollux (he was the prince of boxers). After their death, so the myth goes, because of their brotherly love, they were translated by Zeus into the heavens where they became the constellation we call Gemini. Neptune also wanted to honor them, and so gave them power over the winds and the waves so that they might assist shipwrecked sailors. Castor and Pollux thus came to be known as the tutelary gods of sailors. This eyewitness detail that Luke mentions in passing reminds us of the continual trial Jews and Christians must have faced as they saw signs of idolatry all around them, even in the common actions of everyday life.

[38] See map at the back of the book for these details of the Straits of Messina.

is about 180 miles, the ship clearly was making good headway before the south wind.[39] Puteoli, modern Pozzuoli,[40] is located on the northern shore of the Bay of Naples. Cape Misenum stretches out into the bay on the west side of Puteoli and forms one side of a smaller horseshoe-shaped cove which opens on the south. This was the harbor for unloading the Alexandrian grain ships for it was the closest harbor to Rome that could accommodate the deep draft of these heavily laden grain ships.

As the ship came in toward the harbor, Paul would have seen some of the well-known beauties of the Bay of Naples. The imperial fleet had its anchorage at Cape Misenum, and just to the west of the cape were the isles of Ischia and Procida. To enter the bay from the south they would have sailed past the isle of Capri, and if he looked to the east at that moment, he could see Mt. Vesuvius and the city of Pompeii to the south of the volcano. The modern city of Napoli (Naples; in Paul's day it was called Neapolis) to the east of Puteoli was just a small village in the 1st century.

Since the people of Italy depended so heavily on the grain from Egypt for their bread, the arrival of the grain ships was eagerly awaited and welcomed. Seneca gives a vivid description of the arrival of these grain ships.[41] All other ships except the grain ships were required to strike their topsails (*suppara* – see the little triangular shaped sails above the main yard arm in the picture of the ship on the cover of the book) as they entered the harbor. The grain ships were allowed to carry the topsails so as to speed their arrival. When one of the grain ships hove into sight, it was immediately recognizable by those topsails, and the whole population of Puteoli went out to see them sail into the harbor and to celebrate the arrival of more grain from Alexandria.

28:14 – *There we found some brethren, and were invited to stay with them for seven days; and thus we came to Rome.*

There we found some brethren. There were Christians in Puteoli. How much the teachings of Jesus have been spreading through the empire is indicated by notes like this. We can only conjecture which evangelists brought the gospel here and planted the church.[42] There is an interesting note in Ramsay that Christianity had made its way to Pompeii (which was destroyed in AD 79) and was discussed there by gossiping loungers in the street.[43] So it would not be surprising that there was a church in the important commercial center of Puteoli. The gospel had been preached for some time in Italy, and congregations established in many towns, before Paul ever arrived in that country.

---

[39] Earlier in the voyage it had taken "many days" to cover 150 miles from Myra to Cnidus (Acts 27:6-7).

[40] Puteoli is derived from the Latin word for the "springs" (*putei*) which abound there. The place was celebrated for its warm baths as well as for the mineral springs.

[41] Seneca, *Epistle 77*.

[42] In comments at the close of chapter 18, we noted the conjecture of some that Apollos was the author of Hebrews. Those who think he wrote it that epistle often suggest he wrote it from Puteoli. The theory is based on two slim bits of evidence. One is the phrase "those of Italy" (Hebrews 13:24), which it is said cannot refer to Christians in Rome, but might fit those of Puteoli. The second is that the destination of the Hebrews epistle is thought (by those who think Apollos wrote it) to be Alexandria (Apollos' hometown), and there was a connection between Alexandria with its grain ships and Puteoli.

[43] Ramsay, *St. Paul the Traveller and Roman Citizen*, p.346.

And were invited to stay with them for seven days. These seven days, like those before at Troas (Acts 20:6) and at Tyre (Acts 21:4), would have included at least one Lord's Day. The brethren invited Paul to stay with them, that they might hear Paul teach them (we suppose), and Paul would have been pleased to have opportunity to observe the Lord's Supper with these brethren. That the centurion Julius consented to so long a delay indicates a high degree of sympathy with Paul. Perhaps by this time he also had become a Christian. If we cannot attribute his granting permission to Paul to this reason, at least we can see another example of the same kind of kindness which he showed to the apostle at the beginning of the voyage (Acts 27:3).

And thus we came to Rome. Here is a place where the KJV seems to better capture the sense. It reads, "And so we went toward Rome." The KJV preserves a sequence that goes from Puteoli (verse 14) to the gates of Rome (verse 16) and integrates an account of several delightful meetings on the road between the two cities.[44] Rome was approximately 150 miles by the Appian highway from Puteoli. The journey would take them from Puteoli to Capua, a distance of 33 miles. Here they would come upon the Appian Way, which ran from Rome to Brundisium. At Capua they would turn north, passing through Formica (modern Formia), Fundi (modern Fondi), and come soon to Terracina, a distance of 57 miles. At Terracina they would have to choose between two possible ways to continue their journey northward. They could take the circuitous road around the Pontine Marshes, or they could take one of the mule drawn boats down the canal through the Marshes. Both routes came out at Appii forum[45] ("Market of Appius," NASB), about 18 miles from Terracina. From there they would continue up the Appian Way until they reached Rome.

Roman antiquity provides several illustrations to help us get the feel of Paul's final miles to Rome. We may think of the great Appius Claudius, who, as censor in 312 BC, planned the road and supervised the building of part of it. Both the road and Appii forum are named after him.[46] Or we might remember that Horace wrote about the overcrowded canal boat, with its brawling sailors, the coarse vice and rude revelry and the scoundrel innkeepers at the wretched little town of Appii forum.[47]

For Paul, however, as he comes up the road toward Rome, his mind is filled with thoughts about how he will be received. Will the brethren be ashamed of him because he is a prisoner? Will his opportunity to preach and share with the Christians there be greatly curtailed or prohibited altogether? Entering Rome as a prisoner was not exactly what Paul had anticipated when he wrote to them, some years earlier, about his desire to visit them, and then be helped by them as he departed to enter a new field of evangelism.[48]

---

[44] No completely satisfactory harmonization of verses 14 and 16 has been discovered by this commentator when verse 14 is translated as the NASB does it. One attempt is to make "Rome" in verse 14 mean the State of Rome, and the "Rome" of verse 16 mean the City of Rome. Another attempt says that after Luke says they arrived at Rome, he goes back in time to relate one particularly exciting part of the trip.

[45] When the word is "forum" (lower-case "f") rather than "Forum" (capital "F"), it speaks of a little town. Forum" (capital "F") speaks of the "business district and government offices" in the larger cities.

[46] Livy, IX.29.

[47] Horace, *Odes*, III.29.62-64.

[48] Acts 19:21; Romans 15:23.

"Thus we went to Rome," Luke writes, meaning "after the seven day visit with the brethren at Puteoli." The long journey that began with his being grabbed and nearly killed by some Asian Jews, that entailed two years of imprisonment at Caesarea, and that included the perils of the storm and shipwreck, now would take only a few days longer, and they would be there. Very probably the hearts of both Paul and Luke beat more quickly as they begin the final leg of the journey to Rome.

j. At the Market of Appius and the Town of Three Inns. 28:15

28:15 – *And the brethren, when they heard about us, came from there as far as the Market of Appius and Three Inns to meet us; and when Paul saw them, he thanked God and took courage.*

And the brethren, when they heard about us. The seven days at Puteoli had given ample time for word to be taken to Rome that the apostle had arrived in Italy, and soon would be on his way up the highway toward Rome. If the summary that was given of Aristarchus' travels is correct,[49] for some time the Roman Christians have been anticipating his arrival. Now a messenger comes from Puteoli saying that Paul is getting close. Two different groups of Roman Christians immediately set southward along the Appian Way to meet Paul and escort him back to Rome. Among these "brethren" we would expect to find Aquila and Priscilla and some of the other Christians addressed by name in chapter 16 of Romans – Epanaetus, Andronicus and Junias, some of the household of Narcissus, and others. Ever since they had received the Roman epistle through the hands of Phoebe these Christians have been looking forward to his visit. Some can't wait to see him, so they hurry down the road to meet the apostle they loved the sooner.

Came from there as far as the Market of Appius and Three Inns to meet us. The practice of going some miles from the city to meet someone in order to honor him was common.[50] One group of Christians got as far as Appii forum, some 45 miles from Rome. There was an obvious reason for the one group not going farther than Appii forum, for they could not tell whether Paul would come by the canal or by the road. Appii forum was a convenient place for travelers on the Appian Way to stop for refreshment, which is why it was called the "Market of Appius." On the day when the Christians from Rome and Paul met there, the town, which was in general notorious for its vileness, was the scene of a prayer meeting, with thanksgivings and praises pouring forth from rejoicing hearts.

The second group got as far as Three Inns, about 33 miles from Rome. "Three Inns" is a better rendering of the name of the town than "Three Taverns," a rendering used in some of the older versions. "Tavern" is a wrong connotation. The Latin word "tavern" means a "shop of any kind," which is a different meaning than the English word.[51] Three Inns was a small village in Paul's day, and is near the modern Cisterna.

---

[49] See notes at Acts 27:2

[50] Josephus, *Antiquities*, XVII.12.1; Tacitus, *Annals*, III.5; Cicero, *pro Sext.* 63, *in Pison.* 22.

[51] It would be necessary to add an adjective such as *diversoria* or *cauponaria* before *Tabarnae* if this were to mean "tavern" in today's English sense of the word.

And when Paul saw them, he thanked God and took courage. The words imply a previous tendency toward anxiety and discouragement. Evidently, it has been some time since Paul had heard any word from the brethren at Rome. Would the friends he addressed in the Roman letter welcome him, or would he have to enter Rome as a criminal, with no one to escort him but the soldiers under the command of Julius? Were those Roman disciples still sound in the faith, or had persecutions driven them from their homes, or had the Judaizers (about whom he warned them in the Roman letter) perverted their beliefs? To questions like these the coming of the brethren from Rome gave a full and satisfying answer, and Paul resumed his journey with an eager and buoyant hope.

5. Paul's First Roman Imprisonment. 28:16-31

   a. Paul arrives at Rome. 28:16

28:16 – *And when we entered Rome, Paul was allowed to stay by himself, with the soldier who was guarding him.*

And when we entered Rome. Given the use of the pronoun "we," it is evident that Luke is accompanying Paul from Puteoli to Rome. Traveling the Appian Way from Three Inns, they would have come to Arica (now Ariccia), where they would probably have stopped for the night. From that point as they neared the city of Rome, the Appian Way would have presented to Paul and Luke some of the features that modern visitors to Rome still are shown. There were the tall milestones, the stately tombs[52] lining either side of the road which give the traveler the feeling he is walking through one long cemetery, and then the cemetery of the Jews of Rome,[53] lying on the east side of the Appian Way. To the east, Paul could have seen the beginnings of the Catacombs; here, in later years, the Christians, who would not burn their dead and who were excluded from the cemetery of the Jews, laid their dead to sleep in peace and to await the final resurrection. Continuing their journey, they could look across about a half-mile of flat land to the west and see the pyramid of Caius Cestius near the Ostian Gate.[54] Next they would have passed through the Appian Gate (also called the Porta di S. Sebastian) which pierces the outer of the two walls around the southern part of the city of Rome. Walking on toward the center of the city, they would have passed through the Arch of Drusus, and after a while would have come to the Capuan Gate (Porta Capena) which pierces the inner wall. On their right, once through this gate, they would have seen the Caelian Hill rising above them. On their left was the Circus Maximus (where in just a few years many Christians would be dying as they are torn by the lions). Immediately in front of them was the Palatine Hill, with the Palace of the Caesars crowning its top. Just beyond the Palatine Hill was the Roman Forum.

Interestingly, this is the last use of "we" in Acts. This means that for a time Luke and Paul were separated. However, we know that Luke did not leave Rome; he is present

---

[52] One example of which is the tomb of Caecilia Matella, the wife of Crassus.

[53] The cemetery of the Jews of Rome has been discovered and explored in the last 150 years.

[54] The map of Rome at the back of this volume locates the places spoken of in the next several sentences.

with Paul when the letters to Philemon and to the church at Colossae were written,[55] and those letters were, according to all indications, written from this first Roman imprisonment.

But once they were separated, what happened to Paul? The KJV at this place reads, "When we entered into Rome, the centurion handed his prisoners over to the Captain of the Guard (*stratopedarchē*), but Paul was suffered to dwell by himself with a soldier that kept him." This reading is supported both by the Byzantine text and by the Western text, and these details may in fact be correct. But just who is the "Captain of the Guard"?

- He may be the "captain of the Peregrini." One Old Latin manuscript (Gigas) reads that the prisoners were handed over to the *princeps peregrinorum*. The Peregrini were the corps of officer-couriers who helped Caesar keep in close contact with his far-flung legions.[56] The headquarters of the Peregrini, and the place where they resided when in Rome between missions, was on the Caelian Hill. In favor of this interpretation. it may be said that the Old Latin was the work of a translator who, being a Roman, presumably had accurate knowledge and used the precise technical term to translate Luke's (?) *stratopedarchē*. Against this interpretation are these two problems: (a) There is no clear evidence of the title *princeps peregrinorum* before the reorganization by Septimus Severus (c. AD 200). (b) There is evidence that prisoners from the provinces were delivered to the care of the *praefectus praetorio*.[57]

- He may be the "Captain of the Praetorian Guard." This is the interpretation most commentators prefer. The captain of Caesar's body guard, the men who protected Caesar's palace on the Palatine Hill, would be the natural one to whom to deliver prisoners, like Paul, who have appealed to Caesar, and prisoners like the others, some of whom have been condemned to die in the Circus Maximus. The fact that the Greek is definite, "*the* captain," has also been held to be significant. Usually there were two prefects (captains) in the Praetorian Guard. But between the years AD 51 and 62 there was just one prefect; his name was Afranius Burrus;[58] before and after his time there were the usual two prefects. If the Byzantine text which supports the KJV's wording can be accepted,[59] the way Luke speaks of "*the* prefect" may indeed help fix the date of Paul's arrival in Rome.

The Praetorian camp, where the other prisoners would be kept, lay to the northeast of the city, outside the Porta Viminalis.

Paul was allowed to stay by himself. Paul was treated differently than the other prisoners. He was given unusual courtesy; instead of being placed in the common military prison, Paul was permitted to dwell in whatever home he wished, with no restraint other than that of having a single soldier to guard him.

---

[55] Philemon 24; Colossians 4:14.

[56] See notes at Acts 27:1.

[57] Trajan, *ad Pliny*, 57.

[58] Tacitus, *Annals*, XII.42.1.

[59] The entire clause "the centurion handed his prisoners over to the Captain of the Guard" is not found in Codices *Aleph*, A, B, nor in the Syriac or Vulgate, nor in most critical editions of the Greek text. Hence, we should be careful how much stress is put on the ideas contained in it.

How is this special courtesy to be explained? Paul was no ordinary prisoner, brought to Rome to entertain the bloodthirsty crowds by fighting wild beasts or the gladiators in the Circus Maximus. He came as an unconditioned Roman, who had appealed to Caesar. The presentation of his case in the letter from Festus, as well as a good word from Julius concerning Paul's conduct on the voyage to Rome, must all have contributed to Paul's relatively mild confinement.

Paul first retired to a friend's house (verse 23; perhaps Aquila and Priscilla's), and then later rented an apartment for himself (verse 30). Many commentators suggest that Paul would have had his residence in the Jewish quarter of the city, on the west side of the Tiber River.[60]

With the soldier who was guarding him. The arrangement where he was chained to a soldier, but yet had the freedom of living in the dwelling of his choice, was technically called *custodia libera*. Paul speaks of his "chain,"[61] of being a "prisoner,"[62] and of being "an ambassador in chains."[63] More than likely, the guard would be changed from time to time. Each guard would have to listen as Paul spoke to those who came to visit him. It would have been in this way that the apostle's bonds, and the story of his sufferings on account of Christ, would become known throughout the whole Praetorian camp.[64]

    b.   Paul preaches to the Jews. 28:17-29

28:17 – *And it happened that after three days he called together those who were the leading men of the Jews, and when they had come together, he* **began** *saying to them, "Brethren, though I had done nothing against our people, or the customs of our fathers, yet I was delivered prisoner from Jerusalem into the hands of the Romans.*

And it happened that after three days. He has hardly settled in his temporary quarters before he begins his missionary activities. Here is Paul, a man now perhaps in his early sixty's, going at a pace that would keep many a younger man hurrying to keep up. In these few hours since his arrival he has renewed acquaintances with his old friends and brethren who had been requested, more than three years before, to strive together with him in prayer to God that he might come to them.[65] Now he has arrived, but in a way very different than he had expected. Instead of coming as a free man, able to move about through the streets of the city to visit in homes and reason in the synagogues, he had been marched in between

---

[60] Tradition has pointed to a spot now covered by the vestibule of the church of St. Mary Major, located at the junction of the Via Lata and the Corso, as the site of his rented dwelling. However, the validity of this traditional site is doubtful. In Paul's time this location formed part of the Flaminian Way, and so likely would have been occupied by arches and public buildings.

[61] Acts 28:20.

[62] Ephesians 3:1, 4:1.

[63] Ephesians 6:20; Philippians 1:7,13,17; Colossians 4:18.

[64] Philippians 1:13.

[65] Romans 15:24,30-32.

files of soldiers, presented to the authorities as a prisoner awaiting trial, and was now kept under military guard night and day. He may not be able to go to them, but there is nothing to keep men from coming to him. Those old friends of his here in the imperial city can be his arms and legs and help him reach out to the masses in the city who need the gospel. In harmony with his regular practice of preaching to the Jews first,[66] Paul immediately begins efforts to contact his countrymen, beginning with their leaders.

He called together those who were leading men of the Jews. The expression "leading men" would include such people as the rulers and elders of the synagogues[67] and the heads of the principal Jewish families that had settled in Rome.[68]

The fact that there are Jews in the city causes some commentators to express surprise. Remembering the edict of Claudius which banned Jews from the city,[69] they suppose that there would no longer be a Jewish population living in Rome. But in fact the edict of Claudius had been allowed to expire. Now, some ten years later, the Jews have long since returned and settled in their old quarters on the west side of the Tiber river. As we listen to what the Jewish leaders say to Paul in the verses below, it seems that the church has made no significant contact with the Jews. This is entirely understandable, at least from the Jewish standpoint. If they had been expelled because of constant strife about "one Christ" (Acts 18:2), once they had returned to the city the Jews would be slow to hear anything at all about the Christ, lest they be expelled again.

And when they had come together, he *began* saying to them. It is likely that some of Paul s friends had served as messengers to carry the invitation to the Jewish leaders. These leaders have responded and have arrived where Paul is staying. Paul now begins teaching.

"Brethren. He uses the same opening address that he had used when addressing the leading men at Jerusalem (Acts 23:1). In this address, Paul is chiefly concerned with showing that although he is a prisoner, he is actually guilty of no crime. There would be several reasons Paul would want to establish his innocence in their eyes. One is that unless he does, he can hardly expect the Jewish leaders and people to pay any attention to his message about Christ. The other is that he doesn't need any Jews at Rome putting pressure on the government leaders against him, like had been done at Caesarea.

Though I had done nothing against our people, or the customs of our fathers. "I" is emphatic in the Greek. He may be a prisoner, but he insists he had done nothing to deserve such treatment, either against the Jewish people[70] or in violation of the customs that have been observed by the Jews for generations.[71] By these words Paul intimates that the Jews

---

[66] Romans 1:16.

[67] There were no less than seven different synagogues in Rome.

[68] Josephus uses the expression "leading men" to signify all the leaders of a neighborhood or district.

[69] Acts 18:2.

[70] See notes at Acts 24:14-16, 20-21; and 25:8.

[71] See notes at Acts 6:14 and 21:21.

in Judea had something to do with his continuing imprisonment; he would have been a free man if they had not kept pressure on the Roman authorities. It is also true that the Roman authorities had something to do with his continuing imprisonment, for Paul's not being freed when he should have been. Paul is actively disclaiming the substance of the rumors which James had told him had been spread about him.[72]

Yet I was delivered prisoner from Jerusalem into the hands of the Romans. This is Paul's brief summary of what is recorded in Acts 21:30ff.

28:18 – *"And when they had examined me, they were willing to release me because there was no ground for putting me to death.*

And when they had examined me. Paul here summarizes the judicial proceedings that transpired under both Felix and Festus. It is possible that Luke gives only an abbreviated version of a much longer explanation by Paul of all that had happened between his arrest in the temple and his appeal to the emperor.

They were willing to release me. These words are strictly true of Festus and Agrippa II,[73] who decided that Paul might have been released if he had not appealed to Caesar. Perhaps they are true of Felix, too, who we are told left Paul in custody to please the Jews.[74]

Because there was no ground for putting me to death. No Roman magistrate in Judea – neither Lysias, nor Felix, nor Festus, nor Agrippa II – had ever condemned Paul. They could not find him guilty of the things the Jews charged. Paul had used this same expression concerning Jesus as he spoke to the Jews in Pisidian Antioch.

28:19 – *"But when the Jews objected, I was forced to appeal to Caesar; not that I had any accusation against my nation.*

But when the Jews objected. The verdict of the Roman authorities in each case was that Paul was not guilty of any crime worthy of death or imprisonment. They wished to release him, but the Jews "objected," Paul says, using a very mild word to describe their bitter enmity against him. When we add this detail (which was not specifically stated) to what is recorded in chapter 25, it helps us to understand what was going on in Festus' mind when he proposed they go to Jerusalem for a trial. As was have noted there, Festus apparently had determined to free the prisoner, but the Jews cried out against. Thus, the proposal that Festus made at Acts 25:9 was offered in consequence of their opposition, in an effort to conciliate them, to meet them half-way.

I was forced to appeal to Caesar. The word "forced" is emphasized. "I was *forced* to appeal to Caesar," says Paul.[75] To appeal to Caesar was something distasteful to the Jews,

---

[72] Acts 21:21,28.

[73] Acts 26:32.

[74] Acts 24:27.

[75] On Paul's appeal to Caesar, see Acts 25:8-11.

for they were turning away from their own religious court and asking a heathen judge to decide their case. It was a surrender of Jewish independence. So Paul emphasizes that he was *forced* to appeal to Caesar; it was unavoidable, the only way to avoid being handed over to a prejudiced tribunal (i.e., the Sanhedrin) or to assassination plots (like Acts 25:3).

Not that I had any accusation against my nation. In these words, Paul assures his Jewish audience that when his case is heard by Caesar, he will not say anything inflammatory against the Jews, for that would only cause the government to bring more hardships on the Jews. He knew of the anti-Jewish feelings that often lay just beneath the surface in this 1st century world; he knew the hardships his people had suffered in Rome, and that at different times they had been banished from their homes there. He assures his listeners that he would not do like many appellants before him had done and make counteraccusations against the Jews. All he was interested in was having his innocence established.

Paul speaks with kindness and courtesy to these Jews in Rome about the opposition of the Judean Jews against him. He uses conciliatory words and phrases such as "brethren," "our people," "our fathers," "the hope of Israel," and "not that I had any accusation ...." Paul exhibits the long-suffering and lack of retaliation that Jesus expects of His followers as he tells how he cherished no unkind feelings towards those who had done him wrong.

28:20 – *"For this reason therefore, I requested to see you and to speak with you, for I am wearing this chain for the sake of the hope of Israel."*

For this reason therefore, I requested to see you and to speak with you. Paul now shares with them the exact reason he invited them to come speak with him. He desired to clear himself of whatever false reports may have been sent to Rome, or that the Jews visiting Jerusalem from Rome might have heard about him there. Because Paul is a prisoner in chains, he must explain his circumstances to their satisfaction before they will ever listen to the gospel.

For I am wearing this chain for the sake of the hope of Israel." This is not the first time in these closing chapters of Acts that Paul has invoked Israel's "hope;" he has spoken of it on at least two previous occasions.[76] He does this to emphasize that the message he proclaims, far from undermining the cherished beliefs and customs of Israel, was its divinely-appointed fulfillment. Paul's whole address to the Jewish leaders was calculated to win their sympathy. It was no uncommon thing for Jews to be persecuted, especially because they cherished the hope they did. Paul even speaks of "this chain" to show that he is sharing the common experience of many Jews.[77]

How much this Jewish audience permitted him to enlarge on this topic of "hope" before they replied to the general defense of his circumstances that he has just given, cannot be determined. But on another day, when they return, Paul will have opportunity to explain that what they still look for in the future, he knows has already happened – that Messiah has come, has set up His kingdom, and now offers life and immortality to all.

---

[76] Acts 23:6, 26:6-7.

[77] The singular "chain" agrees with verse 16, that Paul was entrusted to the keeping of a single soldier.

28:21 – *And they said to him, "We have neither received letters from Judea concerning you, nor have any of the brethren come here and reported or spoken anything bad about you.*

And they said to him. After hearing Paul's explanation of his own personal situation, some of the Jewish leaders spoke up and assured him that they had little information about him, and no official information against him had come to them.

We have neither received letters from Judea concerning you. "Letters" is from the Greek *grammata*, and in this case must mean official documents from the Sanhedrin containing charges against Paul. These men do not say that they have never heard of Paul, or of Paul's religion. What they do affirm is that no official charges have been sent out against him by the Sanhedrin.

Such official letters were often sent by the Sanhedrin to outlying Jewish communities, to inform them of official decisions or to warn them of doctrinal deviations or teachers to be avoided. At first sight it may seem surprising that no letters have been sent about Paul, either before or after his departure from Caesarea to Rome. Perhaps during his two years' imprisonment, the Jews in Judea felt secure in the thought that if he ever walked out of Roman custody and protection, he would not walk far until he was dead, so they sent no warning letters to the synagogues. When Paul did finally appeal to Caesar, it was late in the sailing season, and the Jews would have had difficulty getting a letter to Rome before Paul himself got there.

Nor have any of the brethren come here and reported or spoken anything bad about you. Paul has just explained to these Jewish leaders what has happened to him the past two years, including the charges brought against him by the Jews in Judea. The leaders now assure Paul that no one has come from Judea and spoken against him concerning these matters. Again, the Jews do not say they have heard absolutely nothing about Paul, but only that those who had come had spoken "nothing bad" against him. They clearly had heard enough of this prisoner to identify him with the Christians (verse 22). Since Paul himself came on one of the first boats to reach Italy this sailing season, all of this probably implies that whatever news or information the Jews in Rome have heard about Paul was gleaned before his appeal to Caesar.

28:22 – *"But we desire to hear from you what your views are; for concerning this sect, it is known to us that it is spoken against everywhere."*

But we desire to hear from you what your views are. That is, "Although we have heard nothing against you that would invalidate your statements of the cause of your imprisonment, Paul, we have heard of the religion which you have been preaching." The word "desire" literally means "we think it right." "Your views" must not be pressed to mean that Paul taught a special "view" of Christianity different than, say, Peter or John taught. But Christianity was different than the views the synagogue and community leaders among the Jews at Rome held. These Jewish leaders are certainly being very open and fair in their dealings with Paul. They will hear from Paul himself before they make up their minds, rather than being influenced simply by what they hear second-hand from others.[78]

For concerning this sect. On "sect" see notes at Acts 24:5,14. Paul did not regard Christianity as a "sect" in the way that the Jews regarded it. To him, Christianity was not a split off the Jewish religion, but was the rightful fulfillment of their whole religion; the old foretold this new; the hopes of the old centered in the very Messiah he was preaching. Paul had introduced this subject by his reference to "the hope of Israel." Now the Jews say, "We want to hear what you have to say about the predicted Messiah having come and having set up His kingdom."

It is known to us that it is spoken against everywhere. The context would lead us to suppose the Jewish leaders mean that Christianity is spoken against *by Jews*. It is not difficult to see why this would be the view held by the Jews in Rome. If the edict of Claudius was due to a disturbance about Christ, once the edict expired, the Jews who returned would tell each other to watch out for those Christians, or they would find themselves banished again.[79] Outside of Rome, too, Christianity was spoken against by the Jews. Pilgrims from Rome going to Jerusalem for the feast would hear rumors. The language used by Tertullus when he called Christians "the *sect* of the Nazarenes" clearly indicates that the Jews had a contemptuous name for these Christians.[80] Indeed, the Jewish leaders at Rome would know that among Jews, Christianity had a bad name.

There is a further possibility that "everywhere spoken against" is true of what many *Gentiles* thought of Christianity. There are records almost contemporary to Paul's first Roman imprisonment which document some of the things Gentiles were saying about Christians. When the Christians are suffering under Nero, Tacitus describes them as holding "a destestable superstition," and guilty of "atrocious and shameful crimes, convicted by the hatred of mankind."[81] Speaking of the same general persecution, Suetonius writes that the Christians are "a race of men holding a new and criminal superstition."[82] And a few years after Paul's time, there were calumnies – e.g., stories of Thyestean (i.e., cannibal) banquets and licentious orgies[83] – against the Christians, and possibly even in Paul's day were whispered from ear to ear by wicked men. Christians would already have been known as worshiping One who had been crucified. Because of this association, in Tertullian's time the name *Asinarii* ("ass-worshipers") was used of

---

[78] If these leading Jews of Rome in Paul's time had acted as many do today, they would have refused to hear Paul at all because of the evil report heard everywhere about this "sect." But the fact that they had heard second-hand information that was prejudicial did not keep them from hearing first-hand from Paul. Perhaps they had refused to have much to do with Christians since the Jews had returned to Rome, but the courteous manner in which Paul invited them to his lodging, and the conciliatory manner of his address to them, had won them to a better feeling.

[79] This statement should not be construed as saying that there was no Christian church in Rome at this time. Both the epistle addressed to the Romans and the word "brethren" at Acts 28:15 indicate there was such a church here before Paul came.

[80] Acts 24:5.

[81] Tacitus, *Annals*, XV.44.

[82] Suetonius, *Nero*, c.16.

[83] Compare notes at Acts 20:8.

Christians. Some present-day writers think this name had already been given to Christians by the contemptuous masses in Paul's time. That title had earlier been given to Jews,[84] but evidence shows that it came to be applied to Christians. A caricature of a Christian convert named Alexamenos kneeling before a figure hanging on a cross – that is, the figure of a man with the head of an ass – bears the inscription, "Alexamenos worships his god."[85]

28:23 – *And when they had set a day for him, they came to him at his lodging in large numbers; and he was explaining to them by solemnly testifying about the kingdom of God, and trying to persuade them concerning Jesus, from both the Law of Moses and from the Prophets, from morning until evening.*

And when they had set a day for him. Before the Jews departed that first day, they and Paul agreed on a date mutually suitable to both when they would come again and give his gospel a full hearing. His explanation of his imprisonment had been satisfactory in their minds, so they have no hesitation on that account to hear Paul's explanation of the hope of Israel.

They came to him at his lodging in large numbers. This phrase suggests that Paul is staying as a guest in someone's home, for the word "lodging" is the same one used at Philemon 22 of a place where a guest is entertained.[86] Aquila and Priscilla have returned to Rome,[87] and it would be completely natural for them to provide a room for their old friend and brother in Christ. The Greek for "large numbers" is a comparative adjective, implying a larger attendance than might have been looked for.

And he was explaining to them. "Explained" is a verb used before in Acts.[88] And was true before, the word implies a detailed and comprehensive explanation. The evidences for Christianity were studied and discussed. Luke does not give us anything more than the barest outline of the things which were discussed that day, or the evidences that Paul presented to the Jews. But it can be assumed that Paul used a line of argument similar to what he has used previously in Acts,[89] and which is given fuller treatment in several of Paul's epistles (e.g., Romans, Galatians, and Hebrews).

By solemnly testifying about the kingdom of God. Included would be an explanation of how the church is the fulfillment of the prophecies of a coming kingdom.[90] Also included would be the great doctrines of justification, sanctification, and glorification through Jesus

---

[84] Josephus, *Against Apion*, II.7.

[85] Tacitus, *History*, V.4; Tertullian, *Apology*, c.16.

[86] The word for "lodging" here is different than the word used of Paul's residence in verse 30. Though there is no way to show absolutely that the variance in wording denotes a change of housing, this is the likely explanation for why the different words are used.

[87] Romans 16:3.

[88] Acts 11:4, 18:26.

[89] Acts 13:17ff, 17:2ff, 26:22ff.

[90] Compare Daniel 2:44, Acts 1:3, and Special Study #1, "Diverse Opinions About the Kingdom of God."

Christ.[91] As Paul spoke of the "kingdom of God" he would not have been speaking of any of those temporal, earthly notions that many Jews held, but he would have been telling about the spiritual nature of the kingdom.[92]

And trying to persuade them concerning Jesus. "Persuade" (*peithō*) suggests he was reasoning with them and trying to convince them that Jesus of Nazareth was the Messiah to which the Law and Prophets looked forward. What Paul wants is not only conviction, but obedience.[93]

From both the Law of Moses and from the Prophets. Paul labored to prove to them that the gospel of Christ was the true and necessary fulfillment of Israel's religion, of Old Testament history and prophecy. His text was the whole volume of Hebrew Scripture, interpreted by the events of the advent, passion, and triumph of Jesus of Nazareth. The same Old Testament passages that have been appealed to a number of times in Acts[94] would have been studied, and more as well. We can imagine that Paul appealed to the ordinances, sacrifices, priesthood, and prophecies of the Mosaic dispensation in their significance as preparatory for the coming of Christ. Just as Jesus had done years before with two men on the road to Emmaus,[95] and with the disciples in the upper room,[96] Paul now begins with Moses and the Prophets and expounds to them all the things concerning Jesus.

From morning until evening. It is unlikely that Paul did all the talking through this whole day; instead, there were likely questions and answers, followed by further teaching, and appeals made to additional passages in the Old Testament. Every separate proposition was supported by appeal to the proper verses of Scripture. If "morning until evening" seems like a long meeting, we should remember that these people were not bound to timepieces as modern Americans are, and the topic under discussion was one that had to do with both time and eternity. The audience permits Paul sufficient time to place his whole teaching before them in some detail.

28:24 – *And some were being persuaded by the things spoken, but others would not believe.*

And some were being persuaded by the things spoken, but others would not believe. The gospel made its customary division between believers and unbelievers. Some of the hearers were receptive to the truth; they were in the process of being persuaded. Given time they might throw their lot with the Christians. Others who did not wish to accept the responsibilities that the gospel lays on a person found reasons to reject it. It seems that the people who came to hear Paul on this set day were evenly divided in their response. The

---

[91] Romans 3:8.

[92] Throughout Acts, the kingdom of God has been presented in its spiritual significance, with the exception of Acts 14:22, where the reference is to the church triumphant.

[93] See notes on *peithō* in Special Study #16, "The Faith That Saves."

[94] Acts 2:16ff, 2:25ff, 2:34ff, 3:22ff, 4:25ff, 8:23ff, 13:13ff, 26:23.

[95] Luke 24:25ff.

[96] Luke 24:44ff.

implication of the following verses is that the ones who were being persuaded had enough conviction to begin arguing with the unbelievers that what Paul had presented must be right.

28:25 – *And when they did not agree with one another, they* **began** *leaving after Paul had spoken one* **parting** *word, "The Holy Spirit rightly spoke through Isaiah the prophet to your fathers,*

And when they did not agree with one another. "Did not agree" is from the Greek *asumphōnoi,* which means "without symphony, out of harmony, dissonant, discordant." Yet it is difficult to determine for sure who was out of harmony with whom.

- It may mean that all the Jews were out of harmony with Paul, including even those who were somewhat inclined to be persuaded.
- It may mean that the persuaded Jews were out of harmony with the Jews who would not believe.

Perhaps this latter idea is the one we should adopt, and picture the audience taking up the argument amongst themselves, much as happened among the Pharisees and Sadducees at Jerusalem a couple of years earlier.[97] These present unbelievers spoke with such stridency that Paul applied to them the condemnation of God against those who refused His message. It may even be that the disagreement led to some altercation, and to the exhibition of the usual bigotry and prejudice and bitter opposition on the part of the unbelieving Jews.

They *began* **leaving after Paul had spoken one parting word.** Knowling suggests that this parting word was addressed to all the Jews, who, he thinks, suppressed their differences after some time, and for the sake of an outward show of unity (lest they be charged again with "tumults over one Christ") began leaving in a body.[98] However, it does not seem likely that after all his efforts at conciliation and winning a hearing for the gospel that Paul would apply these words from Isaiah to even those who "were being persuaded." Thus, we prefer to think of these next words as addressed in particular to the unbelieving Jews.

Throughout this whole day, Paul has been turning to passages from the Old Testament to show that what had happened in the coming of Jesus and the beginning of the kingdom of God was just as God had predicted it would be. Very appropriately, he turns to one more passage in their Scriptures, and shows that even what had happened this day was just as God had said it would be.

"The Holy Spirit rightly spoke. Here the apostle Paul distinctly asserts the inspiration of the Old Testament prophet Isaiah.[99] "Rightly" represents *kalos,* "well, beautiful." What the Spirit led Isaiah to record fits this situation beautifully!

Through Isaiah the prophet to your fathers. The words Paul quotes are from Isaiah 6:9-10. The words originally formed part of what God gave Isaiah to preach after one of his

---

[97] Acts 23:7.

[98] Knowling, *op. cit.*, p.550.

[99] See also Special Study #5, "The Doctrine of Inspiration."

calls to the ministry. Paul is reminding his hearers that this for a long time has been God's estimate of the Jewish people; namely, that they have a characteristic to reject the testimony sent to them by God Himself through inspired messengers.

28:26 – *saying, 'GO TO THIS PEOPLE AND SAY, "YOU WILL KEEP ON HEARING, BUT WILL NOT UNDERSTAND; AND YOU WILL KEEP ON SEEING, BUT WILL NOT PERCEIVE;*

Saying, 'GO TO THIS PEOPLE AND SAY, "YOU WILL KEEP ON HEARING, BUT WILL NOT UNDERSTAND; AND YOU WILL KEEP ON SEEING, BUT WILL NOT PERCEIVE. Paul is quoting the Septuagint almost verbatim. This Isaiah passage is quoted a number of times in the New Testament. Jesus quoted it the day He preached his sermon in parables,[100] and John's Gospel alludes to it just after he has recorded Jesus' last public sermon preceding his crucifixion.[101] Thus we can say that what had been the response of the Jews 700 years before Christ to a message from God, what had been the response of the Jews to God's own Messiah, has become almost a national characteristic.[102] Paul now sees this same response repeated in these Jews at Rome. There was a willful blindness and a willful deafness to that which ought to have produced conviction and conversion. This willfulness is specifically pointed out in the phrases from Isaiah which follow. Observe that God does not say "to My people;" He says "to this people." God was speaking in displeasure as He gave the message to Isaiah.

28:27 – *FOR THE HEART OF THIS PEOPLE HAS BECOME DULL, AND WITH THEIR EARS THEY SCARCELY HEAR, AND THEY HAVE CLOSED THEIR EYES; LEST THEY SHOULD SEE WITH THEIR EYES, AND HEAR WITH THEIR EARS, AND UNDERSTAND WITH THEIR HEART AND RETURN, AND I SHOULD HEAL THEM.'"*

FOR THE HEART OF THIS PEOPLE HAS BECOME DULL. "Become dull" in the Hebrew is imperative (in the prophetic style), and it means "made fat" or "shut." They have deliberately shut their hearts (i.e., their minds) to the truth.

AND WITH THEIR EARS THEY SCARCELY HEAR. This speaks of a willful deafness.

AND THEY HAVE CLOSED THEIR EYES. This also speaks of a willful closing. In rather pointed language, Paul is saying (in the words of God to Isaiah) that there are none so deaf as those who refuse to hear, and there are none so blind as those who refuse to see.

LEST THEY SHOULD SEE WITH THEIR EYES, AND HEAR WITH THEIR EARS, AND UNDERSTAND WITH THEIR HEART. If they were to see, and hear, and understand, they would have to give up the pleasures of sin they are currently enjoying, their selfish living,

---

[100] Matthew 13:14.

[101] John 12:40.

[102] In his extended treatment of the problem of Israel's unbelief in Romans 9-11, Paul quotes this same Isaiah passage (see Romans 11:8). The Jews refusal to heed the gospel resulted from their own willfulness and lack of interest in repentance.

and their wicked ways. Because this is the very thing these Jewish hearers in Rome did not want to do, they harden their hearts to the gospel.

The words of Isaiah are true of numbers of people who are not Jews, too. Herein is the true explanation of why the gospel seemingly fails to win some who hear it. They just don't want to obey; they just don't want to repent!

This passage from Isaiah illustrates once more from the book of Acts that the doctrine of a first work of grace is at variance with the Divine Record.[103] If that doctrine were true, it would follow that the reason these Jews didn't believe is because there had been no direct and immediate regenerative work by the Holy Spirit on these men's hearts; it would follow that some of Paul's hearers went away unbelievers because a divine influence was withheld from them while it was granted to others. But what does the Acts record say? The real reason some believed and others disbelieved is that those who disbelieved deliberately plugged their ears and shut their eyes. Just as they closed their eyes and ears voluntarily, they had the power to keep them open. And it is implied that had they done so, the result would have been reversed. The reason the gospel was or was not received rested with the will of the hearers, rather than on a direct work of the Spirit on their hearts.

AND TURN AGAIN, AND I SHOULD HEAL THEM. "Turning again" would include repentance and obedience.[104] They did not allow themselves to be convinced by what Paul was sharing with them about the Messiah because they didn't want to repent. It is as simple, and as tragic, as that! One writer has noted the interesting fact that Luke the physician, as almost one of the last words of volume two of his history, cites a prophecy that ends with the word "heal." Included in God's healing from sin is its forgiveness, with the corresponding result that the broken relationship with God is restored; and when sin's hurts are healed, men find that their relationships with each other can be restored, too.

28:28 – *"Let it be known to you therefore, that this salvation of God has been sent to the Gentiles; they will also listen."*

Let it be known to you therefore. Here Paul sadly sounds a note of warning to these willfully disbelieving Jews. The words are not said in a tone of condemnation. When we remember how Paul loved his Jewish kinsmen, how he had great sorrow and unceasing grief in his heart because of their refusal to come to Christ,[105] we can understand why he tells them of his plans to turn to the Gentiles so quickly. It is not that he is giving up on these Jews after only one sermon, but that by speaking of how the Gentiles will respond, he is hoping to provoke the Jews to emulation.[106]

That this salvation of God has been sent to the Gentiles. What Paul had said before in Pisidian Antioch (Acts 13:46), at Corinth (Acts 18:6), and elsewhere, he now says with reference to Rome. From that time on, in Rome, the Gentiles would have priority in re-

---

[103] Compare also footnote #42 in chapter 8.

[104] Acts 3:19.

[105] Romans 9:1ff.

[106] Romans 11:14.

ceiving the message of salvation.[107] "This salvation" is the salvation promised in Isaiah's word "heal" just quoted, the salvation that Messiah Himself was to usher in. The very method of deliverance which God gave in fulfillment of the Old Testament prophecy would be embraced by the Gentiles. Yet while the Jews might reject God's way of saving men for themselves, that would not destroy the kingdom of God nor prevent Messiah from reigning over His kingdom! He would reign over the hearts of Gentiles who responded to His gracious offer of salvation, proffered on the condition of an obedient faith.

They will also listen." We might paraphrase this, "They will really listen!" The very thing the Jews willfully refused to do – namely, hear and repent so that God could heal them – the Gentiles would do! The Gentiles, who knew they were sick and in need of a Physician, would embrace God's means of saving men, if only they were given the opportunity to hear about it. Paul's hope was this: that perhaps when the Jews saw the blessings of Messianic salvation being enjoyed by all those Gentiles, they would be led to want those blessings, too, and then they would be ready to hear and turn.

28:29 – *[And when he had spoken these words, the Jews departed, having a great dispute among themselves.]*

[And when he had spoken these words, the Jews departed, having a great dispute among themselves.] This whole verse is not found in codices *Aleph,* A, B, E, and most modern critical texts; hence, it appears in the margin of the NASB. These words likely are an accurate description what happened after Paul had his closing word with them. Perhaps the verse was written on the margin of some ancient manuscript to relieve the apparent abruptness of the account in verses 28 and 30 if it is omitted. Later, a scribe seeing it in the margin, supposed it had been omitted from the text, and when he made a copy of Acts, included it in the text of his new copy.

       c. Paul spends two years in custody. 28:30-31

28:30 – *And he stayed two full years in his own rented quarters, and was welcoming all who came to him,*

And he stayed two full years in his own rented quarters. Since the word for "rented quarters" differs from the word used in verse 23, it seems that Paul has changed dwellings, from someone's home in which he was a guest to these quarters that he rents. "Quarters" is probably a better translation than "house," for the Greek seems to speak of an apartment rather than a whole house. Money to pay rent likely came via help from Paul's friends, like the missionary offering from Philippi that had been brought from the brethren there by Epaphroditus.[108] Doubtless, Paul is still in the custody of a soldier, chained to him day and

---

[107] This passage does not at all support the Dispensational idea that at this juncture the Jews are finally rejected by God, and so the "stopgap measure" called the "Church" becomes necessary until God can work with the Jews to bring in the earthly millennial kingdom as He had all along intended to, if only the Jews would have allowed Him to.

[108] Philippians 4:10ff.

night,[109] and so the Gospel continues to spread through the whole Praetorian camp.

From these rented quarters during these two years will issue five of the epistles which are now contained in our New Testaments – the epistles to the Ephesians, Colossians, Philippians (a thank-you letter for that missionary offering), Philemon, and probably Hebrews.

The verb tense behind "stayed" and the words "two whole years" both seem to be indicative of more than first meets the eye. The verb tense seems to imply that when Luke wrote there had been a change of condition; that is, the staying in the rented quarters is over. What happened? The "two whole years" supplies the clue to this question. The Introductory Studies documented the fact that two years was the limit of time a man had to wait for his prosecutors to arrive to press charges.[110] We think that at the time Luke writes Acts, Paul's two years' wait are just over, his accusers have not come, and so Paul automatically has been set at liberty.

And was welcoming all who came to him. Paul is a prisoner during these two years, and so was limited as to where he himself might go; he would not be allowed to go to the synagogues, or to the "churches," or to the houses of this or that disciple, or to homes where teaching was needed to win converts. On this surface, this limitation might seem to be a hindrance to his evangelistic work. But what at first seemed a hindrance, as he himself afterwards acknowledged, turned out "for the greater progress of the gospel."[111] For he was not limited as to who might come and visit with him, just as the leaders of the Jewish community already had done. His presence in Rome stimulated others to renewed evangelistic activity.[112]

"All" indicates that both Jews and Gentiles were welcome, and it also implies he had many visitors. Many of them were likely Christian brethren who were evangelizing in the city, and would return for further directions concerning location and work to be entered next. Others would be new converts brought to meet Paul. Still others would be acquaintances who came to Rome from the provinces, and would look up Paul. Among these latter, we suppose, was Onesimus, a run-away slave from Colossae, who was converted to Christ by Paul in Rome, and then was sent back home along with the letter to Philemon his master.

From the letters he wrote during these two years, it is evident that Paul had a number of faithful co-workers and helpers alongside him during this two-year period. Luke the beloved physician, who had shared the perils of the voyage from Caesarea to Rome, was his constant co-worker.[113] Timothy, who was last mentioned by name during the carrying of the offering to Jerusalem,[114] is united with him in the salutations of Colossians, Philemon, and Philippians, so must have come to Paul while he was in custody in Rome.

---

[109] See notes at verse 16, and also Philippians 1:13.

[110] See page *xxxvi* where this matter of Roman jurisprudence is documented.

[111] Philippians 1:12.

[112] Philippians 1:14ff.

[113] Colossians 4:14.

[114] Acts 20:4.

Mark, who once quit as a helper during the first missionary journey, was back in Paul's good graces, had come to him in Rome, and was about to be sent off on a distant journey at Paul's request.[115] Aristarchus has joined Paul in Rome.[116] Demas, who some years later will forsake Paul because "he loved this present world," was still by Paul's side at this time.[117] Epaphras, a preacher who served with several congregations in the Lycus River valley of Asia, has come to Rome in the capacity of messenger for those congregations at Colossae, Laodicea, and Hierapolis.[118] Tychicus, the Ephesian, who had gone with Paul to Jerusalem, had also found his way to Rome.[119] A Jew named Jesus, who also was named Justus, was also among Paul's fellow workers at Rome.[120]

A number of things happened in connection with Epaphroditus, whose special mission from Philippi to Paul has already been noted. In addition to bringing an offering from the church, he was to serve Paul in whatever capacity he could, giving him the loving attention he would get from the Philippians if they could have been there to bestow it themselves. But while at Rome, or on the way to Rome, Epaphroditus had become sick nigh unto death.[121] Some visitor to Philippi after this told the Philippians about Epaphroditus' sickness, and news of the church's resulting concern made its way back to Paul at Rome. Now that Epaphroditus is fully recovered, Paul sends him home to Philippi, along with instructions that the Philippians are to look on him as a hero for the way he represented their interests and helped Paul.[122]

28:31 – *preaching the kingdom of God, and teaching concerning the Lord Jesus Christ with all openness, unhindered.*

Preaching the kingdom of God, and teaching concerning the Lord Jesus Christ. "Preaching" would be public heralding of the gospel, while "teaching" would be individual instruction given to those who came to his quarters for that instruction. The preaching (if the word is used here as elsewhere in Acts) would be mostly to unbelievers, while teaching would be especially to those who were already Christians. Even while a prisoner, Paul fulfilled the preaching and teaching functions commanded in the Great Commission.[123]

With all openness, unhindered. Thus, the ministry that seemed to have been brought to an end with Paul's arrest was actually continued under Roman protection. While he was in Rome, Paul was saved the hardships, persecutions, and afflictions that had often attended

---

[115] Colossians 4:10.

[116] Philemon 24.

[117] Colossians 4:14.

[118] Colossians 4:12.

[119] Ephesians 6:21; Colossians 4:7.

[120] Colossians 4:10-14.

[121] Philippians 2:27.

[122] Philippians 2:25-30.

[123] Matthew 28:18-20

his preaching in the cities of Greece, Macedonia, and Asia Minor.[124]

> During this period the gospel was proclaimed freely in Rome through the lips of its chief messenger. The apologetic value of the fact mentioned in the last words of the book was considerable. Luke is suggesting that it is unlikely, that if the gospel were illegal and subversive propaganda, it could have been taught for two years in the heart of the empire without hindrance, and that by a Roman citizen who had appealed to Caesar, and was waiting under guard for his case to be heard. The authorities must have known what Paul was doing all along, and yet they put no obstacle in his way. Acts is brought to a close, then, on this triumphant note. The Kingdom of God and the story of Jesus are openly proclaimed and taught in Rome itself ....[125]

And so ends this lively, beautiful, faithfully rendered sketch of the world's greatest missionary. As we read Acts, we see that Paul's own statement – "in far more labors, in far more imprisonments, beaten times without number, often in danger of death"[126] – is no empty boast, but a simple statement of truth. "I do not consider my life of any account as dear to myself, in order that I may finish my course, and the ministry which I received from the Lord Jesus, to testify solemnly of the gospel of the grace of God"[127] is the true description of Paul's life.[128]

Our brief glance over those "two whole years" with which this record closes fills us with amazement at the work done for the Lord during that time. In addition to what we are told, there are things which we can imagine. Think of the gatherings of holy men and women within the walls of those "rented quarters." Think of the prayer meetings, the expositions of the Word of God, the descriptions of the kingdom of God, and the anticipations of the day when the Church will be taken to be with the Lord! Think of the loving exhortations, the words of sympathy, and the joy in the hearts of the preachers as well as rejoicing by the angels in heaven over the souls won! Think of the contribution to the literature of the kingdom of heaven that is to be found in the epistles to the Ephesians, Colossians, Philippians, Hebrews, and Philemon! "Truly, they were two years of infinite moment to the church of God!"[129]

---

[124] Philippians 1:15,17 indicate that Paul did have some opposition from the very ones who should have been his friends. but there was no reason to fear bodily harm such as often was a worry in many of the towns where he went to evangelize.

[125] Bruce, *op. cit.*, p.535.

[126] 2 Corinthians 11:23.

[127] Acts 20:24.

[128] Hervey, *op. cit.*, p.325

[129] Hervey, *op. cit.*, p.326.

Drawing by Horace Knowles
from the British and Foreign Bible Society

EPILOGUE
The Last Labors and Letters of Paul

Having finished this study of Acts, someone may ask, "What happened to Paul?" Luke doesn't tell us, but there are some other sources of information.[1]

If we accept the Pastoral Epistles[2] as genuine, and we do, they cannot be fitted into Paul's life and travels as recorded in Acts.[3] Therefore, the Pastoral Epistles depict labors accomplished by Paul and are letters written after the first Roman imprisonment had ended.

In the year AD 63, Paul was released from the first Roman imprisonment, just as the Prison Epistles anticipated.[4]

If Paul fulfilled the wishes that the Prison Epistles intimate, upon being released from custody in Rome he went to Philippi, and from there he passed over into Asia Minor to visit the churches of the Lycus Valley (i.e., Colossae, Hierapolis, Laodicea).

Tradition has it that Paul visited Spain and possibly Britain. If he did (which this commentator doubts), it would have been after he visited the churches of the Lycus Valley.[5]

At some time in the five-year period between his release and his death, he visited Ephesus, leaving Timothy there, and then went on over to Macedonia, from whence 1 Timothy was written.[6] We date 1 Timothy about AD 65.

Some time between his two Roman imprisonments, perhaps toward the close of the five-year interval (if the winter spoken of in Titus 3:12 and in 2 Timothy 4:20 is the same winter), Paul visited Crete. Upon leaving the island, he left Titus behind to set things in order.[7]

The departure from Crete begins the trip that will eventually bring Paul back to Rome, and to his martyrdom. Leaving Crete, he went to Miletus, perhaps by way of Corinth.[8] Trophimus was left behind at Miletus because he was sick. From Miletus, Paul went to Ephesus, where he spent time with Timothy. During this visit, he received the ministrations of Onesiphorus.[9] Most commentators believe the epistle to Titus was written

---

[1] In the Introductory Studies, under the paragraph about the "Date of Writing," see information concerning the alleged "abrupt ending" to Acts, wherein are stated several ideas that are attempts to explain what happened to Paul, none of which is satisfactory.

[2] 1 and 2 Timothy and Titus have been called "Pastoral Epistles" for the last 200 or so years,

[3] Some have attempted to fit these into the Acts record, but not satisfactorily or successfully.

[4] Philippians 1:26, 2:24; Philemon 22. Compare notes also at Acts 28:30.

[5] The evidences alleged to show a trip to Spain include 1 Clement 5:7; Muratorian Canon; Eusebius, *Church History*, II.22.1,2; Theodoret, *in Phil.*, I.25; Jerome, *Illustrious Men*, V; Cyril of Jerusalem, *Catechetical Lectures*, XVII.26; Epiphanius, *Heresies*, XXVII.6.

[6] 1 Timothy 1:3, 3:14-15.

[7] Titus 1:5.

[8] 2 Timothy 4:20.

[9] 2 Timothy 1:18.

from Ephesus during this same visit. From Ephesus, Paul traveled north to Troas, where he stored some things in the home of Carpus.[10] At length, Paul came to Nicopolis, in the province of Epirus, just across the sea from the heel of Italy, where he intended to spend the winter.[11]

Nicopolis, a Roman colony, would offer a certain safety against tumultuary violence. But at the same time, Paul would be more open to arrest by Roman authorities. Knowing that he intended to pass the winter in Nicopolis, and that very shortly after that he was a prisoner in Rome, the natural inference is that Paul was arrested by the authorities in Epirus, and by them was sent to Rome for trial.

Since Paul's release from the first Roman imprisonment, a great change had come over the polity of the imperial court at Rome. Afranius Burrus[12] was no longer the adviser of Nero. In his place the influence of the base, brutal, and cruel Tigellinus was altogether dominant. Poppaea, with her tendency to protect the Jews, and probably the "Christians in Caesar's household," had died by the brutality of Nero in AD 65. The great fire of AD 64 had broken out at the foot of the Caelian and Palatine Hills, after an entertainment which Nero had given in the gardens of Agrippa.[13] The fire was almost controlled when it broke out anew in the Aemilian district of the city where Tigellinus had large estates, and in a week's time, the whole city of Rome had burned. People had suspicions that Nero and Tigellinus were deeply implicated, and so that suspicion had to be stamped out. The Christians of Rome, especially those whose presence in the palace disapproved the vices of Tigellinus and the Emperor, were accused. Many of the better people in Rome knew the Christians were not guilty,[14] but the populace, excited, rushed upon the members of the "sect everywhere spoken against"[15] with a ferocious eagerness. Fanaticism can be contagious; and though there was as yet no formal or organized persecution in the empire, old enmities revived, and the opportunities for acting on them were utilized.

It was in this context that Paul's second Roman imprisonment began. There is not the slightest hint in Scripture, or in any history, as to the place or circumstances of Paul's arrest, but it is conceivable that a warrant was issued by Tigellinus for the arrest of the leaders of Christianity, including Paul. Tigellinus must have known that for two years Paul had been the central figure among the Christians of Rome, and that he was on terms of friendship with the officers of the Augustan Band and the Praetorian Guard. While Paul had left the city before the fire, could it be insinuated that he had planned it, or even suggested the idea, and left others to work it out, in order to make the charges stated in the warrant sound plausible? From Nicopolis, Paul, after being arrested, would be sent to Rome to stand trial, for the crime was alleged to have been committed in Rome.

---

[10] 2 Timothy 4:13. It is also at this place that some place a visit to Corinth (2 Timothy 4:20), rather than putting it on the way from Crete to Miletus

[11] Titus 3:12.

[12] See notes at Act 28:16.

[13] Tacitus, *Annals*, XV.37-40.

[14] Juvenal, *Satires*, I.155.

[15] Acts 28:22.

Paul's second Roman imprisonment is dated AD 67-68. In Rome this second time, his imprisonment would be much more severe and restricting than the first.[16] The Roman tradition that he was confined in the lower dungeon of the Mamertine prison, dark and damp, with no opening but a hole through which the prisoners were let down, is not improbable. On the other hand, the tradition that Peter and Paul were imprisoned together in the Mamertine prison has been rejected even by Catholic scholars, perhaps because there is evidence that the Christians at Rome managed to keep in touch with Paul. Eubulus, Pudens, Linus, and Claudia are some of the brethren who send greetings to Timothy, as did "all the brethren," which likely is evidence of the continued communication between the Christians at Rome and Paul the prisoner.[17]

Compared with the number of friends who constantly streamed through his hired quarters during the first imprisonment, this second imprisonment was a lonelier one. Old friends had either left him, or were away on missionary activities. Demas forsook him,[18] and many of his Asiatic friends avoided him.[19] Crescens had gone to Galatia (hopefully on evangelistic work).[20] Titus, having come to Rome, had been sent off to Dalmatia on evangelistic work.[21] Tychicus had been sent to Ephesus,[22] and Priscilla and Aquila have moved back to Ephesus.[23] Of his usual companions, only the faithful Luke remained with him.[24] He had a longing to see Timothy and Mark,[25] and Timothy is urged to bring his cloak, and books and parchments,[26] and to get to Rome before winter.[27]

Paul's first trial before the Roman magistrates, and a delay in the final sentencing, are recorded in 2 Timothy 4:16-18. That first hearing filled Paul with the conviction that the end was near, and so he penned his second epistle to Timothy, an epistle filled with hope and joy at seeing the crown of righteousness at last within his reach.[28] We date 2 Timothy in the summer or fall of AD 67.

Paul's confinement probably lasted for several months after his first hearing. During this time, according to tradition, Peter joined Paul in Rome, also having been arrested (perhaps after he comes to Rome).[29] From Rome, Peter writes his two epistles, urging the

---

[16] 2 Timothy 2:9.

[17] 2 Timothy 4:21.

[18] 2 Timothy 4:10.

[19] 2 Timothy 1:15.

[20] 2 Timothy 4:10.

[21] 2 Timothy 4:10.

[22] 2 Timothy 4:12.

[23] 2 Timothy 4:19.

[24] 2 Timothy 4:11.

[25] 2 Timothy 4:9,21.

[26] 2 Timothy 4:13.

[27] Whether Timothy arrived in Rome before Paul's execution is not known.

[28] 2 Timothy 4:8.

[29] See Special Study #14, "Was Peter Ever in Rome?"

brethren to be faithful to Christ, even though in the midst of persecutions.[30] 1 Peter is dated AD 67, and 2 Peter is dated AD 68.

The death of Paul. There is traditional evidence that Paul suffered martyrdom in the last year of Nero's reign.[31] This would put his death in the spring of AD 68. Again, tradition has it that Peter and Paul were at last tried and condemned together. For the last time his Roman citizenship saved Paul from prolonged agony. Paul, tradition has it, was beheaded on the Ostian Way.[32] But Peter, the fisherman from Galilee, was to be subjected to the suffering of crucifixion.[33] His request was granted that he be crucified head-downward, since he felt he was not worthy to suffer as his Master had suffered.[34] Tradition locates the place of Peter's crucifixion as the Hill of Janiculum. Tradition regarding the burial places of the bodies of the two apostles are mixed and contradictory.[35]

Wherever Paul died, his soul is with Jesus. And where that body rested at last, which he labored "to keep in subjection"[36] and which was to him (before he became a Christian) so much the source of conflict and sin,[37] is a matter of little consequence. It will be guarded by the eye of that Savior whom he served, and will be raised up to eternal life. In his own inimitable language, it was "sown in corruption, it shall be raised in incorruption; it was sown in dishonor, it shall be raised in glory; it was sown in weakness, it shall be raised in power; it was sown a natural body, it shall be raised a spiritual body."[38] To Paul now, what are his sorrows, and persecutions, and toils in the cause of his Master? They are a source of thanksgiving that he was permitted thus to labor to spread the gospel through the world.

"And so we bid [Paul] adieu till the resurrection morning, well pleased that the course of the narrative on which we have been commenting has kept us for so long a time in his company."[39] So may we too live – imitating his life of zeal, and self-denial, and faithfulness, that when we also arise from the dead, we may participate with him in the glories of the resurrection of the just.

---

[30] 1 Peter 2:12; 3:17; 4:1,12-16; 5:8-9.

[31] See Special Study #14, "Was Peter Ever in Rome?"

[32] Tradition has the site of Paul's beheading at the third milestone out on the Ostian Way, at a place now called Tre Fontane (i.e., Three Springs). Compare Conybeare and Howson, *op. cit.*, p.782.

[33] See John 21:18-19.

[34] See Special Study #14, "Was Peter Ever in Rome?"

[35] Theodore Zahn, *Introduction to the New Testament* (Grand Rapids: Kregel, 1953), Vol. 2, p.78, note 9.

[36] 1 Corinthians 9:27.

[37] Romans 7:5-23.

[38] 1 Corinthians 15:42-44.

[39] McGarvey, *op. cit.*, p.292.

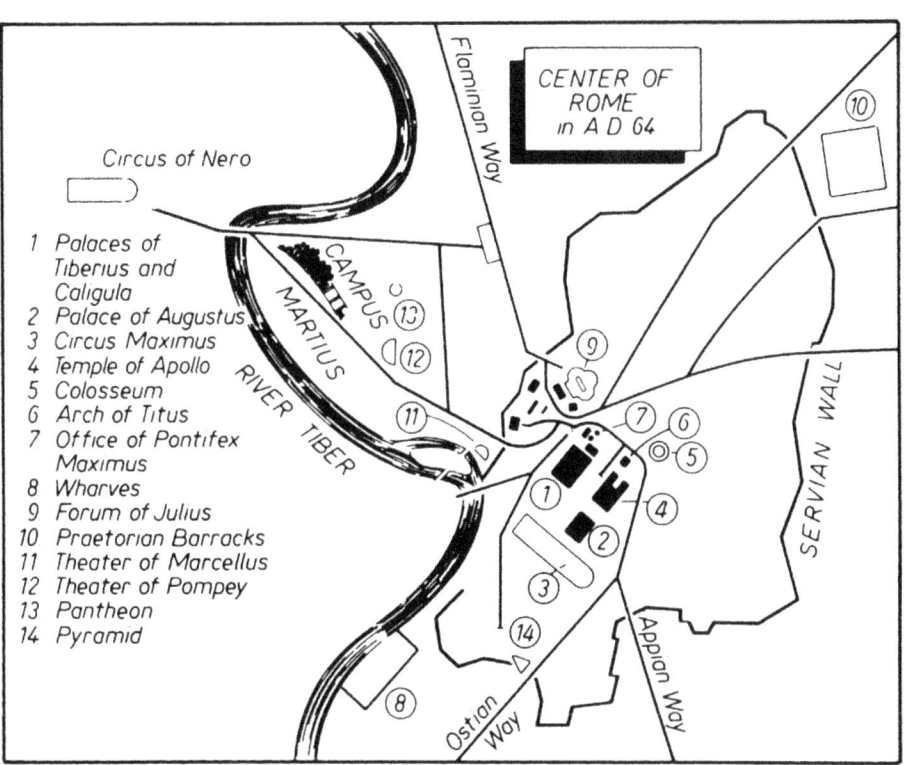

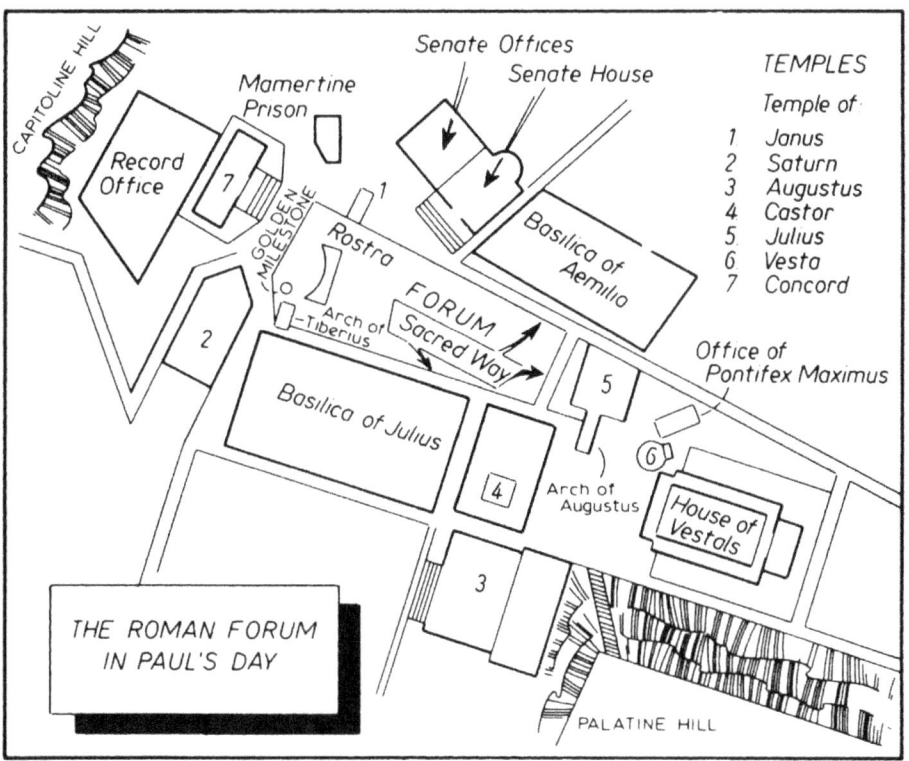

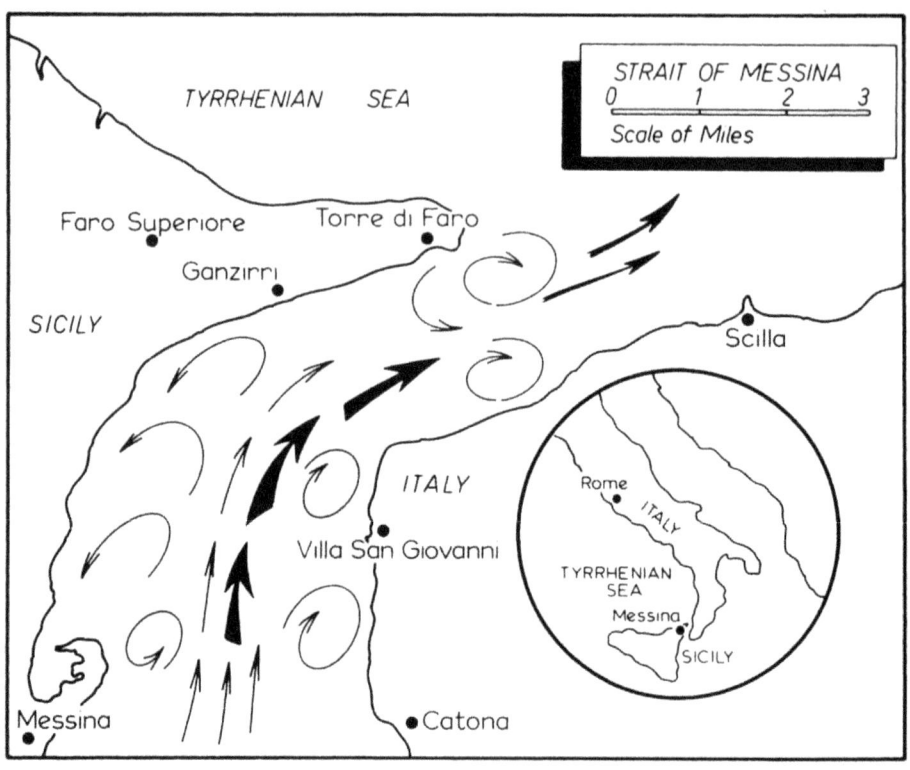

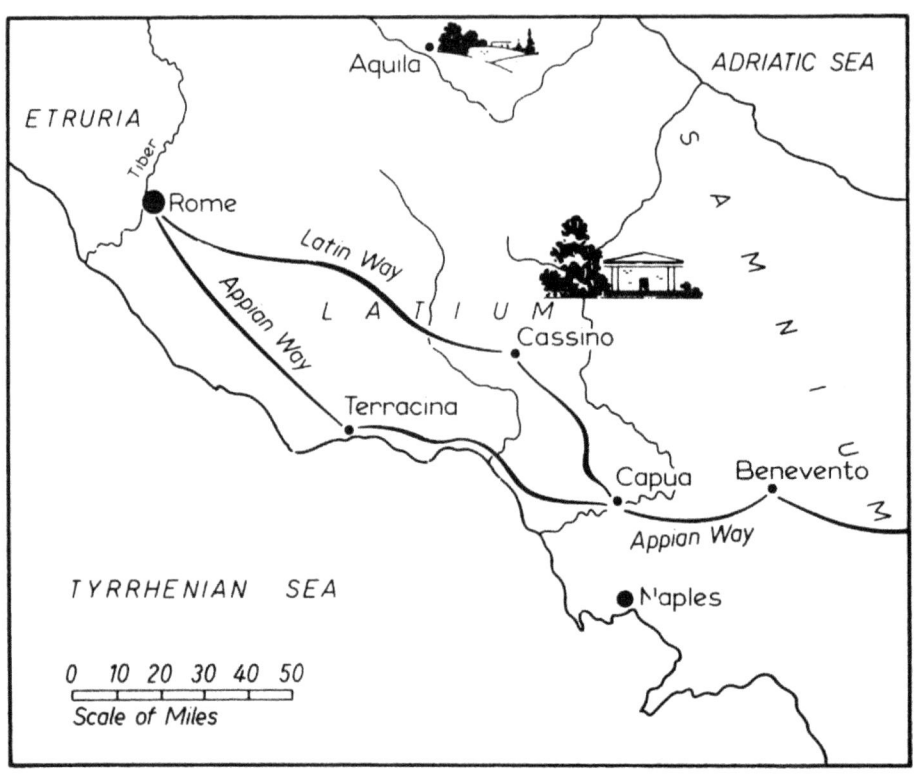

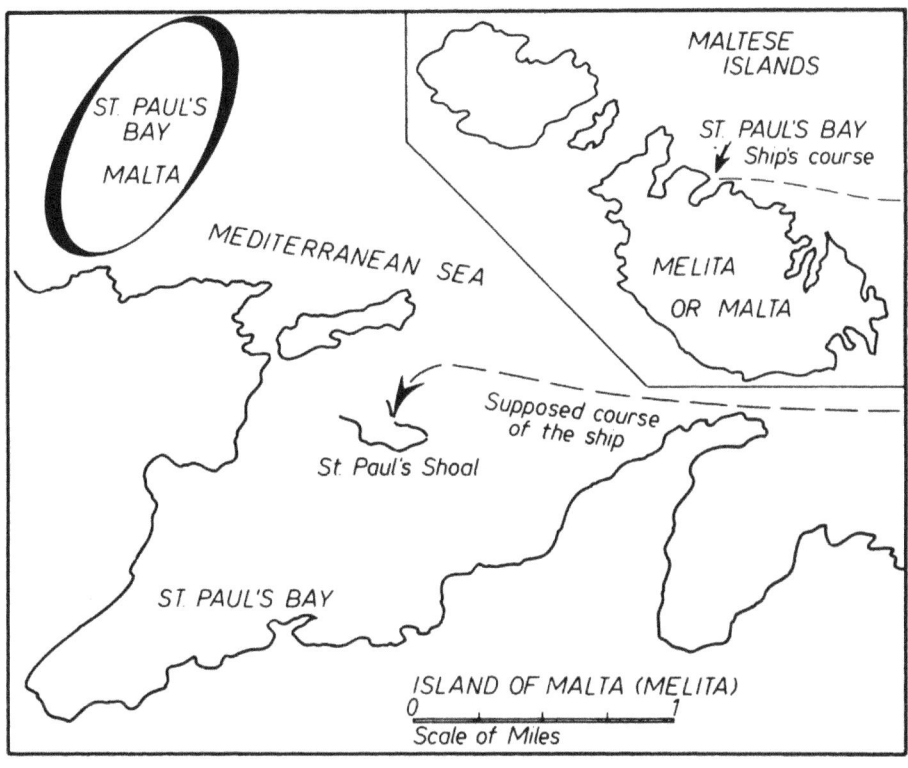

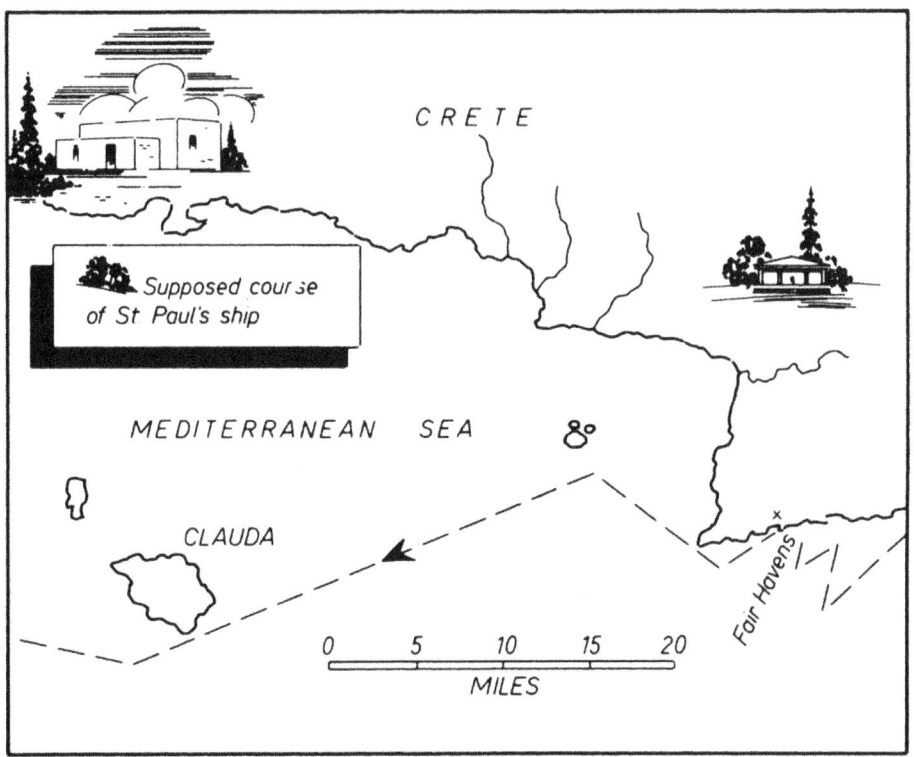

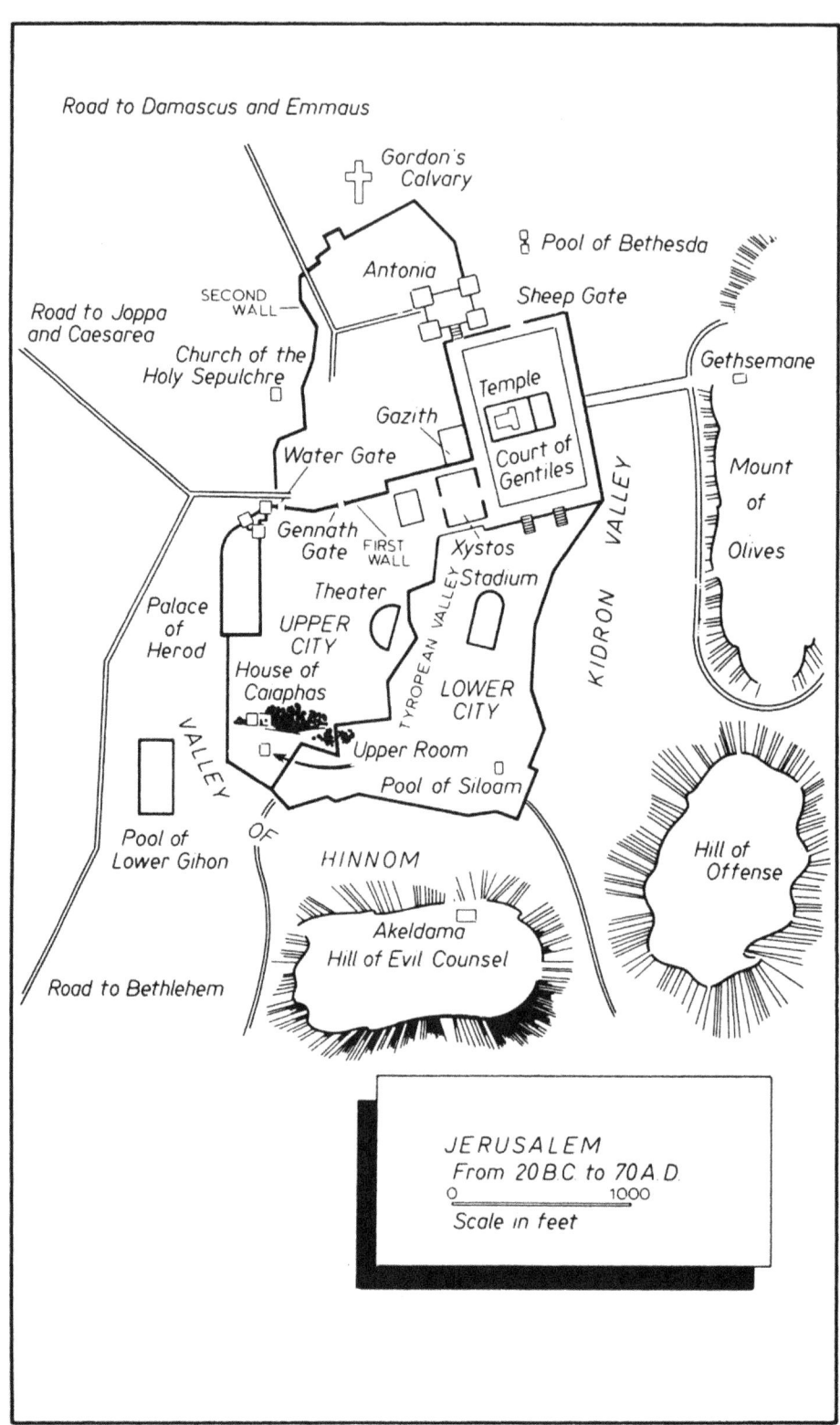

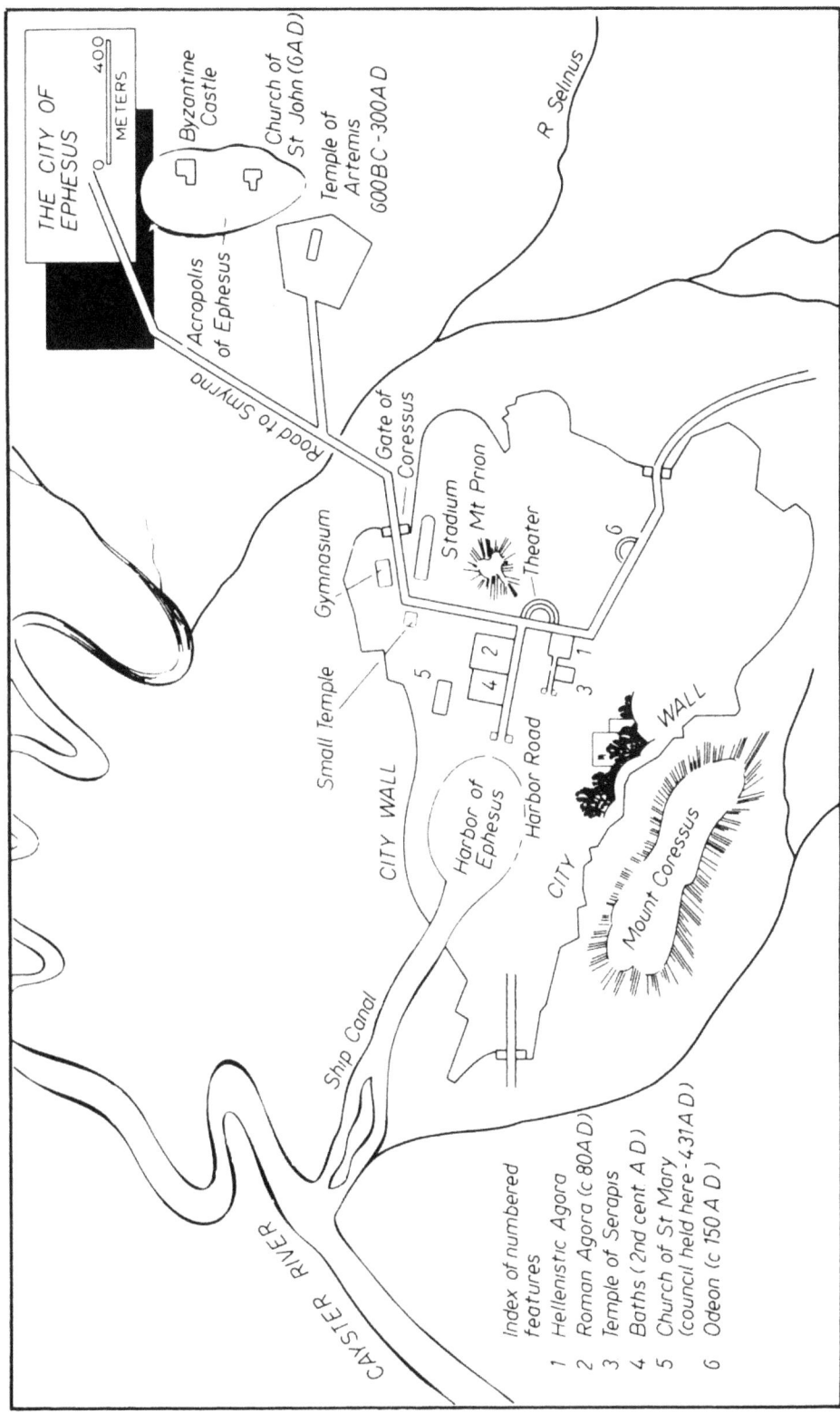

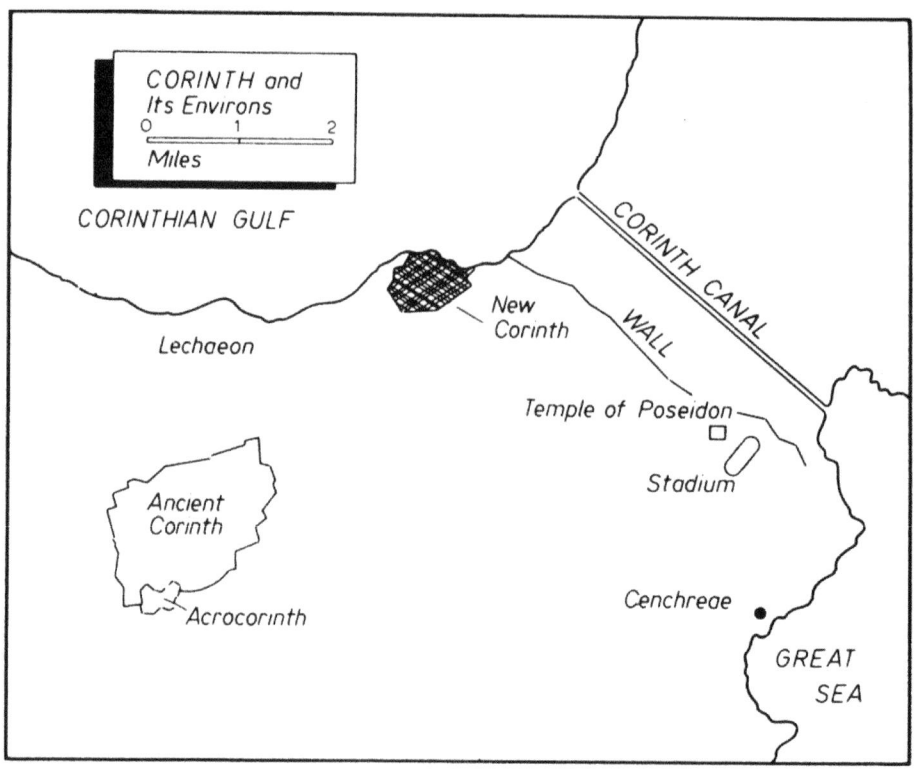

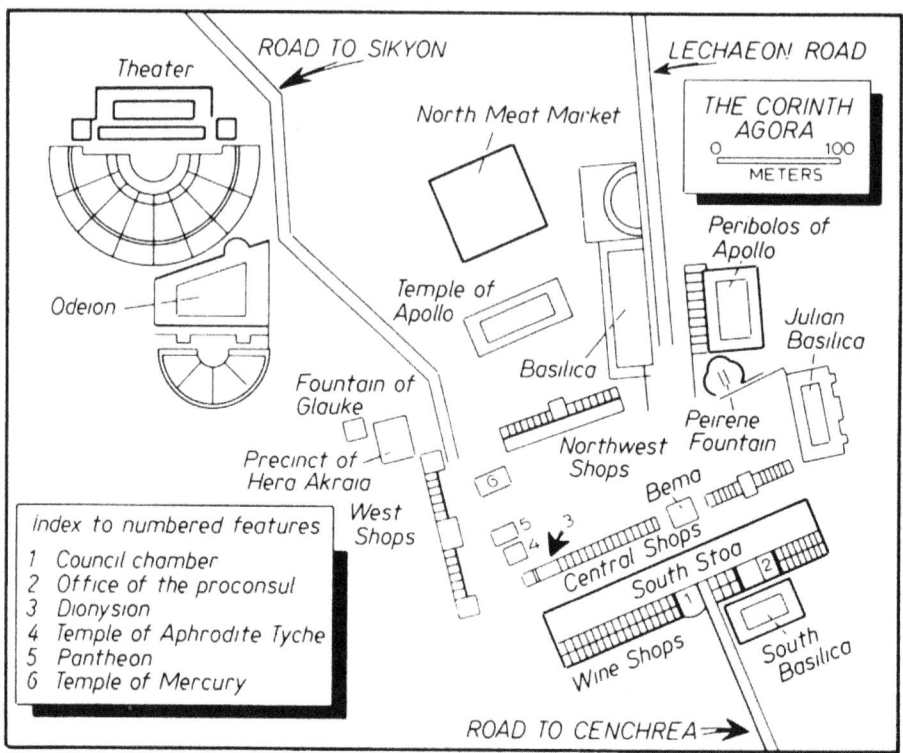

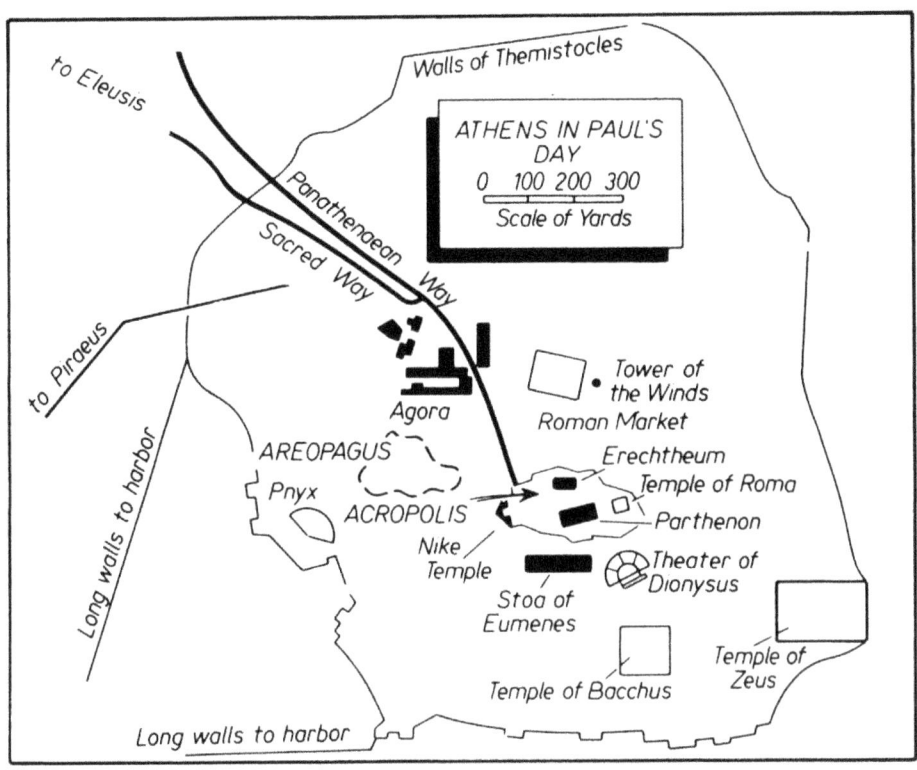
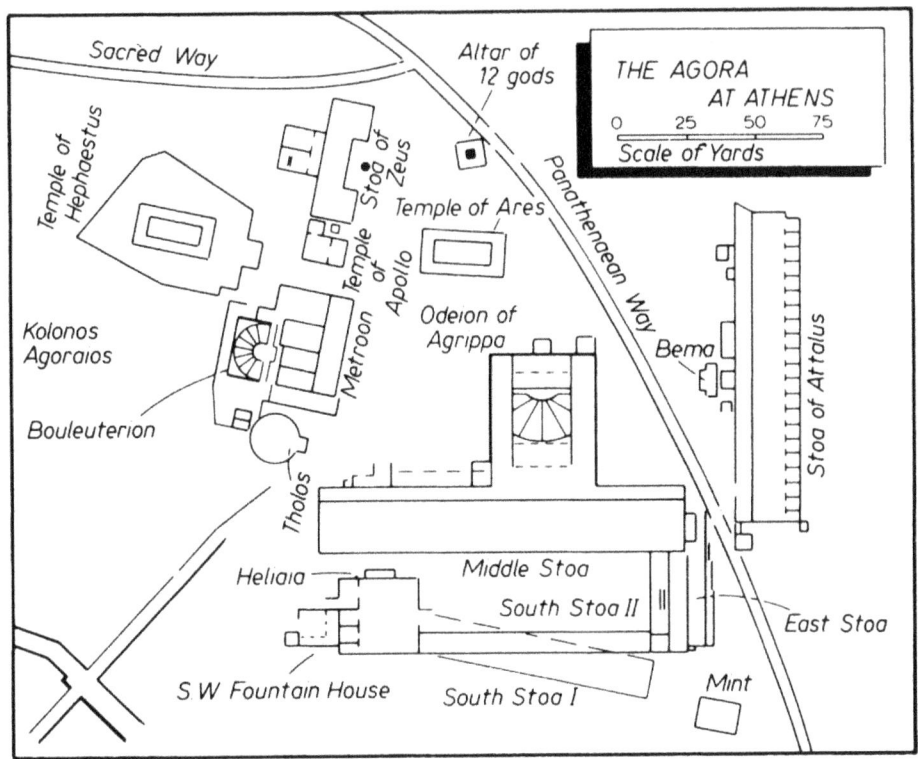

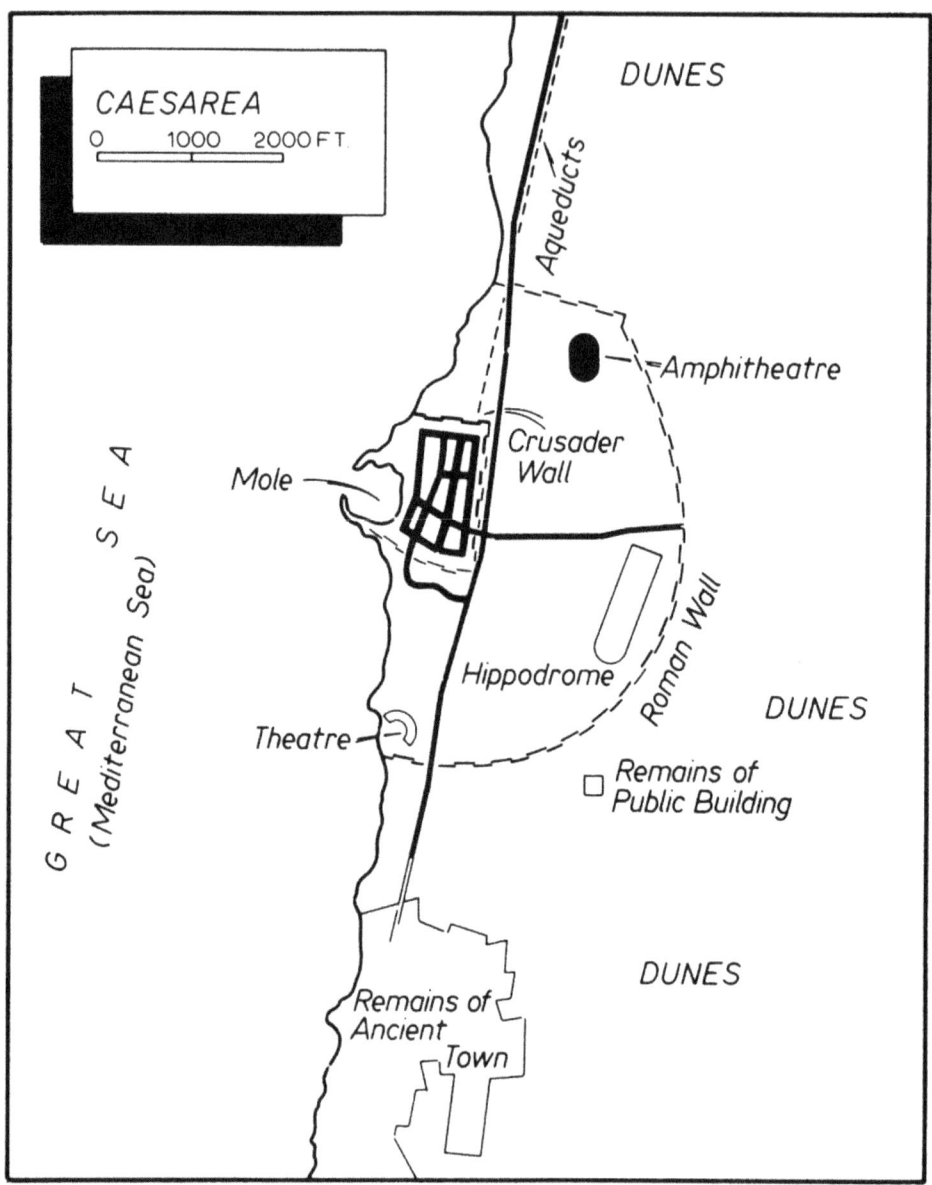

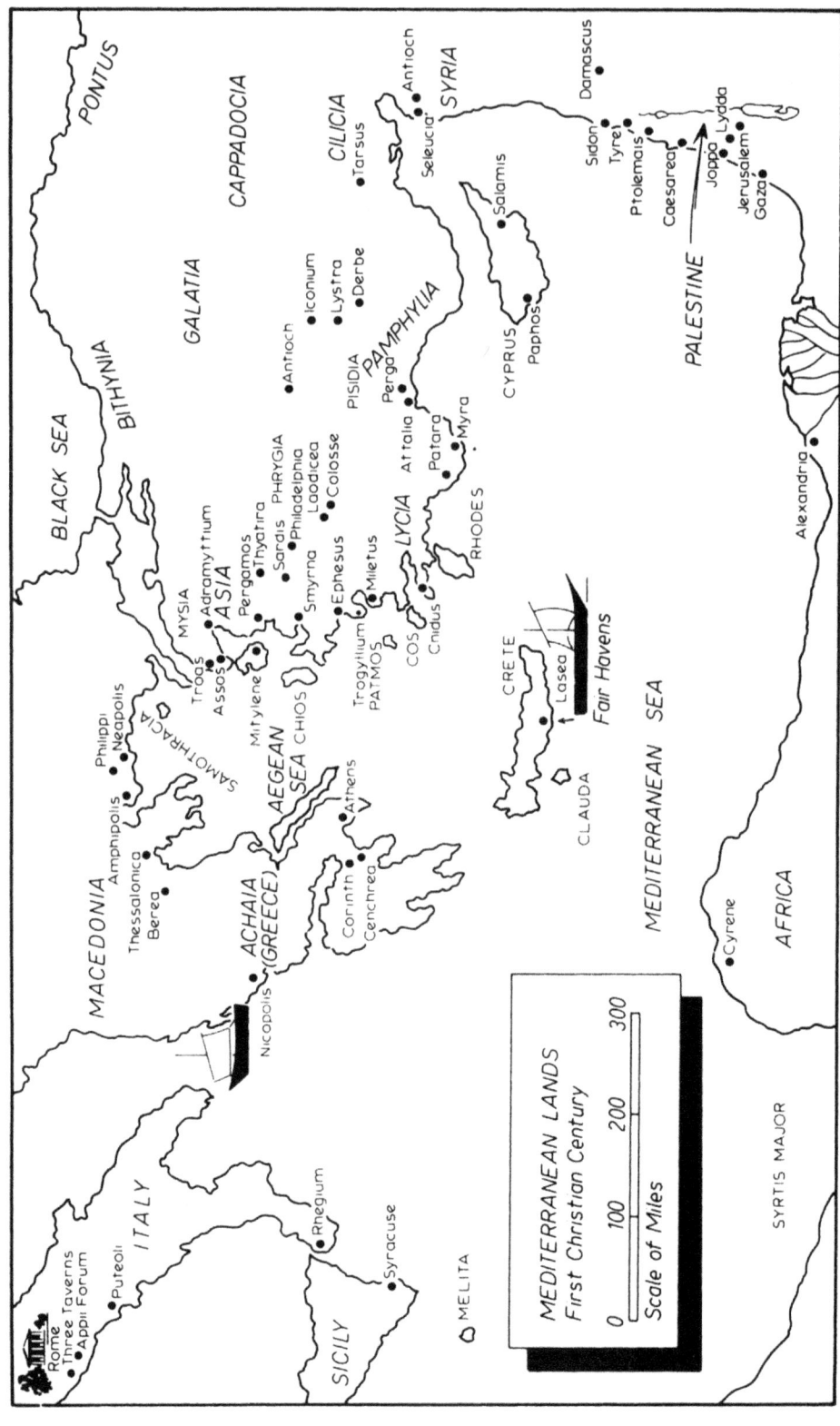

MEDITERRANEAN LANDS
First Christian Century

INDEX OF AUTHORS, IDEAS & TOPICS IN ACTS

(Roman numerals refer to materials found in the Introductory Studies. Arabic numbers refer to comments on the text. Arabic numbers followed by ff. refer to the pages following. Arabic numbers followed by n refer to footnotes found on that page.)

Aaron – 194, 281, 291, 300, 306
Abaddon – 138
Abana River – *see* River
Abibas – 228
Abijah, course of – *iv*
Abimelech – 588
Ablutions – 236
Abraham – 158, 167, 170, 271-275, 287, 470, 476, 496, 712, 875
   believed God – 603
   call from Ur – 272
   not the oldest son of Terah – 306, 307
   father of Isaac – 275, 476
   purchased a tomb at Shechem – 311
Abrahamic covenant – 548
Abstain from four things – *see* Jerusalem Conference
Abyss – 138, 239
Accho – *see* Acre
Accommodation – 242
Accusative case – 395, 400, 421
Achaia – 571, 638, 647, 684, 729
   how used by Luke – 647
   interchangeable with "Greece – 662, 728
   first converts in – 637, 638
Achan – 31, 705
Acre
   formerly Ptolemais – 782, 783
   ancient Accho – 782
Acropolis
   at Athens – 620
   at Corinth – 638
Acts of Paul and Thecla – 505
Acts, Introductory Studies
   alleged contradictions in – *xxv*, 354, 399, 405, 472, 588
   authorship – *xxiv-xxvi*, 731, 948. *See also* Luke
   characteristics – *xxxvii*
   criticism – 224, 289, 405, 464, 502, 574, 615, 626, 744, 781, 793, 871, 872, 921
   date of writing – *xxxv*, 626
   dependence – *xxxiii*
   destination – *xxxvi*
   integrity – *xxxvii*, 785
   language – *xxxv*
   outline – *xxxix-xlii*, 12, 13
   place of writing – *xxxvi*
   purpose – *xxii-xxiv*, 832, 887, 938
   sources – *xxxiii*, 301, 409, 434, 455, 464, 781, 783, 785
   title – *xxii*
   trustworthiness – *xxvi*, 224, 502, 562, 682, 744, 806
   unity of –785
   value of introductory studies – *xxxvii*
   why ended so abruptly – *xxxv*, 951
Acupuncture – 703
Adam – 130, 167, 236, 578, 629, 712
Adamic covenant – 548
Added to the Lord – 419
Admonish – 754
Adoptionist heresy – 396
Adramyttium – 891, 892
Adriatic Sea – 574, 908, 909, 914, 919
Adultery – 546, 850, 852
Aegean Sea – 53, 54, 570, 573, 574, 654, 666, 667, 748, 778, 895
Aeneas – 371-373
Aesculapius – 925
Africa – 824, 908
Agabus – *xiii*; 423, 453, 747, 787, 789, 823
Agag – 474
Agape (love feast) – *see* Love Feast
Agnomen – 643, 647
Agora – *see* Forum
Agricultural missions – *see* Missionary methods, 20th century
Agrippa I – 424, 797, 850, 893
   history – *vi*, *xiii*, *xiv*, 426
   his family – 426, 831
   his character – 427, 428
   account of his imprisonment at Rome – 426
   circumstances of his death – *x*, 441- 444, 850, 851
   year of his death – 444

Agrippa II
  his history – *x, xvi-xviii* 444, 831, 857, 863, 867, 877, 884
  and Bernice – *see* Bernice
  his control of Jewish worship – 863, 867, 873
  object of his visit to Caesarea – *xviii*, 863, 867
  relationship with Festus – 887, 888
  believed the Prophets – 603, 884, 885
  Paul's defense before – 863-888
  Paul's appeal to – 352, 884-886
Agrippina – 424, 698
Ahaziah, king of Israel – 737
Ahithophel – 588
Ahmes – 280
Akeldama
  used to bury strangers – 24, 205
  its location – 25
  Judas' body found there – 24, 25
Alabarch – 176, 259
Albania – 574
Albinus – *xvii*, 888
Aclimus – 198
Alexamenos – 941
Alexander
  the Jewish religious leader – 175
  the Jewish defender – 693-694, 745
  the coppersmith – 694
Alexander Jannaeus – 196, 198
Alexander the Great – *xxii,* 43, 247, 331, 570, 571, 574, 620, 658, 689, 782
Alexandra – 196
Alexandria – 251, 259, 328, 345, 658, 659, 660, 892, 894, 919, 929, 930, 931
Alexandrian grain ships – *see* Ships
Alger of Liege – 768
Alleged contradictions – *see* Acts, alleged contradictions
Allegorical method of interpretation – 659
"All things to all men" – *xxix,* 566, 799
Alms – 153, 194, 379, 381, 395, 425, 495, 502, 669, 846, 854
Alms distributors
  cause of their appointment – 247-250
  qualifications of – 251
  not called deacons, but perhaps were – 249
  also found in synagogues – 252, 495
Altar – 627
Amalek – 474

Ambrose of Milan – 334, 766
Ambush – 825, 826, 829, 858
Amillennialism – 37
Ammon – 505
Ammonites – 293
Amorites – 296, 472
Amos – 293, 294, 541-543
Amphipolis – 574, 611
  on the Egnatian Way through Macedonia – 611
Amram – 281, 309
Amulets – 236, 293, 682, 687, 711, 715
Ananias (husband of Sapphira – *xxxiii,* 85, 201
  nature of his sin – 202, 203
  death of – 204
  why punished with such severity – 204
  burial of – 205
  a Sanhedrin member – 210
Ananias (high priest)
  son of Nebedaeus – *x, xv,* 808, 814, 816, 824, 836, 847, 857
  to be distinguished from Annas – 816
Ananias of Damascus – 315, 357-362, 610, 868, 872
Anathema – 824, 825
Anchors – 900, 903, 904, 909, 910, 911, 916
Ancyra –567, 568
Andrew, apostle – 253
Andriaca – 894
  port of Myra – 894
Androcydes – 682
Andronicus – 892, 933
Andronicus Livius – 620
Angel of Jehovah – 214, 286, 330
Angelology, an elaborate system of doctrine – 198
Angels – 820, 821, 906, 907, 950
  appear and disappear –383, 432, 724, 820
  appear at time of Jesus' ascension – 15
  appearance of – 292, 392, 432
  appeared to Paul – 906, 907
  gave the Law – 290, 300
  help in man's salvation – 330, 382
  guardian angels – 432, 438
  helped Moses – 287. 289
  delivered Peter – 432-434

released apostles from jail – 214, 215, 220
talked to Cornelius – 380, 410, 412, 537
smote Herod – 443, 444
some once sinned – 139, 238
Animals – 385. *See also* Names, for names of people taken from animals
Anna – 473
Annas (high priest) – *iv*, *vii*, *x*, 175, 187, 213
Annihilation – 67, 198
Anselm – 131
Antichrist – 34-38
Antigonus – *ii*, 571
Antioch, several cities so named – 413 414, 468
Antioch of Syria – 413, 453, 516, 564 572, 651
  church there – *see* Churches, at Antioch
  history – 414
  harbor – 414
  hometown of Luke? – 1, 254, 572
  hometown of Nicholas – 254
  Barnabas and Saul at – *see* Paul and Barnabas
  Judaizers at – 527-528, 551, 554
  visited by Paul four times – 523, 656
  Peter's hypocrisy at – 558, 656
  seat of missionary operations – 446, 523, 657
  seat of Roman government of the province – 370
Antioch of Pisidia – 414, 468, 491, 512, 561, 564, 666, 839, 879, 938, 946
  history – 468, 469
  location – 468
  church there – *see* Churches, at Antioch of Pisidia
  discourse of Paul in the synagogue – 469-485, 744
  visited on second missionary tour – 466-569
Antiochus Sidetes – 69
Antiochus the Great (Epiphanes) – 196, 198, 414, 468, 469, 496, 795
Antipater—834

Antipatris – 344
  identification (Kefr Saba?) – 833, 834
  Paul brought to – 833, 834
Antisemitism – *xxviii*, 64, 938
Antonia, mother of Claudius – 830
Antonia, tower of – 171, 434, 788, 804, 805, 814, 822, 823, 825, 834, 836, 840, 850
  location – 803
  iron gate – 433, 805
  Paul's speech from the stairs of – 313, 805-809
Antony, Mark – *vii*, 574, 575, 803, 812, 830
Aorist tense – 420, 560, 569, 654, 668, 737
  signification – 324, 811
  epistolary aorist – 553, 676
  historical aorist – 833
Aphrodite – 460, 461, 621, 638
Apis – 292
Apocryphal Gospels – 39, 757
Apollo – 580, 581, 621, 628, 687, 704, 925
Apollonia – 611
Apollos
  at Ephesus – 658-663, 665
  his talents – 659
  at Corinth – 87, 232, 663-665, 666, 667
  alleged author of Hebrews – 665, 931
Apologetics – 512
Apostasy from Christ – 254, 753
Apostates – 826
Apostles of Christ – 784, 792
  chosen by Jesus – 4
  qualifications of an apostle – 12, 27, 792
  apostles' teaching – 82, 172
  main point of their testimony – 12, 28, 193
  last mention in the New Testament of many of them – 19, 41
  Matthias selected – 21-33, 248
  empowered and led by the Holy Spirit – 184, 193, 388, 409, 412, 420, 459, 524, 530, 553, 569, 684, 747, 780-781, 841, 842, 898. *See also* Baptism with the Holy Spirit
  Paul selected – *see* Paul
  "Twelve" original named – 4, 248
  not limited to twelve – 500, 507
  miracles worked by – *see* Miracles, done by apostles

tasks – 744
arrested by religious leaders – 218
in Jerusalem during and after the persecution (Stephen's) – 314, 407, 479, 529, 530, 532, 792
were empowered to confer the Spirit – 184
See also names of individual apostles, viz., Paul, Peter, John, etc.
See also Witness
Apostles of the church – 27, 507, 784
Apostolic constitutions – 766
Apostolic succession – 268, 519, 750, 775
Apparitions – 380
Appeal to Caesar – 861, 862, 863, 865, 866, 870, 890, 935, 940, 949
Appian – 864
Appian Way – 574, 675, 931, 933, 934
Appius, Market of – 932, 933
Appius, Claudius – 932
Apport – 342, 465, 682, 718, 720, 724
Aprons – 677
Aquarius – 702
Aquila (husband of Priscilla) – 638, 647
  where he was converted – 638
  why named after his wife – 639, 640, 652
  Paul's labors with him – 640, 756
  his connection with Apollos – 232, 661-662, 667, 669
  moves to Corinth – *xiv*, 639
  moves to Ephesus – 639, 652, 654, 655, 663, 666, 744
  moves to Rome – 667, 684, 692, 933, 935, 942
  moves back to Ephesus – 953
Aquinas, Thomas – 131, 588, 598
Arabia – 54
Arabian Peninsula – 285
Arabia, Paul's visit to – *see* Paul, trip to Arabia
Arabic – 463, 673, 920
Aramaic – 25, 52, 373, 376, 495, 4%, 807
Aratus, a poet – 632
Arbella – 420
Archelaus – *ii, v*, 455
Areopagus – *xxxi*, 865
  location – 620, 621
  was Paul tried before the court of this name? – 624, 625
  outline of Paul's speech there – 633

Areopagites – 624, 625, 636
Ares – 628
Aretas IV
  king of Damascus – *vi, xii, xiii*, 366
  joined Jews in an effort to arrest Paul – *xii*, 365
Argument – *see* Dispute
Aries – 702
Arimathea – 344, 359
Aristarchus – 613, 691, 692, 696, 892 932, 948
  accompanied Paul to Jerusalem – 693, 730, 889, 892
  in what sense a "fellow prisoner" – 692, 892
Aristobulus – 198, 426
Aristotle – 199, 615, 629, 883
Ark of the Covenant – 294, 296
Armageddon – *see* Battle of Armageddon
Armenia – 53
Arminianism – 132
Arnobius – 448
Artemis of Ephesus – 414, 677, 686- 687, 713
  use made of her shrines – 687
  her temple in Paul's time – 654, 666, 676, 689
  how extensively worshiped – 666, 676, 689, 690
  repeating her name was a religious act – 691, 695
  tradition as to the origin of her image – 696, 699
Artemision – 686, 688, 693, 710
Article, definite – 851
  article of previous reference – 738, 782
  absence of – 876
Ascension of Jesus – *see* Christ Jesus, ascension
Ashdod – 344
Ashtoreth – 687
Asian Jews – 258, 259, 790, 800, 804, 823, 824, 844, 847, 879, 932
Asia Minor – 531, 561, 568, 570, 572, 573, 654, 666, 785, 791, 795, 831, 839, 894, 895, 896, 949, 951
Asia, Proconsular – 440, 467, 568, 569, 570, 577, 578, 654, 685, 690, 731, 742, 892, 894
  how much it included – 53, 260

Index of Authors, Ideas and Topics

evangelization of – 446, 569, 570, 676, 688, 692, 744
Asiarchs – 879
   position – *xxxi*, 692
   friendship for Paul – 693
Askelon – 344
Assembly
   lawful – 208, 614, 691, 693, 695 698, 806
   of Sanhedrin – 820
Assassins – *xvii*, 806, 824, 826, 829, 837, 858
Assos – 740, 741
Assumption of Mary – *see* Mary, mother of Jesus
Assyrians – 438
Astarte – 687
Astral projection – 320, 721
Astrologers – *xiv*, 682
Astrology – 707
   ancient – 282, 293, 294, 320, 636
   modern – 683, 702, 724
Athame – 711
Athanasius – 451
Athene – 297
Athens – 345, 584, 619, 620, 638, 673, 690, 728, 744, 746
   location – 620
   extent of its idolatry – 620, 621, 627
   intellectual center of the world – 620, 626
   Acropolis and Parthenon – 620
   sought news of new things – 625, 626
   philosophers at – 622, 623
   origin of its "altar to an unknown god" – 627
   church at – 637, 657
Atmos – 831
Atonement – 476, 629
Attalia
   location – 523
   Paul and Barnabas at – 523
Attalus Philadelphus – 523
Attorney (Roman – 833, 836, 837, 859
Augury – 707
Augustan cohort – 891
Augustine – 40, 87, 130, 131, 174, 334, 577, 588, 649, 652, 766
Augustus, Caesar – *i*, v, *xii,* 195, 258, 351, 378, 426, 443, 460, 462, 469, 501, 568, 575, 698, 812, 866, 870, 891

Authority – 525, 529
Authorship of Acts
   external evidence - *xxiv*
   internal evidence - *xxv*
Azizus, king - 831, 850
Azotus – 344
Azuza Street Mission – 103

Baal – 293
Babbler – 623
Babel – 49, 703
Babylonia – 52, 294, 505
Babylonian captivity – 294, 494, 542, 576, 875
Backsliding – 254, 745
Ba'Hai faith – 722
Baptism
   cases of baptism in Acts
      3000 on Pentecost – 74-82, 671
      the Samaritans – 321, 322
      the Ethiopian eunuch – 341-342
      Paul – 358, 362
      the Philippian jailer – 591-592
      Lydia – 578, 638
      Cornelius – 403-406, 579
      of Corinthian believers – 644, 645
   household baptisms – 579, 644
   infant – *see* Infant sprinkling
   John's – 7, 74, 396, 475, 660, 661, 667, 669, 670, 672
   mode – 59, 75, 81, 256, 341, 403, 404, 579, 592, 672, 774
   origin of the ordinance – 74
   proselyte – 74
   purpose – 6, 8, 101, 339, 362, 482, 518, 537, 578, 607, 610, 668, 669, 776, 809, 878
   same hour of the day – 578, 579, 592
   subjects – 8, 74, 412
   administrator – 9, 81, 101, 358, 404, 644
   necessity of, for salvation – 56, 76- 78, 164, 317, 339, 402-406, 482, 604, 609, 670, 671, 672, 774, 809
   validity of – 672
Baptismal formula – 76, 324, 405, 661, 669, 671, 672
Baptismal regeneration – 607

Baptisms in the New Testament, chart
   John's – 7, 27, 396, 475, 660, 661, 669, 670, 762
   suffering – 7
   with Holy Spirit – *see* Holy Spirit
   with fire – 9
   chart concerning - 8
   of the Great Commission - 9, 10, 101, 660, 671, 927. *See also* Baptism
Barabbas – 159, 478, 529
Barak – 142
Barbarian – *see* Natives
Bar-Jesus – 461-466, 725, 816
Barnabas – 790
   a Levite – 194, 463
   Cyprus, his home – 194, 366
   significance of his name – 195, 367, 560
   "a good man" – 418
   his contribution to the poor at Jerusalem – 194, 195, 201
   his influence at Jerusalem – 195
   introduced Paul to the Jerusalem disciples – 367, 419
   his work at Antioch – *xxi*, 416-422, 454, 559
   on the first missionary journey – 454-526
   in what sense called an "apostle" – 419, 457, 792
   appearance – 505
   at the Jerusalem Conference – 528, 529, 539, 554
   his disagreement with Paul – *xxv, xxxiii*
   his relationship with Paul after the first missionary journey – 562
   traditions as to his later life – 562
Barracks – *see* Antonia, tower of
Barsabbas
   see Joseph Barsabbas
   see Judas Barsabbas
Barth, Karl – 132
Bartholomew – 41
Basil – 766
Basket – 366
Battle of Armageddon – 34-38
Baucis – *see* Philemon and Baucis
Baur, Ferdinand C – *xxiii*
Bay of Acre – 782, 783
Bay of Naples – 930
Beaten with rods – *see* Rods
Beautiful Gate – *see* Gates of Jerusalem

Beckon with the hand - 807, 841, 872
   Alexander - 684
   Peter - 439
   Paul - 470
Bed – *see* Pallets
Beelzebub – 243
Belief – *see* Faith
Believers – 210, 420
Bellomancy – 705
Belus – 505
Benediction – 496
Benevolence – 152, 194, 248, 375, 381, 425
Ben-Hadad – 708
Benjamin – 277, 345, 473
Berea – 613, 617-619, 637, 641, 730, 747
   location – 617
   noble converts – 617
   Sosipater of Berea – *see* Sopater
   church there – *see* Churches
Berengarius of Tours – 767
Bernice (wife of Agrippa II)
   her history – *xvii*, 850, 863
   Paul's defense before – *xviii*, 863-888
Bernice (wife of Aristobulus) – 426
Bethany – 17, 18
Beth Horon – 834
Bethlehem – 212, 441, 867
Bethpage – 17
Bethsoron – 338
Beza, Codex – *see* Manuscripts
Bibliomancy – 703
Birds – 385, 706, 707, 797
Bishop – 26, 792
   synonymous with elder – *see* Elders, Christian
Bithynia
   evangelized by Peter – 451, 570
   not entered by Paul – 570, 578
Black Sea – 570
Blasphemy – 477, 697, 700
   against Moses – 261, 271-272, 428, 500, 513, 808
   against Christ - 349, 487, 488, 642
Blastus - 442
Blessed - 170, 757, 875
Blessings - 470, 480-482, 495
Blind - 356, 466, 677, 872
Blood - 61, 544, 547, 548, 554, 643, 674, 751, 767, 769, 770, 772, 773, 774, 776, 798
Blood, field of - *see* Akeldama
Body-Soul-Spirit - 67, 143, 196, 444, 505,

552, 621, 635, 660, 684, 781, 820, 821, 954
Boldness – 499, 616
    of Peter and John – 181
    of apostles – 190
    of Paul – 367, 488, 498, 501, 745, 851, 883, 884
Bond (surety) – 616
Bonds (imprisonment) – 747, 787, 788, 803, 823, 832, 886, 887
Bondage of iniquity – 328
Books – 953
Books of magic and occult practices – 461, 682, 712, 716
    Book of Shadows – 682, 710
    Book of the Dead – 682
    Book of Venus – 682
    Books of Moses, 6th and 7th – 682
Boundaries of nations – 630
Breaking of bread
    common meal – 83, 86, 737, 738, 739, 914
    Lord's Supper – *see* Lord's Supper
Breath – 629
Brethren
    Peter's use of the term before Pentecost – 21
    conciliatory use, speaking to non-Christians – 360, 815, 817, 937, 940
    in what sense, speaking of Christians – 230, 389, 420, 439, 498, 527, 540, 551, 596, 619, 620, 654, 663, 667, 783, 788, 794
Bribe – *xxvii*, 261, 854
Britain – 443, 875, 951
British Israelism – 875
Brook Kidron – *see* Valley of Kidron
Brothers of Jesus – 18, 20, 39-42, 792
Brundisium – 574, 919, 932
Brunner, Emil – 132
Brutus – 574, 575
Buddhism – 506, 582, 721
Bundle of sticks – 921, 922
Burial
    of Jesus - *see* Christ Jesus, burial of
    Stephen - *see* Stephen, burial of
    preparation for - 205, 374
    hastened in the East - 205, 374
    outside city walls - 208
Burning bush - 282, 286, 289
Burning of Rome - *see* Rome

Burrus, Afranius – 862, 952
    prefect at Rome – 862, 935
Butcher shop – *see* Meat market
Byzantine text – 655, 833, 840, 934
Byzantium – 690

Cabala – 712
Cabirian Mystery Religion – *see* Mystery Religions
Caesar – 443, 837, 862, 863, 867, 890, 907
    see Appeals to Caesar
    see Augustus; Nero; Claudius; Tiberius; Caligula; Julius Caesar
Caesarea – 329, 344, 372, 373, 378, 383, 402, 413, 441, 655, 783, 785, 787, 789, 790, 829, 831, 834, 843, 850, 855, 857, 859, 861, 865, 878, 889, 892
    history – 373, 378, 379
    seaport of Judea – 368, 369, 373, 655
Caesarea Philippi – *vii*, 290, 536, 863, 888
Caiaphas, Joseph – *iv, vii, x,* 175, 187, 213, 271, 350, 808
Caleb – 295
Calendar, Dionysian – *i*
Calf
    worshiped by Egyptians – 292
    worshiped by Hebrews – *see* Golden Calf
Caligula – *vi, xii, xiii, xiv,* 228, 370, 424, 426, 443, 850, 870
Call
    invitation to salvation – *see* Invitation
    to preach – 573
    on the name of the Lord – 62, 76, 304, 359, 362
Calliphron – 689
Calvinistic Doctrines – *see* Five Points of Calvinism; Predestination, Calvinistic
Calvin, John – 599, 601, 759, 765, 770
Campbell, Alexander – 75, 234, 245, 534, 771, 774, 844
Campbell, Thomas – 325
Cana – 396
Canaan – 273, 275, 277, 279, 295, 308, 471, 687
Canal
    in Greece - *see* Diolkos
    through the Pontine Marshes - 932, 933

Candace – *x*
   name of a dynasty – *xi,* 332
Canon
   Muratorian – *see* Muratorian Canon
   New Testament – *see* New Testament Canon
   Old Testament – *see* Old Testament Canon
Cape
   Cape Lectum – 741
   Cape Malea – 638
   Cape Matala – 897, 900, 901
   Cape Misenum – 930
   Cape Salmone – 896
Capena, Porta – *see* Gates, Rome
Capernaum – 372
Capital punishment – 175, 227, 304, 428, 593, 699, 801, 861
Cappadocia – 53, 451
Captain of the ship – 898, 899, 906, 911, 926
Captain of the Temple Guard – 171, 172, 217, 218, 228
Captivity
   Babylonian – *see* Babylonian Captivity
   Egyptian – *see* Egyptian Captivity
Captivity led captive – 141, 142
Capua – 931, 932
Caria – 53, 468, 568, 894, 895
Carlstadt – 769
Carpus – 951
Carthage – 257, 902
Cartomancy – 704
Caspian Sea – 52
Cassander – 611
Cassius – 575, 812
Casting of lots – *see* Lots, casting of
Castle of Antonia – *see* Antonia, tower of
Castor and Pollux - 926
   mythology - 926
   figurehead on a ship - 926
Catacombs - 786, 934
Catholic Pentecostalism - 104
Cauda - *see* Clauda
Cave of Machpelah - 273, 278, 311
Cayce, Edgar - 703
Cayster River - *see* River
Celer – 698
Celibacy – 785, 786
Cemetery
   Jewish – 205, 934

catacombs used by Christians – 934
Cenchrea – 638, 647, 652, 653, 654, 728
Centaurs – 621
Center of evangelism – 414
   moves from Jerusalem to Antioch – 414, 446
   moves from Antioch toward Rome – 684, 932
Centurions – 803, 811, 827, 828, 829, 849, 889, 891, 894, 911, 912, 917, 918
   always mentioned favorably in New Testament – 891
   see Cornelius; Julius
Ceremonial defilement – 797, 798
Ceres – 696
Cestrus River – see River
Chains – 432, 804, 807, 813, 849, 884, 886, 893, 936, 939, 947
   how fastened to prisoners – 431, 587, 886, 923
   unfastened by earthquake – 587
Chaldeans – 273, 484
Chamberlain – 442
Chapel of the Ascension – 17
Chapters, New Testament divided into – 389
Chariot – 333
Charismatic gifts – see Spiritual gifts
Charismatic movement – 102-126, 222, 324, 668
Charms – 461, 678, 681, 682, 683, 687, 710, 711, 715
Cheiromancy – 702, 704
Cherubim – 292
Chief priest(s) – 187, 217, 359, 364, 814, 825, 845, 857, 859, 864,
Children – 781
Chiliarch – *see* Commander
Chios – 741, 742
Chiun – 294
Chloe – 645, 685
Choice by lot – *see* Lots, casting of
Chosen instrument – 359, 360
Chrestus – xiv, 640, 649
Christ Jesus
   accused of being mistaken – 241
   agony in the Garden – 150, 398
   anointed – 189, 397
   ascension - 3, 4, 5, 10-16, 68, 135, 141, 166, 220, 378, 489, 660, 661, 674, 724

birth, date of – *i, iv,* 866
birth, virgin – 480
baptism – 75, 396
baptism, date – *iv*
blasphemy of – *see* Blasphemy
burial – 478, 510, 660, 661
chronological outline of life of Christ – 475
creator – 723
crucifixion – 4, 61, 64, 72, 178, 219, 261, 337, 366, 379, 394, 398, 456, 470, 476, 478, 761, 762, 866, 867, 881, 953. *See also* Crucifixion, who was responsible for
Davidic lineage – 474
death, date of – *ix*
death, necessary for man's salvation – 337, 476, 591, 612, 618, 734, 762, 770, 775, 776
deity of – 10, 63, 67, 337, 606, 751, 878
descent into Hades – 140-142
eternality of – 723
exaltation – 220, 302, 480, 485, 570, 734, 876, 880
fulfilled prophecies – 6, 157, 168, 178, 189, 338, 470, 478, 538, 612, 866, 876, 878, 883, 884, 943, 944
glorification – 45, 220, 363, 674, 877
incarnation – 91, 480, 512
intercessor – 14
"Jesus," meaning of name – 63, 178
judge, final, of the world – 14, 394, 399, 634
king – 615, 772, 881
Lord – *see* Lord
mediator – 168
Messiah – *see* Messiah
ministry, dates of – 398
ministry, last week of – 398, 661, 945
ministry, length of – *ix*, 2, 63
ministry, summary of – 394-398, 823
miracles done by - 183, 397, 503
miracles wrought in His name – 154, 161, 190, 191
post-resurrection appearances – 4, 5, 14, 15, 142, 343, 360, 383, 394, 398, 478, 609, 821
pre-existence – 290
Prophet, the – *see* Prophet, the
Prince and Savior – 159, 221

public knowledge of Jesus' ministry – 894
resurrection of – 4, 28, 45, 65, 68, 69, 70, 92, 160, 172, 173, 178, 182, 193, 215, 220, 361, 363, 394, 398, 399, 430, 432, 470, 478-482, 485, 486, 507, 510, 512, 539, 591, 609, 613, 624, 625, 634, 635, 636, 660, 661, 734, 738, 819, 832, 845, 866, 876, 877, 880, 881, 882, 883, 884
righteous one – 361
Savior – 417, 474, 477, 479, 486, 591, 624, 659, 774, 879
sayings not recorded in the Gospels – 757
second advent of – *see* Second Coming
sinless – 219
Son of God – 341, 363, 379, 391, 405, 477, 480
Son of man – 302
subordination to the Father – 786
suffering servant – 158, 163, 189, 220, 335, 612, 771, 772, 880, 881
temptation – 396
transfiguration – 15, 150
trials of – 150, 158, 176, 336, 435, 455, 477, 478, 861, 867
triumphal entry – 398
worshiped as God – 14, 16, 304, 586, 941
Christian Baptism – *see* Baptisms in the New Testament, Great Commission
Christianity – 590, 839, 844, 845, 848, 862
  only valid world religion – 180, 582, 819, 884
  origin of, not in pagan religious practices – 252
  how it differs from world's religions – 629
Christian liberty – *xxix*, 151, 184, 528, 533, 555-556, 559, 566, 652, 653, 732, 762, 794, 796, 798, 799, 803, 804. *See also* Paul, his use of Christian liberty
Christian life – 489, 509, 661, 878
Christians – 744, 780, 781, 790, 819, 826, 834, 850, 851, 873, 886, 890, 893, 931, 940, 943
  disciples first called, at Antioch – 420, 885
  origin and import of the name - 180, 420, 421, 645

who is a Christian – 774
used by Agrippa – 885
sect everywhere spoken against – 940, 941, 952
in Caesar's household – 952
blamed for the burning of Rome – 952
Chronology
gospel age – *i-ix*
apostolic age – *x-xxi,* 365, 369, 415- 416, 426, 441, 444, 445, 514, 525, 560, 647, 657, 676, 686, 727, 728, 732, 806, 831, 855, 856, 861, 897, 928, 935, 951, 952, 953
Chrysostom – 45, 120, 174, 240, 258, 375, 451, 458, 505, 616, 637, 640, 641, 698, 751, 780
Church – 519, 694, 749, 750, 751, 753, 756, 774, 950
biblical uses of the word – 208, 422, 699
established at Pentecost – 12, 21
erroneous ideas as to its time of beginning – 534
in the wilderness – 290
daily additions to – 87
patterned after the synagogue in some respects – 733
divine pattern for – 750, 775
local – 370
universal – 370
Church and state – 185
Church age
predicted in the Old Testament - 166, 169, 338, 400, 844, 946
Church buildings – 86, 150, 420, 628, 675
Church discipline – 201, 208, 210, 559, 694
Special Study – 230-234
Churches (in specific cities)
at Antioch
of Syria – 413-425, 446, 453-458, 524, 527, 551, 554
of Pisidia – 489-493, 516-522, 566-569
at Berea – 618, 619, 657, 727
at Caesarea – 344, 788
at Colossae – 676
at Corinth – 402, 546, 644, 646, 657, 663, 675
at Damascus – 351, 357
at Ephesus – 248, 661, 663, 682, 684, 692, 743, 752
at Iconium – 498, 565, 569
at Jerusalem – 194, 250, 416, 439, 445, 530, 531, 532, 558, 791
at Joppa – 248, 344, 373-376
at Lydda – 344, 371-373
at Lystra – 515, 565
at Philippi – 458, 580, 596, 657, 727, 730, 732, 947, 949
at Puteoli – 931
at Rome – 54, 251, 579, 728, 931, 933, 941, 952, 953
at Sidon – 893
at Thessalonica – 612, 617, 657, 727
at Troas – 572, 732, 733-741
Churches (in specific countries)
in Achaia – 637, 684
in Asia – 731
in Ethiopia – 343
in Galatia – 468-522, 657, 730, 734
in Galilee – 370
in Judea – 212, 370, 445, 783, 849
in Macedonia – 684
in Samaria – *see* Samaria
in Syria and Cilicia – 369, 551, 563
Church government – 417, 519, 521, 784
three kinds – 518
temporary and permanent officers – 557, 784
Church growth – 371, 419, 420, 445, 567
Church letters – *see* Letters of commendation
Church membership – 87, 517, 520
Church, names for – 422, 751
Church of the Brethren – 759, 770, 771
Church of Satan – 701, 709, 713
Church officers – 517, 750
selection of – *see* Elders; Deacons
Cicero – 584, 594, 595, 629, 696, 706, 837, 933
Cilicia – 260, 417, 467, 523, 551, 564, 632, 779, 806, 835, 894
Jews living there – 260
tent-making a common trade in – 346, 641
sea of – *see* Sea of Cilicia
Paul's labors there – *see* Paul
Cilician Gates – 501, 516, 564, 657
Cilicium – 346
Circumcision – 263, 299, 345, 400, 497, 527-529, 554, 555, 661, 795, 844
conference on – *see* Jerusalem Conference

covenant of – 275, 528
   of Timothy – 565, 566
   refused for Titus – 535, 565
   word sometimes used to designate Jewish Christians – 389, 402, 410
Circus Maximus – 934, 935
Citizenship, Roman – 346, 469, 575, 584, 806
   immunities which it secured – 227, 594, 595, 596, 811, 953
   seldom claimed falsely – 594, 812
   how acquired – 346, 414, 812, 813
Citta Vecchia (in Malta) – 925
Clairaudience – 707, 719
Clairvoyance – 707, 719
Claros – 581
Clauda – 901, 909
Claudia – 953
Claudius, emperor – *xii, xiv, xvi, xviii,* 176, 228, 329, 424, 426, 443, 447, 448, 462, 595, 640, 782, 812, 830
   famine in his reign - *x. xiii,* 423
   his edict banishing the Jews - *x, xiv,* 54, 576, 584, 615, 638, 639, 640, 647, 675, 936, 940
   restored Achaia to the Senate - 647
Claudius Lysias – *see* Lysias
Clean and unclean foods – 383-387, 406, 408, 527, 794
Cleanthes, a poet – 632
Clement of Alexandria – *iv, xxiv, xxv,* 152, 240, 314, 428, 451, 682
Clement of Rome – 119, 450, 750, 951
Cleopatra – 812, 830
Clergy and laity – 317
Clothes – 755, 798, 809, 921, 928, 953
Cloud, clouds – 14, 15, 16, 707
Cnidus – 778, 895, 896, 930
Coasting vessel – 741, 778, 779, 893, 928
Coats – 373
Cognomen – 643
Cohort – 803, 868, 891
Coins – 574, 729, 837
   of Damascus – *xiii*
   of Cyprus – 462
   of Ephesus – 691, 695
Collection for the saints at Jerusalem – *see* Offering for the poor at Jerusalem

Colony, Roman – 571, 575, 583, 584, 614, 782, 812, 951
   privileges enjoyed by – 575
   six Roman colonies named in Acts – 575
Colophon – 692
Colossae – 676, 948, 949, 951
   whether visited by Paul – 658, 666, 951
   epistle to – 263, 450, 658, 892, 934, 947, 948, 950
Colossus of Rhodes – 788
Columbarium – 253, 675
Comforter – *see* Holy Spirit
Commagne – 831
Commander (tribune) – 803, 804, 805, 806, 809, 810, 811, 812, 813, 822, 825, 827, 828, 829, 868, 886
   Lysias – *see* Lysias
Commemoration – 769, 770, 771, 776
Commendation, letters of – *see* Letters of commendation
Common fund – 249
Communion – *see* Lord's Supper
Communiora – 586
Communism – 85, 193, 199, 203
Community of goods – *xxxii,* 85, 154, 192-195
Comparative religion – 506
Compass – 905
Conference at Jerusalem – *see* Jerusalem Conference
Confession – 913
   of Christ – 56, 76, 256, 340, 341, 378, 603, 709, 724, 907
   of sin – 444, 681, 724, 771
Confidence – *see* Boldness
Confirmation – 324, 517, 563
Conscience – 353, 430, 538, 643, 815, 816, 846, 848, 853, 854
Conservation of converts – *see* Training of new converts
Conspiracies against Paul – *see* Plots by the Jews
Constantine, emperor – 734
Constantine Porphyrogenitus – 919
Consubstantiation – 766, 769
Consummation – 72, 634
Contention – 561, 562, 822
Converts, training of – *see* Training of new converts
Conversion – 416, 445, 746, 884, 886

Conversion, cases of
   of 3000 – 81, 82
   of 5000 – 173
   of Samaritans – 321-322
   of Cornelius – 254, 378-412, 536
   of Gentiles – 413, 416, 531
   of Paul – 357-362, 609, 610, 875, 877
   of Eunuch – 330-344
   of Sergius Paulus – 467
   of Apollos – 664, 665
   of Crispus – 644
Conversion, a process or instantaneous? – 81, 88, 164, 354
Coptic Version – 294, 308
Corinth – 685, 739, 747, 764, 786, 858, 879, 946, 951
   location – 638
   history – 638
   commercial capital of the world – 620, 638
   Paul's evangelization there - 420, 550, 641-651, 673, 675
   Silas and Timothy join Paul there - 620
   Apollos at – *see* Apollos
   an intermediate trip made to Corinth – *see* Intermediate trip to Corinth
   Paul's third visit to Corinth – 726, 727, 728
   participation in offering for Jerusalem – *see* Offering for the poor at Jerusalem
   epistles to – 368, 450, 637, 639, 647, 676, 685, 692, 726, 727, 729, 731, 734, 745, 786, 796
   church at Corinth – *see* Churches
Cornelius – 378-413, 415, 438, 528, 655, 656, 788, 878
   not a Jewish proselyte – 333, 379
   homage offered to Peter rebuked – *xxxii*, 390
   baptized of the Holy Spirit – 93, 324, 668
   date of his conversion – 415, 416
   first convert from the Gentiles – 254, 378, 379, 427
   Peter's defense of his visit to Cornelius – 407-413
Cornerstone – 179
Cos – 778
Cosmological changes at Second Coming – 61
Cots – 211
Cotyaeum – 569

Council, Jewish – *see* Sanhedrin
Council, Roman governor's – 862, 863, 870
Council at Jerusalem – *see* Jerusalem Conference
Councils
   Council of Agatha – 764, 765
   Council of Antioch – 764
   Council of Braga – 763
   Council of Chalcedon – 344
   Council of Constantinople – 372
   Council of Ephesus – 373
   Council of Illiberus – 764
   Council of Lateran – 767
   Council of Lydda – 372
   Council of Neo-Caesarea – 251
   Council of Nicea – 344, 372
   Vatican II – 556
Course – 475, 747
Courses of priests – *see* Priests, Old Testament
Court
   of Israel – 150-153, 175, 798, 801 802, 812
   of the Gentiles – 150-153, 156, 175, 802, 814
   of the Priests – 150, 151
   of the Women – 150-153
Courts of law—697, 700
Coven – 710, 713
Covenant – 169, 528, 548, 844. *See also* Adamic; Mosaic; Noahic; Abrahamic; Davidic covenants
Covenant of circumcision – *see* Circumcision, covenant of
Covetousness – 233, 755
Crassus – 934
Creation – 235, 543, 629, 630
Crescens – 953
Crete – 54, 505, 627, 632, 731, 895, 896, 897, 900, 906, 909, 919, 951
Crispus – 644, 650
Cross – 220, 398
Crystallomancy – 703
Crucifixion – *see* Christ Jesus, crucifixion
Crucifixion, Roman citizens exempt from – 595
Crucifixion, who was responsible for? – 64, 190, 219, 220, 300, 337, 398, 470, 476, 477, 478, 805
Crusades – 782, 783
Ctesiphon - 689

Cultural Anthropology – 121
Cumanus – *xiii, xvi,* 842
Curse – 828
Cuspius Fadus – *xiii,* 223, 424, 443
Custodia libera – 936
Custody – 849, 858, 940
Customs – 584, 795, 796, 799, 842, 873, 937
Customs handed down by Moses – 263, 429, 527, 873, 937
Cybele – 687
Cydnus River – *see* River
Cyprian – 340
Cyprus – 415, 523, 622, 831
    location – 194, 413, 467
    Jews settled there – 194, 460
    Barnabas' home – 194, 366, 460
    visited by Paul on his first tour – 195, 460-467
    visited by Barnabas and Mark – *xxv,* 413, 562
    governed by a proconsul – 462
    bypassed on voyage to Jerusalem – 779
    bypassed on voyage to Rome – 893- 894
    Mnason's home – 790
Cyrene – 53, 258, 259, 415, 444, 454, 902, 908
Cyril of Jerusalem – 766, 951
Cythera – 896

Dagon – 344
Daily ministration – 247-250
Dalmatia – 919, 953
Damaris – 637
Damascus – 294, 350, 755
    history – *xii, xiii,* 351, 414
    location – 351
    road to – *see* Paul's Damascus Road experience
    labors of Paul there – 363, 365, 413
    escape of Paul from – *xii, xx,* 365- 366
Daniel – 438, 446, 716, 786
Daphne, groves of – 414
Daphnis of Miletus – 689
Darius – 440
Darkness – 356
Date of writing of new Testament books – *xxxvii,* 478, 550, 553, 641, 676, 685, 727, 796, 855, 947, 951, 953. *See also* the names of individual books of the New Testament in this index
Dative case – 472, 482, 539, 603, 612
Daughters of men – 237, 240
David – 10, 26, 66, 71, 137, 152, 198, 296, 472, 474, 480-482, 486, 541, 542, 613, 705, 810
    son of Jesse – 474
    called a patriarch – 68
    his tomb – 69
    was inspired – 22, 69, 188
    would build the temple – 296
David's throne – *see* Throne of David
Day, activities commenced early in the East – 215
Day of Atonement – 44, 897, 921, 928
Day of Pentecost – *see* Feasts of the Jews
Day of the Lord – *see* Judgment
Deacons – 743, 750, 771, 775
    "young men" may have been deacons – 205
    selection of, method – 250, 264-270, 371, 446, 519
    duties of – 205, 252
    qualifications of – 251, 265
    See also Alms distributors
Dead Sea Scrolls – 200
Death – 862
    definition – 204
    as viewed by Christians – 144, 431, 720
    "falling asleep" – 305, 481
    of Christ – *see* Christ, crucifixion
    of Eutychus – 737
    of Herod Agrippa I – *see* Agrippa I
    of Stephen – see Stephen, death
    of five stages of dying – 431
Debate – 528, 529, 536
Decalogue – 291, 606
Deceit – 465
Decree of Jerusalem Conference – *see* Jerusalem Conference
Dedication, Feast of – *see* Feasts of the Jews
Deliberate sin – 162
Delos – 581
Delphi – 580, 647
Demas – 948, 953
Demetrius – 667, 676, 686-688, 696- 699, 725, 726, 742, 745, 802, 879
    a silversmith – 687
    his artful speech – 688-690

Demons
- identification – 235-238, 623, 701, 820
- often called evil spirits – 212, 513, 582, 627, 678-680, 709, 717
- often called unclean spirits – 212, 319
- sphere of operation – 239
- deliverance from – 213, 245, 509, 582, 583. 636. 681, 682, 723-724
- possession – 235-246, 397, 580, 581
- possession distinguished from illness or insanity – 212, 240, 242, 319, 397, 678
- demon possessed slave girl at Philippi – 238, 580-583, 725
- duration of demon possession – 244
- destiny of demons – 239
- doctrines of demons – 244, 582, 701, 720-724
- powers available from – 176-179, 677, 680
- worshiped by Gentiles – 238, 239, 621, 623, 627
- Special Study - 235-246, 701

Demosthenes – 624, 625
Demotic – 53
Dependence – *see* Acts, Introductory Studies
Derbe – 561, 564, 657, 730
- location of – 501, 515
- Paul and Barnabas flee here – 501, 515
- why named before Lystra – 564

Desert – 231
Destruction of Jerusalem – *see* Jerusalem, destruction of
Determined plan and foreknowledge of God – 64. *See also* Purpose, God's
Deuteronomy, quoted by Paul – 471
Devil – 202, 235, 243, 245, 292, 321, 397, 461, 463, 615
- binding of – 34
- demons, agents of – 235
- dominion of – 356, 518
- influence of – 465

Devil's compensation – 719
Devout – 379
- men – 50, 315, 427
- women – *see* Women, devout
- meaning of term – 379, 383

Diana – 467, 687. *See also* Artemis
Didache, the – *xxiv,* 456, 750
Difficulties in Acts 7 – 306-312
Dio Cassius – 595, 812

Diogenes – 623, 627
Diognetus, epistle to – *xxiv*
Diolkos – 638
Dionysius (a Greek god) – 620
Dionysius of Corinth – 451
Dionysius of Halicarnasus – 595
Dionysius, the Areopagite – 636, 637
Dioscuri – *see* Twin Brothers
Dinner – *see* Meals
Discerning of spirits – 202, 207, 325, 503
Disciple(s) – 363, 366, 420, 424, 515, 516, 667, 670, 675, 692, 726, 753, 771, 774, 780, 789, 881
Disciples of Christ – 773
Disciples of John – *see* John the Baptist, his disciples; Twelve disciples of John at Ephesus
Diseases – 678, 927
Disitheus – 328
Dispensationalism – 36, 169, 400, 488, 748, 946
Dispensations – 11
Dispersion (Diaspora) – 45, 50, 247, 258, 316, 451, 485, 639, 795
Dispute – 260, 367, 664
Dissension – 528, 822
Districts – *see* Provinces, Roman
Dium – 619
Divination – 581, 682, 701, 720, 723
- spirit of divination – 580-582
- modern methods of divination – 702-707

Diving rod – 705
Dixon, Jeanne – 703
Doberus – 730
Doctrine – 82, 395
Doctrines of demons – *see* Demons
Dorcas – *xxxii,* 373-376, 926
Domitian, emperor – *xii, xviii*
Dorylaeum – 569
Dreams – 46, 60, 282, 380, 682, 706, 708
Drugs – 713, 720
Drunkenness – 57, 58, 233
Drusilla – 830, 850-853
- her history – 830, 850, 856
- wife of Felix – *xvii,* 848, 850

Dry season – 47
Dualism – 722
Dust
- shook off feet or garments - 492, 493, 642, 643
- thrown into the air - 810

duumviri - 583
Dyrrhachium - 574, 919
Dysentery - 926

Early Christian Literature – *xxiv*, 254, 588, 734, 764, 765, 855
Early church – 598, 763, 764, 774, 786
Earth-mother (goddess) – 687
Earthquake – 191, 587, 590, 592, 593
"Easter" – 430, 764
Eastern religions – 226, 673
Ebionites – 762
Eckankar – 721
Eclipse – *ii*, 706
Ecstasy – 49, 380, 384, 580
Ecumenical movement – 84
Edessa – 420
Edict of Claudius – *see* Claudius
Edom – 53, 542
Edomites – 345
Education – 659
Education, Paul's – *see* Paul, education
Educational missions – *see* Missionary methods, 20th century
Egnatian Way, the – 574, 597, 611, 617, 727, 892
Egypt – 53, 274, 278, 279, 291, 308, 505, 523, 779, 782, 824, 894, 898
Egyptian captivity – 288, 471, 486
  duration – 274, 307-309, 472
  deliverance from – 284, 288, 471
Egyptian imposter – *x*, 805, 806
  referred to by Lysias – *xv*, 806
  Luke's account compared with Josephus' – 805, 806
Eirenikon – *xxiii, xxxiv*
Elam – 52
El Belka – 365
Elders, Christian – 425, 758, 778, 784, 792, 800, 843
  first selection of – 250, 446, 743
  selection of, method – 264-270, 370, 750, 784
  qualifications of – 264, 521
  same as bishops – 425, 521, 743, 750, 792
  plurality of in each congregation – 521
  their function – 230, 425, 454, 743, 750, 753, 775, 791
  appointed in every church – 519, 784
  involved in Jerusalem Conference – 530, 532, 534, 549, 551
  Paul's address to Ephesian elders – 743-757
  financial support of – 755, 928
Elders, Jewish – 174, 187, 216, 808, 825, 836, 845, 859, 864
  See also Senate
Election – 360, 490, 646
Elements – 716
Eleusinian mystery religions – *see* Mystery religions
Eliashib – 198
Eliezer – 285
Elijah – 342, 645, 737
Elisha – 737
Elogium – 835
Eloquent – 659
Elymas, the sorcerer – *see* Bar-Jesus
Emesa – 830
Emmaus – 212, 433, 834, 943
Enchantment – 708
End of the world – 548
Enoch – 169
Enrollments – *i*, 225
Epaenetus – 933
Epaphras – 948
Epaphroditus – 947, 949
Ephesian letters – 682, 715
Ephesians, epistle to – 450, 749, 757, 794, 799, 827, 947, 950
Ephesus – 569, 657, 658, 660, 666, 677, 696, 730, 742, 748, 752, 754, 756, 758, 785, 786, 800, 802, 804, 839, 879, 951, 953
  famous for magical arts – 682
  location – 570, 654, 666, 676
  Apollos at – *see* Apollos
  Paul's first visit there – 654-655
  Paul's evangelization there – 420, 666-700, 726, 756
  church there – *see* Church at Ephesus
  twelve disciples of John – *see* Twelve disciples of John at Ephesus
Ephraim – 310
Epicureans - 622, 632, 634, 635, 636
  their beliefs - 622, 628, 630, 631
Epilepsy - 242, 505, 506
Epimenides of Crete - 627, 632

Epiphanes – 831
Epiphanian view – 28, 39
Epiphanius – 120, 253, 951
Epirus – 951
Epistle of the Churches of Vienne and Lyon – *xxiv*
Epistle of James – *see* James, epistle of
Epistle of Jude – *see* Jude, epistle of
Epistles of Paul – *see* Paul, epistles of. *See also* names of individual letters
Epistolary aorist – *see* Aorist tense
Erasmus – 340, 652
Erastus – 645, 685
Esbath – 710, 713
Esdraelon, plain of – *see* Plain of Esdraelon
Essenes – 226, 687
    origin of the party – 199
    beliefs – 199
    were Jesus, John, and apostles Essenes? – 199
Eternal generation – 480
Eternal life – 180, 215, 488-490, 670, 671, 755, 772, 954
Eternal purpose, God's – 543, 749, 845, 947
Eternal security – 82, 322, 326
Eternity – 72
Etesian winds – 732, 894, 896
Ethiopia – 633
    location – 332
    history of church there – *see* Church in Ethiopia
Ethiopian Eunuch – 330-344, 669, 724, 785
    his country and rank – 332
    a proselyte – 333
    reading the prophet Isaiah – 333
    traditional place of his baptism – 331, 338, 339
Ethiopic Church – *see* Church in Ethiopia
Ethiopic version – 6, 673
Ethnarch – *xiii*
Eubulus – 953
Eucharist – *see* Lord's Supper, names of
Euodia – 576
Eunice – 514, 564
Eunuch, Ethiopian – *see* Ethiopian Eunuch
Euphrates River – *see* River
Euraquilo – 901, 903
Europe – 378, 446, 560, 570, 571
Eusebius of Caesarea – *xxiv*, 235, 314, 333, 338, 343, 428, 444, 447, 448, 451, 572, 636, 766, 785, 794, 810

Euthanasia – 489
Eutychus – *xxxii*, 736-740, 781, 926
Evangelism – 459
Evangelist – 662, 786, 931
    how appointed – 784
    meaning of the term – 783, 784
    relation to offices of apostle, prophet, and elder – 256, 743, 784
    tasks – 230, 784
Evangelistic methods – 420, 572
    visiting synagogues – 260, 363, 469, 611
    house to house – 420, 646, 745, 746, 936, 949
    Paul's – 491, 497, 501, 516, 612, 622, 638, 642, 654, 658, 676, 684, 936, 948, 949.
    See also Missionary methods in Acts
    personal evangelism – *see* Personal Evangelism
    See also Center of evangelism
Evangelistic missions – *see* Missionary methods, 20th century
Eve – 236
Evening – 173
Evidences of Christianity – 512, 942
Evil spirits – *see* Demons
Excommunication
    from the church – *see* Church discipline
    from the synagogue – 603, 694
Exhortation – 195, 728
Exodus – 43, 307, 473
    date of – 280
Exorcism, Exorcists – 237, 238, 678- 680, 682, 701, 716
Expediency – 555
Experience connected with salvation – 342
Extortion – 233
Extraordinary miracles - *see* Miracles, extraordinary
Extreme unction - *see* Roman Catholic church doctrines
Eyewitness - 855
Ezekiel - 749
Ezra - 174, 198

Face of an angel - 265
Fadus - *see* Cuspius Fadus

Fair Havens – 896, 897, 899, 900, 906, 907, 908, 928
Faith – 56, 173, 225, 463, 517, 674, 746, 772, 851, 946
   definition of – *xxxviii,* 598-600
   full of faith – 253, 418
   justification by – 256, 400, 483, 524, 590, 598, 670
   comes by hearing – 173, 209, 361, 382, 467, 497, 537, 591, 601, 618
   miraculous "faith" – 161, 601-602
   faith to be healed – 155, 161, 162, 503
   saving faith – 161, 256, 400, 602-605, 655, 670, 946
   body of doctrine – 256, 419, 517, 602, 675, 875
   obedient faith – 342, 343, 400, 467, 491, 497, 533, 537, 593, 636, 644, 663, 667, 668, 670, 681, 746, 794, 851, 947
   Special Study – 598-610
   continue in, exhortation to – 517
Faith and reason – 618
Faith healers – 96, 97, 152, 161, 162, 213, 325
"Faith only" doctrine – 76, 81, 256, 342, 400, 405, 497, 590-591, 599, 603, 604, 607-609, 809
Fall – 243
False messiahs – 224
False prophets – 461, 581, 752
False teachers – 752, 753
False witnesses – 262, 271, 301, 303, 477, 841
Familiar spirits – 328, 717, 719
Famine in Egypt – 277
   worldwide, predicted by Agabus – 422-424, 426, 445
Farewell
   to Ephesian elders – 757, 758, 778, 782
   to Troas church – 792
Fasces – 593
Fast, the – *see* Day of Atonement
Fasting – 357, 609, 669
   as a Christian exercise – 455, 456, 522
   connected with ordination services – 269, 457, 522
   during the voyage to Rome – 905, 913
Fatalism – 198
Fates, the – 505, 622, 628
Fathers – 538, 808, 844, 845, 875, 944

Fathom – 909, 910
Fear – 208, 371, 379, 394, 589, 645, 680, 727, 745, 853, 854, 907.
   See also God fearers
Feasts of the Jews – 888, 940
   attendance at – 45, 50, 475, 806
   Dedication – 157
   Passover – *ix,* 43, 150, 159, 396, 429- 431, 479, 528, 651, 655, 685, 732, 761, 762, 763, 771, 790, 897
   Pentecost – *xi,* 43-45, 56, 58, 174, 195, 253, 324, 333, 378, 401, 410, 411, 651, 655, 668, 685, 726, 742, 748, 764, 779, 783, 787, 790, 791, 794, 799, 800, 824, 826, 847
   Tabernacles – 44, 253, 857, 897
Feet, fall at one's – 390
Felix, governor – *x, xxiii,* 803, 805, 806, 824, 830, 831, 832, 837, 840, 841, 842, 844, 847, 850-857, 858, 861, 864, 865, 938
   history and character – *xvi,* 830, 837, 838, 853
   how long he was governor – *xvii,* 842
   his knowledge of Christianity – 848
   sought a bribe from Paul – *xxviii,* 848, 849, 854, 890
   recalled to stand trial before Nero – XVII, 838, 855, 856
Fellowship – 83, 193, 367, 411, 417, 424, 535, 670, 772, 773
Festus, Porcius – *x, xxiii,* 832, 855, 859, 861, 862, 865, 867, 868, 879, 880, 882, 883, 887, 888, 889, 890, 891, 893, 938
   date of his accession – *xxxvi,* 855
   history and character – *xvii,* 855, 857
   Paul's appeal before – 352, 857-863
   relationship with Agrippa II – 887, 888
   See also Agrippa II
Fever – 926
Fighting against God – 227
Final judgment – *see* Judgment
Finney, Charles G. – 102
Fire – 921, 924
Fire, baptism of – *see* Baptism in the New Testament
Fire, tongues as – *see* Tongues as of fire
First day of the week – *see* Lord's Day
First missionary journey – *see* Missionary journeys

First persecution of the church – *see* Persecution of early church
First work of grace – 87, 98, 539, 577, 578, 945
Fish – 385, 577, 620
Five points of Calvinism – 322
    T-otal Depravity – 322, 577, 578, 601, 607
    U-nconditional Election – 130, 646, 945
    L-imited Atonement – 322
    I-rresistible Grace – 87, 164, 577, 664
    P-erseverance of the Saints – *see* Eternal Security
Flaminian Way – 935
Fondi/Fundi– 932
Food – 905, 912, 913, 914
Footstool – 72
Foot washing – 770, 771
Foreknowledge of God – 64, 130-134
Foreign deities – 623, 624, 636
Foresail – *see* Sails, *Artemona*
Forgiveness – 56, 73-77, 327, 343, 356, 362, 367, 400, 470, 482, 488, 493, 510, 528, 578, 605, 609, 664, 672, 776, 853, 875, 881, 946.
See also Sin, remission of
Formica – 932
Fornication – 233, 544, 546, 548, 554, 638, 798
Fortress of Antonia – *see* Antonia, tower of
Fortune telling – 320, 461, 463, 580, 581
Forum – *see* Market place
Forum of Appius – *see* Market of Appius
France – 567
Frankincense – 381
Fraud – 465
Free city – 414, 570, 614, 812
Freedman – 253, 639, 675, 730, 731
    who they were – 257, 258
    synagogue of – 257
Free will – 24, 130-134, 147, 196, 198, 747, 877
Fruit of the vine – *see* Lord's Supper, names for; Lord's Supper, cup
Frumentarii – 891
Fulfilled prophecy – 58, 163, 908.
See also Christ Jesus, fulfilled prophecies
Fulfilled Scripture – 22, 163, 844, 845.
See also Christ Jesus, fulfilled prophecies

Full Gospel Business Men's Fellowship – 105
Fumigations – 236, 237
Fundamentalism – 181, 659
Funeral services, among Jews – 315
Future punishment – 196, 198, 484
See also Hell

Gabinus – 344
Gadarene demoniac – 242, 679, 701
Gaius – 691, 692, 696
    different persons of this name – 691
    Gaius Julius Caesar – *see* Augustus
Gaius of Corinth – 643, 644, 691, 728
Gaius of Derbe – 516, 691, 730
Gaius of Rome – 451, 785
Galatia – 451, 752
    area included under this name – 493
    churches of – *see* Churches
    visited on Paul's first mission – 468, 493
    visited on Paul's second mission – 564-569
    visited on Paul's third mission – 657, 658, 666, 727
Galatians, epistle to – 450, 483, 511, 558, 568, 569, 657, 658, 727, 796, 942
Galatic and Phrygian region – 567-569, 657, 659, 666
Galen – 214, 257
Galilee – 442, 454, 478, 863, 953
    gospel spreads to – 317
    Jesus' ministry there – 396
Galileans – *xv*, 51, 53
Gall – 327, 328
Gallio, proconsul at Corinth – *x, xiv, xv, xxiii*, 638, 646-651, 653, 832, 858
Gamaliel – *xi, xxxii*, 184, 228, 314, 315, 346, 808, 817, 822, 874
Gambling – 31
Gangites River – *see* River
Garden of Eden – 511
Garden of Gethsemane – 7, 17
Garlands - *see* Oxen and garlands
Garments – 373, 375, 433, 680, 787, 868.
See also Robes

Gates
- of houses – 387, 436
- of Jerusalem Beautiful – 150, 567
  - Nicanor – 152
  - Susan – 153
  - Huldah – 153
  - Golden – 153
- of Lystra – 502, 506,
- of Philippi – 575
- of Rome
  - Ostian Gate – 934
  - Porta Capena – 934
  - Porta San Sebastiano – 934
  - Porta Viminalis – 935
- Cilician – *see* Cilician Gates

Gathered to his people – *see* Hades
Gaul – 567, 856
Gaza – 314, 331
- when destroyed by the Romans – 331
- the roads which lead there from Jerusalem – *see* Roads

Gazith – 218, 262, 814, 825
Gemara – 337, 345
Gehenna – *see* Hell
Gelasius I – 766
Gemini – *see* Twin Brothers
Genitive case – 539
Gentiles – 355, 407, 411, 415, 484,485, 487, 488, 511, 533, 541, 543, 630, 795, 797, 802, 808, 809, 846, 868, 878, 879, 946
- described as "far off" – 80
- guilt in crucifixion of Jesus – 188, 189
- have sufficient light to create obligation – 511
- acknowledge blindly the existence of God – 627, 628, 631
- have no excuse for their idolatry – 632, 633
- must repent to be prepared for the judgment – 537, 633, 634, 878
- their acceptance of gospel predicted in Old Testament – 378, 488-489, 540-543, 880, 881, 946
- God showed Peter that Gentiles are to be offered salvation – 401, 410, 411, 537

Gens – 639
Gergesa – 351
Gerizim – *see* Mt. Gerizim
Germany – 567

Gershom – 194, 285
Gessius Florus – 888
Gideon – 241, 706
Gift of the Holy Spirit – *see* Holy Spirit
Gift of tongues – 323, 493, 672, 836
- how conferred on the day of Pentecost – 49
- conferred on Cornelius' household – 403, 579
- object of the endowment – 49, 108, 403
- nature of the miracle - 49-54, 96, 107, 109-116, 191, 403
- interpretation of - 108, 504
- how long did they continue, once granted? - 403

Girgashites - 296, 472
Giving of thanks - 913, 914, 933
Glorify God - 411, 444, 793
Glory of God - *see* Shekinah
Glossalalia - 49
- Special Study - 102-126
- *See also* Gift of tongues

Gnashing of teeth - 301
Gnosticism - 5, 328, 598, 721, 752
Goad - 352, 353
God – 907, 908
- attributes – 90, 226, 393, 432, 628, 852
- creator – 188, 298, 509, 628, 629, 630, 635, 852, 907
- eternal purpose of – *see* Eternal purpose
- impartial – 394, 401
- just and righteous – 634
- living – 509, 511, 628, 844, 846, 913
- names of – 220, 818
- nature of – 632
- omnipotent – 766
- omnipresence – 90, 632
- omniscience – 90.
  See also Knower of hearts
- personal – 723
- sovereignty – *see* Sovereignty,
- divine wrath of – 590, 670, 824

Goddesses – 624
God fearers – 470, 476, 486, 577, 613, 621.
  See also Proselytes
Godhead – 90, 125, 397, 405, 672
Gods, mythological – 504-508
Gog and Magog – 35-38
Golden calf – 292, 707
Golden Gate - *see* Gates

Golden rule – 547
Good deeds (good works) – *see* Alms; Benevolence
Good news – *see* Gospel
Goshen – 283
Gospel – 55, 479, 509, 524, 571, 602, 645, 668, 670, 673, 674, 727, 733, 748, 754, 755, 784, 851, 866, 884, 886, 927, 928, 931, 937, 939, 950
    preached to Jews first – 378, 460, 469, 488, 612, 641, 673, 936
    universality of its design – 392, 394, 510, 746, 787
        See also Salvation is for all
    first time it was offered to the Gentiles – 378, 536
    gospel in a nutshell – 483
    divides hearers – 499, 636, 674, 745, 853, 873, 943
    sources of opposition to – 583
Gospel of Luke – *see* Luke, gospel of
Gospel of Mark – *see* Mark, gospel of
Gospel of Matthew – *see* Matthew, gospel of
Gospel of Peter – 39
Gossip – 795
Government – 185, 473, 490, 511, 544, 575, 614, 818, 868, 889, 923
Governor – iii, iv, v, ix, xv, xvi, xvii, xviii, 648, 830, 831, 837, 842, 857, 862, 863, 866, 868, 880, 883, 888.
    See also Procurators
Grace – 193, 256, 353, 417, 418, 486, 498, 499, 513, 517, 523, 535, 539, 562, 577, 586, 601, 663, 664, 748, 754, 760, 776, 809, 877, 950
    See also First work of grace
    second work of grace – 102
Grain – 277, 780, 891, 894, 904, 914, 915, 919, 931
Graphology – 706
Gratitude – *see* Giving of thanks
Grave – 67, 135-136
Great commission – 3, 5, 9, 185, 231, 314, 378, 399, 405, 459, 489, 646, 660, 670, 949
Great day of questions – 287, 821
Great fire of Rome – *see* Rome
Great tribulation – 35-38
Great white throne judgment – *see* Judgment
Greece – 424, 440, 657, 728, 839, 895, 896, 908, 949

Greek language – 511, 805, 806, 807, 812, 836, 876, 901, 920
    prepositions – *see* Prepositions, Greek
    used with great purity by Luke – *xxxv*
    the language of business among the nations – 504
    See also Accusative case; Aorist tense; Article, definite; Dative case; Imperfect tense; Perfect tense; Sharp's rule of grammar
Greek Orthodox Church – 762, 766
Greeks – 415, 497, 801
Gregory Nazianzen – 766
Gregory of Nyssa – 766
Growth of the early church – 173, 210-211, 247, 255
Guardian angels - *see* Angels
Guards, prison - 217, 431, 432
Guilds, trade - 577, 688
Gulf of Adramyttium - 741
Gulf of Adria - 909
Gulf of Corinth - 638

Habakkuk – 484
Hades – 67, 70, 198, 481, 687, 820
    "gathered to his people," "laid to his people" – 137, 481
    Special Study – 135-144
Hadrian, emperor – 69, 462, 891
Hagar – 307, 768
Hagiographa – 484
Haifa – 782
Hall of Hewn Stones – *see* Gazith
Halloween – 711
Ham – 306
Hamaxitos – 620
Hamor, sons of – 278, 279, 311
Handkerchiefs – 677
Hand, motion with the – *see* Beckon with the hand
Hand of the Lord – 416, 465
Hands, laying on of – *see* Laying on of hands
Haphtara – 496
Haran – 272, 279, 306, 420
Hardening of heart – 674, 853, 854, 945
Haruscopy – 705
Harvest - 43, 44

Hasidim – 196
Hatshepsut – 282
He goats – 237
Healing – 493, 504, 592, 677, 946
    done by Jesus – 397
    no defects after miraculous healings –
        361, 516
    of lame man at gate Beautiful – 150
    of sick by Peter – 212
    of Aeneas – 372
    of demon possessed man – 213
    of Paul's blindness – 361
    of lame man at Lystra—502-515
    of Maltese residents – 926, 927, 928
Heart – 66, 73, 192, 202, 327, 334, 382,
    418, 474, 512, 537, 578, 581, 635, 704,
    771, 853, 945, 947
    Lord opens the heart of Lydia – 577,
        578, 788
    See also Hardness of heart
Heathen – *see* Gentiles
Heathen poets – *see* Poets, heathen
Heaven – 5, 16, 135, 301, 356, 381, 628,
    755
Heavens, Three – 143, 166, 368, 514
Hebraisms – 825
Hebrew language – 271, 352, 600, 807, 808,
    810, 812, 814, 836, 920
Hebrew parallelism – 189
Hebrews, epistle to – 947
    author—*xxxvii*, 450, 665, 855, 931
    message of – 261, 286, 799, 897, 942,
        950
Hebron – 212, 278, 311, 314, 331, 338
Helena, queen of Adiabene – 424
Heliopolis – 292
Helius – 698
Hell – 9, 30, 135, 239, 484, 485, 489, 490,
    589, 643, 815
Hellenists – *xxxiii*, 247, 253, 258, 313, 354,
    368, 372, 415
    how distinguished from Greeks – 247,
        415
Hellenistic names – 568
Hellenization – 196, 259
Hellespont – 568
Helvidian view – 39
Henry VIII – 769
Hepatoscopy – 705, 708
Hermeneutics – *xxxviii*, 46, 198, 209, 335,
    607, 659, 755, 943

Hermes – 504, 621, 907
Hermes, Paul called – 505, 925
Hermogenes – 7 53
Herod Agrippa I – *see* Agrippa I
Herod Agrippa II – *see* Agrippa II
Herod Antipas
    tetrarch of Galilee – *iv, vi,* 158, 189, 426,
        454, 477
    his war with Aretas IV – *vi, xii*
    his exile – *ii, vi,* 426, 454
Herod of Chalcis – *iv, xvii, xviii*
Herod Philip – 253
Herod the Great – *ii, xiv,* 69, 195, 224, 225,
    318, 373, 378, 414, 426, 443, 444, 460,
    803, 824, 834, 835, 843
Herodians - *vi,* 200
Herodias - *vi,* 426
Herodotus - 289, 696, 706, 762
Herostratus - 689
Hesychius – 716
Hetairai – 636
Hex – 463, 713
Hexagram – 712
Hezekiah – 137, 438
Hierai – 687
Hierapolis – 658, 666, 676, 785, 949 951
Hieroglyphics – 282
Hieronymian view – 40
High priest – *viii, xvi,* 175, 176, 215, 218,
    350, 477, 817, 836, 847, 857
    See also Chief priest(s)
Highways
    Damascus road – *see* Paul
    see Egnatian Way; Appian Way; Ostian
        Way; Way of the Sea; Way of the
        Kings, Way of the Patriarchs;
        Hamaxitos; Flaminian Way
Hildebert of Tours – 767
Hillel – *xi,* 181, 223
Hinduism – 506, 721
Hippocrates – 257, 466, 926
Hippolytus – 448
His own place – *see* Judas, the traitor
Hittites – 296, 472
Hivites – 296, 472
Holiness movement – 102
Holy kiss – 656, 757, 783
Holy Place – 150, 151
Holy of Holies – 150, 151

Holy Spirit
   activities of Holy Spirit, chart on the – 101
   Special Study – 89-101
   Comforter – 371
   Deity of – 90, 204
   person and work – 89-101, 323, 334, 423, 750, 766
   names of – 89, 207, 570
   in the Old Testament – 90, 91, 944
   in the ministry of Jesus – 3, 91-92, 397
   procession of – 570
   promised to the apostles – 6, 7, 9
   in conversion – 73, 94, 98-99, 147, 334, 382, 397, 578, 601, 607, 851, 854, 945
   indwelling gift – 74, 78-79, 97-98, 124, 125, 165, 221, 325, 361, 363, 401, 402, 489, 555, 563, 592, 661, 667, 668, 669, 684, 716, 852
   baptism with – 9, 10, 12, 46-50, 58, 76, 92-94, 105, 161, 209, 222, 324, 361, 363, 401-406, 411, 464, 537, 668
   spirit baptism does not take the place of baptism in water – 402
   spiritual gifts – *see* Spiritual gifts
   filled with – 48, 124, 177, 191, 251, 253, 301, 304, 360-361, 418, 464, 493
   measures of the Holy Spirit – 59, 411
   unknown to John's disciples – 660, 661
   grieving (rejecting) the Holy Spirit – 99, 124
   lying to the Holy Spirit – 202
   resisting – 299, 301, 780-781, 854
   blasphemy of – 487
   direct leading in the case of the apostles – *see* Apostles
   leads men to a knowledge of truth – 412
   fruit of the spirit – 419
Homage – 390
Homer – 235, 504, 577, 706
Honorarium – 927, 928
Hope – 539, 772, 819, 845, 876, 878, 879, 886, 905, 939
Hope of Israel – 939, 942
Horace – 932
Horeb – *see* Mt. Sinai
Horoscope – 702, 703
Horsemen – 829, 834
Horses – 789, 830

Hospitality – 579, 580, 615, 728, 783, 785, 790, 920, 921, 926
Host of Heaven – *see* Astrology
Hours of prayer – *see* Prayer
House to house
   worshiping from – 86
   evangelizing – *see* Evangelistic work
Household – 379, 579, 591-593, 637, 644, 781
Household baptism - *see* Baptism
Household servants - *see* Slaves
Housetop - 384, 401
Huguenots - 121
Humility – 743, 744, 745
Hunger – 384, 386
Huss, John – 131
Hyksos kings – 280
Hymenaeus and Alexander – 753
Hymns – 586
Hypnotism – 708
Hypocrisy – 201, 558-559, 816, 817
Hyrcanus, John – 69, 196, 198, 318, 803

I Ching - 705
Ibis – 282
Iconium – 512, 565, 657, 839
   location – 493, 500, 501
   church at – *see* Churches
   Paul and Barnabas visit – 493, 497- 501, 516, 561
   Paul and Silas visit – 565, 566
Ides – 897
Idolatry – 237, 370, 426, 509, 544, 548, 569, 629, 633, 635, 689, 697, 929
   Christians dissuaded from – 233, 509, 545-547, 553, 689, 774, 793
   forbidden to Jews – 391, 474, 694
   pollutions of – 414, 545, 798
   degrading to worshiper's morals – 546
   foolish – 292, 509, 628
   ideas of the gods' appearance – 633
   at Athens – 620, 621
   at Lystra – 504, 505
   in Egypt – 291
   1st century people dissatisfied with – 379
Idol worship – 292
Idols, things sacrificed to – 385

Ignatius, bishop of Antioch – 30, 451, 686, 750, 765
Ignorance – 157, 162, 476, 627.
   See also Uneducated and untrained
Illissus – 621
Illumination – 128, 335, 412
Illyricum – 525, 727
Images – 294, 633, 687
Immersion – *see* Baptism, mode
Immortality – 196, 198, 508, 622, 635, 820, 939
Impanation – 770
Imperfect tense – 502, 527, 539, 560, 641, 650, 660, 681, 742, 757, 789, 809, 854, 867, 927
Imposters – 716
Imprecatory prayer – 190, 326, 643, 816
Imprisonment
   Peter and John's – 171
   apostles' – 213
   Peter's – *see* Peter
   Paul's – 781
      at Philippi – 585-596
      at Jerusalem – 813, 822, 827
      at Caesarea – *see* Paul, Caesarean imprisonment
      at Rome – 574, 933-950, 952, 953
   release from, Roman practice – *xxxvi*, 450, 948
Incantation – 678, 679, 682, 710, 712, 716
Incest – 546
Incubation – 706, 708
Independent missionaries – 458
India – 53
Indigenous churches – 521
Infant sprinkling – 10
   poor Scriptural proof for – 79, 324, 533, 579, 591, 593, 844
Infralapsarianism – 133
Inheritance – 755
Inner prison – *see* Jail
Innocent III, pope – 767
Inscriptions that corroborate Luke's history
   at Abilene – vii
   at Cyprus – *xxx,* 462
   at Delphi – xv. 647
   at Ephesus – 695, 697
   at Jerusalem – 801
   at Malta – 920, 925
   at Piraeus – 902
   at Thessalonica – xxx, 615

Insects – 385
Inspiration – xxiv, xxv, 22, 49, 60, 66, 69, 127-129, 163, 167, 177, 188, 213, 260, 290, 363, 380, 412, 419, 421, 423, 428, 480, 487, 497, 529, 543, 544, 545, 553, 606, 680, 781, 786, 944
   did not result in omniscience – 535
Intermarriage with pagan nations – 391
Intermediate place of the dead – 67, 135-144, 198, 431, 820, 821
Intermediate trip to Corinth – 685, 686, 726, 728
International Church of the Foursquare Gospel – 104
Interpreter – 495, 496, 810
Interpretation – *see* Hermeneutics
Interpretation of tongues – *see* Gift of tongues
Introductory Studies to Acts – *see* Acts, Introductory Studies
Invination – 769
Invitation – 56, 80, 401, 411, 787, 809, 853
Irenaeus – *xxiv, xxv,* 119, 254, 320, 329, 340, 343, 448, 451, 527, 751, 765
Isaac – 158, 275, 285, 306, 307, 470, 472, 496, 608
Isaiah
   Jesus' quotation of – 945
   John the Baptist's use of – 349, 659
   John the apostle's use of – 945
   Paul's quotations of – 471, 480, 604, 882, 944-946
   Peter's use of – 328, 604
   Philip's use of – 333, 338
Ish-Bosheth – 473
Ishmael, son of Abraham – 306, 307
Ishmael, son of Fabi – *xvi*, 857
Islam – *see* Mohammedanism
Israel – 72, 178, 180, 470, 474, 475, 875
Italian cohort – 379
   why so named – 379
   why stationed at Caesarea – 379
   how long at Caesarea – 396, 397

Jacob – 136, 137, 158, 275, 278, 287, 311, 470, 496, 508
   where buried – 278, 279, 311
   number of his family descending into Egypt – 278, 310

Jail – 173, 214-215, 316, 349, 429, 585
   three sections to a Roman jail—586
Jailer, Philippian – *see* Philippian jailer
Jairus' daughter – 150, 375
James, apostle – 40, 427
   son of Zebedee – 40, 427
   martyred – 426-428, 435, 867
James, epistle of – 18, 20, 527, 791
James, Lord's brother – 18, 40, 329, 406, 439, 540, 794, 850
   risen Lord appears to him – 5
   apostle at Jerusalem – 367, 413, 439, 530, 534, 791, 792, 843
   speech at Jerusalem Conference – 540-549
   advice to Paul – 793-798, 937
   martyrdom of – 888
   epistle of – *see* James, epistle of
James, the son of Alphaeus – 18, 40, 439
Jannes and Jambres – 753
Japheth – 306
Jason
   high priest – 198
   a Christian – 614-616, 620
Jealousy – 214, 487, 491, 614
Jebusites – 296, 472
Jehovah's Witnesses – 67
Jeremiah – 586
Jericho – 212, 471, 805
Jerome – *xxiv, xxv,* 40, 53, 338, 343, 372, 447, 448, 451, 572, 751, 786, 951
Jerusalem – 6, 13, 16, 153, 175, 323, 329, 373, 422, 446, 478, 742, 779, 783, 787, 788, 789, 790, 791, 799, 802, 824, 844, 848, 857, 858, 859, 861, 864, 866, 869, 874, 879, 939, 944
   pools at – 81
   destruction of – *xiii, xvi, xviii, xxi,* 44, 50, 58, 61, 200, 262, 379, 484, 485, 794, 824, 837, 888
   how often visited by Paul after his conversion – 531, 846
   offering for the poor at – *see* Offering for the poor at Jerusalem
Jerusalem Conference – 151, 254, 330, 427, 428, 440, 449, 525, 527- 556, 558, 566, 791, 792, 793, 794, 795, 846
   date of – *xix,* 525, 530
   public and private meetings at – 534
   decree of - 544, 546, 549, 550-554, 559, 563, 565, 566, 791, 798
   still binding - 546, 553, 797, 798
   not an example for delegate conventions - 556, 557
Jesse – 474
Jesus Christ – *see* Christ Jesus
Jesus Justus – 949
Jesus People – 104
Jethro – 174, 285
Jews
   meaning of the term – 54, 828
   of the Dispersion – *see* Dispersion
   Asian Jews – *see* Asian Jews
   asked for a king – 473
   God's dealings with – 510
   numerous in Antioch of Pisidia – 469, 486
   numerous in Bithynia – 570
   numerous in Cilicia – 259
   numerous in Cyprus – 194
   numerous in Damascus – 351
   numerous in Egypt – 258, 259, 658
   numerous in Ephesus – 654, 680, 694
   numerous in Ethiopia – 333
   numerous in North Africa – 258, 259
   numerous in Pontus – 639
   numerous in Rome – 54, 258, 888, 936, 937
   Roman domination of Israel – 10, 175, 380
   believed salvation was for Jews only – 394, 401, 489
   enjoyed religious toleration – 259
   loved to hear their history recounted – 272, 470
   expelled from Rome – 54, 258, 937
   persecution of – 938, 939
   prejudiced against non-Jews – 487, 794, 809, 855, 879
   involved in the death of Jesus – *see* Crucifixion, who was responsible for
   leaders often violently opposed to Christianity – 87, 172, 173, 213, 257, 487, 492, 498, 512, 513, 614, 618, 645, 646, 647, 657, 674, 824, 839, 841, 869, 941, 944
   plots of, to kill Paul – *see* Plots of the Jews
   social segregation from and hostility to non-Jews – 318, 391, 548, 614, 791, 794, 809, 938

God's rejection of the Jews – 612, 643, 946
zealous for the Law – 795, 796
rebellion to Rome – 837, 860, 888
Jezebel – 720
Job – 137
Jochebed – 281, 284, 308, 309
Joel, prophecy of – 46, 58-63, 79, 402
Johanan Ben Zakki – 175
John, apostle – *xxvi*, 330, 406, 782
traditions concerning his writing several New Testament books – 330
traditions concerning his death – 427, 428
at Jerusalem Conference – 534
epistles of – 691, 752
Gospel of – 752, 754, 757, 855, 945
John Hyrcanus – *see* Hyrcanus, John
John Mark – *see* Mark
John of Damascus – 766
John the Baptist – 349, 396, 411, 428, 455, 475-477, 659, 660, 667, 669, 681, 746, 795
his disciples – 150, 328, 605, 659, 660, 670.
See also Twelve disciples of John at Ephesus
confessed inferiority to Christ – 167, 475
nature of his baptism – 7, 475, 670, 671, 672
by whom martyred – *vi*, 426, 454, 867
his rebuke of Jewish religious leaders – 197
John, the Jewish religious leader – 175
Jonah – 383, 705
Jonathan, high priest – *xvi*, 199, 837
Jonathan, son of Saul – 705, 706
Joppa – 212, 314, 344, 372, 373, 382, 383, 402, 410, 413, 833
church there – *see* Church at Joppa
Jordan River – *see* River
Joseph Barnabas – *see* Barnabas
Joseph Barsabbas – 28, 550
Joseph, patriarch – 280, 423, 708, 763
sold into Egypt – 276, 299
made governor of Egypt – 276, 471
made known to his brothers – 277
where buried – 278, 311
Joseph Caiaphas – *see* Caiaphas, Joseph
Joseph of Arimathea - 359, 478
Joseph the carpenter – 20, 881

Josephus
accounts that supplement Bible statements – 176, 199, 237, 259 310, 379, 414, 473, 625, 639, 648, 705, 763, 797, 824, 831, 834, 856, 861, 891, 897, 903
accounts that parallel Luke's accounts – *ii, vii, xi, xxiv*, 197, 224, 225, 307, 348, 424, 441- 444, 626, 654, 678, 691, 797 801, 803, 806, 820, 842, 849, 855, 868, 890, 914, 933, 937, 941
explanation of Old Testament accounts – 44, 281, 282, 284, 294, 309, 310, 472
owned lands near Jerusalem – 195
his shipwreck in the Sea of Adria – 908, 914
Joshua – 273, 295, 300, 331, 472
Joy – 493, 531. *See also* Rejoicing
Judah, patriarch – 276
Judaizers – *xxxiii*, 407, 412, 413, 527, 530, 544, 548, 549, 551, 552, 566, 656, 657, 658, 727, 728, 752, 762, 795, 796, 933
claim to come from Jerusalem church – 412, 527, 528, 551
their teaching – 527-530, 533
Judas Barsabbas – 550, 553, 554-558
Judas of Antioch – 358
Judas of Galilee – 225
his place of birth – 225
reason for his opposition to Rome – *ii*, 225
Judas, the traitor – 22, 23, 477, 774
selected by Jesus to be an apostle – 24
his suicide at Jerusalem – 18, 24, 29, 30
remorse, not repentance – 148
meaning of "Iscariot" – 16
his office filled by Matthias – 21-33, 248, 519
no inconsistency in the different accounts of his death – 24, 25
went to his own place – 30
See also Akeldama
Judea – 13, 53, 370, 396, 424, 425, 726, 742, 787, 842, 849, 874, 878, 888, 908, 938, 940
part of province of Syria – *i*, 857
church spreads to – 314, 407
relief sent to – *see* Offering for the poor at Jerusalem
Jude, epistle of - 20

Judges, period of the – 472, 473, 486
Judgment, final
    day of – 62, 238, 510, 634, 821, 851, 852
    purpose of – 144
    to be universal – 399, 634, 635
    for the righteous and wicked – 144
    moral effect of looking for – 148, 852, 853
    sheep and goat judgment – 34
    great white throne – 34
    judgment seat of Christ – 852
Judgment, human – 560, 898
Judgment seat – 583, 648, 650, 859, 865
Julius, a centurion – 891, 892, 895, 906, 911, 926, 933
    why he favored Paul – 889, 893, 917, 931, 935
Julius Caesar – 351, 575, 638, 643, 654, 812, 867, 910
Julius Cordus – *xiv*
Junias – 892, 933
Jupiter – *see* Zeus
Justification – 165, 256, 275, 400, 470, 483, 601, 603, 605, 607-609, 661, 670, 796, 852, 942
Justinian, emperor – 690
Justin Martyr – 119, 328, 329, 330, 448, 763, 765
    his testimony concerning the Lord's Day – 764
    his testimony concerning demons – 239, 678
Justice – 584, 593, 594, 923, 924
Justus – *see* Joseph Barsabbas, or, Titus Justus
Juvenal – 576, 916, 952

Kefr Saba (Antipatris site?) – *see* Antipatris
Kerygma and *Didache* – 229
Keturah – 285, 307
Key of Solomon – 712
Keys of the kingdom – 56, 378, 382, 536, 748
Khartoum – 332
Kidron – *see* Valley of Kidron
King – 868, 869, 880

Kingdom of God – 5, 405, 542, 606, 616, 674, 701, 746, 748, 749, 774, 785, 881, 939, 940, 942, 946, 949, 950
    synonymous with "kingdom of heaven" – 5
    sometimes refers to the church – 5, 6, 34, 321, 942
    sometimes refers to heaven – 5, 492, 518, 748, 942
    earthly one anticipated – 10, 11, 942
    diverse opinions about – 34-38
    spiritual nature of – 12, 14, 670, 942.
    See also Millennial kingdom
Kiss, holy – *see* Holy kiss
Knower of hearts – 29, 537
Knowledge – 598, 602, 631, 663, 807
Knox, John – 132
Kohath – 194, 281, 308, 309
Kosher – 547
Koura, a point at the entrance of St. Paul's Bay – 909, 916, 917
Krishna – 506, 721
Krishna consciousness – 721

Laban – 294, 687
Lactantius – 451
Laid to his fathers – *see* Hades
Laity
    clergy and laity – 317
    laity denied the cup by Catholics – 768
Lamb's Book of Life – 87
Lame man healed at Samaria – 319
    by Peter – *xxxii*, 150-156, 173, 567
    by Paul – *xxxii*, 502-515
Lamentation – 315, 375
Lammas – 710
Lamps – 735, 736, 737
Laodicea – 658, 666, 676, 949, 951
Lasea – 896, 899
Last days – 58, 62
Latin – 54, 554, 677, 730, 836, 901, 920
Latin Vulgate – 6, 171, 309, 600, 651, 652, 658, 840, 935
Laurium – 633
Law and Gospel – 524, 530, 533, 534, 537, 547, 794, 795, 799, 879, 897

Law of Moses – 223, 291, 300, 353, 391, 400, 408, 444, 469, 483, 484, 510, 527, 553, 606, 649, 670, 817, 832, 845, 860, 863, 873 897
    abrogated – 150, 261, 294, 386, 544, 606, 652, 653, 661, 672, 794, 799
    not kept by Jews – 301, 538
    studied by Paul – 348
    penalty for teaching others to disobey the Law – 313, 513
    read in the synagogue services – 469, 471, 495, 496, 548, 549, 807
    Sadducees' "Bible" – 198
    could not save – 482, 483, 794
    not essential to salvation – 794, 796
    intended to "lead" men to Christ for salvation – 538, 578, 611, 673, 795, 796, 875, 943
    some precepts observed by early Christians – 150, 151, 794
Lawrence of Arabia – 772
Law, two kinds in New Testament – 555, 556
Lawyers (Jewish) – *see* Scribes Lawyers (Roman) – *see* Attorney
Laying on of hands – 96, 110, 213, 255, 257, 268, 318, 324, 325, 359, 360, 401, 456, 457, 521, 563, 565, 601, 672, 784
Lazarus – 18, 140, 183, 205
Leading man (on Malta) – 925, 926
Leading men among the brethren – 550
Leading men of the city – 492, 618, 868
Leading men of the Jews – 857, 859, 868, 936, 937, 941, 942
Leading women – 613, 618, 637
Lebanon Mountains – 413, 414
Lechaeum – 638
Lectionaries – 471
Leda – 929
Lee, Mother Ann - 121
Legalism - 197, 418
Legates - *iii, v, xii,* 647, 857, 925, 927
Legions - 370, 379, 803, 891, 934.
    See also Soldiers, Roman
Lesbos – 741, 892
Letter
    form of 1st century letters – 550
    from Sanhedrin – 350, 357, 939, 940
    of Jerusalem Conference – 544, 549, 551-554
    of Lysias to Felix – 831-833, 837
    from Festus and Agrippa II to Caesar – 870, 871, 887, 935
    Paul's – *see* names of individual New Testament books
Letters of commendation – 367, 663, 665, 667, 727
Levi – 308, 309
Levitation – 465, 682, 711, 720, 722, 724
Levites – 281, 455, 888
    as a temple guard – 171, 802
    their right to property – 195
Liberalism, religious – *xxii, xxxiii, xxxiv, xxxv,* 48, 181, 214, 241, 351, 352, 444, 569, 572, 599, 676, 744, 752, 761, 793, 819, 832, 871, 872, 921, 922
Liberality
    of early Christians – 192-195, 201
    of the believers at Antioch – 424, 425
    See also Offering for the poor at Jerusalem
Libertina – 257, 258
Libertines – *see* Freedmen
Liberty, Christian – *see* Christian liberty
Libra – 702
Libya – 53, 332
Lictors – 585, 593, 595, 650, 810
Life – 215, 412, 629, 939
"Lift the voice" – 187
Light – 881, 882
Lightning – 432
Linguistics – 122
Linus – 953
Liturgy – 455, 760
Livia, Columbarium of Empress – 675
Living link missionaries – 13, 458, 531
Living oracles – 291
Livy – 932
Local autonomy – 21, 532
Located ministry – 420, 597, 646, 677
Lois – 514
Lombard, Peter – 131
Lord – 71, 87, 183, 187, 211, 606, 628, 629, 709, 756, 771, 822, 823, 878, 950
    Lordship of Jesus preached to Gentiles – 394, 396, 416, 591
    meaning and uses of this title – 10, 72, 187, 189, 327, 358, 368, 381, 434, 498, 499, 645, 674, 870
Lord's Day – 44, 430, 549, 732, 733, 734, 738, 743, 764, 765, 780, 931

Lord's Supper – 83, 84, 733-734, 738, 739, 914, 931
   bread at – 83, 86, 739, 759, 760, 762, 765, 769
   cup, contents of – 759, 762-765, 769
   institution of – 150, 355, 398, 435, 661, 759, 761-762, 774, 776
   who may officiate at – 455, 456, 775
   who may partake – 760, 768, 774-775
   frequency – 83, 86, 430, 734, 735, 739, 764, 765, 771
   names for – 83, 759-761
   self-examination precedes – 775, 776
   theology of – 738, 765-776
   Special Study – 759-777
Lot – 139, 472
Lots, casting of – 31, 704, 705
Love Feast – 86, 738, 739, 765, 771
Lower parts of the earth – *see* Intermediate place of the dead
Lucian – 621
Lucius of Cyrene – 259, 454
Lucifer – 136
Luke
   Gospel of – *xxiv*, 757, 783, 855, 889, 927
   hometown – 571.
      See also Antioch of Syria
   writer of Acts – *xxvi*, 1, 454, 731.
      See also "We" sections
   peculiarities of his style – *xxx*, 194
   sketch of his life – 572, 731, 890
   physician – 257, 502, 503, 572, 580, 737, 889, 890, 922, 946
   examples of his historical accuracy – *xxx*, *xxxi*, 462, 501, 574, 615, 647, 695, 909, 922
   planted church at Troas – 572
   his first connection with Paul – 518,
   ministry in Philippi – 583, 597, 646, 677, 732
   visit to Corinth? – 727
   carries Philippian offering to Jerusalem – 730
   writes as an eyewitness – *xxvi, xxxiv*, 791, 859, 868, 882, 929
   his use of geographical terms – 567- 570
   has correct nautical terms – *xxxi*, 779, 889, 890, 909, 916
   his activities while Paul is prisoner in Caesarea – 830, 850, 855, 889
   with Paul in Rome – 450, 933, 934, 948, 953
Luna – 687
Lunch – *see* Meals
Lutheran Church – 517
Luther, Martin – 132, 171, 342, 599, 608, 759, 768, 769
Lutro – 899, 900
Lycaonia – 493, 501, 568, 657
   its extent – 493, 501
   cities of – 657
   dialect of – 52, 53, 504
Lycia – 467, 581, 788, 894, 895
Lycus River – *see* River
Lydda – 212, 314, 344, 471
Lydia – 53, 568, 570
Lydia, purple seller – 576-580
   her name – 576, 577
   baptized – 479
   members of her household – 579
   hospitality extended to missionaries – 579, 596
Lysanias, tetrarch – iv, *vii*, 426
Lysias, Claudius
   commander of Roman garrison – *xvi*, 803, 804, 806, 807, 811, 812, 822, 825, 827, 828, 832, 833, 836, 840, 841, 843, 847, 849, 858, 879, 890
   his letter – 831-833, 837, 847, 849
   his misrepresentation – 832
Lystra – *xxxii*, 501-517, 561, 564, 565, 657, 744, 879, 925
   healing of lame man – 502-515
   no synagogue there – 502
   visited by Zeus and Hermes – 504, 505

Maccabees – 196, 198, 199, 344, 496, 824, 860, 887
Macedonia – 458, 571, 611, 641, 642, 647, 684, 949
   location – 571
   how used by Greeks – 574
   its Roman signification – 571, 574
   Timothy and Erastus sent to – 685
   Paul visits – 571-619, 726, 727, 728, 729, 731
Macedonian call, the – *xxv*, 571
Macpelah, Cave of – *see Cave* of Macpelah
Madness, Paul accused of - 883

Magic and magical arts – 236, 320, 321, 326, 461-466, 677, 678, 681, 682, 701, 709-716
Magician – 463, 831
Magistrates – *xxx,* 583, 585, 593-5%
Malaria – 468
Malta – *see* Melita, Sicilius
Malta fever – 926
Mamertine Prison – 586, 952
Manaen – 432, 454
Manasseh – 310, 333
Manna – 289, 471
Man of Macedonia – 571, 572
Man of sin – 34
Mantic – 701, 702
Manuscripts, New Testament
    Codex Alexandrinus – 308, 318, 472, 751, 935, 947
    Codex Beza – *xxii,* 14, 434, 506, 509, 572, 658, 662
    Codex Claromontanus – 751
    Codex Ephraemi – 472, 751
    Codex Sinaiticus – *xxii,* 279, 318, 472, 658, 751, 754, 797, 833, 929, 935, 947
    Codex Vaticanus – *xxii,* 279, 308, 318, 472, 751, 797, 929, 935, 947
Manuscript variations - 6, 53, 281, 327, 340, 370, 413, 423, 471, 472, 484, 485, 506, 532, 543, 551, 558, 560, 619, 642, 650, 652, 655, 656, 660, 673, 691, 698, 731, 751, 754, 783, 787, 797, 822, 828, 833, 840, 864, 875, 886, 896, 904, 909, 914, 929, 934, 947
    conjectural emendations – 878, 880
    chapter and verses not in old manuscripts – 46
Maps – 955
    Hellenistic – 567-569
    Roman provincial – 567-569
Marathon, battle of – 622
Marcion – 238
Marcus Junius Silanus – 698
Mark – *xxxiv,* 435, 445, 485
    his relationship to Barnabas – 435, 560
    his mother's home in Jerusalem – 187, 430, 435
    "attendant" to Paul – *xxv,* 435, 460
    his abrupt departure from the mission – 467, 468, 523, 524, 561, 948

    quarrel of Paul and Barnabas concerning – *xxxiii,* 559-562
    regained the apostle's confidence – 468, 562, 948, 953
Mark, Gospel of – 757, 855, 927
    author – 435
    wrote what Peter preached – 396, 435
Market place – 620, 667, 691
    the resort of loafers – 614
    courts held in them – 583, 584, 697
    preaching done in them – 502, 622
Marriage
    repudiated by Essenes – 199
    mixed, prohibited to Jews – 564
Martyrs
    first Christian martyr – *see* Stephen
Mars – 704
Mars Hill – *see* Areopagus
Mary and Martha – 18, 19
Mary Magdalene – 4, 19, 41, 142
Mary, mother of Jesus – 20, 767, 881
    assumption of – 20
    doctrine of perpetual virginity – 39, 40
    worship of – 20
Mary, mother of John Mark – 187, 430, 435
Mary, wife of Clopas – 40, 41
Masada – 824
Mass – 712
Matala, Cape of – *see* Cape Matala
Materializations – 465, 717, 720, 722, 724
Mathematics – 282
Matter viewed as eternal – 509, 510, 622, 628
Matthew, Gospel of – 405, 438, 550, 754, 757, 855
Matthias, apostle – 28-33, 57, 248, 507, 705
Matthias, Maccabean – 824
Mauritania – 830
Maximinus – 444
Meals, two per day – 384
Meander River – *see* River
Meaning of *eis* at Acts 2:38 – *see* Prepositions, Greek
Meat market – 545
Media – 52
Medical missions – *see* Missionary methods, 20th century
Medical terms – 466, 502, 893, 897, 902, 905, 923, 925, 926, 927, 928, 946
Medicine – 282, 466, 675, 778, 927

Mediterranean Sea – 53, 54, 194, 373, 413, 467, 728, 729, 732, 748, 779, 780, 782, 894, 897, 898, 902, 908, 909, 922, 928
Mediums – 461, 581, 703, 707, 715, 717-720
Melanchthon – 132
Melissai – 687
Melita Illyrica – 919
    not the island where Paul was wrecked – 919
Melita, Sicilius – *xviii*, 908, 909, 916, 925, 927, 928
    why not recognized by the sailors – 915
    island where Paul was wrecked – 919
        See also St. Paul's Bay
    part of the province of Sicily – 919, 920, 925
    timber not now found on the island – 921
Mellierai – 687
Memorial – 381, 770
Memphis – 292
Menahem – 454
Menelaus – 198
Mental assent - 598, 599, 602, 603
Merari - 194
Mercury - *see* Hermes
Mesmerism – *see* Hypnotism
Mesopotamia – 53, 272, 279, 420
Messalina – 812
Messiah – 10, 163, 166, 178, 182, 259, 260, 302, 362, 364, 470, 475, 476, 479, 485, 487, 489, 533, 613, 622, 642, 649, 660, 664, 667, 670, 772, 832, 845, 874, 875, 876, 878, 939, 943, 944
    Jewish ideas about coming Messiah – 335, 474, 881
    Messiahship of Jesus preached to Jews – 416, 474, 475, 477, 613, 670, 674, 807, 876, 877, 879, 880, 881, 882, 939, 940
Messianic age – 165
Messianic prophecies – 163-167, 290, 300, 337, 364, 400, 475, 542, 612, 613, 879, 880, 943
Messianic Psalms – *see* Psalms, Messianic
Messianism, political – 839, 860
Messina – 594
Messina, straits of – *see* Straits of Messina
Meteorites – 696
Methodists – 102, 121, 765
Methods used to convert people – 851, 852

Michael – 712
Midian – 285, 299
Midnight – 586, 735, 739, 778, 909
Midrash – 345
Mighty works – *see* Miracles
Miletus – 726, 741, 743, 748, 757, 758, 778, 780, 782, 951
    location – 742
    address of Paul there to Ephesian elders – *see* Elders, Christian
    Trophimus left here sick – 731, 951
Millennial kingdom – 5, 166, 946
Millennial theories – 35-38
Minister – 355, 495
Ministering to the Lord – 455
Ministry – 29, 252, 523, 579, 662, 748, 755, 793, 850
Ministry, Christian – 181, 467, 565, 743
Ministry, located – *see* Located ministry
Minuscules – 751, 754
Miracles
    admitted by enemies – 182, 183, 441
    no deception practiced – 187, 736
    doubted by a scientific age – 257, 444
    definition of – 91
    credentialled the messenger – 55, 63, 95, 119, 154, 178, 210, 221, 318, 373, 376, 466, 467, 499, 503, 540, 613, 677, 678, 681, 683, 740, 923
    done after an indication from God to work them – 375, 737, 926
    how designated, signs, wonders, mighty works – 54, 61, 63, 84, 209, 257, 539
    effect on bystanders – 156, 923-927
    lying miracles – 179, 322, 677, 678, 681, 711
    not everyday happenings – 91
    done through apostles – 12, 84, 150, 154, 208, 315, 376, 419, 499, 539, 737, 925, 926
    done by other than the apostles – 257, 289, 318, 416, 432, 471
    instantaneous – 155, 372, 504, 515, 740
    no lingering after-effects – 516, 740
    extraordinary at Ephesus – *xxxii*, 677
    at Jerusalem – *xxxii*, 211, 212
    for the infancy of the church – 823, 403, 898, 927
    part of very warp and woof of Bible account - 906, 926

Miriam – 281
Mirror mantic – 703
Mishna – 255, 345, 653, 763, 814
Missionary journeys of Paul – 846, 878
    first – *xiv, xxi,* 445-526, 552, 790
    second – *xxi,* 550, 559-657, 793
    third – *xxi,* 577, 657-791, 793
    voyage to Rome – *xxi,* 889-933
Missionary methods suggested in Acts – 13, 330, 456, 458, 461, 491, 516, 520, 524, 525, 531, 560, 565, 619, 654, 684, 728, 793.
    See also Evangelism, Paul's method
Missionary methods, 20th century – 572
Missionary offerings - 580, 617, 640, 642
Missions, Holy Spirit's work in – 456, 457, 458, 523, 569, 570, 684
Missions, support of – 579, 580, 612 640, 756
Mist – 466
Mitylene – 741
Mnason of Cyprus – 85, 790, 791, 826 850
Mnevis – 292
Modernism – *see* Liberalism, religious
Modin – 795, 824
Mohammedanism – 582, 722
Molina – 131
Moloch – *see* Tabernacle of Moloch
Monarchical episcopate – 791, 792
Money-changers – 249
Montanism – 120
Moon – 61, 703, 704
Morality does not save – 146, 381
Mormons – 121, 534
Mortality – 508
Moses – 167, 168, 174, 261, 275, 279- 286, 306, 674, 712, 722, 753, 874, 880
    how like Christ – 168, 284, 289, 290
    infancy in Egypt – 281
    fled to Midian – 282, 285, 299
    his age – 283, 286
    killed an Egyptian – 283-285
    his leadership rejected – 284, 288, 291
    his eloquence – 282
    instructed in the wisdom of Egypt – 282
    married Zipporah – 285
    received the Law – 291
    ruler and deliverer – 288
    radiance of appearance – 263
    worked miracles – 289
    never crossed the Jordan into the Promised Land – *v,* 295
    his death – 481
    author of Pentateuch – *see* Pentateuch; Law of Moses
Moslem Mosques – 288, 690
Most excellent – 1, 831, 838, 883
Most High God – 581, 582, 590, 630
Mother
    influence of Moses' – 282
    influence of Timothy's – 564, 565
Motion with the hand – *see* Beckon with the hand
Mountain Peak prophecies – 62
Mount
    Carmel – 373, 782, 783
    Gerizim – v
    Ida – 505, 901
    Messogis – 666
    of Olives – *viij,* 17, 805
    Pangaeus – 574
    Parnassus – 580
    Pentelicus – 633
    Sinai – 275, 286, 290, 292, 295, 365, 768
    Vesuvius – 831, 930
    Zion – 7, 69
Mourning – 315, 737
Muratorian Canon – *xxii, xxiv, xxv,* 951
Murder – 544, 547, 923
Murmurings – 247
Music – 282
Myra – 778, 779, 892, 893, 894, 895, 898, 930
Mysia – 53, 568, 569, 570, 891, 893
Mystery religions – 573, 636
Mysticism – 598
Myth in the Bible – 241
Mythology, pagan – 123, 504-506, 580, 633, 636, 923, 924, 925, 929

Nahor – 307
Naked – 680
Name of Saul changed to Paul – *see* Paul, two names
Name of the Lord, in the – 155, 161, 190, 314, 405, 582, 669, 671, 701, 927.
    See also Baptismal formula

Names
- of God – *see* God, names of
- common names among the Jews – 42, 201, 679
- used among the Romans – 643
- taken from animals – 373
- taken from flowers – 437

Narcissus – 933
Nathan – 69
Nations
- God determines their rise and fall – 630

"Natives" – 919, 920, 923
Naturalism – *see* Liberalism, religious; Acts, criticism
Natural theology – 512, 631
Navigation
- on the Mediterranean – 573
- open and closed, times of – *see* Sailing season
- how regulated at a distance from the land – 905

Nazarene
- how applied to Christ – 178, 182, 263, 348, 396, 470, 487, 612, 839, 877
- sect of the Nazarenes – 839, 842

Nazarite vow – 653, 656, 796, 797, 843, 846, 847, 850
- rules to which they were subject – 653
- how long a Nazarite vow continued – 653, 797
- their expenses often defrayed by others – 427, 797
- provisions if time of the vow expired away from Jerusalem – 653

Neapolis
- in Italy – 930
- in Samaria – 351
- in Macedonia – 573, 574, 732

Nebuchadnezzar – 440, 705
Necromancy – 707, 708, 715, 717, 720
Needy, care for – 248
Negative Higher Criticism of Acts – *see* Acts, Introductory Studies, criticism. *See also* Religious liberalism
Negeb – 332, 833
Negroes – 333
Nehemiah – 198
Neo-liberalism – 752
Neo-orthodoxy – 132, 599, 752
Neo-Pentecostalism – 102-126, 191, 404
Neo-Platonism – 598

Neptune – 929
Nero, Caesar – *xii, xiii, xv,* 351, 448, 451, 689, 695, 855, 856, 860, 862, 866, 867, 870, 871, 879, 887, 888, 941, 952, 953
Nerva, emperor – *xii*
Nestorians – 763
New Testament accounts supplement Old Testament – 272
New Testament canon
- *See also* Date of writing of New Testament
- books collection – *xxii, xxvii,* 754
- completed – 119

New Testament text – 423
New Covenant – 260
Nicanor, one of the Seven – 253
Nicodemus – 228, 315, 359, 478
Nicolas, proselyte from Antioch – 254
Nicolaitans – 254, 752
Nicopolis – 951, 952
Night – 570, 645, 813, 822, 833
Nile River – *see* River
Nineveh – 383, 420
Nisan – 43, 732
Noah – 139, 306
Noahic Covenant – 544, 545, 548
North Africa – 902
North Galatia – 567-569, 666
Nostradamus – 703
Numerology – 703

Oath – 69, 279, 477, 824, 825
Obedience – 256, 362, 371, 400, 403, 474, 478, 483, 589, 598, 600, 601, 602, 604, 609, 610, 638, 646, 669, 670, 672, 754, 796, 816, 821, 851, 877, 878, 943, 946, 947
Occult practices – 245, 320, 326, 342, 461, 467, 547, 581, 582, 680, 681, 690
- deliverance from – 681, 682, 683, 723-724
- Special Study – 701-725

Octavian – *see* Augustus, Caesar
Offering for the poor at Jerusalem – *xxvii,* 85, 194, 425, 445, 456, 507, 516, 684, 685, 726-732, 757, 788, 791, 792, 793, 794, 802, 823, 846, 892, 948
Officers, Jewish - 216, 816, 817

Old Latin Version – 935
Old Testament
   See also Law of Moses
   canon – 883
   chronology – 472.
      See also Egyptian captivity, duration of
   threefold division of – 293, 484, 786
Olives – 620
Olivet – see Mount of Olives
Olympiads – i
Omens – 444, 706, 708, 712
"Once saved, always saved" – see Eternal security
One mind – 19
Oneiromancy – 706
Onesiphorus – 951
Onesimus – 948
Onkelos – 309, 639
Open membership – 87
Oracle of Delphi – see Delphi
Oracles – 462, 580, 708.
   See also Living oracles
Oral tradition – 511, 545, 659, 754, 755, 757
Ordination – 317, 490, 519-520, 750
   of the Seven? – 255
   of elders and deacons – 266-269, 519-520
   of Paul and Barnabas – 456, 457
   of Timothy – 566
Oriental religions – see Eastern religions
Origen – 39, 120, 240, 451, 466, 598, 766
Ornithomancy – 706
Orontes River – see River
Orphans – 247, 456
Osiris – 292, 505
Ostian Gate – see Gates, Rome
Ostian Way – 953
Ouija board – 320, 719
Overseer – see Bishop
Oxen and garlands – 506, 507
Ozman, Agnes - 103

Pacifism – 199
Pagan – 799
Palestine – 779, 806, 838, 853, 855, 857, 875, 884

Palladium – 696
Pallas – 830, 853, 855, 856
Pallets – 211, 372
Palmistry – 704
Pamphylia – 53, 467, 522, 523, 894
Pantheism – 632
Pantheon – 623
Papacy – 323, 391, 408, 447, 540
Paphos – 461-467, 779
Papias – 254, 451, 785
Paraclete – see Holy Spirit
Paradise – 141, 143.
   See also Intermediate place of the dead
Paralysis – 242, 319, 372
Parapet – 384
Parchments – 953
Parham, Charles F. – 103
Parierai – 687
Parmenas, one of the Seven – 253
Parthenon – 620, 621, 628
Parthia – 52
"Passed through" – 684, 727
Passing through the fire – 708
Passover – see Feasts of the Jews
Pastoral Epistles – 752, 753, 951
   what letters so called – 951
   when written – 951-953
Pastoral shepherding programs – 750
Pastors – see Elders
Patara – 581, 735, 778, 779, 780, 790, 893
Patriarchs – 68, 275, 548
Patron – xxxvi, 2, 505
Paul and Barnabas
   at Antioch of Syria – 369, 419-425, 572
   sent to Judea (Jerusalem) – 425-446, 878
   on Cyprus – 461-466, 779
   in Perga – 467-468, 522, 523
   at Pisidian Antioch – 468-492
   flight to Iconium – 497-500
   flight to Lystra and Derbe – 501-516
   called "apostles" – 500, 507
   at the Jerusalem Conference – 527- 556
   quarrel between over Mark – 559- 562
Paul and Silas
   co-workers on second missionary journey – 550, 562, 564, 576
   before magistrates at Philippi – 583- 585
   at Thessalonica – 611-617
   at Berea – 617-619

Paul
- apostle to Gentiles - 355, 366, 419, 748, 808, 809, 869, 872, 877, 950
- early life – 197, 345, 806, 808
- education, Jewish or Greek? – 345, 346, 362
- family – 345, 826
- physical appearance – 464, 505, 506, 727
- eyesight – 361, 465, 818
- Pharisee by belief – 197, 345, 819, 872, 874
- hometown – 260, 345, 812
- trade he learned – 346, 580, 638, 640
- rabbinic training in Jerusalem – 184, 346, 348, 640, 808, 817, 826, 874
- not a personal witness of Jesus' ministry – 347
- member of Sanhedrin? – 348-350
- two names, Paul and Saul – 259, 463, 464
- persecution of the church – 313-316, 348-350, 815, 874, 877
- guarded garments of those who stoned Stephen – 256, 304
- Damascus road experience – *xxvi*, 351-357, 606, 609, 645, 748, 808, 821, 823, 872, 877
- qualifications to be an apostle – 27, 353-355, 877
- blinded by light – 356, 872
- Ananias visits him in Damascus – *xx*, 357-362
- conversion completed in baptism – *xxi*, 355-362
- date of Paul's conversion – *xx*, 365, 369
- preaches in synagogues – *xix*, 469- 491
  - at Damascus – 363, 365, 878
  - at Jerusalem – 367
  - on missionary journeys – 460, 469, 487, 497, 611, 617, 621, 641, 673, 744, 754, 800
- trip to Arabia – 363-365
- revelations made to Paul – 365, 366, 493, 528, 645
- escape from Damascus – xii, xx, 365-366
- visits
  - to Jerusalem – xx, xxviii, 195, 366, 367, 425, 645, 655, 656, 808, 846, 878
  - to Syria and Cilicia – *xx*, 368, 369
- suffered the loss of all things – 369, 826
- with Barnabas in Antioch – 369, 419-425
- Jesus appears to Paul – 368, 645, 823, 889, 907
- the prisoner – 827, 899, 905, 921, 932, 936, 937, 939, 953
- first missionary journey – *xx*, *xxi*, 453-526, 552
  - name changed from Saul to Paul – 463, 464
  - visits Galatia because of sickness – 468, 568
  - first recorded sermon to Jewish audience – 469-486
  - healing of lame man at Lystra – *xxxii*, 502-515
  - first recorded sermon to Gentile audience – 508-512
  - stoning of Paul at Lystra – *xxxii*, 513, 514, 879
- at Jerusalem Conference – *xx*, 527-556. *See also* Jerusalem Conference
- his use of Christian liberty
  - circumcised Timothy and not Titus – 565
  - Nazarite vow – *see* Nazarite vow
  - pays for sacrifices of Jewish Christians – *xxix*
  - all things to all men – *xxix*, 569, 799
- second missionary journey – *xx*, *xxi*, *xxv*, 550, 559-657
  - sermon on the Areopagus – *see* Areopagus
  - trial before Gallio – 646-651
  - letters written from – 450, 641, 651
- third missionary journey – *xx*, *xxi*, 313, 657-791
  - intermediate trip to Corinth – 685, 686
  - change of itinerary – 726
  - offering for poor at Jerusalem – *see* Offering for the poor at Jerusalem
  - address to Ephesian elders - *see* Elders, Christian
  - letters written from – 450, 685, 846
  - warned that bonds and imprisonment awaited him – 747
  - disobeyed the Spirit's leading? – 780-781

arrested in temple at Jerusalem – *xxi*,
731, 787, 800-805, 839, 872, 879,
887, 889, 937
  defense from steps of tower of
    Antonia – 313, 805-809
  trial before Sanhedrin – 814-823
  Roman citizenship – 588, 594, 812-
    814, 832, 953
Caesarean imprisonment – *xxi*, 785, 834-
  888
  two years' long – 855, 857, 889, 893,
    932, 940
  trial before Felix – 835, 836-850, 937
  sermon to Felix and Drusilla – 850-
    856
  trial before Festus – 857-863, 937
  defense before Agrippa II—863 –
    888
  appeal to Caesar – 862, 863, 866, 870,
    887, 889, 935, 937, 938, 940, 949
voyage to Rome – *xxi*, 681, 823, 824,
  889, 933
  shipwreck at Malta – 916-918, 928,
    932
  bitten by a viper—922-925, 927
  heals Publius' father—926, 927
first Roman imprisonment – *xviii*, 450,
  574, 677, 731, 748, 887, 892, 933-
  950
  Paul lives in his own hired house –
    935, 942, 947, 950
  preaches to Jews – 936-947
  letters from – 450, 730, 855, 892,
    934, 947
  two years' long – 947, 950
release from first Roman imprisonment –
  xxxvi, 450, 948, 951
  travels – 450, 748, 951-953
  journey to Spain? – *see* Spain, Paul's
    journey to
  letters written from – 450, 951
second Roman imprisonment – 450, 731,
  952, 953
  letters written from – 450, 953
  trials – 953
death of Paul – *xxxii, xxxv, xxxvi* 451,
  452, 953, 954
Paul and Thecla, acts of – *see* Acts of Paul
  and Thecla
Paulus Aemelius – 574
Pausanius – 621, 626, 627, 690

Pavement, the – 814, 822
Peace – 370, 395, 442, 584, 593, 609, 615,
  669, 804, 837, 838, 839, 842, 853, 860,
  865, 886
Peducaeus Priscinus – 695
Pelagius – 372
Pelagonia – 574
Pella
  in Macedonia – 574
  in Perea – 63
Penates – 687
Pendulum – 705
Pentagram – 712
Pentateuch – 820, 880
  authorship of – 167
  divided into pericopes – 496
Pentecost – *see* Feasts of the Jews
Pentecostalism – 102-126, 668
People – 479, 541, 646, 846, 882, 937
Perea – 63, 454, 863
Peregrini – 891, 895, 934
Perfect tense – 15, 681, 755
Perga
  location in Pamphylia – 467, 522, 523
  Word preached there – 522, 523
Pergamum – 546, 676, 690
Perizzites – 296, 472
Persecution – 759, 953
  of early church – 154, 171, 183, 213,
    256, 301, 313, 314, 349, 359, 426-
    429, 816
  arising about Stephen – 256, 259, 313,
    407, 413, 783, 893
  first Gentile persecution of church – 583
  of Paul - 583, 619, 645, 949.
    See also Plots of the Jews
  of Paul and Silas by Jews from
    Thessalonica - 614, 618, 619
  of Christians in Rome by Jews - 933
  of Christians by Nero - 941, 952
  of Jews - *see* Jews, persecution of
  See also Pharisees; Sadducees; Paul
Perseverance of the saints – *see* Eternal
  security
Persia – 52
Personal evangelism – 335, 469, 669, 746,
  851
Person and work of the Holy Spirit
  Special Study – 89-101
  See also Holy Spirit

Pessinus – 567, 568
Peter
   his family – 155
   his confession at Caesarea Philippi – 340
   his rebuke of Jesus – 881
   his denials of Jesus – 177
   an affinity between his speeches and his epistles – *xxxi, xxxiii*
   risen Lord appears to him – 5
   leads out in the selection of Matthias – 21, 32
   preaches on Pentecost – 46-70, 671, 799
   Peter and John associated together – 150, 323
   Peter and John heal the lame man at Gate Beautiful – 150-157
   Peter's second address – 157-170
   Peter and John arrested – 172-174
   defense before the Sanhedrin – 174-180
   Ananias and Sapphira's experience with Peter – 201-208
   extraordinary miracles worked by Peter – *xxxii,* 211, 677
   arrested a second time – 213
   Peter and John visit Samaria, Simon Magus confronted – *xxxii,* 323-329
   Peter heals Aeneas – 371-373
   Peter raises Dorcas from the dead – *xxxii,* 373-376
   Peter's vision of the sheet – *xxxii,* 384-387
   preaches to Cornelius – *xxxii,* 378-406, 429, 536-537
   justifies his preaching to Gentiles – 401, 407-413, 528
   arrested by Agrippa I, and released – *xxxii,* 429-435, 791, 813, 850, 867
   was Peter ever in Rome? – 329, 440, 447-452
   addresses the Jerusalem Conference – 536-539, 541
   hypocrisy at Antioch – 232, 449, 539, 558-559
   missionary visit to Corinth – 440, 450, 550, 642
   death by crucifixion, tradition of – 450-452, 539, 952, 953
   epistles of – 449, 452, 539, 550, 570, 752, 953
Petra – *xii,* 365

Petrine vs. Pauline element in the church – *see Eirenikon;* F.C. Baur; Theology
Petronius – 370, 621
Pharisees – 44, 71, 175, 223, 226, 227, 345, 492, 527, 544, 816, 818, 819, 820, 822, 825, 845, 873, 874, 877, 944
   origin of the party – 196
   their beliefs – 196, 197, 819, 820
   zealousness for traditions of the elders – *see* Traditions of the Pharisees
   synagogue leaders – 257, 262
   persecution of the church – 223, 257
   schools of Hillel and Shammai – *xi,* 181
Pharaoh – 43, 276, 716
   his policy toward the Hebrews – 278, 280
   knew not Joseph – 280
   hardened heart – 674
Pharaoh's daughter – 281. *See also* Hatshepsut
Pheretime of Cyrene – 444
Phidias – 633, 689
Philadelphia – 676
Philemon – 666
Philemon and Baucis – 504, 505
Philemon, epistle to – 450, 692, 756, 827, 892, 934, 942, 947, 948, 950
Philetus – 694, 753
Philip, apostle – 253, 317, 785
Philip, evangelist – *xxxiv,* 59, 371, 374, 458, 724, 783, 790, 834, 848, 855
   chosen to serve tables - 253, 318, 785
   had spiritual gifts – 96, 318
   his preaching in Samaria – 253, 317-323, 402, 413, 785
   lacked ability to pass on spiritual gifts – 325
   his residence at Caesarea – 344, 382, 646, 655, 676, 783, 784, 848
   why he was called an evangelist – 253, 318
   and the eunuch – 330-344, 387, 669, 785
   four virgin daughters – 59, 785, 786
Philip of Macedon – 571, 574, 625
Philip, the tetrarch – *ii, iv, vi, xiii,* 426
Philippi – 571, 573, 619, 727, 730, 731, 747, 780, 854, 879, 947, 951
   history – 574
   its port – 573
   its rank as a city – 574
   few Jews living there - 575

its magistrates – 583, 585, 593-596
Paul's evangelism there – *xxv,* 574- 597
the church there – *see* Churches
Philippians, epistle to – 574, 575, 576, 577, 815, 854, 947, 948, 950
Philippian jailer – 579, 585-596, 605, 606, 607, 853
Philip's fountain – *see* Bethsoron
Philistines – 331, 344, 474, 706
Philo – 175, 237, 259, 282, 310, 897
Philosophers – *see* Epicureans; Stoics
Philosophy, failure of human – 635
Philostratus – 627
Phoebe – 653, 933
Phoenicia – 779, 780, 878, 920
    how extensive – 413
    churches there – 330, 413, 531, 554, 780-782, 893
Phoenix – 899, 900, 901, 906
    its location disputed – 899, 900
    direction its harbor opened to – 899, 900
Phygelus – 758
Phrygia – 53, 493, 567-569, 659, 687
Phylacteries – 236
Piety – 158
Pike, James A. – 104
Pilate – *see* Pontius Pilate
Pilot – 898, 899, 901, 906, 911, 926
Piraeus – 620, 638, 902
Pisces – 702
Pisidia, province of – 467, 468, 475, 578, 657
Place of prayer – 575, 576, 580, 582
Plagues in Egypt – 274, 282, 289, 471
Plain
    of Esdraelon – 531
    of Philistia – 331, 344
    of Sharon – 212, 344, 372
Plato – 123, 235, 422
Pledge – *see* Bond
Pliny the elder – 689, 896, 928
Pliny the younger
    his letters – 688, 764
    hymns sung to Jesus as to God – 304
Plots by the Jews
    at Berea – 618, 619
    at Caesarea – 841, 849, 860, 869, 937, 938
    at Corinth – *xxvi,* 728, 729
    at Damascus – 365
    at Ephesus – 745, 800
    at Iconium – 500
    at Jerusalem – 788, 800, 802, 824- 833, 836, 843, 857, 858, 870, 879, 887, 890, 937, 940
    at Lystra – 513
    at Thessalonica – 613, 614
Plutarch – *xxxi, xxxii,* 236, 581, 682
Poets, heathen – 510, 632
Point of contact – 627
Polemo, king of Cilicia – *xvii*
Politarchs – *xxx,* 615-617, 648
Political messianism – *see* Messianism, political
Pollux – *see* Castor and Pollux
Polycarp of Smyrna – 870
Polycletus – 689
Polycrates – 785
Pomp – 868, 869
Pompeii – 831, 930
Pompey – 258, 351
Pontine marshes – 932
Pontius Pilate – *iv, v, ix,* 64, 158, 188, 189, 340, 477, 478, 835, 836, 860, 861
Pontus – 53, 451, 639
Pools at Jerusalem – *see* Jerusalem, pools at
Poor at Jerusalem - *see* Offering for the poor at Jerusalem
Poppaea – 888, 952
Porch – *see* Gates of houses
Porcian Law – 594
Porcius Festus – *see* Festus, Porcius
Porta Capena – *see* Gates, Rome
Porters – *see* Temple guard
Possession, demon – *see* Demons
Postmillennialism – 35
Post-resurrection appearances – *see* Christ Jesus
Potter's field – *see* Akeldama
Poverty – 194, 195, 372, 756, 793
Praetorian camp – 935, 936, 947
Praetorian guard – 862, 891, 935
Praetorium
    at Caesarea – 835, 837, 843, 849, 860, 868
    at Rome – 935
Praise – 87, 155, 412, 418
Prayer
    angels assist in answering – 438
    asking for wrong things – 9
    at what hours offered by Jews - 46, 58, 150, 151, 171, 379

imprecatory – *see* Imprecatory prayer
was addressed to Christ – 29, 304
nature of – 724
posture when praying – 83, 376, 737, 757, 781
Stephen's dying prayer – *see* Stephen, his dying prayer
Archaic language not necessary – 188
public – 83, 187-190, 252, 522, 777
for others – 328, 757, 782
for guidance – 571, 744

Prayers
in synagogue service – 496
of apostles before Pentecost – 19
at the selection of Matthias – 28-30
of the early Christians – 83, 86, 252, 430, 781
by apostles after their release – 187-191
Paul's, after Damascus Road experience – 358
as part of an ordination service – 457
of Paul and Silas in Philippian jail – 586
Paul's – 737, 823
by Paul on voyage to Rome – 905, 906, 907, 914
sinner's prayers, does God hear? – 380
thanksgiving for food – 913, 914

Preaching Jesus – 338, 416
the kingdom of God – 949
the Word – 252, 317, 329, 662, 777, 784, 872, 949
forbidden by men – 184
house to house – 229, 745

Precepts – 555
Predestination – 30, 64, 69, 130-134, 190, 490
Calvinistic doctrine of – 30, 80, 489, 490
Prefect – 414, 862, 891, 934 Prejudice – 408, 415, 584, 794, 942, 944

Premillennialism
historic – 35
modern – 36
See also Dispensationalism

Prenomen – 643
Preparation – 723
Prepositions, Greek
apo – 797
dio – 539
en – 76, 604
eis – 76-78, 604, 851
epi – 416, 603, 797
meta – 416, 524, 744

Presbyters – *see* Elders
Preservation – 907, 911, 914, 918
Previous letter – 676
Priests, Old Testament – 799, 943
divided into courses – *iv*, 171, 187, 256, 857, 859
distinguished from Levites – 194
service in the temple – 171, 287, 455, 653, 887
functioned as teachers – 172
other tasks – 705, 798
many converted – 184, 256

Priests, pagan – 294, 506, 507, 545, 580, 687
Priests, Roman Catholic – *see* Roman Catholic Church
Priests (witchcraft) - 682, 710, 713
Priscilla - 638, 639, 652, 654, 661-662, 666, 669, 684

Prison Epistles – 730, 951
what letters so called – 676
when written – 676, 855, 947
where written – 676, 8M, 855, 947

Prison house – *see* Jail
Prisoner, Paul – *see* Paul, the prisoner
Prisoners, of Rome – 917, 927, 948
in what manner they were chained – *see* Chains
subject to different punishments – 214
sent from provinces to Rome – 863, 889, 890, 895
attendants or slaves, allowed to accompany their master – 889
committed into keeping of Praetorian prefect – 934, 935

Private meeting – *see* Jerusalem Conference
Private property – 193, 203
Prochorus, one of the Seven – 253
Proclus – 235
Proconsuls – *xv, xx,* 462, 647, 648, 695, 698, 779
Procrastination – 636, 853, 854
Procurators – *v, xv,* 803, 836, 837, 925
Progressive revelation – 279
Prohibitions – 555
Promise – 79, 754, 875, 876, 912
Property and possessions – 85
Prophecy, fulfilled – *see* Fulfilled prophecy
Prophecy, Messianic - *see* Messianic prophecies

Prophesy, prophesying – 59, 60, 80, 581, 672
"Prophet, The" – 167, 290
Prophetess – 786, 787
Prophets, Old Testament – 394, 473, 484, 485, 510, 541, 787, 844, 845, 880
   were persecuted – 300
   read in the synagogue services – 469, 477, 549
   sons of the – *see* School of the Prophets
   believed by Agrippa II – 603
Prophets, New Testament – 48, 111, 371, 422, 453, 456, 493, 557, 569, 747, 780, 784, 786, 787
   how related to teachers – 453, 454
   Agabus – *see* Agabus
   Silas – *see* Silas
   temporary office – 557
Proselytes – 253, 254, 315, 333, 395, 405, 446, 485, 489, 492, 497, 564, 578, 579, 733, 801, 888
   meaning of the term – 54
   different classes – 54
   of the gate – 54, 379, 486, 497, 544, 576, 577, 613, 641, 642, 644
   of righteousness – 54, 379
   initiation ceremonies – 345
Proselyte baptism – *see* Baptism
Proserpine – 687
Prostitution – 546, 687
Protevangelium Jacobi – 39
Proverbs, examples of – 913
Providence – 3, 91, 131, 170, 207, 215, 276, 334, 353, 387, 445, 470, 512, 562, 564, 569, 578, 591, 622, 623, 628, 629, 630, 631, 632, 645, 655, 709, 794, 837, 879, 890, 898, 918, 927
Provinces, Roman – 835, 857
   divided into imperial and senatorial - *xv*
   divided into districts (regions) – 491, 501, 574, 727
Psalms, Messianic – 26, 66, 71, 178, 179, 480, 482
Psalms, quoted in Acts – 26, 187-189, 479-481
Psammetichus – 333, 344
Pseudo-Clementine Homilies – 240, 328
Pseudo-Clementine Recognitions – 329
Psychokinesis – 320, 720

Ptolemais – 370, 531, 782, 783
   See also Acre
   location – 782, 783
Ptolemy (Claudius Ptolemaeus) – 908
Ptolemy Lagus – 258, 259
Ptolemy Philadelphus – 259
Ptolemy Soter – 782
Publius – *xi*, *xviii*, *xxxi*, 925, 926, 927
Pudens – 953
Punic dialect – 920
Punishment – 810, 811, 824, 862, 923, 924
   temporal – 466, 484, 485, 768, 781, 924
   eternal – *see* Hell
Purification – 797, 798, 800
Purified in the temple – 847
Purgatory – *see* Roman Catholic Church Doctrines
Purple – 576, 577
Purpose of God – *see* Eternal purpose, God's
Puteoli – 895, 908, 919, 929
   location – 930
   entry-port for wheat ships – 898, 928, 929, 930, 931
   brethren at – 931
Pyramid – 934
Pyromancy – 706
Pythagoras – 235
Python spirit – 580

Quadratus – *xv*
Quail – 289
Quakers – 121
Quartus – 645, 730
Quaternion – 429
Qubeiba – 834
Queen
   Candace – *x*, *xi*, 332
   of Adiabene – 424
Quicksands – *see* Syrtis
Quinctilius Varus – *iii*
Quinquennalia – 443
Quirinius – *i*, *iii*, *viii*, 200, 225
Quotations
   from the Old Testament, how applied in the New Testament - 26

Rabbi, Rabban, Rabboni – 223
Rabbinical writings – 68, 236
Races of men – 630
Rachel – 294, 687
Radbertus, Paschasius – 766
Rahab – 608
Railing – 233
Rains – 511, 920
Rameses II – 280, 283
Raphael – 712
Rapture – 399
Readings, various – *see* Manuscript variations
Reason – 199, 643
Reasoning from the Scriptures – 612, 621, 641, 654, 673, 735
Rebaptism – 672
Receiving the Word – 81, 407
Reconciliation – 395, 771, 776
Redemption – 337, 417, 509, 511, 660, 774, 776
Red Sea – 54, 274, 285, 289, 332, 471
Reef – 916
Reformation – 599
Refreshing, times of – 165
Reincarnation – 197, 623, 712, 720, 721, 723, 820
Rejoicing – 342, 343, 489, 531, 555, 579, 591-592
Relief sent to Judea – 425, 445
Religio illicita – 498, 584, 839, 841, 844, 845, 848, 860
Religio licita – 584, 650, 844
Religious – 626, 627, 865
Religious liberalism – *see* Liberalism, religious
Remission of sins – *see* Sin, remission of
Remnant – 542
Remotest parts of the earth – 13
Remphan – *see* Rompha
Renan, Ernest – 48
Repentance – 56, 206, 256, 357, 466, 475, 591, 592, 628, 635, 645, 646, 668, 670, 674, 726, 727, 746, 748, 851, 879, 925, 946, 947
    to be preached – 6, 412, 660
    required – 74, 157, 163, 233, 327, 510, 537, 606, 633-634, 672, 746-775, 878
    different than remorse – 23
    a gift – 221, 412
    Special Study – 145-149
Rephan – *see* Rompha
Restoration Movement – *xxxviii*, 105, 125, 256, 572, 577, 759, 770, 771, 772
Restoration of a repentant brother – 233
Restoration, period of – 166
Resurrection –
    See also Christ Jesus, resurrection
    proofs of – 4, 400, 634
    confidently asserted by apostles – 4
    of righteous and wicked – 144, 375, 376, 753, 845, 848, 881, 882, 954
    denied by Sadducees – 198
    excited ridicule in Athens – 624, 635
    an article of Jewish belief – 196, 882
    discussed at Paul's trial – 845, 848, 875
Resurrection bodies – 399, 755, 766, 818, 819, 820, 821, 954
Retaliation – 939
Reuben – 276
Revelation, book of – *xviii, xxi,* 330, 752
Revelation (God's) – 127, 287, 355, 365, 380, 412, 423, 512, 529, 545 , 548 , 631, 633 , 635, 733, 781, 799, 808, 898, 906, 907
Revisiting young churches – 329, 791
Revolt of Jews against Rome – *see* Jews, rebellion to Rome
Rhabdomancy – 702, 705, 708
Rhegium – 919, 929, 930
Rhoda – 436, 437
Rhodes – 595, 778, 895
Rich young ruler – 606
Right hand of God – 66, 70, 71
Righteous – 389, 845
Righteousness – 465, 851, 852
Riot at Jerusalem – 802, 814, 844
Riot of Demetrius – *see* Demetrius
River
    Abana and Parphar – 362
    Andriacus – 894
    Cayster – 655, 666
    Cestrus – 467, 523
    Cnydus – 345
    Euphrates – 53, 272
    Gangees – 816
    Gangites – 575
    Jordan – 27, 224, 295, 351, 475, 660
    Lycus – 658, 666, 948, 951
    Meander – 468, 666, 742

Nile – 53, 281, 332, 658
Orontes – 195, 414, 459
Strymon – 611
Tiber – 329, 414, 935, 936
Tigris – 53, 272
Roads
   from Jerusalem to Gaza – 331, 338, 339, 785
   See also Highways
Robbers – 468, 837, 838
Robbers of temples – 697, 700
Robes – 868
   torn in expression of horror – 508
   torn off prisoners – 585
Rods – 585, 593, 611, 810
Roofs, how built – 384
Roman Catholic Church Doctrines – 534, 739, 766
   assumption of Mary – *see* Mary, mother of Jesus
   calendar of special days – 427, 430
   canonization of saints – 359
   church councils – 556.
      See also Councils
   church is infallible interpreter of Scriptures – 335
   confirmation – 517
   extreme unction – 776
   faith – 598
   indulgences – 342, 849
   Limbo – 131
   Mary
      worship of – *see* Mary, mother of Jesus
      perpetual virginity of – *see* Mary, mother of Jesus
   mass – 759, 760, 762, 763, 768, 775
   meritorious works – 342
   priesthood – 455, 766, 768
   primacy of Peter – 21, 408, 536, 540.
      See also Papacy
   purgatory – 768
   sisterhoods – 786
   twenty-five-year ministry of Peter in Rome – 447
Roman citizenship – *see* Citizenship, Roman
Roman colony – *see* Colony, Roman
Roman empire – 50, 423, 839, 884
Roman Imperial chronology – *xii*
Roman jurisprudence – 835, 948

Roman laws – 836, 861, 862, 870, 871, 948
   concerning penalty for allowing prisoners to escape – 440, 441, 587, 588, 917
   beating of Roman citizens not allowed – 594, 811, 813
   prohibiting introduction of new religions – 584, 615, 839, 844
   no prisoner condemned before he had a trial – 859, 864, 865
Roman provinces – *see* Provinces, Roman
Romans, epistle to – 54, 450, 454, 483, 653, 667, 692, 727, 728, 729, 730, 793, 796, 818, 892, 933, 941 942
Rome – 329, 424, 657, 684, 730, 742, 748, 823, 824, 861, 887, 889, 891, 892, 896, 907, 931, 949
   evangelization of – 54, 446, 684, 941
   founding of – *i*
   gates of – *see* Gates, Rome
   political center of the world – 620
   burning of – *xviii, xxi,* 650, 952
   description of features, hills, buildings – 934, 935, 952, 953
   Jewish population – 54, 258, 935
Rompha – 294
Rosicrucianism – 722
Royal porch – 157
Rudders – 895, 901, 903, 909, 916
Rule of faith and practice – 226
Rulers of the Jews – *see* Sanhedrin
Ruler(s) of the synagogue – *see* Synagogue, officers
Runes – 704

Sabaism – 293
Sabbat – *see* Witches' sabbath
Sabbath – 44, 235, 263, 469, 477, 485, 487, 549, 575, 612, 641, 661, 673, 733, 735
Sabbath day's journey – 17
Sabbath versus Lord's Day – 549, 641, 734, 735
Sacraments – 760, 768
Sacrifice, human – 460, 687, 708, 712
Sacrifices (Jewish) – 61, 199, 215, 293, 380, 381, 427, 483, 653, 773, 794, 797, 798, 799, 800, 846, 847, 887
Sacrifices (pagan) – 492, 506-508, 512, 545, 547, 553, 795

Saddoc – *see* Zadok
Sadducees – 44, 172, 175, 213-215, 226, 227, 818, 820, 822, 825, 845, 873, 874, 876, 877, 880, 944
   origin of the party – 197
   their beliefs – 172, 198, 219, 820, 821, 822, 880
   ruling party in the New Testament times – 198, 262, 345, 427
   persecution of apostles – 172, 824
   persecution of the church – 213, 257, 427
Sailing season – 45, 651, 652, 655, 729, 732, 742, 855, 892, 893, 894, 896, 897, 899, 928, 940
Sailors – 827, 895, 902, 903, 907, 909, 911, 912, 913, 915, 916, 921
Sails – 895, 903
   artemona – 916
   suppara – 930
Saints – 349, 359, 371, 376, 420, 890, 905
Salamis – 195, 460
Salmone – *see* Cape Salmone
Salmonetta – 916
Salome – *vi, vii*, 19, 40, 41
Salvation – 55, 56, 62, 63, 80, 88, 177, 178, 179, 215, 220, 354, 382, 458, 463, 476, 527, 528, 552, 553, 555, 582, 591, 646, 661, 734, 745, 749, 754, 755, 772, 776, 846, 853, 905, 913, 927, 928, 946, 947
   available to all men – 80, 392, 394, 396, 400, 406, 412, 417, 418, 487, 489, 510, 537, 635, 879, 880, 881
   God's part and man's part – 80, 221, 403
   God's initiative in – 578, 646
   is man active or passive in? – 164, 170, 171, 601
   available only in Christ – 179, 180, 482, 582
   instantaneous or a process – *see* Conversion, instantaneous or a process?
   divine help given – 380, 511
   human agency in – 382
   not by deeds of Law – 524, 530, 535, 539, 540, 555, 608
   circumcision not necessary for – 527-529, 554, 565, 566
   steps of – 55, 56, 404, 419, 578, 590-592, 607, 644, 645, 746, 809
   See also Justification; Redemption

Samaria – 13, 318, 672, 785, 831, 842, 849, 853, 878, 891
   church spreads to – 314, 329, 330 446, 849
   Philip in – *see* Philip, evangelist
   Peter and John visit – 323, 329
   churches visited by Paul – 330, 531 554
   Simon the sorcerer born there – 328
Samaritan Pentateuch – 306, 308
Samaritans – *v, xv, xvi*, 96, 318
   Jews have no dealings with – 318
Samaritan woman at the well – 262, 279, 297, 322
Samos – 741, 742
Samothrace – *xxv*, 573
Samson – 588
Samuel – 169, 473
Sanctified – 102, 356, 754, 755, 878, 942
Sandals – 287, 433, 476
Sanhedrin – *xvi*, 156, 177, 215, 228, 302, 349, 428, 603, 808, 818, 822, 825, 828, 832, 833, 843, 848, 857, 858, 859, 861, 862, 938, 939, 940
   its organization – 174
   its history – 174
   its jurisdiction – 175, 304, 350, 351, 940
   time of meeting – 174, 216
   Gazith, its place of meeting – *see* Gazith
   different names for – 174, 189
   prisoners ordered outside of council room (so judges may confer) – 182, 223
   qualifications for membership in – 348, 350
   prime movers behind Jesus' crucifixion – 163, 261, 476
   opposition to the gospel – *see* Persecution
   Peter's address to – 218-222
   Gamaliel's speech to – 222-227
   Stephen's defense before – *see* Stephen, his defense
   Paul's defense before – 814-822, 847, 848, 879, 938
Sapphira – 201, 373
   agreed to lie – 201, 202, 206
   smitten dead – 207
   her burial – 208
Sarah – 307
Sardinia – 258
Sardis – 569, 676

Index of Authors, Ideas and Topics

Saronic Gulf – 638
Satan – *see* Devil
Satanism – *see* Witchcraft, black
Saturn – 294, 505, 704, 707
Satyrs – 237
Saul, king – 26, 31, 296, 463, 472-474, 486, 588, 720
Saul of Tarsus – *see* Paul
Scales – 360, 361
Scapegoat – 31, 705
Sceva, seven sons of – 679-680
School of the Prophets – 169
School
    of Tyrannus – *see* Tyrannus, school
    of Scientology – 721
Scott, Thomas – 765
Scourging – 810
    of Jesus – 228
    of Jews at Caesarea – 855
    of all the apostles – 227
    of Paul, attempted – 810-812, 832
    difference between Jewish and Roman – 227, 585, 810
Scribes (Jewish) – 174, 223, 261, 808, 821
Scribes (Roman) – *see* Attorney
Scriptures fulfilled – *see* Fulfilled Scripture
Scripture, appealed to by preachers – 394, 400, 488, 664
Scripture, examined by hearers – 617, 618
Scripture, mighty in the – 659
Scripture, reading of – 333
Scylla and Charybdis – 930
Seances – 320, 717, 724
Sea of Adria – *see* Mediterranean Sea
Sea of Cilicia – 894
Sea of Galilee – 150, 351, 371
Second Coming – 11, 16, 61, 107, 137, 156, 616, 777
Second missionary journey – *see* Paul, missionary journeys
Second work of grace – *see* Grace
Sect – 532, 839, 844, 874, 940, 941
    various meanings of the word – 213
    sects of the Jews – 196-200
    sect of the Nazarenes – *see* Nazarenes
Secundus – 613, 730
Seed – 170
Selene – 830
Seleucia – 459, 523
Seleucids – 414
Seleucis Nicator – 414, 459, 468

Self-control – 508, 555, 851, 852
Self-preservation – 555
Semitisms – *xxxii*
Senate (Jewish) – 216, 808, 825, 859.
    See also Elders, Jewish
Senate (Roman) – 462, 831
Seneca – 647, 649, 862, 930
Sentius Saturninus – *iii*
Separation – 675
Septinus Severus – 935
Septuagint version – 208, 235, 236, 259, 271, 286, 291, 294, 308, 309, 333, 336, 481, 541, 581, 639, 904, 945
Sergius Paulus – *x, xxiii*, 462-467, 817
    his office – *xiv*, 462
    his title confirmed as correct – *xxx*, 462
Sermon – 496, 508, 794, 872
Sermon on the Bread of Life – 767
Sermon on the Law – 534
Sermon on the Mount – 5
Serpents – 924
    in Egypt – 282, 283
    in wilderness – 289
Servants – 383, 579
Servant, title for Messiah – 158, 170, 488, 489.
    See also Suffering Servant Poems
Serve tables – 248-250, 785
Servius Tullus – 689
Seven nations in Canaan – 471, 472
Seven, the – 249-255, 785
Seven sons of Sceva – Sceva, seven sons of
Seventy, the – 28, 253
Shadow of Peter – 211, 212
Shake off dust – *see* Dust
Shakers – 121
Shalmaneser – 875
Shambles – *see* Meat market
Shammai – *xi*, 181
Sharon, plain of – *see* Plain of Sharon
Sharp's rule of grammar – 569
Sheba – 332
Shechem – 278, 279, 311
Sheep and goat judgment – *see* Judgment
Sheet – 384
Shekinah – 15, 272, 294, 302
Shem – 306
Shema – 495
Sheol – *see* Hades
Shepherd Kings – *see* Hyksos Kings
Shimei – 810

Ships, ancient – 890, 906, 913
   their size – 895, 914
   their rigging – *see* Sails
   how they were undergirded – 902
   could anchor by the stern – 910
   steered by two rudders – 895, 901, 916
   had figureheads – 929
   how rapidly they could sail – 780, 895, 909, 930
   "ship's boat" towed astern – 902, 911, 912
   ship of Adramyttium – 891, 892
   ship of Alexandria – 894, 929
   Alexandrian grain ships – 894, 895, 902, 928, 929
   See also Navigation; Coasting vessel
Shipwreck – 903, 916-918, 919, 920, 925, 927
   scene of Paul's – *see* St. Paul's Bay; Melita Sicilius
Shook off the dust – *see* Dust
Shrines – *see* Artemis
Sicarrii – *see* Assassins
Sicily – 594, 696, 895, 896, 908, 929
Sickness – 211, 212, 374, 468, 568, 677, 756, 823, 926, 927, 928, 949
Sidon – 413, 889, 892, 893
   its harbor – 442
   Herod angry with – 442
   Paul refreshes himself here – 893
Signs and wonders – *see* Miracles
Silas, Silvanus – 550, 553, 554, 555, 594, 656, 657, 823
   Silas and Paul
      visit Antioch – 555
      chosen by Paul for missionary companion – 558, 562
      imprisoned – 585
      sang hymns at midnight – 586
   Silas and Timothy – 619
      join Paul at Corinth – 620, 641, 642
   Silas and Peter – 550, 642
Silver and gold – 154, 755
Silver, 50,000 pieces of – 683
Silver shrines of Artemis – 687
Silversmiths – 687, 694, 696
Simeon, looking for consolation of Israel – 315, 489, 881
Simeon, called Niger – 454
Simeon, son of Gamaliel – 175

Simon Magus
   the sorcerer – *xxxii*, 239, 319-322, 329, 720
   his conversion – 322
   his desire for ability to lay on hands – 325-327
   exposure of his pretensions – 320-324
   traditions concerning, after Acts' accounts – 328, 329, 448
   traditions concerning his manner of death – 329
Simon of Cyrene – 259, 454
Simon Peter – *see* Peter
Simon the tanner – 377, 382, 387, 389, 393
Simon the Zealot – 41, 200
Simony – 326
Sin – 768, 772, 816, 954
   bondage of – 328, 567, 581
   original – 131.
      See also Fall
   willful – 162, 207
   universality – 633
   in ignorance – 162
   guilt and penalty of – 854
   three things involved in any act of sin – 202-204
   God does not condone sin – 633
   remission of – 6, 164, 179, 221, 327, 402, 403, 482, 483, 660, 776, 853.
      See also Forgiveness
   separates man from God – 391, 511
Sinai – *see* Mount Sinai
Sinaiticus, Codex – *see* Manuscripts
Sinless perfection – 776
Singing – 84, 586, 587, 777, 823
Sirhan Sirhan – 703
Slaves – 383, 436, 476, 580, 584, 638, 639, 730, 731, 734, 830, 889, 893, 921
Sleep – 430, 736, 737
Sleep, a type of death – *see* Death
Smite on the mouth – 816, 817, 818
Smith, "Raccoon" John – 132
Smyrna – 569, 676, 692
Snake – 708, 713, 716.
   See also Viper
Social gospel – 249
Socrates – 624, 689
Sodom and Gomorrah – 139, 907

Index of Authors, Ideas and Topics

Soldiers
    Jewish – 218, 354.
        See also Temple guard
    Roman – *v*, 354, 379, 429, 440, 803, 804, 805, 807, 810, 812, 814, 820, 822, 823, 826, 829, 830, 833, 834, 858, 887, 888, 891, 911, 912, 917, 918, 923, 926, 933, 939, 947.
        See also Legions
Solomon – 10, 69, 237, 2%, 472, 534, 613
Solomon's Porch – 150, 156, 171, 209, 228
Soothsaying – 461, 707
Sons of God – 237
Sopater (Sosipater) – 618, 730
Sorcery – 320, 513, 681, 709, 710, 715, 720
Sorrow, Godly – 146
Sosthenes – 650, 651, 653
Soul – *see* Body-Soul-Spirit
Soul sleep – 305
Southern Galatia – 567-569, 572, 657
Sovereignty, divine – 130, 190
Spain – 647
Spain, Paul's journey to – 684, 728, 748, 951
Speaking in tongues – *see* Gift of tongues
Spearman – 829, 830
Speech psychology – 122
Spells – 462, 463, 678, 679, 681, 682, 709, 710
Spirit – *see* Holy Spirit
Spirit, human – *see* Body-Soul-Spirit
Spiritism – 320, 461, 701, 702, 707, 715, 716-720
Spirit of divination – *see* Divination
Spiritual death – 752
Spiritual gifts – 9, 49, 58, 59, 95-97, 102-126, 244, 251, 255, 257, 260, 268, 323-326, 359, 401, 402, 423, 457, 493, 521, 602, 668, 672, 673, 750, 784
    duration – 107, 117-121, 325, 454, 601, 898, 927
    given by laying on of apostles' hands – *see* Laying on of hands
    not received by all Christians – 324, 325
    purpose of – 101, 325, 684
Spiritual life – 159, 215, 878
Spirit writing – 718
Sponsor – *see* Patron
Spurling, Richard G. – 103
St. Paul's Bay – 909, 915, 921, 925
    described – 915, 916, 917
    place of Paul's shipwreck – 915

Star of Bethlehem – *iii*
Stephanas—579, 637
Stephen – *xxxii*
    choosing of – 252
    his earlier history – 252, 253
    arrested and falsely accused – 256- 263, 271, 801
    his defense – 262, 271-300, 808, 809, 815, 820
    his rebuke of the Sanhedrin – 298, 299
    alleged mistakes – 273, 274, 278, 279, 306-312
    full of Holy Spirit – 253, 301, 304
    probably a Hellenist – 253, 310
    death of – 13, 301-305, 893
    place of stoning – 366
    first Christian martyr – 252
    his dying prayer – 304, 305
    not the only Christian who was martyred in Paul's persecution – 348
    his burial – 228, 315
Stephen, Robert – 389
Stewardship, Christian – 424, 735
Stocks – 586, 587
Stoics – 509, 598, 622, 623, 628, 630, 632, 634, 635, 861
Stoning – 218, 428, 500
    of Stephen – *see* Stephen, death of
    of Paul – 513, 514, 879
Strabo – 462
Straight course – 573, 778
Straight, street called – 358
Straits of Gibraltar – 920
Straits of Messina – 930
Strangled – 547, 554
Strauss, David Friedrich – 241
Streets – 211, 502
Strengthening the churches – 517, 557, 563, 567, 658
Strymon River – *see* River
Suetonius – *xi*, *xiv*, 640 640, 812, 830, 870, 941
Suffering – 7, 9
Suffering Servant Poems – 158, 336
Suicide – 30, 31, 588, 589
Suidas – 258
Sulpicius Severus – 451
Sun – 466, 703, 905
    darkened – 61
Sunday – *see* Lord's Day

Superstition – 627, 923-925.
　See also Religious
Support of missions – see Missions, support of
Supralapsarianism – 133
Susan Gate – see Gates
Susanna – 19
Sweet wine – 56, 763
Sword – 428, 499, 587, 588, 912
Sychar – 321.
　See also Samaritan woman at the well
Synagogues – 345, 469, 487, 521, 617, 640, 641, 644, 654, 661, 673, 675, 733, 745
　at Damascus – 350, 363
　numerous at Jerusalem – 46, 258
　ten family heads needed – 575
　of the Freedmen – see Freedmen, synagogue of
　their officers – 469, 494, 495, 500, 644 650 936
　services – 363, 469, 477, 487, 495, 496, 548
　used through the week – 345, 485
　punishments inflicted in them – 495
　numerous in Rome – 936
　attended by Christians – 661
　Special Study – 257, 494-496
Synoptic gospels – 761
Syntyche – 576
Syracuse – 919, 929, 930
Syria – i, 370, 413, 442, 523, 728, 779, 780, 831, 835
Syria and Cilicia – 369, 563
Syriac – 53, 461
Syriac Version – 6, 171, 309, 593, 652, 673, 698, 751, 840, 935
Syrtis – 902, 903, 909, 919

Tabernacle
　of David – 541-542
　of Moloch – 293, 707, 708
　Old Testament place of worship – v, 293-295, 542
Tabernacles, Feast of – see Feasts of the Jews
Tabitha – see Dorcas
Tables of stone – 291, 294

Tacitus – xi, xiv, 241, 258, 378, 690, 691, 698, 810, 830, 842, 856, 864, 870, 891, 933, 935, 941, 952
Tackle and rigging – 895, 902, 904.
　See also Sails
Talisman – 293, 711, 773
Talmud – xi, 74, 346, 705, 828
Tanner – see Simon the tanner
Targums – 30, 68, 639
Tarot cards – 704
Tarsus – 345, 358, 368, 419, 425, 516, 564, 657, 806, 812, 835
　history – 260
　political importance – 806, 807
　educational center – 345, 571
Tartarus – 135, 137-139
Taurus Mountains – 414, 516
Tavium – 567, 568
Taxes (customs) – 812
Teacher, office of, in New Testament – 453-456
Teacher of the Law – see Scribes
Tears – 745, 754, 788
Telekinesis – 465, 682, 711
Telepathy – 724
Tell – 782, 833
Temple guard – 171, 216, 354
Temple, Herod's – 798, 843, 874, 881, 887
　diagram of – 151
　building begun in 19 BC – viii
　cleansed by Jesus – 396, 398
　meeting place for the early church – 46, 47, 215, 228
　completed in AD 66 – viii, 888
　its destruction foretold – 261, 262, 485, 661
　Beautiful Gate – see Gate, Beautiful
　courts of – see Court
　Holy of Holies – see Holy of Holies
　Holy Place – see Holy Place
　Roman attempts to set an idol in – 370, 426
　porches
　　Solomon's – see Solomon's Porch
　　Royal – see Royal Porch
　profaned – 800, 801, 802, 839, 840, 842, 843, 846, 847, 848, 860, 873, 879, 888
　treasury – xviii
Temple, Solomon's – 157, 472, 542, 628
Temple, Zerubbabel's – 157, 705

Index of Authors, Ideas and Topics

Temple of Apollo – *see* Apollo
Temple of Artemis – *see* Artemis of Ephesus
Temples, pagan – 506, 545, 622, 627, 628
Temptation – 202-204, 206, 418, 517, 852
Ten Commandments – *see* Decalogue
Ten lost tribes – 875
Tent-makers – 659
    Aquila – 638, 640
    Paul – 346, 580, 612, 638, 640, 642, 654, 673, 675, 677
Terah – 273, 306, 307, 309
Teraphim – 708
Terracina – 932
Terrorists – *see* Assassins
Tertius – 730
Tertullian – *xxiv, xxv,* 119, 329, 448, 451, 527, 736, 764, 870, 941
Tertullus – 836, 837, 844, 849, 859, 940
    an orator – 836, 859
    his gross flattery – 837, 838
    his charges against Paul – 838-841, 844, 846, 848, 860
Testament of the Twelve Patriarchs – 311
Testimonies – 880, 881
Thanatos Inscription Stones – 801
Thanks, giving of – *see* Giving of thanks
Thaumaturgy – 711
Theaters
    used among the Greeks for public business – 691, 698
    at Caesarea – 443, 444
    at Ephesus – 666, 667, 691, 745
Thebes – 581
Theism – 511, 512
Theocracy – 473, 518, 815
Theology
    Pauline – *xxiii, xxix,* 561
    alleged development of Paul's theology? – 369, 535, 798, 799
    harmony between Paul's and other apostles' – 479, 529, 535, 655, 791, 793, 940
    Petrine – *xxiii,* 561
Theophilus
    Luke's books addressed to – *xxv, xxxvi,* 1, 19, 659
    his rank and country – 1
    "most excellent" – 1
    high priest's brother – 1
Theosophy – 721

Therma – 611
Theseus – 621, 628
Thessalonians, epistles to – 550, 612, 616, 641, 642, 685
Thessalonica – *xxx,* 611, 648, 727, 730, 747, 839, 879, 892
    location – 611
    history of – 574
    Paul's labors there – 611-617, 642
    miracles wrought there – 613
Theudas
    insurrection led by – 224
    not mentioned by Josephus – 224
Thieves – 505, 544
Third heaven – *see* Heavens, Three
Thirty-nine lashes – 227
Thomas, apostle – 41
Thorn in the flesh, Paul's – 747
Thotmes I – 280
Three Inns – 932, 933
Thrace – 574, 633
Throne of David – 69, 70, 72, 480, 541-543, 674
Thucydides – 241, 529, 626
Thyatira – 546, 577, 676
Tiberius Alexander – *xiii,* 226
Tiberius Caesar – *v, xii, xiii,* 426, 647, 867, 870
Tiber River – *see* River
Tigellinus – 952
Tigris River – *see* River
Time
    Jewish method of counting – 57, 733, 738, 829, 857, 897
    Roman method of counting – 733
Times and epochs – 11
Times of ignorance – 510, 633
Times of refreshing – *see* Refreshing, times of
Timon, one of the Seven – 253
Timothy – 340, 583, 727, 730, 784, 953
    native of Lystra – 502, 515, 564, 730
    youthfulness – 515, 564
    converted by Paul – 515, 564
    taken along as a helper on second missionary journey – 564, 569, 657
    why required to be circumcised – 565, 566, 795
    his ministry in Macedonia – 576, 597, 617, 619

joined Paul at Athens and Corinth – 620, 641
sent to Thessalonica – 620, 641, 685
had spiritual gifts – 96, 566
sent into Macedonia from Ephesus – 685
ministry in Ephesus – 951
not the author of Acts – *xxvi,* 731
with Paul in Rome – 948
epistles addressed to – 450, 452, 515, 676, 753, 951, 953

Tishri – 897
Titius Justus – 643, 644, 675
Titus, the evangelist – 519, 602, 685, 686, 726, 727, 731, 733, 784, 795, 953
not named in Acts – *xxvi,* 643, 731
at Jerusalem Conference – 529-535, 554
ministry in Crete – 951
epistle to – 519, 676, 731, 951
Titus, emperor – *xii, xviii,* 50, 175, 892
Tobit – 237
Tomb of Caecilia Matella – 934
Tongues as of fire – 47, 48
Tongues, gift of – *see* Gift of tongues
Torches – 589, 736
Tower of Antonia – *see* Antonia, tower of
Tower of Babel – *see* Babel
Town clerk
at Ephesus – *xxxi,* 695
his speech – 695-699
Trade guilds – *see* Guilds, trade
Tradition – 447, 511, 915, 927, 952, 953. *See also* Oral tradition
Traditions of the Jews
concerning the tomb of the Patriarchs – 311
concerning the origin of the magical *Key of Solomon* – 712
concerning the length of Saul's reign – 473
of the Pharisees – 197, 348, 408, 538, 874
Training of new converts – 322, 406, 417, 420, 460, 467, 516, 646
Trajan, emperor – *xii,* 688, 690, 935
Trance – 380, 717, 718, 722, 808
Peter's – 384-387
Paul's – 368
Transcendental meditation – 722
Transmigration of souls – *see* Reincarnation
Transubstantiation – 760, 766-769
Tribulation – 492, 517, 518, 748

Tribute – 575
Tribunal – *see* Judgment seat
Tribune – *see* Commander
Trinity – *see* Godhead
Tripolis – 329, 413
Troas – *xxv,* 523, 567, 569-573, 685, 696, 726, 729, 731, 732-741, 747, 748, 764, 780, 931, 951
Trogyllium – 742
Trophimus – 730, 731, 798, 800, 801, 802, 840, 951
Trustworthiness of Acts – *see* Acts, Introductory Studies
Tubingen School—*xxiii*
Tullianium – 586
Tunic – 375, 680
Turkey – 467, 469
Turn to the Lord – 164, 373, 416, 509, 543, 878, 879, 946
Tutelary angels – *see* Angels, guardian
Tutelary gods—929
Twelve, the – *see* Apostles
"Twelve days," how figured? – 842, 843
Twelve disciples of John at Ephesus – 402, 662, 666-673, 744
Twelve tribes – 875
Twin Brothers – 929
Two evenings – *see* Evening
Tychicus – 727, 730, 949, 953
Tyrannus, school of – *x, xv,* 675, 676, 745, 754
Tyre – 329, 790, 893, 931
location – 413
gospel preached there early – 413, 414
Herod's displeasure at – 442
Paul's seven days' stay there – 779-782
Tyropean Valley – 814

Uncircumcision – 298, 299
Unclean – *see* Clean and unclean meats
Unclean spirits – *see* Demons
Uneducated and untrained – 181
Undergirding – *see* Ships, ancient
Unity
in the early church – 84, 192
of the human race – 629
religious, a plea for – 422, 684, 729, 730, 772, 773, 794

Index of Authors, Ideas and Topics

Unity School of Christianity – 722
Universal salvation – 167
Unknown God – 509, 627, 635
Unlawful – 391
Unleavened bread – 43, 429, 762, 773, 797
Unpardonable sin – 327
Upper country – 666
Upper room – 18, 187, 375, 736-738, 943
Urim and Thummim – 380, 705
Ur of Chaldees – 272

Vain things – 509
Valerian Law – 594, 595
Valerius Gratus – *viii*
Valetta – 915, 929
Valley
   of Elah – 331, 338, 339
   of Hinnom – 81
   of Kidron – 17, 153
Valona – 574
Vatican II Council – *see* Councils
Vaticanus, Codex – *see* Manuscripts
Vegetius – 897, 928
Venom – 328, 922, 923, 924
Ventriloquism – 581, 679
Venus – *see* Aphrodite
Verisimilitude – *xxx*
Verres, governor of Sicily – 594
Verses, New Testament divided into – 389
Vespasian – *xii, xvii, xviii,* 615
Vesuvius – *see* Mt. Vesuvius
Via Appia – *see* Appian Way
Via Egnatia – *see* Egnatian Way
Victor, Bishop of Libertina – 258
Victorious of Petau – 254
Vintage, time of in Palestine – 56
Violence – 218, 225, 500, 649, 805, 822, 840, 861, 952
Viper – 922, 923, 924, 925, 927
   ideas of, in demonology – 236
   why extinct in Malta – 922
Virgil – 123, 504, 584
Virgin daughters of Philip – *see* Philip, the evangelist
Vision – *xxxii,* 46, 60, 358, 359, 380, 387, 401, 412, 433, 570-573, 645, 821, 872, 877, 898

Vitellius, emperor – *vi, viii, xiii,* 891
Voodoo – 713
Vote – 349, 899
Vow – 652, 798, 843, 846
   Is Acts 18:18 Paul's or Aquila's? – 652, 654
   paying charges for a vow – 427, 796
   See also Nazarite vow
Voyages – 889, 893, 908, 928
   distance covered in an hour – 780, 895, 909
Vulcan – 628
Vulgate – *see* Latin Vulgate

Wailing – 737
Waldensians – 452
Warfield, Benjamin B. – 119
Way from Jerusalem to Gaza – *see* Roads
Way of the Kings – 351
Way of the Patriarchs – 351, 834
Way of the Sea – 351, 369
Way, those of the – 349, 674, 686, 844, 848, 851
Weak – 756
Weeping – 375, 737, 757, 788, 823
"We" sections – *xxv, xxvi, xxxiv,* 423, 518, 572, 597, 731, 732, 889, 902, 903, 904, 934.
   See also Acts, authorship
Wesley, John – 102, 765
Western text – *xxxv,* 407, 420, 423, 547, 554, 589, 593, 595, 596, 644, 655, 675, 742, 778, 779, 789, 790, 840, 850, 856, 894, 934
White clothing – 15
Widows – 247, 373, 375, 456
Wild beasts, Paul's fight with – 686
Wilderness wanderings – 174, 289, 293, 471
Will, free – *see* Free will
Will of God – 411, 528, 543, 655, 789, 821
Will of God, how to know it – 32, 33, 411
Windows
   how made in Eastern houses – 736
   Eutychus falls from one – 737
Winds – 890, 893, 896, 897, 900, 916, 929, 930
   Etesian – *see* Etesian winds
   Euraquilo – *see* Euraquilo
   rushing, mighty wind – 47

Wine – 762, 763, 778, 780
Wine, sweet – *see* Sweet wine
Winter – 728, 928, 953
Wisdom – 251, 260
Wiseman – 441
Witchcraft – 320, 414, 461, 463, 547, 683, 687, 690, 701, 702, 709- 716
    black – 709, 712-713
    white – 709, 710-712
Witches' ladder – 711, 713, 715
Witches' sabbath – 710
Witness – 12, 27, 70, 80, 160, 221, 355, 363, 378, 394, 397, 398, 479, 489, 742, 823, 884
Witnesses, false – *see* False witnesses
Wizards – 461, 710, 715
Wolves – 752
Women
    activities in early church – 59, 662, 786, 787
    followed Jesus from Galilee – 19, 479
    witnesses of Jesus' crucifixion – 40, 41
    wives of apostles – 20
    devout and prominent – 492
    converted to Christianity – 211, 321
    leading women – *see* Leading women
    heathen, converts to Judaism – 492, 888
    ordination to church offices – 786
    persecuted – 316
    attitude toward, in 1st century – 546, 613, 640
Wonders and signs – *see* Miracles
Word of God – 460 463, 487, 488-490, 591, 646, 649, 676, 683, 744, 754, 755, 770, 774, 775, 776, 851
Work ethic – 756
Works – 598, 608, 609
World Council of Churches – 773
World-view – 629, 883
World-wide Communion Sunday – 774
Worms – 444
Worship – 776, 843, 844, 865, 876, 941
    begun at dawn in the temple – 215
    Jewish – 155, 333, 348, 474, 492, 575-576, 641, 648, 874, 876
    pagan – 507, 545, 580, 584, 627, 629
    at riverside locations – 575, 576
    place of meeting – 150, 187
    in the early church – *xxii*, 44, 82-84, 314, 315, 420, 549, 734, 735, 738, 761, 764
    day of worship in the New Testament – 44, 549
    of angels forbidden – 438, 439
    of men forbidden – *xxxii*, 390, 444
    ordained by God – 185
    not limited to temple at Jerusalem – 279, 295, 298, 485, 808
    in the synagogue – *see* Synagogue, services
    in the Catholic Church – 760
    Roman laws concerning – 648
    See also – *Religio Licita* and *Religio Illicita*
Worship of Idols – *see* Idol worship
Wounded – 680
Wrath – *see* God, wrath of
Wycliffe – 46, 131

Xanthus – 778
Xenoglossia – 122, 719
Xenophanes – 633
Xenophon – 1, 690, 691

Yoga – 722
Yoke, Jewish – 538
Young man
    used of Saul – 304, 827, 874
    used of Eutychus – 736, 740, 827
    used of Paul's nephew – 827, 828
Young men – 204, 207

Zacchaeus – 74
Zadok – 197
Zealots – 226, 824
    origin of the party – 200
    beliefs – 200
    rebellion against Rome – 200
Zeal
    of Jews – 795, 796, 807
    of Paul as a Pharisee – 348
    of Paul for conversion of the Jews – 807

Zechariah, father of John the Baptist – *iv*
Zenas – 665
Zen Buddhism – 721
Zeno of Cyprus – 622, 623
Zeus – 297, 504, 506, 507, 580, 622, 628,
    632, 633, 687, 696, 924, 929
   priest of – 506
   Barnabas called – 505
Zimri – 588
Zion – 333
Zion, Mount – *see* Mount Zion
Zipporah – 285
Zoan-abaris – 283
Zodiac – 702
Zoroastrianism – 582
Zwingli, Huldrich – 132, 759, 769, 770

OTHER BOOKS BY GARETH L. REESE

New Testament Epistles: *Romans* (097-176-5200)

New Testament Epistles: *1 Corinthians* (097-176-5251)

New Testament Epistles: *2 Corinthians and Galatians* (097-176-5278)

New Testament Epistles: *Paul's Prison Epistles* (099-845-1800)

New Testament Epistles: *1 & 2 Thessalonians* (099-845-186X)

New Testament Epistles: *1 & 2 Timothy and Titus* (097-176-5227)

New Testament Epistles: *Hebrews* (097-176-5219)

New Testament Epistles: *1 & 2 Peter and Jude* (097-176-5243)

New Testament Epistles: *James and 1,2,3 John* (097-176-526X)

Order from:
Scripture Exposition Books
803 McKinsey Place
Moberly, MO, 65270
www.reesecommentaries.com

www.ingramcontent.com/pod-product-compliance
Lightning Source LLC
LaVergne TN
LVHW080741250326
834688LV00006B/163